Fromm

France

**by Darwin Porter
& Danforth Prince**

Macmillan • USA

ABOUT THE AUTHORS

France is a "second home" to **Darwin Porter,** a native of North Carolina, and **Danforth Prince,** who lived in France for many years. Porter, who worked in television advertising and as a bureau chief for the *Miami Herald,* wrote the original edition of this book back in 1971. Prince, who began his association with Porter in 1982, worked for the Paris bureau of *The New York Times* between renovations of a historic building in the Loire Valley. Both these writers know their destination well, for they've made countless annual trips through the countryside and lived and worked in provinces from Brittany to Provence.

MACMILLAN TRAVEL

A Simon & Schuster Macmillan Company
1633 Broadway
New York, NY 10019

ISBN 0-02-860629-9
ISSN 0899-3351

Editor: Ron Boudreau
Map Editor: Douglas Stallings
Production Editor: Kathleen Varanese
Design by Michele Laseau
Digital cartography by Devorah Wilkenfeld and Ortelius Design

Front cover photo: Château d'Azay-le-Rideau, Loire Valley

SPECIAL SALES

Bulk purchases (10+ copies) of Frommer's Travel Guides are available to corporations at special discounts. The Special Sales Department can produce custom editions to be used as premiums and/or for sales promotion to suit individual needs. Existing editions can be produced with custom cover imprints such as corporate logos. For more information write to: Special Sales, Simon & Schuster, 1633 Broadway, New York, NY 10019.

Manufactured in the United States of America.

Contents

Appendix: Menu Savvy   687

Index   693

List of Maps

AN INVITATION TO THE READER

In researching this book, we discovered many wonderful places—hotels, restaurants, shops, and more. We're sure you'll find others. Please tell us about them, so we can share the information with your fellow travelers in upcoming editions. If you were disappointed with a recommendation, we'd love to know that, too. Please write to:

Darwin Porter/Danforth Prince
Frommer's France '96
Macmillan Travel
1633 Broadway
New York, NY 10019

AN ADDITIONAL NOTE

Please be advised that travel information is subject to change at any time—and this is especially true of prices. We therefore suggest that you write or call ahead for confirmation when making your travel plans. The authors, editors, and publisher cannot be held responsible for the experiences of readers while traveling. Your safety is important to us, however, so we encourage you to stay alert and be aware of your surroundings. Keep a close eye on cameras, purses, and wallets, all favorite targets of thieves and pickpockets.

WHAT THE SYMBOLS MEAN

✪ Frommer's Favorites

Hotels, restaurants, attractions, and entertainment you should not miss.

⑨ Super-Special Values

Hotels and restaurants that offer great value for your money.

The following abbreviations are used for credit cards:

AE	American Express	EU	Eurocard
CB	Carte Blanche	JCB	Japan Credit Bank
DC	Diners Club	MC	MasterCard
DISC	Discover	V	Visa
ER	enRoute		

The Best of France

France presents visitors with an embarrassment of riches—and you may find yourself bewildered at all the choices you'll have to make when planning your trip. We've tried to make the task easier for you by compiling a list of our favorite experiences and discoveries. In the following pages you'll find the kind of candid advice we'd give our close friends.

1 The Best Travel Experiences

- **Making a Pilgrimage to Normany's D-Day Beaches.** On June 6, 1944, the largest armada ever assembled departed under cover of rough seas and dense fog from the English coast. Its success was anything but guaranteed, and for about a week the future of the civilized world hung in a bloody and brutal balance between the Nazi and Allied armies. Today you'll see only the sticky sands and wind-torn, gray-green seas of a rather chilly beach. With just a bit of imagination, you can tap into the collective unconscious of an army that established a bulkhead on the Nazi-occupied continent of Europe at a terrible price.
- **Touring the Loire Valley.** Examining the châteaux scattered among the valley's rich fields and forests will familiarize you with the French Renaissance's architectural aesthetics. Nothing evokes the aristocratic *ancien régime* more evocatively than a leisurely tour of their legendary châteaux.
- **Holiday-Making on the Côte d'Azur.** Until Edwardian escapists "discovered" it about a century ago, the Provence coastline was dotted with a series of sleepy fishing villages. Today the Azure Coast figures prominently in the fantasies of every sybarite, and despite its desperate overcrowding (and impossible traffic jams) it continues to be the place where every French person most wants to be.
- **Touring Burgundy During the Grape Gathering.** The harvests in Burgundy are permeated with medieval lore and legend. During the harvest, thousands of workers (armed with vintner's shears and baskets) radiate over the rolling hills to gather the ripened grapes that make the classified wines of Burgundy so famous. As you'd expect, area restaurants prepare Burgundian specialties flawlessly and always stock impressive collections of the local wines.

- **Shopping in Paris's Upscale Boutiques.** The French ferociously guard their self-image as Europe's most stylish people. The citadels of Right Bank *grand bourgeois* chic are firmly entrenched along rue du Faubourg-St-Honoré and its extension, rue St-Honoré. The most glamorous shops sprawl for about a mile along these interconnected narrow streets, which stretch between the Palais Royal (to the east) and Palais de l'Elysée (to the west). Follow in the footsteps of Coco Chanel for a shopper's tour of a lifetime.
- **Hunting Antiques.** The 18th- and 19th-century French aesthetic was gloriously different from that of England and North America, and many worthwhile objects bear designs with mythological references to the French experience. It's estimated that there are more than 13,000 antiques shops throughout the country. Stop wherever the sign ANTIQUAIRE or BROCANTE is displayed.
- **Cruising the Interior.** Take a leisurely cruise on the waterways of Burgundy, Brittany, Alsace, Languedoc, the Dordogne, or Provence. Many barges (for lumber, coal, or grain) have been upgraded into luxury craft with fine dining and comfortable accommodations. Contact Première Selections, a division of the Kemwell Company, 106 Calvert St., Harrison, NY 10528 (☎ 800/234-4000). Costs for a six-night/seven-day barge cruise (all meals included) begin at $1,680 per person.
- **Dining Out.** Despite the encroachment of dinners on the run and the fast-food restaurants sprouting up in urban landscapes throughout France, the art of fine dining is still considered serious business in this nation of gastronomes. Even meals at bistros are likely to include fresh (seasonal) ingredients used in time-tested recipes. Part of the fun in ordering dinner involves understanding how radical the chef was in combining unexpected ingredients into new combinations and how rigorously he or she remained faithful to the standards of 19th-century cuisine. Food here is as cerebral as it is sensual.
- **Touring the Riviera's Modern-Art Museums.** Since the 1890s, when Signac, Bonnard, and Matisse discovered St-Tropez, artists and their patrons have been drawn to the French Riviera. You can enjoy an unforgettable trip by driving across southern Provence, interspersing museum visits with relaxed meals, people-watching, and stops at the area's architectural and artistic marvels. Highlights include Aix-en-Provence (Cézanne's studio and the Vasarély Museum), Biot (the Léger museum), Cagnes-sur-Mer (the Museum of Modern Mediterranean Art), Cap d'Antibes (the Grimaldi Château's Picasso collection), Fréjus (a chapel containing unfinished murals by Jean Cocteau), La Napoule (the Henry Clews Museum), and Menton (the Cocteau Museum). If this isn't enough, Nice, St-Paul-de-Vence, and St-Tropez all have impressive modern-art collections.
- **Cycling in the Countryside.** The country that invented La Tour de France—the world's most impassioned bicycle race—offers thousands of options for

Impressions

The country seems to me as beautiful as Japan for clarity of atmosphere and gay color effects. Water forms patches of lovely emerald or rich blue in the landscape, just as we see it in the crêpe prints. The pale orange of the sunsets make the fields appear blue.

—Vincent van Gogh, *Letters* (1888)

leisurely cycling. For a modest charge, trains throughout France will carry your bicycle to any point you specify, allowing cyclers to avoid the urban congestion of Paris or other large cities. North America's oldest specialist is Bike Tour France, 5523 Wedgewood Dr., Charlotte, NC 28210-2432 (☎ **704/ 527-0955**). Best suited for tours through the Loire Valley, Provence, and the Southwest, the company provides a technically sophisticated bicycle plus hotel accommodations as part of the price of tours that last 5 to 30 days. Routes are carefully selected for maximum exposure to monuments and natural beauty.

2 The Most Romantic Getaways

- **La Baule.** Consider an escape with your Significant Other to La Baule, a coastal resort in southern Brittany. The salt air, Atlantic pensiveness, and belle époque architecture here help justify the name of its five-mile beach as La Côte d'Amour.
- **Les Baux de Provence.** During the Middle Ages, troubadours in southern Europe were encouraged to present their courtly love ballads to audiences at the craggy fortress of Les Baux. The romantic tradition continues today, with escapists from all over congregating in the weirdly eroded, rocky, arid Les Baux landscapes. The town contains an abundance of romantic hideaways to satiate your worldly needs.
- **Deauville.** Using the site to propel herself to stardom, Coco Chanel added greatly to its sense of glamour and romance. Play your hand at the casinos, if that's your thing; ride horses; stroll along what's probably the world's most discreetly elegant boardwalk; or simply revel in the exaggerated style and nostalgia of *La Belle Epoque.*
- **St-Tropez.** Somehow, any blond manages to look like Brigitte Bardot in the fair-weathered context of St-Tropez, and the sheer number of satyrs and nymphs who run through town in midsummer could perk up the most sluggish libido. The real miracle here is that the charm of the place actually manages to survive both its own hype and the hordes of visitors who check into its highly tolerant hotels.
- **Talloires.** A bracing climate, a history that goes back to the early Middle Ages, and a Gallic nonchalance by local innkeepers contribute to the almost-tangible sense of well-being visitors to Talloires sometimes feel. Accommodations include everything from a converted medieval monastery to less glamorous (and less expensive) B&Bs. The cuisine is world-class, as is the opportunity for quiet, relaxed romance.

3 The Most Dramatic Countryside Drives

- **Route des Grandes Alpes.** One of the most panoramic alpine drives in Western Europe stretches southward from the lakefront town of Evian to the coastal resort of Nice. En route, alpine uplands, larch forests, glaciers, and the foothills of Mont Blanc are sheathed in mountain scenery. Plan on spending anywhere from two to six days for the excursion, stopping for R&R in such towns as Thonon, Morzine-Avoriaz, Chamonix, and Megève. The route covers about 460 miles and crosses about 20 of France's dramatic mountain passes. Some sections are passable only in midsummer.

- **Route des Crêtes (The Crest Road).** The Vosges are one of the oldest mountain ranges in France and for many years formed one of the country's boundaries with Germany. Richly forested with tall hardwood trees and firs, they skirt the western edge of the Rhine and bear many similarities to the (better-known) Black Forest of Germany. Some areas comprise the closest thing in France to a wilderness. During World War I, a road (La Route des Crêtes) was chiseled out of the mountains as a supply line. Later, some horrifying strife took place over this jagged upland. It begins just west of Colmar, at the Col du Bonhomme. High points include Münster (home of the famous cheese), Col de la Schlucht (a resort with sweeping panoramas as far as the Jura and the Black Forest), and Markstein. At any point of this route, you can stop and strike out along some of the well-marked hiking trails.

- **The Gorges of the Ardèche.** The river that carved these canyons (the Ardèche, a tributary of the Rhône) is probably the most temperamental of any French waterway. The resulting ebbs and flows between its banks have created the "Grand Canyon of France." Riddled with alluvial deposits, canyons sometimes more than 950 feet deep, grottos, and caves, the valley is one of the country's most unusual pieces of geology. A panoramic road (D290) runs along one rim of these canyons, providing views over an arid landscape of grasses, toughened trees, and drought-resistant shrubs. Plan to park at many of the belvederes scattered along the route and walk for a few minutes along some of the well-marked footpaths radiating from the parking areas beside them. The route, which can be traversed in a day even if you stop frequently for sightseeing, stretches in a southeast-to-northwest trajectory between the towns of Vallon-Pont-d'Arc and Pont St-Esprit.

- **Burgundy's Côte d'Or.** Stretching from Santenay to Dijon, only 37 miles, this route is lushly evocative for anyone who ever memorized names on a French-language wine list. Rows of carefully terraced vines rise in tiers above the D122/N74/D1138 highways (La Route des Grands Crus), passing through the wine hamlets of Puligny-Montrachet, Volnay, Beaune, Nuits-St-Georges, Vosne-Romanée, Gevrey-Chambertin, and Marsannay-la-Côte. Many who experience this drive comment on the sense of timelessness they feel. Proceed leisurely, stopping wherever you like for purchases and *dégustations* of the noble vintages whose growers are identified by signs sprouting from the sides of the highway.

4 The Best Offbeat Experiences

- **Riding in a Hot-Air Balloon.** One company can carry you aloft over the ancient vineyards of Burgundy in a wildly exhilarating style: Between April and November, Air Escargot, 71150 Chagny (☎ **85-87-12-30**), offers two daily departures of about one hour each. Passengers can be retrieved from whatever Burgundian hotel they stay at, ride high over the countryside, and eventually be picked up by a light truck (which follows the balloon's route). The voyage is celebrated with a glass or two of local wine.

- **Touring Brittany's Celtic Dolmens.** Stonehenge might indeed be larger, but the Celtic coast of Brittany offers thousands of dolmens erected thousands of years ago. One of the greatest concentrations of stones is at Carnac, 302 miles southwest of Paris. Here a field of megaliths is the most important prehistoric find in northern France, their arrangement and placement still a mystery.

- **Exploring Provence's Perched Villages.** After the collapse of Roman rule in Provence, Gallo-Romans here banded into communities for mutual protection. In fortified villages perched atop rocky crags they survived for centuries despite frequent sieges by marauders. Many were abandoned during the 1700s as residents migrated toward cities and towns. These villages have enjoyed a Renaissance thanks to increased tourism, rising real estate values, and newfound fascination with the ancient premises that prompted their construction. Most of the perched villages are filled with stone-sided buildings topped by terra-cotta–tiled roofs, a cobbled central square with a fountain, narrow streets, and sweeping views over olive groves and arid fields. Examples include elegant eagle's-nest eyries above the Mediterranean: Eze, Roquebrune, Ste-Agnès, St-Paul-de-Vence, Gordes, Roussillon, Gorbio, and Crestet.
- **Inspecting the Auvergne.** Despite its weird beauty and wealth of romanesque churches, the Auvergne is one of France's least-visited regions. Perched atop the Massif Central, it boasts occasional pockets of fertility, dramatic volcanic rock formations, and *charcuterie*. Esplanade Tours (the North American sales agent for London-based Swan Hellenic Tours), 581 Boyleston St., Boston, MA 02116 (☎ 800/426-5492), offers in-depth tours to this isolated province. Originating and ending in London, the tours include insights into natural and cultural history, a guest lecturer who expounds on everything *auvergnat*, and overnight lodgings and meals. Prices, which include airfare from London, begin at $2,000 per person for an eight-day/seven-night intensive tour.

5 The Best Ski Resorts

- **Courchevel.** Chalets in the nearby forest routinely sell for up to $4 million each, and even the most ardent skier will most likely want to linger amid the well-heeled socialites, parvenus, scoundrels, ski rats, and millionaires who flock here for fun, diversion, and even skiing. There's something invigorating and stylish about Courchevel—perhaps it's all that flesh carefully bundled against the alpine chill. Know before you arrive that the resort consists of four communities, each named Courchevel and each marked by its elevation above sea level in meters. Thus, you'll pass the relatively unfashionable Courchevel 1300, 1550, and 1650 on your way uphill to the most desirable core, Courchevel 1850.
- **Chamonix.** Separated from its twin resort, Courmayeur (across the Italian border, on the opposite side of Mont Blanc), Chamonix first became famous during the 1924 Winter Olympics. Much of the resort's architecture is charmingly old-fashioned, but hidden beneath the woodsy surfaces is a high-tech infrastructure with chair lifts and cable cars leading to ski trails extending in uninterrupted runs of more than 10 miles. In recent years, the resort's charming sense of isolation has been affected by its position near one end of the Mont Blanc Tunnel, a seven-mile-long year-round link between France and Italy that's now one of Europe's strategic highways.
- **Megève.** Built around a 13th-century core, Megève is nostalgic, charming, and elegantly rustic and acts as a magnet for loyal and often stylish French people who return year after year. Skiing here is admittedly not as superb as in such competing resorts as Courchevel and Chamonix, but the charm lives on partly through a phalanx of hotels and restaurants that cater to the demands of the *enfants terribles* who check in with disconcerting regularity.

• **Morzine-Avoriaz.** Since this resort lies confusingly close to the Swiss border, internationalists delight in schussing languidly between the two countries as part of their adventures on the slopes. Consisting of two villages, Morzine (an older village set in a valley at 3,000 feet) and the more modern Avoriaz (on a windswept snowy plateau at 5,400 feet), the resort offers amenities suitable for either solo travelers or family groups. Cars are not allowed on the streets, and the cable cars leading up to many ski runs make Avoriaz especially desirable.

• **Flaine.** Isolated in a high alpine valley adjacent to the Arve and Carrozd'Araches rivers, this resort winds uphill between altitudes of 5,300 and 8,900 feet above sea level. It's one of the highest, most modern, and most frequently snowbound of the resorts of the French Alps, a fact much beloved by skiers and cold-weather athletes. What this small resort lacks in terms of nightlife, boutiques, and exotic restaurants is amply compensated by the more than 80 lifts servicing 150 miles of ski runs.

6 The Best Châteaux & Palaces

• **Château de Versailles.** This is the most spectacular palace in the world, inspiring awe (yet not necessarily affection) in the eyes of all who see it. Its construction was riddled with ironies and tragedies, and its hyperinflated costs can be partly blamed for the bloodbath that destroyed the *ancien régime*. Ringed with world-class gardens and a network of canals whose excavations required an army of laborers, the site also contains the Grand and Petit Trianons as well as miles of ornate corridors lined with the spoils of a vanished era.

• **Château de Chambord.** Despite the incorporation (probably by Michelangelo) of feudal trappings in its layout, this château was designed exclusively for pleasure—a manifestation of the political and military successes of a 21-year-old king, François I. Begun in 1519 as the Loire Valley's most opulent status symbol, Chambord heralded the end of the feudal age and the debut of the Renaissance. Ironically, after military defeats in Italy, a much-chastened François opted to live in châteaux closer to Paris and rarely visited here.

• **Palais de Fontainebleau.** Since the time of the earliest Frankish kings, the forest here was recognized for its abundant game. Various royal dwellings had been erected for medieval kings in the heart of the forest, but in 1528 François I commissioned the core of the building that would be enlarged, expanded, and embellished by subsequent monarchs, including Henri II, Henri III, Catherine de Medici, Charles IX, and Louis XIII. Napoléon declared it his favorite château, delivering an emotional farewell to his troops from its horseshoe-shaped staircase just after his 1814 abdication.

• **Château d'Azay-le-Rideau.** Many visitors consider this château among their three or four favorites, thrilling to its fairy-tale proportions and innate sense of beauty. Poised above the waters of the Indre (a tributary of the Loire), it boasts purely decorative remnants of medieval fortifications and an allure that prefigured the Renaissance embellishments of subsequent Loire Valley châteaux. For a glimpse of Azay-le-Rideau, see the front cover of this book.

• **Château de Chantilly.** This palace was begun in 1528 by Anne de Montmorency, a Constable of France who gave her advice to six monarchs. To save costs, she ordered that her new building be placed atop the foundations of a derelict building completed in 1386. Her descendants enlarged and embellished the premises, added the massive stables for which the place is admired today, and hired Le Nôtre to design gardens that later inspired Louis XVI to create similar (though larger) ones at Versailles.

- **Château de Chenonceau.** Its builders daringly placed this palace on arched stone vaults above the rushing Cher, a tributary of the Loire. Built between 1513 and 1521, Chenonceau was later fought over by two of France's most influential women, each of whom imposed her will on Renaissance politics and the château's design. Henri II gave the palace to his mistress, Diane de Poitiers, whose allure, it was rumored, was kept alive by milk baths, morning horseback rides, and witchcraft. After the king's death, his scheming, unloved widow, Catherine de Medici, ousted Diane to a less prestigious château nearby (Chaumont), thoroughly humiliating her in the process.
- **Château de Vaux-le-Vicomte.** Vaux-le-Vicomte symbolizes the dangers for status-seekers who refuse to curb themselves. It was built in 1661 for Nicolas Fouquet, Louis XIV's finance minister, and its lavishness made many wonder if some of the money for its construction had been pilfered from the treasury—which it had. This act did not amuse the Sun King, who had Fouquet jailed and his château confiscated. As a backhanded compliment to Fouquet, Louis swiftly hired the complex's designers (Mansard, Le Nôtre, LeBrun, Girardon, and de Legendre) to design a palace and gardens at Versailles.
- **Château de Villandry.** Built in 1538, Villandry is a truly dignified palace. Most of its aesthetic thrill, however, derives from its 17 acres of formal gardens; brought to their full magnificence after 1906 by the noted French scholar Dr. Carvallo, they're a not-to-be-missed stopover on any gardener's tour of France.

7 The Best Museums

- **Musée du Louvre,** Paris. Graced with an exterior that's a triumph of grandiloquent French architecture, its stately premises suffer from an embarrassment of artistic riches, with more paintings (around 300,000) than can be displayed at any one time. The collection somehow manages to retain its dignity despite the thousands of visitors who trail through the corridors every day. In the 1980s, the grandeur of its Cour Carrée was neatly offset by I. M. Pei's notoriously controversial Great Pyramid.
- **Musée d'Orsay,** Paris. The spidery glass-and-iron canopies of an abandoned railway station were adapted into one of Europe's most thrilling museums. Devoted exclusively to 19th-century art, it contains most of the paintings of the French impressionists, as well thousands of sculptures and decorative objects whose design changed forever the way Europe interpreted line, movement, and color between 1848 and 1914.
- **Centre Georges Pompidou,** Paris. Despite its astounding collection of 20th-century art, few people can decide whether they like or loathe the exterior of this place. Debate has raged over the center's aesthetics since its 1977 opening on the plateau Beaubourg. The building's "exoskeleton" bristles with brightly painted (and highly impractical) pipes and tubes, allowing an open interior free of fixed partitions.
- **Musée de la Tapisserie de Bayeux,** Bayeux. This museum's star exhibit is a 900-year old tapestry named in honor of medieval Queen Mathilda. Housed in a glass case, the Bayeaux tapestry is a long, narrow band of linen embroidered with depictions of the war machine that sailed from Normandy to conquer England in 1066.

- **Musée Lorrain,** Nancy. Few other French museums reflect a specific province as pointedly as this one. Its eclectic collections include 16th-century engravings, 17th-century masterpieces by local painters, exhibits devoted to Jewish history in eastern France, antique furniture, wrought iron, and domestic accessories.
- **Musée Ingres,** Montauban. This museum, housed in a 17th-century archbishop's palace, was created in 1867 when Jean-Auguste-Dominique Ingres (one of the most admired classicists since the Revolution) bequeathed the city more than 4,000 drawings and paintings.
- **Musée Toulouse-Lautrec,** Albi. The crippled artist whose work this museum commemorates was born in Albi in 1864. Much to his family's horror, he opted to move to a scandalous neighborhood in Paris, where his affectionate and amused depictions of the belle époque's demimonde are considered priceless treasures today. Also on view here are works by Degas, Bonnard, and Matisse.
- **Musée Fabré,** Montpellier. This museum occupies a historic villa where Molière once presented some of his plays. Today it boasts one of the worthiest collection of French, Italian, and Spanish paintings in the south of France.
- **Musée Ile de France,** St-Jean-Cap-Ferrat. This breathtaking villa is loaded with paintings and furniture that have remained more or less in their original positions since the donor's death in 1934. The source of the museum's obsessive ostentation was the Baronne Ephrussi, scion of the Rothschilds, who scoured Europe in pursuit of her treasures.
- **Fondation Maeght,** St-Paul-de-Vence. Established as a showcase for modern art by 20th-century collectors Aimé and Marguerite Maeght, this museum is an avant-garde compendium of works by Giacometti, Chagall, Braque, Miró, Matisse, and Barbara Hepworth. Built on many levels in a design by fabled architect José Luís Sert, it boasts glass walls that allow views over the surrounding ancient arid landscapes of Provence.

8 The Best Cathedrals

- **Notre-Dame de Paris.** This is a triumph of medieval French architecture, its gray stone walls symbolizing the power of Paris in the Middle Ages and the country that eventually radiated outward from the island on which it sits. Begun in 1163, Notre-Dame is the cathedral of the nation. It's especially dazzling in the early morning and at sunset, when its image is reflected in the Seine.
- **Notre-Dame de Chartres.** No less a talent than Rodin declared that the cathedral of Chartres was a French acropolis. The site it occupies was considered holy by both the prehistoric Druids and the ancient Romans. One of the first High Gothic cathedrals, the first to use flying buttresses, Chartres is the third-largest cathedral in the world (after St. Peter's in Rome and Canterbury in England). It also contains what might be the finest stained-glass windows in history, more than 3,000 square yards of glass whose vivid hues and patterns of light are truly mystical.

Impressions

All the steam in the world could not, like the Virgin, build Chartres.
                    —Henry Adams, *The Education of Henry Adams* (1906)

- **Notre-Dame de Rouen.** Consecrated in 1063 and rebuilt after a fire in 1200, this cathedral was immortalized in the late 19th century when Monet spent hours painting a series of moody impressions of the facade at various times of day. Some sections of the cathedral are masterpieces of the flamboyant gothic style; others are plainer though equally dignified.
- **Notre-Dame de Reims.** One of France's first Christian bishops, St. Remi, baptized the pagan king of the Franks, Clovis, on this site in 496, thereby elevating Reims to one of the holiest sites in northern Europe. The cathedral celebrating that event was conceived as a religious sanctuary where the French kings would be anointed and was suitably large, spectacular, and (in our eyes) rather cold. The coronation of every king between 1137 and 1825 was celebrated here. Damaged by World War I bombings, the cathedral was largely restored by American donations during the 1920s and 1930s.
- **Notre-Dame de Strasbourg.** One of the largest buildings in the Christian world, this is also one of the most architecturally harmonious gothic cathedrals of the Middle Ages. Built of russet-colored stone between 1176 and 1439, it's a perfect symbol of Alsatian pride and one of our favorite cathedrals. The monument's 16th-century astrological clock is a showstopper, gathering crowds daily for its 12:30pm exhibition of allegorical figures from myth and fable.

9 The Best Vineyards & Wineries

One of the best-respected sources for information about French wines is the **CIDD (Centre d'Information, de Documentation, et de Dégustation)**, 45 rue Liancourt, 75014 Paris (☎ 1/43-27-67-21; fax 1/43-20-84-00). Throughout the year this self-funded school, organized in 1982, presents about a dozen courses addressing all aspects of wine tasting, producing, buying, and merchandising. Conducted in French and English, they're tailored to wine merchants, wine growers, and restaurant-industry professionals. The organization is a gold mine of information for anyone anticipating a tour of the vineyards.

- **Champagne Taittinger,** 9 place St-Nicaise, 51100 Reims (☎ 26-85-45-35; fax 26-82-30-13). Taittinger is a *grand marque* of French champagne, one of the few whose ownership is controlled by members of the family that founded it in 1930. It's one of the most visitor-friendly of the champagne houses. The romanesque cellars were dug from the site of Gallo-Roman chalk mines between the 4th and 13th centuries. Tours last about an hour, including a film presentation, a guided cellar tour, and a surprisingly rich set of anecdotes about Reims, the champagne-making process, and Taittinger family lore. Tours cost 18 F ($3.40) and are conducted Monday to Friday from 9:30am to noon and 2 to 4:30pm, Saturday and Sunday from 9 to 11am and 2 to 5pm. There are no weekend tours during January and February.
- **Société Antonin Rodet,** 71640 Mercurey (☎ 85-46-22-22). This distinctive vineyard is one of the most influential in central France. Established in 1875, it includes more than 320 acres of prestigious Burgundy vineyards, most scattered over four locations in the district. There are prominent signs posted throughout Mercurey. The company's *centre de dégustation* is in the turn-of-the-century house once occupied by the founder. Glasses of its famous wines are offered free, along with discourses on the products aging in the 600-year-old

Bordeaux is . . . dedicated to the worship of Bacchus in the most discreet form.
—Henry James, *A Little Tour of France* (1882)

cellars. Two miles away, the Château Féodale de Rully (☎ 85-87-20-42), a 12th-century stronghold of the comtes de Ternay, can be visited from June to September. Advance appointments are necessary; although groups of visitors are preferred, exceptions are sometimes made for individuals. The cost is 25 F ($4.75) per person.

- **Domaines Schlumberger,** 100 rue Théodore-Deck (BP 40), 68500 Guebwiller (☎ 89-74-27-00). These vineyards are open for public visits Monday to Friday from 8am to noon and 2 to 5pm (closed the first two weeks of August). The cellars are an unusual combination of early 19th-century brickwork and modern stainless steel, but a visit will go far in enhancing your understanding of the subtle differences between rieslings, gewürtztraminers, muscats, silvaners, and the pinots (blancs, gris, and noir) produced with enduring success by the Schlumberger vineyards.

- **Couly-Dutheil,** 12 rue Diderot, 37500 Chinon (☎ 47-93-05-84). This company's cellars are suitably medieval, many carved into the rock undulating through the area's forests. Most of this company's production involves Chinon wines (mostly reds), though two that they're justifiably proud of are Borgeuil and St-Nicolas de Borgeuil, whose popularity in the North American market has grown stronger in recent years. Tours of the *caves* and a *dégustation des vins* require an advance phone call and cost around 20 F ($3.80) per person. Visits are usually conducted Monday to Friday from 8am to noon and 1:45 to 5:45pm.

- **The wine-growing region around Bordeaux.** This region is among the most glamorous in France, with a strong English influence thanks to centuries of wine buying from London- and Bristol-based dealers. One of the region's prestigious growers is Société Duboscq, Château Haut-Marbuzet, 33180 St-Estephe (☎ 56-59-30-54), which welcomes visitors daily from 9am to noon and 2 to 6pm. Free visits to the cellars are followed by a free *dégustation des vins* of whatever of the company's products a client requests. A relative newcomer whose prestige has grown rapidly, Duboscq offers excellent opportunities for studying the ancient fermentation process in its modern poured-concrete and stainless-steel forms. No appointments are necessary for the tours and visits.

10 The Best Hotels

- **Grand Hôtel du Cap-Ferrat,** St-Jean-Cap-Ferrat. A destination in its own right, the Grand Hôtel occupies 14 prime acres on one of the world's most exclusive peninsulas. It's housed in a belle époque "palace" and since the turn of the century has been the temporary home for royals, aristocrats, and wealthy wannabes.

- **Hôtel du Cap–Eden Roc,** Cap d'Antibes. Built during the grand Second Empire and set on 22 acres of splendidly landscaped gardens, this hotel is one of Europe's most legendary. Swimmers will revel in a pool blasted from the dark rock of the mythically glamorous coastline of Cap d'Antibes.

- **Trianon Palace,** Versailles. Built around 1900, with grounds abutting Louis XIV's gardens at Versailles, this hotel was the site of the conference that crafted the Treaty of Versailles ending World War I. Edward VIII and Wallis Simpson selected this spot for their honeymoon. Today it's easy to confuse the opulence of the place with that of the Grand Trianon in the nearby park.
- **Le Ritz,** Paris. This hotel occupies a palace overlooking the octagonal borders of one of the most aesthetically perfect plazas in France: place Vendôme. The decor is pure *ancien régime*. Marcel Proust wrote parts of *Remembrance of Things Past* in an apartment here, and Georges-Auguste Escoffier perfected many of his recipes in its kitchens.
- **Hôtel de Crillon,** Paris. This hotel's majestic exterior was designed by 18th-century architect Jacques-Ange Gabriel and forms part of the symmetrical backdrop for place de la Concorde. The decor encompasses the reigns of Cardinal Richelieu and Marie Antoinette, and nearly every surface is polished weekly by a battalion of well-trained attendants.
- **Hôtel Le Prieuré,** Villeneuve-lèz-Avignon. Ivy entwines around the 14th-century stone facade of this place in Provence, adjacent to a village church. The furnishings evoke a carefully maintained country estate: rustic, idiosyncratic, and old-fashioned. Built for a cardinal and enlarged in the 1980s with a modern annex, the hotel provides charming accommodations not as stratospherically expensive as those at the other hotels on this list.
- **Hôtel du Palais,** Biarritz. Delectably beautiful, this place was built in 1845 as a pink-walled summer palace for Napoléon III and his empress, Eugénie. Adept at housing such guests as Edward VII of England, Alfonso XIII of Spain, and Edward VIII, duke of Windsor, the hotel is a belle époque fantasy.
- **Hôtel Negresco,** Nice. Built in 1913 as a layered wedding cake in the château style, the Negresco has embraced the holiday needs of some of the Edwardian age's most respected and most notorious figures. Among them was actress Lillie Langtry, the long-term mistress of Britain's Edward VII. After her fall from grace, she sat in the Negresco's lobby, swathed in veils, refusing to utter a word. Following tasteful renovations, the hotel is better now than it was even during its Jazz Age heyday.
- **Hôtel du Donjon,** Carcassonne. The town that is home to this hotel is considered one of France's most perfect examples of a medieval fortified site. Built into its solid bulwarks is this small-scale hotel whose luxurious furnishings provide a stunning contrast to their crude stone shell. A stay here truly allows you personal contact with a site that often provoked bloody battles between medieval armies.
- **Ostellerie du Vieux-Pérouges,** Pérouges. This hotel, often described as a museum of the 13th century, is one of the most significant in central France. Composed of a group of much-restored 13th-century buildings, with low ceilings and thick walls, it vividly evokes the France of another day.

11 The Best Restaurants

- **Joël Robuchon,** Paris. Culinary artists rank him in the same league as Escoffier and cite his gastronomic flair (and basic good sense) as one of France's most brilliant products. His work blends the excesses of *nouvelle cuisine* with the staid tenets of *cuisine bourgeoise*. The happy result he helped develop—

cuisine moderne—makes ample use of flavoring from meat, fish, and vegetable stocks.

• **Taillevent,** Paris. Dining here is still the social and gastronomic high point of a Paris visit. Its premises (an antique house near the Arc de Triomphe laden with flowers and reminders of the *ancien régime*) are suitably grand and its cuisine appropriately stylish to the Jackie O lookalikes who sometimes dine here.

• **Boyer-les-Crayères,** Reims. This restaurant's setting is a lavish but dignified château with soaring ceilings and a flawless French Empire decor. Built in 1904 as the home of the Pommery family (of champagne fortune) and surrounded by a 14-acre park, it's maintained by an impeccably trained staff who appreciate the nuances of elaborate service rituals. Guests can retire directly to their overnight accommodations after consuming a bottle or two of the region's famous bubbly.

• **L'Auberge de l'Ill,** near Colmar. After a meal here you'll understand why France and Germany fought so bitterly for control of Alsace. Set amid well-tended farmland on the edge of the River Ill, this half-timbered manor house presents an almost-idyllic setting. The food and wine served are rich, lush, and firmly rooted in the vineyards surrounding the place.

• **Auberge du Père Bise,** Talloires. A mysterious alchemy eventually transformed what was a simple lakeside chalet into an illustrious restaurant. Set beside Lac d'Annecy in eastern France, it's outfitted like the prosperous provincial home of local gentry yet serves sublimely elegant food favored by many generations of such clients as the Rothschilds.

• **A la Côte St-Jacques,** Joigny. On the edge of Burgundy, beside the River Yonne, this is the quintessential *restaurant avec chambres.* Indulge your taste for supremely well prepared food and wine, then totter off to one of about a dozen carefully furnished guest rooms scattered over several buildings in this historic compound. One of our favorite dishes is cassolette of morels and frogs' legs, especially sublime when consumed with a half bottle of fine red burgundy.

• **Espérance,** Vézelay. Housed in an antique farmhouse at the base of a hill (La Colline de Vézelay) considered a holy site for thousands of years, Espérance is run by one of Europe's most famous chefs, Marc Meneau, and his wife, Françoise. The place combines country comforts with world-class sophistication.

• **Paul Bocuse,** Collonges-au-Mont-d'Or, near Lyon. This dining citadel's namesake was known as the *enfant terrible* of French gastronomy throughout most of his youth. Today Paul Bocuse is the world's most famous living chef, catering to Europe's hardest-to-please customers. Beware of saying anything gastronomically gauche—superb as it is, the staff judges its clientele with the same microscopic zeal that the clientele uses to judge the legendary food.

• **Hôtel des Frères-Troisgros,** Roanne. The setting here is the dining room of a once-nondescript hotel near a Loire Valley railway terminus. The cuisine, however, is a joyfully lush celebration of the agrarian bounty of France. Mingling

specialties from all the regions, it attracts diners from as far away as Paris and Brussels. Years after they dine here, many people speak reverently of their meal.
- **Le Moulin de Mougins,** Mougins. Occupying a 16th-century olive mill in a Provence pine forest, this restaurant is the creation of chef Roger Vergé, probably the most sophisticated media genius in the French culinary world.

12 The Best Shopping

- **Porcelain & Stoneware.** For delicate porcelains, head for Limoges (in the Limousin). We prefer the more robust stoneware of Quimper (in Brittany) and Lunéville (in Lorraine). In each of those towns, dozens of outlets sell every imaginable form of plate, cup, saucer, and porringer, painted in the strong, bright colors of their respective manufacturers' provincial origins. If driving to the French provinces doesn't suit your itinerary, head for rue de Paradis in Paris.
- **Perfumes.** Grasse (in Provence) is known for its perfume distilleries and rows of boutiques where *flacons* of scent, freshly distilled from tons of pressed roses and wildflowers, are sold. In Paris try any of the perfume outlets recommended in Chapter 8, where intensely marketed name brands of the scents that keep the French smelling sweet are sold, sometimes at discounts.
- **Wines & Liqueurs.** Searching out unusual vintages from small vintners is great fun. Any wine outlet in France inventories an overwhelming choice of wines from Bordeaux, Burgundy, Alsace, the Rhône valley, and Champagne. You'll find lots of sales outlets for exotic burgundy in and around Beaune, Brouilland, Montbard, and Gevrey-Chambertin, and any wine store in Dijon will be amply stocked. If bubbly is your thing, head for Epernay and Reims, where all sorts of champagne are sold at good prices. Alsace, Provence, and the Bordeaux region retain thousands of cases of their local vintages for sale (at favorable prices). Bottles of unusual cognacs, often with labels scrawled in the shaky script of an old vintner, are for sale in out-of-the-way corners throughout southwestern France. And if after-dinner liqueurs are your thing, you'll find bottles of Calvados (the region's famous apple-based liqueur) everywhere in Normandy.
- **Kitchenware.** Don't be hasty in acquiring any of the new-fangled machines you'll see being promoted, because their electricity requirements are *not* compatible with your household electricity in North America. The ubiquitous copper-lined casseroles and thick-walled roasters you'll see, however, might last a lifetime once you recover from the initial shock of their prices. If you happen to be touring Normandy and want to pick up some of the best copper-lined saucepans available, head for the hamlet of Villedieu-les-Poêles, 22 miles south of St-Lô. Copper-lined cookware has been manufactured here since the 1700s, and dozens of stores along the main street sell huge amounts of the stuff every year.
- **Crystal.** A worthy collection of multifaceted lead crystal is one of the status symbols of modern France. To learn about how it's manufactured, head for the factories of Baccarat, in eastern France, where a local museum illustrates the glass-making process. For a wide choice of purchasing options, go to rue de Paradis in central Paris, where a vast array of the shimmering product can be bought, wrapped, and shipped anywhere.

2 | Celebrating the Bounty of France

France remains one of the world's most hyped, talked about, and written about destinations. It can inspire a masterpiece—and has on countless occasions. Even the cantankerous James McNeill Whistler would allow his masterpiece, a portrait of his mother, to hang in no other city save Paris.

Although not large by North American standards (about the size of the U.S. state of Texas or about the size of Britain and the re-united Germany combined), France is densely packed with attractions. Even better, it's permeated with style and known for its *joie de vivre*.

During the Middle Ages, France's monastic traditions radiated from such points as Paris and Cluny to affect workaday and ecclesiastical cultures from the western tip of Iberia to the eastern edge of Europe. France claims credit for the development of gothic architecture and the cathedrals that are legacies of soaring stone for future generations. Everything from palaces to subway stations has drawn at least some inspiration from designs inaugurated here. However, despite the thrilling architectural monuments peppering the country's landscapes, it would be wrong to assume that the culture's main contribution to the world is derived from stone, mortar, stained glass, and gilt. Its contributions to painting, literature, cuisine, fashion, and *savoir-faire* are staggering.

When other parts of Europe were slumbering through the Dark Ages, Provence was alive with creativity as Provençal poetry evolved into a truly lyrical, evocative, and (in some cases) erotic verse form. Despite the frequent absences of its monarchs, who sequestered themselves with their entourages in remote Loire Valley châteaux, Renaissance Paris developed into one of Europe's most cosmopolitan cities, embellishing itself with majestic buildings and sculpture.

The passionate French tradition of scholarship helped build Europe's university system, synthesized the modern world's interpretation of human rights, helped topple one of the most powerful monarchies of all time, and justified the role of a postrevolutionary emperor (Napoléon) as conqueror of most of Europe.

As for style, it has always been foolhardy to try to compete (on their terms) with the French. The theatrical backdrops of the sometimes-silly Gallic monarchs have been interpreted by latter-day aesthetes as history's crowning achievement when it comes to conspicuous displays of wealth and prestige.

In politics and ideology, France has always been a leader: Fueled by Enlightenment writings, whose most articulate voices were French, the 1789 Revolution toppled Europe's most deeply entrenched regime and cracked the foundations of dozens of other governments. After a period of murky maneuverings by diverse coalitions of strange bedfellows, postrevolutionary Paris became a magnet for the greatest talents of the 19th and early 20th centuries in many fields of endeavor.

Newcomers have commented (sometimes adversely) on the cultural arrogance of the French. But despite its linguistic and cultural rigidity, France has received more immigrants and political exiles than any other European country. (Until recent strains overtaxed the system, newcomers' talents and virtues were more or less gracefully assimilated.) Part of this might derive from France's status, per square kilometer, as one of Europe's least densely populated nations, part of it from the tendency of the French to *laissez-faire des autres* until their actions become either dangerous or obnoxious, not necessarily in that order.

This guidebook represents our effort to introduce first-time visitors to France's subtle pleasures and—if possible—to open new doors to those who might already have spent time here. We've set for ourselves the formidable task of seeking out France at its finest and condensing that information so you can access it easily. But the best need not always be the most expensive or the most chic or widely publicized. Our ultimate aim—beyond that of familiarizing you with France's cultural banquet—is to stretch your dollar power . . . to reveal that you need not always pay scalpers' prices for memorable charm, top-grade comfort, or gourmet food.

1 The Regions in Brief

Though France covers only 212,741 square miles, no other country concentrates such a fabulous diversity of sights and scenery into so compact an area. France encompasses each of the natural characteristics that make up Europe: the north's flat, fertile lands; the central Loire Valley's rolling green hills; the east's snowcapped alpine ranges; the southwest's towering Pyrénées; the Massif Central's plateaux and rock outcroppings; and the southeast's lushly semitropical Mediterranean coast. And even more noteworthy than geography are the strong cultural and historic differences defining each region.

And all these contrasts beckon within easy traveling range. The train trip from Paris is just four hours to Alsace, five to the Alps, seven to the Pyrénées, and eight to the Côte d'Azur. France's National Railroads (SNCF) operate one of the

Impressions

I tried to think it out. Why did Paris still draw us to its fascination, why did it draw those who felt themselves creative—talent or no talent? Why had it been, since Franklin, that all of us felt that we were freer there than elsewhere? Why did art, literature, and sex, and the feeding and drinking seem more genuine there? Generations of Americans had run a whole gamut of desires, hopes in Paris—all so opposite to those they had found at home, on the farm, in the city.

—Stephen Longstreet, *We All Went to Paris* (1972)

finest lines in the world, with impressively fast service to and from Paris (though trains tend to crawl on routes unconnected with the capital).

You'll find some 44,000 miles of roadway at your disposal, most in good condition for fast long-distance driving. *Tip:* Try not to stick to the Route Nationale network all the time. Nearly all France's scenic splendors lie along secondary roads, and what you'll lose in mileage you'll more than make up for in enjoyment.

A "grand tour" of France is nearly impossible for the average visitor. It would take you at least two weeks to tour each major province. You're going to be faced with hard choices about where to go given your time limit, interests, and budget. With this in mind, we've summarized the highlights of each region.

THE ILE DE FRANCE   The Ile de France is an island only in the sense that its boundaries (following approximately a 50-mile radius from the center of Paris) are delineated by rivers with such odd-sounding names as Essonne, Epte, Aisne, Eure, and Ourcq, plus a handful of canals. It was from this temperate basin that the boundaries of France radiated to encompass the modern nation. Though this region's spectacular attractions include Versailles, Fontainebleau, and Chartres, it also incorporates endless waves of dreary suburbs. Despite creeping industrialization, pockets of verdant charm remain, including the forests of Rambouillet and Fontainebleau and the artist's hamlet of Barbizon.

THE LOIRE VALLEY   This area includes two ancient provinces, Touraine (centered around Tours) and Anjou (centered around Angers)—both ringed with the spires, turrets, and pepper-pot chimneys of magnificent Renaissance châteaux. Irrigated by the waters of the longest river in France, the Loire, and its many tributaries, this region produces many superb reasonably priced wines.

NORMANDY   This region will be forever be linked to the 1944 D-Day invasion. Normandy boasts 372 miles of coastline and a firmly entrenched maritime tradition. Normandy is a popular weekend getaway from Paris, and many glamorous hotels and restaurants thrive here, especially around the belle époque casino town of Deauville. This area has hundreds of half-timbered houses reminiscent of medieval England, such charming seaports as Trouville, and such mighty ports as Le Havre, set where the Seine flows into the English Channel. Normandy's great abbeys and churches include Rouen cathedral in the "city of one hundred spires," the abbey of Jumièges, and medieval Bayeux. Some readers of past editions of this guide have considered their visit to the D-Day beaches the most emotionally worthwhile part of their trip to France.

BRITTANY   Jutting out into the Atlantic, the westernmost (and one of the poorest) regions of France is known for its rocky coastlines, Celtic roots, frequent rains, and ancient dialect akin to the Gaelic tongues of Wales and Ireland. For many years isolated and shunted aside from the development projects that raised the standard of living of other parts of the country, the province is amazingly folkloric. Brittany has one of the most sought-after seacoasts in France (rivaled only by the Côte d'Azur), partly because of its sandy beaches, high cliffs, and relatively modest prices (by French standards). Highlights of the region include Carnac (home to a dense concentration of ancient Celtic dolmens and burial mounds) and such atmospheric fishing ports as Quimper, Quiberon, Quimperlé, and Concarneau. The region's most sophisticated resort, La Baule, lies near some of southern Brittany's best beaches.

The Regions of France

ENGLAND
English Channel
Strait of Dover
BELGIUM
Calais
Boulogne
Lille
Arras
THE ARDENNES
LUXEMBOURG
GERMANY
Cherbourg
Le Havre
Amiens
Rouen
ÎLE DE FRANCE
Reims
Metz
Golfe de Saint-Malo
Caen
Versailles
PARIS
Marne
ALSACE-LORRAINE
Nancy
Strasbourg
Brest
Quimper
BRITTANY
NORMANDY
Seine
CHAMPAGNE
Troyes
Colmar
Rennes
Chartres
LOIRE VALLEY
Le Mans
Orléans
BURGUNDY
Mulhouse
Belle-Île
St-Nazaire
Angers
Nantes
Loire
Tours
Indre
Bourges
Yonne
Dijon
Besançon
SWITZERLAND
ATLANTIC
OCEAN
La Rochelle
Île d'Oléron
Poitiers
Loire
Saône
Lake Geneva
Bay of Biscay
Gironde
Limoges
Angoulême
Périgueux
Clermont-Ferrand
Vichy
Lyon
Rhône
St-Étienne
RHÔNE VALLEY
Annecy
Mont Blanc
Bordeaux
Dordogne
MASSIF CENTRAL
Grenoble
FRENCH ALPS
ITALY
Golfe de Gascogne
THE DORDOGNE & PÉRIGORD
BORDEAUX & THE ATLANTIC COAST
Lot
Agen
Cahors
Montauban
Garonne
Valence
Rhône
Isère
Biarritz
Pau
BASQUE COUNTRY
Lourdes
Toulouse
Albi
Tarn
Montauban
Nîmes
Avignon
Durance
PROVENCE
Nice
MONACO
Cannes
Carcassonne
LANGUEDOC/ROUSSILLON
Montpellier
Marseille
FRENCH RIVIERA
Toulon
Golfe du Lion
MEDITERRANEAN SEA
ANDORRA
SPAIN

CORSICA
Bastia
Calvi
Corte
Golo
Ajaccio
Propriano
Sartène
Porto-Vecchio
Bonifacio

0   100 mi.
     160 km
N

1398

REIMS & CHAMPAGNE   Every French monarch since A.D. 496 has legitimatized his rule with a coronation at Reims. Much of Merovingian and Carolingian France's history has revolved around this holy site and the fertile hills ringing it. Joan of Arc was burned at the stake thanks partly to her efforts to lead her dauphin through enemy lines to his coronation at Reims. Lying directly in the path of any invader wishing to occupy Paris, both Reims and the fertile Champagne district have been awash in more blood than any other region in France. Famous Champagne battle sites that still evoke shudders from residents include the Somme and Marne (World War I). There are industrial sites concentrated among patches of verdant forest and the steep sides of valleys sheathed in vineyards. The 78-mile road from Reims to Vertus takes in a trio of wine-growing regions that produce 80% of the bubbly used for celebrations around the world.

THE ARDENNES & NORTHERN BEACHES   France's northern region is often neglected by North Americans. In summer, French families arrive by the thousands to visit such Channel beach resorts as Le Touquet–Paris-Plage. Comprising the medieval provinces of Picardy and Artois, this district is heavily industrialized and (like neighboring Champagne) has always been horribly wartorn. The region's best-known port, Calais, was a bitterly contested English stronghold on the French mainland for hundreds of years. Ironically, Calais functions today as the port of disembarkation for the ferryboats, hydrofoils, and Channel Tunnel arrivals from Britain. Notre-Dame Cathedral in Amiens, medieval capital of Picardy, is considered a treasure, with a 140-foot-high nave—the highest in France.

ALSACE-LORRAINE & THE VOSGES   Between Germany and the forests of the Vosges is the most Teutonic of France's provinces: Alsace, with cosmopolitan Strasbourg as capital. Celebrated for its cuisine, particularly foie gras and choucroute (sauerkraut), this area is home to villages whose half-timbered designs evoke the Black Forest at its most charming and old-fashioned. Travel the Route de Vin (Wine Road) and visit such historic towns as Colmar, Riquewihr, and Illhaeusern, all famous to Europe's gastronomes. Lorraine, birthplace of Joan of Arc and site of the industrial center of Mulhouse, witnessed countless bloody battles during the world wars. Its capital, Nancy, is proud guardian of a flawlessly proportioned 18th-century plaza—place Stanislaus. The much-eroded peaks of the Vosges forest, the closest to a wilderness left in France, make for a rewarding hiking district.

THE FRENCH ALPS   This area's resorts rival those of neighboring Switzerland and contain some incredible scenery—snowcapped peaks, glaciers, and alpine lakes. Chamonix is a world-famous ski resort facing Mont Blanc, Western Europe's highest mountain. Courchevel and Megève are more chic, though. During summer in the Alps you can enjoy such spa resorts as Evian and the calm and restful 19th-century resorts ringing Lake Geneva.

BURGUNDY   Few trips will prove as rewarding as a five-day trek through Burgundy. Great wines and vineyards and splendid old cities like Dijon make this a visitor's mecca. Besides being famous for its renowned cuisine (boeuf and escargots à la bourguignonne, for example), the district contains a series of wine hamlets along the Côte d'Or whose names (Mercurey, Beaune, Puligny-Montrachet, Vougeot, and Nuits-St-Georges, among others) excite the salivary glands of well-heeled oenophiles.

LYON & THE UPPER RHONE VALLEY   A fertile area of alpine foothills and sloping valleys in eastern and southeastern France, the upper Rhône Valley ranges from the cosmopolitan French suburbs of the Swiss city of Geneva to the northern borders of Provence. The district is thoroughly French, unflinchingly bourgeois, and dedicated to preserving the gastronomic and cultural traditions that have produced some of the most celebrated chefs in French history.

Only two hours by train from Paris, the region's cultural centerpiece, Lyon, is France's "second city." North of here, visitors travel the Beaujolais trail or head for Bresse's ancient capital, Bourg-en-Bresse, a gastronomic center said to produce the finest poultry in the world. The Rhône Valley can be explored en route from northern climes to Provence and the south. Try to visit the little medieval villages of Pérouges and Vienne, 17 miles south of Lyon, the latter known for its Roman ruins.

THE MASSIF CENTRAL   The rugged heartland of south-central France, this underpopulated district contains ancient cities, unspoiled scenery, and an abundance of black lava that comprises much of the area's building material. According to world-weary Parisians, the Massif Central is provincial with a vengeance—and the locals work hard to keep it that way. The largest cities here are historic Clermont-Ferrand and Limoges—the medieval capitals of the provinces of the Auvergne and the Limousin, respectively. Bourges, a gateway to the region and once capital of Aquitaine, has a beautiful gothic cathedral.

THE DORDOGNE & PERIGORD   The land of foie gras and truffles is also the site of some of the oldest prehistoric settlements in Europe. In Périgord, traces of Cro-Magnon settlements are evidenced by the cave paintings at Les Eyzies. Dordogne is the second-largest *département* and includes parts of the old provinces of Limousin and Quercy. Some of France's most unusual châteaux were built in the valley of the Dordogne during the early Middle Ages. The region is, unfortunately, no longer undiscovered, as retirees from abroad (often England) have moved into the elegant stone manor houses dotting the banks of the many rivers. For cycling or pursuing gastronomic pleasure, the region is among the most fashionable in the country. Tourist highlights are the ancient towns whose names are spelled with the archaic orthography of medieval France: Périgueux, Les Eyzies-de-Tayac, Sarlat-le-Canéda, Beynac-et-Cazenac, and Souillac.

BORDEAUX & THE ATLANTIC COAST   Flat, fertile, and frequently ignored by North Americans, this region incorporates towns pivotal in French history (Saintes, Poitiers, Angoulême, and La Rochelle) and wine- and liquor-producing villages (Cognac, Margaux, St-Emilion, and Sauternes) whose names are celebrated around the world. Bordeaux itself, the district's largest city, has an economy firmly based on wine merchandising and contains a truly grand accumulation of l8th-century architecture.

BASQUE COUNTRY & THE PYRENEES   Since prehistoric times the rugged Pyrénées have formed a natural boundary between France and Spain. Sheltered within the mountain valleys flourished one of Europe's most unusual cultures: the Basques. In the 19th century, resorts like Biarritz and St-Jean-de-Luz attracted the French aristocracy—Empress Eugénie's palace at Biarritz is now a celebrated hotel. The Parc National des Pyrénées is suitably crisscrossed with panoramic hiking trails, and four million faithful Catholics find much of interest every year in the pilgrimage city of Lourdes. In the isolated villages and towns of the Pyrénées, the old folkloric traditions, strongly permeated with Spanish influences, continue to thrive.

LANGUEDOC, ROUSSILLON & THE CAMARGUE   Languedoc is less chic but less frenetic than Provence, enjoying fewer visitors and (at least in the past) lower prices. Roussillon is the rock-strewn arid French answer to ancient Catalonia, just across the Spanish border. The Camargue is the name given to the steaming marshy delta formed by two arms of the Rhône River. Rich in bird life, it's famous for its flat expanses of tough grasses and for such fortified medieval sites as Aigues-Mortes. Also appealing are Auch, capital of Gascony; Toulouse, bustling pink capital of Languedoc; and the "red city" of Albi, birthplace of Toulouse-Lautrec. Carcassonne, a marvelously preserved walled city with fortifications begun around A.D. 500, is the region's sightseeing highlight.

PROVENCE   One of France's most fabled regions flanks the Alps and the Italian border along its eastern end and incorporates a host of sites the rich and famous have long frequented. Premier tourist destinations include Aix-en-Provence, associated with Cézanne; Arles, "the soul of Provence," captured so brilliantly by van Gogh; Avignon, 14th-century capital of Christendom during the papal schism; and Marseille, a port city established by the ancient Phoenicians (in some ways more North African than French). Special Provence gems are the small villages, such as Les Baux, Gordes, and St-Rémy-de-Provence, birthplace of Nostradamus. The strip of glittering coastal towns along Provence's southern edge is known as the Côte d'Azur (the French Riviera).

THE FRENCH RIVIERA   The fabled gold-plated Côte d'Azur has become hideously overbuilt and spoiled by tourism. Even so, the names of its resorts still evoke glamour and excitement: Cannes, Monaco, St-Tropez, Cap d'Antibes, St-Jean-Cap-Ferrat. July and August are the most crowded, but spring and fall can be a delight. There are some sandy beaches, but many are rocky or pebbly. Topless bathing is common, especially in St-Tropez, and some of the restaurants there are fabled citadels of conspicuous consumption. This is not just a place for sun and fun, though—dozens of artists and their patrons have littered the landscape with world-class galleries and art museums.

CORSICA   The third-largest island in the Mediterranean, more Italian than French, Corsica is arid and rocky, far removed from the mainstream of French life. It's the home of a fervently devoted nationalist movement that rejects the authority of Paris and preaches the virtues of self-determination and is infamous for some of the most vicious and enduring vendettas in Mediterranean history. Few North Americans visit the island. The largest port is Bastia; Ajaccio, birthplace of Napoléon, is the capital. The real charm, though, lies in its mountains and rock-built coastal villages, many of which appear not to have changed much since the turn of the century.

2 France Today

It seems as if modern France is being perpetually punished for whatever long-dissipated rewards it extracted from its overseas colonies. In 1986, partly as a reflection of smoldering ethnic tensions, the National Front (FN) emerged with an unashamedly racist platform. Headed by Jean-Marie Le Pen (whose slogan "La France pour les français" was intended as a protest against Arab, black African, and Third World immigration), the movement gained a noteworthy 10% of the popular vote and major publicity around Europe. Not all Le Pen's complaints are unjustified: French unemployment remains at a anxiety-inducing 12%.

France retains a bitter legacy of revolutions in Indochina and Algeria. Foremost among these are the problems caused by, and the reactionary backlash against, hundreds of thousands of Arabs who've transformed the urban landscape. Even Edouard Balladur, an aristocratic politician whose support derives mostly from the comfortable side of the income curve, cites modern-day France as "a raw and difficult society in which too many people have lost out." The "raw deal" of modern French life is felt especially hard by the thousands of North African immigrants whose presence in slums from Lille to Marseille has caused some of the greatest domestic strife in recent French memory.

Examples of ethnic conflicts are obvious wherever you look. In 1994, French police arrested 95 Muslim radicals whom Interior Minister Charles Pasqua cited as members of support networks that Algeria-based fundamentalist guerrillas are forming in Europe and North America. Tensions between France and the United States have stemmed from this, as the French accuse Americans of harboring guerrillas who've contributed to the deaths of more than 11,000. Pasqua has publicly stated his fears that the Algerian revolt could spread to France's large Algerian community, fanned by the flames of growing adherence to fundamentalist Muslim doctrines. Contributing to the rancor are the continuing dissatisfaction with rule from Paris of Corsica and, to a lesser extent, Brittany.

All, however, is not gloom and doom on France's horizon. In 1988, Edith Cresson was elected the first female premier, and she governed for four years before stepping down, the subject of mixed reviews. (One of the many controversies during her term involved her public statement that most Englishmen were closet gays, which evoked the immediate wrath of London's tabloid press on "Madame Frog.")

Other women have been equally successful at breaking down the establishment's gender barriers. In the 1980s, Marguerite Yourcenar was elected to the Académie Française, and in 1995, after aggressive campaigning by women's-rights groups, Marie Curie's ashes were reinterred in the Panthéon, which hitherto had been reserved exclusively for the "great men" of France.

Like a beacon guiding pilgrims through a treacherous swamp, the enduring belief in the superiority of their culture can do much to comfort French citizens in their moments of doubt. In keeping with the advances in its own technologies, France has permeated its ancient landscapes with a radical new look: This includes the construction of high-speed RER trains, space rockets, nuclear reactors, and some of the most dramatic modern architecture in Europe. Many of these glittering urban monuments are tastefully isolated from districts of gothic or neoclassical grandeur; others, such as I. M. Pei's glass pyramid rising from the Louvre's Cour Carrée in Paris, are deliberately superimposed on venerated architecture.

Regardless of how far modern France advances with its new ethics, perspectives, and realities, it remains firmly committed to the rich culture and enduring traditions on which its modern-day priorities are based.

French & the Creeping English Influx

Despite the allure of the French language, its critics maintain that since the nation's unification, French has been wielded as a political weapon, an instrument of cultural coercion, and a vehicle for the exclusion of free enterprise.

Some of its syntactical rigidity derives from Louis XIV's Académie Française, an august body whose goal was codifying the rules of French syntax, grammar, and vocabulary. Its efforts linguistically unified a disparate group of duchys and provinces and helped establish the French language as one of the most splendid on earth. But all these efforts weren't done only for cultural glory: When the Académie was formed, the greatest perceived threat to French unity was the widespread use of dialects like Provençale, Breton, Alsatian, and Basque. As a sign of the Académie's success, these dialects are weaker today than at any other time in their histories.

Recently, however, French-speaking purists have become enraged. The newest assault is from North America, and the language is youthful, international, and well acquainted with the often-awkward phrases needed to describe scientific and computer-related jargon in French. In recent speeches delivered to an audience in Armenia, French Culture Minister Jacques Toubon condemned the "savage Americanization which is destroying the basis of national culture in many nations of the former Soviet bloc." Toubon has reason to be afraid: France has lost the global war for linguistic superiority, and in a nation increasingly awash with Coca-Cola, Levi's, McDonald's, and American-derived entertainment, the linguistic purity and cultural hegemony of France is being eroded every minute.

Ninety percent of French citizens rally to the newest call to arms: Since 1976, a "language law" has imposed stiff fines ($10,000—or imprisonment in some cases) on anyone thoughtless enough to phrase a classified ad, newspaper announcement, or billboard using a syntax other than that endorsed by the Académie Française. Though the widespread use of Arabic is perceived as a threat, a greater fear is the creeping influx of English-language phrases engendered by the computer, electronics, entertainment, and publishing industries.

Advocates of linguistic controls claim they want to protect a national treasure. Such respected actors as Gérard Depardieu and Jeanne Moreau have voiced support of the anti-English laws. The war is fueled, however, by well-paid lobbyists from France's entertainment industry, for whom the war is a market-share struggle. If expressions of American popular culture are suppressed, the field will be open for French entrepreneurs.

Under Toubon (called "Mr. All-Good" by his enemies), France maintains carefully policed quotas for the presentation of U.S. movies and TV shows and—even more disastrously—requires that French instead of English be used for the presentation of most scientific papers. Significantly, the only other government exhibiting such overwhelming distress at the perceived corruption of their language is that of French-speaking Québec in Canada, where similar anti-English laws have been in effect for years.

3 A Look at the Past: France from Caesar to Chirac

EARLY GAUL When the ancient Romans considered France part of their empire, their boundaries extended deep into the forests of the Paris basin and up to the edges of the Rhine. Part of Julius Caesar's early fame derived from his defeat of the Gallic king Vercingetorix at Alésia in 52 B.C., a victory he was quick to publicize in one of the ancient world's literary masterpieces, *The Gallic Wars*. That same year, the Roman colony of Lutetia (Paris) was established on an island in the Seine (Ile de la Cité).

As the Roman Empire declined, its armies retreated to the flourishing colonies that had been established along a strip of the Mediterranean coast—among others, these included Orange, Montpellier, Nîmes, Narbonne, and Marseille, which retain some of the best Roman monuments in Europe.

As one of their legacies, the Roman armies left behind the Catholic church, which, for all its abuses, was probably the only real guardian of civilization during the anarchy following the Roman decline. A form of low Latin was the common language, and it slowly evolved into the archaic French that both delights and confuses today's medieval scholars.

The form of Christianity adopted by many of the chieftains was considered heretical by Rome. Consequently, when Clovis (king of northeastern Gaul's Franks and founder of the Merovingian dynasty) astutely converted to Catholicism, he won the approval of the pope, the political support of the powerful archbishop of Reims, and the loyalty of the many Gallic tribes who had grown disenchanted with anarchy. (Clovis's baptism is viewed as the beginning of a collusion between the Catholic church and the French monarchy that would flourish until the beginning of the 1789 Revolution.) At the 486 Battle of Soissons, Clovis defeated the last vestiges of Roman power in Gaul. Other conquests that followed included expansions westward to the Seine, then to the Loire. After a battle in Dijon in 500, he became the nominal overlord of the king of Burgundy. Seven years later,

Dateline

- 121 B.C. The Romans establish the province of Gallia Narbonensis to guard overland routes between Spain and Italy; its borders correspond roughly to today's Provence.
- 58–51 B.C. Julius Caesar conquers Gaul (north-central France).
- 52 B.C. The Roman city of Lutetia, later Paris, is built on a defensible island in the Seine.
- 2nd century A.D. Christianity arrives in Gaul.
- 485–511 Under Clovis I, the Franks defeat the Roman armies and establish the Merovingian dynasty.
- 511 on Confusion and disorder; feudalism and the power of the Catholic church grow.
- 768 Charlemagne (768–814) becomes Frankish king and establishes the Carolingian dynasty; from Aix-la-Chapelle (Aachen) he rules lands from northern Italy to Bavaria to Paris.
- 800 Charlemagne is crowned Holy Roman Emperor in Rome.
- 814 Charlemagne dies and his empire breaks up.
- 1066 William of Normandy (the Conqueror) invades England; his Conquest is completed by 1087.

continues

- 1140 St-Denis Cathedral, the first example of gothic architecture, is built.
- 1270 Louis IX (St. Louis), along with most of his army, dies in Tunis on the Eighth Crusade.
- 1309 The papal Schism— Philip the Fair establishes the Avignon Papacy, which lasts nearly 70 years; two popes struggle for domination.
- 1347–51 Bubonic plague (the Black Death) kills 33% of the population.
- 1431 The English burn Joan of Arc at the stake in Rouen for resisting their occupation of France.
- 1453 The French drive the English out of all of France except Calais; the Hundred Years' War ends.
- 1515–47 France captures Calais after centuries of English rule.
- 1562–98 The Wars of Religion: Catholics fight Protestants; Henri IV converts to Catholicism and issues the Edict of Nantes, granting limited rights to Protestants.
- 1643–1715 The reign of Louis XIV, the Sun King; France develops Europe's most powerful army, but wars in Flanders and court extravagance sow seeds of decline.
- 1763 The Treaty of Paris effectively ends French power in North America.
- 1789–94 Revolution: The Bastille is stormed on July 14, 1789; the Reign of Terror follows.
- 1793 Louis XVI and Marie Antoinette are guillotined.
- 1794 Robespierre and the leaders of the Terror are guillotined.

continues

after the battle of Vouillé, his armies drove the Visigoths into Spain, giving most of Aquitaine, in western France, to his newly founded Merovingian dynasty. Trying to make the best of an earlier humiliation, Anastasius, the Byzantium-based emperor of the Eastern Roman Empire, finally gave the kingdom of the Franks his legal sanction.

After Clovis's death in 511, his kingdom was split among his squabbling heirs. The Merovingian dynasty, however, managed to survive in fragmented form for another 250 years. During this period, the power of the bishops and the great lords grew, firmly entrenching the complex hierarchies and preoccupations of what we today know as feudalism. Although apologists for the Merovingians are quick to point out their achievements, the feudalistic quasi-anarchy of their tenuous reign has been (not altogether unfairly) identified by many historians as the Dark Ages.

THE CAROLINGIANS   From the wreckage of the intrigue-ridden Merovingian court emerged a new dynasty: the Carolingians. One of their leaders, Charles Martel, halted a Muslim invasion of northern Europe at Tours in 743 and left a much-expanded kingdom to his son, Pepin. The Carolingian empire eventually stretched from the Pyrénées to a point deep in the German forests (the River Elbe), encompassing much of modern France, Germany, and northern Italy. The heir to this vast land was Charlemagne. Crowned emperor in Rome on Christmas in 800, he returned to his capital at Aix-la-Chapelle (Aachen) to found the Holy Roman Empire. Charlemagne's rule saw a revival of interest in scholarship, art, and classical texts, defined by scholars as the Carolingian Renaissance. Though illiterate, Charlemagne funded efforts to preserve the battered texts of ancient Greece and requested that excerpts from St. Jerome's Latin Bible be read to him every night during dinner.

Despite Charlemagne's magnetism, cultural rifts formed in his sprawling empire, most of which was eventually divided between two of Charlemagne's three squabbling heirs. Charles of Aquitaine annexed the western region; Louis of Bavaria took the east. Historians credit this division with the development of modern France and Germany as separate nations. Shortly after Charlemagne's death, his empire, fragmented into parcels, was invaded by

Vikings from the north, Muslim Saracens from the south, and Hungarians from the east.

THE MIDDLE AGES   When the Carolingian dynasty died out in 987, Hugh Capet, comte de Paris and duc de France, officially began the Middle Ages with the establishment of the Capetian dynasty. In 1154, the annulment of Eleanor of Aquitaine's marriage to Louis VII of France and subsequent marriage to Henry II of England placed the western half of France under English control, and vestiges of their power would remain for centuries. Meanwhile, vast forests and swamps were cleared for harvesting (often by the Middle Ages' hardest-working ascetics, Cistercian monks), the population grew, great gothic cathedrals were begun, and monastic life contributed to every level of a rapidly developing social order. Fortuitous marriages among the ruling families more than doubled the size of the territory controlled from Paris, a city that was increasingly recognized as the country's capital. Philippe II, reigning from 1179 to 1223, infiltrated more prominent families with his genes than anyone else in France, successfully marrying members of his family into the Valois, Artois, and Vermandois. He also managed to win Normandy and Anjou back from the English.

Louis IX (St. Louis) emerged as the 13th century's most memorable king, though he ceded most of the hard-earned military conquests of his predecessors back to the English. Somewhat of a religious fanatic, he died of illness (along with most of his army) in 1270 in a boat anchored off Tunis. The vainglorious and not-very-wise pretext for his trip was the Eighth Crusade. At the time of his death, Notre-Dame and the Sainte-Chapelle in Paris had been completed and the arts of tapestry-making and stone-cutting were flourishing.

During the 1300s the struggle of French sovereignty against the claims of a rapacious Roman pope tempted Philip the Fair to encourage support for a pope based in Avignon. (The Roman pope, Boniface VIII, whom Philip publicly insulted and then assaulted in his home, is said to have died of the shock.) During one of the most bizarre episodes in medieval history, two popes ruled simultaneously, one from Rome and one from Avignon. They competed fiercely for the spiritual and fiscal control of Christendom, until years of political

- **1799** Napoléon enters Paris and unites diverse factions; his military victories in northern Italy solidify his power in Paris.
- **1804** Napoléon crowns himself emperor in Notre-Dame de Paris.
- **1805–11** Napoléon and his armies successfully invade most of Europe.
- **1814–15** Napoléon abdicates after the failure of his Russian campaign; exiled to Elba, he returns; on June 18, 1815, finally defeated at Waterloo, he is exiled to St Helena, where he dies in 1821.
- **1830–48** The reign of Louis-Philippe.
- **1848** A revolution topples Louis-Philippe; Napoléon III (nephew of Napoléon I) is elected president.
- **1851–71** President Napoléon declares himself Emperor Napoléon III.
- **1863** An exhibition of paintings marks the birth of impressionism.
- **1870–71** The Franco-Prussian War: Paris falls; France cedes Alsace-Lorraine but aggressively colonizes North Africa and Southeast Asia.
- **1873** France loses Suez to the British; financial scandal wrecks an attempt to dredge the canal.
- **1889** The Eiffel Tower built for Paris's Universal Exhibition and the Revolution's centennial; architectural critics howl with disgust.
- **1914–18** World War I; French casualties exceed five million.

continues

■ 1923 France occupies
the Ruhr, Germany's
industrial zone,
demanding (and
collecting) enormous
war reparations.

■ 1929 France retreats
from the Ruhr and the
Rhineland and constructs
the Maginot Line, dubbed
"impregnable."

■ 1934 The Depression;
a political crisis is
spurred by clashes
of left and right.

■ 1936 Germans march
into the demilitarized
Rhineland; France
takes no action.

■ 1939 France and Britain
guarantee to Poland,
Romania, and Greece
protection from
aggressors; Germany
invades Poland; France
declares war.

■ 1940 Paris falls on June
14; Marshal Pétain's
Vichy government
collaborates with the
Nazis; General de Gaulle
forms a government-in-
exile in London to direct
the maquis (French
resistance fighters).

■ 1944 On June 6 the Allies
invade the Normandy
beaches; other Allied
troops invade from
the south; Paris is
liberated in August.

■ 1946–54 War in
Indochina; the French
withdraw from Southeast
Asia; North and South
Vietnam created.

■ 1954–58 The Algerian
revolution and subsequent
independence from
France; refugees flood
France; the Fourth
Republic collapses.

continues

intrigue turned the tables in favor of Rome and Avignon relinquished its claim in 1378.

The 14th century saw an increase in the wealth and power of the French kings, an increase in the general prosperity, and a decrease in the power of the feudal lords. The death of Louis X without an heir in 1316 prompted more than a decade of intrigue before the eventual emergence of the Valois dynasty.

The Black Death began in the summer of 1348, killing an estimated 33% of the population of Europe, decimating the population of Paris, and setting the stage for the eventual exodus of the French monarchs to safer climes in such places as the Loire Valley. A financial crisis, coupled with a series of ruinous harvests, almost bankrupted the nation.

During the Hundred Years' War, the English made sweeping inroads into France in an attempt to grab the throne. At their most powerful, they controlled almost all the north (Picardy and Normandy), Champagne, parts of the Loire Valley, and the huge western region called Guyenne. Peasant-born charismatic visionary Joan of Arc rallied the dispirited French troops as well as the timid dauphin (crown prince), whom she managed to have crowned as Charles VII in the cathedral at Reims. As threatening to the Catholic church as she was to the English, she was declared a heretic and burned at the stake in Rouen in 1431. Led by the newly crowned king, a barely cohesive France initiated internal reforms that strengthened its finances and vigor. After compromises among the quarreling factions, the French army drove the discontented English out, leaving them only the Norman port of Calais.

In the late 1400s Charles VIII married Brittany's last duchess, Anne, for a unification of France with its Celtic-speaking western outpost. In the early 1500s the endlessly fascinating François I, through war and diplomacy, strengthened the monarchy, rid it of its dependence on Italian bankers, coped with the intricate policies of the Renaissance, and husbanded the arts into a form of patronage French monarchs would continue to endorse for centuries.

Meanwhile, the growth of Protestantism and the unwillingness of the Catholic church to tolerate it led to intense civil strife. In 1572 Catherine de

Médici reversed her policy of religious tolerance and ordered the St. Bartholomew's Day Massacre of hundreds of Protestants. Henri IV, tired of the bloodshed and fearful that a fanatically Catholic Spain would meddle in the religious conflicts, converted to Catholicism as a compromise in 1593. Just before being fatally stabbed by a half-crazed monk, he issued the Edict of Nantes in 1598, granting freedom of religion to Protestants in France.

THE PASSING OF FEUDALISM By now France was a modern state, rid of all but a few of the vestiges of feudalism. In 1624 Louis XIII appointed a Catholic cardinal, the duc de Richelieu, his chief minister. Amassing enormous power, Richelieu virtually ruled the country until his death in 1642. His sole objective was investing the monarchy with total power—he committed a series of truly horrible acts trying to attain this goal and paved the way for the eventual absolutism of Louis XIV.

Though he ascended the throne when he was only nine, with the help of his Sicilian-born chief minister, Cardinal Mazarin, Louis XIV was probably the most powerful monarch Europe had seen since the Roman emperors. Through first a brilliant military campaign against Spain and then a judicious marriage to one of its royal daughters, he expanded France to include the southern provinces of Artois and Roussillon. Later, a series of diplomatic and military victories along the Flemish border expanded the country toward the north and east. The estimated population of France at this time was 20 million, as opposed to 8 million in England and 6 million in Spain. French colonies in Canada, the West Indies, and America (Louisiana) were stronger than ever. The mercantilism that Louis' brilliant finance minister, Colbert, implemented was one of the era's most important fiscal policies, hugely increasing France's power and wealth. The arts flourished, as did a sense of aristocratic style that's remembered with a bittersweet nostalgia today. Louis' palace of Versailles is the perfect monument to the most flamboyantly consumptive era in French history.

Louis' territorial ambitions so deeply threatened the other nations of Europe that, led by William of Orange (the Dutch-born English king), they united to hold him in check. France entered a series of expensive and demoralizing wars that, coupled with high taxes and bad harvests, engendered much civil discontent. England was viewed as a threat both within Europe and in the global rush for lucrative colonies. The great Atlantic ports, especially Bordeaux, grew and prospered because of France's success in the West Indian slave and sugar trade. Despite the

- 1958 De Gaulle initiates the Fifth Republic, calling for a France independent from the United States and Europe.
- 1960 France tests its first atomic bomb.
- 1968 Students riot in Paris; de Gaulle resigns.
- 1981 François Mitterrand becomes the first Socialist president since World War II.
- 1986 The National Front articulates anti-immigrant rage, eventually gathering 10% of the popular vote.
- 1988 Mitterrand is reelected.
- 1989 The bicentenntial of the French Revolution and the centennial of the Eiffel Tower.
- 1991 France joins its allies in a war against Iraq.
- 1993 Conservatives topple the Socialists, as Edouard Balladur becomes premier.
- 1994 The Channel Tunnel opens to link France with England.
- 1995 The conservative mayor of Paris, Jacques Chirac, wins the French presidency on his third try, with 52% of the vote; he declares war on unemployment.

country's power, the total number of French colonies diminished thanks to the naval power of the English. The rise of Prussia as a militaristic neighbor posed an additional problem.

THE REVOLUTION   Meanwhile, the Enlightenment was training a new generation of thinkers for the struggle against absolutism, religious fanaticism, and superstition. Europe was never again the same after the Revolution of 1789, although the ideas that engendered it had been brewing for more than 50 years. On August 10, 1792, troops from Marseille, aided by a Parisian mob, threw the dim-witted Louis XVI and his tactless Austrian-born queen, Marie Antoinette, into prison. After months of bloodshed and bickering among violently competing factions, the two thoroughly humiliated monarchs were executed.

France's problems got worse before they got better. In the ensuing bloodbaths, both moderates and radicals were guillotined in full view of a bloodthirsty crowd that included voyeurs like Dickens's Madame Defarge, who brought her knitting every day to place de la Révolution (later renamed place de la Concorde) to watch the beheadings. The drama surrounding the collapse of the *ancien régime* and the beheadings of Robespierre's Reign of Terror provides the most heroic and horrible anecdotes in the history of France. From all this emerged the "Declaration of the Rights of Man," an enlightened document published in 1789; its influence has been cited as a model of democratic ideals ever since. The implications of the collapse of this firmly entrenched aristocracy shook the foundations of every monarchy in Europe.

THE RISE OF NAPOLEON   It required the militaristic fervor of Napoléon Bonaparte to unite France once again. A political and military genius who appeared on the landscape at a time when the French were thoroughly sickened by the anarchy following their Revolution, he restored a national pride that had been severely tarnished. He also established a bureaucracy and a code of law that has been emulated in other legal systems around the world. In 1799, at the age of 30, he entered Paris and was crowned First Consul and Master of France. Soon after, a decisive victory in his northern Italian campaign solidified his power at home. A brilliant politician, he made peace through a compromise with the Vatican, moderating the atheistic rigidity of the earliest days of the Revolution.

Napoléon's victories made him the envy of Europe. Beethoven dedicated his Eroica symphony to Napoléon—but later retracted the dedication when Napoléon committed what Beethoven considered atrocities. Just as he was poised on the verge of conquering all Europe, Napoléon's famous retreat from Moscow during the winter of 1812 reduced his formerly invincible army to tatters, as 400,000 Frenchmen died in the Russian snows. Napoléon was then defeated at Waterloo by the combined armies of the English, Dutch, and Prussians. Exiled to the British-held island of St. Helena in the South Atlantic, he died in 1821, probably the victim of an unknown poisoner.

THE BOURBONS   In 1814, following the destruction of Napoléon and his dream, the Congress of Vienna took a step back in time and redefined the map of Europe. The new geography was an approximation of the boundaries that had existed in 1792, prior to Napoléon's military campaigns. The Bourbon monarchy was reestablished, with reduced powers for Louis XVIII, an arch-conservative, and a changing array of leaders who included the prince de Polignac and, later, Charles X. A renewal of the ancien régime's oppressions, however, did not sit well in a France that had already spilled so much blood in favor of egalitarian causes.

In 1830, after censoring the press and dissolving Parliament, Louis XVIII was removed from power after yet more violent uprisings. Louis-Philippe, duc d'Orléans, was elected king under a liberalized constitution. His reign lasted for 18 years of calm prosperity during which England and France more or less collaborated on matters of foreign policy. The establishment of an independent Belgium and the French conquest of Algeria (1840–47) were to have resounding effects on French politics a century later. It was a time of wealth, grace, and the expansion of the arts for most French people, though the industrialization of the north and east produced some of the 19th century's most horrific poverty.

THE SECOND EMPIRE   A revolution in 1848, fueled by a financial crash and disgruntled workers in Paris, forced Louis-Philippe out of office. That year, Napoléon I's nephew, Napoléon III, was elected president. Appealing to the property-protecting instinct of a nation that hadn't forgotten the violent upheavals of less than a century before, he initiated a repressive right-wing government in which he was awarded the totalitarian status of emperor in 1851. Rebounding from the punishment they'd received during the Revolution and the minor role they'd played during the First Empire, the Second Empire's clergy enjoyed great power, especially in the countryside. Steel production was begun and a railway system and Indochinese colonies were established. New technologies fostered new kinds of industry and the bourgeoisie flourished. And Baron Georges-Eugène Haussmann radically altered Paris, laying out the boulevards the world knows today.

By 1866 an industrialized France began to see the Second Empire as more of a hindrance than an encouragement to its expansion. The dismal failure of colonizing Mexico and the increasing power of Austria and Prussia were setbacks to the empire's prestige. In 1870 the Prussians defeated Napoléon III at Sedan and held him prisoner with 100,000 of his soldiers. Paris was besieged by an enemy who only just failed to march its vastly superior armies through the capital.

After the Prussians withdrew, a violent revolt ushered in the Third Republic and its elected president, Marshal MacMahon, in 1873. Peace and prosperity slowly returned, France regained its glamour, a mania of building occurred, the impressionists made their visual statements, and writers like Flaubert redefined the French novel into what today is regarded the most evocative in the world. As if as a symbol of this period, the Eiffel Tower was built as part of the 1889 Universal Exposition.

By 1890 a new corps of satirists (including Zola) had exposed the country's wretched living conditions, the cruelty of the country's vested interests, and the underlying hypocrisy of late 19th-century French society. The 1894 Dreyfus Affair exposed the corruption of French army officers who had destroyed the career and reputation of a Jewish colleague (Albert Dreyfus) falsely and deliberately punished—as a scapegoat—for treason. The ethnic tensions identified by Zola led to further divisiveness in the rest of the 20th century.

THE WORLD WARS   International rivalries, thwarted colonial ambitions, and conflicting alliances led to World War I, which, after decisive German victories for two years, degenerated into the mud-slogged horror of trench warfare. Mourning between four and five million casualties, Europe was inflicted with psychic scars that never healed. In 1917 the United States broke the European deadlock by entering the war. Immediately after the Allied victory, grave economic problems caused by inflation and the devastation of much of northern France, plus the demoralization stemming from years of fighting, encouraged the growth of socialism and communism. The French government, led by a vindictive Clemenceau, demanded every centime of reparations it could wring from a crushed Germany. The humiliation associated with this has often been cited as the origin of the German nation's almost-obsessive determination to rise from the ashes of 1918 to a place in the sun.

The worldwide Great Depression had devastating repercussions in France. Poverty and widespread bankruptcies weakened the Third Republic to the point where successive coalition governments rose and fell with alarming regularity. The crises reached a crescendo on June 14, 1940, when Hitler's armies arrogantly marched down the Champs-Elysées, and newsreel cameras recorded Frenchmen openly weeping. Under the terms of the armistice, the north of France was occupied by the Nazis and a puppet French government was established at Vichy under the authority of Marshal Pétain. The immediate collapse of the French army is viewed as one of the most significant humiliations in modern French history.

Pétain and his regime cooperated with the Nazis in ways that are today considered unbearably shameful. Not the least of their errors included the deportation of more than 75,000 French Jews to German work camps. Pockets of resistance fighters (*le maquis*) waged small-scale guerrilla attacks against the Nazis throughout the course of the war, and free-French forces continued to fight with the Allies on battlegrounds like North Africa. Charles de Gaulle, the pompous and irascible giant whose personality is forever associated with the politics of his era, established himself as the head of the French government-in-exile, operating first from London and then from Algiers.

The scenario was radically altered on June 6, 1944, when the largest armada in humankind's history successfully established a bulkhead on the beaches of Normandy. Paris rose in rebellion even before the Allied armies arrived, and on August 26, 1944, Charles de Gaulle entered the capital as head of the government. The Fourth Republic was declared even as pockets of Nazi snipers continued to shoot from scattered rooftops throughout the city.

THE POSTWAR YEARS   Plagued by the bitter residue of colonial policies France had established during the 18th and 19th centuries, the Fourth Republic witnessed the rise and fall of 22 governments and 17 premiers. Many French soldiers died on battlefields as once-profitable colonies in North Africa and Indochina rebelled. It took 80,000 lives, for example, to put down a revolt in Madagascar. After suffering a bitter defeat in 1954, France ended the war in Indochina and freed its former colony. It also granted internal self-rule to Tunisia and (under slightly different circumstances) Morocco.

Algeria was to remain a greater problem, partly because Algerian soil was considered an integral part of France and partly because of the vast investment there from sources throughout the French mainland. The advent of the 1958 Algerian revolution, along with the widely publicized massacres and atrocities committed

Impressions

The French will only be united under the threat of danger. Nobody can simply bring together a country that has 265 kinds of cheese.

—Charles de Gaulle

by both sets of antagonists, signaled the end of the much-maligned Fourth Republic. De Gaulle was called back from retirement to initiate a new constitution, the Fifth Republic, with a stronger set of executive controls than those of its doomed predecessor. To nearly everyone's dissatisfaction, de Gaulle ended the Algerian war in 1962 by granting the country full independence in the wake of a national referendum. Screams of protest resounded long and loud, but the sun had set on most of France's far-flung empire. Internal disruption followed the referendum as vast numbers of *pieds-noirs* (French-born residents of Algeria recently stripped of their lands) flooded back into metropolitan France, often into makeshift refugee camps in Provence and Languedoc.

In 1968 major social unrest and a violent coalition hastily formed between the nation's students and blue-collar workers eventually led to the collapse of the government. De Gaulle resigned when his attempts to placate some of the marchers were defeated. The reigns of power passed to his second-in-command, Georges Pompidou, and his successor, Valerie Giscard d'Estaing, both of whom continued de Gaulle's policies emphasizing economic development and protection of France as a cultural resource to the world.

THE 1980s & 1990s   In 1981 François Mitterrand was elected the first Socialist president of France (with a close vote of 51%) since World War II. In almost immediate response, many wealthy French decided to transfer their assets out of the country, much to the delight of banks in Geneva, Monaco, and Vienna. Although reviled by the rich and ridiculed for personal mannerisms that often seemed inspired by Louis XIV, Mitterrand was reelected in 1988.

In 1989 France celebrated the bicentennial of the French Revolution and the centennial of the Eiffel Tower with much fanfare, focusing some of its celebrations on the then-newest musical force in Paris—the Opéra de la Bastille.

In July 1992 France played a leading role in the development of the European Union (EU), 13 countries that will eventually abolish all trade barriers among themselves. More recent developments include France's interest in developing a central European bank for the regulation of a shared intra-European currency, a ruling politicians have interpreted as another block in the foundation of a united Europe.

In 1994 President Mitterrand and Elizabeth II of Britain co-inaugurated the opening of the Channel Tunnel, an ambitious structure that will erode even further the traditional barriers between the two rival nations.

Diagnosed with terminal prostate cancer near the end of his second term, Mitterrand bravely continued to represent France with dignity, despite his physical deterioration and hair loss from chemotherapy. Just prior to leaving office, his popularity was at an all-time high, in marked contrast to the 1993 opinion polls that showed his administration as universally unpopular.

In April 1993, French voters had dumped the long-ruling Socialists and installed a new conservative government, with a huge parliamentary majority. Polls cited corruption scandals, rising unemployment, and urban insecurity as reasons for this defeat. Conservative premier Edouard Balladur had to "cohabit" the government with Mitterrand, whom he blamed for the country's growing economic problems. The battle over who would succeed the ailing Mitterrand was waged against Balladur with epic public rancor by Jacques Chirac, tenacious survivor of many terms as mayor of Paris. Their public discord was among the most venomous electoral diatribe since the days of Pétain.

On his third try, on May 7, 1995, Chirac won the presidency with 52% of the vote. He defeated Lionel Jospin, former education minister, who had hoped to succeed fellow Socialist Mitterrand. Chirac immediately declared war on unemployment. Mitterrand turned over the reins of government on May 17. Chirac's seven-year term will lead France into the 21st century.

4 France's Art & Architecture: From Pre-Roman to Postmodern

Much of France's identity comes from the art and architecture that has been produced in abundance on its soil. Annually, vast sums of money are earmarked for salvaging, cleaning, restoring, and documenting national treasures. Today, many of the great buildings of Paris and the provinces look as good as when they were first built.

The foundations of French art began with the Romans, who imported their monumental sense of symmetry and grandeur (and their engineering techniques) deep into the forests of northern France. But despite the strategic importance of Roman military bases like Lutetia (Paris), only the southernmost region of France was considered of any commercial or artistic merit. This region, through trade with the architecturally sophisticated Mediterranean, was quick to adopt the building techniques that were common in the Roman world. Regarding architecture, it has been said that the Romans' triumphal arches, rhythmically massive aqueducts, and mausoleums fixed themselves in the French aesthetic for all time. Today, some of the best-preserved ruins of the classical world are scattered though such Provençal towns as Nîmes, Orange, Saintes, and Arles.

ROMANESQUE As Christianity made its way toward the Celtic tribes on the northern edges of Gaul, an abbreviated and naïve kind of naturalism permeated the old Roman ideals, resulting in a crude, often-bulky aesthetic of geometric carvings and primitive masses. Some were influenced by eastern motifs from Byzantium. Many purists consider romanesque architecture a symbol of the growing power of the 11th- and 12th-century church, which in many areas was the only constant amid shifting feudal alliances. The earliest romanesque buildings resembled thick-walled fortresses and often served as refuges during times of invasion. At first they were unembellished, relying on rounded arches and narrow windows for ornamentation.

Many critics consider the echoing simplicity of the Cistercians—a reform-minded offshoot of the Benedictines—to be among the more spiritually alluring styles of the era. (Clairvaux and Fontenay are the best remaining examples.)

By the 1100s, notably in Poitou, the facades and sections of the interiors of some romanesque churches were almost completely covered with sculptures whose forms emphasized the architecture rather than served as separate works of art. Although many more visible romanesque sculptures are unyielding and lifeless, the capitals topping massive columns are often charming, the most natural representations that can be found.

The first French romanesque church was built around 1002 in Dijon (St-Bénigne Monastery). The flowering of the style appeared in the vast ecclesiastical complex of Cluny in Burgundy, which was begun in 1089 and then destroyed by zealous townspeople just after the Revolution.

Contemporaneously with the 10th- and 11th-century construction of churches, the era produced secular fortresses whose crenellations and thick walls often concealed dank, drafty, cramped quarters where cooped-up occupants barely managed to stay sane during times of war. Often, when a fortress was destroyed during a pillage, the survivors rebuilt it in a more fashionable form. In this way, some of the greatest châteaux of France were built, altered, upgraded, and transformed into the sometimes-elegant domiciles preserved today as symbols of the Renaissance.

GOTHIC   About 400 years before the great châteaux of the Loire Valley reached their present form, the architects of the royal abbey of St-Denis, outside Paris, completed the first section of a radically new architectural style—gothic. The cathedrals of Noyon, begun a year later in 1145, and Laon, launched in 1155, almost immediately exemplified the new principles, as did Notre-Dame de Paris when construction was undertaken in 1163. Gothic churches usually included a choir, a ring-around ambulatory, radiating chapels, pointed arches, clustered (rather than monolithic) columns, and ceilings held aloft by ribbed vaulting. Probably most important is the presence of wide, soaring windows occupying the space that in a romanesque church would have been devoted to thick stone walls. This new design usually required the addition of exterior flying buttresses to support the weight of the heavy roof and ceiling.

It was at Chartres, 60 miles southwest of Paris, that an adaptation of earlier gothic principles developed for the first time into a flamboyant High Gothic when a section of the existing cathedral was destroyed in a fire. The tendency toward increased elevation was more fully developed until the cathedrals of Reims and Amiens reached heights so dizzying that medieval man couldn't help but be awed by the might and majesty of God.

The ecclesiastical sculpture that ornamented the portals and facades of gothic churches progressed from a static kind of stern rigidity to a more fluid, more relaxed, often coquettish kind of naturalism. By the 14th century, ecclesiastical and especially secular carvings attained a kind of international refinement and courtliness that was appreciated and copied in aristocratic circles throughout Europe.

THE RENAISSANCE   It wasn't long, however, before the Renaissance helped the French realize that the glass-and-stone marvels erected to the glory of God were also fine examples of the skill and imagination of the humans who had built them. When the 14th-century papal schism led to the recognition of Avignon, not Rome, as the legitimate seat of the papacy, a fortress that would also be a palace was required. No longer were aristocratic residences designed as gloomy, dank fortresses: Although defense was still a priority, the windows and doors were enlarged and interiors were adorned with tapestries, paintings, elaborate religious artifacts (including triptychs), and music. Many of the new châteaux were inspired by Italian models—François I imported many designers, including Leonardo da Vinci, from Italy, whose influence changed French aesthetics forever; Chambord, the Renaissance king's hunting château, is a good example. Religious themes were abandoned as French painting modeled itself first after Flemish and then northern Italian examples. To an increasing degree, artists began to distance themselves from church dictates.

BAROQUE   The early 17th century witnessed the architectural burgeoning of Paris, whose skyline bristled with domes in the restrained baroque of the Italianate style. Louis XIV employed Le Vau, Perrault, both Mansarts, and Bruand for his buildings, with Le Nôtre in charge of the rigidly intelligent layouts of his gardens at Versailles. Meanwhile, court painters like Boucher depicted allegorical shepherdesses and cherubs at play and Georges de la Tour used techniques of light and shadow (chiaroscuro) inspired by Caravaggio. The châteaux built during this era included the lavishly expensive Vaux-le-Vicomte, whose excesses led to the imprisonment of its owner, and the even more lavishly expensive royal residence of Versailles, whose excesses helped destroy the ancien régime.

NEOCLASSICISM   Following the 1789 collapse of the monarchy, French architects returned to a dignified form of classicism that suited postrevolutionary ideals. Public parks in Metz, Bordeaux, Nancy, and Paris were laid out, sometimes requiring the demolition of acres of twisted medieval sections of cities. Styles inspired by the aesthetics of ancient Rome became the rage in painting, sculpture, and dress, although a brief fling with Egyptology followed the discovery of the Rosetta Stone during Napoléon's campaign in Egypt. The revolutionary school of David came and went, and, within the new order, Ingres strove for a kind of classical calm.

THE 19TH CENTURY   Around 1850 a new school of eclecticism combined elements from scattered eras of the past into new, sometimes-inharmonious wholes. Between 1855 and 1869 Napoléon III and his chief architect, Baron Haussmann, demolished much of crumbling medieval Paris to lay out the wide avenues that today connect the various monuments in well-proportioned broad vistas. New building techniques were developed, including the use of iron as the structural support of bridges, viaducts, and buildings such as the National Library, completed in 1860. Naturally, this opened the way for Eiffel to design and erect the most frequently slurred building of its day, the Eiffel Tower, for the 1889 Universal Exposition.

Among sculptors, the only authentic giant to emerge from the 19th century was Rodin. His human figures were vital, passionate, and lifelike, and he became known for such works as *The Thinker* and *The Kiss*.

Delacroix became the greatest name in French Romantic painting, showing great skill as a colorist. In the mid-19th century landscape painting rose in prominence, and no one was better at this than Corot, of the Barbizon school. To many critics the first modern painter in France was Manet; he painted portraits and scenes of everyday life but could also create a scandal (*Picnic on the Grass*) by depicting nudes among dressed figures. Manet is not to be confused with Monet, a great innovator known for his series of paintings of water lilies and of Rouen cathedral. Renoir became celebrated for his sensuously rounded nudes in pearl white, and Degas turned to ballet dancers and scenes of racing and the theater for his inspiration.

Outside all movements, but equally important, was Toulouse-Lautrec. Satiric but amused, his style was exemplified by the posters and sketches of music-hall life he depicted. His interest was in the demimonde of his day.

THE 20TH CENTURY   In the early 20th century, the Fauves ("wild beasts") attracted the most attention, and the greatest of their lot was Matisse. He became known for his bright colors and flattened perspective.

Throughout the 20th century exquisite beaux-arts buildings continued to be erected throughout Paris, most at roughly the same height, giving the city an evenly spaced skyline and rhythmically ornate facades that have caused it to be deemed the most beautiful city in the world. The art nouveau movement added garlands of laurel and olive branches to the gray-white stone of elegant apartment buildings and hotels throughout France. In the 1920s and 1930s art deco's simplified elegance captivated sophisticated sensibilities. Braque defined cubism and Picasso worked at his mission of turning the art world upside down. Le Corbusier developed his jutting, gently curved planes of concrete, opening the door for a new but often less talented school of modern French architects.

Critics have not been kind to the rapidly rusting exposed structural elements of Paris's notorious Centre Pompidou. In the 1980s, an obsolete railroad station beside the Seine was transformed into the truly exciting Musée d'Orsay and an expanse of dreary 19th-century slaughterhouses was transformed into a site of tourist worth by the addition of a hypermodern science museum. In the 1990s, the Opéra de la Bastille brought new life to the decaying eastern edge of the Marais but, predictably, sparked a controversy regarding its iconoclastic design. And the screams of outrage could be heard throughout France when I. M. Pei's glass pyramid was built as the postmodern centerpiece of one of the Louvre's most formal 17th-century courtyards.

Mitterrand inaugurated the Grande Arche de la Défense on France's bicentennial on July 14, 1989. This 35-story office complex shaped like a hollow cube is the endpoint of the *voie triomphale* (triumphal way) begun in 1664 at the Tuileries Gardens; its roof covers $2^1/_2$ acres (it's estimated that Notre-Dame could fit into its hollow core). The latest addition to the architectural scene (opened 1995) is the Cité de la Musique, designed by architect Christian de Portzamparc as a complex of interconnected post-cubist shapes.

5 France's *Cousin* Cuisines

As any French person will tell you, French food is the best in the world. That's as true today as it was during the 19th-century heyday of master chef Escoffier. A demanding patriarch who codified the rules of French cooking, he ruled the kitchens of the Ritz in Paris, standardizing the complicated preparation and presentation of *haute cuisine*. Thanks to Escoffier's legendary flare-ups and his French-born colleagues whose kitchen tantrums have been the bane of many a socialite's life, the French chef for years has been considered a temperamental egomaniac, bearing singlehandedly the burden of diffusing French civilization into the kitchens of the Anglo-Saxon world.

The demands of these chefs, however, are not as far-fetched as they might seem, considering the intense scrutiny that has surrounded every aspect of France's culinary arts since the start of the Industrial Revolution.

Until the early 1800s the majority of French citizens did not eat well. Many diets consisted of turnips, millet, fruits, berries, unpasteurized dairy products, and whatever fish or game could be had. Cooking techniques and equipment were unsanitary and crude, and starvation was a constant threat. Fear of famine was one

Impressions

Frivolity and lightheartedness are proverbial characteristics of the French.
—Henry Wadsworth Longfellow

Dining Details

France's restaurants, especially those in Paris, are reputed to be ultra-expensive. Its internationally famous ones—like La Tour d'Argent and Maxim's—are not so much restaurants as temples of gastronomy, memorials to the glory of French cuisine. La Tour d'Argent, for example, boasts the finest wine cellar in the world. In these culinary cathedrals, you pay and pay for not only the superb decor and regal service but also the art of celebrated chefs.

A vast array of expensive restaurants has opened to cater almost exclusively to tourists. The food may be indifferent or even bad, but they have iced water and ketchup to anesthetize your tastebuds, trilingual waiters, and quadrilingual menus. Luckily, there are hundreds of others. Paris, said to have more restaurants than any other city, contains many impressive reasonably priced ones.

By law, French restaurants add a service charge of 12% to 15% to your bill (*service compris*), meaning you don't have to leave a tip—however, it's customary to leave something extra.

In many less expensive places, the menu will be handwritten in French only, but don't be intimidated (see the Appendix for common menu terms). You needn't be timid about ordering dishes without knowing precisely what they are—you'll get some delightful surprises. Relax and enjoy your restaurant experience as an art form and an intricate social ritual.

The French regard vegetables as a separate course and eat them apart from meat or poultry. We wouldn't advise you to order them specially, unless you're an exceptionally hearty eater. Most main courses come with a small garni of vegetables anyway.

As a rule, it's better to order an apéritif—often the house will have a specialty—rather than a heavy drink before a classic French dinner. Vodka or scotch can assault your palate, destroying your tastebuds for the festive repast to come. Allow plenty of time for a gourmet dinner. Orders are often prepared individually, and it takes time to absorb the wine and flavors. Sometimes sorbet (a sherbet) is served midway through your meal to cleanse your palate, although many modern gastronomes consider that a frivolous nicety and sometimes prefer to avoid it.

Most French meals consist of several small courses. You can begin, for example, with hors d'oeuvres or a light potage (soup), though chefs don't serve soups as frequently as they used to. The classic restaurant used to serve fish (a small order) after the appetizer, then the meat or poultry. Nowadays it's likely to be either fish or meat. A salad follows the main course, then a selection of cheese, and finally a dessert, often a fruit concoction or a sorbet.

Making reservations is important, as is showing up on time. Too many Americans make reservations and then become a "no-show," and this creates ill-will, especially since many nine-table restaurants must fill completely every night in order to make a profit. If you're window-shopping for a restaurant, you'll find the menu most often displayed outside. Most French people have their main meal during the day, and when in France you, too, may want to follow that custom, dining more lightly in the evening.

of the rallying cries of the Revolution—everyone knows Marie Antoinette's "Let them eat cake" response to cries that the poor could not afford bread.

At the foundation of virtually every culinary theory ever developed within France is a deep-seated respect for the *cuisine des provinces* (also known as *cuisine campagnarde*). Ingredients usually included only what was produced locally, and the rich and hearty result was gradually developed over several generations of *mères cuisinières*. Springing from an agrarian society with a vivid sense of nature's cycles, the cuisine provided appropriate nourishment for bodies that had toiled through a day in the open air. Specific dishes and cooking methods were as varied as the climates, terrains, and crops of France's many regions.

CUISINE BOURGEOISE & HAUTE CUISINE Cuisine bourgeoise and its pretentious cousin, haute cuisine, were refinements of country cooking that developed from the increased prosperity and urbanization brought on by 19th-century industrialization. As France grew more affluent, food and the rituals involved in its preparation and presentation became one of the hallmarks of culture and civilization. And as refrigerated trucks and railway cars carried meats, fish, and produce from one region to the other, associations were formed and entire industries spawned, revolving around specific ingredients produced in specific districts. Like the country's wines (demarcated with "Appellation d'Origine Contrôlée"), lamb from the salt marshes of Pauillac, poultry from Bresse in Burgundy, and melons, strawberries, apples, and truffles from specific districts command premiums over roughly equivalent ingredients produced in less-legendary neighborhoods.

France often names a method of preparation (or a particular dish) after its region of origin. Dishes a menu describes as *à la Normande* are likely to be prepared with milk, cream, or cheese or with Calvados, in honor of the dairy products and apple brandy produced in abundance within Norman borders. *Cassoulet* (a stewed combination of white beans, duck, pork, onions, and carrots) will forever be associated with Toulouse, where the dish originated in the dim shadows of culinary prehistory. And who doesn't know that something cooked *à la Bordelaise* has probably been flavored with ample doses of red bordeaux (along with bone marrow, shallots, tarragon, and meat juices)?

Other than caviar (which the French consume in abundance but do not produce), the world's most elegant garnish is truffles, an underground fungus with a woodsy, oaky smell. Thousands of these are unearthed yearly from the Dordogne or Périgord forests, so if your menu proclaims a dish is *à la Périgourdine*, you'll almost certainly pay a premium for the truffles and foie gras forming part of its ingredients.

And what's all the fuss about *foie gras?* It comes from either a goose or a duck (the rose-hued goose liver is the greater delicacy). The much-abused goose, however, has a rough life, being force-fed about a kilogram (2.2 lb.) of corn every day in a process the French call *gavage*. In about 22 days the animal's liver is swollen to about 25 ounces (in many cases far more than that). When prepared by a Périgourdine housewife (some of whom sell the livers directly from their farmhouses to passing motorists) it's truly delicious. Foie gras is most often served with truffles; otherwise, it's called *au naturel*.

Bouillabaisse, developed as a staple for fisherfolk along the Provence coast, has been elevated into one of the world's greatest dishes. Purists claim that key ingredients are rascasse (hogfish), a species found only in the Mediterranean; garlic-based aïoli; and a medley of specific Provençal herbs—without these, the resulting stew simply isn't bouillabaisse.

What this means for diners is that a rebirth of *cuisine du terroir* has returned to France with a vengeance. *Chefs de cuisine* (especially the younger ones) are making creative statements, many as cerebral as they are sensual. Never has there been such an emphasis on fresh and authentic ingredients derived locally or from specific regions and provinces. Some chefs (including one we know in Bordeaux) have been known to shut down their restaurants for the day if they cannot find exactly what they want in the marketplace that morning.

The competition for clients and prestige among chefs has heated up almost to the boiling point. And as the specific tastes and rituals associated with French food are disseminated around the globe, French-born chefs hired to prepare banquets as far away as Tokyo have been known to haul kegs of their own butter and cream halfway across the world as a guarantee that the flavors they create at the edge of the Pacific rim are equivalent to those produced in the Ile de France.

CUISINE MODERNE & CUISINE MINCEUR   The anti-Escoffier revolution has been raging for so long that many early rebels are returning to the old style, as exemplified by boeuf à la bourguignonne, blanquette de veau, and pot-au-feu. Yet the unfashionable expression *nouvelle cuisine* (even if it isn't that "new") remains a viable part of the dining scene. Unlike another revolution, the battle between haute and nouvelle cuisine didn't begin in Paris. The romantic in us would like to think it started when Michel Guérard's beautiful wife, Christine, murmured in his ear, "Vous savez, Michel, mon cher—if you would lose some weight, you'd look vraiment fantastique."

For a man who loves food as much as Guérard, that was a formidable challenge. However, he set to work and ultimately invented cuisine minceur, a way to cook good French food without the calories. You can sample it in Guérard's restaurant, at Eugénie-les-Bains in the Landes, just east of the Basque country. His *Cuisine Minceur* became a best-seller in North America, and food critic Gael Greene hailed him as "the brilliant man who is France's most creative chef." Cuisine minceur is more of a diet cuisine than nouvelle or any of its later permutations. However, the "new cuisine," like cuisine minceur, represents a major break with haute cuisine. Rich sauces, for example, are eliminated; cooking times that can destroy the best of fresh ingredients are considerably shortened. The aim is to release the natural flavor of food without covering it with layers of butter and cream. New flavor combinations in this widely expanding repertoire are often inspired.

Many chefs, including some of France's finest, dislike the word *nouvelle* when applied to cuisine. They call theirs *moderne*, which blends the finest dishes of the classic repertory with that of the nouvelle. Although widely defined, cuisine moderne basically means paying homage to the integrity of ingredients, certainly fresh ones, and working to bring out natural flavors and aromas.

6 By the Glass or Bottle: Burgundy, Bordeaux & Beyond

French cookery achieves palate perfection only when accompanied by wine, considered neither a luxury nor even an addition but an integral part of every meal. Certain rules about wine drinking have been long established, but no one except traditionalists seems to follow them anymore. For example, if you're having a roast, a steak, or game, a good burgundy might be your choice. If it's chicken, lamb, or veal, perhaps you might choose a red from Bordeaux; a full-bodied red is perfect with a cheese like Camembert, as is a blanc de blanc with oysters. A light rosé (beaujolais) can go with almost anything.

Let your own good taste and your budget determine your wine choice. Most wine stewards, called *sommeliers*, are there to help you, and only in the most dishonest of restaurants will they push you toward the most expensive selections. Of course, if you prefer only bottled water or beer, then be firm and order either without embarrassment. In fact, bottled water might be a good idea at lunch if you're planning to drive later. Some restaurants include a beverage in their menu rates (*boisson compris*), but that's only in the cheaper places. Some of the most satisfying wines we've drunk in France came from unlabeled house bottles or carafes, called a *vin de la maison*. Unless you're a connoisseur, for the most part you need not worry about labels and vintages.

You can rarely go wrong with a good burgundy or bordeaux, but you may want to be more experimental. That's when the sommelier (who is likely to be a woman) can help, particularly if you tell him or her your taste in wine (semidry or very dry, for example). State frankly how much you're willing to pay and what you plan to order for your meal. If you're dining with others, you may want to order two or three bottles, selecting a wine to suit each course. However, even the French at most informal meals (especially if there are only two people dining) select only one wine to go with all their platters from hors d'oeuvres to cheese.

Note: Most readers don't need to be told this, but under no circumstances should you order Coca-Cola or any soft drink with your meal. It just isn't done. Chances are you'll alienate the chef and staff and probably receive amused but disdainful glances from any other client who happens to have heard you make one of the few gross cultural gaffes left in a country that's familiar with multicultural tastes.

WINE LABELS   Since the late 19th century, French wine (at least French wine served in France) has been labeled. The general label is known as "Appellation d'Origine Contrôlée" (often abbreviated AC). These controls, for the most part, are designated by region. These simple, honest wines can be blended from grapes grown at any place in the region; some are composed of the vintages of different years.

The more specific the label, the greater the wine is (in most cases). For example, instead of a bordeaux, the wine might be labeled a Médoc, which is an intensely prestigious triangle of land extending some 50 miles north from Bordeaux. Wine labels can be narrowed down to a particular vine-growing property, such as a Château Haut-Brion, one of the greatest red wines of Bordeaux (this château produces only about 10,000 cases per year).

On some burgundies, you're likely to see the word *clos* (pronounced *clo*). Originally that meant a walled or otherwise enclosed vineyard, as in Clos de Beze, a celebrated Burgundian vineyard producing a superb red wine. *Cru* (pronounced *crew* and meaning "growth") suggests a wine of superior quality when it appears on a label as a *vin de cru*. Wines and vineyards are often divided into crus. A Grand Cru or Premier Cru should, by implication, be an even more superior wine.

Labels are only part of the story. It's the vintage that counts. Essentially, a vintage refers to a specific year's grape harvest and the wine made from those grapes.

Therefore, any wine can be a vintage wine unless it was blended. Like people, there are good vintages and bad. The variation between wine produced in a "good year" and wine produced in a "bad year" can be major, even to the neophyte palate.

Finally, champagne is the only wine that can be correctly served through all courses of a meal—but only to those who can afford its astronomical prices. Frankly, we consider champagne an overrated pleasure and usually prefer a mellow burgundy or a sophisticated bordeaux.

Planning Your Trip to France

3

This chapter is devoted to the where, when, and how of your trip. It covers everything from what you'll need to do before leaving home and how you'll get to France to where you can go for an adventure like ballooning over the countryside or barging along its waterways.

1 Information, Required Documents & Money

SOURCES OF VISITOR INFORMATION

IN THE U.S. Your best source of information—besides this guide, of course—is the **French Government Tourist Office,** at 444 Madison Ave., 16th Floor, New York, NY 10022; 676 N. Michigan Ave., Suite 3360, Chicago, IL 60611-2819; or 9454 Wilshire Blvd., Suite 715, Beverly Hills, CA 90212-2967. To request information at any of these offices, call the **France on Call** hotline (☎ 900/990-0040); each call costs 50¢ per minute.

The French Government Tourist Office publishes *France Insider's News,* a quarterly newspaper with the latest news and best deals on charming hotels, cultural happenings, restaurants worth every franc, and other fascinating discoveries in both Paris and the provinces. It's edited by journalist David Doty, who's an expert on travel to France. Free subscriptions are available by calling the France on Call hotline (above) or writing to the French Government Tourist Office at the New York City address.

IN CANADA Write to Maison de la France/French Government Tourist Office, 1981 av. McGill College, Tour Esso, Suite 490, Montréal, PQ H3A 2W9 (☎ 514/288-4264); or 30 St. Patricks St., Suite 700, Toronto, ON M5T 3A3 (☎ 416/593-4723).

IN BRITAIN Write to Maison de la France/French Government Tourist Office, 178 Piccadilly, London, W1V 0AL (☎ 0171/491-7622).

IN AUSTRALIA Write to the French Tourist Office, in the B.N.P. Building, 12th Floor, 12 Castlereagh St., Sydney, NSW 2000 (☎ 02/231-5244).

IN IRELAND Write to the Maison de la France/French Government Tourist Office, 35 Lower Abbey St., Dublin 1, Ireland (☎ 01/703-4046).

Monaco on Your Mind?

Information on travel to Monaco (which retains some degree of autonomy from the rest of France) is available from the **Monaco Government Tourist and Convention Bureau,** 845 Third Ave., New York, NY 10022 (☎ 212/759-5227, or 800/753-9696). Although most of its facilities (along with its consulate) are in New York at the above address, Monaco maintains a branch office at 542 S. Dearborn Ave., Chicago, IL 60605 (☎ 312/939-7863), and at 1001 Genter, Suite 4E, La Jolla, CA 92037 (☎ 619/459-8912). In London, the office is at 3/18 Chelsea Garden Market, Chelsea Harbour, London SX10 OXE (☎ 0171/352-9962). Visa requirements for travel to Monaco are exactly the same as those for travel to France, and there are virtually no border patrols or passport formalities at the Monegasque frontier.

IN NEW ZEALAND   There's no representative in New Zealand, so citizens should contact the Australian representative.

REQUIRED DOCUMENTS

PASSPORT   All foreign (non-French) nationals need a valid passport to enter France (check its expiration date).

VISA   As of July 1, 1989, the French government no longer requires visas for **U.S. citizens,** providing they're staying in France for less than 90 days. For longer stays, U.S. visitors must apply for a long-term visa, residence card, or temporary-stay visa. Each requires proof of income or a viable means of support in France and a legitimate purpose for remaining in the country. Applications are available from the Consulate Section of the French Embassy, 4101 Reservoir Rd. NW, Washington, DC 20007 (☎ 202/944-6015), or from the visa section of the French Consulate at 935 Fifth Ave., New York, NY 10021 (☎ 212/606-3653).

Visas are generally required for **citizens of other countries,** although Canadian, Swiss, and Japanese citizens and citizens of EU countries are exempt from the visa requirement (but check with your nearest French consulate, as the situation can change overnight).

DRIVER'S LICENSE   U.S. and Canadian driver's licenses are valid in France, but if you're going to tour Europe by car you may want to invest in an **International Driver's License.** Apply at any branch of the American Automobile Association (AAA). You must be 18 years old and include two 2- by 2-inch photographs, a $10 fee, and your valid U.S. driver's license with the application. If AAA doesn't have a branch in your hometown, send a photograph of your driver's license (front and back) with the fee and photos to AAA, 1000 AAA Dr. (P.O. Box 28), Heathrow, FL 32746-5063 (☎ 407/444-4300, or 800/222-4357). Always carry your original license with you to Europe, however.

In Canada, you pay $10 Canadian and apply to the Canadian Automobile Association (CAA), 2 Carlton St., Toronto, ON M5B 153 (☎ 416/593-6119).

INTERNATIONAL INSURANCE CERTIFICATE   In Europe, you must have an international insurance certificate, called a green card (*carte verte*). The car-rental agency will provide one if you're renting.

MONEY

CASH/CURRENCY   The basic unit of French currency is the **franc (F),** worth about 19¢ U.S. (about 5.26 francs = $1 U.S.). One franc breaks down into 100 **centimes.** Coins are issued in units of 5, 10, 20, and 50 centimes, plus 1, 2, 5, and 10 francs. Bills come in 10, 20, 50, and 100 francs. The franc and the dollar, like all world currencies, fluctuate on the market. That means the franc-to-dollar conversions given in parentheses throughout this book are not exact; they're presented only to give you a rough idea of the price you'll pay in U.S. dollars. There's no way to predict exactly what the rate of exchange will be when you visit France. Check with your bank for up-to-the-minute quotations.

TRAVELER'S CHECKS   Most large banks sell traveler's checks, charging fees of 1% to 2% of the value of the checks, though some out-of-the-way banks have charged as much as 7%. If your bank wants more than a 2% commission, it sometimes pays to call the traveler's check issuers directly for the address of outlets where this commission will be less.

   American Express (☎ 800/221-7282 in the U.S. and Canada) doesn't charge a commission to AAA members or holders of certain types of American Express cards. For questions or problems arising outside the United States or Canada, contact any of the company's regional representatives. There's also **Citicorp** (☎ 800/ 645-6556 in the U.S. and Canada, or 813/623-1709, collect, from elsewhere). **Thomas Cook** (☎ 800/223-7373 in the U.S. and Canada, or 609/987-7300, collect, from elsewhere) issues MasterCard traveler's checks. And **Interpayment Services** (☎800/221-2426 in the U.S. and Canada, or 212/858-8500, collect, from elsewhere) sells Visa checks issued by a consortium of member banks and the Thomas Cook organization.

   Each of these agencies will refund your checks if they're lost or stolen, provided you have sufficient documentation. Of course, carry your documentation in a safe place—never along with your checks. When purchasing checks from one of the banks listed, ask about refund hotlines; American Express and Bank of America have the most offices around the world.

   Sometimes you can purchase traveler's checks in the currency of the country you're planning to visit, thereby avoiding a conversion fee. American Express, for example, issues checks in French francs. Foreign banks may ask up to 5% to convert your checks into French francs. Note, also, that you always get a better rate if you cash traveler's checks at the banks issuing them.

CREDIT & CHARGE CARDS   Credit and charge cards are useful in France. Both **American Express** and **Diners Club** are widely recognized. The French equivalent for Visa is **Carte Bleue.** A **Eurocard** sign on an establishment means it accepts MasterCard.

   With American Express and Visa not only can you charge purchases in shops and restaurants that take the card but you can also withdraw francs from bank cash machines at many locations in France. Check with your credit/charge-card company before leaving home.

   Of course, you may make a purchase with a credit or charge card thinking it will be at a certain rate, only to find that the U.S. dollar or British pound has declined by the time your bill arrives and you're actually paying more for an item than you bargained for. But those are the rules of the game. It also can work in

The French Franc

For American Readers At this writing, $1 = approximately 5.26 francs (or 1 franc = 19¢), and this was the rate of exchange used to calculate the dollar values given in this book, rounded to the nearest nickel.

For British Readers At this writing, £1 = approximately 8 F (or 1 F = 12.5p), and this was the rate of exchange used to calculate the pound values in the table below.

Note: Because the exchange rate fluctuates from time to time, this table should be used only as a general guide:

F	U.S.$	U.K.£	F	U.S.$	U.K.£
1	.19	.13	150	28.52	18.75
2	.38	.25	200	38.02	25.00
3	.57	.38	250	47.53	31.25
4	.76	.50	300	57.03	37.50
5	.95	.63	350	66.54	43.75
6	1.14	.75	400	76.05	50.00
7	1.33	.88	450	85.55	56.25
8	1.52	1.00	500	95.05	62.50
9	1.71	1.13	600	114.07	75.00
10	1.90	1.25	700	133.08	87.50
15	2.85	1.88	800	152.09	100.00
20	3.80	2.50	900	171.10	112.50
25	4.75	3.13	1,000	190.11	125.00
50	9.51	6.25	1,250	237.64	156.25
75	14.26	9.38	1,500	285.17	187.50
100	19.01	12.50	2,000	380.23	250.00

your favor if the dollar or pound should unexpectedly rise after you make a purchase.

WHAT WILL YOUR TRIP COST?

France is one of the world's most expensive destinations. But, to compensate, it often offers top-value food and lodging. Part of the problem is the value-added tax (VAT), which tacks about 6% to 33% on top of everything. It's expensive to rent and drive a car in France (gasoline is costly, too), and flying within France costs more than flying within the United States. Train travel is relatively inexpensive, though, especially if you purchase a rail pass. Inflation has stayed at 2% during the mid-1990s.

Remember that prices in Paris and on the Riviera will be higher than those in the provinces. Three of the most touristed parts of France—Brittany, Normandy, and the Loire Valley—have reasonably priced hotels and scads of restaurants offering superb food at medium prices.

What Things Cost in Paris	U.S.$
Taxi from Charles de Gaulle Airport to the city center	38.00
Taxi from Orly Airport to the city center	32.30
Public transportation for an average trip within the city from a Métro *carnet* (packet) of 10	.78
Local telephone call	.33
Double room at Le Ritz (very expensive)	665.00
Double room at Lord Byron (moderate)	165.30
Double room at the Hôtel Opal (inexpensive)	91.20
Lunch for one, without wine, at Chez Georges (moderate)	49.40
Lunch for one, without wine, at Le Drouot (inexpensive)	13.30
Dinner for one, without wine, at Le Grand Véfour (very expensive)	142.50
Dinner for one, without wine, at Chez André (moderate)	34.20
Dinner for one, without wine, at Aux Charpentiers (inexpensive)	28.00
Glass of wine	3.00
Coca-Cola	3.50
Cup of coffee	3.10
Roll of ASA 100 film, 36 exposures	7.00
Admission to the Louvre	6.75
Movie ticket	8.50
Theater ticket (at the Comédie-Française)	25.00

2 When to Go

July and August are the worst months—that's when there are the most tourists. Parisians desert their city in August, leaving it to the tourists and the businesses that cater to them. Paris has an uncommonly long springtime, lasting through April, May, and June, and an equally extended fall, September through November. The climate, however, is temperate throughout the year.

The best time to come to Paris is off-season, in the early spring or late autumn, when the tourist trade has trickled to a manageable flow and everything is easier to come by—hotel rooms, Métro seats, even good-tempered waiters.

Don't come to Paris in the first two weeks of October without a confirmed hotel reservation. The weather's fine, but the place is jammed for the annual motor show when the French indulge their passion for cars.

CLIMATE France's weather varies considerably from region to region and sometimes from town to town as little as 12 miles apart. Despite its north latitude, Paris never gets very cold. Snow is a rarity. The hands-down winner for wetness is Brittany, where Brest (known for the mold that adds flavor to its blue cheeses—probably caused by the constant rainfall) receives a staggering amount of rain between October and December. The rain usually falls in a kind of steady, foggy drizzle and rarely lasts more than a day. May is considered the driest month.

The Mediterranean coast of the south has the driest climate. When it does rain, it's usually heaviest in spring and autumn. (Surprisingly, Cannes sometimes receives more annual rainfall than Paris.) Summers are comfortably dry—beneficial to humans but deadly to much of the vegetation, which (unless it's irrigated) often dries and burns up in the parched months.

Provence dreads *le mistral* (an unrelenting, hot, dry, dusty wind from North Africa), which most often blows in winter for a few days, but which can blow for up to two weeks.

Regional Rain- & Snowfall   An alpine climate, with heavy snowfall, prevails in the French Alps; a mild Atlantic climate prevails in the southwest near the Garonne delta. In the east, when it does rain it's likely to come down in heavy thundershowers, though rarely strong enough to do any serious damage to riverbanks or houses. On France's central plateau, the elevated altitude causes more snow to remain on the ground than you'll find in most of the rest of the country.

Weather Forecasts   For up-to-the-minute weather forecasts in the United States, dial 900/WEATHER, at a cost of 95¢ per minute. This report comes from the cable TV station Weather Channel. Listen to the recorded menu, pressing the appropriate buttons on your Touch-Tone phone after dialing the 900 number given above. The 24-hour service reports on conditions in Paris and several other large cities throughout France.

HOLIDAYS (*JOURS FERIES*)   In France, holidays are known as *jours feriés*. Shops and many businesses—banks and some museums and restaurants—close on holidays, but hotels and emergency services remain open.

The main holidays—a mix of both secular and religious ones—include New Year's Day (Jan 1), Shrove Tuesday (the Tues before Ash Wednesday), Good Friday, Easter Sunday, Ascension Day (40 days after Easter), Pentecost Sunday (seventh Sun after Easter), Whit Monday, Labor Day (May 1), V-E Day in Europe (May 8), Bastille Day (July 14), Assumption of the Blessed Virgin (Aug 15), All Saints' Day (Nov 1), Armistice Day (Nov 11), and Christmas (Dec 25).

FRANCE CALENDAR OF EVENTS

January
  Monte Carlo Motor Rally. The world's most venerable car race. Usually mid-January.

February
  ✪ **Carnival of Nice.** Float processions, parades, confetti battles, boat races, street music and food, masked balls, and fireworks are all part of this ancient celebration. The climax follows a 130-year-old tradition where King Carnival is burned in effigy, an event preceded by Les Batailles des Fleurs (Battles of the Flowers), during which members of opposing teams pelt one another with flowers.
    Where: Nice, especially on promenade des Anglais. **When:** Late February to early March. **How:** Come with proof of a hotel reservation. For information, contact the Comité des Fêtes, 5 promenade des Anglais, 06000 Nice (☎ 92-14-60-60; fax 93-87-56-10).

April
  • **Son-et-Lumière (Sound-and-Light) Shows**, Loire Valley. April to September.

May

- **Mai Musicale,** Bordeaux. Music festival with operas, recitals, and concerts. Final two weeks of May.
- ✪ **Cannes Film Festival.** Movie madness transforms this city into the kingdom of the media-related deal, with daily melodramas acted out in cafés, on sidewalks, and in hotel lobbies. Great for voyeurs.

    Where: Cannes. **When:** May 17–28. **How:** Reserve early and make a deposit. Getting a table on the Carlton Hotel terrace is even more difficult than procuring a room. Admission to some of the prestigious films is by invitation only. There are box-office tickets for the less important films, which play 24 hours. For information, contact Direction du Festival International du Film, 99 bd. Malesherbes, 75008 Paris (☎ 1/42-66-92-20; fax 1/45-61-97-60). Two weeks before the festival, the event's administration moves en masse to the Palais des Festivals, Esplanade Georges-Pompidou, 06400 Cannes (☎ 93-39-01-00).
- **Monaco Grand Prix,** Monaco. Hundreds of cars race through narrow streets and winding corniche roads in a surreal blend of high-tech machinery and medieval architecture. May 25–28.
- **St-Guilhem Music Season,** St-Guilhem le Désert (Languedoc). A festival of baroque organ and choral music held in a medieval monastery. Mid-May to mid-August. For information, call 67-63-14-99.

June

- **Spectacle de Puy du Fou,** *son-et-lumière* at the Château du Puy du Fou, Les Epesses (Vendée). With a cast of 650 actors, dozens of horses, laser-based light shows, and a soundtrack by famous actors, it celebrates the achievements of the Middle Ages. Mid-June to early September. For information, call 51-64-11-11.
- **The 24-Hour Le Mans Car Race.** June 17–18.
- **Les Nocturnes du Mont-St-Michel.** This is a sound-and-light tour through the maze of stairways and corridors of one of the most impressive medieval monuments of Europe. Every evening from late June to mid-September.

July

- **Le Tour de France.** The world's most famous (and most difficult) bicycle race catalyzes the ardor and patriotism of France. July 1–23.
- **Colmar International Music Festival,** Colmar. Different musical concerts are held in various public buildings of one of the most folkloric towns in Alsace. First two weeks of July.
- ✪ **Festival d'Aix-en-Provence.** A musical event par excellence, featuring everything from Gregorian chant to melodies composed on computerized synthesizers. The audience sits on the sloping lawns of the 14th-century papal palace for operas and concertos. Local recitals are performed in the medieval cloister of the Cathédrale St-Sauveur.

    Where: Aix-en-Provence, Bouches-du-Rhône. **When:** July 11–30. **How:** Make advance hotel reservations and take a written confirmation with you when you arrive. Expect heat, crowds, and traffic. For information, contact the Festival International d'Art Lyrique et de Musique, Palais de l'Ancien Archévêche, 13100 Aix-en-Provence (☎ 42-17-34-00; fax 42-96-12-61).
- **Bastille Day.** Dances, drinking, and fireworks take place around France to celebrate the storming of the Bastille and the start of the French Revolution in 1789. July 14.

○ **Grand Parade du Jazz (Nice Jazz Festival).** This is the biggest, flashiest, and most prestigious jazz festival in Europe, with world-class entertainers. Concerts begin in early afternoon and go until late at night (sometimes all night in the clubs) on in the Arènes de Cimiez, a hill above the city.

   Where: Nice. **When:** 10 days in mid-July. **How:** Reserve hotel rooms way in advance. For information, contact the Grand Parade du Jazz, c/o Hôtel Abela, 223 promenade des Anglais, 06200 Nice, or Office de Tourisme, avenue Thiers, 06000 Nice (☎ **93-87-07-07**).

• **Les Chorégies d'Orange**, Orange. One of southern France's most important lyric festivals presents oratorios and choral works by master performers whose voices are amplified by the ancient acoustics of France's best-preserved Roman amphitheater. Mid- to late July. For information, call 90-51-83-83.

○ **Festival d'Avignon.** One of France's most prestigious theater events, this world-class festival has a reputation for exposing new talent to critical acclaim. The focus is usually on avant-garde works in theater, dance, and music by groups from around the world. Mime, too.

   Where: Avignon. **When:** Mid-July to early August. **How:** Make hotel reservations early. For information, call 90-82-67-08 or fax 90-85-09-32.

August

• **Festival Inter-Celtique de Lorient.** Traditional Celtic verse and lore are celebrated in the Celtic heart of France, Brittany. The event includes 4,500 classical and folkloric musicians, dancers, singers, and painters from all over. Throughout July and August, traditional Breton *pardons* (religious processions) take place in this once-independent maritime duchy. For information, call 99-28-44-30.

September

○ **Festival International de Folklore et Fête de la Vigne (Les Folkloriades).** At the International Festival of Folklore and Wine, in Dijon, dance troupes from around the world perform, parade, and participate in folkloric events to help to celebrate the famous wines of Burgundy.

   Where: Dijon, Beaune, and about 20 villages of the Côte d'Or. **When:** Early September. **How:** For information, contact the Festival de Musique et Danse Populares, 27 bd. de la Tremouille, 21025 Dijon (☎ **80-30-37-95;** fax 80-30-23-44).

October

• **Perpignan Jazz Festival.** Musicians from everywhere jam in what many visitors consider Languedoc's most appealing season. For information, call 68-35-37-46.

November

○ **Les Trois Glorieuses.** The country's most important wine festival is celebrated in three Burgundian towns. Although you may not gain access to many of the gatherings, there are enough wine tastings and other amusements to keep you occupied.

   Where: Clos-de-Vougeot, Beaune, and Meursault. **When:** Third week in November. Festivities include wine auctions from some of the district's most historic cellars. **How:** Reserve early or visit as part of day trips from any of several nearby villages. Confirm information by contacting the Comité Régional du

Tourisme, place Darcy, 21035 Dijon (☎ **80-43-42-12**), or Office de Tourisme, rue de l'Hôtel-Dieu, 21200 Beaune (☎ **80-22-24-51**).

December

- **Christmas Fairs,** Alsace (especially Strasbourg). More than 35 Alsatian villages celebrate a traditional Christmas. The events in Strasbourg have continued for nearly 430 years. Other towns with noteworthy celebrations are Munster, Selestat, Riquewihr, and Kaysersberg. Late December.

PARIS CALENDAR OF EVENTS

January

- **International Ready-to-Wear Fashion Shows** (Le Salon International de Prêt-à-porter), Parc des Expositions, Porte de Versailles, 15e (Métro: Porte-de-Versailles). Various couture houses, such as Lanvin and Courrèges, present their own shows at their respective headquarters. Here you'll see what the public will be wearing in six months. Mid-January to mid-February.

March

- **Foire du Trône,** on the Neuilly Lawn of the Bois de Vincennes. This mammoth amusement park operates daily from 2pm to midnight. End of March to June.

April

- **Paris Marathon.** Runners from around the world compete. Weekend of April 2.
- **City of Paris's Festival of Sacred Art.** A dignified series of concerts held in five of the oldest (or most recognizable) Paris churches. For information, call 45-61-54-99.

May

- **End of World War II.** Although the capitulation of the Nazis was signed on May 7, 1945, the celebration lasts from May 5 to 8 in Paris and even more visibly in Reims.
- Illuminated fountains at Versailles. May to September.
- **French Open Tennis Championship,** Stade Roland-Garros. May 29–June 11.

June

- **Festival Juin.** This is a month of music, art exhibitions, and drama set for the most part in Paris's 16th arrondissement. For information, call 45-03-21-16.
- **Le Prix du Jockey Club** (June 4) and the **Prix Diane-Hermès** (June 11), Hippodrome de Chantilly. Phone 49-10-20-30 for information on this and all other equine events in this calendar.
- **Paris Air Show,** Le Bourget Airport. Early June in alternate years only (next air show is 1997).
- **Festival Chopin.** Here you'll find everything you've ever wanted to hear from the Polish exile who lived most of his life in Paris. Piano recitals are given in the Orangerie de Bagatelle. For information, call 45-00-22-19. June 16–July 14.
- **Grand Steeplechase de Paris,** Auteuil racetrack in the Bois de Boulogne. Mid-June.
- **Festival de Musique de St-Denis.** Music in the burial place of the French kings. Call 48-13-12-12 for information. Mid-June to mid-July.
- **Grand Prix de Paris,** Longchamp racetrack. Late June.

July
- **Festival "Weekend" de Musique en l'Ile.** A spectrum of classical music and oratorios are presented in four historic churches, including the Sainte-Chapelle. For information, call 44-62-70-90. July 1–September 5.
- ✪ **Bastille Day.** Celebrating the birth of modern-day France, the nation's festivities reach their peak in Paris with street fairs, pageants, fireworks, and feasts. The day begins with a parade down the Champs-Elysées and ends with fireworks at Montmartre. **When:** July 14. **Where:** Bars, restaurants, streets, and private homes throughout Paris. **How:** Hum the "Marseillaise"; outfit yourself with a beret, a pack of Gauloises, a bottle of cheap wine, and a baguette; leave your hotel; and stamp around the neighborhood.
- **Paris Quartier d'Eté.** This movable feast of concerts, art exhibitions, and dance recitals is held at four locations in and around central Paris. For information, call 40-28-40-33. July 15–August 15.
- **Le Grand Tour de France.** Europe's most visible bicycle race decides its winner at a finish line drawn across the Champs-Elysées. Late July.

September
- **Festival d'Automne.** Concentrating mainly on modern music, ballet, theater, and modern art, this is the most eclectic of the festivals. For details, write to the Festival d'Automne, 156 rue de Rivoli, 75001 Paris (☎ 1/42-96-96-94). Late September until just before Christmas.
- **International Ready-to-Wear Fashion Shows** (Le Salon International de Prêt-à-porter), Parc des Expositions, Porte de Versailles, 15e (Métro: Porte-de-Versailles). Late September.

October
- **Festival d'Automne.** All month.
- ✪ **Paris Auto Show.** Glistening metal, glitzy attendees, lots of hype, and the latest models from world automakers, this is the showcase for European car design. **Where:** Parc des Expositions, near the Porte de Versailles in western Paris. **When:** 10 days in early October. **How:** Check *Pariscope* for details or contact the French Government Tourist Office (see "Information, Required Documents, and Money," earlier in this chapter).
- **Prix de l'Arc de Triomphe.** This is France's most prestigious horse race. Early October.

November
- **Festival d'Automne.** All month.
- **Armistice Day.** The signing of the controversial document that ended World War I is celebrated with a military parade from the Arc de Triomphe to the Hôtel des Invalides. November 11.

December
- **Festival d'Automne.** Through late December.
- **The Boat Fair** (Le Salon International de la Navigation de Plaisance), Parc des Expositions, Porte de Versailles, 15e (Métro: Porte-de-Versailles). This is Europe's most visible exposition of what's afloat.
- **Fête de St-Sylvestre** (New Year's Eve). It's most boisterously celebrated in the Quartier Latin around the Sorbonne. At midnight, the city explodes. Strangers

kiss strangers, and boulevard St-Michel and the Champs-Elysées become virtual pedestrian malls. December 31.

3 Health & Insurance

STAYING HEALTHY   If you need a doctor, your hotel will locate one for you. You can also obtain a list of English-speaking doctors from the **International Association for Medical Assistance to Travelers (IAMAT):** in the United States, at 417 Center St., Lewiston, NY 14092 (☎ **716/754-4883**); in Canada, at 40 Regal Rd., Guelph, ON N1K 1B5 (☎ **519/836-0102**). Getting medical help is relatively easy. Don't be alarmed, even in rural areas. Competent doctors can be found in all parts of the country.

INSURANCE   Insurance needs for the traveler abroad fall into three categories: (1) health and accident, (2) trip cancellation, and (3) lost luggage.

First, review your present policies—you may already have adequate coverage between them and what's offered by your credit/charge-card companies. Many card companies insure their users in case of a travel accident, providing the ticket was purchased with their card. Sometimes fraternal organizations have policies protecting members in case of sickness or accidents abroad.

Incidentally, don't assume that Medicare is the answer to illness in France. It covers only U.S. citizens who travel south of the border to Mexico or north of the border to Canada.

Many homeowners' insurance policies cover theft of luggage during foreign travel and loss of documents—your Eurailpass, passport, or airline ticket, for instance. Coverage is usually limited to about $500 U.S. To submit a claim on your insurance, remember that you'll need police reports or a statement from a medical authority that you did suffer the loss or experience the illness for which you're seeking compensation. Such claims, by their very nature, can be filed only when you return from France.

Some policies (and this is the type you should have) provide advances in cash or transfers of funds so you won't have to dip into your precious travel funds to settle medical bills.

If you've booked a charter fare, you'll probably have to pay a cancellation fee if you cancel a trip suddenly, even if the cancellation is caused by an unforeseen crisis. It's possible to get insurance against such a possibility. Some travel agencies provide this coverage, and often flight insurance against a canceled trip is written into the cost of tickets paid for by credit/charge cards from such companies as Visa and American Express. Many tour operators and insurance agents provide this type of insurance.

The following companies offer such policies:

Access America, 6600 W. Broad St., Richmond, VA 23230 (☎ **804/ 285-3300,** or 800/284-8300), offers a comprehensive travel insurance/assistance package, including medical and on-the-spot hospital payments, medical transportation, baggage insurance, trip cancellation/interruption insurance, and collision-damage insurance for a car rental. Their 24-hour hotline connects you to multilingual coordinators who can offer advice on medical, legal, and travel problems. Packages begin at $27.

Wallach & Co., 107 W. Federal St. (P.O. Box 480), Middleburg, VA 22117-0480 (☎ **703/687-3166,** or 800/237-6615), offers a policy called Healthcare

Abroad (MEDEX). It covers 10 to 90 days at $3 per day; the policy includes accident and sickness coverage to the tune of $100,000. Medical evacuation is also included, along with $25,000 dismemberment and/or death compensation. Provisions for trip cancellation and lost or stolen luggage can also be written into the policy at a nominal cost.

Travel Guard International, 1145 Clark St., Stevens Point, WI 54481 (☎ **800/826-1300**), offers a comprehensive seven-day policy that covers basically everything for $52: emergency assistance, accidental death, trip cancellation/interruption, medical coverage abroad, and lost luggage. However, there are restrictions you should understand before accepting the coverage.

4 Special Accommodations in France

French hotels are rated by stars: from four-star luxury and four-star deluxe, down through three-star (first class), two-star (good-quality tourist hotel), and one-star (budget) hotels. In some of the lower categories, the rooms may not have private baths; instead, many have what the French call a *cabinet de toilette* (hot and cold running water and a bidet), while others have only sinks. In such hotels, bathrooms are down the hall. Nearly all hotels in France today have central heating, but, in some cases, you might wish the owners would turn it up a little on a cold night.

Most hotel rates quoted in France are for double occupancy, since most rooms are doubles; if you're traveling solo, be sure to ask about rates for a single. Some of these rooms contain twin beds, but most have double beds, suitable for one or two.

RELAIS & CHATEAUX

Now known worldwide, this organization of deluxe and first-class hostelries began in France for visitors seeking the ultimate in hotel living and dining, most often in a traditional atmosphere. Numbering some 150 establishments, Relais & Châteaux hotels are found throughout the country. Former castles, abbeys, and manor houses have been converted into hostelries or small inns and elegant hotels. They always have a limited number of rooms, so reservations are imperative. Sometimes these owner-run establishments have pools and tennis courts. The Relais part of the organization refers to inns called *relais*, meaning "posthouse." These tend to be less luxurious than the châteaux, but they're often quite charming for those seeking a traditional atmosphere. Top-quality restaurants are *relais gourmands*.

For reservations or an illustrated catalog of these establishments, send $10 to **Relais & Châteaux,** 11 E. 44th St., Suite 704, New York, NY 10017 (for information about and descriptions of individual Relais & Châteaux, call 212/856-0115).

BED-&-BREAKFASTS

Called *gîtes-chambres d'hôe* in France, these accommodations may be one or several bedrooms on a farm or in a village home. Many of them offer one main meal of the day as well (lunch or dinner).

There are at least 6,000 of these accommodations listed with **La Maison du Tourisme Vert Fédération Nationale des Gîtes Ruraux-de-France,** 35 rue Godet-de-Mauroy, 75009 Paris (☎ **1/49-70-75-75**). Sometimes these B&B accommodations aren't as simple as you might think: Instead of a barebones farm room, you might be housed in a mansion deep in the French countryside.

In the United States, a good source for this type of accommodation is **The French Experience,** 370 Lexington Ave., New York, NY 10017 (☎ 212/986-3800). It also rents fully furnished houses with pools for as short a period as one week. Many of these are on scenic hills overlooking the French Riviera.

Listings of more than 300 Paris homes and apartments ranging from $30 to $55 can be secured from **Bed & Breakfast 1,** 73 rue Notre-Dame-des-Champs, 75006 Paris (☎ 1/43-25-42-97).

CONDOS, VILLAS, HOUSES & APARTMENTS

If you can stay for at least a week and don't mind cooking your own meals and cleaning house, you might want to rent a long-term accommodation. The local French Tourist Board might help you obtain a list of real estate agencies that represent this type of rental (which tends to be especially popular at ski resorts). In France, one of the best agencies for this is the **Fédération Nationale des Agents Immobiliers,** 129 rue du Faubourg St-Honoré, 75008 Paris (☎ 1/44-20-77-00).

In the United States, **At Home Abroad,** 405 E. 56th St., Apt. 6H, New York, NY 10022-2466 (☎ 212/421-9165; fax 212/752-1591), specializes in villas on the French Riviera and in the Dordogne as well as places in the Provençal hill towns. Rentals usually are for one or two weeks. For a $25 registration fee (applicable to any rental), photographs of the properties and a newsletter will be sent to you.

A worthwhile competitor is **Vacances en Campagne,** British Travel International, P.O. Box 299, Elkton, VA (☎ 800/327-6097). Its directory, which sells for $4, contains information on more than 700 potential rentals across Europe, including France.

If renting an apartment in Paris is what you're looking for, the **Barclay International Group,** 150 E. 52nd St., New York, NY 10022 (☎ 212/832-3777, or 800/845-6636), can give you access to about 1,000 apartments ranging from modest modern units to among the most stylish. Rentals range from one night to up to a year; all have color TVs and kitchens, and many have concierge staffs and lobby-level security. The least-expensive units cost around $100 a night, double occupancy. Incremental discounts are granted for a stay of one week or three weeks. Rentals must be prepaid in U.S. dollars.

HOMESTAYS

Friends in France, Ltd., 40 E. 19th St., Suite 8, New York, NY 10003 (☎ 212/269-9820; fax 212/228-0576), arranges homestays in over 50 private residences, ranging from farmhouses to manors and châteaux, in every region of France. The host families have been carefully selected to assure you the friendliest and most comfortable stay. The program's 90-page *Guide to Host Families* describes the homes, the hosts, and other necessary details; it's available by sending a check for $12 (including postage) to the above address. The staff will also personally assist you in selecting just the right hosts to match your interests and needs. The cost is between $55 and $120 for a room for two, including breakfast.

HOTEL ASSOCIATIONS

Hometours International, Inc., P.O. Box 11503, Knoxville, TN 37939 (☎ 615/588-8722, or 800/367-4668), established in 1982, offers moderately priced apartments as well as apartment hotels and B&Bs in Paris. On the Riviera, beautiful villas, all with pools, can be rented at reasonable rates.

For budget travelers, the organization offers a prepaid voucher program for the Campanile hotels, a chain of about 350 two-star family-run hotels throughout France. Rates begin as low as $69 per night double. This is an excellent alternative to B&B hotels, since all chain members provide a buffet breakfast for only 30 F ($5.70) per person.

Others wanting to trim costs might want to check out the **Mercure** chain—an organization of simple but clean and modern hotels offering attractive values throughout France. Even at the peak of the tourist season, a room at a Mercure in the heart of Paris rents for about $100 per night. For more information on Mercure hotels and a copy of their 100-page directory, call RESINTER (☎ **800/ 221-4542** in the U.S.).

Formule 1 hotels are bare-bones and basic though clean and safe, offering rooms for up to three people at around $25 a night. Built from prefabricated units, these air-conditioned soundproof hotels are shipped to a site and reassembled, often on the outskirts of such cities as Paris (27 in the suburbs alone). In addition, there's a coterie of 150 of these low-budget hotels throughout the rest of France. (Formule 1, a member of the French hotel giant Accor, recently purchased the Motel 6 chain in the United States, to which Formule 1 bears a resemblance.)

While a reservation at any member of the Accor group can be made through the RESINTER number above, if you wish to try the Formule 1 group make reservations through Best Western (☎ **800/528-1234** in the U.S. and Canada). Be warned that Formule 1 properties have almost none of the Gallic charm for which some country inns are famous, but you can save some money by planning your itinerary at Formule 1 properties. For a directory, write to Formule 1/ETAP Hotels, 29 promenade Michel Simon, 93166 Noisy-le-Grand CEDEX, France. (There's no phone, but faxes can be sent to 1/43-05-31-51.)

Other worthwhile economy bets, sometimes with a bit more charm, are the hotels and restaurants belonging to the **Féderation Nationale des Logis de France,** 83 av. d'Italie, 75013 Paris (☎ **1/45-84-70-00**). This is a marketing association of more than 5,000 hotels, usually simple country inns especially convenient for motorists, most rated one or two stars. The association publishes an annual directory, priced in France at 70 F ($13.30), or around $22, depending on the merchant, at bookstores outside of France. Copies are available from the French Government Tourist Office, Maison de France, 444 Madison Ave., 16th Floor, New York, NY 10020-2452 (☎ **212/838-7800**), and also from stores specializing in travel publications, including the Traveller's Bookstore, 22 W. 52nd St., New York, NY 10019 (☎ **212/664-0995**).

5 Tips for Special Travelers

FOR DISABLED TRAVELERS

Facilities for the disabled are certainly above average in Europe, and nearly all modern hotels in France now provide rooms designed for the disabled. However, older hotels (unless they've been renovated) may not provide such important features as elevators, special toilet facilities, or ramps for wheelchair access.

The new high-speed trains are wheelchair accessible; older trains have special compartments for wheelchair boarding. On the Paris Métro, handicapped persons are able to sit in wider seats provided for their comfort. Guide dogs ride free. Some stations don't have escalators or elevators, so these present problems.

There are agencies in the United States and France that can provide advance-planning information. Knowing in advance which hotels, restaurants, and attractions are wheelchair accessible can save you a lot of frustration—firsthand accounts by other disabled travelers are the best.

The **Association des Paralysés de France,** 17 bd. Auguste-Blanqui, 75013 Paris (☎ 1/40-78-69-00), is a privately funded organization that provides wheelchair-bound persons with documentation, moral support, and travel ideas. In addition to the central Paris office, it maintains an office in each of the 90 *départments* of France and can help find accessible hotels, transportation, sightseeing, house rentals, and (in some cases) companionship for paralyzed or partially paralyzed persons.

The **Travel Information Service,** Moss Rehab Hospital, 1200 W. Tabor Rd., Philadelphia, PA 19141 (☎ 215/456-9600), can give you an overview of facilities in Paris and provide toll-free numbers for airlines with special lines for the hearing impaired.

"Air Transportation of Handicapped Persons," prepared by the U.S. Department of Transportation, can be obtained by writing to Free Advisory Circular No. AC12032, Distribution Unit, U.S. Department of Transportation, Publications Division, M-4332, Washington, DC 20590.

The **Society for the Advancement of Travel for the Handicapped,** 347 Fifth Ave., New York, NY 10016 (☎ 212/447-7284), can provide a list of companies operating tours for disabled travelers. Yearly membership dues are $45, $25 for seniors and students.

You might also consider the **FEDCAP Rehabilitation Service,** 154 W. 14th St., New York, NY 10011 (☎ 212/727-4200; fax 212/727-4374), offering summer tours for members, who pay $4 annually.

The **Information Center for Individuals with Disabilities,** Fort Point Place, 27–43 Wormwood St., Boston, MA 02210 (☎ 617/727-5540; fax 617/345-5318), is another good source. It has lists of travel agents who specialize in tours for the disabled.

One of the best organizations serving the needs of the disabled (wheelchairs and walkers) is **Flying Wheels Travel,** 143 W. Bridge (P.O. Box 382), Owatoona, MN 55060 (☎ 507/451-5005, or 800/535-6790), which offers various escorted tours and cruises internationally.

For a $20 annual fee, consider joining **Mobility International USA,** P.O. Box 10767, Eugene, OR 97440 (☎ 503/343-6812). It answers questions about the facilities for the handicapped at various destinations and offers discounts on videos, publications, and the programs it sponsors.

Finally, the bimonthly *Handicapped Travel Newsletter* keeps you current on accessible sights worldwide. To order a $15 annual subscription, call 903/677-1260 or fax 903/677-1260.

FOR GAY & LESBIAN TRAVELERS

Paris vies with London and Amsterdam for the title of Europe's gay and lesbian capital. France is one of the world's most tolerant countries toward gays and lesbians. Paris, of course, is the center of gay life in France, though gay and lesbian establishments exist through the provinces as well.

The following information may be helpful before you leave home. For specific information about Paris networks and resources for gays and lesbians, see the end of Chapter 4. And for hotels and restaurants that are particularly gay- and lesbian-friendly, see the "Staying 'Out'" box in Chapter 5 and the "Dining 'Out'" box in Chapter 6.

PUBLICATIONS Before going to France, men can order *Spartacus*, the international gay guide ($29.95) or *Guia Gay*, a bilingual (English/Italian) guidebook published in Italy ($12.50). Also helpful is *Odysseus, the International Gay Travel Planner* ($25). Both lesbians and gays might want to pick up *Places of Interest: World* ($16). David Andrusia's *Gay Europe* (1995) includes France in its Europe survey but lacks details and specifics. These books and others are available from **A Different Light Book Store,** 151 W. 19th St., New York, NY 10011 (☎ 212/ 989-4850, or 800/343-4002), or **Giovanni's Room,** 1145 Pine St., Philadelphia, PA 19107 (☎ 215/923-2960).

Our World, 1104 N. Nova Rd., Suite 251, Daytona Beach, FL 32117 (☎ 904/ 441-5367), is a magazine about gay and lesbian travel worldwide; it costs $35 for 10 issues. *Out & About,* 8 W. 19th St., Suite 401, New York, NY 10011 (☎ 800/ 929-2268), has been hailed for its "straight" reporting about gay travel. It profiles the best gay or gay-friendly hotels, gyms, clubs, and other places, with coverage ranging from Key West to Paris. Its cost is $49 per year for 10 information-packed issues. Aimed at the more upscale gay traveler, it's been praised by everybody from *Travel & Leisure* to the *New York Times.*

ORGANIZATIONS The **International Gay Travel Association (IGTA),** P.O. Box 4974, Key West, FL 33041 (☎ 305/292-0217, or voice mail 800/448-8550), is an international network of travel-industry businesses and professionals who encourage gay/lesbian travel worldwide. With around 1,000 members, it offers quarterly newsletters, marketing mailings, and a membership directory that's updated quarterly. Membership often includes gay or lesbian businesses but is open to individuals for $125 yearly, plus a $25 administration fee for new members. Members are kept informed of gay or gay-friendly hoteliers, tour operators, and airline and cruise line representatives, plus such ancillary businesses as the contacts at travel guide publishers and gay-related travel clubs.

UNI (International Network, Inc.), 7231 Radio Rd., Suite 203, Naples, FL 33942 (☎ 800/468-5864), is an exclusive 24-hour national and international telephone line providing members with information on gay events as well as gay-friendly hotels, clubs, restaurants, and bookstores. Membership also offers discounts on services like greens fees at golf courses, dental plans, hotels, and floral arrangements. Annual membership is $99 per person or $139 per couple. Student membership is $79.

Travel Agencies A company called **Our Family Abroad,** 40 W. 57th St., Suite 430, New York, NY 10019 (☎ 212/459-1800, or 800/999-5500), operates escorted tours that include about a dozen Europe itineraries. In California, a leading gay-friendly option for travel arrangements is **Above and Beyond,** 3568 Sacramento St., San Francisco, CA 94118 (☎ 415/922-2683, or 800/397-2681).

Also in California, **Skylink Women's Travel,** 746 Ashland Ave., Santa Monica, CA 90405 (☎ 310/452-0506, or 800/225-5759), runs about two international trips for lesbians yearly.

FOR SENIORS

Many discounts are available in France for seniors—men and women who've reached the "third age," as the French say. For more information, contact the French Government Tourist Office (see "Information, Required Documents, and Money," earlier in this chapter).

DISCOUNT RAIL CARD At any rail station in the country, seniors (men and women age 60 and older—with proof of age) can obtain a *Carte Vermeil* (silver-gilt card). There are two types of Carte Vermeil: The *Carte Vermeil Quatre Temps* costs 150 F ($28.50) and allows a 50% discount on four rail trips per year. A *Carte Vermeil Plein Temps* costs 275 F ($52.25) and is good for a 50% discount on unlimited rail travel throughout the course of a year.

There are some restrictions on Carte Vermeil travel, such as between 3pm Sunday and noon on Monday and from noon on Friday until noon on Saturday. There's no Carte Vermeil discount on the Paris network of commuter trains. Holders of the Plein Temps card sometimes receive discounts of up to 30% on rail trips to many other countries of Western Europe. Carte Vermeil also delivers reduced prices on certain regional bus lines, as well as theater tickets in Paris and half-price admission at state-owned museums.

AIRFARE DISCOUNTS The French domestic airline Air Inter honors "third agers" by offering a 25% to 50% reduction on its regular nonexcursion tariffs. Restrictions do apply, however. Also, discounts of around 10% are offered on selected Air France flights to passengers 62 or over. These include some flights between Paris and Nice, as well as many international flights, including some on the Concorde.

ORGANIZATIONS The **American Association of Retired Persons (AARP)**, 601 E St. NW, Washington, DC 20049 (☎ 202/434-AARP), is the best organization in the United States for seniors, offering discounts on car rentals and hotels.

Elderhostel, 75 Federal St., Boston, MA 02110 (☎ 617/426-7788), arranges numerous study programs around Europe, including France. Most courses, lasting about three weeks, represent great value since they include airfare, accommodations in student dormitories or modest inns, all meals, and tuition. The courses involve no homework, are ungraded, and often focus on the liberal arts. They're not luxury vacations, but they are fun and fulfilling. Participants must be 56 or older. Write or call for a free newsletter and a list of upcoming courses and destinations.

Mature Outlook, 6001 N. Clark St., Chicago, IL 60660 (☎ 800/336-6330; fax 312/764-4871), is a travel organization for people over 50. Members are offered discounts at ITC-member hotels and receive a bimonthly magazine. Annual membership is $9.95, which entitles members to discounts and often free coupons for discounted merchandise from Sears Roebuck. Savings are also offered on selected auto rentals and restaurants.

SAGA International Holidays, 222 Berkeley St., Boston, MA 02116 (☎ 800/343-0273), is well known for its all-inclusive tours for those 50 and older. Insurance is included in the net price of their tours.

The **National Council of Senior Citizens,** 1331 F St. NW, Washington, DC 20005 (☎ 202/347-8800), a nonprofit organization, offers a monthly newsletter (part of which is devoted to travel tips) and discounts on hotel and auto rentals; annual dues are $12 per person or couple.

FOR STUDENTS

Research is the key for students who want to take advantage of budget travel and study abroad. There are organizations and publications that will provide you with all the details of programs available specifically for students—see also "Educational and Study Travel," below. You should carry an **International Student Identity Card (ISIC)**—good for discounts on travel fares and attractions. Youth hostels provide an inexpensive network of accommodations while you trek through the country.

Council Travel is the largest travel service for students and provides details about budget travel, study abroad, work permits, and insurance. For $16 the organization (a subsidiary of the Council on International Educational Exchange) issues an ISIC to bonafide students. Their *Student Travel Catalogue* is available free. Discounted international and domestic air tickets are available from Council Travel with special prices for student and youth travelers. Eurotrain rail passes, YHA passes, weekend packages, overland safaris, and hostel/hotel accommodations are all bookable from Council Travel.

This organization also sells a number of publications, like *Work, Study, Travel Abroad: The Whole World Handbook; Volunteer: The Comprehensive Guide to Voluntary Service in the U.S.A. and Abroad;* and *The Teenager's Guide to Study, Travel, and Adventure Abroad.*

Council Travel has offices throughout the United States. Call 800/GET-AN-ID to find the location nearest you. The main office is at 205 E. 42nd St., New York, NY 10017 (☎ 212/661-1450; fax 212/972-3231).

The **IYHF (International Youth Hostel Federation)** was designed to provide bare-bones accommodations for serious budget travelers. Regular membership costs $25 annually; those under 18 pay $10 and those over 54 pay $15. For information, contact American Youth Hostels (AYH)/Hostelling International, 733 15th St. NW, Suite 840, Washington, DC 20005 (☎202/783-6161).

6 Special Travel Programs: Cultural, Educational & Recreational

Note: Under no circumstances is the inclusion of an organization in this section to be interpreted as a guarantee of its credit-worthiness or competency. Information about the organizations is intended only as a preliminary preview, to be followed up by your own investigation should you be interested.

EDUCATIONAL TRAVEL

LEARNING THE LANGUAGE   The **Alliance Française,** 101 bd. Raspail, 75270 Paris CEDEX 06 (☎ 1/45-44-38-28)—a state-approved nonprofit organization with a network of 1,200 establishments in 107 countries—offers French-language courses to some 350,000 students. The international school in Paris is open all year, and you can enroll for a minimum of a one-month session. Fees tend to be reasonable, and the school offers numerous activities and services. Write for information and application forms at least one month before your departure. In North America, the largest branch is the Alliance Francaise, 22 E. 60th St., New York, NY 10022 (☎ 212/355-6100).

A clearinghouse for information on French-language schools is **Lingua Service Worldwide,** 2 W. 45th St., Suite 500, New York, NY 10036 (☎ 212/768-2728, or 800/394-5327; fax 212/921-7666). Its programs cover not only Paris but also Antibes, Aix-en-Provence, Avignon, Bordeaux, Cannes, Juan-les-Pins, Megève, Montpelier, Nice, Strasbourg, and Tours. Courses can be both long- or short-term, the latter consisting of 20 lessons per week.

The **National Registration Center for Studies Abroad (NRCSA),** 823 N. 2nd St. (P.O. Box 1393), Milwaukee, WI 53201 (☎ 414/278-0631), has a catalog ($3) of schools in France. They'll register you at the school of your choice, arrange for room and board, and make your airline reservations—all for no extra fee. Contact them and ask for a free copy of their newsletter.

LEARNING TO COOK   If you've always wanted to learn to cook *à la française*, you can take those all-important lessons from **Maxime and Eliane Rochereau** at their hotel/restaurant, Le Castel de Bray-et-Monts, Brehemont, 37130 Langeais (☎ 47-96-70-47).

Before settling on the banks of the Loire, the Rochereaux spent 15 years living and working in the United States—Maxime as chef de cuisine at Chicago's Ritz Carlton and Palm Beach's Breakers, Eliane as a caterer for the Palm Beach jet set. In the charming vineyard village of Brehemont, Maxime now offers classes in classic French cooking at an 18th-century manor surrounded by a magnificent garden and stream.

A week's accommodation and full board included, the price is $1,100 per person, double occupancy. Maxime devotes mornings to the preparation of an intricate French meal (from apéritif to dessert), allowing students to observe the service rituals of a working restaurant. Afternoons are usually unscheduled, allowing time for explorations of the nearby châteaux of the Loire Valley. Classes are conducted from February 15 to November 20.

The famous/infamous Georges-Auguste Escoffier (1846–1935) taught the Edwardians how to eat. Today, Le Ritz, once the site of many of Escoffier's meals, maintains the **Ritz-Escoffier Ecole de Gastronomie Française,** 75001 Paris (☎ 1/43-16-30-50, or 800/966-5758 in the U.S.), offering daily demonstration classes of the master's techniques. Courses last 1 to 12 weeks and are taught in French and English.

Le Cordon Bleu, 8 rue Léon-Delhomme, 75015 Paris (☎ 1/48-56-06-06, or 800/457-2433 in the U.S.), was established in 1895 and is probably the most famous French cooking school. Its best-known courses last 10 weeks, at the end of which certificates of competence are issued. Many readers, however, prefer a less intense immersion and opt for either a four-day workshop or a three-hour demonstration class. Enrollment in either of these is on a first-come, first-served basis and costs around 200 F ($38) for a demonstration and around 4,590 F ($872.60) for the four-day workshop. Also of interest to professional chefs (or wannabes) are the two- and five-week courses in catering; they're offered twice a year and attract avid business hopefuls. Any of these programs, even the three-hour quickies, offer unexpected insights into the culinary subculture of Paris.

LEARNING ABOUT THE ARTS & ARCHITECTURE   France contains more world-class art treasures than can be absorbed during one trip. Acting as the North American agent for London-based Swan Hellenic Tours, **Esplanade Tours,** 581 Boyleston St., Boston, MA 02116 (☎ 617/266-7465, or 800/426-5492), recognizes this and offers guided lecture-tours of clearly designated regions of France lasting between 8 and 12 days. Each focuses on all aspects of art and architecture in the Dordogne, Languedoc and the Pyrénées, Provence, and the Auvergne. Tours include lectures, usually by Britain-based authorities on gothic and romanesque architecture, and touch on the geological makeup of the territories.

LEARNING TO PAINT   Amateur watercolor enthusiasts can join an "Arts in the South of France" trip, sponsored by **Art Trek,** P.O. Box 807, Bolinas, CA

94924 (☎ 415/868-1836, or 800/786-1830). Tours, led by art instructors familiar with both the techniques and the traditions of French art, take you to medieval hill towns and such legendary artists' refuges as Antibes, Nice, St-Paul-de-Vence, and Paris. Tours always take place in June and July, when the Mediterranean sunlight is at its intense impressionistic best. The average cost, including airfare from the West Coast, is $4,455 per person. Each tour lasts 16 days, with half board included in accommodations based on double occupancy.

SPA PROGRAMS

To restore the well-being of mind and body, **Spa Trek Travel,** 475 Park Ave. S., New York, NY 10016 (☎ 212/779-3480, or 800/272-3480), offers spa programs at such sites in France as Evian, Thalasso Dinard, and La Baule, as well as stays at such "beauty farms" as the Hôtel Trianon Palace at Versailles and the Thalassoleil Resort in Nice. You can sign up for a week's deluxe accommodations, medical consultation, two or three treatments a day (depending on your personalized program), and exercise.

OPERA TOURS

On a cultural note, **Dailey-Thorp Travel,** 330 W. 58th St., Suite 610, New York, NY 10019-1817 (☎ 212/307-1555), is probably the best-regarded organizer of music and opera tours in America. Because of its "favored" relations with European box offices, the company can purchase blocks of otherwise unavailable tickets to Paris operas and other events and festivals all across Europe. Tours range from 7 to 21 days and include first-class or deluxe accommodations and meals in top European restaurants.

ADVENTURE TOURS

BIKE TOURS A well-recommended company that has led cyclists through the provinces since 1979 is California-based **Backroads,** 1516 5th St., Berkeley, CA 94710 (☎ 510/527-1555, or 800/462-2848). Its well-organized bike tours of Alsace, Burgundy, the Dordogne, the Loire Valley, and Provence last between five and eight days and come in a degree of luxury that includes everything from well-upholstered stays in Relais & Châteaux hotels to simple campgrounds. (In even the camping tours, a staff member is on hand to prepare evening meals.) All tours are "van-supported" and include an accompanying vehicle that provides liquid refreshments and assists in the event of breakdowns. Per-person rates range from $900 to $3,000, depending on the territory, the duration, and the degree of luxury.

Holland Bicycling Tours, Inc., P.O. Box 6485, Thousand Oaks, CA 91359 (☎ 800/852-3258; fax 805/495-8601), is the North American representative for a Dutch-based company that leads 12-day bicycle tours through the flat and richly historic landscapes of the Loire Valley. Frequent stopovers manage to encompass many of the most glorious châteaux and palaces en route, tracing the Loire, Cher, and Indre rivers over mostly flat terrain. Great efforts are expended to create itineraries that for the most part follow secondary roads with very little traffic. The price of the land portion (without airfare) of this tour is $1,675 per person, double occupancy, including all meals, accommodations, and the services of a tour leader. Occupants of single rooms pay a supplement of $300 per person.

BARGE TOURS Before the advent of the railways, many of the crops, building supplies, raw materials, and finished products of France were barged through a series of rivers, canals, and estuaries. Many of these are still graced with their old-fashioned locks and pumps, allowing shallow-draft barges easy access through some of the most idyllic countryside.

Several companies offer tours: **French Country Waterways,** P.O. Box 2195, Duxbury, MA 02331 (☎ **617/934-2454,** or 800/222-1236), leads tours focusing on Burgundy and Champagne. More unusual is **Le Boat,** 215 Union St., Hackensack, NJ 07601 (☎ **201/342-1838,** or 800/992-0291). In business since 1979, it focuses on regions of France not covered by the itineraries of many other barge operators. The company's pair of barges are luxury craft, altered in Rotterdam to a size and shape that fit through the relatively narrow canals and locks of La Camargue, Languedoc, and Provence. Each tour contains no more than 10 passengers in five cabins outfitted with mahogany and brass, plus elegant meals prepared by a Cordon Bleu chef. Itineraries include waterborne transit from Sete to Homps (a port near Carcassone) and wine country tours along the Garonne, through the Médoc region, between Toulouse and Bordeaux. Some tours focus on upgraded food and wine and are directed by seasoned world-class chefs. (The day's purchases of culinary ingredients in outdoor markets is one of the aesthetic experiences of each day.)

HOT-AIR BALLOONING   The world's largest balloon operator is **Buddy Bombard Balloon Adventures,** 855 Donald Ross Rd., Juno Beach, FL 33408 (☎ **407/775-0039,** or 800/862-8537). It maintains about three dozen hot-air balloons, some stationed in the Loire Valley and Burgundy. The five-day/four-night tours incorporate food and wine tasting and include all meals, lodging in Relais & Châteaux hotels, sightseeing attractions, rail transfers to and from Paris, and a daily balloon ride over vineyards and fields. Lunches are served in the best restaurants in the district; dinners are elegant picnics served huntboard-style after a daily late-afternoon balloon ride.

EQUESTRIAN TOURS   A California-based clearinghouse for at least eight French stables is **FITS (Fun in the Saddle) Equestrian Tours,** 685 Lateen Rd., Solvang, CA 93463 (☎ **805/688-9494,** or 800/666-3487). It can arrange cross-country treks through such regions as the Pyrénées, Périgord, Brittany, Quercy, and the Loire Valley, with overnight stops en route in colorful country inns, private homes, and farmhouses. Rides last between five and seven hours a day, with routes carefully engineered to avoid as much traffic as possible. Luggage and the ingredients for daily picnics follow in vans. Prices range from $750 to $2,200 per person, all-inclusive.

HIKING TOURS   Established in 1979, **Backroads,** 1516 5th St., Berkeley, CA 94710-1740 (☎ **510/527-1555,** or 800/462-2848; fax 510/527-1444), specializes in hiking tours with a basic daily routine that includes covering from 6 to 10 miles, with 3 to 6 hours a day of walking. Longer or shorter options are available, and a follow-up van rescues tired, injured, or uninspired walkers. Participants are free to walk alone or as a group through the rolling hills of some of the most fertile terrain in France's southwest. Hiking is almost always along footpaths or quiet dirt roads and incorporates stays at upscale Relais & Châteaux hotels, canoe rides on the Dordogne, visits to artists' hamlets and 13th-century villages (like Sarlat, Les Eyzies, Domme, and La Roque-Gageac), and the gastronomic citadel of Brive. The six-day/five-night tours begin and end in Bordeaux. Double-occupancy (meals, lodging, and a trek leader included) costs are $1,900 per person.

CANOEING TOURS   Between May and early July, **Journeys Beyond,** P.O. Box 7511-FF, Jackson, WY 83001 (☎ **307/733-9615**), offers guided canoe tours on two of southwestern France's most scenic rivers, the Dordogne and the Tarn. Each lasts between five and eight days and includes breakfast, dinner, and overnight accommodations in riverside inns as part of the net price, which ranges from $1,300 to $1,600 per person, double occupancy (without airfare). Canoes are equipped to carry participants' luggage inside, all paddling is downstream, and inns are adjacent to the riverbanks. No more than 12 miles is covered per day. Itineraries on the Tarn include some sections with whitewater.

ALPINE TOURS   Travelers who prefer the high alpine grandeur of France's southeast can contact **Wilderness Travel,** 801 Allston Way, Berkeley, CA 94710 (☎ **510/548-0420,** or 800/368-2794). One of the most spectacular offerings is a 16-day hike between Chamonix (France) and Zermatt (Switzerland), through the region where mountaineering and alpinism were first developed in the 19th century. Accommodations in alpine dormitories and family-run inns, as well as most meals and guide fees, are included in prices that begin around $2,200, double occupancy.

Equally challenging is the company's "Tour du Mont-Blanc," a 14-day circumnavigation of one of the most distinctive granite massifs in the world, complete with visits to seven of the outwardly radiating valleys. The tour traverses rugged territory belonging to France, Switzerland, and Italy and climbs to a maximum of no more than 9,000 feet above sea level. Prices begin at $1,995 per person, double occupancy.

The company also offers 12-day tours through the lush historic valley of western France's Dordogne and the ancient and richly evocative landscapes of Provence.

7 Getting to France from North America

BY PLANE
Nonstop flights to Paris (sometimes on airlines you might not have automatically thought of) are available from such North American hubs as Atlanta, Chicago, Cincinnati, Houston, Miami, New York, and St. Louis.

Flying time to Paris from New York is about 7 hours; from Chicago, 9 hours; from Los Angeles, 11 hours; from Atlanta, 8 hours; from Miami, $8^1/_2$ hours; and from Washington, D.C., $7^1/_2$ hours.

Most airlines divide their year roughly into seasonal slots with the lowest fares between November 1 and March 13. Shoulder season, the period between the high and low seasons, is only slightly more expensive and includes all of October, which many veteran tourists consider the ideal time to visit France. It also extends from mid-March to mid-June.

MAJOR U.S. CARRIERS
American Airlines (☎ 800/433-7300) offers daily flights to Paris (Orly Airport) from Dallas/Fort Worth, Chicago, and New York City's JFK. **Delta Airlines** (☎ 800/221-4141) is one of the best choices for passengers flying to Paris from both the southeastern United States and the Midwest. In fact, Delta offers the greatest number of flights to Paris from the United States. From such cities as New Orleans, Phoenix, Columbia (S.C.), and Nashville, Delta flies to Atlanta,

connecting every evening with a nonstop flight to Orly in Paris. Delta also operates flights to Orly from Cincinnati four times a week nonstop and seven flights a week that stop briefly en route in Atlanta. There are also daily flights to Paris's Orly from New York City's JFK. All these flights depart late enough in the day to permit easy transfer from much of Delta's vast North American network.

Continental Airlines (☎ 800/231-0856) provides nonstop flights to Orly from Newark and Houston. Flights from Newark depart daily, while flights from Houston depart four to seven times a week, depending on the season.

TWA (☎ 800/221-2000) operates daily nonstop service to Charles de Gaulle Airport from Boston, New York City's JFK, and (in summer) several nonstop flights a week from Washington, D.C.'s Dulles Airport. In summer, TWA also flies to Paris from St. Louis several times a week nonstop and to Paris from Los Angeles three times a week nonstop. In winter, flights from Los Angeles and Washington, D.C., are suspended and flights from St. Louis are direct, with brief touchdowns in New York or Boston en route to Paris.

USAir (☎ 800/428-4322) offers daily nonstop service from Philadelphia International Airport to Paris's Charles de Gaulle.

FRENCH NATIONAL CARRIERS

Aircraft belonging to the **Air France Group** (☎ 800/237-2747) fly frequently across the Atlantic. Formed from a recent merger combining three of France's largest (and completely nationalized) airlines, the conglomerate offers routes that until the merger were maintained separately by Air France, UTA (Union des Transports Aériens), and France's internal domestic airline, Air Inter. In the process, many transatlantic routes that previously flew nonstop into France's provincial capitals were abandoned.

The airline offers daily or several-times-a-week flights between Paris's Orly and Newark, N.J.; Washington, D.C.'s Dulles; Miami; Chicago; Houston; San Francisco; Los Angeles; Montréal; Toronto; Mexico City; and Los Angeles. Flights to Paris from Los Angeles originate in Papeete, French Polynesia, very far from *la France métropolitaine.*

THE MAJOR CANADIAN CARRIER

Canadians usually choose the **Air Canada** (☎ 800/776-3000 in the U.S. and Canada) flights to Paris from Toronto and Montréal. Nonstop flights from Montréal depart every evening for Paris, while flights from Toronto to Paris are nonstop six days a week, and direct (with a touchdown in Montréal en route) one day a week. Two of the nonstop slights from Toronto are shared with Air France and feature Air France aircraft.

OTHER GOOD-VALUE CHOICES

Consolidators (known as "bucket shops") act as clearinghouses for blocks of tickets that airlines discount and consign during normally slow periods of air travel.

Tickets are usually priced 20% to 35% below the full fare. Terms of payment vary—from 45 days before departure to last-minute sales. Tickets can be purchased through regular travel agents, who usually mark up the ticket 8% to 10%, maybe more, thereby greatly reducing your discount. But using such a ticket doesn't qualify you for an advance seat assignment, so you're likely to be assigned a "poor seat" at the last minute.

Most flyers estimate their savings at around $200 per ticket off the regular price. Nearly a third of the passengers reported savings of up to $300 off the regular price. But—and here's the hitch—many people who booked consolidator tickets reported no savings at all, as the airlines will sometimes match the consolidator ticket by announcing a promotional fare. The situation is a bit tricky and calls for some careful investigation to determine how much you're saving.

Bucket shops abound from coast to coast. Look for their ads in your local newspaper's travel section; they're usually very small and a single column in width. (*Note:* Since dealing with unknown bucket shops might be a little risky, it's wise to call the Better Business Bureau in your area to see if complaints have been filed against the company from which you plan to purchase a ticket.)

Here are some recommendations:

One of the biggest U.S. consolidators is **Travac**, 989 Sixth Ave., New York, NY 10018 (☎ 212/563-3303, or 800/TRAV-800 in the U.S.), which offers discounted seats from throughout the United States to most cities in Europe on airlines that include TWA, United, and Delta. Another Travac office is at 2601 E. Jefferson St., Orlando, FL 32803 (☎ 407/896-0014).

In New York, try **TFI Tours International**, 34 W. 32nd St., 12th Floor, New York, NY 10001 (☎ 212/736-1140, or 800/745-8000 in the U.S. outside New York State). This tour company offers services to 177 cities worldwide.

For the Midwest, explore the possibilities of **Travel Avenue**, 10 S. Riverside Plaza, Suite 1404, Chicago, IL 60606 (☎ 800/333-3335 in the U.S.), a national agency. Its tickets are often cheaper than most shops', and it charges the customer only a $25 fee on international tickets, rather than taking the usual 10% commission from an airline. Travel Avenue rebates most of that back to the customers— hence, the lower fares.

In New England, a possibility is **TMI (Travel Management International)**, 39 JFK St. (Harvard Square), 3rd Floor, Cambridge, MA 02138 (☎ 800/245-3672 in the U.S.), which offers a wide variety of discounts, including youth fares, student fares, and access to other kinds of air-related discounts.

BY OCEAN LINER

The era of sailing to Paris in the 1950s style of Marilyn Monroe and Jane Russell is long gone. The only ocean liner now making scheduled transatlantic crossings is the *Queen Elizabeth 2* (*QE2*), the flagship of the British **Cunard Line.** The *QE2*'s most frequent trip is between New York and the Channel port of Southampton. From Southampton, you can go by ferryboat or hovercraft to France; or you can take a train to London—perhaps taking in some plays, museums, and shopping before flying to Paris.

Cruise hopefuls should remember that Cunard offers greater numbers of eastbound routes into England than it does into France but that several of its westbound crossings depart for North America directly from the northern French coast rather than from England. This policy makes it especially convenient for travelers to fly directly from their home airports to Paris, then to return to North America by ship directly from Cherbourg. Many passengers appreciate the leisure this gives them to relax and "decompress" at the end of their travels through France.

On board, you'll find four pools, a sauna, nightclubs, a movie theater, boutiques (like the only seagoing Harrods), four restaurants, paddle-tennis courts, and a children's playroom staffed with English nannies. There's also an on-board branch of California's Golden Door Health Spa, a computer learning center with a battery of IBM personal computers, seminars by experts on everything from astrology to French cuisine, and meetings with an array of visiting celebrities.

Fares are extremely high, depending on your cabin and season of sailing. Call your travel agent or a Cunard representative (☎ **212/880-7500,** or 800/ 221-4770).

BY PACKAGE TOUR

Travel Concepts, 62 Commonwealth Ave., Suite 3, Boston, MA 02116-3029 (☎ **617/266-8450**), specializes in art-history and cultural tours to less traveled regions, such as the Dordogne (with side trips to the prehistoric caves at Lascaux), lesser-known wineries in Burgundy and Chablis, and distilleries in Cognac and Armagnac. Since tours are usually custom-designed for groups of 10 or more, this company is a favorite of alumni(ae) groups and special-interest groups whose members are traveling together. If collecting butterflys in Provence, watching birds in Brittany, or following in the footsteps of Nostradamus in southern France interests you, then get a group of like-minded people together. In rare instances, individuals or individual couples can latch onto some other group's prearranged tour, but this company is best used as a vehicle to arrange a tour for groups with a common interest.

Delta Airlines, for example, through its tour division (Delta Dream Vacations; ☎ 800/872-7786), offers a land package (without airfare) to the Ile de France that includes six nights at a good hotel in Paris, with guided tours of the monuments, an excursion to Versailles, breakfasts, taxes, a five-day public transportation pass, and a three-day museum pass. The cost varies from $949 to $1,169 per person, double occupancy, depending on the hotel you stay in. (Single occupancy for the same package costs $1,619.) Other add-ons are usually available for excursions to the Riviera, Geneva, and the rest of Europe at prices that are lower (sometimes significantly so) than if you had arranged each component of the package yourself.

The French Experience, 370 Lexington Ave., New York, NY 10017 (☎ **212/ 986-3800**), offers several fly-drive programs using different types and price categories of hotels. It also takes reservations for about 30 hotels in Paris, arranges short-term apartment rentals, and offers prearranged package tours of various regions. Any of these can be adapted and altered to suit your individual needs.

American Express Vacations (as represented by Certified Vacations, Inc.), P.O. Box 1525, Fort Lauderdale, FL 33302 (☎ **800/446-6234** in the U.S. and Canada), is perhaps the world's most instantly recognizable tour operator. Its offerings in France and the rest of Europe are truly comprehensive. If you have a clear idea of what you want (and it's not already available), it can arrange an individualized itinerary for you.

8 Getting to France from the U.K.

BY PLANE

From London, **Air France** (☎ 0181/742-6600), **British Airways** (☎ 0181/ 897-4000), and **Caledonian Airways** (☎ 0181/897-4000), a charter division of BA, fly regularly and frequently to Paris (trip time is one hour). Air France and British Airways alone operate up to 17 flights daily from Heathrow, one of the busiest air routes in Europe. Air France also flies four or five times a day from Gatwick to Charles de Gaulle, the main airport outside Paris. Many commercial travelers also use regular flights originating from the London City Airport in the Docklands.

In addition, there are direct flights to Paris from many regional British airports, departing from such major cities as Birmingham, Edinburgh, Glasgow, Manchester, and Southampton. Some U.K. flights (check with a travel agent) will take you to a regional French city, if that's where you're going—thus letting you avoid a changeover in Paris. Destinations in France include Bordeaux, Caen, Clermont-Ferrand, Lyon, Marseille, Montpellier, Nantes, Nice, Quimper, and Toulouse.

Flying from England to France is often very expensive, even though the distance is short. That's why most Brits depend on a good travel agent to get them the lowest possible transportation costs. Good values are offered by a number of companies, such as **Nouvelles Frontières,** 1–2 Hanover St., London W14 9WB (☎ 0171/629-7772). If you don't want to use a travel agent, an APEX ticket might be the way to keep costs trimmed. These tickets must be reserved in advance. However, this ticket offers a discount without the usual booking restrictions. You might also ask the airlines about a "Eurobudget ticket," which has restrictions or length-of-stay requirements.

The newspapers are always full of classified ads touting "slashed" fares from London to other parts of the world. One good source for data is *Time Out* magazine. London's *Evening Standard* maintains a daily travel section, and the Sunday editions of virtually any newspaper in the British Isles will run many ads. Though competition is fierce, one well-recommended company that consolidates bulk ticket purchases and then passes the savings on to its consumers is **Trailfinders** (☎ 0171/937-5400 in London). It offers access to tickets on such carriers as British Airways, KLM, and SAS.

BY TRAIN

Paris is one of Europe's busiest railway junctions, with trains arriving at and departing from its many stations every few minutes. If you're already in Europe, you may want to go to Paris by train, particularly if you have a Eurailpass. Even if you don't, the cost is relatively low—especially in comparison to renting a car. Incidentally, you don't have to go to Paris from London. For example, there are direct trains from London to such places as the Côte d'Azur (French Riviera), the Alps, Strasbourg (capital of Alsace), Lyon (in wine-rich Burgundy), and the Pyrénées bordering Spain.

FARES The one-way fare from London to Paris by train (including the Channel crossing) is $154 in first class and $123 in second class; from Rome to Paris, depending on the route and the time of travel, the one-way fare ranges from $191 to $251 in first class and $125 to $161 in second class; and from Madrid to Paris the one-way fare is $162 in first class and $109 in second class.

Visitors from Britain may want to consider a British/French joint rail pass, linking the two most popular vacation spots in Europe. Called **BritFrance Railpass,** it's available to North Americans, providing unlimited train travel in both Britain and France. (Unlike in previous years, it doesn't include passage by boat or hovercraft across the Channel.)

The pass comes in two options, offering either 5 days of travel in any consecutive month or 10 days of travel in any consecutive month on both the British and French rail networks. Adult first-class fares for the less comprehensive of the above options are $359 in first class and $259 in second class. For the 10-day option the

A Note on British Customs

On January 1, 1993, the borders between European countries were relaxed as the European markets united. When you're traveling within the EU, this will have a big impact on what you can buy and take home with you for personal use.

If you buy your goods in a duty-free shop, then the old rules still apply—you're allowed to bring home 300 cigarettes and 2 liters of table wine, plus 1 liter of spirits or 2 liters of fortified wine. But now you can buy your wine, spirits, or cigarettes in an ordinary shop in France or Belgium, for example, and bring home *almost* as much as you like. (U.K. Customs and Excise does set theoretical limits.) If you're returning home from a non-EU country, the allowances are the standard ones from duty-free shops. You must declare any goods in excess of these allowances. British Customs tends to be strict and complicated in its requirements.

For details, get in touch with Her Majesty's Customs and Excise Office, New King's Beam House, 22 Upper Ground, London, SE1 9PJ (☎ 0171/382-5468).

---

price is $539 in first class and $399 in second class. When they're accompanied by an adult holder of either of the passes described above, children 4 to 12 travel for half the adult fare, and those under 4 travel free. The pass is activated the first time you use it, but be warned that holders must validate their pass at a railway station's ticket counter prior to boarding a train.

Some of the most popular passes, including Inter-Rail and EuroYouth, are offered only to travelers under 26 years, entitling them to unlimited second-class travel in 26 European countries.

Rail passes as well as individual rail tickets in Europe are available at most travel agents, at any **RailEurope** office (☎ 800/848-7245 in the U.S.), or at **BritRail Travel International** (☎ 800/677-8585). In New York City, call 212/575-2667. You might also want to stop in at the **International Rail Centre,** Victoria Station, London SW1V 1JY (☎ 0171/834-2345).

In London, an especially convenient place to buy railway tickets to virtually anywhere is just opposite Platform 2 in Victoria Station, London SW1V 1JY. **Wasteels, Ltd.** (☎ 0171/834-7066) will provide railway-related services and discuss the pros and cons of various types of fares and rail passes; its staff will probably spend more than the usual amount of time with you while planning your itinerary. Depending on circumstances, Wasteels sometimes charges a £5 fee, but for the information provided the fee might be worth it.

BY BUS

Bus travel to Paris is available from London as well as from many other cities on the Continent. In the early 1990s, the French government established strong incentives for long-haul buses not to drive into the center of Paris. The arrival and departure point for Europe's largest bus operators, **Eurolines France,** is a 35-minute Métro ride from central Paris, at the terminus of Métro line 3 (Métro: Gallieni), in the suburb of Bagnolet. Despite this inconvenience, many people prefer bus travel. Eurolines France is at 28 av. du Général-de-Gaulle, 93541 Bagnolet (☎ 1/49-72-51-51).

Because Eurolines does not have a U.S.–based sales agent, most people wait until they reach Europe to buy their tickets. Any European travel agent can arrange for these purchases. If you're traveling to Paris from London, you can contact **Eurolines U.K.**, Victoria Coach Station (the continental check-in desk) or call 01582/40-45-11 for information, or 0171/73-03-499 for credit-card sales.

BY FERRY

About a dozen companies run hydrofoils, ferries, and hovercraft across La Manche ("the sleeve," as the French call the Channel)—all of which now face competition from the Channel Tunnel (below).

Services operate day and night. Most ferries carry cars, but some hydrofoils carry passengers only. Hovercraft and hydrofoils make the trip in just 40 minutes, while slower-moving ferries might take hours, depending on conditions. The major routes are between Dover or Folkestone and Calais or Boulogne (about 12 trips a day). It's important to make reservations, as vessels are always crowded. Prices and timetables can vary depending on weather conditions.

There are three main carriers. The most frequently used are Sealink (conventional ferryboat service) and Hoverspeed (travel on motorized catamarans, Seacats, which skim along a few inches above the water). Cars can usually be taken on both vessels, though rates are probably lower for conventional ferryboats. The shortest and busiest route between London and Paris is the one from Dover to Calais. By ferryboat, the trip takes about 90 minutes, though a Seacat can make the run in about 35 minutes. The Seacat also crosses from Folkestone to Boulogne in about 55 minutes. Each crossing is carefully timed to coincide with the arrival and departure of trains from London and Paris, since passengers and their luggage get off the trains a short walk from the piers. The U.S. sales agent for the above-mentioned lines is **Britrail** (☎ 212/575-2667, or 800/ 677-8585).

Another opportunity to travel by ferryboat from England to France (including the vital link between Dover and Calais) is offered by **P&O Channel Lines** (☎ 0181/575-8555 in London). It offers 20 to 25 ferryboat crossings a day, depending on the season, between the busy harbors of Dover and Calais. The crossing can take as little as an hour and a quarter, depending on the craft.

If you plan to take a rented car across the Channel, check carefully with the rental company about license and insurance requirements before you leave.

BY THE CHANNEL TUNNEL

Elizabeth II and former President François Mitterrand officially opened the Channel Tunnel (Chunnel) in 1994, and the *Eurostar Express* began twice-daily passenger service between London and both Paris and Brussels. The $15-billion tunnel, one of the great engineering feats of all time, is the first link between Britain and the Continent since the Ice Age. The 31-mile journey between Great Britain and France takes 35 minutes, though the actual time spent in the Chunnel is only 19 minutes.

Rail Europe (☎ 800/94-CHUNNEL for information) sells tickets for the *Eurostar* direct train service between London and Paris or Brussels. A round-trip fare between London and Paris, for example, is $312 in first class and $248 in second class. But you can cut costs to $152 with a second class, 14-day advance-purchase (nonrefundable) round-trip ticket. In London, make reservations for *Eurostar* at 01345/300003; in Paris at 44-51-06-02; and in the United States, at 800/387-6782.

The tunnel also accommodates passenger cars, charter buses, taxis, and motorcycles under the English Channel from Folkestone, England, to Calais, France. It operates 24 hours, 365 days a year, running every 15 minutes during peak travel times and at least once an hour at night. Tickets may be purchased at the toll booth. With *Le Shuttle*, gone are weather-related delays, seasickness, and the need for advance reservations.

Motorists drive onto a half-mile-long train and then travel through an underground tunnel built beneath the seabed through a layer of impermeable chalk marl and sealed with a reinforced-concrete lining.

Before boarding *Le Shuttle*, motorists stop at a toll booth and then pass through Immigration for both countries at one time. During the ride, motorists stay in air-conditioned carriages, remain inside their cars, or step outside to stretch their legs. When the trip is completed, they simply drive off toward their destinations—in our case, to Paris. Total travel time between the French and English highway system is about one hour. Once on French soil, Britain-based drivers must, obviously, begin driving on the right-hand side of the road.

Stores selling duty-free goods, restaurants, and service stations are available to travelers on both sides of the Channel. A bilingual staff is on hand to assist travelers at both the French and the British terminals.

9 Suggested Itineraries

Normandy & Brittany in Four Days

Day 1   Strike out for Normandy and Brittany, the two old provinces that North Americans generally find the most intriguing (see Chapters 12 and 13). Head first for Rouen, 84 miles northwest of Paris, to view the site of Joan of Arc's 1431 death and the famous Rouen Cathedral.

Day 2   Continue east toward Caen, 150 miles from Paris. Stay overnight there or travel 17 miles west to Bayeux to see the cathedral and the Bayeux Tapestry.

Day 3   Based in either Bayeux or Caen, spend the day exploring the D-Day beaches. The highlights are described in Chapter 12.

Day 4   Continue west, heading toward Mont-St-Michel, one of the great sightseeing attractions of Europe, lying at the border of Normandy and Brittany, 209 miles from Paris. For an overnight stopover, consider those enchanting resort towns in Brittany, St-Malo and Dinard, on the northwest coast. St-Malo, an ancient pirates' stronghold and walled fishing village, lies 53 miles from Mont-St-Michel. Dinard has a gambling casino and sheltered beach, along with golf and tennis.

Those with the time can explore the entire peninsula of Brittany, with its 600 miles of coast and chains of beaches, rustic fishing ports, and fantastic seafood.

The Loire Valley in Six Days

Day 1   From Paris, take the autoroute to Chartres, 60 miles south. See the fabulous cathedral and stay overnight.

Day 2   Drive to Tours, 144 miles southwest of Paris. It's your best base in the châteaux country because it has a diversified selection of hotels. However, Tours is a big city and many people stay in Amboise, 15 miles east of Tours, which is also a good center for exploring.

Day 3   Based in either Tours or Amboise, head for the southwest's major attractions: Azay-le-Rideau, 17 miles from Tours (a private residence during the Renaissance), and Chinon, 30 miles from Tours, one of the oldest fortress-châteaux in France.

Day 4   Again based in Tours, head for Amboise, with its memories of Leonardo da Vinci, and Chenonceaux, 21 miles southeast of Tours, forever linked to the legend of the dames de Chenonceau.

Day 5   Leave Tours or Amboise, heading east along the autoroute to Blois, seat of the comtes de Blois. Spend the morning sightseeing at Chaumont, with its memories of Diane de Poitiers. Spend the night in Blois.

Day 6   Leave the next morning, heading east to Orléans, but stop first at Chambord, former seat of François I. Stay overnight in Orléans, forever associated with the Maid of Orléans.

The French Riviera in Seven Days

Days 1–3   Head for Nice, 577 miles south of Paris, for three nights. Spend Day 1 getting there and settling into your hotel. Spend Day 2 exploring St-Paul-de-Vence, with its Maeght Foundation, and Vence, with its Matisse Chapel. Nice has many attractions of its own (and you'll also want some sun), so spend Day 3 on home ground.

Day 4   Drive to Monte Carlo, at least for a night, going along to St-Jean-Cap-Ferrat on the same day if you have time. This is one of the poshest parts of southern France. Monaco is 12 miles from Nice along the Moyenne Corniche.

Days 5–6   Head for Cannes, 20 miles east of Nice. Spend Day 5 enjoying Cannes itself and Day 6 exploring at least some of the attractions in its environs, including the Lerins Islands off its shoreline (linked to the Man in the Iron Mask).

Day 7   Visit chic St-Tropez, 46 miles east of Cannes, our last stopover. St-Tropez is strictly for fun and won't dazzle you with a lot of attractions—except bikini-clad ones of both sexes.

Languedoc & Provence in Seven Days

Days 1–2   Spend Day 1 settling into Marseille and Day 2 exploring the attractions of the second-largest city of France. Spend part of your day visiting Château d'If, an island used as a setting for *The Count of Monte Cristo*.

Day 3   It's an easy 19-mile drive to Aix-en-Provence, northeast of Marseille. Aix-en-Provence, the old capital city of Provence, linked with Cézanne, makes a good overnight stopover, and you can spend the day sightseeing there.

Day 4   Leave Aix-en-Provence in the morning and go to Les Baux, 54 miles from Marseille. Spend part of the day exploring this "nesting place for eagles," then travel to Arles, 47 miles west of Aix-en-Provence, to discover why it cast a spell over van Gogh. Spend the night there.

Day 5   Continue on to Avignon, surrounded by ancient ramparts, 24 miles from Arles. Arrive early because you'll have a busy day of sightseeing.

Day 6   Two of the most charming cities in the region are Nîmes and Montpellier. Nîmes contains the most impressive Roman remains in France, including an arena and the Temple of Diana. Montpellier is the center of southern wine production and is surrounded by unsurpassed beauty. These cities are only 31 miles apart and can be visited in one busy day. Nîmes should be viewed first, as it lies 27 miles west of Avignon. Stay overnight in Montpellier.

Day 7 For a wrap-up, head for one of the major attractions of France, Carcassonne, the greatest fortress city of Europe, 57 miles southeast of Toulouse. It's linked to Montpellier by autoroute. Spend the night in Carcassonne after enjoying a platter of cassoulet.

Burgundy in Six Days

Day 1 Drive toward Burgundy from Paris, spending the night at Auxerre, 103 miles southeast of the French capital. Make an afternoon visit to the cathedral and wander through the town's medieval streets.

Day 2 Detour 12 miles east to the winemaking town of Chablis, perhaps buying a souvenir bottle of whatever vintage appeals to you. Continue on to Vézelay for a trek through the ancient hamlet and a visit to its legendary romanesque church. Spend the night in Vézelay or continue on for overnight lodgings in the quiet but scenic town of Avallon.

Day 3 Drive cross-country through Burgundy, stopping at such historic towns as Montbard and Saulieu. Spend the night in Autun and visit the monuments erected there by the ancient Romans.

Day 4 Devote a day to meandering through the scattered villages of the Côte d'Or, exploring towns like Mercurey, Nuits-St-Georges, and Gevrey-Chambertin. Stay overnight in Beaune, one of the most famous wine centers of France.

Day 5 Drive on to Dijon for a view of its distinctive medieval architecture and fine cuisine.

Day 6 Spend the morning in Dijon, visiting whatever sights you missed the day before, before continuing on elsewhere.

Alsace in Five Days

Day 1 Plan your Alsatian debut in one of the crown jewels of eastern France: Strasbourg, 303 miles east of Paris, near the banks of the Rhine. Wander beside the town's many canals and through the medieval streets, which radiate outward from the russet-colored cathedral. Dine that night on sauerkraut (*choucroute*), one of the region's most distinctive specialties, accompanied by a mug of beer or a bottle of local riesling.

Day 2 Meander 44 miles southwest to Colmar, which evokes some of the most charming folklore of Germany's Black Forest. En route, stop in at such folkloric wine hamlets as Rosheim, Obernai, and Illhausern. (Illhausern is the site of what might be the province's best restaurant.) Spend the night in Colmar.

Day 3 Travel to one of the centers of France's industrial revolution, medieval Mulhouse, site of prestigious railway and automobile museums. En route, detour through such winemaking hamlets as Riquewihr and Guebwiller.

Day 4 Driving northeast, enjoy one of the most panoramic routes in Alsace— La Route des Crêtes—stopping at Baccarat (site of the crystal factories) and Lunéville (site of the folkloric porcelain) on your way to Nancy, the capital of Lorraine, where you can spend the night.

Day 5 Visit Nancy to see its place Stanislaus and intriguing museums. If time allows, continue another 32 miles northwest to Verdun, a folkloric town permeated with the memories of some of the most destructive battles of World War II.

10 Getting Around France

BY PLANE

The French domestic airline **Air Inter** (☎ 1/45-39-25-25, or 800/AF-PARIS in the U.S.) flies to 30 major French centers, with an average of 300 flights a day that crisscross the country in an average flight time of one hour. Air Inter flies in and out of both Orly and Charles de Gaulle airports, servicing such major cities as Bordeaux, Lille, Lyon, Marseille, Montpellier, Nantes, Nice, Strasbourg, Toulouse, and Mulhouse and Basel (Switzerland).

The **Air Inter Air Pass** offers 7 days of flying within the borders of France (including flights to and from Corsica), which must be used in a 30-day period, for $329 per person. These passes must be reserved and purchased in North America.

BY TRAIN

With some 50 cities in France linked by the world's fastest trains, Paris is connected to many areas of the country by a trip of just a few hours. With 24,000 miles of track and about 3,000 stations, SNCF (French National Railroads) is fabled throughout the world for its on-time performance. You can travel either first or second class by day, and in couchette or sleeper by night. Many trains carry dining facilities, which range from cafeteria to formal dinners.

INFORMATION

If you plan much travel on European railroads, get the latest copy of the *Thomas Cook European Timetable of Railroads.* This comprehensive 500-plus-page timetable documents all Europe's mainline passenger rail services with detail and accuracy. It's available exclusively in North America from the **Forsyth Travel Library,** P.O. Box 2975, Shawnee Mission, KS 66201 (☎ 800/367-7984), at a cost of $25.95 plus $4 postage (priority airmail to the U.S. and $5 U.S. for shipments to Canada).

IN THE UNITED STATES   For more information and to purchase rail passes (see below) before you leave, contact Rail Europe, Inc., at 226–230 Westchester Ave., White Plains, NY 10604 (☎ 800/438-7245).

IN CANADA   Rail Europe, Inc., offices are at 2087 Dundas St. E., Suite 105, Mississauga, ON L4X 1M2 (☎ 905/602-4195, or 800/361-7245).

IN LONDON   SNCF maintains offices at 170 Piccadilly, London W1 OBA (☎ 0171/493-9731).

IN PARIS   The SNCF administrative offices are at 10 place Budapest, 75436 Paris (☎ 1/42-85-60-00), but for information about railway departures, the most efficient way to handle information is to call or visit the nearest railway station, where staffs are on hand to assist with ticket sales and inquiries. Paris railway stations include the Gare de l'Est, Gare du Nord, Gare St-Lazare, Gare Montparnasse, Gare d'Austerlitz, and Gare de Lyon.

FRENCH RAIL PASSES

Working cooperatively with SNCF, Air Inter, and Avis, Rail Europe offers three flexible, cost-saving rail passes that can reduce travel costs considerably.

The **France Railpass** provides unlimited rail transportation throughout France for three days, to be used within one month. It costs $185 in first class and $145 in second class. Up to six additional days can be purchased for an additional fee. Costs are even more reasonable for two adults traveling together: $150 per person for first class and $115 for second class.

The **France Rail 'n Drive Pass,** available only in North America, combines good value on both rail travel and car rentals and is best used in conjunction with arriving at a major rail depot, then striking out to explore the countryside by car. It includes the rail pass above, along with unlimited mileage on a car rental. Costs are lowest when two or more people travel together. It can be used during five nonconsecutive days in one month and includes three days of travel on the train and two days' use of a rental car. If rental of the least expensive car is combined with first-class rail travel, the price is $179 per person; if rental of the least expensive car is combined with second-class travel, the price is $149 per person. Cars can be upgraded for a supplemental fee. The above-mentioned prices apply to two people traveling together; solo travelers pay from $259 for first class and $219 for second class.

The **France Fly, Rail, 'n Drive Pass** is an arrangement whereby air, rail, and car transportation in France are combined into one all-encompassing discounted purchase. You fly to any destination in metropolitan France on Air Inter, the French domestic airline; then travel any three days by train and any two days by car—all in any month-long period. When two people travel together, each pays an all-inclusive $279 for first-class travel and $245 for second-class. When a solo adult travels alone, the price rises to $349 for first-class and $309 for second-class travel.

EURAILPASSES

For years, many in-the-know travelers have been taking advantage of one of Europe's greatest travel bargains—the **Eurailpass,** which permits unlimited first-class rail travel in any country in Western Europe except the British Isles (good in Ireland). Passes are purchased for periods as short as 15 days or as long as three months and are strictly nontransferable.

The pass is sold only in North America. Vacationers in Europe for 15 days can purchase a Eurailpass for $498; a pass for 21 days costs $648, and a 1-month pass costs $798. A two-month pass goes for $1,098, a three-month pass for $1,398. Children 3 and under travel free providing they don't occupy a seat (otherwise they're charged half fare); children 3 to 11 are charged half fare. If you're under 26, you can purchase a **Eurail Youthpass,** entitling you to unlimited second-class travel for 15 days for $398, or for one or two months, costing $578 and $768, respectively.

Seat reservations are required on some trains. Many of the trains have couchettes (sleeping cars), for which an additional fee is charged. Obviously, the two- or three-month traveler gets the greatest economic advantages; the Eurailpass is ideal for such extensive trips. Passholders can visit all of France's major sights, from Normandy to the Alps, then end their vacation in Norway, for example.

Fourteen-day or one-month voyagers have to estimate rail distance before determining if such a pass is to their benefit. To obtain full advantage of the ticket for 15 days or 1 month, you'd have to spend a great deal of time on the train. Eurailpass holders are entitled to considerable reductions on certain buses and ferries.

Travel agents in all towns and railway agents in such major cities as New York, Montréal, and Los Angeles sell all these tickets. A Eurailpass is available at the

North American offices of CIT Travel Service, the French National Railroads, the German Federal Railroads, and the Swiss Federal Railways.

The **Eurail Saverpass** is a money-saving ticket offering discounted 15-day travel, but only if groups of three people travel constantly and continuously together between April and September or if 2 travel constantly and continuously together between October and March. The price of a Saverpass, valid all over Europe, good for first class only, is $430 for 15 days, $550 for 21 days, and $678 for one month.

The **Eurail Flexipass** allows passengers to visit Europe with more flexibility. It's valid in first class and offers the same privileges as the Eurailpass. However, it provides a number of individual travel days that can be used over a much longer period of consecutive days. That makes it possible to stay in one city and yet not lose a single day of travel. There are three passes: 5 days of travel in 2 months for $348, 10 days of travel in 2 months for $560, and 15 days of travel in 2 months for $740.

With many of the same qualifications and restrictions as the previously described Flexipass is a **Eurail Youth Flexipass.** Sold only to travelers under age 26, it allows 5 days of travel within 2 months for $255, 10 days of travel within 2 months for $398, and 15 days of travel within 2 months for $540.

BY CAR

The most charming châteaux and best country hotels always seem to lie away from the main cities and train stations. You'll find that renting a car is usually the best way to travel once you get to France, especially if you plan to explore in depth and not stick to the standard route, such as the Paris–Nice run.

Driving time in Europe is largely a matter of conjecture, urgency, and how much sightseeing you do along the way. Driving time from Geneva to Paris is 5¹/₂ hours minimum. Rouen to Paris requires 2¹/₂ hours; Nantes to Paris, 3¹/₂ hours; Lyon to Paris, 4 hours. The driving time from Marseille to Paris is largely a matter of national pride, and tall tales abound about how rapidly the French can do it. With the accelerator pressed to the floor, you might conceivably make it in seven hours, but we always make a two-day journey of it.

But frankly, Europe's rail networks are so well developed, and (compared to the cost and anxiety of driving) so inexpensive we recommend you rent a car only for exploring rural areas little serviced by rail lines, such as Brittany, rural Burgundy, and the Dordogne.

CAR RENTALS   Renting a car in France is easy. You'll need to present a valid driver's license and be at least 23 for the cheaper models and at least 25 for the more expensive vehicles. Renters must also present a valid passport and a valid credit or charge card unless payment is arranged in North America before leaving. It usually isn't obligatory, but certain companies, perhaps the smaller ones, have at times asked for the presentation of an international driver's license.

Note: The best deal is usually a weekly rental with unlimited mileage. All car-rental bills in France are subject to a 22% government tax, among the highest in Europe.

Unless it's already factored into the rental agreement, an optional collision-damage waiver (CDW) carries an additional charge of 72 to 95 F ($13.70 to $18.05) a day for the least expensive cars. Buying this extra insurance will usually eliminate all except 1,000 F ($190) of your responsibility in the event of accidental damage to the car. Because most newcomers are not familiar with local driving customs and conditions, we highly recommend that you buy the CDW, though certain credit/charge-card issuers will compensate a renter for any accident-related liability to a rented car if the imprint of their card appears on the original rental contract. At some of the companies (including Hertz) the CDW will not protect you against the theft of a car, so if this is the case, ask about buying additional theft protection. This cost is 38 F ($7.20) extra per day.

At all four of the big car-rental companies, the least expensive car will probably be either a Ford Fiesta, a Renault Clio, a Peugeot 106, or an Opel Corsa, usually with manual transmission, no air conditioning, and few frills. Depending on the company and the season, prices may range from $186 to $201 per week, with unlimited mileage (but not tax or CDW) included. Discounts are sometimes granted for rentals of two weeks or more. Automatic transmission is regarded as a luxury in Europe, so if you want it you'll probably have to pay dearly. All the agencies allow clients to prepay their rentals in U.S. dollars, though the benefits of prepayment vary from case to case and company to company, depending on what's included as part of the proposed prepayment. Of course, if your intention is to remain within the city limits of Paris, a rental of virtually any kind is not recommended.

Budget Rent-a-Car (☎ 800/527-0700) maintains about 30 locations inside Paris, including its largest branch at 81 av. Kléber, 16e (☎ 1/47-55-61-00). For rentals of more than seven days, cars can be picked up in one French city and dropped off in another with no additional charge. Drop-offs in cities within an easy drive of the French border (including Geneva and Frankfurt) incur no additional charges either; however, drop-offs in other non-French cities can be arranged for a reasonable surcharge. Be aware that Budget doesn't allow its French cars to be driven anywhere in Britain.

Hertz (☎ 800/654-3001) maintains about 15 locations in Paris, including at the city's airports. The main office is at 27 rue St-Ferdinand, 17e (☎ 1/45-74-97-39). Be sure to ask about any promotional discounts.

Avis (☎ 800/331-1084) has offices at both Paris airports, as well as an inner-city headquarters at 5 rue Bixio, 7e (☎ 1/44-18-10-50), near the Eiffel Tower.

National Car Rental (☎ 800/227-3876) is represented in Paris by Europcar, whose largest office is at 145 av. Malakoff, 16e (☎ 1/45-00-08-06). It also has offices at both Paris airports and at about a dozen other locations. Any of its offices can rent you a car on the spot, but to qualify for the lowest rates it's best to reserve in advance from North America.

GASOLINE   Known in France as *essence,* gasoline is extraordinarily expensive for the visitor used to North American prices. All but the least expensive cars usually require an octane rating that the French classify as *essence super,* the most expensive variety offered. At press time, *essence super* sold for about 6.15 F ($1.15) per liter, which works out to around 23.30 F ($4.45) per U.S. gallon. (Certain smaller engines might get by on *essence ordinaire,* which costs a fraction less than *super.*) Depending on your car, you'll need either leaded (*avec plomb*) or unleaded (*sans plomb*). To fill a tank of a medium-sized car will cost between $40 and $65.

Beware of the mixture of gasoline and oil sold in certain rural communities called *mélange* or *gasoil;* this mixture is for very old two-cycle engines.

Note: Sometimes you can drive for miles in rural France without encountering a gas station, so don't let your tank get dangerously low.

DRIVING RULES   Everyone in the car, in both the front and the back seats, must wear seat belts. Children under 12 must ride in the back seat. Drivers are supposed to yield to the car on their right, except where signs indicate otherwise, as at traffic circles. If you violate the speed limits, expect a big fine. Those limits are about 130kmph (80 m.p.h.) on expressways, about 100kmph (60 m.p.h.) on major national highways, and 90kmph (56 m.p.h.) on small country roads. In towns, don't exceed 60kmph (37 m.p.h.).

MAPS   Before setting out on a country tour of France, pick up a good regional map of the district you plan to explore. If you're visiting a town, ask at the local tourist office for a town plan, usually given away free.

For France as a whole, most motorists opt for the Michelin map 989. For regions, Michelin publishes a series of yellow maps that are quite good. Big travel-book stores in North America carry these maps, and they're commonly available in France (at lower prices). One useful feature of the Michelin map (in this age of congested traffic) is its designations of alternative *routes de dégagement*, which let you skirt big cities and avoid traffic-clogged highways.

BREAKDOWNS/ASSISTANCE   A breakdown is called *une panne* in France, and it's just as frustrating there as anywhere else. Call the police at 17 anywhere in France and they'll put you in touch with the nearest garage. Most local garages have towing services. If your breakdown should occur on an expressway, find the nearest roadside emergency phone box, pick up the phone, and put a call through. You'll immediately be connected to the nearest breakdown service facility.

FAST FACTS: France

For information specifically about Paris, see "Fast Facts: Paris" in Chapter 4.

Auto Clubs   The Association Française des Auto Clubs, 9 rue Anatole-de-la-Forge, 75017 Paris (☎ 1/42-27-82-00), provides some limited information to members of U.S. auto clubs such as the AAA.

Business Hours   Business hours here are erratic, as befits a nation of individualists. Most **banks** are open Monday to Friday from 9:30am to 4:30pm. Many, particularly in smaller towns or villages, take a lunch break at varying times. Hours are usually posted on the door. Most **museums** close one day a week (often Tuesday), and they're generally closed on national holidays. Usual hours are 9:30am to 5pm. Some museums, particularly the smaller and less-staffed ones, close for lunch from noon to 2pm. Most French museums are open on Saturday; many are closed Sunday morning but open Sunday afternoon. Again, refer to the individual museum listings.

Generally, **offices** are open Monday to Friday from 9am to 5pm, but always call first. In Paris or other big French cities, **stores** are open from 9 or 9:30am (often 10am) to 6 or 7pm without a break for lunch. Some shops, particularly those operated by foreigners, open at 8am and close at 8 or 9pm. In some small stores the lunch break can last three hours, beginning at 1pm. This is more common in the south than in the north.

Currency & Exchange   See "Information, Required Documents, and Money," earlier in this chapter.

Customs   Customs restrictions differ for citizens of the European Union and for citizens of non-EU countries. Non-EU nationals can bring in duty-free 200 cigarettes or 100 cigarillos or 50 cigars or 250 grams of smoking tobacco. This amount is doubled if you live outside Europe. You can, as well, bring in 2 liters of wine and 1 liter of alcohol over 22 proof and 2 liters of wine 22 proof or under. In addition, you can bring in 50 grams of perfume, a quarter liter of toilet water, 500 grams of coffee, and 200 grams of tea. Those 15 and over can bring in 300 F ($57) of other goods; for those 14 and under the limit is 150 F ($28.50).

Visitors from EU countries can bring in 300 cigarettes or 150 cigarillos or 75 cigars or 400 grams of smoking tobacco. The limit for "spirits" is 5 liters of table wine, $1^1/2$ liters of alcohol over 22 proof, and 3 liters of alcohol 22 proof or under. In addition, visitors can bring in 75 grams of perfume, three-eighths of a liter of toilet water, 1,000 grams of coffee, and 80 grams of tea. Passengers 15 and over can bring in 4,200 F ($798.45) of merchandise duty-free; those 14 and under can bring in 1,000 F ($190.10) worth.

Items destined for personal use, including bicycles and sports equipment, already in use, whether or not contained in personal luggage, are admitted without formality providing the quantity or the type of goods imported does not indicate the owner's intention to carry out a commercial transaction. They cannot be sold or given away in France and must be reexported.

Documents Required   See "Information, Required Documents, and Money," earlier in this chapter.

Driving Rules   See "By Car" under "Getting Around France," earlier in this chapter.

Drugstores   If you need one during off-hours, have your concierge get in touch with the nearest Commissariat de Police. An agent there will have the address of a nearby pharmacy open 24 hours a day. French law requires that the pharmacies in any given neighborhood display the name and location of the one that will remain open all night.

Electricity   In general, expect 200 volts and 50 cycles, though you'll encounter 110 and 115 volts in some older establishments. Adapters are needed to fit sockets. Many hotels have two-pin (in some cases, three-pin) sockets for electric razors. It's best to ask your hotel concierge before plugging in any appliance.

Embassies/Consulates   In case you lose your passport or have some other emergency, here's a list of addresses and phone numbers: The Embassy of **Australia** is at 4 rue Jean-Rey, 75015 Paris (☎ 1/40-59-33-00; Métro: Bir-Hakeim), open Monday to Friday from 9am to noon and 2 to 5pm. The Embassy of **Canada** is at 35 av. Montaigne, 75008 Paris (☎ 1/44-43-29-00; Métro: Franklin-D. Roosevelt or Alma-Marceau), open Monday to Friday from 9 to 10:30am and 2 to 3pm; the Canadian Consulate is at the same address. The Embassy of the **United Kingdom** is at 35 rue du Faubourg St-Honoré, 75383 Paris CEDEX (☎ 1/42-66-91-42; Métro: Concorde or Madeleine), open Monday to Friday from 9am to noon and 2 to 5pm. The Embassy of **New Zealand** is at 7 ter rue Léonard-de-Vinci, 75116 Paris (☎ 1/45-00-24-11; Métro: Victor-Hugo), open Monday to Friday 9am to 1pm and 2 to 5:30pm.

The Embassy of the **United States** is at 2 av. Gabriel, 75008 Paris (☎ 1/42-96-12-02; Métro: Concorde), open Monday to Friday from 9am to 4pm. Passports are issued at its annex at 2 rue St-Florentin (☎ 1/42-96-12-02, ext. 2613; Métro: Concorde). Getting a passport replaced costs about $42. In addition to its embassy and consulate in Paris, the United States maintains the following consulates: 22 cours du Maréchal-Foch, 33080 Bordeaux (☎ **56-52-65-95**); 12 bd. Paul-Peytral, 13286 Marseille (☎ **91-54-92-00**); and 15 av. d'Alsace, 67082 Strasbourg (☎ **88-35-31-04**).

Emergencies   In an emergency while at a hotel, contact the front desk. Most staffs are trained in dealing with a crisis and will call the police, summon an ambulance, or do whatever is necessary. But if it's something like a stolen wallet, go to the police station in person. Otherwise, you can get help anywhere in France by calling 17 for police, 18 for the fire department (*pompiers*). For roadside emergencies, see "By Car" under "Getting Around France," earlier in this chapter.

Gasoline   See "By Car" under "Getting Around France," earlier in this chapter.

Holidays   See "When to Go," earlier in this chapter.

Information   See "Information, Required Documents, and Money," earlier in this chapter.

Language   The world's best-selling phrase books are published by Berlitz—*French for Travellers* has everything you'll need.

Legal Aid   The French government advises foreigners to consult their embassy or consulate (see "Embassies/Consulates," above) in case of a dire emergency, such as an arrest. Even if a consulate or embassy declines to offer financial or legal help, the staff can generally offer advice as to how you can obtain help locally. For example, they can furnish a list of attorneys who might represent you. Most arrests are for illegal possession of drugs, and the U.S. embassy and consular officials cannot interfere with the French judicial system. A consulate can only advise you of your rights.

Mail   Most post offices in France are open Monday to Friday from 8am to 7pm and Saturday from 8am to noon. Allow five to eight days to send or receive mail from your home. Airmail letters to North America cost 4.30 F (80¢) for 20 grams or 7.90 F ($1.50) for 30 grams. Letters to the U.K. cost 2.80 F (55¢) for up to 20 grams. An airmail postcard to North America or Europe (outside France) costs 3.80 F (70¢).

If you don't have a hotel address in France, you can receive mail c/o American Express (see "Fast Facts: Paris," in Chapter 4). However, you may be asked to show an American Express card or traveler's check when you go to pick up your mail. Another option is to send your mail *Poste Restante* (general delivery) in care of the major postal office in whatever town you plan to visit. You'll need to produce a passport to pick up mail, and you may be charged a small fee for the service.

You can also exchange money at post offices. Many hotels sell stamps, as do local post offices and cafés displaying a red TABAC sign outside. Mailboxes are clearly marked.

Maps   See "By Car" under "Getting Around France," earlier in this chapter.

Medical Emergencies   If you're ill and need medicine, go to a *pharmacie* (drugstore). At night and on Sunday, the local Commissariat de Police will tell you the location of the nearest drugstore that's open or the address of the nearest doctor on duty. The police will also summon an ambulance if you need to be rushed to a hospital. Seek assistance first at your hotel desk if language is a problem.

Newspapers/Magazines   Most major cities carry copies of the *International Herald Tribune, USA Today,* and usually a major London paper or two. Nearly all big-city newsstands—at least in areas that cater to tourists—also sell copies of *Time* and *Newsweek.*

Passports   See "Information, Required Documents, and Money," earlier in this chapter.

Police   Call **17** anywhere in France.

Restrooms   If you're in dire need, duck into a café or brasserie to use the lavatory. It's customary to make some small purchase if you do so. Paris Métro stations and underground garages usually contain public lavatories, but the degree of cleanliness varies. France still has many "hole-in-the-ground" toilets, so be forewarned.

Safety   Much of the country, particularly central France, the northeast, Normandy, and Brittany, remains relatively safe, even though no place in the world is crime-free. Those intending to visit the south of France, especially the French Riviera, should exercise extreme caution—robberies and muggings there are commonplace. It's best to check your baggage into a hotel and then go sightseeing instead of leaving it unguarded in the trunk of a car, which can easily be broken into. Marseille is among the most dangerous cities.

Taxes   *Watch it:* You could get burned. As a member of the European Union France routinely imposes a value-added tax (VAT) on many goods and services—currently 6% to 33.3%.

Telephone   All phone numbers in France require eight digits; these eight digits include the **area code.** For example, the telephone number for the Hôtel Carlton (93-68-91-68) contains the area code for Cannes. If you were anywhere in France, to call the Carlton all you would have to dial is this eight-digit number. When calling from outside France, all you would have to dial is the country code for France and then the eight-digit number.

This system is complicated by only one factor: Calls destined for Paris or the *région parisienne* from outside the *région parisienne* require the addition of a "1" before the eight digits.

Note that if you're in Paris or the *région parisienne,* to call the Hôtel de Crillon in Paris all you would do is dial the eight digit number 42-65-24-24. If you're in France but outside Paris or the *région parisienne,* dial 1/42-65-24-24 to call the Hôtel de Crillon in Paris. If you're calling the Hôtel de Crillon from outside France, dial the country code and then 1/42-65-24-24.

Public **phone booths** are found in cafés, restaurants, Métro stations, post offices, airports, and train stations and occasionally on the streets. Some of these booths work with tokens called *jetons,* which can be purchased at the post office or from the cashier at any café. (It's usually customary to give a small tip if you buy them at a café.) Pay telephones accept coins of $^1/_2$, 1, 2, and 5 F; the minimum charge is 1 F (20¢). Pick up the receiver, insert the *jeton* or coin(s), and dial when you hear the tone, pushing the button when there's an answer.

The French also use a ***télécarte,*** a telephone debit card, which can be purchased at rail stations, post offices, and other places. Sold in two versions, it allows callers to use either 50 or 120 charge units (depending on the card) by inserting the card into the slot of most public telephones. Depending on the type of card you buy, they cost 40 to 96 F ($7.60 to $18.25).

If possible, avoid making calls from your hotel, as some French establishments double or triple the charges on you.

When you're calling **long distance** within France, dial 16, wait for the dial tone, and then dial the eight-digit number of the person or place you're calling. To call the United States or Canada, first dial 19, listen for the tone, then slowly dial 1, the area code, and the seven-digit number. To place a collect call to North America, dial 19-33-11 and an English-speaking operator will assist you. Dial 19-00-11 for an American AT&T operator.

For information, dial 12.

Time   The French equivalent of daylight saving time lasts from around April to September, which puts it one hour ahead of French winter time. Depending on the time of year, France is six or seven hours ahead of eastern standard time in the United States.

Tipping   This is practiced with flourish and style in France, and as a visitor you're expected to play the game. All bills, as required by law, are supposed to say *service compris*, which means that the tip has been included.

Here are some general guidelines: For **hotel staff** tip 5 to 10 F (95¢ to $1.90) for every item of baggage the porter carries on arrival and departure. You're not obligated to tip the concierge (hall porter), doorman, or anyone else—unless you use his or her services. In cafés, **waiter** service is usually included. **Porters** have an official scale of charges—it's usual to give about 5 F (95¢) per bag, depending on the number of bags. Tip **taxi drivers** 10% to 15% of the amount shown on the meter. In theaters and restaurants, give **cloakroom attendants** at least 5 F (95¢) per item. Give **restroom attendants** about 2 F (40¢) in nightclubs and such places. Give **cinema and theater ushers** about 2 F (40¢). Tip the **hairdresser** about 10%, and don't forget to tip the person who gives you a shampoo or a manicure 10 F ($1.90). For **guides** for group visits to museums and monuments, 5 F (95¢) is a reasonable tip.

Visas   See "Information, Required Documents, and Money," earlier in this chapter.

Water   Drinking water is generally safe, though it's been known to cause diarrhea. If you ask for water in a restaurant, it'll be served bottled (for which you'll pay) unless you specifically request tap water (*l'eau du robinet*).

Yellow Pages   As in North America, the *Yellow Pages* are immensely useful. Your hotel will almost certainly have a copy, but you'll need the help of a French-speaking resident before tackling the French Telephone Company's (P.T.T.'s) *Yellow Pages*.

Paris: City of Light 4

Stroll along the broad tree-lined boulevards stopping to browse through the chic shops and relax at the sidewalk cafés; visit the world-renowned art museums, monuments, and gothic cathedrals; sample the meticulously prepared cuisine; and enjoy the hot nightlife. From the smoky cafés to the River Seine, Paris always manages to live up to its reputation as one of the world's most romantic cities.

Ernest Hemingway referred to the many splendors of Paris as a "moveable feast" and wrote, "There is never any ending to Paris, and the memory of each person who has lived in it differs from that of any other." It is this personal discovery of the city that's always been the most compelling reason for coming to Paris. And perhaps that's why France has been called *le deuxième pays de tout le monde*—everyone's second country.

1 Getting to Know Paris

ARRIVING
BY PLANE
Paris has two major international airports: Aéroport d'Orly, 8^1/$_2$ miles south, and Aéroport Roissy–Charles de Gaulle, 14^1/$_4$ miles northeast of the city. A shuttle operates between the two airports about every 30 minutes, taking 50 to 75 minutes to make the journey.

CHARLES DE GAULLE AIRPORT (ROISSY)   At Charles de Gaulle Airport (☎ **1/48-62-22-80**), foreign carriers use Aérogare 1 and Air France uses Aérogare 2. From Aérogare 1, you take a moving walkway to the passport checkpoint and the Customs area. The two terminals are linked by a shuttle bus (*navette*).

The free shuttle bus connecting Aérogare 1 with Aérogare 2 also transports passengers to the Roissy rail station, from which fast **RER trains** leave every 15 minutes heading to such Métro stations as Gare du Nord, Châtelet, Luxembourg, Port-Royal, and Denfert-Rochereau. A typical fare from Roissy to any point in central Paris is 40 F ($7.60).

You can also take an **Air France shuttle bus** to central Paris for 48 F ($9.10). It stops at the Palais des Congrès (Port Maillot), then continues on to place de l'Etoile, where subway lines can carry you farther along to any other point in Paris. That ride, depending on traffic, takes between 45 and 55 minutes. The shuttle departs about every 12 minutes between 5:40am and 11pm.

Another option is the **Roissybus,** departing from the airport daily from 5:45am to 11pm and costing 35 F ($6.65) for the 45- to 50-minute ride. Departures are about every 15 minutes, and the bus will take you near the corner of rue Scribe and place de l'Opéra in the heart of Paris.

A **taxi** from Roissy into the city will cost about 200 F ($38). At night (from 8pm to 7am), fares are 35% higher. Long queues of both taxis and passengers form outside each of the airport's terminals and are surprisingly orderly.

ORLY AIRPORT   Orly Airport (☎ 1/49-75-15-15) also has two terminals—Orly Sud (south) for international flights and Orly Ouest (west) for domestic flights. They're linked by a free shuttle bus.

Air France buses leave from Exit E of Orly Sud and from Exit F of Orly Ouest every 12 minutes between 5:45pm and 11pm, heading for Gare des Invalides. At Exit D you can board **bus no. 215** for place Denfert-Rochereau in central Paris. Passage on any of these buses costs 32 F ($6.10).

An alternative method for reaching central Paris involves taking a free shuttle bus that leaves both of Orly's terminals at intervals of approximately every 15 minutes for the nearby Métro and RER train station (Pont-de-Rungis/Aéroport-d'Orly), from which **RER trains** take 30 minutes for rides into the city center. A trip to Les Invalides, for example, costs 34 F ($6.50). (When you're returning to the airport, buses leave the Invalides terminal heading either to Orly Sud or Orly Ouest every 15 minutes, taking about 30 minutes.)

A **taxi** from Orly to the center of Paris costs about 170 F ($32.30) and is higher at night. Don't take a meterless taxi from Orly Sud or Orly Ouest—it's much safer (and usually cheaper) to hire a metered cab from the lines, which are under the scrutiny of a police officer.

BY TRAIN

There are six major train stations in Paris: **Gare d'Austerlitz,** 55 quai d'Austerlitz, 13e (servicing the southwest with trains to the Loire Valley, the Bordeaux country, and the Pyrénées); **Gare de l'Est,** place du 11 Novembre 1918, 10e (servicing the east, with trains to Strasbourg, Nancy, Reims, and beyond to Zurich, Basel, Luxembourg, and Austria); **Gare de Lyon,** 20 bd. Diderot, 12e (servicing the southeast with trains to the Côte d'Azur, Provence, and beyond to Geneva,

Impressions

Paris is still monumental and handsome. Along the rivers where its splendours are, there's no denying its man-made beauty. The poor, pale little Seine runs rapidly north to the sea, the sky is pale, pale jade overhead, greenish and Parisian, the trees of black wire stand in rows, and flourish their black wire brushes against a low sky of jade-pale cobwebs, and the huge dark-grey palaces rear up their masses of stone and slope off towards the sky still with a massive, satisfying suggestion of pyramids. There is something noble and man-made about it all.

—D. H. Lawrence

Lausanne, and Italy); **Gare Montparnasse,** 17 bd. Vaugirard, 15e (servicing the west, with trains to Brittany); **Gare du Nord,** 18 rue de Dunkerque, 15e (servicing the north with trains to Holland, Denmark, Belgium, and the north of Germany); and **Gare St-Lazare,** 13 rue d'Amsterdam, 8e (servicing the northwest, with trains to Normandy).

For general train information and to make reservations, call 45-82-50-50 from 7am to 8pm daily. Buses operate between the stations.

Note: The stations and the surrounding areas are usually seedy and frequented by pickpockets, hustlers, hookers, and drug addicts. Be alert, especially at night.

Each of these stations also has a Métro stop, making the whole city easily accessible. Taxis are also available at every station at designated stands. Look for the sign that says TETE DE STATION.

BY BUS

Most buses arrive at **Gare Routière Internationale du Paris-Gallieni,** avenue du Général-de-Gaulle, Bagnolet (☎ 1/49-72-51-51; Métro: Gallieni).

BY CAR

Driving a car in Paris is definitely not recommended. Parking is difficult and traffic dense. If you do drive, remember that Paris is encircled by a ring road called the *périphérique.* Always obtain detailed directions to your destination, including the name of the exit on the périphérique (exits are not numbered). Avoid rush hours.

Few hotels, except the luxury ones, have garages, but the staff will usually be able to direct you to one nearby.

The major highways into Paris are A1 from the north (Great Britain and Benelux); A13 from Rouen, Normandy, and other points of northwest France; A109 from Spain, the Pyrénées, and the southwest; A7 from the French Alps, the Riviera, and Italy; and A4 from eastern France.

VISITOR INFORMATION

The main **tourist information office** is at 127 av. des Champs-Elysées, 8e (☎ 1/49-52-53-54), where you can secure information about both Paris and the provinces. The office is open daily (except May 1) from 9am to 8pm.

Welcome Offices in the city's railway stations (except the Gare St-Lazare) will also give you free maps, brochures, and *Paris Selection,* a monthly French-language listing of all current events and performances.

CITY LAYOUT

Paris is surprisingly compact. Occupying 432 square miles (6 more than San Francisco), it's home to more than 10 million people. The River Seine divides Paris into the **Right Bank (Rive Droite)** to the north and the **Left Bank (Rive Gauche)** to the south. These designations make sense when you stand on a bridge and face downstream, watching the waters flow out toward the sea—to your right is the north bank; to your left the south. Thirty-two bridges link the Right Bank and the Left Bank, some providing access to the two small islands at the heart of the city, **Ile de la Cité**—the city's birthplace and site of Notre-Dame—and **Ile St-Louis,** a moat-guarded oasis of sober 17th-century mansions. These islands can cause some confusion to walkers who think they've just crossed a bridge from one bank to the other, only to find themselves caught up in an almost-medieval maze of narrow streets and old buildings.

Those Americans in Paris

- In the spring of 1922 **Edna St. Vincent Millay** dined at the Café de la Rotonde almost daily with her mother. Writing home, she recorded her first impression of French food: "Mummie & I about live in this here kafe. We feed on *choucroute garnie*, which is fried sauerkraut trimmed with boiled potatoes, a large slice of ham & a fat hot dog—yum, yum, werry excillint. Mummie & I come every day & eat the stinkin' stuff, & all our friends hold their noses & pass us by till we've finished."

- Living in a Paris apartment in 1925, **F. Scott Fitzgerald** owed $6,200 to his publisher, Scribner's. Though *The Great Gatsby* had sold 20,000 copies (a huge total then), Fitzgerald was disappointed. At the height of his fame, Fitzgerald launched the year with "1,000 parties and no work." His drunken bouts sometimes lasted for a week. He'd show up at the *Chicago Tribune* office on rue Lamartine, staggering and shouting for reporters to get out "the goddamn paper." After being evicted from the offices, he'd visit bars until lapsing into unconsciousness. One couple reported taking him home only to hear Zelda yell down: "You bastard. Drunk again!"

- Newspaper tycoon **William Randolph Hearst** visited Paris in September 1928 with his mistress, actress Marion Davies. Upon returning to America, Hearst revealed in his newspaper a confidential memorandum exposing a Franco-British pact to increase the strength of their navies. When he returned to Paris in 1930, along with Ms. Davies and a dozen of her girlfriends from Hollywood, a French official greeted him and asked him—"as an enemy of France"—to leave the country at once. Hearst and his entourage hastened over to the Savoy in London. The yellow-press baron later wrote that he could endure being persona non grata in France "without loss of sleep."

MAIN ARTERIES & STREETS   Between 1860 and 1870 Baron Georges-Eugène Haussmann, at the orders of Napoléon III, forever changed the look of Paris by creating the legendary *grands boulevards*: St-Michel, St-Germain, Haussmann, Sébastopol, Magenta, Voltaire, and Strasbourg.

The "main street" on the Right Bank is, of course, the **avenue des Champs-Elysées**, beginning at the Arc de Triomphe and running to **place de la Concorde.** Haussmann also created avenue de l'Opéra and the 12 avenues that radiate star-like from the Arc de Triomphe, giving it its original name, place de l'Etoile (*étoile* means "star"). It was renamed place Charles-de-Gaulle following the general's death; today it's often referred to as **place Charles-de-Gaulle–Etoile.**

Haussmann also cleared the Ile de la Cité of its medieval buildings, transforming it into a showcase for Notre-Dame. Finally, he laid out the two elegant parks on the western and southeastern fringes of the city: Bois de Boulogne and Bois de Vincennes.

FINDING AN ADDRESS   Paris is divided into 20 municipal wards called *arrondissements*, each with its own mayor, city hall, police station, and central post office; some even have remnants of market squares. Most city maps are divided by arrondissement, and all addresses include the arrondissement number (written in Roman or Arabic numerals and followed by "e" or "er"). Paris also has its own version of a ZIP Code. Thus the proper mailing address for a certain hotel is written as, for example, "75014 Paris." The last two digits, 14, indicate that the address is in the 14th arrondissement, in this case, Montparnasse.

Numbers on buildings running parallel to the Seine usually follow the course of the river—east to west. On perpendicular street, numbers on buildings begin low closer to the river.

MAPS If you're staying more than two or three days, purchase an inexpensive, pocket-size book that includes the *plan de Paris* by arrondissement, available at all major newsstands and bookshops. Most of these guides provide you with a Métro map, a foldout map of the city, and maps of each arrondissement, with all streets listed and keyed.

ARRONDISSEMENTS IN BRIEF

Each of Paris's 20 arrondissements possesses a unique style and flavor. You'll want to decide which district appeals most to you and find a place to stay there (note, however, that in this guide we cover only those hotels in central Paris; for accommodations in the outer arrondissements, see *Frommer's Paris '96*).

1er One of the world's greatest art museums, the Louvre lures hordes of visitors to the 1st arrondissement. Here are many elegant addresses, rue de Rivoli, and the Jeu de Paume and Orangerie museums. Walk through the formal Jardin des Tuileries, laid out by Le Nôtre, Louis XIV's gardener. Pause to take in the classic beauty of place Vendôme. Jewelers and art dealers are plentiful, and the memories of Chopin are evoked at no. 12 on the square where he died. Zola's "belly of Paris" (Les Halles) is no longer the food-and-meat market but has become Forum des Halles, a center of shopping, entertainment, and culture.

2e Home to the Bourse (stock exchange), this Right Bank district lies mainly between the *grands boulevards* and rue Etienne-Marcel. On weekdays, the shouts of brokers echo across place de la Bourse until it's time for lunch. The movers and shakers of capitalism continue their hysteria in the district's restaurants. Much of the eastern end of the 2nd (Le Sentier) is devoted to the garment district, where thousands of garments are sold to buyers from stores all over Europe. If you explore this district, you'll find gems amid the commercialism—none finer than the Musée Cognacq-Jay, at 25 bd. des Capucines. Ernest Cognacq created the Samaritaine chain of stores and collected exquisite art from Watteau to Fragonard.

3e This district embraces much of Le Marais (the swamp), one of the best loved of the old Right Bank neighborhoods. Allowed to fall into decay for decades, it has come back, though it will never recapture its aristocratic heyday. Over the centuries, kings have called Le Marais home, and its salons have echoed with the witty, often devastating remarks of Racine, Voltaire, Molière, and Mme de Sévigné. One of its chief draws today is the Musée Picasso, a great repository of 20th-century art.

4e It seems as if the 4th has it all: Not only the Ile de la Cité with Notre-Dame and the Conciergerie but also the Ile St-Louis with its aristocratic town houses, courtyards, and antiques shops. Ile St-Louis, a former cow pasture and dueling ground, is home to 6,000 lucky *Louisiens*, its permanent residents. Of course, the whole area is touristy and overrun. Seek out its two gems of gothic architecture: the Sainte-Chapelle and Notre-Dame.

The heart of medieval Paris, the 4th evokes memories of Danton and Robespierre, even of Charlotte Corday stabbing Marat in his bath. You get France's finest bird and flower markets, plus the Centre Pompidou, now one of the top three attractions of France. After all this pomp and glory, you can retreat to place des Vosges, a square of perfect harmony where Victor Hugo penned many masterpieces from 1832 to 1848.

5e The Quartier Latin (Latin Quarter) is the intellectual soul of Paris. Bookstores, schools, churches, smoky jazz clubs, student dives, Roman ruins, publishing houses, and chic boutiques characterize the district. With the founding of the Sorbonne in 1253, the quarter got its name because all the students and professors spoke Latin. As the traditional center of "bohemian Paris," it formed the setting for Henry Burger's novel *La Vie bohème* (and later the Puccini opera *La Bohème*).

For sure, the old Latin Quarter is gone. Changing times have brought Greek, Moroccan, and Vietnamese immigrants, among others, hustling everything from couscous to fiery-hot spring rolls and souvlaki. The 5th borders the Seine, so you'll want to stroll along quai de Montebello, where vendors sell everything from antique Daumier prints to yellowing copies of Balzac's *Père Goriot*. The 5th also stretches to the Panthéon, the resting place of Rousseau, Zola, Hugo, Braille, Voltaire, and Jean Moulin, the Resistance leader who was tortured to death by the Gestapo.

6e This heartland of Paris publishing is, for some, the most colorful Left Bank quarter. Waves of earnest young artists can be seen emerging from the Ecole des Beaux-Arts. To stroll the boulevards of the 6th, including St-Germain, has its own rewards, but the secret of the district lies in discovering its narrow streets and hidden squares. To be really "authentic" you should stroll these streets with an unwrapped loaf of country sourdough bread from the wood-fired ovens of Poilâne, 8 rue du Cherche-Midi. Everywhere you turn you'll encounter famous historical and literary associations, none more so than on rue Jacob, where Racine, Wagner, Ingres, and Hemingway once lived at various times. Today's "big name" is likely to be filmmaker Spike Lee checking into his favorite, La Villa Hôtel, at 29 rue Jacob.

7e Paris's most famous symbol, the Eiffel Tower, dominates the Left Bank 7th. The tower is now one of the most recognizable landmarks in the world, though many Parisians hated it when it was unveiled in 1889. Many imposing monuments are in the 7th, including the Hôtel des Invalides, which contains Napoléon's Tomb and the Musée de l'Armée. But there's much hidden charm as well. Your predecessors on these often-narrow streets include Picasso, Manet, Baudelaire, Wagner, de Beauvoir, Sartre, and even Truman Capote, Gore Vidal, and Tennessee Williams,

Even visitors with no time to discover the 7th at least rush to the Musée d'Orsay, the world's premier showcase of 19th-century French art and culture. The museum is housed in the old Gare d'Orsay, which Orson Welles used in 1962 as a setting for his *The Trial.*

8e The 8th is the heart of the Right Bank and its prime showcase is avenue des Champs-Elysées, linking the Arc de Triomphe with the delicate Egyptian obelisk on place de la Concorde. Here you'll find the fashion houses, the most elegant hotels, expensive restaurants and shops, and fashionably attired Parisians. By the 1980s it had become a garish strip, with too much traffic and too many fast-food joints. But in the 1990s the Gaulist mayor of Paris (now president of France), Jacques Chirac, launched a massive cleanup and improvement. The major change has been in broadened sidewalks, with new rows of trees planted. The old glory is perhaps gone forever, but what an improvement!

Paris by Arrondissement

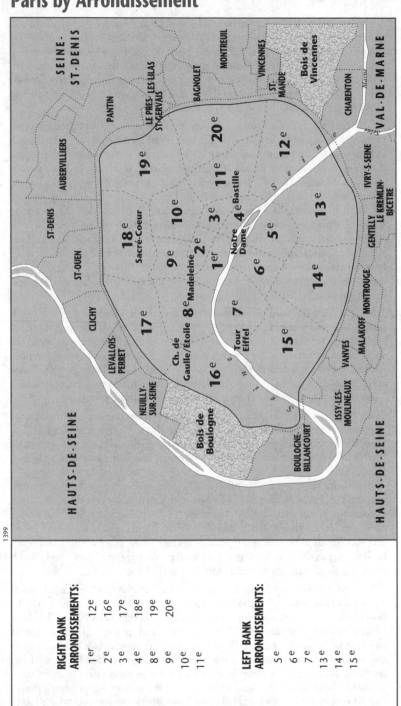

1399

RIGHT BANK ARRONDISSEMENTS:

1er	12e
2e	16e
3e	17e
4e	18e
8e	19e
9e	20e
10e	
11e	

LEFT BANK ARRONDISSEMENTS:

5e
6e
7e
13e
14e
15e

The area is known for having either the world's or France's best, grandest, and most impressive: the best restaurant (Taillevent), the sexiest strip joint (Crazy Horse Saloon), the most splendid square (place de la Concorde), the best rooftop café (at La Samaritaine), the grandest hotel (the Crillon), the most impressive triumphal arch (Arc de Triomphe), the most expensive residential street (avenue Matignon), the oldest Métro station (Franklin-D.-Roosevelt), and the most ancient monument (Obelisk of Luxor, 3,300 years old).

9e Everything from the Quartier de l'Opéra to the strip joints of Pigalle (the infamous "Pig Alley" for the GIs of World War II) falls within the 9th. The 9th was radically altered by Baron Haussmann's 19th-century urban redevelopment, and the *grands boulevards* here are among the most obvious of his labors. The 9th continues on, even if fickle fashion now prefers other addresses. Boulevard des Italiens is the site of the Café de la Paix, opened in 1856 and once the meeting place of the Romantic poets, like Théophile Gautier and Alfred de Musset. Later, de Gaulle, Dietrich, and two million Americans started showing up.

Other major attractions include the Folies-Bergère, where cancan dancers have been kicking since 1868 and such entertainers as Mistinguett, Piaf, and Chevalier have appeared, along with American Josephine Baker. More than anything, it was the Opéra (now the Opéra Garnier) that made the 9th the last hurrah of Second Empire opulence.

10e The Gare du Nord and Gare de l'Est, along with movie theaters and porno houses and dreary commercial zones, make the 10th one of the least desirable arrondissements for living, dining, and sightseeing. We always try to avoid the 10th, except for two longtime favorite restaurants, Brasserie Flo, 7 cour des Petites-Ecuries (go for its *la formidable choucroute*—a heap of sauerkraut garnished with everything), and Julien, 16 rue du Faubourg St-Denis (called the poor man's Maxim's because of its belle époque interiors and moderate prices).

11e For many years this quarter seemed to sink lower and lower. However, the 1989 opening of the Opéra de la Bastille has given it a new lease on life. The "people's opera house" now stands on the landmark place de la Bastille, where on July 14, 1789, 633 Parisians stormed the fortress, seized the ammunition depot, and released the few prisoners.

Even when the district wasn't fashionable, visitors flocked to the most famous brasserie in Paris, Bofinger, 5–7 rue de la Bastille, to sample its Alsatian choucroute. (Technically Bofinger lies in the 4th arrondissement, but it has always been associated with place de la Bastille.) What charms exist in the 11th? Whatever is there has to be sought out, including the Marché place d'Aligre, a secondhand market in the Middle Eastern food market. Everything is cheap, and though you must search hard for treasures, you'll often find them.

12e Few out-of-towners came here until a French chef opened Au Trou Gascon. Then the whole world started showing up at the door. The major attraction is the Bois de Vincennes, a sprawling park on the eastern periphery of Paris. It has been a longtime favorite of families who enjoy its zoos and museums, its royal château and boating lakes, and the Parc Floral de Paris, whose springtime rhododendrons and autumn dahlias are among the city's major lures. The dreary Gare de Lyon lies in the 12th, but going there's worthwhile even if you don't have to take a train. The attraction is Le Train Bleue, a restaurant in the station, whose ceiling frescos and art nouveau decor are classified as national artistic treasures. (And the food's good, too.) The 12th, a once-depressing neighborhood, has been slated for a multi-million-dollar resuscitation, including new housing, shops, gardens, and restaurants.

13e Centering around the grimy Gare d'Austerlitz, the 13th might have its devotees, though we've yet to meet one. British snobs who flitted in and out of the train station were among the first foreign visitors, and they in essence wrote the 13th off as a "dreary working-class district—but then London has its East End." Certainly there remain more fashionable places to be seen, but there's at least one reason to go here: Manufacture des Gobelins, 42 av. des Gobelins, which made the word *Gobelins* world famous.

14e The northern end of this district is Montparnasse, home of the Lost Generation. One of its major monuments, helping set the tone of the neighborhood, is the Rodin statue of Balzac at the junction of boulevard Montparnasse and boulevard Raspail. At this corner are famous literary cafés like La Rotonde, Le Sélect, La Dôme, and La Coupole. Perhaps only Gertrude Stein didn't come here (she loathed cafés), but all the other American expatriates, including Hemingway and Fitzgerald, arrived for a drink or four. At 27 rue de Fleurus Stein and Toklas collected their paintings and entertained T. S. Eliot and Matisse. At its southern end, the 14th contains residential neighborhoods filled with well-designed apartment buildings, many built between 1910 and 1940.

15e A mostly residential district beginning at the Gare Montparnasse, the 15th stretches to the Seine. It's the largest quarter but attracts few tourists and has few attractions, except for the Parc des Expositions and Institut Pasteur.

16e Highlights of the 16th include the Bois de Boulogne, Jardin du Trocadéro, Musée de Balzac, Musée Guimet (famous for its Asian collections), and Cimetière de Passy, resting place of Manet, Talleyrand, Giraudoux, and Debussy. One of the largest of the arrondissements, it's known for its well-heeled bourgeoisie, upscale rents, and posh residential boulevards. Prosperous and suitably conservative addresses include avenue d'Iéna and avenue Victor-Hugo; also prestigious is avenue Foch, the widest boulevard, with homes that at various periods were maintained by Onassis, the shah of Iran, Debussy, and Prince Ranier of Monaco. The 16th also includes the best place in Paris to view the Eiffel Tower from afar: place du Trocadéro.

17e Flanking the northern periphery of Paris, the 17th incorporates bourgeois neighborhoods in its western end with more pedestrian neighborhoods in its eastern end. Highlights include the Palais des Congrès (which will be of interest only if you're attending a convention or special exhibit) and the Porte Maillot Air Terminal, no grand distinction. More exciting than either of those are two great restaurants: Guy Savoy and Michel Rostang (see Chapter 6).

18e The 18th is the most famous outer quarter, embracing Montmartre, associated with such legendary names as the Moulin Rouge, Basilica of Sacré-Coeur, and place du Tertre. Utrillo was its native son, Renoir lived here, and Toulouse-Lautrec adopted the area as his own. Today, place Blanche is known for its prostitutes, and Montmartre is filled with honky-tonks, souvenir shops, and terrible restaurants. Go for the attractions and *mémoires*. The Marché aux Puces de Clignancourt flea market is another landmark.

19e Visitors come here to what was once the village of La Villette to see the much-publicized angular Cité des Sciences et de l'Industrie, a spectacular science museum/park built on a site that for years was devoted to slaughterhouses. Mostly residential and not at all upscale, the district is one of the most ethnic in Paris, home of workers from all parts of the former Empire. A highlight is Les Buttes-Chaumon, a park where kids can enjoy puppet shows and donkey rides.

20e   This district's greatest landmark is the Père-Lachaise Cemetery, resting place of Piaf, Proust, Wilde, Duncan, Stein, Bernhardt, Colette, Jim Morrison, and many others. Nostalgia buffs sometimes visit Piaf's former neighborhood, Ménilmontant-Belleville, but it has been almost totally bulldozed and rebuilt. The district is now home to many Muslims and hundreds of members of Paris's Jew-ish (Sephardic) community, many of whom fled from Algeria or Tunisia. With turbaned men selling dates and grains on the street, this arrondissement seems more North African than French.

2 Getting Around

Paris is a city for strollers whose greatest joy is rambling through unexpected al-leys and squares. Given a choice of conveyance, try to make it your own two feet whenever possible.

DISCOUNT PASSES   You can purchase a **Paris-Visite,** a tourist pass valid for three or five days on the public transportation system, including the Métro, buses, and RER (Réseau Express Régional) trains. (The RER has both first- and second-class compartments, and the pass lets you travel in first class.) As a bonus, the funicular ride to the top of Montmartre is also included. The cost is 95 F ($18.05) for three days or 150 F ($28.50) for five. The card is available at RATP (Régie Autonome des Transports Parisiens), tourist offices, or the main Métro stations.

There are other discount passes as well, though most are available only to French residents with government ID cards and proof of taxpayer status. One available to temporary visitors is **Formule 1,** which allows unlimited travel on all bus, subway, and RER lines during a one- or two-day period. A one-day pass costs 28 F ($5.30); a two-day pass costs 38 F ($7.20). Ask for it at any Métro station.

BY METRO

Easy to use, the Métro (☎ 1/43-46-14-14 for information) is the most efficient and fastest means of transportation in Paris. Each line is numbered, and the final destination of each line is clearly marked on subway maps, in the underground passageways, and on the train cars.

The Métro runs daily from 5:30am to around 1:15am. It's reasonably safe at any hour, but beware of pickpockets.

METRO MAPS   Most stations display a map of the Métro system at the en-trance. By studying the map, figure out the route to your destination; it's impor-tant to note the station (or stations) where you'll have to change trains. To make sure you catch the correct train, find your destination, then follow the rail line it's on to the end of the route and note the name of the final destination—this final stop is the *direction.* To find your train in the station, follow the signs labeled with your direction in the passageways until you see your direction labeled on a train.

Transfer stations are known as *correspondances*—some require long walks, Châtelet is the most difficult—but most trips will require only one transfer. When transferring, follow the bright-orange CORRESPONDANCE signs until you reach the proper platform. Don't follow a SORTIE sign ("Exit") or you'll have to pay another fare to resume your journey.

Many of the larger stations have easy-to-use maps with pushbutton indicators that light up your route when you press the button for your destination.

FARES   On the urban lines, it costs the same to any point. One ticket costs 7 F ($1.35). On the Sceaux, Boissy–St-Léger, and St-Germain-en-Laye lines serving the suburbs, fares are based on distance. When purchasing Métro tickets, a *carnet* is the best buy—10 tickets for 41 F ($7.80).

TICKET PROTOCOL   At the turnstile entrances to the station, insert your ticket in the turnstile and pass through. At some exits tickets are also checked, so hold on to your ticket. There are occasional ticket checks on the trains, platforms, and passageways, too.

BY BUS

Buses are much slower than the subway. Most buses run from 7am to 8:30pm (a few operate until 12:30am, and a handful operate during the early-morning hours). Service is limited on Sunday and holidays. Bus and Métro fares are the same and you can use the same *carnet* tickets on both. Most bus rides require one ticket, but there are some destinations requiring two (never more than two within the city limits).

At certain bus stops signs list the destinations and numbers of the buses serving that point. Destinations are usually listed north to south and east to west. Most stops along the way are also posted on the sides of the buses. To catch a bus, wait in line at the bus stop. Signal to the driver to stop the bus and board in order. During rush hours you may have to take a ticket from a dispensing machine, indicating your position in the line.

If you intend to use the buses a lot, pick up an RATP bus map at the office on place de la Madeleine, 8e, or at the tourist offices at RATP headquarters, 55 quai des Grands-Augustins, 75006 Paris; or you can write ahead of time. For detailed information on bus and Métro routes, call 43-46-14-14.

BY TAXI

It's impossible to secure one at rush hour, so don't even try. Taxi drivers are strongly organized into an effective lobby to keep their number limited to 14,300.

Watch out for the common rip-offs. Always check the meter to make sure you're not paying the previous passenger's fare. Beware of cabs without meters, which often wait for tipsy patrons outside nightclubs—or settle the tab in advance. Regular cabs can be hailed on the street when their signs read LIBRE. Taxis are easier to find at the many stands near Métro stations.

The flag drops at 12 F ($2.30), and you pay 5.20 F ($1) per kilometer. At night, expect to pay 7 F ($1.35) per kilometer. On airport trips you're not required to pay for the driver's empty return ride.

You're allowed several small pieces of luggage free if they're transported inside and don't weigh more than 5kg (11 lb.). Heavier suitcases carried in the trunk cost 6 F ($1.15) apiece. Tip 12% to 15%— the latter usually elicits a *merci*. For radio cabs, call 42-41-50-50, 42-70-41-41, 49-36-10-10, or 47-39-47-39— note that you'll be charged from the point where the taxi begins the drive to pick you up.

Paris Métro

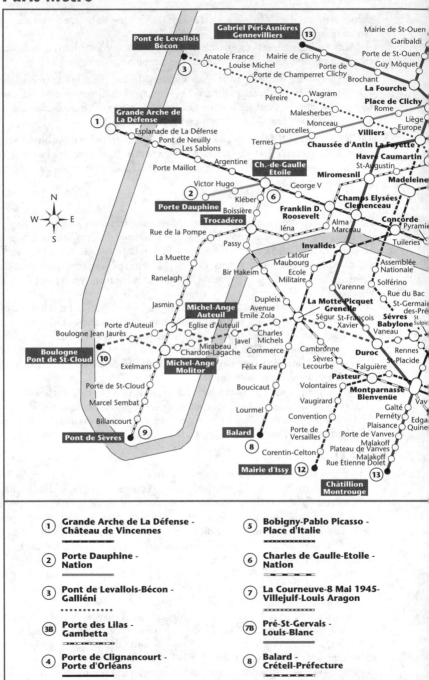

1 Grande Arche de La Défense -
Château de Vincennes

2 Porte Dauphine -
Nation

3 Pont de Levallois-Bécon -
Galliéni

3B Porte des Lilas -
Gambetta

4 Porte de Clignancourt -
Porte d'Orléans

5 Bobigny-Pablo Picasso -
Place d'Italie

6 Charles de Gaulle-Etoile -
Nation

7 La Courneuve-8 Mai 1945-
Villejuif-Louis Aragon

7B Pré-St-Gervais -
Louis-Blanc

8 Balard -
Créteil-Préfecture

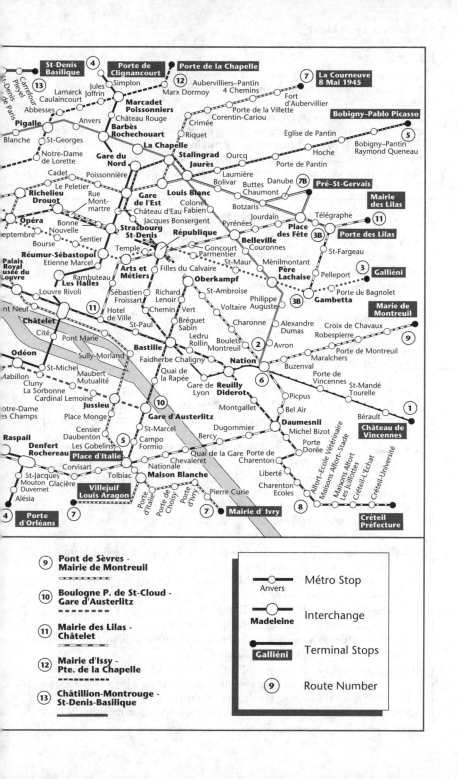

St-Denis Basilique ④ Porte de Clignancourt Porte de la Chapelle
⑬ Carrefour Pleyel Simplon ⑫ Aubervilliers–Pantin 4 Chemins ⑦ La Courneuve 8 Mai 1945
Lamarck Caulaincourt Jules Joffrin Marx Dormoy
Abbesses Château Rouge Fort d'Aubervillier
Pigalle Anvers Marcadet Poissonniers Porte de la Villette Bobigny–Pablo Picasso
Blanche St-Georges Barbès Rochechouart Crimée Corentin-Cariou
Notre-Dame de Lorette La Chapelle Riquet Eglise de Pantin ⑤ Bobigny–Pantin Raymond Queneau
Cadet Gare du Nord Stalingrad Ourcq Hoche
Poissonnière Jaurès Porte de Pantin
Le Peletier Laumière Bolivar Buttes Chaumont Danube ⑦ᴮ Pré-St-Gervais
Richelieu Drouot Rue Mont-martre Louis Blanc Colonel Fabien Mairie des Lilas
Opéra Bonne Nouvelle Gare de l'Est Château d'Eau Jacques Bonsergent Botzaris Télégraphe ⑪
eptembre Sentier Strasbourg St-Denis République Jourdain Pyrénées Place des Fête ③ᴮ Porte des Lilas
Bourse Temple Belleville St-Fargeau
Réaumur-Sébastopol Etienne Marcel Goncourt Couronnes
Palais Royal usée du ouvre Rambuteau Arts et Métiers Filles du Calvaire Parmentier St-Maur Mènilmontant Père Lachaise Pelleport ③ Galliéni
Les Halles Oberkampf Gambetta ③ᴮ Porte de Bagnolet
Louvre Rivoli Sébastien Froissart Richard Lenoir St-Ambroise Mairie de Montreuil
nt Neuf ⑪ Hotel de Ville Chemin Vert Voltaire Philippe Auguste Croix de Chavaux
Châtelet St-Paul Bréguet Sabin Charonne Alexandre Dumas Robespierre ⑨
Cité Pont Marie Ledru Rollin Boulets Montreuil ② Avron Porte de Montreuil
Odéon Sully-Morland Bastille Faidherbe Chaligny Nation Maraîchers
St-Michel Quai de la Rapée ⑥ Buzenval Porte de Vincennes St-Mandé Tourelle
labillon Maubert Mutualité Gare de Lyon Reuilly Diderot Picpus ①
Cluny La Sorbonne Cardinal Lemoine Montgallet Bel Air Bérault
otre-Dame es Champs Jussieu Gare d'Austerlitz Dugommier Daumesnil Château de Vincennes
Place Monge St-Marcel Michel Bizot
Raspail Censier Daubenton ⑤ Campo Formio Bercy Porte Dorée
Denfert Rochereau Les Gobelins Quai de la Gare Porte de Charenton
Corvisart Chevaleret Liberté Alfort-Ecole Vétérinaire Maisons Alfort-Stade Maisons Alfort Les Juillottes Créteil-L'Echat Créteil-Université
St-Jacques Mouton Duvernet Glacière Tolbiac Place d'Italie Nationale Maison Blanche Charenton Ecoles ⑧
Alésia Villejuif Louis Aragon Pierre Curie Créteil Préfecture
④ Porte d'Orléans ⑦ Porte d'Italie Porte de Choisy Porte d'Ivry ⑦ Mairie d'Ivry

⑨ **Pont de Sèvres - Mairie de Montreuil**
- - - - - - - -

⑩ **Boulogne P. de St-Cloud - Gare d'Austerlitz**
- - - - - - - -

⑪ **Mairie des Lilas - Châtelet**
━━━━━━━

⑫ **Mairie d'Issy - Pte. de la Chapelle**
- - - - - - - -

⑬ **Châtillion-Montrouge - St-Denis-Basilique**

━━◯━━ Métro Stop
Anvers

◯ Interchange
Madeleine

■◯■ Terminal Stops
Galliéni

⑨ Route Number

BY CAR

Don't even consider driving in Paris. The streets are narrow and parking is next to impossible. Besides, most visitors don't have the nerve, skill, and ruthlessness required.

If you insist on ignoring this advice, here are a few tips: Get an excellent street map and ride with a co-pilot because there'll be no time to think at intersections. *Zone Bleue* means you can't park without a parking disc, obtainable from garages, police stations, and hotels. Parking is unlimited in these zones on Sunday and holidays. Attach the disc to your windshield, setting its clock to show the time of

---

Raves for Our Paris Faves

- **Peltier,** 66 rue de Sèvres, 7e (☎ 1/47-34-06-62; Métro: Vaveau or Duroc), prepares the best *tarte au chocolat* of any Paris pâtisserie.
- **Le Carrousel,** 194 rue de Rivol, 1er (☎ 1/42-60-63-28; Métro: Palais-Royal), makes a *croque monsieur* (grilled sandwich with cheese and ham) that's the most authentic in Paris.
- **Chez Joséphine,** 117 rue du Cherche-Midi, 6e (☎ 1/45-48-52-40; Métro: Croix-Rouge), is a 19th-century bistro that whips up an *omelette aux truffes* worth crossing town to eat.
- **Lili la Tigresse,** 98 rue Blanche, 9e (☎ 1/48-74-08-25; Métro: Blanche), is a Pigalle bar featuring the hippest live revue in town. If you go, be Parisian, not provincial.
- **Le Ritz,** 15 place Vendôme, 1er (☎ 1/42-60-38-30; Métro: Opéra), is our all-time favorite Paris movie locale, where *Love in the Afternoon*, starring Audrey Hepburn and Gary Cooper, was shot.
- **L'Assommoir,** 12 rue Girardon, 18e (☎ 1/42-64-55-01; Métro: Lamarck), is the most authentic bistro in touristy Montmartre (we dare to say this even though the owner threatened that if his restaurant's name is published in a travel guide we'd never be allowed back). The *tripes* (calf stomach) *à la mode de Caen* is almost as good as that served at Pharamond in Les Halles. The owner makes the *terrine de foies de volailles* (chicken-liver terrine) himself. Don't bother to ask for his *fondant au chocolat* recipe.
- **Café Cosmos,** 101 bd. du Montparnasse, 6e (☎ 1/43-26-74-36; Métro: Vavin), boasts an ultramodern interior and is patronized by the French film colony. Black tables, black leather chairs, and black clothing in winter are just a backdrop for smoked salmon with toast (does anybody eat anything else?).
- **L'Arlequin,** 76 rue de Rennes, 6e (☎ 1/45-44-28-80; Métro: St-Sulpice), is an *art-et-essai* movie house where you slip away for a revival showing of an oldie but goodie on a rainy Paris afternoon. Many films are shown in their *version originale*, which most often means English.
- **Le Queen,** 102 av. des Champs-Elysées, 8e (☎ 42-89-31-32; Métro: Franklin-D.-Roosevelt), is perfect for when you want to experience New York in Paris. Follow the flashing purple sign on the city's "main street." When you see drag queens dancing on the tables, you'll know you're in the right place.

arrival. From 9am to noon and 2:30 to 5pm you may park for 1 hour, between noon and 2:30pm for 2¹/₂ hours.

The driver and all passengers (front and back) must wear seat belts. Children under 12 must ride in the back seat. Drivers are supposed to yield to the car on the right, except where signs indicate otherwise, as at traffic circles.

Watch for the gendarmes, who lack patience and consistently countermand the lights. Horn-blowing is forbidden except in dire emergencies.

To take advantage of the discounts offered by the major U.S.–based firms, rent your car before your trip. See "By Car" under "Getting Around France," in Chapter 3, for details.

BY BICYCLE

It's tough to negotiate the traffic-clogged narrow streets filled with mean-spirited motorists who don't look kindly upon tourists on bikes. Save your cycling for the Bois de Boulogne or another park.

Bicyclub, 8 place de la Porte-Champerret, 17e (☎ 1/47-66-55-92; Métro: Porte-de-Champerret), rents bicycles by the hour, charging from 28 F ($5.30) per hour depending on the bike. Deposits of 1,000 to 2,000 F ($190.10 to $380.20) must be posted. Bikes are rented July to September, daily from 9am to 7pm; October to June, Monday to Friday from 9am to 7pm and Saturday from 9am to 1pm and 2 to 7pm.

FAST FACTS: Paris

For additional practical information, see "Fast Facts: France," in Chapter 3.

American Express   With a grand Paris office, American Express, 11 rue Scribe, 9e (☎ 1/47-77-77-07; Métro: Opéra, Chaussée-d'Antin, or Havre-Caumartin; RER: Auber), is extremely busy with customers buying and cashing traveler's checks (not the best rates for exchange transactions), picking up mail, and solving travel problems. It's open Monday to Friday from 9am to 6:30pm; the bank is also open Saturday (same hours), but the mail pickup window is closed. Less busy American Express offices are at 5 rue de Chaillot, 16e (☎ 1/47-23-72-15; Métro: Alma-Marceau or Iéna); 83 bis rue de Courcelles, 17e (☎ 1/47-66-03-00; Métro: Courcelles); and 38 av. de Wagram, 8e (☎ 1/42-27-58-80; Métro: Ternes).

Area Code   Paris's telephone area code is 1, followed by an eight-digit number. No other provinces have area codes. However, to dial long distance anywhere within France, first dial 16.

Babysitters   There are several agencies available, but verify that the sitter and your child speak the same language before you commit yourself. The Institut Catholique, 21 rue d'Assas, 6e (☎ 1/45-48-31-70), runs a service staffed by students. The price is 32 F ($6.10) per hour. The main office is open Monday to Friday from 9am to noon and 2 to 6pm.

Car Rentals   See "By Car" under "Getting Around France," in Chapter 3.

Climate   See "When to Go," in Chapter 3.

Currency Exchange   American Express can fill most of your banking needs. Most banks in Paris are open Monday to Friday from 9am to 4:30pm, but only a few are open Saturday; ask at your hotel for the location of the one nearest you. For the best exchange rate, cash your traveler's checks at banks or foreign-exchange offices, not at shops and hotels. Most post offices will also change traveler's checks or convert currency. Currency exchanges are also found at Paris airports and train stations. One of the most central currency-exchange branches is at 154 av. des Champs-Elysées, 8e (☎ 1/42-25-93-33; Métro: George-V or Charles-de-Gaulle–Etoile). It's open Monday to Friday from 9am to 5pm and Saturday and Sunday from 10:30am to 6pm. A small commission is charged.

Dentist   For emergency dental service, call 43-37-51-00 Monday to Friday from 8pm to 8am. On holidays and weekends you can call this number 24 hours. The American Hospital, 63 bd. Victor-Hugo, Neuilly (☎ 1/46-41-25-41; Métro: Pont-de-Levallois or Pont-de-Neuilly; Bus: 82), operates a bilingual (English-French) dental clinic, open 24 hours.

Doctor   Some large hotels have a doctor on staff. If yours doesn't, try the American Hospital, 63 bd. Victor-Hugo, Neuilly (☎ 1/46-41-25-41; Métro: Pont-de-Levallois or Pont-de-Neuilly; Bus: 82), which operates a 24-hour emergency service. Blue Cross and other American insurance are accepted by their bilingual staff.

Drugstores   After regular hours, have your concierge contact the Commissariat de Police for the nearest 24-hour pharmacy. French law requires that one pharmacy in any given neighborhood stay open 24 hours. You'll find the address posted on the doors or windows of all other drugstores. One of the most central all-night pharmacies is Pharmacy Dhery, 84 av. des Champs-Elysées, 8e (☎ 1/45-62-02-41; Métro: George-V).

Embassies/Consulates   See "Fast Facts: France," in Chapter 3.

Emergencies   For the police, call 17; to report a fire, call 18. For an ambulance, call the fire department at 45-78-74-52; a fire vehicle rushes cases to the nearest emergency room. S.A.M.U. (☎ 1/45-67-50-50) is an independently operated, privately owned ambulance company. You can reach the police at 9 bd. du Palais, 4e (☎ 1/42-60-33-22; Métro: Cité).

Eyeglass Repair   Lissac Brothers (Frères Lissac) is one of the city's largest chains, with at least 18 branches in greater Paris. On the Right Bank, go to 112–114 rue de Rivoli, 1e (☎ 1/42-33-44-77; Métro: Louvre), and on the Left, to 207 bd. St-Germain, 7e (☎ 1/45-48-16-76; Métro: Rue-du-Bac). There's a surcharge for same-day service. Always carry an extra pair.

Holidays   See "When to Go," in Chapter 3.

Hospitals   The American Hospital, 63 bd. Victor-Hugo, Neuilly (☎ 1/46-41-25-41; Métro: Pont-de-Levallois or Pont-de-Neuilly; Bus 82), operates 24-hour emergency service. The direct line to its emergency service is 47-47-70-15.

Information   See "Visitor Information" under "Getting to Know Paris," earlier in this chapter.

Laundry/Dry Cleaning   Ask at your hotel for the nearest laundry or dry-cleaning establishment. Expensive hotels provide this service, but it costs a lot. Instead, consult the Yellow Pages under "laveries automatiques"; for dry cleaning, look under "nettoyage à sec."

Mail   See "Post Office," below.

Newspapers/Magazines English-language newspapers, including the latest editions of *Time, Newsweek, USA Today,* and the *International Herald Tribune* (published Monday to Saturday) are available at nearly every newsstand. They're generally open daily from 8am to 9pm.

Photographic Needs All types of film are available in Paris at fairly modest prices. Unless you're going to be in the country for an extended period, we don't recommend you process your film here, for it takes time. Ask at your hotel for the nearest camera and photographic accessory store.

Police In an emergency call 17. The principal Prefecture is at Place Baudoyer 4e (☎ 1/42-77-67-21; Métro: Hôtel-de-Ville).

Post Office The main post office (P.T.T.) for Paris is Bureau de Poste, 52 rue du Louvre, 75001 Paris (☎ 1/40-28-20-00; Métro: Louvre). Your mail can be sent here Poste Restante (general delivery) for a small fee. Take an ID, such as a passport, if you plan to pick up mail. It's open daily from 8am to 7pm for most services, 24 hours for telegrams and phone calls. For postage rates, see "Fast Facts: France," in Chapter 3.

Restrooms See "Fast Facts: France," in Chapter 3.

Safety Especially beware of child pickpockets. They roam the capital, preying on tourists around such sites as the Louvre, Eiffel Tower, Notre-Dame, and Montmartre, and they especially like to pick pockets in the Métro, often blocking the entrance and exit to the escalator. A band of these young thieves can clean out your pockets even while you try to fend them off. They'll get very close, sometimes ask for a handout, and deftly help themselves to your money, passport, or whatever. Women should hang on to their purses with both hands. Gendarmes advise tourists to carry umbrellas and to keep anyone who looks like a pickpocket an umbrella's length away.

Taxes France's VAT (value-added tax) should already be included in the cost of items you buy. The rate varies depending on the item—it can be as high as 33.33%. You can get a tax refund on purchases of more than 2,000 F ($380.20) in a single store. Ask the shopkeeper to make out an export sales invoice (bordereau), which you show to the French Customs officer when you leave the country (at the airport, on the train, at the highway border post). In a number of weeks the shop will send you a check for the amount of the refund. Not all shops participate in the program. Ask before you buy.

Telegrams/Telex Telegrams may be sent from any Paris post office during the day (see "Post Office," above) and anytime from the 24-hour central post office. In telegrams to the United States, the address is counted in the price, there are no special rates for a certain number of words, and night telegrams cost less. If you're in Paris and wish to send a telegram in English, call 42-33-44-11. The 24-hour public Telex office in Paris is at 103 rue de Grenelle, 7e (☎ 1/45-60-34-34; Métro: Rue-du-Bac). By phone, you dictate a Telex by calling 42-47-12-12. You can also send Telexes and faxes at the main post office in each arrondissement.

Transit Information For information on public transportation, stop in at either of the two offices of the Services Touristiques de la RATP—at 53 bis quai des Grands-Augustins, 6e (Métro: St-Michel), or place de la Madeleine, 8e (Métro: Madeleine)—or call 43-46-14-14.

Weather Call 36-69-00-00.

3 Networks & Resources

FOR STUDENTS   One privately run establishment catering most of the year to students is the **Maison d'Etudiants J. de Ruiz de Lavison,** 18 rue Jean-Jacques-Rousseau, 75001 Paris (☎ **1/45-08-02-10;** Métro: Palais-Royal–Musée-du-Louvre). It offers inexpensive lodgings for about 50 male students, usually French-born men from the provinces ages 18 to 23, for about 9 months during the academic year. From mid-June to late August it opens its doors to nonstudents, male and female, and houses them in simple rooms with one or two beds. (About 70 beds are available, and the minimum stay is reduced to four days.) With breakfast included, overnight rates for a single are 200 F ($38); for a double, 260 F ($49.40) per night. Advance reservations are essential. The building is owner-managed by Mme Michelle Bensier and has a small but charming garden in back.

   Foyer International des Etudiantes, 93 bd. St-Michel (☎ **1/43-54-49-63;** Métro: Luxembourg), stands across from the Jardin du Luxembourg, welcoming students from all over the world. From October to June, it accepts women only, charging 133 F ($25.25) in a single or 82 F ($15.60) in a double, including breakfast. From July to September, both men and women are accepted, paying 155 F ($29.45) in a double or 105 F ($19.95) in a double, including breakfast. This place is popular and you must write at least two months in advance for the reservation, paying a 200-F ($38) deposit if space is confirmed. Facilities are available for cooking and laundry, and there's a TV lounge. Some accommodations have their own balconies.

FOR GAYS & LESBIANS   "Gay Paree," with one of the world's largest homosexual populations, has dozens of clubs, restaurants, organizations, and services. Other than publications (see below), one of the best sources of information on gay and lesbian activities is the **Centre Gai & Lesbien,** 3 rue Keller, 11e (☎ **1/43-57-21-47;** Métro: Bastille). Well equipped to dispense information and coordinate the activities and meetings of gay people from virtually everywhere, it's open daily from 2 to 8pm. On Sunday it adopts a format known as Le Café Positif, featuring music, cabaret, and information about AIDS and the care for (and prevention of) sexually transmitted diseases.

   A gay hot line, theoretically designed as a way to creatively counsel persons with gay-related problems, is **SOS Ecoute Gay** (☎ **1/48-06-19-11**). Someone will respond to calls Monday to Friday from 6 to 10pm. A separate hot line, specifically intended for victims of homophobia or gay-related discrimination, is **SOS Homophobie** (☎ **1/48-06-42-41**), where a panel of French-trained lawyers and legal experts will offer advice and counsel Monday to Friday from 8 to 10pm.

   Another helpful source is **La Maison des Femmes,** 8 Cité Prost, 11e (☎ **1/43-48-24-91;** Métro: Charonne), offering information about Paris for lesbians and bisexual women. Sometimes, informal dinners and get-togethers are sponsored at irregular intervals. Call any Monday, Wednesday, or Friday from 3 to 8pm for further information.

   A publication, *Gai Pied*'s **Guide Gai** (revised annually) is the best source of information on gay and lesbian clubs, hotels, organizations, and services—even restaurants. Lesbians or bisexual women might also like to pick up a copy of **Lesbia,** to check ads if for no other reason. These publications and others are available at Paris's largest and best-stocked gay bookstore, **Les Mots à la Bouche,** 6 rue Ste-Croix-de-la-Bretonnerie, 4e (☎ **1/42-78-88-30**). It's open Monday to Saturday from 11am to 11pm and Sunday from 2 to 8pm. French- and English-language publications are inventoried.

FOR WOMEN   The leading feminist bookstore is **La Librairie des Femmes,** 74 rue de Seine, 6e (☎ 1/43-29-50-75; Métro: Odéon), open Monday to Saturday from 11am to 7pm. It features a vast collection of women's literature, much of it in English.

In 1993, the French government initiated a nationwide service for counseling any victim of physical and/or mental assault and/or cruelty, including victims of domestic violence. If it's your bad luck to be a victim of any form of attack (including rape) during your sojourn in Paris, call **Paris Aide aux Victimes** (☎ 1/45-88-18-00) daily from 11am to 6pm. Queries of a less urgent, more academic nature are best addressed to the **Centre National d'Information et de Documentation des Femmes et des Familles (CNIDFF),** 7 rue du Jura, 75013 Paris (☎ 1/43-31-12-34). This government-sponsored agency offers a wealth of data and scientific studies and is a good point of departure for anyone embarking on a study of women's issues in France and the rest of Europe.

5 Paris Accommodations

In 1995 it was estimated that Paris contains 2,000 hotels—with about 80,000 guest rooms—spread across its 20 arrondissements. These range from palaces with opulent interiors to dives so low that even the late George Orwell, author of *Down and Out in Paris and London*, wouldn't have considered checking in. Naturally, you'll find none of the latter in this guide.

We've focused our 1996 recommmendations solely on central Paris, where most people wish to stay to be in the midst of the action; the outer districts are too far removed to attract the average visitor.

THE HOTEL SCENE By now the Paris "season" has almost ceased to exist. Most visitors, at least from North America, come in July and August. Since many French are on vacation then and trade fairs and conventions come to a halt, there are usually plenty of hotel rooms at that time, even though these months have traditionally been the peak season for European travel. In most hotels February is just as busy as April or September.

The 1990s have seen major changes in Paris hotels as more and more have been upgraded, both inside and out. Old-fashioned charm—at least an attempt at it—characterizes many of the new hotels, which have turned their backs on the sterility of the 1960s and 1970s.

Since hot weather doesn't last long in Paris, most hotels, except the deluxe ones, don't provide air conditioning. If you're trapped in a Paris garret on a hot summer night, you may have to sweat it out. To avoid the noise problem when you have to open windows, request a room in the back when making a reservation.

Most hotels offer a continental breakfast of coffee, tea, or hot chocolate; a freshly baked croissant and roll; and limited quantities of butter and jam or jelly. Though nowhere near as filling as a traditional English or American breakfast, it does have the advantage of being quick to prepare—it'll be at your door moments after you call down for it and can be served at almost any hour. The word *breakfast* in the following entries refers to this continental version.

Note: Service and value-added tax are included in the rates quoted below unless otherwise specified. Also, unless otherwise specified, all rooms come with a private bath.

PRICE CATEGORIES Classifying Paris hotels by price is quite a task. For example, it's possible to find a moderately priced room in an otherwise "very expensive" hotel or an expensive room in an "inexpensive" hostelry. Most hotel rooms—at least in the older properties—are not standardized, so the range of rooms goes from super-deluxe suites to the "maid's pantry" now converted into a small room. At some hotels, in fact, you'll find rooms that are moderate, expensive, and very expensive under one roof.

The following price categories are only for a quick general reference. When we've classified a hotel as moderate, it means the average room is moderately priced—not necessarily *all* the rooms. Also note that Paris is one of the most expensive cities in the world for hotels; what might be viewed as expensive in your hometown could be seen as inexpensive in Paris.

In general, hotels we've rated "Very Expensive" charge 2,000 to 4,470 F ($380.20 to $849.80) for a double room—and far beyond that for suites. Doubles in "Expensive" hotels might begin at 1,155 F ($219.60) and go up to 2,400 F ($456.30), the latter only for the most select rooms. "Moderate" doubles begin at around 600 F ($114.05) and could go to 1,600 F ($304.20). "Inexpensive" doubles begin at 170 F ($32.30) and climb fast to 990 F ($188.20) for those few exceptionally good rooms some inexpensive hotels offer.

1 City Center: Left Bank

5TH ARRONDISSEMENT

MODERATE

Hôtel le Colbert
7 rue de l'Hôtel-Colbert, 75005 Paris. ☎ **1/43-25-85-65.** Fax 1/43-25-80-19. 36 rms, 2 suites. MINIBAR TV TEL. 1,007 F ($191.45) double; 1,600–1,900 F ($304.20–$361.20) suite. Breakfast 50 F ($9.50) extra. AE, DC, MC, V. Métro: Maubert-Mutualité or St-Michel.

Not only is this centuries-old inn a minute from the Seine, but it provides a fine view of Notre-Dame from many rooms. There's even a small courtyard to set it apart from the Left Bank bustle. Built during the 18th century, the building was converted into a hotel in 1966. You enter a tasteful lobby, with marble floors and antique furniture. The rooms are well designed and tailored, most providing comfortable chairs and a breakfast area. Those on the uppermost (fifth) floor seem like garrets, and some (the suites) feature old exposed beams. The hotel restaurant, Le Clos Bruneau, serves traditional French cooking (closed Saturday at lunch and Sunday). Facilities include a private garage, a sauna, a Jacuzzi, and a fitness room. Some rooms are handicapped-accessible.

INEXPENSIVE

Agora St-Germain
42 rue des Bernardins, 75005 Paris. ☎ **1/46-34-13-00.** Fax 1/46-34-75-05. 39 rms. MINIBAR TV TEL. 680 F ($129.25) double. Breakfast 45 F ($8.55) extra. AE, DC, MC, V. Parking 110 F ($20.90). Métro: Maubert-Mutualité.

One of the best of the district's moderately priced hotels, the building Agora St-Germain occupies was built in the early 1600s, probably to house a group of guardsmen protecting the brother of the king at his lodgings on nearby rue Monsieur-le-Prince. The hotel offers compact soundproof rooms, each comfortably furnished and equipped with an alarm clock, hairdryer, and safety-deposit box. Room service is provided daily from 7:30 to 10:30am.

Staying "Out"

Any hotel recommended in this guide is friendly to (or at least tolerant of) same-sex couples, but the following are probably more willing than the norm to welcome gays and lesbians.

Hôtel Central, 33 rue Vieille-du-Temple, 75004 Paris (☎ 1/48-87-99-33; fax 1/42-77-06-27; Métro: Hôtel-de-Ville), is the most visibly gay hotel in Paris. The seven rooms (one with bath) are on the third, fourth, and fifth floors of this 18th-century building, which contains Le Central, Marais's major gay bar. Women are welcome but rare. Rates are 460 F ($87.45) double, without or with bath. MasterCard and Visa are accepted.

Le Saint-Hubert, 27 rue Traversière, 75012 Paris (☎ 1/43-43-39-16; fax 1/43-43-35-32; Métro: Gare-de-Lyon), occupies a five-story 18th-century town house on a quiet residential street. The 15 rooms are simple and functional but clean. The gay bars of the eastern Marais are a 10-minute walk to the west. Rates are 315 to 335 F ($59.85 to $63.65) double. American Express, MasterCard, and Visa are accepted.

The pleasures of the Marais are a 15-minute walk west of the **Iris Hôtel,** 80 rue de la Folie-Regnault, 75011 Paris (☎ 1/43-57-73-30; fax 1/47-00-38-29; Métro: Père-Lachaise). About a quarter of the guests here are gay or lesbian. In 1988 the Iris was totally modernized and its 33 rooms were given a facelift. Rates are 430 F ($81.75) double and 520 F ($98.85) triple. MasterCard and Visa are accepted.

Le 55 Guest House, 55 av. Reille, 75014 Paris (☎ 1/45-89-91-82; fax 1/45-89-91-83; Métro: Porte-d'Orléans; RER: Cité-Universitaire), is an upscale B&B offering two monochromatic suites accented with oak paneling and art deco furnishings. Rates (including breakfast) are 900 to 1,200 F ($171.10 to $228.10) double. No credit cards are accepted.

Tucked away in a maze of medieval streets, the stone-and-timbered **Relais-Hôtel du Vieux Paris,** 9 rue Gîte-le-Coeur, 75006 Paris (☎ 1/43-54-41-66; fax 1/43-26-00-15; Métro: St-Michel), boasts 13 rooms and 7 suites, all elegant with upholstered walls and reproductions of 19th-century antiques. Rates are 1,070 to 1,270 F ($203.40 to $241.40) double and 1,370 to 1,600 F ($260.45 to $304.15) for a suite. American Express, MasterCard, and Visa are accepted.

Hôtel Elysa-Luxembourg

6 rue Gay-Lussac, 75005 Paris. ☎ **1/43-25-31-74.** Fax 1/46-34-56-27. 30 rms. MINIBAR TV TEL. 580–720 F ($110.25–$136.85) double; 830 F ($157.80) triple. Breakfast buffet 45 F ($8.55) extra. AE, DC, MC, V. Parking 50 F ($9.50). Métro: Odeon or St-Michel. RER: Luxembourg.

One of the best choices in the heart of the Latin Quarter, this hotel is near the Luxembourg Gardens. The completely renovated rooms in this 19th-century structure are spacious and soundproof; some are reserved for nonsmokers. Guests may use the sauna. This is a "gay friendly" hotel—though listed in some gay guides, it's not exclusively a gay hotel.

Ⓢ Hôtel le Jardin des Plantes

5 rue Linne, 75005 Paris. ☎ **1/47-07-06-20.** Fax 1/47-07-62-74. 33 rms. MINIBAR TV TEL. 470–640 F ($89.35–$121.65) double. Breakfast 40 F ($7.60) extra. MC, V. Métro: Jussieu. Bus 67 or 89.

This hotel lies in the academic section, near the Panthéon and across from the Jardin des Plantes. It offers well-equipped rooms, some with flowered terraces, as well as a vaulted basement lounge, a sauna, and a roof terrace. Breakfast is served in the brasserie/snack bar.

Ⓢ Hôtel Moderne St-Germain

33 rue des Ecoles, 75005 Paris. ☎ 1/43-54-37-78. Fax 1/43-29-91-31. 45 rms. TV TEL. 590–840 F ($112.15–$159.70) double. Rates include continental breakfast. AE, DC, MC, V. Parking 100 F ($19). Métro: Maubert-Mutalité or St-Michel.

Near Notre-Dame and the Panthéon in the Latin Quarter, the Hôtel Moderne successfully blends the Paris of yesterday with that of today. Its charming owner, Mme Gibon, provides a warm welcome and rents comfortably furnished spotless rooms. Double-glazed windows in the rooms fronting rue des Ecoles create a quiet atmosphere.

Hôtel Résidence St-Christophe

17 rue Lacépède, 75005 Paris. ☎ 1/43-31-81-54. Fax 1/43-31-12-54. 31 rms. MINIBAR TV TEL. 750 F ($142.55) double. Breakfast 50 F ($9.50) extra. AE, DC, MC, V. Métro: Place-Monge.

This hotel has a gracious English-speaking staff and a location in one of the undiscovered but charming districts of the Latin Quarter. It was created in 1987 when a derelict hotel was connected to a butcher shop. Millions of francs later, the result is clean and comfortable, with traditional furniture and wall-to-wall carpeting. The hotel serves only breakfast, though the staff offers good advice about neighborhood restaurants.

Hôtel Serotel Lutèce

2 rue Berthollet, 75005 Paris. ☎ 1/43-36-26-30. Fax 1/43-31-08-21. 46 rms, 1 suite. MINIBAR TV TEL. 620–690 F ($117.80–$131.15) double; 1,200 F ($228.10) suite. Breakfast 50 F ($9.50) extra. AE, MC, V. Métro: Censier-Daubenton.

Near the pont Royal in a quiet residential neighborhood, this hotel was built late in the 19th century. A complete renovation in the early 1990s modernized many of the rooms, equipping them with wall-to-wall carpeting, pastel color schemes, comfortable beds, and simple furniture. The baths have adequate (but slightly cramped) shower stalls and a handful of pleasant amenities. Some rooms overlook a courtyard dotted with jardinières and flowers. Breakfast (the only meal served) is presented in a basement room that resembles a bright cave.

6TH ARRONDISSEMENT
EXPENSIVE

L'Hôtel

13 rue des Beaux-Arts, 75006 Paris. ☎ 1/43-25-27-22. Fax 1/43-25-64-81. 24 rms, 3 suites. A/C MINIBAR TV TEL. 1,050–1,300 F ($199.60–$247.15) small double, 1,800–2,400 F ($342.20–$456.25) large double; from 4,000 F ($760) suite. Breakfast 100 F ($19) extra. AE, DC, MC, V. Métro: St-Germain-des-Prés.

L'Hôtel was once a 19th-century "fleabag" called the Hôtel d'Alsace, and its major distinction was that Oscar Wilde, broke and in despair, died here. However, today's guests aren't exactly on poverty row: Through the lobby march many show-business and fashion personalities. L'Hôtel is the creation of French actor Guy-Louis Duboucheron, who's responsible for establishing the intimate atmosphere of super-sophistication in this "jewel box." You'll feel like a movie star when you bathe in your tub of rosy-pink imported Italian marble. Throughout the building is an eclectic collection of antiques that includes Louis XV and Louis XVI, Empire, and Directoire pieces.

Dining/Entertainment: Breakfast is served in a stone cellar, which in the evening becomes a tavern for intimate dinners. Le Bélier is a luxurious piano bar/restaurant.

Services: Concierge, 24-hour room service, babysitting, laundry, valet.

Hôtel Lutétia-Paris

45 bd. Raspail, 75006 Paris. ☎ **1/49-54-46-46,** or 800/888-4747 in the U.S. Fax 1/49-54-46-00. 241 rms, 29 suites. A/C MINIBAR TV TEL. 1,250–1,650 F ($237.60–$313.65) double; from 1,950 F ($370.70) suite. Breakfast 125 F ($23.75) extra. AE, DC, MC, V. Parking 120 F ($22.80). Métro: Sèvres-Babylone.

This is the largest and one of the most unusual hotels on the Left Bank, richly associated with Paris's literary history and restored to its original grandeur. Early in its history the hotel attracted such luminaries as Cocteau, Gide, Picasso, and de Gaulle, who spent part of his honeymoon at the Lutétia. The hotel offers comfortable lodgings and a distinct flavor of the Roaring '20s; it attracts a knowledgeable clientele of repeat visitors. The high-ceiling rooms are tastefully subdued and soundproof.

Dining/Entertainment: The hotel's most famous restaurant, Le Paris, has a decor of black lacquer and amber designed by fashion designer Sonia Rykiel, who was inspired by the great days of the transatlantic ocean liners. Less expensive is the old-fashioned Brasserie Lutétia, where waiters wear black vests and aprons and carry steaming platters of well-flavored bistro food. The Bar Lutèce is in a darkened but amiable cubbyhole adjacent to the art deco main lobby.

Services: Concierge, 24-hour room service, babysitting, laundry/dry cleaning.

Facilities: Business center, private conference facilities.

✪ Relais Christine

3 rue Christine, 75006 Paris. ☎ **1/43-26-71-80.** Fax 1/43-26-89-38. 38 rms, 13 duplex suites. A/C MINIBAR TV TEL. 1,630–1,720 F ($309.85–$326.95) double; 2,250–3,000 F ($427.75–$570.30) suite. Breakfast 95 F ($18.05) extra. AE, DC, MC, V. Free parking. Métro: Odéon.

The Relais Christine welcomes guests into what was a 16th-century Augustinian cloister. You enter from a narrow cobblestone street, first into a symmetrical courtyard and then into an elegant reception area dotted with baroque sculpture and a scattering of Renaissance antiques. The breakfast room is in a vaulted cellar; the ancient well and massive central stone column are part of the cloister's former kitchen. Each room is uniquely decorated with wooden beams, marble baths, and Louis XII–style furnishings.

Dining/Entertainment: Off the reception area is a paneled sitting room/bar area ringed with 19th-century portraits and comfortable leather chairs.

Services: 24-hour room service, laundry, babysitting.

Relais St-Germain

9 carrefour de l'Odéon, 75006 Paris. ☎ **1/43-29-12-05.** Fax 1/46-33-45-30. 22 rms, 4 suites. A/C MINIBAR TV TEL. 1,500–1,650 F ($285.15–$313.65) double; 1,900 F ($361.15) suite. Rates include breakfast. AE, DC, MC, V. Métro: Odéon.

The Relais St-Germain is an oasis of charm and comfort, a tall, slender hotel adapted from a 17th-century building. Its decor is a medley of traditional and modern. Of course, all the necessary amenities were tucked in under the beams, including private safes and soundproofing. Four rooms feature a kitchenette, and two of the suites come with a terrace.

Hotels: 5th & 6th Arrondissements

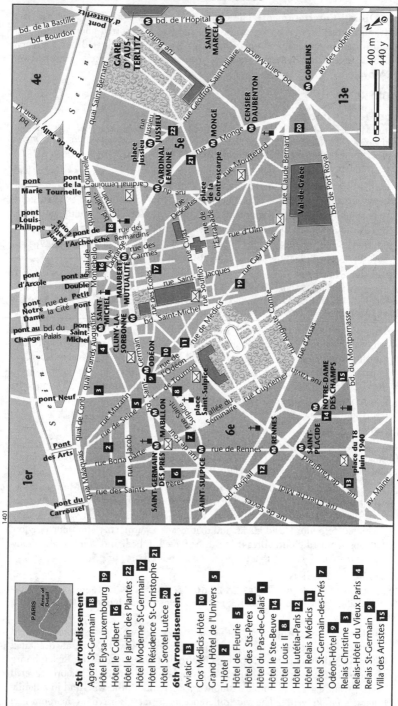

Church ✝ Post Office ⊠ Métro Ⓜ

5th Arrondissement
Agora St-Germain **18**
Hôtel Elysa-Luxembourg **19**
Hôtel le Colbert **16**
Hôtel le Jardin des Plantes **22**
Hôtel Moderne St-Germain **17**
Hôtel Résidence St-Christophe **21**
Hôtel Serotel Lutèce **20**

6th Arrondissement
Aviatic **13**
Clos Médicis Hôtel **10**
Grand Hôtel de l'Univers **5**
L'Hôtel **2**
Hôtel de Fleurie **5**
Hôtel des Sts-Pères **6**
Hôtel du Pas-de-Calais **1**
Hôtel le Ste-Beuve **14**
Hôtel Louis II **8**
Hôtel Lutétia-Paris **12**
Hôtel Relais Médicis **11**
Hôtel St-Germain-des-Prés **7**
Odéon-Hôtel **9**
Relais Christine **3**
Relais-Hôtel du Vieux Paris **4**
Relais St-Germain **9**
Villa des Artistes **15**

Dining/Entertainment: The Comptoir du Relais, a bistro/wine bar, is a delightful retreat where you can order such dishes as potted goose pâté, pork-and-pistachio sausage, and any number of sandwiches with traditional French bread, including "Rosette" sausage from Lyon and smoked salmon from Norway.

MODERATE

Clos Médicis Hôtel

54 rue Monsieur-le-Prince, 75006 Paris. ☎ **1/43-29-10-80.** Fax 1/43-54-26-90. 37 rms, 1 duplex. A/C MINIBAR TV TEL. 706–906 F ($134.20–$172.20) double; 1,206 F ($229.25) duplex for one or two. Breakfast 60 F ($11.40) extra. AE, DC, MC, V. Metro: Odéon.

In 1994, the neighborhood's newest hotel opened on the premises of what had been a private home in 1860 and most recently had been a bookstore and a run-down boarding house. You'll find a verdant garden with lattices and exposed stone walls, a lobby with modern spotlights and simple furniture, and a multilingual staff. Its location, adjacent to the Luxembourg Gardens in the heart of the Latin Quarter, is one of the establishment's major advantages. The warmly colored rooms are uncomplicated and comfortable. Breakfast is the only meal served.

Hôtel des Sts-Pères

65 rue des Sts-Pères, 75006. ☎ **1/45-44-50-00.** Fax 1/45-44-90-83. 39 rms, 3 suites. MINIBAR TV TEL. 706–962 F ($134.20–$182.85) double; 1,500 F ($285.15) suite. Breakfast 50 F ($9.50) extra. AE, MC, V. Métro: St-Germain-des-Prés or Sèvres-Babylone.

The best recommendation for this old favorite off boulevard St-Germain is the long list of famous guests, including Edna St. Vincent Millay, who enjoyed the camellia-trimmed garden. Designed by Louis XIV's architect, the hotel is decorated in part with antique paintings, tapestries, and mirrors. The most-sought room is the *chambre à la fresque,* which has a 17th-century painted ceiling. The modernized rooms face a quiet courtyard accented in summer with potted plants. Breakfast is sometimes served there.

Hôtel le Ste-Beuve

9 rue Ste-Beuve, 75006 Paris. ☎ **1/45-48-20-07.** Fax 1/45-48-67-52. 23 rms, 1 suite. MINIBAR TV TEL. 700–1,000 F ($133.05–$190.10) double; 1,250 F ($237.60) suite. Breakfast 80 F ($15.20) extra. AE, MC, V. Métro: Vavin.

The Ste-Beuve is the answer to a dream: a small restored hotel in Montparnasse, with its memories of long-gone but still-fabled personalities. Around the corner from Rodin's famous statue of Balzac, this is a charmer. Its decor was created by celebrated decorator David Hicks, and that means a warm, cozy atmosphere, aglow with rose-colored chintz. Breakfast can be served in bed, and you can also enjoy the intimate lobby bar with a fireplace. Each room has a safe.

Hôtel Relais Médicis

23 rue Racine, 75006 Paris. ☎ **1/43-26-00-60.** Fax 1/40-46-83-39. 16 rms. A/C MINIBAR TV TEL. 980–1,480 F ($186.30–$281.35) double. Rates include breakfast. AE, DC, MC, V. Métro: Odéon.

Until its radical overhaul in 1991, this place was a well-worn two-star hotel favored by students, indigent artists, and visiting professors. Today it's a lavishly decorated romantic hideaway adjacent to the Théâtre de l'Odéon, near the Luxembourg Gardens. The soundproof rooms are richly upholstered and include fabric-covered walls, private safes, and an old-fashioned patina you'd otherwise find in a family homestead in Provence. The wide difference in the rates is based on the room size;

some are quite large. There's a small bar near the public rooms; breakfast is the only meal served.

Hôtel St-Germain-des-Prés

36 rue Bonaparte, 75006 Paris. ☎ 1/43-26-00-19. Fax 1/40-46-83-63. 28 rms, 2 suites. MINIBAR TV TEL. 750–900 F ($142.55–$171.10) double; 1,300–1,600 F ($247.15–$304.15) suite. Rates include breakfast. MC, V. Métro: St-Germain-des-Prés.

Most of this hotel's attraction comes from its enviable location in the Latin Quarter—behind a well-known Left Bank street near many shops. Janet Flanner, the legendary correspondent for *The New Yorker* in the 1920s, lived here for a while. Each room is small but charming, with antique ceiling beams and a private safe. The public areas are severely elegant, with dentil moldings, Louis XIII furnishings, and exposure of the building's original stonework. Air conditioning is available in most rooms for a 100-F ($19) daily supplement.

Odéon-Hôtel

3 rue de l'Odéon, 75006 Paris. ☎ 1/43-25-90-67. Fax 1/43-25-55-98. 34 rms. TV TEL. 850–1,100 F ($161.60–$209.10) double. Breakfast 55 F ($10.45) extra. AE, DC, MC, V. Métro: Odéon.

Near both the Théâtre de l'Odéon and boulevard St-Germain, this hotel stands on what in 1779 was the first Paris street to have pavements and gutters. At the turn of the century this area began attracting such writers as Gide, Joyce, Eliot, Fitzgerald, Stein, and Hemingway. Today, with its exposed beams, rough stone walls, high crooked ceilings, and tapestries mixed with contemporary fabrics, mirrored ceilings, and black leather furnishings, the Odéon is reminiscent of a modernized Norman country inn. After modern plumbing was added, each room was individually designed.

INEXPENSIVE

Aviatic

105 rue de Vaugirard, 75006 Paris. ☎ 1/45-44-38-21. Fax 1/45-49-35-83. 43 rms. MINIBAR TV TEL. 590–790 F ($112.15–$150.15) double. Rates include continental breakfast. AE, DC, MC, V. Parking 120 F ($22.80). Métro: Montparnasse-Bienvenue.

This is a bit of old Paris, with a modest inner courtyard and a vine-covered lattice on the walls. It has been a family-run hotel of character and elegance for a century. The reception lounge, with its marble columns, brass chandeliers, antiques, and petit salon, provides an attractive traditional setting. Completely remodeled, the hotel is in an interesting section of Montparnasse, surrounded by cafés frequented by artists, writers, and jazz musicians. The staff speaks English.

⑤ Grand Hôtel de l'Univers

6 rue Grégoire-de-Tours, 75006 Paris. ☎ 1/43-29-37-00. Fax 1/40-51-06-45. 34 rms. MINIBAR TV TEL. 850 F ($161.60) double. Breakfast 40 F ($7.60) extra. AE, DC, MC, V. Métro: Odéon.

This building was constructed in the 1400s as the home of a member of the then-emerging bourgeoisie. The massive ceiling beams, the thick stone walls, and the facade's incised "logo" of a loincloth-clad barbarian with a club have been retained. Some of the pleasantly renovated rooms enjoy a panoramic view over the neighborhood's crooked rooftops. One of the most amusing rooms is "La Bonbonnière," an all-pink concoction whose name translates as "the candy box." Breakfast, the only meal served, is presented beneath the 500-year-old stone vaults of a handsome cellar.

Hôtel de Fleurie

32 rue Grégoire-de-Tours, 75006 Paris. ☎ **1/43-29-59-81.** Fax 1/43-29-68-44. 29 rms. A/C MINIBAR TV TEL. 810–1,200 F ($154–$228.10) double or twin. Breakfast 50 F ($9.50) extra. AE, DC, MC, V. Métro: Odéon.

Just off boulevard St-Germain on a colorful little street, the Fleurie is one of the best of the "new" old hotels. Restored to its former glory in 1988, the facade is studded with statuary spotlit by night, recapturing its 17th-century elegance. The stone walls have been exposed in the reception salon, with its refectory desk where guests check in. An elevator takes you to the well-furnished modern rooms, each with a private safe; a spiral staircase leads down to the breakfast room.

Hôtel du Pas de Calais

59 rue des Sts-Pères, 75006 Paris. ☎ **1/45-48-78-74.** Fax 1/45-44-94-57. 41 rms. TV TEL. 790 F ($150.15) double. Rates include continental breakfast. AE, MC, V. Métro: St-Germain-des-Prés or Sèvres-Babylone.

This 17th-century building has housed many celebrities since it was converted into a hotel in 1815, including Chateaubriand (who lived here before it became a hotel) and Maurice Béjart, the dancer/choreographer/stage designer. The hotel has also played host to Sartre as well as many singers, actors, and writers. Guests may enjoy afternoon drinks or breakfast on the small patio. The modernized rooms are well maintained and comfortable.

Hôtel Louis II

2 rue St-Sulpice, 75006 Paris. ☎ **1/46-33-13-80.** Fax 1/46-33-17-29. 22 rms. MINIBAR TV TEL. 480–700 F ($91.25–$133.10) double; 850 F ($161.60) triple. Breakfast 42 F ($8) extra. AE, DC, MC, V. Métro: Odéon.

Housed in what was a neglected 18th-century building, this hotel provides well-decorated rustic accommodations. Afternoon drinks and morning coffee are served in the reception salon, where gilt-framed mirrors, fresh flowers, and well-oiled antiques add a provincial feeling. Upstairs, the cozy rooms boast exposed beams and wide expanses of mellowed patina contrasting with chintz coverings and plush carpeting. Many repeat visitors request the romantic attic rooms. TVs are available upon request.

Villa des Artistes

9 rue de la Grande-Chaumière, 75006 Paris. ☎ **1/43-26-60-86.** Fax 1/43-54-73-70. 60 rms. TV TEL. 760–860 F ($144.50–$163.50) double. Rates include continental breakfast. AE, DC, MC, V. Métro: Vavin.

This hotel derived its name from the dozens of art students who lodged here while pursuing their art at the nearby schools of painting. White-fronted, the simple five-story Villa des Artistes offers much-modernized rooms, each renovated in 1990. Breakfast is the only meal served, though coffee and snacks can usually be procured throughout the day beneath the greenhouse-style roof of the breakfast area. Adjacent to the breakfast area is an outdoor courtyard.

7TH ARRONDISSEMENT
EXPENSIVE

Le Duc de Saint-Simon

14 rue de St-Simon, 75007 Paris. ☎ **1/44-39-20-20.** Fax 1/45-48-68-25. 29 rms, 5 suites. TEL. 1,365–1,515 F ($259.55–$288) double; 1,865–1,965 F ($354.55–$373.55) suite. Breakfast 80 F ($15.20) extra. No credit cards. Métro: Rue-du-Bac.

Hotels: 7ᵗʰ Arrondissement

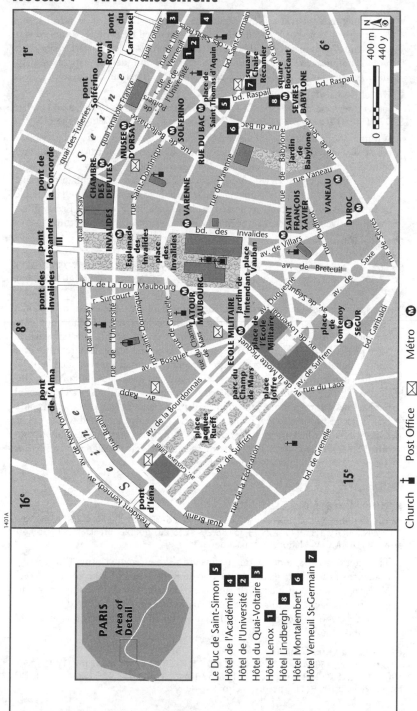

PARIS
Area of Detail

Le Duc de Saint-Simon **5**
Hôtel de l'Académie **4**
Hôtel de l'Université **2**
Hôtel du Quai-Voltaire **3**
Hôtel Lenox **1**
Hôtel Lindbergh **8**
Hôtel Montalembert **6**
Hôtel Verneuil St-Germain **7**

Church ╬   Post Office ⊠   Métro Ⓜ

On a quiet residential street, this small villa has a tiny front garden and an 1830s decor with trompe-l'oeil marble panels and a frescoed elevator. The vaulted cellar contains an intimate bar with an adjacent Louis XIII–style breakfast room. Each room is unique, though sure to include at least one antique. The service, perhaps the best reflection of the owner's extensive training, is helpful but reserved.

✪ Hôtel de l'Université
22 rue de l'Université, 75007 Paris. ☎ **1/42-61-09-39.** Fax 1/42-60-40-84. 28 rms. TV TEL. 1,300 F ($247.10) double. Breakfast 50 F ($9.50) extra. V. Métro: St-Germain-des-Prés.

Within walking distance of boulevard St-Germain, this hotel is an attractive place near the Seine. The 300-year-old town house has been reconstructed by M. and Mme Bergmann, who have added modern conveniences. The rooms, many with antiques and courtyard views, are sophisticated and unique; 12 contain minibars. Room 54 is a favorite for its combination of period pieces and rattan and its marble bath. Drinks and light food are served in the lounge in the evening. Reservations are imperative. It's well worth the money if you want a glamorous setting.

✪ Hôtel Montalembert
3 rue de Montalembert, 75007 Paris. ☎ **1/45-49-68-68.** Fax 1/45-49-69-49. 46 rms, 5 suites. A/C MINIBAR TV TEL. 1,625–2,080 F ($308.85–$395.40) double; 2,750–3,600 F ($522.80–$684.41) suite. Breakfast 100 F ($19) extra. AE, DC, MC, V. Parking 110 F ($20.90). Métro: Rue-du-Bac.

Unusually elegant for the Left Bank, the Montalembert was erected in 1926 in a venerable beaux arts style. In 1989 the hotel, much in need of renovation, was bought by a Hong Kong–based chain, the Leo group, whose directors immediately hired one of France's premier architectural designers, Christian Liaigre. After millions of dollars' worth of discreet improvements, the hotel was reopened in 1992 and hailed as one of the capital's most successful and imaginative restorations. Inside, you'll find a sophisticated modern interpretation that borrows elements of Bauhaus design and postmodernism in a palette of honey beiges, creams, and golds. Half the guest rooms follow the architectural patterns established in the public rooms; the other half are stylishly but conservatively decorated in a staid but dignified Louis-Philippe style. The baths are sheathed in gray Portuguese marble. The Restaurant Montalembert is appropriately elegant.

MODERATE

Hôtel de l'Académie
32 rue des Sts-Peres, 75007 Paris. ☎ **1/45-48-36-22.** Fax 1/45-44-75-24. 34 rms. A/C MINIBAR TV TEL. 990–1,290 F ($188.20–$245.20) double. Breakfast 50 F ($9.50) extra. AE, DC, MC, V. Métro: St-Germain-des-Prés.

The exterior walls and old ceiling beams are all that remain of this 17th-century residence of the private guards of the duc de Rohan. In 1983 the hotel was completely renovated to include an elegant reception area. The comfortably up-to-date guest rooms have Directoire beds, an Ile-de-France decor upholstered in soft colors, and views over the 18th- and 19th-century buildings of the neighborhood. The staff speaks English.

⑤ Hôtel du Quai-Voltaire
19 quai Voltaire, 75007 Paris. ☎ **1/42-61-50-91.** Fax 1/42-61-62-26. 32 rms. TV TEL. 590–690 F ($112.15–$131.15) double; 800 F ($152.10) triple. Breakfast 42 F ($8) extra. AE, DC, MC, V. Parking 100 F ($19) nearby. Métro: Rue-du-Bac.

Built in the 1600s as an abbey, then transformed into a hotel in 1856, the Quai-Voltaire is best known for its illustrious guests, who have included Wilde, Baudelaire, and Wagner, who occupied Rooms 47, 56, and 55, respectively. Many rooms in this modest inn have been renovated and most overlook the bookstalls and boats of the Seine. Guests can have drinks in the bar or the small salon, and simple meals (such as omelets and salads) can be prepared for guests who prefer to eat in.

Hôtel Lenox

9 rue de l'Université, 75007 Paris. ☎ **1/42-96-10-95.** Fax 1/42-61-52-83. 30 rms, 2 duplex suites. TV TEL. 590–780 F ($112.15–$148.30) double; 960 F ($182.50) suite. AE, DC, MC, V. Métro: Rue-du-Bac.

The Lenox is a favorite for tourists seeking reasonably priced attractive accommodations in St-Germain-des-Prés. In 1910 T. S. Eliot spent a summer here "on the old man's money" when the hotel was just a basic pension. Today this much-improved hotel offers a helpful staff and cramped but still comfortable rooms, some with elaborate ceiling molding. Many returning guests request the attic duplex with its tiny balcony and skylight. The hotel bar, the watering hole for members of the fashion industry, is open daily from 5:30pm to 1:30am.

Hôtel Lindbergh

5 rue Chomel (off bd. Raspail), 75007 Paris. ☎ **1/45-48-35-53.** Fax 1/45-49-31-48. 26 rms. TV TEL. 450–580 F ($85.55–$110.25) double; 700 F ($133.10) triple; 760 F ($144.50) quad. Breakfast 40 F ($7.60) extra. AE, DC, MC, V. Parking 150 F ($28.50). Métro: Sèvres-Babylone or St-Sulpice.

In a prosperous, conservative neighborhood, this hotel is named after the American aviator who made a historic solo transatlantic flight from New York to Paris in 1927. The Lindbergh was built early in the 19th century; modernized most recently in the early 1990s, it contains streamlined comfortable rooms. A TV salon and a lounge are on the premises.

Hôtel Verneuil St-Germain

8 rue de Verneuil, 75007 Paris. ☎ **1/42-60-82-14.** Fax 1/42-61-40-38. 26 rms. TV TEL. 700–950 F ($133.10–$180.60) double. Rates include breakfast. AE, DC, MC, V. Métro: Rue-du-Bac or St-Germain-des-Prés.

A three-star hostelry a few steps from the Seine, the Verneuil St-Germain was built in the 1700s as a private home. Completely renovated in 1992, the hotel offers rustically elegant rooms, usually with fabric-upholstered walls and exposed structural beams; each has a marble-tiled bath. Guests may order their breakfast in the stone-walled basement breakfast room and have drinks in the French provincial bar.

2 City Center: Right Bank

1ST ARRONDISSEMENT
VERY EXPENSIVE

Hôtel Lotti

7–9 rue Castiglione, 75001 Paris. ☎ **1/42-60-37-34,** or 800/221-2626 in the U.S., 800/237-0319 in Canada. Fax 1/40-15-93-56. 127 rms, 6 suites. A/C MINIBAR TV TEL. 2,600–3,300 F ($494.30–$627.35) double; 4,900 F ($931.55) suite. Breakfast 120 F ($22.80) extra. AE, DC, MC, V. Parking 160 F ($30.40). Métro: Opéra or Tuileries.

This hotel is a less pretentious and less expensive version of its neighbor, Le Ritz. Well respected since 1910, it's today one of the most luxurious members of the Jolly hotel group, an Italy-based chain. The Lotti's elegant atmosphere is enhanced by an 18th-century decor and high ceilings. The public rooms contain fine old tapestries, marble-and-gilt tables, and fresh flowers. The guest rooms boast mahogany desks, rosewood chests, gilt chairs, silk-damask draperies, and tufted slipper chairs.

Dining/Entertainment: The distinguished Le Lotti restaurant serves classic French cuisine. Set lunches cost 150 F ($28.50); set dinners, 220 F ($41.80).

Services: Room service, laundry, babysitting.

Hôtel Meurice

228 rue de Rivoli, 75001 Paris. ☎ **1/44-58-10-10.** Fax 1/44-58-10-15. 152 rms, 28 suites. A/C MINIBAR TV TEL. 2,550 F ($484.80) double; from 6,000 F ($1,140.70) suite. Breakfast 140 F ($26.60) extra. For stays of two or more nights, 2,300 F ($437.25) double (including breakfast). AE, DC, MC, V. Parking 90 F ($17.10). Métro: Tuileries or Concorde.

The Meurice offers romantic 18th-century surroundings. Its gilded salons were copied from those at Versailles, complete with huge crystal chandeliers, ornate tapestries, and Louis XIV, XV, and XVI furniture. Built in 1907, the hotel is just off rue de Rivoli and the Tuileries Gardens (you can see the Louvre from the upper floors). The lounge has a circular "star"-studded ceiling. The rooms are soundproof and richly furnished with some period and modern pieces.

Dining/Entertainment: The Meurice Restaurant serves haute cuisine. The Pompadour cocktail lounge is ideal for cocktails and tea, and the Meurice Bar offers drinks in an elegant atmosphere.

Services: Concierge, 24-hour room service, telex/fax.

Paris Inter-Continental

3 rue de Castiglione, 75001 Paris. ☎ **1/44-77-11-11,** or 800/327-0200 in the U.S. and Canada. Fax 1/44-77-14-60. 451 rms, 15 suites. A/C MINIBAR TV TEL. 2,300–2,600 F ($437.25–$494.25) double; 3,100–3,900 F ($589.35–$741.40) suite. Breakfast 100–150 F ($19–$28.50) extra. AE, DC, MC, V. Parking 120–150 F ($22.80–$28.50). Métro: Concorde.

The Inter-Continental is a mixture of tradition, Gallic know-how, and 20th-century modernism. Opened in 1878 as "The Continental," it has welcomed many famous guests, including Empress Eugénie of France and Jean Giraudoux. The main lounge has Persian carpets, period furnishings, bronze sconces, and marble cocktail tables. The rooms and suites are among the finest in Paris, boasting a classic French decor including paneled walls, crystal, and Louis XVI reproductions. Some suites come with a Jacuzzi.

Dining/Entertainment: The Terrasse Fleurie is an elegant gourmet restaurant in the interior courtyard. The Café Tuileries serves breakfast, snacks, light meals, informal suppers, cocktails, and French pastries. In fair weather, lunch, tea, and drinks are served in the courtyard under a canopy. There's also a coffee shop.

Services: Concierge, 24-hour room service, secretarial service, fax, CNN news service.

✪ Le Ritz

15 place Vendôme, 75001 Paris. ☎ **1/43-16-30-30.** Fax 1/43-16-36-68. 142 rms, 45 suites. A/C MINIBAR TV TEL. 3,500–4,170 F ($665.40–$792.75) double; from 5,120 F ($973.35) suite. Breakfast 170 F ($32.30) extra. AE, DC, MC, V. Parking 150 F ($28.50). Métro: Opéra.

The Ritz is the greatest hotel in Europe. This enduring symbol of elegance stands on one of the most beautiful and historic squares in Paris. César Ritz, the "little

Hotels: 1st & 2nd Arrondissements

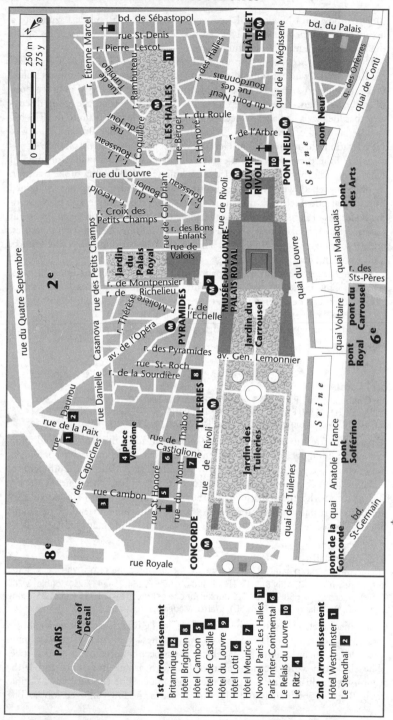

1st Arrondissement
Britannique 12
Hôtel Brighton 8
Hôtel Cambon 5
Hôtel de Castille 3
Hôtel du Louvre 9
Hôtel Lotti 6
Hôtel Meurice 7
Novotel Paris Les Halles 11
Paris Inter-Continental 6
Le Relais du Louvre 10
Le Ritz 4

2nd Arrondissement
Hôtel Westminster 1
Le Stendhal 2

Church ✝   Métro M

shepherd boy from Niederwald," converted the private Hôtel de Lazun into a luxury hotel that he opened in 1898. With the help of culinary master Escoffier, the Ritz became a miracle of luxury living.

During Paris's occupation, on August 25, 1944, Ernest Hemingway "liberated" the Ritz. Armed with machine guns, "Papa" and a group of Allied soldiers pulled up to the hotel in a Jeep, intent on capturing Nazis and freeing, if only symbolically, the landmark. After a sweep from the cellars to the roof, the group discovered that the Nazis had already fled. Hemingway then led his team to the Ritz bar to order a round of dry martinis. In commemoration of the 50th anniversary of the liberation, the renovated Bar Hemingway reopened on August 25, 1994.

In 1979 the Ritz family sold the hotel to Egyptian businessman Mohamed Al Fayed, who refurbished it and added a cooking school. The Ritz broke tradition by providing a bath with every guest room. Two town houses were annexed, joined by a long arcade lined with miniature display cases representing 125 of the leading boutiques of Paris. The salons are furnished with museum-caliber antiques: gilt pieces, ornate mirrors, Louis XV and Louis XVI furniture, hand-woven tapestries, and 10-foot-high bronze candelabra. The decor of the baths is impeccably French, with wood and marble, antique chests, and crystal lighting.

Dining/Entertainment: The Espadon grill room is one of the finest in Paris. The Ritz Club includes a bar, a salon with a fireplace, a restaurant, and a dance floor. Drinks can be ordered in either the Bar Vendôme or the Bar Hemingway.

Services: Concierge, 24-hour room service, laundry, valet.

Facilities: Luxury health club with pool and massage parlor, florist, shops, squash court.

EXPENSIVE

Hôtel Cambon

3 rue Cambon, 75001 Paris. ☎ **1/42-60-38-09.** Fax 1/42-60-30-59. 43 rms, 1 suite. A/C MINIBAR TV TEL. 1,380 F ($262.35) double; 1,880 F ($357.40) suite. Breakfast 75 F ($14.25) extra. AE, MC, V. Parking in nearby lot 150 F ($28.50) per 24 hours. Métro: Concorde.

On a stylish street in the heart of Paris's monument zone, this stone-fronted 19th-century building recently was completely renovated in a comfortable contemporary decor. The public rooms are richly furnished with 19th- and 20th-century sculptures and paintings, including the cozy street-level bar, where guests can usually converse with the genial owners, the Simeones. The rooms are individually decorated, usually with fabric wallcoverings, marble-sheathed baths, and much exposed wood. The staff seems especially helpful; many of them speak English.

Hôtel de Castille

37 rue Cambon, 75001 Paris. ☎ **1/44-58-44-58.** Fax 1/44-58-44-00. 70 rms, 3 junior suites, 14 duplexes. A/C MINIBAR TV TEL. 1,390–2,300 F ($264.25–$437.25) double; 3,200 F ($608) junior suite; 2,650 F ($503.50) duplex for one or two. Breakfast 115 F ($21.85) extra. AE, DC, MC, V. Parking 150 F ($28.50). Métro: Madeleine.

This quiet hotel, across from the "back door" of Le Ritz, is close to major shops, museums, and busy boulevards, just a few minutes' walk from place Vendôme, place de la Concorde, and the Madeleine. It has been restored in a Venetian style. The black-and-white facade is embellished with ornate stonework and 19th-century wrought-iron detailing on the upper floors. The entrance has a double arch. Beige marble panels and big mirrors adorn the low-ceilinged lobby. The sunny streamlined art deco rooms are done in pastels. In-room movies are provided.

Dining/Entertainment: Off the lobby is Il Cortile, an Italian restaurant opening onto a glassed-in conservatory. Two lunch menus are offered, at 150 F ($28.50) and 180 F ($34.20); a fixed-price dinner costs 180 F ($34.20).

Services: 24-hour room service, secretarial services, babysitting, laundry/dry cleaning.

Hôtel du Louvre

Place André-Malraux, 75001 Paris. ☎ 1/44-58-38-38, or 800/888-4747 in the U.S. Fax 1/44-58-38-01. 178 rms, 22 suites. A/C MINIBAR TV TEL. 1,400–1,800 F ($266–$342) double; 2,500–4,000 F ($475–$760) suite. Breakfast 90–140 F ($17.10–$26.60) extra. Midwinter promotions available. AE, DC, MC, V. Métro: Louvre.

When this hotel was inaugurated in 1855 by Napoléon III, French journalists described it as "a palace of the people, rising adjacent to the palace of kings." In 1897 Camille Pissarro moved into one of its rooms, using the view to inspire many of his Parisian landscapes. Between the Louvre and the Palais Royal, the hotel has a decor of soaring marble, bronze, and gilt. The rooms are quintessentially Parisian—cozy, soundproof, and filled with souvenirs of the belle époque.

Dining/Entertainment: Le Bar "Defender" is a cozy, masculine hideaway, with mahogany trim, overtones of Scotland, and a collection of single-malt whiskies; a pianist plays after dusk. There's also the French Empire Brasserie du Louvre, whose tables extend to the terrace during fine weather.

Services: Concierge, 24-hour room service, babysitting, laundry, valet.

Facilities: Business center.

MODERATE

Hôtel Brighton

218 rue de Rivoli, 75001 Paris. ☎ 1/42-60-30-03. Fax 1/42-60-41-78. 70 rms, 1 suite. MINIBAR TV TEL. 650–870 F ($123.50–$165.40) double; 1,360 F ($258.55) suite. Rates include continental breakfast. AE, DC, MC, V. Métro: Tuileries or Louvre.

Despite its English-sounding name, this is a very French hotel, on one of Paris's major shopping streets, across from the Louvre. The clean and comfortable rooms are furnished traditionally, often with brass beds. The front rooms have a view of the museum and the Tuileries Gardens; a few have tiny balconies that offer views of the Seine and the Eiffel Tower. Breakfast is the only meal served, but salads and sandwiches can be ordered in a tea salon.

Novotel Paris Les Halles

Place Marguerite-de-Navarre, 75001 Paris. ☎ 1/42-21-31-31, or 800/207-2542 in the U.S. Fax 1/40-26-05-79. 271 rms, 14 suites. A/C MINIBAR TV TEL. 915 F ($173.95) double; 1,200–1,500 F ($228.10–$285.15) suite. Buffet breakfast 60 F ($11.40) extra. AE, DC, MC, V. Métro: Les Halles.

Beside the beaux arts lattices of place des Halles, this hotel is one of the best Novotels in its worldwide network. Built in 1986, the futuristic Paris Les Halles has a mirrored facade and sloping skylights. The lobby boasts a small-scale copy of the Statue of Liberty and a stylish bar on a dais. The guest rooms contain a no-nonsense but comfortable decor, each with one double bed and one sofa (which can serve as a single bed); in-room movies are provided. The best rooms overlook Les Halles with its fountains, shrubbery, and carousel. The greenhouse Sun Deck Grill overlooks the ancient Church of St. Eustache.

Le Relais du Louvre

19 rue des Prêtres, 75001 Paris. ☎ **1/40-41-96-42.** Fax 1/40-41-96-44. 18 rms, 2 suites. MINIBAR TV TEL. 800–900 F ($152.10–$171.10) double; 1,280–1,450 F ($243.30–$275.65) suite. Breakfast 50 F ($9.50) extra. AE, MC, V. Métro: Louvre or Pont-Neuf.

One of the neighborhood's newest hotels was inaugurated in 1991, set midway between the wings at eastern end of the Louvre, overlooking the gargoyles and high windows of the nearby church of St-Germain-l'Auxerrois. Nostalgia buffs are usually impressed with the building's history: Between 1800 and 1941 its upper floors sheltered the printing presses that recorded the goings-on in Paris's House of Representatives. Its street level held the Café Momus, favored by Voltaire, Hugo, and many intellectuals of the day. And when Puccini created his plot for *La Bohème*, he set one of the pivotal scenes in that legendary café. Today the rooms are painted in bright, strong colors, with bold patterns, well-chosen fabrics, modern conveniences, soundproof windows, and reproductions of antique French furniture.

INEXPENSIVE

Britannique

20 av. Victoria, 75001 Paris. ☎ **1/42-33-74-59.** Fax 1/42-33-82-65. 40 rms. MINIBAR TV TEL. 720–830 F ($136.80–$157.70). Breakfast 49 F ($9.30) extra. AE, DC, MC, V. Parking 80 F ($15.20). Métro: Châtelet.

After a complete renovation, the Britannique has been rated three stars. It's in the heart of Paris, near Les Halles, the Pompidou Centre, and Notre-Dame. The rooms may be small but they're clean, comfortable, and adequately equipped. The TV satellite receiver picks up U.S. and U.K. programs. The building was a Quaker mission in World War I, offering shelter to U.S. and British volunteers from 1914 to 1918.

🏨 Family-Friendly Hotels

In addition to the **Novotel Paris Les Halles** *(see p. 115)*, where the rooms offer couches that convert to beds and breakfast is an all-you-can-eat buffet, the following hotels are particularly good for families:

Hôtel le Warwick, 5 rue de Berri, 75008 Paris (☎ 1/45-63-14-11; fax 1/45-63-75-81; Métro: George-V), is perfect for the affluent family seeking a smart Right Bank address. This first-class hotel is inviting. The management welcomes children (in English) and lets those under 12 stay free in their parents' room. Rates are 2,650 F ($503.80) double and 3,100–8,500 F ($589.35–$1,615.95) for a suite.

Madeleine-Plaza, 33 place de la Madeleine, 75008 Paris (☎ 1/42-65-20-63; fax 1/42-65-22-30; Métro: Madeleine), is between the Tulieries and the Opéra and offers many rooms suitable as triples or quads, ideal for small families. Many major Paris attractions are within walking distance. Rates are 470 F ($89.35) double and 620 F ($117.85) triple.

Hôtel de Neuville, 3 place Verniquet, 75017 Paris (☎ 1/43-80-26-30; fax 1/43-80-38-55; Métro: Pereire), is a former private house in a quiet neighborhood near the Arc de Triomphe; it has a policy of providing an extra bed (for 100 F/$19) for children sharing a room with their parents—a great way to save money if you don't mind a little crowding. Rates are 700 F ($133.05) double.

2ND ARRONDISSEMENT

VERY EXPENSIVE

Hôtel Westminster

13 rue de la Paix, 75002 Paris. ☎ 1/42-61-57-46. Fax 1/42-60-30-66. 102 rms, 18 suites. A/C MINIBAR TV TEL. 2,000 F ($380.20) double; 3,600–4,300 F ($684.40–$817.50) suite. Breakfast 110 F ($20.90) extra. AE, DC, MC, V. Métro: Opéra.

This hotel was built during Baron Haussmann's reorganization of Paris in 1846 and declared a national monument in 1907. At the turn of the century the Westminster was purchased and renovated by M. Bruchon, who brought his famous collection of clocks, now on display in the lobby. In 1981 it was acquired by Warwick International, which added all the modern comforts. Its cousin hotel is the contemporary Le Warwick in the 8th arrondissement. The rooms are uniquely decorated in pastels, with rich paneling, molded ceilings, and marble-top fireplaces; many have Louis XIV antiques. We recommend the hotel's bar/ gourmet restaurant, Le Celadon. Room service is available around the clock. Babysitting and laundry/valet can also be arranged.

EXPENSIVE

Le Stendhal

22 rue Danielle-Casanova, 75002 Paris. ☎ 1/44-58-52-52. Fax 1/44-58-52-00. 17 rms, 3 suites. A/C MINIBAR TV TEL. 1,310–1,510 F ($249–$287) double; 1,610–1,910 F ($306–$363.10) suite. Breakfast 55–80 F ($10.45–$15.20) extra. AE, DC, MC, V. Métro: Opéra.

Occupying a six-story white building best known as the site of the 1842 death of French novelist Marie-Henri Beyle (Stendhal), this hotel was established in 1992. Its decor mingles a medley of styles into a hip and deliberately iconoclastic mix of old and new. Its location, near glamorous jewelry stores and place Vendôme, couldn't be more grand. The rooms, accessible via a tiny elevator, are outfitted in one of three vivid color schemes, with the exception of the red-and-black Stendhal Suite, whose hues pay nostalgic homage to its namesake's classic, *Le Rouge et le noir*. Other than breakfast, there's no formal restaurant service, but simple platters can be served in the rooms daily from 3 to 11pm.

3RD & 4TH ARRONDISSEMENTS

EXPENSIVE

✪ Le Pavillon de la Reine

28 place des Vosges, 75003 Paris. ☎ 1/42-77-96-40. Fax 1/42-77-63-06. 30 rms, 17 duplexes, 15 suites. A/C MINIBAR TV TEL. 1,700 F ($323.20) double; 2,100 F ($399.20) duplex for one or two; 2,700–3,200 F ($513.30–$608.35) suite. Breakfast 95 F ($18.05) extra. AE, DC, MC, V. Free parking. Métro: Bastille.

Built in 1986, this cream-colored neoclassical villa blends in perfectly in an area that was once home to Victor Hugo. Guests enter the hotel through a tunnel that opens onto a small formal garden. Inside, the Louis XIII decor evokes the heyday of place des Vosges. Wing chairs with flame-stitched upholstery combined with iron-banded Spanish antiques create a rustic feel. Each room is unique; some are duplexes with sleeping lofts set above cozy salons. All have a warm decor of weathered beams, reproductions of famous oil paintings, and marble baths.

MODERATE

✪ Hôtel de Lutèce

65 rue St-Louis-en-l'Ile, 75004 Paris. ☎ **1/43-26-23-52.** Fax 1/43-29-60-25. 23 rms. TV TEL. 830 F ($157.80) double; 980 F ($186.30) triple. Breakfast 45 F ($8.55) extra. No credit cards. Métro: Pont-Marie.

Walking into this hotel is much like walking into a country house in Brittany. The lounge is graciously furnished with antiques, original tile floors, an old fireplace, and contemporary paintings. Each of the individualized rooms comes furnished with antiques, adding to the sort of refined atmosphere that attracts many famous guests, including the duke and duchess of Bedford.

Hôtel des Deux-Iles

59 rue St-Louis-en-l'Ile, 75004 Paris. ☎ **1/43-26-13-35.** Fax 1/43-29-60-25. 17 rms. TV TEL. 830 F ($157.80) double. Breakfast 45 F ($8.55) extra. No credit cards. Métro: Pont-Marie.

The Hôtel des Deux-Iles was impeccably restored by Roland Buffat, the designer who worked on the Hôtels St-Louis and de Lutèce. This 17th-century building is the largest and most glamorous of his creations. The collection of furnishings is eclectic, mostly bamboo and reed, blended with period pieces and the occasional cage of white doves or antique painting. Downstairs is a rustic tavern with an open fireplace; the lounge has a central garden of plants and flowers. Like the public rooms, the guest rooms are decorated with bamboo and reed.

INEXPENSIVE

Hôtel de Nice

42 rue de Rivoli, 75004 Paris. ☎ **1/42-78-55-29.** Fax 1/42-78-36-07. 23 rms. TEL. 370–390 F ($70.30–$74.10) double; 465 F ($88.40) triple. Rates include breakfast. MC, V. Métro: Hôtel-de-Ville.

This hotel prides itself on the kind of decor your favorite (art-conscious) aunt might have used for her bohemian studio. Rising seven stories from a position beside a small park opposite the Mairie (Town Hall) of the 4th arrondissement, it's owned/managed by Mme Vaudoux, who welcomes you with charm and bilingual skill. There's a parlor with boldly patterned Oriental rugs, oversize portraits from the Edwardian Age, and personalized memorabilia. The high-ceilinged guest rooms are idiosyncratic, deliberately old-fashioned, and very Parisian. Breakfast is the only meal served.

Ⓢ Hôtel St-Louis

75 rue St-Louis-en-l'Ile, 75004 Paris. ☎ **1/46-34-04-80.** Fax 1/46-34-02-13. 21 rms. TEL. 685–785 F ($130.20–$149.20) double. Breakfast 45 F ($8.55) extra. MC, V. Métro: Pont-Marie.

This small hotel occupies a 17th-century town house romantically positioned on the Ile St-Louis. Guy Record discovered this hotel and did a good job refurbishing it. Along with his wife, Andrée, he maintains a charming family atmosphere that's becoming harder to find in Paris. Many of the upper-level rooms offer views over the rooftops. We prefer those on the fifth floor, which have the most atmosphere and are decorated with old wood and attractive furniture. Antiques enhance the small reception lounge. Beneath the cellar's stone vaulting are a breakfast room and a lounge.

Hotels: 3rd & 4th Arrondissements

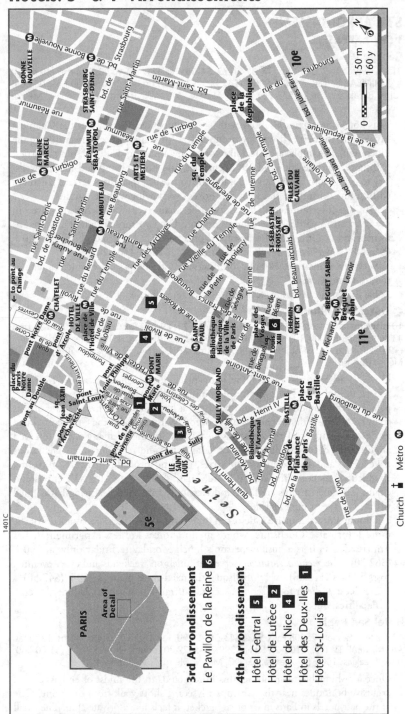

PARIS

Area of Detail

3rd Arrondissement
Le Pavillon de la Reine 6

4th Arrondissement
Hôtel Central 5
Hôtel de Lutèce 2
Hôtel de Nice 4
Hôtel des Deux-Îles 1
Hôtel St-Louis 3

Church ✝ ■   Métro Ⓜ

1401C

8TH ARRONDISSEMENT
VERY EXPENSIVE
George V

31 av. George-V, 75008 Paris. ☎ **1/47-23-54-00.** Fax 1/47-20-40-00. 228 rms, 40 suites. A/C MINIBAR TV TEL. 2,500–3,900 F ($475.25–$741.40) double; from 5,700 F ($1083.65) suite. Breakfast 130 F ($24.70) extra. AE, DC, MC, V. Parking 100 F ($19). Métro: George-V.

This hotel offers grandiose luxury on a tree-lined avenue between the Champs-Elysées and the Seine. It was the headquarters for General Eisenhower during the Liberation. The public areas feel like rooms in a museum, with rich old tapestries, paintings from the 18th and 19th centuries, and Pompeiian inlaid-marble walls. Try to get a room or suite overlooking the courtyard; these have terrace balconies with summer furniture plus urns and boxes overflowing with geraniums.

Dining/Entertainment: In good weather, haute cuisine lunches are served in the courtyard's garden-style café/restaurant. The two formal restaurants are Les Princes and Le Grill. The cheapest fixed-price menu at Les Princes begins at 240 F ($45.60), and à la carte meals at Le Grill start at 180 F ($34.20).

Services: Concierge, 24-hour room service, CBS news service, video movies in rooms, laundry, valet.

Facilities: Beauty salon, tearooms, florist, gift shop.

✪ Hôtel de Crillon

10 place de la Concorde, 75008 Paris. ☎ **1/44-71-15-00.** Fax 1/44-71-15-02. 120 rms, 43 suites. A/C MINIBAR TV TEL. 2,800–4,000 F ($532.30–$760.45) double; from 4,900 F ($931.55) suite. Breakfast 150 F ($28.50) extra. AE, DC, MC, V. Parking 150 F ($28.50). Métro: Concorde.

One of Paris's greats, the Crillon is on place de la Concorde, across from the American Embassy. The 200-year-old building, designed by Gabriel, was once the palace of the duc de Crillon and has been a hotel since the first decade of this century. Its most famous guest was Woodrow Wilson. Today the Crillon is owned by Jean Taittinger of the champagne family. Inside are many well-preserved architectural details and both authentic antiques and reproductions. The salons have 17th- and 18th-century tapestries, gilt-and-brocade furniture, glittering chandeliers, niches with fine sculpture, inlaid desks, and Louis XVI chests and chairs. The guest rooms are large and classically furnished, featuring baths lined with travertine or pink marble.

Dining/Entertainment: Guests can dine at the elegant Les Ambassadeurs or the more informal L'Obelisque, where menu choices are less experimental. Les Ambassadeurs offers a businessperson's lunch Monday to Friday only, at 330 F ($62.70). The *menu dégustation,* served at lunch on weekends and every evening, costs 590 F ($112.10). At L'Obélisque, the fixed-price menu is 250 F ($47.50).

Services: 24-hour room service, secretarial/translation service, laundry, valet.

Facilities: Shops.

Hôtel San Régis

12 rue Jean-Goujon, 75008 Paris. ☎ **1/43-59-41-90.** Fax 1/45-61-05-48. 33 rms, 12 suites. A/C MINIBAR TV TEL. 2,100–2,750 F ($399.20–$522.80) double; from 5,300 F ($1,007.60) suite. Breakfast 100 F ($19) extra. AE, DC, MC, V. Métro: F.-D.-Roosevelt.

Once a fashionable town house, this hotel stands in the midst of embassies and exclusive boutiques near the Champs-Elysées, a short walk from the Seine. One of the best hotels in Paris in its price bracket, it feels like a private club. The small

Hotels: 8th Arrondissement

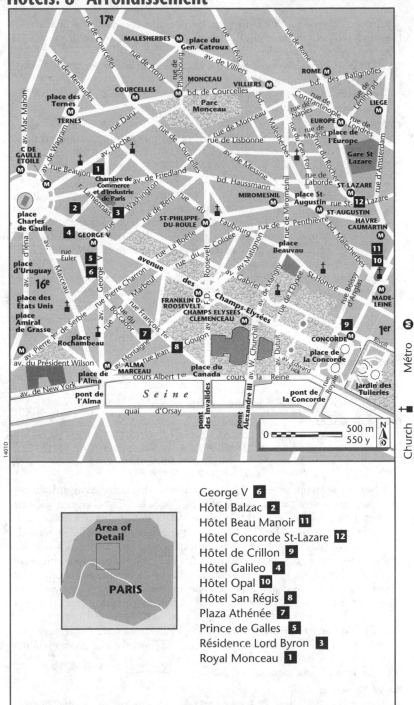

George V **6**
Hôtel Balzac **2**
Hôtel Beau Manoir **11**
Hôtel Concorde St-Lazare **12**
Hôtel de Crillon **9**
Hôtel Galileo **4**
Hôtel Opal **10**
Hôtel San Régis **8**
Plaza Athénée **7**
Prince de Galles **5**
Résidence Lord Byron **3**
Royal Monceau **1**

attentive staff will quickly learn your whims and make you feel at home. Each room is uniquely and tastefully decorated; a few have a separate sitting room and many overlook a side garden.

Dining/Entertainment: The hotel has an elegant restaurant serving formal French cuisine. There's also a winter garden.

Services: 24-hour room service, laundry, valet, babysitting.

Facilities: Car-rental desk.

✪ Plaza Athénée

25 av. Montaigne, 75008 Paris. ☎ **1/47-23-78-33.** Fax 1/47-20-20-70. 211 rms, 42 suites. A/C MINIBAR TV TEL. 3,010–4,470 F ($572.24–$849.80) double; from 6,430 F ($1,222.40) suite. Breakfast 150 F ($28.50) extra. AE, DC, MC, V. Parking 110 F ($20.90). Métro: F.-D.-Roosevelt.

About half the celebrities visiting Paris have been pampered in this palatial hotel; in the old days Mata Hari used to frequent the place. The hotel is halfway between the Champs-Elysées and the Seine on a shady avenue. Liveried attendants greet guests at the formal entrance below a glass shelter. You check in at a Louis XVI desk, facing a rare Flemish tapestry. The finest public room is the Montaigne Salon, paneled in rich grained wood and dominated by a marble fireplace. The best guest rooms overlook a courtyard with awnings and parasol-shaded tables; they have ample closet space and the large tiled baths have double basins and shower.

Dining/Entertainment: La Régence is a pink, peach, and gold room of handsome period furniture. The food is superb—try the lobster soufflé. For lunch, the Grill Relais Plaza is the meeting place of dress designers and personalities from the worlds of publishing, cinema, and art. The Bar Anglais is a favorite spot for a late-night drink (open until 1:30am).

Services: 24-hour room service, sophisticated concierge, laundry, Reuters telex with international stock quotes.

Facilities: Beauty parlor/hairdresser, massage parlor.

Prince de Galles

33 av. George-V, 75008 Paris. ☎ **1/47-23-55-11,** or 800/323-3535 in the U.S. Fax 1/47-20-06-61. 140 rms, 30 suites. A/C MINIBAR TV TEL. 2,500–3,300 F ($475.85–$627.35) double; 4,500–12,000 F ($855.50–$2,280.35) suite. Breakfast 135–170 F ($25.65–$32.30) extra. AE, DC, MC, V. Parking 80 F ($15.20). Métro: George-V.

When this hotel opened in 1927, its art deco/neo-Byzantine courtyard was the meeting place for the highest levels of Paris's social life. The courtyard walls are covered with elaborate mosaics that glisten like the background of a Klimt painting. Recently restored by ITT Sheraton, the palace maintains its impeccable Parisian standards with a hint of American efficiency. The "Prince of Wales" is a short walk from the Champs-Elysées, the Arc de Triomphe, and the boutiques of avenue Montaigne. The guest rooms are elegant, spacious, and sunny, with in-room movies provided; the quietest ones overlook the famous courtyard. The comfortable baths have Edwardian/art deco tilework patterned after the hotel's facade.

Dining/Entertainment: The bar, with its leather replicas of 18th-century armchairs, is one of the great hotel bars of Paris. The paneled dining room overlooks the garden-style courtyard with restaurant service.

Services: 24-hour room service, concierge, babysitting.

Royal Monceau

35–39 av. Hoche, 75008 Paris. ☎ **1/45-61-98-00.** Fax 1/42-99-89-90. 180 rms, 39 suites. A/C MINIBAR TV TEL. 2,600–3,200 F ($494.30–$608.35) double; 3,500–13,000 F

($665.40–$2,471.45) suite. AE, DC, MC, V. Breakfast 135–185 F ($25.65–$35.15) extra. AE, DC, MC, V. Métro: Charles-de-Gaulle–Etoile.

This graceful hotel is in an upscale neighborhood, with a view of the Arc de Triomphe. In the center of the airy lobby is an oval dome covered with murals of heavenly skies and fluffy clouds. The grand scale of the guest rooms was maintained in a sympathetic restoration completed in 1992. Some of the accommodations are the largest hotel rooms in Paris. Sometimes an elegant four-poster bed will be set in an alcove; at other times the walls will be hung with moiré silk. The baths are done in marble, of course.

Dining/Entertainment: Le Jardin restaurant is a glassed-in gazebo with rounded walls combining space-age construction with French neoclassicism. In the surrounding courtyard are double tiers of plants, including a 20-foot magnolia and dozens of flowering shrubs. In addition, guests can dine at Le Carpaccio, with one of Paris's most acclaimed chefs.

Services: Concierge, 24-hour room service, secretarial service, laundry, valet.

Facilities: State-of-the-art health club/gym with sauna, pool, balneotherapy (hydrotherapy), and massage parlor; solarium; golf practice room; hairdressing salon; conference rooms.

EXPENSIVE

✪ Hôtel Balzac

6 rue Balzac, 75008 Paris. ☎ **1/45-61-97-22,** or toll free 800/44-UTELL in the U.S. Fax 1/42-25-24-82. 70 rms, 14 suites. A/C MINIBAR TV TEL. 1,830–2,200 F ($347.90–$418.25) double; 3,200 F ($608.35) suite. Breakfast 90 F ($17.10) extra. AE, DC, MC, V. Parking 150 F ($28.50). Métro: George-V.

The Balzac is a fine addition to the 19th-century grandeur of the neighborhood. Popular with the cognoscenti, it's a few steps from the Champs-Elysées, near the Arc de Triomphe. A team of French and Lebanese designers have created public rooms that include elements of art deco, Palladian revival, and neo-Byzantine. The lobby has a sunny atrium with an alcove covered by hand-painted tendrils and vines. A glass-walled elevator transports guests up past yards of Turkish-patterned carpeting. The soundproof rooms were recently restored, with marble baths. We recommend the Bice restaurant. The breakfast room has the same art deco styling as the Bice. Laundry and 24-hour room service are available.

Hôtel Beau Manoir

6 rue de l'Arcade, 75008 Paris. ☎ **1/42-66-03-07,** or 800/528-1234 for reservations in the U.S. and Canada. Fax 1/42-68-03-00. 29 rms, 3 suites. A/C MINIBAR TV TEL. 1,155 F ($219.55) double; suite 1,465 F ($278.50). Rates include breakfast. AE, MC, V. Métro: Madeleine.

Open since March 1994, this four-star hotel prides itself on its 19th-century nostalgia and decorative zest. The lobby boasts the trappings of a private living room, with walnut reproductions of 18th- and 19th-century antiques, Aubusson tapestries, and fresh flowers. Breakfast is served beneath the chiseled stone vaults of a very old cellar, and the guest rooms are charming and very French. Each contains a safe for valuables, soundproofing, a marble bath, and the conveniences you'd expect. The suites often have exposed beams and/or sloping garret-style ceilings.

✪ Hôtel Concorde St-Lazare

108 rue St-Lazare, 75008 Paris. ☎ **1/40-08-44-44,** or 212/752-3900 in New York State, 800/888-4747 in the U.S. and Canada, 0171/630-1704 in London. Fax 1/42-93-01-20. 277 rms, 23 suites. A/C MINIBAR TV TEL. 1,160–1,260 F ($220.50–$239.50) double; 2,450–3,500 F

($465.75–$665.40) suite. Breakfast 90 F ($17.10) extra. AE, DC, MC, V. Parking 100 F ($19). Métro: St-Lazare.

Across from the St-Lazare railway station, the St-Lazare was built in 1889 as lodging for the visitors who flocked to the Universal Exposition. In the 1990s the St-Lazare's main lobby (a carefully protected historic monument) was restored under the supervision of the Concorde chain. The guest rooms were elevated to modern standards of comfort, redecorated, and soundproofing.

Dining/Entertainment: The hotel has a gilt-and-russet room worthy of J. P. Morgan that's devoted to French billiards—the only room of its kind in any hotel in Paris. An American bar, Le Golden Black, bears fashion designer Sonia Rykiel's signature decor of black lacquer with touches of gold and amber. The Café Terminus bristles with turn-of-the-century accessories and daily brasserie service from noon to 11pm. The Bistrot 108 offers provincial dishes with great vintages that can be ordered by the glass.

Services: Concierge, 24-hour room service, babysitting, laundry, valet, currency exchange.

MODERATE

Hôtel Galileo
54 rue Galilée, 75008 Paris. ☎ **1/47-20-66-06.** Fax 1/47-20-67-17. 27 rms. A/C MINIBAR TV TEL. 950–980 F ($180.60–$186.30) double. Breakfast 50 F ($9.50) extra. AE, MC, V. Parking 100–150 F ($19–$28.50). Métro: George-V.

About two blocks from the Arc de Triomphe and a block from the Champs-Elysées, this is a streamlined modern 1992 restoration of an elegant older building. Its facade has all the neoclassical carved-stone details and ornate wrought iron you'd expect in this neighborhood, but the inside is well lit, warmly decorated, and comfortable. There's a small garden on the premises. Breakfast in the basement breakfast room is the only meal served.

Résidence Lord Byron
5 rue de Chateaubriand, 75008 Paris. ☎ **1/43-59-89-98.** Fax 1/42-89-46-04. 31 rms, 6 suites. MINIBAR TV TEL. 870–970 F ($165.40–$184.40) double; from 1,320 F ($250.95) suite. Breakfast 60 F ($11.40) extra. MC, V. Métro: George-V. RER: Etoile.

You can feel proud to stay here and recommend it to your friends. It's just off the Champs-Elysées, on a gently curving street. The owner, Mme Françoise Coisne, who moved to Paris from the Ile de France, has added many personal touches. Throughout are framed prints of butterflies and historic French scenes. The furnishings are good reproductions of antiques or restrained modern pieces. Breakfast is served in the dining room or, in fair weather, in a shaded inner garden.

INEXPENSIVE

⊛ Hôtel Opal
19 rue Tronchet, 75008 Paris. ☎ **1/42-65-77-97.** Fax 1/49-24-06-58. 36 rms. MINIBAR TV TEL. 480–590 F ($91.25–$112.15) double. Breakfast 40 F ($7.60) extra. Additional bed 90 F ($17.10) extra. AE, MC, V. Parking 120 F ($22.80). Métro: Madeleine.

This rejuvenated hotel is a real find in the heart of Paris, behind the Madeleine near the Opéra Garnier. The guest rooms are somewhat cramped but very clean and comfortable. Those on the top floor are reached by a narrow staircase; some have skylights. The reception desk will make arrangements for parking at a nearby garage.

Paris Dining 6

Paris boasts more restaurants than any other city in the world. We suggest you follow Parisians, who save their trips to the temples of *haute gastronomie*—from today's legends, like Joël Robuchon, Michel Rostang, and Bernard Pacaud, to yesterday's, like Taillevent, Maxim's, and La Tour d'Argent—for special occasions. An array of other choices awaits you, including moderate and even inexpensive restaurants, cafés, bistros, and brasseries that serve every cuisine from every province of France and from all the former colonies, such as Morocco.

THE DINING SCENE   The big change on the Paris scene today is that you might actually get a reservation. Blame it on the recession (*le crise*). In the heady late 1980s if you spoke only English or English-accented French, you likely would've been refused.

One question we're often asked is if you can you dine badly in Paris. The answer is an emphatic yes, and increasingly so. We repeatedly get complaints from visitors who cite haughty service and mediocre food dispensed at "outrageous" prices. Often these complaints are about places catering almost solely to tourists. We'll help you avoid them by sharing our favorite off-the-beaten-track discoveries. Considering the prices charged, view your culinary pursuit as an investment. While others are fighting it out for a table at one of the less-than-wonderful places along the Champs-Elysées, you might be seeking finer fare at some well-recommended choice farther away.

Other changes are in the air. In the past, no man would have thought of dining out, even at a neighborhood bistro, without a suit and tie and no woman would have let herself be seen without a smart dress or suit. That dress code has become more relaxed now, except in first-class and *luxe* establishments. Relaxed doesn't mean sloppy jeans and jogging attire, however. Parisians still value style, even when dressing informally. And note that it's now considered provincial to request *l'addition* (the bill). Chic Parisians ask for *la note*.

Establishments are still required by law to post their menus outside, so peruse them carefully. The prix-fixe (fixed-price) menu still remains an admirable choice if you want to have some idea of what your *la note* will be when it's presented by the waiter (whom, by the way, you should call *monsieur*, not *garçon*).

WHAT THE LISTINGS MEAN   Restaurants we've classified as "Very Expensive" charge 550 F ($104.55) and up, plus drinks, for dinner. That's per person, too. In "Expensive" restaurants, dinner ranges from 300 to 550 F ($57 to $104.50); "Moderate" restaurants charge 175 to 300 F ($33.25 to $57). Anything under 175 F ($33.25) per person is considered "Inexpensive," though such a price tag means luxurious dining in most parts of the world.

Note that the tax and tip are included in all prices (look for *service compris* or *prix nets* on the menu). In simple bistros, the small change is left on the table; in *luxe* or first-class establishments, patrons often add another 5% to the bill.

In France, lunch (as well as dinner) tends to be a full-course meal with meat, vegetables, salad, bread, cheese, dessert, wine, and coffee. It may be difficult to find a restaurant that serves the type of light lunch North Americans are accustomed to. Cafés, however, may be the answer, since they offer sandwiches, soup, and salads in a relaxed setting.

Coffee is served after the meal and carries an extra charge. The French consider it absolutely barbaric to drink coffee during the meal, and unless you specifically order it with milk (*au lait*) the coffee will be served black. In the more conscientious establishments, it's prepared as the traditional *filtre*, a slow but rewarding filtered style that takes a bit of manipulating.

In the addresses below, designations like "1er" and "12e," which follow the name of the street, refer (in French form) to the arrondissement in which the establishment is located.

1 City Center: Left Bank

5TH ARRONDISSEMENT
VERY EXPENSIVE

✪ La Tour d'Argent
15–17 quai de la Tournelle, 5e. ☎ 1/43-54-23-31. Reservations required. Main courses 290–395 F ($55.10–$75.05); fixed-price lunch 385 F ($73.15). AE, DC, MC, V. Tues–Sun noon–2:30pm and 8–10:30pm. Métro: Maubert-Mutualité or Sully-Morland. FRENCH.

Since the 16th century there's always been a restaurant on this spot. The restaurant became famous, though, when it was owned by Frédéric Delair, who purchased the wine cellar of the Café Anglais and began issuing certificates to diners who ordered the house specialty, pressed duck (*caneton*). Today this restaurant is under the direction of the debonair Claude Terrail.

A gastronomic museum now surrounds the restaurant. On the top floor, facing the Left Bank, the glass enclosure provides a panoramic view of the 17th-century houses along the quays of the Ile St-Louis. At night, you can see the illuminated flying buttresses of Notre-Dame.

The cuisine is classically French. New diners often order the duck—it's sensational. Other selections include filets de sole cardinal and filet Tour d'Argent. Begin with the potage Claudius Burdel made with sorrel, egg yolks, fresh cream, chicken broth, and butter whipped together. For dessert, the pêches flambées is marvelous.

MODERATE

Auberge des Deux Signes
46 rue Galande, 5e. ☎ 1/43-25-46-56. Reservations required for dinner. Main courses 170–320 F ($32.30 $60.80); fixed-price meal 140 F ($26.60) at lunch, 230 F ($43.70) at dinner.

Impressions

Frédéric [Frédéric Delair, former owner of La Tour d'Argent] was preparing the duck in a special way. He got two servings (and two lots of profit) out of it, one pressed, the other grilled. Although they are both equally delicious, I think I still prefer the grilled version. Frédéric was really quite a sight, with his lorgnon, his graying side-whiskers and his imperturbably serious expression, as he cut up his plump quack-quack, already trussed and flambéed, threw it into the saucepan and made his sauce, salting and peppering just as Claude Monet painted.

—Léon Daudet, *Paris Vécu* (1929)

AE, DC, MC, V. Sun 12:30–2pm, Mon–Fri 12:30–2pm and 7:30–10:30pm, Sat 7:30–10:30pm. Closed Aug. Métro: Maubert-Mutualité or St-Michel. FRENCH.

This medieval building once served as the chapel of St. Blaise. Auvergne-born Georges Dhulster has this place well under control, and many visitors come here in the evening to enjoy the view of floodlit Notre-Dame and St-Julien-le-Pauvre (without having to pay Tour d'Argent's prices). Try for a table upstairs, with a view of the garden.

The cuisine of Auvergne is given a *moderne* twist here, with fresh ingredients used in all the dishes. Be prepared, at times, for a wait. Try the veal medallions with morels, beef from the Aurillac in central France, or goose confit with flap mushrooms.

Au Pactole

44 bd. St-Germain, 5e. ☎ 1/43-26-92-28. Reservations recommended. Main courses 130–152 F ($24.70–$28.90); fixed-price menu 149 F ($28.30). AE, MC, V. Sun–Fri noon–2:45pm and 7:15–10:45pm, Sat 7:15–10:45pm. Métro: Maubert-Mutualité. FRENCH.

Former French President François Mitterrand and German Prime Minister Helmut Kohl used to meet here for lunch. Jacques Chirac, the new president, has been known to show up as well. In this modern dining room done in tones of burnt orange and yellow, you can do what the statesmen do and order, among others, terrine of saltwater fish flavored with algae, ragoût of scallops with wild mushrooms, filet of roebuck with red-wine sauce, or a meli-melo of codfish with salmon.

ⓢ Rôtisserie du Beaujolais

19 quai de la Tournelle, 5e. ☎ 1/43-54-17-47. Reservations recommended. Main courses 75–160 F ($14.25–$30.40). MC, V. Tues–Sun noon–2:30pm and 7:30–10:30pm. Métro: Pont-Marie. FRENCH/SPIT-ROASTED.

Though it offers uncomplicated cuisine at reasonable prices, this restaurant was founded by Claude Terrail, owner of the ultra-expensive La Tour d'Argent. Set at the edge of the Seine overlooking the Ile St-Louis, the Rôtisserie contains a stone, zinc, and wood-inlaid antique bar imported from the Beaujolais region; comfortable banquettes; checkered napery; and a relaxed atmosphere inspired by the best brasseries in the provinces. Appetizers include a fricassée of wild mushrooms, a gâteau of chicken livers, and salads. Main courses are usually roasted on spits in the kitchen and come, savory and steaming, with a garnish of mashed potatoes in the old-fashioned style. Examples are spit-roasted chicken, duck, and pigeon, as well as non spit-roasted coq au vin and côte de boeuf for two. The wine list is deliberately unpretentious, with many beaujolais vintages.

INEXPENSIVE

Brasserie Balzar

49 rue des Écoles, 5e. ☎ 1/43-54-13-67. Reservations recommended. Main courses 90–115 F ($17.10–$21.85). AE, MC, V. Daily noon–midnight. Métro: Cluny–La Sorbonne. FRENCH.

During France's 1968 civil unrest, Paris's students, in alliance with the country's factory workers, came close to overthrowing the government. Head here if you'd like to experience a dining room where some of those alliances were debated. Established in 1898, it's gruff but cheerful and makes almost no concessions to experimental modern cuisine. Menu items include steak au poivre, sole meunière, sauerkraut with ham and sausage, pig's feet, and calf's liver. Be warned that if you want just coffee or a drink, you probably won't be awarded a table during meal hours. Former patrons have included both Sartre and Camus (who often got into arguments), William Shirer, James Thurber, professors from the nearby Sorbonne, and a bevy of English and American journalists who claimed the place in the days prior to the Vichy government.

Campagne et Provence

25 quai de la Tournelle, 5e. ☎ 1/43-54-05-17. Reservations recommended. Main courses 89–99 F ($16.90–$18.80); fixed-price lunch 99 F ($18.80). AE, MC, V. Mon 8–11pm, Tues–Fri 12:30–2pm and 8–11pm, Sat 8–11pm. Métro: Maubert-Mutualité. PROVENÇAL.

Beside the quai across the Seine from the Ile de la Cité, this restaurant celebrates the traditions of Provençal cuisine. Its cream walls are decorated with bouquets of dried flowers; the upholstery is the color of the Provençal sky. Best of all, the prices are kept deliberately modest and food items include all the savor of the south. Examples include a brandade of codfish with aüoli, an ethnic dish known as pieds et paquet (lamb's feet with lamb tripe in a white-wine sauce), ragoût of stockfish, and roasted rabbit stuffed with olives. Desserts might include a spice-flavored savarin with fennel-flavored ice cream.

Chez René

14 bd. St-Germain, 5e. ☎ 1/43-54-30-23. Reservations recommended. Main courses 72–160 F ($13.70–$30.40). MC, V. Mon–Fri 12:15–2:15pm and 7:45–11pm. Métro: Cardinal-Lemoine. FRENCH.

Skip the greasy Middle Eastern and mediocre Asian restaurants of the 5th arrondissement and head here for an old-fashioned corner bistro, the kind Paris used to have so many of before they became pizzerias. The dining room isn't fancy, but a steady clientele frequents the place for the good, reliable food, especially the *plats du jour* (daily specials). At mealtimes, service can be rushed and a tad hysterical. For an appetizer, if featured, try fresh wild mushrooms laced with butter and garlic and perhaps a platter of country-style sausages. You'll find such reliable fare as boeuf à la bourguignonne and a dish of the day that might be pot-au-feu or blanquette de veau (veal in white sauce). Enjoy it all with a bottle of beaujolais.

Moissonnier

28 rue des Fosses St-Bernard, 5e. ☎ 1/43-29-87-65. Reservations required for dinner. Main courses 80–140 F ($15.20–$26.60). MC, V. Tues–Sat noon–2:30pm and 7–9:15pm, Sun noon–2:30pm. Closed Aug. Métro: Jussieu or Cardinal-Lemoine. LYONNAISE.

Come here for true French country cooking, the kind that many discriminating palates visit Paris just to sample. Big portions of solid old-fashioned food are served, beginning with saladiers, large glass salad bowls filled with a selection of charcuterie.

Restaurants: 5th & 6th Arrondissements

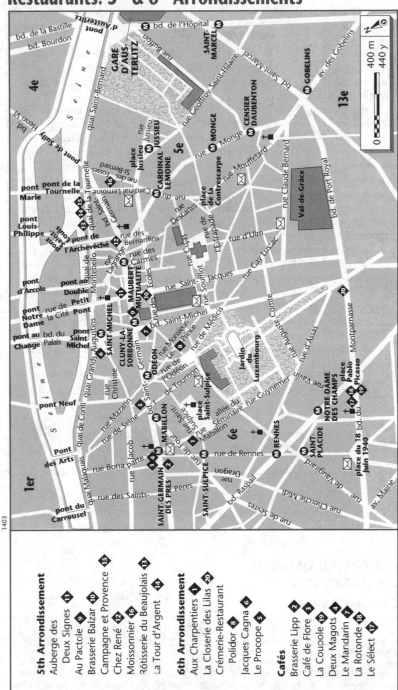

1403

5th Arrondissement

Auberge des
Deux Signes   ◆ 11
Au Pactole   ◆ 9
Brasserie Balzar   ◆ 10
Campagne et Provence   ◆ 15
Chez René   ◆ 12
Moissonnier   ◆ 16
Rôtisserie du Beaujolais   ◆ 13
La Tour d'Argent   ◆ 14

6th Arrondissement

Aux Charpentiers   ◆ 1
La Closerie des Lilas   ◆ 20
Crémerie-Restaurant
Polidor   ◆ 8
Jacques Cagna   ◆ 6
Le Procope   ◆ 5

Cafés

Brasserie Lipp   ◆ 2
Café de Flore   ◆ 3
La Coupole   ◆ 19
Deux Magots   ◆ 4
Le Mandarin   ◆ 7
La Rotonde   ◆ 18
Le Sélect   ◆ 17

Church ✝▬   Post Office ⊠   Métro Ⓜ

Dining "Out"

Parisian maître d'hôtels are famous for their skill at welcoming a wide array of dining companions. Although same-sex couples and groups will usually be treated courteously in every restaurant, here's a list of places where the clientele is primarily gay and lesbian.

Established in 1870 on the Ile de la Cité, **Au Rendezvous des Camionneurs,** 72 quai des Orfèvres, 1er (☎ 1/43-54-88-74; Métro: Pont-Neuf), has the look, feel, cuisine, and service of a traditional bistro—with the distinct difference that 80% of its clientele is gay. Its well-prepared meals are reasonably priced. Au Rendezvous is open daily from noon to 2:30pm and 7 to 11:30pm (last order).

Bleu-Marine, 28 rue de Léopold-Bellan, 2e (☎ 1/42-36-92-44; Métro: Sentier or Bourse), serves mostly fish to a clientele that's about 40% gay. In the pedestrian zone near the headquarters of *Le Figaro,* the restaurant was founded in 1988 by gregarious Louis Marion, whom everyone calls simply "Marion." Bleu-Marine is open Monday to Saturday from noon to 3pm and 8 to 10:30pm.

Established a decade ago in the heart of the Marais, **L'Amazonial,** 3 rue Ste-Opportune, 1er (☎ 1/42-3-53-13; Métro: Châtelet), is one of Paris's most popular gay restaurants, offering South American/French cuisine. It occupies a 19th-century building with a flowered terrace extending onto the sidewalk and is open daily from noon to 3pm and 7pm to 1am (last order).

Le Gai Moulin, 4 rue St-Merri, 4e (☎ 1/42-77-60-60; Métro: Hôtel-de-Ville), near the Centre Pompidou, is about 99% gay (as its name suggests). Only three-course fixed-price menus are offered, each served to only 28 diners at a time. Le Gai Moulin is open Wednesday to Friday from noon to 2pm and Wednesday to Monday 7:30 to 11pm.

L'Imprimerie, 101 rue Vieille du Temple, 3e (☎ 1/42-77-93-80; Métro: Filles-du-Calvaire), welcomes members of the Marais art community, many of whom happen to be gay. The setting is reminscent of a brick-lined bistro in New York City's Greenwich Village, and menu items include a conservative array of French-inspired dishes. L'Imprimerie is open daily from noon to 3pm and 8pm to 1am.

You might also select some excellent terrines, perhaps Lyonnais sausages. The specialties, from Burgundy and Lyon, include main courses like duck with turnips and rack of herb-flavored lamb.

6TH ARRONDISSEMENT
VERY EXPENSIVE

✪ Jacques Cagna
14 rue des Grands-Augustins, 6e. ☎ 1/43-26-49-39. Reservations required. Main courses 230–360 F ($43.70–$68.40); fixed-price meal 260 F ($49.40) at lunch, 480 F ($91.25) at dinner. AE, DC, MC, V. Mon–Sat noon–2pm and 7:30–10:30pm. Closed Aug. Métro: St-Michel. FRENCH.

In a 17th-century town house, Jacques Cagna is a place where both the clientele and the food are among the grandest in Paris. Its pinkish-beige interior is filled with massive timbers, plus 17th-century Dutch paintings. A specialty here is the

Aberdeen Angus beef, aged for three weeks, which chef Cagna imbues with a rich shallot-flavored sauce. You might begin with a salad of prawn fritters and artichoke chips with a gazpacho sauce or a scallop-and-lobster puff pastry in a cream sauce with sea urchins. Other specialties include milk-fed veal with a ginger-and-lime sauce and Challans duck roasted in a burgundy sauce. The desserts are overwhelmingly tempting.

EXPENSIVE

La Closerie des Lilas (Pleasure Garden of the Lilacs)
171 bd. du Montparnasse, 6e. ☎ **1/43-26-70-50.** Reservations required. Main courses 180–230 F ($34.20–$43.70) in the restaurant, 70–120 F ($13.30–$22.80) in the brasserie. AE, DC, V. Restaurant, daily 12:30–2:30pm and 7:30pm–12:30am; brasserie, daily noon–1am. Métro: Port-Royal or Vavin. FRENCH.

The number of famous people who've dined at the Closerie watching the fallen leaves blow along the Montparnasse streets is almost countless: Stein and Toklas, Ingres, Henry James, Chateaubriand, Lenin and Trotsky, Proust, Sartre and de Beauvoir, and Whistler. To get a seat in the "bateau" (brasserie) section is difficult. However, you may enjoy waiting at the bar and ordering the best champagne julep in the world. In the bateau, you can select such rustic dishes as poached haddock, beef with a salad, and steak tartare. In the chic restaurant inside the Closerie, the cooking is classic. Try the escargots façon Closerie for openers. Of the main-course selections, the rognons de veau à la moutarde (veal kidneys with mustard) and ribs of veal in cider sauce are highly recommended. Both sections are on street level—the brasserie faces boulevard Montparnasse, while the restaurant looks out onto boulevard du Port-Royal.

INEXPENSIVE

⊗ Aux Charpentiers
10 rue Mabillon, 6e. ☎ **1/43-26-30-05.** Reservations required. Main courses 78–180 F ($14.80–$34.20); fixed-price menu 120 F ($22.80) at lunch, 150 F ($28.50) at dinner. AE, DC, MC, V. Mon–Sat noon–3pm and 7:30–11:30pm. Métro: Mabillon. FRENCH.

Aux Charpentiers used to be the rendezvous of master carpenters, whose guild was next door. Nowadays it's where the youth of St-Germain-des-Prés take their dates for inexpensive meals at a bistro established more than 130 years ago. Though not especially imaginative, the food is well prepared in the best tradition of *cuisine bourgeoise*. Appetizers include pâté of duck and rabbit terrine. Especially recommended as a main course is the roast duck with olives. Each day a different *plat du jour* is offered, with time-tested French home-cooking: petit salé aux lentilles, pot-au-feu, and boeuf à la mode are among the main dishes. The chef suggests the platters of

Impressions

The Closerie des Lilas had once been a café where poets met more or less regularly and the last principal poet had been Paul Fort whom I had never read. But the only poet I ever saw there was Blaise Cendrars, with his broken boxer's face and his pinned-up empty sleeve, rolling a cigarette with his one good hand. He was a good companion until he drank too much and, at that time, when he was lying, he was more more interesting than many men telling a story truly.

—Ernest Hemingway, *A Moveable Feast* (1964)

fresh fish. There's a large choice of Bordeaux wines direct from the châteaux, including Château Gaussens. Reader reaction to this restaurant has been mixed over the years, ranging from "How dare you send me to that dive!" to "We took all our meals here—and how good they were!"

✪ Crémerie-Restaurant Polidor

41 rue Monsieur-le-Prince, 6e. ☎ **1/43-26-95-34.** Reservations not accepted. Main courses 40–69 F ($7.60–$13.10); fixed-price lunch (Mon–Fri) 50 F ($9.50); fixed-price menu 100 F ($19). No credit cards. Mon–Sat noon–2:30pm and 7pm–12:30am, Sun to 11pm. Métro: Odéon. FRENCH.

This little bistro serves *cuisine familiale.* Frequented by students and artists, it opened in 1930 and has changed little since. The restaurant's name still contains the word *crémerie*, referring to its specialty: frosted crème desserts. This has become one of the Left Bank's most established literary bistros; it was André Gide's favorite. Lace curtains and brass hat racks, drawers in the back where repeat customers lock up their cloth napkins, and clay water pitchers on the tables create an old-fashioned atmosphere. Overworked but smiling waitresses serve grandmother's favorite dishes, such as pumpkin soup, snails from Burgundy, rib of beef with onions, rabbit with mustard sauce, and veal in white sauce. Desserts include raspberry and lemon tarts.

Le Procope

13 rue de l'Ancienne-Comédie, 6e. ☎ **1/43-26-99-20.** Reservations recommended. Main courses 83–150 F ($15.75–$28.50). AE, DC, MC, V. Daily 8am–1am. Métro: Odéon. FRENCH.

The oldest café in Paris, Le Procope was opened in 1686 by a Sicilian named Francesco Procopio dei Coltelli. The art of coffee drinking was popularized here, probably brought from Italy. Along the walls are portraits of former patrons—Franklin, Rousseau, Robespierre, Danton, Marat, Bonaparte, and Balzac, among others. The café is more of a restaurant today than it was originally. There are two levels for dining: the spacious upstairs section and the more intimate street-level room. Fresh oysters and shellfish are served from a refrigerated display. Well-chosen classic French dishes include baby duckling with spices, "drunken chicken," and "green coffee."

7TH ARRONDISSEMENT
VERY EXPENSIVE

✪ L'Arpège

84 rue de Varenne, 7e. ☎ **1/47-05-09-06.** Reservations required. Main courses 280–340 F ($53.20–$64.60); fixed-price lunch 390 F ($74.10); *menu dégustation* 790 F ($150.20). AE, DC, MC, V. Sun–Fri noon–1:30pm and 7:30–9:45pm. Métro: Varenne. FRENCH.

One of the most talked about restaurants in Paris, L'Arpège is where Alain Passard prepares many of his charming culinary specialties. It's in a prosperous residential neighborhood, on the site of what for years was the world-famous L'Archestrate, where Passard once worked in the kitchens. Amid a cultivated decor of etched glass, burnished steel, and monochromatic paintings, you can enjoy specialties that've been heralded as truly innovative: like crabmeat-stuffed cabbage and game cock with chicken livers and herbed onions. Or you can try the John Dory with celery juice and sage-flavored asparagus. The chocolate beignets and sugared tomato with vanilla stuffing make superb desserts. The wine list is something to write home about.

Restaurants: 7th Arrondissement

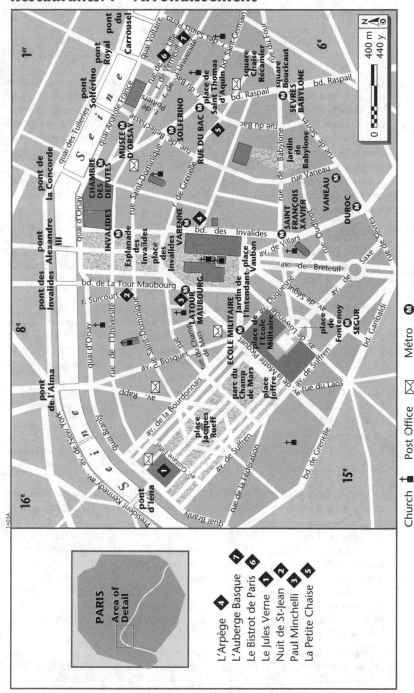

PARIS
Area of
Detail

L'Arpège **4**
L'Auberge Basque **7**
Le Bistrot de Paris **6**
Le Jules Verne **1**
Nuit de St-Jean **2**
Paul Minchelli **3**
La Petite Chaise **5**

Church ✝   Post Office ⊠   Métro Ⓜ

Le Jules Verne

In the Tour Eiffel, Champ-de-Mars, 7e. ☎ **1/45-55-61-44**. Reservations required. Main courses 210–430 F ($39.90–$81.70); fixed-price lunch (Mon–Fri) 290 F ($55.10); *menu dégustation* 690 F ($131.10). AE, DC, MC, V. Daily 12:15–2pm and 7:30–9:30pm. Métro: Trocadéro, Ecole-Militaire, or Bir-Hakeim. FRENCH.

Only a handful of restaurants enjoy so sweeping a view of the City of Light. Set on the second platform of the Eiffel Tower, the Jules Verne is reached by a private elevator from the south foundation (*le pilier sud*) of the monument. A piano bar offers a relaxing spot for a before-dinner drink, after which you'll be ushered to a table in a darkened room whose indirect lighting shows the glitter of Paris to its maximum advantage. The menu, which changes seasonally, might include chartreuse of asparagus with red snapper and a brandade of codfish, carpaccio of raw marinated tuna and salmon with a slice of warm foie gras, or cassolette of fresh oysters with cucumbers. The *menu dégustation* is available at night and at lunch on Saturday and Sunday.

EXPENSIVE

Le Bistrot de Paris

33 rue de Lille, 7e. ☎ **1/42-61-16-83**. Reservations recommended. Main courses 85–98 F ($16.15–$18.60). MC, V. Mon–Fri noon–2pm and 7:15–10:30pm, Sat 7:15–10:30pm. Métro: Rue-du-Bac. FRENCH.

Chef Michel Oliver knows the secret of making discriminating diners zero in on his chic little, sophisticated bistro. He's the son of Raymond Oliver, one of France's great restaurateurs, who ruled supreme for a long time at the prestigious Grand Véfour. We'll never forget the sweetbreads flavored with orange that Michel served us. The specialties may have changed over the years, but the cooking has remained superb and the wine list is impressive. Today's specialties include "three herb" lamb—a slow-cooked shoulder of lamb that's been marinated with rosemary, thyme, and garlic. Another delight is brochette of Bresse chicken marinated with lime, coriander, and cumin, served with artichokes.

Paul Minchelli

54 bd. de la Tour-Maubourg, 7e. ☎ **1/47-05-89-86**. Reservations required. Main courses 200–300 F ($38–$57). AE, MC, V. Tues–Sat noon–3pm and 8–11pm. Métro: La-Tour-Maubourg. SEAFOOD.

Established in 1994 on the street level of an 1860 building, this restaurant immediately made a splash on the Paris dining scene. Much of the allure derives from the chef's refusal to indulge in gratuitously pretentious rituals. The restaurant's namesake is Marseille-born Paul Minchelli, whose cuisine is described even by his financial backers as "marginal," not following the tried-and-true methods of many Parisian chefs. Part of his inspiration derives from Provençal techniques he learned from his parents. Very little meat is offered, and at least part of the seafood is scooped from an aquarium just before it's cooked. Seated in a yellow-walled dining room outfitted with modern furniture and round seascapes evocative of ship portholes, you can order such dishes as raw saltwater fish served with olive oil, salt, and pepper; merlan Colbert; and bar filet steamed in seaweed.

⊗ La Petite Chaise

36–38 rue de Grenelle, 7e. ☎ **1/42-22-13-35**. Reservations recommended. Fixed-price menu 170 F ($32.30). MC, V. Daily noon–2:15pm and 7–11pm. Métro: Sèvres-Babylone. FRENCH.

This is the oldest restaurant in Paris, established by the baron de la Chaise in 1680 as an inn at the edge of what was then a large hunting preserve. (The baron, according to the restaurant's lore, maintained a series of upstairs bedrooms for midafternoon dalliances.) Very Parisian, La Petite Chaise invites you into a world of cramped but attractive tables, very old wood paneling, and ornate wall sconces. The only option available is a cost-conscious four-course set menu with a large choice of dishes. Samplings from the menu might be veal scallops with Camembert sauce, magrêt of duck with tarragon sauce, mignon of pork with lettuce-flavored cream sauce, and gigotin of sea bass.

MODERATE

L'Auberge Basque

51 rue de Verneuil, 7e. ☎ 1/45-48-51-98. Reservations recommended. Main courses 80–120 F ($15.20–$22.80); fixed-price meal 120 F ($22.80) at lunch, 180 F ($34.20) at dinner. MC, V. Mon–Sat noon–2:30pm and 7:30–10:30pm. Métro: Rue-du-Bac. FRENCH.

The fixed-price meal of the day offered here depends on the *cuisine du marché* (whatever is fresh at the market that day). Owners M. and Mme Rourre come from the Basque country near the Spanish border, and their meals reflect the rich cuisine of that region. Among their satisfied diners are some famous sports figures and French TV stars. You might begin with their Basque pâté, then follow with a piperade, a regionally famous omelet. They also prepare magrêt and confit of canard (duck). Various fresh fish dishes also are served, along with a selection of cheese and fresh-fruit tarts. The wines are well chosen.

INEXPENSIVE

Nuit de St-Jean

29 rue Surcouf, 7e. ☎ 1/45-51-61-49. Reservations recommended. Main courses 80–90 F ($15.20–$17.10); fixed-price menu 120 F ($22.80). AE, DC, MC, V. Mon–Fri noon–2:30pm and 7:30–10:30pm, Sat 7:30–10:30pm. Métro: Invalides. FRENCH.

One of the smallest and most charming restaurants in the well-heeled residential Les Invalides area is this enclave of cuisine from France's southwest. Containing only 30 seats and warmly decorated with ceiling beams and a conservative modern design, it features such dishes as cassoulet, smoked haddock in ginger sauce, tripe and ouillette, lamb curry with rice, lime-marinated chicken, and rascasse (scorpion fish) in champagne-cream sauce. The desserts are tempting, freshly made concoctions like fondant au chocolat à la crème anglaise. Though the restaurant has been here since the early 1950s, it was given new life when owners from Toulouse took it over in the mid-1980s.

2 City Center: Right Bank

1ST ARRONDISSEMENT
VERY EXPENSIVE

✪ Carré des Feuillants

14 rue de Castiglione, 1er. ☎ 1/42-86-82-82. Reservations required. Main courses 198–240 F ($37.60–$45.60); fixed-price meal 280 F ($53.20) at lunch, 560 F ($106.45) at dinner. AE, DC, MC, V. Mon–Fri noon–2pm and 7:30–10:30pm, Sat 7:30–10:30pm. Closed Aug. Métro: Tuileries, Concorde, Opéra, or Madeleine. FRENCH.

When leading chef Alain Dutournier converted this 17th-century convent into a restaurant, in the platinum location near place Vendôme and the Tuileries, it was an overnight success. The interior is like a turn-of-the-century bourgeois house with several small salons opening onto a skylit interior courtyard, across from which is a glass-encased kitchen where you can watch the chefs perform magic. Dutournier likes to call his brand of French cooking *cuisine du moment,* the product of an imaginative mind—specialties are likely to include cream of pheasant with fresh chestnuts or roasted red mullet with an oyster dressing. He prefers a light, healthy cuisine, working with farmers who supply him with the freshest produce possible. His beef comes from one of the oldest cattle breeds in France, the *race bazadaise,* and his lamb is raised in Pauillac. The exciting wine cellar contains several little-known wines and a fabulous Armagnac collection.

✪ Le Grand Véfour

17 rue de Beaujolais, 1er. ☎ **1/42-96-56-27.** Reservations required. Main courses 230–380 F ($43.70–$72.20); fixed-price meal 305–750 F ($57.95–$142.50) at lunch, 750 F ($142.50) at dinner. AE, DC, MC, V. Mon–Fri 12:30–2:15pm and 7:30–10:15pm. Métro: Louvre. FRENCH.

Since the reign of Louis XV this has been a restaurant, though not always under the same name. Though the exact date of its opening as the Café de Chartres is not known, this historical treasure is more than 200 years old. It was named after owner Jean Véfour, a former chef to a member of the royal family in 1812. Since then, Napoléon, Danton, Hugo, Colette, and Cocteau, among others, have dined here—as the brass plaques on the tables testify. Jean Taittinger of the champagne family (who also own the Crillon) purchased the restaurant, and the meticulous restoration, overseen by the Department of Historical Monuments, has improved its former glories.

Dining here is an experience. Specialties, served on Limoges china, include terrine of half-cooked roe salmon with "smoked milk" (you heard right), bouillon of asparagus with truffles, and deboned poached filet of sole Grand Véfour (stuffed with duxelle of mushrooms and served with mustard-flavored mousseline sauce). The desserts are often grand, as exemplified by the gourmandises au chocolate, served with a chocolate sorbet. The dining room is under the watchful eye of peerless maître d' Christian David.

EXPENSIVE

Escargot-Montorgueil

38 rue Montorgueil, 1er. ☎ **1/42-36-83-51.** Reservations required. Main courses 105–150 F ($19.95–$28.50); fixed-price meal 180 F ($34.20) at lunch, 190–250 F ($36.10–$47.50) at dinner. AE, DC, MC, V. Daily noon–2:30pm and 7:30–11pm. Closed two weeks in Aug. Métro: Les Halles. FRENCH.

No wonder the "divine Sarah" Bernhardt took many of her meals here. (That ceiling mural of cherubic chefs is said to have come from her summer home on an island off the Brittany coast.) The building dates from the time of Henri II and Catherine de Médici, but it wasn't a restaurant until the early 19th century. Owner Mme Saladin-Terrail, known as Kouikette, has improved the style without disturbing the atmosphere. The original Louis-Philippe decor is carefully preserved—two

Restaurants: 1st Arrondissement

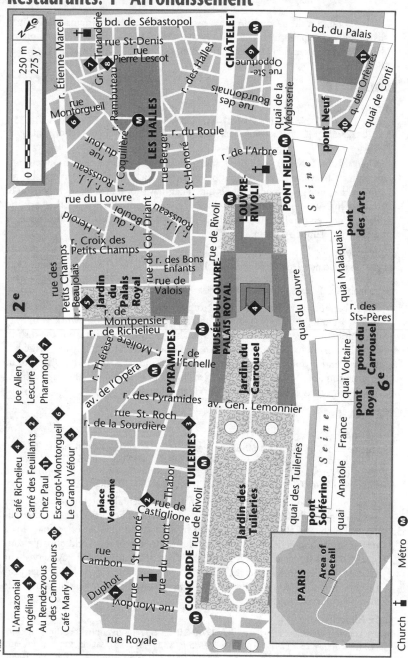

L'Amazonial 9
Angélina 3
Au Rendezvous
des Camionneurs 10
Café Marly 4

Café Richelieu 4
Carré des Feuillants 2
Chez Paul 11
Escargot-Montorgueil 6
Le Grand Véfour 5

Joe Allen 8
Lescure 1
Pharamond 7

250 m
275 y
0

bd. de Sébastopol
rue St-Denis
rue Pierre Lescot
rue St-Denis
r. Truanderie
Gr. Truanderie
r. Rambuteau
rue Montorgueil
r. Étienne Marcel
LES HALLES
r. des Halles
r. du Roule
rue Berger
rue du Jour
r. Coquillière
r. J. J. Rousseau
rue du Louvre
r. Hérold
r. Croix des Petits Champs
rue des Petits Champs
r. Beaujolais
Jardin du Palais Royal
r. de Montpensier
r. de Richelieu
rue de Valois
rue de Col. Driant
r. des Bons Enfants
r. du Bouloi
r. J. J. Rousseau
r. St-Honoré
r. de l'Arbre
rue de Rivoli
PONT NEUF
LOUVRE-RIVOLI
CHÂTELET
rue Ste-Opportune
quai de la Mégisserie
PARIS
Area of Detail

bd. du Palais
q. des Orfèvres
quai de Conti
Pont Neuf
pont des Arts
Seine

MUSÉE-DU-LOUVRE
PALAIS ROYAL
PYRAMIDES
r. de l'Echelle
r. Molière
r. Thérèse
av. de l'Opéra
r. des Pyramides
rue St-Roch
r. de la Sourdière
rue Thabor
place Vendôme
rue de Castiglione
rue Cambon
St Honoré
rue du Mont Thabor
rue Duphot
rue Mondovi
rue Royale
CONCORDE
rue de Rivoli
TUILERIES
Jardin du Carrousel
av. Gen. Lemonnier
Jardin des Tuileries
quai des Tuileries
pont Solférino
quai Anatole France
pont Royal
pont du Carrousel
quai Voltaire
quai du Louvre
quai Malaquais
r. des Sts-Pères
Seine

2ᵉ
6ᵉ

M Métro
✝■ Church

dining rooms on the ground floor have starched Breton lace curtains and gaslight fixtures on the sepia-toned walls. The escargot (snail) of Les Halles reigns supreme here. We also recommend the feathery turbot soufflé. The dessert specialty is crêpes flambées.

MODERATE

⑨ Chez Paul
15 place Dauphine, 1er. ☎ 1/43-54-21-48. Reservations required. Main courses 88–135 F ($16.70–$25.65). MC, V. Tues–Sun noon–2:30pm and 7:30–10:15pm. Métro: Pont-Neuf. FRENCH.

When this century was young this address was given with strictest confidence to first-time Paris visitors. Since then it has become a cliché for the hidden little bistro, serving the same good food it always did. That may—or may not—be what you're looking for. Why not sample the chicken liver grandmother style, then try the filet mignon en papillote (cooked in parchment)? The dessert specialty is baba à la confiture flambé au rhum.

Pharamond
24 rue de la Grande-Truanderie, 1er. ☎ 1/42-33-06-72. Reservations required. Main courses 90–150 F ($17.10–$28.50). AE, DC, MC, V. Mon 7:30–10:45pm, Tues–Sat 12:30–2:30pm and 7:30–10:45pm. Métro: Les Halles. FRENCH.

The restaurant, part of an 1832 neo-Norman structure, sits on a Les Halles street once frequented by the vagabonds of Paris. For an appetizer, work your way through half a dozen Breton oysters (available October to April). But the dish to order here is tripes à la mode de Caen, served over a charcoal burner. Tripe is a delicacy, and if you're at all experimental you'll find no better introduction to it. Try the coquilles St-Jacques au cidre (scallops in cider) if you're not up to tripe. Another specialty is the grillade du feu de bois for two.

INEXPENSIVE

Angélina
226 rue de Rivoli, 1er. ☎ 1/42-60-82-00. Reservations accepted for lunch, not for teatime. Pot of tea for one 31 F ($5.90); sandwiches and salads 35–58 F ($6.65–$11); *plats du jour* 90–115 F ($17.10–$21.85). AE, MC, V. Daily 9:30am–7pm (lunch 11:45am–3pm). Closed most of Aug. Métro: Tuileries. TEA, SANDWICHES, SALADS, PLATTERS.

In the high-rent district near the Paris Inter-Continental Hotel, this *salon de thé* combines glitter, bougeois respectability, and hysteria. The carpets are red, the ceilings are high, and the gilded accessories have the right amount of patina—for a view (over tea and delicate sandwiches) of the lionesses of the world of haute couture, this place has no equal. Overwrought waitresses bearing silver trays serve light platters, pastries, drinks, and tea or coffee at tiny marble-top tables. Lunch usually offers a salad and a daily *plat du jour*. Examples are chicken salad, sole meunière, and poached salmon.

Café Richelieu
In the Louvre's Richelieu Wing, 1er. ☎ 1/40-20-53-63. Reservations recommended for meals. Café au lait 23 F ($4.35); pastries 20–65 F ($3.80–$12.35); salads, sandwiches, and platters 30–75 F ($5.70–$14.25). AE, DC, MC, V. Mon and Wed 9am–10pm, Tues and Thurs–Sun 9am–6pm. Métro: Palais-Royal–Musée-du-Louvre. INTERNATIONAL.

While in the Louvre admiring its collection, consider stopping for a pick-me-up in the most unusual museum restaurant in Europe. Occupying three grandiose rooms of the premises formerly occupied by the French finance minister, the café boasts lavish 19th-century adornments and a view over the forecourt's glass pyramid. It's officially defined as a *café de haute gamme* (upscale café) rather than a restaurant, and the menu is limited to coffees, pastries (by legendary pastrymaker Lenôtre), salads, sandwiches, and simple platters. Far more interesting, however, is the arch and often witty chit-chat you'll overhear in this setting rife with art politics, cultural pride, and bureaucratic intrigue. The carpets, tables, chairs, and computer-generated artworks are deliberately modern contrasts (by well-known designer Jean-Michel Wilmotte and photographer Francis Giacobetti) to the ornate historic walls they hang on. Note that a visit here requires you to pay the Louvre's admission charge—hopefully, you'll also soak in some of the art on your way to and from the café.

Joe Allen

30 rue Pierre-Lescot, 1er. ☎ **1/42-36-70-13.** Reservations recommended for dinner. Main courses 53–134 F ($10.05–$25.45). AE, MC, V. Daily noon–2am. Métro: Les Halles. AMERICAN.

Joe Allen long ago invaded Les Halles with his hamburger. Though the New York restaurateur admits "it's a silly idea," it works. After he set the place up, most of his work went into creating the American burger, easily the best in Paris. While listening to the jukebox, you can order the savory black-bean soup, spicy chili, juicy sirloin steak, barbecued spareribs, or apple pie. And try the spinach salad topped with creamy roquefort dressing and sprinkled with crunchy bits of bacon and fresh mushrooms.

Joe claims that his saloon is the only place in Paris that serves an authentic New York cheesecake or real pecan pie. Thanks to French chocolate, he feels the brownies here are better than those made in the States. Giving the brownies tough competition is the California chocolate-mousse pie, along with the strawberry Romanoff and coconut-cream pie. Thanksgiving dinner here is becoming a tradition (you'll need a reservation way in advance). On a regular night, if you haven't made a reservation for dinner, expect to wait at the New York bar for at least 30 minutes.

Ⓢ Lescure

7 rue de Mondovi, 1er. ☎ **1/42-60-18-91.** Reservations not accepted. Main courses 38–100 F ($7.20–$19); four-course fixed-price menu 100 F ($19). MC, V. Mon–Fri noon–2:15pm and 7–10pm. Closed two weeks in Aug. Métro: Concorde. FRENCH.

This mini-bistro, open since 1919, is a major discovery because reasonably priced restaurants near place de la Concorde are difficult to find. The tables on the sidewalk are tiny and there isn't much room inside, but what this place does have is rustic charm. The kitchen is wide open, and the aroma of drying bay leaves, salami, and garlic pigtails hanging from the ceiling fills the room. Expect *cuisine bourgeoise*

Impressions

Where shall I begin with the endless delights
Of this Eden of milliners, monkies and sights—
This dear busy place, where there's nothing transacting
But dressing and dinnering, dancing and acting?

—Thomas Moore (1818)

here—nothing overly thrilling, just substantial, hearty fare. Perhaps begin with a pâté en croûte. Main-course house specialties include confit de canard and salmon in green sauce. A favorite dessert is one of the fruit tarts.

2ND ARRONDISSEMENT
MODERATE

Chez Georges
1 rue du Mail, 2e. ☎ **1/42-60-07-11.** Reservations required. Main courses 130–150 F ($24.70–$28.50). AE, MC, V. Mon–Sat 12:30–2pm and 7:30–10pm. Métro: Bourse. FRENCH.

This bistro is something of a local landmark, established in 1964 in the neighborhood of the Bourse. Naturally, at lunch it's heavily patronized by stock-exchange members. The owner serves what he calls *la cuisine typiquement bourgeoise*—"food from our grandmère in the provinces." Waiters bring around bowls of appetizers, such as celery remoulade, to get you started. You can follow with pot-au-feu (beef simmered with vegetables), classic cassoulet, or beef braised in red wine. Beaujolais goes great with this hearty yet not imaginative food.

INEXPENSIVE

⑤ Le Drouot
103 rue Richelieu, 2e. ☎ **1/42-96-68-23.** Reservations accepted only for groups of 20 or more. Main courses 35–60 F ($6.65–$11.40). MC, V. Daily 11:45am–3pm and 6:30–10pm. Métro: Richelieu-Drouot. FRENCH.

One of the best budget restaurants in the 2nd arrondissement, Le Drouot is usually packed with economy-minded Parisians who know where to go for well-prepared food. Almost in the tradition of the famous bouillons at the turn of the century, a breadman comes around to see that your plate is full. For an appetizer, you might try ham from the Ardennes or artichoke bottom vinaigrette. Among the main courses, we'd recommend pepper steak with french fries or the filet of turbot in hollandaise. Chocolate mousse is the favored dessert. The service is hectic and not always friendly, but the regulars expect that.

3RD ARRONDISSEMENT
EXPENSIVE

L'Ami Louis
32 rue de Vertbois, 3e. ☎ **1/48-87-77-48.** Reservations required. Main courses 180–270 F ($34.20–$51.30). AE, MC, DC, V. Wed–Sun noon–2pm and 8–11pm. Closed July 10–Aug 25. Métro: Temple. FRENCH.

The neighborhood is among Paris's least fashionable and the restaurant's facade has seen better days, but L'Ami Louis has always fulfilled a yearning in the Parisian soul for a return to country virtues. It was established in 1924 by someone named Louis, who sold the bistro in the 1930s to M. Antoine, who became a legend for intimidating the grandest of his guests. Under his direction, L'Ami Louis became one of Paris's most famous brasseries because of its excellent food, copious portions, and earthy old-fashioned decor. The Master died in 1987, but his traditions are fervently maintained here. Amid a "brown gravy" decor whose walls retain the smoky patina no one has scrubbed off since their construction in the 1920s, you'll dine at marble-top tables. Menu items include suckling lamb, pheasant, venison, confit of duckling, and foie gras.

Restaurants: 2nd Arrondissement

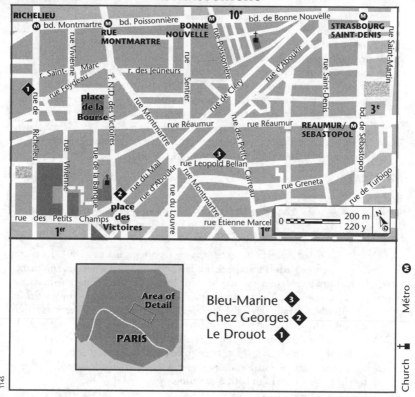

Bleu-Marine **3**
Chez Georges **2**
Le Drouot **1**

Métro **Ⓜ**

Church **✚■**

INEXPENSIVE

L'Ambassade d'Auvergne

22 rue de Grenier St-Lazare, 3e. ☎ **1/42-72-31-22.** Reservations recommended. Main courses 82–120 F ($15.60–$22.80). MC, V. Daily noon–2pm and 7:30–11pm. Métro: Rambuteau. FRENCH.

In an obscure district, this rustic tavern serves the hearty *cuisine bourgeoise* of Auvergne. You enter through a busy bar, with heavy oak beams, hanging hams, and ceramic plates. Rough wheat bread is stacked in baskets, and rush-seated ladderback chairs are placed at tables covered with bright cloths, stemware, mills to grind your own salt and pepper, and a jug of mustard. Specialties include cassoulet with lentils, pot-au-feu, confit de canard, and codfish casserole. Some specials are featured on one day of the week only. For a side dish, we recommend aligot, a medley of fresh potatoes, garlic, and Cantal cheese.

4TH ARRONDISSEMENT
VERY EXPENSIVE

✪ L'Ambroisie

9 place des Vosges, 4e. ☎ **1/42-78-51-45.** Reservations required. Main courses 190–380 F ($36.10–$72.20). AE, MC, V. Tues–Sat noon–1:30pm and 8–9:30pm. Métro: St-Paul. FRENCH.

Bernard Pacaud is one of the most talented chefs in Paris. He trained at the prestigious Vivarois before deciding to strike out on his own, first on the Left Bank and now at this ideal location in Le Marais. The restaurant occupies an early 17th-century town house built for the duc de Luynes. You'll dine in either of two dining rooms with high ceilings and a decor vaguely inspired by an Italian palazzo. In summer, there's outdoor seating as well. The dishes change seasonally but may include feuillantine of crayfish tails with sesame seeds and curry sauce; filet of turbot braised with celery and celeriac, served with a julienne of black truffles; and one of our favorites, poulard de Bresse demi-deuil hommage à la Mère Brazier, roasted with black truffles and truffled vegetables. An award-winning dessert is tarte fine sablée served with bitter chocolate and mocha-flavored ice cream.

MODERATE

Bofinger
5–7 rue de la Bastille, 4e. ☎ 1/42-72-87-82. Reservations recommended. Main courses 76–146 F ($14.45–$27.75). AE, DC, MC, V. Mon–Fri noon–3pm and 6:30pm–1am, Sat–Sun noon–1am. Métro: Bastille. FRENCH/ALSATIAN.

This is Paris's oldest Alsatian brasserie, tracing its origins back to 1864. Its decor is such a part of the Paris landscape that it has been classified a historic landmark. At night, many opera-goers venture here for beer and sauerkraut. The brasserie offers not only excellent Alsatian fare but also hearty portions served by waiters in floor-length white aprons. The chef prepares a different main dish every day; one Wednesday night the special was savory stew in casserole (cassolette toulousain). Most guests order the choucroute formidable (sauerkraut), complete with sausages, smoked bacon, and pork chops. The fixed-price menu is the most appealing in the neighborhood, containing such choices as foie gras and magrêt de canard. For dessert, try the apple tart or fresh berries of spring.

Marc-Annibal de Coconnas
2 bis place des Vosges, 4e. ☎ 1/42-78-58-16. Reservations required. Main courses 85–145 F ($16.15–$27.55); fixed-price menu 160 F ($30.40). AE, DC, MC, V. Wed–Sun noon–2pm and 7:45–10:15pm. Métro: Bastille or St-Paul. FRENCH.

Named after a French rake whose peccadillos with members of the royal family once scandalized place des Vosges, this restaurant features a Louis XIII decor of high-backed chairs and elegantly rustic accessories. Chef Claude Terrail (who also owns La Tour d'Argent) serves a superb cuisine. Menu items change frequently but might include a soup of scallops with anise; foie gras; a pastillade of crayfish; rack of veal en papillote with crème fraîche, white wine, and mushrooms; and turbot poached in essence of almonds and served on a bed of fennel.

INEXPENSIVE

Le Brise-Miche
10 rue Brise-Miche, 4e. ☎ 1/42-78-44-11. Reservations recommended. Main courses 59–115 F ($11.20–$21.85); fixed-price menu 70–145 F ($13.30–$27.55). AE, DC, MC, V. Daily 8am–midnight (full menu available daily noon–midnight). Métro: Rambuteau, Hôtel-de-Ville, or Châtelet–Les Halles. FRENCH.

Whimsical, sometimes chaotic, and firmly entrenched in the avant-garde aesthetic that surrounds its neighbor, the Centre Pompidou, this is one of the most appealing low-cost restaurants in the district. In nice weather, tables and chairs overlook the dozen or so spinning, spitting, and bobbing characters in the waters of the Stravinsky fountain. Each table is provided with a round loaf of bread, crayons,

Restaurants: 3rd & 4th Arrondissements

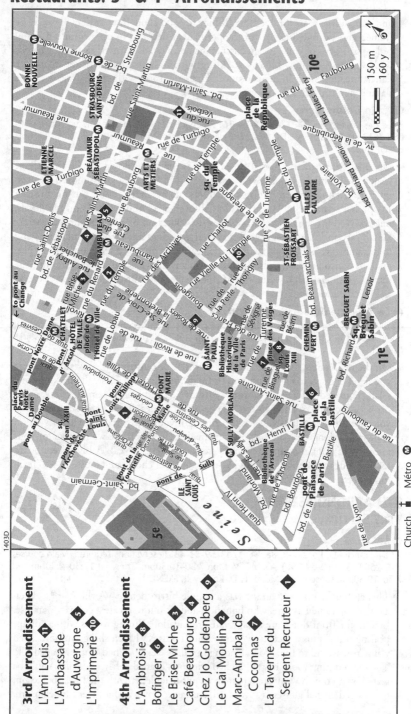

3rd Arrondissement

L'Ami Louis
L'Ambassade
d'Auvergne 5
L'Imprimerie 10

4th Arrondissement

L'Ambroisie 8
Bofinger 6
Le Brise-Miche 3
Café Beaubourg 4
Chez Jo Goldenberg 9
Le Gai Moulin 2
Marc-Annibal de
Coconnas 7
La Taverne du
Sergent Recruteur 1

Church   Métro

and paper place mats for doodling (if they're good enough, your drawings may be framed and exhibited as part of the permanent decor). No one will mind if you order just a glass of wine. Menu choices include a range of "maxi salads," tagliatelle with smoked salmon, filet of duckling with peaches, half chicken roasted à l'ancienne, and steak in pepper sauce. The tarte Tatin with crème fraîche can be flambéed in Calvados if you wish.

Chez Jo Goldenberg

7 rue des Rosiers, 4e. ☎ **1/48-87-20-16.** Reservations recommended. Main courses 70–85 F ($13.30–$16.15). AE, DC, MC, V. Daily noon–1am. Métro: St-Paul. JEWISH/CENTRAL EUROPEAN.

On this "Street of the Rose Bushes" this is the best-known restaurant. Albert Goldenberg, the doyen of Jewish restaurateurs in Paris, long ago moved to a restaurant in choicer surroundings (at 69 av. de Wagram, 17e), but his brother Joseph has remained at the original establishment. Dining here is on two levels, one reserved for nonsmokers. Look for the collection of samovars and the white fantail pigeon in a wicker cage. Interesting paintings and strolling musicians add to the ambience. The carpe farcie (stuffed carp) is a preferred selection, but the beef goulash is also good. We also like the eggplant moussaka and the pastrami. The menu also offers Israeli wines, but M. Goldenberg admits that they're not as good as French wine.

⑤ La Taverne du Sergent Recruteur

41 rue St-Louis-en-l'Ile, 4e. ☎ **1/43-54-75-42.** Reservations recommended. All-you-can-eat menu 185 F ($35.15). AE, MC, V. Mon–Sat 7pm–midnight (last order). Métro: Pont-Marie. FRENCH.

On the main street of the Ile St-Louis is this 17th-century–style restaurant where you'll get enough to eat to last you through the next day. First, the makings of a salad are placed before you: carrots, radishes (red and black), fennel, celery, green peppers, cucumbers, and hard-boiled eggs. Next comes a huge basket of sausages—you slice off as much as you wish. A bottle of wine (rosé, red, or white) is set on your table, along with a crock of homemade pâté. Then the waiter asks for your selection of a main course—perhaps steak, chicken, or veal. A big cheese board follows. But that's not the end of it—you can select chocolate mousse or ice cream for dessert.

8TH ARRONDISSEMENT
VERY EXPENSIVE

✪ Lasserre

17 av. Franklin-D.-Roosevelt, 8e. ☎ **1/43-59-53-43.** Reservations required. Main courses 190–250 F ($36.10–$47.50). AE, MC, V. Mon 7:30–10:30pm, Tues–Sat 12:30–2:30pm and 7:30–10:30pm. Closed Aug. Métro: F.-D.-Roosevelt. FRENCH.

This elegant deluxe restaurant was a simple bistro before World War II. Then along came René Lasserre, who bought it and set out to create a culinary paradise. Behind the front doors are two private ground-floor dining rooms with a "disappearing wall," plus a reception lounge with Louis XVI furnishings and brocaded walls. You ascend to the second landing in a little elevator lined with brocaded silk. The main dining room has tall arched windows draped softly with silk. You'll be seated on a Louis XV salon chair at an exquisite table set with the finest porcelain, gold-edged crystal glasses, a silver bird, a ceramic dove, and a silver candelabrum.

Restaurants: 8th Arrondissement

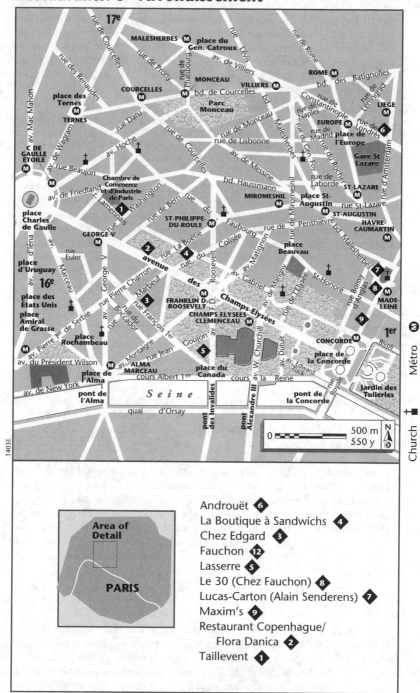

Androuët 6
La Boutique à Sandwichs 4
Chez Edgard 3
Fauchon 12
Lasserre 5
Le 30 (Chez Fauchon) 8
Lucas-Carton (Alain Senderens) 7
Maxim's 9
Restaurant Copenhague/
   Flora Danica 2
Taillevent 1

The ceiling, painted blue with fleecy-white clouds, is pulled back in fair weather to reveal the sky. We suggest you begin with the blanc de sandre (zander) à la nage d'estrilles. From among the fish dishes, choose the rissolles of crayfish with essence of green tomatoes. For dessert, try a parfait aux noisettes (hazelnuts) grillées, with a honey-flavored sabayon. The wine cellar, with some 180,000 bottles, is one of Paris's most remarkable.

✪ Lucas-Carton (Alain Senderens)
9 place de la Madeleine, 8e. ☎ **1/42-65-22-90.** Reservations required several days ahead for lunch, several weeks ahead for dinner. Main courses 300–700 F ($57–$133); fixed-price lunch 375 F ($71.25); *menu dégustation* 1,500–1,900 F ($285–$361). AE, MC, V. Mon–Fri noon–2:30pm and 8–10:15pm, Sat 8–10:15pm. Closed three weeks in Aug. Métro: Madeleine. FRENCH.

This landmark restaurant was designed by an Englishman named Lucas and a talented French chef, François Carton. Since Senderens has taken over as restaurateur, he's added some welcome modern touches. The two dining rooms downstairs and the private rooms upstairs are decorated with mirrors, fragrant bouquets, and wood paneling that's probably been polished weekly since 1900. Every dish is influenced by the creative flair of Alain Senderens. Menu items change seasonally and include ravioli aux truffes, foie gras with cabbage, vanilla-flavored lobster, duckling Apicius (roasted with honey and spices), pastillade of rabbit, and a wonderful millefeuille with vanilla sauce. Senderens is always searching for new creations, so by the time you visit there'll probably be fresh additions. His *menu dégustation* includes a selection of grand French wines—hence the high tab.

Maxim's
3 rue Royale, 8e. ☎ **1/42-65-27-94.** Reservations required. Main courses 250–490 F ($47.50–$93.10). AE, DC, MC, V. Mon–Sat 12:30–2pm and 7:30–11:30pm. Métro: Concorde. FRENCH.

Maxim's is the world's most legendary restaurant. It even has clones in cities like New York, Beijing, and Tokyo. It preserves the era of belle époque decor and was a favorite of Edward VII, then the prince of Wales. The restaurant was the setting for *The Merry Widow*, so you can be sure the orchestra will play that tune at least once each evening. Much later, Louis Jourdan took Leslie Caron to the restaurant in the musical *Gigi*. Today, rich tourists from around the world are likely to occupy once-fabled tables where Onassis wooed Callas. Clothing industry giant Pierre Cardin took over the restaurant in 1981. Although not always available, Billi-By Soup, made with mussels, white wine, cream (of course), chopped onions, celery, parsley, and coarsely ground pepper is a classic opener. Another favorite is sole Albert (named after the late maître d'hôtel), flavored with chopped herbs and breadcrumbs, plus a large glass of vermouth. For dessert, try the tarte Tatin.

✪ Taillevent
15 rue Lamennais, 8e. ☎ **1/45-63-39-94.** Reservations required weeks, even months, in advance for lunch and dinner. Main courses 220–380 F ($41.80–$72.20). AE, DC, MC, V. Mon–Fri noon–2:30pm and 7–10pm. Closed Aug. Métro: George-V. FRENCH.

Dine in grand 18th-century style in this town house just off the Champs-Elysées. In 1946, when owner Jean Claude Vrinat's father opened the doors, he established one of Paris's outstanding restaurants. The wines are superb and the service is impeccable. Under the direction of chef Philippe Legendre, menus are deftly balanced between traditional and modern cuisine. You might begin with aspic de foie gras

> ### 🎪 Family-Friendly Restaurants
>
> **Androuët**   *(see p. 147)* If your kids love cheese, they'll get the fill of a lifetime at this longtime favorite. Here cheese is cooked in all the dishes—especially delectable is the ravioli stuffed with goat cheese.
>
> **La Boutique à Sandwichs**   *(see p. 148)* Here you'll find the largest selection of sandwiches in Paris. Concoctions come in almost every known variety.
>
> **Joe Allen**   *(see p. 139)* Joe Allen delivers everything from chili to chocolate-mousse pie. This place in Les Halles serves real American cuisine, including hamburgers.
>
> **Crémerie-Restaurant Polidor**   *(see p. 132)* One of the most popular restaurants on the Left Bank, this reasonably priced dining room is so family-friendly it even calls its food *cuisine familiale.* This might be the best place to introduce your child to French cuisine.

(dices of liver and veal sweetbreads in aspic jelly with fine slivers of carrots and truffles). Main-dish specialties may include cassolette de langoustines, agneau aux trois cuissons (feet, breast, and tenderloin of lamb with various sauces), followed by fondant aux deux parfumes (an almond-toffee Bavarian cream covered with chocolate). Taillevent's wine list is one of the best in the city.

EXPENSIVE

Restaurant Copenhague / Flora Danica

143 av. des Champs-Elysées, 8e. ☎ 1/43-59-20-41. Reservations recommended. Main courses 130–280 F ($24.70–$53.20). AE, DC, MC, V. Restaurant Copenhague, Mon–Sat noon–2pm and 7:15–10:30pm (closed Aug and Jan 1–7); Flora Danica, daily noon–2pm and 7:15–11pm. Métro: George-V. DANISH.

The specialties of Denmark are served with style and flair at the "Maison du Danemark." In many ways, this is probably the best restaurant along the Champs-Elysées, with a terrace for midsummer dining. There are two dining areas: the street-level Flora Danica and the more formal Restaurant Copenhague upstairs. Try aquavit as an apéritif and ignore the wine list in favor of Carlsberg or Tuborg. Menu items include a terrine of foie gras, smoked salmon, a selection of fresh shrimp, and open-face sandwiches. The house specialty is a platter of délices Scandinaves, composed of the many seafood and dairy specialties the Danes prepare perfectly.

MODERATE

Androuët

41 rue d'Amsterdam, 8e. ☎ 1/48-74-26-93. Reservations required. Main courses 90–280 F ($17.10–$53.20); fixed-price meal 230 F ($43.70) at lunch, 195 F ($37.05) at dinner; *dégustation de fromages* 250 F ($47.50). AE, DC, MC, V. Mon–Sat noon–3pm and 7:30–10pm. Métro: St-Lazare or Liège. FRENCH.

Brightly lit and decorated in pastels, this is one of the most unusual restaurants in the world, because cheese is the basic ingredient in most dishes. It all began in World War I, when founder M. Androuët started inviting favored guests down to his cellar to sample cheese and good wine. The idea caught on. Today Androuet isn't merely chic—it's an institution. Cheese experts, of course, flock here; we've heard one claim that he could tell what the goat ate by the cheese made from its milk. For a first course, the ravioles de chèvre frais (ravioli stuffed with fresh goat cheese) is wonderful. A good main dish is filet de boeuf cotentin (beef filet with roquefort sauce, flambéed with Calvados). True cheese-lovers order the dégustation de fromages affinés dans nos caves (a sampling of cheese from our cellars). There are as many as 120 varieties.

Chez Edgard

4 rue Marbeuf, 8e. ☎ **1/47-20-51-15.** Reservations required. Main courses 95–180 F ($18.05–$34.20). AE, DC, MC, V. Mon–Sat noon–3pm and 7pm–12:30am. Métro: F.-D.-Roosevelt. FRENCH.

Chic residents regard this as their favorite neighborhood place, and ebullient owner Paul Benmussa makes it a point to welcome them during their frequent visits as if they were members of his extended family. (If you're not known here, you might merit a weak smile.) Conversation in this scarlet-and-black restaurant can be noisier than in less expensive restaurants. Specialties include breast of duckling, rouget with basil in puff pastry, salmon tartare, and several terrines. There's also a range of well-prepared meat dishes. In winter, seafood and oysters are shipped from Brittany. The ice-cream sundaes (listed with other desserts on a special menu) are particularly delectable.

Le 30 (Chez Fauchon)

30 place de la Madeleine, 8e. ☎ **1/47-42-56-58.** Reservations recommended, especially at lunch. Main courses 130–220 F ($24.70–$41.80). AE, DC, MC, V. Mon–Sat 12:15–2:30pm and 7:30–10:30pm. Métro: Madeleine. FRENCH.

In 1990, one of Europe's most legendary delicatessens (Fauchon) transformed one of its upper rooms into an elegant pastel-colored showplace dotted with neo-Grecian columns and accessories. It caught on immediately as the preferred lunch restaurant for many of the bankers, stockbrokers, and merchants in the neighborhood. Menu items, prepared with the freshest ingredients available from the displays downstairs, might include cassoulet of lobster with a basil-flavored shellfish sauce, curried fried sweetbreads, suprême of sea bass with fennel, and luscious cheeses and pastries. This is our favorite of the four restaurants Fauchon operates along place de la Madeleine. Other choices include La Trattoria (no. 26) for upscale Italian food; Le Bistro du Caviar (no. 30), where a *chariot de caviar* dispenses epicurean samples of foie gras and smoked salmon for 190 F ($36.10) to 350 F ($66.50) and every imaginable type of caviar for between 300 F ($57) and 550 F ($104.50) per portion. Fauchon also operates a seafood bistro, Bistro de la Mar, at no. 6. All three share the same phone number: 47-42-60-11.

INEXPENSIVE

Ⓢ La Boutique à Sandwichs

12 rue du Colisée, 8e. ☎ **1/43-59-56-69.** Reservations recommended. Main courses 36–75 F ($6.80–$14.25); sandwiches from 15 F ($2.85). MC. Mon–Sat 11:45am–1am. Closed Aug 1–20. Métro: F.-D.-Roosevelt. FRENCH.

Run by Alsatian brothers Hubert and Claude Schick, La Boutique is a good place to order delectable sandwiches in many imaginative varieties. You'll find this marriage of American and French tastes a quarter of a block from the Champs-Elysées, with bare wooden tables and colored mats. There are at least two dozen sandwich concoctions on the menu, as well as light snacks or "plate meals," some with distinctly Swiss and Alsatian overtones. Special hot plates include pickelfleisch raclette valaisanne à gogo—a wheel of cheese (part of it melted) is taken to your table and scraped right onto your plate; accompanying it are pickles and boiled potatoes. For dessert, try the apple strudel.

3 Elsewhere in Paris

LEFT BANK
14TH ARRONDISSEMENT
Moderate

La Cagouille

Rue de l'Ouest at place Constantin-Brancusi, 14e. ☎ 1/43-22-09-01. Reservations required. Main courses 110–175 F ($20.90–$33.25); fixed-price menus 150–250 F ($28.50–$47.50). AE, DC, MC, V. Daily 12:30–2pm and 7:30–10pm. Closed Dec 15–Jan 1. Métro: Gaité. SEAFOOD.

Near the Tour du Montparnasse, Gérard Allemandou, a native of Cognac, creates his specialties in this thriving restaurant. You can sample a splendid selection of cognacs from small properties, but that's not why everyone comes here: The major draw is some of the freshest and most reasonably priced fish in Paris. The fish, such as salmon steak, is usually slightly underdone and served without a sauce (a dieter's dream come true). The huge red mullet is grilled to perfection. Ungar-nished barnacles, grilled snapper, mussels sautéed in a cast-iron pan—it's all here. Peppered butter and sea salt are trademarks of the place. Two specialties are escabeche de petits poissons (a stewpot of fresh fish) and effilochée de raie avec sauce gribiche (a filet of stingray with a vinaigrette, capers, and fines herbes sauce).

RIGHT BANK
9TH & 10TH ARRONDISSEMENTS
Expensive

Restaurant Opéra

In the Grand Hotel Inter-Continental, place de l'Opéra, 9e. ☎ 1/40-07-30-10. Reservations recommended. Main courses 158–235 F ($30–$44.65); fixed-price menu 325 F ($61.75). AE, DC, MC, V. Mon–Fri noon–2:30pm and 7–11pm. Métro: Opéra. FRENCH.

If you opt for a meal here, your predecessors will have included Dalí, Josephine Baker, Dietrich, Chevalier, Callas, and Chagall, who often came here while working on the famous ceiling of the nearby Opéra Garnier. On August 25, 1944, de Gaulle placed this restaurant's first food order in a newly freed Paris—a cold plate to go. Today you can enjoy a before-dinner drink in a lavishly ornate bar before heading for a table in what some diners compare to a gilded jewel box. Appetizer choices might include lobster bisque with champagne or deep-fried frogs' legs with tomato and cauliflower in the Greek style. Among the fish selections are lightly salted cod with green-olive cream and filet of sea bass with herb-flavored crust. Main dishes may be breast of Challans duckling and roast rack of veal for two. The desserts are sumptuous, like chestnut cake with a hazelnut milk sauce.

Restaurants: Elsewhere on the Right Bank

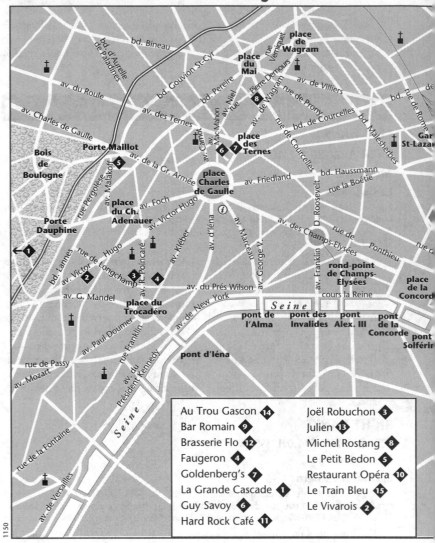

Au Trou Gascon ⓮

Bar Romain ❾

Brasserie Flo ⓬

Faugeron ❹

Goldenberg's ❼

La Grande Cascade ❶

Guy Savoy ❻

Hard Rock Café ⓫

Joël Robuchon ❸

Julien ⓭

Michel Rostang ❽

Le Petit Bedon ❺

Restaurant Opéra ❿

Le Train Bleu ⓯

Le Vivarois ❷

Moderate

Bar Romain

6 rue de Caumartin, 9e. ☎ 1/47-42-98-04. Reservations recommended for lunch and late-night suppers; otherwise, not required. Main courses 100–120 F ($19–$22.80). AE, DC, MC, V. Mon–Sat noon–1am. Métro: Opéra or Madeleine. FRENCH.

This began in 1905 as a wine bar where the chic and important mingled with the actors and comedians from the arrondissement's cabarets and music halls. The bar

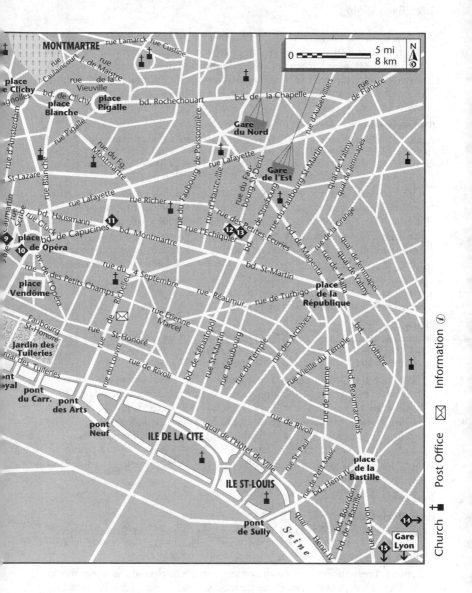

was richly fitted with Carrara marble, mahogany paneling, and 13 murals by Surand, winner of the coveted Grand Prix de Rome. Seven of these panels remain, fixed in their turn-of-the-century gloom above the bar. The clientele that bustles around below includes loyal neighborhood bankers and merchants, a scattering of fashion models, and many of the musical stars and agents involved at the Théâtre de l'Olympia around the corner. After 5pm the street level is reserved exclusively for drinking and diners move into a basement room outfitted like a dining car on

Church ■   Post Office ⊠   Information ⓘ

a turn-of-the-century train. Run by brother and sister Jacques and Monique Bescond, Bar Romain serves savory platters that emerge miraculously from probably the smallest kitchen in Paris. Most dishes seem to be from time-honored recipes handed down by someone's grandmother and include smoked salmon, chateaubriand, entrecôte, soup of the day, terrine maison, and a specialty version of steak tartare.

Brasserie Flo

7 cour des Petites-Ecuries, 10e. ☎ 1/47-70-13-59. Reservations recommended. Main courses 96–113 F ($18.25–$21.45); fixed-price menu 185 F ($35.15); fixed-price late-night supper (served only after 10pm) 109 F ($20.70). AE, DC, MC, V. Daily noon–3pm and 7pm–1:30am. Métro: Château-d'Eau or Strasbourg–St-Denis. FRENCH.

This restaurant in a remote area is a bit hard to find, but once you arrive (after walking through passageway after passageway), you'll see that fin-de-siècle Paris lives on. The restaurant was established in 1860 and has changed its decor very little since. You may expect high prices, but you'll be pleasantly surprised. The house specialty is la formidable choucroute (a heaping mound of sauerkraut surrounded by boiled ham, bacon, and sausage) for two. Look for the *plats du jour*, ranging from roast pigeon to fricassée of veal with sorrel. Escargots are a traditional appetizer. Other specialties include fricassée of chicken with morels and foie gras served with apples in the Normandy style.

Julien

16 rue du Faubourg St-Denis, 10e. ☎ 1/47-70-12-06. Reservations required. Main courses 100–130 F ($19–$24.70); fixed-price lunch (and after 10pm) 109 F ($20.70). AE, DC, MC, V. Daily noon–3pm and 7pm–1:30am. Métro: Strasbourg–St-Denis. FRENCH.

This is one of the most sumptuous restaurants in Paris. The building was conceived in 1889 for the Universal Exposition, though it didn't open until 1903. Until 1976 it was a famous working-class eatery. Today it has been restored to its former elegance. The food is *cuisine bourgeoise*, but without the heavy sauces once used. The excellent appetizers include smoked salmon rillettes, duckling foie gras, and snails à la bourguignonne. Mussels poached in riesling also make a savory beginning. Then perhaps try grilled lobster flambéed with whisky, cassoulet, or fricassée of capon with morels.

Inexpensive

Hard Rock Café

14 bd. Montmartre, 9e. ☎ 1/42-46-10-00. Reservations not accepted. Sandwiches, salads, and platters 57–99 F ($10.85–$18.80); fixed-price lunch 69 F ($13.10). AE, MC, V. Daily 11:30am–2am. Métro: Rue-Montmartre or Richelieu-Drouot. AMERICAN.

Parisian Americaphiles soak up the ambience and nostalgia of the recent past at this French branch of what might be the most successful restaurant chain ever. Like its counterparts, which now stretch from London to Reykjavik, the Hard Rock Café offers a collection of rock 'n' roll classics. These are pumped out at reasonable levels at lunch and at less reasonable levels at night. The crowds love both the music and the juicy steaks, hamburgers, veggie burgers, salads, and heaping platters of informal French-inspired food. As you dine, scan the high-ceilinged room for such venerated objects as the tuxedo worn by Buddy Holly, Jim Morrison's leather jacket, Jimi Hendrix's psychedelic vest, and the black-and-gold bustier worn by Madonna during a Paris concert.

12TH ARRONDISSEMENT
Expensive
Au Trou Gascon

40 rue Taine, 12e. ☎ **1/43-44-34-26.** Reservations required. Main courses 158–220 F ($30–$41.80); fixed-price menus 180–380 F ($34.20–$72.20). AE, DC, MC, V. Mon–Fri noon–2pm and 7:30–10pm. Closed Aug. Métro: Daumesnil. FRENCH.

This popular spot's chef has an interesting story. One of the most acclaimed chefs in Paris, Alain Dutournier launched his career in southwestern Gascony, working in the kitchen with his mother and grandmother. His parents mortgaged the inn they owned to allow him to open a turn-of-the-century bistro in a rather unchic part of the 12th arrondissement. Soon word spread that Dutournier was a true artisan who practiced authentic modern French cooking. Today he has opened another restaurant in Paris. The owner's wife, Nicole, is there to greet you, and Dutournier has distinguished himself for his extensive cellar containing several little-known wines along with an array of Armagnacs. It's estimated that the cellar has some 700 varieties of wine. Here you get the true cuisine of Gascony—cassoulet, wild salmon with smoked bacon, foie gras, and Gascon ham farmer's style.

Moderate
Le Train Bleu

In the Gare de Lyon, 12e. ☎ **1/43-43-09-06.** Reservations recommended. Main courses 140–190 F ($26.60–$36.10); fixed-price menus 195–260 F ($37.05–$49.40). AE, DC, MC, V. Daily noon–2pm and 7–9:45pm (last order). Métro: Gare de Lyon. FRENCH.

To reach this restaurant, climb the ornate double staircase that faces the Gare de Lyon's grimy platforms. Both the restaurant and the station were built with the Grand Palais, Petit Palais, and pont Alexandre III for the 1900 World Exhibition. The station's architects designed a restaurant whose decor is now classified as a national artistic treasure. Inaugurated by the French president in 1901 and renovated and cleaned at great expense in 1992, the restaurant displays an army of bronze statues, a lavish frescoed ceiling, mosaics, mirrors, and old-fashioned banquettes. Each of the 41 belle époque murals celebrates the distant corners of the French-speaking world—the depictions of Marseille, Algiers, and the North African port of Sousse are particularly appealing. The service is attentive and efficient in case you must catch a train. The formally dressed staff brings steaming platters of soufflé or brill, escargots in chablis sauce, steak tartare, loin of lamb provençal, veal kidneys in mustard sauce, and rib of beef for two, followed by rum baba.

16TH ARRONDISSEMENT
Very Expensive
✪ Faugeron

52 rue de Longchamp, 16e. ☎ **1/47-04-24-53.** Reservations required. Main courses 180–260 F ($34.20–$49.40); fixed-price meal 290–650 F ($55.10–$123.50) at lunch, 550–650 F ($104.55–$123.55) at dinner. AE, MC, V. Mon–Fri 11:30am–2pm and 7:30–10pm, Sat 7:30–10pm. Closed Aug and Sat Oct–Mar. Métro: Trocadéro. FRENCH.

Chef Henri Faugeron is an inspired master of classic French cooking. He and his Austrian wife, Gerlinde, entertain a faithful list of gourmets, including artists, diplomats, and business executives. Faugeron established this restaurant many years ago in the Trocadéro district. Calling his cuisine "revolutionary," he is somewhat of a culinary researcher, and his menu always has one or two platters like leg of lamb baked seven hours or rack of hare in traditional French style. Much of his cooking depends on the season and whatever is fresh at the market.

✪ Joël Robuchon

59 av. Raymond-Poincaré, 16e. ☎ 1/47-27-12-27. Reservations required six to eight weeks in advance. Main courses 260–520 F ($49.40–$98.80); fixed-price menus 900–1,200 F ($171–$228). AE, DC, MC, V. Mon–Fri 12:30–2:30pm and 7:30–10:30pm. Closed July. Métro: Trocadéro. FRENCH.

This is where chef Joël Robuchon basks in his reputation as the country's most innovative cook. He's a master of *cuisine moderne*, sometimes called *cuisine actuelle*. Foods produced here are light and delicate, with outstanding flavors. He even bakes his own bread fresh daily and is known to spend long hours testing (or inventing) new recipes. He has fish and shellfish shipped from Brittany so it doesn't linger at the Rungis wholesale market. Early in 1994 the restaurant moved into new premises: a 1920s town house where guests climb a monumental staircase to reach a trio of carefully decorated dining rooms. Among the delectable offerings have been such dishes as kidneys and sweetbreads diced and sautéed with mushrooms, canette rosée (roasted and braised duckling flavored with spices like ginger, nutmeg, cinnamon, and other Chinese-influenced touches), shellfish-filled ravioli steamed in cabbage leaves, and chicken poached in a pig's bladder (for two). His mashed potatoes, once labeled "the silliest dish in the world," are a masterpiece.

Expensive

La Grande Cascade

In the Bois de Boulogne, 16e. ☎ 1/45-27-33-51. Reservations required. Main courses 190–250 F ($36.10–$47.50); *menu d'affaires* (lunch only) 285 F ($54.15). AE, DC, MC, V. Daily noon–3pm and 7:30–10:30pm. You must take a taxi or drive; there's no Métro stop nearby. FRENCH.

In the 17th century this indoor/outdoor restaurant was a hunting lodge for Napoléon III, but its fame as a restaurant dates from the early 20th century. Opposite the Longchamp racecourse, Grande Cascade serves the best food in this fashionable park and was named after the waterfall of the Bois de Boulogne; it's a perfect spot for a long lunch or fashionable tea. If the sun is shining, most guests ask for a table on the front terrace. Inside, you'll dine to the soft sounds of the nearby cascade in a room lit by tall frosted lamps. The restaurant features à la carte selections like duckling foie gras, fish poached in seaweed and basil, filet of red snapper in truffle sauce, and veal sweetbreads in truffle-flavored butter. The crêpes soufflés à l'orange make a stunning finish.

✪ Le Vivarois

192–194 av. Victor-Hugo, 16e. ☎ 1/45-04-04-31. Reservations required. Main courses 220–280 F ($41.80–$53.20); fixed-price lunch 345 F ($65.55). AE, DC, MC, V. Mon–Fri noon–2pm and 8–10pm. Closed Aug. Métro: Pompe. FRENCH.

Gourmet magazine once hailed this "the most exciting, audacious, and important restaurant in Paris today." Opened in 1966, it retains its original standards thanks to the supremely talented owner/chef, Claude Peyrot. He does a most recommendable coquilles St-Jacques (scallops) en crème and a pourpre de turbot Vivarois. His winning dish is rognons de veau (veal kidneys). Mme Peyrot, one of the finest maîtres d's in Paris, guides you beautifully through wine selections to perfectly complement her husband's sublime cuisine.

Moderate

Le Petit Bedon

38 rue Pergolèse, 16e. ☎ **1/45-00-23-66.** Reservations required. Main courses 160–190 F ($30.40–$36.10); fixed-price menus 240–600 F ($45.60–$114.05). AE, DC, MC, V. Mon–Fri noon–2pm and 7–10:30pm, Sat–Sun 7–10:30pm. Métro: Argentine. FRENCH.

The 14-table dining room is decorated simply but is warm and inviting. The cuisine is traditional yet innovative, and the menu changes frequently. You might begin with cured and smoked salmon, thinly sliced and seasoned with South American black pepper. If you visit in early spring, you can order milk-fed lamb from the Dordogne. The lamb is delicate and tender perfection. The kitchen is also known to do marvelous twists with Challons duckling. A masterpiece of desserts is the plate of mixed sorbets.

17TH ARRONDISSEMENT

Very Expensive

Guy Savoy

18 rue Troyon, 17e. ☎ **1/43-80-40-61.** Reservations required a week in advance. Main courses 180–300 F ($34.20–$57); fixed-price meal 650 F ($123.55) at lunch, 750 F ($142.55) at dinner. AE, MC, V. Mon–Fri noon–2pm and 7:30–10:30pm, Sat 7:30–10:30pm. Closed last three weeks in July. Métro: Charles-de-Gaulle–Etoile. FRENCH.

Guy Savoy is among Europe's hottest chefs. Both the restaurant and the cuisine bear his signature style. His cooking almost always takes its inspiration from the market. Save your appetite and order his nine-course *menu dégustation.* Perhaps you'll get red mullet and wild asparagus, cassoulet of snails flavored with tarragon, or chicken quenelles with chicken livers and cream, garnished with black truffles. Depending on when you visit, you may have the pleasure of tasting Savoy's masterfully prepared mallard, venison, or game birds. He's fascinated with mushrooms and has been known to serve as many as a dozen types, especially in autumn.

✪ Michel Rostang

20 rue Rennequin, 17e. ☎ **1/47-63-40-77.** Reservations required a week in advance. Main courses 200–290 F ($38–$55.10); set menus 520–720 F ($98.85–$136.85). AE, MC, V. Mon–Fri 12:30–2:30pm and 8–10:30pm, Sat 8–10:30pm. Closed two weeks in Aug. Métro: Ternes. FRENCH.

Michel Rostang is a creative fifth-generation chef from one of France's most distinguished "cooking families." From Grenoble, Rostang eventually came to the 17th arrondissement, where the world soon came to dine at what he modestly calls his "boutique restaurant" seating up to 70. Your menu choices may include ravioli filled with goat cheese and sprinkled with chervil bought fresh from the market as well as Bresse chicken, the finest in France. From October to March he prepares quail eggs with a coque of sea urchins. On occasion he also prepares a delicate fricassée of sole or duckling cooked in its own blood. Wines from the Rhône are available, like Châteauneuf du Pape and Hermitage.

Moderate

Goldenberg's

69 av. de Wagram, 17e. ☎ **1/42-27-34-79.** Reservations required. Main courses 100–160 F ($19–$30.40); fixed-price menu 98 F ($18.60). V. Daily 9am–midnight. Métro: Ternes or Charles-de-Gaulle–Etoile. JEWISH/DELI.

This is the best place around the Champs-Elysées for deli food. Albert Goldenberg opened his first delicatessen in Montmartre in 1936, and it's been tempting Parisians ever since with cabbage borscht, blinis, stuffed carp, and pastrami. Naturally, Jewish rye bread comes with almost everything. The menu even offers Israeli wines. The front half of the deli is for take-out, the rear for in-house dining. There's also a large room downstairs.

Paris Attractions

Paris may be an old city, but it's *au courant* as well, trying to be the style-setter of the world. Fads come and go here with such rapidity that only New York City and London could harbor so much fickleness.

Even though we glorify monumental Paris, blessed with such incredible art and architecture, such fashionable promenades and beautiful gardens, the city's top attraction is and has always been the Parisians themselves. They're a unique breed, as even a brief visit will prove. The French from the provinces regard Parisians with interest, detachment, and often outright envy.

The best way to discover Paris is on foot—and it won't cost you a franc to explore the streets of the City of Light. Walk along the grand avenue des Champs-Elysées, tour the quays of the Seine, wander around Ile de la Cité and Ile St-Louis, browse through the countless shops and stalls, wander through the famous squares and parks. Each turn will open a new vista. If you're an early riser, a stroll through Paris at dawn can be wonderful as you see the city coming to life: Shopfronts are washed clean for the new day, cafés begin serving hot coffee and warm croissants, and vegetable vendors begin setting up their stalls and arranging their produce.

For detailed walking tours with accompanying maps, see *Frommer's Paris* and especially *Frommer's Walking Tours: Paris, 2nd Edition,* which contains 14 memorable strolls.

SIGHTSEEING STRATEGIES FOR THE FIRST-TIME VISITOR

If You Have One Day

The most practical way to see Paris in a day is to take a guided tour, since you can't possibly master the city on your own in such a short time. Start the day by ordering a café au lait or café crème and croissants at a sidewalk café. At 9:30am the Cityrama tour's double-decker bus leaves for its two-hour ride around the city, past such sights as Notre-Dame and the Eiffel Tower (see "Organized Tours," below). After the tour, have lunch and go to the Louvre for a guided tour of its most important works.

With what's left of the afternoon, stroll along the banks of the Seine, ending up at Notre-Dame as the sun sets over Paris. If you have an early dinner at a nearby bistro, you may still have the time and energy to attend the Lido or Folies-Bergère (see "The Club and Music Scene," in Chapter 9).

If You Have Two Days

For your first day, follow the suggestions above. Start your second day by taking a Bateaux-Mouche cruise on the Seine (see "Organized Tours," below), with departures from pont de l'Alma at place de l'Alma on the Right Bank (Métro: Alma-Marceau). Then go to Jules Verne in the Eiffel Tower for lunch with a panoramic view (see Chapter 6).

Next head for the Arc de Triomphe, a perfect place to begin a stroll down the Champs-Elysées, the main boulevard, until you reach the Egyptian obelisk at place de la Concorde. This grand promenade is one of the most famous long walks in the world. That night, visit a Left Bank boîte or jazz club.

If You Have Three Days

Spend your first two days as outlined above. On your third morning explore the Sainte-Chapelle and the Conciergerie. Have lunch, perhaps on the Ile St-Louis, then take a walking tour of that island in the Seine. Afterward, spend two or three hours at the Musée d'Orsay. Before the day is over, head for the Cimetière du Père-Lachaise and pay your respects to Edith Piaf, Jim Morrison, Richard Wright, Oscar Wilde, and Gertrude Stein. In the early evening go for a walk along rue des Rosiers, the heart of the Jewish community, then dine at a bistro in the Marais.

If You Have Five Days or More

Follow the itineraries above for your first three days. On your fourth day, go on your own or take an organized tour to Versailles, 13 miles south of Paris. Then head back to the city for an evening stroll through the Latin Quarter, perhaps dining in a Left Bank bistro. With a good map, try walking along some of the livelier streets, such as rue de la Hachette and rue Monsieur-le-Prince.

On your fifth day, spend the morning roaming the Marais. By all means, pay a visit to the Picasso Museum and have lunch near the historic place des Vosges. Afterward, you might want to head toward Montmarte to explore. Try to time your visit so you'll be at Sacré-Coeur at sunset, where you can promise yourself a return to Paris. Cap the evening by heading for one of the famous cafés of Montparnasse, La Rotonde or Le Sélect, then follow in the footsteps of everyone from Dalí to Picasso and enjoy your final Parisian meal at La Coupole.

ORGANIZED TOURS

BY BUS   Before plunging into more detailed sightseeing on your own, you might like to take the most popular get-acquainted tour in Paris: **Cityrama,** 4 place des Pyramides, 1er (☎ 1/44-55-60-00; Métro: Tuileries). On a double-decker bus with enough windows for the Palace of Versailles, you're taken on a leisurely

---

Impressions

Paris is the greatest temple ever built to material joys and the lust of the eyes.
—Henry James

⭐ Frommer's Favorite Paris Experiences

Window-Shopping Along the Faubourg St-Honoré   In the 1700s this was home to the wealthiest of Parisians; today it's home to the stores that cater to them. Even if you don't purchase anything, you'll enjoy some great window-shopping with all the big names, like Hermès, Larouche, Courrèges, Cardin, Saint-Laurent, and Lagerfeld.

Spending a Languid Afternoon in a Café   The Parisian café is an integral part of life. Even if it means skipping a museum, spend some time at a café. Whether you have one small coffee or the most expensive cognac in the house, nobody will hurry you.

Taking Afternoon Tea at Angélina   Drinking tea in London has its charm, but the Parisian *salon de thé* is unique. Skip London's cucumber-and-watercress sandwiches and get down to the business of rich, luscious desserts like Mont Blanc, that creamy purée of sweetened chestnuts. Try the grandest Parisian tea salon of them all: Angélina, 226 rue de Rivoli, 1er (Métro: Concorde).

Attending the Ballet   Renoir may have hated the ostentation of the building, but a night at the Opéra Garnier is still one of the highlights of any trip to Paris. The Opéra Garnier, at place de l'Opéra, is now the major center for ballet in Paris (the Opéra de la Bastille is for opera), and an evening here will take you back to the Second Empire world of gilt and grand staircases, all sheltered under a controversial ceiling by Chagall. (Alas, the Opéra is currently closed for renovations; when you arrive, call to see if it has reopened.)

Going to the Races   Paris has eight racetracks, some within the boundaries of the city. The most famous (and classiest) is Longchamp, in the Bois de Boulogne, 16e. The site of the Prix de l'Arc de Triomphe and Grand Prix, Longchamp is the longest racetrack in the world. If it's a major social event, you'll have to dress up, of course. Take the Métro to Porte d'Auteuil, then a special bus from there to the track. *Paris-Turf*, the racing paper, has details about racing times and special events.

Strolling Along rue des Rosiers   In the 4th arrondissement, the Street of the Rosebushes is anything but. One of Paris's most evocative streets, it's at the heart of the old Jewish quarter. The Star of David shines here, Hebrew letters flash (in neon, no less), restaurants serve strictly kosher meals, and signs appeal for Jewish liberation. This is also the place to pick up the sausage stuffed in a goose neck that you've been dreaming about.

---

two-hour ride through the city. Since you don't go inside any attractions, you must settle for a look at the outside of such places as Notre-Dame and the Eiffel Tower.

The language barrier is overcome as individual earphones are distributed with a canned commentary in 10 languages. Tours depart daily at 9:30, 10:30, and 11:30am and 1:30, 2:30, and 3:30pm. The cost is 150 F ($28.50). Another Cityrama offering, a tour of the nighttime illuminations, leaves daily at 10pm in summer, daily at 8:45pm in winter. The cost is 150 F ($28.50).

BY BOAT   A boat tour on Seine provides sweeping views of the riverbanks and some of the best views of Notre-Dame. Many of the boats have open sun decks, bars, and restaurants.

Bateaux-Mouche cruises (☎ 1/42-25-96-10 for information and reservations; Métro: Alma-Marceau) depart from the Right Bank of the Seine, adjacent to pont de l'Alma, and last about 75 minutes each. Tours depart every day, at 30-minute intervals between 10am and 8:30pm and at 15-minute intervals between 9 and 11pm. Lunch cruises depart at 1pm; dinner cruises at 8:30pm (jackets and ties are required for men on the dinner cruises).

Fares are 40 F ($7.60) for adults and 20 F ($3.80) for children. Luncheon cruises cost 350 F ($66.50) Monday to Saturday and 400 F ($76) Sunday; a dinner cruise goes for 500 to 650 F ($95 to $123.50), depending on the menu you select.

1 The Top Attractions

THE TOP MUSEUMS

✪ Musée du Louvre

Quai du Louvre, 1er. ☎ 1/40-20-53-17, 40-20-51-51 for recorded information, 40-20-52-09 for hours of tours in English. Admission 40 F ($7.60) before 3pm, 20 F ($3.80) after 3pm and all day Sun; free for children 17 and under. Mon and Wed 9am–9:30pm, Thurs–Sun 9am–6pm. 90-minute English-language tours Mon and Wed–Sat at 10am, 11:30am, 2pm, and 3:30pm for 33 F ($6.25) adults, 22 F ($4.20) children 13–18; 12 and under free with museum ticket. Métro: Palais-Royal–Musée-du-Louvre.

The Louvre is the world's largest palace and the world's largest and greatest museum. You'll have no choice but to miss certain masterpieces here because you won't have the time or stamina to see everything—the Louvre's collection is truly staggering. People on one of those "Paris-in-a-day" tours try to break track records to glimpse the two most famous ladies here: the *Mona Lisa* and the *Venus de Milo*. Those with an extra five minutes go in pursuit of *Winged Victory*, that headless statue discovered at Samothrace and dating from about 200 B.C.

To enter the Louvre, you pass through the controversial 71-foot I. M. Pei glass pyramid in the courtyard. Commissioned by former President Mitterrand and completed in 1990, it has received mixed reviews. The pyramid allows sunlight to shine on an underground reception area and shelters a complex of shops and restaurants. The renovation also increases the Louvre's gallery space by an astonishing 80% and provides underground garages for the tour buses that used to jam rue de Rivoli. Automatic ticket machines help relieve the long lines of yesteryear.

The collections are divided into six departments: Egyptian, Oriental, and Greek and Roman antiquities; sculpture; painting; and furniture and art objects. Those with little time should go on one of the guided tours (in English), which last about 1¼ hours.

Our favorites include *Ship of Fools* by Hieronymous Bosch (tucked in the Flemish galleries)—no one can depict folly and greed more vividly than Bosch; *Four Seasons* by Nicolas Poussin, the canonical work of French classicism; Eugène Delacroix's *Liberty Leading the People*, perhaps the ultimate endorsement of revolution (Louis-Philippe purchased the painting and hid it during his reign); and Veronese's gigantic *Wedding Feast at Cana*, showing (if nothing else) how stunning colors can be when used by a master.

The Richelieu Wing, inaugurated in 1993, houses the museum's collection of northern European and French paintings, along with decorative arts, French sculpture, Oriental antiquities (a rich collection of Islamic art), and the grand salons of

The Louvre

The Pyramid

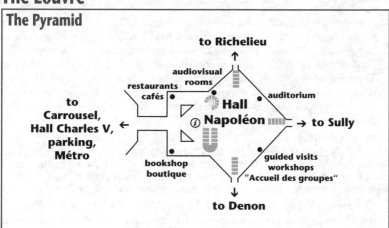

to Richelieu

audiovisual rooms

restaurants cafés

auditorium

Hall Napoléon

to Carrousel, Hall Charles V, parking, Métro

to Sully

bookshop boutique

guided visits workshops "Accueil des groupes"

to Denon

The Levels

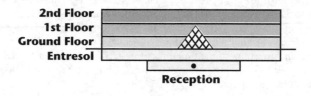

2nd Floor
1st Floor
Ground Floor
Entresol

Reception

The Wings

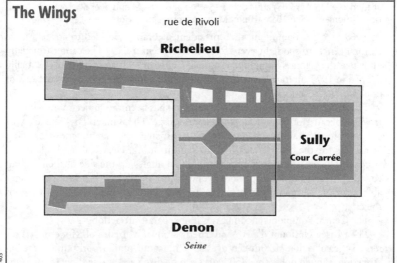

rue de Rivoli

Richelieu

Sully
Cour Carrée

Denon

Seine

Napoléon III. Originally constructed from 1852 to 1857, the Richelieu Wing has recently been virtually rebuilt, adding some 230,000 square feet of exhibition space. In this wing's 165 rooms, plus three covered courtyards, some 12,000 works of art are displayed. Of the Greek and Roman antiquities, the most notable (aside from *Venus* and *Winged Victory*) are fragments of the Parthenon's frieze.

If you have limited time to explore the Louvre, perhaps take the two tours—one of sculpture, one of painting—detailed in *Frommer's Walking Tours: Paris, 2nd Edition.*

✪ Musée d'Orsay

1 rue de Bellechasse or 62 rue de Lille, 7e. ☎ **1/40-49-48-14,** 40-49-48-48 for the information desk. Admission 35 F ($6.65) adults, 24 F ($4.55) ages 18–24 and seniors, free for children 17 and under. Tues–Wed and Fri–Sat 10am–6pm, Thurs 10am–9:45pm, Sun 9am–6pm. June 20–Sept 20, museum opens at 9am. Métro: Solférino. RER: Musée-d'Orsay.

The defunct but handsome neoclassical Gare d'Orsay railway station has been transformed into one of the greatest art museums in the world. Across the Seine from the Louvre and the Tuileries, it's a repository of 19th-century art and civilization. The museum houses thousands of sculptures and paintings spread across 80 galleries, plus belle époque furniture, photographs, objets d'art, architectural models, and even a cinema.

One of Renoir's most joyous paintings is here—*Moulin de la Galette* (1876). Another celebrated work is by American James McNeill Whistler—*Arrangement in Gray and Black: Portrait of the Painter's Mother.* Perhaps the most famous piece in the museum is Manet's 1863 *Déjeuner sur l'herbe* (Picnic on the Grass), which created a scandal when it was first exhibited; it depicts a nude woman nonchalantly picnicking with two fully clothed men in a forest. Two years later his *Olympia,* lounging on her bed wearing nothing but a flower in her hair and high-heeled shoes, met the same response.

✪ Centre Pompidou

Place Georges-Pompidou (or plateau Beaubourg), 4e. ☎ **1/42-77-12-33,** 44-78-40-86 for information. One-day pass to all exhibits, 60 F ($11.40) adults, 40 F ($7.60) ages 18–24 and over 60, free for children 17 and under, free for everyone Sun 10am–2pm. Musée National d'Art Moderne, 35 F ($6.65) adults, 24 F ($4.55) ages 18–24 and over 60. Mon and Wed–Fri noon–10pm, Sat–Sun 10am–10pm. Métro: Rambuteau or Hôtel-de-Ville.

In 1969 Georges Pompidou, then president of France, decided to create a large cultural center to spotlight every form of 20th-century art. The center (officially known as the Georges Pompidou National Center for Art and Culture) was finally opened in 1977 on the plateau Beaubourg, amid a huge pedestrian district east of boulevard de Sébastopol.

The structure, towering over a festive plaza, has been the subject of much controversy because of its radical exoskeletal design. The Tinker Toy–like array of colorful pipes and tubes surrounding the transparent shell are functional, serving as casings for the center's heating, air-conditioning, electrical, and telephone systems. The great wormlike tubes crawling at angles up the side of the building contain escalators. Inside, each floor is one vast room, divided as necessary by movable partitions. From the top of the center you can enjoy one of the best views of the city.

The Centre Pompidou encompasses four separate attractions:

The **Musée National d'Art Moderne** (National Museum of Modern Art) offers a large collection of 20th-century art. With some 40,000 works, this is the big attraction, though only some 850 works can be displayed at one time. If you want

> ## ❷ Did You Know?
>
> - The Eiffel Tower outraged critics in its day, especially novelist Emile Zola, who denounced it as a "tower of Babel" and a "dishonor to Paris."
> - The most valuable painting in the world, Leonardo's *Mona Lisa*, was estimated at $100 million—too expensive for the French government to insure.
> - In 1985 Bulgarian-born artist Christo wrapped the oldest bridge in Paris, pont Neuf, in 440,000 square yards of polyamide fabric and 42,900 feet of rope.
> - The Louvre sells five million postcards a year.
> - Underground Paris has 112 miles of tunnels through which the Métro runs.
> - Paris is home to nearly 54,000 people per square mile.
> - Hitler ordered the burning of Paris, but the Nazi general in charge refused to obey because he didn't want to go down in history as the man who burned Paris.

to view some real charmers, see Alexander Calder's *1926 Josephine Baker*, one of his earliest versions of the mobile, an art form he invented. Marcel Duchamps' *Valise* is a collection of miniature reproductions of his fabled Dada sculptures and drawings; they're displayed in a carrying case. Every time we visit Paris we have to see Salvador Dalí's *Portrait of Lenin Dancing on Piano Keys* (exhibited on the fourth floor). It makes our day!

In the **Public Information Library** the public (for the first time in Paris's history) has free access to one million French and foreign books, periodicals, films, records, slides, and microfilms in nearly every area of knowledge. The **Center for Industrial Design** emphasizes the contributions made in the fields of architecture, visual communications, publishing, and community planning. The **Institute for Research and Coordination of Acoustics/Music** brings together musicians and composers interested in furthering the cause of music, both contemporary and traditional. Concerts, workshops, and seminars are frequently open to the public.

✪ Musée Picasso

In the Hôtel Salé, 5 rue de Thorigny, 3e. ☎ **1/42-71-25-21.** Admission 27 F ($5.15) adults, 17 F ($3.25) ages 18–24 and over 60, free for children 17 and under. Apr–Sept, Wed–Mon 9:30am–6pm; Oct–Mar, Wed–Mon 9:30am–5:30pm. Métro: St-Paul, Filles-du-Calvaire, or Chemin-Vert.

When it opened in the beautifully restored Hôtel Salé (salt mansion, built in 1656 for Aubert de Fontenay, who collected the dreaded salt tax), a state-owned property in Le Marais, the press hailed it as a "museum for Picasso's Picassos," meaning those he chose not to sell. Almost overnight it became—and continues to be—one of the most popular attractions in Paris. The greatest Picasso collection in the world, acquired by the state in lieu of $50 million in inheritance taxes, consists of 203 paintings, 158 sculptures, 16 collages, 19 bas-reliefs, 88 ceramics, and more than 1,500 sketches and 1,600 engravings, plus 30 notebooks. These works span some 75 years of Picasso's life and changing styles.

The range of paintings includes a remarkable 1901 self-portrait and embraces such masterpieces as *Le Baiser* (The Kiss), painted at Mougins in 1969. Another masterpiece is *Reclining Nude and the Man with a Guitar*. It's easy to stroll through seeking your own favorite work (ours is a delightfully wicked one, *Jeune Garçon à la Langouste*, "young man with a lobster," painted in Paris in 1941). The Paris museum owns several intriguing studies for *Les Demoiselles d'Avignon*, the painting that launched cubism.

✪ Musée de l'Orangerie des Tuileries

In the Jardin des Tuileries, 1er. ☎ **1/42-97-48-16.** Admission 27 F ($5.15) adults, 18 F ($3.40) ages 18–25 and over 60, half price on Sun; free for children 17 and under. Wed–Mon 9:45am–5pm. Métro: Concorde.

This museum is a gem. Often set aside for special exhibits, it has an outstanding collection of art and one celebrated display: Claude Monet's exquisite *Nymphéas*, executed between 1890 and 1921, a light-filtered tangle of lily pads and water, paneling the two ground-floor oval rooms whose construction was supervised by the artist himself.

Creating his effects with hundreds of minute brushstrokes (one 19th-century critic called them "tongue lickings"), Monet achieved unity and harmony, as he did in his Rouen cathedral series. See his lilies and feel the mood and melancholy as he experienced them so many years ago. Monet continued to paint his water landscapes right up until his death in 1926, though he was greatly hampered by failing eyesight.

The renovated building also contains the Walter-Guillaume collection, which includes more than 24 Renoirs, of which the most important is *Young Girl at a Piano*. Cézanne is represented by 14 works, notably *The Red Rock*, and Matisse by 11. The star of Rousseau's nine works is *The Wedding*, and of the dozen Picassos the most brilliant is *The Female Bathers*.

ON OR NEAR THE GRAND PROMENADE

✪ Arc de Triomphe

Place Charles-de-Gaulle–Etoile, 8e. ☎ **1/43-80-31-31.** Admission 32 F ($6.10) adults, 21 F ($4) ages 18–25 and over 60, 10 F ($1.90) children 12–17, free for children 11 and under. Apr–Sept, daily 9:30am–4:30pm; Oct–Mar, daily 10am–4:30pm. Closed Jan 1, May 1 and 8, July 14, Nov 11, and Dec 25. Métro: Charles-de-Gaulle–Etoile.

At the western end of the Champs-Elysées, the Arc de Triomphe is the largest triumphal arch in the world, about 163 feet high and 147 feet wide. To reach it, don't try crossing the square, the busiest traffic hub in Paris (death is certain!). Instead, take the underground passage. With a dozen streets radiating from the "Star," the traffic circle was called by one writer "vehicular roulette." After de Gaulle's death, the government—despite anti-Gaullist protests—voted to change the name of place de l'Etoile to place Charles-de-Gaulle–Etoile.

The triumphal arch has witnessed some of France's proudest moments—and some of its more humiliating defeats, notably those of 1871 and 1940. The memory of German troops marching under the arch that had come to symbolize France's glory is still painful to the French. And who could forget the 1940

Impressions

To the Arc de Triomphe de l'Etoile
raise yourself all the way to the heavens, portal of victory
That the giant of our glory
Might pass without bending down.

—Victor Hugo

1st Arrondissement

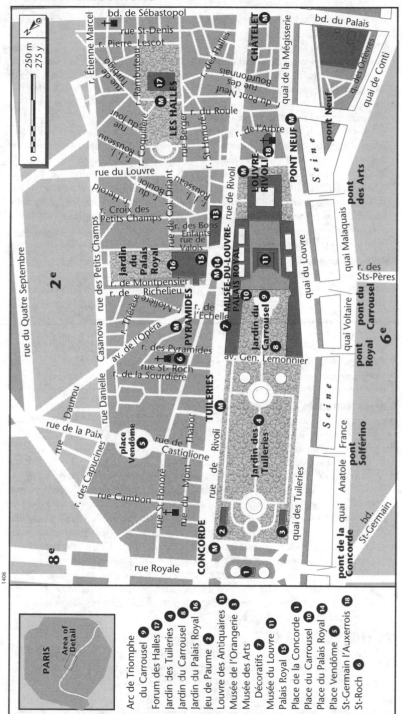

Arc de Triomphe du Carrousel **9**
Forum des Halles **17**
Jardin des Tuileries **4**
Jardin du Carrousel **8**
Jardin du Palais Royal **16**
Jeu de Paume **2**
Louvre des Antiquaires **13**
Musée de l'Orangerie **3**
Musée des Arts Décoratifs **7**
Musée du Louvre **11**
Palais Royal **15**
Place de la Concorde **1**
Place du Carrousel **10**
Place du Palais Royal **14**
Place Vendôme **5**
St-Germain l'Auxerrois **18**
St-Roch **6**

newsreel of the Frenchman standing on the Champs-Elysées openly weeping as the Nazi stormtroopers goose-stepped through Paris?

Commissioned by Napoléon in 1806 to commemorate his Grande Armée's victories, the arch wasn't completed until 1836, under Louis-Philippe. Four years later Napoléon's remains—brought from his grave on St-Helena—passed under the arch on their journey to his tomb at the Invalides. Since then it has become the focal point for state funerals. It's also the site of the tomb of the unknown soldier, where an eternal flame is kept burning.

Of the sculptures decorating the monument, the best known is Rude's *Marseillaise*, also called *The Departure of the Volunteers*. J. P. Cortot's *Triumph of Napoléon in 1810* and the *Resistance of 1814* and *Peace of 1815*, both by Etex, also adorn the facade. The arch is engraved with the names of hundreds of generals (those underlined died in battle) who commanded troops in Napoléonic victories.

You can take an elevator or climb the stairway to the top. Up there is an exhibition hall, with lithographs and photos depicting the arch throughout its history. From the observation deck you have a magnificent view of the Champs-Elysées as well as such landmarks as the Louvre, Eiffel Tower, and Sacré-Coeur.

Palais de l'Elysée
Rue du Faubourg St-Honoré, 8e. Métro: Miromesnil.

The "French White House" occupies a block along fashionable Faubourg St-Honoré. It's now occupied by the president of France and cannot be visited by the public without an invitation. Built in 1718 for the comte d'Evreux, the palace had many owners before it was purchased by the Republic in 1873. Once it was owned by Mme de Pompadour. When she "had the supreme delicacy to die discreetly at the age of 43," she bequeathed it to the king. After her divorce from Napoléon, Joséphine also lived here. A grand dining hall was built for Napoléon III and an orangerie (now a winter garden) was built for the duchesse du Berry.

Galerie Nationale du Jeu de Paume
In the Jardin des Tuileries at place de la Concorde, 1er. ☎ **1/47-03-12-50.** Admission 35 F ($6.65) adults, 25 F ($4.75) students, free for children 12 and under. Tues–Fri noon–7pm, Sat–Sun 10am–7pm. Métro: Concorde.

In the northeast corner of the Tuileries Garden, the Jeu de Paume was ordered constructed by Napoléon III as a court on which to play *jeu de paume,* a precursor to tennis. For years it was one of Paris's treasured addresses, displaying some of the finest works of the impressionists. In 1986 this collection was hauled off to the Musée d'Orsay, much to the regret of many. Following a $12.6-million facelift, the Second Empire building has been transformed into a new art gallery with state-of-the-art display facilities and a video screening room. There's no permanent collection housed here, and each two or three months a new show is mounted. Sometimes the works of little-known contemporary artists are on display; at other times the exhibition features such established artists as Jean Dubuffet. Even when established artists are featured, the tendency of the directors is to focus on "unexplored" aspects of their work.

ON THE ILE DE LA CITE
Medieval Paris, that architectural blending of grotesquerie and gothic beauty, began on this island in the Seine. Explore as much of it as you can, but if you're in a hurry, try to visit at least Notre-Dame, the Sainte-Chapelle, and the Conciergerie.

✪ Cathédrale Notre-Dame de Paris

6 place du Parvis Notre-Dame, 4e. ☎ 1/43-26-07-39. Cathedral, free; towers, 35 F ($6.65) adults, 20 F ($3.80) ages 18–24 and over 60, 7 F ($1.35) children 7–17, free for children 6 and under; treasury, 15 F ($2.85) adults, 10 F ($1.90) ages 18–24 and over 60, 5 F (95¢) children 7–17, free for children 6 and under. Cathedral, daily 8am–6:45pm (closed Sat 12:30–2pm); towers and crypt, daily 9:30am–7:30pm (10am–4:30pm Oct–Mar); museum, Wed and Sat–Sun 2:30–6pm; treasury, Mon–Sat 9:30am–5:45pm. Six masses are celebrated on Sunday, four on weekdays, and one on Saturday. Free organ concerts Sun at 5:30pm. Métro: Cité or St-Michel.

This cathedral ranks near the top as one of the world's most famous houses of worship. For six centuries it has stood as a fabled gothic masterpiece of the Middle Ages. Though many may disagree, we feel Notre-Dame is more interesting outside than in. You'll have to walk around the entire structure to appreciate this "vast symphony of stone" more fully. Better yet, cross the bridge to the Left Bank and view it from the quay.

From square Parvis, you can view the trio of 13th-century sculptured portals. On the left, the Portal of the Virgin depicts the signs of the Zodiac and the Virgin's coronation. The restored central Portal of the Last Judgment is divided into three levels: the first shows Vices and Virtues; the second, Christ and his Apostles; the third, Christ in triumph after the Resurrection. On the right is the Portal of St. Anne, depicting such scenes as the Virgin enthroned with Child. It's the most perfect piece of sculpture in Notre-Dame. Over the central portal is a remarkable rose window, 31 feet in diameter, forming a showcase for a statue of the Virgin and Child. Equally interesting (though often missed) is the Portal of the Cloisters (around on the left), with its dour-faced 13th-century Virgin, a unique survivor of the many that originally adorned the facade. Unfortunately, the Child she's holding is decapitated.

If possible, see the interior at sunset. Of the three giant medallions that warm the austere cathedral, the north rose window in the transept, dating from the mid-13th century, is best. The interior is typical gothic, with slender, graceful columns. The carved-stone choir screen from the early 14th century depicts such biblical scenes as the Last Supper. Near the altar stands the highly venerated 14th-century Virgin and Child. Behind glass in the treasury is a display of vestments and gold objects, including crowns. Notre-Dame is especially proud of its relic of the True Cross and the Crown of Thorns.

To visit those grimy gargoyles immortalized by Victor Hugo you have to scale steps leading to the twin square towers, rising to a height of 225 feet. Once there, you can closely inspect those devils (some sticking out their tongues), hobgoblins, and birds of prey.

From October to May, history or theology lectures are given on Sunday at 4:45pm, followed by a free organ recital at 5:30pm and a mass at 6:30pm. During these hours, visitors are not encouraged to circulate in the cathedral.

Approached through a garden behind Notre-Dame is the **Memorial des Martyrs Français de la Déportation de 1945,** jutting out on the tip of the Ile de la Cité. This memorial honors the French martyrs of World War II, who were deported to camps like Auschwitz and Buchenwald. In blood-red are these words: "Forgive, but don't forget." It may be visited from 10am to noon and 2 to 7pm. Admission is free.

✪ Sainte-Chapelle

4 bd. du Palais, 1er. ☎ 1/43-54-30-09. Admission 27 F ($5.15) adults, 18 F ($3.40) ages 18–25 and over 60, 10 F ($1.90) ages 12–17, free for children 11 and under. Apr–Sept, daily 9:30am–6:30pm; Oct–Mar, daily 10am–5pm. Closed Jan 1, May 1, Nov 1 and 11, and Dec 25. Métro: Cité, St-Michel, or Châtelet. RER: St-Michel.

The Sainte-Chapelle is Paris's second most important monument of the Middle Ages (after Notre-Dame)—erected in the flamboyant gothic style to enshrine relics from the First Crusade. These included what was believed to have been the Crown of Thorns, two pieces from the True Cross, and even the Roman lance that pierced the side of Christ. St. Louis (Louis IX) acquired the relics from the emperor of Constantinople and is said to have paid heavily for them, raising money through unscrupulous means.

Viewed on a bright day, the 15 stained-glass windows vividly depicting Bible scenes seem to glow ruby red and Chartres blue. The walls consist almost entirely of the glass. Built in only five to seven years, beginning in 1246, the chapel has two levels. You enter through the lower chapel, supported by flying buttresses and ornamented with fleur-de-lis. The lower chapel was used by the servants of the palace, the upper chamber by the king and his courtiers; the latter is reached by ascending a narrow spiral staircase.

Conciergerie

1 quai de l'Horloge, 1er. ☎ 1/43-54-30-06. Admission 27 F ($5.15) adults, 18 F ($3.40) ages 18–24, 6 F ($1.15) children 17 and under. Apr–Sept, daily 9:30am–6:30pm; Oct–Mar, daily 10am–5pm. Métro: Cité, Châtelet, or St-Michel. RER: St-Michel.

The Conciergerie has been called the most sinister building in France. Though it had a long regal history before the Revolution, it's visited today chiefly by those wishing to bask in the Reign of Terror's horrors. The Conciergerie conjures images of the days when tumbrils pulled up daily to haul off the fresh supply of victims to the guillotine.

You approach the Conciergerie through its landmark twin towers, the Tour d'Argent and Tour de César, though the 14th-century vaulted Guard Room is the actual entrance. Also from the 14th century—and even more interesting—is the vast, dark, foreboding Salle des Gens d'Armes (People at Arms), chillingly changed from the days when the king used it as a banqueting hall.

Few of the prisoners in the Conciergerie's history endured the tortures of Ravaillac, who assassinated Henry IV in 1610. He got the full treatment—pincers in the flesh as well as hot lead and boiling oil poured on him like bath water. Also, this was where Marie Antoinette, in failing health and in shock, was brought to await her "trial" and eventual beheading.

ON THE ILE ST-LOUIS

As you walk across the iron footbridge from the rear of Notre-Dame, you descend into a world of tree-shaded quays, aristocratic town houses and courtyards, restaurants, and antiques shops.

The sister island of the Ile de la Cité is primarily residential; its denizens fiercely guard their heritage, privileges, and special position. It was originally two "islets," one named Island of the Heifers. The two islands were ordered joined by Louis XIII. The number of famous people who've occupied these patrician mansions is now a legend. Plaques on the facades make it easier to identify them. Madame Curie, for example, lived at 36 quai de Bethune, near ponte de la Tournelle, from 1912 until her death in 1934.

Ile de la Cité & Ile St-Louis

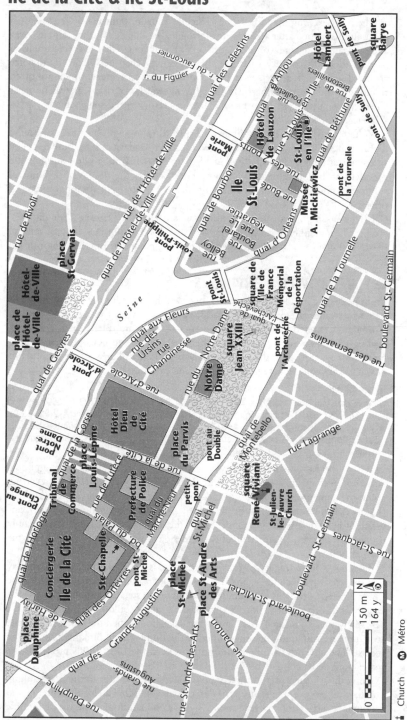

square Barye

Hôtel Lambert

pont de Sully

r. du Figuier

quai des Célestins

r. du Fauconnier

rue de Bretonvilliers

quai de Béthune

rue d'Anjou

Hôtel Quai de Lauzon

quai d'Orléans

St-Louis en l'Ile

Musée A. Mickiewicz

pont de la Tournelle

pont Marie

rue des deux ponts

rue Budé

Ile St-Louis

rue de Bourbon

rue le Regrattier

rue de Béthune

rue Poulletier

St-Louis-en-l'Ile

quai de la Tournelle

rue de Rivoli

place St-Gervais

pont Louis-Philippe

quai de l'Hôtel-de-Ville

rue de l'Hôtel-de-Ville

rue Belloy

rue Boutarel

square de l'Ile de France

Mémorial de la Déportation

boulevard St-Germain

Hôtel-de-Ville

place de l'Hôtel-de-Ville

quai de Gesvres

Seine

quai aux Fleurs

rue des Ursins

rue Chanoinesse

pont St-Louis

quai de l'Archevêché

pont de l'Archevêché

rue des Bernardins

pont d'Arcole

rue d'Arcole

rue du Notre Dame

Notre Dame

square Jean XXIII

quai de Montebello

rue Lagrange

Hôtel Dieu de Cité

place du Parvis

pont au Double

square René Viviani

St-Julien-le-Pauvre Church

pont Notre-Dame

rue de la Corse

place Louis-Lépine

rue de la Cité

rue de Lutèce

Préfecture de Police

quai du Marché-Neuf

petit-pont

rue St-Jacques

pont au Change

quai de l'Horloge

Tribunal de Commerce

bd. du Palais

quai des Orfèvres

pont St-Michel

St-Michel

place St-Michel

place St-André des Arts

boulevard St-Germain

Conciergerie

Ile de la Cité

Ste-Chapelle

r. de Harlay

place Dauphine

quai des Grands-Augustins

rue des Grands-Augustins

rue St-André-des-Arts

rue Danton

boulevard St-Michel

rue Dauphine

N

150 m

164 y

0

✝ Church   Ⓜ Métro

The most exciting mansion is the Hôtel de Lauzun, built in 1657, at 17 quai d'Anjou; it's named after a 17th-century rogue, the duc de Lauzun, famous lover and on-again/off-again favorite of Louis XIV. French poet Charles Baudelaire lived here in the 19th century with his "Black Venus," Jeanne Duval. Baudelaire attracted such artists as Delacroix and Courbet to his apartment, which was often filled with the aroma of hashish. Occupying another apartment was novelist Théophile Gautier ("art for art's sake"), who's remembered today chiefly for his *Mademoiselle de Maupin.*

Voltaire lived in the Hôtel Lambert, 2 quai d'Anjou, with his mistress, Emilie de Breteuil, the marquise du Châteley, who had an "understanding" husband. The mansion was built by Louis Le Vau in 1645 for Nicolas Lambert de Thorigny, the president of the Chambre des Comptes. For a century the *hôtel* was the home of the royal family of Poland, the Czartoryskis, who entertained Chopin, among others.

Farther along, at no. 9, is the house where Honoré Daumier, the painter/sculptor/lithographer, lived between 1846 and 1863. From here he satirized the petite bourgeoisie. His caricature of Louis-Philippe netted him a six-month jail sentence.

THE EIFFEL TOWER & ENVIRONS

From place du Trocadéro, you can step between the two curved wings of the Palais de Chaillot and gaze out on a breathtaking view. At your feet lie the Jardins du Trocadéro, centered by fountains. Directly in front, pont d'Iéna spans the Seine, leading to the the iron immensity of the Tour Eiffel. And beyond, stretching as far as your eye can see, is the Champ-de-Mars, once a military parade ground but now a garden with arches, grottoes, lakes, and cascades.

✪ Tour Eiffel

In the Parc du Champ-de-Mars, 7e. ☎ **1/45-50-34-56.** First landing, 20 F ($3.80); second landing, 38 F ($7.20); third landing, 55 F ($10.45); stairs to second landing, 12 F ($2.30). Sept–June, daily 9:30am–11pm; July–Aug, daily 9am–midnight (in fall and winter the stairs close at 6:30pm). Métro: Trocadéro, Ecole-Militaire, or Bir-Hakeim. RER: Champ-de-Mars–Tour-Eiffel.

Except for perhaps the Leaning Tower of Pisa, this is the single most recognizable structure in the world—the symbol of Paris. Weighing 7,000 tons but exerting about the same pressure on the ground as an average-size person sitting in a chair, the tower was never meant to be permanent. It was built for the Universal Exhibition of 1889 by Gustave-Alexandre Eiffel, the engineer whose fame rested mainly on his iron bridges. (Incidentally, he also designed the framework for the Statue of Liberty.)

The tower, including its 55-foot TV antenna, is 1,056 feet tall. On a clear day you can see it from some 40 miles away. An open-framework construction, the tower ushered in the almost-unlimited possibilities of steel construction, paving the way for the 20th century's skyscrapers. Skeptics said it couldn't be built, and Eiffel actually wanted to make it soar higher. For years it remained the tallest man-made structure on earth, until such skyscrapers as the Empire State Building usurped the record. The advent of wireless communication in the early 1890s preserved the tower from destruction.

You can visit the tower in three stages: Taking the elevator to the first landing, you have a view over the rooftops of Paris. Here you'll find a cinema museum and restaurants and a bar open year-round. The second landing provides a panoramic

3rd & 4th Arrondissements

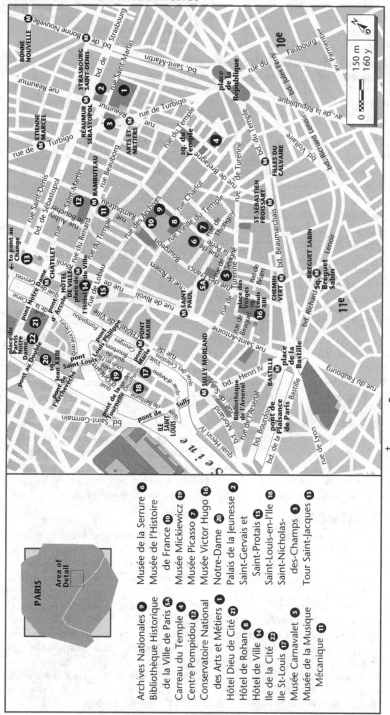

PARIS

Area of
Detail

Archives Nationales **9**
Bibliothèque Historique
de la Ville de Paris **5A**
Carreau du Temple **4**
Centre Pompidou **12**
Conservatoire National
des Arts et Métiers **1**
Hôtel Dieu de Cité **21**
Hôtel de Rohan **8**
Hôtel de Ville **14**
Île de la Cité **22**
Île St-Louis **17**
Musée Carnavalet **5**
Musée de la Musique
Mécanique **11**

Musée de la Serrure **6**
Musée de l'Histoire
de France **10**
Musée Mickiewicz **19**
Musée Picasso **7**
Musée Victor Hugo **16**
Notre-Dame **20**
Palais de la Jeunesse **2**
Saint-Gervais et
Saint-Protais **15**
Saint-Louis-en-l'Île **18**
Saint-Nicholas-
des-Champs **3**
Tour Saint-Jacques **13**

Church **✝**   Métro **Ⓜ**

look at the city. The third landing gives the most spectacular view, allowing you to identify monuments and buildings. On the ground level, in the eastern and western pillars, you can visit the 1899 elevator machinery when the tower is open.

Hôtel des Invalides (Napoléon's Tomb)

Place des Invalides, 7e. ☎ **1/44-42-37-72.** Admission (good for two consecutive days for the Musée de l'Armée, Napoléon's Tomb, and the Musée des Plans-Reliefs) 35 F ($6.65) adults, 24 F ($4.55) children 7–18, free for children 6 and under. Apr–Sept, daily 10am–6pm (Napoléon's Tomb open until 7pm June–Aug); Oct–Mar, daily 10am–5pm. Closed Jan 1, May 1, Nov 1, and Dec 25. Métro: Latour-Maubourg, Varenne, or Invalides.

The glory of the French military lives on here in the Musée de l'Armée, the world's greatest army museum. It was the Sun King who decided to build the "hotel" to house soldiers who'd been disabled. It wasn't entirely a benevolent gesture, since these veterans had been injured, crippled, or blinded while fighting Louis's battles. Louvois was ordered in 1670 to launch this massive building program. Eventually the building was crowned by a Jules Hardouin-Mansart gilded dome.

The best way to approach the Invalides is by walking from the Right Bank across the turn-of-the-century pont Alexandre III. Among the collections (begun by a French inspector in 1794) are Viking swords, Burgundian bacinets, 14th-century blunderbusses, Balkan khandjars, American Browning machine guns, war pitchforks, salamander-engraved Renaissance serpentines, musketoons, and grenadiers. As a sardonic touch, there's even General Daumesnil's wooden leg. Outstanding are the suits of armor—especially in the new Arsenal—worn by kings and dignitaries, including Louis XIV. The famous "armor suit of the lion" was made for François I. The showcases of swords are among the finest in the world.

Crossing the Court of Honor, you'll come to the Eglise du Dôme, designed by Hardouin-Mansart for Louis XIV. He began work on the church in 1677, though he died before its completion. The dome is Paris's second-tallest monument. In the Napoléon Chapel is the hearse used at the emperor's funeral on May 9, 1821.

To accommodate the Tomb of Napoléon—of red porphyry, with a green granite base—the architect Visconti had to redesign the high altar in 1842. First buried at St. Helena, Napoléon's remains were returned to Paris in 1840 and then locked inside six coffins. Surrounding the tomb are a dozen amazonlike figures representing his victories. Almost lampooning the smallness of the man, everything is made awesome: You'd think a real giant was buried here, not a symbolic one. The statue of Napoléon in his coronation robes stands 8$^1/_2$ feet tall.

IN MONTMARTRE

From the 1880s to just before World War I, Montmartre enjoyed its golden age as the world's best-known art colony. *La vie de bohème* reigned supreme. Following World War I the pseudo-artists flocked here in droves, with camera-snapping tourists hot on their heels. The real artists had long gone to such places as Montparnasse.

Before its discovery and subsequent chic, Montmartre was a sleepy farming community, with windmills dotting the landscape. Since it's at the highest point in the city, visitors who find it too much of a climb will want to take the miniature train along the steep streets: **Le Petit Train de Montmartre,** which passes all the major landmarks, seats 55 passengers who can listen to the English commentary. Board at place du Tertre (at the Eglise St-Pierre) or place Blanche (near the Moulin Rouge). Trains run daily from 10am to 7pm. For information, contact Promotrain, 131 rue de Clignancourt, 18e (☎ **1/42-62-24-00**).

Impressions

The kid will come from Nebraska or Heidelberg, from Poland or Senegal, and Paris will be born again—new, brand new and unexpected, and the Arch of Triumph will rise again, and the Seine will flow for the first time, and there will be new areas, unknown and unexplored, called Montmartre and Montparnasse . . . and it will all be for the first time, a completely new city, built suddenly for you and you alone.

—Romain Gary

The simplest way to reach Montmartre is to take the Métro to Anvers, then walk up rue du Steinkerque toward the funicular. Funiculars run to the precincts of Sacré-Coeur every day from 6am to 11pm. Except for Sacré-Coeur, Montmartre has only minor attractions. It's the historic district itself that's compelling.

Specific attractions to look for include the **Bateau-Lavoir** (Boat Warehouse), place Emile-Goudeau. Though gutted by fire in 1970, it has been reconstructed. Picasso once lived here and, in the winter of 1905–6, painted one of the world's most famous portraits, *The Third Rose* (Gertrude Stein).

The **Espace Montmartre Salvadore Dalí,** 11 rue Poulbot (☎ 1/42-64-40-10), presents Dalí's phantasmagorical world, featuring 300 original works that include his 1956 *Don Quixote* lithograph. It's open daily from 10am to 6pm, charging 35 F ($6.65) for adults and 10 F ($1.90) for children.

One of the most famous churches here is the **Eglise St-Pierre,** rue du Mon-Cenis, originally a Benedictine abbey. The church was consecrated in 1147; two of the columns in the choir stall are the remains of a Roman temple. Among the sculptured works, note a nun with the head of a pig, a symbol of sensual vice. At the entrance are three bronze doors sculpted by Gismondi in 1980: The middle door depicts the life of St. Peter; the left is dedicated to St. Denis, first bishop of Paris; and the right is dedicated to the Holy Virgin.

The **Musée de Vieux Montmartre,** 12 rue Corot (☎ 1/46-06-61-11), exhibits a wide collection of mementos. This 17th-century house was once occupied by Dufy, van Gogh, Renoir, and Suzanne Valadon and her son, Utrillo. It's open Tuesday to Sunday from 11am to 6pm. Admission is 25 F ($4.75) for adults and 15 F ($2.85) for children.

✪ Basilique du Sacré-Coeur

Place St-Pierre, 18e. ☎ 1/42-51-17-02. Basilica, free; dome, 15 F ($2.90) adults, 8 F ($1.50) students 6–25; crypt, 10 F ($1.90) and 5 F (95¢), respectively. Basilica, daily 7am–10:30pm. Dome and crypt, Apr–Sept, daily 9:15am–7pm; Oct–Mar, daily 9:15am–6pm. Métro: Abbesses; then take the elevator to the surface and follow the signs to the funiculaire, which takes you up to the church for the price of one Métro ticket.

Montmartre's crowning achievement is the Basilique du Sacré-Coeur, though the view of Paris from its precincts takes precedence over the basilica itself. Like other Parisian landmarks, it has always been the subject of much controversy. One Parisian called it "a lunatic's confectionery dream." Zola declared it "the basilica of the ridiculous." Sacré-Coeur's supporters include Jewish poet Max Jacob and artist Maurice Utrillo. Utrillo never tired of drawing and painting it, and he and Jacob came here regularly to pray.

In gleaming white, it towers over Paris—its five bulbous domes suggesting some 12th-century Byzantine church and its campanile inspired by Roman-Byzantine art. After France's defeat by the Prussians in 1870, the basilica was planned as an offering to cure the country's misfortunes. Both rich and poor contributed money to build it. Construction began in 1873, but the church was not consecrated until 1919. On a clear day the vista from the dome can extend for 35 miles. You can also walk around the inner dome of the church, peering down like a pigeon (a few will likely be there to keep you company).

IN THE MARAIS

When Paris began to overflow the confines of the Ile de la Cité in the 13th century, the citizenry settled in Le Marais, the marsh that used to be flooded regularly by the high-rising Seine. By the 17th century the Marais had reached the pinnacle of fashion, becoming the center of aristocratic Paris. At that time, the majority of its great *hôtels particuliers* (mansions)—many already restored or being restored—were built by the finest craftsmen in France.

In the 18th and 19th centuries, the fashionable deserted the Marais in favor of the expanding Faubourg St-Germain and Faubourg St-Honoré. Industry eventually took over the quarter, and the once-elegant *hôtels* were turned into tenements. There was talk of demolishing this blighted sector, but in 1962 the alarmed Comité de Sauvegarde du Marais banded together and saved the district.

As you stroll the Marais, you might want to seek out the following *hôtels:* The **Hôtel de Rohan,** 87 rue Vieille-du-Temple, was once occupied by the fourth Cardinal Rohan, who was involved in the diamond necklace scandal that implicated Marie Antoinette. The first Cardinal Rohan, the original occupant, was reputed to be the son of Louis XIV. The interior is open to the public only when exhibitions are on. The main attraction is the amusing 18th-century Salon des Singes (Monkey Room). In the courtyard (open Monday to Friday from 9am to 6pm) is a stunning bas-relief of a nude Apollo and four horses against exploding sunbursts.

At 47 rue Vieille-du-Temple is the **Hôtel des Ambassadeurs de Hollande,** where Beaumarchais wrote *The Marriage of Figaro.* It's one of the most splendid mansions in the area—and was never occupied by the Dutch embassy. It's not open to the public.

Though the facade of the 17th-century **Hôtel de Beauvais,** 68 rue François-Miron, was badly damaged during the Revolution, it remains one of the most charming in Paris. A plaque commemorates the fact that Mozart inhabited the mansion in 1763. To visit inside, speak to the Association du Paris Historique, on the ground floor of the building, any afternoon.

The **Hôtel de Sens,** a landmark at 1 rue de Figuier (☎ 1/42-78-14-60), was built from the 1470s to 1519 for the archbishops of Sens. Along with the Hôtel de Cluny on the Left Bank, it's the only domestic architecture remaining from the 15th century. Long after the archbishops had departed in 1605, it was occupied by the scandalous Queen Margot, wife of Henri IV. Her "younger and more virile" new lover slew the discarded one as she looked on in amusement. Today the mansion houses the Bibliothèque Forney. In the courtyard you can see the ornate stone decoration—the gate is open Tuesday to Saturday from 1:30 to 8pm.

Work began on the **Hôtel de Bethune-Sully,** 62 rue St-Antoine (☎ 1/42-74-22-22), in 1625. In 1634 it was acquired by the duc de Sully, who had been Henri IV's minister of finance before the king was assassinated in 1610. After a straitlaced life, Sully broke loose in his later years, adorning himself with diamonds and garish rings—and a young bride who had a preference for very young men. The *hôtel* was acquired by the government after World War II and now contains the

National Office of Historical Monuments and Sites. Recently restored, the relief-studded facade is especially appealing. You can visit the interior with a guide, on Saturday or Sunday at 3pm, depending on the program. There's daily admittance to the courtyard and the garden that opens onto place des Vosges.

The most characteristic street in the district is **rue des Rosiers** (Street of the Rosebushes), one of the most colorful of the streets remaining from the old Jewish quarter. The Star of David shines here, Hebrew letters flash (in neon), couscous is sold from the shops run by Moroccan or Algerian Jews, bearded old men sit in doorways, restaurants serve strictly kosher meals, and signs appeal for Jewish liberation.

Musée Carnavalet

23 rue de Sévigné, 3e. ☎ 1/42-72-21-13. Admission 35 F ($6.65) adults, 25 F ($4.75) ages 18–24 and over 60, free for children 17 and under. Tues–Sun 10am–5:40pm. Métro: St-Paul or Chemin-Vert.

The history of Paris comes alive here in intimately personal terms—right down to the chessmen Louis XVI used to distract his mind in the days before he went to the guillotine. A renowned Renaissance palace, the *hôtel* was built in 1544 by Pierre Lescot and Jean Goujon; later it was acquired by Mme de Carnavalet. The great François Mansart transformed it between the years 1655 and 1661. Its best-known memories concern one of history's most famous letterwriters, Mme de Sévigné, who moved into the house in 1677. Fanatically devoted to her daughter (until she had to live with her), she poured out nearly every detail of her life in letters, virtually ignoring her son. A native of the Marais, she died at her daughter's château in 1696. It wasn't until 1866 that the city acquired the mansion and turned it into a museum.

IN THE LATIN QUARTER

This is the Left Bank precinct of the University of Paris (often called the Sorbonne), where students meet and fall in love over coffee and croissants. Rabelais called it the Quartier Latin, because of the students and professors who spoke Latin in the classrooms and on the streets. The sector teems with belly dancers, exotic restaurants (from Vietnamese to Balkan), sidewalk cafés, bookstalls, and *caveaux*.

A good starting point might be place St-Michel (Métro: Pont-St-Michel), where Balzac used to get water from the fountain when he was a youth. This center was the scene of much Resistance fighting in the summer of 1944. The quarter centers around boulevard St-Michel, to the south (the students call it "Boul Mich").

Musée National du Moyen Age / Thermes de Cluny (Musée de Cluny)

6 place Paul-Painlevé, 5e. ☎ 1/43-25-62-00. Admission 27 F ($5.15) adults, 18 F ($3.40) ages 18–24, free for children 17 and under. Wed–Mon 9:15am–5:45pm. Métro: Cluny–La Sorbonne.

There are two reasons to go here: The museum houses the world's finest collection of art from the Middle Ages, including jewelry and tapestries, and it's all displayed in a well-preserved manor house that was constructed on top of Roman baths. In the cobblestone Court of Honor you can admire the flamboyant gothic building with its clinging vines, turreted walls, gargoyles, and dormers with seashell motifs. Along with the Hôtel de Sens in Le Marais, this is all that remains in Paris of domestic medieval architecture. Originally the Cluny was the mansion of a 15th-century abbot. By 1515 it was the residence of Mary Tudor, teenage widow of Louis XII and daughter of Henry VII of England and Elizabeth of York.

Seized during the Revolution, it was rented in 1833 to Alexandre du Sommerard, who adorned it with medieval works of art. Upon his death in 1842, both the building and the collection were bought back by the government.

Most people come primarily to see the Unicorn Tapestries, the world's most outstanding tapestries. A beautiful princess and her handmaiden, beasts of prey, and just plain pets—all the romance of the age of chivalry lives on in these remarkable yet mysterious tapestries. They were discovered only a century ago in the Château de Boussac in Auvergne. Five seem to deal with the five senses (one depicts a unicorn looking into a mirror held by a dour-faced maiden). The sixth shows a woman under an elaborate tent, her pet dog resting on an embroidered cushion beside her. The lovable unicorn and his friendly companion, a lion, hold back the flaps. The background in red and green forms a rich carpet of spring flowers, fruit-laden trees, birds, rabbits, donkeys, dogs, goats, lambs, and monkeys. Downstairs are the ruins of the Roman baths, dating from around A.D. 200. You wander through a display of Gallic and Roman sculptures and an interesting marble bathtub engraved with lions.

The Sorbonne
Bd. St-Michel, 5e. Métro: St-Michel.

The University of Paris—everybody calls it the Sorbonne—is one of the most famous institutions in the world. Founded in the 13th century, it had become the most prestigious university in the West by the 14th century, drawing such professors as Thomas Aquinas. Reorganized by Napoléon in 1806, the Sorbonne is today the premier university of France. At first glance from place de la Sorbonne, it may seem architecturally undistinguished. It was rather indiscriminately reconstructed at the turn of the century. Not so the Eglise de la Sorbonne, built in 1635 by Le Mercier, which contains the marble tomb of Cardinal Richelieu, a work by Girardon based on a Le Brun design. At his feet is the remarkable statue *Science in Tears.*

The Panthéon
Place du Panthéon, 5e. ☎ **1/43-54-34-52.** Admission 27 F ($5.15) adults, 18 F ($3.40) ages 18–25 and over 60, 10 F ($1.90) children 12–17, free for children under 12. Apr–Sept, daily 10am–6:30pm; Oct–Mar, daily 10am–5:30pm. Métro: Cardinal-Lemoine or Maubert-Mutualité.

Some of the most famous men in the history of France (Hugo, for one) are buried here in austere grandeur, on the crest of the mount of St. Geneviève. In 1744 Louis XV made a vow that if he recovered from a mysterious illness he'd build a church to replace the decayed Abbeye de St-Geneviève. When he recovered, Madame de Pompadour's brother hired Soufflot for the job. He designed the church in the form of a Greek cross, with a dome reminiscent of that of St. Paul's Cathedral in London. Soufflot died, and the work was carried out by his pupil, Rondelet, who completed the structure nine years after his master's death.

Following the Revolution the church was converted into a "Temple of Fame"—ultimately a pantheon for the great men of France. The body of Mirabeau was buried here, though his remains were later removed. Likewise, Marat was only a temporary tenant. However, Voltaire's body was exhumed and placed here—and allowed to remain. In the 19th century the building changed roles so many times—a church, a pantheon, a church—that it was hard to keep its function straight. After Hugo was buried here it became a pantheon once more. Other notable men entombed here include Rousseau, Soufflot, Zola, and Braille.

5th & 6th Arrondissements

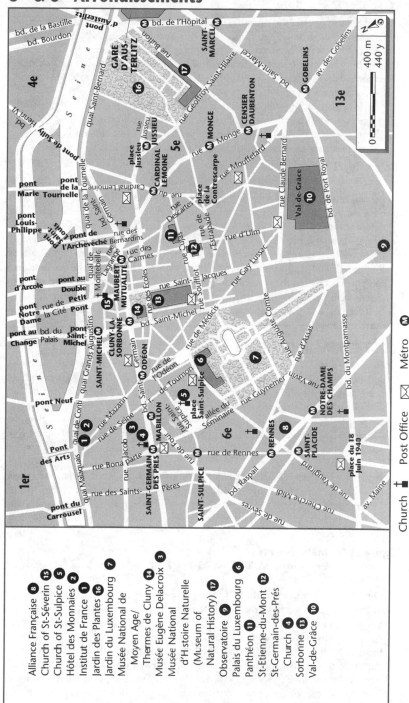

Alliance Française 8
Church of St-Séverin 15
Church of St-Sulpice 5
Hôtel des Monnaies 2
Institut de France 1
Jardin des Plantes 16
Jardin du Luxembourg 7
Musée National de Moyen Age/Thermes de Cluny 14
Musée Eugène Delacroix 3
Musée National d'Histoire Naturelle (Museum of Natural History) 17
Observatoire 9
Palais du Luxembourg 6
Panthéon 11
St-Etienne-du-Mont 12
St-Germain-des-Prés 4
Church
Sorbonne 13
Val-de-Grâce 10

Church ✝   Post Office ⊠   Métro Ⓜ

In the spring of 1995, the ashes of scientist Marie Curie were entombed at the Panthéon, "the first lady so honored in our history for her own merits," in the words of François Mitterrand. Another woman, Sophie Bertholet, was buried there first, but only alongside her chemist husband, Marcellin, and not as a personal honor to her. Madame Curie was once denied membership in the all-male Academy of Sciences because she was a woman.

The finest frescoes—the Puvis de Chavannes—are at the end of the left wall before you enter the crypt. One illustrates St. Geneviève bringing supplies to relieve the victims of the famine. The best depicts her white-draped head looking out over moonlit medieval Paris, the city whose patroness she became.

Palais Royal

Place du Palais-Royal on rue St-Honoré, 1er. Métro: Louvre.

At the demolished Café Foy in the Palais Royal, outraged Camille Desmoulins once jumped up on a table and shouted for the mob "to fight to the death." The date was July 13, 1789. The renown of the Palais Royal goes back even further. The gardens were planted in 1634 for Cardinal Richelieu, who presented them to Louis XIII. In time the property became the residence of the ducs d'Orléans. Philippe-Egalité, a cousin of Louis XVI, built his apartments on the grounds and subsequently rented them to prostitutes. By the 20th century those same apartments were rented by such artists as Cocteau and Colette. (A plaque at 9 rue Beaujolais marks the entrance to her apartment, which she inhabited until her death in 1954.)

IN ST-GERMAIN-DES-PRES

Sometime after World War II, long-haired Juliette Greco (in black slacks, sweater, and sandals) drifted into this neighborhood. She arrived in the heyday of the existentialists, when all the world revolved around Sartre, de Beauvoir, and Camus. The Café de Flore, Brasserie Lipp, and Café Deux Magots were the settings for the postwar bohemians who came there to "existentialize." In time Sartre eulogized Mme Greco ("She has millions of poems in her throat"); her black outfit was adopted from Paris to California; and eventually she earned the title of "la muse de St-Germain-des-Prés."

In the 1950s new names appeared, like Françoise Sagan, Gore Vidal, and James Baldwin. By the 1960s tourists had become more prevalent at the cafés. In the 1990s the old days are gone, but St-Germain-des-Prés remains an interesting quarter of nightclubs in "*caves*," publishing houses, bookshops, galleries, bistros, and coffeehouses.

Eglise St-Germain-des-Prés

3 place St-Germain-des-Prés, 6e. ☎ 1/43-25-41-71. Admission free. Daily 8am–7:30pm. Métro: St-Germain-des-Prés.

Outside it's a handsome early 17th-century town house. However, inside it's one of Paris's oldest churches, going back to the 6th century, when a Benedictine abbey was founded here. The marble columns in the triforium are all that remains from that period. Restoration of the St. Symphorien Chapel—the site of a pantheon for Merovingian kings, at the entrance of the church—began in 1981. During that work, romanesque paintings were discovered on the chapel's triumphal arch. Its romanesque tower, topped by a 19th-century spire, is the most enduring landmark in the village of St-Germain-des-Prés. Its church bells, however, are hardly noticed by the patrons of Deux Magots across the way.

The Normans were fond of destroying the abbey and did so at least four times. The present building has a romanesque nave and a gothic choir with fine capitals. Among the people interred at the church are Descartes and Jean-Casimir, the king of Poland who abdicated his throne. When you leave the church, just turn right in rue de l'Abbaye and have a look at the 17th-century pink Palais Abbatial.

Eglise St-Sulpice

Rue St-Sulpice, 6e. ☎ 1/46-33-21-78. Admission free. Daily 7:30am–7:30pm. Métro: St-Sulpice.

Pause first on the 18th-century place St-Sulpice. On the 1844 fountain by Visconti are sculpted likenesses of four 18th-century bishops: Fenelon, Massillon, Bossuet, and Flechier. Napoléon, then a general, was given a stag party here in 1799. He liked the banquet but not the square, so when he was promoted he changed it. Work began on the church in 1646; the facade, "bastardized classic," was completed in 1745, though one of the two towers was never completed. Many architects, including Le Vau, worked on the building. Some were summarily fired; others, such as the Florentine Servandoni, were discredited. One of the most notable treasures inside the 360-foot-long church is Servandoni's rococo Chapel of the Madonna, with a marble statue of the Virgin by Pigalle. The church contains one of the world's largest organs, with more than 6,500 pipes. Chalgrin designed the organ case in the 18th century.

The main draw at St-Sulpice are the Delacroix frescoes in the Chapel of the Angels (first on your right as you enter). Seek out his muscular Jacob wrestling (or dancing?) with an angel. On the ceiling St. Michael has his own troubles with the Devil, and another mural depicts Heliodorus being driven from the temple. Painted in the final years of his life, the frescoes were a high point in the career of the baffling, romantic Delacroix.

IN MONTPARNASSE

For the Lost Generation, life centered around the literary cafés here. Hangouts such as the Dôme, Coupole, Rotonde, and Sélect became legendary. Artists, especially U.S. expatriates, turned their backs on "too touristy" Montmartre. Picasso, Modigliani, and Man Ray came this way, and Hemingway was a popular figure. So was Fitzgerald when he was poor (when he was in the chips, he hung out at the Ritz). Faulkner, Isadora Duncan, Miró, Joyce, Ford Madox Ford, and even Trotsky came here.

The life of Montparnasse still centers around its cafés and nightclubs, many only a shadow of what they used to be. Its heart is at the crossroads of boulevards Raspail and du Montparnasse, one of the settings of *The Sun Also Rises*. Rodin's controversial statue of Balzac swathed in a large cape stands guard over the prostitutes who cluster around the pedestal. Balzac seems to be the only one in Montparnasse who doesn't feel the impact of time and change.

IN LA DEFENSE

Grande Arche de la Défense

1 place du Parvis de la Défense, 18e. ☎ 1/49-07-27-57. Admission 40 F ($7.60) adults, 30 F ($5.70) children 4–18, free for children 3 and under. Apr–Sept, daily 9am–7pm; Oct–Mar, daily 9am–6pm. RER: La Défense.

Designed as the centerpiece of the sprawling futuristic satellite suburb of La Défense, this massive steel-and-masonry arch rises 35 stories. It was built with the

The Mother of the Lost Generation

"So Paris was the place that suited those of us that were to create the twentieth century art and literature, naturally enough." Gertrude Stein, who made this pronouncement, wasn't known for her modesty. In the 1920s she and her lover, Alice B. Toklas, became the most famous expatriates in Paris. To get an invitation to call on Lovey and Pussy (nicknames for Gertrude and Alice) at 27 rue de Fleurus, in the heart of Montparnasse, was to to be invited into the innermost circle of expatriate Paris. Though Gertrude didn't achieve popular success until the 1933 publication of her *Autobiography of Alice B. Toklas*, she was known and adored by many members of the Lost Generation—all except Ernest Hemingway, who later turned against her, libeling her in *A Moveable Feast*, published post-humously. But to the young sensitive man, often gay, arriving from America in the 1920s, La Stein was "The Mother of Us All." These young fans hung on her every word, while Alice baked her notorious hashish brownies in the kitchen.

At rue de Fleurus, Gertrude and Alice lived in a world filled with modern paintings, including a nude by Vallotton, a Toulouse-Lautrec, Picassos, Gauguins, and Matisses. Gertrude had paid $1,000 for her first Matisse, $30 for her first Picasso. Matisse had, in fact, first met Picasso at Gertrude's studio. The Saturday-night soirées here became a Montparnasse legend.

Not all visitors came to worship. Gertrude was denounced by many, including avant-garde magazines of the time, which called her a "fraud, egomaniac, and publicity seeking." Braque called her claim to have influenced art in Paris "nonsense."

In spite of the attacks, the jokes, the lurid speculation, Stein, at least in public, kept her ego intact. Bernard Fay once told her he'd met three people in his life who ranked as a genius: Gide, Picasso, and Stein herself.

"Why include Gide?" Stein asked.

blessing of François Mitterrand and ringed with soaring office buildings and a circular avenue (*périphérique*), the design of which imitates the traffic circle surrounding the Arc de Triomphe. This deliberately overscale archway is one of the latest major landmarks to dot the Paris skyline, along with the Cité de la Musique in the northwestern section of the city. High enough to shelter Notre-Dame below its canopy, the monument was designed as an extension of the panorama that interconnects the Louvre, Arc du Carroussel, Champs-Elysées, Arc de Triomphe, avenue de la Grande-Armée, and place du Porte-Maillot into a magnificent straight line. An elevator carries visitors to an observation platform from which you can see the carefully conceived geometry of the surrounding street plan.

IN LES HALLES

For eight centuries Les Halles was the major wholesale fruit, meat, and vegetable market of Paris. The smock-clad vendors, the carcasses of beef, the baskets of the most appetizing vegetables in the world—all that belongs to the past. Today the action has moved to the modern steel-and-glass structure at Rungis, a suburb near Orly Airport: Le Forum des Halles (Métro: Les Halles; RER: Châtelet–Les Halles),

7th Arrondissement

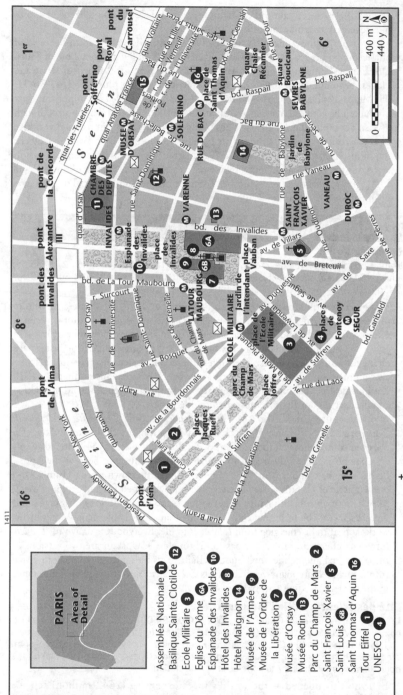

PARIS

Area of Detail

Assemblée Nationale **11**
Basilique Sainte Clotilde **12**
Ecole Militaire **3**
Eglise du Dôme **6A**
Esplanade des Invalides **10**
Hôtel des Invalides **8**
Hôtel Matignon **14**
Musée de l'Armée **9**
Musée de l'Ordre de
  la Libération **7**
Musée d'Orsay **15**
Musée Rodin **13**
Parc du Champ de Mars **2**
Saint François Xavier **5**
Saint Louis **6B**
Saint Thomas d'Aquin **16**
Tour Eiffel **1**
UNESCO **4**

Church ✝   Post Office ⊠   Métro Ⓜ

0   400 m
     440 y

opened in 1979, is a complex, much underground, containing dozens of shops, plus several restaurants and movie theaters.

For many visitors a night on the town is still capped by the traditional bowl of onion soup in Les Halles, usually at Au Pied de Cochon ("Pig's Foot") or Au Chien Qui Fume ("Smoking Dog"), in the wee hours. There's still much to see in Les Halles, beginning with the **Eglise St-Eustache,** 2 rue du Jour (☎ 1/42-36-31-05; Métro: Les Halles). In the old days cabbage vendors came here to pray for their produce. The gothic-Renaissance church dates from the mid-16th century, though it wasn't completed until 1637. It has been known for its organ recitals ever since Liszt played here in 1866. Inside is the black marble tomb of Jean-Baptiste Colbert, the minister of state under Louis XIV. A marble statue of the statesman rests on top of his tomb, which is flanked by Coysevox's *Abundance* (a horn of flowers) and J. B. Tuby's *Fidelity*. There's another entrance on rue Rambuteau. The church is open daily from 7:30am to 7:30pm.

2 More Museums

✪ Musée Rodin

In the Hôtel Biron, 77 rue de Varenne, 7e. ☎ **1/44-18-61-10.** Admission 27 F ($5.15) adults, 18 F ($3.40) ages 18–25, free for ages 17 and under. Apr–Sept, Tues–Sun 9:30am–5:45pm; Oct–Mar, Tues–Sun 9:30am–4:45pm. Métro: Varenne.

The most beautiful museum in Paris, this house and its gardens are a repository of the work of Auguste Rodin (1840–1917), the undisputed master of French 19th-century sculpture. These days Rodin is acclaimed as the father of modern sculpture, but in a different era his work was labeled obscene. Artistic tastes have changed, and in due course the government purchased his gray-stone 18th-century mansion in Faubourg St-Germain, where Rodin had his studio from 1910 until his death. The rose gardens were restored to their original splendor, making a perfect setting for Rodin's most memorable works.

In the courtyard are three world-famous creations: *The Gate of Hell, The Thinker,* and *The Burghers of Calais.* Rodin's first major public commission, *The Burghers* commemorated the heroism of six burghers who in 1347 offered themselves as hostages to Edward III in return for his ending the siege of their port. Perhaps the best-known work, *The Thinker,* in Rodin's own words, "thinks with every muscle of his arms, back, and legs, with his clenched fist and gripping toes." Inside the mansion, the sculptures, plaster casts, reproductions, originals, and sketches reveal the freshness and vitality of that remarkable man. Many of his works appear to be emerging from marble into life. Everybody is drawn to *The Kiss* (of which one critic wrote, "the passion is timeless"). Upstairs are two versions of the celebrated and condemned nude of Balzac, his bulky torso rising from a tree trunk. Included are many versions of his *Monument to Balzac* (a large one stands in the garden), Rodin's last major work.

Cité des Sciences et de l'Industrie

La Villette, 30 av. Corentin-Cariou, 19e. ☎ **1/40-05-80-00.** Cité Pass (entrance to all exhibits), 45 F ($8.55) adults, 35 F ($6.65) ages 7–25, free for children 6 and under; Géode, 55 F ($10.45) adults, 40 F ($7.60) children 17 and under. Tues and Thurs–Fri 10am–6pm, Wed noon–9pm, Sat–Sun and holidays noon–8pm. Show times at Géode, Tues–Sun on the hour 10am–9pm. RER: Line 7 to Porte de la Villette station.

In 1986 this opened as the world's most expensive ($642 million) science complex designed to "modernize mentalities" as a first step in the process of

8th Arrondissement

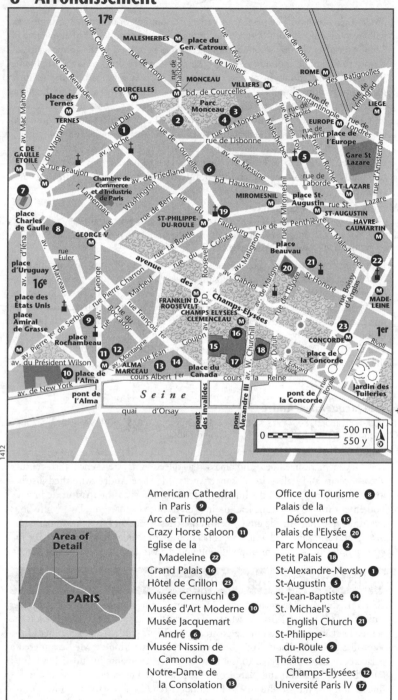

modernizing society. The place is so vast, with so many options, that a single visit will give you only an idea of its scope. Some exhibits are couched in an overlay of Gallic humor, including seismographic activity as presented in the comic-strip adventures of a jungle explorer. Among others is the silver-skinned Geodesic Dome (the Géode) that shows the closest thing to a 3-D cinema in Europe on the inner surfaces of its curved walls. It's a 112-foot sphere with a 370-seat theater. Explora, a permanent exhibit, is spread over the three upper levels; its displays revolve around four themes: the universe, life, matter, and communication. The Cité also has a multimedia library and a planetarium. An "inventorium" is for children.

The Cité is in La Villette park, Paris's largest city park, with 136 acres of greenery—twice the size of the Tuileries. Here you'll find a belvedere, a video workshop for children, and information about exhibitions and events, along with a café and restaurant.

Musée des Arts Décoratifs

In the Musée du Louvre, 107 rue de Rivoli, 1er. ☎ **1/42-60-32-14.** Admission 25 F ($4.75) adults, 16 F ($3.05) ages 5–24, free for children 4 and under. Wed–Sat 12:30–6pm, Sun noon–6pm. Métro: Palais-Royal or Tuileries.

In the northwest wing of the Louvre's Pavillon de Marsan, this museum holds a treasury of furnishings, fabrics, wallpaper, objets d'art, and other items displaying living styles from the Middle Ages to the present. Notable on the first floor are the 1920s art deco boudoir, bath, and bedroom done for couturier Jeanne Lanvin by designer Rateau, plus a prestigious collection of the works donated by Jean Dubuffet. Decorative art from the Middle Ages to the Renaissance is on the second floor, while rich collections from the 17th, 18th, and 19th centuries occupy the third and fourth floors. The fifth has specialized centers, such as wallpaper and drawings, and documentary centers detailing fashion, textiles, toys, crafts, and glass trends.

Musée Jacquemart-André

158 bd. Haussmann, 8e. ☎ **1/42-89-04-91.** Admission 10 F ($1.90). Wed–Sun 1–5:30pm. Closed Aug. Métro: Miromesnil or St-Philippe-du-Roule.

This is the best decorative arts museum in Paris. Edouard André and his wife, artist Nélie Jacquemart, lived here and amassed a collection of rare French 18th-century decorative art and Italian Renaissance works. Madame André, who died just before World War I, willed the building and its contents to the Institut de France. You enter through an arcade leading into an enclosed courtyard. Two white lions guard the doorway. Inside are Gobelin tapestries, Houdon busts, Savonnerie carpets, grand antiques, and a rich art collection that includes Rembrandt's *The Pilgrim of Emmaüs.* The salons drip with gilt and the winding staircase is truly elegant.

3 Historic Gardens & Squares

GARDENS   Bordering place de la Concorde, the statue-studded **Jardin des Tuileries** (☎ **1/42-60-38-01;** Métro: Tuileries) are as much a part of Paris as the Seine. They were designed by Le Nôtre, Louis XIV's gardener and planner of the Versailles grounds. About 100 years before that, Catherine de Médici ordered a palace built here, connected to the Louvre; other occupants included Louis XVI (after he left Versailles) and Napoléon. Twice attacked by enraged Parisians, it was finally burnt to the ground in 1871 and never rebuilt. The gardens, however, remain. Like the orderly French mind, the trees are arranged according to designs.

Even the paths are straight, as opposed to the winding ones in English gardens. Breaking the sense of order and formality are bubbling fountains.

Seemingly half of Paris can be found in the Tuileries on a warm spring day, listening to the chirping birds and admiring the daffodils and tulips. As you walk toward the Louvre, you'll enter the **Jardins du Carrousel,** dominated by the Arc de Triomphe du Carrousel, at the Cour du Carrousel. Pierced with three walkways and supported by marble columns, the monument honors Napoléon's Grande Armée, celebrating its victory at Austerlitz on December 5, 1805. The arch is surmounted by statuary, a chariot, and four bronze horses.

Hemingway told a friend that the ✪ **Jardin du Luxembourg,** 6e (☎ 1/43-29-12-78; Métro: Odéon; RER: Luxembourg), "kept us from starvation." He related that in his poverty-stricken days in Paris, he wheeled a baby carriage through the gardens because it was known "for the classiness of its pigeons." When the gendarme left to get a glass of wine, the writer would eye his victim, then lure it with corn and snatch it. "We got a little tired of pigeon that year," he confessed, "but they filled many a void."

Before it became a feeding ground for struggling artists in the 1920s, the Luxembourg Gardens knew greater days. But they've always been associated with artists, though students from the Sorbonne and children predominate nowadays. The gardens are the best on the Left Bank (if not in all of Paris). Marie de Médici, the much-neglected wife and later widow of the roving Henri IV, ordered the Palais du Luxembourg built on this site in 1612. She planned to live here with her "witch" friend, Leonora Galigaï. A Florentine by birth, the regent wanted to create another Pitti Palace, as she informed architect Salomon de Brosse. She wasn't entirely successful, though the overall effect is Italianate.

The queen didn't get to enjoy the Luxembourg Palace for very long after it was finished. She was forced into exile by her son, Louis XIII, after he discovered she was plotting to overthrow him. She died in Germany in poverty, quite a comedown from the luxury she'd known here. (Incidentally, the 21 paintings she commissioned from Rubens that glorified her life were intended for her palace, though they're now in the Louvre.) The palace isn't normally open to visitors; however, you can be granted permission to visit it if you apply to the Caisse Nationale des Monuments Historiques, 62 rue St-Antoine, 75004 Paris (☎ 1/44-61-21-70). If permission is granted, you can visit on the first Sunday of any month at 10:30am.

But the main draw here are the gardens, not the palace. For the most part, they're in the classic French style: well groomed and formally laid out, the trees planted in designs. The large central water basin is encircled by urns and statuary—one statue honors Ste. Geneviève, the patroness of Paris, depicted with pigtails reaching her thighs.

SQUARES In **place de la Bastille** on July 14, 1789, a mob Parisians attacked the Bastille and thus sparked the French Revolution. Nothing remains of the historic Bastille, built in 1369, for it was torn down. Many prisoners—some sentenced by Louis XIV for "witchcraft"—were kept within its walls, the best known being the "Man in the Iron Mask." When the fortress was stormed, only seven prisoners were discovered (the marquis de Sade had been transferred to the madhouse 10 days earlier). Authorities had discussed razing it anyway. So the attack was more symbolic than anything else. What it symbolized, however, and what it started will never be forgotten. Bastille Day is celebrated with great festivity on each July 14. In the center of the square is the Colonne de Juillet (July Column), but

Where the Royal Heads Rolled

In the east, avenue des Champs-Elysées begins at place de la Concorde, an octagonal traffic hub ordered built in 1757 to honor Louis XV and one of the world's grandest squares. The statue of the king was torn down in 1792 and the name of the square changed to place de la Révolution. Floodlit at night, it's dominated now by an Egyptian obelisk from Luxor, the oldest man-made object in Paris; it was carved circa 1200 B.C. and presented to France in 1829 by the viceroy of Egypt.

During the Reign of Terror, Dr. Guillotin's invention was erected on this spot and claimed thousands of lives—everybody from Louis XVI, who died bravely, to Mme du Barry, who went kicking and screaming all the way. Before the leering crowds, Marie Antoinette, Robespierre, Danton, Mlle Roland, and Charlotte Corday lost their heads here. (You can still lose your life on place de la Concorde—if you try to chance the frantic traffic and cross over.)

For a spectacular sight, look down the Champs-Elysées—the view is framed by Coustou's Marly horses, which once graced the gardens at Louis XIV's Château de Marly (these are copies—the originals are in the Louvre). On the opposite side, the gateway to the Tuileries is flanked by Coysevox's winged horses. On each side of the obelisk are two fountains with bronze-tailed mermaids and bare-breasted sea nymphs. Gray-beige statues ring the square, honoring the cities of France. To symbolize that city's fall to Germany in 1871, the statue of Strasbourg was covered with a black drape that wasn't lifted until the end of World War I. Two of the palaces on place de la Concorde are today the Ministry of the Marine and the deluxe Hôtel de Crillon. They were designed in the 1760s by Jacques-Ange Gabriel.

it doesn't commemorate the Revolution. It honors the victims of the 1830 July Revolution, which put Louis-Philippe on the throne. The tower is crowned by a winged nude, the *God of Liberty,* a star emerging from his head.

✪ **Place des Vosges,** 4e (Métro: St-Paul or Chemin-Vert), is Paris's oldest square and was once the most fashionable. In the heart of the Marais, it was called the Palais Royal in the days of Henri IV, who planned to live here—but his assassin, Ravaillac, had other intentions for him. Henry II was killed while jousting on the square in 1559, in the shadow of the Hôtel des Tournelles. His widow, Catherine de Médici, had the place torn down. Place des Vosges, once a major dueling ground, was one of the first planned squares in Europe. Its *grand siècle* red-brick houses are ornamented with white stone. Its covered arcades allowed people to shop at all times, even in the rain—quite an innovation at the time. In the 18th century chestnut trees were added, sparking a controversy that continues to this day: Critics say that the addition spoils the perspective.

Always aristocratic and often royal, **place Vendôme,** 1er (Métro: Opéra, Tuileries, Concorde, or Madeleine), enjoyed its golden age during the Second Empire. Fashion designers—the great ones, such as Worth—introduced the crinoline there. Louis Napoléon lived here, wooing his future empress, Eugénie de Montijo, at the Hôtel du Rhin. In its halcyon days Strauss waltzes echoed across the plaza. However, in time they were replaced by cannon fire. The square is dominated today by a column crowned by Napoléon. There was a statue of the Sun King here until the Revolution, when it was replaced briefly by *Liberty*.

Then came Napoléon, who ordered that a sort of Trajan's Column be erected in honor of his victory at Austerlitz. It was made of bronze melted from captured Russian and Austrian cannons. After Napoléon's downfall, the statue was replaced by one of Henri IV, everybody's favorite king and every woman's favorite man. Later Napoléon surmounted it again, this time in uniform and without the pose of a Caesar.

The Communards of 1871, who detested royalty and the false promises of emperors, pulled down the statue. Courbet is said to have led the raid. For his part in the drama, he was jailed and fined the cost of restoring the statue. He couldn't pay it, of course, and was forced into exile in Switzerland. Eventually, the statue of Napoléon, wrapped in a Roman toga, finally won out.

4 Historic Parks & Cemeteries

PARKS   One of the most spectacular parks in Europe is the ✪ **Bois de Boulogne,** Porte Dauphine, 16e (☎ 1/40-67-97-02; Métro: Les-Sablons, Porte-Maillot, or Porte-Dauphine). Horse-drawn carriages traverse it, but you can also drive through. Many of its hidden pathways, however, must be discovered by walking. If you had a week to spare, you could spend it all in the Bois de Boulogne and still not see everything. Porte Dauphine is the main entrance, though you can take the Métro to Porte Maillot as well. West of Paris, the park was once a forest kept for royal hunts. In the late 19th century it was in vogue. Carriages bearing elegant Parisian damsels with their foppish escorts rumbled along avenue Foch. Nowadays it's more likely to attract middle-class picnickers.

When Napoléon III gave the grounds to the city in 1852, they were developed by Baron Haussmann. Separating Lac Inférieur from Lac Supérieur is the Carrefour des Cascades (you can stroll under its waterfall). The Lower Lake contains two islands connected by a footbridge. From the east bank, you can take a boat to these idyllic grounds, perhaps stopping at the café/restaurant on one of them. Restaurants in the Bois are numerous, elegant, and expensive. The Pré-Catelan contains a deluxe restaurant of the same name and a Shakespearean theater in a garden said to have been planted with trees mentioned in the bard's plays.

The Jardin d'Acclimation at the northern edge of the Bois de Boulogne is for children, with a small zoo, an amusement park, and a narrow-gauge railway (see "Especially for Kids," later in this chapter). Two racetracks, Longchamp and Auteuil, are also in the park. The annual Grand Prix is run in June at Longchamp (site of a medieval abbey). The most fashionable Parisians turn out, the women in their finest haute couture. Directly to the north of Longchamp is Grand Cascade, the artificial waterfall of the Bois de Boulogne.

In the Bois de Boulogne's 60-acre **Bagatelle Park,** the comte d'Artois (later Charles X), brother-in-law of Marie Antoinette, made a bet with her that he could erect a small palace in less than three months—and he won. If you're here in late April, go to the Bagatelle to look at the tulips, if for no other reason. In late May one of the finest and best-known rose collections in all of Europe is in full bloom. *Note:* Beware of muggers and prostitutes at night.

An American expatriate once said that all babies in the **Parc Monceau,** 8e (☎ 42-27-39-56; Métro: Monceau or Villiers), were respectable. Whether or not babies like the park, at least their mothers and/or nurses are fond of wheeling their carriages through it. Much of the park is ringed with 18th- and 19th-century mansions, some of them evoking Proust's *Remembrance of Things Past.* The park was opened to the public during Napoléon III's Second Empire. It was built in 1778 by the duc d'Orléans, or Philippe Egalité, as he became known. Carmontelle designed the park for the duke, who was the richest man in France.

Parc Monceau was laid out with an Egyptian-style obelisk, a medieval dungeon, a thatched alpine farmhouse, a Chinese pagoda, a Roman temple, an enchanted grotto, various chinoiseries, and a waterfall. Most of these fairy-tale touches are gone, except for a pyramid and an oval *naumachie* fringed by a colonnade. Many of the former fantasies have been replaced by solid statuary and monuments, one honoring Chopin. In spring, the red tulips and magnolias are worth the airfare to Paris.

CEMETERIES   The ✪ **Cemetière du Père-Lachaise,** 16 rue de Repos, 20e (☎ 1/43-70-70-33; Métro: Père-Lachaise), is Paris's largest and contains more illustrious dead than any other. When it comes to name-dropping, this cemetery knows no peer—it's been called the "grandest address in Paris." Everybody from Sarah Bernhardt to Oscar Wilde (his tomb by Epstein) was buried here. So were Balzac, Delacroix, and Bizet. Colette's body was taken here in 1954, and her black granite slab always sports flowers (legend has it that cats replenish the red roses). In time, the "little sparrow," Edith Piaf, followed. The lover of George Sand, poet Alfred de Musset, was buried under a weeping willow. Napoléon's marshals, Ney and Masséna, were entombed here, as were Chopin and Molière. Marcel Proust's black tombstone rarely lacks a tiny bunch of violets.

Some tombs are sentimental favorites—that of Jim Morrison, the American rock star who died in 1971, reportedly draws the most visitors. The great dancer Isadora Duncan is reduced to a "pigeon hole" in the Columbarium, where bodies have been cremated and then "filed." If you search hard enough you can find the tombs of star-crossed Abélard and Héloïse, the ill-fated lovers of the 12th century. At Père-Lachaise they've found peace at last. Lovers of a different kind can also be found here: One stone is marked GERTRUDE STEIN on one side and ALICE B. TOKLAS on the other.

More than 40 acres, Père-Lachaise was acquired by the city in 1804. Nineteenth-century French sculpture abounds, for each family tried to outdo the others in ornamentation and cherubic ostentation. Some French socialists still pay tribute at the Mur des Fédérés, the anonymous grave site of the Communards who were executed on May 28, 1871. The French who died in the Resistance or in Nazi concentration camps are also honored by a monument. A guide at the entrance may give you a map outlining some of the well-known grave sites. (For a detailed walk of the cemetery, see *Frommer's Walking Tours: Paris, 2nd Edition.*)

The cemetery is open Monday to Friday from 8am to 6pm, Saturday from 8:30am to 6pm, and Sunday from 9am to 6pm (closes at 5:30pm November 6 to March 14).

In the shadow of the Tour Montparnasse, the **Cimetière Montparnasse,** 3 bd. Edgar Quinet, 6e (☎ 1/44-10-36-50; Métro: Edgar-Quinet), though debris-littered and badly maintained, is a burial ground of yesterday's celebrities. A map (available to the left of the main gateway) will direct you to the most famous occupants: the shared gravesite of Simone de Beauvoir and Jean-Paul Sartre. Others who were buried here include Samuel Beckett, Guy de Maupassant, Alfred Dreyfus, auto tycoon André Citroën, Ossip Zadkine, Camille Saint-Saëns, and Man Ray. The cemetery is open Monday to Friday from 7:30am to 6pm, Saturday from 8:30am to 6pm, and Sunday from 9am to 6pm.

West of the Butte and north of boulevard de Clichy, the **Cimetière de Montmartre,** 30 av. Rachel, 18e (☎ 1/43-87-64-24; Métro: La Fourche), is the resting place of famous composers, writers, and artists. Everybody from novelist Alexandre Dumas fils to Russian dancer Vaslav Nijinsky was interred here. The great Stendhal was buried here, as were lesser literary lights, including Edmond and Jules de Goncourt. Others bured here include Hector Berlioz, Heinrich Heine, Edgar Degas, Jacques Offenbach, and even François Truffaut. We like to pay our respects at the tomb of Alphonsine Plessis, the courtesan on whom Dumas based his Marguerite Gautier in *La Dame aux camélias,* and Madame Récamier, who taught the world how to lounge. Emile Zola was interred here, but his corpse was exhumed and taken to the Panthéon in 1908. In the tragic year of 1871, the cemetery became the site of the mass burials of victims of the Siege and the Commune. It's open Monday to Friday from 8am to 6pm, Saturday from 8:30am to 6pm, and Sunday from 8am to 7pm, closing at 5:30pm in winter.

5 Especially for Kids

If you're staying on the Right Bank, take your children strolling through the **Jardin des Tuileries** (above), where there are donkey rides, ice-cream stands, and a marionette show; at the circular pond you can rent a toy sailboat. On the Left Bank, similar delights exist in the **Jardin du Luxembourg** (above). After a visit to the **Eiffel Tower,** you can take the kids for a donkey ride in the nearby Champ-de-Mars gardens (above). **Puppet shows** are worth seeing for their enthusiastic, colorful productions—they're a genuine French child's experience. At the Jardin du Luxembourg, you'll see puppet productions with sinister plots set in gothic castles and Oriental palaces; some young critics say the best puppet shows are held in the Champ-de-Mars (performance times at the Luxembourg Gardens and Champs-de-Mars vary). In the Tuileries there are shows on Wednesday, Saturday, and Sunday at 3:15pm all summer long.

On Sunday afternoons, French families head up to the **Butte Montmarte** to bask in the fiesta atmosphere. You can join in the fun: Take the Métro to Anvers and walk to the Funiculaire de Montmarte (the silver cable car that carries you up to Sacré-Coeur). Once up top, follow the crowds to place du Tertre, where a band will usually be blasting off-key and where you can have the kids' picture sketched by local artists. You can take in the views of Paris from the various vantage points and treat the kids to ice cream in an outdoor café.

A Zoo

Parc Zoologique de Paris

In the Bois de Vincennes, 53 av. de St-Maurice, 12e. ☎ 1/44-75-20-10. Admission 40 F ($7.60) adults; 20 F ($3.80) ages 4–16, students 16–25, and over 60; free for children 3 and under. May–Sept, daily 9am–6:30pm; Oct–Apr, Mon–Sat 9am–5pm, Sun 9am–5:30pm. Métro: Porte-Dorée or Château-de-Vincennes.

There's a modest zoo in the Jardin des Plantes, near the natural history museum. But without a doubt the best Paris zoo is in the Bois de Vincennes—it's on the outskirts but quickly reached by subway. This modern zoo's animals live in settings similar to their natural habitats. The lion has an entire veldt to itself, and you can view one another across a deep protective moat. On a concrete mountain reminiscent of Disneyland's Matterhorn, lovely Barbary sheep leap from ledge to ledge or pose gracefully for hours watching the penguins in their pools at the mountain's foot. The animals seem happy here and are consequently playful. Keep well back from the bear pools.

AN AMUSEMENT PARK

Jardin d'Acclimation

Bois de Boulogne, 16e. ☎ **1/40-67-90-82.** Admission 10 F ($1.90) adults, 5 F (95¢) children 3–10, free for children 2 and under. Daily 10am–6:30pm. Métro: Les-Sablons.

The definitive Paris children's park is the Jardin d'Acclimation, a 25-acre amusement park on the northern edge of the Bois de Boulogne. The visit starts with a ride from Porte Maillot to the garden's entrance, through a stretch of wooded park, on a jaunty green-and-yellow narrow-gauge train. Inside the gate is an easy-to-follow layout map. The park is circular—follow the road in either direction and it'll take you all the way around and bring you back to the train at the end. En route you'll find a house of funny mirrors, an archery range, a miniature-golf course, zoo animals, an American-style bowling alley, a puppet theater (performances only on Thursday, Saturday, Sunday, and holidays), a playground, a hurdle-racing course, and a whole conglomeration of junior-scale rides, shooting galleries, and waffle stalls.

You can trot the kids off on a pony or join them in a boat on a lagoon. Also fun to watch is "La Prévention Routière," a miniature roadway operated by the Paris police. The youngsters drive through in small cars equipped to start and stop and are required by two genuine Parisian gendarmes to obey all street signs and light changes.

MUSEUMS

In Paris's largest park, the **Cité des Sciences et de l'Industrie,** is one of the best museums for kids, with special areas dedicated to them (see "More Museums," earlier in this chapter).

Musée de l'Homme

In the Palais de Chaillot, 16e. ☎ **1/44-05-72-72.** Admission 25 F ($4.75) adults, 15 F ($2.85) children 7–18, free for children 6 and under. Daily 9:45am–5:15pm. Métro: Trocadéro.

This museum is devoted to the history of people and their way of life. The most important exhibit is the Cro-Magnon "Menton man," discovered in 1872 in the Grimaldi grottoes on the Riviera. Among the replicas are South African and Sahara cave paintings. One long gallery depicts African cultures, with some of the best-known pieces of African art. Then follow Ethiopia, with a rare set of church paintings; North Africa; the Middle East; and Europe. The upstairs galleries are filled with representative artifacts from the Arctic, Asia, Oceania, and the Americas. The North American section contains some of the oldest Plains Indian pieces in existence. Of particular note are the shaman costumes from Siberia, the renewed exhibits dealing with Laos and Cambodia, a complete set of door carvings from New Caledonia, some of the best-known carvings from Polynesia, and pre-Columbian art from South and Central America.

16th Arrondissement

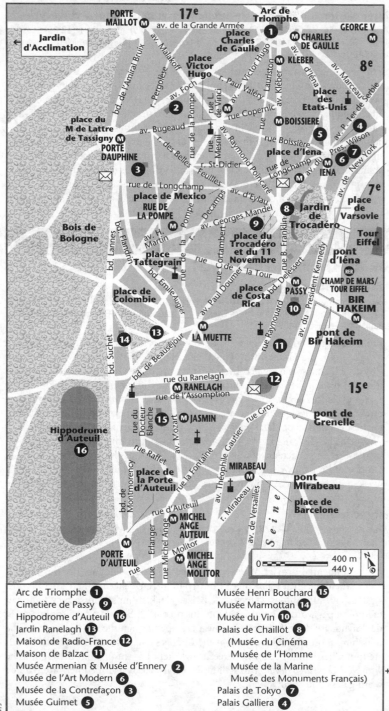

Jardin d'Acclimation

PORTE MAILLOT Ⓜ
17ᵉ
Arc de Triomphe ❶
av. de la Grande Armée
place Charles de Gaulle
GEORGE V Ⓜ
Ⓜ CHARLES DE GAULLE
8ᵉ
Ⓜ KLEBER
av. Marceau
av. d'léna
place des Etats-Unis
av. P. 1er de Serbie
av. de la Grande Armée
av. Foch
place Victor Hugo
r. Paul Valéry
av. Victor Hugo
Lauriston
av. Kléber
r. de Vinci
rue Copernic
Ⓜ BOISSIERE ❺ ❹
rue Boissière
place d'léna
❼ ❻ av. Pres. Wilson
Ⓜ IENA
av. du New York
7ᵉ
place du M de Lattre de Tassigny
Ⓜ PORTE DAUPHINE
av. Bugeaud
r. des Belles Feuilles
r. Mesnil
r. St-Didier
av. Raymond Poincaré
av. de Longchamp
✉
place de Varsovie
Tour Eiffel
❸
✉
rue de Longchamp
place de Mexico
RUE DE LA POMPE
Decamps
av. d'Eylau
av. Georges Mandel
❽ Jardin de Trocadéro
pont d'léna
bd. de l'Amiral Bruix
r. Pergolèse
r. de la Pompe
av. H. Martin
place Tattegrain
bd. Lannes
bd. Flandrin
r. de la r. de la Pompe
rue Cortambert
❾
place du Trocadéro et du 11 Novembre
rue de la Tour
rue B. Franklin
bd. Delessert
RER CHAMP DE MARS/ TOUR EIFFEL
BIR HAKEIM Ⓜ
Bois de Bologne
place de Colombie
bd. Emile Augier
av. Paul Doumer
place de Costa Rica
Ⓜ PASSY
❿
pont de Bir Hakeim
bd. Suchet
bd. de Beauséjour
⓭
Ⓜ LA MUETTE
av. du Président Kennedy
⓮
rue Raynouard
⓫
15ᵉ
rue du Ranelagh
Ⓜ RANELAGH
rue de l'Assomption
✉
⓬
pont de Grenelle
Hippodrome d'Auteuil
⓰
rue du Docteur Blanche
⓯ Ⓜ JASMIN
av. M.ozart
rue Gros
rue Raffet
bd. de Montmorency
place de la Porte d'Auteuil
rue la Fontaine
av. Théophile Gautier
MIRABEAU Ⓜ
pont Mirabeau
place de Barcelone
rue d'Auteuil
Ⓜ MICHEL ANGE AUTEUIL
r. Mirabeau
av. de Versailles
Seine
rue Erlanger
rue Michel Ange
Molitor
Ⓜ MICHEL ANGE MOLITOR
Ⓜ PORTE D'AUTEUIL
rue

0 ━━━━ 400 m / 440 y

Ⓜ Métro
✉ Post Office
✝ Church

Arc de Triomphe ❶	Musée Henri Bouchard ⓯
Cimetière de Passy ❾	Musée Marmottan ⓮
Hippodrome d'Auteuil ⓰	Musée du Vin ❿
Jardin Ranelagh ⓭	Palais de Chaillot ❽
Maison de Radio-France ⓬	(Musée du Cinéma
Maison de Balzac ⓫	Musée de l'Homme
Musée Armenian & Musée d'Ennery ❷	Musée de la Marine
Musée de l'Art Modern ❻	Musée des Monuments Français)
Musée de la Contrefaçon ❸	Palais de Tokyo ❼
Musée Guimet ❺	Palais Galliera ❹

1413

Musée National d'Histoire Naturelle (Museum of Natural History)

57 rue Cuvier, 5e. ☎ 1/40-79-30-30. Admission 25 F ($4.75) adults, 15 F ($2.85) ages 18–24, 6 F ($1.15) ages 17 and under. Wed–Fri 10am–5pm, Sat 11am–6pm. Métro: Jussieu or Gare-d'Austerlitz.

This museum's history dates back to 1635, when it was founded as a scientific research center by Guy de la Brosse, physician to Louis XIII, but that period is a fleeting moment compared to the eons of history covered inside the huge complex. The building was reopened after a $90-million restoration, and today an 85-foot whale skeleton greets visitors. In the galleries of paleontology, anatomy, and mineralogy, your kids can trace the evolution of life on earth, wondering at the massive skeletons of dinosaurs and mastodons and staring fascinated at the two-headed animal embryos floating in their pickling jars. A display is dedicated to endangered or vanished species. On the museum grounds are tropical hothouses containing thousands of species of unusual plant life along with small animal life in simulated natural habitats.

6 Special-Interest Sightseeing

FOR THE LITERARY ENTHUSIAST

Maison de Victor Hugo

6 place des Vosges, 4e. ☎1/42-72-10-16. Admission 27 F ($5.15) adults, 19 F ($3.60) ages 7–17, free for children 6 and under. Tues–Sun 10am–5:40pm. Closed holidays. Métro: St-Paul, Bastille, or Chemin-Vert.

From 1832 to 1848 the novelist/poet lived on the second floor at 6 place des Vosges, in the old Hôtel Rohan Guéménée, built in 1610 on what was then place Royale. His maison is owned by the city, which has taken over two additional floors. A leading figure in the French Romantic movement, Hugo is known for such novels as *The Hunchback of Notre-Dame* and *Les Misérables*. The museum owns some of Hugo's furniture as well as pieces that once belonged to Juliette Drouet, the mistress with whom he lived in exile on Guernsey, one of the Channel Islands.

Worth the visit are Hugo's 450-plus drawings illustrating scenes from his own works. See, in particular, his *Le Serpent*. Mementos of the great writer abound: samples of his handwriting, his inkwell, first editions of his works, and the death mask in his bedroom. A painting of his funeral procession at the Arc de Triomphe in 1885 is on display.

Maison de Balzac

47 rue Raynouard, 16e. ☎ 1/42-24-56-38. Admission 17.50 F ($3.30) adults, 9 F ($1.70) children 18 and under, free for seniors over 60. Tues–Sun 10am–5:45pm. Métro: Passy or La-Muette.

In the residential district of Passy, near the Bois de Boulogne, sits this modest house where the great Balzac lived from 1840 to 1847. Fleeing there after his possessions and furnishings were seized, Balzac cloaked himself in secrecy (you had to know a password to be ushered into his presence). Should a creditor knock on the Raynouard door, Balzac could always escape through the rue Berton exit. The museum's most notable memento is the Limoges coffee pot (the novelist's initials are in mulberry pink) that his "screech-owl" kept hot throughout the night as he wrote *La Comédie Humaine* to stall his creditors. Also enshrined here are Balzac's writing desk and chair.

FOR THE UNDERGROUND ENTHUSIAST

Catacombs

1 place Denfert-Rochereau, 14e. ☎ **1/43-22-47-63.** Admission 27 F ($5.15) adults, 15 F ($2.85) students, free for children under 6. Tues–Fri 2–4pm, Sat–Sun 9–11am and 2–4pm. Métro: Denfert-Rochereau.

Every year an estimated 50,000 tourists explore some 1,000 yards of tunnel in these dank Catacombs to look at some six million skeletons arranged in artistic skull-and-crossbones fashion. It's called the empire of the dead. First opened to the public in 1810, the Catacombs are now illuminated with overhead electric lights for their entire length. In the Middle Ages the Catacombs were quarries, but in 1785 city officials decided to use them as a burial ground—so the bones of several million persons were moved here from their previous resting places, the overcrowded cemeteries being considered health menaces. In 1830 the prefect of Paris closed the Catacombs to the public, considering them obscene and indecent. He maintained that he couldn't understand the morbid curiosity of civilized people who wanted to gaze upon the bones of the dead. During World War II the Catacombs were the headquarters of the French Underground.

Les Egouts de Paris (The Sewers)

Pont de l'Alma (at the corner of quai d'Orsay and place de la Résistance), 7e. ☎ **1/47-05-10-29.** Admission 25 F ($4.75) adults, 20 F ($3.80) ages 6–14 and over 60, free for children 5 and under. Tours begin on the Left Bank at pont de l'Alma, where a stairway leads into the bowels of the city. May–Oct, Sat–Wed 11am–6pm; Nov–Apr, Sat–Wed 11am–pm. Closed three weeks in Jan for maintenance. Métro: Alma-Marceau. RER: Pont-de-l'Alma.

Some say Baron Haussmann will be remembered mainly for the vast, complicated network of sewers he erected. The *égouts* of the city, as well as telephone and telegraph pneumatic tubes, were built around a quartet of principal tunnels, one 18 feet wide and 15 feet high. It's like an underground city, with the street names clearly labeled. Further, each branch pipe bears the number of the building to which it's connected. These underground passages are truly mammoth, containing pipes bringing in drinking water and compressed air as well as telephone and telegraph lines. You often have to wait in line as much as half an hour. Visiting times might change when there's bad weatas a storm can make the sewers dangerous. The tour consists of seeing a movie on sewer history, visiting a small museum, and then taking a short trip through the maze.

FOR VISITING AMERICANS

The American Center

51 rue de Bercy, 12e. ☎ **1/44-73-77-77.** Admission free; films, concerts, and special exhibitions, 50–100 F ($9.50–$19). Wed–Sat noon–8pm, Sun noon–6pm. Métro: Bercy or Gare-de-Lyon.

The American Center was designed as a showcase for the vast output of culture and art from America. From a now-defunct premises at 226 bd. Raspail, it evolved from a social club for students to a Nazi headquarters during World War II. The new American Center opened in 1994 on the eastern fringe of Paris, near the Gare de Lyon in the Parc de Bercy. Designed by Frank O. Gehry, the eight-story postmodern structure consists of two separate buildings (identified as "colliding forms")—one stark and monolithic, the other animated and more complex. They're linked by a free-form atrium. The entrance, covered with a tin roof evocative of the garret studios inhabited by expatriate artists in the 1920s and 1930s, has been compared by its architect to a "ballerina lifting her tutu."

Head here for bilingual film and theater presentations, dance programs, art exhibitions, and anything else celebrating the complexities and wealth of the American cultural experience. There's a 400-seat theater, a 100-seat cinema, lots of exhibition space, an audiovisual center, a restaurant/café, classrooms, and 24 apartments for resident artists.

Paris Shopping

Are there any good buys in Paris you shouldn't pass up? Is there any item here you can't find back home? Yes, certain items unique to France aren't easily available in other countries and make great gifts. In addition, you can bring back home memories of strolling along the chic boulevards, window-shopping, browsing in the smart boutiques, and finally finding that special "something from Paris."

1 The Shopping Scene

SHOPPING AREAS   The **1st and 2nd arrondissements,** where you'll find the famous rue de Rivoli, are filled with shops. Rue St-Honoré, parallel to rue de Rivoli, is also renowned for its many stores, which become less elegant as you head toward the Louvre and more upscale as you approach the 8th arrondissement. The 1st is the site of one of the best family department stores in Paris, Samaritaine, and Forum des Halles, the city's biggest shopping mall. A stroll along avenue de l'Opéra will bring you to the chic boutiques on place de l'Opéra. The great jewelry stores are clustered on the prestigious place Vendôme.

From the chic avenue Montaigne to rue du Faubourg St-Honoré, the **8th arrondissement** is where the international elite goes to buy haute couture. The 8th also includes the Champs-Elysées, although its former elegance has long since been replaced by rampant commercialism.

Most of the *grands magasins* (department stores), including Galeries Lafayette and Le Printemps, are found in the **9th arrondissement.** The nearby boulevards Haussmann, des Italiens, and des Capucines are also good for browsing. If you're looking for crystal and china, however, your best bet is rue de Paradis in the **10th arrondissement.** Rue de Passy is lined with stores catering to the wealthy residents of the **16th arrondissement.**

We recommend the Marais, in the **3rd and 4th arrondissements,** if you're interested in antiques. Place des Vosges, of Victor Hugo fame, is the place for old engravings and curios. From there you can head to rue des Francs-Bourgeois, where, as you progress toward the Centre Pompidou, you'll find the neighborhood packed with old galleries, boutiques, and antiques shops.

On the Left Bank, the **5th and 6th arrondissements** contain charming specialty shops, boutiques, and bookstores. Boulevard

St-Germain is the main venue, while boulevard St-Michel is filled with souvenir and fast-food shops. Shopping is usually better in the 6th, with its stylish fashions and expensive antiques. On rue du Bac in the **7th arrondissement** you'll find countless art galleries and pricey fashion boutiques.

SHIPPING There are restrictions on what merchandise can be shipped. Customs regulations change, so when in doubt it's best to check before you buy so that your purchase doesn't show up on a "prohibited" list.

If you buy something at a Parisian department store or an upscale boutique, ask the clerk about reliable shippers. Most major hotel desks also maintain up-to-date lists of shipping companies. Many shoppers even talk to their local shipping companies before they go. Remember, however, that there's always some degree of risk involved in shipping goods.

Check with the shipper in Paris to make sure you understand the arrangement you've made and ask about insurance. Don't forget to ask about duties and clearance fees in your home country, what kind of packing will be used, and whether there'll be warehouse penalties if you can't pick up the item right away.

BUSINESS HOURS Shops are *usually* open Tuesday to Saturday from 9am to 7pm, but the hours can vary greatly. Small shops sometimes take a two-hour lunch. The flea market and some other street markets are open on Saturday, Sunday, and Monday. That intriguing sign on shop doors reading ENTREE LIBRE means you may browse at will. SOLDES means "sale." SOLDES EXCEPTIONELLES means they're pushing it a bit.

VAT REFUNDS Tourists staying in France for less than six months are entitled to a refund on the value-added tax (VAT) on certain purchases, but only under carefully defined conditions. These refunds usually average around 13% to 15.7%, are allowed only on purchases of more than 2,000 F ($380.20) made in a single store, and apply only to citizens of non-EU countries. The refund, however, is not automatic (some forms and paperwork need to be completed at the time of purchase), and food, wine, and tobacco don't count. Procedures for receiving the refund are slightly different for merchandise you carry with you outside of France than for merchandise you have shipped, although any reputable merchant will have the necessary forms and paperwork.

You must take several steps to receive your refund. First, show the clerk your passport to prove your eligibility. You'll then be given an export sales document in triplicate (two pink sheets and a green one), which you must sign, as well as an envelope addressed to the store. Arrive at your departure point as early as possible to avoid lines at the *détaxe* (refund) booth at French Customs. If you're traveling by train, go to the détaxe area in the station before boarding—you can't get your refund documents processed on the train. The refund booths are outside the passport checkpoints, so you must handle your refund before you proceed with the passport check.

Only the person who signed the documents at the store can present them for refund. Give the three sheets to the Customs official, who'll countersign and give you the green copy. (Save it in case any problems arise.) Give the official the stamped envelope addressed to the store. One of the processed pink copies will be mailed to the store for you. Your reimbursement will be either mailed by check (in convertible French francs) or credited to your credit/charge-card account. In some cases you may get the refund immediately, paid at an airport bank window. If you don't receive your tax refund in four months, write to the store, giving the date of purchase and the location where the forms were given to Customs. Include a photocopy of your green refund sheet.

BEST BUYS   Perfumes and cosmetics, including such famous brands as Guerlain, Chanel, Schiaparelli, and Jean Patou, are almost always cheaper in Paris than in the United States. Paris is also a good place to buy Lalique and Baccarat **crystal.** They're expensive but still priced below international market value.

Of course, many visitors come to Paris just to shop for **fashions.** From Chanel to Yves Saint-Laurent, from Nina Ricci to Sonia Rykiel, the city overflows with fashion boutiques, ranging from haute couture to the truly outlandish. Fashion accessories, such as those designed by Louis Vuitton and Céline, are among the finest in the world.

Lingerie is another great French export. All the top lingerie designers are represented in boutiques as well as in the major department stores, Galeries Lafayette and Le Printemps.

AIRPORT TAX-FREE BOUTIQUES   You're better off buying certain products at the airport. In the duty-free shops at Orly and Charles de Gaulle, you'll get a minimum discount of 20% on all items and up to 50% on liquor, cigarettes, and watches. Among the items on sale are crystal, cutlery, chocolates, luggage, wines and whiskies, pipes and lighters, lingerie, silk scarves, perfume, knitwear, jewelry, cameras and equipment, cheeses, and antiques. The drawbacks of airport shopping are that the selections are limited and you must carry your purchase onto the plane.

2 Shopping A to Z

ANTIQUES

La Cour aux Antiquaires
54 rue du Faubourg St-Honoré, 8e. ☎ **1/42-66-58-77.** Métro: Concorde or Madeleine.

This elegant Right Bank arcade contains 18 independent shops offering a variety of antiques, paintings, and objets d'art (usually from the 16th to the 20th century). Open Monday from 2 to 6:30pm and Tuesday to Saturday from 10:30am to 6pm.

✪ Le Louvre des Antiquaires
2 place du Palais-Royal, 1er. ☎ **1/42-97-27-00.** Métro: Palais-Royal–Musée-du-Louvre.

This is Europe's largest antiques center, stocking everything from Russian icons to art deco pieces. It houses 250 dealers in its $2^1/_2$ acres of well-lit modern salons. Customers must go down an enormous flight of stairs and pass the café/reception area. Open Tuesday to Sunday from 11am to 7pm.

ART

Carnavalette
2 rue des Francs-Bourgeois, 3e. ☎ **1/42-72-91-92.** Métro: St-Paul.

Carnavalette sells one-of-a-kind engravings, plus satirical 19th-century magazines and newspapers. Open daily from 10:30am to 6:30pm.

Galerie Documents
53 rue de Seine, 6e. ☎ **1/43-54-50-68.** Métro: Odéon.

Galerie Documents contains an original collection of old posters. Many are inexpensive, though you could easily pay dearly for an original. The store will mail your poster home. Open Tuesday to Saturday from 10:30am to 7pm.

Galerie Maeght

12 rue St-Merri, 4e. ☎ **1/42-78-43-44.** Métro: Rambuteau or Hôtel-de-Ville.

This gallery sells excellent contemporary artwork—painting, sculpture, and photographs. Open Tuesday to Saturday from 10am to 1pm and 2 to 7pm.

Galerie 27

27 rue de Seine, 6e. ☎ **1/43-54-78-54.** Métro: St-Germain-des-Prés.

Galerie 27 sells lithographs by some of the most famous artists of the early 20th century, including Picasso. The inventory ranges from art posters to original paintings by Chagall, Miró, Picasso, and Léger. Open Monday to Saturday from 10am to 1pm and 2:30 to 7pm.

Maeght Editeur & Adrien Maeght Gallery

42 rue du Bac, 7e. ☎ **1/45-48-31-01.** Métro: Rue-du-Bac.

This gallery has an interesting collection of posters and pictorial books by important artists, like Matisse. Exhibits include modern sculpture and engravings by established and unknown artists. Open Tuesday to Saturday from 10am to 1pm and 2 to 7pm.

Schmock Broc

15 rue Racine, 6e. ☎ **1/46-33-79-98.** Métro: Odéon.

This is a specialty shop run by one of the city's leading collectors of jewelry from the 1940s and 1950s, paintings, and drawings. Open Monday from 3 to 7:30pm and Tuesday to Saturday from 10:30am to 1:30pm and 2:45 to 7:30pm.

BOOKS

Brentano's

37 av. de l'Opéra, 2e. ☎ **1/42-61-52-50.** Métro: Opéra.

Brentano's is one of the leading English-language bookstores in Paris, offering guides, maps, novels, and nonfiction. Open Monday to Saturday from 10am to 7pm.

The Village Voice

6 rue Princesse, 6e. ☎ **1/46-33-36-47.** Métro: Mabillon.

Literary icons from America, including Edmund White and Raymond Carver, have given readings at this favorite venue for expat Yanks. There's also a collection of feminist literature, even copies of *The Village Voice* newspaper. Open Monday from 2 to 8pm and Tuesday to Saturday from 11am to 8pm.

W. H. Smith and Son

248 rue de Rivoli, 1er. ☎ **1/44-77-88-99.** Métro: Concorde.

Across from the Tuileries Gardens, this is Paris's best English bookstore. *The New York Times* is available every Monday. The store stocks many American magazines as well as a fine selection of maps, reference books, language books, and children's books. Open Monday to Saturday from 9:30am to 7pm.

CHINA & CRYSTAL

✪ Baccarat

30 bis rue de Paradis, 10e. ☎ **1/47-70-64-30.** Métro: Château-d'Eau, Poissonière, or Gare-de-l'Est.

Purveyor to kings and presidents since 1764, Baccarat produces world-renowned full-lead crystal for an international clientele. Everyone's welcome to look at the company's historical models in the Baccarat museum. Open Monday to Friday from 10am to 6:30pm and Saturday from 10am to 5pm.

Galerie d'Amon

28 rue St-Sulpice, 6e. ☎ **1/43-26-96-60.** Métro: Odéon, St-Sulpice, or Mabillon.

In St-Germain-des-Prés, Amon has a large permanent exhibition of glasswork from both France and abroad. Madeleine and Jean-Pierre Maffre display items in blown glass, blown engraved glass, sculptures, and paperweights by top glassworkers. Open Tuesday to Saturday from 11am to 7pm.

Lalique

11 rue Royale, 8e. ☎ **1/42-65-33-70.** Métro: Concorde.

Lalique is run by Marie-Claude Lalique, the granddaughter of its original founder, silversmith René Lalique. Known around the world for its glass sculpture and decorative lead crystal, the shop sells a wide range of merchandise at prices slightly lower than those abroad. Open Monday to Saturday from 9:30am to 6:30pm.

Limoges-Unic

12 and 58 rue de Paradis, 10e. ☎ **1/47-70-54-49.** Métro: Gare-de-l'Est or Poissonnière.

Limoges-Unic sells an extensive stock of Limoges china—such as Ceralane, Haviland, and Bernardaud—as well as Baccarat, Dior, Villeroy & Boch, Hermès, Lanvin, Lalique, and Sèvres crystal. Open Monday to Saturday from 10am to 6:30pm.

CHOCOLATES

Dalloyau

99–101 rue du Faubourg St-Honoré, 8e. ☎ **1/43-59-18-10.** Métro: Champs-Elysée–Clemenceau.

When Dalloyau was established in 1802, the bourgeoisie rushed to its doorstep to sample its chocolates, pastries, petits-fours, and cakes. Today this store, near some of the most fashionable boutiques in Europe, will ship its elegantly packaged confections anywhere in the world. Open daily from 8:30 to 9pm.

La Maison du Chocolat

225 rue du Faubourg St-Honoré, 8e. ☎ **1/42-27-39-44.** Métro: Champs-Elysée–Clemenceau.

This place boasts a subtle decor containing racks and racks of chocolates, priced individually or by the kilo. Each is made from a blend of as many as six kinds of South American chocolate, flavored with about everything imaginable. All the merchandise, including the chocolate pastries, is made in the supermodern cellar facilities. Open daily from 8:30am to 9pm.

CRAFTS

Boutique du Musée des Arts Décoratifs

In the Palais du Louvre, 107 rue de Rivoli, 1er. ☎ **1/42-61-04-02.** Métro: Palais-Royal or Tuileries.

This boutique offers attractive household goods, some museum replicas. Craftspeople have copied museum pieces in faïence and molded crystal, jewelry and porcelain boxes, and even scarves. There's also a selection of the work of young French artists in ceramic, jewelry, and glass. Open daily from 10:30am to 6:30pm.

Le Printemps
64 bd. Haussmann, 9e. ☎ 1/42-82-50-00. Métro: Havre-Caumartin. RER: Auber.

In addition to its other merchandise, Le Printemps offers one of the largest selections of handcrafts in Paris. See "Department Stores," below.

DEPARTMENT STORES

Galeries Lafayette
40 bd. Haussman, 9e. ☎ 1/42-82-34-56. Métro: Chausée-d'Antin or Opéra. RER: Auber.

A landmark in the Parisian fashion world, Galeries Lafayette is one of the world's leading department stores. An entrance marked WELCOME directs you to English-speaking hostesses available to assist you. Finish your shopping day with an exceptional view of Paris on the rooftop terrace. Open Monday to Wednesday and Friday and Saturday from 9:30am to 6:45pm, Thursday from 9:30am to 9pm.

✪ Le Printemps
64 bd. Haussmann, 9e. ☎ 1/42-82-50-00. Métro: Havre-Caumartin. RER: Auber.

This is the city's largest department store, with three stores connected by bridges on the second and third floors. Brummell offers men's clothing, while Printemps de la Mode sells clothes for women, juniors, and children. Printemps de la Maison is mainly for records, books, furniture, and housewares. The ground floor has a large perfumerie, as well as cosmetics, gifts, and handcrafts. Interpreters at the ground-floor Welcome Service will help you claim your discounts and guide you. Open Monday to Wednesday and Friday and Saturday from 9:35am to 7pm, Thursday from 9:35am to 10pm.

La Samaritaine
19 rue de la Monnaie, 1er. ☎ 1/40-41-20-20. Métro: Pont-Neuf.

La Samaritaine, much less expensive than Galeries Lafayette and Le Printemps, is a family-oriented store. It offers some good buys in clothing and a little bit of everything. Open Monday to Wednesday and Friday and Saturday from 9:30am to 7pm, Thursday from 9:30am to 10pm.

DISCOUNT SHOPPING

At each of the stores below at least one employee speaks English.

⑤ Anna Lowe
35 av. Matignon, 8e. ☎ 1/43-59-96-61. Métro: Miromesnil.

This is the premier Paris boutique for high-quality clothing at discount prices. All items sold by former model Anna Lowe have the designer's label still attached, including Chanel, Valentino, Givenchy, Ungaro, and Lacroix. The merchandise from last season's collection of famous designs doesn't contain factory rejects or seconds, though some clothes are models' samples. Alterations are done for a normal price, often within two or three days. Open Monday to Saturday from 10:30am to 7pm.

⑤ Mendes (Saint-Laurent)
65 rue Montmartre, 2e. ☎ 1/42-36-83-32. Métro: Les Halles.

Many fashion- and budget-conscious Parisian women come to Mendes to buy Saint-Laurent sportswear. Sometimes discounts on last season's clothing average as much as 50%. There are no dressing rooms, no alterations, and no exchanges or refunds. Clothes from the winter collection are available at reduced prices after mid-January, and clothes from the summer collection become available after mid-July. None of the clothing has been worn. Open Monday to Thursday from 10am to 6pm and Friday and Saturday from 10am to 5pm.

Réciproque
89–123 rue de la Pompe, 16e. ☎ **1/47-04-30-28.** Métro: Pompe.

For the perfect (used) accessory for that night out in Paris, visit these five stores set side by side. Réciproque has been accepting the used garments of locals since 1980. No. 101 sells only menswear; no. 95 is the most chic, selling used clothing from Chanel, Lacroix, Hermès, and the like; no. 89 sells used tablecloths, silverware, and porcelain; the other two storefronts are a mishmash of everything else. Open Tuesday to Saturday from 10:30am to 7pm.

FASHION
For Children
Bonpoint
15 rue Royale, 8e. ☎ **1/47-42-52-63.** Métro: Concorde.

Bonpoint is part of a well-known children's haute couture chain whose clothing is well tailored and expensive. The shop sells clothes for boys and girls 1 day to 16 years. It specializes in formal and confirmation dresses as well as elegant long baptism robes. Open Monday to Saturday from 10am to 7pm.

For Women
Céline
24 rue François-1er, 8e. ☎ **1/47-20-22-83.** Métro: F.-D.-Roosevelt.

Céline is one of the best choices for ultraconservative well-made clothes. There's also a selection of elegant shoes and handbags. Open Monday to Saturday from 10am to 7pm.

✪ Chanel
31 rue Cambon, 1er. ☎ **1/42-86-28-00.** Métro: Concorde or Tuileries.

Chanel is a haute couture landmark where prices are naturally astronomical. It also sells accessories, perfumes, cosmetics, and watches. Open Monday to Friday from 9:30am to 6:30pm and Saturday from 10am to 6:30pm.

Chanel
42 av. Montaigne, 8e. ☎ **1/47-23-74-12.** Métro: F.-D.-Roosevelt.

This Chanel boutique offers somewhat reasonably priced ready-to-wear clothes. Here customers will find classic designs and accessories. Open Monday to Friday from 9:30am to 6:30pm and Saturday from 10am to 6:30pm.

Christian Dior
28–32 av. Montaigne, 8e. ☎ **1/40-73-54-44.** Métro: F.-D.-Roosevelt.

Christian Dior offers a wide selection of women's and men's sportswear and accessories. There are separate salons for shoes and leather goods, furs, children's clothing, and jewelry. Open Monday to Friday from 9:30am to 6:30pm and Saturday from 10am to 6:30pm.

✪ Hermès
24 rue du Faubourg St-Honoré, 8e. ☎ **1/40-17-47-17.** Métro: Concorde.

Paris Finds & Faves

Laine en Couleur Vegétale, place Dauphine, 6e (☎ 1/40-51-72-65; Métro: Pont-Neuf). Anne Rieger specializes in a technique of dying wools from natural substances found in vegetables. For example, her distinctive red comes from red cabbage; her brilliant yellow yarn gets its color from the leaves of chestnut trees outside her door.

L'Epicerie, 51 rue St-Louis-en-l'Ile, 4e (☎ 1/42-25-20-14; Métro: Pont-Marie). You'll forget Fauchon when you shop for delicacies at this store that lures gourmet chefs from all over the city with rabbit pâté, foie gras, mustard made from champagne, and some of the world's most succulent jams.

La Tuile à Loup, 35 rue Daubenton, 5e (☎ 1/47-07-28-90; Métro: Censier-Daubenton). Packed to the ceiling, this overstuffed store gently peddles some of the finest regional arts and crafts—earthenware bowls, toys, glassware, whatever. Owners Michel Joblin and Marie-France will be glad to help you find what you want.

Annick Goutal, 12 place St-Sulpice, 6e (☎ 1/46-33-03-15; Métro: St-Sulpice). Men or women can follow the scent to this boutique filled with some of Paris's finest soaps, oils, lotions, and even original perfumes. It's an amazing treasure created by Mother Nature herself.

Marché St-Pierre, 2 rue Charles-Nodier, 18e (☎ 1/46-06-92-25; Métro: Anvers). This is the city's best-known fabric discount house, though it's not familiar to most visitors. In the garment district, it's a bazaar that feels as if it stretches over acres. At times it seems like a souk in North Africa.

La Maison du Miel, 24 rue Vignon, 8e (☎ 1/47-42-26-70; Métro: Madeleine). The House of Honey has been a family tradition since before World War I. The entire store is devoted to products made from honey: Honey oil, honey soap, and certainly various honeys to eat, including one made from heather, owe a debt to the busy bee.

Legendary Hermès is noted for its silk scarves printed with antique motifs. Ties, fragrances, clothing, and other items also are available. Hermès leather goods, such as reindeer hide, kid, and doeskin gloves, are known worldwide. Handbags are crafted on the premises. Open Monday to Saturday from 10am to 6:30pm.

Lanvin

22 rue du Faubourg St-Honoré, 8e. ☎ 1/44-71-33-33. Métro: Concorde.

Lanvin specializes in women's fashions and accessories. On the second floor, haute couture dresses are presented in the salon. On the first floor, customers will find chic and contemporary prêt-à-porter (ready-to-wear) dresses and ensembles. Open Monday to Saturday from 10am to 6:45pm.

Pierre Cardin Couture

27 av. Marigny, 8e. ☎ 1/42-66-92-25. Métro: Champs-Elysée–Clemenceau.

Pierre Cardin boutiques seem to be on every corner. The ready-to-wear styles for women range from conservative to ultramodern. Open Monday to Saturday from 10am to 7pm.

For Men
Alain Figaret
21 rue de la Paix, 2e. ☎ 1/42-65-04-99. Métro: Opéra.

Alain Figaret has one of Paris's best selections of men's shirts in a broad range of fabrics. The store prides itself on selling cotton (never silk) shirts and all-silk (never synthetic) neckties. It also sells men's underwear and elegant pajamas. Open Monday to Saturday from 10am to 7pm.

Lanvin
15 rue du Faubourg St-Honoré, 8e. ☎ 1/44-71-33-33. Métro: Concorde.

This elegant shop is just one of many Lanvin boutiques throughout the city. Specializing in "the latest" conservative but stylish fashion, Lanvin also sells a handsome collection of shirts and ties (and custom-makes shirts and suits). Open Monday to Saturday from 10am to 7pm.

Pierre Cardin Boutique Hommes
59 rue du Faubourg St-Honoré, 8e. ☎ 1/42-66-92-25. Métro: Champs-Elysée–Clemenceau.

Pierre Cardin carries a large assortment of sophisticated men's clothing and some of the finest accessories available, including an unusual selection of shoes. As you'd expect, everything is expensive. Open Monday to Saturday from 10am to 7pm.

FOOD

✪ Fauchon
Place de la Madeleine, 8e. ☎ 1/47-42-60-11. Métro: Madeleine.

Vast Fauchon is one of the most popular city sights. The window display, often including plump chickens or lamb filled with fresh vegetables, entices passersby. English-speaking clerks help you choose from the incredible selection. The fruit-and-vegetable department offers such items as rare mushrooms and *fraises des bois* (wild strawberries). The confectionery features pastries and especially good candies. Also on the premises are a self-service stand-up bar, a cocktail department, a gifts department, a selection of porcelain and table settings, and an impressive collection of wines. Open Monday to Saturday from 9:40am to 7pm. A "mini-Fauchon" selling mainly foods is open Monday to Saturday from 7 to 9pm.

HATS

E. Motsch
42 av. George-V, 8e. ☎ 1/47-23-79-22. Métro: George-V.

Since 1887, E. Motsch has been one of the most distinguished outlets for classic handmade hats for both men and women, from berets to Scottish tam-o'-shanters. The women's section contains some of the most stylish, albeit conservative, hats in Paris. Open Monday and Saturday from 10am to 1pm and 2:15 to 6:30pm, Tuesday to Friday from 10am to 6:30pm.

JEWELRY

Van Cleef & Arpels
22 place Vendôme, 1er. ☎ 1/42-61-58-58. Métro: Opéra or Tuileries.

Established at the turn of the century, Van Cleef & Arpels is world renowned. This exclusive shop is known for its special settings and carries a range of deluxe watches. Open Monday to Friday from 10am to 6:30pm.

LEATHER GOODS

Gucci

2 rue du Faubourg St-Honoré, 8e. ☎ **1/42-96-83-27.** Métro: Concorde.

This Gucci store is one of the world's largest showcases for the Milan-based designer. Gucci makes outstanding shoes and handbags, as well as other accessories, including wallets, handbags, gloves, and clothing. This branch also has an excellent selection of scarves, two-piece ensembles, and sweaters. Open Monday to Saturday from 9:30am to 6:30pm.

LINGERIE & SWIMWEAR

Cadolle

14 rue Cambon, 1er. ☎ **1/42-60-94-94.** Métro: Concorde or Madeleine.

The store's original owner, Herminie Cadolle, invented the brassiere in 1889. Today the store is managed by Herminie's descendants, Alice and Poupie Cadolle, who offer made-to-order and ready-to-wear lingerie. Custom-made whalebone corsets are still available, and the nightgowns range from the demure to the scandalous. There's also a collection of swimwear. Open Monday to Saturday from 9:30am to 1pm and 2 to 6pm.

MALLS

Le Carrousel du Louvre

99 rue de Rivoli, 1er. Métro: Palais-Royal–Musée-du-Louvre.

This prestigious complex next to the Louvre's new entry hall opened in 1993. All sorts of shops and services tempt you, and many branches are open on Sunday. You can also purchase show and theater tickets here. There are 60 boutiques, plus four halls dedicated to fashion shops, exhibitions, and seminars.

Forum des Halles

1–7 rue Pierre-Lescot, 1er. ☎ **1/42-96-68-74.** Métro: Etienne-Marcel.

Once the great old vegetable markets, Les Halles is now a vast crater in the middle of Paris, selling (among other things) clothing, accessories, food, and gifts.

Montparnasse Shopping Center

Between rue de l'Arrivée and rue du Départ, 14e. Métro: Montparnasse-Bienvenue.

Boutiques in this center offer men's and women's fashions, jewelry, perfume, cosmetics, gifts, shoes, art, wool, records, glasses, and children's wear. Shoppers will also find a branch of Galeries Lafayette, restaurants, a travel agent, and even a pool.

MARKETS

Marché aux Puces

Av. de la Porte de Clignancourt. Métro: Vanves.

The Marché aux Puces—flea market—has an enormous mixture of vintage bargains and old junk. It's estimated that the complex has 2,500 to 3,000 open stalls spread over half a mile. Monday is traditionally the day for bargain hunters, and negotiating is a must. Once you arrive at Porte de Clignancourt, turn left and cross boulevard Ney, then walk north on avenue de la Porte de Clignancourt. You'll pass stalls offering cheap clothing, but continue walking until you see the entrances to the first maze of flea-market stalls on the left. Open Saturday and Sunday from 6:30am to 4:30pm.

Marché aux Timbres

Off the Champs-Elysées. Métro: Champs-Elysée–Clemenceau.

This market draws avid stamp collectors to its nearly two dozen stalls set up on a permanent basis under shady trees on the eastern edge of the Rond-Point. Generally open Thursday, Saturday, and Sunday from 10am to 7pm.

✪ Marché aux Fleurs and Marché aux Oiseaux

Place Louis-Lépine, Ile de la Cité, 4e. Métro: Cité.

The Flower Market has always provided inspiration for artists and a breath of fresh air for tourists. The stalls burst with color. The Bird Market is also here. Even if you're not in the market for a rare bird, have a look. The stalls run along the Seine, from the Louvre to the Hôtel de Ville. The Flower Market is open daily from 8am to 4pm; the Bird Market, Sunday from 9am to 7pm.

MUSIC

✪ Virgin Megastore

52–60 av. des Champs-Elysées, 8e. ☎ 1/49-53-50-00. Métro: F.-D.-Roosevelt.

Paris's largest music store opened in 1988 and quickly became a social phenomenon. A number of dedications, exhibitions, and performances (with Jessye Norman, Sting, Plácido Domingo, Tina Turner, Claudio Abbado, and others) have taken place here. Open Monday to Thursday from 10am to midnight, Friday and Saturday from 10am to 1am, and Sunday from noon to midnight.

PERFUMES

Freddy of Paris

3 rue Scribe, 9e. ☎ 1/47-42-63-41. Métro: Auber or Opéra.

Freddy of Paris offers discounts of up to 40% on all name-brand perfumes, creams, novelties, gifts, top handbags, scarves, ties, and costume jewelry. Open Monday to Friday from 9am to 6:30pm.

Michel Swiss

16 rue de la Paix, 2e. ☎ 1/42-61-61-11. Métro: Opéra.

Michel Swiss looks like the other ultra-chic boutiques near place Vendôme. But once you're inside (there's no storefront window), you'll see the major brands of luxury perfumes, makeup, leather bags, pens, neckties, accessories, and giftware, all discounted 25%, plus an additional tax discount for non-EU residents amounting to 15.7%. Open Monday to Saturday from 9am to 6:30pm.

Parfumerie Fragonard

9 rue Scribe, 9e. ☎ 1/47-42-93-40. Métro: Opéra. RER: Auber.

In a Napoléon III mansion, this perfume house contains a more edited version of the museum of perfume in Grasse. This Parisian shop is an outlet for the scent factories in Eze and Grasse. Open Monday to Saturday from 9am to 6pm and Sunday from 9:30am to 4pm.

SHOES

Maud Frizon

81–83 rue des Saints-Pères, 73. ☎ 1/45-49-20-59. Métro: Sèvres-Babylone.

Exotic leathers are used to create some of the fanciest exclusive shoes for men. If the prices are too high here, go next door to the Maud Frizon Club, where the shoes are machine made and go for about one-third the price. Open Monday to Saturday from 10:30am to 7pm.

Stéphane Kélian

23 bd. de la Madeleine, 1er. ☎ **1/42-96-01-84.** Métro: Bourse.

Kélian is acclaimed as one of the most creative designers of women's shoes. A selection of men's shoes is also sold. Not all shoes are flamboyant; many appeal to conservative customers. Open Monday to Saturday from 10am to 7pm.

SOUVENIRS & GIFTS

Eiffel Shopping

9 av. de Suffren, 7e. ☎ **1/45-66-55-30.** Métro: Bir-Hakeim.

Eiffel Shopping offers a free glass of cognac while you browse through the designer collection of handbags, ties, scarves, watches, sunglasses, jewelry, perfumes, Lalique crystal, and much more. This tax-free center offers top-quality merchandise at discounts. All salespeople are bilingual. Open Monday to Friday from 9:15am to 8pm, Saturday from 9:15am to 8pm, and Sunday from 11am to 8pm.

Papeterie Moderne

12 rue de la Ferronnerie, 1er. ☎ **1/42-36-21-72.** Métro: Châtelet–Les Halles.

This unique little shop has signs both old and new. *Rue* signs, bakery signs, butcher shop signs (including one advertising horse meat), and lots more wait for you. Copies of anything on sale can be ordered. Open Monday to Thursday and Saturday from 7:30am to noon and 1 to 8pm, Friday from 10:30am to noon and 1 to 8pm.

STATIONERY

Cassegrain

422 rue St-Honoré, 8e. ☎ **1/42-60-20-08.** Métro: Concorde.

Cassegrain, which has another store at 81 rue des Sts-Pères, 6e (☎ **1/42-22-04-76**; Métro: Sèvres), opened right after World War I and is the city's premier stationery shop. It offers beautifully engraved traditional stationery, as well as business cards and gift items. Both stores are open Monday to Saturday from 10am to 7pm.

TABLEWARE & BED LINEN

Au Bain Marie

10 rue Boissy-d'Anglas, 8e. ☎ **1/42-66-59-74.** Métro: Concorde.

This is one of the best choices for new, antique, and embroidered table and bed linen. The store also sells virtually everything for a dining table, including antique and modern tableware and about 5,000 English and French books on food and wine. A mail-order catalog is available. Open Monday to Saturday from 10am to 7pm.

TOYS

Au Nain Bleu

406 rue St-Honoré, 8e. ☎ **1/42-60-39-01.** Métro: Concorde.

In business since 1836, the Blue Dwarf is filled with toy soldiers, stuffed animals, games, model airplanes, technical toys, model cars, and puppets. France's oldest toy shop has attracted such customers as Sarah Bernhardt and Marcel Proust. Open Monday to Saturday from 9:45am to 6:30pm.

Rigodon

13 rue Racine, 6e. ☎ **1/43-29-98-66.** Métro: Odéon.

This store has one of the most varied puppet and marionette collections anywhere hanging from its ceiling: angels, witches on broomsticks, bat women with feathered wings, and delicate re-creations of porcelain dolls in 18th-century costumes. About half the inventory is fabricated by French subcontractors near Paris; others come from Italy and Southeast Asia. Open Monday from 2 to 7pm and Tuesday to Saturday from 10:30am to 7pm.

9 Paris After Dark

Parisians tend to do everything later than their Anglo-American counterparts. Once the workday is over, people head straight to the café to meet up with friends, and from there they go to the restaurant or bar and finally to the nightclub.

1 The Cafés of Paris

To a Parisian a café is a combination club/tavern/snack bar. You can read a newspaper, meet a lover or a friend, do your homework, or write your memoirs in a café. You can nibble at a hard-boiled egg or drink yourself into oblivion. Often people meet at cafés to relax and talk before going to a show.

Cafés aren't restaurants, though the larger ones may serve complete and excellent meals. They aren't bars either, though they do offer a variety of alcoholic drinks. And they aren't coffeehouses in the American sense because you can order a bottle of champagne just as readily as an iced chocolate.

The texture of classic cafés changes radically over the course of a day. Considered the living rooms and unofficial salons of many neighborhood residents, they thrive during the workday, when their premises burgeon with clients and activities. They adopt a less hurried aura at night, when wine and brandy replace café au lait as the drink of choice and the dark shadows and bright lights give life a different perspective.

Brasserie Lipp
151 bd. St-Germain, 6e. ☎ 1/45-48-53-91. Métro: St-Germain-des-Prés.

The Lipp is known as the "rendezvous for *le tout Paris*." Picasso and de Gaulle patronized this St-Germain-des-Prés landmark, as did Sartre, Gide, Man Ray, de Beauvoir, Joyce, and James Baldwin. After the 1944 Liberation, Hemingway was the first to return to the café. Today you might see Catherine Deneuve sitting on a mole-skin banquette. An Alsatian named Lipp opened the café after the Franco-Prussian War in 1871. He preferred not to live in Germany but couldn't do without Alsatian beer, still served today.

There's an upstairs dining room, but it's more fashionable to sit in the back room. For breakfast, order the traditional black coffee and croissants. At lunch or dinner, the house specialty is pork and choucroute (sauerkraut)—the best in Paris. Open daily from 9am to 2am—it's fashionable to arrive late.

Café Beaubourg

100 rue St-Martin, 4e. ☎ **1/48-87-63-96.** Métro: Rambuteau or Hôtel-de-Ville.

Across the pedestrian plaza from the Centre Pompidou, this avant-garde café boasts soaring concrete columns and a minimalist decor by noted architect Christian de Portzamparc. In summer tables are set on the sprawling terrace, providing a panoramic view of the neighborhood's goings-on. Open Sunday to Thursday from 8am to 1am and Saturday and Sunday from 8am to 2am.

Café de Flore

172 bd. St-Germain, 6e. ☎ **1/45-48-55-26.** Métro: St-Germain-des-Prés.

Sartre, the granddaddy of existentialism, often came here during the war and was a key figure in the Resistance. Wearing a leather jacket and beret, he sat at his table and wrote his trilogy, *Les Chemins de la liberté* (The Roads to Freedom). Camus, Picasso, and Apollinaire also frequented the Flore. The café is still going strong, although the famous folks have moved on. Open daily from 7am to 1:30am (closed July).

Café de la Paix

Place de l'Opéra, 9e. ☎ **1/40-07-30-12.** Métro: Opéra.

This has been a popular American enclave since the Yankee troops marched down the street in their victory parade after World War I. Famous visitors have included Zola, Wilde, Edward VII, de Maupassant, Chevalier, Caruso, and Chagall. No one can remember Charles de Gaulle dining here, but a messenger arrived and ordered a "tinned" ham for the general's first supper when he returned at the Liberation. Open daily from 10am to 1:30am.

Café Marly

In the Cour Napoléon du Louvre, 93 rue de Rivoli, 1er. ☎ **1/49-26-06-60.** Métro: Palais-Royal–Musée-du-Louvre.

In 1994 the government granted permission for a café/restaurant to open in one of the Louvre's most historic courtyards. It's accessible only from a point close to the famous glass pyramid and so has become a favorite refuge for Parisians escaping the roar of traffic just outside. Anyone is welcome to sit for a café au lait (anytime between 8am and 2am daily, whenever meals are not being served). More substantial fare is the norm here, served in one of three Louis-Philippe–style dining rooms. Menu items include club sandwiches, fresh oysters and shellfish, steak au poivre, sole meunière, and an array of upscale bistro food. In summer, outdoor tables overlook views of the majestic courtyard. Open daily from noon to 3pm and 8 to 11pm.

La Coupole

102 bd. Montparnasse, 14e. ☎ **1/43-20-14-20.** Métro: Vavin.

This Montparnasse café is so well known that some tourists stop here with suitcases in tow for a beer or coffee before searching for a hotel. The clientele ranges from artists' models to young men dressed like Rasputin. In 1928 Fraux and Lafon—two waiters at the Café du Dôme—opened La Coupole. At first the café was unwelcome; now it's a landmark. Perhaps order a coffee or cognac VSOP at one of the sidewalk tables. The dining room looks like a railway station but serves surprisingly good food. Try the sole meunière, curry d'agneau (lamb), or cassoulet.

The fresh oysters and shellfish are popular. A buffet breakfast is served Monday to Friday from 7:30 to 10:30am. Open daily from 7:30am to 2am.

Deux Magots

170 bd. St-Germain, 6e. ☎ **1/45-48-55-25**. Métro: St-Germain-des-Prés.

This legendary café/brasserie is still the hangout for the sophisticated neighborhood residents and a tourist favorite in summer. Deux Magots was once a gathering place of intellectuals, including Sartre, de Beauvoir, and Giraudoux. Inside are two large Oriental statues that give the café its name. The crystal chandeliers are too brightly lit, but the regulars seem used to the glare. Open daily from 7:30am to 1:30am.

Fouquet's

99 av. des Champs-Elysées, 8e. ☎ **1/47-23-70-60**. Métro: George-V.

Founded at the turn of the century, this is the premier sidewalk café on the Champs-Elysées. It has attracted Chaplin, Chevalier, Dietrich, Mistinguett, and even Churchill and Roosevelt. Outside tables are separated from the sidewalk by a barricade of potted flowers. Inside is an elegant grill room with leather banquettes and rattan furniture, as well as private banquet rooms and a restaurant. The café and grill room are open daily from 8am to midnight; the restaurant and banquet rooms are open Monday to Friday from 8am to midnight.

Le Mandarin

148 bd. St-Germain, 6e. ☎ **1/46-33-98-35**. Métro: Odéon or Mabillon.

This elegant corner café is always packed with a young Left Bank crowd and visitors to St-Germain-des-Prés. Fine wines and coffee are served at the brass bar. Bentwood chairs are scattered over several raised platforms and spill out onto the sidewalk in warm weather. The decor includes lace-covered hanging lamps, brass trim, and lots of exposed wood. The specialties are punch and onion soup auvergnat. Open Sunday to Thursday from 8am to 2am, Friday to 3am, and Saturday to 4am.

La Rotonde

105 bd. du Montparnasse, 6e. ☎ **1/43-26-68-84**. Métro: Vavin.

Once patronized by Hemingway, the original Rotonde has faded into history. Lavishly upgraded, this reincarnated restaurant/café has art deco paneling and shares the original hallowed site with a movie theater. Prices are lower if you stand at the bar. Open Sunday to Thursday from 7:30am to 2am and Friday and Saturday from 7:30am to 3am.

Le Sélect

99 bd. du Montparnasse, 6e. ☎ **1/45-48-38-24**. Métro: Vavin.

In *The Sun Also Rises*, Hemingway's Jake Barnes walks past the "sad tables" of the Rotonde to the Sélect. Not much has changed since Jean Cocteau was a patron. The literary café basks in its former glory and continues to flourish, impervious to fads. There are 40 whiskies and 20 cocktails to choose from. Open Sunday to Thursday from 8am to 2:30am and Friday and Saturday from 8am to 3:30am.

2 The Performing Arts

Announcements of shows, concerts, and even the opera programs are plastered on kiosks all over town. Listings of what's playing can be found in *Pariscope,* a weekly entertainment guide, or the English-language *Paris Passion.* Performances start later in Paris than in London or New York City—anywhere from 8 to 9pm—and Parisians tend to dine after the theater. You may not want to do the same since many of the less expensive restaurants close as early as 9pm.

There are many ticket agencies in Paris, but most are found near the Right Bank hotels. *Avoid them if possible.* The cheapest tickets can be purchased at the theater box office. Remember to tip the usher who shows you to your seat in a theater or movie house 3 F (55¢).

DISCOUNTS   Several agencies sell tickets for cultural events and plays at discounts of up to 50%. One outlet for discount tickets is the **Kiosque Théâtre,** 15 place de la Madeleine, 8e (no phone; Métro: Madeleine), offering leftover tickets for about half price on the day of performance. Tickets for evening performances are sold Tuesday to Friday from 12:30 to 8pm and Saturday from 2 to 8pm. If you'd like to attend a matinée, buy your ticket Saturday from 12:30 to 2pm or Sunday from 12:30 to 4pm.

For discounts of 20% to 40% on tickets for festivals, concerts, and theater performances, try one of two locations of the **FNAC** department store chain: 136 rue de Rennes, 6e (☎ **1/44-09-18-00;** Métro: Montparnasse-Bienvenue), or in the Forum des Halles, 1–7 rue Pierre-Lescot, 1er (☎ **1/40-41-40-00;** Métro: Châtelet–Les Halles).

THEATER

Comédie-Française
2 rue de Richelieu, 1er. ☎ **1/40-15-00-15.** Tickets 50–200 F ($9.50–$38). Métro: Palais-Royal–Musée-du-Louvre.

Those with a modest understanding of French can still delight in a sparkling production of Molière at this national theater, established to keep the classics alive and promote the most important contemporary authors. Nowhere else will you see the works of Molière and Racine so beautifully staged. In 1993, a much-neglected wing of the building was renovated and launched as Le Théâtre du Vieux Colombier. The box office is open daily from 11am to 6pm; closed August 1 to September 15.

OPERA

Opéra-Comique
Place Boildieu, 2e. ☎ **1/42-60-04-99,** or 42-86-88-83 for reservations. Tickets 50–490 F ($9.50–$93.15). Métro: Richelieu-Drouot.

For light-opera productions, try the Opéra-Comique. If possible, make arrangements two weeks before the performance. The box office is open Monday to Saturday from 11am to 7pm; closed July and August.

✪ Opéra de la Bastille
Place de la Bastille, 120 rue de Lyon. ☎ **1/44-73-13-00.** Tickets 60–670 F ($11.40–$127.35). Métro: Bastille.

The controversial building was designed by Canadian architect Carlos Ott, with curtains created by Japanese fashion designer Issey Miyake. The showplace was inaugurated in July 1989 (for the Revolution's bicentennial), and on March 17, 1990, the curtain rose on Hector Berlioz's *Les Troyens.* Since its much-publicized opening, the opera house has presented masterworks like Mozart's *Marriage of Figaro* and Tchaikovsky's *Queen of Spades.* The main hall is the largest of any French opera house, with 2,700 seats. The building contains two additional concert halls, including an intimate room, usually used for chamber music, with only

250 seats. Both traditional opera performances and symphony concerts are presented here.

Several concerts are presented free, in honor of certain French holidays. Write ahead for tickets to the Opéra de la Bastille, 120 rue de Lyon, 75012 Paris.

Théâtre Musical de Paris (Théâtre du Châtelet)

1 place du Châtelet, 1er. ☎ **1/40-28-28-40.** Tickets, 80–580 F ($15.20–$110.25) for opera, 80–300 F ($15.20–$57) for concerts, 80–200 F ($15.20–$38) for ballet. Métro: Châtelet.

The Théâtre Musical de Paris, whose prices are usually lower than those of other theaters, occupies a neoclassical building near the City Hall. Built in 1862 on the site of an ancient Roman stadium, it's largely subsidized by the government of Paris and known for its superb acoustics. Closed in July and August.

CLASSICAL MUSIC

Numerous concerts are presented throughout the year, with daily listings taking up full columns in the newspaper. Organ recitals are featured in churches (the largest organ is in St-Sulpice); and jazz is played at the modern-art museum.

Cité de la Musique

221 av. Jean-Jaurès, 19e. ☎ **1/44-84-45-00,** or 44-84-44-84 for ticket sales and information. Tickets 60–160 F ($11.40–$30.40); entrance during nonconcert hours free. At press time, admission costs to the museum weren't determined. Métro: Porte-de-Pantin.

Of the half-dozen *grands travaux* conceived by the Mitterrand administration, this testimony to the power of music has been the most widely applauded and (in some ways) the most intangible and innovative. At the city's northeastern edge, in what used to be a rundown neighborhood, it incorporates a network of concert halls, a library/research center for the categorization and study of all kinds of music from around the world, and a museum.

Designed as an interconnected complex of bulky post-cubist shapes by noted architect Christian de Portzamparc, the Cité has targeted as its audience Paris's growing low-income multicultural population. Its directors envision it as a kind of Centre Pompidou of music, with archives documenting folk songs from Brittany and Siberia, classical music from North Africa, jazz, and unusual interpretations of French baroque. Buildings for viewing are open Wednesday to Sunday from noon to 6pm; the museum is open Tuesday to Sunday (hours not set at press time); concerts are held Wednesday to Saturday at 8pm and Sunday at 4:30pm.

Radio France Salle Olivier Messiaen

116 av. Président-Kennedy, 16e. ☎ **1/42-30-15-16.** Tickets 50–190 F ($9.50–$36.10) for Orchestra National de France, 120 F ($22.80) for Orchestre Philharmonique. Métro: Passy-Ranelagh.

This mammoth auditorium boasts fine acoustics that were carefully planned during its 1963 construction. It's home to both the Orchestra National de France and the Orchestre Philharmonique.

Salle Pleyel

252 rue du Faubourg St-Honoré, 8e. ☎ **1/45-61-53-00.** Tickets 50–350 F ($9.50–$66.50). Métro: Ternes.

The Salle Pleyel is host to the Orchestre de Paris, whose season runs from September to Easter. Tickets are sold daily from 11am to 6pm on the day of concerts.

Théâtre des Champs-Elysées

15 av. Montaigne, 8e. ☎ **1/49-52-50-00.** Tickets 70–640 F ($13.30–$121.65). Métro: Alma-Marceau.

Operas, concerts, and ballets are performed here by national and international companies. The box office is open Monday to Saturday from 11am to 7pm; closed in August.

Théâtre National de Chaillot
Place du Trocadéro, 16e. ☎ **1/47-27-81-15.** Tickets 50–160 F ($9.50–$30.40). Métro: Trocadéro.

One of the largest concert halls in Paris, this theater is part of the complex of buildings preceding the upward thrust of the Eiffel Tower. Programs are announced on big showboards out front.

BALLET

✪ Opéra Garnier
8 rue Scribe, 9e. ☎ **1/40-01-17-89.** Métro: Opéra.

The rococo Opéra Garnier is the premier stage for ballet and musical productions. Since the competition from the Opéra de la Bastille, the original opera has made great efforts to present more up-to-date works, including choreography by Jerome Robbins, Twyla Tharp, Agnes de Mille, and Georges Balanchine. This architectural wonder was designed as a contest entry by a young architect, Charles Garnier, in the heyday of Napoléon III's Second Empire. The facade is adorned with marble and sculpture, including *The Dance* by Carpeaux.

Note: At press time the Opéra was closed for renovations. When you arrive in Paris, call to see if it has reopened.

3 The Club & Music Scene

Paris is still a mecca for night owls, though some of the once-unique attractions now glut the market. The fame of Parisian nights was established in those distant days of innocence when Anglo-Americans still gasped at the sight of a bare bosom in a chorus line. The fact is that contemporary Paris has less nudity than London, less vice than Hamburg, and less drunkenness than San Francisco.

Nevertheless, both the quantity and the variety of Paris nightlife still beat those of any other metropolis. Nowhere else will you find such a huge and mixed array of clubs, bars, discos, cabarets, jazz dives, music halls, and honky-tonks.

A MUSIC HALL

Olympia
28 bd. des Capucines, 9e. ☎ **1/47-42-82-45.** Tickets 150–600 F ($28.50–$114.05). Métro: Opéra.

Charles Aznavour and other big names make frequent appearances in this cavernous hall. The late Yves Montand appeared once—and the performance was sold out four months in advance. A typical lineup might include an English rock group, a showy group of Italian acrobats, a well-known French singer, a dance troupe, an American juggler/comedy team (doing much of their work in English), plus the featured star. A witty emcee and an on-stage band provide a smooth transition between acts. Performances usually begin Tuesday to Sunday at 8:30pm; Saturday matinees are at either 2:30 or 5pm.

FOLK SONGS & CHANSONNIERS

The *chansonniers* (literally "songwriters") provide a bombastic musical satire of the day's events. This combination of parody and burlesque is a time-honored Gallic

La Miss & Maurice

Except for Edith Piaf, no figure has shone as brightly or as long in the French music hall as the legendary **Mistinguett.** Born in 1876 to a mattress-maker father and a feather-dresser mother who named her Jeanne Bourgeois, "Miss" went on to enchant Paris with her witty tongue and shapely legs that never grew tired or old even after 60 years on stage. In time she became almost a symbol of the city itself, like the Eiffel Tower.

Her career was launched in 1893, and her final show was in 1950 at the age of 75, when she danced bebop nightly for 12 minutes nonstop. She would walk down spiral staircases with 15 pounds of plumes on her head. Behind her stretched 7 yards of feathers, perhaps in memory of her mother's former profession. All the world learned the songs she introduced, ranging from "Valencia" to "Mon homme." She's been called "the true originator of the Spectacular Revue."

Her male equivalent was **Maurice Chevalier,** who became far better known in America. Born in 1888 to a house-painter father and a braid-trimmer mother called *La Louque,* Maurice was a carpenter and metal engraver before his show-business break came at 13. Star of such films as *Ariane* and *Gigi,* he loved many women, none more so than Mistinguett. Wearing or carrying his famous straw hat, he enchanted audiences around the world. Though he never sang very well, he always pulled off a song with his familiar refrains, including "Thank Heaven for Little Girls" and "I Remember It Well," both from *Gigi.*

Both entertainers came from the streets. Although they later acquired much polish and sophistication, they never lost their ability to relate to the ordinary "street people" in their audience. Mistinguett and Maurice Chevalier reigned like a queen and king over what the French call *Le Music-Hall,* a tradition that flourished between the wars.

amusement and a Parisian institution. Songs are often created on the spot, inspired by the "disaster of the day."

Au Caveau de la Bolée
25 rue de l'Hirondelle, 6e. ☎ **1/43-54-62-20.** No cover with fixed-price dinner, 230 F ($43.70); 100 F ($19) without dinner. Métro: St-Michel.

This cellar, built in 1317 as part of the historic St-André Abbey, has been both a prison and a literary club. Paul Verlaine and Oscar Wilde both drank potent absinthe here. Balladeers, poets, and storytellers perform, and the audience is encouraged to join in. You won't understand the jokes and references made in the show unless your French is good. A fixed-price dinner is served Monday to Saturday at 8:30pm, followed by at least four entertainers, usually comedians. The cabaret starts at 10:30pm. On Sunday a jazz show begins at 10:30pm. This caveau is on a tiny street off the western edge of place St-Michel.

✪ Au Lapin Agile
22 rue des Saules, 18e. ☎ **1/46-06-85-87.** Cover 110 F ($20.90), including first drink. Métro: Lamarck.

Picasso and Utrillo once patronized this little cottage near the top of Montmartre, formerly known as the Café des Assassins. It has been painted by numerous artists, known and unknown, including Utrillo. For many decades it's been the heartbeat of French folk music. You'll sit at carved wooden tables in a dimly lit room with walls covered by bohemian memorabilia. Songs include French folk tunes, love ballads, army songs, sea chanteys, and music-hall ditties. You're encouraged to sing along, even if it's only the *"oui, oui, oui—non, non, non"* refrain of "Les Chevaliers de la Table Ronde." The best sing-alongs are on weeknights after tourist season ends. Open Tuesday to Sunday from 9pm to 2am.

Caveau des Oubliettes

11 rue St-Julien-le-Pauvre, 5e. ☎ 1/43-54-94-97. Cover 140 F ($26.60), including first drink. Métro: St-Michel.

This caveau presents French *chansons* (sentimental or bawdy love songs) from the 11th to the 20th century sung by performers in costumes from various eras. After the show, a guide takes you through the museum, where a chastity belt, arms and armor, and thumbscrews are on display. This caveau was opened by Marcel François in 1920, under Notre-Dame's subterranean vaults that many centuries ago were connected to the fortress prison of the Petit Châtelet. It's best to reserve a table. Open Monday to Saturday from 9pm to 2am.

NIGHTCLUBS/CABARET

While decidedly expensive, these places give you your money's worth by providing some of the most lavishly spectacular floor shows anywhere.

✪ Crazy Horse Saloon

12 av. George-V, 8e. ☎ 1/47-23-32-32. Cover 290–530 F ($55.10–$100.75), including two drinks; third drink from 50 F ($9.50). Métro: George-V.

Alain Bernardin's stripteasery is no ordinary cabaret. It's a French parody of a western saloon, which became the first emporium in France where the strippers tossed their G-strings to the winds, throwing up their hands for the big "revelation."

The management invites you to "Be cool! Do it yourself! We dig English like Crazy!" and indeed the place is always packed with out-of-towners. Between acts vaudeville skits are performed. Shows are Sunday to Friday at 8:45 and 11:15pm and Saturday at 8 and 10:20pm and 12:50am.

✪ Folies-Bergère

32 rue Richer, 9e. ☎ 1/44-79-98-98. Cover 150–280 F ($28.50–$53.20); dinner and show 600 F ($114). Métro: Rue-Montmartre or Cadet.

The Folies-Bergère is a Paris institution. Since 1886 foreigners have been flocking here for the performances, the excitement, and the scantily clad dancers. The risqué spectacle is probably as famous for its elaborate costumes as it is for nudity. From the towering plumes to the bushy tails, there can be thousands of costumes worn in each show. Josephine Baker, the African-American singer who used to throw bananas into the audience, became "the toast of Paris" at the Folies-Bergère. According to legend, the first G.I. to reach Paris at the 1944 Liberation asked for directions to the club.

In this age of more advanced (and permissive) sexuality, the Folies has radically changed its context into a less titillating, more conventional format. It often presents bemused, lighthearted French-language comedies and musical comedies, many derived from London or New York productions. Recent examples include *Fou des Folies* (a coy memorial to the theater's raunchy old days) and *Les Années Twist* (a Gallic version of an American homage to rock 'n' roll). Performances are Tuesday to Sunday, as announced.

✪ Lido Cabaret Normandie

116 bis av. des Champs-Elysées, 8e. ☎ **1/40-76-56-10.** Cover 150 F ($28.50); dinner/dance (including half bottle of wine) 760–940 F ($144.40–$178.60). Métro: George-V.

Sitting in the panoramic Lido, the audience is overwhelmed with glamour and talent. The permanent attractions are the Bluebell Girls, a precision ensemble of lovely long-legged international women. The show, visible from any seat, is subject to change. A dinner/dance begins at 8pm, with the revue at 10pm and midnight daily.

Milliardaire

68 rue Pierre-Charron, 8e. ☎ **1/42-89-88-09.** Show and two drinks 450 F ($85.50). Métro: F.-D.-Roosevelt.

The stylish Milliardaire is off the Champs-Elysées, reached through a backyard that's hardly as plush as the interior. Many beautiful women appear in the show, their nudity interspersed with international humor and comedy acts. Two different shows are staged nightly, at 9:30 and 11:30pm. The place maintains a popular and discreet piano bar open every night after the last show from 1:45 to 4am. During July and August no shows are presented on Sunday, and in January and August only one show is presented (at 11pm).

✪ Moulin Rouge

Place Blanche, 18e. ☎ **1/46-06-00-19.** Cover 495 F ($94.05), including champagne; dinner and revue, 720 F ($136.80). Métro: Place-Blanche.

The Moulin Rouge was immortalized in the paintings of Toulouse-Lautrec. Colette created a scandal here by offering an on-stage kiss to Madame de Morny. Today the shows still have shock value. The revue itself is stunning, with elaborate feather costuming and the best cancan in France. Once a nude couple jumped into a tank for some underwater recreation; or you may be treated to a ballet—with a slightly bawdy twist, of course. Try to get a table, as the view is much better on the main floor than from the bar. Reservations are essential. The bar opens 15 minutes before each show. There's no minimum if you sit at the bar. The club is open nightly, serving dinner at 8pm, with the revue beginning at 10pm.

Le Paradis Latin

28 rue Cardinal-Lemoine, 5e. ☎ **1/43-25-28-28.** Cover 465 F ($88.40) including half a bottle of champagne, 670 F ($127.30) including dinner. Métro: Jussieu or Cardinal-Lemoine.

Built by Alexandre-Gustave Eiffel with the same metallic skeleton as his famous tower, Le Paradis Latin represents the architect's only venture into theater design. The theater itself is credited with introducing vaudeville and musical theater to Paris. In 1903 the building functioned as a warehouse. In the 1970s, however, it was transformed into an amazingly successful cabaret. The master of ceremonies speaks in French and English. Performances are Wednesday to Monday: Dinner is at 8:30pm, and the revue is at 9:45pm.

Villa d'Este

4 rue Arsene-Houssaye, 8e. ☎ **1/42-56-14-65.** One-drink minimum, 140 F ($26.60). Métro: Charles-de-Gaulle–Etoile.

In the past this club booked Amalia Rodrígues, Portugal's leading *fadista*, and French chanteuse Juliette Greco. Today you're more likely to hear French singer François de Guelte or other top talent from Europe and America. The Villa d'Este has been around for a long time, and the quality of its offerings remains high. The doors open at 8pm, with an orchestra playing from 8:30pm. A comedy/cabaret/magic act lasts until midnight, with dancing until 2am. Reservations are necessary. Every Sunday a tea dance with a live orchestra is presented from 3 to 7pm.

JAZZ CLUBS

The great jazz revival that long ago swept America is still going strong here, with Dixieland or Chicago rhythms being pounded out in dozens of jazz cellars, mostly called *caveaux*. The majority of the jazz clubs are crowded into the Left Bank near the Seine, between rue Bonaparte and rue St-Jacques, which makes things easy for syncopation-seekers.

Le Bilboquet

13 rue St-Benoit, 6e. ☎ 1/45-48-81-84. Cover 120 F ($22.80), including first drink.

This restaurant/jazz club/piano bar offers some of the best music in Paris. The film *Paris Blues* was shot here. Jazz is played on the upper level in Le Bilboquet restaurant, a wood-paneled room with a copper ceiling, brass-trimmed sunken bar, and Victorian candelabra. The menu is limited but classic French, specializing in carré d'agneau, fish, and beef. Open nightly from 8pm to 2:45am. Live music is presented from 10:45pm to 2:45am.

Under separate management is the downstairs Club St-Germain disco, open Tuesday to Saturday from 11:30pm to 5am. Entrance is free, but drinks cost 90 F ($17.10). Clients can walk from one club to the other but have to buy a new drink each time they change venues.

Caveau de la Huchette

5 rue de la Huchette, 5e. ☎ 1/43-26-65-05. Cover 60 F ($11.40) Sun–Thurs, 70 F ($13.30) Fri–Sat; students, 50 F ($9.50) Sun–Thurs, 60 F ($11.40) Fri–Sat. Métro and RER: St-Michel.

This celebrated jazz cave, reached by a winding staircase, draws a young crowd, mostly students, who dance to the music of well-known jazz combos. In pre-jazz days this caveau was frequented by Robespierre and Marat. Open Sunday to Friday from 9:30pm to 3am and Saturday and holidays from 9:30pm to 4am.

Jazz Club Lionel Hampton

In the Hôtel Méridien, 81 bd. Gouvion-St-Cyr, 17e. ☎ 1/40-68-34-34. Cover 135 F ($25.65), including first drink. Métro: Porte-Maillot.

Some of the world's jazz greats, including Lionel Hampton, have performed in the Hôtel Méridien's central courtyard. The hotel is near the Champs-Elysées and the Arc de Triomphe. Open daily from 10:30pm to 2am or later, depending on business.

New Morning

7–9 rue des Petites-Ecuries, 10e. ☎ 1/45-23-51-41. Cover 120–180 F ($22.80–$34.20). Métro: Château-d'Eau.

Jazz maniacs come here to drink, talk, and dance. The high-ceilinged loft, formerly a newspaper office, was turned into a nightclub in 1981. Many styles of music are played and performed, except disco. The place is especially popular with jazz groups from Central and South Africa. It might be open at 8:30pm or closed just any night, but when it's in business, closing (except on salsa nights) is at 1:30 or 2am. If a well-known performer can be booked on a Sunday, the place is open on Sunday. A phone call will let you know what's going on the night you plan to visit. No food is served. Shows usually begin at 8:30 or 9:30pm.

Slow Club

130 rue de Rivoli, 1er. ☎ **1/42-33-84-30.** Cover 60 F ($11.40) Tues–Thurs, 75 F ($14.30) Fri–Sat and holidays. Métro: Châtelet.

One of the most famous jazz cellars in Europe, the Slow Club features the well-known French jazz band of Claude Luter, who played 10 years with the late Sidney Bechet. Open Tuesday to Thursday from 10pm to 3am and Friday, Saturday, and holidays from 10pm to 4am.

Trois Mailletz

56 rue Galande, 5e. ☎ **1/43-54-42-94.** Cellar cover, 40–70 F ($7.60–$13.30); restaurant and piano bar, free. Métro: Maubert-Mutualité.

This medieval cellar once housed the masons who built Notre-Dame, many of whom carved their initials into the walls. Today it attracts jazz aficionados from all over the world. It's one of the few places where students don't predominate. Celebrities appearing here have included Memphis Slim, Bill Coleman, and Nina Simone. It's open nightly from 10:30pm to "whenever"; the piano bar, daily from 6pm to 5am. Traditional French meals are served in a restaurant adjacent to the piano bar. Reservations are recommended on weekends.

DANCE CLUBS/DISCOS

The nightspots below are a few of the hundreds of places where people go chiefly to dance—distinct from others where the main attraction is the music. The area opposite and around the Eglise St-Germain-des-Prés is full of dance dives. They come and go so quickly that many could be hardware stores by the time you get there—but new ones will spring up to take their place.

Les Bains

7 rue du Bourg-l'Abbé, 3e. ☎ **1/48-87-01-80.** Cover 140 F ($26.60), including first drink. Métro: Réaumur-Sébastopol.

This chic enclave has been pronounced "in" and "out" of fashion, but lately it's very "in," attracting some of the better-looking Parisians. Sometimes the dress the customer wears is more for show than for comfort. The name Les Bains comes from the place's old function as a Turkish bath attracting gay clients, none more notable than Marcel Proust. Sometimes it may be hard to get in if the bouncer doesn't like your looks. Open daily from 11pm to 6am.

La Balajo

9 rue de Lappe, 11e. ☎ **1/47-00-07-87.** Cover 100 F ($19), including first drink. Métro: Bastille.

This club is practically a national shrine to the famous French chanteuse Edith Piaf, who used to perform here frequently. The place is still popular, drawing the young and young at heart, but the music is recorded now. It's a good place to go after the Opéra de la Bastille. Afternoon openings are Saturday and Sunday from 3 to 6:30pm; evening dances are Monday, Thursday, and Friday from 11pm to 5am and Sunday from 9pm to 5am.

Club Zed

2 rue des Anglais, 5e. ☎ **1/43-54-93-78.** Cover 50–100 F ($9.50–$19), including first drink. Métro: Maubert-Mutualité.

This popular nightspot in what was a bakery may surprise you with its mix of musical offerings: samba from Rio, rock, 1960s pop tunes, or jazz. Open Wednesday to Saturday from 10:30pm to 5am.

La Coupole

102 bd. Montparnasse, 14e. ☎ **1/43-20-14-20.** Ballroom cover, Sat matinee 60 F ($11.40), Sun matinée 80 F ($15.20), Fri–Sat nights 90 F ($17.10). Métro: Vavin.

This landmark café has a basement ballroom that's a popular place to waltz and tango to orchestra music as well as bump and grind to "disco retro" (the best disco tunes of the 1960s, 1970s, and 1980s). The upstairs café is previewed separately. The ballroom is open for dancing on Friday from 9:30pm to 4am and Saturday and Sunday from 3 to 7pm and 9:30pm to 4am.

Le Palace

8 rue du Faubourg-Montmartre, 9e. ☎ **1/42-46-10-87.** Cover 100 F ($19) until 6am, 60 F ($11.40) after 6am. Métro: Montmartre.

One of the leading Paris nightclubs, La Palace re-creates 1940s Hollywood glamour. It's designed in the spirit and allure of a Roman or Greek amphitheater, with four bars scattered over three levels. Music is recorded, and there's plenty of room to dance. In 1992 it was acquired by Régine, empress of the Paris night, who plans to retain its youthful ambience. The management doesn't allow sneakers or jeans with holes pierced in indiscreet places. For the gay men's tea dance, see "Gay and Lesbian Bars," later in this chapter. The club is open Tuesday to Sunday from 11:30pm to 6am.

Rex Club

5 bd. Poissonière, 2e. ☎ **1/42-36-83-98.** Cover 50–100 F ($9.50–$19), including first drink. Métro: Bonne-Nouvelle.

Set in a deep cellar at the edge of the garment district, Rex welcomes a youngish clientele on the fringe of Paris nightlife who enjoy acting and dressing as weirdly as possible. Go here for a glimpse of fast music, jaded night owls, and a sense that social anarchy is alive and thriving. Different evenings feature different types of music (rap, Eurodisco, live bands, reggae, acid rock, or whatever). Sometimes special events are scheduled on Wednesday. Open Thursday to Sunday from 11:30pm until dawn.

Riverside Club

7 rue Grégoire-de-Tours, 6e. ☎ **1/43-54-46-33.** Cover 75–90 F ($14.25–17.10), including first drink. Métro: St-Michel or Odéon.

There's usually a line at the door to this typical Left Bank cellar disco with an interesting international crowd. Some dance *comme des foux* (like lunatics) to the rock music. Open daily from 11pm to 6am.

4 The Bar Scene

WINE BARS

Many Parisians now prefer the wine bar to the traditional café or bistro. The food is often better and the ambience more inviting.

Au Sauvignon

80 rue des Sts-Pères, 7e. ☎ **1/45-48-49-02.** Métro: Sèvres-Babylone.

This tiny wine bar has tables overflowing onto a covered terrace. Wines served here range from the cheapest beaujolais to the most expensive Puligny-Montrachet. To go with your wine, choose an Auvergne specialty, including goat cheese and terrines. The fresh Poilane bread is ideal with the ham, pâté, or goat cheese. The place is decorated with old ceramic tiles and frescoes done by Left Bank artists. Open Monday to Saturday from 8:30am to 10:30pm.

La Tartine

24 rue de Rivoli, 4e. ☎ **1/42-72-76-85.** Métro: St-Paul.

Mirrors, brass detail, and frosted-globe chandeliers make La Tartine look like a movie set of Old Paris. At least 60 wines are offered at reasonable prices, including 7 kinds of beaujolais and a large selection of bordeaux, all served by the glass. We recommend the light wine Sancerre and goat cheese from the Loire Valley. Open Thursday to Monday from 8am to 10pm and Wednesday from noon to 10pm (closed two weeks in August).

Willi's Wine Bar

13 rue des Petits-Champs, 1er. ☎ **1/42-61-05-09.** Métro: Bourse or Palais-Royal–Musée-du-Louvre.

Journalists and stockbrokers patronize this increasingly popular wine bar in the center of the financial district. It's run by two Englishmen, Mark Williamson and Timothy P. Johnson. About 250 kinds of wine are offered, including a dozen "wine specials" you can taste by the glass. Lunch is the busiest time—on quiet evenings, you can better enjoy the warm ambience and 16th-century beams. Daily specials are likely to include lamb brochette with cumin or lyonnaise sausage in truffled vinaigrette, plus a spectacular dessert like chocolate terrine. Open Monday to Saturday from noon to 2:30pm and 7 to 11pm.

BARS & PUBS

These "imported" establishments try to imitate American cocktail bars or masquerade as British pubs—most strike an alien chord. But that doesn't prevent fashionable Parisians from bar-hopping (not to be confused with café-sitting).

Le Bar

10 rue de l'Odéon, 6e. ☎ **1/43-26-66-83.** Métro: Odéon.

Each evening, university students crowd this popular bilevel Left Bank hangout. The walls are decorated with posters and a jukebox keeps the place jumping. Many people speak English, but French is still helpful. Open daily from 5:30am to 2am.

Bar Anglais

In the Hôtel Plaza Athénée, 25 av. Montaigne, 8e. ☎ **1/47-23-78-33.** Métro: Alma-Marceau.

This elegant bar, on the hotel's lower level, has a classical Anglo-Saxon decor. The service is French, and the drinks—priced from 80 F ($15.20) before 11pm, from 100 F ($19) after 11pm—are international. Open daily from 11am to 1:30am.

Bar Obelisque

In the Hôtel de Crillon, 10 place de la Concorde, 8e. ☎ **1/44-71-15-00.** Métro: Concorde.

The bar is just as famous as the luxury hotel that houses it. Recent patrons have included Madonna, Tom Cruise and Nicole Kidman, Debra Winger, and upper-level staff of the U.S. Embassy. Classified as a historic monument, the hotel was recently refurbished by fashion designer Sonia Rykiel. Open daily from noon to 2am.

The China Club

50 rue de Charenton, 12e. ☎ **1/43-43-82-02.** Métro: Bastille.

Close enough to the Opéra de la Bastille to attract an après-opera crowd, this is a bar that appeals to Paris's night denizens of the fashion and arts communities. Decorated in a mostly red palette with overtones of the French colonial empire in Asia, it features a Chinese restaurant on the street level, a clam bar and a quiet bar upstairs (with a scattering of chessboards), and a more animated bar in the cellar. No one dances, but everyone seems to talk. The restaurant is open daily from 7pm to 12:30am; the bar, daily from 7pm to 1:30am.

Hemingway Bar

In Le Ritz, 15 place Vendôme, 1er. ☎ 1/42-60-38-30. Métro: Opéra.

Fifty years after Hemingway "liberated" the Ritz in 1945 (see the hotel entry in Chapter 7), the bar named after him is still going strong. The decor consists of warm wood paneling and leather chairs. Book promotions and signings and literary conferences are frequently organized here, and daily newspapers, magazines, and a selection of books are always available. Black-and-white photos of famous writers who frequented the Ritz hang on the walls. Open Tuesday to Saturday from 5pm to 1am.

Pub St-Germain-des-Prés

17 rue de l'Ancienne-Comédie, 6e. ☎ 1/43-29-38-70. Métro: Odéon.

This is the only pub in the country to offer 24 draft beers and 500 international beers. The decor consists of leather niches that render drinking discreet, gilded wall mirrors, hanging gaslamps, and a stuffed parrot in a gilded cage. There are nine rooms and 500 seats, which makes the pub the largest in France. The atmosphere is quiet, relaxed, and rather posh. Genuine Whitbread beer is sold, and Pimm's No. 1 is featured. You can also order snacks or complete meals. In the evening there's band entertainment, both rock and variety. Open daily 24 hours.

Renault

53 av. des Champs-Elysées, 8e. ☎ 1/42-25-28-17. Métro: F.-D.-Roosevelt.

If you like to combine your hamburgers with shopping for a Renault, you'll be at the right place if you drop in here. At first you'll think you've come to an automobile showroom—and you have. But proceed to the rear, where a bar of "horseless carriages" is waiting. Here you can order either a fixed-price menu, an à la carte meal, or just a drink. Open daily from 11am to 1:30am.

5 Gay & Lesbian Bars

Gay life is centered around Les Halles and Le Marais, with the greatest concentration of gay and lesbian clubs, restaurants, bars, and shops between the Hôtel-de-Ville and Rambuteau Métro stops. Gay discos come and go so fast that even a magazine devoted somewhat to their pursuit, *Gay Pied*, has a hard time keeping up. That magazine is sold at many news kiosks, as is *Lesbia*, a monthly national lesbian magazine.

Banana Café

13 rue de la Ferronnerie, 1er. ☎ 1/42-33-35-31. Métro: Châtelet–Les Halles.

This is a ritualized stopover for European homosexuals (mostly male but also female) visiting or doing business in Paris. Set on two floors of a 19th-century building, it has walls the color of an overripe banana, dim lighting, and a well-known happy hour where the price of drinks is reduced daily between 4:30 and 7pm. The street level features just a bar, where you're likely to meet virtually anyone, some of them rather well known. The cellar level puts forth music that alternates between a live pianist and recorded disco, and patrons have been known to dance. It's at its most animated every night after 11:30pm. Thursday, Friday, and Saturday nights, go-do dancers of virtually any orientation and sexual persuasion perform from spotlit platforms in the cellar. Open daily from 4:30pm to 5am.

Le Bar Central

33 rue Vielle-du-Temple, 4e. ☎ 1/48-87-99-33. Métro: Hôtel-de-Ville.

Le Bar Central is one of the leading bars for men in the Hôtel-de-Ville area. Open daily from 4pm to 2am. The club has opened a small hotel upstairs. Both the bar and its hotel are in a 300-year-old building in the heart of the Marais. The hotel caters mostly to gay men, less frequently to lesbians.

La Champmeslé

4 rue Chabanais, 2e. ☎ 1/42-96-85-20. Métro: Pyramides.

With dim lighting, background music, and comfortable banquettes, La Champmesle offers a cozy and discreet meeting place for women, though men are welcome. The club is in a 300-year-old building, decorated with exposed stone and heavy ceiling beams, with 1950s-style furnishings. Every Thursday one of the premier lesbian events is the cabaret beginning at 10pm. The entrance and drinks prices are the same on Thursday as any other time. Open daily from 6pm to 2am.

Madame Arthur

75 bis rue des Martyrs, 18e. ☎ 1/42-54-40-21. Cover 165 F ($31.35), including first drink. Métro: Abbesses.

Madame Arthur is one of the leading female-impersonator cabarets of Europe. This place Pigalle showplace, drawing both straights and gays, is directed by Madame Arthur, who is no lady. The joke is, this place has been around so long it welcomed the invading armies of Julius Caesar—and it's still going strong. You can visit just to drink or to dine from a choice of fixed-price menus. Reservations are a good idea. The show begins nightly at 11pm.

Le New Monocle

60 bd. Edgar-Quinet, 14e. ☎ 1/43-20-81-12. Cover 150 F ($28.50), including first drink. Métro: Edgar-Quinet.

In the center of Montparnasse, Le New Monocle has been a traditional lesbian hangout since the days of Gertrude and Alice. It's a *disco féminin*, but does admit gay male couples. Inside is a bar, plus a dance floor ringed with seats and banquettes and 1950s-look accessories. Live entertainment is interspersed with disco music. Open Monday to Saturday from 3pm to 4am.

Le Palace Gay Tea Dance

8 rue du Faubourg-Montmartre, 93. ☎ 1/42-46-10-87. Cover 40 F ($7.60) before 6pm, 60 F ($11.40) after 6pm. Métro: Rue-Montmartre.

If you're gay, this is *the* gathering place in Paris on a Sunday afternoon. You're welcome in this chatty, gossipy, fun place whether you've come to dance or not. It's an international crowd, and if you don't want to drink beer or liquor you can sip coffee. For more details about Le Palace, see "Dance Clubs/Discos," above, and Le Privilège, below. Open Sunday from 4 to 11pm.

Le Piano Zinc

49 rue des Blancs-Manteaux, 4e. ☎ 1/42-74-32-42. Métro: Rambuteau or Hôtel-de-Ville.

This ever-popular place is unusual. Founded about 12 years ago by a German-born francophile named Jürgen, it's a piano bar/cabaret, filled with singing patrons who belt out old French chansons with humor and gusto. It defines itself as a gay bar, "but you can happily bring your grandmère, as some of our clients do," the management assures us. The place is on three floors of a building, with the cabaret presented in the basement nightly at 10pm for no charge. Open Tuesday to Sunday from 6pm to 2am.

Le Privilège

In the basement of Le Palace, 8 rue du Faubourg-Montmartre. ☎ **1/47-70-75-02.** Métro: Rue-Montmartre.

Set in the basement of Le Palace (above), this bar is one of the most popular watering holes in Paris for lesbians, who arrive wearing everything from leather and sunglasses to silk scarves and lipstick. It's most alive between midnight and around 4am, after which it's usually relinquished to a crowd of mostly gay men. You may be rather intensely "screened" at the door before being allowed inside.

6 Literary Haunts

La Closerie des Lilas

171 bd. du Montparnasse, 6e. ☎ **1/43-26-70-50.** Métro: Pont-Royal.

Hemingway, Picasso, Gershwin, and Modigliani all loved the Closerie, and it has once again become one of the hottest bars in Paris. Look for the brass nameplate of your favorite Lost Generation artist along the banquettes or at the well-oiled bar. Open daily from noon to 2am.

✪ Harry's New York Bar

5 rue Daunou, 2e. ☎ **1/42-61-71-14.** Métro: Opéra or Pyramides.

Harry's, Europe's best-known bar and the most popular American watering hole in Paris, has spawned a host of imitators. Famous patrons have included Fitzgerald, Faulkner, Steinbeck, Stein, Ford Madox Ford, and Ring Lardner. It was also the birthplace of the Bloody Mary. Primo Carnera hung up his gloves at Harry's in 1929, after losing the world's heavyweight championship; they're still there, dangling from a wooden monkey. In 1932 J. H. Cochrane set the world's drinking-speed record here, downing 4.4 pints in 11 seconds.

A Scotsman named Harry opened the bar on Thanksgiving Day 1911 and ran the place until he died in 1958. Today the bar is managed by his son, Duncan C. Mac Elhone. The IBF (International Bar Flies Association) meets here regularly. A variety of whiskies is sold, including a 1965 MacAllan single-malt scotch. Open daily from 10:30am to 4:30am; there's piano music from 10:30pm to 4am.

Rosebud

11 bis rue Delambre, 14e. ☎ **1/43-35-38-54.** Métro: Vavin.

This place—whose name is reminiscent of Orsen Welles's classic, *Citizen Kane*, and Otto Preminger's flop, *Rosebud*—is a coffeehouse/bar/social center. It's not unusual to see some of the patrons dressed 1920s style. The walls are lined with wine bottles, the tables crowded, and the shades drawn. Open daily from 7pm to 2am.

7 Films

Paris has had a love affair with film for years. You can find English-language films listed in *Pariscope* and in the papers. The letters *V.O.* stand for *Version Originale*, indicating that the soundtrack is in the original language and the film is subtitled, not dubbed, in French. Movies run daily from 2pm to midnight with several breaks. You often have to stand in line at the theater even in the middle of the week. Many of the major first-run theaters are along the Champs-Elysées.

Cinémathèque Française, 7 av. Albert-de-Mun, 16e (☎ 1/47-04-24-24; Métro: Trocadéro), is a government-supported theater that's a favorite of Parisian film aficionados. Foreign films are often shown in their original language, with French subtitles. Up to five films are shown Tuesday to Sunday at theaters including Palais de Chaillot, 7 av. Albert-de-Mun, 16e (Métro: Trocadéro); and Palais de Tokyo, avenue du Président-Wilson, 16e (Métro: Iéna). Admission ranges from 28 to 40 F ($5.30 to $7.60). Call the number above for schedules of both theaters.

The largest cinema is **Le Grand Rex,** 1 bd. Poissonnière, 2e (☎ 1/42-36 -83-93; Métro: Bonne-Nouvelle), seating 2,800. First-run films, in their original language, are featured. It contains seven theaters. Seats range from 35 to 44 F ($6.65 to $8.35).

The Ile de France 10

The Château de Versailles, the Palais de Fontainebleau, and the Cathédrale Notre-Dame de Chartres draw countless tour buses. They're the stars of the Ile de France and need no selling from us. However, the lesser-known spots in this green belt around Paris do.

Everything we include in this chapter is a day trip from Paris. You can, for example, wander through the archeological garden of medieval Senlis in the morning, thrill to the Château de Chantilly in the afternoon, and enjoy the show at the Moulin Rouge back in Paris that evening.

Most people's knowledge of the "Island of France" is through the paintings of Corot, Renoir, Degas, Monet, and Cézanne. Here you'll find everything from romanesque ruins, gothic cathedrals, and feudal castles to splendid 18th-century châteaux, enormous forests like Fontainebleau and Chantilly, sleepy villages, and even an African game reserve. To top it off, there's Disneyland Paris. And the many regional restaurants will introduce you to the provincial cooking of France.

EXPLORING THE REGION BY CAR

Here's how to link together the best of the region if you rent a car.

Day 1   Leave Paris via A13, driving west about 3 miles beyond the *périphérique* encircling Paris, to the Château de Versailles. Reserve time for a stroll in the sprawling gardens after you tour the château. Overnight in the town of Versailles.

Day 2   Depart from Versailles via N10, then A11, heading for one of the holiest sites in France: the medieval Cathédrale Notre-Dame de Chartres. Plan to stop for a meal in Rambouillet at La Poste, 101 av. du Géneral-de-Gaulle, Rambouillet (☎ **34-83-03-01**). The town's 14th-century château has housed François I, Louis XV, Marie Antoinette, and Napoléon. Recently, Rambouillet has been the country retreat for France's presidents. The château can be visited unless it's being used for government purposes.

Continue your drive south to Chartres. Visit the magnificent cathedral and wander through the town's twisted medieval streets.

Day 3   Head eastward, driving in a wide loop south of Greater Paris along A11 and N191, stopping in Milly-la-Forêt (40 miles east

---

What's Special About the Ile de France

Great Towns
- Barbizon, famed for its 19th-century school of painting.
- Senlis, former home to royalty from Clovis to Louis XIV.

Gardens
- Giverny, where Claude Monet lived for 43 years and in which he "invented light."

Castles & Palaces
- Château de Versailles, where French art reached its zenith in the 17th and 18th centuries.
- Palais de Fontainebleau, where Napoléon bid farewell to France.
- Malmaison, home of Martinique-born Joséphine, first wife of Napoléon Bonaparte.

Architectural Highlights
- Cathédrale Notre-Dame de Chartres, a gem of medieval stone carving—its stained glass gave the world "Chartres blue."
- The 236-foot-long Hall of Mirrors at Versailles, where the treaty ending World War I was signed.
- Château de Vaux-le-Vicomte, north of the Fontainebleau forest, built in 1656 by the finance minister to Louis XIV—a monument to the *grand siècle*.

Events
- Versailles Spectacle, evening fireworks and illuminated fountains throughout the summer.
- Versailles Grandes Eaux Musicales, a display of fountains in the park on summer Sundays, with classical music.

Top Attraction
- Disneyland Paris, the spectacular entertainment park 20 miles east of Paris—everything from Frontierland to Adventureland.

---

of Chartres) for a view of Jean Cocteau's murals in the 12th-century chapel of St-Blaise (☎ 64-98-96-68); then continue on to Barbizon or Fontainebleau to spend the night. (Both lie around 56 miles east of Chartres and 3¹/₂ miles from each other.) Stroll among the art galleries of Barbizon's core and, even more compelling, visit the Palais de Fontainebleau.

Day 4 Drive north from Fontainebleau along N36, stopping at one of our favorite sites, the Château de Vaux-le-Vicomte, 12¹/₂ miles north of Fontainebleau along N152, before continuing your northward trek for an additional 12 miles to Disneyland Paris, where you can spend two nights.

Day 5 Devote the day to exploring France's interpretation of the Wild West and Main Street, USA, before retiring to any of Disneyland's megahotels.

Day 6 Head northward from Disneyland Paris 28 miles on N330 to the soaring Cathédrale de Senlis, site of one of the early Roman settlements and one of the best-preserved medieval towns of this region. Then continue for 6 miles west along a narrow well-signposted road to Chantilly for a view of another extravagant château (with extravagant stables). Spend the night in Chantilly.

Paris & the Ile de France

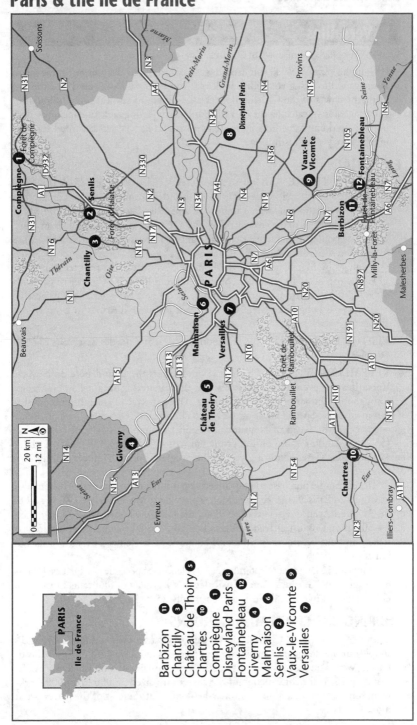

Barbizon **11**
Chantilly **3**
Château de Thoiry **5**
Chartres **10**
Compiègne **1**
Disneyland Paris **8**
Fontainebleau **12**
Giverny **4**
Malmaison **6**
Senlis **2**
Vaux-le-Vicomte **9**
Versailles **7**

1 Versailles

13 miles SW of Paris, 44 miles NE of Chartres

Back in the *grand siècle,* all you needed was a sword, a hat, and a bribe for the guard at the gate. Providing you didn't look as if you had smallpox, you'd be admitted to the precincts of the Château de Versailles, there to stroll through salon after glittering salon—watching the Sun King at his banqueting table or dancing or flirting or even doing something far more personal. Louis XIV was accorded about as much privacy as an institution.

ESSENTIALS

GETTING THERE   To get to Versailles, catch RER line C5 at the Gare d'Austerlitz, St-Michel, Musée d'Orsay, Invalides, Pont-de-l'Alma, Champ-de-Mars, or Javel station and take it to the Versailles Rive Gauche station, from which there's a shuttle bus to the château. The 35-F ($6.65) trip takes about half an hour; Eurailpass holders travel free. A regular train also leaves from the Gare St-Lazare to the Versailles Rive Gauche RER station.

If you go by Métro, get off at the Pont-de-Sèvres stop and transfer to bus no. 171. The trip takes 15 minutes. To get there from Paris, it's cheaper to pay with three Métro tickets from a *carnet.* You'll be let off near the gates of the palace.

If you're driving, take Rte. N10 and park on place d'Armes in front of the château.

VISITOR INFORMATION   The tourist office is at 7 rue des Réservoirs (☎ 39-50-36-22).

VERSAILLES EVENTS   The tourist office offers the **Grand Fête de Nuit de Versailles,** an evening of fireworks and illuminated fountains, several times throughout summer, usually on Saturday. These spectacles are announced a season in advance. Spectators sit on bleachers clustered at the boulevard de la Reine entrance to the Basin of Neptune. The most desirable front seats cost 185 F ($35.15); standing room on the promenoir costs 70 F ($13.30); children under 10 enter free. Gates admitting you to the program open 1¹/₂ hours before show time.

Tickets can be purchased in advance at the tourist office (above). You can also buy them in Paris at Agence Perrossier, 6 place de la Madeleine, 8e (☎ 1/42-60-58-31), and Agence des Théâtres, 78 av. des Champs-Elysées, 8e (☎ 1/43-59-24-60). If you've just arrived in Versailles, you can take a chance and purchase tickets an hour before show time on boulevard de la Reine. The show lasts 1¹/₂ hours.

From early May to late September, a less elaborate spectacle is staged each Sunday. Called the **Grandes Eaux Musicales,** it's a display of fountains in the park choreographed to classical music and costs only 23 F ($4.35).

TOURING THE CHATEAU & GARDENS

Within 50 years the ✪ **Château de Versailles** was transformed from Louis XIII's simple hunting lodge into an extravagant palace, a monument to the age of absolutism. What you see today is the greatest living museum of a vanished way of life. Begun in 1661, the construction of the château involved 32,000 to 45,000 workmen, some of whom had to drain marshes—often at the cost of their lives—and move forests.

Enraged that his finance minister, Fouquet, lived better at Vaux-le-Vicomte than he did at Fontainebleau, Louis XIV set out to create a palace that would awe all Europe (after arranging to have Fouquet arrested for embezzling from the country's treasury, Louis hired the designers Fouquet had used for Vaux-le-Vicomte). He created a symbol of pomp and opulence that was to be copied, yet never quite duplicated, all over Europe and even in America.

So he could keep an eye on the nobles of France (and with good reason), Louis XIV summoned them to live at his court. There he amused them with constant entertainment and lavish banquets. To some he awarded such tasks as holding the hem of his ermine-lined robe. While the aristocrats frivolously played away their lives, often in silly intrigues and games, the peasants back on the estates sowed the seeds of the Revolution.

Peaches & Peas Fit for a King

Between 1682 and 1789, the Versailles palace housed a royal entourage whose population, except for eight years during the minority of Louis XV, remained constant at 3,000. To feed them, the sprawling kitchens employed a permanent staff of 2,000. Without benefit of running water or electricity, they labored over the banquets that became day-to-day rituals at the most glorious court since the collapse of ancient Rome.

The fruits and vegetables that arrayed the royal tables were produced on-site, in Les Potagers du Roi (King's Kitchen Garden). Surprisingly, the gardens have survived and can be found a 10-minute walk south of the château's main entrance, at 6 rue du Hardy, behind an industrial-looking gate. Twenty-three acres of fertile earth are arranged into parterres and terraces as formal as the legendary showcases devoted, during the royal tenure, to flowers, fountains, and statuary.

Meals at Versailles were quite a ritual. The king almost always dined in state, alone, at a table visible to hundreds of observers and, in some cases, other diners, who sat in order of rank. Fortunately for gastronomic historians, there are many detailed accounts about what Louis XIV enjoyed and how much he consumed: Devoted to salads, he ate prodigious amounts of basil, purslane, mint, and wood sorrel. He loved melons, figs, and pears. With him apples were not particularly popular, but he found peaches so desirable that he rarely waited to cut and peel them, preferring to let the juices flow liberally down his royal chin. The culinary rage, however, was peas, whose newest cultivar were imported from Genoa for the first time in 1660. According to Mme de Maintenon, Louis XIV's second wife, the entire court was obsessed with "impatience to eat them."

Today, Les Potagers du Roi are maintained by about half a dozen gardeners under the direction of the Ecole Nationale du Paysage. It manages to intersperse the fruits and vegetables once favored by the monarchs with experimental breeds and hundreds of splendidly espaliered fruit trees. Lecture tours, conducted only in French, are offered between April 1 and November 15 Wednesday to Sunday at 2:30pm and Saturday and Sunday at 4:30pm. They begin at 6 rue Hardy and cost 40 F ($7.60) for adults, 20 F ($3.80) for children 7 to 18, and free for children 6 and under. For information, call 39-49-99-91.

When Louis XIV died in 1715, he was succeeded by his great-grandson, Louis XV, who continued the outrageous pomp, though he is said to have predicted the outcome: *"Apres moi, le déluge"* ("After me, the deluge"). His wife, Marie Leczinska, was shocked at the blatant immorality at Versailles. When her husband tired of her, she lived as a nun, while the king's attention wandered to Mme de Pompadour, who was accused of running up a debt for her country far beyond that of a full-scale war. On her death, Mme du Barry replaced her in the king's affections.

Louis XVI found his grandfather's behavior scandalous—in fact, upon gaining the throne he ordered that the "stairway of indiscretion" (secret stairs leading into the king's bedchamber) be removed. This rather dull, weak king and his queen, Marie Antoinette, were at Versailles on October 6, 1789, when they were notified that mobs were marching on the palace. As predicted, *le déluge* had arrived.

Napoléon stayed at Versailles but never seemed fond of it. Louis-Philippe (reigned 1830–48) prevented the destruction of Versailles by converting it into a museum dedicated to the glory of France. To do that, he had to surrender some of his own not-so-hard-earned currency. Many years later, John D. Rockefeller contributed heavily toward the restoration of Versailles and work continues to this day.

The six magnificent **Grands Appartements** are in the Louis XIV style, each taking its name from the allegorical painting on its ceiling. The best known and largest is the Hercules Salon, with a ceiling painted by François Lemoine, depicting the *Apotheosis of Hercules*. The artist worked on that ceiling from 1733 to 1736, completing it in time for his suicide. Louis XV was delighted (by the painting, not the suicide). In one of these apartments, the Mercury Salon (with a ceiling by Jean-Baptiste Champaigne), the body of Louis XIV was put on display in 1715; his was one of the longest reigns in history: 72 years.

The War Salon (with a ceiling by Le Brun) contains a bas-relief by Coysevox depicting a triumphant Sun King on horseback trampling his enemies (or victims). The most famous room at Versailles is the 236-foot-long **Hall of Mirrors.** Begun by Mansart in 1678 in the Louis XIV style, it was decorated by Le Brun with 17 large arched windows matched by corresponding beveled mirrors in simulated arcades. On June 28, 1919, the treaty ending World War I was signed in this corridor. Ironically, the German Empire was also proclaimed there in 1871.

The royal apartments were for show, but Louis XV and Louis XVI retired to the **Petits Appartements** to escape the demands of court etiquette. Louis XV died in his bedchamber in 1774, a victim of smallpox. In a second-floor apartment, which can be visited only with a guide, he stashed away first Mme de Pompadour and then Mme du Barry. Also shown is the apartment of Mme de Maintenon, who was first the mistress and then the wife of Louis XIV. Attempts have been made to return the Queen's Apartments to their appearance in the days of Marie Antoinette, when she played her harpsichord in front of specially invited guests.

Her king, Louis XVI, had an impressive **Library,** designed by Gabriel, which was sumptuous. Its panels are delicately carved, and the room has been restored and refurnished. The **Clock Room** contains Passement's astronomical clock, encased in gilded bronze. Twenty years in the making, it was completed in 1753. The clock is supposed to keep time until the year 9999. At the age of seven Mozart played in this room for the court.

Gabriel designed the **Opéra** for Louis XV in 1748, though it wasn't completed until 1770. The bas-reliefs are by Pajou. In its heyday it took 3,000 powerful

Versailles

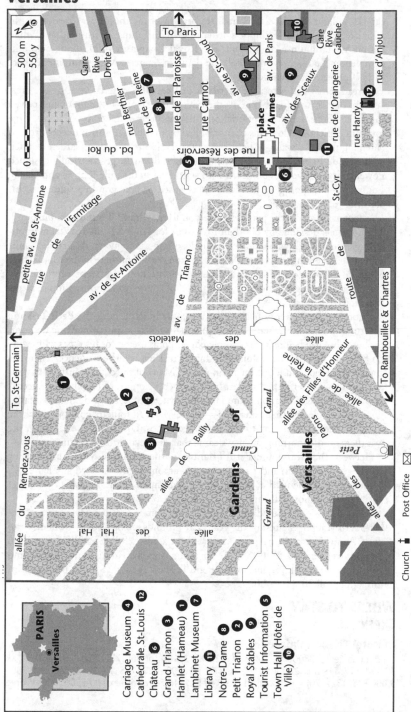

500 m
550 y

To Paris

To St-Germain

To Rambouillet & Chartres

Gare Rive Droite

Gare Rive Gauche

rue d'Anjou

rue Berthier

bd. de la Reine

rue de la Paroisse

rue Carnot

av. de St-Cloud

av. de Paris

av. des Sceaux

rue de l'Orangerie

rue Hardy

bd. du Roi

rue des Réservoirs

place d'Armes

St-Cyr

route de

petite av. de St-Antoine

rue de l'Ermitage

av. de St-Antoine

av. de Trianon

des Matelots

Gardens of

Versailles

Grand Canal

Petit Canal

allée de la Reine

allée des Filles d'Honneur

allée de Bailly

allée du Rendez-vous

allée des Hal Hal

allée des paons

allée des

PARIS

Versailles

Carriage Museum ④

Cathédrale St-Louis ⑫

Château ⑥

Grand Trianon ③

Hamlet (Hameau) ①

Lambinet Museum ⑦

Library ⑪

Notre-Dame ⑧

Petit Trianon ②

Royal Stables ⑨

Tourist Information ⑤

Town Hall (Hôtel de Ville) ⑩

Church ✝   Post Office ⊠

candles to light the place. The final restoration of the theater was carried out in 1957, replacing Louis-Philippe's attempt at refurbishing. With gold-and-white harmony, Hardouin-Mansart built the **Royal Chapel** in 1699, dying before its completion. Louis XVI, when still the dauphin, married Marie Antoinette there in 1770. Both were teenagers.

Spread across 250 acres, the **Gardens of Versailles** were laid out by the great landscape artist André Le Nôtre. At the peak of their glory, 1,400 fountains spewed forth. *The Buffet* is an exceptional one, having been designed by Mansart. One fountain depicts Apollo in his chariot pulled by four horses, surrounded by tritons emerging from the water to light the world. Le Nôtre created a Garden of Eden in the Ile de France, using ornamental lakes and canals, geometrically designed flower beds, and avenues bordered with statuary. On the mile-long Grand Canal, Louis XV—imagining he was in Venice—used to take gondola rides with his "favorite" of the moment.

A long walk across the park will take you to the **Grand Trianon,** in pink-and-white marble, designed by Hardouin-Mansart for Louis XIV in 1687. Traditionally, it's been a place where France has lodged important guests, though de Gaulle wanted to turn it into a weekend retreat. Nixon once slept there in the room where Mme de Pompadour died. Madame de Maintenon also slept there, as did Napoléon. The original furnishings are gone, of course, with mostly Empire pieces there today.

Gabriel, the designer of place de la Concorde in Paris, built the **Petit Trianon** in 1768 for Louis XV. Actually, its construction was inspired by Mme de Pompadour, who died before it was completed. So Louis used it for his trysts with Mme du Barry. In time, Marie Antoinette adopted it as her favorite residence. There she could escape the rigid life at the main palace. Many of the current furnishings, including a few in her rather modest bedchamber, belonged to the ill-fated queen.

Behind the Petit Trianon is the **Hamlet,** that collection of little thatched farmhouses—complete with a water mill—where Marie Antoinette could pretend she was a shepherdess, tending to her perfumed lambs. Lost in a bucolic world, she was there on the morning the news came that the Revolution was launched.

Between the Grand and Petit Trianons is the **Carriage Museum,** housing coaches from the 18th and 19th centuries—among them one used at Charles X's coronation and one used at Napoléon I's wedding to Marie-Louise. (Your ticket to the Petit Trianon will admit you to see these *voitures.*)

The palace is open Tuesday to Sunday: from 9am to 6:30pm May 2 to September 30, to 5:30pm the rest of the year. The grounds are open daily from dawn to dusk. Admission to the palace is 42 F ($8) for adults, 28 F ($5.30) for ages 18 to 24 and over 60, and 28 F ($5.30) for all on Sunday. Admission to the Grand Trianon is 23 F ($4.35) and to the Petit Trianon is 13 F ($2.45). For more information, call 30-84-74-00.

WHERE TO STAY
EXPENSIVE

✪ Hôtel Trianon Palace
1 bd. de la Reine, 78000 Versailles. ☎ **30-84-38-00,** or 800/772-30-41 in the U.S. Fax 39-49-00-77. 179 rms, 20 suites. MINIBAR TV TEL. 900–1,800 F ($171–$342) double; 2,700–3,000 F ($513–$570) suite. Breakfast 75–140 F ($14.25–$26.60) extra. AE, DC, MC, V. Free parking.

In 1919 this was the headquarters of the Peace Conference where Woodrow Wilson, Lloyd George, Georges Clemenceau, and national leaders from Italy and Belgium gathered. A stay here is almost like living at the Grand Trianon. A classically designed palace with stately charm, it's set in a five-acre garden bordering those of the Trianons at Versailles. Japanese owners have restored the place to the tune of $60 million. Guests stay in either the palace or the new Hôtel Trianon, separated from the palace by a garden and connected to it by an underground tunnel. Though many of the dignified rooms are old-fashioned, others (in the new wing) are modern. They're decorated traditionally with subdued colors, antiques, and many fine reproductions. The Japanese suites are the ultimate in luxury.

Dining/Entertainment: Breakfast is served in the sumptuous Salle Clemenceau, where the Treaty of Versailles was negotiated. Chef Gérard Vié, the finest in Versailles, has moved his world-class Les Trois Marches (see "Where to Dine," below) here to an 18th-century-style glass veranda overlooking the park. Guests can dine less expensively by ordering a *menu du jour* in the Brasserie La Fontaine. A Japanese restaurant overlooks a zen garden. After 5pm daily, you can relax and listen to good music in the Marie-Antoinette Piano Bar.

Services: 24-hour room service, babysitting, laundry.

Facilities: Sports/health center, spa, indoor pool, tennis courts.

MODERATE

Novotel Versailles le Chesnay

4 bd. St-Antoine, 78150 le Chesnay. ☎ **39-54-96-96.** Fax 39-54-94-40. 105 rms. A/C MINIBAR TV TEL. 565 F ($107.40) double. Breakfast 55 F ($10.45) extra. Children under 16 stay free in parents' room. AE, DC, MC, V. Parking 40 F ($7.60) indoors, free outdoors.

A 15-minute walk north from one of the side wings of the Château de Versailles, this hotel, built in 1988 as part of a nationwide chain, has a modern facade with columns and large windows. The rooms are practical and identical; four are equipped for the disabled.

INEXPENSIVE

Hôtel Bellevue

12 av. de Sceaux, 78000 Versailles. ☎ **39-50-13-41.** Fax 39-02-05-67. 24 rms. MINIBAR TV TEL. 450 F ($85.55) double. Breakfast 40 F ($7.60) extra. AE, DC, MC, V. Parking 12 F ($2.30).

On one of the city's grandest tree-lined avenues, this hotel is only a three-minute walk from the château entrance. Built in 1850, the hotel was renovated in 1990 but needs a rejuvenation. The lobby is simple and modern, and the worn but soundproof rooms are done in Louis XV or Louis XVI style.

Hôtel la Résidence du Berry

14 rue Anjou, 78000 Versailles. ☎ **39-49-07-07.** Fax 39-50-59-40. 38 rms. TV TEL. 400–470 F ($76.05–$89.35) double. Breakfast 40 F ($7.60) extra. AE, DC, MC, V. Parking free.

Built as a five-story town house in the 1600s, this is one of the only small three-star hotels in Versailles. Each of its slightly cramped and functional rooms has a hairdryer and radio. Breakfast is the only meal served. The hotel's just five minutes from the château. From one of three nearby terminals you can easily get back to Paris.

WHERE TO DINE
EXPENSIVE

Le Rescatore
27 av. St-Cloud. ☎ **39-50-23-60.** Reservations required. Main courses 115–140 F ($21.85–$26.60); fixed-price meal 235 F ($44.65). AE, MC, V. Mon–Fri 12:30–2pm and 7:30–10pm, Sat 7:30–10pm. SEAFOOD.

The decor here is classic, with high ceilings and tall French doors overlooking a busy avenue. Chef Jacques Bagot's specialties include a cassoulet of fish, pot-au-feu of seafood with sweet garlic, and Orient et Occident Porte de Versailles, a ragoût of turbot cooked with potatoes in chicken stock and garnished with cumin, curry, and warmed slices of foie gras. Only about three of his main courses contain meat.

✪ Restaurant les Trois Marches
In the Hôtel Trianon Palace, 1 bd. de la Reine. ☎ **30-84-38-01.** Reservations required. Main courses 175–300 F ($33.25–$57); set menus 260 F ($49.40) (available only at lunch Tues–Fri) and 395–750 F ($75.05–$142.60). AE, DC, MC, V. Tues–Sat noon–2pm and 7:30–10pm. BOURGEOISE.

The food here is sublime, and so are the prices. Chef Gérard Vié is now known for the inventiveness of his *cuisine bourgeoise.* His soaring greenhouse-inspired dining room is remarkable for both its generous expanses of glass and its intimate size (only 55 seats). In summer the front terrace is adorned with a canopy and additional tables, as well as formal flower and vegetable beds. Menu specialties may include flan of foie gras, roast pigeon in a garlic-and-cream sauce, and a modern interpretation of Toulouse-style cassoulet. Note that some people have found the staff a bit too stiff and patronizing.

MODERATE

Le Potager du Roy
1 rue du Maréchal-Joffre. ☎ **39-50-35-34.** Reservations required. Main courses 95–160 F ($18.05–$30.40); fixed-price meal 165 F ($31.35). MC, V. Tues–Sat noon–2:30pm and 7:30–10:30pm. FRENCH.

Philippe Le Tourneur used to work for Gérard Vié (above) before setting up his own attractive restaurant. In three warmly decorated modern dining rooms he offers a fixed-price menu or comparably priced à la carte meals. You might begin with a lamb terrine with raisins and pistachios or a terrine of pot-au-feu; you can follow with duckling with baby turnips, roast lamb en papillote, or steamed filet of sole with summer vegetables. Some critics have faulted him for "lack of imagination," but he knows what he can do and does so excellently.

⑤ Le Quai No. 1
1 av. de St-Cloud. ☎ **39-50-42-26.** Reservations required. Main courses 80–100 F ($15.20–$19); fixed-price meals 115–160 F ($21.85–$30.40). MC, V. Tues–Sun noon–2pm and 7:30–10:30pm. FRENCH.

New owners Dominique de Ravel and Marc Le Loup have breathed new life into this longtime favorite, overlooking the château's western facade. Decorated with lithographs and wood paneling, the restaurant also has a summer terrace. Its fixed-price menus make it a dining bargain in high-priced Versailles. Specialties include seafood sauerkraut, bouillabaisse, and home-smoked salmon. Care and imagination seem to go into the cuisine, and the service is more than professional—it's also polite.

INEXPENSIVE

La Flottille

In the Parc du Château. ☎ **39-51-41-58.** Reservations recommended. Restaurant, main courses 85–115 F ($16.15–$21.85); fixed-price menu 128 F ($24.30). Brasserie, snacks 30–60 F ($5.70–$11.40). MC, V. Brasserie, daily 8:30am–7pm for coffee, ice cream, and snacks; restaurant, daily noon–3:30pm. FRENCH.

This place was built around 1896 as a bar for the laborers who maintained the gardens surrounding the château. Today the only restaurant inside the park, it occupies an enviable position at the head of the Grand Canal, with a sweeping view over some of Europe's most famous landscaping. There are outside tables for lunching in warm weather and a charming pavilion-inspired dining room. Throughout the day, a brasserie/snack bar serves sandwiches, omelets, crêpes, salads, and ice cream. At lunch most diners, however, prefer the dining room, where unpretentious menu specialties include assiette La Flottille (several kinds of raw marinated fish with olive oil and anise), roast rack of lamb with herbs, and filet of sole with baby vegetables.

2 Fontainebleau

37 miles S of Paris, 46 miles NE of Orléans

Napoléon called the Palais de Fontainebleau the house of the centuries. Much of French history has taken place within its walls, perhaps no moment more memorable than when Napoléon stood on the horseshoe-shaped exterior stairway and bade farewell to his army before his departure to exile on Elba. That scene has been the subject of seemingly countless paintings, including Vernet's *Les Adieux.*

ESSENTIALS

GETTING THERE   Trains to Fontainebleau depart from the Gare de Lyon in Paris, and the trip takes 35 minutes to an hour. The Fontainebleau station is just outside the town in Avon, a suburb of Paris; a local bus makes the 2-mile trip to the château every 10 to 15 minutes Monday to Saturday (every 30 minutes on Sunday).

VISITOR INFORMATION   The Office de Tourisme is at 31 place Napoléon-Bonaparte (☎ **64-22-25-68**).

SEEING THE CHATEAU & GARDENS

Napoléon joined in the grand parade of French rulers who used the **Palais de Fontainebleau** as a resort, hunting in its magnificent forest. Under François I the hunting lodge here was enlarged into a royal palace (as at Versailles under Louis XIV), much in the Italian Renaissance style the king admired. The style got botched up, but many artists, including Cellini, came from Italy to work for the French monarch.

Under François I's patronage, the School of Fontainebleau (led by painters Rosso Fiorentino and Primaticcio) increased in prestige. These two artists adorned one of the most outstanding rooms at Fontainebleau: the 210-foot-long **Gallery of François I.** (The restorers under Louis-Philippe did not completely succeed in ruining it.) Surrounded by pomp, François I walked the length of his gallery while artisans tried to tempt him with their wares, job seekers asked favors, and scented courtesans tried to lure him from the duchesse d'Etampes. The stucco-framed panels depict such scenes as Jupiter (portrayed as a bull) carrying off Europa, the *Nymph of Fontainebleau* (with a lecherous dog peering through the reeds), and the monarch holding a pomegranate, a symbol of unity. However, the frames compete with the pictures. Everywhere is the salamander, symbol of the Chevalier King.

If it's true that François I built Fontainebleau for his mistress, then Henri II, his successor, left a fitting memorial to the woman he loved, Diane de Poitiers: Sometimes called the Gallery of Henri II, the **Ballroom** is in the mannerist style, the second splendid interior of the château. The monograms H & D are interlaced in the decoration (the king didn't believe in keeping his affection for Diane a secret). At one end of the room is a monumental fireplace supported by two bronze satyrs, made in 1966 (the originals were melted down in the Revolution). A series of frescoes, painted between 1550 and 1558, depicts mythological subjects.

An architectural curiosity is the richly adorned **Louis XV Staircase.** Originally the ceiling was decorated by Primaticcio for the bedroom of the duchesse d'Etampes. When an architect added the stairway, he simply ripped out her bedroom floor and used the ceiling to cover the stairway. Of the Italian frescoes that were preserved, one depicts the Queen of the Amazons climbing into Alexander's bed.

When Louis XIV became king, he neglected Fontainebleau because of his preoccupation with Versailles. However, he wasn't opposed to using it to house guests—specifically, such unwanted ones as Queen Christina, who'd abdicated the throne of Sweden. Apparently thinking she still had "divine right," she ordered the brutal murder of her lover, Monaldeschi, who had ceased to please her.

Fontainebleau found renewed glory under Napoléon. You can wander around much of the palace on your own, but the **Napoléonic Rooms** are accessible by guided tour only. Most impressive are his throne room and his bedroom (look for his symbol, a bee). You can see where the emperor signed his abdication (the one exhibited is a copy). The furnishings in the grand apartments of Napoléon and Joséphine evoke the imperial heyday.

The interior (☎ **60-71-50-70**) is open Wednesday to Monday from 9:30am to 12:30pm and 2 to 5pm. In July and August, it's open Wednesday to Monday from 8:30am to 6pm. A combination ticket allowing visits to the *grands appartements*, the Napoleonic Rooms, and the Chinese Museum costs 31 F ($5.90) for adults and 20 F ($3.80) for students 18 to 20; under 18 free. A ticket allowing access to the *petits appartements* goes for 15 F ($2.85) for adults and 10 F ($1.90) for students 18 to 20; under 18 free.

After your long trek through the palace, visit the gardens and, especially, the carp pond; the gardens, however, are only a prelude to the Forest of Fontainebleau.

WHERE TO STAY
EXPENSIVE

✪ Hôtel de l'Aigle-Noir (The Black Eagle)

27 place Napoléon-Bonaparte, 77300 Fontainebleau. ☎ **64-22-32-65.** Fax 64-22-17-33. 57 rms, 6 suites. A/C MINIBAR TV TEL. 950–1,200 F ($180.60–$228.13) double; 1,500–2,000 F ($285.17–$380.20) suite. Breakfast 85 F ($16.15) extra. AE, DC, MC, V. Parking 50 F ($9.50).

Once the home of the Cardinal de Retz, this mansion opposite the château was built with a formal courtyard entrance, using a high iron grille and pillars crowned

Fontainebleau

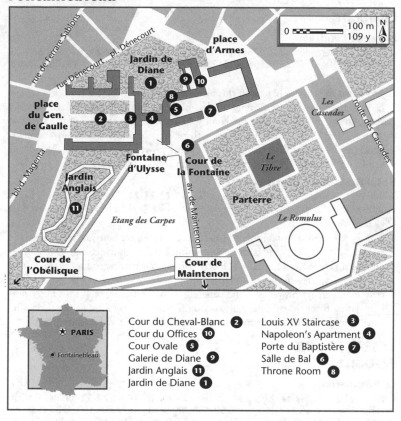

Cour du Cheval-Blanc ②		Louis XV Staircase ③	
Cour du Offices ⑩		Napoleon's Apartment ④	
Cour Ovale ⑤		Porte du Baptistère ⑦	
Galerie de Diane ⑨		Salle de Bal ⑥	
Jardin Anglais ⑪		Throne Room ⑧	
Jardin de Diane ①			

by black eagles. It was converted into a hotel in 1720 and has recently been remodeled, making it the finest lodgings in Fontainebleau. The rooms are decorated with Louis XVI, Empire, or Restoration antiques or reproductions. The Napoléon III–style piano bar is fabulous. Facilities here include an indoor pool, a gymnasium, a sauna, and an underground garage.

Napoléon

9 rue Grande, 77300 Fontainebleau. ☎ **64-22-20-39.** Fax 64-22-20-87. 56 rms, 1 suite. MINIBAR TV TEL. 700 F ($133.05) double; 990 F ($188.20) suite. Breakfast 60 F ($11.40) extra. AE, DC, MC, V. Parking 50 F ($9.50).

This classically designed hotel is a short walk from the château. The lobby has Oriental rugs, big arched windows overlooking the street, and a garden tea room. An inviting bar off the reception area has an ornate oval ceiling, Louis-Philippe chairs, and a neoclassical fireplace. The rooms are filled with reproductions of antiques and eye-catching flowered headboards. All are comfortable, but those facing the courtyard are larger and more tranquil. Since the Napoléon is so close to the château, many visitors patronize its first-class restaurant, La Table des Maréchaux—the food is among the finest served in Fontainbleau.

MODERATE

Hôtel de Londres

1 place du Général-de-Gaulle, 77300 Fontainebleau. ☎ **64-22-20-21.** Fax 60-72-39-16. 22 rms. TV TEL. 350–650 F ($66.50–$123.55) double. Breakfast 55 F ($10.45) extra. AE, DC, MC, V.

Attractive and modestly priced, this hotel is conveniently across from the palace. It dates from the Second Empire but has been substantially modernized over the years. In the mid-1990s half the hotel was restored. Ask for one of the renewed chambers, as they tend to be larger with new baths and soundproof windows. Much of the old furniture from 1830 remains, however. You can order food and drinks on the terrace; fixed-price meals begin at 80 F ($15.20).

Hôtel-Restaurant Legris et Parc

36 rue Paul-Séramy, 77300 Fontainebleau. ☎ **64-22-24-24.** Fax 64-22-22-05. 25 rms, 2 suites. TV TEL. 590 F ($112.15) double; from 610 F ($115.95) suite. Breakfast 45 F ($8.55) extra. MC, V.

This is our favorite hotel in its price range, on a country lane just steps from the château. Part of the facade is art nouveau, unusual for Fontainebleau, and another wing is much older. The classical lobby contains elegant reproduction furniture, marble floors, a few antiques, and gold-and-blue fabric-covered walls. Some of the cozy rooms are freshly painted and papered, with a scattering of 17th-century timbers dating from the original construction. There's a restaurant across the courtyard from the lobby. In summer, lunch and dinner are served in the garden.

WHERE TO DINE

EXPENSIVE

Le Beauharnais

In the Hôtel de l'Aigle-Noir, 27 place Napoléon-Bonaparte. ☎ **64-22-32-65.** Reservations required. Main courses 110–160 F ($20.90–$30.40); fixed-price meals 180–450 F ($34.20–$85.55). AE, DC, MC, V. Daily noon–2pm and 7:30–9:30pm. Closed Dec 23–30. FRENCH.

This is the most beautiful restaurant in town, occupying a former courtyard; the refined interior boasts Empire furniture and potted palms. Try to avoid it if a conference is in town, as its usually fine atmosphere often becomes raucous and service falls off considerably. Some courses have been memorable, namely the salmon mariné with cucumbers and caviar-filled blinis, but the Rouen duckling is often dry. The desserts are sumptuous.

Le François-1er

3 rue Royale. ☎ **64-22-24-68.** Reservations required. Main courses 80–110 F ($15.20–$20.90); fixed-price meals 150–200 F ($28.50–$38). AE, DC, MC, V. Mon–Sat 12:30–2pm and 7:30–9:30pm. FRENCH.

The premier dining choice for Fontainebleau has Louis XIII decor. Try to sit on the terrace overlooking the château and the cour des Adieux. In game season the menu includes hare, roebuck, duck liver, and partridge. Other choices may be pavé de saumon with cèpes (mushrooms), rognon de veau (veal kidneys) with a mustard sauce, and a salad of baby scallops with crayfish. The cuisine is meticulous, with an undeniable savoir-faire. The only reader who wrote in with a complaint alleged that he found fellow diners "stuffy." Watch for certain winter closings, usually on Sunday night and all day Tuesday.

INEXPENSIVE

Le Caveau des Ducs

24 rue de Ferrare. ☎ **64-22-05-05.** Reservations recommended. Main courses 85–135 F ($16.15–$25.65); fixed-price menus 95–230 F ($18.05–$43.70). AE, MC, V. Daily noon–2pm and 7–10pm. FRENCH.

Deep underground, this reasonably priced restaurant occupies what once was a storage cellar for the nearby château. Candles flicker against the vaulted stone ceiling; the decor is traditional and the staff helpful. Menu specialties include snails in garlic butter, sole and salmon on a bed of pasta, rumpsteak filet served with Brie sauce, and roast leg of lamb with garlic-and-rosemary sauce. An excellent dessert is tarte fine aux pommes. The cuisine is good, competent, and plentiful.

3 Vaux-le-Vicomte

29 miles SE of Paris, 12 miles NE of Fontainebleau

The ✪ **Château de Vaux-le-Vicomte,** 77950 Maincy (☎ **64-14-41-90**), was built in 1656 for Nicolas Fouquet, Louis XIV's ill-fated finance minister. Louis was not at all pleased that Fouquet was able to live so extravagantly here, hosting banquets that rivaled the king's. Then Louis discovered Fouquet had financed this château with funds embezzled from the treasury—Louis was not amused. Fouquet was swiftly arrested, and then Louis hired the same artists and architects who had built Vaux-le-Vicomte to begin the grand task of creating Versailles. Visitors will see the striking similarities between the two monuments to the *grand siècle*. To get here, take a 45-minute train ride from Gare de Lyon in Paris to Melun, then a direct bus ride.

The view of the château from the main gate will reveal the splendor of 17th-century France. On the south side, a majestic staircase sweeps toward the formal gardens, designed by Le Nôtre. The grand canal, flanked by waterfalls, divides the lush greenery. The château's interior, now a private residence, is completely furnished and decorated with 17th-century pieces. The great entrance hall leads to 12 state rooms, including the oval rotunda. Many of the rooms are hung with Gobelin tapestries and decorated with painted ceiling and wall panels by Le Brun, with sculpture by Girardon. A tour of the interior also includes Fouquet's personal suite, the huge basement with its wine cellar, the servants' dining room, and the copper-filled kitchen.

A Carriage Museum is housed in the stables. The carriages are of three types—country, town, and sports and hunting. Some 25 perfectly restored 18th- and 19th-century carriages are on exhibit, with mannequin horses and people.

From May to October, candlelight evenings are held every Saturday from 8:30 to 11pm, when the château can be visited by the light of more than a thousand candles. On those evenings, the Ecureuil cafeteria and Carriage Museum stay open until midnight. On the second and last Saturday of each month the fountains of the 13 main pools bubble from 3 to 6pm.

Admission is 56 F ($10.65) for adults and 46 F ($8.75) for children 15 and under (5 and under free). It's open only from May 1 to October 31, daily from 10am to 6pm. In summer special exhibitions of the fountains are staged the first and third Saturdays of the month and candlelight visits are every Saturday from 8:30 to 11pm.

WHERE TO DINE

Restaurant l'Ecureuil

At the Château de Vaux-le-Vicomte. ☎ **60-66-97-09.** Reservations not required. Fixed-price menus 100–150 F ($19–$28.50); children's menu 49 F ($9.30). No credit cards. Sun–Fri 11:30am–6pm, Sat 11:30am–11pm. Closed Nov–Apr. FRENCH.

The only place to eat in the village is this dull self-service eatery near the château's entrance, in what was the stables. You can order suprême of chicken in white-wine sauce, steaks in red-wine sauce with gratinéed potatoes, and filet of sole with butter-and-parsley sauce. For more formal meals, try the nearby town of Melun.

4 Barbizon

35 miles SE of Paris, 6 miles NW from Fontainebleau

In the 19th century the Barbizon school of painting gained world renown. On the edge of the Forest of Fontainebleau, the village was a refuge for artists like Rousseau, Millet, and Corot, many of whom could not find acceptance in the more conservative Paris salons. In Barbizon they turned to nature for inspiration and painted more realistic pastoral scenes, without nude nymphs and dancing fauns. These artists attracted a school of lesser painters, including Daubigny and Diaz. Charles Jacques, Decamps, Paul Huet, Ziem, Troyon, and many others followed. Today, Barbizon's chic attracts some of the most fashionable Parisians with its celebrated inns. Some complain about its outrageous prices, but others just enjoy Barbizon's sunshine and clean air.

Along the Grande-Rue you can visit the ateliers of some of the noted painters, such as Millet. Their main center was **L'Auberge du Père-Gannes,** 92 Grande-Rue (closed for restoration). Millet, Charles Jacques, Corot, Rousseau, Bonheur, and even Delacroix and Ingres used to drop in. Writers were welcome as well: Verlaine, Robert Louis Stevenson, and George Sand with her effete lover, poet Alfred de Musset. Other studios include the **Musée Municipal de l'Atelier de Théodore Rousseau,** 55 Grande-Rue (☎ **60-66-22-38**), a showcase for the man who founded the Barbizon school. Rousseau began painting landscapes directly from nature (novel at the time) and settled in Barbizon in the 1840s. The gallery is open April to September, Wednesday to Monday from 10:30am to 12:30pm and 2 to 6pm; October to March, to 5pm. Admission is 15 F ($2.85).

Another atelier/museum is the **Maison et Atelier de Jean-François Millet,** 27 Grande-Rue (☎ **60-66-21-55**), devoted to the best-known painter, who settled in Barbizon in 1849. He painted religious, classical, and especially peasant subjects. See his etching of *The Man with the Hoe,* as well as some of his original furnishings. The atelier is open Wednesday to Monday from 9:30am to 12:30pm and 2 to 5:30pm. Admission is free.

ESSENTIALS

GETTING THERE   You can take the train from Paris to Fontainebleau (above) and then continue on to Barbizon via a connecting bus. Several buses run between Fontainebleau and Barbizon daily.

VISITOR INFORMATION   The Office de Tourisme is at 41 Grande-Rue (☎ **60-66-41-87**).

WHERE TO STAY
EXPENSIVE

✪ Hotellerie du Bas-Bréau

22 Grande-Rue, 77630 Barbizon. ☎ **60-66-40-05.** Fax 60-69-22-89. 12 rms, 8 suites. TV TEL. 1,300–1,500 F ($247.15–$285.15) double; from 1,800 F ($342.20) suite. Breakfast 90 F ($17.10) extra. AE, DC, MC, V. Parking free.

This is one of the great old inns of France, set amid shade trees and courtyards. In the 1830s, when it was known as M. Siron's auberge, many famous artists stayed here. When Napoléon III and Eugénie came here for a day in 1868 to purchase some paintings from the Barbizon school, the inn became known as the Hôtel de l'Exposition. It's furnished in lustrous provincial antiques and fantastic reproductions. In the colder months, guests gather around the brick fireplace in the living room. The guest rooms (each a double or suite) of this Relais & Châteaux are furnished in part with antiques. The rear building's rooms open directly onto semi-private terraces.

Dining/Entertainment: Whether in an old-world dining room or the court yard, you can enjoy specialties like filet de charolais en feuilleté and soufflé chaud aux framboises (raspberries). In summer, you can order wonderful fish courses flavored with herbs from the hotel's own garden. During the brisk autumn you'll find wild game on the menu, none finer than the specialty of the house: pâté chaud de grouse (a gamey Scottish grouse pâté that's been wrapped in puff pastry and coated with a clear brown sauce). Meals begin at 450 F ($85.55).

MODERATE

Hostellerie les Pléiades

21 Grande-Rue, 77630 Barbizon. ☎ **60-66-40-25.** Fax 60-66-41-68. 23 rms, 1 suite. TV TEL. 320–550 F ($60.80–$104.55) double; 650 F ($123.55) suite. Breakfast 50 F ($9.50) extra. AE, DC, MC, V. Parking free.

Les Pléiades combines antique decor with modern comforts in the former home of landscape painter Charles Daubigny. It's the seat of a monthly conference to which important politicians, artists, and writers are invited. The establishment is run and directed by the town's local historian, Roger S. Karampournis, and his wife, Yolande. Before Karampournis bought the place 12 years ago, he was a dish-washer near the fish piers in Boston and later managed several PX operations for U.S. soldiers in Europe. Today he's one of the best-known chefs in Barbizon; his cuisine has flair and style. Meals cost 150 to 280 F ($28.50 to $53.20). Reservations are recommended.

WHERE TO DINE

⑤ Le Relais

2 av. Charles-de-Gaulle, 77630 Barbizon. ☎ **60-66-40-28.** Reservations recommended weekends. Main courses 82–120 F ($15.60–$22.80); fixed-price menus 145–185 F ($27.55–$35.15). V. Tues noon–2:15pm, Wed 7:30–9:30pm, Thurs–Mon noon–2:15pm and 7:30–9:30pm. Closed last two weeks of Aug. FRENCH.

Many prefer this down-to-earth, comfortable restaurant to the more pricey inns. Le Relais is a corner tavern in a venerable building boasting 300-year-old walls, with a provincial dining room centering around a small fireplace. In sunny weather, tables are set in the rear yard, with a trellis, an arbor, and trees. Typical courses include quenelle de brochet, roast quail with prunes, and grilled beef.

5 Chartres

60 miles SW of Paris, 47 miles NW of Orléans

Many observers feel that the architectural aspirations of the Middle Ages reached their highest expression in the **Cathédrale Notre-Dame de Chartres,** 11 rue des Lisses (☎ 37-21-32-33). Come here to see its architecture, its sculpture, and—perhaps most important—its stained glass, which gave the world a new color, Chartres blue.

ESSENTIALS

GETTING THERE   From Paris's Gare Montparnasse, trains run directly to Chartres, taking less than an hour and passing through the sea of wheatfields that characterize Beauce, the granary of France.

VISITOR INFORMATION   The Office de Tourisme is on place de la Cathédrale (☎ 37-21-50-00).

SEEING THE CATHEDRAL

Reportedly, Rodin once sat for hours on the edge of the sidewalk, admiring the cathedral's romanesque sculpture. His opinion: Chartres is the French Acropolis. When it began to rain, a kind soul offered him an umbrella—which he declined, so transfixed was he by the magic of his precursors.

The cathedral's origins are uncertain; some have suggested that it grew up over an ancient Druid site that had later become a Roman temple. As early as the 4th century it was a Christian basilica. A fire in 1194 destroyed most of what had then become a romanesque cathedral, but it spared the western facade and the crypt. The cathedral you see today dates principally from the 13th century, when it was built with the combined efforts and contributions of kings, princes, churchmen, and pilgrims from all over Europe. One of the greatest of the world's High Gothic cathedrals, it was the first to use flying buttresses. In size, it ranks third in the world, bowing only to St. Peter's in Rome and the Canterbury Cathedral in Kent, England.

French sculpture in the 12th century broke into full bloom when the Royal Portal was added. A landmark in romanesque art, the sculptured bodies are elongated, often formalized beyond reality, in their long flowing robes. But the faces are amazingly (for the time) lifelike, occasionally betraying *Mona Lisa* smiles. In the central tympanum, Christ is shown at the Second Coming, while his descent is depicted on the right, his ascent on the left. Before entering, you should stop to admire the Royal Portal and then walk around to both the north and south portals, each dating from the 13th century. They depict such biblical scenes as the expulsion of Adam and Eve from the Garden of Eden.

Inside is a celebrated choir screen; work on it began in the 16th century and lasted until 1714. The niches, 40 in all, contain statues illustrating scenes from the life of the Madonna and Christ—everything from the massacre of the innocents to the coronation of the Virgin.

But few of the rushed visitors ever notice the screen—they're too transfixed by the light from the stained glass. Covering an expanse of more than 3,000 square yards, the glass is without peer in the world and is truly mystical. It was spared in both World Wars because of a decision to remove it painstakingly piece by piece. Most of the stained glass dates from the 12th and 13th centuries.

See the windows in the morning, at noon, in the afternoon, at sunset—whenever and as often as you can. They constantly change like a kaleidoscope. It's difficult to single out one panel or window of special merit; however, an exceptional one is the 12th-century *Vierge de la belle verrière* (Our Lady of the Beautiful Window) on the south side. Of course, there are three fiery rose windows, but you couldn't miss those even if you tried.

The nave—the widest in France—still contains its ancient maze. The wooden *Virgin of the Pillar*, to the left of the choir, dates from the 14th century. The crypt was built over two centuries, beginning in the 9th. Enshrined within is *Our Lady of the Crypt*, a 1976 Madonna that replaced one destroyed during the Revolution.

Try to get a tour conducted by Malcolm Miller, an Englishman who has spent three decades studying the cathedral and giving the tours in English. His rare blend of scholarship, enthusiasm, and humor will help you understand and appreciate the cathedral. He usually conducts tours at noon and 2:45pm Monday to Saturday. The cathedral is open daily from 7:30am to 7:30pm.

After your visit, stroll through the episcopal gardens and enjoy yet another view of this remarkable cathedral.

EXPLORING THE OLD TOWN

If time remains you may want to explore the medieval cobbled streets of the **Vieux Quartiers** (Old Town). At the foot of the cathedral, the lanes contain gabled houses. Humped bridges span the Eure River. From the Bouju Bridge, you can see the lofty spires in the background. Try to find rue Chantault, which boasts houses with colorful facades; one is eight centuries old.

One of the highlights of your visit might be the **Musée des Beaux-Arts de Chartres,** 29 Cloître Notre-Dame (☎ **37-36-41-39**), which is open April to October, Wednesday to Monday from 10am to 1pm and 2 to 6pm; off-season, Wednesday to Monday from 10am to noon and 2 to 5pm. Next door to the cathedral, this museum of fine arts charges 20 F ($3.80) for adults and 10 F ($1.90) for children. Installed in a former episcopal palace, the building at times competes with its exhibitions. One part dates from the 15th century and encompasses a courtyard. The permanent collection of paintings covers mainly the 16th to the 19th century, offering the works of such old masters as Zurbarán, Watteau, and Brosamer. Of particular interest is David Ténier's *Le Concert.* There are also rare modern works, such as Bernard Rancillac's *Portrait of Giacometti*, an acrylic on canvas (1966). Special exhibitions are often mounted.

WHERE TO STAY
MODERATE

Le Grand Monarque Best Western
22 place des Epars, 28005 Chartres. ☎ **37-21-00-72**, or 800/528-1234 in the U.S. Fax 37-36-34-18. 49 rms, 5 suites. MINIBAR TV TEL. 630–730 F ($119.75–$138.75) double; 1,055–1,280 F ($200.55–$243.35) suite. Rates include continental breakfast. AE, DC, MC, V. Parking 40 F ($7.60).

The leading hotel of Chartres is housed in a classical building enclosing a courtyard. Functioning as an inn almost since its original construction and greatly expanded over the centuries, it still attracts guests who enjoy its old-world charm—such as art nouveau stained glass and Louis XV chairs in the dining room. The

To Taste a Madeleine

"And suddenly the memory returns. The taste was that of the little crumb of madeleine which on Sunday mornings at Combray (because on those mornings I did not go out before church-time), when I went to say good day to her in her bedroom, my aunt Léonie used to give me, dipping it first in her own cup of real or of lime-flower tea."

—Marcel Proust, *Remembrance of Things Past*

Illiers-Combray, a small town 54 miles southwest of Paris and 15 miles southwest of Chartres, was once known simply as Illiers. Then tourists started to come and signs were posted: ILLIERS, LE COMBRAY DE MARCEL PROUST. Illiers was and is a real town, but Marcel Proust in his imagination made it world famous as Combray in his masterpiece, *A la recherche du temps perdu* (*Remembrance of Things Past*). So today the town is known as Illiers-Combray.

It was the taste of a madeleine that launched Proust on his immortal recollection. To this day hundreds of his readers from all over the world flock to the pastry shops in Illiers-Combray to eat a madeleine or two dipped in limeflower tea. Following the Proustian labyrinth, you can explore the gardens, streets, and houses he wrote about so richly and had frequently visited until he was 13. The town is epitomized by its Eglise St-Jacques, where Proust as a boy placed hawthorn on the altar.

Some members of Proust's family have lived at Illiers for centuries. His grandfather, François, was born here on rue du Cheval-Blanc. At 11 place du Marché, just opposite the church, he ran a small candle shop. His daughter, Elisabeth, married Jules Amiot, who ran a shop a few doors away. Down from Paris, young Marcel would visit his aunt at 4 rue du St-Esprit, which has been renamed rue du Docteur-Proust, honoring Marcel's grandfather.

The **Maison de Tante Léonie,** 4 rue du Docteur-Proust (☎ 37-24-30-97), is a museum, charging 25 F ($4.75) for admission. In the novel this was Aunt Léonie's home; filled with antimacassars, it's typical of the solid bourgeois comfort of its day. Upstairs you can visit the bedroom where the young Marcel slept; today it contains souvenirs of key episodes in the novel. The house can be visited Tuesday to Sunday at 2:30, 3:30, and 5:30pm.

In the center of town, a sign will guide you to further Proustian sights.

---

rooms are decorated with reproductions of antiques; most have sitting areas. The hotel also has a restaurant, where set menus cost 140 to 250 F ($26.60 to $47.50). One local critic found the kitchen trapped in an *"ancien régime* time warp."

Hôtel Mercure

6–8 av. Jehan-de-Beauce, 28000 Chartres. ☎ **37-21-78-00.** Fax 37-36-23-01. 48 rms. TV TEL. 420–490 F ($79.80–$93.10) double. Third person 60 F ($11.40) extra. Breakfast 48 F ($9.10) extra. AE, DC, MC, V. Parking free.

Though this 1982 hotel is one in a chain, it has many traditional touches, and the rooms are inviting, with reproductions of Louis XV and Louis XVI furniture. Most accommodations face a garden, and many windows open out to a panoramic cathedral view. In chilly weather, guests gather around the log fire. Breakfast is the only meal served, but there are numerous restaurants nearby.

INEXPENSIVE

⑤ Hôtel de la Poste

3 rue du Général-Koenig, 28003 Chartres. ☎ **37-21-04-27.** Fax 37-36-42-17. 58 rms. TV
TEL. 290–310 F ($55.10–$58.90) double. Breakfast 39.50 F ($7.50) extra. AE, DC, MC, V.
Parking 37 F ($7.05).

A Logis de France, this hotel offers one of the best values in Chartres—even though
it's short on charm. It's located in the center of town, across from the main post
office. The rooms are soundproof and comfortably furnished and have wall-to-wall
carpeting. A fixed-price dinner in the restaurant costs 78 F ($14.80), 105 F
($19.95), or 175 F ($33.25). There's an in-house garage.

WHERE TO DINE

Le Buisson Ardent

10 rue au Lait. ☎ **37-34-04-66.** Reservations recommended. Main courses 100–200 F ($19–
$38); fixed-price menu 108 F ($20.50). AE, DC, MC, V. Mon–Sat 12:30–2pm and 7:30–
9:30pm, Sun 12:30–2pm. FRENCH.

In a charming house in the most historic section of town, this establishment is one
floor above street level in the shadow of the cathedral. From its location you might
expect it to be a tourist trap, but it isn't, though the food rarely rises above bistro
level. Try the stuffed mushrooms with garlic butter, followed by fresh codfish flavored with coriander and served with parsley flan. A dessert specialty is crispy hot
apples with sorbet and a Calvados-flavored butter sauce.

NEARBY ACCOMMODATIONS & DINING

✪ Château de Blanville

Saint Luperce, 28190 Courville-sur-Eure. ☎ **37-26-77-36.** Fax 37-26-78-02. 5 rms, 2 suites.
700–800 F ($133–$152) double; 900 F ($171) suite. Rates include breakfast. AE. From
Chartres, head west along N23 for 6 miles, following the signs to Courville; then follow the
signs to the Château de Blanville.

Built in the Louis XIII style in 1643 and acquired in 1738 by the ancestors of the
present owners, this château is a testament to the accomplishments of many generations of the Cossé-Brissac family. Since 1992 they've rented some of their well-
furnished rooms to visitors who announce their arrival in advance. Ringing the
building are about 275 acres of forest and parkland, little changed since the
building's construction. The guest rooms are high-ceilinged reminders of another
age. None contains a TV or telephone, but shared facilities are available in one of
three guest lounges.

An experience here is best appreciated during dinner, when your hostess, Lisa
(a Cordon Bleu–trained chef), prepares three-course meals, with wine, coffee, and
before-dinner drinks included, for 300 F ($57) per person. Reservations at least a
day in advance are required, and few other experiences convey in as personal a way
the preoccupations, grace, and problems of *la vie de château.*

Le Manoir des Prés du Roy

Saint-Prest, 28300 Chartres ☎ **32-22-27-27.** Fax 37-22-24-92. 18 rms. MINIBAR TV TEL.
350–550 F ($66.50–$104.50) double. Continental breakfast 45 F ($8.55) extra. AE, MC, V.
Parking free. Closed Jan 2–15. From Chartres, take the road to Maintenon, following the vallée
de l'Eure.

Lying 4¹/₂ miles north of Chartres and 50 miles south of Paris, this former private
dwelling has lots of architectural character. It's a retreat for those wanting to

escape touristy Chartres. The manor house is set in a 36-acre park along the River Eure with a private tennis court. The tile-roofed rustic building has been enlarged over the years and is covered with ivy and graced with gables and chimneys. The rooms are comfortably old-fashioned. Many Chartres residents visit to sample the cooking of Gilles Morel, who uses fresh products. Dinner is served nightly, costing 135 to 250 F ($25.65 to $47.50). The restaurant closes in winter on Sunday night and Monday.

6 Malmaison

10 miles W of Paris, 3 miles NW of St-Cloud

The **Musée National du Château de Malmaison,** avenue du Château, 92500 Rueil-Malmaison (☎ 47-49-20-07), boasts lots of history. In the 9th century Normans landed in this area and devastated the countryside—hence the name of this suburb of Paris: Malmaison ("bad house"). Construction on the château here, which was used as a country retreat far removed from the Tuileries or Compiègne (other Napoléonic residences), began in 1622. It was purchased in 1799 by Joséphine Bonaparte, Napoléon's wife, who had it restored and fashionably decorated as a love nest. She then enlarged the estate (but not the château). Popular references to Malmaison as having been a leper's sanitorium are unfounded.

To get here, take the RER A-1 line from place Charles-de-Gaulle–Etoile to La Défense. Transfer to bus no. 158A for the 6-mile run to the country house—the bus stop is Rueil, le Château.

Today Malmaison is filled with mementos and Empire furnishings. The veranda and council room were obviously inspired by the tent Napoléon occupied on his military campaigns. His study and desk are exhibited in the library. Marie-Louise, his second wife, took Napoléon's books with her when she left France; however, these books were purchased by an English couple who presented them to the museum here. Most of the furnishings are the originals; some came from the Tuileries and St-Cloud. Napoléon always attached a sentimental importance to Malmaison, and he spent a week here before his departure for St-Helena.

Many of the portraits and sculpture immortalize a Napoléonic deity—see, for example, David's equestrian portrait of the emperor and also a flattering portrait of Joséphine by Gérard.

In 1809, following her divorce because she could not bear Napoléon an heir, Joséphine retired here and was passionately devoted to her roses until her death in 1814 at the age of 51. The roses in the garden today are a fitting memorial. The bed in which Joséphine died is exhibited, as is her toilette kit, including her toothbrush.

Also here is the small **Château de Bois-Préau** (follow the signs through the park from the main building). The château is a museum/shrine to the emperor, the ground floor devoted to a review of his life (with some death masks) and the upper floor to his death on St-Helena. (In case you're interested—as one woman was about President Clinton—all is revealed here: Napoléon wore boxer shorts.)

Admission to both châteaux on Monday and Wednesday to Saturday is 27 F ($5.15); on Sunday, 18 F ($3.40). Children 17 and under enter free. The museum is open in summer Wednesday to Monday from 10am to noon and 1 to 5pm; in winter it closes at 4:30pm.

7 Senlis

32 miles S of Paris, 62 miles S of Amiens

Today Senlis is a quiet ancient Roman township surrounded by forests. Barbarians no longer threaten its walls as they did in the 3rd century; royalty is gone, too—all those kings of France, from Clovis to Louis XIV, who either passed through or took up temporary residence here. A visit to this northern French town can be tied in with a trek to nearby Chantilly. Today the core of Vieux Senlis is an archeological garden that attracts visitors from all over the world.

The **Cathédrale Notre-Dame de Senlis,** on place Parvis Notre-Dame in the town center, has a graceful 13th-century spire that towers 256 feet and dominates the countryside for miles around. The severe western facade contrasts with the flamboyant gothic southern portal. A fire swept over the building in 1504 and much rebuilding followed—so the original effect is lost. A 19th-century decorative overlay was applied to the original gothic structure, which was begun in 1153. Before entering, walk around to the western porch to see the sculptures. Depicted in stone is an unusual calendar of the seasons, along with scenes showing the ascension of the Virgin and the entombment. The builders of the main portal imitated the work at Chartres. Inside, the airy feeling of gothic echoes the words of a critic who said it was "designed so that man might realize that he was related to the infinite and the eternal." In the forecourt are memorials to Joan of Arc and Marshal Foch.

The **Château Royal et Parc** are a short walk away. Built on the ruins of a Roman palace, the castle followed the outline of the Gallo-Roman walls, some of the most important in France owing to their state of preservation. Once inhabited by such monarchs as Henri II and Catherine de Médici, the château (now in ruins) encloses a complex of buildings. Of the 28 towers originally constructed against the Gallo-Roman walls, only 16 remain. One ruin houses the King's Chamber, the boudoir of French monarchs since the time of Clovis. In the complex is the Priory of St. Mauritius, which not only honors a saint but also was founded by one, Louis IX.

The **Musée de la Vénerie** (Hunting), in the Château Royal, is housed in an 18th-century prior's building in the middle of the garden. It presents hunting-related works of art from the 15th century to the present. Paintings, drawings, engravings, old hunting suits, arms, horns, and trophies are exhibited. The Hunting Museum and the Royal Castle garden are open Wednesday from 2 to 6pm and Thursday to Monday from 10am to noon and 2 to 6pm (closed mid-December to January). Admission is 15 F ($2.85) for adults and 10 F ($1.90) for children. For information, call 44-53-00-80.

ESSENTIALS

GETTING THERE   Take a train from Paris's Gare du Nord to Chantilly; then a one-hour bus ride will bring you to Senlis.

VISITOR INFORMATION   The Office de Tourisme is on place Parvis Notre-Dame (☎ **44-53-06-40**).

WHERE TO STAY

Hostellerie de la Porte Bellon

51 rue Bellon, 60300 Senlis. ☎ **44-53-03-05.** Fax 44-53-29-94. 19 rms, 5 with shower only, 14 with bath; 1 suite. MINIBAR TV TEL. 200–210 F ($38–$39.90) double with shower only,

360–400 F ($68.40–$76) double with bath; 990 F ($188.10) suite suitable for up to six. Breakfast 35 F ($6.65) extra. MC, V. Parking free.

This hotel/restaurant is on a quiet cobblestone street with an adjacent parking lot. The 300-year-old building was a former abbey and is designed with three floors of big windows, shutters, and flower boxes filled with pansies. Five rooms are cramped, with only small showers (no toilets), and are suitable only for those without too much luggage. The ground floor contains a bar area. The adjacent restaurant is accented with flowered wallpaper, charmingly rustic accessories, and a massive fireplace. Fixed-price meals run 115 to 189 F ($21.85 to $35.90).

WHERE TO DINE

Les Gourmandins

3 place de la Halle. ☎ **44-60-94-01.** Reservations required on weekends. Fixed-price meals 210–310 F ($39.90–$58.90); fixed-price lunch (Mon and Wed–Fri only) 120 F ($22.80). MC, V. Wed–Thurs 7-10pm, Fri–Sun noon–2pm and 7–10pm. FRENCH.

In a 16th-century building a five-minute walk from the cathedral, this is one of the most reliable restaurants in Senlis. Amid a conservatively modern decor you can appreciate the modernized French cuisine and delectable seafood of Sylvain Knecht, who's ably assisted in the dining room by his wife, Marie-Christine. Specialties include terrine of foie gras with apples and celery; chartreuse of scallops with lobster in anise sauce; croustillant of "little birds" (pigeon, quail, and hen) beneath phyllo pastry in a brown sauce, with baby vegetables; and roast guinea fowl with foie gras and cinnamon. The cuisine is fresh and clever, and most of the wine list is reasonable, especially the bordeaux.

8 Compiègne

50 miles N of Paris, 20 miles NE of Senlis

A visit to this Oise River valley town is usually tied in with an excursion to Senlis. The most famous dance step of all time was photographed in a forest about 4 miles from town: Hitler's "jig of joy" on June 22, 1940, which heralded the ultimate humiliation of France and shocked the world.

ESSENTIALS

GETTING THERE   There are frequent rail connections from Gare du Nord in Paris. The ride takes 50 minutes. The station is across the river from the town center.

If you're driving, take the northern Paris–Lille motorway (E3) for 50 miles.

VISITOR INFORMATION   The Office de Tourisme is on place Hôtel-de-Ville (☎ 44-40-01-00).

SEEING THE CHATEAU & TOWN

At the peak of his power, Hitler forced the vanquished French to capitulate in the same railway coach where German plenipotentiaries signed the Armistice on November 11, 1918. The coach was transported to Berlin, where it was destroyed. A replica, the **Wagon du Maréchal Foch,** Forêt de Compiègne (☎ **44-40-09-27**), can be visited Wednesday to Monday from 9am to 12:30pm and 2 to 6:30pm. Three-dimensional slides showing scenes from the Great War are projected on a screen. Admission is 10 F ($1.90) for adults and 5 F (95¢) for children 7 to 14. The Glade, as it's known, is on the Soissons Road.

But you don't come to Compiègne—which the French call *la ville de l'armistice*—just for war memories. In the town's heyday, royalty and the two Bonaparte emperors flocked here.

Life at Compiègne centered around what's now the **Musée National du Château de Compiègne,** place du Palais (☎ 44-38-47-00). But this wasn't always a place of pagentry. Louis XIV supposedly once said: "In Versailles, I live in the style befitting a monarch. In Fontainebleau, more like a prince. At Compiègne, like a peasant." But the Sun King returned again and again. His successor, Louis XV, started rebuilding the château, based on plans by Gabriel. The king died before work was completed, but Louis XVI and Marie Antoinette continued to expand it.

Marie-Louise arrived at Compiègne to marry Napoléon I, and in a dining room you can visit on a guided tour she had her first meal with him. Accounts maintain that she was paralyzed with fear of this older man (Napoléon was in his 40s). After dinner, he seduced her and is said to have only increased her fears.

It wasn't until the Second Empire that Compiègne reached its pinnacle of success. Under Napoléon III and Eugénie the autumnal hunting season was the occasion for gala balls and parties, some, according to accounts, lasting 10 days without a break. It was the "golden age": Women in elegant hooped gowns danced with their escorts to Strauss waltzes; Offenbach's operas echoed through the chambers and salons; and Eugénie, who fancied herself an actress, performed in the palace theater for her guests.

On the guided tour you'll see the gold-and-scarlet Empire Room, where Napoléon I spent many a troubled night. His library, known for its "secret door," is also on the tour. In the Queen's Chamber, the "horn of plenty" bed was used by Marie-Louise. The furniture is by Jacob, and the saccharine nude on the ceiling by Girodet. Dubois decorated the charming Salon of Flowers, and the largest room, the Ball Gallery, was adorned by Girodet. In the park, Napoléon ordered the gardeners to create a green bower to remind his new queen, Marie-Louise, of the one at Schönbrunn in Austria.

One wing of the château houses the **National Automobile and Touristic Museum,** which exhibits about 150 vehicles: everything from *Ben Hur* chariots to bicycles to a Citroën "chain-track" vehicle. Also try to see the **Musée du Second-Empire,** which has a fine collection of paintings, sculpture, and furniture, including works by Carpeaux; and the **Musée de l'Impératrice** has souvenirs from the imperial family.

The château is open Wednesday to Monday from 9:15am to 6:15pm. Admission is 31 F ($5.90). You can also visit the other museums in the château with this ticket.

The *picantins* strike the hours at the **Hôtel de Ville,** built in the early 16th century with a landmark belfry. Nearby is a **Museum of Historical Figurines,** place de l'Hôtel-de-Ville (☎ 44-40-72-55), a unique collection of about 100,000 tin soldiers, from a Louis XIV trumpeter to a soldier from World War II. The Battle of Waterloo is depicted here. This museum can be visited Tuesday to Sunday from 9am to noon and 2 to 6pm (closes earlier off-season). Admission is 12 F ($2.30).

A **statue of Joan of Arc,** who was taken prisoner at Compiègne by the Burgundians on May 23, 1430, before she was turned over to the English, stands in the town square.

WHERE TO STAY

The restaurant under "Where to Dine," below, also rents rooms.

Hostellerie du Royal-Lieu

9 rue de Senlis, 60200 Compiègne. ☎ **44-20-10-24.** Fax 44-86-82-27. 20 rms, 3 suites. TV TEL. 450 F ($85.50) double; 550 F ($104.50) suite. Breakfast 43 F ($8.15) extra. AE, DC, MC, V. Parking free.

This hotel is about 1¼ miles from town. Monsieur and Madame Bonechi have carefully decorated the guest rooms in this rambling two-story annex. They have names like Madame Pompadour, Madame Butterfly, and La Goulue; less fancifully named units include rooms done in a representative scattering of different "Louis" periods or Empire style. Both the rooms and the terrace of the restaurant look out over an immaculate garden.

Meals in the elegantly rustic dining room might include a four-fish stew with red butter, scallops with endive, and filet of beef with morels in cream sauce or with foie gras. Dessert soufflés are available if you order them 30 minutes in advance. Meals cost 160 to 360 F ($30.40 to $68.40).

WHERE TO DINE

Rôtisserie du Chat Qui Tourne

In the Hôtel de France, 17 rue Eugène-Floquet, 60200 Compiegne. ☎ **44-40-02-74.** Fax 44-40-48-37. Reservations recommended. Main courses 75–95 F ($14.25–$18.05); fixed-price menus 90–215 F ($17.10–$40.85). MC, V. Daily noon–2pm and 7:15–9pm. FRENCH.

The name, "Inn of the Cat That Turns the Spit," dates from 1665. The bar and a traditional country inn–style dining room are downstairs. Madame Robert, the proprietor, believes in judicious cooking and careful seasoning and prices her table d'hôte menus to appeal to a wide range of budgets. The *menu gastronomique* is likely to include terrine de canard (duck), then trout meunière, followed by poulet rôti (roast chicken) à la broche, and finally a dessert.

Madame Robert also rents 20 clean rooms, each with bath, TV, and phone. Doubles are 300 to 350 F ($57 to $66.50), plus another 42 F ($8) for breakfast.

9 Chantilly

26 miles N of Paris, 31 miles SE of Beauvais

This is a resort town for Parisians who want a quick weekend getaway. Known for its frothy whipped cream and black lace, it also draws visitors for its racetrack and château. The first two Sundays in June are the highlight of the turf season, bringing out an exceedingly fashionable crowd.

ESSENTIALS

GETTING THERE   Trains depart frequently for Chantilly from the Gare du Nord in Paris; the ride takes about an hour.

VISITOR INFORMATION   The Office de Tourisme is at 23 av. du Maréchal-Joffre (☎ 44-57-08-58).

TOURING THE CHATEAU & MUSEUMS

Once the seat of the Condé, the **Château de Chantilly** (☎ **44-54-04-02**) and Musée Condé are on an artificial carp-stocked lake. You approach via the same forested drive that Louis XIV, along with hundreds of guests, rode along for a banquet prepared by Vatel, one of the best-known French chefs. One day when the fish didn't arrive on time, Vatel committed suicide. The château is French Renaissance, with gables and domed towers, but part was rebuilt in the 19th century. It's skirted by a romantic forest once filled with stag and boar.

In 1886 the château's owner, the duc d'Aumale, bequeathed the park and palace to the Institut de France, along with his fabulous art collection and library. The château houses sumptuous furnishings as well as works by artists like Memling, van Dyck, Botticelli, Poussin, Watteau, Ingres, Delacroix, Corot, Rubens, and Vernet. See especially Raphael's *Madonna of Lorette, Virgin of the House d'Orléans*, and *Three Graces* (sometimes called the *Three Ages of Woman*). The foremost French painter of the 15th century, Jean Fouquet, is represented here by a series of about 40 miniatures. A copy of the rose diamond that received worldwide attention when it was stolen in 1926 is on display in the jewel collection. Try not to miss one of the most celebrated Condé library acquisitions, *Les Très riches heures du duc de Berri*, a 15th-century illuminated manuscript illustrating the months of the year.

The petit château was built about 1560 by Jean Bullant for one of the members of the Montmorency family. The stables (see below), a hallmark of French 18th-century architecture, were built to house 240 horses with adjacent kennels for 500 hounds. If you have time, take a walk in the garden laid out by Le Nôtre. A hamlet of rustic cottages and the Maison de Sylvie, a graceful building constructed in 1604 and rebuilt by Maria-Felice Orsini, are in the park.

The château is open March to October, Wednesday to Monday from 10am to 6pm; November to February, Wednesday to Monday from 10:30am to 12:45pm and 2 to 5pm. Admission is 37 F ($7.05) for adults and 27 F ($5.15) for children.

The **Musée Vivant du Cheval,** rue du Connétable (☎ **44-57-40-40**), occupies the restored Grandes Ecuries, the stables built between 1719 and 1735 for Louis-Henri, duc de Bourbon and prince de Condé, who occupied the château. Besides being fond of horses, he believed in reincarnation and expected to come back as a horse in his next life; therefore he built the stables fit for a king.

The stables and an adjoining kennel fell into ruins over a couple of centuries, but they've now been restored as a museum of the living horse, with thoroughbreds housed alongside old breeds of draft horses, Arabs and Hispano-Arabs, and farm horses. Yves Bienaimé, the certified riding instructor who established the museum, presents exhibitions tracing the horse's association with humans, as well as a blacksmith shop and displays of saddles, equipment for the care of horses, and horse-race memorabilia. In April, September, and October, it's open Wednesday to Monday from 10:30am to 5:30pm; in May and June, daily from 10:30am to 5:30pm; in July and August, Wednesday to Monday from 10:30am to 5:30pm and Tuesday from 2 to 5:30pm; and November to March, Wednesday to Monday from 2 to 4:30pm. Closed December 1 to 15. There are three equestrian displays April to October, at 11:30am, 3:30pm, and 5:15pm; the rest of the year, there's one display, at 3:30pm. These last about half an hour and explain how the horse is ridden and trained.

WHERE TO STAY

Hôtel Campanile

Route de Creil, R.N. 16, 60600 Chantilly. ☎ **44-57-39-24.** Fax 44-58-10-05. 17 rms. TV TEL. 270 F ($51.30) double. Breakfast 30 F ($5.70) extra. AE, DC, MC, V. Parking free.

Less than a mile north of Chantilly, this two-story hotel is tranquil. Its well-furnished rooms are unpretentious but restful. The hotel operates a reasonably priced restaurant, featuring set menus priced at 85 F ($16.15) and 105 F ($19.95). The cuisine is rich and often consumed by the racing set, who seem more intent on talking about the horses than the rather routine food spread before them.

WHERE TO DINE

Le Relais Condé
42 av. du Maréchal-Joffre. ☎ **44-57-05-75.** Reservations recommended. Main courses 105–145 F ($19.95–$27.55); fixed-price menus (Wed–Fri only) 180–280 F ($34.20–$53.20). AE, DC, V. Mon noon–2:30pm, Wed–Sun noon–2:30pm and 7–10pm. FRENCH.

This is a popular restaurant for fans of the nearby racetrack and tourists coming only to visit the château. Once a 19th-century Anglican chapel, this building was expanded to serve the gourmet demands of today's horse-loving clients—many of whom inhabit villas in the surrounding countryside. The owner has provided a somber setting for his traditional dishes, including appetizers like duckling foie gras, cassoulet of snails Burgundy style, and lobster terrine. Main courses include shellfish-stuffed ravioli flavored with herb butter, lamb cutlets, and veal kidneys. For dessert, try the black-chocolate mousse. Some courses may come with too much cream for modern tastes. The unremarkable wine list includes some vintages from throughout France, and the service is attentive. There's also a garden for outdoor dining.

Le Tiperrary
6 av. du Maréchal-Joffre. ☎ **44-57-00-48.** Reservations recommended. Main courses 90–150 F ($17.10–$28.50); fixed-price menus 95–155 F ($18.05–$29.45). AE, DC, MC, V. Daily noon–2pm and 7–9:30pm. FRENCH.

The owners here welcome you to their traditional establishment in a 19th-century town house. There are also café tables outdoors, where you can enjoy an apéritif. To begin, try the specialty: ravioli stuffed with snails and shrimp. Other courses likely to be featured are scallops sautéed in an endive-flavored cream sauce, rabbit à la Marseillaise (with a concasse of tomatoes and garlic), fricassée of sweetbreads flavored with port, Barbary duckling in a sauce flavored with the herbs of Provence, and a salad of crayfish tails. Some of the courses are pleasing in their simplicity while others are "overdressed."

NEARBY ACCOMMODATIONS & DINING

Château de Chaumontel
21 rue André-Vassord-Chaumontel 95270 Luzarches. ☎ **34-71-00-30.** Fax 34-71-26-97. 18 rms, 2 suites. TV TEL. 900–920 F ($171–$174.80) double; 1,120 F ($212.80) suite for two. Rates include half board. AE, MC, V. Parking free.

Northeast of Luzarches, about 4 miles south of Chantilly, is this hotel/restaurant dating from the late 16th century. It has had many aristocratic owners and was once the hunting lodge of the prince de Condé, who lived at Chantilly. By 1956 it was turned into a hotel, with well-furnished rooms. Surrounded by a moat and a verdant landscape dotted with wildflowers, the château is about as evocative a site as any found in this region. The rustic dining room serves excellent food, offering such specialties as roast lamb and poached turbot. Fixed-price meals start at 159 F ($30.20), running up to 380 F ($72.20) for a gourmet repast.

10 Château de Thoiry

25 miles W of Paris

The ✪ **Château et Parc Zoologique de Thoiry,** 78770 Thoiry-en-Yvelines
(☎ **34-87-52-25**), is a major tourist attraction that in one year drew more visitors than the Louvre or Versailles. The 16th-century château, owned by the
vicomte de La Panouse family (now run by son Paul and his wife, Annabelle), displays two unpublished Chopin waltzes, antique furniture, more than 343 handwritten letters of French or European kings, as well as the original financial records
of France from 1745 to 1750. But these are not as much a draw as the game reserve.

The château's grounds have been turned into a game reserve with elephants,
giraffes, zebras, monkeys, rhinoceroses, alligators, lions, tigers, kangaroos, bears,
and wolves—more than 1,000 animals and birds roam at liberty. The reserve and
park cover 300 acres, though the estate is on 1,200 acres.

In the French gardens you can see llamas, Asian deer and sheep, and many types
of birds, including flamingos and cranes. In the tiger park a promenade has been
designed above the tigers. In addition, in the *caveau* of the château is a vivarium.
Paul and Annabelle are also restoring the 17th-, 18th-, and 19th-century gardens
as well as creating new ones.

To see the animal farm you can drive your own car, providing it isn't a convertible—an uncovered car may be dangerous. Anticipating troubles, the owners carry
thousands of francs' worth of insurance.

The park is most crowded on weekends, but if you want to avoid the crush, visit
on Saturday or Sunday morning. The park is open from April to October, Monday to Saturday from 10am to 6pm and Sunday from 10am to 6:30pm; November to March, daily from 10am to 5pm. The cost is 97 F ($18.45) for adults and
77 F ($14.65) for children 3 to 12; 2 and under free. The château is open April
to October, daily from 2 to 6pm; off-season, daily from 2 to 5pm. Admission is
30 F ($5.70) for adults and 25 F ($4.75) for children 3 to 12; 2 and under free.

To get here, take the Autoroute de l'Ouest (A13) toward Dreux, exiting at Bois-
d'Arcy. Then take N12, following the signs on D11 to Thoiry.

WHERE TO STAY & DINE

Hôtel de l'Etoile
78770 Thoiry. ☎ **34-87-40-21.** Fax 34-87-49-57. 12 rms. TEL. 315 F ($59.85) double.
Breakfast 40 F ($7.60) extra. AE, DC, MC, V. Parking free.

Built centuries ago, this rustic three-story inn has a stone-and-timber garden sitting room for guests. The guest rooms are comfortably furnished and well maintained. A dolphin fountain decorates one of the walls, and the pleasant restaurant
has masonry trim. Meals consist of fairly routine homemade French dishes.
Expect to pay 65 to 165 F ($12.35 to $31.35) for a fixed-price meal.

11 Giverny

50 miles NW of Paris

On the border between Normandy and the Ile de France, the ✪ **Claude Monet
Foundation,** rue Claude-Monet (☎ **32-51-28-21**), is where Claude Monet lived
for 43 years. The restored house and its gardens are open to the public. Born in
1840, the French impressionist painter was a brilliant innovator, excelling in

Impressions

I am entirely absorbed by these plains of wheat on a vast expanse of hills like an ocean of tender yellow, pale green, and soft mauve, with a piece of worked (farmed) land dotted with clusters of potato vines in bloom, and all this under a blue sky tinted with shades of white, pink, and violet.   —Vincent van Gogh (1890)

presenting the effects of light at different times of the day. In fact, some critics claim that he "invented light." His series of paintings of Rouen cathedral and of the water lilies, which one critic called "vertical interpretations of horizontal lines," are just a few of his masterpieces.

Monet came to Giverny in 1883. While taking a small railway linking Vetheuil to Vernon, he discovered the village at a point where the Epte stream joined the Seine. Many of his friends used to visit him here at Le Pressoir, including Clemenceau, Cézanne, Rodin, Renoir, Degas, and Sisley. When Monet died in 1926, his son, Michel, inherited the house but left it abandoned until it decayed into ruins. The gardens became almost a jungle, inhabited by river rats. In 1966 Michel died and left it to the Académie des Beaux-Arts. It wasn't until 1977 that Gerald van der Kemp, who restored Versailles, decided to work on Giverny. A large part of it was restored with gifts from American benefactors, especially the late Lila Acheson Wallace, former head of *Reader's Digest*, who contributed $1 million.

You can stroll through the garden and view the thousands of flowers, including the nymphéas. The Japanese bridge, hung with wisteria, leads to a dreamy setting of weeping willows and rhododendrons. Monet's studio barge was installed on the pond.

The foundation is open only April to October, Tuesday to Sunday from 10am to 6pm, charging 35 F ($6.65) for adults and 25 F ($4.75) for children. You can visit just the gardens for 25 F ($4.75).

ESSENTIALS

GETTING THERE   If you're going by train, take the Paris–Rouen line (Paris–St-Lazare) to the Vernon station. A taxi can take you the 3 miles to Giverny.

Bus tours are operated from Paris by American Express and Cityrama.

If you're driving, take the Autoroute de l'Ouest (Port de St-Cloud) toward Rouen. Leave the autoroute at Bonnières, then cross the Seine on the Bonnières Bridge. From there, a direct road with signs will bring you to Giverny. Expect about an hour of driving and try to avoid weekends.

Another way to get to Giverny is to leave the highway at the Bonnières exit and go toward Vernon. Once in Vernon, cross the bridge over the Seine and follow the signs to Giverny or Gasny (Giverny is before Gasny). This is easier than going through Bonnières, where there aren't many signs.

WHERE TO DINE

Auberge du Vieux Moulin
21 rue de la Falaise. ☎ **32-51-46-15.** Reservations not required. Main courses 65–120 F ($12.35–$22.80); fixed-price menus 100–180 F ($19–$34.20). MC, V. Tues–Sun noon–3pm and 7:30–10pm. Closed Jan. FRENCH.

This is a convenient lunch stop for visitors at the Monet house. The Boudeau family maintains a series of cozy dining rooms filled with original paintings by the impressionists. Since you can walk here from the museum in about five minutes, leave your car in the museum lot. Specialties include appetizers like seafood terrine with baby vegetables. Main courses include escalope of salmon with sorrel sauce and auiguillettes of duckling with peaches. The kitchen doesn't pretend the food is any more than it is: good, hearty country fare. The charm of the staff helps a lot, too. The stone building is ringed with lawns and has a pair of flowering terraces.

12 Disneyland Paris

20 miles E of Paris

After evoking some of the most enthusiastic and controversial reactions in recent French history, the multimillion-dollar Euro Disney Resort opened in 1992 as one of the world's most lavish theme parks. Conceived on a scale rivaling that of Versailles, the project did not begin auspiciously: European journalists delighted in belittling it and accusing it of everything from cultural imperialism to the death-knell of French culture. But after goodly amounts of public relations and financial juggling, the resort is now on track, welcoming visitors at prices that've been reduced by around 20% from those at the initial opening.

Situated on a 5,000-acre site (about one-fifth the size of Paris) in the suburb of Marne-la-Vallée, the park incorporates the most successful elements of its Disney predecessors—but with a European flair. In 1994 its name was unofficially changed to Disneyland Paris.

ESSENTIALS

GETTING THERE   The resort is linked to the RER commuter express rail network (Line A), which maintains a stop within walking distance of the theme park. Board the RER at such inner-city Paris stops as Charles-de-Gaulle–Etoile, Châtelet–Les Halles, or Nation. Get off at Line A's last stop, Marne-la-Vallée/Chessy, a 45-minute ride from central Paris. The round-trip fare from central Paris is 75 F ($14.25). Trains run every 10 to 20 minutes, depending on the time of day.

Each hotel in the resort is connected by shuttlebus to and from Orly and Charles de Gaulle airports. Buses depart from both at intervals of 30 to 45 minutes, depending on the time of day and day of the year. One-way transport to the park from either of the airports costs 75 F ($14.25) per person.

If you're driving, take the A4 highway east from Paris, getting off at Exit 14 where it's marked PARC EURO DISNEYLAND. Guest parking at any of the thousands of spaces begins at 40 F ($7.60). An series of interconnected moving sidewalks speeds up pedestrian transit from the parking areas to the entrance of the park. Parking for guests of any of the hotels in the resort is free.

VISITOR INFORMATION   All the hotels recommended below offer general information about the theme park, but for specific information in all languages, contact the Disneyland Paris office, in City Hall on Main Street, U.S.A. (☎ 64-74-30-00).

FAST FACTS   Coin-operated lockers can be rented for 10 F ($1.90) per use, and larger bags can be stored for 15 F ($2.85) per day. Children's strollers and wheelchairs can be rented for 30 F ($5.70) per day, with a 20-F ($3.80) deposit. Babysitting is available at any of the resort's hotels if 24-hour notice is given.

SPENDING A DAY AT DISNEY

Disneyland Paris is conceived as a total vacation destination, clustering into one enormous unit the Disneyland Park with its five "lands" of entertainment, six massive well-designed hotels, a campground, an entertainment center (Festival Disney), a 27-hole golf course, and dozens of restaurants, shows, and shops.

Visitors from virtually every country in Europe stroll amid an abundance of flower beds, trees, reflecting ponds, fountains, and a large artificial lake flanked with hotels (see below). An army of smiling employees and Disney characters—many of whom are multilingual, including Buffalo Bill, Mickey and Minnie Mouse, and French-born Caribbean pirate Jean Laffitte—are on hand to greet and delight the thousands of children.

Main Street, U.S.A., is replete with horsedrawn carriages and street-corner barbershop quartets. Steam-powered railway cars embark from the Main Street Station for a trip through a Grand Canyon Diorama to **Frontierland,** with its paddlewheel steamers reminiscent of Mark Twain's Mississippi River. Other attractions include a petting zoo called Critter Corral at the Cottonwood Creek Ranch and the Lucky Nugget Saloon, whose inspiration comes from the gold-rush era; the steps and costumes of the cancan show here originated, ironically, in the cabarets of turn-of-the-century Paris.

The park's steam trains chug past **Adventureland**—with its swashbuckling 18th-century pirates, treehouse of the Swiss Family Robinson, and reenacted *Arabian Nights* legends—to **Fantasyland.** Here you'll find the park's symbol, the Sleeping Beauty Castle (Le Château de la Belle au Bois Dormant), whose soaring pinnacles and turrets are an idealized (and spectacular) interpretation of the châteaux of France. Parading in its shadow are time-tested but Europeanized versions of Blanche Neige et les Sept Nains (Snow White and the Seven Dwarfs), Peter Pan, Dumbo, Alice (from Wonderland), the Mad Hatter's Tea Cups, and Sir Lancelot's Magic Carousel.

Visions of the future are exhibited at **Discoveryland,** whose tributes to human invention and imagination are drawn from the works of Leonardo da Vinci, Jules Verne, H. G. Wells, the modern masters of science fiction, and the *Star Wars* series.

In addition to the theme park, Disney maintains the **Festival Disney** entertainment center. Illuminated inside by a spectacular gridwork of lights suspended 60 feet aboveground, the complex contains dance clubs, shops, restaurants (one of which offers a dinner spectacle, "Buffalo Bill's Wild West Show"), bars for adults trying to escape from their children for a while, a French Government Tourist Office, a post office, and a marina.

Admission: For one day, depending on the season, 150–195 F ($28.50–$37.05) adults, 120–150 F ($22.80–$28.50) children 3–11 (2 and under free); for two days, 285–370 F ($54.15–$70.30) adults, 230–285 F ($43.70–$54.15) children. Peak season is mid-June to mid-September as well as Christmas and Easter weeks. Entrance to Festival Disney is free, though there's usually a cover charge to enter the dance clubs.

Open: June 12–Sept 12, daily 9am–11pm; Sept 13–June 11, Mon–Fri 9am–7pm, Sat–Sun 9am–11pm. Opening and closing hours vary with the weather and the season. It's usually good to phone the information office (see above).

Tours: Guided tours can be arranged for 50 F ($9.50) for adults and 35 F ($6.65) for children 3 to 11. Lasting 3¹/₂ hours and including 20 or more people, the tours offer an opportunity for a complete visit. In view of the well-marked paths leading through the park and the availability of printed information in virtually any language, guided tours are not recommended.

WHERE TO STAY

The resort contains six hotels, each evoking a different theme but all sharing a reservations service. For more information in North America, call 407/W-DISNEY (407/934-7639). For information or reservations in France, contact the **Central Reservations Office,** Euro Disney S.C.A., B.P. 105, F-77777 Marne-la-Vallée CEDEX 4 (☎ **60-30-60-30**). In correspondence, Euro Disney Resort—not Disneyland Paris—remains the official designation.

EXPENSIVE

✪ Disneyland Hotel

Euro Disney Resort, B.P. 105, F-77777 Marne-la-Vallée CEDEX 4. ☎ **60-45-65-00.** Fax 60-45-65-33. 479 rms, 21 suites. A/C MINIBAR TV TEL. 1,650–1,990 F ($313.70–$378.30) room for one to four; 2,900–12,500 F ($551.30–$2,376.40) suite. Continental breakfast 75 F ($14.25) extra for adults, 35 F ($6.65) for children. AE, DC, MC, V.

The flagship hotel of the resort, positioned at the entrance to the park, this establishment resembles a massive Victorian resort hotel, with red-tile turrets and jutting balconies. The guest rooms are plushly and conservatively furnished and contain private safes. On the "Castle Club" floor, free newspapers, all-day beverages, and access to a well-equipped private lounge are provided.

Dining/Entertainment: The hotel has three restaurants (the California Grill is recommended under "Where to Dine," below) and two bars.

Services: Room service, laundry, babysitting.

Facilities: Health club with indoor/outdoor pool, whirlpool, sauna, private dining and banqueting rooms.

Hotel New York

Euro Disney Resort, B.P. 105, F-77777 Marne-la-Vallée CEDEX 4. ☎ **60-45-73-00.** Fax 60-45-73-33. 537 rms, 36 suites. A/C MINIBAR TV TEL. 1,025–1,225 F ($194.85–$232.85) room for one to four; from 2,100 F ($399.20) suite. Continental breakfast 75 F ($14.25) extra for adults, 35 F ($6.65) for children. AE, DC, MC, V.

Inspired by the Big Apple at its best, this hotel was designed around a nine-story central "skyscraper" flanked by the Gramercy Park Wing and the Brownstones Wing. At the edge of Lake Disney, the hotel includes an ornamental pool that's transformed in winter into a lookalike version of the Rockefeller Center skating rink. The guest rooms are comfortably appointed with art deco accessories and New York–inspired memorabilia.

Dining/Entertainment: The hotel has a diner, a cocktail and wine bar, and a jazz club.

Services: Room service, laundry, babysitting.

Facilities: Indoor/outdoor pool, two outdoor tennis courts, health club.

MODERATE

Newport Bay Club

Euro Disney Resort, B.P. 105, F-77777 Marne-la-Vallée CEDEX 4. ☎ **60-45-55-00.** Fax 60-45-55-33. 1,083 rms, 15 suites. A/C MINIBAR TV TEL. 825–1,075 F ($156.80–$204.35) room for one to four; 1,400–2,000 F ($266.15–$380.20) suite. Continental breakfast 55 F ($10.45) extra for adults, 35 F ($6.65) for children. AE, DC, MC, V.

This hotel is designed with a central cupola, jutting balconies, a large front porch with comfortable rocking chairs, and a color scheme of blue and cream inspired by a harborfront New England hotel. It's ringed by verdant lawns. Each nautically decorated guest room receives closed-circuit TV movies. The upscale Yacht Club and less formal Cape Cod restaurants are the dining choices. Facilities include a lakeside promenade, a croquet lawn, a glassed-in pool pavilion, an outdoor pool, and a health club with sun beds and a sauna.

Sequoia Lodge

Euro Disney Resort, B.P. 105, F-77777 Marne-la-Vallée CEDEX 4. ☎ **60-45-51-00.** Fax 60-45-51-33. 997 rms, 14 suites. A/C MINIBAR TV TEL. 525–975 F ($99.80–$185.35) room for one to four; 1,500–1,700 F ($285.15–$323.20) suite. Continental breakfast 55 F ($10.45) extra for adults, 35 F ($6.65) for children. AE, DC, MC, V.

Built of gray stone and roughly textured planking and capped with a gently sloping green copper roof, this hotel evokes a rough-hewn but comfortable lodge in a remote section of the Rocky Mountains. At the edge of the resort's lake, the Sequoia consists of a large central building with five chalets (each containing 100 rooms) nearby. The guest rooms are comfortably rustic—a departure from the glossiness of other sections of the resort. By the light of an open fireplace, the Hunter's Grill serves juicy portions of spit-roasted meats. Less formal is the Beaver Creek Tavern. Facilities include an indoor pool and a health club.

INEXPENSIVE

Hôtel Cheyenne and Hôtel Santa Fé

Euro Disney Resort, B.P. 115, F-77777 Marne-la-Vallée CEDEX 4. ☎ **60-45-62-00** (Cheyenne) or 60-45-78-00 (Santa Fé). Fax 60-45-62-33 (Cheyenne) or 60-45-78-33 (Santa Fé). 2,000 rms. TV TEL. Hotel Cheyenne, 400–675 F ($76.05–$128.30) room for one to four. Hotel Santa Fé, 300–500 F ($57–$95.05) room for one to four. Continental breakfast 40 F ($7.60) extra for adults, 25 F ($4.75) for children. AE, DC, MC, V.

Adjacent to each other, these are the least expensive places to stay at the resort (except for the campgrounds). They're near a re-creation of Texas's Rio Grande and evoke the Old West. The Cheyenne accommodates visitors in 14 2-story buildings along Desperado Street, while the Santa Fé, sporting a desert theme, encompasses 4 "nature trails" winding among 42 adobe-style pueblos. The guest rooms are basic. The only disadvantage of these hotels, according to some parents, is the lack of a pool. Tex-Mex specialties are offered at La Cantina (Santa Fé), while barbecue and smokehouse specialties predominate at the Chuck Wagon Café (Cheyenne).

WHERE TO DINE

Within the resort are at least 45 restaurants and snack bars.

Auberge de Cendrillon

Fantasyland. ☎ **64-74-24-02.** Reservations not required. Main courses 95–125 F ($18.05–$23.75); fixed-price menus 110–260 F ($20.90–$49.40). AE, DC, MC, V. Fri–Tues 11:30am–11pm. FRENCH.

The major French restaurant at the resort is a fairy-tale version of Cinderella's sumptuous country inn, with a glass couch in the center. A master of ceremonies, in a plumed tricorne hat and an embroidered tunic and lace ruffles, welcomes you. Try the warm goat-cheese salad with lardons or the smoked-salmon platter for an appetizer. If you don't choose one of the good fixed-price meals, you can order from the limited but excellent à la carte menu. Perhaps you'll settle happily for poultry in a pocket (puff pastry), loin of lamb roasted with mustard, or sautéed médaillons of veal.

Key West Seafood

In the Festival Disney Building. ☎ **60-45-70-60.** Reservations required. Main courses 78.50–130 F ($14.90–$24.70); children's menus 45 F ($8.55). AE, DC, MC, V. Daily 5:30–11pm. SEAFOOD.

Evocative of a Florida Keys seafood place, this restaurant regales European diners with exposed timbers and an amply stocked oyster bar. Drinks include a spice-laden Bloody Mary and a margarita made with a mixture of tequilas. Your meal might consist of a sand digger's bucket brimming with steamed mussels; crabs served either steamed or fried with garlic; Islamorada clam chowder; garlic crabs; heaping platters of shrimp, oysters, and clams; and dessert pies made either from Key limes or southern pecans.

Walt's, An American Restaurant

Main Street, U.S.A. ☎ **64-74-24-08.** Reservations not accepted. Main courses 80–125 F ($15.20–$23.75); fixed-price menu 145 F ($27.55); children's menu 75 F ($14.25). AE, DC, MC, V. Fri–Tues 11:30am–11pm. AMERICAN.

This popular family restaurant honors Walt Disney. On the ground floor is a well-decorated bistro and upstairs is a restaurant divided into small dining rooms. The decor consists, in part, of photographs tracing Disney's career. Each dining room evokes one of the theme-park lands. Begin your meal with an appetizer like seafood in a pastry shell and follow it with veal Oscar, grilled breast of chicken with barbecue sauce, or grilled New York steak. Hot apple cobbler with ice cream is among the dessert offerings.

11 The Loire Valley

Bordered by vineyards, the winding Loire Valley cuts through the land of castles deep in France's heart. Crusaders returning to their medieval quarters here brought news of the opulence of the East, and soon they began rethinking their surroundings. Later, word came from neighboring Italy of a great artistic flowering led by Leonardo de Vinci and Michelangelo. So when royalty and nobility built châteaux throughout this valley during the French Renaissance, sumptuousness was uppermost in their minds. An era of excessive pomp reigned here until Henri IV moved his court to Paris, marking the Loire's decline.

The Loire is blessed with abundant attractions—ranging from medieval, Renaissance, and classical châteaux to romanesque and gothic churches to treasures like the Apocalypse Tapestries. There's even the castle that inspired the fairy tale "Sleeping Beauty."

REGIONAL CUISINE   Patricia Wells, author of *The Food Lover's Guide to France*, has said that the Loire's cuisine reminds her "of the daffodil days of spring and blue skies of summer." Particularly superb are rose-fleshed salmon caught in the Loire River, often served with sorrel. The region's rivers are stocked with other fish as well, including pike, carp, shad, and mullet.

Various types of rillettes (potted pork) begin most meals. Gourmets highly prize pâté d'alouettes (lark pâté) and matelote d'anguille (stewed eel). From the mushroom-rich Sologne emerges wild boar, along with deer, miniature quail, hare, pheasant, and mallard duck. Two popular poultry dishes are chicken casserole in red-wine sauce and spit-roasted capon.

The valley's Atlantic side produces an astonishing variety of grapes used to make wines ranging from dry to lusciously sweet and from still to sparkling and fruity. The best whites are Vouvray (ideal with Loire salmon) and Montlouis. Red Anjou wines, including Rouge de Cabernet and Saumur-Champigny, have a slight raspberry flavor. Dry Sancerre wines, with plenty of backbone, are wonderful with the Loire's fabled goat cheese and whitewater fish.

EXPLORING THE REGION BY CAR

The Loire Valley's finest châteaux are relatively isolated, so here's how to link together the best of the region if you rent a car.

What's Special About the Loire Valley

Ancient Monuments
- Chinon, the oldest fortress-château in the Loire Valley, where Joan of Arc changed the course of history.
- Fontevraud-l'Abbaye, the burial abbey for the Plantagenet kings of England.

Gardens
- The spectacular Renaissance gardens at Villandry, laid out in three cloisters with a water garden.

Castles
- Château de Chambord, the largest of the Loire châteaux and François I's favorite.
- Château d'Amboise, where Charles VII and François I lived and Leonardo da Vinci died.
- Château de Blois, seat of the comtes de Blois in the 13th century and later briefly capital of France.
- Chaumont-sur-Loire, the medieval fortress to which Diane de Poitiers was banished after Henri II's death.
- Château de Chenonceau, an architectural masterpiece of the Renaissance, fought over by Diane de Poitiers and Catherine de Médici.
- Château d'Azay-le-Rideau, whose beauty and expense was said to have destroyed its original owners.

Events
- *Son-et-lumière* (sound-and-light) shows each summer bring to life the royal past of the Loire Valley.

Day 1   Depart early from Paris or Chartres, driving southwest along A10 and N10, heading for Châteaudun (64 miles from Paris and 27 miles from Chartres). Stop at the town of Vendôme (25 miles to the south via N10) before visiting its well-known château. The town might be a suitable place for a meal at Le Petit Bilboquet, route de Tours (☎ 54-77-16-60). Continue along N10 for 34 miles and stay overnight in Tours.

Day 2   With Chinon as your final destination, drive southwest from Tours on D7 for 28 miles, stopping to admire the architecture of Luynes, Montbazon, Villandry, and Langeais—all along the south bank of the Loire, on either side of D7. Make a special effort to detour for a view of Azay-le-Rideau. Spend the night in Chinon.

Day 3   Backtrack to the northwest for 6 miles on secondary roads and visit the Château d'Ussé (it's signposted from Chinon). Return to Chinon, then drive west for 14 miles on secondary roads to one of the premier romanesque churches here: Fontevraud-l'Abbaye. Visit the Château de Saumur, 7¹/₂ miles to the northwest, before heading west on D952 for 25 miles to Angers, where you can stay the night.

Day 4   Head due east on A11 and then D766, bypassing Tours and stopping for a view of Amboise (71 miles from Angers) and Chaumont-sur-Loire (84 miles from Angers). Drive another 19 miles northeast to Blois, where you can stay overnight.

Day 5   Visit the Château de Blois before departing for Cheverny (7¹/₂ miles southeast) and finally the Château de Chambord (9¹/₂ miles east). Drive northeast another 28 miles to spend the night in Orléans.

1 Châteaudun

64 miles SW of Paris, 27 miles SW of Chartres

The first château you'll come to is the **Château de Châteaudun,** place Jean de Dunois (☎ **37-45-22-70**). Austere and foreboding, it rises on a stonebound table over a tributary of the Loire.

Though begun in the Middle Ages, the château is a mix of medieval and Renaissance architecture, with towering chimneys and dormers. After a fire in the 18th century, Hardouin, Louis XV's architect, directed the town's near-total reconstruction and indiscreetly turned the castle over to the homeless, who stripped it of its finery. In 1935 the government acquired the fortress and launched a major restoration. Even today it's not richly furnished, but fine tapestries depicting scenes like the worship of the golden calf now cover its walls. The château's most admirable features are two carved staircases. Inside the Sainte-Chapelle, a keep dating from the Middle Ages, are more than a dozen 15th-century robed statues.

The château is open daily: April to September, from 9:30 to 11:45am and 2 to 6pm; October to March, from 10 to 11:45am and 2 to 4pm. Admission is 32 F ($6.10), half price on Sunday and holidays.

ESSENTIALS

GETTING THERE   Buses run frequently from Chartres.

VISITOR INFORMATION   The Office de Tourisme is at 1 rue de Luynes (☎ 37-45-22-46).

WHERE TO STAY

Hôtel de Beauce

50 rue Jallans, 28200 Châteaudun. ☎ **37-45-14-75.** Fax 37-45-87-53. 24 rms, 18 with bath. TV TEL. 180 F ($34.20) double without bath, 300 F ($57) double with bath. Breakfast 30 F ($5.70) extra. MC, V. Parking 26 F ($4.95). Closed Dec 16–Jan 10.

This hotel is clean, modern, and simple, and though it lacks a restaurant, it does have a small cocktail lounge for guests only. It's about a two-minute walk from the heart of town, on a quiet street. The rooms are furnished in an uncomplicated style.

Hôtel Saint-Michel

28 place du 18-Octobre and 5 rue Péan, 28200 Châteaudun. ☎ **37-45-15-70.** Fax 37-45-83-39. 19 rms, 14 with bath (tub or shower). TV TEL. 220 F ($41.80) double without bath, 330 F ($62.70) double with bath. Breakfast 30 F ($5.70) extra. AE, MC, V. Parking free.

Monsieur and Madame Halbout own this hotel on the main square of town. The rooms are simply furnished, with hot- and cold-water basins; nine have minibars. Breakfast is served in the lounge, in your room, or in the winter garden (there's no restaurant). The hotel's facilities include a sauna and solarium.

2 Tours

144 miles SW of Paris, 70 miles SW of Orléans

Though it doesn't boast a major château, Tours is the traditional center for exploring the valley, at the junction of the Loire and Cher rivers. The devout en route to Santiago de Compostela in northwest Spain once stopped off here to pay homage at the tomb of St. Martin, the Apostle of Gaul, who'd been bishop of Tours

The Loire Valley

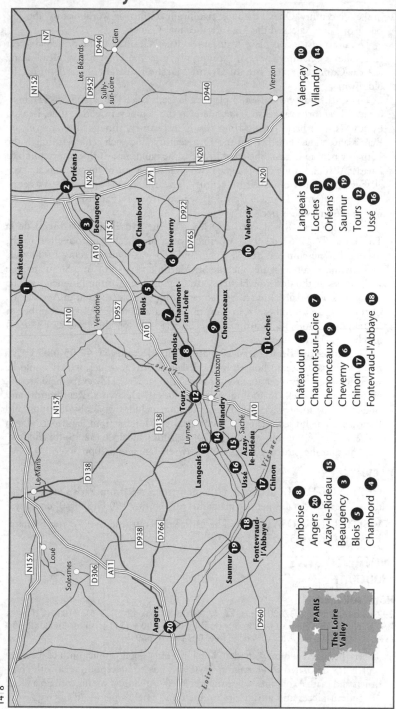

Valençay **10**
Villandry **14**

Langeais **13**
Loches **11**
Orléans **2**
Saumur **19**
Tours **12**
Ussé **16**

Chaumont-sur-Loire **7**
Châteaudun **1**
Chenonceaux **9**
Cheverny **6**
Chinon **17**
Fontevraud-l'Abbaye **18**

Amboise **8**
Angers **20**
Azay-le-Rideau **15**
Beaugency **3**
Blois **5**
Chambord **4**

PARIS
The Loire
Valley

in the 4th century. One of the most significant conflicts in world history, the 732 Battle of Tours, checked the Arab advance into Gaul.

The heart of town is place Jean-Jaurès. Rue Nationale is the principal street (the valley's Champs-Elysées), running north to the Loire River. Head along rue du Commerce and rue du Grand-Marché to reach *la vieille ville* (the old town).

The **Cathédrale St-Gatien,** 5 place de la Cathédrale (☎ **47-05-05-54**), honors a 3rd-century evangelist. Its facade is in the flamboyant gothic style, flanked by towers with bases dating from the 12th century, though the lanterns are Renaissance. The choir is from the 13th century, and each century through the 16th saw new additions. Sheltered inside is the handsome 16th-century tomb of Charles VIII and Anne de Bretagne's two children. Some of the glorious stained-glass windows are from the 13th century. The cathedral is open daily: Easter to September from 7:15am to 7pm; off-season, from 7:15am to noon and 2 to 6:45pm. Admission is free.

In the Château Royal, quai d'Orléans, is the **Musée de l'Historial de la Touraine** (☎ **47-61-02-95**). A perfect (yet a bit kitschy) introduction to the region, this museum features 30 scenes and 165 wax figures tracing 1,000 years of Touraine history. Figures include St. Martin and Joan of Arc. Simulated are such scenes as the death of Henry V and the hanging of the Huguenots. The museum is open daily: June to September, from 9am to 6:30pm; in April, May, October, and November, from 9am to noon and 2 to 6:30pm; December to March, from 2 to 5:30pm. Admission is 29 F ($5.50) for adults and 22 F ($4.20) for children 15 and under.

The **Musée des Beaux-Arts,** 18 place François-Sicard (☎ **47-05-68-73**), is a fine provincial museum housed in the Palais des Archevêques, which would be worth visiting just to see its lovely rooms and gardens. However, there are old masters here as well, including works by Degas, Delacroix, Rembrandt, and Boucher. The impressive sculpture collection includes works by Houdon and Bourdelle. The museum is open Wednesday to Monday from 9am to 12:45pm and 2 to 6pm. Admission is 30 F ($5.70) for adults and 15 F ($2.85) for children. You can tour the gardens for free daily between 7am and 8:30pm.

ESSENTIALS

GETTING THERE   Tours is a 2½-hour train ride from Paris's Gare d'Austerlitz. Nearly 22 trains per day make this run, costing 190 F ($36.10) one way.

VISITOR INFORMATION   The Office de Tourisme is at 78 rue Bernard-Palissy (☎ **47-70-37-37**).

WHERE TO STAY
MODERATE

Hôtel Alliance
292 av. de Grammont, 37000 Tours. ☎ **47-28-00-80.** Fax 47-27-77-61. 110 rms, 6 suites. A/C MINIBAR TV TEL. 450 F ($85.50) double; from 600 F ($114) suite. Breakfast 60 F ($11.40) extra. AE, DC, MC, V. Parking free. Bus 1, 2, 5, or 9.

This is the largest and most modern hotel in Tours, about a mile south of the town center. It's decorated in *grand siècle* style and boasts a reception area with chandeliers and marble columns. The bright-colored soundproof rooms contain a blend of modern pieces and antique reproductions. There's plenty of open space, a

French garden, and a pool. Breakfast and drinks are served in a sitting area. The hotel has a distinguished restaurant with a terrace; full meals cost 225 to 250 F ($42.75 to $47.50), and the fixed-price menu is 150 F ($28.50).

Hôtel de l'Univers

5 bd. Heurteloup, 37000 Tours. ☎ **47-05-37-12.** Fax 47-61-51-80. 85 rms. TV TEL. 780 F ($148.20) double. Breakfast 65 F ($12.35) extra. AE, DC, MC, V. Parking 50 F ($9.50).

This highly regarded hotel on the main artery of Tours is the oldest in town and has hosted Edison, Hemingway, and the former kings of Spain, Portugal, and Romania. The rooms are decorated partly with modern pieces and partly with art deco pieces. La Touraine, the main dining room (open Sunday to Friday), serves excellent meals, with fixed-price menus ranging from 100 to 170 F ($19 to $32.30).

INEXPENSIVE

⊕ Le Central

21 rue Berthelot, 37000 Tours. ☎ **47-05-46-44.** Fax 47-66-10-26. 43 rms, 38 with bath, 2 with shower only, 3 with wash basin and bidet only. TEL. 180 F ($34.20) double with wash basin and bidet only, 310 F ($58.90) double with shower only, 360 F ($68.40) double with bath. Breakfast 40 F ($7.60) extra. AE, DC, MC, V. Parking 35 F ($6.65). Bus 1, 4, or 5.

Off the main boulevard, this old-fashioned hotel is within walking distance of the river and cathedral, surrounded by gardens, lawns, and trees. The Tremouilles family offers comfortable rooms (38 with TVs and minibars) at reasonable rates, as well as two salons with reproductions of 18th- and 19th-century pieces. A garage is available.

WHERE TO DINE
EXPENSIVE

✪ La Roche le Roy

55 route St-Avertin. ☎ **47-27-22-00.** Reservations recommended. Main courses 110–160 F ($20.90–$30.40); fixed-price meal 150–330 F ($28.50–$62.70) at lunch, 200–330 F ($38–$62.70) at dinner. AE, MC, DC, V. Mon–Fri 12:15–1:45pm and 7:15–10pm, Sat 7:15–10pm. Closed first three weeks in Aug. FRENCH.

One of Tours's hottest chefs, Alain Couturier, blends new and old culinary techniques at this restaurant, housed in a 15th-century manor 2 miles south of the town center. Couturier's repertoire includes red mullet gazpacho with two sauces, crayfish sautéed with vanilla and mint, and fraicheur of lobster with roe-enhanced vinaigrette. His masterpiece is suprême of pigeon with a "roughly textured" sauce. For dessert, try his mélange of seasonal fruit with sabayon made from Vouvray Valley wine.

MODERATE

Rôtisserie Tourangelle

23 rue du Commerce Tours. ☎ **47-05-71-21.** Reservations required. Main courses 115–140 F ($21.85–$26.60); fixed-price menus 98 F ($18.60), 145 F ($27.55), and 190 F ($36.10). AE, DC, MC, V. Tues–Sat 12:15–1:45pm and 7:30–9:45pm, Sun 12:15–1:45pm. Bus 1, 4, or 5. FRENCH.

This is a local favorite. You can dine on a terrace in summer, but there's not much to see. It's better to concentrate on the food, which might include homemade foie gras, snails in red-wine sauce, and white fish caught in the Loire served with beurre blanc (white butter sauce). Regional ingredients mix well with the local wines, as exemplified by pike-perch with sabayon and aiguillettes de filet de canard (duckling), followed in summer by strawberry parfait with raspberry coulis. If only the service were a little better.

Les Tuffeaux

19 rue Lavoisier. ☎ **47-47-19-89.** Reservations required. Main courses 85–96 F ($16.15–$18.25); fixed-price menus 110 F ($20.90), 140 F ($26.60), 150 F ($28.50), and 260 F ($49.40). MC, V. Mon 7–9:30pm, Tues–Sat noon–1:45pm and 7–9:30pm. Bus 1, 4, or 5. FRENCH.

This 18th-century house contains one of the best restaurants in Tours. A meal might consist of thyme-flavored langoustines soup, suprême of pike-perch, filet of sole with asparagus, roast pigeon with pink grapefruit, and sumptuous desserts. Although the 110-F ($20.90) fixed-price menu is not available on Saturday night, try this bargain meal on any other night, as it's the best value in town. Chef Gildas Marsollier faithfully prepares the classics but also experiments, especially when each new season brings an array of fresh ingredients.

INEXPENSIVE

Le Relais Bure

1 place de la Résistance. ☎ **47-05-67-74.** Reservations not required. Main courses 60–98 F ($11.40–$18.60). AE, DC, MC, V. Daily noon–3pm and 7pm–midnight. Bus 1, 4, or 5. FRENCH.

A five-minute walk east of the center of Tours, this brasserie specializes in shellfish and regional recipes, though is somewhat unimaginative. It has a busy bar and a front terrace, with tables scattered inside on the street level and mezzanine. Menu items include six well-flavored versions of sauerkraut, a wide choice of grilled meats (including a peppery steak au poivre), foie gras and smoked salmon (both prepared in-house), and a tempting array of desserts.

NEARBY ACCOMMODATIONS & DINING

✪ Château d'Artigny

Route d'Azay-le-Rideau, 37250 Montbazon. ☎ **47-26-24-24.** Fax 47-65-92-79. 51 rms, 2 suites. TV TEL. 945–1,575 F ($179.55–$299.25) double; 3,150 F ($598.50) suite. Breakfast 85 F ($16.15) extra; half board 905–1,220 F ($171.95–$231.80) per person extra. MC, V. Parking free. Closed Nov 26–Jan 13. From Tours, take N10 south for 7 miles to Montbazon, then take D17 a mile southeast.

This château was built for perfume king François Coty, who lived and entertained lavishly here. The drawing room and corridors are classically furnished, with fine antiques, Louis XV–style chairs, and bronze statuary. There are acres of private park, as well as a large formal garden with a reflecting pool. Among the trees is a flagstone-edged pool. The guest rooms are furnished in various periods, with many antiques. Weekend soirees and musical evenings are popular. Another reason to stay here is the superb cuisine served in the gilded dining room.

Château de Beaulieu

37300 Joué-les-Tours. ☎ **47-53-20-26.** Fax 47-53-84-20. 19 rms. A/C MINIBAR TV TEL. 380–750 F ($72.20–$142.50) double. Breakfast 50 F ($9.50) extra. Half board (minimum three days) 770–1,160 F ($146.30–$220.40) for two. AE, MC, V. Parking free. Take D86 from Tours, then D207 for Beaulieu, 4¹/₂ miles southwest of Tours. Bus 3.

At this secluded 18th-century country estate's restaurant and three-star hotel you can experience the lifestyle of another era. Beyond the formal entrance, a double curving stairway takes you to the reception hall. The rooms are furnished with mahogany and chestnut pieces, fireplaces, and good plumbing; nine are in the château (these are preferred), and the others are more sterile, in a pavilion nearby.

Owner Jean-Pierre Lozay is an excellent chef, so at least try to visit for a meal. The dining room's French windows open onto views of the gardens, with two public pools (open July to September) and four tennis courts; a terrace also overlooks the garden. Fixed-price meals run 195 to 420 F ($37.05 to $79.80), and à la carte meals are available. Reservations are required.

3 Azay-le-Rideau

162 miles SW of Paris, 13 miles SW of Tours

Its machicolated towers and blue-slate roof pierced with dormers shimmer in the moat, creating a reflection like one in a Monet painting. But the defensive medieval look is all for show. The ✪ **Château d'Azay-le-Rideau,** 37190 Azay-le-Rideau (☎ **47-45-42-04**), was created as a private residence during the Renaissance at an idyllic spot on the Indre River (for a glimpse of the château, see the front cover of this book). Gilles Berthelot, François I's finance minister, commissioned the castle and his spendthrift wife, Philippa, supervised its construction. So elegant was the creation that the Chevalier King grew immensely jealous. In time, Berthelot was forced to flee and the château reverted to the king. He didn't live there, however, but granted it to "friends of the Crown." It became the property of the state in 1905.

Before entering, circle the château, enjoying the perfect proportions of the crowning achievement of the Renaissance in Touraine. Its most fancifully ornate feature is a bay enclosing a grand stairway with a straight flight of steps. The Renaissance interior is a virtual museum.

From the second-floor Royal Chamber, look out at the gardens. This bedroom, also known as the Green Room, is believed to have sheltered both Louis XIII and Louis XIV. The adjoining Red Chamber contains a portrait gallery that includes a *Lady in Red* (erroneously attributed to Titian) and Gabrielle d'Estrées (Henri IV's favorite) in her bath.

The château is open daily: in July and August from 9am to 6pm, April to June and in September from 9:30am to 6pm, and October to March from 9:30am to 12:30pm and 2 to 5pm. Admission is 31 F ($5.90) for adults and 20 F ($3.80) for children. From May to July, *son-et-lumière* performances are staged at 10:30pm; in August and September, at 10pm. Tickets cost 50 F ($9.50) for adults and 40 F ($7.60) for children.

ESSENTIALS

GETTING THERE   Seven trains a day arrive from Tours (trip time: 30 min.), costing 27 F ($5.15) for a one-way ticket.

VISITOR INFORMATION   The Syndicat d'Initiative (tourist office), at place de l'Europe (☎ **47-45-44-40**), is open from March 15 to September.

WHERE TO DINE

L'Aigle d'Or

10 av. Adélaïde-Riché. ☎ **47-45-24-58.** Reservations recommended. Main courses 85–240 F ($16.15–$45.60); fixed-price meal 88 F ($16.70) at lunch, 140–265 F ($26.60–$50.35) at

Balzac: An Androgynous Genius

Honoré de Balzac (he added the "de" once he tasted some success) has been re-ferred to as not only the greatest novelist of France but also the greatest novelist of all time, so prolific that he wrote the 14,000-word *Illustrious Gaudissart* in a single evening. (Latter-day biographers estimate that's an average of 33.3 words per minute, scrawled by lamplight under the influence of crushing debts and floods of coffee.)

Ironically, Balzac composed the work that best exemplifies the pitfalls of social climbing in Paris (*Le Père Goriot*) in the Loire Valley near Azay-le-Rideau, at the Château de Saché, which was owned by powerful friends.

Balzac's relationship with the Loire began early: Born in Tours in 1799, he moved to Paris in 1814, just in time to witness Napoléon's fall. Reared by foster parents for his first four years (a common practice for the children of the well-to-do), he eventually became—in the words of one biographer—"one of the best-dressed bankrupts in Paris." He was also one of the most socially voracious, drinking life in great gulps as he created a wealth of amazingly lifelike characters (more than 2,000) that included whores, hostesses, clerics, publishers, aristocrats, and criminals.

As his debts piled up ("A debt is a work of the imagination which no tax col-lector can understand," he once wrote), Balzac continued his flamboyant life, frequenting all classes of Paris society and mining them for new characters and situations. He sometimes got lost in the gray area between fiction and reality and puzzled over his characters' dilemmas as if they were those of real people. And his binges—eating, writing, having sex, and spending, interspersed with smok-ing opium and falling prey to suicidal depressions—were legendary.

Biographer Graham Robb has described *La Peau de Chagrin* as "one of the finest novels that exhaustion ever produced." Balzac referred to himself in letters as an "androgynous genius" with "maternal instincts." His empathy transcended age, class, and sex, qualities that led, in hideaways like the Château de Saché, to the creation of a body of about 100 astounding works.

dinner. V. Thurs–Tues 12:30–2pm and 7:30–9:30pm. Closed Feb 5–Mar 5, Sept 4–11, and Dec 15–25. FRENCH.

This restaurant is one of the most enduring favorites of everyone visiting the château. The service is professional, the welcome often charming, but the food (in our opinion) is not what it used to be. Courses are likely to include stingray with artichokes or minced lamb with zucchini flan. A specialty is rabbit with Vouvray wine. The chef needs to perk up the flavors a bit.

4 Villandry

157 miles SW of Paris, 20 miles NE of Chinon, 11 miles W of Tours, 5 miles E of Azay-le-Rideau

The extravagant 16th-century–style gardens of the Renaissance ✪ **Château de Villandry,** 37510 Joué-les-Tours (☎ 47-50-02-09), are celebrated throughout the Touraine. Forming a trio of superimposed cloisters, with a water garden on the highest level, the gardens were purchased in a decaying state and restored by Span-ish doctor/scientist Joachim Carvallo, the present owner's grandfather.

The grounds contain 10½ miles of boxwood sculpture, which the gardeners must cut to style in only two weeks in September. Every square of the gardens seems like a geometric mosaic. The borders represent the many faces of love: tender, tragic (with daggers), or crazy, the last evoked by a labyrinth that doesn't get you anywhere. Pink tulips and dahlias suggest sweet love; red, tragic; and yellow, unfaithful. Crazy love is symbolized by all colors. The vine arbors, citrus hedges, and shady walks keep six men busy full-time. One garden contains all the common French vegetables except the potato, which wasn't known in France in the 16th century.

Originally a feudal castle stood at Villandry, but in 1536 Jean Lebreton, the chancellor of François I, built the present château, whose buildings form a U and are surrounded by a two-sided moat. Near the gardens is a terrace from which you can see the small village and its 12th-century church.

Admission to the gardens with a tour of the château is 40 F ($7.60). Visiting the gardens separately without a guide costs 26 F ($4.95). The château is open from mid-March to mid-November, and guided tours are conducted daily from 9am to 6:30pm. The gardens are open from 9am to sunset.

Unfortunately, Villandry doesn't have bus service from Tours. Rent a bike and ride along the Cher or go by car.

WHERE TO STAY & DINE

Le Cheval Rouge

Villandry, 37510 Joué-les-Tours. ☎ 47-50-02-07. Reservations recommended. Fax 47-50-08-77. Fixed-price menus 85–180 F ($16.15–$34.20). MC, V. Tues–Sun noon–2pm and 7:30–9pm. Closed Jan 10–Mar 10, and Sun night and Mon Mar–Apr and Sept–Oct. FRENCH.

This is the major luncheon venue near the château in spite of the uptight management and their stiff welcome. Many of the famous gardens of the château are visible from the dining room windows, and the Cher flows 100 yards from the hotel. Specialties include fresh grilled salmon, farm-bred pigeon with garlic, and filet of pork with plums. The food is competent enough, but chances are this won't be one of your most memorable meals in the Loire.

This inn also rents 20 comfortable rooms, 18 with private bath. A double rents for 295 F ($56.05) and a triple costs 400 F ($76), plus 35 F ($6.65) for breakfast.

5 Loches

160 miles SW of Paris, 25 miles SE of Tours

Forever linked to legendary beauty Agnès Sorel, Loches is the *cité médiévale* of the valley, in the hills on the banks of the Indre. Known as the acropolis of the Loire, the château and its satellite buildings form a complex called the ✪ **Cité Royale.** The House of Anjou, from which the Plantagenets descended, owned the castle from 886 to 1205. The kings of France occupied it from the mid-13th century until Charles IX became king in 1560.

The **Château de Loches,** 5 place Charles-VII (☎ 47-59-01-32), is remembered for the *belle des belles* (beauty of beauties), Agnès Sorel. Inside is her tomb—two angels guard her velvet cushion. In 1777 her tomb was opened; inside the coffin was a set of dentures and some locks of hair—all that remained of the most dazzling beauty of the 15th century. Maid of honor to Isabelle de Lorraine, she was singled out by Charles VII to be his mistress. She had great influence with the king until her mysterious death. Afterward, Fouquet painted her as a practically topless Virgin Mary, with a disgruntled Charles VII looking on. (Antwerp owns the original masterpiece, but the château has a copy.) The château also contains the oratory of Anne de Bretagne, decorated with sculptured ermine tails. One of its most outstanding treasures is *The Passion* triptych from the Fouquet school (1485).

You can visit the apartments without a guide from June to September, daily from 9am to noon and 2 to 6pm (at other times a guide is required); off-season it's open daily from 9am to noon and 2 to 5pm. The dungeon opens and shuts 30 minutes after the castle. One ticket for both costs 26 F ($4.95) for adults and 19 F ($3.60) for children. A *son-et-lumière* depicting the exploits of Joan of Arc is presented on the second and fourth Friday and Saturday in July at 10:30pm and on every Friday and Saturday in August at 10pm. The show lasts 1 1/2 hours and costs 60 F ($11.40).

The ancient **keep** (donjon), reached along the Mail du Donjon, of the comtes d'Anjou can also be visited during the same hours as the château. The **Round Tower** of Louis XI contains rooms formerly used for torture; a favorite method was to suspend the victim in an iron cage. In the 15th century the duke of Milan, Ludovico Sforza, was imprisoned in the **Martelet,** and he painted frescoes on the walls to pass the time; he died here in 1508.

Nearby, the romanesque **Collegiate Church of St-Ours,** 1 rue Thomas-Pactius (☎ 47-59-02-36), spans the 10th to the 15th century. Its portal is richly decorated with sculptured figures, unfortunately damaged but still attractive. Monumental stone pyramids (*dubes*) surmount the nave. The carving on the west door is exceptional. The church is open daily from 8am to 7pm.

Finally, you may want to walk the **ramparts** and enjoy the view of the town, including a 15th-century gate and Renaissance inns.

ESSENTIALS

GETTING THERE   Six buses a day arrive here from Tours (trip time: 50 min.); a one-way ticket costs 41 F ($7.80).

VISITOR INFORMATION   The Office de Tourisme is near the bus station on place Wermelskirchen (☎ 47-59-07-98).

WHERE TO STAY & DINE

George Sand

39 rue Quintefol, 37600 Loches. ☎ **47-59-39-74.** Fax 47-91-55-75. 20 rms. TV TEL. 250–600 F ($47.50–$114.05) double; 450–650 F ($85.55–$123.55) triple. Breakfast 35 F ($6.65) extra. MC, V. Bus 10.

Loaded with faithful reproductions of medieval tapestries, this tastefully redecorated inn dates from the 17th century and is a few steps from the base of the château. George Sand used to stash her luggage here before trekking up the hill to visit her lover, Chopin, who resided in a nearby château. The inn, owned by M. and Mme Fortin, has just been completely renovated. Several of the rooms look out over a tributary of the Indre River; the quieter ones are at the rear.

This Logis de France hotel has a restaurant with a view of the Indre. A la carte courses feature Touraine cuisine, including fondue of goat with confit of leeks, filet of pike-perch (a river fish) in beurre blanc, and breast of duck George Sand.

ⓢ Grand Hôtel de France

6 rue Picois, 37600 Loches. ☎ **47-59-00-32.** Fax 47-59-28-66. 19 rms. TV TEL. 215–340 F ($40.85–$64.60) double. Breakfast 32 F ($6.10) extra. DC, MC, V. Parking 24 F ($4.55). Closed Jan 7–Feb 15. Bus 10.

Charmingly French, this hotel has an inner courtyard, which many rooms overlook. The rates are low for the area, and English is spoken. There's a petite dining room with paneling and crystal, and you can also dine under parasols in the courtyard. Three fixed-price meals are offered: for 83 F ($15.75), 110 F ($20.90), and 157 F ($29.85). The restaurant is open daily in July and August, but closed Sunday night and Monday the rest of the year.

6 Amboise

136 miles SW of Paris, 22 miles E of Tours

On the banks of the Loire, Amboise is in the center of vineyards known as Touraine-Amboise. Leonardo da Vinci, the quintessential Renaissance man, spent his last years in this city. Dominating the town is the ⊙ **Château d'Amboise** (☎ 47-57-14-47), the first in France to reflect the Italian Renaissance. A combination of both gothic and Renaissance, this 15th-century château is mainly associated with Charles VIII, who built it on a rocky spur separating the valleys of the Loire and the Amasse.

You enter via a ramp, opening onto a panoramic terrace fronting the river. At one time this terrace was surrounded by buildings and fêtes were staged in the enclosed courtyard. At the time of the Revolution, the castle declined and only a quarter or even less remains of this once-sprawling edifice. First you come to the flamboyant gothic Chapel of St. Hubert, distinguished by its lacelike tracery. It allegedly contains Leonardo's remains; actually the great artist was buried in the castle's Collegiate Church, which was destroyed between 1806 and 1810. During the Second Empire, excavations were done there and bones discovered were "identified" as Leonardo's.

Today the walls of the château are hung with tapestries and the rooms furnished grandly. The Logis du Roi (king's apartment) escaped destruction and can be visited. It was built against the Tour des Minimes ou des Cavaliers and was known for its ramp that horsemen could ride up. The other notable tower is the Hurtault, which is broader than the Minimes, with thicker walls.

The château is open daily: in July and August from 9am to 6:30pm, April to June from 9am to noon and 2 to 6:30pm, and September to March from 9am to noon and 2 to 5pm. Admission is 28 F ($5.30) for adults, 18 F ($3.40) for students, and 12 F ($2.30) for children.

You might also wish to visit **Clos-Lucé,** 2 rue de Clos-Lucé (☎ 47-57-62-88), a 15th-century brick-and-stone manor. In what had been an oratory for Anne de Bretagne, François I installed "the great master in all forms of art and science," Leonardo da Vinci. Venerated by the Chevalier King, Leonardo lived there for three years, dying at the manor in 1519. (Those paintings of Leonardo dying in François's arms are probably symbolic; the king was supposedly out of town at the time.) The manor's rooms are well furnished, some with reproductions from Leonardo's time.

Clos-Lucé is open March to October, daily from 9am to 7pm; in November, December, and February, daily from 9am to 6pm. Admission is 30 F ($5.70) for adults and 22 F ($4.20) for children.

ESSENTIALS

GETTING THERE Amboise lies on the main Pairs–Blois–Tours rail line, with a dozen trains per day arriving from both Tours and Blois. Trip time from Tours is only 20 minutes and a one-way ticket costs 27 F ($5.15); trip time from Blois is just 15 minutes and a one-way ticket costs 32 F ($6.10). Seven trains arrive daily from Paris (trip time: $2^1/_2$ hr.), at a one-way fare of 140 F ($26.60).

In Tours, Les Rapides de Touraine (call 47-37-81-81 in Tours for information) operates six buses a day to Amboise (trip time: 25 min.), costing 25 F ($4.75) one way.

VISITOR INFORMATION The Office de Tourisme is on quai du Général-de-Gaulle (☎ 47-57-01-37).

WHERE TO STAY
EXPENSIVE

✪ Le Choiseul

36 quai Charles-Guinot, 37400 Amboise. ☎ **47-30-45-45.** Fax 47-30-46-10. 32 rms, 4 suites. MINIBAR TV TEL. 540–990 F ($102.65–$188.20) double; 1,200–1,600 F ($228.10–$304.15) suite. Breakfast 80 F ($15.20) extra. AE, DC, MC, V. Parking free. Closed Nov 26–Jan 15.

This 18th-century hotel's rooms, 15 of which are air-conditioned, are luxurious; though recently modernized, they've retained their old-world charm. On the grounds is a garden with flowering terraces. This hotel is set in the valley between a hillside and the Loire River, close to the château. The formal dining room has a view of the Loire and welcomes nonguests who phone ahead. It's open daily from noon to 2pm and 7 to 9:30pm; fixed-price menus are 220 F ($41.80), 290 F ($55.10), and 390 F ($74.10). It serves some of the finest food in the Touraine. Even the bread is homemade, and the service is impeccable. Hotel facilities include an outdoor pool and a tennis court.

Hostellerie du Château-de-Pray

Route de Chargé (D751), 37400 Amboise. ☎ **47-57-23-67.** 19 rms, 1 suite. TEL. 580 F ($110.25) double; 720 F ($136.85) suite. Breakfast 50 F ($9.50) extra; half board 195 F ($35.10) extra. AE, DC, MC, V. Parking free. Closed Jan 2–27.

From its position above parterres surveying the Loire in a park about a mile east of the town center, this château resembles a tower-flanked castle on the Rhine. Inside, you'll find antlers, hunting trophies, venerable antiques, and a paneled drawing room with a fireplace and a collection of antique oils. The guest rooms are stylishly conservative and comfortable—if they're in the main building. Try to avoid the four rooms in the annex. Open to nonguests, the hotel restaurant offers fixed-price menus for 130 to 250 F ($24.70 to $47.50). In summer, tables are placed on a terrace overlooking formal gardens. The menu might include grilled salmon with beurre blanc, lobster cannelloni, or roast rabbit with wine sauce.

MODERATE

Belle-Vue

12 quai Charles-Guinot, 37400 Amboise. ☎ **47-57-02-26.** Fax 47-30-51-23. 34 rms. TV TEL. 300 F ($57) double. Breakfast 35 F ($6.65) extra. MC, V. Parking free. Closed Dec–Mar 15.

This inn lies at the bridge crossing the Loire at the foot of the château. It has rows of French doors and outside tables on two levels shaded by umbrellas in summer. The interior lounges are well maintained, and the modernized guest rooms are comfortable, with traditional French pieces. Try to stay here and not in the annex across the river. Breakfast is the only meal served.

WHERE TO DINE

Le Manoir St-Thomas

Place Richelieu. ☎ **47-57-22-52.** Reservations required. Main courses 90–125 F ($17.10–$23.75); fixed-price menu 165–295 F ($31.35–$56.05). AE, DC, MC, V. Tues–Sat 12:15–2:30pm and 7:15–9:30pm, Sun 12:15–2:30pm. Closed Jan 15–Mar 15. FRENCH.

The best food in town is served at this Renaissance house, in the shadow of the château. The restaurant is in a pleasant garden, and the elegant dining room is richly decorated with a polychrome ceiling and a massive stone fireplace. Owner/chef François Le Coz's specialties include lamb filet with port, duck-liver confit with Vouvray sauce, and red mullet filet with cream of sweet-pepper sauce. The tender saddle of hare is perfectly flavored.

7 Blois

112 miles SW of Paris, 37 miles NE of Tours

A wound in battle had earned him the name Balafré (Scarface), but he was quite a ladies' man. In fact, on that cold misty morning of December 23, 1588, the duc de Guise had just left a warm bed and the arms of one of Catherine de Médici's lovely "flying squadron" girls. His archrival, Henri III, had summoned him. The king's minions were about. That was nothing unusual—Henri was always surrounded with attractive young men these days. Then it happened. The guards moved menacingly toward him with daggers. Wounded, the duke was still strong enough to knock a few down. He made for the door, where more guards awaited him. Staggering, he fell to the floor in a pool of his own blood. Only then did Henri emerge from behind the curtains. "*Mon Dieu,*" he is reputed to have exclaimed, "he's taller dead than alive!" The body couldn't be shown: the duke was too popular. Quartered, it was burned in a fireplace. Then Henri's mother, Catherine de Médici, was told the "good news."

The murder of the duc de Guise is only one of the memories evoked by the ✪ **Château de Blois** (☎ **54-78-06-62**), begun in the 13th century by the comtes de Blois. Charles d'Orléans (son of Louis d'Orléans, assassinated by the Burgundians in 1407) lived at Blois after his release from 25 years of English captivity. He'd married Mary of Cleves and brought a "court of letters" to Blois. In his 70s, Charles became the father of the future Louis XII, who was to marry Anne de Bretagne. Blois was then launched in its new role as a royal château. In time it was to be called the second capital of France, with Blois the city of kings.

However, Blois soon became a palace of banishment. Louis XIII got rid of his interfering mother, Marie de Médici, by sending her there; but this plump matron escaped by sliding into the moat down a mound of dirt left by the builders. Then in 1626 the king sent his conspiring brother, Gaston d'Orléans, there; he stayed.

If you stand in the courtyard, you'll find the château's like an illustrated storybook of French architecture. The Hall of the Estates-General is a beautiful 13th-century work; the Charles d'Orléans gallery was actually built by Louis XII from 1498 to 1501, as was the Louis XII wing. The Gaston d'Orléans wing was built by Mansart between 1635 and 1637. The most remarkable is the François I wing, a masterpiece of the French Renaissance, containing a spiral staircase with elaborately ornamented balustrades and the king's symbol, the salamander. In the

Louis XII wing, seek out paintings by Antoine Caron, Henri III's court painter, depicting Thomas More's persecution.

The château is open daily: April to October from 9am to 6pm; November to March from 9am to noon and 2 to 5pm. Admission is 30 F ($5.70) for adults and 25 F ($4.75) for children. A *son-et-lumière* presentation (in French) is sponsored daily at 10:30pm from June to September, costing 60 F ($11.40).

ESSENTIALS

GETTING THERE   The Paris–Austerlitz line via Orléans delivers eight trains per day from Paris (trip time: 1 hr.), costing 117 F ($22.25) one way. From Tours, 14 trains arrive per day (trip time: 1 hr.), costing 49 F ($9.30) one way, and from Amboise, 9 trains per day arrive (trip time: 20 min.), a one-way ticket costing 32 F ($6.10).

VISITOR INFORMATION   The Office de Tourisme is at Pavillon Anne-de-Bretagne, 3 av. Jean-Laigret (☎ 54-74-06-49).

WHERE TO STAY

L'Horset Lavallière
26 av. Maunoury, 41000 Blois. ☎ **54-74-19-00.** Fax 54-74-57-97. 78 rms. MINIBAR TV TEL. 495 F ($94.10) double. American buffet breakfast 55 F ($10.45) extra. AE, DC, MC, V. Children 11 and under stay free in parents' room. Parking free. Bus 1.

This leading hotel has all the modern amenities as well as a respect for traditional charm. A three-star hotel, it's a member of a small but widely respected French-based chain. The rooms are furnished with contemporary flair. There's a good restaurant, where meals go for 105 F ($19.95), 125 F ($23.75), 145 F ($27.55), and 260 F ($49.40). Children's meals are available. The hotel is more reliable than exciting.

Mercure Centre
28 quai St-Jean, 41000 Blois. ☎ **54-56-66-66.** Fax 54-56-67-00. 96 rms. MINIBAR TV TEL. 495–600 F ($94.10–$114.05) double. Breakfast 54 F ($10.25) extra. AE, DC, MC, V. Parking 35 F ($6.65). Quayside bus marked PISCINE.

This is the newest and best-located hotel in Blois, beside the quays of the Loire, a five-minute walk from the château. Three stories of reinforced concrete, with big windows, it contains larger-than-expected rooms filled with contemporary furniture and soothing color schemes. The greenhouse-style lobby leads into a pleasant restaurant where unimaginative meals are served daily.

WHERE TO DINE

Le Médicis
2 allée François-1er. ☎ **54-43-94-04.** Fax 54-42-04-05. Reservations required. Main courses 50–120 F ($9.50–$22.80); fixed-price menus 98 F ($18.60), 148 F ($28.10), and 198 F ($37.60). AE, DC, MC, V. Daily 12:30–2pm and 7–10pm. Closed Jan 1–15. Bus 149. FRENCH.

Christian and Annick Garanger maintain the most sophisticated inn in Blois—ideal for a gourmet meal or an overnight stopover. Fresh fish is the chef's specialty. Typical main courses include asparagus in mousseline sauce, scampi ravioli with saffron sauce, suprême of perch with morels, and thinly sliced duck breast with Cassis sauce. Chocolate in many manifestations is the dessert specialty. Some courses are not recommended for those with high cholesterol levels.

In addition, the Garangers rent 12 elegant rooms, each with private bath. Charges are 420 to 550 F ($79.80 to $104.55) daily in a double, plus 42 F ($8) for breakfast.

✪ Rendezvous des Pêcheurs

27 rue du Foix. ☎ **54-74-67-48.** Reservations recommended. Main courses 88–120 F ($16.70–$22.80); fixed-price menu 140 F ($26.60). AE, MC, V. Mon 7:30–9:30pm, Tues–Sat 12:30–2pm and 7:30–9:30pm. FRENCH.

This restaurant is in an old building beside the quays of the Loire. The chef makes sure that the fish is always fresh and well prepared. As a result, some dishes may seem overly simple, but the result is usually a taste sensation. Only fish, not shellfish of any kind, is served. The menu changes daily according to the availability of fish in the markets; sea urchins raw from the shell is a favorite. Other specialties include a filet of Loire valley sandre (zander) in wine-and-butter sauce and crayfish-stuffed cabbage. You can also order dishes other than fish—for example, sautéed foie gras with warm potatoes.

8 Chaumont-sur-Loire

124 miles SW of Paris, 25 miles E of Tours

On the morning when Diane de Poitiers crossed the drawbridge, the ✪ **Château de Chaumont** (☎ **54-20-97-76**) looked fiercely grim with its battlements and pepper-pot turrets crowning the towers. Henri II, her lover, had recently died. The king had given her Chenonceau, but his widow, Catherine de Médici, banished her from her favorite château and sent her into exile at Chaumont. Inside, portraits reveal that Diane truly deserved her reputation as forever beautiful. Another portrait—of Catherine looking like a devout nun—invites unfavorable comparisons.

Chaumont (Burning Mount) was built during the reign of Louis XII by Charles d'Amboise. Overlooking the Loire, it's approached by a long walk up from the village through a tree-studded park. It was privately owned and inhabited until it was acquired by the state in 1938. The castle spans the period between the Middle Ages and the Renaissance. Its prize exhibit is a rare collection of medallions by Nini, an Italian artist. A guest of the château for a while, he made medallion portraits of kings, queens, and nobles—even Benjamin Franklin, who once visited. In the bedroom once occupied by Catherine de Médici is a rare portrait, painted when she was young. Superstitious Catherine always kept her astrologer, Cosimo Ruggieri, at her beck and call, having him housed in one of the tower rooms (a portrait of him remains). It's reported that he foretold the disasters awaiting her sons, including Henri III. In Ruggieri's room is a most unusual tapestry depicting Medusa with a flying horse escaping from her head.

The château is open daily: April to September from 9:30am to 6:30pm; October to March from 10am to 5pm. Admission is 30 F ($5.70) for adults and 20 F ($3.80) for children. You can ride around Chaumont in horse-drawn carriages, costing 30 F ($5.70) per person.

ESSENTIALS

GETTING THERE   From Blois, Chaumont is reached by 12 trains per day (trip time: 10 min.), costing 19 F ($3.60) one way. A dozen trains also arrive from Tours (trip time: 35 min.), costing 14 F ($2.65) one way. The train station is in Onzain, 1¹/₂ miles north of the château, a pleasant walk.

VISITOR INFORMATION　The Office de Tourisme is on rue du Maréchal-Leclerc (☎ 54-20-91-73).

WHERE TO STAY & DINE

Hostellerie du Château

2 rue du Maréchal-de-Lattre-Tassigny, 41150 Chaumont-sur-Loire. ☎ **54-20-98-04.** Fax 54-20-97-98. 13 rms, 2 suites. TEL. 350–400 F ($66.50–$76) double; 480 F ($91.20) suite. Breakfast 40 F ($7.60) extra. V. Parking free.

This early 20th-century house has the kind of exposed timbers and black-and-white facade you'd expect to find in Normandy. A 10-minute walk downhill from the château, in a village of no more than 900, it has a small garden and a pool. The hotel has a kind staff, comfortable but rather dull rooms, and the best and most reasonably priced restaurant in the village. Regional specialties are served, with fixed-price meals priced at 80 F ($15.20), 150 F ($28.50), and 180 F ($34.20).

9　Chambord

118 miles SW of Paris, 11 miles E of Blois

When François I used to say, "Come on up to my place," he meant the ✪ **Château de Chambord**, 41250 Bracieux (☎ 54-20-98-03), not Fontainebleau or Blois. Some 2,000 construction workers began to piece together "the pile" in 1519. What emerged after 20 years was the pinnacle of the French Renaissance, the largest château in the Loire Valley. It was ready for the visit of Charles V of Germany, who was welcomed by nymphets in transparent veils gently tossing wildflowers in his path. French monarchs like Henri II and Catherine de Médici, Louis XIII, and Henri III came and went from Chambord, but none developed an affection for it to match François I's. The state acquired Chambord in 1932.

The château is in a park of more than 13,000 acres, enclosed within a wall stretching some 20 miles. Looking out a window in one of the 440 rooms, François is said to have carved these words on a pane with a diamond ring: "A woman is a creature of change; to trust her is to play the fool." Chambord's facade is dominated by four monumental towers. The keep has a spectacular terrace the ladies of the court used to stand on to watch the return of their men from the hunt.

The three-story keep also encloses a corkscrew staircase, superimposed so one person may descend at one end and a second ascend at the other without ever meeting. The apartments of Louis XIV, including his redecorated bedchamber, are also in the keep.

The château is open daily: mid-June to mid-September from 9:30 to 5:45pm; mid-September to mid-June from 9:30 to 11:45am and 2 to 4:45pm. Admission is 31 F ($5.90) for adults and 20 F ($3.80) for students. At the tourist office you can pick up tickets for the *son-et-lumière* presentation in summer, called *Jours et Siècles* (Days and Centuries), but check the times.

ESSENTIALS

GETTING THERE　It's best to travel to Chambord by car. Otherwise, you could rent a bicycle in Blois and cycle the 11 miles to Chambord or take one of the organized tours to Chambord leaving from Blois in summer.

VISITOR INFORMATION   The Office de Tourisme is on place St-Michel (☎ 54-20-34-86).

WHERE TO STAY & DINE

Hôtel du Grand-St-Michel

103 place St-Michel, 41250 Chambord, Bracieux. ☎ **54-20-31-31.** Fax 54-20-36-40. 39 rms. TV TEL. 320–450 F ($60.80–$85.50) double. Breakfast 38 F ($7.20) extra. MC, V. Parking free. Closed Nov 14–Dec 20.

Across from the château, this inn is about the only one in town. Try for a front room overlooking the château, which is dramatic when floodlit at night. The rooms are plain but comfortable, with provincial decor. The staff is rather blasé and inarticulate even in French. Most visitors arrive for lunch, which in summer is served on an awning-shaded terrace. The regional dishes rarely match the Loire wines, with set menus costing 130 F ($24.70).

10 Beaugency

93 miles SW of Paris, 53 miles NE of Tours

On the right bank of the Loire, the town of Beaugency boasts a bridge dating from the 14th century. It's unusual in that each of its 26 arches is in a different style. The heart of this ancient Loire Valley town is an archeological garden called the **City of the Lords,** named after the counts who enjoyed great power in the Middle Ages. A major event in medieval Europe took place here: the 1152 annulment of the marriage of Eleanor of Aquitaine to Louis VII. Eleanor sought an annulment on the grounds of consanguinity: They were cousins in the fourth degree and so forbidden to marry. This remarkable woman later became queen consort of Henry II of England, bringing southwestern France as her dowry. She was also the mother of Richard the Lion-Hearted.

The 15th-century **Château Dunois,** 2 place Dunois (☎ 38-44-55-23), floodlit at night, contains a folklore museum of the Orléans district. Exhibiting artifacts discovered in the district, the collection embraces antique toys, hairpieces, furniture, costumes, paintings, and sculpture. The museum is open Wednesday to Monday from 10am to noon and 2 to 5pm (closes at 6:30pm in summer). Admission is 20 F ($3.80) for adults and 10 F ($1.90) for children 6 to 17; 5 and under free. Near the château is **St. George's Vault,** a gate of the former castle of the Lords of Beaugency, which opened from the fortress onto the Rû Valley and the lower part of town.

The **Church of Notre-Dame** would have been a good example of 12th-century romanesque architecture if gothic touches hadn't been added. Originally it was attached to a Benedictine abbey. Nearby is **St. Firmin's Tower,** all that remains of a church that once stood on place St-Firmin. A trio of bells is sheltered in this tower, whose spire rises 180 feet. From here you'll have a panoramic view of the river valley.

In the archeological garden, the **Hôtel-Dieu** (hospital) is one of the oldest buildings in Beaugency, having been erected in the 11th century. **St. Etienne's Church,** also from the 11th century, is one of the oldest churches of France, and **Caesar's Tower** is a fine example of the period's military art.

ESSENTIALS

GETTING THERE   About 15 trains per day run between Beaugency and either Blois or Orléans, each trip taking 20 minutes and costing 26 F ($4.95) one way.
From Orléans there are about 10 buses a day making the trip to Beaugency.

VISITOR INFORMATION   The Office de Tourisme is at place de l'Hôtel-de-Ville (☎ **38-44-54-42**).

WHERE TO STAY & DINE

L'Abbaye de Beaugency

2 quai de l'Abbaye, 45190 Beaugency. ☎ **38-44-67-35.** 18 rms. TV TEL. 550 F ($104.50) double. Breakfast 42 F ($8) extra. AE, DC, MC, V. Parking free.

This ancient building offers rooms with views of the Loire and the old bridge. The large, sunny rooms were recently renovated, and the baths are spacious and modern. The restaurant is known for classic courses such as coq au vin and (in season) game is a specialty. Fixed-price menus begin at 185 F ($35.15).

La Tonnellerie

12 rue des Eaux-Bleues, Tavers, 45190 Beaugency. ☎ **38-44-68-15.** Fax 38-44-10-01. 20 rms, 8 suites. TEL. 740–890 F ($140.65–$169.20) double; from 880 F ($167.30) suite. Breakfast 55 F ($10.45) extra. MC, V. Parking free. Take N152 about 2 miles from Beaugency.

This is a longtime favorite in town. A pleasant old house with comfortable rooms, it's run by the Pouey family, who'll arrange cruises on the Loire or point out the best hiking trails in the area. The rooms are soothingly traditional. The inn is also known for its food, with Loire salmon a specialty.

11 Cheverny

119 miles SW of Paris, 12 miles SE of Blois

The *haut monde* still come to the Sologne area for the hunt as if the 17th century had never ended. However, 20th-century realities like taxes are *formidable* here—hence the **Château de Cheverny** (☎ **54-79-96-29**) must open some of its rooms for inspection by paying guests. At least that keeps the tax collector at bay and the hounds fed in winter.

The town of Cheverny is best reached by car along D765 southeast of Blois or on an organized bus tour from nearby Blois.

Unlike most of the Loire châteaux, Cheverny is actually lived in by the descendants of the original owner, the vicomte de Sigalas. The family's lineage can be traced back to Henri Hurault, the son of the chancellor of Henri III and Henri IV, who built the first château here in 1634. Upon finding his wife, Françoise, carrying on with a page boy, he killed the boy and offered his spouse two choices: She could swallow poison or have his sword plunged into her heart. She elected the less bloody method. Perhaps to erase the memory, he had the castle torn down and the present one built for his second wife. Designed in classic Louis XIII style, it boasts square pavilions flanking the central pile.

Inside, the antique furnishings, tapestries, decorations, and objets d'art are quite impressive. A 17th-century French artist, Jean Mosnier, decorated the fireplace with motifs from the legend of Adonis. In the Guards' Room is a collection of medieval armor. Also displayed is a Gobelin tapestry depicting the abduction of Helen of Troy. In the king's bedchamber, another Gobelin tapestry traces the trials of Ulysses. Most impressive, however, is a stone stairway of carved fruit and flowers.

The château is open daily: June to September 15 from 9:15am to 6:45pm; September 16 to May from 9:15am to noon and 2:15 to 5:30pm. Admission is 30 F ($5.70) for adults and 20 F ($3.80) for children. In July and August, a daily *son-et-lumière* show called *Rêves en Sologne* (Dreams in Sologne) is presented at 10pm for 80 F ($15.20) per ticket.

WHERE TO DINE

Saint-Hubert
Rue Nationale, 41700 Cour-Cheverny. ☎ **54-79-96-60.** Reservations not required. Fax 54-79-21-17. Main courses 90–140 F ($17.10–$26.60); fixed-price menus 95–250 F ($18.05–$47.50). MC, V. Thurs–Tues 12:15–1:15pm and 7:30–8:45pm. Closed Jan 15–Feb 28. FRENCH.

About 800 yards from the château, this roadside inn was built in the old provincial style. Chef Jean-Claude Pillaut is the secret of the Saint-Hubert's success. The least expensive menu might include terrine of quail, pike-perch with beurre blanc, a selection of cheese, and a homemade fruit tart. The most expensive menu might offer lobster or fresh spring asparagus. Game is featured here in season. Though you can eat well here, the staff is brusque and often not pleased to see another table fill with tourists.

Most visitors pass through Cour-Cheverny on a day trip, but it's also possible to spend the night. The Saint-Hubert offers 20 rooms with bath, charging 280 to 300 F ($53.20 to $57) for a single or double, plus 35 F ($6.65) for breakfast.

Les Trois Marchands
Place de l'Eglise, 41700 Cour-Cheverny. ☎ **54-79-96-44.** Reservations not required. Fax 54-79-25-60. Fixed-price menus 105 F ($19.95), 190 F ($36.10), and 310 F ($58.90). AE, DC, MC, V. Daily noon–2pm and 7:30–9pm. Closed Mon Oct–June. FRENCH.

This much-renovated coaching inn has been handed down for many generations from father to son. Today Jean-Jacques Bricault owns the three-story building that sports awnings, a mansard roof, a glassed-in courtyard, and sidewalk tables with bright umbrellas. In the large tavern-style dining room, the menu might include frogs' legs, fresh asparagus in mousseline sauce, or cassoulet of lobster.

The inn also rents 38 rooms. A single or double costs 240 to 330 F ($45.60 to $62.70), with breakfast priced at 40 F ($7.60) per person extra.

12 Valençay

145 miles SW of Paris, 35 miles S of Blois

One of the Loire's handsomest Renaissance châteaux, the **Château de Valençay** (☎ **54-00-10-66**) was acquired in 1803 by Talleyrand on the orders of Napoléon, who wanted his shrewd minister of foreign affairs to receive dignitaries in great style. In 1838 Talleyrand was buried at Valençay, the château passing to his nephew, Louis de Talleyrand-Périgord. Before the Talleyrand ownership, Valençay was built in 1550 by the d'Estampes family. The dungeon and great west tower are of this period, as is the main body of the building; but other wings were added in the 17th and 18th centuries. The effect is grandiose, almost too much so, with domes, chimneys, and turrets.

The private apartments are open to the public; they're sumptuously furnished, mostly in the Empire style but with Louis XV and Louis XVI trappings as well. In the main drawing room is a star-footed table said to have been the one on which the Final Agreement of the Congress of Vienna was signed in June 1815 (Talleyrand represented France).

Visits to Valençay usually last longer than those to other châteaux in the valley, about 45 minutes. The Museum of Talleyrand that used to stand on the premises is now closed, but some of the collection is displayed in the new rooms of the castle. In the park is a museum of 60 antique cars (ca. 1890 to 1950). After your visit to the main buildings, you can walk through the garden and deer park. On the grounds are many exotic birds, including flamingos.

Admission to the castle, car museum, and park is 30 F ($5.70) for adults, 25 F ($4.75) for seniors age 60 or over, and 18 F ($3.40) for children 17 and under. It's open mid-March to mid-November, daily from 9am to noon and 2 to 7pm; mid-November to mid-March, Saturday and Sunday from 9am to noon and 1:30 to 4:30pm.

ESSENTIALS

GETTING THERE   There are frequent SNCF rail connections from Blois.

VISITOR INFORMATION   The Office de Tourisme is on route de Blois (☎ 54-00-04-42).

WHERE TO STAY & DINE

✪ Hôtel d'Espagne

9 rue du Château, 36600 Valençay. ☎ **54-00-00-02.** Fax 54-00-12-63. 8 rms, 6 suites. TV TEL. 450–700 F ($85.55–$133.05) double; from 1,000 F ($190.10) suite. Breakfast 75 F ($14.25) extra. AE, DC, MC, V. Parking 25 F ($4.75). Closed Jan–Feb.

This former coaching inn has a wide-arched entrance leading to a U-shaped building and a flagstone courtyard. M. and Mme Fourré and their family provide an old-world ambience combined with a first-class kitchen; the family has maintained a smooth operation since 1875. The unique guest rooms have names—yours might have an authentic Empire, Louis XV, or Louis XVI decor. The hotel has a cluster of adjoining buildings. Lunch is served in the dining room or gardens Tuesday to Sunday. The specialties include noisettes of lamb in tarragon, sweetbreads with morels, and délicieuse au chocolat. Fixed-price menus begin at 200 F ($38), with a spectacular à la carte meal, including wine, costing 350 F ($66.50) and up. The restaurant is open daily from June to September; off-season, it's closed Monday.

13 Chenonceaux

139 miles SW of Paris, 16 miles E of Tours

A Renaissance masterpiece, the **Château de Chenonceau** (☎ 47-23-90-07) is best known for the dames de Chenonceau who've occupied it. (Note that the town is spelled with a final **x** but the château is not.) Originally it was owned by the Marqués family, but its members were far too extravagant. Deviously, Thomas Bohier, the comptroller-general of finances in Normandy, began buying up land around the château. The Marqués family was forced to sell to Bohier, who tore down Chenonceau, preserving only the keep and building the rest in the emerging Renaissance style.

Many of the château's walls are covered with Gobelin tapestries, including one depicting a woman pouring water over the back of an angry dragon, another of a three-headed dog and a seven-headed monster. The chapel contains a delicate marble *Virgin and Child*, plus portraits of Catherine de Médici in her traditional black and white. There's even a portrait of the stern Catherine in the former bedroom of her rival, Diane de Poitiers. In François I's Renaissance bedchamber the most interesting portrait is that of Diane de Poitiers as the huntress Diana.

The history of Chenonceau is related in 15 tableaux in the wax museum, which charges 10 F ($1.90). Diane de Poitiers, who, among other accomplishments, introduced the artichoke to France, is depicted in three tableaux. One portrays Catherine de Médici tossing out her husband's mistress.

The château is open daily: mid-March to mid-September from 9am to 7pm, mid-September to October from 9am to 6pm, in November from 9am to 5pm, December to January from 9am to noon and 2 to 4pm, and February to mid-March from 9am to noon and 2 to 5pm. Admission is 40 F ($7.60) for adults and 25 F ($4.75) for children 7 to 15; 6 and under free. A *son-et-lumière* spectacle, *In the Old Days of the Dames of Chenonceau*, is staged daily in summer at 10:15pm; admission is 40 F ($7.60).

ESSENTIALS

GETTING THERE   There are three daily trains from Tours to Chenonceaux (trip time: 45 min.); a one-way ticket costs 32 F ($6.10). The train deposits you half a mile from the château.

VISITOR INFORMATION   The Syndicat d'Initiative (tourist office) is at 13 bis rue du Château (☎ 47-23-94-45), open Easter to September.

WHERE TO STAY

Hôtel du Bon-Laboureur et du Château

6 rue du dr. Bretonneau Chenonceau, 37150 Bléré. ☎ **47-23-90-02.** Fax 47-23-82-01. 32 rms, 1 suite. TEL. 320–700 F ($60.80–$133.05) double; 800–1,000 F ($152.–$1900) suite. AE, DC, MC, V. Parking free. Closed Jan 2–Feb 15 and Nov 15–Dec 15.

This country inn, with an ivy-covered facade and tall chimneys, is within walking distance of the château. The rear garden has a little guesthouse, plus formally planted roses. The owner and chef is Louis-Claude Jeudi. Founded in 1880, the hotel maintains the flavor of that era, but modern baths have been added to the rooms, 10 of which contain TVs. In fair weather, request a table in the courtyard, under a maple tree. The fixed-price menus in Le Bon Laboureur run 160 to 320 F ($30.40 to $60.80). You can also order grill specialties in a second restaurant, Les Gourmandises de Touraine, where meals begin at 120 F ($22.80). There's also an outdoor heated pool.

La Roseraie

Chenonceaux, 37150 Blois. ☎ **47-23-90-09.** Fax 47-23-91-59. 16 rms. TV TEL. 255–465 F ($48.45–$88.40) double. Breakfast 38 F ($7.20) extra. AE, DC. Parking free. Closed Nov 15–Feb 15.

This is a traditional French inn, in a leafy setting with a rear garden, a short walk from the château. The rooms are furnished in classic boudoir style and offer much comfort at reasonable rates. Some of the finest meals in town are served in the restaurant with its steakhouse. Good regional specialties are featured, and meals can also be served out on a terrace in the garden. Complete dinners cost 98 to 148 F ($18.60 to $28.10).

Les Dames de Chenonceau

Chenonceau has been called the most feminine château in the Loire because its history has involved six lionesses known as the dames de Chenonceau.

Occupied with military campaigns, Thomas Bohier left the reconstruction of his prize to his wife, Catherine. She added the features that made the place perfect for entertaining, such as straight rather than curved stairways and public rooms radiating from central vestibules, which facilitated the service rituals. Bohier and his wife died two years apart; then François I seized the property, turning it into a royal castle.

In 1547 Henri II gave Chenonceau to his mistress, Diane de Poitiers, 20 years his senior. For a time this remarkable woman was virtually queen of France, infuriating Henri's dour wife, Catherine de Médici. Apparently Henri's love for Diane continued unabated, though she was in her 60s when he died in a jousting tournament in 1559. Diane's critics accused her of using magic to preserve her celebrated beauty and keep Henri's attentions from waning.

Upon Henri's death, Catherine became regent of France (her eldest son was still a boy) and wasted no time in forcing Diane to return the jewelry Henri had given her and abandon her beloved Chenonceau for grim Chaumont, which she didn't want. Catherine added her own touches to Chenonceau, building a two-story gallery across the bridge—obviously inspired by her native Florence.

One of Catherine's sons, Henri III, sponsored an infamous fête at Chenonceau. As described by historian Philippe Erlanger: "Under the trees of this admirable park the King presided over the banquet, dressed as a woman. He wore a gown of pink damask, embroidered with pearls. Emerald, pearl, and diamond pendants distended the lobes of his ears, and diamonds shone in his hair which, like his beard, was dyed with violet powder." After Henri was assassinated, Chenonceau was occupied by his widow, Louise de Lorraine. Even though the king had preferred his "curly-haired minions" to her, she mourned his death for the rest of her life, earning the name La Reine Blanche (White Queen).

In the 18th century Mme Dupin, grandmother of George Sand, acquired the château. A lady of the aristocracy, she was the wife of the "farmer-general" of France. She's said to have brought the "talents of the époque" to her château, employing Rousseau as a tutor for her sons. However, when he declared his undying love for her, she asked him not to return. Rousseau is said to have fallen "sick with humiliation."

In the 19th century Mme Pelouse took over the château and began the task of restoring it to its original splendor. That duty is still being admirably carried out by the present owners, the chocolate-making Menier family.

WHERE TO DINE

⑤ Au Gateau Breton

16 rue Bretonneau. ☎ **47-23-90-14.** Reservations required July–Aug. Fixed-price menus 64–108 F ($12.15–$20.50). MC, V. Tues 7–9:30pm, Wed 11:30am–2pm, Thurs–Mon 11:30am–2pm and 7–9:30pm. Closed mid-Nov to mid-Dec. FRENCH.

The sun-terrace dining area in back of this Breton-type inn, a short walk from the château, is a refreshing place for dinner or tea. Gravel paths run among beds of pink geraniums and lilacs, and the red tables have bright canopies and umbrellas.

The chef provides home-cooking and a cherry liqueur—a specialty of the region. In cool months meals are served in the rustic dining rooms. Specialties include small chitterling sausages of Tours, chicken with Armagnac sauce, and coq au vin. The médaillons of veal with mushroom-cream sauce are excellent, though you may want to skip the blood sausage with apples, highly touted locally. Tasty pastries are sold in the front room.

14 Orléans

74 miles SW of Paris, 45 miles SE of Chartres

Orléans suffered heavy damage in World War II, so those visiting who hope to see how it looked when the Maid of Orléans was there are likely to be disappointed. However, reconstruction has been planned, and there are many rewarding sights for visitors.

Orléans is the chief town of Loiret, on the Loire. Joan of Arc relieved the city in 1429 from the attacks of the Burgundians and the English. That deliverance is celebrated every year on May 8, the anniversary of her victory. An equestrian **statue of Joan of Arc** stands in place du Martroi, which was created by Foyatier in 1855. From that square you can drive down rue Royal—rebuilt in the 18th-century style—across the pont George-V, erected in 1760. After crossing the bridge you'll have a good view of the town. A simple cross marks the site of the Fort des Tourelles, which Joan of Arc and her men captured.

Back in the heart of town, you can go to the **Cathédrale Ste-Croix,** place Ste-Croix (☎ **38-66-64-17**), begun in 1287 in the High Gothic period, though burned by the Huguenots in 1568. The first stone on the present building was laid by Henri IV in 1601, and work continued until 1829. The cathedral boasts an excellent 17th-century organ and some magnificent woodwork from the early 18th century in its chancel, the masterpiece of Jules Hardouin-Mansart and other artists of Louis XIV. You'll need a guide to tour the chancel and the crypt and to see the treasury with its Byzantine enamels, goldwork from the 15th and 16th centuries, and Limoges enamels. There's no admission fee, but you should tip the guide. It's open daily from 9am to noon and 2 to 6pm. Take bus J or G.

To the northwest of the cathedral is the **Hôtel Groslot,** place de l'Etape (☎ **38-79-22-30**). This Renaissance mansion was begun in 1550 and embellished in the 19th century. François II (first husband of Mary, Queen of Scots) lived in it during the fall of 1560 and died here on December 5. On a lighter note, it was here that Charles IX met his lovely Marie Touchet. The statue of Joan of Arc praying (at the foot of the flight of steps) was the work of Louis-Philippe's daughter, Princesse Marie d'Orléans. In the garden you can see the remains of the 15th-century chapel of St. Jacques. Admission is free, and it's open Sunday to Friday from 10am to 6:30pm.

Another church of much interest is the **Eglise St-Aignan,** place St-Aignan, consecrated in 1509. Its choir and transept remain, but the nave was burned by the Protestants. In a gilded carved-wood shrine are the remains of the church's patron saint. The crypt, completed in 1029, is intriguing, containing some decorated capitals. This surely must be one of the earliest vaulted hall crypts in France. It's open daily from 8am to noon and 2:15pm to dusk. Take bus J or G.

The **Musée des Beaux-Arts,** 1 rue Paul-Belmondo (☎ **38-79-21-83**), is mainly a picture gallery of French works from the 16th to the 20th century. Some of the works once hung in Cardinal Richelieu's château. Other pieces include busts by

Pigalle and a fine array of portraits, including one of Mme de Pompadour. A few foreign works are also displayed, including a lovely Velásquez. The museum is open Wednesday to Monday from 10am to noon and 2 to 6pm. Admission is 16 F ($3.05) for adults and 8 F ($1.50) for children.

ESSENTIALS

GETTING THERE   Nine trains per day arrive from Paris's Gare d'Austerlitz (trip time: 1¹/₄ hours), plus there are a dozen connections from Tours (trip time: 1¹/₄ hours). One-way tickets from either Paris or Tours cost 84 F ($15.95).

VISITOR INFORMATION   The Office de Tourisme is on place Albert (☎ 38-53-05-95).

WHERE TO STAY

Hôtel Mercure Orléans

44–46 quai Barentin, 45000 Orléans. ☎ **38-62-17-39.** Fax 38-53-95-34. 108 rms. A/C MINIBAR TV TEL. 495 F ($94.10) double Sun–Thurs, 445 F ($84.60) Fri–Sat. Breakfast 55 F ($10.45) extra. AE, DC, MC, V. Parking free. Bus J or G.

Along the river at pont Joffre, this modern eight-floor bandbox structure with a relatively anonymous format is within walking distance of place du Martroi and its statue of Joan of Arc. The restaurant/bar, Le Gourmandin, serves regional specialties. A table d'hôte menu with wine costs 98 to 130 F ($18.60 to $24.70). The hotel also has a big heated pool.

Novotel Orléans la Source

2 rue Honoré-de-Balzac, 45100 Orléans La Source. ☎ **38-63-04-28.** Fax 38-69-24-04. 119 rms. A/C MINIBAR TV TEL. 475 F ($90.30) double. Breakfast 48 F ($9.10) extra. AE, DC, MC, V. Parking free. Follow N20 south of Orléans for 7 miles.

This two-story hotel, in a beautiful park, offers such diversions as pétanque (French bowling), golfing, swimming, and tennis. The hotel is nine miles south of the center of Orléans at the edge of La Sologne, a district known for its natural beauty. The rooms are comfortable and tastefully decorated. The hotel's grill offers a fixed-price meal for only 90 F ($17.10).

WHERE TO DINE

✪ Les Antiquaires

2–4 rue au Lin. ☎ **38-53-52-35.** Reservations required. Main courses 75–140 F ($14.25–$26.60); fixed-price menus 190–280 F ($36.10–$53.20). AE, DC, MC, V. Tues–Sat noon–2pm and 7:30–10pm. Closed Apr 18–24, Aug 1–22, and Dec 24–Jan 1. Bus J or G. FRENCH.

This rustically elegant mansion on a small street near the river was built before the Renaissance and retains its original ceiling beams. Most of the emphasis is on well-grounded French cuisine, using seasonal ingredients from the region. Specialties include petit rôti of turbot, nage of sea bass with baby vegetables, and charlotte of sweetbreads with foie-gras sauce. You might want to sample the sautéed veal chops with essence of fresh morels. Your dessert might be a warm soufflé with Grand Marnier sauce.

✪ La Poutrière

8–10 rue de la Brêche. ☎ **38-66-02-30.** Reservations required. Main courses 95–220 F ($18.05–$41.80); fixed-price menus 150–310 F ($28.50–$58.90). AE, DC, MC, V. July 15–Aug 27, daily noon–2pm and 7:30–10pm; off-season, Tues–Sat noon–2pm and

Orléans

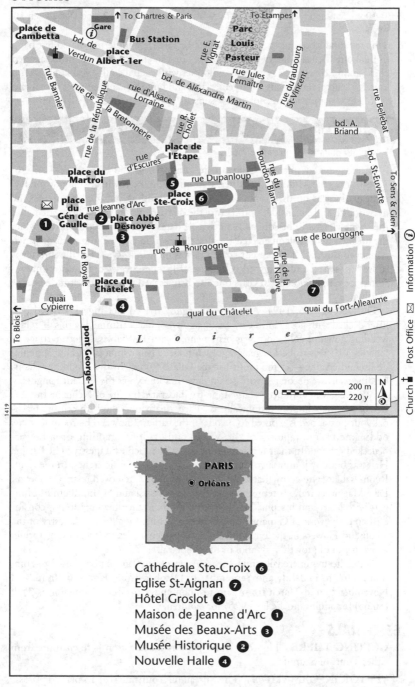

place de Gambetta

Gare

bd. de Verdun

place Albert-1er

Bus Station

To Chartres & Paris

To Etampes

Parc Louis Pasteur

rue E. Vignat

rue Jules Lemaître

rue du faubourg St-Vincent

bd. de Aléxandre Martin

rue Bannier

rue de la République

rue de la Bretonnerie

rue d'Alsace-Lorraine

rue R. Cholet

bd. A. Briand

rue Bellebat

bd. St-Euverte

To Sens & Gien

rue d'Escures

place de l'Etape

place du Martroi

rue Dupanloup

place Ste-Croix

rue du Bourdon Blanc

Information

place du Gén de Gaulle

rue Jeanne d'Arc

place Abbé Désnoyes

rue de Bourgogne

Post Office

rue Royale

rue de Bourgogne

rue de la Tour Neuve

place du Châtelet

quai Cypierre

quai du Châtelet

quai du Fort-Alleaume

To Blois

pont George-V

L o i r e

0   200 m   220 y

N

Church   Post Office   Information

1419

PARIS

Orléans

Cathédrale Ste-Croix **6**
Eglise St-Aignan **7**
Hôtel Groslot **5**
Maison de Jeanne d'Arc **1**
Musée des Beaux-Arts **3**
Musée Historique **2**
Nouvelle Halle **4**

7:30–10pm, Sun noon–2pm. Closed Apr 25–May 2, Aug 29–Sept 12, and Dec 24–Jan 10. FRENCH.

This restaurant occupies a farmhouse on the relatively underpopulated left bank of the Loire. Beneath heavy ceiling beams, you can enjoy specialties from talented chef Simon Lebras, such as a gâteau of lobster with chervil coulis, veal kidneys with sauterne sauce, salmon with Bourgeuil wine, and Loire fish and game. It's been said that Lebras's approach to cooking is "sensual."

15 Langeais

161 miles SW of Paris, 16 miles W of Tours

A formidable gray pile, the **Château de Langeais,** 37130 Langeais (☎ 47-96-72-60), is a true Middle Ages fortress, dominating the town. It's one of the few châteaux located on the Loire. The facade is forbidding, but once you cross the drawbridge and go inside, you'll find the apartments so richly decorated that the severe effect will be softened. The castle dates back to the 9th century, when the dreaded Black Falcon erected the first dungeon in Europe, the ruins of which remain to this day. The present structure was built in 1465. That the interior is so well preserved and furnished is because of Jacques Siegfried, who not only restored it over a period of 20 years but also bequeathed it to the Institut de France in 1904.

On December 6, 1491, Anne de Bretagne "arrived at Langeais carried in a litter decked with gold cloth, dressed in a gown of black trimmed with sable. Her wedding gown of gold cloth was ornamented with 160 sables." Her marriage to Charles VIII was to be Langeais's golden hour. Their symbols—scallops, fleurs-de-lis, and ermine—set the motif for the Guard Room. In the Wedding Chamber, the walls are decorated with seven tapestries known as the Valiant Knights.

At the château entrance, a large tapestry illustrates the life of Nebuchadnezzar. In a bedchamber known sardonically as "The Crucifixion," the 15th-century black-oak four-poster bed is reputed to be one of the earliest known. The room takes its odd name from a tapestry of the Virgin and St. John standing on a flower-bedecked ground. In the Monsieur's Room is a rare Flemish tapestry. The Chapel Hall was built by joining two stories under a ceiling of gothic arches. In the Luini Room is a large fresco by that artist, dating from 1522, removed from a chapel on Lake Maggiore, Italy. It represents St. Francis of Assisi and St. Elizabeth of Hungary with Mary and Joseph. The Byzantine Virgin in the drawing room is considered an early work of Cimabue, the Florentine artist. Finally, the Tapestry of the Thousand Flowers in the Drawing Room is like an ageless celebration of spring, a joyous riot of growth, a symbol of life's renewal.

The château is open daily: mid-July to August from 9am to noon and 2 to 7pm, mid-March to mid-July and September to October, from 9am to 6:30pm, and November to mid-March from 9am to noon and 2 to 5pm. Admission is 35 F ($6.65) for adults and 17 F ($3.25) for children.

ESSENTIALS

GETTING THERE Eighteen trains per day make a stop here en route from either Tours or Saumur.

VISITOR INFORMATION The Bureau du Tourisme is at 15 place de Brosse (☎ 47-96-58-22).

WHERE TO STAY & DINE

La Duchesse Anne

10 rue de Tours, 37130 Langeais. ☎ **47-96-82-03.** Fax 47-96-68-60. 15 rms, 10 with bath (tub or shower). TV TEL. 220–250 F ($41.80–$47.50) double without bath, 280–295 F ($53.20–$56.05) double with bath. Breakfast 35 F ($6.65) extra. MC, V. Parking free.

On the eastern outskirts of town, this hotel served as a coaching inn during the 18th century, and its white-painted facade still has its covered carriage passageway, leading to a courtyard. The rooms are simply furnished but comfortable. Garden tables are set out for dining, and there's a holding tank for the fresh trout that's one of the house specialties. Other courses include fresh Loire Valley salmon with beurre blanc and thigh of guinea fowl with Bourgueil wine sauce. Fixed-price menus cost 90 to 180 F ($17.10 to $34.20).

Hosten et Restaurant Langeais

2 rue Gambetta, 37130 Langeais. ☎ **47-96-82-12.** Fax 47-96-56-72. 11 rms, 1 suite. 340–550 F ($64.60–$104.55) double; 600 F ($114.05) suite. Breakfast 50 F ($9.50) extra. Parking free. AE, DC, MC, V. Closed Jan 10–Feb 10 and July 1–15.

This country inn has an informal atmosphere and excellent food. The restaurant is expensive (and has received many honors), but the hotel is reasonable, with well-furnished comfortable rooms (all doubles). Besides the dining room, there are tables set in the open courtyard under umbrellas and flowering trees. The *menu de prestige* includes blanquette de soles et turbots, escalope de saumon à l'oseille (sorrel), and homard (lobster) Cardinal. The desserts are likely to include classic soufflé au Grand-Marnier and charlotte au coulis de framboises (raspberries). A meal costs 160 to 380 F ($30.40 to $72.20). The restaurant is open for lunch Wednesday to Monday and dinner Wednesday to Sunday.

16 Ussé

183 miles SW of Paris, 9 miles NE of Chinon

At the edge of the hauntingly dark forest of Chinon, the **Château d'Ussé** (☎ 47-95-54-05) was the inspiration behind Perrault's legend of "The Sleeping Beauty" ("La Belle au Bois Dormant"). On a hill overlooking the Indre River, it's a complex of steeples, turrets, towers, chimneys, and dormers. Conceived as a medieval fortress, Ussé was erected at the dawn of the Renaissance. Two powerful families—the Bueil and d'Espinay—lived here in the 15th and 16th centuries. The terraces, laden with orange trees, were laid out in the 18th century. When the need for a fortified château had passed, the north wing was demolished, opening up a greater view. The château is best visited by car or an organized bus tour from Tours.

In time the château was owned by the duc de Duras and later by Mme de la Rochejacquelin, before being acquired by its present owner, the marquis de Blacas. The marquis has opened many rooms to the public. The guided tour begins in the Renaissance chapel, with its sculptured portal and handsome stalls. Then you proceed to the royal apartments, furnished with tapestries and antiques, like a four-poster bed draped in red damask. One gallery displays an extensive collection of swords and rifles. A spiral stairway leads to a tower with a panoramic view of the river and a waxwork Sleeping Beauty waiting for her prince to come.

The château is open daily: March to October from 9am to noon and 2 to 7pm and November to February from 10am to noon and 2 to 6pm. Admission is 54 F ($10.25) for adults and 22 F ($4.20) for children.

17 Chinon

176 miles SW of Paris, 30 miles SW of Tours, 19 miles SW of Langeais

Remember in the film *Joan of Arc* when Ingrid Bergman sought out the dauphin as he tried to conceal himself among his courtiers? The action in real life took place at the Château de Chinon, one of the oldest fortress-châteaux in France. Charles VII, mockingly known as the King of Bourges, centered his government at Chinon from 1429 to 1450. In 1429, with the English besieging Orléans, the Maid of Orléans, that "messenger from God," prevailed upon the weak dauphin to give her an army. The rest is history. The seat of French power stayed at Chinon until the Hundred Years' War ended.

On the banks of the Vienne, the **town of Chinon** retains a medieval atmosphere. It consists of winding streets and turreted houses, many built in the 15th and 16th centuries in the heyday of the court. For the best view, drive across the river, turning right onto quai Danton. From that vantage point you'll have the best perspective, seeing the castle in relation to the village and the river. The gables and towers make Chinon look like a toy village. The most typical street is **rue Voltaire,** lined with 15th- and 16th-century town houses. At no. 44, Richard the Lion-Hearted died on April 6, 1199, after being mortally wounded while besieging Chalus in Limousin. In the heart of Chinon, the **Grand Carroi** was the crossroads of the Middle Ages.

The most famous son of Chinon, Rabelais, the Renaissance writer, walked these streets. He was born at La Devinière, on D17 near N751, now the **Musée Rabelais.** It's open mid-March to September, daily from 9am to noon and 2 to 6pm; off-season it closes at 5pm and on Wednesday. Admission is 18 F ($3.40).

The **Château de Chinon** (☎ 47-93-13-45) is three separate strongholds, badly ruined. Some of the grim walls remain, although many of the buildings—including the Great Hall where Joan of Arc sought out the dauphin—have been torn down. Some of the most destructive owners were the heirs of Cardinal Richelieu. Now gone, the Château de St-Georges was built by Henry II of England, who died there in 1189. The Château de Mileu dates from the 11th to the 15th century, containing the keep and the clock tower, where a Museum of Joan of Arc has been installed. Separated from the latter by a moat, the Château du Coudray contains the Tour du Coudray, where Joan of Arc stayed during her time at Chinon. In the 14th century the Knights Templar were imprisoned there (they're responsible for the graffiti) before meeting their violent deaths.

The château is open February to November only, daily from 9am to 6pm, charging 25 F ($4.75) for adults and 17 F ($3.25) for children.

ESSENTIALS

GETTING THERE   There are two trains daily from Tours (trip time: 1 hr.). A one-way ticket costs 45 F ($8.55).

VISITOR INFORMATION   The Office de Tourisme is at 12 rue Voltaire (☎ 47-93-17-85).

WHERE TO STAY

Chris' Hôtel

12 place Jeanne-d'Arc, 37500 Chinon. ☎ **47-93-36-92.** Fax 47-98-48-92. 40 rms. TV TEL. 350–400 F ($66.50–$76.05) double. Breakfast 40 F ($7.60) extra. AE, DC, MC, V. Parking free.

This well-run hotel is housed in a 19th-century building near the town's historic district. Many of the rooms offer views of the castle and river; most are furnished in a Louis XV style and all have modern amenities. Breakfast is the only meal served.

Hostellerie Gargantua

73 rue Voltaire, 37500 Chinon. ☎ **47-93-04-71.** 7 rms, 6 with bath. TEL. 160 F ($30.40) double without bath, 380–540 F ($72.20–$102.65) double with bath. Breakfast 50 F ($9.50) extra. MC, V. Parking 20 F ($3.80). Closed mid-Nov to Feb 1.

This 15th-century town mansion features a terrace with a château view. Try to stop here at least for a meal—they're formally served in a stylish medieval hall, and on weekends the staff dons medieval attire. You can sample Loire sandre prepared with Chinon wine or magrêt of duckling with dried pears and smoked lard, followed by a medley of seasonal red fruits in puff pastry. Set menus cost 140 F ($26.60). We're not as fond of the cookery here as we once were, but it's recommendable to first-time visitors.

WHERE TO DINE

✪ Au Plaisir Gourmand

2 rue Parmentier. ☎ **47-93-20-48.** Reservations required. Main courses 115–140 F ($21.85–$26.60); fixed-price menus 75–330 F ($14.25–$62.70). MC, V. Tues–Sat noon-2pm and 7:30-9:30pm, Sun noon-2pm. Closed Jan–Feb. FRENCH.

This is the premier restaurant in the area, owned by Jean-Claude Rigollet, who used to direct the chefs at Les Templiers in Les Bézards. His restaurant offers an intimate dining room with a limited number of tables in a charming 18th-century building. Menu items are likely to include roast rabbit in aspic with foie-gras sauce, sandre in beurre blanc, and sautéed crayfish with a spicy salad. The chef turns out a cuisine that's refined and subtle.

NEARBY ACCOMMODATIONS & DINING

✪ Château de Marcay

Marcay, 37500 Chinon. ☎ **47-93-03-47.** Fax 47-93-45-33. 38 rms, 3 suites. TV TEL. 520–1,575 F ($98.85–$299.40) double; from 1,650 F ($313.65) suite. Additional bed 150 F ($28.50) extra. Half board 680–1,180 F ($129.25–$224.30) per person. AE, DC, MC, V. Parking free. Take D116 for 4¹/₂ miles southwest of Chinon.

This Relais & Châteaux was a 15th-century fortress and remained untouched by the region's civil wars. It's sumptuously decorated throughout. Menu specialties change with the season, and the chef works hard to maintain standards. Some dishes have won high praise from readers; others have cited disappointments. There's a panoramic view from the garden terrace and dining room, where the accessories are elegantly rustic. A la carte meals start at 350 F ($66.50); fixed-price menus run 250 to 370 F ($47.50 to $70.30).

Manoir de la Giraudière

Beaumont-en-Veron, 37420 Avoine. ☎ **47-58-40-36.** Fax 47-58-46-06. 20 rms, 5 suites. TV TEL. 200–390 F ($38–$74.10) double; 420 F ($79.80) suite. Breakfast 35 F ($6.65) extra. AE, DC, MC, V. Parking free. Head 3 miles west of Chinon along D749 toward Bourgueil.

In a 6-acre park, this 17th-century family-run manor offers classic decor and modern comforts. The hotel restaurant—not the hotel itself—closes from December to February; otherwise, it's open daily except Tuesday and Wednesday at lunch.

A daily fixed-price menu is offered for 160 to 230 F ($30.40 to $43.70). Local products are featured, including fresh asparagus in spring, pike-perch, duck stew, goat cheese, and pear charlotte dripping with strawberry sauce.

18 Fontevraud-l'Abbaye

189 miles SW of Paris, 10 miles SE of Saumur

In the **Abbaye Royale de Fontevraud** (☎ **41-51-71-41**) you'll find the Plantagenet dynasty of England buried. You may ask, Why here? These monarchs, whose male line vanished in 1499, were also the comtes d'Anjou, and they left instructions that they be buried on their native soil.

In the 12th-century romanesque church—boasting four Byzantine domes—are the remains of the two English kings or princes, including Henry II of England, the first Plantagenet king, and his wife, Eleanor of Aquitaine, the most famous woman of the Middle Ages. Her crusading son, Richard the Lion-Hearted, was also entombed here. The Plantagenet line ended with the death of Richard III at the 1485 Battle of Bosworth. The tombs fared badly in the Revolution, as mobs invaded the church, desecrating the sarcophagi and scattering their contents on the floor.

More interesting than the tombs, however, is the octagonal **Tour d'Evraud,** the last remaining romanesque kitchen in France. Surrounding the tower is a group of apses crowned by conically roofed turrets. A pyramid tops the conglomeration, capped by an open-air lantern tower pierced with lancets.

The abbey was founded in 1099 by Robert d'Arbrissel, who'd spent much of his life as a recluse. His abbey was like a public-welfare commune, liberal in its admission policies. One part, for example, was filled with aristocratic ladies, many banished from court, including discarded mistresses of kings. The four youngest daughters of Louis XV were educated there as well.

The abbey is open daily: June to September from 9am to 7pm and October to May from 9:30am to 12:30pm and 2 to 6pm. Admission is 26 F ($4.95) for adults and 17 F ($3.25) for children.

ESSENTIALS

GETTING THERE　Three buses leave daily from Saumur, taking 30 minutes and costing 18 F ($3.40) for a one-way ticket.

If you're driving, take N147 about $2^1/_2$ miles from the village of Montsoreau.

VISITOR INFORMATION　The Office de Tourisme is at Chapelle Sainte-Catherine (☎ **41-51-79-45**), open May 15 to September.

WHERE TO STAY

Hotellerie du Prieuré St-Lazare

49590 Fontevraud-l'Abbaye. ☎ **41-51-73-16.** Fax 41-51-75-50. 50 rms. MINIBAR TV TEL. 430 F ($81.70) double; 580 F ($110.25) triple. Breakfast 48 F ($9.15) extra. AE, MC, V. Parking free.

This is probably one of the most unusual hotels in Europe. Set on 11th-century foundations, it's in what functioned long ago as cells for penitent monks. As part of the continuing restoration of the world-famous abbey, one of its four-story wings was transformed into a conference center in the 1970s. In 1990 those facilities were turned over to a private management company, which today maintains them as a hotel. The guest rooms are well maintained and monastically simple, with white walls and modern furniture. On the premises is a big-windowed restaurant, Le Cloître, built as a panoramic enclosure of the 11th-century medieval cloister. Fixed-price menus cost 98 to 230 F ($18.60 to $43.70) and are served daily. Despite the lack of plushness, most guests appreciate the abbey's meditative atmosphere.

WHERE TO DINE

✪ La Licorne

Allée Ste-Catherine. ☎ **41-51-72-49.** Reservations required. Main courses 90–150 F ($17.10–$28.50); fixed-price menus 100–300 F ($19–$57) (weekdays only) and 150–300 F ($28.50–$57). AE, MC, V. June to mid-Sept, daily noon–1:30pm and 7–9pm; mid-Sept to May, Tues–Sat noon–1:30pm and 7–9pm, Sun noon–1:30pm. FRENCH.

A visit to the nearby abbey and a meal at this restaurant are the perfect combination of medieval history and sensuality. With only 30 seats, the restaurant lies along a sycamore-lined pedestrian walkway stretching between the abbey and a nearby parish church. It was built in the 1700s, and its neoclassical pilasters and proportions are quite beautiful. During summer, tables are set in a flowered garden as well as in the elegantly rustic dining room. The meals are prepared by one of the region's best-trained chefs, Michel Lecomte, and may include lobster couscous with lima beans, crayfish-stuffed ravioli with morel sauce, filet of salmon with vanilla sauce, and luscious desserts like warm chocolate tart with pears and lemon-butter sauce.

19 Saumur

186 miles SW of Paris, 33 miles SE of Angers

Where the Loire separates to encircle an island, Saumur is set in a region of vineyards. The town is famous as the birthplace of couturière Coco Chanel. Founded in 1768, its Cavalry School and riding club, the Black Cadre, are world renowned. Its horsemen are among the finest in Europe (to see a rider carry out a *curvet* is a thrill). The townspeople have even created a **Musée du Cheval,** a museum devoted to the history of the horse down through the ages, complete with stirrups, antique saddles, and spurs.

The museum is housed in the **Château de Saumur** (☎ **41-51-30-46**), towering from a promontory over the Loire. In the famous *Les Très riches heures du duc de Berri* at Château de Chantilly, a 15th-century painting shows Saumur as a fairy-tale castle of bell turrets and gilded weathercocks. However, these adornments are largely gone, leaving a stark and foreboding fortress.

Under Napoléon the castle became a prison, then eventually a barracks and munitions depot. The town of Saumur acquired it in 1908 and began restoration. Now an interesting regional museum, the **Musée des Arts Décoratifs,** has been installed. The museum is noted mainly for its ceramics, dating from the 16th through the 18th century. A series of 13th-century enamel crucifixes from Limoges is remarkable.

The château and its museums are open June 15 to September 15, daily from 9am to 7pm (until 10pm Wednesday and Saturday in July and August); April to June 14 and September 16 to 30, daily from 9am to noon and 2 to 6pm;

October to March, Wednesday to Monday from 10am to noon and 2 to 5pm. Admission is 35 F ($6.65) for adults and 23 F ($4.35) for children.

ESSENTIALS

GETTING THERE Trains run frequently between Tours and Nantes, with stopovers at Saumur. Eleven trains per day arrive from Tours (trip time: 45 min.), costing 51 F ($9.70) one way; 11 trains per day also arrive from Angers (trip time: 30 min.), a one-way ticket costing 38 F ($7.20).

The train station is on the north side of town. Most major points of interest, including the château, are on the south bank. From the station, take bus A into town.

VISITOR INFORMATION The Office de Tourisme is on place de la Bilange (☎ 41-51-03-06).

WHERE TO STAY

Hôtel Anne d'Anjou

32 quai Mayoud, 49400 Saumur. ☎ **41-67-30-30.** Fax 41-67-51-00. 50 rms. TV TEL. 410–520 F ($77.90–$98.85) double. Breakfast 48 F ($9.10) extra. AE, DC, MC, V. Parking 50 F ($9.50).

This building was constructed in the 18th century as a family home. The magnificent stairwell below a trompe-l'oeil ceiling is classified a historic monument. The rooms in the back overlook the château, while the front facade faces the Loire. Five rooms still have their original decor, ranging from Louis XVI to Empire. Former famous guests have included actor Jean Marais, the late Ginger Rogers, and Prince Albert of Monaco. The hotel also operates one of the most prestigious restaurants in Saumur, Les Menestrels.

Le Roi René

94 av. du Général-de-Gaulle, 49400 Saumur. ☎ **41-67-45-30.** Fax 41-67-74-59. 39 rms. TV TEL. 250–410 F ($47.50–$77.90) double. Breakfast 30 F ($5.70) extra. AE, MC, V. Parking 25 F ($4.75). Closed Nov 23–Dec 23.

This traditional favorite is on a quiet square overlooking the Loire. Many comforts have been added recently, and it remains a serviceable but unexciting choice. The rooms are well furnished and have double-pane windows. The inn serves good food daily.

WHERE TO DINE

Délices du Château

Les Feuquières, Château de Saumur. ☎ **41-67-65-60.** Reservations required. Main courses 100–150 F ($19–$28.50); fixed-price menus 130–330 F ($24.70–$62.70). AE, DC, MC, V. June–Oct, daily 12:30–2pm and 1:30–10:30pm; Jan–May, and Nov, Tues–Sat 12:30–2pm and 7–10:30pm, Sun 12:30–2pm. Closed Dec. Bus 6. FRENCH.

This elegant restaurant, in a restored 12th-century house on the château grounds, has a large fireplace and antique furnishings; from the flowery terrace you'll have panoramic views of the city and the Loire. Pierre Millon is the outstanding chef—his food is classic but personalized. Try the filet of beef sautéed with duck liver and essence of truffles, shrimp with red currants and cucumbers, or bavarois of lobster. A newer specialty is zander encased in a shell of puréed potatoes and served with a coulis of a local wine (Saumur Champigny). The cheapest of the fixed-price menus is one of the dining bargains in Saumur.

L'Escargot

30 rue du Maréchal-Leclerc. ☎ **41-51-20-88.** Reservations required. Main courses 50–110 F ($9.50–$20.90); fixed-price menus 73–165 F ($13.85–$31.35). AE, DC, MC, V. Daily noon–2:30pm and 7–10pm. Closed Wed Sept–May. Bus A. FRENCH.

This typical French bistro contains two mellow dining rooms in a 19th-century house. The fixed-price menus include hors d'oeuvres, a fish and meat course, plus dessert (service and drinks extra). Here you'll find Loire Valley bistro cooking the way it used to be, including many old favorites, certainly the ubiquitous filet of sandre in beurre blanc. In honor of its namesake, the chef prepares a cassoulet of snails in garlic butter. Other courses include sausage made with brochet, a freshwater Loire white fish.

NEARBY ACCOMMODATIONS & DINING

Hostellerie du Prieuré

Chênehutte-les-Tuffeaux, 49350 Gennes. ☎ **41-67-90-14.** Fax 41-67-92-24. 35 rms, 2 suites. MINIBAR TV TEL. 550–1,360 F ($104.55–$258.55) double; 1,350–1,750 F ($256.65–$332.70) suite. Breakfast 80 F ($15.20) extra. AE, MC, V. Closed Jan 5–Mar 5. Parking free. Take D751 4 miles west of Saumur.

This 12th-century priory has a steep roof, dormer windows, and a large peaked tower. It's set in a 60-acre park. This Relais & Châteaux offers graciously comfortable rooms; two of the most beautiful rooms are in a 10th-century chapel. The least expensive ones are in a simple outlying pavilion and are less desirable. The Grand Salon has an ornately carved stone fireplace, crystal chandeliers, oak furniture, and a bar with a fleur-de-lis motif. M. Doumerc is the director. The dining room has one of the finest views of the Loire, spanning 40 miles—truly beautiful at sunset. The rognons de veau sautés à la moutarde (sautéed veal kidneys in a mustard sauce) is heavenly. Fixed-price meals cost 220 to 400 F ($41.80 to $76). Facilities include a miniature-golf course and a heated pool.

20 Angers

179 miles SW of Paris, 55 miles E of Nantes

Once the capital of Anjou, Angers straddles the Maine River. Though it suffered extensive damage in World War II, it has been considerably restored, somehow blending provincial charm with the suggestion of sophistication. The town is often used as a base for exploring the château district to the west.

The moated **Château d'Angers** (☎ **41-87-43-47**), dating from the 9th century, was once the home of the comtes d'Anjou. The notorious Black Falcon lived here, and in time the Plantagenets also took up residence. After the castle was destroyed, it was reconstructed by St. Louis. From 1230 to 1238 the outer walls and 17 massive towers were built, creating a formidable fortress well prepared to withstand invaders. The château was favored by Good King René, during whose reign a brilliant court life flourished here until he was forced to surrender Anjou to Louis XI. Louis XIV turned the château into a prison, dispatching his finance minister, Fouquet, to a cell here. In the 19th century the castle again became a prison, and during World War II it was used by the Nazis as a munitions depot. Allied planes bombed it in 1944.

The castle should be visited if for no other reason than to see the ✪ **Apocalypse Tapestries,** one of the masterpieces of art from the Middle Ages. This series of tapestries wasn't always so highly regarded—they once served as a canopy for orange trees to protect the fruit from unfavorable weather and at another time to cover the damaged walls of a church. They were made by Poisson beginning in 1375 for Louis I of Anjou. In the 19th century they were purchased for only a nominal sum. Seventy-seven pieces of them stretch a distance of 335 feet, the series illustrating the book of St. John. One scene is called *La Grande Prostituée*, and another shows Babylon invaded by demons; yet another is a peace scene with two multiheaded monsters holding up a fleur-de-lis.

After seeing the tapestries, you can tour the fortress, including the courtyard of the nobles, prison cells, ramparts, windmill tower, 15th-century chapel, and royal apartments. The château is open daily: June to September 15 from 9am to 7pm and September 16 to May from 9:30am to 12:30pm and 2 to 6pm. Admission is 32 F ($6.10) for adults, 21 F ($4) for seniors 60 or over, and 6 F ($1.15) for children 7 to 17; 6 and under free.

The **Cathédrale St-Maurice,** place Freppel (☎ 41-87-58-45), is mostly from the 12th and 13th centuries; the main tower, However, is from the 16th century. The statues on the portal represent everybody from the Queen of Sheba to David at the harp. On the tympanum is depicted Christ Enthroned; the symbols, such as the lion for St. Mark, represent the Evangelists. The stained-glass windows from the 12th through the 16th century have made the cathedral famous. The oldest one illustrates the martyrdom of St. Vincent (the most unusual is of former St. Christopher with the head of a dog). Once all the Apocalypse Tapestries were shown here; now only a few remain. The 12th-century nave is a landmark in cathedral architecture, a clear, coherent plan that's a work of harmonious beauty, covered with Angevin vaulting. It's open daily from 8am to 5pm.

ESSENTIALS

GETTING THERE   From Saumur it's a 30-minute train trip to Angers, a one-way ticket costing 54 F ($10.25); from Tours, it's 1 hour for a one-way cost of 82 F ($15.60). Trains also leave Paris-Austerlitz for the 2³/₄-hour trip, costing 192 F ($36.50) one way. The train station at place de la Gare is a convenient walk from the château.

VISITOR INFORMATION   The Office de Tourisme is on place du Président-Kennedy (☎ 41-23-51-11).

WHERE TO STAY

Hôtel d'Anjou

1 bd. Foch, 49100 Angers. ☎ **41-88-24-82.** Fax 41-87-22-21. 53 rms, 46 with bath. MINIBAR TV TEL. 355 F ($67.50) double without bath, 600 F ($114.05) double with bath. Breakfast 57 F ($10.85) extra. Tax 6 F ($1.15) per person extra. AE, DC, MC, V. Parking 45 F ($8.55).

The prices are reasonable at this four-story hotel on the main boulevard, next to a large park. The clean rooms are comfortably furnished with traditional pieces, and guests are politely welcomed and cared for. The hotel restaurant, La Salamandre, is one of the better ones in town, offering regional specialties and fresh fish courses. Try the sole in tomato sauce and filets of duck with spring turnips. Fixed-price meals cost 120 F ($22.80), 150 F ($28.50), and 190 F ($36.10).

Hôtel de France

8 place de la Gare, 49100 Angers. ☎ **41-88-49-42.** Fax 41-86-76-70. 57 rms. MINIBAR TV TEL. 550 F ($104.55) double. Breakfast 50 F ($9.50) extra. AE, DC, MC, V. Parking 40 F ($7.60).

One of the most respected in town, this 19th-century hotel has been run by the Bouyers since 1893. It's the preferred choice near the railway station. The rooms are soundproof, but only four are air-conditioned (it can get hot on a summer night in Angers). The restaurant, Les Plantagenets, serves reliable fixed-price meals beginning at 95 F ($18.05).

WHERE TO DINE

Provence Café

9 place du Ralliement. ☎ **41-87-44-15.** Reservations recommended. Main courses 65 F ($12.35); fixed-price menus 85 F ($16.15). AE, MC, V. Mon 7–10pm, Tues–Sun noon–2pm and 7–10pm. PROVENÇAL.

This restaurant opened in 1994 celebrating the herbs, spices, and seafood of Provence. The decor includes bundles of herbs, bright colors, and souvenirs of the Mediterranean, and the ambience is unstuffy and sunny. Menu items include a risotto with asparagus and basil, grilled salmon with provençal herbs, and a ballotine of chicken with ratatouille.

Le Toussaint

7 place du Président-Kennedy. ☎ **41-87-46-20.** Reservations recommended. Main courses 65–140 F ($12.35–$26.60); fixed-price menus 125–200 F ($23.75–$38). AE, MC, V. Tues–Sat noon–2pm and 7:45–9:30pm, Sun noon–2pm. FRENCH.

This leading restaurant, on the same street as the cathedral, serves the imaginative cuisine of well-known chef Michel Bignon. The second-floor dining room boasts a sweeping château view. The recipes include only the freshest ingredients, and specialties include foie gras with Layon wine, farm-bred pigeon stuffed with foie gras, and an array of fresh fish and shellfish. The dessert specialty is a soufflé glacé with Cointreau.

NEARBY ACCOMMODATIONS & DINING

Château de la Jaillière

44370 La Chapelle St-Sauveur, at Varades. ☎ **40-98-62-54.** 4 rms, 1 suite. 660–840 F ($125.40–$159.60) double; 4,800 F ($912) suite for six per week. Rates include continental breakfast. No credit cards. Parking free. Closed Oct 15–May 15. Take D6 22 miles west of Angers; D6 intersects with N23 midway between Angers and Nantes.

Heavily embellished, this 19th-century château contains dozens of marble fireplaces, tapestries, and period furniture. It's owned by the comtesse d'Anthenaise, who's well-versed in the region's history. The rooms (all doubles) are beautifully furnished with antiques. Well-prepared dinners begin at 200 F ($38). You'll also find gardens, expansive lawns, a tennis court, and a pool.

12 Normandy

Ten centuries have passed since the Vikings invaded the province of Normandy. The early Scandinavians might've come to ravish the land, but they stayed to cultivate it. The Normans produced great soldiers, none more famous than William the Conqueror, who defeated the forces of King Harold at Battle Abbey in 1066. The English and the French continued to do battle on and off for 700 years—a rivalry that climaxed at the 1815 Battle of Waterloo.

Much of Normandy was later ravaged in the 1944 invasion that began on a June morning when airborne troops parachuted down into Ste-Mère-Eglise and Bénouville-sur-Orne. The largest armada ever assembled was responsible for a momentous saga: the reconquest of continental Europe from the Nazis. Today, many come to Normandy just to see the D-Day beachheads.

Some of this province may remind you of a Millet landscape, with cattle grazing sleepily in verdant fields and quaint wood-framed houses existing alongside modern buildings. Not far from the Seine you'll come on the hamlet where Monet painted his water lilies. Here and there you can still find stained-glass windows and gothic architecture miraculously spared from the bombardments heaped on Normandy; however, many great buildings were leveled to the ground. And Normandy's wide beaches may attract families, but in August the Deauville sands draw the chicest of the chic from Europe and North America.

REGIONAL CUISINE   Normandy is the land of the three Cs: cider, Calvados, and Camembert. Butter, cream, and other dairy products with such accompaniments as pear or apple cider and fiery apple brandy make up a large part of the diet. Norman cream is velvety in texture and ivory in color. The region's *sauce normande* might be called a plain white sauce anywhere else, but here it takes on added allure because of its richer taste.

Certain Norman towns and regions are associated with certain courses—tripe in the mode of Caen, sole from Dieppe, duck from Rouen, and soufflélike omelets from Mont-St-Michel. Auge Valley chicken, though not as highly praised as that of Bresse, also has a place in the diet. Locals adore andouillet (tripe sausage) from Vire, mussels from Isigny, oysters from Courseulles, cockles from

Normandy

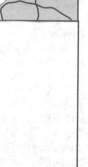

English Channel

Channel
Islands

Baie de la Seine

Dieppe

Fécamp

Montvilliers

Le Havre

Cherbourg

Iles St-Marcouf

Grandcamp-
les-Bains

Port-
en-Bessin

Arromanches-
les-Bains

Carteret

Granville

Mont-
St-Michel **8**

Dol

Pontorson

Antrain

Fougères

Avranches

St-Hilaire-
du-Harc.

Mayenne

Domfront

Flers

Tinchebray

Vire

Villedieu

St-Lô

Coutances

Carentan

Thebray

Clécy

Falaise

Argentan

Pré-en-Pail

Alençon

Séez

Mortagne

Bellême

l'Aigle

Conches

Bernay

Orbec

Lisieux

Pont l'Évêque

Honfleur **2**

Trouville **3**
Deauville **4**

Cabourg

Caen **5**

Bayeux **6**

Grandcamp-
les-Bains **7**

St-Wandrille

Rouen **1**

Jumièges

Caudebec-
en-Caux

Pont-Audemer

Elbeuf

Louviers

Les
Andelys

Vernon

Evreux

Nonancourt

Bayeux **6**
Caen **5**
D-Day Beaches **7**
Deauville **4**
Honfleur **2**
Mont-St-Michel **8**
Rouen **1**
Trouville **3**

Normandy
PARIS

Airport ✈

40 km
50 mi

Honfleur, and lobsters from La Hague. Highly prized lamb (*pré salé*) is raised on the salt meadows of Normandy.

The supple, fragrant cow's-milk Camembert, sold in a wooden box since 1880, is joined by other cheeses of the area, including Pont-L'Evêque. Brillat-Savarin, with a high fat content of 75%, was invented in the 1930s by cheese merchant Henri Androuët.

Normans consume cider at nearly every meal. *Bon bère* is the term for true cider, and sometimes it's so strong that it must be diluted with water. It takes 12 to 15 years to bring Calvados to taste perfection (in America Calvados may be called apple jack). Many a Norman finishes a meal with black coffee and a glass of this strong drink, which is also used to flavor main courses.

EXPLORING THE REGION BY CAR

Here's how to link together the best of the region if you rent a car.

Day 1   Begin in Rouen, 84 miles from central Paris along the A13 superhighway, allowing a full afternoon and part of the following morning for an exploration of the city's half-timbered central core and cathedral. After a hearty Norman dinner, retire for the night.

Day 2   The following morning, drive 44 miles west along A13 to Honfleur, for a view of an antique seaport whose charm inspired Flaubert and a string of lesser luminaries. If you have enough time, opt to spend the night here; otherwise, continue westward for 9 miles on the coastal road to Deauville. Stroll along the town's boardwalk, imagining Coco Chanel making her fashion debut at this dignified resort just after the turn of the century. Perhaps try your hand at the casino, then dine Norman style and opt for a drink at a cocktail lounge or pub.

Day 3   Begin your day with an excursion to the earthier resort of Trouville, then make a literary pilgrimage to Marcel Proust's favorite coastal resort, Cabourg, $7^1/_2$ miles to the west, if only for a view over the mists of the English Channel. Continue driving another $12^1/_2$ miles to the west along D513, a route that will bring you to Caen, the Athens of Normandy. Caen contains twin abbeys founded by William the Conqueror and Queen Mathilda, as well as a university established in the 1400s. It has a long history of imperial grandeur. Fortunately, some remains despite the devastation of World War II. Stay the night here.

Day 4   Head northwest to Bayeux, 16 miles away via E46 for an overnight. After a morning visit to the cathedral, go to the Musée de la Tapisserie to see the Bayeux tapestry: It's the most extraordinary embroidery ever produced in Europe—a needlepoint chronicle of one of the most pivotal battles of the Middle Ages. In the early afternoon, depart for a 5-mile excursion to the colorful coastal town of Port-en-Bessin and wander along its harborfront. Consider having lunch at Le Chenevière, a mile from the port, at Port-en-Bessin-Huppain (☎ **31-21-47-96**). The beaches of the D-Day invasion, as well as the American cemetery, are a 15-minute drive away. Spend the night here or return to Bayeux for the night.

Day 5   The following morning, get an early start for your 60-mile southwest drive along D972, D999, and N175 to one of Europe's premier attractions: Mont-St-Michel. Throughout most of the 14th century it stood as the lone bulwark against what could've been a complete invasion of France by the English army. Its position atop "the archangel's mountain" was one of the most secure in the Middle

What's Special About Normandy

Beaches
- Corniche Normande, a 9-mile coastline of Normandy's grandest resorts: Deauville, Trouville, and Honfleur, with sandy beaches, the *haut monde*, gambling, the works.
- D-Day beaches, where Allied troops landed on June 6, 1944.
- Côte Fleurie, a 12-mile stretch of sand from Deauville-Trouville to Cabourg of Marcel Proust fame.

Great Towns
- Bayeux, for a glimpse of Queen Mathilda's magnificent tapestry.
- Rouen, capital of Upper Normandy, forever associated with Joan of Arc's burning at the stake.

Ancient Monuments
- Mont-St-Michel, a wonder of the Western world.
- Cathédrale Notre-Dame de Rouen, a stunning example of French gothic.
- Cathédrale Notre-Dame de Bayeux, the Reims of Normandy.

Architectural Highlights
- Abbaye aux Hommes (in Caen), built in Norman romanesque style, site of William the Conqueror's tomb.
- Jumièges, one of the greatest ruins in France.

Festivals
- Grande Fête Normande (Festival of Normandy), Etretat (Ascension weekend).

Ages, partly because of the roaring tides that periodically engulf the surrounding tidal flats. Despite the crowds, this site is one of the most memorable anywhere.

1 Rouen

84 miles NW of Paris, 55 E of Le Havre

Capital of Normandy, Rouen is the second most important tourist center in the north. It's also a hub of commerce, the third-largest port in France. Victor Hugo called it "the city of a hundred spires." Half of it was destroyed during World War II, mostly by Allied bombers, and many Rouennais were killed. In the reconstruction of the old quarters some of the almost-forgotten crafts of the Middle Ages were revived. On the Seine, the city is rich in historical associations: William the Conqueror died here in 1087, and Joan of Arc was burned at the stake on place du Vieux-Marché in 1431.

The Seine, as in Paris, splits Rouen into a Rive Gauche (Left Bank) and Rive Droite (Right Bank). The old city is on the right bank.

ESSENTIALS

GETTING THERE   From Paris's Gare St-Lazare, trains leave for Rouen about once every hour (trip time: 70 min.), costing 97 F ($18.45) one way.

VISITOR INFORMATION   The Office de Tourisme is at 25 place de la Cathédrale (☎ 32-08-32-40).

SEEING THE TOP ATTRACTIONS

Start your exploration with the ✪ **Cathédrale Notre-Dame de Rouen,** place de la Cathédrale. This cathedral was immortalized by Monet in a series of impressionistic paintings of the three-portal facade with its galaxy of statues. The main door is embellished with sculptures (some decapitated) depicting the Tree of Jesus. It's flanked by the 12th-century Porte St-Jean and Porte St-Etienne. Consecrated in 1063, the cathedral, a symphony of lacy stonework, was last reconstructed after the bombings of World War II. Two soaring towers distinguish it—the Tour de Beurre (Tower of Butter) was financed by the faithful willing to pay money in exchange for the privilege of eating butter at Lent, and it's a masterpiece of flamboyant gothic style. Containing a carillon of 56 bells, the three-story lantern tower—built in 1877 and utilizing 740 tons of iron and bronze—rises to almost 500 feet.

The cathdral's interior is fairly uniform. The nave has 11 bays and a sexpartite vault, and the choir is a masterpiece of harmony, with a delicate triforium and 14 soaring pillars. The Booksellers' Stairway, in the north wing of the transept, is adorned with a large rose window with stained glass that dates in part from the 1500s. The 13th-century chancel is beautiful, with relatively simple lines. Especially interesting is the Chapelle de la Vierge, adorned with the Renaissance tombs of the cardinals d'Amboise as well as Jean de Brézé. Also entombed inside was the heart of Richard the Lion-Hearted, a token of his affection for the people of Rouen.

The cathedral is open daily but closed Monday to Saturday from noon to 2pm and Sunday from 1 to 3pm. Admission is free.

Behind the cathedral is the **Archbishop's Palace,** bombed in the war. Now it stands naked against the sky. The broken arches and rosette windows witnessed the trial of Joan of Arc in 1431. At this same spot her rehabilitation was proclaimed in 1456.

A lane running between the cathedral and place du Vieux-Marché is called **rue du Gros-Horloge** (Street of the Great Clock). Now a pedestrian mall, it's named for an ornate gilt Renaissance clock mounted on an arch, Rouen's most popular monument. The arch bridges the street and is connected to a Louis XV fountain with a bevy of cherubs and a belltower. At night the bells still toll a curfew. Visitors who purchase a ticket at the Musée des Beaux-Arts (below) are entitled to visit the belfry to see the iron clockworks and the bells. It's open only Easter to mid-September, Wednesday from 2 to 6pm and Thursday to Monday from 10am to noon and 2 to 6pm.

Place du Vieux-Marché (Old Marketplace) is where Joan of Arc was executed for heresy. Tied to a stake, she was burned alive on a pyre set by the English on May 30, 1431. Kissing a cross while being chained, she's reported to have called out "Jesus!" as the fire was set. Her ashes were gathered and tossed into the Seine. In the center of a monumental complex in the square is a modern church displaying stained-glass windows from St-Vincent. Beside it a bronze cross marks the position of St. Joan's stake.

Nearby, at 15 place de la Pucelle (Square of the Maid), is the gothic-inspired **Hôtel de Bourgtheroulde** (☎ 35-08-64-00). It dates from the 16th century and was built by William the Red. The inside yard is exceptional. Once in the courtyard, look back at the gothic building with its octagonal stair tower. The left gallery is entirely Renaissance. A bank uses the hôtel now, and access is free during

Rouen

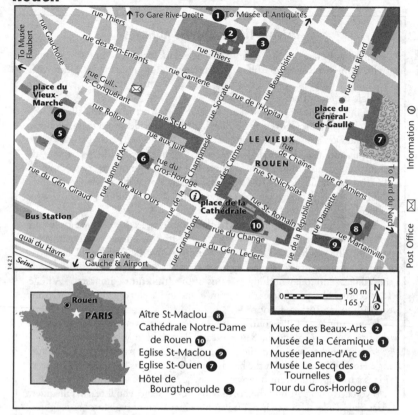

Aître St-Maclou 8
Cathédrale Notre-Dame de Rouen 10
Eglise St-Maclou 9
Eglise St-Ouen 7
Hôtel de Bourgtheroulde 5

Musée des Beaux-Arts 2
Musée de la Céramique 1
Musée Jeanne-d'Arc 4
Musée Le Secq des Tournelles 3
Tour du Gros-Horloge 6

working hours. On Saturday and Sunday you can visit by ringing a bell and asking for the porter.

MORE CHURCHES

Rouen has two other churches worth exploring. One is the **Eglise St-Maclou,** behind the cathedral, at 3 rue Dutuit (☎ 35-71-71-72). It was built in the florid gothic style, with a step-gabled porch and handsome cloisters, and is known for the remarkable 16th-century panels on its doors. Our favorite (to the left) is the Portal of the Fonts. The church was constructed in 1200, rebuilt in 1432, and finally consecrated in 1521, though its lantern tower is from the 19th century. It sits on a square of old Norman crooked-timbered buildings. Inside, pictures dating from June 4, 1944, document St-Maclou's destruction. It's open daily from 10am to noon and 2 to 6pm; closed May 1 and July 14.

If you walk from rue de la République to place du Général-de-Gaulle, you'll be at the **Eglise St-Ouen,** the outgrowth of a 7th-century Benedictine abbey. Flanked by four turrets, its 375-foot octagonal lantern tower, in the gothic style, is called "the ducal crown of Normandy." One of the best-known gothic buildings in France, the church represents the work of five centuries. Its nave is from the 15th century, its choir from the 14th (but with 18th-century railings), and its remarkable stained glass from the 14th to the 16th. On May 23, 1431, Joan of Arc was

Driving the Route des Abbayes

Beginning at Rouen, the Seine winds through black forests and lush green countryside along the Route des Abbayes, eventually ending at Le Havre. Filled with the ruins of monasteries and châteaux, this is one of the most evocative and nostalgic routes in France.

Ten minutes after leaving Rouen (via D982), you arrive at the 11th-century **abbey church of St. George,** in St-Martin de Boscherville. From there, go along D982 and D65 around the Seine for 12 miles to Jumièges. One of France's most beautiful ruins, the **Abbaye de Jumièges** was founded by St. Philbert in the 7th century and rebuilt in the 10th century. The abbey church was consecrated in 1067 by the archbishop of Rouen in the presence of William the Conqueror. The 100-foot-high nave is complete, and the porch is surrounded by two towers 150 feet high.

Another 10 miles along the right bank of the Seine leads to St-Wandrille, 33 miles northwest of Rouen (reached via D982 from Jumièges). The **Abbey of St-Wandrille** was founded in 649 by Wandrille, an official of King Dagobert's court. Over the centuries the abbey has suffered various attacks, including from the Vikings, and today nothing remains of the 7th-century monastery. A huge 18th-century blue gate frames the entrance, and inside you can visit cloisters from the 14th to the 16th century.

From Saint-Wandrille, continue for 2 miles or so to **Caudebec-en-Caux,** set in an amphitheater along the Seine. Nearly destroyed in World War II, it has a gothic church that dates from the 15th century and was spared in the war bombings. Henri IV considered it the handsomest chapel in his kingdom. On its west side is a trio of flamboyant doorways, crowned by a rose window.

If you drive west around the north bank of the Seine, you'll reach Villequier, a tranquil hamlet with a château. It was here that Victor Hugo lost his daughter, along with her husband, in a seasonal tidal wave. The **Musée Victor Hugo,** on quai Victor-Hugo, can be visited. It has the manuscript of his poem "Contemplations," a lament.

Some 33 miles to the west, along D81 and N182, you reach **Le Havre,** France's major Atlantic port. The city was the target of more than 170 bombings during World War II, and its recovery has been amazing. Boat tours are possible from here to Trouville and Deauville, those competitive resorts for the chic at heart.

taken to the cemetery here, where officials sentenced her to be burnt at the stake unless she recanted. An abjuration was signed by her, thus condemning her to life imprisonment; that sentence was later revoked. It's open Wednesday to Monday from 10am to noon and 2 to 5pm; closed from November 1 to March 15.

MUSEUMS

The **Musée des Beaux-Arts,** place Verdel (☎ 35-71-28-40), is one of the most important provincial museums in France, with portraits by David, plus works by Delacroix and Ingres (seek out his *La Belle Zélie*). A Gérard David retable, *La Vierge et les Saints* (The Virgin and the Saints), is a masterpiece. One salon is devoted to Géricault, including a portrait of Delacroix. Other works are by Veronese,

Velásquez, Caravaggio, Rubens, Poussin, Fragonard, Ingres, and Corot. There's even a version of Monet's *Rouen Cathedral.* The museum is open Wednesday to Monday from 10am to noon and 2 to 6pm. Admission is 20 F ($3.80) for adults and 10 F ($1.90) for children.

One of the greatest treasures in the 17th-century **Musée de la Céramique,** 1 rue Faucon (☎ 35-07-31-74), is the Rouen faïence, which pioneered a special red in 1670. The exhibits provide a showcase for the talents of Masseot Abaquesne, the premier French artist in faïence. In time, his position was usurped by Louis Poterat. An exceptional showcase is devoted to chinoiseries dating from 1699 to 1745. The museum is open Thursday to Monday from 10am to noon and 2 to 6pm. Admission is 13 F ($2.45) for adults; children enter free.

The **Musée Le Secq des Tournelles** (Wrought Ironworks Museum), rue Jacques-Villon (☎ 35-71-28-40), is housed in the 15th-century Eglise St-Laurent. Its collection ranges from what the press once called "forthright masculine forging to lacy feminine filigree, from Roman keys to the needlepoint balustrade that graced Mme de Pompadour's country mansion." A Parisian aristocrat, Le Secq des Tournelles began the collection in 1870. So passionately was he devoted to it that his wife divorced him, charging alienation of affection. Donated to the city of Rouen, the collection now has some 14,000 pieces. The museum is open Thursday to Monday from 10am to noon and 2 to 6pm. Admission is 20 F ($3.80) for adults and 10 F ($1.90) for children.

In the Hôtel-Dieu is the **Musée Flaubert et d'Histoire de la Médécine,** 51 rue de Lecat (☎ 35-15-59-95). Gustave Flaubert, author of *Madame Bovary,* was born in the director's quarters of Rouen's public hospital (his father was the director). Flaubert spent his first 25 years in the city, and the room where he was born in 1821 is still intact. In addition, family furniture and medical paraphernalia are displayed. Only a glass door separated the Flauberts from the ward and its moaning patients. The museum is open Tuesday to Saturday from 10am to noon and 2 to 6pm; it's closed holidays. Admission is free.

The life and martyrdom of Joan of Arc, France's national heroine, are traced at the **Musée Jeanne-d'Arc,** 33 place du Vieux-Marché (☎ 35-88-02-70). It's on the old market square where Joan was executed. In a vaulted cellar are waxworks depicting the main stages of her life—from Domrémy, where she was born, to the stake. The museum is open May to October, daily from 9:30am to 6:30pm; November to April, Tuesday to Sunday from 10am to noon and 2 to 6pm. Admission is 22 F ($4.20) for adults and 10 F ($1.90) for children.

WHERE TO STAY
EXPENSIVE

Mercure Centre
Rue Croix-de-Fer, 76000 Rouen. ☎ **35-52-69-52.** Fax 35-89-41-46. 121 rms, 4 suites. A/C MINIBAR TV TEL. 520 F ($98.80) double; 800 F ($152) suite. Breakfast 55 F ($10.45) extra. AE, DC, MC, V. Parking 40 F ($7.60). Métro: Place Foch.

This is a good choice for value and modern comfort, bought by the nationwide Mercure chain in 1992. The location's unbeatable—at the cathedral and rue du Gros-Horloge. The functionally designed rooms are clean and well maintained, though perhaps a tad small. There's a bar on the premises, but breakfast is the only meal served.

MODERATE

Hôtel de Dieppe

Place Bernard-Tissot, 76000 Rouen. ☎ **35-71-96-00,** or 800/528-1234 in the U.S. and Canada. 41 rms. TV TEL. 495–595 F ($94.10–$113.10) double. Breakfast 45 F ($8.55) extra. AE, DC, MC, V. Parking free. Bus 1, 3, 5, 7, or 10.

This hotel across from the train station has been run by the Gueret family since 1880. Though modernized, this is still a traditional French inn. The only problem might be the noise, but the double-glazed windows help; after 10pm the last train from Paris arrives and the area quiets down. The rooms are done in either period or contemporary styling and are fairly compact. In the adjoining rôtisserie, Le Quatre Saisons, you can select a fixed-price menu for 135 F ($25.65) or à la carte dishes like duckling à la presse and sole poached in red wine.

INEXPENSIVE

Hôtel de la Cathédrale

12 rue St-Romain, 76000 Rouen. ☎ **35-71-57-95.** 24 rms. TV TEL. 300–355 F ($57–$67.50) double. Breakfast 35 F ($6.65) extra. MC, V. Parking 35 F ($6.65) nearby. Bus 1, 3, 5, 7, or 10.

Built around a timbered courtyard, the hotel is on a pedestrian street midway between the cathedral and the Eglise St-Maclou, opposite the Archbishop's Palace where Joan of Arc was tried. The recently remodeled rooms are clean, accessible by both stairs and an elevator. Breakfast is the only meal served.

⑤ Hôtel le Viking

21 quai du Havre, 76000 Rouen. ☎ **35-70-34-95.** Fax 35-89-97-12. 38 rms. TV TEL. 255–320 F ($48.45–$60.80) double. Breakfast 35 F ($6.65) extra. AE, MC, V. Parking 45 F ($8.55). Bus 1, 3, 5, 7, or 10.

On a riverbank overlooking the Seine, this seven-story hotel is in a white-sided concrete building. Though the traffic noise can be bad at times, the front rooms open onto charming views of the river. In July and August reserve at least two weeks in advance, as demand for rooms here is great then. The rooms are a little small but still comfortable. Breakfast is the only meal served.

WHERE TO DINE

EXPENSIVE

✪ Gill

9 quai de la Bourse. ☎ **35-71-16-14.** Reservations recommended. Main courses 145–170 F ($27.55–$32.30); fixed-price menus 195–370 F ($37.05–$70.30) Mon–Fri; 280–370 F ($53.20–$70.30) Sat–Sun. AE, DC, MC, V. May–Sept, Mon–Sat noon–2:15pm and 7–9:45pm; Oct–Apr, Tues–Sat noon–2:15pm and 7–9:45pm, Sun 7–9:45pm. Métro: Théâtre des Arts. FRENCH.

One of the city's most talked-about upper-bracket restaurants is beside the traffic of the Seine's quais. The uncluttered modern decor with high-tech accessories is an appropriate backdrop for the sophisticated subtle cuisine of Gilles Tournadre. Menu items change seasonally but may include chutney-roasted crayfish with red peppers, turbot roasted with fondue of endive, sliced duck liver with leeks, and North Atlantic lobster stew. The desserts may include millefeuille nature, which in M. Tournadre's hands becomes an elegant work of art.

MODERATE

Maison Dufour

67 bis rue St-Nicholas. ☎ **35-71-90-62.** Reservations required. Main courses 80–130 F ($15.20–$24.70); fixed-price menus 120–230 F ($22.80–$43.70). AE, MC, V. Tues–Sat noon– 2pm and 7–9:30pm, Sun noon–2pm. Closed Aug 2–23. Métro: Théâtre des Arts. NORMAN.

One of Normandy's best-preserved 15th-century inns, the Maison Dufour contains several dining rooms decorated with copper pots, wood carvings, and engravings. The food is so outstanding it's hard to single out specialties. However, the home-smoked salmon, canard (duckling) rouennais, John Dory in cider sauce, and sole normande are standouts. And so is the Calvados-flavored soufflé.

INEXPENSIVE

⑤ Brasserie de la Grande Poste

43 rue Jeanne-d'Arc. ☎ **35-70-08-70.** Reservations not required. Main courses 53–65 F ($10.05–$12.35); fixed-price menus 60–85 F ($11.40–$16.15). AE, MC, V. Daily 8am– 11:30pm. Bus 1, 3, 5, 7, or 10. FRENCH.

Boasting a decor that's changed little since the place was established in the 1880s, this is one of the most popular brasseries in Rouen. It offers a tiny terrace (good for drinks) and a large interior staffed by veteran waiters. Menu items include hardboiled eggs with mayonnaise, steak au poivre, sole meunière, and entrecôte with french fries. These are the same dishes served when Bardot was making *And God Created Woman*. The wine list is reasonably priced.

⑤ Pascaline

5 rue de la Poterne. ☎ **35-89-67-44.** Reservations recommended. Main courses 48–95 F ($9.10–$18.05); fixed-price menus 75–95 F ($14.25–$18.05). V. Daily noon–2:30pm and 7:30–11:30pm. Métro: Place-Foch. FRENCH.

The cheapest fixed-price menu here is the best bargain in town. This informal bistro has a turn-of-the-century decor and is often filled with regulars. The à la carte menu offers fresh seafood, tenderloin steaks, and cassoulet toulousain. Desserts are an ice-cream lover's delight. Don't come here for refined cuisine—stop in to be filled up with hearty old favorites.

NEARBY ACCOMMODATIONS & DINING

Novotel Rouen-Sud

Le Madrillet, 76800 Saint-Etienne-du-Rouvray. ☎ **35-66-58-50.** Fax 35-66-15-56. 134 rms. A/C MINIBAR TV TEL. 490 F ($93.10) double. Children 15 and under stay free in parents' room. Breakfast 50 F ($9.50) extra. AE, DC, MC, V. Parking free.

About 4 miles south on N138, facing the Parc des Expositions, this hotel is designed for ease of accessibility and businesslike convenience. You get no surprises, but few disappointments either. There are two tennis courts, an outdoor pool, a bar that serves exotic drinks, and a modern grill open from 6am to midnight. You wheel your own luggage to one of the comfortable rooms—each uninspired, with one single bed, one double bed, and a desk.

2 Caen

148 miles NW of Paris, 74 miles SE of Cherbourg

On the banks of the Orne, the port of Caen suffered great damage in the Allied invasion of Normandy in 1944. Nearly three-quarters of its buildings, 10,000 in all, were destroyed, though the twin abbeys founded by William the Conqueror and his wife, Mathilda, were spared. The city today is essentially modern and has many broad avenues and new apartment buildings.

Founded by William and Mathilda, the **Abbaye aux Hommes,** Esplanade Jean-Marie-Louvel (☎ **31-30-42-01**), is adjacent to the Eglise St-Etienne, which you enter on place Monseigneur-des-Hameaux. During the height of the Allied invasion, denizens of Caen flocked to St-Etienne for protection from the bombardment. The church is dominated by twin 276-foot romanesque towers. Its 15th-century spires helped earn for Caen the appellation of "a city of spires." A marble slab inside the high altar commemorates the site of William's tomb. The Huguenots destroyed the tomb in an uprising in 1562, save for a hipbone that was recovered. However, during the Revolution the last of William's dust was scattered to the wind.

Conducted tours (in French) of the abbey are given daily at 9:30 and 11am and 2:30 and 4pm, costing cost 10 F ($1.90). The hand-carved wooden doors and elaborately sculpted wrought-iron staircase are exceptional. From the cloisters you get a good view of the two towers of St-Etienne. Part of the former abbey houses municipal offices.

On the opposite side of town, the **Abbaye aux Dames,** place de la Reine-Mathilde (☎ **31-06-98-98**), was founded by Mathilda and embraces the Eglise de la Trinité, which is flanked by romanesque towers. Destroyed in the Hundred Years' War, its spires weren't rebuilt. In the 12th-century choir is the tomb of Queen Mathilda; note the ribbed vaulting. To see the choir, transept, and crypt, take a free guided tour (in French), offered daily at 2:30 and 4pm. The abbey is open daily from 8am to 6pm.

If time remains, you can visit the **Château de Guillaume-le-Conquérant,** near the Relais des Gourmets; the gardens afford a fine view over Caen. The approach ramp is from the front of the Eglise St-Pierre. The château is open daily: May to September from 6am to 9:30pm and October to April from 6am to 7:30pm. Entrance is free.

ESSENTIALS

GETTING THERE From Paris's Gare St-Lazare, five to seven trains per day arrive in Caen (trip time: 2¹/₂ hr.), costing 150 F ($28.50) one way. There are also four trains from Fouen (trip time: 1¹/₂ hr.), costing 113 F ($21.45) one way.

VISITOR INFORMATION The Office de Tourisme is on place St-Pierre (☎ 31-86-27-65).

WHERE TO STAY
MODERATE

Holiday Inn
Place du Maréchal-Foch, 14000 Caen. ☎ **31-27-57-57.** Fax 31-27-57-58. 92 rms. TV TEL. 460–580 F ($87.45–$110.25) double. Breakfast 50 F ($9.50) extra. AE, DC, MC, V. Parking free. Bus 1, 3, 4, 10, or 11.

Across from the racecourse and opposite an angel-capped monument to a military hero, this Holiday Inn was enlarged/modernized in 1991. It offers a cozy bar favored by Americans visiting the D-Day beaches, plus a restaurant, Le Rabelais, where fixed-price menus cost 118 F ($22.40), 175 F ($33.25), and 230 F ($43.70). The rooms are predictable, comfortable, and well maintained.

Les Relais des Gourmets

15 rue de Geôle, 14300 Caen. ☎ **31-86-06-01.** Fax 31-39-06-00. 28 rms, 7 suites. MINIBAR TV TEL. 520 F ($98.80) double; from 770 F ($146.30) suite. Breakfast 50 F ($9.50) extra. AE, DC, MC, V. Bus 1, 3, 4, 10, or 11.

At the foot of the château is this charming four-star hotel. Many antiques and re-productions adorn the lounges and reception area. The personalized rooms are generally spacious, many with views of the garden or château. You can dine in the terraced garden, where excellent seafood—like lobster, oysters, and the fish of the Channel—is served. Meals cost 145 to 240 F ($27.55 to $45.60).

INEXPENSIVE

Bristol

31 rue du 11-Novembre, 14000 Caen. ☎ **31-84-59-76.** Fax 31-52-29-28. 20 rms. TV TEL. 230–260 F ($43.70–$49.40) double. Breakfast 30 F ($5.70) extra. V. Parking free. Bus 1, 3, 4, 10, or 11.

Renovated in 1992, this hotel is on a block of modern apartments and shops, not far from the park. Consider the Bristol more as a stopover hotel than a charming inn. The price is fair, however. A continental breakfast is the only meal served.

⑤ Hôtel des Quatrans

17 rue Gémare, 14300 Caen. ☎ **31-86-25-57.** Fax 31-85-27-80. 32 rms. TEL. 245–255 F ($46.55–$48.45) double. Breakfast 30 F ($5.70) extra. MC, V. Parking free. Bus 1, 3, 4, 10, or 11.

This agreeable hostelry is one of Caen's best bargains. The rooms are simply fur-nished and offer basic amenities. Breakfast is the only meal served.

WHERE TO DINE

✪ Le Bourride

15–17 rue du Vaugueux. ☎ **31-93-50-76.** Reservations required. Main courses 133–195 F ($25.25–$37.05); fixed-price meal 190–470 F ($36.10–$89.35) at lunch, 332–470 F ($63.10–$89.35) at dinner. AE, DC, MC, V. Tues–Sat 12:30–2pm and 7:15–10pm. Closed Jan 3–19 and Aug 16–Sept 3. Bus 1, 3, 4, 10, or 11. NORMAN.

This restaurant has the best food in Caen. As the name implies, there's indeed a bourride served here, concocted from five kinds of fish, delicately seasoned and cooked under the expert eye of Michel Bruneau. The restaurant occupies a beau-tiful 17th-century house near the château, and its dining room has thick stone walls and a magnificent Renaissance fireplace. The service, directed by Françoise Bruneau, includes tactful advice on wines to accompany any of the specialties, such as foie gras of Norman duckling and roast lamb with onion confit. The desserts, which often depend on fruits in season, are excellent, as is the Calvados sorbet.

Le Dauphin

29 rue Gémare, 14300 Caen. ☎ **31-86-22-26.** Fax 31-86-35-14. Reservations required. Main courses 95–130 F ($18.05–$24.70); fixed-price menu (Mon–Fri only) 95 F ($18.05); fixed-price dinners 165–310 F ($31.35–$58.90). AE, DC, MC, V. Sun–Fri noon–2:30pm and 7–9:30pm, Sat 7–9:30pm. Closed Jan 23–Feb 7 and July 24–Aug 8. Bus 1, 3, 4, 10, or 11. FRENCH.

This restaurant was originally a medieval priory. The menu is wisely limited, and all ingredients are market fresh; alas, the chef/owner, Robert Chabredier, doesn't measure up to Bruneau at La Bourride (above). However, interesting items appear on the menu, including ragoût of lobster with fresh pasta, sweetbreads forester style, and oysters stuffed with leeks and asparagus.

Le Dauphin also offers 22 guest rooms with bath (tub or shower), costing 370 to 390 F ($70.30 to $74.10) in a double or 610 F ($115.95) for one of two suites; breakfast is 50 F ($9.50) extra.

Les Echevins
35 route de Trouville. ☎ **31-84-10-17.** Reservations required. Main courses 85–165 F ($16.15–$31.35); fixed-price menus 165–340 F ($31.35–$64.60). AE, DC, MC, V. Daily noon–2:30pm and 7:30–9:30pm. Closed July 31–Aug 27. FRENCH.

This restaurant is about two miles east of the town center on the Deauville–Cabourg road. It has two dining rooms and a lounge bar, plus a garden. Owner/chef Patrick Regnier prepares meals with the flair he showed at an exclusive Paris restaurant before he moved here. His specialties include morel-stuffed veal cutlet, truffle-stuffed pigeon, and lobster-and-scallop salad. Regional dishes include Caen-style tripe and marmite dieppoise, with a Calvados soufflé for dessert.

NEARBY ACCOMMODATIONS & DINING

Relais Château d'Audieu
14250 Audrieu. ☎ **31-80-21-52.** Fax 31-80-24-73. 21 rms, 9 suites. TV TEL. 950–1,600 F ($180.60–$304.15) double; 1,950 F ($370.70) suite. Breakfast 80 F ($15.20) extra. AE, MC, V. Parking free. Closed Dec–Feb. From Caen, take N13 for 11 miles, then D158 for 2 miles to Audrieu.

This château in a 50-acre park offers some of the most luxurious accommodations in the environs of Caen. Built at the beginning of the 18th century, it was a private home until 1976. The rooms are lovely and well appointed, often with antiques. Many well-heeled Caen residents drive here for dinner, which may include bouillon of duckling with cider or croustade of oysters with beet-flavored vinaigrette. Fixed-price menus range from 240 to 450 F ($45.60 to $85.55).

NEARBY DINING

✪ Le Manoir d'Hastings
14970 Bénouville. ☎ **31-44-62-43.** Fax 31-44-76-18. Reservations required. Main courses 85–190 F ($16.15–$36.10); fixed-price lunch (Mon–Fri only) 120 F ($22.80); fixed-price menus 160–390 F ($30.40–$74.10). AE, DC, MC, V. July–Aug, daily 12:30–2pm and 7–9:30pm; Sept–June, Tues–Sat 12:30–2pm and 7–9:30pm, Sun 12:30–2pm. From Caen, follow the signs north for Ouistreham, then go 6¹/₂ miles after turning off for Bénouville; the manor is next to the village church. FRENCH.

This restaurant occupies a converted 17th-century priory and has an enclosed Norman garden. Its owners, José and Carole Aparicio, serve *cuisine moderne*. The chef has developed his own style, as reflected by cider-cooked lobster and delicately flavored sea bass. For dessert, try the tart normand flambé with Calvados. Of the fixed-price menus, the most expensive is a *menu gourmand* with seven *petits plats dégustation*, based on the best available at the market.

The manor also offers 15 handsome rooms facing a garden, each with bath. A double goes for 500 to 800 F ($95.05 to $152.10), plus 50 F ($9.50) for breakfast.

3 Bayeux

166 miles NW of Paris, 16 miles NW of Caen

The ducs de Normandie sent their sons to this Viking settlement to learn the Norse language. Bayeux has changed a lot since, but miraculously it was spared from bombardment in 1944. This was the first French town liberated, and the citizens of Bayeux gave de Gaulle an enthusiastic welcome when he arrived on June 14. Today the sleepy town is filled with timbered houses, stone mansions, and cobbled streets.

ESSENTIALS

GETTING THERE   Five trains per day arrive from Paris (trip time: $2^1/_2$ hr.), costing 161 F ($30.60) one way; a dozen trains from Caen pull in (trip time: 20 min.), costing 29 F ($5.50) one way.

VISITOR INFORMATION   The Office de Tourisme is at pont St-Jean (☎ 31-92-16-26).

SEEING THE TOP ATTRACTIONS

The **Cathédrale de Bayeux,** 5 rue Maitrise (☎ 31-92-01-85), was consecrated in 1077 and partially destroyed in 1105. Left from an earlier church, its romanesque towers rise on the western side, and the central tower is from the 15th century, with an even later top. The nave is a fine example of the Norman romanesque style. Rich in sculpture, the 13th-century choir has handsome Renaissance stalls. To see the crypt and 13th-century chapter house, ask the sexton. (The crypt was built in the 11th century and then sealed; its existence remained unknown until 1412.) The cathedral is open in July and August, Monday to Saturday from 8am to 7pm and Sunday from 9am to 7pm; September to June, Monday to Saturday from 8:30am to noon and 2:30 to 7pm and Sunday from 9am to 12:15pm and 2:30 to 7pm.

At the ✪ **Musée de la Tapisserie de Bayeux,** Centre Guillaume-le-Conquérant, rue de Nesmond (☎ 31-92-05-48), you'll find the Bayeux tapestry—the most famous tapestry in the world. Actually, it's not a tapestry—it's an embroidery on a band of linen, 231 feet long and 20 inches wide, depicting some 58 scenes in 8 colors. Contrary to legend, it wasn't made by Queen Mathilda but was probably commissioned in Kent and made by unknown embroiderers between 1066 and 1077. The first recorded mention of the embroidery was in 1476, when it was explained that it was used to decorate the nave of the Cathédrale de Bayeux.

Housed in a glass case, the embroidery tells the story of the conquest of England by William the Conqueror, including such scenes as the coronation of Harold as the Saxon king of England, Harold returning from his journey to Normandy, the surrender of Dinan, Harold being told of the apparition of a comet (a portent of misfortune), William dressed for war, and the death of Harold. The decorative borders include scenes from Aesop's Fables.

Admission is 30 F ($5.70) for adults and 13 F ($2.45) for children 10 and under. The museum is open mid-May to mid-September, daily from 9am to 7pm; mid-Mar to mid-May and mid-September to mid-October, daily from 9am to 12:30pm and 2 to 6:30pm; and mid-October to mid-March, daily from 9:30am to 12:30pm and 2 to 6pm.

The **Musée Memorial de la Bataille de Normandie,** boulevard Fabian-Ware (☎ **31-92-93-41**), across from the cemetery, deals exclusively with the military and human history of the Battle of Normandy (June 6 to August 22, 1944). Inside are about 440 feet of window and film displays, plus a diorama. Wax soldiers in their uniforms, along with the tanks and guns used to win the battle, are exhibited. Admission is 24 F ($4.55) for adults and 11 F ($2.10) for children. The museum is open daily: June to August from 9am to 7pm and September to May from 10am to 12:30pm and 2 to 6pm.

WHERE TO STAY & DINE
MODERATE
✪ Le Lion d'Or
71 rue St-Jean, 14400 Bayeux. ☎ **31-92-06-90.** Fax 31-22-15-64. 26 rms, 2 suites. TV TEL. 450 F ($85.55) double; 850 F ($161.60) suite. Breakfast 55 F ($10.45) extra. AE, DC, MC, V. Parking free. Closed Dec 20–Jan 20. Bus 3.

This old-world hotel has a large open courtyard, with lush flower boxes decorating the facade. The personalized guest rooms are set back from the street. One meal is required of overnight guests. The traditional cuisine is inspired by the region's bounty, like homemade Normandy sausage, mushroom-stuffed chicken with creamy Pommeau sauce, and sole filet with cider-butter sauce. Of course, Normandy cheese or warm apple tart with a creamy Calvados sauce perfectly tops off a meal. There are lots of reasonably priced wines. Fixed-price menus cost 100 F ($19), 150 F ($28.50), 180 F ($34.20), 210 F ($39.90), and 320 F ($60.80).

Luxembourg
25 rue Bouchers, 14403 Bayeux. ☎ **31-92-00-04,** or 800/528-1234 in the U.S. and Canada. Fax 31-92-54-26. 19 rms, 3 suites. MINIBAR TV TEL. 450–500 F ($85.55–$95.05) double; from 1,200 F ($228.13) suite. Breakfast 55 F ($10.45) extra. Half board 400–410 F ($76.05–$77.95) per person daily. AE, MC, V. Parking free. Bus 3.

This is the finest hotel in the area. The completely restored interior has terrazzo floors and a decor combining neoclassical and art deco. The Luxembourg contains a richly decorated bar, an elegant restaurant, and a basement disco open until 4am. Fixed-price menus cost 99 F ($18.80), 128 F ($24.30), 158 F ($30), 210 F ($39.90), and 295 F ($56.05).

INEXPENSIVE
☻ Family Home
39 rue du Général-de-Dais, 14400 Bayeux. ☎ **31-92-15-22.** Fax 31-92-55-72. 13 rms. 220 F ($41.80) double. Rate includes continental breakfast. AE, MC, V. Bus 3.

In the town center, this 16th- and 17th-century presbytery, now a private house, encompasses four interconnected buildings. The rooms are simply furnished, and you can cook your own meals in the kitchen. Mme Lefèvre also serves copious and varied meals at a long communal table for 65 F ($12.35), including wine and service charge. The wine served is a smooth Anjou produced by Mme Lefèvre's family at their own vineyards.

Hôtel d'Argouges
21 rue St-Patrice, 14402 Bayeux. ☎ **31-92-88-86.** Fax 31-92-69-16. 25 rms. MINIBAR TEL. 270–420 F ($51.30–$79.85) double. Breakfast 35 F ($6.65) extra. AE, DC, MC, V. Parking free. Bus 3.

Monsieur and Madame Auregan have handsomely restored this 18th-century hotel. In fair weather, you can enjoy sipping drinks in the garden. The rooms are comfortable, 18 with TVs. Breakfast is the only meal served; however, five restaurants line the plaza outside.

4 The D-Day Beaches

Arromanches-les-Bains, 169 miles NW of Paris, 6¹/₂ miles NW of Bayeux; Grandcamp-Maisy (near Omaha Beach), 186 miles NW of Paris, 35 miles NW of Caen

From June 6 to July 18, "the longest day" was very long indeed. The greatest armada ever known—soldiers and sailors, warships, landing craft, tugboats, Jeeps, whatever—assembled along the southern coast of England in late spring 1944. At 9:15pm on June 5, the BBC announced to the French Resistance that the invasion was imminent, signaling the underground to start dynamiting the railways. Before midnight, Allied planes began bombing the Norman coast fortifications. By 1:30am on June 6, members of the 101st Airborne were parachuting to the ground on German-occupied French soil. At 6:30am the Americans began landing on the beaches code-named Utah and Omaha. An hour later British and Canadian forces made beachheads at Juno, Gold, and Sword.

The Nazis had mocked Churchill's promise in 1943 to liberate France "before the fall of the autumn leaves." When the invasion did come, it was swift, sudden, and a surprise to the formidable "Atlantic wall." Today aging veterans from Canada, the United States, and Britain walk with their children and grandchildren across the beaches where "Czech hedgehogs," "Belgian grills," pillboxes, and "Rommel asparagus" once stood.

ESSENTIALS

GETTING THERE   Out of Bayeux, bus service is a bit uneven and sometimes involves long delays. Bus Verts head for Port-en-Bessin and points west along the coast, and no. 74 buses offer service to Arromanches and other targets in the east.

It's best to explore the coast by car and not have to depend on public transportation.

VISITOR INFORMATION   The Office de Tourisme is at 4 rue du Maréchal-Joffre, Arromanches-les-Bains (☎ 31-21-47-56), open April to September.

EXPLORING THE BEACHES

The exploration of the D-Day Beaches begins at the modest seaside resort of **Arromanches-les-Bains.** In June 1944 it was a fishing port, until it was taken by the 50th British Division. Towed across the English Channel, a mammoth prefabricated port known as Winston was installed to supply the Allied forces. "Victory could not have been achieved without it," said Eisenhower. The wreckage of that artificial harbor—known as Mulberry—lies right off the beach, *la plage du débarquement.* The **Musée du Débarquement,** place du 6-Juin (☎ 31-22-34-31), features relief maps, working models, a cinema, and photographs. A diorama of the landing, with an English commentary, is featured. Admission to the museum is 30 F ($5.70). It's open daily: April to May 7 from 9 to 11:30am and 2 to 6pm, May 8 to September 4 from 9am to 6:30pm, and September 5 to March from 9 to 11:30am and 2 to 5:30pm.

Moving along the coast, you arrive at **Omaha Beach,** where you can still see the war wreckage. "Hanging on by their toenails," the men of the 1st and 29th American Divisions occupied the beach that June day. The code-name Omaha became famous throughout the world, though up to then the beaches had been called St-Laurent, Vierville-sur-Mer, and Colleville. A monument commemorates the heroism of the invaders. Covering some 173 acres at Omaha Beach, the **Normandy American Cemetery** (☎ **31-22-40-62**) is filled with crosses and stars of David in Lasa marble. The remains of 9,386 American military dead were buried here on territory now owned by the United States, a gift from the French nation. The cemetery is open daily from 9am to 5pm.

Farther along the coast you'll see the jagged lime cliffs of the **Pointe du Hoc.** A cross honors a group of American Rangers led by Lt.-Col. James Rudder, who scaled the cliff using hooks to get at the pillboxes. The scars of war are more visible here than at any other point along the beach.

Much farther along the Cotentin Peninsula is **Utah Beach,** where the 4th U.S. Infantry Division landed at 6:30am. The landing force was nearly 2 miles south of their intended destination, but, fortunately, Nazi defenses were weak at this point. By midday the infantry had completely cleared the beach. A U.S. monument commemorates their heroism.

Nearby you can visit **Ste-Mère-Eglise,** which not many people had heard of until the night of June 5 and 6, when parachutists were dropped over the town. They were from the 82nd U.S. Airborne Division, under the command of Gen. Matthew B. Ridgeway. Members of the 101st U.S. Airborne Division, commanded by Gen. M. B. Taylor, were also involved. Also in Ste-Mère-Eglise is Kilometer "0" on the Liberty Highway, marking the first of the milestones the American armies reached on their way to Metz and Bastogne.

More fervently than residents of any other region of France, Normans spent most of the summer of 1994 celebrating the 50th anniversary of D-Day. Representatives of 11 nations participated in the countless ceremonies, the most visible of which was held on Omaha Beach on June 6, when President Clinton, Queen Elizabeth II, and President Mitterrand shared the spotlight. Less elaborate observances were held in 1995 commemorating the 50th anniversary of the end of World War II in Europe.

WHERE TO DINE

Hôtel Duguesclin

4 quai Crampon, 14450 Grandcamp-Maisy. ☎ **31-22-64-22.** Reservations recommended. Fax 31-22-34-79. Fixed-price menus 85–170 F ($16.15–$32.30). MC, V. Daily noon–2pm and 7–9pm. Closed Jan 15–Feb 6. FRENCH.

We recommend this typical Norman inn for lunch or even for an overnight stay. The fish soup and Norman sole (if available) are excellent. Everything tastes better with the country bread and Norman butter.

The hotel rents 31 simple but comfortable rooms, 25 with bath (tub or shower) and all with TVs. A double without bath costs 150 F ($28.50) and a double with bath costs 265 F ($50.35); breakfast is 25 F ($4.75) extra.

La Marée

5 quai Chéron. ☎ **31-22-60-55.** Reservations required. Main courses 133–250 F ($25.25–$47.50); fixed-price menus 90–220 F ($17.10–$41.80). MC, V. Apr–Oct, daily 12:30–2:30pm and 7–9:30pm; Nov–Mar, Tues 12:30–2:30pm, Thurs–Mon 12:30–2:30pm and 7–9:30pm. NORMAN.

At the port, this small restaurant in a 1920s building is perfect for seafood devotees. The fish, always fresh and savory, is often bought from the boats that gathered the harvest. First try the fresh oysters, then perhaps the medley of monkfish, morels, and sweetbreads cooked in the same dish. Meals are served in the rustic dining room or on the outdoor terrace.

5 Mont-St-Michel

201 miles W of Paris, 80 miles SW of Caen, 47 miles E of Dinan, 30 miles E of St-Malo

One of Europe's great sightseeing attractions, ✪ **Mont-St-Michel** is surrounded by massive walls measuring more than half a mile in circumference. Connected to the shore by a causeway, it crowns a rocky islet at the border between Normandy and Brittany. The rock is 260 feet high.

You'll have a steep climb up Grande Rue, lined with 15th- and 16th-century houses, to reach the **abbey** (☎ **33-60-14-14**). Those who make it to the top can begin their exploration of the Marvel of the West. In the 8th century an oratory was founded on the spot by St. Aubert, the bishop of Avranches. It was replaced by a Benedictine monastery, founded in 966 by Richard I. That met with destruction by fire in 1203. Large parts of the abbey were financed by Philip Augustus in the 13th century.

Ramparts encircle the church and its ensemble of buildings, a part of which includes the **Merveille** (Marvel), one of the most important gothic masterpieces in Europe. One of these, the Salle des Chevaliers is most graceful. Begun in the 11th century, the abbey church consists of a romanesque nave and transept, plus a choir in the flamboyant gothic style. The rectangular refectory is from 1212, the cloisters with their columns of pink granite from 1225.

The abbey is open daily (with mass daily at 12:15pm): May 15 to September 15 from 9:30am to 6pm, February 16 to May 14 and September 16 to November 10 from 9:30 to 11:45am and 1:45 to 5pm, and November 11 to February 15 from 9:30 to 11:45am and 1:45 to 4:15pm. Guided tours, leaving every 15 minutes, are 45 minutes long. Tours in English are conducted daily at 10 and 11am, noon, and 1:30, 2:30, 3:30, 4:30, and 5:30pm—no tours in English are conducted on Friday. After the tour, you can enter the abbey gardens. The cost is 36 F ($6.80) for adults, 23 F ($4.35) for ages 18 to 25 and over 60, and 27 F ($5.10) for children 17 and under.

You can also visit the **Logis Tiphaine** (☎ **33-60-23-34**), the home of Tiphaine de Raguenel, wife of Bertrand Duguesclin, constable of France in the 16th century. From mid-February to mid-November only, it's open daily from 9am to 6:30pm; admission is 20 F ($3.80) for adults, 10 F ($1.90) for students, and 5 F (95¢) for children 11 and under.

ESSENTIALS

GETTING THERE   Mont-St-Michel can be reached by train from Paris (Gare Montparnasse); take the train to Dol and then transfer to Pontorson, the closest rail station.

From Pontorson, there's bus service to Mont-St-Michel, 6 miles away. Bus schedules are somewhat erratic, so you may have to take a taxi.

VISITOR INFORMATION   The Office de Tourisme is in the Corps de Garde des Bourgeois (the Old Guard Room of the Bourgeois), at the left of the town gates (☎ **33-60-14-30**). The office is open from February to November.

TIDES Mont-St-Michel historically has been noted for its tides, the highest on the Continent, measuring at certain times of the year a 50-foot difference between high and low tide. Unsuspecting tourists wandering across the sands (notorious for quicksands) have been trapped as the sea rushes toward the Mont at a speed comparable to that of a galloping horse. However, the bay around the abbey has silted not only because of the causeway but because of various barriers and dikes erected. Today tides engulf the island less and less frequently. France will spend $110 million over the next few years replacing the milelong causeway with a bridge so water can lap freely around the Mont. Parking lots will be moved farther away from the abbey, and both the causeway and as-yet-unbuilt bridge will be closed to visitors. Bridge construction and other engineering works will be launched in 1996.

PARKING It's free to park your car on the causeway-bridge, but spaces are tight as you approach the Mont. There are also some small free lots near the end of the causeway. The largest of the public parking lots charges 15 F ($2.85) per day—note that this lot becomes flooded at high tide and cars make a scramble to get out before the waters arrive; there's ample time warning for drivers, however.

WHERE TO STAY

Hôtel du Mouton-Blanc
Grande Rue, 50116 Mont-St-Michel. ☎ **33-60-14-08.** Fax 33-60-05-62. 22 rms. TEL. 300–600 F ($57–$114.05) double. Breakfast 50 F ($9.50) extra. MC, V.

This inn stands halfway between the sea and the famous basilica. The lower floors contain the restaurant; the simple double rooms available for guests are upstairs. Tables are set in a Norman-style dining room and on a terrace overlooking the sea. As in most restaurants here, omelets are offered, along with fruits de mer (fruits of the sea). Local specialties are mussels in cream sauce and several preparations of lobster. Fixed-price menus are 70 F ($13.30) and 250 F ($47.50). A crêperie is also on site.

Les Terrasses Poulard
Grande Rue, 50116 Mont-St-Michel. ☎ **33-60-14-09.** Fax 33-60-37-31. 29 rms. MINIBAR TV TEL. 300–950 F ($57–$180.60) double. Breakfast 60 F ($11.40) extra. AE, DC, MC, V.

This inn was formed when two village houses—one medieval, the other built in the 1800s—were united. Today the establishment is one of the best in town, with an English-speaking staff. The rates depend on the view: of the pedestrian traffic on the main street, a pleasant garden, or the medieval ramparts. The largest and most expensive rooms have fireplaces. The restaurant offers a sweeping view over the bay and seafood and regional specialties. Fixed-price meals cost 69 to 150 F ($13.10 to $28.50).

WHERE TO DINE

La Mère Poulard
Grande Rue, 50116 Mont-St-Michel. ☎ **33-60-14-01.** Reservations recommended. Main courses 150–180 F ($28.50–$34.20); fixed-price menus 350–450 F ($66.50–$85.55). AE, DC, MC, V. Daily noon–2pm and 7–9pm. NORMAN.

This country inn is a shrine to those who revere the omelet that Annette Poulard created in 1888 when the hotel was founded. Her "secret" has been passed on to the inn's operators: The beaten eggs are cooked over an oak hearth fire in a long-handled copper skillet. The frothy mixture really creates more of an open-fire soufflé than an omelet. Other specialties include lamb (agneau du pré salé) raised on the saltwater marshes near the foundations of the abbey and an array of fish, including lobster.

The inn also rents 27 rooms. A double ranges from 650 to 950 F ($123.55 to $180.60), with breakfast 60 F ($11.40) extra.

NEARBY ACCOMMODATIONS & DINING

⑤ La Verte Campagne

Hameau Chevalier par Trelly, 50660 Quettreville. ☎ 33-47-65-33. 7 rms, 4 with bath. TEL. 220–260 F ($41.80–$49.40) double without bath, 380 F ($72.20) double with bath. MC, V. Parking free. Closed Jan 6–31 and Dec 1–8. Take D7 north from Avranches to Lengronne and follow the signs 2¹/₂ miles north from Trelly.

This 1717 Norman farmhouse is about 30 miles north of Mont-St-Michel, and you'll be welcomed by Mme Bernou and her cats. The farmhouse has been sumptuously decorated with antiques and lots of brass. If you're spending the night, ask for the double room that has red carpeting, curtains, bedcover, and vanity—all in harmony with the pink "Vichy" pattern. In the restaurant, fixed-price menus cost 140 F ($26.60) and 350 F ($66.50); à la carte meals begin at 225 F ($42.75). Specialties include chicken and lamb raised on the property, magrêt of duckling with walnut-butter sauce, and saffron-flavored monkfish. Hours are 12:30 to 2:30pm and 7:30 to 9:30pm; no meals are served Sunday night or Monday in winter or Monday lunch in summer. Nonguests are welcome but should phone ahead for a table.

6 Deauville

128 miles NW of Paris, 29 miles NE of Caen

Deauville has always been associated with the rich and famous. In 1913 Coco Chanel launched her career here by opening a boutique selling tiny hats. The fashion at the time was huge-brimmed hats loaded with flowers and fruit, and Coco asked, "How can the mind breathe under those things?" Today's visitors still put on their best for the evening activities, including concerts, ballets, and the nightclub/casino where some of the biggest names in Europe perform.

Parasols dot the beach and jet setters abound—especially in August. Many chic bathers, with their hangers-on and wannabes, strut the boardwalk just to see and be seen and occasionally stop for an apéritif at Le Bar du Soleil. One French comtesse confided to us that she diets for three months before coming here to sun. Visit the aptly named **Plage Fleurie,** covered with bright flowers.

Trouville (see below), built in the days of Louis-Philippe, was the most fashionable resort until 1859, when the duc de Morny (Napoléon III's half brother) founded Deauville, which quickly took the lead. With its golf courses, casinos, deluxe hotels, La Touques and Clairefontaine racetracks, regattas, yachting harbor, polo grounds, and tennis courts, Deauville is still a formidable contender for the business of the smart set.

Inaugurated in 1912 and site of innumerable elegant comings and goings since, the **Casino de Deauville,** rue Edmond-Blanc (☎ 31-14-31-14), is one of France's premier casinos. Its original belle époque core has been expanded with a theater, a nightclub, three restaurants, and an extensive collection of slot machines (*machines à sous*). Jackets but not ties are required for men.

The Glittering Literati of Normandy

Normandy has been the birthplace of more world-class literature than any other province of France. Some scholars think that the region's deeply entrenched monastic traditions kept learning and literature alive during eras when other parts of Europe slumbered in undistinguished obscurity. Others credit a coastal position beside one of Europe's busiest waterways for a cosmopolitan blend of literary influences from France, England, and Scandinavia.

Madame de Sévigné called Normandy's intellectual center, Caen (site of a university founded in the 1400s), "the source of all of our finest minds." Poet François de Malherbe was born in Caen in 1555 at 126 rue St-Pierre and is honored with a plaque on the building's facade, a lycée named after him, and a prominent statue on place St-Sauveur.

France's first major dramatist, Pierre Corneille, was born at 4 rue de la Pie in Rouen's historic core and educated there by the Jesuits. And though Racine was not from Rouen (or Normandy), both his mistress (actress La Champmeslé, née Marie Desmarest) and his bitterest rival, playwright Pradon, were as Rouennais as canard au sang.

Few writers are as associated with Normandy as Gustave Flaubert. For years, he reconfigured scenes and passages from *Madame Bovary* in his Norman garden, and his depiction of Honfleur is a tribute to the 19th-century aesthetics of the English Channel ports. He was born in Rouen's Hôtel-Dieu (hospital) at 51 rue de Lecat (see the Rouen section at the beginning of this chapter).

Guy de Maupassant moved to Rouen, befriended Flaubert—who helped tighten his often-rambling prose—and drew inspiration for *Boule-de-suif* from a Norman brothel set beside the water in either Fécamp or Rouen.

Marcel Proust spent holidays in Cabourg, where he stayed at the Grand Hôtel, calming his asthma and developing an obsession for a dashing taxi driver named Alfred Agostinelli, whose charm and male flesh were later transmuted into the female character of Albertine in *Remembrance of Things Past*. He combined his memories of Cabourg with visual aspects of Trouville—and, to a lesser extent, Evian—to create the mythic seaside resort of Balbec, site of key events in his masterpiece.

Though they're rarely read outside France, the province has also produced such writers as Lucie Delarue-Mardrus, Jean de la Varende, and Barbey d'Aurevilly.

From July 1 to September 15, the main body of the casino is open daily from 3:30pm to 3am (the area with the slot machines opens at 10am). Off-season, the room with slot machines opens at 11am and the entire casino is open from 3pm to 2am. The most interesting nights here are Friday and Saturday, when all the restaurants and the cabaret theater are open. The theater presents shows at 10:30pm on Friday and Saturday. Entrance costs 120 F ($22.80) per person.

Restaurants Le Banco, the most upscale in the casino, with meals beginning at 325 F ($61.75), and La Dolce Vita (a middle-bracket Italian restaurant) serve dinner only on Friday and Saturday. The Café de la Boule is open daily for both lunch and dinner and is the least formal of the trio. Le Régine's, a newer version of a club patterned on the famous nightclub in Paris, is open only on Friday and Saturday from 10pm until very late. Cover is 130 F ($24.70).

ESSENTIALS

GETTING THERE   There are four rail connections from Paris's Gare St-Lazare (trip time: $2^1/_2$ hr.), costing 138 F ($26.20) one way. The rail depot is between Trouville and Deauville, south of the town.

Bus Verts du Calvados serves the lower Normandy coast from Caen to Le Havre.

VISITOR INFORMATION   The Office de Tourisme is on place Mairie (☎ 31-88-21-43).

SPECIAL EVENTS   For a week in early September, the **Deauville Film Festival** honors movies made in the United States only. Actors, producers, directors, and writers flock here and briefly eclipse the high rollers at the casinos and the horse-race/polo crowd. No prizes are awarded to the films; oddly, a prize for literature is the only one given.

WHERE TO STAY
EXPENSIVE

Hôtel du Golf

At New-Golf, Mont Canisy, St-Arnoult 14800 Deauville. ☎ **31-88-19-01.** Fax 31-88-75-99. 168 rms, 10 suites. MINIBAR TV TEL. 890–1,350 F ($169.10–$256.50) double; 1,800–2,500 F ($342–$475) suite. Breakfast 90 F ($17.10) extra. AE, DC, MC, V. Parking free. Closed Nov–Mar 15. From Deauville, take D278 south for $1^1/_2$ miles.

Sports fans—especially golfers—gravitate to this colossal Norman inn. Rising only four floors, it's one of the few hotels in Normany with its own adjoining golf course. The lobby is old-fashioned. Accommodations come in a wide range of sizes, many with traditional pieces and such amenities as hairdryers; some rooms have balconies. The older rooms aren't as good as the more recently renovated ones; those in back open onto the links, but those in front have better views over the Channel.

Dining/Entertainment: A glass-enclosed dining room encircles a veranda, offering views of the Channel. The food doesn't rate a trip here but is competently prepared in the international style. Poolside barbecues are a summer feature.

Services: Room service, laundry.

Facilities: Heated pool, sauna, three tennis courts, 27-hole golf course.

✪ Normandy

38 rue Jean-Mermoz, 14800 Deauville. ☎ **31-98-66-22.** Fax 31-98-66-23. 276 rms, 25 suites. MINIBAR TV TEL. 890–2,200 F ($169.10–$418) double; from 1,720 F ($326.80) suite. Breakfast 90 F ($17.10) extra. AE, DC, MC, V. Parking free.

Resembling a Norman village, with turrets, gables, and windows piercing sloping roofs, this year-round hotel is near the casino, in a park of well-manicured shrubs and flowers. It's Deaville's best hotel, though certain people prefer the Royal (below). The interior is as warm and comfortable as a rambling country house, with chandeliers and Oriental carpeting. Activities center around the main rotunda, encircled by a marble colonnade. The rooms are in a constant state of refurbishment, with double-glazed windows and mirrored closets setting the tone. Fourth-floor units under sloping ceilings are the most cramped.

Dining/Entertainment: Guests gather in the paneled piano bar before selecting one of three restaurants: a gourmet enclave, the main dining room, or a restaurant dedicated to lighter cooking.

Services: Room service, laundry.
Facilities: Heated indoor pool, sauna, underground garage.

✪ Le Royal

Bd. Eugène-Cornuché, 14800 Deauville. ☎ **31-98-66-33.** Fax 31-98-66-34. 298 rms, 16 suites. A/C MINIBAR TV TEL. 1,250–2,200 F ($237.50–$418) double; 1,800–7,000 F ($342–$1,330) suite. Breakfast 120 F ($22.80) extra. AE, DC, MC, V. Parking free. Closed Nov–Mar.

Le Royal adjoins the casino and fronts a blockwide park between itself and the Channel. An ideal place for a holiday, provided you're well heeled, it rises like a regal palace, with columns and exposed timbers. Accommodations range from sumptuous suites to cozy little nooks. More than two dozen rooms were recently renovated, with designer fabrics and thick rugs. Other rooms seem to languish back in the 1970s. Some of the suites are named for movie stars. Accommodations on the upper floors, of course, open onto the most panoramic views.

Dining/Entertainment: L'Etrier is the chic choice for dining, and Sundays are caviar nights. The chef often creates innovative courses. There's also terrace dining in summer.

Services: Room service, laundry.
Facilities: Heated pool, sauna, two recreation rooms, health club.

MODERATE

⑤ Le Continental

1 rue Désiré-le-Hoc, 14800 Deauville. ☎ **31-88-21-06.** Fax 31-98-93-67. 42 rms, 6 suites. TV TEL. 280–410 F ($53.20–$77.90) double; from 500 F ($95) suite. Breakfast 37 F ($7.05) extra. AE, DC, MC, V. Closed Nov 15–Dec 20.

This simple hotel offers rooms that are comfortably furnished and well kept. Breakfast is the only meal served here, but the hotel has a bar. The owner is usually on hand to assist you. Though the hotel doesn't get a rave, in high-priced Deauville it's an oasis.

⑤ Hôtel Ibis

9 quai de la Marine, 14800 Deauville. ☎ **31-41-50-90.** Fax 31-14-50-05. 95 rms, 11 suites. TV TEL. 305–440 F ($57.95–$83.60) double; 660 F ($125.40) suite. Breakfast 39 F ($7.40) extra. MC, V. Parking 38 F ($7.20).

Part of a nationwide chain, the Hôtel Ibis is scenically located and offers some of the best values of any hotel in Deauville. The modern building overlooks the harbor; the rooms are comfortable but in a rather dull chain format. The hotel restaurant offers a traditional French menu, with meals starting at 79 F ($15).

WHERE TO DINE
EXPENSIVE

✪ Le Ciro's

Promenade des Planches. ☎ **31-88-18-10.** Reservations required. Main courses 95–195 F ($18.05–$37.05); fixed-price meals 190–320 F ($36.10–$60.80). AE, DC, MC, V. Daily noon–2:30pm and 7:15–10pm. FRENCH.

You can't be more chic than Le Ciro's, which serves Deauville's best seafood—expensive but worth it. As you enter, you can make your lobster selection from a tank; the kitchen stocks a wide range of delectable oysters and mussels. If you want a bit of everything, ask for the plateau de fruits de mer, with lobster and various oysters and clams. The most expensive item is grilled lobster. For an elaborate appetizer, we recommend a foie gras of duckling or lobster salad with truffles. Classic French courses like grilled beef filet with béarnaise and grilled lamb cutlets also are offered. The least expensive way to dine here is to order one of the fixed-price meals. The collection of Bordeaux wine is exceptional.

☼ Le Spinnaker

52 rue Mirabeau. ☎ **31-88-24-40.** Reservations required. Main courses 140–270 F ($26.60–$51.30); fixed-price meals 160 F ($30.40), 220 F ($41.80), 250 F ($47.50), and 320 F ($60.80). AE, MC, V. Thurs–Tues 12:30–2:30 and 7:30–10pm. Closed Jan and Wed–Thurs Oct–Mar. NORMAN.

This charming restaurant is in a half-timbered building. Directed by owner/chef Pascal Angenard, it features regional cuisine and is filled with English chintz and white napery. Menu specialties are ultra-fresh and richly satisfying, like terrine of foie gras with four spices, roast lobster with cider vinegar and cream-enriched potatoes, slow-cooked baby veal flank, and a succulent tart with hot apples. A fine array of wines can accompany your meal. There are nights when a dish here or there might not always be sublime, but usually most are excellent.

MODERATE

⑤ Brasserie-Crêperie Deauville-Trouville

90 rue Eugène-Colas. ☎ **31-88-81-72.** Reservations not required. Main-course crêpes 28–48 F ($5.30–$9.10); fixed-price menu 59 F ($11.20). MC, V. Daily Tues–Sun noon–8pm. FRENCH.

This place offers fast food and fast times *à la française*, and its set menu is among the best values in town. Try the tasty cut of beef, onglet, served with shallots or a plat du jour. You can select from the shellfish and fish menus or even order a crêpe. The brasserie also serves velvety ice cream. At the self-service cafeteria downstairs you can order sandwiches and salads. One floor above street level is the more formal brasserie with waiter service. Also on the premises is the English-style Pub 90, open daily from 9pm to 4am.

Chez Miocque

81 rue Eugène-Colas. ☎ **31-88-09-52.** Reservations recommended. Main courses 85–150 F ($16.15–$28.50); fixed price menus 150–200 F ($28.50–$38). MC, V. May–Oct, daily 9am–midnight; Mar–Apr and Nov–Dec, Thurs–Mon noon–3pm and 7pm–midnight. Closed Jan–Feb. FRENCH.

This brasserie/café near the casino and the fashionable boutiques does a bustling business at its sidewalk tables. The owner, known simply as Jack, is an American from New York City who'll welcome you for lunch, dinner, or just drinks. You get hearty brasserie-style food, including mussels, fish, and steaks. The portions are filling, and the atmosphere can be the liveliest in Deauville.

7 Trouville

128 miles NW of Paris, 27 miles NE of Caen

This resort launched the Côte Fleurie—the Flower Coast—at the start of the Second Empire. As the first major seaside resort in France, it was developed during the days of Louis-Philippe and has long been fashionable. It lies across the Touques River from its more sophisticated (and more expensive) rival, Deauville.

Admittedly, Trouville is old, but like a charming countess it wears its years with hautiness, covering a wrinkle with a mere blush. Time was when Trouville was the formal resort; nowadays it gives Deauville that privilege, as it's noisier and more fun for some. When the sea bathers have left Trouville's splendid sands to return to Paris or wherever, Trouville lives. Its hardcore resident population of fisherfolk see to that.

On the seafront Promenade des Planches is a large swimming pool, called the **Piscine Olympique,** and an impressive **casino** (yet not as grand as the one at Deauville).

ESSENTIALS

GETTING THERE   There are rail connections from Gare St-Lazare in Paris to Trouville. See the Deauville section, above.

Bus Verts du Calvados serves the coast from Caen to Le Havre and Bus Inter Normandie serves the region from Caen to Rouen.

VISITOR INFORMATION   The Syndicat d'Initiative (tourist office) is at 32 quai Fernand-Moureaux (☎ **31-88-36-19**).

WHERE TO STAY

Carmen
24 rue Carnot, 14360 Trouville. ☎ **31-88-35-43.** Fax 31-88-08-03. 17 rms, 13 with bath. MINIBAR TV TEL. 430 F ($81.70) double without bath, 580 F ($110.25) double with bath. Rates include half board. AE, DC, MC, V.

This Logis de France consists of two connected late 18th-century villas, one designed by a cousin of Georges Bizet. The management prefers that guests book in on the half-board plan. It's run by the Bude family, whom some guests find a bit bourgeois and smug. The rooms are simply furnished, some overlooking a flower-filled courtyard. The restaurant is closed on Tuesday between January 15 and February 15.

Hôtel St-James
16 rue de la Plage, 14360 Trouville. ☎ **31-88-05-23.** 14 rms. 450 F ($85.55) double. Breakfast 50 F ($9.50) extra. Parking free. MC, V.

Built in 1834 as a private mansion, this is the most interesting place to stay at Trouville, turned into a hotel in 1957 and most recently renovated in 1995. The social center of the hotel is a Louis XIII salon, and each guest room is charmingly decorated. The hotel serves breakfast only, but does operate a bar.

Maison Normande
4 place Maréchal-de-Lattre-Tassigny, 14360 Trouville. ☎ **31-88-12-25.** 20 rms. TEL. 380–345 F ($72.20–$65.55) double. Breakfast 36 F ($6.80) extra. MC, V. Parking free. Closed Oct–Feb.

This little hotel is a good bargain on the resort's main street, a few blocks from the beach. The lounges are cozy, with rustic touches like heavy beams and a fireplace. The rooms are simple but comfortable. Breakfast is the only meal served. This is a clean, safe haven—not a lot else.

WHERE TO DINE

⊕ La Petite Auberge
7 rue Carnot. ☎ **31-88-11-07.** Reservations required. Fixed-price menus 110 F ($20.90), 160 F ($30.40), 180 F ($34.20), and 240 F ($45.60). MC, V. July–Aug, daily noon–2:30pm and 7–10pm; Sept–June, Thurs–Tues noon–2:30pm and 7–10pm. FRENCH.

If you want something inexpensive without sacrificing quality, try this Norman bistro just a block from the casino. We recently enjoyed an excellent meal for 110 F

($20.90). Try the soupe de poissons (fish soup), one of the finest along the Flower Coast, or the seafood pot-au-feu. You can also order grilled beef and roast lamb. Since there are only 30 seats, reservations are vital in summer. Hopefully, there'll be major improvements in the wine carte by the time you visit.

Les Vapeurs

160 bd. Fernand-Moureaux. ☎ **31-88-15-24.** Reservations recommended. Main courses 50–150 F ($9.50–$28.50). AE, V. Daily 12:30pm–1am. FRENCH.

This art deco brasserie, one of the most popular on the Norman coast, is frequented by Parisians on *le weekend.* This has been called the Brasserie Lipp of Normandy. The windows face the port, and in warm weather you can dine at sidewalk tables. Seafood is the specialty, and a wide range of shrimp, mussels laced with cream, crinkle-shelled oysters, and fish is offered. Sauerkraut is also popular. Patrons here seem to have a good time and enjoy the food.

8 Honfleur

125 miles NW of Paris, 39 miles NE of Caen

At the mouth of the Seine, opposite Le Havre, Honfleur is one of Normandy's most charming fishing ports. It's actually 500 years older than Le Havre, dating from the 11th century. Early in the 17th century colonists set out for Québec in Canada. The township has long been favored by artists, including Daubigny, Corot, and Monet. Baudelaire wrote *Invitation au Voyage* here.

From place de la Porte-de-Rouen you can begin your tour of the town, which should take about an hour. Stroll along the **Vieux Bassin,** the old harbor, which has fishing boats and slate-roofed narrow houses. The former governor's house, **Lieutenance,** on the north side of the basin, dates from the 16th century. Nearby is the **Eglise Ste-Catherine,** built entirely of timber in the 15th century by shipbuilders. The church's belfry stands on the other side of the street and is also of wood.

The **Musée Eugène-Boudin,** place Erik-Satie (☎ **31-89-54-00**), has a good collection of the painters who flocked to this port. The largest collection is of the pastels and paintings of Eugène Boudin, of course. It's open March 15 to September, Wednesday to Monday from 10am to noon and 2 to 6pm; October to March 14, Monday and Wednesday to Friday from 2:30 to 5pm and Saturday and Sunday from 10am to noon and 2:30 to 5pm. Admission is 20 F ($3.80).

ESSENTIALS

GETTING THERE Three Bus Verts connect Caen and Honfleur per day (trip time: 2 hr.), costing 65 F ($12.35) one way.

If you're driving in from Pont l'Evêque to the south, D579 leads to the major boulevard, rue de la République. Follow it until the end for the town center.

VISITOR INFORMATION The Office de Tourisme is on place Arthur-Boudin (☎ **31-89-23-30**).

WHERE TO STAY

✪ La Ferme St-Simeon

Route Adolphe-Marais, 14600 Honfleur. ☎ **31-89-23-61.** Fax 31-89-48-48. 38 rms, 4 suites. MINIBAR TV TEL. 1,460–3,000 F ($277.40–$570) double; from 3,510 F ($666.90) suite. Breakfast 95 F ($18.05) extra. MC, V. Parking free.

An old cider press is a focal point in front of this 17th-century Norman wood-and-slate house. The light and shimmering water of the English Channel drew artists to this hilltop inn, said to be the place where impressionism was born in the 19th century. Today the atmosphere is tranquil thanks to owner Roland Boelen. Much of the hotel has terra-cotta floors, carved wood, and copper and faïence touches. The guest rooms are decorated in an 18th-century style. Food is served in the restaurant or on the terrace, with a view of the Seine estuary and Le Havre. The classic yet simple cuisine is superb: Try the chausson of lobster, fricassée of rice and kidneys, or sole normande. Meals run 420 to 550 F ($79.80 to $104.55). The bar is used for drinks and breakfast. Facilities include tennis courts, a heated indoor pool, a sauna, a solarium, massage service, a fitness center, and a whirlpools.

⊗ Hostellerie Lechat

3 place Ste-Catherine, 14600 Honfleur. ☎ **31-89-23-85.** Fax 31-89-28-61. 22 rms, 1 suite. TV TEL. 360–460 F ($68.40–$87.45) double; 700 F ($133.05) suite. Breakfast 45 F ($8.55) extra. AE, DC, MC, V. Parking free. Closed Jan. Bus 20 or 50.

This hotel is run to perfection under the supervision of owner Jean-Luc Blais. The comfortably furnished rooms, though modest, are fine for an overnight stopover at the center of the port. The rustic restaurant offers an array of seafood, like sole, salmon, and turbot, plus lobster (very expensive) and oysters. The chef also does some superb terrines. A fixed-price meal costs 135 to 195 F ($25.65 to $37.05). The restaurant is closed on Wednesday and for lunch on Thursday. The hotel is closed in January except on Saturday night.

WHERE TO DINE

✪ L'Assiette Gourmande

2 quai des Passagers. ☎ **31-89-24-88.** Reservations required. Main courses 90–195 F ($17.10–$37.05); fixed-price menus 160–395 F ($30.40–$75.10). AE, DC, MC, V. Tues–Sun noon–2:15pm and 7–9:45pm. FRENCH.

Beside the medieval port, this is the town's finest restaurant. On the street level of the Cheval Blanc hotel, with which it's not associated, this restaurant is the domain of Gérard and Anne-Marie Bonnefoy, who serve delicious dishes like roasted crayfish with a marinade of two vegetables, roast turbot with essence of chicken, and the house specialty, lobster omelet. The chef has been faulted for his "too active" imagination, as exemplified by his Camembert with a peppery caramel, but he has his fans.

Restaurant l'Absinthe

10 quai de la Quarantaine. ☎ **31-89-39-00.** Reservations required. Main courses 120–210 F ($22.80–$39.90); fixed-price meals 159–248 F ($30.20–$47.10). AE, DC, MC, V. Daily 12:15–2:15pm and 7:15–9:15pm. Bus 20 or 50. FRENCH.

This tavern—named for the drink preferred by many 19th-century writers in Honfleur—is known by practically everyone in town for its beautiful decor, extravagant portions, and well-prepared savory cuisine. It has two dining rooms—one from the 17th century, one from the 15th. Chef Antoine Ceffrey, who apprenticed for many years at Troisgros, will probably make an appearance in the dining rooms before the end of your meal. Menu choices may be veal kidneys with Calvados, baked turbot with pepper sauce, and attractive desserts like assorted fresh fruit with essence of raspberries.

Brittany 13

In their ancient northwestern province, many Bretons stubbornly cling to their traditions. Deep in l'Argoat (the interior), older folks quietly live in stone farmhouses, like their grandparents had, and on special occasions the women still wear the trademark starched-lace headdresses. The Breton language is still spoken, but it's better understood by the Welsh and Cornish than by the French. Sadly, it may die out altogether, in spite of attempts by folklore groups to keep it alive.

Nearly every hamlet has its own *pardon*, a religious festival that sometimes attracts thousands of pilgrims who don traditional dress. The best-known ones are on May 19 at Treguier (honoring St. Yves), on the second Sunday in July at Locronan (honoring St. Ronan), on July 26 at St-Anne-d'Auray (honoring the "mothers of Bretons"), and on September 8 at Le Folgoet (honoring *ar foll coat*—"idiot of the forest").

Traditionally, the province is divided into Haute-Bretagne and Basse-Bretagne. The rocky coastline, some 750 miles long, is studded with promontories, coves, and beaches. Like the prow of a ship, Brittany projects into the sea. The interior, however, is a land of sleepy hamlets, stone farmhouses, and moors covered with yellow broom and purple heather. We suggest that first-time visitors to the craggy peninsula stick to the coast, where salt-meadow sheep can be seen grazing along pastureland whipped by sea breezes. Those leaving Mont-St-Michel in Normandy can use St-Malo, Dinan, or Dinard as a base. Visitors coming from the château country can explore the south Brittany coastline.

REGIONAL CUISINE   Breton cuisine derives its excellence from the flavors and freshness of its ingredients rather than from the skill of its preparation. Seafood is abundant here: oysters, shellfish, barnacles, and crabs from the Breton coastline are famous throughout France. Many are served raw, especially the Belon oysters, as appetizers (served on a bed of seaweed with a lemon/onion sauce and white wine).

Other regional specialties include *homard* (lobster) in cream sauce, grilled, or à l'armoricaine; salmon and brochet; trout and l'alose, excellent with one of the Loire's fruity whites; and lamb and mutton, raised on the salt marshes. *Gigot à la bretonne* (leg of lamb), traditionally served with white beans, is one of France's great dishes.

The ducklings of Nantes and chickens of Rennes are excellent, as are the strawberries of Plougastel.

Brittany is closely associated with crêpes, those wonderful thin pancakes served plain, sweet, or salted and often filled with jam, cheese, ham, salad, or eggs. Most villages have their own crêperie, some of which sell crêpes right on the street.

The only famous wine produced in Brittany is Muscadet, cultivated near Nantes, an excellent complement to seafood.

EXPLORING THE REGION BY CAR

Here's how to link together the best of the region if you rent a car.

Day 1   Visit St-Malo and Dinard, admiring the rocky sea walls and touring the ramparts of those ancient ports, less than 4 miles from each other across the estuary of the Rance River. Spend the night in whichever of the two strikes your fancy.

Days 2–3   Drive south for 12 miles along D766, stopping for midmorning coffee or lunch in Dinan. Then drive west along D766, E401, and E50 for 140 miles. At Brest, head south for 38 miles on E60 to Quimper, one of Brittany's folkloric centerpieces. Spend two nights in the neighborhood, admiring the slate-roofed buildings and crashing seas, stopping in La Forêt-Fouesnant and Concorneau. Plan at least a lunch in a medieval village about a mile south of Locronan: Along the D107 highway is the 17th-century Manoir de Moëllien (☎ 98-92-50-40), where meals are served daily between June and September, and every day except Wednesday the rest of the year, from 12:30 to 2pm and 7:30 to 9pm. The manor also rents 10 rooms in a 19th-century barn.

Days 4–5   These days are for hopping between folkloric towns like Pont-Aven, Riec-sur-Belon, and Hennebont, no more than 10 miles from one another. En route you'll probably want to stop at Quimperlé, at the confluence of the Isole and Ellé rivers, which merge to form the Laïta. There's little to do there than admire the town's mossy charm and visit one of Brittany's most exotic medieval churches, the Eglise de la Sainte-Croix, rue Brémond-d'Art. A worthy place for a meal is the Bistro de la Tour, 2 rue Dom-Morice (☎ 98-39-29-58), open for lunch and dinner daily (except Saturday at lunch and Sunday evening).

Days 6–7   Arise early for a full-day excursion southeast along E60 for about 90 miles to La Baule. Stopovers en route could include the Quiberon Peninsula (site of a noted sardine port) and Carnac (site of thousands of mysterious cromlechs and dolmens erected in misty prehistory). If time is no problem, opt for an overnight stay on the sleepy offshore island of Belle-Ile-en-Mer. Otherwise, spend the night in La Baule and enjoy the next day exploring western France's premier beach resort, on the sands of La Côte d'Amour.

1 Nantes

239 miles SW of Paris, 202 miles N of Bordeaux

Nantes is Brittany's largest town, though in spirit it seems to belong more to the Loire Valley's château country. The mouth of the Loire is 30 miles away, and here it divides into several branches. A commercial/industrial city, Nantes is a busy port that suffered great damage in World War II. The city is best known for the Edict of Nantes, sponsored by Henri IV in 1598, guaranteeing religious freedom to Protestants (it was later revoked). Many famous people have lived here, from Molière to Mme de Sévigné to Stendhal to Michelet.

Brittany

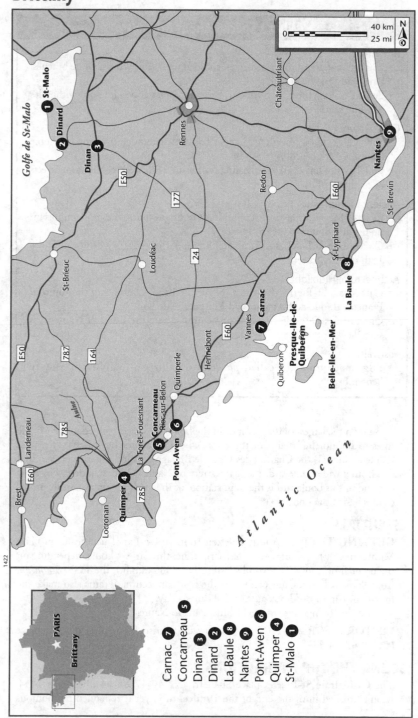

Carnac **7**
Concarneau **5**
Dinan **3**
Dinard **2**
La Baule **8**
Nantes **9**
Pont-Aven **6**
Quimper **4**
St-Malo **1**

What's Special About Brittany

Beaches
- 750 miles of grand rocky coastline, studded with sandy coves, white beaches, bays, and little fishing villages.
- La Baule, along the Côte d'Amour, Brittany's premier beach resort, with miles of white sand.

Great Towns
- Ville-Close, Concarneau, an ancient hamlet surrounded by ramparts, some from the 14th century.
- Old Town, Dinan, a 1¹/₂-mile circuit of walls, with steep cobblestone streets of medieval houses.

Ancient Monuments
- Field of Megaliths at Carnac, hundreds of huge stones, the most important prehistoric find in northern France.
- Château de la Duchesse Anne at Dinan, a 14th-century dungeon and a 15th-century tower.

Architectural Highlights
- Cathédrale St-Pierre at Nantes, begun in 1434, containing the tomb of François II, duc de Bretagne, and Marguerite de Foix.
- Château des Ducs de Bretagne at Nantes, where the Edict of Nantes was signed.

Festivals
- Pilgrimage festivals, called *pardons,* organized usually from May to September.

Built on the largest of three islands in the Loire, the city expanded in the Middle Ages to the northern edge of the river, where its center lies today. The most visible building is the Château des Ducs de Bretagne, which rises several hundred feet from a wide boulevard, the main artery of Nantes—the quai de la Fosse. At one end of this boulevard is the train station; at the other are the waterside promenades beside the Loire.

ESSENTIALS

GETTING THERE   About a dozen trains leave Paris, usually from Gare Montparnasse, for Nantes every day (trip time: three to six hours, depending on the number of stops). The world's fastest train (300 m.p.h.), the TGV *Atlantique* from Paris to Rennes and Nantes, is the best connection. Trains also make the four-hour trip to Bordeaux at least five times a day.

If you're driving, note that A11 links Paris to Nantes.

VISITOR INFORMATION   The Office de Tourisme is on place du Commerce (☎ 40-47-04-51).

SEEING THE TOP ATTRACTIONS

The **Cathédrale St-Pierre,** place St-Pierre (☎ 40-47-84-64), begun in 1434, wasn't finished until the end of the 19th century, yet it remained harmonious

Nantes

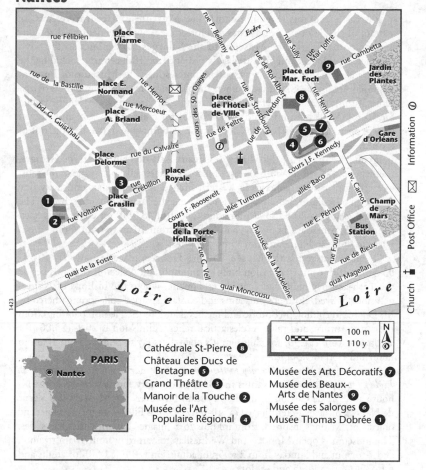

Information	⊕
Post Office	⊠
Church	✠

Cathédrale St-Pierre **8**
Château des Ducs de
  Bretagne **5**
Grand Théâtre **3**
Manoir de la Touche **2**
Musée de l'Art
  Populaire Régional **4**

Musée des Arts Décoratifs **7**
Musée des Beaux-
  Arts de Nantes **9**
Musée des Salorges **6**
Musée Thomas Dobrée **1**

PARIS
● Nantes

0 [   ] 100 m
           110 y
N

architecturally—a rare feat. The facade is dominated by two square towers, but the 335-foot-long interior is more impressive. Its pièce-de-résistance, however, is Michel Colomb's Renaissance tomb of François II, duc de Bretagne, and his second wife, Marguerite de Foix. Another impressive work is the tomb of Gen. Juchault de Lamoricière, a native of Nantes and a great African campaigner; sculptor Paul Dubois completed the tomb in 1879. After a 1972 fire destroyed the roof (rebuilt 1975), the interior was restored. The white walls and pillars contrast with the rich colors of the stained-glass windows. The crypt, from the 11th century, shelters a museum of religions. The cathedral is open daily from 8:45am to 7pm.

Between the cathedral and the Loire is Nantes' second major sight, where the Edict of Nantes was discussed and signed: the **Château des Ducs de Bretagne,** 1 place Marc-Elder (☎ **40-41-56-56**), once the seat of the ducs de Bretagne. The castle was built in the 9th or 10th century, and François II began reconstruction in 1466. It's flanked by large towers and a bastion. The duchesse du Berry was imprisoned here, as was Gilles de Retz, known as "Bluebeard," who confessed to more than 100 murders.

The castle contains three museums. The **Museum of Decorative Arts,** in a room of the Tour du Fer à Cheval (Horseshoe Tower), is dedicated to contemporary textile art. The **Museum of the Salorges** has exhibits on the city's commercial, colonial, and industrial activities since the 18th century, including the slave trade. The ship models are especially interesting. The **Museum of Popular Regional Art** (in the Grand Gouvernement building) presents many aspects of costumes, furniture, and handcrafts of the Bretons. All three museums can be visited for 30 F ($5.70) for adults and 10 F ($1.90) for children. In July and August they're open daily from 10am to noon and 2 to 6pm; closed Tuesday the rest of the year.

If you have time, visit the **Musée des Beaux-Arts de Nantes,** 10 rue Georges-Clemenceau (☎ 40-41-65-65), east of place du Maréchal-Foch. One of the most interesting provincial galleries in western France, it contains an unusually fine collection of sculptures and paintings that accent the French modern schools. The museum, charging 20 F ($3.80) for adults and 10 F ($1.90) for children, is open Monday, Wednesday, Thursday, and Saturday from 10am to 6pm, Friday from 10am to 9pm, and Sunday from 11am to 6pm.

Of minor interest is the **Musée Thomas Dobrée,** place Jean-V (☎ 40-71-03-50), a 19th-century mansion built by an important collector. It stands beside the 15th-century manor of Jean de la Touche, where the bishops of Nantes occasionally lived. Both are museums and contain a varied collection gathered by M. Dobrée, including prehistoric and medieval antiquities, Flemish paintings from the 15th century, and many ecclesiastical relics. Admission is 20 F ($3.80) for adults and 10 F ($1.90) for children; it's open Tuesday to Sunday from 10am to noon and 1:30 to 5:30pm.

Novelist Jules Verne (*Journey to the Center of the Earth, Around the World in Eighty Days*) was born in Nantes in 1828, and literary fans like to seek out his house at 4 rue de Clisson in the Ile-Feydeau. However, the **Musée Jules Verne de Nantes,** 3 rue de l'Hermitage (☎ 40-69-72-52), is filled with memorabilia and objects his writings inspired, from inkpots to a "magic" lantern with glass slides. The museum is open Monday and Wednesday to Saturday from 10am to noon and 2 to 5pm and Sunday from 2 to 5pm; admission is 8 F ($1.50) for adults and 4 F (75¢) for children and seniors.

WHERE TO STAY

✪ Graslin
1 rue Piron, 44000 Nantes. ☎ **40-69-72-91.** Fax 40-69-04-44. 47 rms. TV TEL. 290–360 F ($55.10–$68.40) double. Breakfast 38 F ($7.20) extra. AE, DC, MC, V.

In the center of town, the Graslin is on a steep old street near the harbor. Owners M. and Mme Cassard have given it many homelike touches, so it now offers more for the money than almost any hotel in its price category. The comfortable rooms are decorated with functional simplicity; eight contain minibars.

Mercure Beaulieu
Ile-Beaulieu, 44200 Nantes-Beaulieu. ☎ **40-47-61-03.** Fax 40-48-23-83. 98 rms. A/C MINIBAR TV TEL. 530 F ($100.70) double. Breakfast 50 F ($9.50) extra. AE, DC, MC, V. Parking 20 F ($3.80).

On an island surrounded by the Loire, 2 miles from the center of town, the Mercure offers well-furnished soundproof chambers. This chain hotel is the best place to stay in town for those seeking the most up-to-date amenities. The restaurant/bar, Le Tilbury, offers a wide choice of seafood and fish. Facilities include a heated outdoor pool and tennis courts.

WHERE TO DINE

✪ L'Atlantide
Centre des Salorges, 16 quai E. Renaud. ☎ **40-73-23-22.** Reservations required. Main courses 125–225 F ($23.75–$42.75); fixed-price menus 130 F ($24.70), 220 F ($41.80), 250 F ($47.50), and 330 F ($62.70). V. Mon–Fri noon–2:30pm and 7–10:30pm, Sat 7–10:30pm. Closed Aug 6–28. FRENCH.

The city's most panoramic restaurant serves the finest cuisine. Designer Jean-Pierre Wilmotte created excitement when he set the style for this room, but it's the innovative cooking of Pierre Lecoutre that draws people here. M. Lecoutre uses only market-fresh ingredients and isn't afraid to use spices, some from the far-flung corners of the world. For example, he makes Breton sea bass even more delightful with the use of an exotic ginger. His scallops flavored with Muscadet is sublime. For dessert, only his glace au caramel will do (available September to January). The cellar is known for some of the finest bottles from the Loire, especially rich in Muscadets. The 250-F ($47.50) menu is one of the best dining values in Nantes.

La Cigale
4 place Graslin. ☎ **40-69-76-41.** Reservations recommended. Main courses 75–95 F ($14.25–$18.05); fixed-price meals 69 F ($13.10), 89 F ($16.90), 100 F ($19), and 130 F ($24.70). MC, V. Daily 11:45am–2:30pm and 6:45pm–12:30am. Bus 11 or 34. FRENCH.

This is the most historic brasserie in Nantes, decorated in a belle époque style that's changed very little since the place was established in 1895. Menu items might include heaping platters of fresh shellfish, zander in beurre-blanc sauce, confit des cuisses de canard, an array of grilled steaks, and seasonal specialties.

Villa Mon Rêve
Route des Bords-de-Loire. ☎ **40-03-55-50.** Reservations required. Main courses 108–155 F ($20.50–$29.45); fixed-price menus 98 F ($18.60), 130 F ($24.70), 168 F ($31.90), and 185 F ($35.15). AE, DC, MC, V. May–Aug, daily 12:15–2pm and 7:30–9:30pm; Sept–Apr, Wed 12:15–2pm, Thurs–Mon 12:15–2pm and 7:30–9:30pm. Closed 15 days in late Oct and early Nov (dates vary). Take N751 5 miles east of Nantes. FRENCH.

The people of Nantes have been dining in this parklike setting with a rose garden for years. Chef Gérard Ryngel and his wife, Cécile, took over Mon Rêve in 1979. Monsieur Ryngel's repertoire includes both regional specialties and those of his own creation: Loire salmon steak, wild duck with Bourjeuil sauce, delectable sweetbreads with crayfish, lobster gazpacho, and a coquilles St-Jacques en chemise that deserves a prize. His fixed-price menus are outstanding; if you're rushed at lunch, ask for his *déjeuner rapide*, a quickly served fixed-price meal.

2 La Baule

281 miles SW of Paris, 49 miles NW of Nantes

Founded during the Victorian seaside craze, La Baule remains as inviting as the Gulf Stream that warms the waters of its 5-mile crescent of white-sand beach. Occupying the Côte d'Amour (Coast of Love), it competes with Biarritz as the Atlantic coast's most fashionable resort. But La Baule is still essentially French and draws only a nominal number of foreigners.

Gambler François André founded the casino and major resort hotels here. Pines grow on the dunes, and on the outskirts villas draw the wealthy chic from late June to mid-September; should you arrive at any other time you might have La Baule all to yourself. While the movie stars and flashy rich go to Deauville or Cannes, La Baule draws a more middle-class clientele; however, the more reserved wealthy still come here—as the yachts in the harbor testify.

The town itself is north of a popular stretch of beachfront. The two main boulevards run roughly parallel through the long, narrow town; the one closer to the ocean changes its name six times—at its most famous point it's boulevard de l'Océan.

ESSENTIALS

GETTING THERE   The train trip from Nantes is about an hour. Get off at the most central inner-city station, La Baule–Escoublac, or the more easterly and remote La Baule–Les Pins.

VISITOR INFORMATION   The Office de Tourisme is at 8 place Victoire (☎ 40-24-34-44).

WHERE TO STAY
EXPENSIVE

✪ Castel Marie-Louise
1 av. Andrieu, 44504 La Baule. ☎ **40-11-48-38.** Fax 40-11-48-35. 29 rms. MINIBAR TV TEL. 1,200–1,730 F ($228.10–$328.90) per person. Rates include half board. AE, DC, MC, V. Parking free. Closed mid-Jan to mid-Feb.

This Breton manor offers grand living in an oceanfront pine park. The public rooms, including a salon for drinks, are furnished in French provincial style, with tapestries of stylized animals. Most upper-floor rooms come with a balcony; two are in a tower. Their furnishings reflect several styles: Louis XV, Directoire, and rustic. The excellent chef is reason enough to stay here, and even if you aren't a guest you may want to stop in for a meal. Specialties include lobster and home-smoked salmon. Many diners begin with Breton oysters.

MODERATE

Alexandra
3 bd. René-Dubois, 44500 La Baule. ☎ **40-60-30-06.** Fax 40-24-57-09. 36 rms. TV TEL. 350–650 F ($66.50–$123.55) double. Breakfast 48 F ($9.10) extra. Half board 900–1,200 F ($171.10–$228.10) for two. AE, DC, MC, V. Parking free. Closed Oct–Mar.

The Alexandra boasts eight floors of modern rooms with balconies. There's an open-air terrace with umbrellas and sidewalk tables, plus planters of flowers and greenery. The ninth-floor solarium, where you sit under parasols, is a popular spot for drinks and coffee. Though the dining room has a view of the ocean and the lounge is *intime*, the rooms are the best feature here, as they're roomy and breezy.

Bellevue Plage
27 bd. de l'Océan, 44500 La Baule. ☎ **40-60-28-55.** Fax 40-60-10-18. 35 rms. A/C TV TEL. 490–790 F ($93.15–$150.20) double. Breakfast 50 F ($9.50) extra. AE, DC, MC, V. Parking free. Closed mid-Nov to Feb.

This hotel, which many prefer to the Alexandra (above), occupies a tranquil position in the center of the shoreline curving around the bay. The decor is contemporary, with a rooftop solarium where guests gravitate and a restaurant with a sweeping view. The rooms are frequently renovated and have soundproof windows. You'll find a beach, sailboats for rent, and access to spa facilities. This hotel's more reliable than exciting.

INEXPENSIVE

Ⓢ La Palmeraie

7 allée des Cormorans, 44500 La Baule. ☎ **40-60-24-41.** Fax 40-42-73-71. 23 rms. TV TEL. 430 F ($81.70) double. Breakfast 40 F ($7.60) extra. Half board 360–400 F ($68.40–$76) per person. AE, DC, MC, V. Closed Oct–Mar.

In high-priced La Baule, this is a charmer. Decorated in festive pink and white, it's near a beach and luxuriant with flowers in summer. The rooms are attractively decorated, often with English-style pieces. The only drawback: The soundproof rooms aren't all that soundproof. Half board is obligatory in July and August; the food, though, is hardly in the league of that at the first-class hotels. The management and staff, however, are helpful and even friendly.

WHERE TO DINE

La Marcanderie

5 av. d'Agen. ☎ **40-24-03-12.** Reservations required. Main courses 80–150 F ($15.20–$28.50); fixed-price menus 155 F ($29.45) (Mon–Fri only), 195 F ($37.05), 235 F ($44.65), and 285 F ($54.15). AE, V. July–Aug, Mon 7–9:30pm, Tues–Sun noon–2:30pm and 7–9:30pm; Sept–June, Tues–Sat noon–2:30pm and 7–9:30pm, Sun noon–2:30pm. FRENCH.

Award-winning chef Jean-Luc Giraud has transformed this into one of La Baule's finest restaurants. The dining room is decorated in harmonious pastels, and the cuisine is savory and well prepared, using only the freshest ingredients. Sometimes, particularly if the restaurant is full, you'll have to wait quite a while between courses. Perhaps try the scallops and endive in light cream sauce or the marmite of shellfish with caramelized scalloped potatoes. The welcome is warm, and the wines have been carefully chosen.

3 Carnac

302 miles SW of Paris, 23 miles SE of Lorient, 62 miles SE of Quimper

In May and June the fields here are resplendent with golden broom. Aside from being a seaside resort, Carnac is home to the most important prehistoric find in northern France: the hundreds of huge stones in the ✪ **Field of Megaliths**— their arrangement and placement remain a mystery. At Carnac Ville, the **Musée de Préhistoire,** 10 place de la Chapelle (☎ 97-52-22-04), displays collections from 350,000 B.C. to the 8th century A.D. Charging 32 F ($6.10) for adults and 12 F ($2.30) for children, the museum is open in July and August, Monday to Friday from 10am to 6:30pm and Saturday and Sunday from 10am to noon and 2 to 6:30pm; September to June, Wednesday to Monday from 10am to noon and 2 to 6pm.

Even if Carnac didn't possess these prehistoric monuments, its pine-studded sand dunes would be worth the trip. Protected by the Quiberon Peninsula, **Carnac-Plage** is a family resort.

The center of Carnac is about half a mile from the sea. From the main square, rue du Tumulus leads out of town to the Tumulus St-Michel, a Celtic burial chamber. The beach area, Carnac-Plage, is beside the ocean, alongside the water-front boulevard de la Plage.

ESSENTIALS

GETTING THERE   Public transportation links are possible but inconvenient. Seven TIM buses (☎ 97-47-29-64 in Vannes for schedules) run to Carnac from Quiberon (trip time: 30 min.), costing 21 F ($4) one way. There are also seven TIM buses from Auray to Carnac (trip time: 30 min.), costing 22 F ($4.20) one way. A train will take you as far as Plouharnel, from which you can catch one of seven buses per day (trip time: 5 min.), costing 3 F (55¢) one way.

VISITOR INFORMATION   The Office de Tourisme on avenue des Druides (☎ 97-52-13-52) is open all year.

WHERE TO STAY & DINE

La Diana

21 bd. de la Plage, 56340 Carnac. ☎ **97-52-05-38.** Fax 97-52-87-91. 30 rms, 3 suites. MINIBAR TV TEL. 600–900 F ($114–$171) double; 800–1,500 F ($152–$285) suite. Breakfast 80 F ($15.20) extra. DC, MC. Parking free. Closed Oct 4–Easter.

On the most popular beach, Le Diana offers a terrace where you can sip drinks and watch the crashing waves. The contemporary rooms are spacious and have balconies facing the sea. The hotel has a restaurant, but the food is rather standard.

Hôtel les Alignements

45 rue St-Cornély, 56340 Carnac. ☎ **97-52-06-30.** Fax 97-52-76-56. 27 rms. TV TEL. 280–395 F ($53.20–$75.05) double. Breakfast 39 F ($7.40) extra. MC, V. Parking free. Closed Oct–Easter.

About 200 yards from the famous megaliths, this hotel looks onto a garden, and inside everything's clean and efficient. Some rooms have balconies or loggias; those facing the street have double windows to filter the noise. Nonguests are welcome to dine in the rustic restaurant, where the 95-F ($18.05) fixed-price menu is the best food value in Carnac.

⑤ Lann-Roz

36 av. de la Poste, 56340 Carnac. ☎ **97-52-10-48.** Fax 97-52-03-69. 14 rms. TV TEL. 625–665 F ($118.75–$126.35) double. Rates include half board. AE, DC, MC, V. Closed Jan 5–Feb 10.

Within walking distance of the water, this is an oasis for the budget-minded, built in the Breton manner and surrounded by a garden and lawns. The Lann-Roz is managed by the friendly Mme Le Calvez, who invites you to have a drink on the veranda. In the typical Breton dining room the chef serves generous portions of regional food. You don't have to be a guest to dine here, where meals begin at 120 F ($22.80).

NEARBY ATTRACTIONS

If you take D768 south from Carnac and follow it onto the peninsula (formerly an island) connected to the mainland by a narrow strip of alluvial deposits, you'll come to the port of **Quiberon,** with a white-sand beach. Aside from the beach, the best sight here is the rugged Breton fishers hauling in their sardine catch.

This entire coast—the **Côte Sauvage (Wild Coast)**—is rugged; the ocean breaks with fury against the reefs. Northern winds, especially in winter, lash across the dunes, shaving the short pines that grow here. On the landward side, however, the beach is calm and relatively protected.

Ten miles west of Brittany's shoreline is **Belle-Ile-en-Mer.** Depending on the season, 4 to 12 ferries depart daily for this island from Port Maria in Quiberon.

The trip takes 45 minutes and costs 85 F ($16.15) one way. In summer you must reserve space on board for your car. The ferry docks at Le Palais, a fortified 16th-century port. The storm-wracked Belle-Ile-en-Mer is eerie, with rocky cliffs, a reef-fringed west coast, a **Grotte de l'Apothicairerie,** and a general sense of isolation. Valleys cut through the ravines, wending their way to small ports like Le Palais. A drive around the island's periphery is about 35 miles.

In the days before he was jailed for embezzlment, the Sun King's finance minister, Nicolas Fouquet, erected a château on this island. Much later, the "Divine Sarah" Bernhardt spent many pleasant summers here in a 17th-century fortress that was "always swarming with guests."

WHERE TO STAY & DINE ON BELLE-ILE

You'll find excellent accommodations in **Port de Goulphar**, one of the most charming spots on Belle-Ile. It's on the southern shore, on a narrow inlet framed by cliffs. The Castel Clara is certainly the star on the island.

✪ Castel Clara

Port de Goulphar, 56360 Le Palais. ☎ **97-31-84-21.** Fax 97-31-51-69. 43 rms. TV TEL. 1,260–1,780 F ($239.50–$338.40) double. Rates include half board. MC, V. Parking free. Closed Nov 15–Feb 15.

This Relais & Châteaux hotel/spa is 2 miles from Bangor. There are few places along the coast where guests can enjoy such peace along with ideal service and first-class cuisine. The guest rooms are well furnished and have balconies facing the sea. The chef takes pride in his achievements, and the menu is a good showcase for his talents, especially his seafood selections. Sea bass, for example, might be steamed over seaweed for the aroma, then served with a beurre-blanc sauce from the Loire. The hotel also offers a large terrace with a solarium around a heated seawater pool.

4 Pont-Aven

324 miles W of Paris, 20 miles SE of Quimper, 10 miles S of Concarneau

Paul Gauguin loved this peaceful village with its little white houses along the gently flowing Aven. In the late 19th century many painters followed him here, such as Maurice Denis, Sérusier, and Emile Bernard. This colony of artists became known as the School of Pont-Aven.

Before leaving for Tahiti, Gauguin painted *The Golden Christ* and *The Beautiful Angela* here. You can admire the crucifix that inspired *The Golden Christ* in the **Chapelle de Trémalo,** less than a mile from town. Every year the Société de Peinture organizes an exhibition of paintings by other members of the School of Pont-Aven.

ESSENTIALS

GETTING THERE   From Quimperlé, motorists can continue west along D783 in the direction of Concarneau.

VISITOR INFORMATION   The Office de Tourisme is on place de l'Hôtel-de-Ville (☎ **98-06-04-70**).

WHERE TO DINE

✪ Le Moulin de Rosmadec

29123 Pont-Aven. ☎ **98-06-00-22.** Fax 98-06-18-00. Reservations recommended. Main courses 130–170 F ($24.70–$32.30); fixed-price menu 295 F ($56.05); *menu tradition* (with oysters and lobster) 395 F ($75.10). AE, MC, V. Thurs–Tues 12:30–2pm and 7:30–9pm. Closed Feb, Nov 15–Dec 1, and Sun night in winter. FRENCH.

For a charming setting, this 15th-century reconstructed stone mill has no comparison in Brittany. Meals are served in a bilevel dining room with antique furniture or, in good weather, on a flower-filled "island" terrace. Owners M. and Mme Sebilleau serve wonderful food, with specialties like trout with almonds, homard (lobster) grillé à l'estragon, sole suprême with champagne, and duck breast with cassis. The fish dishes are especially sublime.

The Moulin also rents four comfortable rooms, at 470 F ($89.35) for a double, plus 45 F ($8.55) for breakfast.

5 Concarneau

335 miles W of Paris, 58 miles SE of Brest

This port is a favorite of painters, who never tire of capturing on canvas the subtleties of the fishing fleet in the harbor. It's also our favorite of the coast communities—primarily because it doesn't depend on tourists for its livelihood. In fact, its canneries produce nearly three-quarters of all the "tunny" fish consumed in France. Walk along the quays here, especially in the late evening, and watch the rustic Breton fishers unload their catch; later, join them for a pint of potent cider in their taverns.

The town is built on three sides of a natural harbor whose innermost sheltered section is the Nouveau Port. In the center of the harbor, connected to its westernmost edge by a bridge, is the heavily fortified **Ville-Close,** an ancient hamlet surrounded by ramparts, some from the 14th century. From the quay, cross the bridge and descend into the town. Admittedly, souvenir shops have taken over, but don't let that spoil it for you. You can easily spend an hour wandering the winding alleys, gazing up at the towers, peering at the stone houses, and pausing in the secluded squares. For a splendid view of the port, walk the ramparts; the cost is 5 F (95¢) for adults, half price for children. Walks are possible daily mid-April to mid-June from 10am to 6:30pm and mid-June to mid-September from 10am to 9:30pm.

Also in the old town is a fishing museum, the **Musée de la Pêche,** rue Vauvan (☎ 98-97-10-20). In a 17th-century building, it contains ship models and exhibits tracing the development of the fishing industry throughout the world. You can view the preserved ship *Hemerica*. Admission is 30 F ($5.70) for adults and 20 F ($3.80) for children. You can visit daily: in July and August from 9:30am to 7pm; in other months, from 9:30am to 12:30pm and 2 to 6pm.

After sightseeing, repair to one of the nearby beaches of Les Sables Blancs. Or check into one of the hotels and enjoy the boating, fishing, tennis, golf, horseback riding, and canoeing.

ESSENTIALS

GETTING THERE   Local rail service is limited to freight. The town is 13 miles southeast of Quimper along D783 if you're driving. A Caoudal bus (☎ 98-90-88-89) runs from Quimper to Concarneau (trip time: 40 min.), costing 22 F ($4.20) one way.

VISITOR INFORMATION   The Office de Tourisme is on quai d'Aiguillon (☎ 98-97-01-44).

WHERE TO STAY

☉ Grand Hôtel

1 av. Pierre-Guéguen, 29110 Concarneau. ☎ **98-97-00-28.** 33 rms, 18 with bath. TEL. 155 F ($29.45) double without bath, 320 F ($60.80) double with bath. Breakfast 29 F ($5.50) extra. MC, V. Parking free. Closed Oct 11–Apr 11.

This is the best budget choice in the center of the port. Across from the Ville-Close, the Grand overlooks the fishing fleet and marketplace and has open stalls selling fresh vegetables, fruit, fish, and even clothing. The rooms are simple but suitable for at least a stopover. Breakfast is the only meal served.

WHERE TO DINE

La Coquille

1 rue du Moros, at Nouveau Port. ☎ **98-97-08-52.** Reservations required Sat–Sun and in summer. Main courses 100–150 F ($19–$28.50); fixed-price menus 150 F ($28.50), 190 F ($36.10), and 280 F ($53.20). AE, DC, MC, V. Tues–Sat 12:30–1:30pm and 7:30–9:30pm, Sun 12:30–1:30pm. Closed Jan. FRENCH.

This 30-year-old restaurant occupies one end of a stone-sided harborfront building that was once a fish-processing plant. It contains a trio of dining rooms with exposed stone walls and ceiling beams. La Coquille serves primarily seafood, particularly lobster. Much of the food is simply prepared because the fish is always fresh and succulent. The service is bistro style, no great compliment. The small terrace offers a view of the port during warm weather.

✪ Le Galion

15 rue St-Guénolé, in La Ville-Close, 29110 Concarneau. ☎ **98-97-30-16.** Fax 98-50-67-88. Reservations required. Main courses 110–150 F ($20.90–$28.50); fixed-price menus 110 F ($20.90), 190 F ($36.10), 260 F ($49.40), and 370 F ($70.30). AE, DC, MC, V. Tues–Sat 12:30–2:30pm and 7:30–9:30pm, Sun 12:30–2:30pm. Closed late Oct to Apr 1. FRENCH.

With granite walls and massive timbers, this is one of the best examples of a country inn in Brittany. The hosts/cooks are proud Bretons and the spelling of their name proves it—Gaonac'h. The specialties include blanquette of lobster with asparagus (April to mid-June only), John Dory flavored with rhubarb, and paupiette of sole. The bounty of the sea around Brittany is treated with great respect here. The food is unpretentious, the way it's always been in this part of France.

Across the street in a renovated old granite house called La Résidence des Iles, M. and Mme Gaonac'h rent five comfortable rooms, each with double or twin beds, bath, and kitchenette. The rate is 350 F ($66.50) for a double, plus 40 F ($7.60) extra for breakfast.

NEARBY ACCOMMODATIONS & DINING

On the outskirts of the once-fortified town of Hennebont, 35 miles west of Concarneau, is the most delightful hotel in all of southern Brittany.

✪ Château de Locguénolé

Route de Port-Louis, 56700 Hennebont. ☎ **97-76-29-04.** Fax 97-76-39-47. 20 rms, 4 suites. TV TEL. 894–1,184 F ($169.95–$225.09) per person double; 1,249–1,499 F ($237.45–$284.95) per person suite. Rates include half board. AE, DC, MC, V. Parking free. Closed Jan 2–Feb 8.

This estate in a 250-acre park 3 miles south of Hennebont has been owned by the same family for more than 500 years. Now a Relais & Châteaux, it's filled with antiques, tapestries, and paintings accumulated over the centuries. The rooms vary widely in size and furnishings, but each has floral sprays and harmonious colors. The converted maids' rooms are smaller than the others, yet still charming; some rooms are in a converted Breton cottage. Even if you can't stay here, consider taking a meal in the dining hall. Specialties include filet de boeuf poêle au foie gras, suprême de barbue (brill) with cider and leeks, and grilled salmon. Meals begin at 190 F ($36.10).

6 Quimper

342 miles W of Paris, 127 miles NW of Rennes

The town that pottery built, Quimper is the historic capital of Brittany's most traditional region, La Cornouaille. Its faïence decorates tables from Europe to America. Skilled artisans have been turning out Quimper-ware since the 17th century, using bold provincial designs. You can tour one of the ateliers during your stay at Quimper; inquire at the tourist office (below).

At the meeting of the Odet and Steir rivers in southwestern Brittany, Quimper was the medieval capital of Cornouailles. In some quarters it still maintains its old-world atmosphere, with charming footbridges spanning the rivers. At place St-Corentin, the **Cathédrale St-Corentin** (☎ 98-95-06-19) is a landmark, characterized by two towers that climb 250 feet. The cathedral was built between the 13th and 15th century; the spires weren't added until the 19th. Inside, the 15th-century stained glass is exceptional. It's open daily from 9am to 6:30pm.

Also on the square is the **Musée des Beaux-Arts,** 40 place St-Corentin (☎ 98-95-45-20), with a collection including Rubens, Boucher, Fragonard, Oudry, and Corot. There's also an exceptional exhibit from the Pont-Aven school (Bernard, Sérusier, Lacombe, Maufra, Denis). Admission is 25 F ($4.75) for adults and 15 F ($2.85) for children. The gallery is open in July and August, daily from 9am to 7pm; September to June, Wednesday to Monday from 10am to noon.

ESSENTIALS

GETTING THERE   Two or three regular trains from Paris arrive daily (trip time: 7¹/₂ hr.). The speedier TGV has five trains per day from Paris (trip time: 5 hr.). Fares from Paris are 305 F ($57.95) one way, but it costs 36 to 90 F ($6.85 to $17.10) extra for reservations on the TGV. Eight trains also arrive from Rennes (trip time: 3 hr.), costing 155 F ($29.45) one way.

VISITOR INFORMATION   The Office de Tourisme is on place de la Résistance (☎ 98-53-04-05).

WHERE TO STAY

Novotel

17 rue Dupoher, pont de Poulguinan, 29000 Quimper. ☎ **98-90-46-26.** Fax 98-53-01-96. 92 rms. A/C MINIBAR TV TEL. 460–480 F ($87.45–$91.25) double. Breakfast 50 F ($9.50) extra. AE, DC, MC, V. Parking free.

In a garden about a mile southwest of the town center, this Novotel, despite its blandness, is the best place to stay here. It's also the best business-oriented hotel in the region and is ideal for motoring families in summer. Each of its chain-format rooms has lots of space, plus a writing desk and a single and double bed. When staying with their family, two children 15 and under get free accommodations and breakfast. The food here is prepared competently—and that's it. The pool is a magnet in summer.

⑨ Tour d'Auverge

13 rue Reguaires, 29000 Quimper. ☎ **98-95-08-70.** Fax 98-95-17-31. 43 rms, 38 with bath (tub or shower). TEL. 430–515 F ($81.70–$97.85) double with bath. Breakfast 49 F ($9.30) extra. AE, MC, V.

The rooms here are small and sometimes in need of sprucing up, but they're clean and good value for Quimper. The doubles have a bath; a few bargain singles don't. One of the principal reasons for staying here is the kitchen's Breton specialties. Fixed-price meals cost 89 F ($16.90), 135 F ($25.65), 165 F ($31.35), and 195 F ($37.05). The less expensive menu is invariably good and could include spider crabs with mayonnaise and saddle of rabbit with mustard sauce.

WHERE TO DINE

✪ Le Capucin Gourmand

29 rue des Réguaires. ☎ **98-95-43-12.** Reservations required in summer. Main courses 95–140 F ($18.05–$26.60); fixed-price meals 115 F ($21.85), 160 F ($30.40), 200 F ($38), 280 F ($53.20), and 350 F ($66.50). DC, MC, V. Mon–Fri 12:15–2pm and 7:15–10pm, Sat 7:15–10pm. FRENCH.

This popular restaurant, run by Soisik and Christian Conchon, is a place to fill up on a well-prepared meal without straining your budget. To begin, you might have scallops, oysters, or homemade duck-liver or snail ravioli. You might then try a seafood pot-au-feu, with scallops, scampi, turbot, red mullet, John Dory, and assorted vegetables. You can also order beef filet in garnay de Touraine sauce and duck breast with sherry-vinegar sauce. Crème brûlée or a warm apple tart with vanilla ice cream and Calvados is a great finish. The chef's secret here is giving familiar dishes a new taste sensation by adding a different ingredient or two.

Le Parisien

13 rue Jean-Jaurès. ☎ **98-90-35-29.** Reservations recommended. Main courses 68–84 F ($12.90–$15.95); fixed-price menus 98 F ($18.60), 145 F ($27.55), and 175 F ($33.25). MC, V. Mon–Sat noon–1:30pm and 7:15–9pm. Closed two weeks in Aug (dates vary). FRENCH.

With mahogany accessories and well-set tables, this is one of the best restaurants in the town center. The refined cuisine includes salmon and lobster with zucchini, trout in sorrel-cream sauce, and beef filet with onion confit. Some dishes, obviously, turn out better than others, but so far we've received no complaints. You can dine well by sticking to the least expensive main courses or the most economical fixed-price menu. Sometime during 1996 the restaurant may move a few doors down the street, but the phone number will stay the same (call before going).

NEARBY ACCOMMODATIONS & DINING

In an orchard district 8 miles from Quimper, **La Forêt-Fouesnant** produces the best cider in the province, and one of Brittany's finest manor houses is in this sleepy village. Take N783 and turn off at the clearly indicated sign.

Manoir du Stang

29940 La Forêt-Fouesnant. ☎ **98-56-97-37.** 26 rms. TEL. 500–720 F ($95–$136.80) double. No credit cards. Breakfast 40 F ($7.60) per person extra. Parking free. Closed Sept 20–May 10. The manor's a mile north of the village center, signposted from N783; access is by private road.

To get to this 16th-century ivy-covered manor you travel down a tree-lined avenue and under a stone tower gate into a courtyard. On your right is a formal garden, and raised stone terraces lead to 25 acres of rolling woodland. This is the domain of M. and Mme Guy Hubert, who provide gracious living in period rooms. Guests are lodged either in the main building or in the even older but less desirable annex; the latter has a circular stone staircase. Your room is likely to be furnished with silk and fine antiques, and a maid in a lacy Breton cap will bring your breakfast tray there each morning. The restaurant's specialties are grilled lobster with tarragon, mousseline de turbot, côte de boeuf au poivre vert, fruits de mer (seafood), and oysters house style.

7 Dinan

246 miles W of Paris, 32 miles NW of Rennes

Once a stronghold of the ducs de Bretagne, Dinan is one of the best-preserved towns of Brittany, characterized by houses built on stilts over the sidewalks. The 18th-century granite dwellings contrast with the medieval timbered houses in this walled town with a once-fortified château.

For a panoramic view of the valley, head for the **Jardin Anglais (English Garden)**, a terraced garden huddling up to the ramparts. Spanning the Rance River is a gothic-style bridge that was damaged in World War II but has been restored. Dinan's most typical street is sloping **rue du Jerzual,** flanked with some buildings dating from the 15th century. The street ends at **La Porte du Jerzual,** an ancient gate. **Rue du Petit-Fours** contains a number of 15th-century maisons.

Dominating the old city's medieval ramparts, the **Château de Dinan,** rue du Château (☎ **96-39-45-20**), contains a 14th-century keep and a 15th-century tower, built to withstand lengthy sieges. Within the stones you'll see the space for the portcullis and the drawbridge. Inside, you can see an exhibition of the architecture and art of the city, including locally carved sculpture from the 12th to the 15th century. Admission is 20 F ($3.80) for adults and 10 F ($1.90) for children; the castle is open daily from 10am to 6:30pm.

The old city's **Tour de l'Horloge** (clock tower), on rue de l'Horloge, now classified a historic monument, boasts a clock made in 1498 and a great bell donated by Anne de Bretagne in 1507. You'll have an incredible view of medieval Dinan from the 75-foot belfry. Admission is 13 F ($2.45), and the belfry is open daily from 10am to 7pm.

The heart of Bertrand du Guesclin, who defended the town when the duke of Lancaster threatened it in 1359, was entombed in a place of honor in the **Basilique St-Sauveur,** place St-Sauveur; note the basilica's romanesque portals and ornamented chapels. It's open daily from 8am to 6pm.

ESSENTIALS

GETTING THERE   Six trains per day arrive from Paris via Rennes (trip time: $3^{1}/_{2}$ hr.), costing 275 F ($52.25) one way. TGV trains carry a 36- to 90-F ($6.85 to $17.10) supplement. From St-Malo (below), five trains per day arrive, with a change at Dol (trip time: $1^{1}/_{4}$ hr.), costing 44 F ($8.35) one way.

Ferry service is daily from Dinard and St-Malo.

VISITOR INFORMATION   The Office de Tourisme is at 6 rue de l'Horloge (☎ **96-39-75-40**).

WHERE TO STAY

⑤ Arvor

5 rue Pavie, 22100 Dinan. ☎ **96-39-21-22.** Fax 96-39-83-09. 23 rms. TV TEL. 340 F ($64.60) double. Breakfast 30 F ($5.70) extra. AE, V.

Mr. and Mrs. Bundy from England took over this former convent and made it into one of the most inviting little hotels in town. It's in the old quarter, with its narrow, cobblestone streets. Breakfast is the only meal served here, but many inviting places to eat are a short walk away. Readers' reactions have been favorable, citing the clean and comfortable rooms, which are good value.

⊛ D'Avaugour

1 place du Champs-Clos, 22100 Dinan. ☎ **96-39-07-49.** Fax 96-85-43-04. 27 rms. MINIBAR TV TEL. 520–650 F ($98.85–$123.55) double. Rates include buffet breakfast. AE, DC, MC, V. Parking free. Bus 34, 36, or 96.

Mme Quinton gutted an old building and turned it into the most up-to-date accommodation in Dinan. The rooms are furnished with reproductions and contemporary pieces—half overlook the square and the others face the rear garden. The stylish front lounge has a lot of natural stone and modern furnishings. The Restaurant d'Avaugour is in the garden overlooking the ramparts and is open daily year round; its chef, M. Quinton, prepares excellent food. A summer restaurant is in a former guard's room in a 15th-century tower at the rear of the garden; it specializes in meats grilled on a wood-burning fireplace.

WHERE TO DINE

La Caravelle

14 place Duclos. ☎ **96-39-00-11.** Reservations required. Main courses 150–250 F ($28.50–$47.50); fixed-price menus 130 F ($24.70), 180 F ($34.20), 200 F ($38), and 260 F ($49.40). MC, V. Daily noon–2pm and 7–9:30pm. Closed Nov 12–Dec 3 and Wed Dec–July. Bus 34, 36, or 96. FRENCH.

We used to hail Jean-Claude Marmion as the most inventive chef in Dinan. He still serves wonderful food and his 130-F ($24.70) menu is the best value in town, but he now prepares only time-tested dishes and some of the magic has gone from the place. Specialties include warm oysters with shallots, civet of lobster à la fleur de Bretagne, John Dory with green mustard and red-pepper/cream sauce, and veal kidneys in cider. In season, Marmion prepares fine game dishes, like jugged hare and rabbit. When the first of the spring turnips come in, he uses them with a veal filet often served with onion compote.

⊛ Chez La Mère Pourcel

3 place des Merciers. ☎ **96-39-03-80.** Reservations recommended. Main courses 100–150 F ($19–$28.50); fixed-price lunch (Tues–Fri only) 92 F ($17.50); fixed price dinner 155 F ($29.45), 210 F ($39.90), 280 F ($53.20), and 350 F ($66.50). AE, DC, MC, V. July–Aug, daily noon–2pm and 7:15–10pm; Sept–June, Tues–Sat noon–2pm and 7:15–10pm, Sun noon–2pm. Closed Feb. Bus 34, 36, or 96. FRENCH.

This restaurant enjoys an outstanding reputation for regional food. Most diners prefer the à la carte menu, with choices like consommé with ham- and duckling-stuffed ravioli and mushrooms from the forest with lobster and green butter. For a main course, try a pastry-encased pigeon, red mullet filet with oyster coulis, or chicken suprême with foie gras. The desserts are sumptuous, including cold chocolate soufflé. The extensive wine carte is too expensive for most budgets.

8 Dinard

259 miles W of Paris, 14 miles N of Dinan

Dinard sits on a rocky promontory at the top of the Rance River, opposite St-Malo (below); ferries ply the waters between the two resorts. Turn-of-the-century

Victorian-gothic villas, many now hotels, overlook the sea. Gardens and parks abound.

One of France's best-known resorts, Dinard offers safe, well-sheltered bathing in **La Manche.** During Queen Victoria's time this town became popular with the Channel-crossing English, who wanted a continental holiday that was "not too foreign." Dinard offers a trio of beaches: The main one is **La Grande Plage,** which gets crowded in July and August; another, facing a backdrop of towering cliffs, is **St-Enogat;** the third, honoring a priory that stood nearby in the Middle Ages, is the **Prieuré.**

From June to September there's *musique-et-lumière* along the floodlit seafront **promenade du Clair-de-Lune.** The **New Municipal Casino** in the Palais d'Emeraude is open year round. And about 5 miles from Dinard is the 18-hole golf course at **St-Briac,** one of the finest in Brittany.

ESSENTIALS

GETTING THERE   Between May and September, a ferry makes one daily trip from Dinan. Buses arrive from many large cities in Brittany, including Rennes.

VISITOR INFORMATION   The Office de Tourisme is at 2 bd. Féart (☎ 99-46-94-12).

WHERE TO STAY
EXPENSIVE

Le Grand Hôtel de Dinard

46 av. George-V, 35801 Dinard. ☎ **99-88-26-26.** Fax 99-88-26-27. 63 rms, 3 suites. MINIBAR TV TEL. 490–820 F ($93.15–$155.90) double; from 1,640 F ($311.80) suite. Breakfast 60 F ($11.40) extra. AE, DC, MC, V. Parking free. Closed Oct–Easter.

Dinard's leading hotel commands an excellent view of the harbor, a two-minute walk from the town center. Most rooms have balconies and are decorated with traditional pieces. Decorated invitingly, the bar is a popular spot before and after dinner. Fine meals, with generous portions, are offered in the dignified in-house restaurant, the George V. The hotel has a heated pool.

✪ Reine Hortense

19 rue de la Malouine, 35800 Dinard. ☎ **99-46-54-31.** Fax 99-88-15-88. 8 rms, 2 suites. TV TEL. 490–980 F ($93.15–$186.30) double; 1,500–1,800 F ($285.15-$342.20) suite. Breakfast 60 F ($11.40) extra. DC, MC, V. Parking free.

This hotel was built in 1860 as a retreat for one of the Russian-born courtiers of Holland-based Queen Hortense de Beauharnais, mother of Napoléon III. On the beach, it offers glamorously outfitted public salons and many guest rooms decorated in either Louis XV or Napoléon III style. One high-ceilinged room even has Hortense's silver-plated bathtub, dating from the early 19th century. Breakfast is the only meal served.

Owned by the same management as the Hortense, the six-room Castel Eugénie is next door and charges the same rates. It's about a decade old and well appointed and comfortable.

MODERATE

Hôtel-Restaurant Emeraude Plage

1 bd. Albert-1er, 35802 Dinard CEDEX. ☎ **99-46-15-79.** Fax 99-46-15-79. 65 rms. TV TEL. 250–460 F ($47.50–$87.45) double. Breakfast 38 F ($7.20) extra. V. Closed Oct 3–Easter.

This well-run hotel is near the main beach. Claude Luyer, an area native, speaks English and makes his guests feel welcome. Many of the well-furnished spacious rooms overlook the water. Mme Luyer whips up excellent breakfasts and dinners, the latter costing 90 to 120 F ($17.10 to $22.80)—a good value for the quality.

Printania

5 av. George-V, 35800 Dinard. ☎ **99-46-13-07.** Fax 99-46-26-32. 59 rms. TV TEL. 400 F ($76) double. Breakfast 36 F ($6.85) extra. AE, MC, V. Closed Nov 20–Mar 15.

On August 15, 1944, this Breton hotel was damaged in a bombing raid, but the debris was removed in time for the Allied victory. The Printania draws many repeat guests, among them writers and artists. The sitting room has carved-oak furniture, old clocks, provincial chairs, and lots of antiques. The main villa boasts terraces and a glassed-in veranda with potted palms. Dinner at Printania combines superb cookery with a view of the coast; the restaurant specializes in seafood and various shellfish. The guest rooms are old-fashioned and contain antiques and Breton decorations.

INEXPENSIVE

Hôtel des Dunes

5 rue Georges-Clemenceau, 35800 Dinard. ☎ **99-46-12-72.** Fax 99-88-14-90. 38 rms. TV TEL. 650 F ($123.55) double. Rates include half board. AE, DC, MC, V. Closed Nov–Mar 15.

High on a cliff, this hotel evokes the Edwardian days with French windows and balustraded balconies. The front terrace has garden furniture under parasols, and the rooms are comfortable. A dining room/lounge overlooks the garden terrace.

WHERE TO DINE

Altaïr

18 bd. Féart, 64200 Dinard. ☎ **99-46-13-58.** Reservations recommended. Fax 99-88-20-49. Main courses 100–120 F ($19–$22.80); fixed-price menus 88 F ($16.70), 120 F ($22.80), 160 F ($30.40), and 200 F ($38). Daily noon–2pm and 7–9:30pm. AE, DC, MC, V. Closed Sun dinner and Mon in winter. FRENCH.

Patrick Leménager operates the intimate Altaïr. His excellent cuisine includes sea scallops in puff pastry with coriander sauce, fresh salmon with herbs, and duck breast with an apple-and-honey sauce, followed by a gratin of red fruits. The portions are very generous, and most prices are good value for the area. Service can be appalling or most gracious—impossible to predict. In warm weather you may prefer to dine alfresco on the terrace.

The Altaïr also rents 21 standard rooms with bath (tub or shower) and TV. A double costs 190 to 390 F ($36.10 to $74.10), plus 35 F ($6.65) for breakfast.

⑤ Le Petit Robinson

38 rue de la Gougeonnais, La Richardais. ☎ **99-46-14-82.** Fax 99-16-05-74. Reservations required. Main courses 65–120 F ($12.35–$22.80); fixed-price menus 95 F ($18.05), 120 F ($22.80), 140 F ($26.60), and 180 F ($34.20). AE, DC, MC, V. July–Aug, Mon 7–9:30pm, Tues–Sat noon–1:45pm and 7–9:30pm, Sun noon–1:45pm; Sept–June, Tues–Sat noon–1:45pm and 7-9:30pm, Sun noon–1:45pm. FRENCH.

Two miles southeast of Dinard, this tasteful hotel/restaurant is in a rambling turn-of-the-century seaside manor built, like many others nearby, in the English colonial style. The conservative and well-presented cuisine includes shellfish, filet of John Dory with sage or beurre-blanc sauce, civet of monkfish with sherry and raspberry vinegar, grilled sea bass with fennel, and numerous preparations of lobster. Patrice Nicolle and his family are the well-informed chefs and directors.

The Nicolles also rent seven rooms suitable for either one or two, each with bath (tub or shower) and color TV. Doubles are 280 to 320 F ($53.20 to $60.80), with breakfast an extra 30 F ($5.70).

9 St-Malo

257 miles W of Paris, 43 miles W of Rennes, 8 miles E of Dinard

Built on a granite rock in the Channel, St-Malo is joined to the mainland by a causeway. It's popular with the English, especially those from the Channel Islands, and makes a modest claim to be a bathing resort. The peninsula curves like a boomerang around a natural harbor whose interior has been subdivided into several smaller basins. The walled city, with its château and Cathédrale St-Vincent, is on the peninsula's tip.

For the best view of the bay and the islets at the mouth of the Rance, walk along the ramparts. These walls were built over a period of centuries, some parts of them dating from the 14th century. However, they were mainly rebuilt in the 17th century, then vastly restored in the 19th. You can begin your tour at the 15th-century **Porte St. Vincent.**

At the harbor, you can book tours for the **Channel Islands.** Hydrofoils leave for the English island of Jersey (a passport is necessary, of course).

At low tide, you can take a 25-minute stroll to the **Ile du Grand-Bé,** the site of the tomb of Chateaubriand, "deserted by others and completely surrounded by storms." The tomb—marked by a cross—is simple, unlike the man it honors, but the view of the Emerald Coast from here makes up for it.

Called the Bastille of the West, the **Château de St-Malo,** Porte St-Vincent (☎ 99-40-71-11), and its towers shelter a museum with souvenirs of Duguay-Trouin and Surcouf, the most famous of the St-Malo privateers. The **Musée de St-Malo** is in the donjon (keep). You can visit Wednesday to Monday from 9:40am to noon and 2 to 6pm; admission is 19 F ($3.60) for adults and 9.50 F ($1.80) for students. Guided tours are available in July and August only.

After the castle/ramparts tour, you may have time to explore the cobblestone plazas, flagstone courtyards, narrow streets, fish market, and tall gabled houses. One of the most important Breton *pardons* is held at St-Malo in February: the **Pardon of the Newfoundland Fishing Fleet.**

St-Malo's **Cathédrale St-Vincent** is known for its nave vault dating from 1160, making it one of the oldest in Brittany. It's of the Angevin or Plantagenet style, elegantly marking the transition between romanesque and gothic. The cathedral also has a Renaissance west facade, with additions from the 18th century and a 15th-century tower. The 14th-century choir is surmounted by a triforium with trefoiled arches and flanked by chapels.

In the resort of **St-Servan,** adjoining St-Malo, you can visit the **Musée International du Long-Cours Cap-Hornier** in the Tour Solidor (☎ 99-40-71-11), a tower built in 1382, commanding the Rance estuary. Here a history of voyages around the world by way of Cape Horn from the 16th to 20th century is depicted in exhibits. Maps, manuscripts, ship models, and nautical instruments are on display. It's open from Easter to September, daily from 10am to noon and 2 to 6pm;

An Idyll on an Ile

The Ile de Bréhat is home to some 500 hearty people who live most of the year isolated from others—until the summer hoards arrive to inspect them and their island. The tiny island (actually two islands, Ile Nord and Ile Sud, linked by bridge) is in the Golfe de St-Malo, north of Paimpol. A visit to Bréhat is considered an offbeat adventure, even to the French.

Walking is what you do here, along marked footpaths, and it's possible to stroll around the islands in a day. Cars aren't allowed, except those used by the police and fire departments. Some tractor-driven carts carry visitors on a 5-mile circuit of Bréhat, charging 25 F ($4.75) for the 45-minute jaunt. You'll see a number of places renting bikes, but one isn't necessary.

The rich flora here astonishes many visitors, who get off the ferry expecting a windswept Channel island only to discover a place more evocative of a Mediterranean climate. Flower gardens are in full summer bloom, though everything—the gardens and the houses—appears tiny because of the scarcity of land. At the highest point you'll discover the Chapelle St-Michel and be rewarded with a panoramic view.

If you need information, there's a little summer tourist office (☎ **96-20-04-14**) at Le Bourg, place du Bourg.

To reach the island, take D789 3 miles north of Paimpol, where the peninsula ends dramatically at the pink-granite Pointe de l'Arcouest. A CAT bus from Paimpol (about 5 to 10 per day) makes the 15-minute run to the point for a one-way fare of 11 F ($2.10). Once there, you catch one of the ferries operated by Les Vedettes de Bréhat (☎ **96-55-73-47** for schedules), which will take you to the Ile de Bréhat from June to September—at other times it's too cold. There are departures about every 30 minutes, costing 35 F ($6.65) round-trip. Once at Bréhat, you can take a 45-minute, 60-F ($11.40) cruise of this idyllic Breton retreat.

---

closed Tuesday off-season. Admission is 19 F ($3.60) for adults and 9.50 F ($1.80) for children.

ESSENTIALS

GETTING THERE   From Paris's Gare Montparnasse, three trains per day make the journey (trip time: 5 hr.), costing 236 F ($44.85) one way. TV trains from Paris via Rennes run at the rate of seven to nine per day (trip time: 3 1/2 hr.), costing 236 F ($44.85) one way, plus 36 to 90 F ($6.85 to $17.10) for a reserved seat.

VISITOR INFORMATION   The Office de Tourisme is on esplanade St-Vincent (☎ **99-56-64-48**). A passport is necessary for the hydrofoil or car-ferry trips and tours to the Channel Islands.

WHERE TO STAY

Central

6 Grand Rue, 35400 St-Malo. ☎ **99-40-87-70**. Fax 99-40-87-70. 44 rms. MINIBAR TV TEL. 395–630 F ($75.05–$119.70) double. Breakfast 55 F ($10.45) extra. AE, DC, MC, V. Parking 45 F ($8.55). Bus 1, 2, or 3.

On a street near the harbor, this hotel is the best of a fairly lackluster lot. It's provincial, but in a sophisticated way. The furnishings are contemporary and color coordinated. One of the best reasons for staying here is the food—meals cost 135 to 195 F ($25.65 to $37.05) in La Frégate. Before dinner, you can have a drink in the bar.

Elisabeth

2 rue des Cordiers, 35400 St-Malo. ☎ **99-56-24-98.** Fax 99-56-39-24. 17 rms. TV TEL. 450–620 F ($85.50–$117.80) double. Breakfast 50 F ($9.50) extra. AE, DC, MC, V. Parking 55 F ($10.45). Bus 1, 2, or 3.

Inside the fortress walls of the old city, behind a 16th-century facade near the ferry terminal, the Elizabeth welcomes you with stylish rooms and modern comforts. Breakfast is served in a typical corsair cellar. Guests can use a public sitting room or retreat to the bar.

WHERE TO DINE

✪ A La Duchesse Anne

5 place Guy-La-Chambre. ☎ **99-40-85-33.** Reservations required. Main courses 100–200 F ($19–$38). MC, V. Thurs–Tues 12:15–1:30pm and 7:15–9:15pm. Closed Dec–Jan. Bus 1, 2, or 3. FRENCH.

This leading restaurant was built into the ramparts. In summer, tables are placed under a large canopy amid hydrangeas. Try the fish specialties—the fish soup with chunks of fresh seafood, spiced and cooked in an iron pot, is excellent, as are the Cancale oysters. Main courses include grilled turbot with beurre blanc and pepper steak. The desserts are equally tempting. Year after year the place delivers the finest food in town.

Le Chalut

8 rue de la Corne-de-Cerf. ☎ **99-56-71-58.** Reservations required. Main courses 90–100 F ($17.10–$19); fixed-price menus 90 F ($17.10), 175 F ($33.25), and 265 F ($50.35). AE, MC, V. Tues–Sat 12:30–2pm and 7:30–10pm, Sun 12:30–2pm. Closed mid-Jan to mid-Feb. Bus 1, 2, or 3. FRENCH.

The decor here is nautical—with green and blue throughout. Chef Jean-Philippe Foucat's flavorful cuisine is based on fresh ingredients and includes braised sweetbreads with baby vegetables in tarragon sauce, terrine of scallops, and crayfish in sage-flavored sauce; for dessert there's a gâteau of bitter chocolate served with almond paste or a feuilleté of red seasonal berries. The only complaint we've received is that the place fills up with too many tourists, but that's the curse of St-Malo in general.

Reims & the Champagne Country

In about three days, you can take the the the Autoroute de l'Est (N3) from Paris and explore a region of beautiful cathedrals, historic battlefields, fantastic food, and world-famous vineyards, topping your tour with a heady glass of bubbly. On the "champagne trail," you can go first to the wine-producing center of Epernay, then on to Reims, some 90 miles northeast of Paris. After visiting Reims and its cathedral, you can leave on Rte. 31 east, heading toward Verdun.

REGIONAL CUISINE Champagne's wine overshadows its cuisine, though several culinary specialties are unique to the district. Most are simple, hearty recipes developed over the centuries in country homes, using pork, beef, fish, and the area's fresh vegetables.

The tang and bite of the sparkling wines dissolve—in the most appetizing of ways—some of the flavorful grease and oils that are part of the local charcuteries and pâtés. Specialties include pork or sheep *andouillettes* (chitterlings) from Bar-sur-Aube or Bar-sur-Seine, pig's trotters from Ste-Menehould, and an endless variety of pâtés made from offal—which many North Americans would never consider eating. A *matelote* is a fish stew, usually prepared with freshwater fish and red or white wine. The matelotes here usually employ champagne and such freshwater fish as carp, pike, and trout.

Most of the area's cheeses are made from cows' milk. The most famous are the *maroilles*, aged collectively (where their skins turn a terra-cotta red) in communal cellars. Some maroilles are sprinkled with tarragon, pepper, and paprika and then aged two months to produce the strong, aromatic Boulette d'Avesnes, which the French eat with beer. One cheese enjoying popularity in North America is Brie de Melun or Brie de Meaux—the best varieties are made in Champagne, preferably near Meaux.

The largest champagne producer is Moët et Chandon, though there are excellent smaller vintners like Krug, Roederer, and Böllinger. Some of the still (nonsparkling) wines from the region are famous too, including blanc de blancs.

EXPLORING THE REGION BY CAR

Here's how to link together the best of the region if you rent a car.

Day 1 Begin relatively close to Paris at the romanesque abbey of La Ferté-sous-Jouarre, where you can tour the oldest crypt in France,

What's Special About Reims & the Champagne Country

Great Towns
- Reims, an ancient city where French kings came to be crowned.
- Châlons-sur-Marne, crisscrossed by canals.
- Troyes, an architectural gem and capital of the southern champagne country.

Architectural Highlights
- Cathédrale Notre-Dame de Reims, one of the most famous in the world.
- Abbaye d'Hautvillers at Epernay, a gracious 12th-century abbey that's the burial place of Dom Pérignon, synonymous with great bubbly.
- Basilique St-Rémi, at Reims, with a grand romanesque nave and 13th-century stained glass.
- Basilique de St-Urbain, at Troyes, the Parthenon of Champagne.
- Château de Condé, once home of the marquis de Sade.

Outstanding Museum
- Musée d'Art Moderne, at Troyes, one of France's greatest collections of modern art.

Champagne Cellars
- Moët et Chandon, at Epernay.
- Reims, site of such cellars as Pommery, Taittinger, and Piper-Heidsieck.

Events
- *Son-et-lumière* (sound-and-light) shows, June to September, with illuminations at Reims and Troyes.

a 7th-century cellar built by the Merovingians. Consider a meal at the Auberge de Condé (see later in this chapter) before moving on to Château-Thierry (13 miles northeast along N3). In the twilight, pay your respects to some of the most evocative sites of World War I, where American losses at the Battle of Belleau Wood were appalling. Spend the night in Château-Thierry.

Day 2　Your goal for the day will be the holy city of Reims, 31 miles northeast on E50. Stop for lunch at the Château de Fère, near the ruined castle of Fère-en-Tardenois. (This will be a detour of about 7 miles.) Then backtrack 12 miles south along clearly marked country roads to Condé-en-Brie. Its most famous monument is the château associated with the family of the marquis de Sade. (Be alert to the hours of visits here or call ahead if you have to arrive at other hours—see later in this chapter.) Afterward, continue north to Reims for the night.

Day 3　Spend your morning at the Cathédrale Notre-Dame de Reims and its older romanesque cousin, the Basilique St-Rémi. Follow with a visit to one of the city's champagne houses. If you're up for more tours of champagne cellars, head south from Reims for 15 miles along the Route du Champagne (N51) for a brief visit to the famous wine hamlet (and cellars) of Epernay. After your tour, head east for 21 miles along highway D3 to the half-timbered town of Châlons-sur-Marne, your overnight stop. Though the scene of bloody World War I battles, it's a charming town of churches, French culture, and art.

Day 4　Take highway N77 south (if you're in a hurry take the A26 superhighway) for 51 miles to Troyes, whose Renaissance core is one of the best preserved in northern France. Stay overnight here.

Champagne

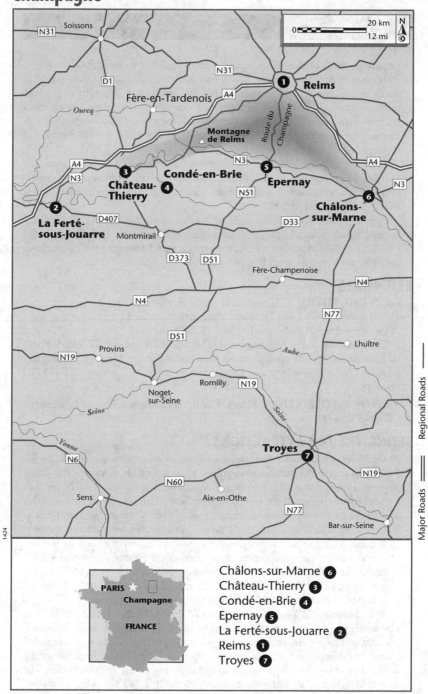

N31 Soissons
N31
D1
Fère-en-Tardenois
A4
Ourcq
1 **Reims**
Montagne
de Reims
Route du Champagne
A4
N3
A4
N3
3
N3
5
Condé-en-Brie
Château-
Thierry **4**
Epernay
2
D407
Châlons-
sur-Marne **6**
La Ferté-
sous-Jouarre
Montmirail
D33
D373 D51
Fère-Champenoise
N4
N51
D51
N77
N19 Provins
Aube
Lhuître
Romilly N19
Noget-
sur-Seine
Seine
Seine
Yonne
N6
Troyes **7**
N60
N19
Sens
Aix-en-Othe
N77
Bar-sur-Seine

0 ▰▰▰ 20 km
12 mi
N

Major Roads ═══ Regional Roads ───

PARIS ★
Champagne
FRANCE

Châlons-sur-Marne **6**
Château-Thierry **3**
Condé-en-Brie **4**
Epernay **5**
La Ferté-sous-Jouarre **2**
Reims **1**
Troyes **7**

1424

1 Epernay

87 miles E of Paris, 16 miles S of Reims

On the left bank of the Marne, Epernay rivals Reims as a center for champagne. Though with only one-sixth of Reims's population, Epernay produces nearly as much champagne as its larger sister. It boasts an estimated 200 miles or more of cellars and tunnels, a veritable rabbit warren, for storing champagne. These caves are vast vaults cut into the chalk rock on which the town is built. Represented in Epernay are such champagne companies as Moët et Chandon (the largest), Pol Roger, Mercier, and de Castellane.

Epernay's main boulevards are the elegant residential avenue de Champagne, rue Mercier, and rue de Reims, all radiating from place de la République. Two important squares in the narrow streets of the commercial district are place Hughes-Plomb and place des Arcades.

Epernay has been either destroyed or burned nearly two dozen times, since it lay in the path of invading armies, particularly the Germans. Thus few of its old buildings are left. However, try to visit **avenue de Champagne** for its neoclassical villas and Victorian town houses.

ESSENTIALS

GETTING THERE   Thirteen trains per day arrive from Paris (trip time: 1¼ hr.), costing 97 F ($18.45) one way; there are also 11 trains per day from Reims (trip time: 20 min.), costing 30 F ($5.70) one way.

The major bus link is operated by SDTM TransChampagne (☎ 26-65-17-07 in Epernay for schedules), operating four buses per day Monday to Saturday between Châlons-sur-Marne and Epernay (trip time: 1 hr.), costing 30 F ($5.70) one way.

VISITOR INFORMATION   The Office de Tourisme is at 7 av. de Champagne (☎ 26-55-33-00).

SEEING THE TOP ATTRACTIONS

At the **Moët et Chandon Champagne Cellars**, 18 av. de Champagne (☎ 26-54-71-11), an expert staff member gives guided tours in English, describing the champagne-making process and also filling you in on champagne lore: Napoléon, a friend of Jean-Rémy Moët, would stop by here for thousands of bottles on his way to the battlefront. The only time he didn't take a supply with him was at Waterloo—and look what happened there! You'll see *remueurs* at work, twisting each bottle a quarter turn so the impurities will settle near the cork. At the end of the tour you're given a complimentary glass of the bubbly. Admission is 20 F ($3.80). The cellars are open April to October, daily from 9:30 to 11:30am and 2 to 4:30pm; November to March, Monday to Friday from 9:30 to 11:30am and 2 to 4:45pm. Closed national holidays. No appointment is necessary.

Since **Mercier,** 73 av. de Champagne (☎ 26-54-75-26), is close to Moët et Chandon, you can visit them on the same day. In the middle of the vineyard, Mercier conducts tours in English of its 11 miles of tunnels from laser-guided trains. Its facilities include a champagne museum. The caves contain one of the world's largest wooden barrels—with a capacity of more than 200,000 bottles. The tour is launched by an audiovisual. Admission is 20 F ($3.80). Mercier is open Monday to Saturday from 9:30 to 11:30am and 2 to 4:30pm and Sunday from

---

Impressions

Brothers, brothers, come quickly! I am drinking stars!

—Dom Pérignon

9:30 to 11:30am and 2 to 5:30pm; closed Tuesday and Wednesday from December to February. No appointment is necessary.

In the 19th-century Château Perrier, the **Musée Municipal,** 13 av. de Champagne (☎ **26-51-90-31**), explores the region's life as reflected in large part by the tools with which locals earned their living—from agricultural tools to wine presses, even old champagne bottles. Admission is 8 F ($1.50). The museum is open April to November, Wednesday to Monday from 10am to noon and 2 to 6pm; closed December to March.

On D386, signposted just north of Epernay, is the **Abbaye d'Hautvillers,** owned by Moët et Chandon; it contains the tomb of monk Dom Pérignon (cellar master at the abbey from 1670 to 1715), who's credited with inventing the process for turning the still wines of the region into sparkling champagne. The abbey has been rebuilt several times since it was founded in the 12th century. When the monks were evicted during the Revolution, the abbey was purchased by the Moët family. Today it's a church again and can be visited free by appointment—call Moët et Chandon at 26-54-71-11. A Moët representative can arrange for you to see the interior gardens with their incomparable view of the champagne vineyards and the Marne Valley.

WHERE TO STAY

Champagne
30 rue Eugène-Mercier, 51200 Epernay. ☎ **26-55-30-22.** Fax 26-51-94-63. 35 rms. TV TEL. 300–350 F ($57–$66.50) double. Breakfast 45 F ($8.55) extra. AE, DC, V. Parking free.

This simple little inn is one of the best of a modest lot in the town itself (the luxurious accommodations are on the outskirts). However, it offers good prices for its well-maintained functional rooms. A generous buffet breakfast is served every morning, and parking is available on the grounds.

WHERE TO DINE

Les Berceaux
13 rue Berceaux, 51200 Epernay. ☎ **26-55-28-84.** Fax 26-55-10-36. Reservations recommended. Main courses 70–150 F ($13.30–$28.50); fixed-price menus 100 F ($19), 140 F ($26.60), 200 F ($38), and 320 F ($60.80). AE, DC, MC, V. Mon–Sat noon–2:30pm and 7–9:30pm, Sun noon–2:30pm. FRENCH.

Owner/chef Luc Maillard (his wife, Jill, is English) serves superior Champenois cookery. The portions are huge, and if you can afford it, wash everything down with champagne. Specialties include turbot au champagne, sole au Berceaux, and pâté de foie gras. The Maillards also operate a wine bar here, with a bistro where customers can order meals for 110 F ($20.90) and up; you can even sample good French wines by the glass. Staff members at Les Berceaux speak English and can arrange your visits to the area champagne houses.

The Maillards rent 29 simply furnished rooms; a double with shower costs 330 F ($62.70) and one with bath goes for 375 F ($71.25), plus 37 F ($7.05) for breakfast.

NEARBY ACCOMMODATIONS & DINING

✪ Royal Champagne

51160 Champillon. ☎ **26-52-87-11.** Fax 26-52-89-69. 30 rms, 3 suites. TV TEL. 870–1,300 F ($165.30–$247) double; 1,500–1,800 F ($285–$342) suite. Breakfast 80 F ($15.20) extra. AE, DC, MC, V. Parking free. Closed Jan. Drive 4 miles from Epernay toward Reims on the Route du Vignoble (RN2051); the hotel is in the hamlet of Champillon.

A Relais & Châteaux, this is the area's best and certainly most scenic hostelry; the windows of the luxurious rooms open onto views of the vineyards. The food is exceptional, with specialties like lobster ragoût, salt cod with mousseline of truffles, and roast lamb with garlic. The chef is known for classic dishes to which he's added some innovative twist. The fixed-price menus cost 260 F ($49.40), 320 F ($60.80), or 400 F ($76); you can expect to spend 500 F ($95) for an à la carte meal.

2 Condé-en-Brie

55 miles E of Paris, 15 miles W of Epernay

West of Epernay, the **Château de Condé** (☎ 23-82-42-25) was inherited in 1814 by the comte de Sade and remained in his family until 1983. The Sade name was besmirched by the infamous marquis, an innovative writer (*Justine, Juliette, The 120 Days of Sodom*) whose sexual practices as described in his works led to the word *sadism*.

If you're traveling between Château-Thierry and Epernay on Rte. 3, head south at Dormans and follow the signs to Condé-en-Brie.

The castle was built in the late 12th century by Enguerran of Coucy. A part of the old keep still remains—two big rooms with great chimneys and thick walls. The castle was rebuilt in the Renaissance style at the beginning of the 16th century by Cardinal de Bourbon, a member of the royal family. His nephew, Louis de Bourbon, called himself prince of Condé, most likely because he had many fond childhood memories of the place. After sustaining damage in the early 18th century, the château was rebuilt yet again—this time for the marquis de La Faye. The Italian architect, Servandoni, invited artists like Boucher and Watteau to do frescoes and paintings (which can still be seen). Servandoni decorated the biggest room, making it a theater hall for music and entertainment. The present castle is an exceptional ensemble, with its paintings, woodwork, chimneys, and so-called Versailles floor.

In 1994 the new owners, the de Rocheforts, discovered several Watteau paintings concealed behind mirrors installed during the 18th century. Now at the push of a button the mirrors open to reveal the previously hidden treasures.

Admission is 28 F ($5.30) for adults and 14 F ($2.65) for children 14 and under. The castle is open for tours June to August, daily at 2:30, 3:30, and 4:30pm; in May and September, on Sunday and French national holidays at 2:30, 3:30, and 4:30pm. It's closed in other months except by advance reservations.

3 Reims

89 miles E of Paris, 28 miles NW of Châlons-sur-Marne

Reims (pronounced Rahns), an ancient Roman city, was important at the time Caesar conquered Gaul. French kings have traditionally come here to be crowned, and it's said that the French nation was born here in A.D. 498. Joan of Arc escorted Charles VII here in 1429, kissing the silly man's feet. But don't let this ancient background mislead you: As you approach Reims you'll pass through prefabricated suburbs that'll make you think of apartment-house blocks in Eastern Europe. There are gems in Reims, including the cathedral (below), of course, but you must seek them out.

Reims is visited chiefly because it's the center of a wine-growing district that gives the world a bubbly with which to make toasts. The champagne bottled in this district is said to be "the lightest and most subtle in flavor of the world's wines." Try to linger here, exploring the vineyards and wine cellars, the gothic monuments, and the battlefields. The Germans occupied Reims in 1870, 1914, and again in 1940.

ESSENTIALS

GETTING THERE   Fifteen trains from Paris arrive daily (trip time: 1½ hr.), costing 104 F ($19.75) one way. There are also seven trains per day from Strasbourg (trip time: 4 hr.), costing 200 F ($38) one way.

VISITOR INFORMATION   The Office de Tourisme is at 2 rue Guillaume-de-Machault (☎ 26-47-25-69).

SEEING THE TOP ATTRACTIONS

On May 7, 1945, the Germans surrendered to General Eisenhower in the **Salle de Reddition,** 12 rue Franklin-Roosevelt (☎ 26-47-84-19), once a little school-house near the railroad tracks. The walls of the room are lined with maps of the rail routes, exactly as they were on the day of surrender. Admission is 10 F ($1.90) for adults and 5 F (95¢) for children. It's open May to September, Wednesday to Monday from 10am to noon and 2 to 6pm; October to April, Wednesday to Monday from 2 to 6pm.

The **Cathédrale Notre-Dame de Reims,** place du Cardinal-Luçon (☎ 26-47-49-37), is one of the most famous cathedrals in the world. After World War I it was restored largely with U.S. contributions; mercifully, it escaped World War II relatively unharmed. Built on the site of a church burned to the ground in 1211, it was intended as a sanctuary where French kings would be anointed—St. Rémi, the bishop of Reims, baptized Clovis, the pagan king of the Franks, here in 496. All the kings of France from Louis VII in 1137 to Charles X in 1825 were crowned here.

Laden with statuettes, its three western facade portals are spectacular. A rose-colored window is above the central portal, which is dedicated to the Virgin. The right portal portrays the Apocalypse and the Last Judgment; the left, Martyrs and Saints. At the western facade's northern door is a smiling angel. Lit by lancet win-dows, the nave is immense, with many bays. Beside the cathedral is the treasury with a 12th-century chalice for the communion of French monarchs and a talis-man that supposedly contains a relic of the True Cross that Charlemagne is said to have worn.

The cathedral is open Monday to Saturday from 7:30am to 7:30pm and Sun-day from 8:30am to 7:30pm. Admission is free.

Though sometimes unfavorably compared to the cathedral above, the **Basilique St-Rémi,** 53 rue St-Simon (☎ 26-85-23-36), is outstanding. Once a Benedictine abbey church, it contains a grand romanesque nave leading to a magnificent choir crowned with massive pointed arches. The nave, the transepts, one of the towers, and the aisles date from the 11th century. The portal of the south transept is in flamboyant early 16th-century style. The apse is made of stained glass, some from the 13th century. The tomb of St. Rémi is elaborately carved with Renaissance figures and columns. The former abbey has been turned into a historical and lapidary museum. In the cloister is a Gallo-Roman sarcophagus said to be that of the consul Jovin (d. 412). There's also a collection of medieval sculpture, mostly romanesque.

Admission is free. The basilica is open Monday to Wednesday, Friday, and Sunday from 8am to 7pm and Thursday and Saturday from 7am to 7pm.

Housed in the 18th-century buildings belonging to the old abbey of St. Denis, the **Musée des Beaux-Arts,** 8 rue Chanzy (☎ **26-47-28-44**), is a fine provincial art gallery that has more than a dozen portraits of German princes of the Reformation by both "the Elder" and "the Younger" Cranach; the museum has owned this remarkable collection since it opened in 1795. In the same hall, the Toiles Peintes (light painting on rough linen) date from the 15th and 16th centuries and depict the *Passion du Christ* and *Vengeance du Christ.* Paintings and fine furniture from the 17th and 18th centuries are in the Salles Diancourt and Jamot-Neveux. In the next room is an excellent series of 26 of Corot's tree-shaded walks. Admission is 10 F ($1.90) for adults; children free. The museum is open Wednesday to Monday from 10am to noon and 2 to 6pm.

EXPLORING THE CHAMPAGNE CELLARS

Many of the vast ✪ **champagne cellars of Reims** extend for miles through chalky deposits. In fact, during the German siege of 1914 and throughout the war, people lived in them and even published a daily paper there. Though the cellars are open all year, they're most interesting during the fall grape harvest. After that, the wine is stored in vats in the caves. While in the chalk caves, a second fermentation of the wine takes place. The wine-growers wait until the sparkle has "taken," as they say, before they remove the bottles to racks or pulpits. For about three months *remueurs* are paid just to turn them a fraction every day, which brings the impurities toward the cork. After aging for a few years, the wines are mixed with a liqueur (wine and sugar) that determines the sweetness of the champagne. The process takes four or five years and is carried out in caves that are usually 100 feet deep and at a constant 50°F.

Among the most visited cellars are those under the gothic-style buildings and spacious gardens of the **House of Pommery,** place du Général-Gouraud (☎ **26-61-62-55**). A magnificent 116-step stairway leads to a maze of galleries, dug into the chalk, that are more than 11 miles long and about 100 feet below the ground. Various stages of champagne-making are shown, and a slide show in English is given at the end of the tour. Admission is free. Open March 15 to October, daily from 10am to 5:30pm; November to March 14, Monday to Friday from 10am to noon and 2 to 5pm.

A visit to **Mumm,** 34 rue du Champ-de-Mars (☎ **26-49-59-70**), includes a video show and a cellar tour. A small museum exhibits ancient tools of a vintner and casks. This is the only cellar in Reims offering a taste of their product; you can purchase their champagne in the gift shop. Tours in English are 20 F ($3.80). Open Easter to October, daily from 9 to 11am and 2 to 5pm; November to Easter, Monday to Friday from 9 to 11am and 2 to 5pm. Closed holidays.

At **Piper-Heidsieck,** 51 bd. Henri-Vasnier (☎ **26-85-01-94**), you explore the cellars in an electric train. The visit includes a video. Admission is 20 F ($3.80). Open May to September, daily from 9 to 11:45am and 1:30 to 6:15pm; in March,

Reims

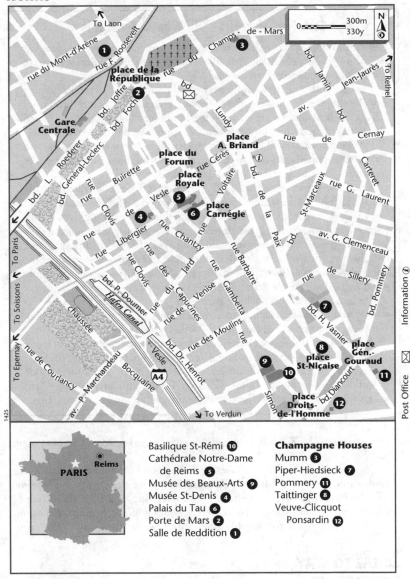

Champagne Houses
Basilique St-Rémi ⑩   Mumm ③
Cathédrale Notre-Dame   Piper-Hiedsieck ⑦
  de Reims ⑤   Pommery ⑪
Musée des Beaux-Arts ⑨   Taittinger ⑧
Musée St-Denis ④   Veuve-Clicquot
Palais du Tau ⑥   Ponsardin ⑫
Porte de Mars ②
Salle de Reddition ①

April, October, and November, daily from 9:45 to 11:45am and 2 to 5:15pm; and December to February, Thursday to Monday from 9 to 11:45am and 2 to 5:15pm.

At **Taittinger,** 9 place St-Niçaise (☎ **26-85-45-35**), you can visit the home of some of the most famous champagne makers, whose underground caverns once formed part of the crypt of an abbey. The guided tours given through five miles of galleries are accompanied by a slide show. You can purchase champagne in the gift shop. Admission is 15 F ($2.85). Open March to November, daily from 9:30am to noon and 2 to 4:30pm and Saturday and Sunday from 9am to noon

Cork Pop, Fizz, Fizz—Oh, What a Treat It Is

Since the Middle Ages everyone from Benedictine monks to *les grands bourgeois de Champagne* have tamed the shale-filled chalky soil of this district into some of the most profitable acreage in Europe.

The love of that effervescent mystery called champagne is certainly nothing new. During the Renaissance, the only thing François I of France and Henry VIII of England could agree on was a preference for bubbly. Napoléon carted along cases of the stuff to his battlefronts. Casanova used it to liven up his legendary seductions, Mme Pompadour employed it to tempt the Sun King, and Tallyrand imported cases of it to the Congress of Vienna for a different sort of seduction—procuring more favorable peace terms.

We all owe a toast or two to Dom Pérignon, that Benedictine monk (1638–1715) who initiated the technique of adding sugar to champagne to cause it, after years of fermentation, to foam. Without a complicated series of additives, double fermentations, and cooling at precise temperatures, champagne is a nonsparkling wine. But without the fizz, where would be the fun? The best champagne grapes are grown in a network of vineyards that meander like narrow ribbons along the bottomlands south of Reims. French vintners refer to the best regions as the Côte des Blancs, Montagne de Reims, and Vallée de la Marne.

The association of this bubbling wine with glamour, romance, and celebration represents one of marketing's most remarkable success stories. Off the record, Burgundy's vintners will remind oeniphiles that it takes a lot more work, with a greater chance of failure from uncontrollable variables, to produce a great bottle of still red than a jeroboam of sparkling Veuve-Clicquot. Nonetheless, the fascination with real champagne remains fervent, as shown by the spectacular increase in worldwide consumption of the stuff since Leslie Caron and Louis Jourdan sang about "The Night They Invented Champagne" in the 1958 movie *Gigi*.

and 2 to 6pm; December to February, Monday to Friday from 9:30am to noon and 2 to 4:30pm.

You can visit part of the 16 miles of underground galleries on fairly routine guided tours at **Veuve-Clicquot Ponsardin,** 1 place des Droits-de-l'Homme (☎ **26-89-54-40**). The highlight is the screening of a film about one of Champagne's grande dames, the Veuve Clicquot (Widow Clicquot). Admission is free. Open April to October only, Monday to Saturday (call for an appointment).

WHERE TO STAY
VERY EXPENSIVE

✪ Boyer-les-Crayères

64 bd. Henry-Vasnier, 51100 Reims. ☎ **26-82-80-80.** Fax 26-82-65-52. 16 rms, 3 suites. A/C MINIBAR TV TEL. 990–1,820 F ($188.10–$345.80) double; from 1,940 F ($368.60) suite. Breakfast 98 F ($18.60) extra. AE, DC, MC, V. Parking free. Closed Dec 25 to mid-Jan.

This hotel occupies one of the finest châteaux in eastern France. Located in a 14-acre private park, it boasts 18-foot ceilings, burnished paneling, and luxurious furnishings. The guest rooms, with terraces and all the amenities, are individually decorated and usually available when a champagne mogul is not in residence;

services include a masseur or hairdresser who can be sent to your room. The hotel's restaurant is one of the greatest in the area. World-famous chef Gérard Boyer imbues each dish with his culinary imprint. One of his masterpieces is salade du Père-Maurice, with green beans, artichoke hearts, lemon, foie gras, truffles, and lobster. Reservations are required a few days in advance for weekday dinners, at least a month in advance for weekend dinners.

EXPENSIVE

L'Assiette Champenoise
40 av. Paul-Vaillant-Couturier, 51430 Tinqueux. ☎ **26-84-64-64.** Fax 26-04-15-69. 60 rms, 2 suites. MINIBAR TV TEL. 545–770 F ($103.60–$146.35) double; 770–1,110 F ($146.35–$211) suite. Breakfast 70 F ($13.30) extra. AE, DC, MC, V. Parking free.

About four miles from the center of Reims, this is the second-best hotel and restaurant in the area. Set among century-old trees, this was once a private Norman estate with a covered pool and terrace. The accommodations are luxurious, of course. Many people come here just to enjoy the cooking of Jean-Pierre Lallement, who is assisted by his wife, Colette. In their elegant country dining room, the cuisine is both classical and innovative. Try the veal kidneys and sweetbreads flavored with star anise, grilled duck liver with fondue of tomatoes, or herb-flavored scallops.

Les Templiers
22 rue Templiers, 51100 Reims. ☎ **26-88-55-08.** Fax 26-47-80-60. 19 rms. A/C MINIBAR TV TEL. 1,500 F ($285.15) double. Breakfast 80 F ($15.20) extra. AE, DC, MC, V.

This hotel a short walk from the cathedral may be small, but it's your best inner-city bet. A restored 1800s mock-gothic house, the place has taste and sensitivity, with antiques, ornate ceilings, and hand-carved woodwork creating an inviting ambience. The guest rooms continue the 19th-century allure, with color-coordinated fabrics and bold print wallcoverings. Breakfast, the only meal served, can be taken in your room or beside an indoor pool.

MODERATE

Mercure Reims Cathédrale
31 bd. Paul-Doumer, 51100 Reims. ☎ **26-84-49-49.** Fax 26-84-49-84. 113 rms, 9 suites. A/C MINIBAR TV TEL. 480 F ($91.25) double; 550–950 F ($104.55–$180.60) suite. Breakfast 51 F ($9.70) extra. AE, DC, MC, V. Parking 40 F ($7.60). Bus G or H.

On the banks of the Marne Canal, a five-minute walk from the town center, this hotel is a member of a national chain with a good reputation. It's near the entrance of the autoroute, so it's easy to find. The good-sized rooms have all the modern conveniences, and some have views of a scenic waterway. Les Ombrages restaurant serves French specialties nightly until 10pm.

ⓢ La Paix
9 rue Buirette, 51100 Reims. ☎ **26-40-04-08.** Fax 26-47-75-04. 105 rms, 1 suite. MINIBAR TV TEL. 420–600 F ($79.80–$114.05) double; 550–700 F ($104.55–$133.05) suite. Breakfast 50 F ($9.50) extra. AE, DC, MC, V. Parking 45 F ($8.55). Bus G or H.

The rooms in this contemporary hotel (between the train station and the cathedral) have comfortable beds, and some have views of the garden, which has a pool and a chapel. Many of the rooms now have air conditioning. The hotel also has a brasserie/taverne that serves excellent meals, including sauerkrauts, fish, grills, oysters, and seafood.

INEXPENSIVE

Grand Hôtel du Nord

75 place Drouet-d'Erlon, 51100 Reims. ☎ **26-47-39-03.** Fax 26-40-92-26. 50 rms. MINIBAR TV TEL. 285–320 F ($54.15–$60.80) double. Breakfast 30 F ($5.70) extra. AE, DC, MC, V. Parking 25 F ($4.75). Bus G or H.

Accessible by the A4 motorway (exit at "Reims-Centre"), this old-fashioned hotel offers comfortably decorated rooms. A TV lounge with a cozy atmosphere is available for guests. Two steps from the drab entrance, the liveliness of place Drouet-d'Erlon, with its boutiques, café terraces, and cinemas, unfolds. You're also near such attractions as the cathedral, the Basilique St-Rémi, and various museums.

WHERE TO DINE

Boyer-les-Crayères and L'Assiette Champenoise (above) both contain excellent restaurants.

Le Drouet

96 place Drouet d'Erlon. ☎ **26-88-56-39.** Reservations not required. Main courses 65–110 F ($12.35–$20.90); fixed-price menu 150 F ($28.50). V. Daily noon–2pm and 7–9:30pm. Bus G or H. FRENCH.

Jean-Pierre and Denise Maillot gained fame in Reims by operating Le Florence, one of the city's finest restaurants. When it closed, they moved a few doors down and opened this deluxe brasserie in an old villa with a terrace and garden. Only fresh products are used, and seafood is a specialty, especially sole cooked in champagne. The care and attention that characterized the cuisine at Le Florence are missing here, but Le Drouet is a brasserie.

Le Vigneron

Place Paul-Jamot. ☎ **26-47-00-71.** Reservations recommended. Main courses 68–140 F ($12.90–$26.60). MC, V. Mon–Fri 11:30am–2:30pm and 5:30–10pm, Sat 5:30–10pm, Sun 11:30am–2:30pm. Closed Dec 23–Jan 2 and Aug 1–16. Bus G or H. FRENCH.

This brasserie is run by Hervé Liegent. The interior of the 17th-century house, behind the cathedral, is filled with old champagne posters, vineyard tools, and antique champagne barrels. The food that accompanies the dozens of brands of champagne includes baked duckling in champagne sauce, garlic sausages (andouillette) with champagne, and champagne-flavored sorbets. The food is hearty but prepared with finesse. Service is geared to a rapid lunch if you want it.

NEARBY DINING

For the most superb restaurant in Champagne, head for Château de Fère on D967. About 1¹/₂ miles north of this hamlet are the ruins of a 12th-century fortified castle—also called the Château de Fère. Take N31 northwest of Reims, pass through Fismes, then turn southwest onto N367.

✪ Château de Fère

Route Forestière (D967), 02130 Fère-en-Tardenois. ☎ **23-82-21-13.** Fax 23-82-37-81. Reservations required. Main courses 160–260 F ($30.40–$49.40); fixed-price menus 290–480 F ($55.10–$91.20). AE, DC, MC, V. Daily noon–2:30 and 7–9:30pm. FRENCH.

Set in a park, this fabulous restaurant occupies a restored 16th-century crenellated château with turrets. During summer, begin your repast in the sunny garden, sipping an apéritif or a glass of champagne with juice from freshly crushed raspberries. The owners oversee every detail and serve imaginative meals, with specialties like champagne-cooked turbot, paupiette of truffles and calves' kidneys, and dégustation des trois mignons (a platter of beef, lamb, and veal). The desserts are mouth-watering, but we prefer to skip them and order the boulette d'Avesnes, a cone of cheese flecked with herbs and crushed peppercorns and coated with paprika.

Also available here are 14 guest rooms and 9 suites—each luxuriously furnished, with bath, minibar, TV, and phone. Doubles are 850 to 1,200 F ($161.50 to $228) and suites are 1,450 to 1,950 F ($275.50 to $370.50), plus 90 F ($17.10) for breakfast.

4 Château-Thierry

56 miles E of Paris, 6 miles SW of Reims

An industrial town on the Maine's right bank, Château-Thierry contains the ruins of a castle believed to have been constructed for Frankish king Thierry IV. Château-Thierry gained fame for being the farthest point reached by the German offensive in the summer of 1918. Under heavy bombardment, French forces were aided by the Second and Third Divisions of the American Expeditionary Force. Battlefields of the Marne are a mile west of town; here, thousands of Allied soldiers who died fighting World War I are buried. Atop Hill 204 stands a monument honoring American troops who lost their lives.

Château-Thierry is also where poet/fable writer Jean de la Fontaine was born in a 16th-century home. The **Musée Jean-de-la-Fontaine,** 12 rue de la Fontaine (☎ 23-69-05-60), contains a small collection of his mementos, including many editions of his works from the Charles-Henri Genot collection, plus paintings and engravings from the 17th to the 20th century. The museum is open July to September, Wednesday to Monday from 10am to noon and 2:30 to 6:30pm; October to March, Wednesday to Monday from 2 to 5pm; April to June, Wednesday to Monday from 10am to noon and 2 to 6pm. Admission is 10 F ($1.90).

If you're interested in seeing some World War I relics, head for the **Bois de Belleau (Belleau Wood).** The Battle of Belleau Wood marked the second clash between American and German troops in World War I and demonstrated the bravery of the U.S. soldiers in modern warfare. The site is 5 miles northwest of Château-Thierry. After a bitter struggle that lasted two weeks, the woods were taken by the Second Division of the U.S. Expeditionary Force under Maj.-Gen. Omar Bundy. Though the Germans suffered many losses and some 1,650 prisoners were taken, U.S. casualties were appalling: Nearly 7,585 soldiers and 285 officers were wounded, killed, or missing in action.

In 1923 the battleground was dedicated as a memorial to the men who gave their lives there. The American cemetery contains 2,288 graves. You'll also see a chapel that was damaged in World War II.

ESSENTIALS

GETTING THERE   There are frequent local trains from Paris and Reims. If you're driving, take N367 southwest from Reims.

VISITOR INFORMATION   The Office de Tourisme is at 12 place de l'Hôtel-de-Ville (☎ 23-83-10-14).

WHERE TO STAY

Hôtel Ile-de-France

Route de Soissons, 02400 Château-Thierry. ☎ **23-69-10-12.** Fax 23-83-49-70. 56 rms, 50 with bath (tub or shower). TEL. 340 F ($64.60) double with bath. Breakfast 38–43 F ($7.20–$8.15) extra. AE, DC, MC, V. Parking free.

This elegant hotel is the leading choice in the area, which has a rather poor selection. Set in a park overlooking the green Marne Valley, the four-story house has balconies and dormers and a view of the town. Part of the Inter-Hôtel chain, the hotel has well-furnished rooms and a fair restaurant. Some singles don't have a bath.

5 La Ferté-sous-Jouarre

41 miles E of Paris, 51 miles SW of Reims

In the hamlet of Jouarre you can visit a 12th-century Benedictine abbey and explore one of the oldest crypts in France. At the **Musée de la Tour de l'Abbaye,** 6 rue Montmorin (☎ **60-22-06-11**), medievalists will appreciate the preserved documents, referring to the history of the Royal Abbey of Jouarre. The stones in its Merovingian crypt strongly evoke the 7th century. There's also a collection of prehistoric artifacts, remnants of the Roman occupation, and sculptural fragments. The crypt and towers are open Wednesday to Monday from 10am to noon and 2:30 to 5pm.

The town lies on the north bank of the Marne, around place de l'Hôtel-de-Ville. The most visited historic monument, the crypt of the abbey, is 2 miles south of town, along D402, toward Jouarre and Coulommiers.

ESSENTIALS

GETTING THERE   If you're driving, take N3 along the Marne.

VISITOR INFORMATION   The Syndicat d'Initiative (tourist office) is at 26 place de l'Hôtel-de-Ville (☎ **60-22-63-43**).

WHERE TO DINE

✪ Auberge de Condé

1 av. de Montmirail. ☎ **60-22-00-07.** Reservations required. Main courses 150–220 F ($28.50–$41.80); fixed-price lunch (weekdays only) 200 F ($38); fixed-price dinner 280 F ($53.20), 330 F ($62.70), and 450 F ($85.50). AE, DC, MC, V. Mon noon–2pm, Wed–Sun noon–2pm and 7–9pm. FRENCH.

This is one of the best restaurants in "the ring around Paris," a mile and a half from the abbey. The inn is old-fashioned, with a lot of provincial character, but serves delectable food worthy of its two-star rating. Manager/chef Pascal Tingaud is the grandson of the famous founder, Emile Tingaud. Perhaps start your meal with feuilleté de truffes et foie gras, then try sweetbreads "des gourmets" or filet of sole Vincent-Bourrel. Another specialty is poulet briarde—Bresse chicken poached in rich stock and served with a sauce of cream, butter, and grainy Meaux mustard. The grand traditional cooking is accompanied by the best champagne.

Auberge Jean-de-la-Fontaine

10 rue des Filoirs. ☎ **23-83-63-89.** Reservations required. Main courses 80–130 F ($15.20–$24.70); fixed-price menus 120 F ($22.80), 160 F ($30.40), and 350 F ($66.50). AE, DC, MC, V. Tues–Sat 12:30–2pm and 7:30–9:30pm, Sun 12:30–2pm. Closed the first two weeks of Jan and the first three weeks of Aug. FRENCH.

This restaurant is filled with engravings dedicated to the fables of Jean de la Fontaine. The menu changes every three weeks but may include such typical courses as foie gras maison en gelée des Sauternes, vinaigrette of crab and salmon (with asparagus-and-tomato coulis), roasted and deboned pigeon with patissons (a kind of turnip) and mustard sauce, and fisherman's salad with several kinds of filet of grilled fish with fresh herbs. It's good bistro cooking and makes no pretensions.

6 Châlons-sur-Marne

102 miles E of Paris, 28 miles SE of Reims, 99 miles NW of Nancy

Intersected by canals of the Marne River, Châlons-sur-Marne is a city of art and churches. The famous and infamous, such as Marie Antoinette, have passed through (her visit is commemorated by a triumphal arch, the Porte Dauphine). An important crossroads, Châlons lies between Reims and Troyes and Paris and Nancy, in the heart of champagne country.

The railway station lies on the western edge of the city, across the Marne from the old town. The city's old town is centered around two churches, the Cathédrale St-Etienne and the Eglise Notre-Dame-en-Vaux. They're connected by a main thoroughfare called rue de la Marne.

ESSENTIALS

GETTING THERE   Since Châlons-sur-Marne is on the main railway line between Strasbourg and Paris, train connections are easy and frequent. Twelve trains per day arrive from Paris (trip time: $1^1/_2$ hr.), costing 112 F ($21.30) one way. From Reims, nine trains per day pull in (trip time: 30 min.), costing 48 F ($9.10) one way; and from Strasbourg, three per day (trip time: $3^1/_2$ hr.), costing 191 F ($36.30) one way.

VISITOR INFORMATION   The Office de Tourisme is at 3 quai des Arts (☎ 26-65-17-89).

SEEING THE TOP ATTRACTIONS

The romanesque/gothic **Eglise Notre-Dame-en-Vaux,** place Tissier (☎ 26-65-63-17), is graced with spires reflected in the city's canals. Begun in 1170, Notre-Dame has one of the greatest chimes on the Continent, with 56 bells; it's also known for its 16th-century stained-glass windows. The church is open Monday to Saturday from 10am to noon and 1:30 to 7pm; admission is free.

While you're there, you can explore the **Musée du Cloître,** rue Nicolas-Durand (☎ 26-64-03-87). The cloister, like the church, dates from 1170 but was destroyed during the Revolution and many of its sculptures were decapitated; however, with the help of recent excavations, the heads and many of the pieces have been restored. The capitals displayed in the museum are richly decorated, some with grotesque scenes. A 12th-century collection, the *Four Evangelists*, the *Marriage in Cana*, and the *Washing of the Feet*, form one of the most enduring works left from 12th-century France. The museum is open Wednesday to Monday from 10am to noon and 2 to 6pm (to 5pm from October to March 3). Admission is 20 F ($3.80) for adults and 13 F ($2.45) for children.

Though consecrated in the 12th century, the **Cathédrale St-Etienne,** rue de la Marne (☎ 26-64-18-30), wasn't completed until the 13th century, then enlarged in the 17th. Unfortunately, it has stood in the way of invading armies—most recently in World Wars I and II. After aerial bombardments, only the north tower remains from the romanesque era. Some rare 12th-century stained-glass windows are in a vaulted room—the bottle-green glass is as celebrated in eastern France as Chartres blue is in the Ile de France. Other stained glass you'll see is from the 13th through the 16th century. You can visit daily from 9am to dusk.

The **Eglise St-Alpin,** off place Foch, was named after a bishop in Attila's time. It's romanesque, though much was altered in the 15th and 16th centuries. The church is best known for its beautiful stained-glass windows—called *en grisaille*— from the 16th century.

The city is filled with *hôtels particuliers* **(mansions)** that date from the 17th and 18th centuries. You may want to wander on your own and explore their facades; or inquire at the tourist office about its guided tour in French.

Beside the town hall is the 17th-century Hôtel des Dubois de Crance, which houses the **Bibliothèque Municipale** (☎ **26-68-54-44**). Its most prized and controversial possession is a prayerbook that may have belonged to Marie Antoinette, in which she wrote her famous "My poor children, adieu, adieu." Some scholars doubt the authenticity of her signature. The library is open Tuesday to Sunday from 9am to noon and 1:30 to 6pm; admission is free.

The **Musée Municipal,** place Godart (☎ **26-69-38-00**), boasts a rich collection of prehistoric Gallo-Roman and Merovingian objects from the surrounding area. Many interesting pieces rescued from the town's churches are in its sculpture section. It's open Wednesday to Monday from 2 to 6pm; admission is free.

WHERE TO STAY & DINE

Hôtel Angleterre et Restaurant Jacky-Michel
19 place Monseigneur Tissier, 51000 Châlons-sur-Marne. ☎ **26-68-21-51.** Fax 26-70-51-67. 18 rms. MINIBAR TV TEL. 490 F ($93.15) double. Breakfast 60 F ($11.40) extra. AE, DC, MC, V. Parking free. Closed Sun.

This is the leading hotel and restaurant, near the town center in a stone-fronted building. The pastel guest rooms are furnished in a "decorator style." The hotel doesn't receive guests on Sunday. Chef Jacky Michel is a culinary artist—try his warm salad of lobster with baby leeks, ragoût of shellfish with baby herbs, or veal kidneys with red-wine sauce and garlic croquettes. The food goes well with some of the grand wines of France. Monday to Friday an excellent fixed-price menu is offered for only 120 F ($22.80); otherwise, fixed-price meals cost as much as 400 F ($76). The restaurant is open Monday to Friday from 12:30 to 2pm and Monday to Saturday from 7:30 to 9:30pm; it's closed July 6 to 31.

NEARBY ACCOMMODATIONS & DINING

Aux Armes de Champagne
51460 L'Epine, 51460 Courtisols. ☎ **26-69-30-30.** Fax 26-66-92-31. 35 rms, 2 suites. MINIBAR TEL. 320–690 F ($60.80–$131.15) double; 1,250 F ($237.60) suite. Breakfast 55 F ($10.45) extra. MC, V. Parking free. Closed Jan 7–Feb 13.

Jean-Paul Pérardel operates this outstanding restaurant/hotel 5 miles from Châlons-sur-Marne, opening onto the facade of "Our Lady of the Thorn." This has become the region's most important restaurant; much care and money went into the improvement of this place, which now has an entrance hall and a garden. The food is delivered straight from the wholesale food market at Rungis twice a week, and the cuisine is of simplified classicism. Fixed-price menus cost 195 F ($37.05) and 270 F ($51.30). The restaurant is open daily from 12:30 to 2pm and

7:30 to 9:30pm; however, from November to March it closes Sunday night and Monday.

7 Troyes

102 miles SE of Paris, 94 miles NW of Dijon

The capital of the southern champagne country, Troyes is filled with Renaissance architectural glories. The comtes de Champagne acquired the town in the 10th century. The historic core of the city is called Bouchon de Champagne, meaning "champagne cork," to which it bears a faint resemblance. However, don't come here for champagne caves—there aren't any.

The town was rebuilt in the Renaissance style after a 1524 fire wiped out much of it, and it was destroyed again in World War II. By 1745, Troyes had become the capital of the knitware industry. The old city lies on the River Seine, but it's the capital of the département of Aube, named for the River Aube.

ESSENTIALS

GETTING THERE   Because French rail lines radiate from Paris, you might have to transfer in the capital if you're coming from Reims or Lille. Once you're in Paris, however, service is frequent and fast from the Gare de l'Est, a total of 12 trains per day, making the 1¹/₂-hour trip for 110 F ($20.90) one way.

VISITOR INFORMATION   The Office de Tourisme is at 16 bd. Carnot (☎ 25-73-00-36).

TOURING THE TOP ATTRACTIONS

CHURCHES   The city has at least nine churches meriting exploration (the tourist office will provide a map). Visiting hours for churches are 10am to noon and 2 to 6pm daily.

Begin your tour at place de la Liberation, where you'll have a view of the gothic **Cathédrale St-Pierre et St-Paul,** 1 place St-Pierre (☎ 25-80-90-12), built primarily in the 13th and 17th centuries. The architecture is remarkably elegant, and the detail in the high stained-glass windows and the two rose windows provides a particularly striking example of the skill of 13th-century artists. Above the richly decorated facade rises the 200-foot St. Peter's Tower. The sumptuous treasury includes enamel work, relics, and alms boxes from the comtes de Champagne and others. From June to September a *son-et-lumière* (sound-and-light) show is presented inside. The facade is floodlit at night.

The cathedral is open daily from 10am to noon and 2 to 6pm; the *son-et-lumière* program is held on Tuesday, Friday, and Saturday at 10:30pm, costing 30 F ($5.70) for adults and 15 F ($2.85) for children. The treasury is open only in summer, Tuesday to Sunday from 2 to 6pm, costing 8 F ($1.50).

The **Eglise Ste-Madeleine,** rue de la Madeleine (☎ 25-73-02-98), is the city's oldest church, dating from the mid-12th century. It was built in the late Roman and early gothic style, with many changes made in the 1500s. The tower is from the 16th and 17th centuries. A charnel house dates from 1525, and its triple-arched rood screen, unique in France, was carved by Jean Galide; it's a fine example of stone tracery. Its stained-glass windows are among the most beautiful examples left from the Champagne school of artisans.

Another church worth exploring is the consummate gothic **Basilique St-Urbain,** rue Clemenceau (☎ 25-73-02-98). Called the Parthenon of

Champagne, the church was founded by Troyes-born Pope Urban IV; construction began in the 13th century. The bold architecture with pillars and tapered mullion windows, harmonious proportions, and elegant sculptures makes this Troyes's greatest monument. The exterior is decorated with sculpted gargoyles. It's open from July 1 to September 15.

Visit the **Eglise St-Jean,** rue Champeaux (☎ **25-73-02-98**), noted for its landmark clock tower. In 1420, the marriage of Catherine de France to Henry V of England took place here after the signing of the Treaty of Troyes. (Incidentally, the treaty led to an English invasion and the Hundred Years' War.)

Note: The three churches above have the same phone number because they share the same presbytery.

MUSEUMS   Troyes is also endowed with many fine museums, including the **Musée d'Art Moderne,** place St-Pierre (☎ **25-80-26-80**), to the right of the cathedral. Housed in a restored bishop's palace from the 16th and 17th centuries, this is a magnificent modern-art collection, from the Pierre and Denise Lévy donation, one of the largest private art collections ever given to France.

The museum owns 350 paintings, 1,300 drawings and sketches, and more than 100 sculptures. A host of famous names—Gauguin, Matisse, Modigliani, Picasso, Cézanne, Degas, and Bonnard—are on display. See, in particular, works by the Fauves (the movement that followed impressionism). It's open Wednesday to Monday from 11am to 6pm; admission is 20 F ($3.80).

The **Musée St-Loup,** 1 rue Chréstien-de-Troyes (☎ **25-42-33-33**), is actually two museums, on the far side of the cathedral square. The museums are in the former abbey of St-Loup, and part of the cloisters can still be seen. One section is devoted to a large natural-history museum and has an outstanding bronze Gallo-Roman statue of Apollo, a collection of Merovingian weapons, gold and garnet jewelry from Attila's time, and medieval sculpture from the 12th to the 15th century. Another section displays paintings from the 15th to the 20th century, including works by Boucher, Fragonard, David, and Watteau. The museum, open Tuesday to Sunday from 10am to noon and 2 to 6pm, costs 15 F ($2.85) for adults and 10 F ($1.90) for children.

The magnificent Hôtel-Dieu (hospital) of Troyes, quai des Comtes de Champagne, has been converted into a university. But it's still possible to visit the **Pharmacie Musée de l'Hôtel-Dieu** (☎ **25-80-98-97**), which has been turned into a museum. It's one of the most unusual apothecary dispensaries in France. The comtes de Champagne founded the hospital in the 12th century. The laboratory contains ancient documents, a collection of pewter in all shapes and sizes, and such items as reliquaries from the 16th century. Painted wooden boxes and pots still hold herbs and other medicines. The museum is open Wednesday to Monday from 10am to noon and 2 to 6pm. Admission is 10 F ($1.90).

Rue Urbain-IV leads to the principal plaza of Troyes, place du Maréchal-Foch, named for the famed World War I general. Here you can enjoy coffee and crêpes at numerous cafés and restaurants while you admire the **Hôtel de Ville** (town hall); from 1624, it's one of the region's few Louis XIII–style buildings.

WHERE TO STAY

Grand Hôtel/Patiotel

4 av. Joffre, 10000 Troyes. ☎ **25-79-90-90.** Fax 25-78-48-93. 102 rms, 2 suites. TV TEL. Grand Hôtel, 445 F ($84.60) double; 750–950 F ($142.55–$180.60) suite. Patiotel,

275–325 F ($52.25–$61.75) single or double. Breakfast 39 F ($7.40) extra. MC, V. Parking 50 F ($9.50).

The core of this hotel/restaurant complex was built on a downtown street corner near the railway station in the 1930s and gained a reputation for comfort and respectability. In 1987, a U-shaped wing was added and the cost-conscious Patiotel, with much less desirable rooms, was opened. Today the Grand Hôtel and its less-expensive sibling share a lobby, breakfast room, covered pool, and garden but maintain completely different price structures.

The rooms at the Grand are conservatively traditional, with minibars. Those at the Patiotel are modern and somewhat cramped, but always have windows opening onto the garden. On the premises are five restaurants. The most elegant is Le Champagne, serving fixed-price meals priced at 130 to 270 F ($24.70 to $51.30). Less expensive are Le Jardin de la Louisiane, the Grill Aquarius, Le Croco (a brasserie), and a pleasant enclave for unpretentious food, La Taverne de l'Ecailler.

Hôtel de la Poste

35 rue Emile-Zola, 10000 Troyes. ☎ **25-73-05-05**. Fax 25-73-80-76. 28 rms. MINIBAR TV TEL. 490–550 F ($93.10–$104.50) double. Breakfast 55 F ($10.45) extra. AE, DC, MC, V.

This four-star hotel offers not only comfortable accommodations but also some of the city's finest dining. The rooms, though, are quite small. In addition to a modern bar, the hotel has three restaurants, including La Pizzeria and La Marée, which features seafood. Its prestigious dining room is La Table Gourmande, where diners enjoy outstanding classical French cooking and the lavish wine menu. The restaurant is closed Sunday night and on Monday.

WHERE TO DINE

Le Bourgogne

40 rue du Général-de-Gaulle. ☎ **25-73-02-67**. Reservations required. Main courses 80–140 F ($15.20–$26.60); fixed-price menu 170 F ($32.30). MC, V. Mon 12:15–1:30pm, Tues–Sat 12:15–1:30pm and 7:15–9:15pm. Closed Aug. FRENCH.

The Dubois brothers, the owners, are from Bresse, said to have the finest poultry in France. Their refined cuisine is made with very fresh ingredients, and their wine cellar contains several treasures. New specialties include duck liver with a raspberry vinaigrette, grilled turbot in beurre blanc, and sweetbreads Florentine style in puff pastry.

Le Valentino

Cour de la Rencontre. ☎ **25-73-14-14**. Reservations not required. Main courses 120–198 F ($22.80–$37.60); fixed-price menus 158–360 F ($30–$68.40). AE, DC, MC, V. Tues–Sat 12:30-1:45pm and 7:30–9:45pm, Sun 12:30-1:45pm. Closed Aug 16–Sept 6. FRENCH.

Chef Alain Vattier operates a distinguished art deco dining room across from the town hall. He serves his *cuisine du marché* (based on market-fresh ingredients) on two terraces. Among the town's restaurateurs, M. Vattier is the seafood expert, and he attends the fish market every morning. Try his lobster with butter sauce flavored with orange juice or salmon cut into ravioli-like pieces and served with caviar and a shallot-flavored butter sauce. He also cooks a young pigeon with candied onions, champagne vinegar, and apples. One food critic deplored the chef's habit of adding "chichi touches" to the plates, but that seems like such a minor quibble about this original and well-balanced cuisine.

15 Alsace-Lorraine & the Vosges

The provinces of Alsace and Lorraine, with ancient capitals at Strasbourg and Nancy, respectively, have been much disputed by Germany and France. Alsace has been called "the least French of French provinces," perhaps more reminiscent of the Black Forest across the Rhine. In fact, it became German from 1870 until after World War I and then was ruled by Hitler from 1940 to 1944. But now both old provinces are under French control, though they are somewhat independent.

In the Vosges you can follow the Crest Road or skirt along the foothills, visiting the wine towns of Alsace. In its cities and cathedrals, the castle-dotted landscape evokes memories of a great past and (in battle monuments or scars) sometimes military glory or defeat. Lorraine is Joan of Arc country, and many of its towns still suggest their heritage from the Middle Ages.

REGIONAL CUISINE The ample use of pork and goose fat in Alsatian dishes gives the cuisine a distinctive flavor. Alsace is a leader in the production of *pâtés*, with more than 40 varieties, so you really must visit a local *charcuterie* (delicatessen). Don't miss the richly flavorful *pâté de foie gras* (goose-liver pâté).

In Lorraine, the joyful excesses of cholesterol are even more exaggerated. In addition to butter and loads of cream, local chefs use large quantities of salted lard. Even local *pot-au-feu* (known as *une potes*) replaces beef with salted lard and locally made pork sausages.

Other regional specialties include *choucroute* (sauerkraut) with sausages, salted ham, pork chops, or (in deluxe versions) truffles; chicken with riesling; trout in cream, with riesling, or simply fried (*au bleu*); Alsatian *kougelhof* (made with almonds, dried raisins, sugar, milk, flour, and eggs); and a simple tart made with flour, milk, and sugar called *un ramequin*.

The most famous Alsatian beer is Kronenbourg, which you'll find in thousands of bars throughout France. There are more than 90 varieties of Alsatian wines, traditionally drunk from slender flutes whose glass is sometimes colored blue or green. The most celebrated Alsatian varieties include Riesling, Gewürztraminer (Traminer), Pinot Blanc, Pinot Gris, Sylvaner, and Muscat Ottonel.

Alsace-Lorraine & the Vosges

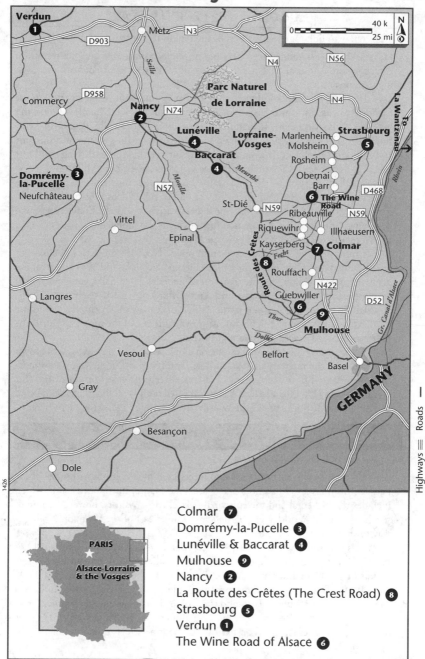

Colmar ⑦
Domrémy-la-Pucelle ③
Lunéville & Baccarat ④
Mulhouse ⑨
Nancy ②
La Route des Crêtes (The Crest Road) ⑧
Strasbourg ⑤
Verdun ①
The Wine Road of Alsace ⑥

Highways ≣ Roads —

EXPLORING THE REGION BY CAR

Here's how to link together the best of the region if you rent a car.

Days 1–2   Begin your tour in Strasbourg, the economic/spiritual center of the Alsace region. A tour of its cultural and artistic treasures more than justifies a two-night stopover.

Day 3   Drive 44 miles southwest on N422 to Colmar, one of the district's most folkloric towns. En route, visit some of the half-dozen wine hamlets lining the highway—like Molsheim, Rosheim, Obernai, Barr, Ribeauville, Riquewihr, and Kayserberg. In Colmar, tour the town's historic core, visiting its famous museum and dining in one of our recommended restaurants. Continue driving south 30 miles on E25 to spend the night in Alsace's second-largest city, Mulhouse.

Day 4   Plan on rising early for a tour of one of the most famous automobile museums in Europe (see "Mulhouse" at the end of this chapter), before backtracking north to Colmar for one of the most scenic drives in eastern France, La Route des Crêtes. Since the final destination for this day is the capital of Lorraine, Nancy, your total driving distance won't exceed 110 miles.

La Route des Crêtes is signposted from beside N83. En route, you'll pass over much-eroded mountain peaks on a road laid out during World War I at great expense in human suffering for the transport of matériel. Eventually, you'll join N59, which passes through Baccarat and Lunéville, known for their crystal and porcelain, respectively—but not particularly for their overnight charms. Continue northeast as far as Nancy, a richly historic town with one of the most graceful 18th-century cores in France. Stay overnight here.

Day 5   Rise early for a 30-mile excursion along secondary highways to the town that sanctifies the memory of Joan of Arc: Domrémy-la-Pucelle (signs will indicate the direction from the center of Nancy). After your visit, continue north for 60 miles along D964 for a visit to Verdun, a town with an authentic medieval core and poignant memories of World War I trench warfare. Spend the night here.

1 Verdun

162 miles E of Paris, 41 miles W of Metz

Built on both banks of the Meuse and intersected by a complicated series of canals, Verdun has an old section called the Ville Haute, on the east bank, which includes the cathedral and the episcopal palace. Most visitors, however, come to see the imfamous World War I battlefields, 2 miles east of the town, off N3 highway toward Metz.

At this garrison town in eastern France, Maréchal Pétain said, "They shall not pass!"—and they didn't. Verdun is where the Allies held out against a massive assault by the German army in World War I. Near the end of the war, 600,000 to 800,000 French and German soldiers died battling over a few miles on the muddy Meuse between Paris and the Rhine. Two monuments commemorate these tragic events: Rodin's *Defense* and Boucher's *To Victory and the Dead*. Today stone houses clustered on narrow cobblestone streets give Verdun a medieval appearance.

A tour of the battlefields is called the **Circuit des Forts**, covering the main fortifications. On the Meuse's right bank, this is a good 20-mile run, taking in

What's Special About Alsace-Lorraine

Great Towns
- Nancy, capital of old Lorraine, full of serene beauty, history, and tradition.
- Strasbourg, capital of Alsace and one of the great cities of France (also capital of pâté de foie gras).
- Colmar, one of the gems of Alsace, filled with medieval and Renaissance buildings.

Architectural Highlights
- Cathédrale Notre-Dame de Stasbourg, an outstanding example of French gothic architecture.
- Place Stanislas in Nancy, which some claim is the grandest square in the world.
- Palais de Rohan at Strasbourg, one of the crowning design achievements in eastern France.

Outstanding Museums
- Musée d'Unterlinden at Colmar, acclaimed for an immense altar screen, the Issenheim Altarpiece.
- Musée de l'Automobile at Mulhouse, the greatest automobile museum in the world.

Wine Routes & Scenic Drives
- The Wine Road of Alsace, 60 miles through charming villages illuminated on summer nights, past medieval towers, feudal ruins, and acres of vineyards.
- The Crest Road, running 150 miles through the Vosges mountain range.

Battlefields
- A tour of Circuit des Forts, outside Verdun, which evokes memories of the bloodiest fighting of World War I.

Pilgrimage Site
- Domrémy-la-Pucelle, the little hamlet that gave the world Joan of Arc.

Fort Vaux, where Raynal staged a heroic defense after sending his last message by carrier pigeon. After passing a vast French cemetery of 16,000 graves, an endless field of crosses, you arrive at the **Ossuaire de Douaumont,** where the bones of those literally blown to bits were embedded. Nearby at the mostly underground **Fort de Douaumont,** the "hell of Verdun" was unleashed. From the roof you can look out at a vast field of corroded tops of "pillboxes." Then you proceed to the **Trench of Bayonets.** Bayonets of French soldiers instantly entombed by a shellburst form this unique memorial.

The other tour, the **Circuit Rive Gauche,** is about a 60-mile run and takes in the **Hill of Montfaucon,** where Americans erected a memorial tower, and the **American Cemetery at Romagne,** with some 15,000 graves.

ESSENTIALS

GETTING THERE   Four trains (sometimes fewer) arrive daily from Paris's Gare de l'Est, after a transfer at Châlons-sur-Marne. Several daily trains also arrive from Metz, after a change at Conflans.

Driving is easy since Verdun is several miles north of the Paris–Strasbourg autoroute (the A4).

VISITOR INFORMATION   The Office de Tourisme, place de la Nation (☎ 29-86-14-18), is closed from mid-December to mid-January.

WHERE TO STAY & DINE

Le Coq Hardi

8 av. de la Victoire, 55100 Verdun. ☎ **29-86-36-36.** Fax 29-86-09-21. 35 rms, 5 suites. TV TEL. 420–750 F ($79.80–$142.50) double; 990 F ($188.10) suite. AE, DC, MC, V. Parking 58 F ($11).

This is our favorite hostelry in Verdun, composed of four attached 18th-century houses near the Meuse. The stone interior contains church pews and antiques, as well as a Renaissance fireplace crowned by a salamander, symbol of François I. Most guest rooms have been decorated in regional style. This hotel serves the best food in town in a dining room with a painted ceiling, Louis XIII chairs, and two deactivated World War I bombshells at its entrance. Menu specialties include salade Coq Hardi with green mustard and pine nuts, Challons duck, cassoulette of snails in champagne, and foie gras from Landes.

NEARBY ACCOMMODATIONS & DINING

Château des Monthairons

Route D334, 55320 Dieue-sur-Meuse. ☎ **28-87-78-55.** Fax 29-87-73-49. 9 rms, 2 suites. MINIBAR TV TEL. 400–750 F ($76–$142.50) double; 950 F ($180.50) suite. AE, DC, MC, V. Drive 7¹/₂ miles south of Verdun on D334.

Amid 30 acres of parkland, this hotel occupies an 1857 château crafted of chiseled blocks of pale stone; it's now operated by the Thouvenin family. The grounds contain a pair of 15th-century chapels, a nesting ground for herons, and ample opportunities for canoeing and fishing in one of eastern France's most historic rivers. The dining room serves meals from noon to 4pm and 7:30 to 9:30pm, Tuesday to Sunday in summer; no meals are served from Sunday night to Tuesday at lunch between November 1 and March 14. Set menus cost 165 F ($31.35) to 380 F ($72.20) and include pigeon soufflé garnished with truffles, scallops with basil-cream sauce, and roast lobster with risotto and Thai herbs.

2 Nancy

230 miles SE of Paris, 92 miles W of Strasbourg

Nancy, in the northeastern corner of France, was the capital of old Lorraine. The city was built around a fortified castle on a rock in the swampland near the Meurthe River. The important canal a few blocks east of the historic center connects the Marne to the Rhine.

The city is serenely beautiful, with a historical tradition, a cuisine, and an architecture all its own. It was once the rival of Paris as a center for art nouveau. Nancy has a triple face: the medieval alleys and towers around the old Ducal Palace where Charles II received Joan of Arc, the rococo golden gates and frivolous fountains, and the spreading dull modern sections with their university and industry. In the city's heart is its most visible monument, place Stanislas. Within a brisk walk in three directions, large inner-city parks and gardens provide lots of breathing space.

ESSENTIALS

GETTING THERE   Trains from Strasbourg arrive every 30 minutes (trip time: 1 hr.), a one-way ticket costing 105 F ($19.95); and trains from Paris's Gare de l'Est pull in about every hour (trip time: 3 hr.), a one-way ticket costing 245 F ($46.55).

VISITOR INFORMATION   The Office de Tourisme is at 14 place Stanislas (☎ 83-35-22-41).

STROLLING THROUGH THE CITY

The heartbeat of the city is **place Stanislas,** named for Stanislas Leczinski, the last of the ducs de Lorraine, ex-king of Poland, and father-in-law of Louis XV. Stanislas turned Nancy into one of Europe's palatial cities. The square stands between the two major sectors—the **Ville-Vieille** in the northwest, with its winding streets, and the **Ville-Neuve** in the southeast, dating from the 16th and 18th centuries, when the streets were made broad and straight.

Place Stanislas was laid out from 1752 to 1760 to the designs of Emmanuel Héré. Its ironwork gates are magnificent. The grilles stand at each corner, and two enclose fountains, the Neptune and the Amphitrite. The most imposing building on the square is the **Hôtel de Ville** (town hall)—try not to miss its inner staircase and 80-foot forged-iron balustrade with a single-piece handrail, the masterpiece of Jean Lamour, who designed the square's screens and fountains. On the eastern side is the **Musée des Beaux-Arts** (below).

The **Arc de Triomphe,** constructed by Stanislas from 1754 to 1756 to honor Louis XV, brings you to the long rectangular **place de la Carrière,** a tree-lined promenade leading to the Palais du Gouvernement, built in 1760. This governmental palace adjoins the **Ducal Palace,** built in 1502 in the gothic style with flamboyant balconies; the much-restored palace contains the Musée Lorrain (below). Alongside the Ducal Palace is the **Eglise des Cordeliers** with its round chapel (below).

The **Musée de l'Ecole de Nancy** attracts art nouveau devotees from all over the world (below). Finally, a short walk from this art museum leads to the **Porte de la Craffe,** Grande-Rue/rue de la Craffe (☎ 83-35-28-41), the oldest building in Nancy, dating from 1360. The interior was a prison during the Revolution and may be visited from mid-June to mid-September, Wednesday to Monday from 10am to noon and 2 to 5pm. Admission is 5 F (95¢).

SEEING THE TOP ATTRACTIONS

The **Eglise des Cordeliers,** 66 Grand Rue (☎ 83-32-18-74), with a round chapel based on a design for Florence's Medici, contains the burial monuments of the ducs de Lorraine. The most notable are those of René II (1509) by Mansuy Gauvain and his second wife, Philippa of Gueldres, by Ligier Richier. The octagonal ducal chapel, built in 1607, holds the baroque sarcophagi. The convent houses the **Musée des Arts et Traditions Populaires,** which has antiques, porcelain, and reconstructed interiors of regional maisons. Admission is 10 F ($1.90) for adults and 7 F ($1.35) for children. The church is open May to September, Tuesday to Sunday from 10am to 6pm; October to April, Tuesday to Sunday from 10am to noon and 2 to 5pm.

Appropriately, in a stunning turn-of-the-century building is the **Musée de l'Ecole de Nancy,** 38 rue Sergent-Blandan (☎ 83-40-14-86), where you can see the works of Emile Gallé, the greatest artist of the Nancy style. See, in particular, Gallé's celebrated "Dawn and Dusk" bed and our favorite, the well-known "mushroom lamp." Works by Eugène Vallin, another outstanding artist, are also on display. Admission is 30 F ($5.70) for adults and 25 F ($4.75) for children. The museum is open April to September, Wednesday to Monday from 10am to noon and 2 to 6pm; October to March, Wednesday to Monday from 10am to noon and 2 to 5pm.

Built in the 1700s, the **Musée des Beaux-Arts,** 3 place Stanislas (☎ 83-85-30-72), boasts a Manet portrait of the wife of Napoléon III's dentist—remarkable because of its brilliance and intensity, as well as because Manet portraits are rare. There are also works by Delacroix, Utrillo, Modigliani, Boucher, and Rubens. The Italians, like Perugino, Caravaggio, Ribera, and Tintoretto, are also represented. In addition to the paintings, the museum exhibits Daum crystal vases and lamps. Admission is 20 F ($3.80) for adults and 15 F ($2.85) for children. The museum is open Monday from noon to 6pm and Wednesday to Sunday from 10:30am to 6pm.

Housed in the Ducal Palace at 64 Grand Rue, the ✪ **Musée Lorrain** (☎ 83-32-18-74) is one of France's great museums; it depicts close to 2,000 years of European history. The first floor devotes an entire room to the work of Jacques Callot, the noted engraver who was born in Nancy in 1592. The Galerie des Cerfs displays excellent tapestries, including the first French flag, representing Henri II's reign. You'll also find a comprehensive collection of 17th-century Lorraine masterpieces, from when the duchy was known as a cultural center. The museum also has a room portraying eastern France's Jewish history. Admission is 20 F ($3.80) for adults and 15 F ($2.85) for children. The museum is open May to September 14, Wednesday to Monday from 10am to 6pm; September 15 to April, Wednesday to Monday from 10am to noon and 2 to 7pm.

WHERE TO STAY

Albert 1er–Astoria
3 rue de l'Armée-Patton, 54000 Nancy. ☎ **83-40-31-24.** Fax 83-28-47-78. 126 rms, 120 with bath (tub or shower). TV TEL. 285 F ($54.15) double without bath, 300–410 F ($57–$77.90) double with bath. Breakfast 39 F ($7.40) extra. AE, DC, MC, V. Parking 30 F ($5.70).

The Albert 1er–Astoria contains an interior garden, a solarium, a sauna, and an English bar called L'Astor. Across from the railway station, the well-equipped hotel is run in a businesslike manner, and the rooms are soberly furnished with built-in units. Guests stay here mainly for the price and central location.

✪ Grand Hôtel de la Reine
2 place Stanislas, 54000 Nancy. ☎ **83-35-03-01,** or 800/777-4182 in the U.S. and Canada. Fax 83-32-86-04. 48 rms, 7 suites. 600–1,300 F ($114–$247) double; 1,200–2,000 F ($228–$380) suite. AE, DC, MC, V. Breakfast 80 F ($15.20) extra.

This 18th-century mansion is exceptional, with Louis XV–style guest rooms boasting draped testers over the beds, Venetian-style chandeliers, and gilt-framed mirrors. The salons are decorated with antique wainscoting. The Stanislas restaurant serves both classic and modern courses, and the waiters are formal and considerate.

Mercure Altea Thiers
11 rue Raymond-Poincaré, 54000 Nancy. ☎ **83-39-75-75.** Fax 83-32-78-17. 192 rms. MINIBAR TV TEL. 625 F ($118.75) double. Breakfast 52 F ($9.90) extra. AE, DC, MC, V.

This is a streamlined hotel for both executives and tourists. The chain-format rooms are first class, and the restaurant, La Toison d'Or, offers Lorraine cuisine. The Mercure also operates a popular brasserie. This place can hardly compare with the more atmospheric Grand Hôtel, yet is "second best" in Nancy.

WHERE TO DINE

Café Foy and Restaurant Le Foy
1 place Stanislas. ☎ 83-32-21-44. Reservations recommended. Main courses 85–150 F ($16.15–$28.50); fixed-price menus 120 F ($22.80), 150 F ($28.50), and 185 F ($35.15). AE, V. Thurs–Tues noon–2pm and 7–9:30pm. Closed Feb and July 14–Aug 1. FRENCH.

A Regency room with ornate ceilings, chandeliers, and enormous windows overlooking the square, this is the most prominent café in town. In summer the outdoor tables offer the best view of the square—the atmosphere becomes more formal, and string music is sometimes played; off-season, the clientele is blue collar. If you'd like to eat in less casual surroundings, you can go up to the Restaurant Le Foy, accessible by a separate staircase opening onto the square. The food is rather regional and heavy on cream and sauces at times; however, it's perfectly acceptable and no place in town has such a supreme location.

✪ Le Capucin Gourmand
31 rue Gambetta. ☎ 83-35-26-98. Reservations required. Main courses 130–240 F ($24.70–$45.60); fixed-price menus 140 F ($26.60) and 230 F ($43.70). V. Tues–Sun 12:30–2pm and 7:30–10pm. Closed Jan 1–7 and Aug 1–21. FRENCH.

Chef Gérard Veissière treats his guests to excellent service and regional cuisine. In homage to Nancy's art nouveau tradition, the restaurant, in an old house, integrates Gallé and Daum glass with Louis Majorelle furniture. You can always order classic quiche Lorraine, but don't overlook the sole cooked with vermouth, duck soup with lentils, fresh foie gras, pigeon casserole, or pêche mignon du Capucin. The featured wine is Gris de Toul. The least expensive fixed-price menu is one of the city's dining bargains.

✪ Le Goéland
27 rue des Ponts. ☎ 83-35-17-25. Reservations imperative. Main courses 150–280 F ($28.50–$53.20); fixed-price menus 165 F ($31.35) and 255 F ($48.45). AE, V. Mon 7–9:30pm, Tues–Sat noon–2:30pm and 7–9:30pm. SEAFOOD/LORRAINE.

Jean-Luc Mengin is all the rave in Nancy, and when it comes to fish and seafood he has no serious contenders in eastern France. The dining room is luxurious and contemporary, and the atmosphere is made all the more inviting by Danièle Mengin, a *sommelière* who almost never fails to please with her suggestions. After trying the John Dory with potatoes and bacon and the sole goujonnettes in tomato coulis, we agree that the chef does indeed work a kind of magic on what might be rather prosaic dishes. The service is flawless, and the wine list well chosen.

3 Lunéville & Baccarat

Lunéville: 208 miles SE of Paris, 22 miles SE of Nancy
Baccarat: 223 miles SE of Paris, 37 miles SE of Nancy

If crystal chandeliers and decanters, along with wineglasses, evoke glamour and glitter for you and you've come this deep into Lorraine, you might spend one of the most enjoyable days of your trip here by visiting Lunéville and Baccarat.

ESSENTIALS

GETTING THERE   The towns are connected with local train service from Nancy and Strasbourg. Six trains per day arrive from Paris (trip time: 4 hr.), costing 210 F ($39.90) one way. There are 4 trains per day from Strasbourg (trip time: 45 min.), costing 85 F ($16.15) one way, and 15 from Nancy (trip time: 20 min.), costing 31 F ($5.90) one way. Once in Lunéville, you'll find that trains to Baccarat run every hour or two daily from 6:30am to 10pm (trip time: 20 min.), costing 24 F ($4.55) one way.

VISITOR INFORMATION   In Lunéville, contact the Office de Tourisme, au Château (☎ 83-74-06-55). In Baccarat, the Syndicat d'Initiative is at Résidence Centre, rue Division-Leclerc (☎ 83-75-13-37), open only from June to September.

LUNEVILLE

Lunéville was a walled town in medieval days. After a decline brought on by war, plague, and famine, it rose again under Dukes Léopold and Stanislas. Lunéville contains factories that produce some of France's best-known porcelain, whose painted patterns are noted for their vivid colors and whimsical designs. For much of the early 18th century this town was the residence of Léopold, duc de Lorraine, who so admired (and wanted to flatter) Louis XIV that he built the Château de Lunéville, a near replica of the one at Versailles, particularly the chapel.

The **Musée du Château,** au Château (☎ 88-76-23-57), is rich in old porcelain, drawings, and paintings, plus military weapons. The museum occupies only part of the Château de Lunéville, which for the most part is in need of repair and off-limits. It's open Wednesday to Monday from 10am to noon and 2 to 6pm (to 5pm in winter). Admission is 10 F ($1.90) for adults and 5 F (95¢) for children.

The baroque **Eglise St-Jacques,** at place St-Jacques (☎ 83-73-04-12), contains a 15th-century pietà of polychrome stone and wood panels carved into Régence detailings. The church is open daily from 7:30am to 12:15pm and 2pm to dusk.

Shops everywhere sell modern examples of the famed dinnerware, which—if you can pack it properly—can become a treasured souvenir.

WHERE TO STAY

Hôtel des Pages
5 quai des Petits-Bosquets, 54300 Lunéville. ☎ 83-74-11-42. Fax 83-74-11-42. 32 rms. TV TEL. 250 F ($47.50) double. Breakfast 29 F ($5.50) extra. AE, DC, MC, V.

This three-story hotel has a central location beside the Château de Lunéville. Its comfortable rooms are simply furnished with functional furniture. There's a cost-conscious restaurant, Le Petit Comptoir, where fixed-price menus begin at 95 F ($18.05).

Hôtel Oasis
3 av. Voltaire, 54300 Lunéville. ☎ 83-73-52-85. Fax 83-73-46-63. 30 rms. TV TEL. 285 F ($54.15) double. Breakfast 35 F ($6.65) extra. AE, DC, MC, V. Parking free.

A 10-minute walk from the town center, this hotel opened in 1990 and has since been considered one of the best in town (though the competition isn't exactly stiff). It contains a bar and breakfast room but no restaurant, and its rooms have well-worn furnishings and big windows. The hotel is owned by the family that owns the Hôtel des Pages (above).

WHERE TO DINE

✪ Château d'Adomenil

Rehainviller, 54300 Lunéville. ☎ 83-74-04-81. Reservations required. Fax 83-74-21-78. Main courses 90–200 F ($17.10–$38); fixed-price menus 240–450 F ($45.60–$85.55). AE, MC, V. Tues 7–9:30pm, Wed–Sat noon–2pm and 7–9:30pm, Sun noon–2pm. Closed Feb 18–Mar 6. FRENCH.

On 16 acres of parkland, containing a 17th-century wine press, the Château d'Adomenil lies about 2¹/₂ miles south of Lunéville. While there are seven rooms for rent—a double costs 730 to 850 F ($138.75 to $161.60)—most people come here to dine. You may begin with cocktails and mini quiches Lorraine in the oak-beamed salon. Dinner is served in an elegant dining room with a view of the expansive lawns, reflecting pools, and peacocks. Outstanding owner/chef Michel Million will often help guide you by suggesting delectable fare like quail wrapped in cabbage leaves, lobster in court bouillon with saffron, filet of lamb en croûte with thyme, and chanterelle-stuffed pigeon. His wife, Bernadette, cheerfully greets guests and sees that they receive impeccable service.

BACCARAT

This small town owes its fame to Baccarat crystal. The company, founded in 1764, was originally a glass manufacturer called La Verrerie Sainte-Anne. In 1817, however, it switched to crystal and became known as the Compagnie des Cristalleries de Baccarat.

In addition to displaying some of the factory's oldest and most noteworthy pieces, the **Musée du Cristal** (☎ 83-76-60-06) has a video in English about crystal manufacturing. You'll learn how lead, potassium, and silica combine to form crystal. The museum is open daily: April to October from 9:30am to 12:30pm and 2 to 6:30pm, November to March from 10am to noon and 2 to 6pm.

A Baccarat shop on the square near the museum is housed in a futuristic rectangular building whose walls are made almost entirely of glass. It's loaded with crystal.

WHERE TO STAY & DINE

Renaissance

31 rue des Cristalleries, 54120 Baccarat. ☎ 83-75-11-31. 19 rms. TEL. 260–290 F ($49.40–$55.10) double. Breakfast 30 F ($5.70) extra. AE, DC, MC, V. Parking free.

This provincial hotel caters to visitors and businesspeople in town to deal with the glass companies. The rooms are functional but well kept. The hotel restaurant does a good business and is open daily in summer; from October to March it closes on Friday night and all day Saturday. Menus cost 80 F ($15.20), 120 F ($22.80), and 180 F ($34.20).

4 Domrémy-la-Pucelle

275 miles SE of Paris, 6¹/₂ miles NW of Neufchâteau

A pilgrimage center attracting tourists from all over the world, Domrémy is a plain hamlet that would be overlooked except for the fact that Joan of Arc was born here in 1412. Here she heard the voices and saw the visions that led her to play out her historic role as the heroine of France.

A residence traditionally considered the Arc family house, near the church, is known as the **Maison Natale de Jeanne d'Arc,** 2 rue de la Basilique (☎ 29-06-95-86). Here you can see the bleak chamber where she was born. A museum beside the house shows a film depicting St. Joan's life. The house can be visited daily: April to September 15 from 9am to 12:30pm and 2 to 7pm, September 16 to March from 9:30am to noon and from 2 to 5pm. Admission costs 6 F ($1.15) for adults and 3 F (55¢) for children 10 to 16; 9 and under free.

Only the tower remains of the church where Joan was baptized. However, above the village, on a slope of the Bois-Chenu, the **Basilique du Bois-Chenu** was commenced in 1881 and consecrated in 1926. The tree that in spring was "lovely as a lily" and believed to be haunted by "faery ladies" no longer exists.

WHERE TO STAY & DINE

Hôtel de la Basilique

Le Bois-Chenu, 88630 Domrémy-la-Pucelle. ☎ **29-06-84-07.** Fax 29-06-84-08. 21 rms. 180–280 F ($34.20–$53.20) double. Breakfast 30 F ($5.70) extra. MC, V. Parking free. Closed Oct–Mar 15, and Sun night and Mon Mar 16–June.

This hotel, run by members of the Vaudron family since 1993, is adjacent to the 19th-century Basilique du Bois-Chenu, about a mile north of the village center. It contains simple rooms, with a communal phone near the reception desk. Most of the hotel's business comes from its restaurant, where fixed-price meals cost 90 to 230 F ($17.10 to $43.70). The restaurant is open daily from noon to 2pm and 7 to 9pm.

Relais de la Pucelle

88630 Domrémy-la-Pucelle. ☎ **29-06-95-72.** 3 rms, none with bath. 100–130 F ($19–$24.70) double. Breakfast 25 F ($4.75) extra. AE, DC, MC, V. Parking free. Closed Mon Nov–Mar.

Facing the Maison Natale, the restaurant here is known for its superb Lorraine pâté and large portions, with full meals costing 70 to 95 F ($13.30 to $18.05). It's open from noon to 2pm and 8 to 10pm. The rooms are modest but clean and old-fashioned; the cheapest have a bidet and the more expensive doubles have only a shower (no toilet). This place, though decent, is definitely for serious Joan of Arc fans only.

5 Strasbourg

303 miles SE of Paris, 135 miles SW of Frankfurt

Capital of Alsace, Strasbourg is one of France's greatest cities and is also the birthplace of pâté de foie gras. And it was in Strasbourg that Rouget de Lisle first sang "La Marseillaise." In June of every year the artistic life of Strasbourg reaches its zenith at the **International Music Festival** held at the Cathédrale Notre-Dame, at the Palais de la Musique et des Congrès, and in the Palais de Rohan's courtyard.

Strasbourg is not only a great university city but also one of France's most important ports, 2 miles west of the Rhine. In addition to being host to the Council of Europe, Strasbourg is the meeting place of the European Parliament, which convenes at the Palais de l'Europe.

In 1871 Strasbourg was usurped by Germany and made the capital of the imperial territory of Alsace-Lorraine, but it reverted to France in 1918. One street is a perfect illustration of the city's identity crisis: More than a century ago it was avenue Napoléon. In 1871 it became Kaiser-Wilhelmstrasse, then turned into boulevard de la République in 1918. In 1940 it became Adolf-Hitler-Strasse, then ended up as avenue du Général-de-Gaulle in 1945.

ESSENTIALS

GETTING THERE The Strasbourg-Entzheim airport (☎ 88-64-67-67), 7 miles southwest of the center, receives daily flights from most European centers—including Paris and Frankfurt. Shuttle buses connect the airport to the city but run only Monday to Friday every 30 minutes during the day, costing 37 F ($7.05) one way.

Strasbourg is a major rail junction. Fourteen trains per day arrive from Paris (trip time: 4 hr.), costing 254 F ($48.25) one way. From Nancy, there are 12 trains per day (trip time: 1½ hr.), costing 101 F ($19.20) one way.

The giant N83 highway, with many lanes, crosses the plain of Alsace, becoming at times the A35 expressway. It links Strasbourg with Colmar and Mulhouse.

VISITOR INFORMATION The Office de Tourisme is on place de la Cathédrale (☎ 88-52-28-28).

RIVER CRUISES One of the most romantic ways to spend your time in Strasbourg is taking an excursion on the Ill River, leaving from the Palais de Rohan near the cathedral. Day excursions operate year-round, and night excursions are offered only from May to October. Those with more time may want to take excursions on the Rhine, which cross the Strasbourg lock. These three- to four-hour cruises on a 300-passenger ship leave from promenade Dauphine May to September only. Meals and cocktails are served on board. Longer excursions along the Rhine can also be booked. Information is provided by the **Strasbourg Port Authority,** 25 rue de la Nuée-Bleue (☎ 88-21-74-74).

EXPLORING THE TOWN

Despite war damage, much remains of old Strasbourg, including covered bridges and towers from its former fortifications, plus many 15th- and 17th-century dwellings with painted wooden fronts and carved beams.

The city's traffic hub is **place Kléber,** dating from the 15th century. Sit here with a tankard of Alsatian beer and slowly get to know Strasbourg. The bronze statue in the center is of J. B. Kléber, born in Strasbourg in 1753, who became one of Napoléon's most noted generals and was buried under the monument. Apparently his presence offended the Nazis, who removed the statue in 1940. However, this Alsatian bronze was restored to its proper place in 1945 at the Liberation.

Next, take rue des Grandes-Arcades to **place Gutenberg,** one of the city's oldest squares and formerly a *marché aux herbes.* The central statue by David d'Angers, dated 1840, is of Gutenberg, who perfected his printing press in Strasbourg in the winter of 1436–37. The former town hall, now the **Hôtel du Commerce,** was built in 1582 and is one of the most significant Renaissance buildings in all Alsace.

Now you can make your way along rue Mercière to place de la Cathédrale to see the city's crowning glory: the ✪ **Cathédrale Notre-Dame de Strasbourg** (☎ 88-24-43-34), which inspired the poetry of Goethe. Today it stands proudly, an outstanding example of gothic architecture, representing a harmonious transition from the romanesque. Construction began on it in 1176. The pyramidal tower in rose-colored stone was completed in 1439 and at 469 feet is the tallest one dating from medieval times.

You can ascend the tower daily: in July and August from 8:30am to 7pm, April to June and in September from 9am to 6:30pm, in March and October from 9am to 5:30pm, and November to February from 9am to 4:30pm. Because of certain structural problems and renovations, visitors are allowed to climb only 329 steps to the platform for a panoramic view—climbing all the way to the spire is forbidden. To make the climb will cost 10 F ($1.90) for adults and 7 F ($1.35) for children.

Four large counterforts divide the main facade into three vertical parts and two horizontal galleries. Note the great rose window, which looks like real stone lace. The facade is rich in sculptural decoration: On the portal of the south transept, the *Coronation and Death of the Virgin* in one of the two tympana is the finest such medieval work. In the north transept, see also the facade of the St. Lawrence Chapel, a stunning achievement of the late-gothic German style.

A romanesque crypt lies under the chancel, which is covered with square stonework. The central stained-glass window is the work of Max Ingrand. The nave is majestic, with windows depicting emperors and kings on the north Strasbourg aisle. Five chapels are grouped around the transept, including one built in 1500 in the flamboyant gothic style. In the south transept stands the Angel Pillar, illustrating the Last Judgment, with angels lowering their trumpets.

The astronomical clock was built between 1547 and 1574. It stopped working during the Revolution and from 1838 to 1842 the mechanism was replaced. The clock is wound once a week. People flock to see its 12:30pm show of allegorical figures. On Sunday Apollo drives his sun horses, on Thursday you see Jupiter and his eagle, and so on. The main body of the clock has a planetarium according to Copernicus. The public is welcome to get a closer view of the clock between noon and 12:30pm. Tickets costing 5 F (95¢) are on sale daily in the south portal at 11:30am.

On the south side of the cathedral, at 2 place du Château, is the **Palais de Rohan** (☎ 88-32-48-95), built from 1732 to 1742, an architectural example of supreme elegance and proportion. It's one of the crowning design achievements in eastern France and is noted for its facades and beautiful rococo interior. On the first floor is a fine-arts museum, with works by Rubens, Rembrandt, van Dyck, El Greco, Goya, Watteau, Renoir, and Monet. There's also a decorative-arts museum exhibiting ceramics and the original machinery of the cathedral's first astronomical clock. The museum, charging 15 F ($2.85) for adults and 8 F ($1.50) for children, is open Monday to Saturday 10am to noon and 1:30 to 6pm and Sunday from 10am to 5pm.

On the southwest corner of place du Château, at no. 3, is the **Musée de l'Oeuvre Notre-Dame** (☎ 88-32-06-39), occupying a collection of ancient houses with wooden galleries. The museum illustrates the art of the Middle Ages and the Renaissance in Strasbourg and surrounding Alsace. Some of the pieces were once displayed in the cathedral, where copies have been substituted. The most celebrated prize is a stained-glass head of Christ from a window said to have been at Wissembourg, dating from about 1070. There's also a stained-glass window depicting an emperor from around 1200. The medieval sculpture is of great interest, as are the works of Strasbourg goldsmiths from the 16th and 17th centuries. The winding staircase and interior are in the pure Renaissance style. The 13th-century hall contains the loveliest sculptures from the cathedral, including the wise and foolish virgins from 1280.

Strasbourg

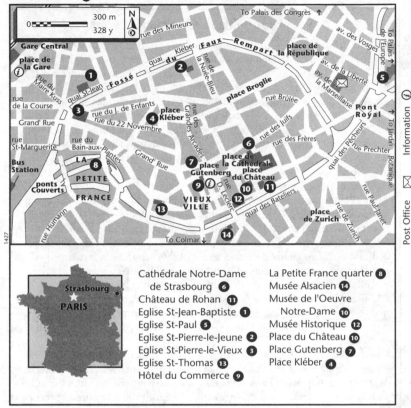

Cathédrale Notre-Dame
de Strasbourg ⑥
Château de Rohan ⑪
Eglise St-Jean-Baptiste ❶
Eglise St-Paul ❺
Eglise St-Pierre-le-Jeune ❷
Eglise St-Pierre-le-Vieux ❸
Eglise St-Thomas ⑬
Hôtel du Commerce ⑨

La Petite France quarter ❽
Musée Alsacien ⑭
Musée de l'Oeuvre
Notre-Dame ⑩
Musée Historique ⑫
Place du Château ⑩
Place Gutenberg ❼
Place Kléber ❹

The museum is open Monday to Saturday from 10am to noon and 1:30 to 6pm and Sunday from 10am to 5pm; admission is 15 F ($2.85) for adults and 8 F ($1.50) for children.

The **Musée Alsacien,** 23 quai St-Nicolas (☎ 88-35-55-36), occupies three mansions from the 16th and 17th centuries and is like a living textbook of the folklore and customs of Alsace, containing arts, crafts, and tools of the old province; it's open Monday and Wednesday to Saturday from 10am to noon and 2 to 6pm and Sunday from 10am to 6pm. Admission is 15 F ($2.85) for adults and 8 F ($1.50) for children.

The **Eglise St-Thomas,** rue Martin-Luther, built between 1230 and 1330, boasts five naves. A Protestant church, it's the most interesting one in Strasbourg after the cathedral and contains the mausoleum of Maréchal de Saxe, a masterpiece of French art by Pigalle, from 1777. The church lies along rue St-Thomas, near pont St-Thomas. It's open daily from 10am to noon and 2 to 6pm (to 5pm in winter).

La Petite France, a long walk from the church down colorful rue des Dentelles, is the most interesting quarter of Strasbourg. Its 16th-century houses are mirrored in the waters of the Ill. In Little France, old roofs with gray tiles have sheltered families for ages, and the crossbeamed facades with their roughly carved rafters are

La Formidable Choucroute

There's no single recipe and no universal preparation, even in Alsace, but *choucroute garnie à l'alsacienne* is the dish most often associated with the province. Best consumed when the leaves start falling, it's a hearty dish intended to fortify hardworking bodies against the coming winter chill. Warnings of autumn appear early in restaurant windows: signs announcing NOUVELLE CHOUCROUTE—the season's first batch of cabbage marinated for weeks in herbs and salt brine, with hints of crunchiness and acidity permeating the healthful fibers. Added zest comes from juniper berries, caraway seeds, freshly ground pepper, *bouquet garni*, bacon fat, and (in truly classic versions) a dollop or two of goose fat.

Choucroute and its perfect accompaniment, riesling, are both products of Alsace. Potatoes and cabbage are produced locally and can be stored in barrels in a cool cellar through a long cropless winter. Since the Middle Ages, local farmers have produced vast amounts of pork products, some traditionally smoked over firwood or cherrywood fires to impart the earthy taste that permeates the shredded cabbage. The sanitized version you'll likely encounter in restaurants will include only the choicest cuts of pork (a variety of chops, sausages, knuckles, and offal keeps even the most jaded diner from growing bored). Earthier, more traditional versions that many Alsatians are likely to remember from their childhoods include pork brains, entrails, feet, ears, tail, and pork-liver dumplings. Regardless of the ingredients, many diners find the result nothing less than *formidable*.

So how does a connoisseur identify a mediocre choucroute? A worthy version is easy to digest, is free of excess grease and/or acidity, and doesn't float on a lake of juices. The dish should be cooked carefully so the potatoes don't turn to mush; and the meat and marinated cabbage should gracefully blend so that they coordinate with the flavors of an Alsatian riesling. (Enjoying it with a hearty glass or two of beer is a dignified alternative, but if you opt for other types of liquid accompaniments you're likely to be labeled an infidel, a gastronomic barbarian.)

How can you tell whether the sauerkraut you're eating is authentically *strasbourgeoise* or the rip-off version served in Germany? The difference is in the sausage, which any *charcutier* within 40 miles of either side of the Rhine could identify as *vraiment alsacienne* or merely frankfurters best consumed with beer and mustard.

in typical Alsatian style. Rue du Bain-aux-Plantes is of particular interest. An island in the middle of the river is cut by four canals—for a good view walk along rue des Moulins, branching off from rue du Bain-aux-Plantes.

WHERE TO STAY
VERY EXPENSIVE

Hilton International Strasbourg
Av. Herrenschmidt, 67000 Strasbourg. ☎ **88-37-10-10,** or 800/445-8667 in the U.S. and Canada. Fax 88-36-83-27. A/C MINIBAR TV TEL. 1,190 F ($226.10) double; from 3,300 F ($627.35) suite. Breakfast 93 F ($17.65) extra. AE, DC, MC, V. Parking 60 F ($11.40). Bus 6, 16, or 26.

The Hilton International includes every luxury associated with its name. The hotel is a five-minute drive from the center of town—take the Strasbourg-Centre exit from the autoroute and follow signs to the Wacken, Palais des Congrès, and the Palais de l'Europe. The seven-story glass hotel looms over a university complex and is opposite the Palais des Congrès. Five kinds of Iberian marble were used in the decor—much of it chosen to resemble the ruddy sandstone of the famous cathedral, visible from the hotel. The rooms contain tasteful artwork and spacious marble-trimmed baths.

Dining/Entertainment: Live music and guests ranging from heads of state to international tourists make the hotel's Bugatti Bar the town's social center. Named for Ettore Bugatti, it opened on the 100th birthday of the Alsatian car manufacturer and contains auto memorabilia. The moderately priced Le Jardin restaurant offers a buffet at all three meals. Some evenings are devoted to special themes, like seafood, Italian, or vegetarian. The Maison du Boeuf restaurant is described under "Where to Dine," below.

Services: 24-hour room service, laundry, dry cleaning.

Facilities: Sauna, health club, massage facilities, boutiques, interpretive/secretarial facilities.

EXPENSIVE

Beaucour

5 rue Bouchers, 67000 Strasbourg. ☎ **88-76-72-00.** Fax 88-76-72-60. 49 rms, 7 suites. A/C TV TEL. 750 F ($142.55) double; from 900 F ($171.10) suite. Breakfast 60 F ($11.40) extra. AE, DC, MC, V. Parking 30 F ($5.70). Bus 10, 20, or 36.

This three-star hotel is geared mainly to business travelers to the city, though many tourists will find it ideal. At the end of a private street a few blocks east of the cathedral, it occupies a 17th-century building with lots of timbered ceilings. Both the rooms and the suites harmoniously blend modern and traditional furnishings. Every room has a whirlpool tub, a fax hookup, and computer connections. The best chambers are a trio of Alsatian suites. The hotel maintains an affiliation with three restaurants a short walk away; the concierge, who seems to know "all the city's secrets," will gladly make reservations for you.

✪ Régent Petite France

5 rue des Moulins, 67000 Strasbourg. ☎ **88-76-43-43,** or 800/223-5652. Fax 88-76-43-76. 72 rms, 11 suites. 950–1,380 F ($180.60–$262.35) double; 1,800–2,200 F ($342.20–$418.25) suite. AE, DC, MC, V.

This hotel occupies a trio of antique-looking buildings. Other than the mellow tile-roofed exterior, the hotel is strikingly modern, boasting color-coordinated rooms with views over a neighborhood known for its charm. The hotel's restaurant, Le Pont Tournant, serves lunch and dinner daily, with a set menu priced at 145 F ($27.55). The menu reflects regional accents, but the chef prefers to chart his own culinary course.

MODERATE

✪ Hôtel des Rohan

17–19 rue du Maroquin, 67000 Strasbourg. ☎ **82-32-66-60.** Fax 88-75-65-37. 36 rms. TV TEL. 350–595 F ($66.50–$113.11) double. Breakfast 50 F ($9.50) extra. AE, MC, V.

In the pedestrian zone, 50 yards from the cathedral, the Hôtel des Rohan is one of the city's best values, in a great location. It offers a choice of rooms, the cheapest of which are small and contain a French bed (called *matrimonial*). Large and more classic rooms have either a large double bed or twins. About half the accommodations are air-conditioned.

⑤ Hôtel Monopole-Métropole
16 rue Kuhn, 67000 Strasbourg. ☎ 88-14-39-14, or 800/528-1234 in the U.S. Fax 88-32-82-55. 94 rms. MINIBAR TV TEL. 480–650 F ($91.20–$123.55) double. Breakfast 65 F ($12.35) extra. AE, DC, MC, V. Parking 45 F ($8.55). Bus 10, 20, or 36.

The Hôtel Monopole-Métropole is on a quiet street corner near the train station and contains a modern lobby with a scattering of antiques, among them a 17th-century carved armoire and a bronze statue of a night watchman. An extension of the salon displays oil portraits of 18th-century Alsatian personalities and glass cases with pewter tankards and brass candlesticks. Breakfast (the only meal served) is presented in the high-ceilinged Alsatian-style dining room. Each room is unique—many contain Louis-Philippe antiques. Léon and Monique Siegel are the proprietors; members of their family have owned this establishment since 1919.

INEXPENSIVE

✪ Hôtel de l'Ill
8 rue des Bateliers, 67000 Strasbourg. ☎ 88-36-20-01. Fax 88-35-30-03. 20 rms. TV TEL. 180–330 F ($34.20–$62.70) double. Breakfast 28–32 F ($5.30–$6.10) extra. MC, V. Bus 10, 20, or 36.

A five-minute walk from the cathedral, this two-star hotel is a good value for Strasbourg. A well-maintained and inviting little place, it offers comfortably furnished and quiet rooms. Each room is unique, though in either a modern or an Alsatian traditional style; both smoking and no-smoking rooms are available. The rooms at the rear contain a private terrace or balcony, opening onto a view of neighboring gardens. Breakfast is served in a room with a cuckoo clock, decorated in Laura Ashley style.

⑤ Hôtel des Princes
33 rue Geiler, Conseil de l'Europe, 67000 Strasbourg. ☎ 88-61-55-19. Fax 88-14-10-92. 43 rms. TEL. 395–480 F ($75.10–$91.25) double. Breakfast 38 F ($7.20) extra. AE, MC, V. Bus 15 or 20.

A 15-minute walk from the center of town, the Hôtel des Princes has received a three-star government rating and is one of the best values in the city. The management is helpful, and the rooms are furnished comfortably but simply. A continental breakfast is the only meal served.

WHERE TO DINE
VERY EXPENSIVE

✪ Au Crocodile
10 rue de l'Outre. ☎ 88-32-13-02. Reservations required. Fixed-price menus 295 F ($56.05), 395 F ($75.05), and 620 F ($117.80). AE, DC, MC, V. Tues–Sat noon–2pm and 7–9:30pm. Closed July 10–31 and Dec 24–Jan 1. Bus 10, 20, or 36. ALSATIAN.

A beautiful skylit restaurant, Au Crocodile serves some of the most inventive food in Strasbourg. Chef Emile Jung offers a wide array of dishes, like salmon-and-eel terrine with tarragon and cucumber and cauliflower à la grecque, pike-perch filet with a timbale of chicken livers and crayfish tails, and truffled goose liver with vegetables and potatoes. The Michelin guide gives M. Jung three stars, its highest accolade. His menu continues to be energized. Our major problem with the place only comes when the check—or *la note*, as the French say—is presented, along with the tab for those high-priced wines.

✪ Buerehiesel

4 parc de l'Orangerie. ☎ **88-61-62-24.** Reservations required. Main courses 154–286 F ($29.25–$54.35); fixed-price meal 290 F ($55.10) at lunch, 320 F ($60.80) at dinner; seven-course *menu dégustation* 630 F ($119.70). AE, DC, MC, V. Thurs–Mon noon–2:30pm and 7–9:30pm, Tues noon–2:30pm. Closed Aug 10–24 and Dec 21–Jan 4. Bus 6, 16, or 26. FRENCH.

Also known as Chez Westermann, Buerehiesel is famous for Antoine Westermann's *cuisine moderne*, as well as the restaurant's prime location—l'Orangerie, a beautiful park at the end of allée de la Robertsau, was planned by landscape artist Le Nôtre, who gave it to Joséphine. Main courses might include sole and lobster à la nage (cooked in court bouillon and flavored with herbs), salmis de pigeon au Bourgogne, steamed spring chicken with cabbage, and braised sweetbreads with truffles. We cannot praise the cuisine too highly: Distantly remembered recipes are brought down from the attic and recycled here in innovative and exciting ways. Even though the place elevates stuffiness to an art form, the movers and shakers of the European Union seem to lap it up.

EXPENSIVE

Maison du Boeuf

In the Hilton International Strasbourg, av. Herrenschmidt. ☎ **88-37-10-10.** Reservations recommended. Main courses 110–172 F ($20.90–$32.70); *menu affaires* (lunch) 180 F ($34.20); *menu dégustation* 280 F ($53.20). AE, DC, MC, V. Mon–Fri noon–2:30pm and 7–10:30pm, Sat 7–10:30pm. Bus 6, 16, or 26. ALSATIAN/INTERNATIONAL.

In a luxurious hotel, the Maison du Boeuf spared no expense becoming one of Strasbourg's best restaurants. The decor includes brass-trimmed doors, etched glass, peacock-blue chairs, and scarlet carpeting. The restaurant was the winner of a national wine-list competition. Specialties include duck-liver terrine, U.S. rib of beef roasted in a salt crust, Caesar salad with lobster chunks, pigeon roasted en cocotte in front of you, and various fresh pastas. The star dessert is crêpes Suzette flambéed in Grand Marnier. The wine list offers a wide variety of Alsatian wines in addition to its impressive array of classical French vintages.

MODERATE

Maison Kammerzell

16 place de la Cathédrale. ☎ **88-32-42-14.** Reservations required. Main courses 67–145 F ($12.75–$27.55). AE, DC, MC, V. Daily noon–3pm and 7pm–1am. Bus 21. ALSATIAN.

The gingerbread Maison Kammerzell is a sightseeing attraction as well as a fantastic restaurant. The carved-wood framework was constructed during the Renaissance; the overhanging stories were built in 1589. We suggest la choucroute formidable (for two), the Alsatian specialty prepared with goose fat and riesling wine, as well as Strasbourg sausages and smoked breast of pork. Owner Guy-Pierre Baumann also offers guinea hen with mushrooms, médaillon of young wild boar, filet of beef Vigneronne with vegetables, and other regional courses.

Maison des Tanneurs

42 rue du Bain-aux-Plantes. ☎ **88-32-79-70.** Reservations required. Main courses 110–150 F ($20.90–$28.50). AE, DC, MC, V. Tues–Sat noon–2:15pm and 7:15–9:30pm. Closed Dec 23–Jan 23 and July 20–Aug 10. Bus 21. ALSATIAN.

This restaurant stands on a typical street in the Petite France quarter. Flowers and Alsatian antiques create a warm atmosphere, while the dining terrace opens onto the canal. The restaurant has been called "La maison de la choucroute," as the sauerkraut-and-pork platter is a specialty, said to be the finest in the area. But the chef prepares many other courses equally well, including the extravagant parfait of foie gras with fresh truffles. Main courses we recommend are crayfish tails à la nage and poulet (coq au riesling) cooked in white wine and served with noodles. Other worthy dishes are duck with black pepper and smoked salmon.

INEXPENSIVE

L'Arsenal
11 rue de l'Abreuvoir. ☎ **88-35-03-69.** Reservations required. Main courses 75–125 F ($14.25–$23.75); fixed-price lunch 130 F ($24.70); fixed-price menus 125–195 F ($23.75–$37.05). AE, DC, MC, V. Mon–Fri noon–2pm and 7:15–11pm, Sat 7:15–11pm. Closed eight days in Feb and three weeks in Aug. Bus 10. FRENCH.

This pleasant Alsatian restaurant is in a historic building and often counts European Parliament members among its patrons. The inventive regional menu changes often but may include breaded pigs' trotters, homemade goose liver, matelote of eel, and calf's head with beer sauce. A specialty of the house is Kougelhopf with escargots; normally it's sweet but the chef here makes it salted with snails.

⑤ Brasserie de l'Ancienne Douane
6 rue de la Douane. ☎ **88-32-42-19.** Reservations recommended. Main courses 37–122 F ($7.05–$23.20); fixed-price menus 65 F ($12.35), 87 F ($16.55), 102 F ($19.40), and 110 F ($20.90); children's menu 47 F ($8.95). AE, DC, MC, V. Daily 11:30am–11pm. Closed Jan 8–22. Bus 21. ALSATIAN.

This is the largest and most colorful dining spot in Strasbourg. Established as part of a historic renovation, it offers 600 seats indoors, plus 200 seats on a terrace. From the outside, along a street in the oldest part of town, you'll see the arcades of the lower floor and the small windows of the stone facade. The high-ceilinged rooms are somewhat formal, with Teutonic chairs and heavily timbered ceilings. Among the Alsatian specialties are the well-known "sauerkraut of the Customs officers" and the foie gras of Strasbourg; chicken in riesling with Alsatian noodles, onion pie, and ham knuckle with potato salad and horseradish also are popular. Next to the brasserie is an old tavern that's now the Quai des Bières, featuring 30 kinds of beer.

NEARBY DINING

Instead of dining in Strasbourg, many motorists prefer to head north for 7¹/₂ miles to the village of La Wantzenau, which has very good restaurants. From Strasbourg, go northeast on D468, which runs along the west bank of the Rhine.

✪ A La Barrière
3 route de Strasbourg. ☎ **88-96-20-23.** Reservations required. Main courses 120–140 F ($22.80–$26.60); fixed-price menus 150–250 F ($28.50–$47.50). AE, DC, MC, V. Thurs–Mon noon–2:30pm and 7–9:30pm, Tues noon–2:30pm. Closed Feb and Aug 7–30. FRENCH.

This restaurant lies a five-minute walk from the center of La Wantzenau. In a restrained art deco interior, Claude Sutter, former pupil of the recently retired master chef/original founder of the place, prepares a sophisticated cuisine. The menu might include filet of sole with scallops and scampi in ginger sauce; roast rack of lamb with gratin dauphinois and garlic en chemise; roast dorado with fennel, celery, and tomatoes; zander in reisling; and salmon steaks with sorrel. In autumn, the game courses (especially pheasant and venison) are excellent.

6 Colmar

273 miles SE of Paris, 87 miles SE of Nancy, 44 miles SW of Strasbourg

One of the most attractive towns in Alsace, Colmar is filled with many medieval and early Renaissance buildings, with half-timbered structures, sculptured gables, and gracious loggias. Tiny gardens and wash houses surround many of the homes. Its old quarter looks more German than French, filled with streets of unexpected twists and turns. As a gateway to the Rhine country, Colmar is a major stopover south from Strasbourg—it's the third-largest town in Alsace, near the vine-covered slopes of the southern Vosges.

ESSENTIALS

GETTING THERE   Railway lines link Colmar to Nancy, Strasbourg, and Mulhouse, as well as to Germany via Freiburg, across the Rhine. Nine trains per day arrive from Paris (trip time: 6 hr.), costing 275 F ($52.25) one way.

If you're driving, take N83 from Strasbourg. Because of Colmar's narrow streets, many motorists park northeast of the railway station, in the Champ-de-Mars, before walking a few blocks east to the heart of the old city.

VISITOR INFORMATION   The Office de Tourisme is at 4 rue d'Unterlinden (☎ 89-20-68-92).

WINE TOURS   For information about free winery tours, contact the **CIVA (Alsace Wine Committee)**, Maison du Vin d'Alsace, 12 av. de la Foire-aux-Vins (☎ 89-24-09-45). The CIVA office is usually open Monday to Saturday from 9am to noon and 2 to 5pm. Make your arrangements far in advance.

SEEING THE TOP ATTRACTIONS

The city's major attraction is the ✪ **Musée d'Unterlinden** (Under the Linden Trees), place d'Unterlinden (☎ 89-41-89-23). It's housed in a former Dominican convent (1232) that was the chief seat of Rhenish mysticism in the 14th and 15th centuries. Converted to a museum around 1850, it has been a treasure house of the art and history of Alsace ever since.

The jewel of its collection is an immense altar screen with two-sided folding wing pieces—designed that way to show first the Crucifixion, then the Incarnation, framed by the Annunciation and the Resurrection. The carved altar screen depicts St. Anthony visiting the hermit St. Paul; it also reveals the Temptation of St. Anthony, the most beguiling part of a work that contains some ghastly misshapen birds, weird monsters, and loathsome animals. The demon of the plague, for example, is depicted with a swollen belly and purple skin, his body blotched with boils, a diabolical grin on his horrible face. One of the most exciting works in the history of German art, the *Issenheim Altarpiece* was created by the Würzburg-born Matthias Grünewald, called "the most furious of realists." His colors glow and his fantasy will overwhelm you.

The museum has other attractions as well, like the magnificent altarpiece of Jean d'Orlier by Martin Schongauer (ca. 1470), a large collection of religious wood-carvings and stained glass from the 14th to the 18th century, and Gallo-Roman lapidary collections, including funeral slabs. Its armory collection includes ancient arms from the romanesque to the Renaissance, featuring halberds and crossbows.

The museum is open April to October, daily from 9am to 6pm; November to March, Wednesday to Monday from 9am to noon and 2 to 5pm. Admission is 28 F ($5.30) for adults and 18 F ($3.40) for children 12 to 17; 11 and under free.

The **Eglise St-Martin,** in the heart of Old Colmar at 1 cours St-Martin, is a collegiate church begun in 1230 on the site of a romanesque church. It has a notable choir erected by William of Marburg in 1350. The church is crowned by a steeple rising to a height of 232 feet. It's open daily from 8am to 5pm.

About two blocks away, opening onto place des Dominicains, is the **Eglise des Dominicains,** which contains one of the most famous artistic treasures of Colmar: Martin Schongauer's painting *Virgin of the Rosebush*, all gold, red, and white, with fluttering birds. Look for it in the choir. Visiting hours are 10am to 6pm daily; closed November to March. Admission is 10 F ($1.90) for adults and 5 F (95¢) for children.

One of the most beautiful houses here is the **Maison Pfister,** 11 rue des Marchands (☎ 89-41-33-61), at the corner of rue Mercière, a civic building erected in 1537 with wooden balconies. On the ground floor is a wine boutique owned by a major Alsace wine grower, Mure, proprietor of the vineyard Clos St-Landelin.

If you take St. Peter's Bridge over the Lauch River, you'll have an excellent view of Old Colmar and can explore the section known as **Petite Venice** because it's filled with canals.

Because of the fame of the Statue of Liberty in New York City, interest continues in sculptor Frédéric-Auguste Bartholdi, who was born in Colmar in 1834. The **Musée Bartholdi,** 30 rue des Marchands (☎ 89-41-90-60), is a small memento-filled museum where there are Statue of Liberty rooms containing plans and scale models, as well as documents in connection with its construction and other works regarding U.S. history. The Paris apartment of Bartholdi, with furniture and memorabilia, has been reconstructed here. The museum supplements its exhibits with displays tracing the history of Colmar. It's open March to December only, daily from 10am to noon and 2 to 6pm. Admission is 20 F ($3.80) for adults and 10 F ($1.90) for children 8 to 18; 7 and under free.

WHERE TO STAY

La Fecht
1 rue de la Fecht, 68000 Colmar. ☎ **89-41-34-08.** Fax 89-23-80-28. 39 rms. MINIBAR TV TEL. 380–470 F ($72.20–$89.30) double. Breakfast 40 F ($7.60) extra. AE, DC, MC, V.

Conveniently set at the edge of the old city, La Fecht is a small hotel with a garden and terrace. The rooms are well designed, and the hotel's restaurant serves well-prepared meals. La Fecht was completely renovated in 1995.

Hostellerie le Maréchal
4–5 place des Six-Montagnes-Noires, 68000 Colmar. ☎ **89-41-60-32.** Fax 89-24-59-40. 30 rms, 6 suites. MINIBAR TV TEL. 550 F ($104.55) double; 1,000–1,500 F ($190.10–$285.15) suite. Breakfast 65 F ($12.35) extra. AE, MC, V.

This hotel was formed when three 16th-century houses were joined. Guests climb a wide staircase to reach the rooms, most of which are air-conditioned. In the east wing there's a small partially timbered room with a sloping ceiling. When Gilbert Bomo set up this hostelry in 1972, he created a winter restaurant with a welcoming fireplace; in summer the restaurant is moved to another part of the complex, so diners have a water view. You can feast on such specialties as stuffed quail, good beef and veal dishes, and lamb provençal—accompanied by Tokay and Alsatian wines.

WHERE TO DINE

✪ Au Fer Rouge

52 Grand' Rue. ☎ **89-41-37-24.** Reservations required. Main courses 180–220 F ($34.20–$41.80); fixed-price menus 295 F ($56.05), 350 F ($66.50), and 470 F ($89.30). AE, DC, MC, V. Tues–Sat noon–2pm and 7–9:30pm, Sun noon–2pm. Closed Jan 6–24. FRENCH.

In a black-and-white-timbered building on a cobblestone square, Au Fer Rouge has stained- and bottle-glass windows and boxes that overflow with geraniums in summer. Inside, carved oak beams and brass and copper decorations provide a traditional setting. Owner Patrick Fulgraff has departed from the typical Alsatian fare in favor of more inventive styles. His specialties include noisettes of lamb with tarragon, quail with shredded cabbage and truffles, roast suckling pig, and wild duck cooked in its own juice, then apples and cinnamon in puff pastry for dessert. The chef rises and falls in popularity as food critics award toques one year, then take one away the next. However, M. Fuklgraff retains his Michelin star— deservedly so.

⑤ Maison des Têtes

19 rue des Têtes. ☎ **89-24-43-43.** Reservations required. Main courses 98–134 F ($18.60–$25.45); fixed-price menus 152 F ($28.90), 165 F ($31.35), 179 F ($34), 216 F ($41.05), and 310 F ($58.90). AE, DC, MC, V. Tues–Sat noon–1:45pm and 7–9:30pm, Sun noon–1:45pm. Closed Dec 26–Jan 1. FRENCH.

This Colmar monument, named for the sculptured heads on its stone facade, is reached via a covered cobblestone drive and an open courtyard. The dining rooms are decorated with aged-wood beams and paneling, art nouveau lighting fixtures, and stained-glass and leaded windows. The food is excellent, like traditional foie gras with truffles, choucroute, seasonal roebuck with morels, and fresh trout or Rhine salmon braised in riesling. The Alsatian wines are sublime.

✪ Schillinger

16 rue Stanislas. ☎ **89-41-43-17.** Reservations required. Main courses 100–280 F ($19–$53.20); fixed-price menus 270–520 F ($51.30–$98.85). AE, DC, MC, V. Tues–Sat noon–2:15pm and 7-9:15pm, Sun noon-2:15pm. Closed July 5–26. FRENCH.

Schillinger—a *belle maison* with Louis XVI–style decor—is the domain of Jean-Yves Schillinger, the most talented chef in competition-rich Colmar. Trained under such greats as Robuchon and Boyer, the chef has forged his own innovative trail, and the results are amazing. Try his foie gras maison, duckling in lemon sauce, ravioli with duckling foie gras, or personal version of Breton lobster. The chef succeeds with each dish he sets out to conquer.

NEARBY ACCOMMODATIONS & DINING

Gourmets flock to Illhaeusern, 11 miles from Colmar, east of the N83 highway, for one important reason—to dine at Auberge de l'Ill, one of France's greatest restaurants. Note that the signs for the restaurant, beside the main highway, are difficult to miss.

✪ Auberge de l'Ill

Route de Collonges. ☎ **89-71-89-00.** Reservations required, sometimes six weeks in advance on midsummer weekends. Main courses 125–490 F ($23.75–$93.10); fixed-price menus 590 F ($112.15) at lunch, 700 F ($133.05) at dinner. AE, DC, MC, V. Mon noon–2pm, Wed–Sun noon–2pm and 7–9pm. Closed Feb. FRENCH.

Run by the Haeberlin brothers in what used to be their family's 19th-century farm-house, L'Auberge de l'Ill combines the finest-quality Alsatian specialties with *cuisine moderne* and classic offerings. You can take your apéritif or coffee under the weeping willows in a beautiful garden, with a river view. The house is furnished with antiques, polished silver hollowware, and Buffet paintings. Chef Paul Haeberlin takes dishes of Alsatian origin and makes them into *grande cuisine*— matelote au riesling, eel stewed in riesling, and an inventive foie gras. His partridge, pheasant, and duckling are among the best in Europe. Sometimes braised slices of pheasant and partridge are served with a winey game sauce, chestnuts, and wild mushrooms and Breton cornmeal. The salmon soufflé is unsurpassed in all France. Some dishes require 24-hour advance notice, so inquire about this when you make reservations.

You can spend the night at the restaurant's air-conditioned Hôtel de Berges (☎ **89-71-87-87;** fax 89-71-87-88) in a delightfully furnished room (11 in all) overlooking the Ill. A double rents for 1,400 F ($266.15), plus 110 F ($20.90) for breakfast.

7 The Wine Road of Alsace

From Strasbourg, motorists heading south for 42 miles to Colmar can take the N83 direct route. However, if you've got time, the famous Wine Road of Alsace makes a truly rewarding experience. For some 60 miles the road passes through charming villages, many illuminated on summer nights for your viewing pleasure. Along the way are country inns if you'd like to sample some of the wine, take a leisurely lunch or dinner, or rent a room for the night.

The Wine Road runs along the Vosges foothills, with medieval towers and feudal ruins evoking faded pageantry. Of course, the slopes are covered with vines, for there's an estimated 50,000 acres of vineyards along this road, sometimes reaching a height of 1,450 feet. Some 30,000 families earn their living tending the grapes. The best time to go is for the vintage in September and October.

Riesling is the king of Alsatian wine, with its exquisitely perfumed bouquet. Other regional wines are Chasselas, Knipperle, Sylvaner, Pinot Blanc (one of the oldest), Muscat, Pinot Gris, Pinot Auxerrois, Traminer, and Gewürztraminer.

The traditional route starts at—

MARLENHEIM

This agreeable wine town—noted for its Vorlauf red wine—lies 13 miles due west of Strasbourg on N4. You might want to visit it even if you can't take the complete route, as it offers an excellent inn (below).

WHERE TO STAY & DINE

✪ Hostellerie du Cerf

30 rue du Général-de-Gaulle, 67520 Marlenheim. ☎ **88-87-73-73.** Fax 88-87-68-08. 15 rms, 2 suites. TEL. 410–550 F ($77.90–$104.55) double; 600 F ($114.05) suite. Breakfast 60–88 F ($11.40–$16.70) extra. AE, MC, V. Parking 10 F ($1.90).

In the heart of the medieval village, occupying a half-timbered building at least 300 years old, this hotel offers 15 pleasantly furnished rooms adjoining an excellent restaurant. Robert Husser and his son, Michel, will feed you specialties like fresh foie gras, cassoulet of lobster, ballotine of quail (autumn only) with sweetbreads, oysters cooked in court bouillon and flavored with herbs, and roast turbot with vegetables. One of the most charming offerings is an all-Alsatian fixed-price meal for 395 F ($75.10). Other fixed-price meals begin at 250 F ($47.50) at lunch during the week. Regular fixed-price menus cost 285 to 485 F ($54.15 to $92.20). The restaurant is closed Tuesday and Wednesday; other days, service hours are noon to 2:15pm and 7 to 9:30pm.

WANGEN

One of the many jewels along the route, Wangen contains a city gate crowned by a tower and twisting narrow streets. It's one of the most typical of the Alsatian wine towns. The road from Wangen winds down to—

MOLSHEIM

One of the 10 free cities of Alsace, called the "Decapolis," Molsheim retains its old ramparts and a gothic/Renaissance church built in 1614 to 1619. Its Alte Metzig (town hall) was erected by the Guild of Butchers and is a most interesting sight, with its turret, gargoyles, loggia, and a belfry housing a clock with allegorical figures striking the hour.

ROSHEIM

Nestled behind medieval fortifications, this old wine-growing town—another of the 10 free Alsatian cities—has a 12th-century romanesque house and the Church of Sts. Peter and Paul, also romanesque, from two centuries later; it's dominated by an octagonal tower. Medieval walls and gate towers evoke its past.

OBERNAI

The patron saint of Alsace, Obernai, was born here. With old timbered houses and a colorful marketplace, place du Marché, this is one of the most interesting stopovers on the wine route. Place de l'Etoile is decked out in flowers, and the 1523 Hôtel de Ville has a delightful loggia (inside you can view the council chamber). An old watchtower, the Tour de la Chapelle, is from the 13th and 16th centuries. The town's six-pail fountain is one of the most spectacular in Alsace. The **Office de Tourisme** is at Chapelle du Beffroi, 67210 Obernoi (☎ **88-95-64-13**).

WHERE TO STAY & DINE

Le Parc

169 rue du Général-Gourand, 67210 Obernai. ☎ **88-95-50-08.** Fax 88-95-37-29. 50 rms. TV TEL. 470–990 F ($89.35–$188.20) double. Breakfast 65 F ($12.35) extra. Half board (with a three-day minimum stay, required in high season) 970 F ($184.40) double. AE, MC, V. Parking free. Closed Dec 5–Jan 6.

This hotel, surrounded by a park, contains three dining rooms, each in a different decor. The food depends on what's available in the local markets and might include monkfish with mushrooms, duckling with apples and cèpes (flap mushrooms), a salad of foie gras, salmon in red-wine sauce, and rich fruit desserts. A la carte dinners cost 300 to 350 F ($57 to $66.50); fixed-price menus are 190 F ($36.10), 280 F ($53.20), and 335 F ($63.65). The dining rooms are closed

Sunday night and Monday. On the premises, owner Marc Wucher rents well-furnished spacious rooms. Facilities include a hot tub, a sauna, and a fitness center.

BARR

The grapes for some of the finest Alsatian wines, Sylvaner and Gewürztraminer, are harvested here. The castles of Landsberg and Andlau stand high above the town. Barr has many pleasant old timbered houses and a charming place de l'Hôtel-de-Ville with a town hall from 1640.

MITTELBERGHEIM

Perched like a stork on a housetop, this is a special village. Its place de l'Hôtel-de-Ville is bordered with houses in the Renaissance style.

WHERE TO STAY & DINE

Winstub Gilg

1 route du Vin, Mittelbergheim, 67140 Barr. ☎ **88-08-91-37.** Fax 88-08-45-17. 10 rms. TV TEL. 250–400 F ($47.50–$76) double. Breakfast 35 F ($6.65) extra. AE, DC, MC, V. Parking free.

This is an excellent inn. Though parts of the building date from 1614, its architectural showpiece is a two-story stone staircase, classified a historic monument, which was carved by the medieval stonemasons who worked on the cathedral at Strasbourg. The rooms are comfortably and attractively furnished. Chef Georges Gilg attracts a loyal following with his regional specialties, such as onion tart, sauerkraut, and foie gras en broche. His main courses include stewed kidneys and sweetbreads and duck with oranges nantaise. In season, he's likely to offer roast pheasant with grapes and filet of roebuck. Fixed-price menus run 125 to 325 F ($23.75 to $61.75). The restaurant is closed Tuesday night and Wednesday and from January 8 to 31.

ANDLAU

This gardenlike resort was once the site of an abbey dating from 887, founded by the disgraced wife of emperor Charles the Fat. It has now faded into history, but a church remains that dates from the 12th century. In the tympanum are noteworthy romanesque carvings.

WHERE TO DINE

Au Boeuf Rouge

6 rue du Dr-Stoltz. ☎ **88-08-96-26.** Reservations recommended. Main courses 95–155 F ($18.05–$29.45); fixed-price menus 160–240 F ($30.40–$45.60). AE, DC, MC, V. Fri–Tues 11:30am–2pm and 6:30–9:30pm, Wed 11:30am–2pm. Closed Jan 3–26 and June 21–July 7. FRENCH.

Once a 16th-century postal relay station, this structure is now occupied by a ground-floor rustic dining room and bar, owned by the Kieffer family for 100 years. It offers classic specialties like homemade terrines, gamecock, fresh fish, a wide array of meats, and a tempting dessert cart. This place doesn't offer the most innovative cookery on the wine trail, but it's reliable and consistent. The chef knows how to impress most palates without reverting to ostentation.

DAMBACH

In the midst of its well-known vineyards, Dambach is one of the delights of the wine route. Its timbered houses are gabled with galleries, and many contain oriels. Wrought-iron shop signs still tell you if a place is a bakery or a butcher shop. The town has ramparts and three fortified gates. A short drive from the town leads to the Saint Sebastian chapel, with a 15th-century ossuary.

Going through Chatenois, you reach—

SELESTAT

This was once a free city, a center of the Renaissance, and the seat of a great school. Towered battlements enclose the town. The **Bibliothèque Humaniste,** 1 rue de la Bibliothèque (☎ **88-92-03-24**), houses a rare collection of manuscripts, including Sainte-Foy's *Book of Miracles*; its open Monday to Friday from 9am to noon and 2 to 6pm and Saturday from 9am to noon. Admission is 8 F ($1.50) for adults and 5 F (95¢) for children.

The gothic **Eglise St-George** has some fine stained glass and a gilded and painted stone pulpit. Finally, see the 12th-century **Eglise Ste-Foy,** built of red sandstone in the romanesque style. One of the town's most noteworthy Renaissance buildings is the Maison de Stephan Ziegler. The **Office de Tourisme** is in La Commanderie, boulevard du Général-Leclerc, 67600 Sélestat (☎ **88-92-02-66**).

WHERE TO DINE

✪ La Couronne

45 rue de Sélestat-Baldenheim. ☎ **88-85-32-22.** Reservations required. Main courses 90–160 F ($17.10–$30.40); fixed-price menus 160–410 F ($30.40–$77.90). AE, MC, V. Tues–Sat noon–2pm and 7–9pm, Sun noon–2pm. Closed the first week in Jan and the last week in July. From Sélestat, go 5 1/2 miles east on D21, and when the road forks, go to the right, taking D209 to the village of Baldenheim. FRENCH.

This family-run establishment serves dishes reflecting the bounty of Alsace, prepared with considerable finesse. A flower-filled vestibule near the entrance leads to a trio of pleasant dining rooms. Menu choices may include noisettes of roebuck (midsummer to Christmas), frogs' legs in garlic, l'omble chevalier (the elusive fish from Lake Geneva) with sauerkraut and cumin-laced potatoes, and traditional matelote ride—zander, brochet, and eel poached in riesling.

A DETOUR TO CHATEAU HAUT-HOENIGSBOURG

From Sélestat you can make an excursion to Château Haut-Koenigsbourg, 67600 Orschwiller (☎ **88-82-50-60**). About 2,500 feet up on an isolated peak, this 15th-century castle—the largest in Alsace—treats you to an eagle's-nest view. It once belonged to the Hohenstaufens. During the Thirty Years' War, the Swedes dismantled the château, but it was rebuilt in 1901 after it was presented to Kaiser Wilhelm II. The château is open daily: June to September from 9am to 6pm, in April and May from 9am to noon and 1 to 6pm, in March and October from 9am to noon and 1 to 5pm, and November to February from 9am to noon and 1 to 4pm. Admission is 31 F ($5.90) for adults and 20 F ($3.80) for children.

BERGHEIM

Renowned for its wines, this town has kept part of its 15th-century fortifications. You can see many timbered Alsatian houses and a gothic church.

RIBEAUVILLE

In September a fair is held here known as the "Day of the Strolling Fiddlers." At the foot of vine-clad hills, the town is charming, with old shop signs, pierced balconies, turrets, and flower-decorated houses. See its Renaissance fountain and Hôtel de Ville, which has a collection of Alsatian tankards known as *hanaps*. Also of interest is the Tour des Bouchers, a "butchers' tower" of the 13th and 16th centuries. The town is noted for its Riesling and Traminer wines. The **Office de Tourisme** is on Grand' Rue, 68150 Ribeauvillé (☎ **89-73-62-22**).

WHERE TO STAY & DINE

Clos St-Vincent

Route de Bergheim, 68150 Ribeauvillé. ☎ **89-73-67-65.** Fax 89-73-32-20. 12 rms, 3 suites. 860 F ($163.50) double; from 990 F ($188.20) suite. MC, V. Parking free.

This Relais & Châteaux is one of the most elegant dining/lodging choices along the Alsatian Wine Road. Most of the individually decorated accommodations have a balcony or terrace, but guests get much more than a lovely view of the Haut-Rhin vineyards and summertime roses. Bertrand Chapotin's food is exceptional—hot duck liver with nuts, turbot with sorrel, roebuck (in season) in hot sauce, and veal kidneys in Pinot Noir. Of course, the wines are smooth, especially the Riesling and Gewürztraminer, which seems to be most popular. Fixed-price menus cost 250 F ($47.50).

RIQUEWIHR

This town, surrounded by some of the finest vineyards in Alsace, appears much as it did in the 16th century. With well-preserved walls and towers and great wine presses and old wells, it's one of the most rewarding targets along the route. You can see many gothic and Renaissance houses, with wooden balconies, voluted gables, and elaborately carved doors and windows. Its most interesting are Maison Liebrich, from 1535; Maison Preiss-Zimmer, from 1686; and Maison Kiener, from 1574. Try to peer into some of the galleried courtyards, where centuries virtually have stopped. The High Gate of Dolder, straddling an arch through which you can pass, is from 1291. Nearby, the pentagonal Tower of Thieves (often called "the robbers' tower") contains a torture chamber. The château, from 1539, offers a minor museum devoted to the history of Alsace.

WHERE TO DINE

✪ Auberge du Schoenenbourg

2 rue de la Piscine. ☎ **89-47-92-28.** Reservations required. Main courses 125–170 F ($23.75–$32.30); fixed-price menus 180 F ($34.20), 235 F ($44.65), 305 F ($57.95), and 370 F ($70.30). AE, MC, V. Daily noon–2pm and 7–9:30pm. Closed Jan 8–Feb 8. FRENCH.

Meals are served in a garden completely surrounded by vineyards at the edge of the village. The cuisine of François Kiener offers a delectable array of tantalizingly prepared courses—foie gras maison, of course, but salmon soufflé with sabayon truffles is an elegant surprise. Perhaps try the panache of fish with sorrel or ravioli of snails with poppy seeds. The place may not be on the cutting edge of fashion, but the cuisine is still highly praised.

KIENTZHEIM

Known for its wine, Kientzheim is one of the three towns to explore in this valley of vineyards, ranking along with Kaysersberg and Ammerschwihr. Two castles, timber-framed houses, and walls that date from the Middle Ages make it an appealing stop. After you've passed through, it's just a short drive to . . .

KAYSERSBERG

Once a free city of the empire, Kaysersberg lies at the mouth of the Weiss Valley, between two vine-covered slopes; it's crowned by a feudal castle that was ruined in the Thirty Years' War. Kaysersberg rivals Riquewihr as one of the most visited towns along the wine route. From one of the many ornately carved bridges, you can see the city's medieval fortifications stretching along the top of one of the nearby hills. Many of the houses are gothic and Renaissance, and most have prominent half-timbering, lots of wrought-iron accents, small leaded windows, and multiple designs carved into the reddish sandstone that seems to have been the principal building material.

In the cafés you'll hear a confusing combination of French and Alsatian. The language is usually determined by the age of the speaker, with the older ones remaining faithful to the dialect of their grandparents. Dr. Albert Schweitzer was born here in 1875, and his house is near the fortified bridge over the Weiss: You can visit the Albert Schweitzer Cultural Center June to October, daily from 10am to noon and 2 to 6pm.

WHERE TO STAY & DINE

Au Lion d'Or

66 rue du Général-de-Gaulle. ☎ 89-47-11-16. Reservations required. Main courses 60–130 F ($11.40–$24.70); fixed-price menus 98 F ($18.60), 145 F ($27.55), 160 F ($30.40), 200 F ($38), and 320 F ($60.80). MC, V. Tues noon–2pm, Thurs–Mon noon–2pm and 7–9:30pm. Closed Jan 1-20 and May 31-Oct. FRENCH.

This restaurant boasts an exceptionally beautiful decor. A carved lion's head is set into the oak door leading into the restaurant, with a beamed ceiling, stone detailing, brass chandeliers, and a massive fireplace. If you eat at an outdoor table, you'll have a view of one of Alsace's prettiest streets. The food, a medley of typical Alsatian courses, is neither as good nor as expensive as that dispensed at Chambard (below), but it's reliable and quite fine. The flavors of Alsace are effectively served up here.

✪ Chambard

9–13 rue du Général-de-Gaulle, 68240 Kaysersberg. ☎ 89-47-10-17. Fax 89-47-35-03. Reservations required. Main courses 140–280 F ($26.60–$53.20); fixed-price menus 300 F ($57), 380 F ($72.20), and 450 F ($85.55). AE, MC, V. Mon–Tues 7–9:30pm, Wed–Sun noon–2pm and 7–9:30pm. Closed Mar 1–21 and Christmas holidays. FRENCH.

The Chambard is the domain of a chef of unusual versatility and imagination. You'll recognize the restaurant—the finest in town—by the gilded wrought-iron sign above the cobblestones. Inside you'll find a rustic ambience, with exposed stone and polished wood. The regional cuisine is so good it's well worth planning your wine tour to include a stopover. Try M. Irrmann's foie gras, turbot in ginger, Bresse chicken sautéed with crayfish tails, or chicken sautéed with riesling.

The Chambard offers a 20-room hotel annex built in 1981 to match the other buildings on the street. It has a massive Renaissance fireplace that was transported from another building. A double is 650 to 750 F ($123.55 to $142.55), plus 60 F ($11.40) for breakfast.

ROUFFACH

One vineyard worth exploring is **Clos St-Landelin** (☎ 89-49-62-19), route du Vin (carrefour RN 83/route de Soultzmatt), 10½ miles south of Colmar. Here the vines grow on little hills at the foot of the Vosges. Rouffach is sheltered by one of the highest of the Vosges mountains, Grand-Ballon, which stops the winds that bring rain. That makes for a dry climate and a special grape. Since 1630 the Muré family has owned the vineyards, and in their cellar is the oldest wine press in Alsace, from the 13th century. They welcome visitors and speak English.

AMMERSCHWIHR

To cap the Wine Road tour, as you move near the outskirts of Colmar stop at Ammerschwihr. Once a free city of the empire, it was almost destroyed in 1944 battles but has been reconstructed in the traditional style. Motorists stop off here in increasing numbers to sample the wine, especially Käferkopf. Check out its trio of gate towers, 16th-century parish church, and remains of early fortifications.

WHERE TO STAY & DINE

A l'Arbre Vert

7 rue des Cigognes, 68770 Ammerschwihr. ☎ **89-47-12-23.** Fax 89-78-27-21. 17 rms. TV TEL. 370 F ($70.30) double. Breakfast 36 F ($6.85) extra. Half board 280–360 F ($53.20–$68.40) per person. AE, DC, MC, V. Parking free. Closed Tues year-round, Feb 10–Mar 25, and Nov 25–Dec 6.

If you don't want to go to Colmar, A l'Arbre Vert is a charming place to stay. Near an old fountain, it's delightfully decorated, though the rooms are rather plain. The inn also serves very good Alsatian specialties in its restaurant, where you can dine even if you aren't staying at the hotel. Meals go for 100 to 310 F ($19 to $58.90).

✪ Aux Armes de France

1 Grande' Rue, 68770 Ammerschwihr. ☎ **89-47-10-12.** Fax 89-47-38-12. Reservations required. Main courses 150–280 F ($28.50–$53.20); fixed-price menus 350–450 F ($66.50–$85.50). AE, DC, MC, V. Thurs 7–9pm, Fri–Tues noon–2pm and 7–9pm. Closed Jan. FRENCH.

While you can rent a room at Aux Armes, the real reason to come here is the food—this is the most superb restaurant along the wine route. In a flower-filled setting, brothers Philippe and François Gaertner receive many French and German gourmets. A specialty of this popular place is fresh foie gras served in its own golden aspic. Main courses include classics with imaginative variations: roebuck (in season) in hot sauce and lobster fricassée with cream and truffles.

There are also rooms for rent, a double costing 360 to 460 F ($68.40 to $87.45), plus 45 F ($8.55) for breakfast.

8 La Route des Crêtes (The Crest Road)

From Basel to Mainz, a distance of some 150 miles, the Vosges mountain range stretches along the west side of the Rhine Valley, bearing a great similarity to the Black Forest of Germany. Many German and French families spend their summer vacation exploring the Vosges. However, those with less time may want to settle for a quick look at these ancient mountains that once formed the boundary between France and Germany. The Vosges are filled with tall hardwood and fir and traversed by a network of twisting roads with hairpin curves. Deep in these mountain forests is the closest that France comes to having a wilderness.

You can explore the mountains by heading west from Strasbourg. But you can take a more interesting route from Colmar. From that ancient Alsatian town, you can explore some of the highest of the southern Vosges with their remarkable beauty. The Route des Crêtes begins at **Col du Bonhomme,** to the west of Colmar. It was devised by the French High Command during World War I to carry supplies over the mountainous front. From Col du Bonhomme you can strike out along this magnificent road, once the object of such bitter fighting but today a series of panoramic vistas, including one of the Black Forest.

By **Col de la Schlucht** you'll have risen a distance of 4,905 feet. Schlucht is a winter/summer resort, one of the best-known beauty spots of the Vosges—with a panoramic vista unfolding of the Valley of Munster and the slopes of Hohneck. As you skirt the edge of this glacier-carved valley, you'll be in the midst of a land of pine groves with a necklace of lakes. You may want to turn off the main road and go exploring in several directions, the scenery is that tempting. But if you're still on the Crest Road, you can circle **Hohneck,** one of the highest peaks at 5,300 feet, dominating the Wildenstein Dam of the Bresse winter sports station.

At **Markstein** you'll come into another pleasant summer/winter resort. From there, take N430 and then D10 to **Münster,** where the savory cheese is made. You go via the Petit-Ballon, a landscape of forest and mountain meadows with lots of grazing cows. Finally, at **Grand-Ballon** you'll have reached the highest point you can go by road in the Vosges, 4,662 feet. From there you can get out of your car and go for a walk. If it's a clear day, you'll be able to see the Jura, with the French Alps beyond, and can gaze upon a panoramic vista of the Black Forest.

WHERE TO STAY & DINE IN MÜNSTER

Au Chene Voltaire

Route du Chêne-Voltaire, at Luttenbach, 68140 Münster. ☎ **89-77-31-74.** 19 rms, 15 with bath. TV. 210 F ($39.90) double without bath, 245 F ($46.55) double with bath. Breakfast 30 F ($5.70) extra. Half board 200–225 F ($38–$42.75) per person. AE, MC. Parking free. Take D10 less than 2 miles southwest from the center of Münster.

This chalet-style inn is in an isolated section of the forest. The modern but no-frills rooms are in a separate building from the rustic restaurant. Unfortunately, you can't dine here unless you're staying at the hotel. Facilities include a sauna and a solarium. View this place only as a much-needed stopover for the night before pressing on your way in the morning.

La Cigogne

4 place du Marché. ☎ **89-77-32-27.** Fax 89-77-28-64. Reservations not required. Main courses 88–100 F ($16.70–$19); fixed-price menu 65 F ($12.35). DC, MC, V. Tues–Sat noon–2pm and 7:30–9pm, Sun noon–2pm. FRENCH.

This historic inn, on the village's main square, was established in the 1870s. It retains its old-fashioned Alsatian rusticity, despite a well-conceived remodeling. Meals are served in either the restaurant or less formally in the brasserie, where simple platters of Alsatian food comprise meals.

On the premises, most in a comfortable new wing, are 22 rooms renting for 400 F ($76), plus 38 F ($7.20) for breakfast.

9 Mulhouse

334 miles SE of Paris; 71 miles SW of Strasbourg; 21 miles NW of Basel, Switzerland

Called Mülhausen by the Germans, this industrial city is topped in size only by Strasbourg in Alsace and lies between the Vosges and the Black Forest. On the same Ill River that flows through Strasbourg, it's the capital of an arrondissement in the Haut-Rhin département. If Mulhouse has an identity problem, it can be forgiven: From 1308 until 1515 it was a free imperial city, but in 1648 it was added to the Swiss confederation. It remained with Switzerland until 1798, when it joined France. However, from 1871 to 1918 it was under German control. Both German and French are spoken here today.

ESSENTIALS

GETTING THERE   Mulhouse has an airport, 17 miles southwest of the city center, which it shares with the Swiss city of Basel, 22 miles away.

Mulhouse is well connected by rail to every other city in the region and to Paris's Gare de l'Est. There's frequent service to Strasbourg, taking one hour and costing 95 F ($18.05) one way.

VISITOR INFORMATION   The Office de Tourisme is at 9 av. du Maréchal-Foch (☎ 89-45-68-31).

SEEING THE TOP ATTRACTIONS

Mulhouse's main square, from which many busy streets radiate, is **place de la République.** For a look at the old town, head for the marketplace, called **place de la Réunion.** The **Hôtel de Ville** (town hall) dates from the 16th century and is much photographed. Its walls are frescoed and it has a covered outside stairway, an example of Rhenish-Renaissance style. Those with time to explore will find some interesting museums here.

The **Musée de l'Automobile,** 192 av. de Colmar (☎ 89-42-29-17), displays the combined collections of the Schlumpf brothers, including more than 400 vintage cars. Some of the displays, most in working order, are the steam-powered Jacquot (1878), custom-made Ferraris, more than 100 Bugattis (including two of the most expensive ever made), and Rolls-Royces. The museum is open May to September, daily from 10am to 6pm; October to April, Wednesday to Monday from 10am to 6pm. Admission is 55 F ($10.45) for adults and 25 F ($4.75) for children 6 to 18; 5 and under free.

Containing more than 10 million swatches, the **Musée de l'Impression sur Etoffes,** 3 rue des Bonnes-Gens (☎ 89-45-51-20), traces the development of printed fabrics from the 1700s. Upstairs you'll find preserved the machines that once were used to print cloth, as well as a collection of old clothing, cloth, and drawings from France, the Far East, and Persia. From June to August printing machines are demonstrated on Monday, Wednesday, and Friday at 3pm. The museum is open May to September, daily from 10am to noon and 2 to 6pm; October to April, Wednesday to Monday from 10am to noon and 2 to 6pm. Admission is 25 F ($4.75) for adults and 7 F ($1.35) for children.

Assembled over about a dozen rail tracks, the **Musée Français du Chemin de Fer,** 2 rue Alfred-de-Glehn (☎ 89-42-25-67), has a noteworthy collection of train engines and cars. Included are a cutaway section of a steam engine—with diagrams explaining how it works—and steam-powered trains that include the car used by

Napoléon III's aides-de-camp in 1856; the interior decor is by Viollet-le-Duc. There's also a collection of 18th-century fire engines and pumps. The museum is open daily: April to September from 9am to 6pm, and October to March from 10am to 5pm. Admission is 28 F ($5.30) for adults and 12 F ($2.30) for children.

WHERE TO STAY

La Bourse

14 rue de la Bourse, 68100 Mulhouse. ☎ 89-56-18-44. Fax 89-56-60-51. 50 rms. TV TEL. 430 F ($81.70) double. Breakfast 52 F ($9.90) extra. AE, DC, MC, V. Bus 4.

La Bourse offers quiet rooms in a convenient location near the stock exchange, train station, and place de la République. The baths are usually modern, even if the decor of the rooms ranges from old-fashioned to contemporary. About half the rooms overlook an inner courtyard. This choice, though satisfying, won't make you want to linger for more than one night.

Hôtel du Parc

26 rue de la Sinne, 68100 Mulhouse. ☎ 89-66-12-22. Fax 89-66-42-44. 73 rms, 3 suites. A/C MINIBAR TV TEL. 800–950 F ($152–$180.50) double; 1,300–2,900 F ($247.10–$551.30) suite. Breakfast 90 F ($17.10) extra. AE, DC, MC, V. Parking 80 F ($15.20). Bus 4.

The Hôtel du Parc is the leading address in town. The beautifully renovated building was designed to recapture the art deco glamour of the 1930s and provide tasteful accommodations. Live music at teatime is one of the house's time-honored traditions. There's a sleek bar called Charlie's, and Park's restaurant offers quality lunches, dinners, and after-theater suppers.

WHERE TO DINE

Le Belvédère

80 av. de la Première-Division-Blindée. ☎ 89-44-18-79. Reservations recommended. Main courses 75–120 F ($14.25–$22.80); fixed-price weekday lunch 68 F ($12.90); fixed-price menus 110 F ($20.90), 165 F ($31.35), 240 F ($45.60), and 300 F ($57). AE, DC, MC, V. Sun-Mon 11:45am–2pm, Wed–Sat 11:45am–2pm and 7–9:45pm. Bus 4. FRENCH.

Le Belvédère is an intimate family-run restaurant, complete with candles and a fireplace. Menu items include a three-fish platter in riesling, salmon tartare in puff pastry, filet of pike-perch in parsley-cream sauce, and, when available, well-prepared sole meunière or amandine. The restaurant offers both fixed-price and à la carte listings, and the dependable cuisine is a good value, particularly if you order from the less expensive set menus.

Le Relais de la Tour

3 bd. de l'Europe, 31st floor. ☎ 89-45-12-14. Reservations required. Main courses 78–120 F ($14.80–$22.80); fixed-price menus 145–165 F ($27.55–$31.35). AE, DC, MC, V. Daily 11:45am–2:30pm and 7–9:30pm. Bus 14. FRENCH.

This restaurant, in the town's tallest office/apartment building, is the only one of its kind in France. An attraction in its own right, it pivots on its base and makes a complete panoramic turn every 75 minutes. As you dine, sweeping views will unfold over the Vosges, the Jura, and Germany's Black Forest. Menu choices include quail stuffed with foie-gras mousse, gratin of seafood, veal Zurich style, and well-flavored filets of duck, beef, and veal.

16 The French Alps

No part of France is more dramatically scenic than the Alps, for the western ramparts of these mountains and their foothills are majestic. From the Mediterranean to the Rhine in the north, they stretch along the southeastern flank of France. The skiing here has no equal in Europe, not even in Switzerland. Some of the resorts are legendary, like Chamonix–Mont Blanc, the historic capital of alpine skiing, with its 12-mile Vallée Blanche run. Mont Blanc is the highest mountain in Western Europe at 15,780 snowy feet.

Most of this chapter covers the area known as Savoy (Savoie), taking in the French lake district, including the largest alpine lake, which the French share with Switzerland. The French call it Lac Léman, but it's known as Lake Geneva in English.

Winter attracts skiers to Chamonix–Mont Blanc, Megève, and Courchevel 1850; summer brings spa devotees to Evian-les-Bains and Aix-les-Bains. The ideal times to visit, then, are January to March for winter sports and July to September for lakeside and mountain touring. Grenoble, the capital of the French Alps, is the gateway. It's just 30 minutes by car from the Grenoble–St-Geoirs airport, 40 minutes from the Lyon-Satolas international airport, and 90 minutes from the Geneva-Cointrin airport. The city is also connected with the Paris–Lyon–Marseille motorway on the west and to the Chambéry–Geneva motorway on the east.

REGIONAL CUISINE The Savoy was economically underdeveloped until early this century, so an elaborate cuisine never developed here. The cuisine that did develop was robust and straightforward, well suited to the lack of cereals and grains and to the active lifestyle of the people. Most indicative are the recipes that depended on the region's superb raw materials: fresh produce, eggs, fish, meats, and—most important—cheese and milk.

Cheesemaking, developed as a process over thousands of years as a means of preserving the proteins and nutrients of milk, was carefully developed in the Savoy (where cows and goats thrived on the grasses of the alpine meadows). The region's most famous cheese is a form of especially savory Gruyère known as beaufort, which—though similar to Emmenthal "Swiss cheese"—has hardly any holes. Aged for up to two years, it's at its best when made from milk produced between June and September, when the aroma of herbs and flowers is especially pungent. Another famous cheese is reblochon, a slightly bitter semihard cheese that gourmets insist must be fermented at high altitude to achieve its full flavor. The capital of the reblochon "empire" is a region scarred by some of the most rugged geography in Europe and whose principal towns, Grand-Bornand and Thones, are almost exclusively engaged in the production of this particular cheese. Another name for reblochon is the one used in Savoyard dialect, tôme (cheese) de Savoie.

Those who appreciate the pungent taste of goat-milk cheese search out the most famous of the Savoyard chevre: St-Marcellin or (as its devoted aficionados call it) petit St-Marcellin. Once made solely from the milk of alpine goats, it's now based on a combination of cows' and goats' milk; its exterior is firm and supple, but its interior runs with sweet creamy goodness. You'll note the presence of a cheese fondue on almost every menu of the region.

The Savoy and its neighbor, the Dauphine, are most famous for the ways in which cheese and milk are used to augment the flavors of other dishes. There's much confusion in the non-French world about the meaning of *au gratin*. A concept developed in some of the most rugged countryside here (the isolated Vercors region southwest of Grenoble), it refers to the crusty top (not the ingredients) formed when certain ingredients are baked in a certain type of flat (usually oval) dish. "Au gratin" might be the most famous culinary concept to come out of the region and is seen today on menus throughout the world. It usually implies the addition of cheese: A gratin dauphinoise, for example, is a baked casserole of sliced potatoes, usually with onions, cream, cheese, and sometimes eggs. A gratin Savoyard substitutes beef bouillon for the cream, omits the eggs, and sometimes adds cheese.

The freshwater lakes and streams of the Savoy have always yielded a healthy catch, like trout, carp, grayling, pike, eel, perch, and a famous regional delicacy found only in the cold alpine lakes of France and Switzerland, omble chevalier. In one recipe for the thousands of unnamed tiny fish, too small to filet, they are seasoned, batter-fried, and served very hot, usually with a white Savoyard wine. As for vegetables, the traditional greens were those that endured a long growing season amid the alpine snows. Most notable were the spikey-leafed cardoon, whose firm flesh provoked many different methods of preparation.

The region's smoked hams, pâtés, and sausages (sometimes served with red lentils) are delicious, and the rich chocolate confections whipped up in elegant bakeries reflect the tastes of citizens who can permit themselves the extra calories—at this high altitude, outdoor activities make calories easy to burn.

As for wines and spirits, the gentle foothills benefiting from southern exposure have produced good wines, though—with one exception—not the world-famous vintages of Burgundy or Bordeaux. The most famous red is the Montmélian, similar to a beaujolais. The best-known white is a sparkling Seyssel, whose best vintages have been favorably compared with champagne. As in many mountain regions of Europe, the alps produce potent eaux-de-vie, which should usually be consumed to top off a full evening meal. Most celebrated is Gentian, which is flavored with a blue alpine wildflower; and the famous Chartreuse, whose herbal green tint has been used for centuries as an adjective to describe a certain color. The local Marc de Savoie is a deceivingly potent residue from the brandy-distillation process guaranteed to give you a hangover.

EXPLORING THE REGION BY CAR

Here's how to link together the best of the region if you rent a car.

Day 1　Begin in Evian-les-Bains, a French city farther east than many points in neighboring Switzerland. For scenic views you can take N5 east along Lac Léman until reaching the Swiss border. Return to Evian for the night.

Day 2　Head west for 28 miles along N5 to Geneva. Maneuvering through the urban landscapes of Geneva is less forbidding than you might think, and border formalities are among the least complicated in Europe. The city's charms include its status as cultural capital of the French-speaking Alps and its role as one of the most orderly large cities in the world. Spend a night in Geneva, where hotels are plentiful and comfortable (for a review of hotels, see *Frommer's Switzerland*). Dine in either of the town's most folkloric restaurants: La Mère Royaume, 9 rue des Corps-Saints (☎ 022/732-70-08), is on the right bank of the Rhône; this paneled restaurant serves delicate French specialties, including a version of fish (omble chevalier) that lives only in a handful of alpine lakes. The second option is Le Restaurant du Palais de Justice, 8 place Bourg-de-Four (☎ 022/310-42-54), a brasserie across from Geneva's most historic courthouse in the Left Bank's medieval core.

Day 3　From Geneva, drive south along N201 and A41 for 22 miles to Annecy, a medieval city boasting a historic core filled with bridges and canals. Spend the night here or detour 7¹/₂ miles southeast along the eastern shore of Lake Annecy for a view of the sleepy but charming lakeside hamlet of Talloires.

Day 4　Continue driving south along A41 for 56 miles to the day's final destination: Grenoble. Suitable stopovers along the way include Aix-les-Bains and Chambéry, site of the Château des Ducs de Savoie and the most famous fountain in the alpine world. (Shaped like an elephant, it was a gift to the town from a native son who made a fortune as a merchant in India.)

Day 5　At this point, you have at least five options. The high-altitude resorts of the French Alps are best suited to stopovers of at least two days, and, depending on your time, you can visit either one or all of them for hill climbing, skiing, or whatever. We recommend that you limit your exposure to just one or two, settle into a hotel, and begin to explore the great outdoors.

Heading north from Grenoble, wind your way along E712 and E70, which will take you through Albertville, the site of the 1992 Winter Olympics. Then you'll have to decide whether to veer southeast to Courchevel or continue northeast to Megève, Flaine, Chamonix, Morzine, and/or Avoriaz. The most distant of these from Grenoble is Avoriaz, and getting there involves driving no more than 120 miles over well-paved roads. While you're reflecting on which resort to grace with your presence, you can dine at the Hôtel Million, 8 place de la Liberté, 73200 Albertville (☎ 79-32-25-15). Fixed-price menus range from 160 to 500 F ($30.40 to $95) and are served daily except Sunday night and all day Monday.

If after your break your intention is to continue southeast to Courchevel, set out from Albertville along N90 for about 25 miles. If your intention is to continue on to any of the other resorts, head northeast along N212 and follow the signs for the resort of your choice.

The French Alps

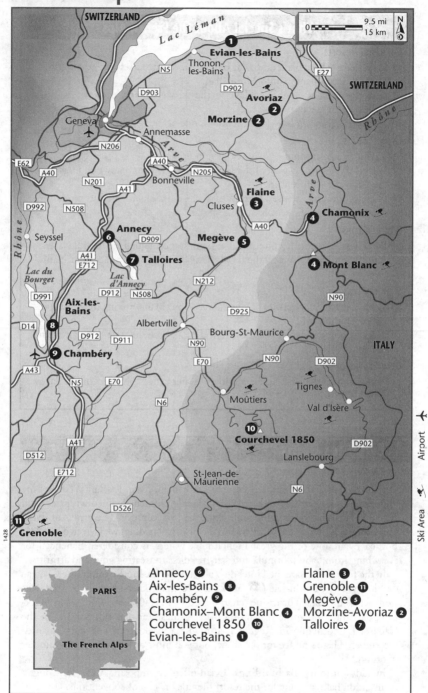

SWITZERLAND

Lac Léman

1 Evian-les-Bains

Thonon-les-Bains

SWITZERLAND

0 ⎯⎯ 9.5 mi
⎯⎯ 15 km
N

D902

2 Avoriaz

D903

Morzine 2

N5

Rhône

Geneva

Annemasse

N206

E62

A40

Arve

N201

A40

N205

A41

Bonneville

Flaine 3

Cluses

Arve

A40

4 Chamonix

D992 N508

Seyssel

6 Annecy

D909

Megève 5

4 Mont Blanc

Rhône

A41
E712

7 Talloires

N212

Lac du Bourget

Lac d'Annecy

N90

D991

D912 N508

Aix-les-Bains

Albertville

D925

8

D14

D912 D911

Chambéry 9

N90

E70

Bourg-St-Maurice

N90

ITALY

A43

N5

E70

D902

Tignes

N6

Moûtiers

Val d'Isère

A41

10

Courchevel 1850

D902

D512

Lanslebourg

E712

St-Jean-de-Maurienne

N6

D526

11 Grenoble

Airport ✈

Ski Area 🎿

★ PARIS

The French Alps

Annecy 6
Aix-les-Bains 8
Chambéry 9
Chamonix–Mont Blanc 4
Courchevel 1850 10
Evian-les-Bains 1

Flaine 3
Grenoble 11
Megève 5
Morzine-Avoriaz 2
Talloires 7

1428

What's Special About the French Alps

Great Ski Resorts
- Chamonix–Mont Blanc, the best of all the French ski resorts, at an altitude of 3,422 feet, opening onto Mont Blanc.
- Courchevel 1850, a chic enclave in the ski world, and part of Les Trois Vallées, with spectacular ski runs.
- Megève, *capitale du ski*—its ski school is one of the best in Europe.

Great Towns
- Talloires, a gastronomic village of eastern France.
- Chambéry, ancient capital of the Duchy of Savoy, with many buildings from the 15th and 16th centuries.
- Grenoble, capital of the Dauphine, with excursions to the old monastery where Chartreuse liqueur is made.

Premier Spas
- Evian-les-Bains, the leading spa of eastern France, famed for its still waters.
- Annecy, on Lac d'Annecy, the jewel of the Savoy Alps and capital of Haute-Savoie.

Scenic Vistas
- Cable cars to the belvederes at Chamonix–Mont Blanc, among the most spectacular in the world.
- Megève, offering a chair hoist to Mont d'Arbois at 6,000 feet for a panorama of Mont Blanc.

Lake Excursions
- Annecy offers the best, across a body of water called the Jewel of the Savoy Alps.

1 Evian-les-Bains

358 miles SW of Paris, 26 miles NE of Geneva

On the château-dotted southern shore of Lac Léman, Evian-les-Bains is one of the leading spa/resorts in eastern France. Its lakeside promenade lined with trees and sweeping lawns has been fashionable since the 19th century. The waters of Evian became famous in the 18th century, and the first spa buildings were erected in 1839. Bottled Evian, one of the great French table waters, is considered beneficial for everything from baby's formula and salt-free diets to treating gout and arthritis.

In the town center are the Hôtel de Ville and the **Casino Royal,** in the Château de Blonay, rive Sud-du-Lac (☎ **50-21-25-10**), patronized heavily by the Swiss from across the lake. The casino, charging 60 F ($11.40) admission, offers blackjack, baccarat, and roulette, among other games, and has floor shows in the Cabaret-Discothèque Le Régent five nights a week from February to mid-December. There's no fee for the show, but you must order a minimum number of drinks.

In addition to its **spa buildings,** Evian offers an imposing Ville des Congrès (convention hall), earning for the resort the title of "city of conventions." In summer the **Nautical Center** on the lake is a popular attraction; it has a 328-foot pool with a diving stage, solarium, restaurant, bar, and children's paddling pool.

The major excursion from Evian is a **boat trip on Lake Geneva** offered by the Compagnie Générale de Navigation. Go to the Office de Tourisme (see "Essentials," below) to pick up a schedule of tariffs and hours—in summer there are also night cruises. If you want to see it all, you can tour both the Haut-Lac and the Grand-Lac. The quickest and most heavily booked of all trips is the crossing from Evian to Ouchy-Lausanne, Switzerland, on the north side.

Crescent-shaped Lake Geneva is the largest lake in central Europe (the name Lac Léman was revived in the 18th century). Taking in an area of approximately 225 square miles, the lake is formed by the Rhône and is noted for its unusual blueness.

ESSENTIALS

GETTING THERE   Evian-les-Bains is easily reached from Geneva by train, car, or ferry.

VISITOR INFORMATION   The Office de Tourisme is on place d'Allinges (☎ 50-75-04-26).

WHERE TO STAY
EXPENSIVE

✪ Hôtel de la Verniaz et ses Chalets

Avenue Verniaz, à Neuvecelle, 74500 Evian-les-Bains. ☎ **50-75-04-90.** Fax 50-70-78-92. 35 rms, 5 suites. MINIBAR TV TEL. 500–1,100 F ($95.05–$209.10) double; 1,500–2,600 F ($285.15–$494.30) suite. Rates include half board. AE, DC, MC, V. Parking free. Closed Nov–Jan.

This glamorous country house stands on a hillside with an amazing view of woods, waters, and the Alps. The rooms (well furnished, with many amenities) are in either the main house or one of the separate chalets; the chalets have their own gardens and privacy, but they're pricey. Since guests stay here on half board, they're usually delighted at the care that goes into the food. The chefs, however, don't believe in innovation; they stick to turning out dishes that've been crowd-pleasers in the past.

✪ Les Prés Fleuris

Route de Thollon, 74500 Evian-les-Bains. ☎ **50-75-29-14.** Fax 50-70-77-75. 12 rms. MINIBAR TV TEL. 850–1,300 F ($161.60–$247.10) double. Breakfast 80 F ($15.20) extra. AE, MC, V. Parking free. Closed Sept to mid-May.

This Relais & Châteaux is a white-painted villa on a lake 4 1/2 miles east of Evian; the glass walls capitalize on the view. Each room is richly furnished, often with antiques or reproductions. Tables and wrought-iron chairs are set under the trees for meals in fair weather. The food served by M. and Mme Roger Frossard is exceptional. Deluxe ingredients are used, including delectable Bresse chicken, whose flavor he enhances with fresh herbs. His fricassée of meadow mushrooms is splendid.

INEXPENSIVE

◎ Les Cygnes

Grande-Rive, 74500 Evian-les-Bains. ☎ **50-75-01-01.** 40 rms, 24 with shower only, 15 with bath. TEL. 310 F ($58.90) double with shower only, 330–350 F ($62.70–$66.50) double with bath. Rates include breakfast. V. Closed Sept 18–June 14.

This is one of the bargains at the spa. The Norman-style villa is characterized by dormer windows, a conical tower, a beam-and-plaster facade, a mansard roof, an entrance courtyard surrounded by flowers and shrubs, and a waterside terrace. This family-run hotel is convenient to use as a base from which to explore Lake Geneva.

WHERE TO DINE

Hôtel-Restaurant le Bourgogne
Place Charles-Cottet, 74500 Evian-les-Bains. ☎ **50-75-01-05.** Fax 50-75-04-05. Reservations required. Restaurant, main courses 88–135 F ($16.70–$25.65); fixed-price menus 128 F ($24.30) at lunch only, and 155–295 F ($29.45–$56.05). Brasserie, platters 45–110 F ($8.55–$20.90); fixed-price menus 45–110 F ($8.55–$20.90). AE, DC, MC, V. Restaurant, daily noon–2pm and 7:30–9:30pm; closed Sun night and Mon in midwinter. Brasserie, daily noon–2pm and 7:30–9:30pm. FRENCH.

This inn near the Congress Hall has many appealing decorative touches. Come here if you want a delectable meal, irreproachable service, an attractive setting, and excellent wine—regional wines featured are Crépy and Rousette. Menu choices are likely to include veal sweetbreads des gourmets, filet of beef in poivrade sauce, and émincé of duckling with caramelized peaches. You have a choice of dining formally in the restaurant or informally in the brasserie. The inn also offers 31 comfortable rooms, costing 466 to 606 F ($88.55 to $115.15) double, plus 39 F ($7.40) for breakfast.

✪ La Toque Royale
In the Casino Royal, Château de Blonay, rive Sud-du-Lac. ☎ **50-75-03-78.** Reservations required. Main courses 140–280 F ($26.60–$53.20); fixed-price menus 185–550 F ($35.15–$104.50). AE, DC, MC, V. Mon–Sat noon–2pm and 7:30–10:50pm. SAVOYARD.

The gourmet restaurant of the Domaine du Royal Club Evian is the most elegant place to eat in Evian. The chefs turn out an array of seasonal dishes with flair and taste, like omble chevalier, the fabled fish of Lake Geneva. Alpine kid appears with polenta and Bresse pigeon with chanterelles. Of course, many people choose the always-reliable côte de boeuf with shallots.

2 Morzine-Avoriaz

370 miles SE of Paris, 25 miles S of Evian

Morzine and Avoriaz are the last stops on an ascending road from Lake Geneva to a dead-end near the Swiss border. Most visitors drive to Morzine, but a bus service from Geneva stops near the center of town. To reach Avoriaz, drive along a 9-mile winding road northeast from Morzine or take a *téléphérique* from the station 3 miles east of the center of Morzine. Since cars are usually not allowed on Avoriaz's innermost streets, many visitors prefer to park at the base of the téléphérique and enjoy the alpine views during their ascent.

In Morzine, the **Office de Tourisme** is on place Crusaz (☎ **50-74-03-72**). In Avoriaz, a tourist office (☎ **50-74-02-11**) is at the last stop on the road before the real mountains begin.

MORZINE

The tourist capital of the Haut-Chablais district, Morzine offers attractions like sleigh rides, beautiful pine forests, ice shows, and more than a dozen cabarets. For years it was known as a summer resort, but now it's also an acclaimed winter ski center. From Morzine, you can visit Lac de Montriond, at an altitude of 3,490 feet. An 18-mile tour of this famous lake takes about two hours.

WHERE TO STAY

La Carlina

Av. Joux-Plane, 74110 Morzine. ☎ **50-79-01-03.** Fax 50-75-94-11. 18 rms. TEL. 450 F ($85.50) double. Breakfast 40 F ($7.60) extra. AE, DC, MC, V. Closed June and Nov 10– Dec 15.

The interior of this informal village chalet is rustic, with several lounges containing open fireplaces. Its guest rooms are pleasantly decorated and comfortable. In summer refreshments can be enjoyed on a street-level terrace with umbrella-shaded tables. In the evening, you can either dance or join in the folk music at the Carlina Club. The least expensive fixed-price menu, which we heartily recommend, costs 145 F ($27.55).

Hôtel Champs-Fleuris

74110 Morzine. ☎ **50-79-14-44.** Fax 50-79-27-75. 45 rms. TEL. 530–790 F ($100.70– $150.10) per person. Rates include half board. V. Parking free. Closed Apr 10–June 25 and Sept 10–Dec 20.

This hotel is as popular in summer as it is in winter. Against a backdrop of forested mountains, it rises a few paces from T-lifts and gondolas. You can sit amid lots of exposed wood softened with earth-toned carpeting and curtains and enjoy the view of the slopes. In summer, hill-climbers appreciate the walking trails that begin nearby. There's also a heated pool near the garden, plus an indoor weight-lifting room with an adjacent sauna, bar, billiard room, café, and restaurant. The rooms are modern and comfortable but nothing to rave about.

AVORIAZ

One of the most modern and sophisticated ski centers of Europe has been developed at Avoriaz. Tucked away above Morzine, it's a village of pine-and-shingle buildings, most of them less than 25 years old, in the midst of an extensive ski terrain set 6,000 feet up in the mountains. The 390 miles of ski trails, reached by some 70 lifts, can usually be used until the third week in April. Astride a series of peaks and valleys called Portes du Soleil (Gates of the Sun), Avoriaz is most easily reached by cable car, and in the village the only transportation is on foot, on skis, or by horse-drawn sleigh. Even if you don't want to stay in one of the hotels here, you may want to take a cable car up for a look and perhaps a meal.

The village of Avoriaz is an interesting outgrowth of the intention of young architects to create a ski-resort community above the Valley of the Slate Quarries (Vallée des Ardoisières) in a style not defacing the mountains. Their accomplishment is notable in the stepped rooflines and geometric balconies on the cylindrical buildings, designed to reflect the sharp lines of the cliffs.

An accredited branch of the French Ski School Federation, the local **ski school** has around 100 experienced instructors, many of whom are proficient in English. Both downhill and cross-country skiing are offered, as well as snowshoeing and indoor activities like aerobic dancing and squash. A feature of this family-oriented ski resort is the **Village des Enfants,** where children as young as 3 are taught skiing.

By cable car or bubble car you can also go to **Le Pléney,** at 5,367 feet, and enjoy a view from its belvedere looking out on Mont Blanc. Through the Dranse Gap a vista of Lake Geneva unfolds.

WHERE TO STAY

Hôtel des Dromonts

Avoriaz 1800, 74110 Morzine. ☎ **50-74-08-11.** Fax 50-74-02-79. 37 rms. TV TEL. 1,700–1,900 F ($323.20–$361.20) double. Rates include half board. AE, DC, MC, V. Parking 40 F ($7.60) outside, 70 F ($13.30) inside. Closed May–June 15 and Sept 15–Dec 12.

With cantilevered architecture, this hotel spreads out to include luxurious apartment villas, boutiques, restaurants, a nightclub, and elaborate playtime facilities. Every facility is here for *le weekend*—Le Solarium, La Taverne, Le Drugstore, Le Roc-Club Disco. Most of the guest rooms are bright with a modern design and natural wood. The hotel is usually filled with a young crowd, and ski runs and lifts are right at the door.

Hôtel des Hauts Forts

Avoriaz 1800, 74110 Morzine. ☎ **50-74-09-11.** Fax 50-74-02-79. 48 rms. TV TEL. 330–995 F ($62.70–$189.15) double. Half board 455–640 F ($86.50–$121.65) per person. V. Parking 30 F ($5.70) outside, 75 F ($14.25) inside. Closed May 2–June 15 and Sept 15–Dec 12.

This hotel has the same cantilevered architecture as des Dromonts (above) and offers most of the same attractions, with well-equipped modern rooms, some irregularly shaped. It also has a good restaurant, with fixed-price meals at 90 F ($17.10), 120 F ($22.80), and 130 F ($24.70), if you're visiting just for the day. Ski lifts are virtually at your doorstep. If bookings don't merit it, the hotel may decide not to have a summer season, so check in advance. In winter, however, it flourishes.

3 Flaine

374 miles SE of Paris, 49 miles E of Annecy, 30 miles from Megève and Morzine

With its superb location, Flaine boasts deep powder snow from November to April. The chalets here, at 5,412 feet, are above the valley of the Arve and the Carroz-d'Araches. From the cable-car station you're whisked up to Les Grandes Platières, where you can admire the Désert de Platé and a panoramic view of Mont Blanc. Skiers have a choice of trails—a thrilling descent in a 4-minute run on the Diamant Noir ski trail or a 60-minute run via the Serpentine trail.

ESSENTIALS

GETTING THERE   Flaine is the last stop on a dead-end mountain road leading into a high alpine valley. The nearest train station is at Les Cluses, 19 miles northwest. From there you can transfer to a bus. Most visitors, however, particularly those with ski equipment, come by car.

VISITOR INFORMATION   The Office de Tourisme is in the Galerie des Marchands (☎ **50-90-80-01**).

WHERE TO STAY & DINE

Le Totem

Flaine, 74300 Cluses. ☎ **50-90-81-10.** Fax 50-90-84-59. 95 rms. TEL. 640–720 F ($121.65–$136.85) double. Rates include half board. AE, MC, V. Closed Apr 19–July 7 and Sept–Dec 17.

This is the most comfortable hotel in town, composed of two four-story hotels. In 1990 they were renovated and linked by a covered corridor, and now they function as a coherent whole. On the premises are a restaurant, a bar, sun terraces, and rows of bay windows offering a panoramic view. Chefs change from season to season, and the cuisine is hearty for those who must go out and face the snow. An indoor pool and tennis courts are within easy reach.

4 Chamonix–Mont Blanc

381 miles SE of Paris, 58 miles E of Annecy

At an altitude of 3,422 feet, Chamonix is the historic capital of alpine skiing. Site of the first winter Olympic Games, in 1924, Chamonix huddles in a valley almost at the junction of France, Italy, and Switzerland. Dedicated skiers all over the world know of its 12-mile Vallée Blanche run, one of Europe's most rugged and certainly its longest. Daredevils also flock here for mountain climbing and hang-gliding.

A charming old-fashioned mountain town, Chamonix has a most thrilling backdrop—✪ **Mont Blanc,** Western Europe's highest mountain, rising to 15,780 feet. When two Englishmen, Windham and Pococke, first visited Chamonix in 1740, they were thrilled with its location and later wrote a travel book that advertised the village around the world. When their guide was published, it was believed that no human foot had yet trod on Mont Blanc. On August 7, 1786, Jacques Balmat became the first man to climb the mountain, destroying the myth that no one could spend a night up there and survive. In the old quarter of town a memorial to this brave pioneer stands in front of the village church.

With the opening of the 7-mile miracle **Mont Blanc Tunnel** (☎ **50-53-06-15**), Chamonix became a major stage on one of the busiest highways in Europe. By going under the mountains, the tunnel provides the easiest way to get past the mountains to Italy; motorists now stop here even if they aren't interested in winter skiing or summer mountain climbing. Toll rates for the tunnel depend on the distance between the axles of the vehicle being taken through. The price for an average car for a one-way transit through the tunnel ranges from 135 to 180 F ($25.65 to $34.20) each way; some very small French cars pay as little as 90 F ($17.10). A car with a camping caravan or trailer almost always costs 180 F ($34.20) each way, unless the trailer is large enough to justify classifying it as an independent vehicle. Round-trip tickets are sold at considerable discounts from the price of two one-way tickets, but be warned in advance that the return portion of those tickets must be used within three days of purchase. Round-trip tickets begin at 115 F ($21.85) for the smallest car and go up to 225 F ($42.75) for the largest.

Because of its exceptional equipment, including gondolas, cable cars, and chair lifts, Chamonix is one of the major sports resorts of Europe, attracting an international crowd.

Chamonix sprawls in a narrow strip along both banks of the Arve River. Its casino, its rail and bus stations, and most of its restaurants and nightlife are in the town center. Cable cars reach into the mountains from the town's edge. Locals refer to Les Praz, Les Bossons, Les Moussoux, and Les Pélerins as satellite villages within Greater Chamonix, though technically Chamonix refers to only a carefully delineated section around its place de l'Eglise.

ESSENTIALS

GETTING THERE   Trains arrive frequently from nearby St-Gervais, where there are connections from Aix-les-Bains, Annecy, Lyon, and Chambéry. There are three connections from Paris per day (trip time: 8 hr.), costing 335 F ($63.65) one way. From Lyon, there are seven rail links per day (trip time: 4 hr.), costing 185 F ($35.15) one way.

In any season, there's at least one daily bus from Annecy and Grenoble. Within Chamonix, a local bus makes frequent runs to many of the téléphériques and villages up and down the valley.

VISITOR INFORMATION   The Office de Tourisme is on place du Triangle-de-l'Amitié (☎ **50-53-00-24**).

WHAT TO SEE & DO

The belvederes that can be reached from Chamonix by cable car or mountain railway are famous. For information about these rides, contact the **Société Touristique du Mont-Blanc,** B.P. 58, 74402 Chamonix CEDEX (☎ **50-53-30-80**).

In the heart of town you can board a cable car heading for the **Aiguille du Midi** and on to Italy—a harrowing journey. The first stage, a 9-minute run to the Plan

---

Mountain Huts at the Heights

France's mountain huts are rustic and aggressively simple, set in high-altitude areas accessible only to mountain goats, climbers with stamina as well as sturdy boots and warm clothing, and four-wheel-drive vehicles. And though some lie a reasonable hike from the terminus of either a cog railway or a gondola, others require ropes, spikes, specialized alpine gear, and/or the services of a helicopter to reach.

So why come to *la belle France* for challenging, nonglamorous activities that make you sweat and freeze in rapid succession? The most obvious benefit is weight loss. Even if you stick to the easier trails, the rate at which you burn calories at these high altitudes is prodigious. (Some campers compare their metabolisms during their climbs to a blast furnace and shovel carbohydrates in at awesome rates.) The agency best equipped to hand out advice and information on France's windswept heights and *refuges de montagne* is the **Club Alpin Français,** 24 av. de la Lumière, 75019 Paris (☎ **1/42-02-68-44**). Kindred mountain spirits dominate the organization, despite its location in the heart of urban Paris.

You'll be tired and physically overwhelmed (almost), and the beauty around you (coupled with the thinness of the oxygen) will leave you breathless—but don't think that bourgeois etiquette won't still be called for. Accommodations in mountain huts often consist of platforms where strangers sleep side-by-side, sardine style, or unisex dormitories where clusters of beds (usually two) are divided by thin partitions or curtains. However, despite the informal conditions, formalities exist: Voices usually remain discreetly hushed throughout the night, blankets and climbing gear are neatly arranged in appropriate places, and hikers work hard to maintain courteous civilities. And though no hiker would consider carrying a bathrobe high into the mountains, there's a naturalistic kind of modesty regarding exposure of too much flesh to cabinmates.

Mountain huts are usually stocked with plenty of blankets, thin Styrofoam mattresses, and pillows, but not sheets or towels, which you should probably bring. The shower you'll need after a day of trekking will probably be supplied by coin-operated hot-water heaters, sometimes fueled by solar generators. Dinners, prepared in cramped kitchens by an on-site monitor, are copious enough to stave off fears of starvation.

des Aiguilles at an altitude of 7,544 feet, isn't so alarming. But the second stage, to an altitude of 12,602 feet, the Aiguille du Midi station, may make your heart sink, especially when the car rises 2,000 feet between towers. At the summit you'll be 1,110 yards from Mont Blanc's peak. The belvedere affords a commanding view of the Aiguilles of Chamonix and Vallée Blanche, the largest glacier in Europe (9.3 miles long and 3.7 miles wide). You also have a 125-mile view of the Jura and the French, Swiss, and Italian Alps.

You leave the tram station along a chasm-spanning narrow bridge leading to the third cable car and the glacial fields that lie beyond. Or you can end your journey at Aiguille du Midi and return to Chamonix. Generally the cable cars operate all year: in summer, daily from 6am to 5pm, leaving at least every half hour; in winter, daily from 8am to 4pm, leaving every hour. The first stage, to Plan des Aiguilles, costs 50 F ($9.50) round-trip, increasing to 160 F ($30.40) per person for a round-trip to Aiguille du Midi.

You then cross over high mountains and pass jagged needles of rock and ice bathed in dazzling light. The final trip to **Pointe Helbronner** in Italy—at 11,355 feet—requires a passport if you wish to leave the station and descend on two more cable cars to the village of Courmayeur. From there you can go to nearby Entrèves to dine at La Maison de Filippo, called a "chalet of gluttony." The round-trip from Chamonix to Pointe Helbronner is 240 F ($45.60); the cable car operates only in summer.

Another aerial cableway takes you up to **Brévent** at 8,284 feet. From here you'll have a first-rate view (frontal) of Mont Blanc and the Aiguilles de Chamonix. The trip takes about 1 1/2 hours round-trip. Cable cars operate from December 16 to October, beginning at 8am and shutting down at 5pm. Summer departures are at least every half hour. A round-trip costs 70 F ($13.30).

Yet another aerial journey is to **Le Montenvers,** at 6,276 feet. From the belvedere at the end of the cable-car run you'll have a view of the Mer de Glace (Sea of Ice, or glacier), which is 4 miles long. The Aiguille du Dru is a rock climb notorious for its difficulty. The trip takes 1 1/2 hours, including a return by rail. Departures are 8am to 6pm in summer, until 4:30pm off-season. The round-trip fare is 60 F ($11.40) per person, and service is usually from May to November.

You can also visit a cave hollowed out of the Mer de Glace; a cable car connects it with the upper resort of Montenvers, and the trip takes just three minutes. Entrance to the cave costs 13 F ($2.45).

WHERE TO STAY
EXPENSIVE

Hôtel Albert-1er et de Milan

119 impasse Montenvers, 74400 Chamonix–Mont Blanc. ☎ **50-53-05-09.** Fax 50-55-95-48. 30 rms. MINIBAR TV TEL. 690–1,500 F ($131.10–$285) double. Breakfast 70 F ($13.30) extra. AE, DC, MC, V. Closed May 7–18 and Oct 23–Dec 5.

This hotel is an enlarged solid alpine chalet, ringed by a garden and private residences. Each of the well-furnished rooms offers a mountain view; several also feature private balconies. You can dine in one of three elegant rooms, with Oriental carpets and 18th-century chests. The chef is a perfectionist who's likely to offer suprême of duckling in puff pastry with lentils, ravioli of truffles with duck far, and sea bass roasted with endive—each worthy of raves. To finish, try some of the delectable mountain cheeses of the Savoy or one of the memorable desserts. There's also a copper-topped bar in the lobby. Facilities include an outdoor pool, tennis court, sauna, and Jacuzzi.

Novotel Chamonix

Vers le Nant, Les Bossons, 74400 Chamonix–Mont Blanc. ☎ **50-53-26-22.** Fax 50-53-31-31. 89 rms, 1 suite. TV TEL. 420–520 F ($79.80–$98.80) double; from 660 F ($125.40) suite. Breakfast 55 F ($10.45) extra, AE, DC, MC, V. Parking 50 F ($9.50).

This well-managed chain hotel 2¹/₂ miles east of the center of Chamonix in Les Bossons combines a mass-market design with a warm ambience. The result is a very comfortable hotel with spacious rooms, each equipped with both a single and a double bed; some open onto Mont Blanc and most have minibars. There's a dining room with a big window, as well as a cozy bar, but the food is only average.

MODERATE

⑤ Au Bon Coin

80 av. de l'Aiguille-du-Midi, 74400 Chamonix–Mont Blanc. ☎ **50-53-15-67.** Fax 50-53-51-51. 20 rms, 16 with bath. TEL. 280 F ($53.20) double without bath, 400 F ($76) double with bath. Rates include continental breakfast. MC, V. Parking free. Closed May–June and Oct–Dec 18.

This two-star hotel is very French. It has comfortable, clean modern rooms, often with views of the mountainside—in autumn, the colors are spectacular. The rooms also contain terraces where you can soak up the sun, even in winter. The chalet is tranquil, and the owner provides private parking as well as a garden.

INEXPENSIVE

⑤ Hôtel Roma

289 rue Ravanel-le-Rouge, 74402 Chamonix. ☎ **50-53-00-62.** Fax 50-53-50-31. 30 rms, 25 with bath (tub or shower). TEL. 430–466 F ($81.70–$88.55) double with bath. Rates include breakfast. AE, DC, MC, V. Parking free. Closed three weeks in June and Oct 15–Dec 20.

Despite renovations completed in 1992, the Roma retains an old-fashioned feeling of alpine charm and simplicity. The English- and Italian-speaking owners, the Quaglia family, welcome guests to their establishment. Breakfast is the only meal served. You'll find this cozy two-star hotel about a five-minute walk south of the town center.

WHERE TO DINE

The Hôtel Albert-1er et de Milan (above) boasts the finest dining rooms in town.

EXPENSIVE

Restaurant Matafan

In the Hôtel Mont-Blanc, 62 allée du Majéstic. ☎ **50-53-05-64.** Reservations required. Main courses 120–180 F ($22.80–$34.20); fixed-price menus 160 F ($30.40), 260 F ($49.40), 280 F ($53.20), and 360 F ($68.40). AE, DC, MC, V. Daily 12:30–2pm and 7:30–9:30pm. Closed Oct 15–Dec 15. FRENCH.

This stellar restaurant has a decor of soft pastels and hand-woven tapestries, arranged around a central pentagonal fireplace. Specialties change seasonally but may include omble chevalier meunière, rack of lamb roasted with herbs (for two), and sinful desserts. Many of the dishes are inspired by Savoy cooking but with a refined touch. In the excellent cellar are more than 500 wines. In summer you can lunch next to the pool in the garden.

INEXPENSIVE

Bartavel

Impasse du Vox. ☎ **50-53-26-51.** Reservations not required. Pizzas 35–45 F ($6.65–$8.55); main courses 48–70 F ($9.10–$13.30). AE, MC, V. Daily noon–midnight. ITALIAN.

Decorated much like a tavern you'd expect to find in Italy, this pizzeria is the domain of Treviso-born Valerio Commazzetto, who prepares 20 kinds of pizza and a wide range of pastas. Other menu items include grilled steaks and chops, escalopes milanese or pizzaiola, and an array of simple desserts. The cooking is as mamma did it back in old Italy. Beer and wine flow liberally, and Bartavel attracts a good share of outdoor enthusiasts, who appreciate its copious portions and reasonable prices.

ⓢ Le Chaudron

79 rue des Moulins. ☎ **50-53-40-34.** Reservations recommended. Main courses 65–125 F ($12.35–$23.75); fixed-price menus 98–130 F ($18.60–$24.70). AE, DC, MC, V. Daily 7pm–midnight. Closed June and Oct–Nov. FRENCH.

Le Chaudron's chef, Pierre Osterberger, cooks right in front of you, and you're sure to appreciate his specialties, like house-style sweetbreads, several robust beef dishes, and fondues, as well as many salads and desserts. There are a lot of fancier places in town, but for good value, honest cooking, and fine mountain ingredients, Le Chaudron emerges near the top of our dining list. The cellar is filled with good wines, including Château Mouton-Rothschild and Château Latour.

5 Megève

372 miles SE of Paris, 43 miles SE of Geneva

A *cité verte*, Megève is famous as a summer resort set amid pine forests, foothills, and mountain streams. But it's even better known as a charming cosmopolitan town, a *capitale du ski*. The old village with its turreted houses gathered around a church dating from the 17th century suggests what Megève looked like at the turn of the century. However, after 1920 the new town came along and started attracting people who like to go to the mountains for fun—especially skiers. Megève was made popular by the baronne de Rothschild.

The interesting center contains place de l'Eglise and its famous hotel, the Mont-Blanc, south of the main arteries that cut through the valley. Some of the resort's hotels and one of its most important cable-car depots are in the village of Mont d'Arbois, about a mile east of the center of Megève, at the end of a steep, narrow, and winding road. In winter, it's unwise to drive up that road without chains on your snow tires.

Tennis, horseback riding, and cable railways add to the attractions, with wide views of the Mont Blanc area from the top of each ski lift. The range of amusements includes a casino, nightclubs, discos, dancing, and shows. Megève is actually one of the best equipped of the French winter-sports resorts and is a social center of international status. In the area are more than 180 miles of runs for skiers plus nearly 50 miles of cross-country trails.

ESSENTIALS

GETTING THERE   Megève, near the Geneva airport, is easy to reach. On weekends, the high-speed Paris–Sallanches train delivers passengers to Megève; on weekdays, the Paris–Bellegarde train makes the same connections.

VISITOR INFORMATION   The Office de Tourisme is on rue Monseigneur Conseil (☎ 50-21-27-28).

WHAT TO SEE & DO

In the environs you can take a chair hoist to **Mont d'Arbois,** at 6,000 feet. Here a panorama unfolds for you, including not only Mont Blanc but also the Fis and Aravis massifs. Cable service operates from July 1 to October 1 every half hour from 9am to 6pm. To reach the station, take the route du Mont-d'Arbois from the resort's center, going past the golf course. The mountain was originally developed in the 1920s by members of the Rothschild family, whose search for solitude led them to this scenic outpost. Today Mont d'Arbois is a pocket of posh in an already posh resort.

From 11am to 6am the center of the old village is closed to traffic, except the pedestrian variety and sledges. You can shop at leisure (some 200 tradespeople await your service, ranging from a cobbler to an antiques dealer, plus many boutiques).

The **Ski School,** 70 impasse du Chamois (☎ 50-21-00-97), is one of Europe's foremost, with 197 instructors for adults and 32 for children. Collective courses include the complete French skiing method, modern ski techniques, monosurf-acrobatic skiing, cross-country skiing, and ski touring. The school is open from December 20 until the end of April, daily from 8:45am to 7pm.

Much improvement has been made in recent years in **sports facilities,** including a Chamois gondola, which takes skiers to the mountain from the center of town; the Rocharbois cable car, linking the two major ski areas of Mont d'Arbois and Rochebrune; and the addition of a gondola and chair lift at the Rochebrune massif.

The **Megève Palais des Sports et des Congrès** (Sports Palace and Assembly Hall) (☎ 50-21-15-71) is for ice sports, swimming, tennis, meetings, and often shows and gala festivals. It's a complex of two pools with a solarium, saunas, an Olympic-size skating rink, a curling track, a body-building room, a dance salon, a bar, a restaurant, a gymnasium, tennis courts, an auditorium, conference rooms, and an exhibition gallery. It's open daily from 9am to 7pm.

WHERE TO STAY
VERY EXPENSIVE

Chalet du Mont-d'Arbois
Route du Mont-d'Arbois, 74120 Megève. ☎ **50-21-25-03.** Fax 50-93-02-63. 20 rms. TV TEL. Winter, 2,140–2,530 F ($406.80–$480.95) double. Off-season, 1,560–2,120 F ($296.55–$403) double. Rates include half board. AE, DC, MC, V. Closed Apr to mid-June and Oct to mid-Dec.

Built in 1928 by a Rothschild matriarch, this chalet houses the best resort on the mountain, with beautiful guest rooms that are worthy of a Relais & Châteaux. The chalet's public rooms are the grandest in Megève, with roaring fireplaces, beamed ceilings, alpine antiques, and silver-plated replicas of alert deer. During part of the season the hotel might be filled with friends of Mme Nadine de Rothschild, whose advice on how a woman should treat her husband became a bestseller in France.

✪ Les Fermes de Marie
Chemin de Riante Colline, 74120 Megève. ☎ **50-93-03-10.** Fax 50-93-09-84. 40 rms, 15 suites, 5 chalets. Winter, 1,400–2,000 F ($266.15–$380.20) double; from 2,000 F

($380.20) suite or chalet for two. Off-season, 1,300–1,900 F ($247.10–$361.20) double; from 1,700 F ($323.20) suite or chalet for two. Rates include half board. AE, MC, V.

In 1989 the Sibuet family inaugurated a style of hotel that had not been seen before in Megève. The architectural remnants of at least 20 antique barns and crumbling chalets were reassembled in a desirable location in the heart of town. The folkloric theme extends to the rooms, which look like attractive alpine cabins. There are three restaurants: Le Gastonomique, Le Restaurant du Fromage (where fondues are served), and a cozy dining room for half-board guests. Also on the premises are a beauty farm and an indoor pool.

MODERATE

Au Vieux Moulin

Av. Ambroise-Martin, 74120 Megève. ☎ **50-21-22-29.** 33 rms. TV TEL. 880–1,360 F ($167.30–$258.55) double. Rates include half board. MC, V. Closed May 7–June 9 and Nov–Dec 2.

This four-story wood-trimmed stucco building is separated from the street by a tiny pool, a lawn, and wrought-iron gates. The rooms and the lobby, with its coffered ceilings and black slate floors, are well maintained, and the hotel also has a pool and a terrace. The place is not exceptional, but many in-the-know local ski guides recommend it to visitors requesting a place where they won't go broke.

✪ Le Fer à Cheval

36 route du Crêt-d'Arbois, 74120 Megève. ☎ **50-21-30-39.** Fax 50-93-07-60. 33 rms, 8 suites. TV TEL. 585–860 F ($111.20–$163.50) per person. Rates include half board. MC, V. Parking free. Closed Apr 8–June and Sept 10–Dec 15.

This is perhaps the finest hotel in the center of the village, filled with skiers in winter and mountain motorists in summer. The restaurant, decked out with wood to evoke an old-fashioned Savoy atmosphere, is open also to nonresidents, with meals beginning at 230 F ($43.70). In summer a pool draws guests to the beautiful garden, and the sauna and Jacuzzi are winter lures. Guests often gather for tea around a wood-and-stone fireplace, where they also can enjoy good-tasting meals.

WHERE TO DINE
EXPENSIVE

Chalet du Mont-d'Arbois

Route du Mont-d'Arbois. ☎ **50-21-25-03.** Reservations required. Main courses 130–200 F ($24.70–$38). AE, DC, MC, V. Daily noon–2pm and 7:30–10pm. Closed Apr to mid-June and Oct to mid-Dec. FRENCH.

Richly accessorized, this restaurant in the above-recommended hotel is one floor below lobby level and has a wood-burning grill. Accumulated mementos of the restaurant's owners, the Rothschilds, are part of the decor. As might be expected from a family connected with some of the greatest vineyards of France, the wine list is overwhelming. Some menu items have been named after the Rothschild image, like vol-au-vent financière; another dish is spit-roasted Bresse chicken.

Les Enfants Terribles

In the Hôtel du Mont-Blanc, place de l'Eglise. ☎ **50-21-20-02.** Reservations required. Main courses 130–265 F ($24.70–$50.35). AE, DC, MC, V. Daily noon–3pm and 7–11pm. Closed mid-Oct to Dec 20. FRENCH.

In the bar adjoining this acclaimed restaurant, Jean Cocteau painted wall frescoes that gave the place its name. Today this restaurant serves a refined menu in a supper-club atmosphere. Menu items include steak Enfants Terribles and Savoy-inspired dishes. Dinner is served indoors or on a covered terrace in warm weather. Some locals predict that after the massive overhaul of this hotel is completed in 1995, this restaurant will not regain its former chic. Stop in and judge for yourself.

⊛ Le Prieuré

Place de l'Eglise. ☎ **50-21-01-79.** Reservations required. Main courses 75–160 F ($14.25–$30.40); fixed-price menus 110 F ($20.90), 139 F ($26.40), and 189 F ($35.90). AE, DC, MC, V. Daily noon–2:30pm and 7–10pm. Closed June 15–July 1, Nov, and on Mon in low season. FRENCH.

The Prieuré offers traditional French cooking, with specialties like foie gras de canard (duckling) and salad made from crab, mussels, and lake fish. An excellent appetizer is fresh melon with locally cured ham, which can be followed by grilled bass filet with fennel or magrêt of duckling flavored with peaches. For dessert, try the apple pie. The restaurant is frequently cited as one of the best dining choices outside the hotels.

MODERATE

La Taverne du Mont-d'Arbois

Route du Mont-d'Arbois. ☎ **50-21-03-53.** Reservations required. Main courses 95–150 F ($18.05–$28.50). V. Daily 12:15–2pm and 7:15–10pm. Closed May 28–June 15. FRENCH.

This is the most visible restaurant in the community of Mont d'Arbois, near a series of ski lifts. Owned by the Rothschilds (and eager to promote the produce of the family's vineyards), the place offers a rustic ambience of blackened timbers and weathered planking. It's so popular that getting a table might be difficult in midwinter. You'll be faced with an array of Savoyard-inspired specialties, including at least three kinds of cheese dishes.

6 Annecy

334 miles SE of Paris, 35 miles SE of Geneva, 85 miles E of Lyon

On Lac d'Annecy, the jewel of the Savoy Alps, the resort of Annecy makes the best base for touring the Haute-Savoie, of which it's the capital. The former seat of the comtes de Genève, and before that a Gallo-Roman town, Annecy opens onto one of the best views of lakes and mountains in the French Alps.

ESSENTIALS

GETTING THERE   Annecy has railway and bus service from Geneva, Grenoble, and Lyon. It's also near a network of highways, so many people drive there. Four trains per day arrive from Grenoble (trip time: 2 hr.), costing 85 F ($16.15) one way. Six TGV trains pull in daily from Paris (trip time: 4 hr.), costing 390 F ($74.10) one way.

VISITOR INFORMATION   The Office de Tourisme is at 1 rue Jean-Jaurès (☎ 50-45-00-33).

WHAT TO SEE & DO

The resort is dominated by the **Château d'Annecy** (☎ 50-45-29-66), with a Queen's Tower dating from the 12th century. It was in this castle that the comtes de Genève took refuge in the 13th century. Go up in the castle and look out on the town's roof and belfries. The museum of regional artifacts is open Wednesday to Monday from 10am to noon and 2 to 6pm. Admission is 20 F ($3.80) for adults and 10 F ($1.90) for children 9 and under.

Built around the River Thiou, Annecy has been called the Venice of the Alps because of the canals cut through the old part of town, **Vieil Annecy.** You can explore the arcaded streets of the old town where Jean-Jacques Rousseau arrived in 1728.

After exploring Annecy, visit **Les Gorges du Fier,** 6 miles from Annecy, 12 minutes by train from the Lovagny station (Aix-les-Bains line). For the latest schedule of daily motorcoach trips, go to the Office de Tourisme (see "Essentials," above). This striking gorge is one of the most interesting sights in the French Alps. A gangway takes visitors through a winding gully, varying from 10 to 30 feet wide. The gully was cut by the torrent through the rock and over breathtaking depths; you'll hear the roar of the river at the bottom. Emerging from this labyrinth, you'll be greeted by a huge expanse of boulders. The gorge is open only Easter to October, daily from 9am to 6pm (to 7pm in July and August). The tour takes less than an hour and costs 22 F ($4.20). Call 50-46-23-07 for more information.

In the area, you can also visit the 13th- and 14th-century **Château de Montrottier** (☎ 50-46-23-02), with a panoramic view of Mont Blanc from its tower. The château contains pottery, Oriental costumes, armor, tapestries, and antiques, as well as some bronze bas-reliefs from the 16th century. The castle is open only from the Sunday before Easter to mid-October, daily from 9am to noon and 2 to 6pm (closed Tuesday June to August). Admission is 25 F ($4.75) for adults and 20 F ($3.80) for children.

Of course, a most interesting excursion is a tour of **Lac d'Annecy,** from Easter until the end of September. Inquire at the tourist office (above) about various possibilities. In July and August there are at least 12 steamers leaving from Annecy. Call 50-51-08-40 for more information.

WHERE TO STAY
EXPENSIVE

Demeure de Chavoire
71 route d'Annecy, 74290 Veyrier-du-Lac. ☎ **50-60-04-36.** Fax 50-60-05-36. 13 rms. MINIBAR TV TEL. 1,000 F ($190.10) double. Breakfast 60 F ($11.40) extra. AE, DC, V.

One of the most charming accommodations is at Chavoires, about 2 miles west of Annecy. Intimate and cozy, it's brightly decorated and homelike, decorated with well-chosen Savoy antiques. Through large doors you can walk down to the gardens overlooking the lake. The rooms aren't numbered but have names, and each is uniquely decorated. Thoughtful extras such as chocolates by the bed make this a deserving selection. It's a more tranquil choice than the accommodations in the center of Annecy. The helpful staff will direct you to nearby restaurants.

MODERATE

Au Faisan Doré
34 av. d'Albigny, 74000 Annecy. ☎ **50-23-02-46.** Fax 50-23-11-10. 40 rms. TV TEL. 300–380 F ($57–$72.20) per person. Rates include half board. MC, V. Parking 50 F ($9.50). Closed Dec 17–Jan 22. Bus 2 or 21.

Near the casino at the end of a tree-lined lakefront boulevard, this hotel is only two minutes by foot from the lake and Imperial Park. A three-star hotel since 1992, it's a member of the Logis de France, a value-oriented hotel catering to the family trade. The hotel has been owned and run by the Clavel family since 1919. The public and private rooms follow the decor of the Haute Savoy. Each guest room is cozily comfortable but a bit plain. The chef serves three fixed-price menus, at 130 F ($24.70), 170 F ($32.30), and 220 F ($41.80).

⑤ Du Nord

24 rue Sommeiller, 74000 Annecy. ☎ **50-45-08-78.** Fax 50-51-22-04. 35 rms. TV TEL. 258–278 F ($49–$52.80) double. Breakfast 34 F ($6.45) extra. V.

A two-star hotel in the center of Annecy, the newly renovated Du Nord is one of the better bargains here. The staff is extremely helpful and speak English. Guests appreciate the cleanliness and modernity of the well-maintained rooms, which have such amenities as soundproofing and direct-dial phones. Breakfast is the only meal served, but the staff will direct you to nearby reasonably priced restaurants.

WHERE TO DINE

✪ Auberge de l'Eridan

13 vieille route des Pensières, 74290 Veyrier-du-Lac. ☎ **50-60-24-00.** Fax 50-60-23-63. Reservations required. Main courses 250–600 F ($47.50–$114.05); fixed-price meals 495–950 F ($94.10–$180.60). AE, DC, MC, V. Mon-Tues and Thurs–Sat noon–2:30pm and 7–9:30pm, Sun noon–2:30pm. Closed Jan 10–31. FRENCH.

Famous throughout France because of the excellent and unusual cuisine of owner Marc Veyrat-Durebex, this world-class restaurant occupies a romanticized version of a château at the edge of the lake in the village of Veyrier-du-Lac, about a mile from Annecy. The dining room is posh, with ceiling frescoes. Menu choices include ravioli of vegetables flavored with rare alpine herbs gathered by M. Veyrat-Durebex and his team in the mountains. Also well recommended are pike-perch sausage, crayfish poached with bitter almonds, and poached sea bass with caviar.

The auberge also rents rooms, charging 1,500 to 6,850 F ($285.15 to $1,302.25) for a double, with suites going for 6,300 to 6,850 F ($1,197.10 to $1,302.25). Breakfast costs an extra 180 F ($34.20).

7 Talloires

342 miles SE of Paris, 20 miles N of Albertville, 8 miles S of Annecy

The charming village of Talloires is old enough to appear on lists of territories once controlled by Lothar II, great-grandson of Charlemagne—it dates back to 866. Chalk cliffs surround a pleasant bay, and at the lower end a wooden promontory encloses a small port. An 18-hole golf course and water sports like skiing, boating, swimming, and fishing make this a favorite spot with French vacationers. Talloires is a also gourmet citadel, boasting one of France's great restaurants, the Auberge du Père-Bise and a Benedictine abbey founded in the 11th century but now transformed into the deluxe Hôtel de l'Abbaye (both below).

ESSENTIALS

GETTING THERE After leaving Annecy (above), you can drive south along N508 (on the eastern shore of Lac d'Annecy) for 8 miles to reach Talloires.

VISITOR INFORMATION The Office de Tourisme is on rue André-Theuriet (☎ 50-60-70-64).

WHERE TO STAY

In addition to the following, the restaurants under "Where to Dine" rent luxurious rooms.

Hôtel de l'Abbaye

Route du Port, 74290 Talloires. ☎ **50-60-77-33.** Fax 50-60-78-81. 28 rms, 4 suites. TEL. 595–1,015 F ($113.10–$192.95) per person. Rates include half board. AE, DC, MC, V. Parking free. Closed Oct 31 to mid-Apr.

This former Benedictine abbey is now a Relais & Châteaux. To enter the abbey, walk through the iron gateway and stroll along shaded walks, bypassing the formal French gardens. The secluded hotel is rich with beamed ceilings, antique portraits, modern deep leather chairs, and richly carved balustrades. The great corridors lead to converted guest rooms—no two alike—and suspended wooden balconies lead to a second level of rooms. The furnishings are distinguished. The dining room, once the monks' dining hall, has large wooden chandeliers. In summer, guests can also dine under the shade trees and enjoy a lake view.

WHERE TO DINE

✪ **Auberge du Père-Bise**

Bord du Lac, 74290 Talloires. ☎ **50-60-72-01.** Fax 50-60-73-05. Reservations required. Main courses 200–300 F ($38–$57); fixed-price menus 480–750 F ($91.25–$142.55). AE, DC, MC, V. Wed 7–9pm, Thurs–Tues noon–2pm and 7–9pm. Closed Nov 15–Feb 12. FRENCH.

This chalet, in a private park, is one of the gastronomic (and astronomically expensive) citadels of France. Père Bise's heirs inherited his secret recipes and carry on his tradition. The dining room is elegant, with sparkling silverware and bowls of flowers, but in fair weather you can dine under a vine-covered pergola and enjoy the view. The cuisine is directed by Sophie Bise, France's only female three-star chef, who offers classic dishes like mousse of goose foie gras, delicate young lamb, and braised pullet with fresh morels.

The inn also offers three suites and 31 guest rooms, each with minibar, TV, and phone; they cost 1,100 to 1,600 F ($209.10 to $304.15) for a double or 300 to 3,800 F ($57 to $722.40) for a suite, plus 95 F ($18.05) for breakfast. It's wise to make reservations at least two months in advance, especially in summer.

⑤ **Villa des Fleurs**

Route du Port, 74290 Talloires. ☎ **50-60-71-14.** Fax 50-60-74-06. Reservations required. Main courses 95–195 F ($18.05–$37.05). MC, V. Daily 12:15–2:30pm and 7:15–9:30pm. Closed Nov 15–Dec 15 and Mon Nov–May. FRENCH.

This attractive *restaurant avec chambres* should be better known, for it's the best establishment in Talloires in this price range. Proprietors Marie-France and Charles Jaegler serve wonderfully prepared meals, which often include veal kidneys, salade landaise with foie gras, and filet of fera, which live only in Lake Geneva. The dining room overlooks the water.

There are also eight rooms for rent here, each with minibar, phone, and Victorian-era decor. Doubles cost 490 F ($93.10); they're at the top of a winding staircase—there's no elevator. Breakfast is 50 F ($9.50) extra.

8 Aix-les-Bains

332 miles SE of Paris, 21 miles SW of Annecy, 10 miles N of Chambéry

On the eastern edge of Lac du Bourget, modern Aix-les-Bains is the most fashionable (and largest) **spa** in eastern France. The hot springs, which offered comfort to the Romans, are said to be useful in the treatment of rheumatism. The spa is well equipped for visitors: It contains flower gardens, a casino (the Palais de

Savoie), a race course, a golf course, and Lac du Bourget, which has a beach. These Thermes Nationaux lie in the center of town, more than 2 miles from the lakeshore, near the casino, the Temple of Diana, and the Hôtel de Ville. Closer to the lake, a long string of flower beds and ornamental shrubs border the town's famous waterside promenades.

Regular steamer service takes you on a four-hour **boat ride on Lac du Bourget**—it's a beautiful trip. For information about departure times (which change seasonally), consult the Syndicat d'Initiative (see "Essentials," below). Boats depart from the landing stage at Grand Port. You can also take a bus ride from Aix to the small town of **Revard,** at 5,080 feet, where you'll be rewarded with a panoramic view of Mont Blanc.

ESSENTIALS

GETTING THERE   Six trains per day arrive from Paris (trip time: 3 hr.), costing 300 F ($57) one way; 12 trains pull in from Annecy (trip time: 20 min.), costing 35 F ($6.65) one way.

VISITOR INFORMATION   The Syndicat d'Initiative (tourist office) is on place Maurice-Mollard (☎ 79-35-05-92).

SEEING THE TOP ATTRACTIONS

The **Abbey d'Hautecombe**, 73310 Chindrieux (☎ 79-54-26-12), the St-Denis of Savoy, is the mausoleum of many of the princes of the House of Savoy. Standing on a promontory jutting out into the lake, the church was rebuilt in the 19th century in what is called the troubadour gothic style. A guided tour in English is offered free to the public, who are also welcome to participate in the mass celebrated daily at noon (Sunday at 9:15am). The Christian community that lives in the abbey organizes religious seminars and perpetuates the tradition of worship maintained on this site since the 12th century. The abbey can be reached by boat, with two to five steamers leaving daily from Easter until September. To board, go to the landing stage at Aix-les-Bains. The price is 50 F ($9.50) for the 2¹/₂-hour trip. The abbey is open Monday and Wednesday to Saturday from 10 to 11:30am and 2 to 5pm and Sunday from 10:30am to noon and 2 to 5pm.

The **Musée Faure,** boulevard des Côtes (☎ 79-61-06-57), is the spa's most interesting museum, with its modern-art collection, including sculptures by Rodin plus works by Degas, Corot, and Cézanne. The location is on a hill overlooking the lake and the town. Admission is 20 F ($3.80). The museum is open Monday and Wednesday to Friday from 9:30am to noon and 1:30 to 5:45pm and Saturday and Sunday from 9:30am to noon and 1:30 to 6:30pm.

The original structure for the **Thermes Nationaux d'Aix-les-Bains,** place Maurice-Mollard (☎ 79-35-05-92), was begun in 1857 by Victor Emmanuel II; the New Baths, launched in 1934, were expanded and renovated in 1972. To visit, go to the caretaker at the entrance opposite the Hôtel de Ville, the former château of the marquises of Aix in the 16th century. Before you enter the baths, you can visit the thermal caves. In the center of the spa are two Roman remains—a Temple of Diana and the 30-foot-high triumphal Arch of Campanus. Tours are 15 F ($2.85) and are given Tuesday to Saturday at 3pm. Closed holidays.

WHERE TO STAY

The restaurants under "Where to Dine" also rent rooms.

Hostellerie le Manoir

37 rue Georges-1er, 73100 Aix-les-Bains. ☎ **79-61-44-00**. Fax 79-35-67-67. 73 rms. TV TEL. 595 F ($113.10) double. Breakfast 50 F ($9.50) extra. DC, MC, V. Parking free. Closed Dec 20–Jan 15.

This charming old building is in the Parc du Splendide-Royal. The white-stucco hotel has shutters and an overhanging roof, with pathways weaving through the old-world gardens in which outdoor furniture has been placed under shade trees. Guests can order breakfast or dinner, weather permitting, on a terrace bordering the garden. Most of the public rooms, as well as the guest rooms, open onto terraces. The decor is traditional, with antique and provincial furniture.

Hôtel Ariana

Av. de Marlioz, à Marlioz, 73100 Aix-les-Bains. ☎ **79-88-08-00**. Fax 79-88-87-46. 60 rms. TV TEL. 410–485 F ($77.90–$92.20) double. Breakfast 58 F ($11) extra. AE, DC, MC, V. Parking free.

The Ariana caters to a spa-oriented clientele who enjoy taking quiet walks through the surrounding park. The stylized loggia-dotted glass exterior opens into a modernized art deco interior highlighted by contrasting metal, wood, and fabrics, plus plenty of white marble and carpeting. Tunnel-like glass walkways connect it to the outbuildings, and there are two indoor pools. The guest rooms are quite comfortable, though small. The Café Adelaïde is one of the finest in town, offering well-prepared classic dishes.

WHERE TO DINE

ⓢ Hôtel Restaurant Davat

Au Grand Port, 73100 Aix-les-Bains. ☎ **79-63-40-40**. Reservations required. Main courses 60–210 F ($11.40–$39.90); fixed-price menus 88 F ($16.70), 130 F ($24.70), 190 F ($36.10), and 260 F ($49.40). AE. Mon noon–2pm, Wed–Sun noon–2pm and 7:30–9:30pm. Closed Jan–Feb. FRENCH.

Diners enjoy the robust cooking, gracious service, and selection of regional wines here. This is not only a leading restaurant but also an excellent moderately priced place to stay, where the chief attraction is the beautiful flower garden. The 20 rooms are simply furnished and begin at 350 F ($66.50) for a double, including breakfast.

Lille

Au Grand Port, 73100 Aix-les-Bains. ☎ **79-63-40-00**. Fax 79-34-00-30. Reservations required. Main courses 90–150 F ($17.10–$28.50); fixed-price menus 95 F ($18.05), 135 F ($25.65), 230 F ($43.70), and 350 F ($66.50). AE, DC, MC, V. Thurs–Mon noon–2pm and 7:30–9pm. Closed Jan 4–Mar 4. FRENCH.

Near the landing stages where the Lac du Bourget steamers depart is one of the best restaurants in Aix-les-Bains, housed in what was a 19th-century private villa. The main courses include pâté en croûte with foie gras, cassoulet of crayfish, and grilled lobster flambé. None of this fare is very innovative, as the owners prefer to present time-tested dishes. Four generations of the Lille family have welcomed guests to their lakeside retreat.

It's also possible to stay overnight in one of 18 simply furnished rooms; doubles cost 350 F ($66.50). Breakfast is 35 F ($6.65) extra. Parking is free.

9 Chambéry

33 miles SE of Paris, 34 miles N of Grenoble, 61 miles SE of Lyon

Chambéry used to be the capital of an ancient sovereign state, the Duchy of Savoy. It's not as important a resort as most nearby towns, but with its handsome streets, good food, and château, it has much to lure visitors. Everywhere you look are reminders of the 15th and 16th centuries.

ESSENTIALS

GETTING THERE   Chambéry has excellent bus and rail service from major cities in eastern France; both depots lie on the western edge of the old city. From Annecy six direct trains arrive per day (trip time: 1½ hr.), costing 46 F ($8.75) one way. There are also two direct trains from Paris per day (trip time: 7 hr.), costing 290 F ($55.10) one way. Eight buses arrive daily from Annecy (trip time: 1 hour), costing 40.50 F ($7.70) one way. The nearby junction of many highways makes driving to Chambéry easy.

VISITOR INFORMATION   The Office de Tourisme is at 24 bd. de la Colonne (☎ 79-33-42-47).

SEEING THE TOP ATTRACTIONS

The residence of the former dukes, the **Château des ducs de Savoie,** rue Basse-du-Château, towers over the city; it was founded in the 14th century and partly rebuilt in the 18th and 19th centuries. Its Sainte-Chapelle contained the Holy Shroud for most of the 16th century, until it was moved to the Cathedral of Turin in Italy. If you're willing to climb nearly 200 steps to the top of the Round Tower, you'll have a fantastic view. Guided tours costing 25 F ($4.75) are obligatory: in July and August, daily at 10:30am and 2:30, 3:30, 4:30, and 5:30pm (none at 10:30am Sunday); in May, June, and September, daily at 2:30 and 4pm; in April and October, Saturday and Sunday at 2:30 and 4pm; and November to March, Saturday and Sunday at 2:30pm.

From the château, you can take rue de Boigne, lined with porticoes, to the **Fontaine des Eléphants,** erected in memory of native son Général de Boigne (1751–1830), who left to his hometown some of the fortune he acquired in India.

In the environs, going up the steep chemin des Charmettes leads to the **Musée des Charmettes** (☎ 79-33-39-44), the handsome 17th-century country house where Jean-Jacques Rousseau lived with Mme de Warens between 1738 and 1740. The property lies 1¼ miles southeast of Chambéry—take rue de la République, which becomes rue J-J-Rousseau. Rousseau's bedroom contains the original furniture, and in the drawing room you can see Mme de Warens's clavichord. Wander in the beautiful garden and enjoy the view of the Chambéry valley from the terrace. Rousseau praised the country house in his *Confessions.* The house is open April to September, Wednesday to Monday from 10am to noon and 2 to 6pm; off-season, to 4:30pm. Admission is 10 F ($1.90).

WHERE TO STAY

Hôtel des Princes

4 rue de Boigne, 73000 Chambéry. ☎ **79-33-45-36.** Fax 79-70-31-47. 45 rms. TV TEL. 390 F ($74.10) double. Breakfast 35 F ($6.65) extra. AE, DC, MC, V.

Beneath 18th-century arcades, this is one of the most pleasant hotels in Chambéry. You register in an elegantly old-fashioned lobby, then are escorted to your comfortably furnished art deco-ish room; most guest rooms have been renovated and all are soundproof. In addition to the bar and lounge, the hotel has one of the city's most attractive restaurants, offering classic French cuisine with a 1990s twist.

Novotel Chambéry
La Motte Servolex, 73000 Chambéry. ☎ **79-69-21-27.** Fax 79-69-71-13. 103 rms. A/C MINIBAR TV TEL. 405 F ($76.95) double. Breakfast 48 F ($9.10) extra. AE, DC, MC, V. Parking free.

This Novotel is 1½ miles north of Chambéry near La Motte Servolex exit from the autoroute between Chambéry and Lyon. For motorists who prefer ease of access to a position in the heart of the city, this might be the ideal but lackluster choice. All the spacious rooms are exactly and efficiently alike. Guests also patronize the bar and the grill restaurant, where they can order food daily from 6am to midnight.

WHERE TO DINE

⊗ La Chaumière
14 rue Denfert-Rochereau. ☎ **79-33-16-26.** Reservations required. Main courses 90–110 F ($17.10–$20.90); fixed-price menus 82 F ($15.60), 110 F ($20.90), and 150 F ($28.50). AE, MC, V. Mon–Sat noon–2pm and 7–10:30pm. FRENCH.

If you want a reasonably priced meal in a cozy room, come here for the best fixed-price dinner in town. The restaurant lies near the Théâtre Dullin on a street with limited traffic access, which makes the front terrace more desirable. The chef is skilled in cooking traditional French dishes; foie gras and duck breast are his specialties, but you might prefer fish, either grilled or steamed in a light sauce. The cellar contains a good range of reasonably priced local wines, including some inexpensive ones.

L'Essentiel
183 place de la Gare. ☎ **79-96-97-27.** Reservations recommended. Main courses 85–260 F ($16.15–$49.40); fixed-price menus 95 F ($18.05), 165 F ($31.35), 185 F ($35.15), 265 F ($50.35), and 340 F ($64.60). AE, MC, V. Mon–Fri 12:30–3pm and 7–10:30pm, Sat 7–10:30pm. Closed Aug 1–15. SAVOYARD/FRENCH.

Beneath a soaring greenhouse-style ceiling, this is the most talked-about restaurant in town, the domain of one of the best-trained chefs in the region, Jean-Michel Bouvier. Ably assisted by members of his family (especially his wife, Catherine, and his sister, Elisabeth), he prepares unusual dishes based strictly on seasonal ingredients. These may include scallops in herb-flavored bouillon, snail-stuffed ravioli, frogs' legs with purée of peas, and caramelized duckling with pine-flavored honey.

10 Grenoble

352 miles SE of Paris, 34 miles S of Chambéry, 64 miles SE of Lyon

Because this city, the ancient capital of the Dauphine, is the commercial, intellectual, and tourist center of the alpine area, it's a major stopover for those exploring the French Alps and for motorists traveling between the Riviera and Geneva. A sports capital in both winter and summer, it also attracts many foreign students—its university has the largest summer-session program in Europe. The university has a modern campus on the outskirts of the city, and many buildings erected for the 1968 Olympics have been put to creative use.

Grenoble lies near the junction of the Isère and Drac rivers. Most of the city is on the south bank of the Isère, though its most impressive monument, Fort de la Bastille, stands in relative isolation on a rocky hilltop on the north bank (a cable car will carry you from the south bank's quai Stéphane-Jay across the river to the top of the fort). The center of Grenoble's historic section is the Palais de Justice and place St-André. The more modern part of town lies southeast and is centered around the contemporary Hôtel de Ville and the nearby Tour Perret.

ESSENTIALS

GETTING THERE   An important rail and bus junction, Grenoble is easily accessible from Paris and all the cities recommended in this chapter. About seven trains per day arrive from Paris (trip time: 3 hr.), costing 330 F ($62.70) one way. Trains arrive almost every hour from Chambéry (trip time: 30 min.), costing 55 F ($10.45) one way. Grenoble's airport is 18 miles northwest of the city center.

VISITOR INFORMATION   The Office de Tourisme is at 14 rue de la République (☎ **76-42-41-41**).

WHAT TO SEE & DO

Begin at **place Grenette,** a lively square filled with flowers in late spring and early summer, where you can enjoy a drink or an espresso. This square enjoys many associations with Grenoble-born Stendhal, who wrote such masterpieces as *The Red and the Black* and *The Charterhouse of Parma*. It was here that Antoine Berthet, supposedly the model for Stendhal's Julien Grel, was executed for attempted murder in 1827.

Next, enjoy a ride on the **Téléférique de la Bastille.** These high-swinging cable cars take you over the Isère River. Most of the year it operates from 9am to midnight, though in winter service stops at 7:30pm; a round-trip costs 20 F ($3.80). For information, phone 76-44-33-65. From the belvedere where you land you'll have a superb view of the city and surrounding mountains. If you want to walk, you can return on foot. Signs point the way to the Parc de la Bastille and Parc Guy-Pape and eventually lead you to the **Jardin des Dauphins,** open daily in summer from 9am to 7:30pm.

If you prefer, from the Belvédère de Grenoble you can take the **Télésiège Bastille–Mont-Jalla** for an even loftier view of the environs. To board the car in Grenoble, head for the Gare de Départ on quai St-Stéphane-Jay, facing the Jardin de Ville.

The **Musée de Peinture et de Sculpture,** 5 place de Lavalette (☎ **76-63-44-44**), was founded in 1796, making it one of the country's oldest art museums. It was the first French museum to concentrate on modern art, a fact appreciated by Picasso, who donated his *Femme Lisant* in 1921. Flemish and Italian Renaissance works are displayed, though it's the impressionist paintings that generate the most interest. Particularly note Matisse's *Intérieur aux Aubergines* and Léger's *Le Remorqueur*. Ernst, Klee, Bonnard, Monet, Rouault—they're all here. Admission is 25 F ($4.75) for adults and 15 F ($2.85) for children and seniors. It's open Wednesday from 11am to 10pm and Thursday to Monday from 11am to 7pm.

If you have time, visit the **Musée Dauphinois,** 30 rue Maurice-Gignoux (☎ **76-87-66-77**), housed in a 17th-century convent and enhanced by the cloister, gardens, and baroque chapel; it's across the Isère in the Ste-Marie-d'en-Haut section. A collection of ethnographical and historical mementos of the Dauphine are displayed, along with folk arts and crafts. It's open Wednesday to Monday from 9am to noon and 2 to 6pm (closed January 1, May 1, and December 25); admission is 15 F ($2.85) for adults and 10 F ($1.90) for children 10 to 16; 9 and under free.

Designed by architect A. Wogenscky and constructed in 1968, the **Maison de la Culture** lies in the new quarter of Malherbe. At the Office de Tourisme (see "Essentials," above), you can pick up a calendar listing the events of the month—they range from impressionist exhibitions to cinema showings, from orchestral concerts to dance. The center is open Tuesday to Saturday from 1 to 6pm and Sunday from 1 to 7pm; it's closed part of August.

WHERE TO STAY

Hôtel d'Angleterre

5 place Victor-Hugo, 38000 Grenoble. ☎ **76-87-37-21.** Fax 76-50-94-10. 66 rms. A/C MINIBAR TV TEL. 580 F ($110.20) double. Breakfast 45 F ($8.10) extra. AE, DC, MC, V.

Behind tall windows and wrought-iron balconies, this hotel has a sparkling contemporary interior. The hotel opens onto a pleasant square with huge chestnut trees in the center of Grenoble. The stylish salons have wood-grained walls and ceilings and tropical plants. The guest rooms have contemporary styling, and some look out on the Vercors Massif. Breakfast is the only meal served.

Hôtel Lesdiguières

122 cours de la Libération, 38000 Grenoble. ☎ **76-96-55-36.** Fax 76-48-10-13. 36 rms. TV TEL. 330 F ($62.70) double. Breakfast 38 F ($7.20) extra. AE, DC, MC, V. Parking 50 F ($9.50). Closed Sat–Sun and all school holidays.

This facility surrounded by a spacious lawn is a training ground for the local hotel school, so the receptionist, bellboys, and restaurant staff are all members of the most recent graduating class. The imposing premises are of gray-brown stucco with white trim and brick accents. The sunny public rooms are filled with Louis XIII chairs and Oriental rugs; the guest rooms are well furnished. Fixed-price menus in the dining room run 100 F ($19), 125 F ($23.75), and 165 F ($31.35).

WHERE TO DINE

Le Berlioz

4 rue Strasbourg. ☎ **76-56-22-39.** Reservations required. Main courses 120–170 F ($22.80–$32.30); fixed-price menus 118 F ($22.40), 158 F ($30), 198 F ($37.60), and 265 F ($50.35). AE, DC, MC, V. Mon–Fri noon–2pm and 7:30–10:30pm, Sat 7:30–10:30pm. Closed Aug. FRENCH.

The chef here offers a gourmet tour of France by featuring a different menu with regional specialties every month. Françoise Legras has won much local acclaim with her talented staff. Try, for example, the fresh codfish with green cabbage and smoked lard, side of beef with baby vegetables in wine sauce, or braised shoulder of lamb with eggplant "cake." If featured, the roast duck in spicy honey sauce is a winner.

Poularde Bressane

12 place Paul-Mistral. ☎ **76-87-08-90.** Reservations required. Main courses 80–165 F ($15.20–$31.35); fixed-price menus 125 F ($23.75), 168 F ($31.90), 198 F ($37.60), 230 F ($43.70), and 280 F ($53.20). AE, DC, MC, V. Mon–Fri noon–2pm and 7:30–9:45pm, Sat 7:30–9:45pm. FRENCH.

Here you'll enjoy superb cuisine in an elegant modern setting. Though the dishes are classical and traditional, contemporary culinary delights have been mastered as well. In honor of the restaurant's namesake, poularde Bressane is the major specialty. The chef's fish pâté is excellent, as is his red mullet flavored with basil. The menu is very much a *cuisine du marché*, based on what's in the market that day. The desserts are delectable, many prepared at the time of request.

NEARBY ATTRACTIONS

Monks have created some of the world's famous wines and liqueurs, but Chartreuse is not one of them, though it was named after the Carthusians. Monks are, however, the custodians of the secret formula, which was given to them in 1605 by Marshal d'Estrées. It was an elixir involving the distillation of 130 herbs, believed to have been originated by an anonymous alchemist.

Eventually the formula found its way to La Grande Chartreuse (charterhouse), founded in 1084 about 20 miles north of Grenoble. The monastery was destroyed and rebuilt many times; the present buildings date from 1688. The Revolution broke up most monastic orders, but somehow the monks held on to their formula, returning to Grenoble in 1816 with the restoration of the monarchy. When they were expelled from France again in 1903 during a period of anticlericalism, they took their recipe with them to Tarragona in Spain, where they continued making their liqueurs. They returned to La Grande Chartreuse again in 1940, shortly before the German attack on France.

The monastery is no longer open to the public, but you're allowed to visit the **Musée de la Correrie,** 38380 St-Pierre-de-Chartreuse (☎ 76-05-81-77), in a 15th-century building at the head of the valley about 1 1/2 miles from the monastery. For 12 F ($2.30) for adults and 6 F ($1.15) for children, the museum can be visited April to October only, daily from 9:30am to noon and 2 to 6:30pm. In this unusual museum you'll get a glimpse of a monk's life; the sound you'll hear is chanting.

Even more interesting is a trip to Voiron, about 20 miles away, where you can visit the **Caves de la Grande Chautreuse,** 10 bd. Edgar-Kofler (☎ 76-05-81-77), the distillery where the famed Chartreuse is made. Free visits are possible in July and August daily from 8am to 6:30pm; Easter to June and in September and October, daily from 8 to 11:30am and 2 to 6:30pm; and November to Easter, Monday to Friday from 8 to 11:30am and 2 to 5:30pm. Dressed in chartreuse green, a guide will show you around, let you view the copper stills, and then take you to the cellar, filled with gargantuan oak casks in which the liqueur matures for several years. At the end of the tour you'll be given a free drink of the yellow or fiery green Chartreuse or of one of the new products. You can also purchase bottles at a shop on the premises. It's said that only three monks and the Father Procurator have access to the formula.

Before you head out into the Massif de la Chartreuse, where the monastery and distillery lie, obtain a good detailed map from the tourist office in Grenoble.

NEARBY ACCOMMODATIONS & DINING

Relais l'Escale

Place de la République, 38761 Varces. ☎ **76-72-80-19.** Fax 76-72-92-58. 7 rms. A/C MINIBAR TV TEL. 490 F ($93.15) double. Breakfast 60 F ($11.40) extra. MC, V. Parking free. Closed Jan–Feb 5. Take N75 8 miles southeast of Grenoble.

A Relais & Châteaux, this hotel/restaurant offers wooden chalets in a lovely garden setting and alfresco dining on a terrace with an alpine garden view. The rooms are well furnished and homelike. At the Restaurant l'Escale, you can enjoy the specialties of chef Frédéric Buntinx, including salmon tartare in herb sauce, young duckling with honey and red fruit, and fresh foie gras. Service hours are 12:15 to 2pm and 7:30 to 9:15pm; closed Tuesday in summer and on Sunday night and Monday off-season. Fixed-price meals cost 125 F ($23.75), 260 F ($49.40), and 295 F ($56.05).

11 Courchevel 1850

393 miles SE of Paris, 32 miles SE of Albertville, 60 miles SE of Chambéry

Courchevel has been called a resort of "high taste, high fashion, and high profile." Skiers and geographers know of it as part of Les Trois Vallées, sometimes called "the skiing supermarket of France" thanks to its conception in 1947 as a resort exclusively for skiing. The resort's 1,400 acres of ski runs employ as many workers in summer as in winter, simply to manicure and maintain the top-notch conditions that won Courchevel the coveted role as a host of the 1992 Winter Olympics.

Believe it or not, Courchevel's origins were rustic. In Savoyard dialect, the name was derived from a place where cows (*vel*) were killed, skinned, and flayed (*écorché*). But that's a forgotten memory to occupants of the $4-million chalets on the pine-covered mountains.

Courchevel maintains three ski schools, with an average staff of 450 instructors, a labyrinth of chair lifts, and more than 200 ski runs, which are excellent in both the intermediate and advanced categories. Included with Courchevel in Les Trois Vallées are the less well known resorts of Méribel, Les Menuires, and Val Thorens, which you should avoid unless you direly need to save money. Courchevel consists of four planned ski towns, each marked by its elevation in meters. Thus there's less fashionable Courchevel 1300 (Le Prez), 1550, and 1650. Crowning them all is Courchevel 1850.

Courchevel 1850 is the most attractive ski mecca in the French Alps, a position once held by Megève. It's also the focal point of a chair-hoist network crisscrossing the region. At the center of one of the largest ski areas in the world, Courchevel was built at the base of a soaring alpine amphitheater whose deep snowfalls last longer than those at most other resorts because it faces the north winds. Courchevel 1850 is also distinguished by having more high-quality restaurants and hotels than any other European resort, so naturally it attracts the international ultra-rich.

ESSENTIALS

GETTING THERE   Courchevel 1850 is the last stop on a steep alpine road that dead-ends at the village center. To go any higher, you'll have to take a cable car from the center of town. Most visitors arrive by car (you'll need snow tires and chains), but some buses link the city to railway junctions farther down the mountain.

VISITOR INFORMATION   The Office de Tourisme is at La Croisette (☎ 79-08-00-29).

WHERE TO STAY

EXPENSIVE

Le Chabichou

Quartier Les Chenus, 73120 Courchevel 1850. ☎ **79-08-00-55.** Fax 79-08-33-58. 34 rms. TV TEL. Winter, 720–1,900 F ($136.85–$361.20) per person. Summer, 570–970 F ($108.35–$184.40) per person. Rates include half board. AE, DC, MC, V. Closed May 10–June 20 and Sept 10–Dec 19.

This is one of the town's finest hotels, with a superb restaurant (see "Where to Dine," below). Le Chabichou is within easy walking distance of many after-dark attractions. In this gingerbread chalet, most of the rooms are large and all are well furnished; their daring modern design might not appeal to everyone, however. The owners, the Rochedy family, would like their rooms to be appreciated as much as their cuisine is, but that's not the case. Facilities include a sauna, a Jacuzzi, and an exercise room.

✪ Hôtel Bellecote

Route de l'Altiport, 73120 Courchevel 1850. ☎ **79-08-10-10.** Fax 79-08-17-16. 56 rms, 2 suites. MINIBAR TV TEL. 1,200–1,700 F ($228.10–$323.20) per person. Rates include half board. AE, DC, MC, V. Closed May–Dec 17.

Beside the Jardin Alpin, this seven-story chalet is known for the quality of its construction and its collection of antiques. Bored with traditional alpine motifs, founder Roger Toussaint scoured the bazaars of Afghanistan and the Himalayas for an array of fascinating objects that lend exotic warmth to the wood-sheathed walls and ceilings of this unusual hotel. Each room contains plush accessories as well as Far or Middle Eastern carved wooden objects. Full meals in the elegant dining room include cassolette of sweetbreads with flap mushrooms, frogs' legs provençal, and chicken with morels. The impressive luncheon buffet table has a dazzling array of seafood, like crayfish and urchins, followed by succulent sauerkraut with pork. The most flavorful fondant au chocolat in the Alps is served here. Meals are offered daily from 12:30 to 2:30pm and 7:30 to 10pm. Facilities include an indoor pool, a fitness center, a hairdresser, and a ski-rental shop.

MODERATE

Les Ducs de Savoie

Au Jardin Alpin, 73120 Courchevel 1850. ☎ **79-08-03-00.** Fax 79-08-16-30. 70 rms. TEL. 730–1,280 F ($138.75–$243.30) per person. Rates include half board. V. Parking 100 F ($19). Closed Apr 22–Dec 16.

This hotel, one of the largest at Courchevel, has elaborately scrolled pinewood and often rows of icicles hanging from the protruding eaves. There's a covered garage, plus an indoor pool with walls intricately chiseled from mountain flagstones. In the lobby bar, the stone base deliberately retains its mountain lichens. Fireplaces add to the conviviality of the good food, drinks, and lively conversation. The hotel has spacious, pleasant rooms, each with a terrace. It lies a few feet from the Téléski of the Jardin Alpin, and guests can ski directly to the hotel's vestibule at the end of the day.

La Sivolière

Quartier Les Chenus, 73120 Courchevel 1850. ☎ **79-08-08-33.** Fax 79-08-15-73. 32 rms. TV TEL. 1,260 F ($239.50) double; 2,500 F ($475.25) suite. Breakfast 75 F ($14.25) extra. MC, V. Parking 90 F ($17.10). Closed late Apr to late Nov.

The secret of La Sivolière's success is owner Madeleine Cattelin, who has a rich knowledge of and appreciation for her native Savoy. Each guest room contains tastefully elegant furnishings and all the modern conveniences. Rooms include free access to the sauna, steambath, and exercise room, as well as an invitation to a richly laden afternoon tea table. In the dining rooms there's no formal menu, and you're likely to get such dishes as filet of John Dory with watercress sauce and sea bass with essence of zucchini. Full meals are served daily from noon to 2:15pm and 7 to 11pm to guests and to nonguests who make reservations.

INEXPENSIVE

⑤ Le Dahu

Près de la Station (near the bus station), 73120 Courchevel 1850. ☎ **79-08-01-18.** Fax 79-08-11-98. 38 rms. TEL. 950 F ($180.60) double. Breakfast 78 F ($14.80) extra. MC, V. Closed Apr 26–Dec 14.

This is one of the resort's most alluring bargains, offering clean and comfortable guest rooms, a charming salon, a bar, and a restaurant. The hotel is named after a mythical alpine goat whose capture by tourists is jokingly encouraged by local guides. The hotel's social center is a flight above the reception, where there's stylish furniture and a long bar. Meals are served in the restaurant daily from 12:30 to 2pm and 7:30 to 8:45pm; nonguests who make reservations are welcome.

WHERE TO DINE
EXPENSIVE

Le Bateau Ivre

In the Hôtel Pomme-de-Pin, quartier Les Chenus. ☎ **79-08-36-88.** Reservations required. Main courses 160–180 F ($30.40–$34.20); fixed-price menus 350 F ($66.50) and 510 F ($96.95). AE, DC, MC, V. Daily 12:30–2:15pm and 7:30–10pm. Closed Apr 15–Dec 15. FRENCH.

This restaurant offers a panoramic view. Its fine reputation is the result of the dedicated efforts of the Jacob family, who run the restaurant and suffer the various changing owners of this hotel property (their restaurant is far more exciting than the hotel that houses it). Full meals might include polenta and escalopes of foie gras in vinaigrette, roast turbot with beignets of artichoke, fricassée of lobster and truffles, and lasagne of oysters and crayfish; especially delectable is succulent rack of lamb with black olives and artichokes. Try one of the superbly crafted desserts with one of four exotic coffees.

✪ Le Chabichou

Quartier Les Chenus. ☎ **79-08-00-55.** Reservations required. Main courses 150–265 F ($28.50–$50.35); fixed-price menus 210 F ($39.90) at lunch, 340 F ($64.60) at dinner. AE, DC, MC, V. Daily noon–2pm and 8–10pm. Closed May 10–June 20 and Sept 10–Dec 19. FRENCH.

The best restaurant in town, Le Chabichou is on the lobby level of the hotel of the same name. Michel and Maryse Rochedy acquired a reputation for their wonderful cuisine at their similarly named place in St-Tropez. The decor includes big windows showcasing a view of the snow and a low but discreetly engineered ceiling with painted fields of geometric colors. The menu lists a number of superlative dishes, like oyster soup with wild mushrooms, tempura of crayfish and rollmops of red mullet with saffron-flavored vegetables, roast pigeon on fresh green cabbage, and succulent aiguillettes of duckling with peaches.

MODERATE

⊜ La Bergerie
Quartier Nogentile. ☎ **79-08-24-70.** Reservations required. Main courses 70–185 F ($13.30–$35.15); fixed-price dinner 300 F ($57). AE, DC, V. Daily noon–3pm and 8–10pm. Closed late Apr to mid-Dec. FRENCH.

Its uneven flagstone steps, stacks of carefully split firewood, and roughly weathered pine logs and planks testify to La Bergerie's 1830s origin as a shepherd's hut. A low-ceilinged dining room on the ground floor contains a dance floor and live entertainment. From mid-December until the end of April, a dinner of alpine specialties is offered for 310 F ($58.90). Upstairs, a lunch restaurant/bar attract daytime drinkers and diners. Typical menu items are scallops in shallot butter, fondue bourguignonne, filet au poivre alpine style, and fricassée of chicken.

⊜ Chalet des Pierres
Au Jardin Alpin. ☎ **79-08-18-61.** Reservations required. Main courses 80–180 F ($15.20–$34.20). AE, MC, V. Daily 11:45am–5pm. Closed late Apr to mid-Dec. FRENCH.

This one is the best of the several lunch restaurants scattered over the ski slopes. Built of fieldstone and weathered planking, it sits in the middle of the Verdon slope, a few paces from the whizzing path of skiers. Lunch is served on a sun terrace, but most visitors gravitate to the rustic two-story interior, where blazing fireplaces, hunting trophies, and "internationally hip" patrons contribute to the allure and excitement. Meals often include an array of air-dried alpine meat and sausages, the best pommes frites in Courchevel, pepper steak, rack of lamb, and *plats du jour.*

AFTER DARK

From casual to sophisticated, après-ski and nighttime diversions in Courchevel are the most varied in the French Alps. **Les Caves de Courchevel,** Porte de Courchevel (☎ **79-08-02-07**), attracts some of the best-heeled patrons in town. Much of its allure comes from a live pianist, who plays nightly in winter from 8pm to 1am. A mock Tyrolean facade of weathered wood hides a club evoking a medieval cloister, with stone arches and columns. Full meals in the restaurant, open nightly from 8pm to 6am, begin at 250 F ($47.50). Drinks cost 60 F ($11.40) and up. It's open December to April only, daily from 6pm to 6am.

La Grange, Rond Point des Pistes (☎ **79-08-07-39**), is the most informal of the resort's leading nightspots, where you can enjoy music and dancing in a sudsy, raucous arena. If a spectacle is being staged on the night of your visit, the doors may open earlier. Drinks start at 95 F ($18.05). It's open December to April only, daily from 10:30pm to 5am.

St-Nicolas, Rond Point des Pistes (☎ **79-08-21-67**), has at its timbered portico a life-size statue of a crozier-carrying St. Nicolas, encouraging you to select between the disco on the left and the Bistrot on the right—the Bistrot's a candlelit room filled with belle époque accessories, where dinner is served nightly from 8pm until "late," beginning at 150 F ($28.50). Drinks run 70 to 95 F ($13.30 to $18.05). It's open December to April only, daily from 8pm to 6am.

Vineyard castles and ancient churches make Bourgogne in eastern France the land of the good life for those who savor fine cuisine and wines served in historic surroundings. Once, Burgundy was an incredibly powerful independent province, its famed Valois dukes spreading their might across all of Europe from 1363 to 1477. To maintain its shaky independence, Burgundy faced many struggles, notably under Charles the Bold, who was always in conflict with Louis XI. When Charles died in 1477, Louis invaded and annexed the duchy. Nonetheless, the Habsburgs still maintained their claims to it. Even after its reunion with France, Burgundy still knew no peace, as it suffered many more upheavals, such as its ravaging in the Franco-Spanish wars beginning in 1636. Peace came in 1678.

At the time of the French Revolution Burgundy disappeared as a political entity, for it was subdivided into the départements of France, Yonne, Saône-et-Loire, and Côte-d'Or. The ducs de Bourgogne are but a dim memory now, but they left a legacy of vintage red and white wines to please and excite the palate. The six major wine-growing regions of Burgundy are Chablis, Côte de Nuits, Côte de Beaune, Côte de Chalon, Mâconnais, and Nivernais.

REGIONAL CUISINE For centuries, the cuisine of Burgundy has been considered excellent for two reasons: the freshness and variety of its ingredients and the skill and finesse of its native chefs. Many Roman historians, Charles VI, Escoffier, and Brillat-Savarin (who was born in the Burgundian town of Bugey) have praised the food and/or wine of Burgundy. There's something about the mild climate, adequate rainfall, and nutrient-rich soil that produces some of the most excellent beef (especially of the rare Charolais breed), mushrooms, grapes, fish, wild game, snails, fruit, and vegetables in Europe. The cuisine seems to have been invented for healthy appetites, and the typical Bourguignon/Bourguignonne has been defined as someone who is both a gourmet and a gourmand.

Any sauce created with a dose of wine added to it (at least in Burgundy) is called *une meurette*, and there are lots listed as accompaniments to main courses on menus in the province. These meurettes, whether bound with butter and flour or strongly spiced with quantities of herbs and (occasionally) the blood of the slaughtered animal, are enormously flavorful and seem to make whatever wine you happen to be drinking taste even better. In the same vein,

What's Special About Burgundy

Great Towns

- Vézelay, a living museum of French antiquity.
- Avallon, shielded behind ramparts with a medieval atmosphere.
- Beaune, capital of the burgundy wine country and a well-preserved medieval city.
- Dijon, the center of the Côte d'Or and ancient capital of Burgundy.

Ancient Monuments

- Basilique Ste-Madeleine at Vézelay, the largest and most famous romanesque church in France.
- Autun, one of the oldest towns in France, called "the other Rome," whose Roman relics include the largest theater in Gaul.

Outstanding Museums

- Musée des Beaux-Arts at Dijon, the premier museum of Burgundy—in the former palace of the ducs de Bourgogne, it's one of the oldest and richest museums in France.

Architectural Highlights

- Château de Gevrey-Chambertin, a thick-walled castle from the 10th century.
- Cathédrale St-Etienne, built in the 13th century at Auxerre, in the flamboyant gothic style.

Gastronomic Pilgrimages

- L'Espérance, outside Vézelay, one of the world's greatest gastronomic shrines.
- A la Côte St-Jacques at Joigny, a sumptuous Relais & Châteaux that attracts Parisians who drive down just for dinner.

Festivals

- Festival International de Folklore et Fête de la Vine (International Folklore and Wine Festival), the first week in September, at Lyon.

any cut of meat prepared *à la bourguignonne* is usually braised and then served with a sauce concocted from wine (usually red), onions, mushrooms, and (except if it's served with fish) lardons.

One major specialty of the region is a succulent species of snails, which are cooked in their shells and flavored with garlic and butter. Other recipes handed down for generations include coq au vin (flavored with red wine, brandy, some of the pulverized liver of the dead animal, and blood); and chicken or ham cooked *en sauce* (made traditionally with white wine and cream) or *au sang* (with blood sauce, lard, and baby onions).

The region also produces fine cheese, samples of which are usually sold in wine bars across Europe, most visibly the goat cheese *crottin de chavignol*, made in the district of Sancerre along with the superb white wine of the same name—the cheese and the wine accompany one another splendidly. Another is the blue-veined Gex, which has a flavor similar to Roquefort, and all of the famous Epoisses cheeses, made in the Yonne valley.

Almost everyone appreciates the flavor of Dijon mustard, called the "king of French condiments," made with ground mustard seeds and slightly fermented wine

Burgundy

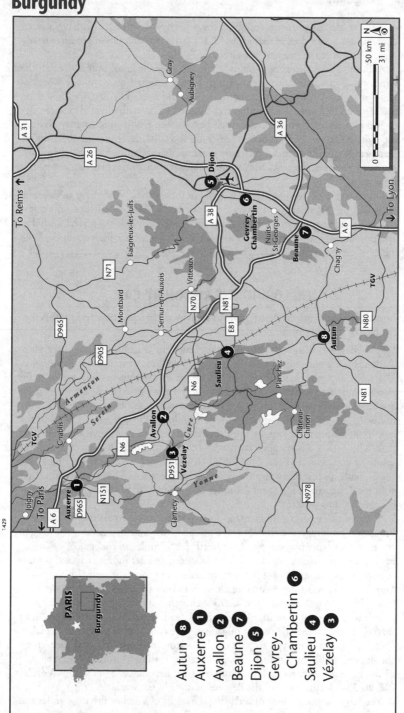

Autun **8**
Auxerre **1**
Avallon **2**
Beaune **7**
Dijon **5**
Gevrey-
Chambertin **6**
Saulieu **4**
Vézelay **3**

Rail Routes +++   Major Roads ▬▬   Regional Roads ▬▬   Airport ✈

or vinegar. Any menu item followed the adjective *dijonnaise* will have a sauce containing a liberal dose of that mustard. It's estimated that Dijon produces nearly three-quarters of the mustard consumed in France.

And, of course, there are Burgundy's wines. Consisting of only 2% of all the wines produced in France (only one-third the production of all the wines of Bordeaux), they include vintages sought the world over. The best are those from the Côte d'Or, a narrow strip of gravel-studded soil usually divided into family-owned plots of less than 40 acres, which lies between Dijon and Santenay. Within the Côte d'Or, the two major categories are the Côte de Nuits and the Côte de Beaune. Other burgundy categories are Gevrey-Chambertin, Chambolle-Musigny, Nuits-St-Georges, Beaune, Meursault, Chassagne-Montrachet, Santenay, and Pommard.

Dr. Lavalle, a noted wine expert, has said of these wines: "They have an exquisite finesse of the bouquet and a flavour at once hot and delicate which lasts a few moments and leaves a sweet and fragrant after-taste, ruby color of perfect limpidity and beneficient action on the digestive organs—such are the high qualities of the wines of the Côte d'Or, the first wines in the world."

EXPLORING THE REGION BY CAR

Burgundy is perhaps the best region to tour by car. Here's how to link together the best of the region if you rent a car.

Day 1   Begin at Burgundy's northwestern edge, in Chablis. Capital of the vine-yards of Basse Bourgogne (Lower Burgundy), Chablis is surrounded by wine fields. The town is more famous for its wine than for its monuments but does contain two interesting churches: the 12th-century Eglise St-Martin and the Eglise St-Pierre, which retains little of its original romanesque design. Chablis is really not worth an overnight stopover, though 9 miles to the east along D965, in the hamlet of Tonnere, is one of the best restaurants in the province: L'Abbaye St-Michel, route St-Michel (☎ 86-55-05-99). Housed in what was a 10th-century monastery, it's open daily for lunch and dinner, and the owners rent nine comfortable rooms; many visitors, however, prefer this as a lunch stopover. After your meal, backtrack for about 15 miles east along D965 (passing through Chablis en route) to Auxerre.

Scene of many pivotal moments in French history, Auxerre is the site of one of France's most impressive churches, the gothic Cathédrale St-Etienne. If you're in the mood for truly fine dining, drive north for 17 miles to the hamlet of Joigny for a dining experience at A La Côte St-Jacques (see later in this chapter). Return to Auxerre for the night or seek accommodations in Joigny if you wish.

Day 2   Drive south from Auxerre along N151 for 32 miles to the hilltop ham-let of Vézelay—if there's any romanesque church in France that's a must-see, this town's is it. Pray for your loved ones or the dead, depending on your beliefs, or marvel at the severe majesty of a pilgrimage site consecrated to Mary Magdalen. Ordinances encourage you to park at the bottom of the village and then climb the sloping cobblestone main street. A luxurious ending to your day is at the base of the hill on which the famous church sits: L'Espérance, St-Père-sous-Vézelay (☎ 86-33-39-10), is one of the best restaurants in the world.

You have the option now of spending the night in Vézelay, driving 6 miles east on D951 to the densely forested town of Avallon, or continuing south for 35 miles on well-signposted country roads to Château-Chinon. (Part of your decision will be determined by the season and occupancy rate of the hotels in the towns.) Wherever you've opted to spend the night, plan on an early-morning departure the following day.

Day 3 From Château-Chinon, drive east 20 miles on D978 for to visit one of the oldest towns in France, Autun. En route, perhaps take a detour: Heading east on D978 toward Autun, turn right (south) at the town of Arleuf, going right onto D500. At a fork, turn right to Glux. After Glux, follow the arrows to Mont Beuvray via D18. You reach the summit through D274. After 2 miles of climbing you'll be at Oppidum of Bibracte, home of the Eduens, a Gallic tribe. At this altitude of 2,800 feet, Vercingetorix organized the Gauls to fight Caesar's legions in A.D. 52. From here you'll have a splendid view of Autun and Mont St-Vincent. If the weather is clear, you can see the Jura and snowy Mont Blanc. Leave Mont Beuvray via D274 and continue northeast to Autun.

At Autun, you'll find a historic town loaded with ruins left by the ancient Romans, as well as a hilltop cathedral built in 1120 to hold the remains of St. Lazarus. Spend the night here.

Day 4 Start your day early, prepared for brief tours of various châteaux, feudal fortresses, vineyards, and other historic sites. Your route will be loaded with appealing detours, so try to be as flexible as possible in negotiating your way through a labyrinth of well-marked country roads leading toward Beaune.

Leave Autun on D973. After 6 miles, turn left onto D326 toward Sully. Here you'll find the Château de Sully, once known as the Fontainebleau of Burgundy; alas, it's closed to the public, though a view from the outside might appeal to you. The gardens are open from Easter to September, daily from 8am to 6pm. Leave Sully, following the road signs to the small village of Nolay and passing through. Three miles past Nolay you'll reach the Château de Rochepot (☎ **80-21-71-37**) with its medieval-style fortress built during the Renaissance. It's open from Palm Sunday to November 1 only, Wednesday to Monday from 10am to noon and 2 to 6pm.

Now head toward Beaune on D973, passing near some of the best-known vineyards: Chassagne-Montrachet, Puligny-Montrachet, Meursault, Auxey Duresses, Volnay, and Pommard. En route, perhaps stop at a restaurant whose setting is as interesting as its food. Chagny, 27 miles east of Autun and 11 miles southwest of Beaune, rarely attracts sightseers, though gourmands from all over stop in for a meal at Lameloise, 36 place d'Armes (☎ **85-87-08-85**). It offers choices like lamb filet in a rice crêpe, Bresse pigeon cooked in a bladder, hot lemon soufflé, and one of the broadest spectrums of burgundies anywhere in France. Reservations are recommended.

Continue north on D974 to Beaune. You'll pass villages like Aloxe-Corton, where Charlemagne once owned vineyards, and Comblanchien. In Vougeot you can visit the Château du Clos-de-Vougeot (☎ **80-62-86-09**), surrounded by the most celebrated vineyards in France. The Renaissance château is associated with the Brotherhood of the Knights of Tastevin, an organization revived in 1934 along medieval lines; they maintain a 12th-century cellar, open for visits daily from 9 to 11:30am and 2 to 7pm (April to September, daily from 9am to 7pm).

Leave N74 for D122, which will take you through the scenic hamlet of Chambolle Musigny, then to Morey St-Denis and the site of your overnight stay, the historic village of Gevrey-Chambertin. It marks the beginning of the Côte de Nuits district, source of some of the world's most prestigious wines.

Days 5–8   Continue north the remaining short distance to Dijon, home to some of the region's most spectacular architecture.

If you have the time, use Dijon as a base and make excursions to sites you may have missed during the first half of your tour. Consider lunch excursions to Aubigny or Saulieu, 20 and 40 miles west of Dijon, respectively (see recommendations later in this chapter). Virtually all the sites around Dijon are best visited by car. Excursions from Dijon should be considered extensions of this driving tour. Here's a rundown:

Leave Dijon on A6, heading toward Paris. You'll be traveling along a good road in the Vallée de l'Ouche, alongside the Burgundy Canal. At pont de Pany, on the outskirts of Sombernon, exit onto a local highway (D905) and continue northwest. On your left lies the artificial lake of Grosbois. The scenery is typical of agricultural France, with isolated farms, woods, and pastures.

You pass through Vitteaux and just before the next village, Posanges, stands a feudal château. You can't visit it, but it's worth a picture. Continue on D905 for a few miles until you come to a railroad crossing. On your left is another old castle, now part of a private farm. The next village you reach along D905 is Pouillenay. Follow the signs for a short detour to the hamlet of Flavigny-sur-Ozerain. Park your car outside the walls and walk through the old streets.

Leave Flavigny and follow the signs for a few miles on country roads to Alise-Ste-Reine, the site of the camp of Alesia, where Caesar wiped out a concentration of Gallic soldiers. Here, Millet sculpted a bronze statue of Vercingetorix. You can explore the excavated ruins of a Roman-Gallic town and visit the Musée Alésia, rue de l'Hôpital (☎ **80-96-10-95**), daily from 9am to 7pm July to September 15; off-season, daily from 10am to 6pm; it's closed November to March.

Alise-Ste-Reine honors a Christian girl who was decapitated for refusing to marry a Roman governor, Olibrius. As late as the 17th century, a fountain at the site of the beheading was said to have curative powers. After Alise-Ste-Reine, you can head back to the village of Les Laumes, a railroad center. Before entering the village, make a U-turn to the right and take N454 to Baigneux-les-Juifs. After the village of Grésigny, on your left is a farm-fortress surrounded by water.

One mile farther, turn right toward the Château de Bussy-Rabutin. Roger de Rabutin, cousin of Mme de Sévigné, ridiculed Louis XIV's court, for which he spent six years in the Bastille. The château, which has two round towers, has survived mostly intact, including the interior decoration. The gardens and park are attributed to Le Nôtre. It's open April to September, Wednesday to Monday from 9am to noon and 2 to 6pm; the rest of the year, Wednesday to Monday from 10am to noon and 2 to 5pm.

Going back to Grésigny, turn right before the farm-fortress, then go left. Outside the village, turn right again toward Menetreux Le Pitois. You're now off the main road and into the real countryside. Once back on D905, head on to Montbard, home town of George-Louis Leclerc, comte de Buffon, one of the 18th century's greatest naturalists, author of *l'Histoire Naturelle*, a 44-volume encyclopedia. The scientist's home is on display, as well as a mini-museum of his life and work. The town is also the site of a pleasant hotel/restaurant, the Hotel de l'Ecu, 7 rue Auguste-Carré (☎ **80-92-11-66**), where moderately priced meals are prepared in what was during the 1700s a postal relay station (see later in this chapter).

Continue east for another 6 miles to Marmagne, then turn left on D32 and head toward the Abbaye de Fontenay (☎ **80-92-15-00**). Isolated in a valley, Fontenay

is one of Europe's most unspoiled 12th-century Cistercian abbeys. It was classified as a site of "Universal Heritage" by UNESCO in 1981 and is open daily from
9am to noon and 2 to 6pm (to 5pm in winter).

1 Auxerre

103 miles SE of Paris, 92 miles NW of Dijon

This town was founded by the Gauls and enlarged by the Romans. On a hill
overlooking the Yonne River, it's the capital of Lower Burgundy and the center
of vineyards, some of which produce chablis. Joan of Arc spent several days here
in 1429. Napoléon met Marshal Ney here on March 17, 1815, on the former
emperor's return from Elba. Louis XVIII had sent Ney to stop Napoléon, but Ney
embraced him and turned his army against the king. For that gesture, Ney was later
shot in Paris.

Pay a visit to the flamboyantly gothic **Cathédrale St-Etienne** (☎ 86-52-
23-29), begun in the 13th century but not completed until the 16th. The front
facade is remarkable, with sculptured portals. The stained glass is famous, some of
it the original from the 13th century. In the crypt, all that remains of the
romanesque church that stood on this site, you can see 11th-century frescoes. The
church is open Monday to Saturday from 9am to noon and 2 to 6pm and Sunday from 2 to 6pm. It costs 10 F ($1.90) to visit the crypt or treasury.

Auxerre used to be a gastronomic relay on the road between Paris and Lyon, but
the Autoroute du Soleil has pretty much ended that. However, **shops** display
interesting regional specialties, including chocolate snails filled with almond
praline, chocolate truffles with rum-soaked grapes, garlic sausage baked in brioche,
and even sourdough bread from wood-fired ovens.

The railway station lies at the eastern edge of town, about a mile from the his-
toric center. Most of Auxerre is on the opposite (western) bank of the Yonne River.
Its heart is between place du Maréchal-Leclerc (where you'll find the Hôtel de
Ville) and the Cathédrale St-Etienne.

ESSENTIALS

GETTING THERE   Many of the trains traveling between Paris and Lyon stop at
Auxerre: 13 per day from Paris (trip time: 2 hr.), costing 115 F ($21.85) one way;
and 9 per day from Lyon (trip time: 4½ hr.), costing 210 F ($39.90) one way.

Many visitors drive here since Auxerre is near A6/E1 (Autoroute du Soleil).

VISITOR INFORMATION   The Office de Tourisme is at 1–2 quai de la
République (☎ 86-52-06-19).

WHERE TO STAY

Hôtel le Maxime

2 quai de la Marine, 89000 Auxerre. ☎ **86-52-14-19.** Fax 86-52-21-70. 25 rms. TV TEL.
430–450 F ($81.70–$85.55) double. Breakfast 45 F ($8.55) extra. AE, DC, MC, V. Parking
15 F ($2.85).

This family-run hotel (with elevator) contains attractive rooms, many with views
of the river or the old city. Guests can take breakfast in their rooms or the quiet
salon, amid Oriental rugs and polished paneling.

Le Normandie

41 bd. Vauban, 89000 Auxerre. ☎ **86-52-57-80.** Fax 86-51-54-33. 47 rms. TV TEL. 260–350 F
($49.40–$66.50) double. Breakfast 32 F ($6.10) extra. AE, DC, MC, V. Parking 24 F ($4.55).

This centrally located hotel offers traditional hospitality, combining antique furnishings with modern amenities. The tranquil and comfortably furnished rooms open onto garden views. There's overnight parking for 30 cars, plus a complete gymnasium.

WHERE TO DINE

Le Jardin Gourmand

56 bd. Vauban. ☎ **86-51-53-52.** Reservations required. Main courses 80–160 F ($15.20–$30.40); fixed-price menus 120 F ($22.80), 190 F ($36.10), 220 F ($41.80), and 260 F ($49.40). AE, MC, V. Tues 7:30–9:30pm, Wed–Sun noon–2pm and 7:30–9:30pm. Closed the first two weeks in Sept. FRENCH.

Le Jardin Gourmand serves *cuisine moderne du marché*, using the freshest ingredients from the markets. Pierre Boussereau is the experienced and subtle chef at this restaurant with seating in the garden or on the terrace during warm weather. The wine list is composed of 330 wines, including 50 selections of chablis and some reasonably priced local burgundies. The discreet personal service makes the place even more alluring.

NEARBY ACCOMMODATIONS & DINING

✪ A La Côte St-Jacques

14 Faubourg de Paris, 89300 Joigny. ☎ **86-62-09-70.** Fax 86-91-49-70. Reservations required. Main courses 230–395 F ($43.70–$75.05); fixed-price *menu gourmand* 690 F ($131.10), 750 F ($142.50), and 840 F ($159.60). AE, DC, MC, V. Daily 12:15–2:45pm and 7:15–9:45pm. From Auxerre, head north on N6 (toward Sens) for 17 miles. FRENCH.

Michel Lorain—with his wife, Jacqueline (a noted sommelière), and their son, Jean-Michel—transformed his family's 300-year-old house into one of the most luxurious Relais & Châteaux in the region. The core of the establishment is a 19th-century building; an annex across the road dates from 1985. On an outdoor terrace or in one of the elegant dining rooms you can enjoy specialties like carp en gelée with spinach buds, cassolette of morels and frogs' legs, and salmon with caviar-cream sauce, as well as an incredible array of desserts. The cuisine sounds a trifle heavy in typical Burgundian style but actually has a light, altogether-delightful aura.

The hotel rents 15 beautiful rooms and 4 luxurious suites, each with air conditioning, TV, minibar, and phone. There's also a heated pool, tennis courts, and a sauna. A double costs 720 to 1,750 F ($136.80 to $332.50), rising to 1,900 to 2,500 F ($361 to $475) for a suite; breakfast is 110 F ($20.90) extra.

Châteay de Prunoy

89120 Charny. ☎ **86-63-66-91.** 13 rms, 6 suites. TEL. 650–700 F ($123.50–$133.00) double; 850–900 F ($161.50–$171) suite. Breakfast 50 F ($9.50) extra. AE, MC, V. Parking free. Closed Jan–Mar 1. From Auxerre, head north on N6 (toward Sens) for 17 miles to Joigny; then drive 12 miles west of Joigny on D950; the hostelry is 2 miles north of Charny.

In 1510, Guillaume de Crève-Coeur (William the Broken-Hearted) built a gothic château on 15,000 acres of parkland. In 1721 parts of the building were demolished and rebuilt in the style then popular. Today the château welcomes diners and overnight guests into a gracious antique world. Surrounded by about 120 acres of forested park, the establishment is calm, quiet, and eminently respectable.

2 Vézelay

135 miles SE of Paris, 32 miles S of Auxerre

Vézelay, a living museum of French antiquity, stands frozen in time. For many, the town is the high point of their trip through Burgundy. Because it contained what was believed to be the tomb of St. Mary Magdalene, that "beloved and pardoned sinner," it was once one of the great pilgrimage sites of the Christian world.

On a hill 360 feet above the countryside, the town is known for its ramparts and houses with sculptured doorways, corbelled staircases, and mullioned windows. The site of Vézelay was originally an abbey founded by Girart de Roussillon, a comte de Bourgogne (troubadours were fond of singing of his exploits). It was consecrated in 878 by Pope John VIII.

On March 31, 1146, St. Bernard preached the Second Crusade there; in 1190 the town was the rendezvous point for the Third Crusade, drawing such personages as Richard the Lion-Hearted and King Philippe-Auguste of France. Later, St. Louis of France came here several times on pilgrimages.

Park outside the town hall and walk through the medieval streets, past flower-filled gardens. After about a quarter of a mile you'll reach the **Basilique Ste-Madeleine** (☎ **86-33-24-36**). The largest and most famous romanesque church in France, this basilica is only 10 yards shorter than Notre-Dame de Paris. The facade was rebuilt by Viollet-le-Duc, who restored Notre-Dame. You enter the narthex, a vestibule of large dimensions, about 4,000 square feet. Look through the main door for a tremendous view of Burgundian-romanesque glory. It's possible to visit the Carolingian crypt, where the tomb of Mary Magdalene formerly rested (today it contains some of her relics). Afterward, you can end your walk by going alongside the ancient walls and back to place du Champ-de-Foire at the lower end of town.

ESSENTIALS

GETTING THERE   Trains travel from Auxerre to nearby Sermizelles, where an infrequent bus makes the run to Vézelay. Another bus arrives in Vézelay late in the day from Avallon. Bus service to Vézelay is Monday through Saturday.

VISITOR INFORMATION   The Syndicat d'Initiative (tourist office) is on rue St-Pierre (☎ **86-33-23-69**), open April to October.

WHERE TO STAY

Le Compostelle

Place du Champ-de-Foire, 89450 Vézelay. ☎ **86-33-28-63.** Fax 86-33-34-34. 18 rms. TV TEL. 250–300 F ($47.50–$57) double. Breakfast 36 F ($6.85) extra. AE, DC, MC, V. Parking free. Closed Jan 15–Feb 15.

This clean, unpretentious, and pleasant hotel is in the center of town, midway up the hill leading to the famous basilica. Despite the building's modernization, many of the old ceiling beams were left intact. There's no restaurant; breakfast is the only meal served.

Poste et Lion d'Or

Place du Champ-de-Foire, 89450 Vézelay. ☎ **86-33-21-23.** Fax 86-32-30-92. 39 rms. TEL. 330–610 F ($62.70–$115.95) double. Breakfast 44 F ($8.35) extra. AE, MC, V. Parking 35 F ($6.65). Closed Nov 15–Apr 1.

Letters, She Wrote

Some writers record majestic accounts of events that shape the course of history. Others record lists of domestic minutiae that, when compiled, help unlock the psyche of an era. France considers the latter great literary artists and reveres their memories as illustrators of the values and priorities of their day.

The 17th century produced the finest example of a writer who triumphed over minutiae: Mme de Sévigné (née Marie de Rabutin-Chantal; 1626–96), who after her husband's 1651 death devoted herself to her two children, especially her daughter, Françoise Marguerite, the not-too-appreciative comtesse de Grignan. To the comtesse, who lived in Provence, she wrote a flood of letters on all aspects of life, full of witty comments. Compiled after Mme de Sévigné's death, these missives have become the elegant apex of the nuanced art of letter-writing. Madame de Sévigné spent her youth at the Château of Bourbilly and is one of the most famous writers associated with Burgundy.

Every French student is introduced to the conversational style of the *ancien régime* through Mme de Sévigné's insightful account of personalities in Paris, at Versailles, or at her country estate in Brittany. Part of the allure of these letters is their use of flawless upper-class French. Equally important is the marquise's delightful point of view about the details of the world of the well-bred of her time: everything from the plumpness of a quail served at a dinner party to gossip about the social embarrassment of a rival. Too clever (and too politically savvy) to express in writing her real opinions about the French kings or any of her powerful peers, the marquise offers a bejeweled account of small-scale domestic concerns.

Madame de Sévigné died at her daughter's château, supposedly from exhaustion after nursing her sick daughter back to health, and was buried in the local chapel. During the Revolution, her body was exhumed and her skull sent to Paris for a phrenological examination. It has never been recovered.

In 1770, just before that revolution, an English noblewoman who made a literary pilgrimage to the grave of her mentor said this: "I am so proud to be here that I feel inclined to sit up all night and write letters, if for no other reason than that they might bear the château's address. My imagination is so filled with Mme de Sévigné that at every moment I expect to see her before me!"

A local monument and former postal station, the Poste et Lion d'Or is a first-class establishment with reasonable rates. The food is exceptional—especially the escargots de Bourgogne in chablis and stuffed trout with herbs. It's classic Burgundian and not experimental at all. Fixed-priced menus cost 115 F ($21.85), 200 F ($38), and 300 F ($57). The restaurant is closed on Monday and Tuesday at lunch.

Résidence Hôtel le Pontot

Place du Pontot, 89450 Vézelay. ☎ **86-33-24-40**. Fax 86-33-30-05. 8 rms, 3 suites. TEL. 600–850 F ($114.05–$161.60) double; 800–950 F ($152.10–$180.60) suite. Breakfast 60 F ($10.80) extra. DC, MC, V. Parking 50 F ($9.50). Closed Nov–Easter.

Near the basilica, this tastefully renovated medieval structure is Vézelay's other leading hotel. The rooms are decorated in a romantic French style—at times not to everyone's taste but a lovely attempt at creating a cozy homelike environment.

It has a charming walled garden for breakfast and bar service but no restaurant. English is spoken.

WHERE TO DINE

✪ L'Espérance

St-Père-sous-Vézelay, 89450 Vézelay. ☎ **86-33-39-10.** Fax 86-33-26-15. Reservations required. Main courses 240–500 F ($45.60–$95); fixed-price menus 630–840 F ($119.75–$159.70). AE, DC, MC, V. May–Nov, Wed 7:30–9:30pm, Thurs–Mon noon–2pm and 7:30–9:30pm; Dec–Apr, Thurs–Mon noon–2pm and 7:30–9:30pm. Closed Feb 15–Mar 15. Take D957 1¼ miles south of Vézelay. FRENCH.

L'Espérance is the most celebrated restaurant in Burgundy, one of the best in the world. Marc and Françoise Meneau began with what had been a family bakery in a stone farmhouse. Marc is the self-taught son of a village harness maker; Françoise helped decorate the exquisite public rooms, the elegant marble guest rooms, and the dining room with its flagstone floors, Oriental rugs, high windows, and garden view. The complex consists of a main building (with the restaurant) and three outbuildings (with 34 rooms and six suites).

In the restaurant you're offered superb fare like cromesquis (liquefied foie gras, which you eat whole) or ambrosia of poultry with truffles and foie gras. As for dessert, you'll beg them for their recipe for orange soufflé pie.

Double rooms cost 660 to 1,400 F ($125.45 to $266.15); suites run 1,650 to 2,800 F ($313.70 to $532.30).

3 Avallon

133 miles SE of Paris, 32 miles SE of Auxerre

This old fortified town is shielded behind its ancient ramparts, upon which you can stroll. A medieval atmosphere still permeates Avallon, and you'll find many 15th- and 16th-century houses. At the town gate on Grande'Rue Aristide-Briand is a **clock tower** from 1460. The romanesque **Eglise St-Lazarus** dates from the 12th century and has two interesting doorways. The church is said to have received the head of St. Lazarus in 1000. This turned Avallon into a pilgrimage site. Today Avallon is mainly visited because it's a gastronomic highlight of Burgundy, as reflected by our following recommendations.

ESSENTIALS

GETTING THERE   Avallon is connected by rail to Paris and the rest of France by about half a dozen daily trains. Seven trains arrive daily from Paris (trip time: 3 hr.), costing 145 F ($27.55) one way, and six trains pull in from Dijon daily (trip time: 3 hr.), costing 150 F ($28.50) one way.

VISITOR INFORMATION   The Office de Tourisme is at 4–6 rue Bocquillot (☎ 86-34-14-19).

WHERE TO STAY & DINE

✪ Château de Vault-de-Lugny

A Vault de Lugny, 89200 Avallon. ☎ **86-34-07-86.** Fax 86-34-16-36. 5 rms, 6 junior suites, 1 suite. TV TEL. 700–1,200 F ($133.05–$228.10) double; 1,500–2,200 F ($285.15–$418.25) suite. Rates include breakfast. AE, V. Parking free. Closed Nov 13–Mar. Take D957 from Avallon; turn right in Pontaubert and follow the signs to the château; Vault-de-Lugny is about 2 miles away.

At this Relais & Châteaux halfway between Avallon and Vézelay, Matherat Audan and his daughter, Elisabeth, welcome you. This 16th-century château is encircled by a grassy moat, and on the grounds are a fortress tower and peacocks. Personal service is a hallmark here (two staff members to every guest). The rooms and suites are often sumptuous, with half-tester or canopied beds and antique furnishings and fireplaces. You order cocktails in an ornate salon, then proceed to dinner by candlelight.

Moulin des Ruats

Vallée du Cousin, 89200 Avallon. ☎ **86-34-07-14.** Fax 86-31-65-47. 24 rms. TEL. 300–650 F ($57–$123.55) double. Breakfast 50 F ($9.50) extra. DC, MC, V. Parking free. Closed Nov 15–Feb 15. Take D427 2 miles outside town.

On the banks of the Cousin, this country inn is enchanting, with rooms that are simultaneously rustic and modern. The elegant restaurant, with a terrace, serves freshwater fish. In addition to the excellent menu, costing 240 F ($45.60), the hostellerie offers a fine wine list. The restaurant is outstanding, certainly more impressive than the hotel it's in. The meals are discreetly balanced, and everything has a certain zest and flavor.

4 Autun

182 miles SE of Paris, 53 miles SW of Dijon, 30 miles W of Beaune

Deep in burgundy country, Autun is one of the oldest towns in France. In the days of the Roman Empire it was often called "the other Rome." Some relics still stand, including the remains of a theater, the **Théâtre Romain,** the largest in Gaul, holding some 15,000 spectators. It was nearly 500 feet in diameter. Outside the town you can see the quadrangular tower of the **Temple of Janus** rising incongruously 80 feet over the plain.

Once Autun was an important link on the road from Lyon to Boulogne, as reflected by the **Porte d'Arroux,** with two large archways used now for cars and two smaller ones for pedestrians. It's in the northwest section, rising 55 feet. Also exceptional is the **Porte St-André** (St. Andrew's Gate), about a quarter of a mile northwest of the Roman theater. Rising 65 feet, it, too, has four doorways and is surmounted by a gallery of 10 arcades.

The crowning achievement, however, is the **Cathédrale St-Lazare,** on the highest point in Autun, built in 1120 to house the relics of St. Lazarus. On the facade, the tympanum in the central portal depicts the Last Judgment—a triumph of romanesque sculpture. Inside, a painting by Ingres depicts the martyrdom of St. Symphorien, who was killed in Autun. In summer you can climb the tower and from there enjoy a good view over the town for 3 F (55¢); it's open daily from 9am to 5pm.

The **Musée Rolin,** 3 rue des Bancs (☎ **85-52-35-71**), is in a 15th-century mansion built for Nicolas Rolin, who became a famous lawyer in his day (b. 1380). An easy walk from the cathedral, the museum displays a fine collection of Burgundian romanesque sculpture, as well as paintings and archeological mementos. From the original Rolin collection are exhibited the *Nativity* by the Maître de Moulins, along with a statue that's a masterpiece of 15th-century work, *Our Lady of Autun.* The museum is open April to September, daily from 9:30am to noon and 1:30 to 6pm; in October, Monday and Wednesday to Saturday from 10am to noon and 2 to 5pm and Sunday from 2 to 5pm; November to March, Monday and

Wednesday to Saturday from 10am to noon and 2 to 4pm and Sunday from 2:30 to 5pm. Admission is 14 F ($2.65) for adults and 7 F ($1.35) for children.

ESSENTIALS

GETTING THERE   Autun has rail and bus connections to the rest of France. Four trains per day arrive from Paris, costing 200 F ($38) one way, and two trains pull in from Lyon, costing 180 F ($34.20) one way. By car, take D3 from St-Léger-sous-Beuvray.

VISITOR INFORMATION   The Office de Tourisme is at 3 av. Charles-de-Gaulle (☎ 85-86-30-00).

WHERE TO STAY & DINE

Hostellerie du Vieux Moulin

Porte d'Arroux, 71400 Autun. ☎ **85-51-10-90.** Fax 85-86-32-15. 16 rms. TEL. 330 F ($62.70) double. Breakfast 65 F ($12.35) extra. AE, MC, V. Parking free. Closed Feb and Dec.

Not only does this hostelry contain the best restaurant in Autun, but also it's a good bargain for lodging. It has a warm ambience, with simple but clean rooms. In summer you can sit at a table overlooking the garden and a tiny millstream. Most guests order the 90-F ($17.10), 150-F ($28.50), or 180-F ($34.20) fixed-price menus, though a huge *gastronomique* special is featured for 250 F ($47.50). The dining room is open Tuesday to Saturday from noon to 2pm and 7:30 to 9pm and Sunday from noon to 2pm.

Ursulines

14 rue Rivault, 71400 Autun. ☎ **85-52-68-00.** Fax 85-86-23-07. 38 rms. TV TEL. 450 F ($85.50) double. Breakfast 60 F ($11.40) extra. AE, DC, V.

The best hotel in Autun, the Ursulines (in a former convent) offers attractively decorated rooms with views of the countryside and the distant Morvan mountains. The hotel is also known for its cuisine, pleasing to both the eye and the palate. The results are sometimes more interesting than the menu suggests. The wine list needs expanding.

5 Beaune

196 miles SE of Paris, 24 miles SW of Dijon

This is the capital of the burgundy wine country and also one of the best-preserved medieval cities in the district, with a girdle of ramparts. Its history goes back more than 2,000 years. Beaune was a Gallic sanctuary, then later a Roman town. Until the 14th century it was the residence of the ducs de Bourgogne. When the last duke, Charles the Bold, died in 1447, Beaune was annexed by Louis XI.

ESSENTIALS

GETTING THERE   Beaune has good railway connections from Dijon, Lyon, and Paris. From Paris, there are two TGV trains per day (trip time: 2 hr.), costing 215 F ($40.85) one way. From Lyon, six trains arrive per day (trip time 2 hr.), costing 110 F ($20.90) one way; and from Dijon, 12 trains per day (trip time: 25 min.), costing 35 F ($6.65) one way.

If you're driving, note that Beaune is a few miles from the junction of four superhighways that fan out—A6, A31, A36, and N6.

VISITOR INFORMATION The Office de Tourisme is on rue de l'Hôtel-Dieu (☎ 80-26-21-30).

SEEING THE TOP ATTRACTIONS

The perfectly preserved 15th-century Hôtel Dieu, on place de la Halle, is one of the world's richest working hospitals, since its vineyards produce renowned wines like Aloxe-Corton and Meursault. (On the third Sunday of November the wines are auctioned.) The gothic building also houses the **Musée de l'Hôtel-Dieu** (☎ 80-24-75-75), which displays Flemish-Burgundian art, such as Roger van der Weyden's 1443 polyptych *The Last Judgment*. In the Chambre des Pauvres (Room of the Poor) you'll find painted, broken-barrel, timbered vaulting, with mostly authentic furnishings. The museum is open daily: April to November 17 from 9am to 6:30pm, and November 18 to March from 9 to 11:30am and 2 to 5:30pm. Admission is 27 F ($5.15) for adults and 21 F ($4) for children.

North of the Hôtel Dieu, the **Collégiale Notre-Dame** is an 1120 Burgundian romanesque church. Some remarkable tapestries illustrating scenes from the life of Mary are displayed in the sanctuary. They may be viewed from Easter to Christmas.

The **Musée des Beaux-Arts et Musée Marey,** in the Hôtel de Ville (town hall) (☎ 80-24-56-92), contains a rich Gallo-Roman archeological section, including burial stones, statuary, and pottery. The main gallery of paintings has works from the 16th to the 19th century, like Flemish primitives. Sculptures from the Middle Ages and the Renaissance are also displayed. A larger part of the museum honors Beaune physiologist Etienne Jules Marey, who discovered the principles of the cinema long before 1895. The museum is open daily: June to September from 9:30am to 1pm and 2 to 6pm, and April, May, and October to November 21 from 2 to 6pm; closed November 22 to March. Admission to this museum is included with the charge to the Musée du Vin (below).

Housed in the former mansion of the ducs de Bourgogne, the **Musée du Vin de Bourgogne,** rue d'Enfer (☎ 80-22-08-19), traces the evolution of the region's wine making. The collection of tools, objets d'art, and documents is contained in 15th- and 16th-century rooms. A collection of wine presses is displayed in a 14th-century press house. The museum is open daily from 9:30am to 6pm (until 5:30pm November to March). Admission is 20 F ($3.80) for adults and 7 F ($1.35) for children.

WHERE TO STAY

⑨ Hostellerie de Bretonnière

43 faubourg Bretonnière, 21200 Beaune. ☎ **80-22-15-77.** Fax 80-22-72-54. 27 rms. TEL. 295–395 F ($56.05–$75.10) double. Breakfast 36 F ($6.85) extra. MC, V. Parking free. Bus 1.

This hotel is the best bargain in town: It's well run, with clean and quiet rooms, 24 of which contain TVs. The rooms in the rear are the cheapest and most tranquil, though most visitors prefer those overlooking the garden. There's no restaurant, but a continental breakfast is available.

Hôtel de la Poste

1 bd. Georges-Clemenceau, 21200 Beaune. ☎ **80-22-08-11.** Fax 80-24-19-71. 23 rms, 7 suites. TV TEL. 500–1,000 F ($95.05–$190.10) double; from 1,200 F ($228.10) suite. Breakfast 65 F ($12.35) extra. AE, DC, MC, V. Parking 50 F ($9.50).

Outside the town fortifications, this traditional hotel has been completely renovated. Some rooms, overlooking either the ramparts or the vineyards, have brass beds, TVs, and air conditioning. Many are just too petite, however. Menu specialties here include chicken fricassée with tarragon and sole in court bouillon with beurre blanc. The bar and restaurant are in the belle époque style.

WHERE TO DINE

✪ Bernard Morillon

31 rue Maufoux. ☎ **80-24-12-06.** Reservations recommended. Main courses 145–230 F ($27.55–$43.70); fixed-price meals 160 F ($30.40), 290 F ($55.10), 380 F ($72.20) and 450 F ($85.55). AE, DC, MC, V. Tues 7:30–10pm, Wed–Sun noon–2:30pm and 7:30–10pm. Closed Jan 28–Mar 5. FRENCH.

You'll dine here, in a Directoire/Louis XV room, on specialties like gratin of cray-fish tails, an unusual version of tournedos made with fish served with a fumet of red wine, sweetbreads with saffron seasoning, and deboned Bresse pigeon stuffed with foie gras and truffles. Bernard Morillon has a distinctive style, and his food always pleases. The desserts are sumptuous.

✪ Relais de Saulx

6 rue Louis-Very. ☎ **80-22-01-35.** Reservations required for large groups. Main courses 110–190 F ($20.90–$36.10); fixed-price menus 110 F ($20.90), 160 F ($30.40), 220 F ($41.80), 285 F ($54.15), and 400 F ($76). MC, V. Tues–Sat noon–2pm and 7:30–9:30pm, Sun noon–2pm. Closed Dec and a week in June. FRENCH.

The Relais de Saulx is decorated with heavy timbers, velvet, and paintings. Chef Jean-Louis Monnoir prepares a sophisticated combination of traditional bour-guignon cuisine and up-to-date adaptations, like salmon with endive and pigeon with foie gras. We still prefer Bernard Morillon (above), though Monnoir richly deserves his Michelin star. His presentation is excellent, and sometimes flavors elicit gasps of delight. The wine list has been carefully chosen.

NEARBY ACCOMMODATIONS & DINING

✪ Hostellerie de Levernois

Route de Verdun-sur-les-Doubs, Levernois, 21200 Beaune. ☎ **80-24-73-58.** Fax 80-22-78-00. Reservations required. Main courses 120–250 F ($22.80–$47.50); fixed-price menus 380–520 F ($72.20–$98.85). AE, DC, MC, V. Wed 7–9:30pm, Thurs–Mon noon–2pm and 7–9:30pm. FRENCH.

Jean Crotet and his sons, Christophe and Guillaume, offer grand cuisine in an idyl-lic setting three miles southeast of Beaune. The kitchen prepares such specialties as salmon smoked on the grounds and snails in puff pastry. Three kinds of fish en papillote are offered as a main course. There's no virtuoso technique demonstrated here, just a powerful knowledge of first-class ingredients and what to do with them. If only the staff didn't act so grand.

The inn rents 14 beautiful rooms—each with TV and phone—in a recently constructed pavilion. Doubles cost 950 F ($180.50). Two suites rent for 1,500 F ($285.15). Breakfast is 90 F ($17.10) extra.

6 Gevrey-Chambertin

194 miles SE of Paris, 17 miles NE of Beaune, 8 miles SW of Dijon

This town was immortalized by writer Gaston Roupnel. Typical of the villages of the Côte d'Or, Gevrey added Chambertin to its name to honor its most famous vineyard.

In the village stands the **Château de Gevrey-Chambertin** (☎ 80-34-36-13), constructed around the 10th century by the lords of Vergy. The castle had fallen into disrepair by the 13th century but was restored and expanded by the powerful monks of Cluny, who retained the corkscrew staircases whose unevenly spaced steps, now polished slick by the passage of thousands of feet, sometimes prove difficult to negotiate. The great hall is impressive, with exposed ceiling beams. The guardsmen's room in the watchtower and the collections of aging wines in the vaulted cellars are part of the château's charm.

Between April 15 and November 15, half-hour guided tours are given in English, daily from 10am to noon and 2 (2:30 on Sunday) to 6pm. In winter, tours are given from 10:30am to noon and 2:30 to 6:30pm. The château is closed Sunday morning. Admission is 20 F ($3.80) for adults and 10 F ($1.90) for children 7 to 12; 6 and under free.

The village church with its romanesque doorway dates from the 14th century.

ESSENTIALS

GETTING THERE   South of Burgundy is the Côte d'Or (golden slope), a famous wine-growing district. Leave Dijon via D122 (grandly called the Route des Grands-Crus) and follow it south until the junction with N74 at Vougeot. Along the way the most notable wine-producing town you'll go through is Gevrey-Chambertin.

VISITOR INFORMATION   The Office de Tourisme, place de la Mairie (☎ 80-34-38-40), is open from May to October only.

WHERE TO STAY

Hôtel Les-Grands-Crus
Route des Grands-Crus, 21220 Gevrey-Chambertin. ☎ **80-34-34-15.** Fax 80-51-89-07. 24 rms. TEL. 430 F ($81.70) double. Breakfast 45 F ($8.55) extra. MC, V. Parking free. Closed Dec–Feb 25.

This charming hotel, near a tiny 12th-century château, is run by helpful Mme Farnier, who speaks English. The rooms, some of which have Louis XV furnishings, provide views of vineyards and a 12th-century church. The hotel does not have a restaurant but serves a continental breakfast. Regional wines also are available.

Les Terroirs
28 route de Dijon, 21220 Gevrey-Chambertin. ☎ **80-34-30-76.** Fax 80-34-11-79. 23 rms. TV TEL. 350–480 F ($66.50–$91.20) double. Breakfast 45 F ($8.55) extra. AE, DC, MC, V.

Les Terroirs is a good value, offering clean and well-furnished rooms in a peaceful establishment. There's a bar, but a generous breakfast is the only meal served. The hotel is open all year.

WHERE TO DINE

✪ Les Millésimes
25 rue de l'Eglise and rue de Meixville. ☎ **80-51-84-24.** Reservations required. Main courses 110–185 F ($20.90–$35.15); fixed-price menu 295 F ($56.05); *menu dégustation* 560 F ($106.40). AE, DC, MC, V. Wed 7:30–9:30pm, Thurs–Mon 12:30–1:30pm and 7:30pm. Closed Dec 25–Jan 25. FRENCH.

Monique Sangoy and her children operate this outstanding restaurant in the courtyard of what used to be a 17th-century warehouse for local wines. House specialties include a salad of foie gras, honey duck flavored with spices, and, for dessert, a soufflé dropped in a fruit syrup. There's a splendid wine list, with more than 2,000 choices. The place has found its groove in town and attracts both local gastronomes and the visiting wine chic from Paris. The cuisine is refined, of the highest quality, and enjoyable. It would be even more enjoyable if the chilly staff would warm up a bit.

La Rôtisserie du Chambertin

Rue Chambertin. ☎ **80-34-33-20.** Reservations required. Main courses 120–160 F ($22.80–$30.40); fixed-price menus 260–410 F ($49.40–$77.90). MC, V. Tues–Sat noon–1:30pm and 7–9pm, Sun noon–1:30pm. Closed Feb and Aug 7–15. FRENCH.

The entrance to this popular regional restaurant is marked only with the menu. Visitors must first pass through a museum devoted to the history of barrel-making, in honor of the owner's great-grandfather, who was the town cooper on this very spot. Once you arrive, be sure to take advantage of the inn's wines. Chambertin has been called "the wine for moments of great decision." Perhaps that's why Napoléon always took it on his campaigns—even to Moscow. Though the wine list is not extensive, it includes the best of recent vintages. The chef prepares the regional classics, including coq au vin. Perhaps you'll order a large sole grilled to perfection on an open wood fire or "winegrower's beef."

7 Dijon

194 miles SE of Paris, 199 miles NE of Lyon

Dijon is known overseas mainly for its mustard. In the center of the Côte d'Or, it's the ancient capital of Burgundy. In this town good food is always accompanied by great wine. Between meals you can enjoy Dijon's art and architecture.

The remains of the Ancien Palais des Ducs de Bourgogne have been turned into the **Musée des Beaux-Arts,** place de la Sainte-Chapelle (☎ **80-74-52-09**). One of France's oldest and richest museums, it contains exceptional sculpture, ducal kitchens from the mid-1400s (with great chimneypieces), a collection of European paintings from the 14th through the 19th century, and modern French paintings and sculptures. Take special note of the Salle des Gardes, the banqueting hall of the old palace built by Philip the Good. The grave of Philip the Bold was built between 1385 and 1411 and is one of the best in France. A reclining figure rests on a slab of black marble, surrounded by 41 mourners. The museum is open Monday and Wednesday from 10am to 6pm, Sunday from 10am to 12:30pm and 2 to 6pm. Admission is 15 F ($2.85).

A mile from the center of town on N5 stands **Chartreuse de Champmol,** the Carthusian monastery built by Philip the Bold as a burial place; it's now a psychiatric hospital. Much of it was destroyed during the Revolution, but you can see the Moses Fountain in the gardens designed by Sluter at the end of the 14th century. The gothic entrance is superb.

Major churches to visit in Dijon include the **Cathédrale St-Bénigne,** a 13th-century abbey church in the Burgundian-gothic style; the **Eglise St-Michel,** in the Renaissance style; and the **Eglise Notre-Dame,** built in the 13th century in the Burgundian-gothic style, with a facade decorated partly with gargoyles. On the Jaquemart clock, the hour is struck by a mechanical family.

ESSENTIALS

GETTING THERE Dijon has excellent air, rail, bus, and highway connections to the rest of Europe. Five TGV trains arrive from Paris each day (trip time: 1^1/$_2$ hr.). Trains arrive from Lyon every hour (trip time: 2 hr.).

VISITOR INFORMATION The Office de Tourisme is at 34 rue des Forges (☎ 80-30-35-39) and at place Darcy (☎ 80-43-42-12).

WHERE TO STAY

Hostellerie du Chapeau-Rouge

5 rue Michelet, 21000 Dijon. ☎ **80-30-28-10**, or 800/528-1234 in the U.S. and Canada. Fax **80-30-33-89**. 31 rms, 1 suite. MINIBAR TV TEL. 635–760 F ($120.70–$144.45) double; from 1,650 F ($313.65) suite. Breakfast 66 F ($12.55) extra. AE, DC, MC, V. Parking 16 F ($3.05).

This is a Dijon landmark, with an acclaimed restaurant. The hotel is filled with 19th-century antiques and boasts rooms with modern conveniences and comfortable furnishings; 10 are air-conditioned. Some of the baths have Jacuzzis. Since no other hotel restaurant here serves comparable food, you may want to visit even if you're not a guest. The hotel has a supercharged chef who serves Burgundian favorites but has broken new ground with mouth-watering fare, the specialties depending on what's good in any given season.

Hôtel Ibis Central

3 place Grangier, 21000 Dijon. ☎ **80-30-44-00.** Fax 80-30-77-12. 90 rms. TV TEL. 370 F ($70.30) double. Breakfast 40 F ($7.60) extra. AE, DC, MC, V. Parking 30 F ($5.70).

On a busy downtown square, this attractive hotel offers comfort in its soundproof rooms, which were recently renovated. The Central Grill Rôtisserie offers candlelit dinner and a panoramic view of Dijon. Meals begin at 190 F ($36.10).

Hôtel Sofitel–La Cloche

14 place Darcy, 21000 Dijon. ☎ **80-30-12-32.** Fax 80-30-04-15. 76 rms, 4 suites. A/C MINIBAR TV TEL. 510–720 F ($96.95–$136.10) double; from 1,290 F ($245.20) suite. Breakfast 60 F ($11.40) extra. AE, DC, MC, V.

This 15th-century historic monument is in the center of town. The sophisticated interior features Oriental rugs and a pink-and-gray marble floor. The lobby bar is one of the most elegant places in town, with a view of the garden shared by an adjoining glassed-in tea room. The much-needed renovation program is proceeding. The staff remains blasé and the service is very slow, but the Sofitel promises changes for the better. The independently run Jean-Pierre Billoux restaurant is recommended below.

WHERE TO DINE

✪ Jean-Pierre Billoux

In the Hôtel Sofitel–La Cloche, 14 place Darcy. ☎ **80-30-11-00.** Reservations required. Main courses 180–250 F ($34.20–$47.50); fixed-price meals 200 F ($38) (lunch only), 350 F ($66.50), and 480 F ($91.25). AE, MC, V. Tues–Sat noon–2pm and 7:30–9:30pm, Sun noon–2pm. Closed two weeks in Feb–Mar. BURGUNDIAN/FRENCH.

One of the finest in Burgundy, this restaurant is in the Sofitel, beneath the soaring stone vaults of an underground wine cellar. Its chef/owner, Jean-Pierre Billoux, prepares deceptively simple meals that have won acclaim throughout Burgundy. Menu items might include roast chicken steeped in liquefied almonds, terrine of

Dijon

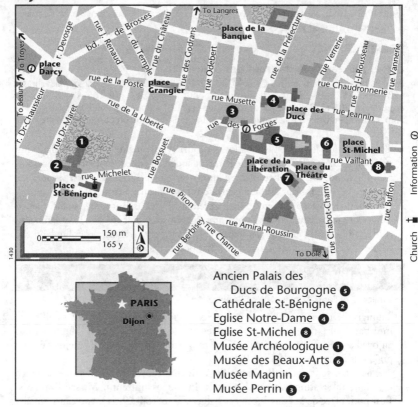

Ancien Palais des
  Ducs de Bourgogne **5**
Cathédrale St-Bénigne **2**
Eglise Notre-Dame **4**
Eglise St-Michel **8**
Musée Archéologique **1**
Musée des Beaux-Arts **6**
Musée Magnin **7**
Musée Perrin **3**

pigeon, guinea fowl with capers, or thick-sliced filet of sole served on a bed of tomato-infused polenta. Some recently sampled and more innovative courses include a gâteau of guinea fowl with artichokes and morels and John Dory with thyme oil and a confit of fennel. The array of wines will be a joy to any connoisseur. *Warning:* The Sofitel is trying to evict the restaurant from its present premises. If it's forced to move, it will have the same phone number—confirm this when making a reservation.

La Toison d'Or

18 rue Ste-Anne. ☎ **80-30-73-52.** Reservations required. Main courses 75–155 F ($14.25–$29.45); fixed-price menus 160 F ($30.40), 195 F ($37.05), and 250 F ($47.50). AE, DC, MC, V. Mon–Sat noon–1:30pm and 7–9:30pm, Sun noon–1:30pm. Closed Aug 8–23. FRENCH.

This elegantly rustic restaurant offers some of the best food in Burgundy. Upon entering you'll be offered a tour (in English) of the adjoining wine museum and medieval buildings. Included are grisly depictions of medieval slayings and Carolingian tortures, as well as a look at everything connected to local wine making. Amid stone walls, Oriental rugs, and Louis XIII chairs, you'll then enjoy specialties like sautéed duck livers and sweetbreads in a spinach salad, incredibly smooth foie gras, half-cooked salmon filet in a delightful bitter sauce, and duckling filet doused in liver sauce with truffles. The classic Burgundian cookery has been updated, with more refined sauces. The wine list is extensive, with many moderately priced vintages.

NEARBY DINING

✪ Joël Perreaut's Restaurant des Gourmets

8 rue Puits-de-Têt, Marsannay-la-Côte. ☎ **80-52-16-32.** Reservations required. Main courses 123–195 F ($23.35–$37.05); fixed-price menus 135–220 F ($25.65–$41.80); *menu dégustation* 380 F ($72.20). AE, DC, MC, V. Tues–Sat 12:15–2pm and 7–9:30pm, Sun 12:15–2pm. Closed Jan. Drive 4 miles south of Dijon, to the first village on Burgundy's Wine Road. FRENCH.

This restaurant is ample justification for journeying outside Dijon to a charming stone village. After Joël and Nicole Perreaut added an annex, modern kitchens, and a dining room, the place became well known as one of Burgundy's best restaurants. (Forget the awful decor and concentrate on the cuisine.) Amid flowers, candles, and original watercolors, enjoy such excellent dishes as Burgundy snails, filet of John Dory in balsamic-vinegar sauce, and filet of roast pigeon. The roast lamb also is marvelous. Joël Perreaut is a remarkable chef. Service is always polite, and the whole place is so discreet—except for that decor.

8 Saulieu

155 miles SE of Paris, 47 miles NW of Beaune

Though the town is fairly interesting, its gastronomy has given this small place international fame. On the boundaries of Morvan and Auxois, the town has enjoyed a reputation for cooking since the 17th century. Even Mme de Sévigné praised it in her letters. So did Rabelais.

The main sight is the **Basilique St-Andoche,** on place de la Fontaine, which has some interesting decorated capitals. In the art museum, **Musée François-Pompon,** place de la Fontaine at rue Sallier (☎ 80-64-19-51), you can see many works by François Pompon, the well-known sculptor of animals. His bull, considered his masterpiece, stands on a plaza off N6 at the entrance to Saulieu. The museum is open Wednesday to Monday from 10am to 12:30pm and 2 to 5:30pm. Admission is 20 F ($3.80) for adults and 15 F ($2.85) for children.

ESSENTIALS

GETTING THERE Saulieu has a railway station (northeast of the town center) linked to the French railway network. If you're driving, take N80 from Montbard.

VISITOR INFORMATION The Maison du Tourisme is at 24 rue d'Argentine (☎ 80-64-00-21).

WHERE TO STAY & DINE

✪ Hôtel de la Côte d'Or

2 rue d'Argentine, 21210 Saulieu. ☎ **80-64-07-66.** Fax 80-64-08-92. 15 rms, 7 suites. TV TEL. 330–980 F ($62.70–$186.30) double; 1,600–1,900 F ($304.15–$361.20) suite. Breakfast 110 F ($20.90) extra. AE, DC, MC, V. Parking free.

This former stagecoach stop is an excellent choice—one of the finest in France. Though chef Alexandre Dumaine, the man who made this a world-famous restaurant, is long gone, inventive Bernard Louiseau now works hard to maintain his standards. (According to most critics, chef Louiseau has surpassed all previous standards, becoming one of the culinary stars of Europe.) The cooking is less traditional, leaning away from heavy sauces toward *cuisine légère*. The emphasis is on bringing out maximum taste with no excess fat or sugar. All the great burgundies are on the wine list. Fixed-price menus cost 580 to 780 F ($110.20 to $148.20), with a fixed-price lunch at 350 F ($66.50).

If you want to stay overnight, you'll find guest rooms with everything from Empire to Louis XV decor. Your bed will be comfortable, though it's likely to be 200 years old.

Hôtel de la Poste

1 rue Grillot, 21210 Saulieu. ☎ **80-64-05-67.** Fax 80-64-10-82. 48 rms. A/C MINIBAR TV TEL. 355–455 F ($67.45–$86.45) double. Breakfast 35 F ($6.65) extra. AE, DC, V. Parking free.

Originally a 17th-century postal relay station, the Hôtel de la Poste has been completely renovated by Guy Virlouvet. The rooms are comfortable and sometimes have courtyard views. In the dining room (open to nonguests as well as guests) specialties include escalope of sea perch with baby vegetables, shrimp with saffron and asparagus tips, filet of Charolais beef with marrow sauce, and kidneys in a sauce of aged mustard. Meals cost 98 F ($18.60), 128 F ($24.30), 148 F ($28.10), and 188 F ($35.70). Service is daily from noon to 2:30pm and 7 to 10:30pm.

NEARBY ACCOMMODATIONS & DINING

Ⓢ Auberge du Vieux Moulin

Porte de la Bourgogne, Aubigney, 70140 Pesmes. ☎ **84-31-61-61.** Fax 84-31-62-38. Reservations recommended. Main courses 115–145 F ($21.85–$27.55); fixed-price menus 100 F ($19), 200 F ($38), and 400 F ($76). AE, DC, V. Daily noon–2pm and 7:30–9pm. Closed Dec 15–Feb 15. From Dijon take D70 northeast toward Gray for 27 miles. FRENCH.

The town of Aubigney has little to recommend save for the Auberge du Vieux Moulin. The property has been in the Mirbey family since the end of the 18th century, and you'll find elegant antiques, gilt-rimmed mirrors, and sparkling table settings. Elisabeth Mirbey is one of France's outstanding *dames cuisinières*, and she (with two other chefs) was the first woman to prepare a meal in the Elysée Palace, where President Mitterrand and Françoise Sagan enjoyed her crêpes de la chandeleur en aumônière à la crème de Grand Marnier. The menu has a regional section that includes chicken suprême in a sauce flavored with Savagnin and cassoulet of Burgundy snails. The terrines are excellent, as are the duckling courses, veal kidneys, rabbit, and sweetbreads. The homemade desserts are light and delicious.

The auberge is also a good place to stay if you prefer to be away from the crowds of Dijon. There are seven rooms, five of which have a bath. A double costs 320 to 350 F ($60.80 to $66.50), plus 45 F ($8.55) for breakfast.

18 The Rhône Valley

The Rhône River is as mighty as the Saône is peaceful, and these two great rivers form a part of the French countryside that's often glimpsed only briefly by motorists rushing south to the Riviera on the thundering Mediterranean Express. But this land of mountains and rivers, linked by a good road network, invites more exploration than that: It's the home of beaujolais country; the gastronomic center of Lyon; Roman ruins, charming villages, and castles; and even the Grand Canyon of France.

It was from the Rhône Valley that Greco-Roman architecture and art made their way to the Loire Valley, the château country, and finally to Paris. The district abounds in time-mellowed inns and wonderful restaurants, offering a cuisine that's among the finest in the world. Our exploration starts in the north, which is really the southern part of Burgundy, and ends in the northern sector of Provence.

REGIONAL CUISINE Lyon and its environs are France's gastronomic capital. The cuisine here has always been more important than the rituals accompanying it. Excellent ingredients are readily available nearby—the best chicken and beef in France (from Bresse and Charolais, respectively), freshwater fish from the high lakes of the Savoy, and game from the dense forests.

Regional specialties include *quenelles de brochet* (pulverized brochet—a local whitefish—fashioned into cigar-shaped cylinders, served with buerre blanc); Lyonnaise sausages; many preparations of chicken, especially one garnished with truffles; and a fully array of pâtes and terrines, often made from wild game. One excellent dish is *pommes de terres lyonnaises* (sautéed potatoes with onions).

As for wines, some of the vineyards along the Rhône are the oldest in France, established by the ancient Greeks. The better wines are sold under the names of the specific villages that produce them: Côtes-du-Rhône-Ardèche, Côtes-du-Rhône Gigondas, Tavel, Châteauneuf-du-Pape, Muscat de Baumes-de-Venise, Condrieu, and Beaujolais. Among them, beaujolais is probably the premier young wine of France. It's intended for early consumption—the annual release of a year's vintage is truly a national event.

The Rhône Valley

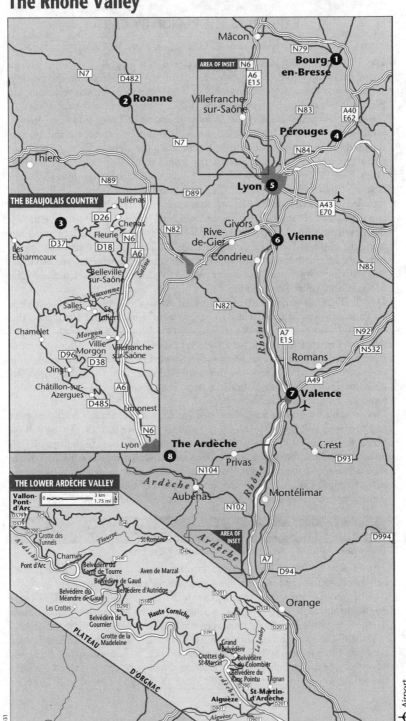

Mâcon

N79

Bourg-en-Bresse **1**

N7

D482

2 Roanne

AREA OF INSET N6

A6
E15

Villefranche-sur-Saône

N7

N83

A40
E62

Pérouges 4

N84

Thiers

N89

D89

Lyon **5**

A43
E70

THE BEAUJOLAIS COUNTRY

Juliénas

3

D26

Chénas

Fleurie

N6

D37

D18

A6

Les Écharmeaux

Belleville-sur-Saône

Vauxonne

Salles

St-Julien

Morgon

Chamelet

Villie-Morgon

Villefranche-sur-Saône

D96

D38

Oingt

Châtillon-sur-Azergues

A6

D485

Limonest

N6

Lyon

8

Givors

Rive-de-Gier

6 Vienne

Condrieu

N82

N82

N85

Rhône

A7
E15

N92

N532

Romans

A49

7 Valence

The Ardèche

Crest

D93

N104

Privas

THE LOWER ARDÈCHE VALLEY

Vallon-Pont-d'Arc

0   3 km
    1.75 mi

N

D579

D4

D579

D290

Grotte des Tunnels

D4

Tiourre

St-Remèze

D4

Ardèche

AREA OF INSET

Aubenas

N102

Montélimar

Rhône

A7

D994

Chames

D490

Pont d'Arc

Belvédère du Serre de Tourre

Aven de Marzal

D94

Belvédère de Gaud

Belvédère d'Autridge

Belvédère du Méandre de Gaud

D590

D201

Orange

Les Crottes

D290

Haute Corniche

Belvédère de Gournier

D690

D358

Grotte de la Madeleine

D290

Grand Belvédère

La Louby

D201

Grottes de St-Marcel

Belvédère du Colombier

D290

Belvédère du Ranc Pointu

Tignan

Ardèche

St-Martin-d'Ardèche

PLATEAU D'ORGNAC

Alguèze

D901

Aiguèze

D901

D201

✈ Airport

1431

EXPLORING THE REGION BY CAR

Here's how to link together the best of the region if you rent a car.

Day 1   Begin in Bourg-en-Bresse and check out its top sights, then stop for lunch at any restaurant we've recommended for a taste of the region's unrivaled poultry. From there, drive southwest along N83 for 35 miles to Lyon, where you should plan to spend two nights—even better, three. Another option is overnighting in the medieval hamlet of Pérouges, 22 miles northeast of Lyon. (Finding Pérouges is difficult, even for old francophiles; remember that it lies beside A42 and 84, near the more visible town of Meximieux.) If spending the night in Pérouges is not an option, plan to visit it as part of a day trip from Lyon.

Days 2–4   Using Lyon as a base, visit such historic/gastronomic shrines as Roanne (site of Hôtel des Frères-Troisgros) and Vienne (site of La Pyramide, founded by the late Raymond Point). Also appealing might be a drive through the vineyards of the beaujolais country, but we usually prefer to do that as part of a day's excursion from Lyon. The district's layout is suited to quick meanderings along the routes radiating east and west from A6. Roads in the district are impossibly rural and marked only with their end destinations. Nonetheless, you can enjoy a day driving toward prosperous wine meccas like Salles, Juliénas, Chenas, Villié-Morgon, and Velleville-sur-Saône.

Day 5   Drive 62 miles south of Lyon along A7 to the former Roman colony of Valence for a view of an Auvernat-romanesque cathedral built in 1095. Take this opportunity to veer west at Valence along D533 for 17 miles to the Ardèche village of Lamastre for a meal (or a night) at the Hôtel du Midi. After your meal, meander about 28 miles south along well-signposted secondary roads through some of France's last wilderness—the northern Ardèche. Opt for a night in Vals-les-Bains. Don't expect sophisticated charm: Here you'll get a taste of the almost-forgotten French provinces of long ago.

Day 6   Head southeast from Vals-les-Bains for a drive through both the upper and the lower valley of the Ardèche. Routes to navigate include driving east on N102, south on D104, and—at Vallons-sur-l'Arc—northwest to southeast for 36 miles along D920 for a high-altitude view of the Gorges of the Ardèche. Where should you spend the night after your communion with the geological awesomeness of nature? Consider the nearby ancient town of Orange, 10 miles from the point where the Gorges of the Ardèche deposit their waters into the swift Rhône.

1 Bourg-en-Bresse

264 miles SE of Paris, 21 miles from Mâcon, 38 miles NE of Lyon

The ancient capital of Bress, this farming/business center lies on the border between Burgundy and the Jura. It's a gastronomic center in the region.

Art lovers are attracted to the **Eglise de Brou,** 63 bd. de Brou (☎ 74-45-39-00), by its magnificent royal tombs. One of France's great artistic heritages, this flamboyant gothic church was built between 1506 and 1532 for Margaret of Austria, the ill-fated daughter of Emperor Maximilian. Over the ornate Renaissance doorway, the tympanum depicts Margaret and her "handsome duke," Philibert, who died when he caught cold on a hunting expedition. The initials of Philibert (sometimes known as "the Fair") and Margaret are linked by love-knots. The nave

What's Special About the Rhône Valley

Great Towns
- Lyon, the gastronomic capital of France.
- Pérouges, a virtual living medieval museum.
- Vienne, a wine center with Roman ruins and medieval monuments.

Architectural Highlights
- Eglise de Brou, at Bourg-en-Bresse, built in the flamboyant gothic style and known for its royal tombs.
- Théâtre Romain, a Roman theater at Lyon, the most ancient in France, built by order of Augustus Caesar in 15 B.C.
- Eglise St-Pierre, at Vienne, from the 5th century, one of the oldest medieval churches of France.
- Vieux Lyon, one of the finest collections of medieval and Renaissance buildings in Europe.

Gastronomic Shrines
- Paul Bocuse, a restaurant outside Lyon, home to one whom many consider the world's greatest chef.
- Hôtel des Frères-Troisgros, at Roanne, one of the major hotel dining rooms of France and part of the nation's culinary lore.
- Restaurant Pic, at Valence, one of the premier three-star restaurants of France.

Wine Routes
- The beaujolais country, 25 miles north of Lyon, with vineyard after vineyard on sunlit hillsides.

Natural Wonders
- The gorges of the Ardèche, where the Ardèche River has carved out the Grand Canyon of France, more than 950 feet deep.

Festivals
- The Biennale Internationale de la Danse, a Lyon dance festival held every two years during the first three weeks of September.

and its double aisles are admirable. Look for the ornate rood screen, decorated with basket-handle arching. Ask a guide for a tour of the choir. Rich in decorative detail, the 74 choir stalls were made out of oak, the work completed in just two years by local craftsmen.

The tombs form the church's treasure. In Carrara marble, the statues are of Philibert, who died in 1504, and Margaret, who remained faithful to his memory until her death in 1530. Another tomb is that of Marguerite de Bourbon, grandmother of François I, who died in 1483. See also the stained-glass windows, inspired by a Dürer engraving, and a retable depicting *The Seven Joys of the Madonna*.

The church is open April to September, daily from 8:30am to noon and 2 to 6pm; October to March, Monday to Friday from 10am to noon and 2 to 4:30pm and Saturday and Sunday from 10am to 12:30pm and 2 to 5pm. Admission is 26 F ($4.95) for adults and 15 F ($2.85) for children.

If time remains, see the **Eglise Notre-Dame,** off place Carriat. Begun in 1505, it contains some finely carved 16th-century stalls. There are some **15th-century houses** on rue du Palais and rue Gambetta, if you'd like to wander around town.

ESSENTIALS

GETTING THERE   The town is linked by rail and autoroute to Lyon, Dijon, and Geneva.

VISITOR INFORMATION   The Office de Tourisme is at 15 av. Alsace-Lorraine (☎ 74-22-43-11).

WHERE TO STAY

Hôtel du Prieuré
49–51 bd. de Brou, 01000, Bourg-en-Bresse. ☎ **74-22-44-60.** Fax 74-22-71-07. 14 rms, 1 suite. TV TEL. 400–550 F ($76–$104.55) double; 720 F ($136.80) suite. Breakfast 45 F ($8.55) extra. AE, DC, MC, V. Parking 60 F ($11.40).

Owned by sisters, Mmes Alby and Guerrin, this is the town's most gracious hotel. Its angled exterior is surrounded by an acre of carefully planned gardens and 400-year-old stone walls. The place is especially alluring in spring, when forsythia, lilacs, roses, and Japanese cherries fill the air with perfume. Most of the guest rooms are large and tranquil, each outfitted in Louis XV, Louis XVI, or French country rustic.

Le Logis de Brou
132 bd. de Brou, 01000 Bourg-en-Bresse. ☎ **74-22-11-55.** Fax 74-22-37-30. 30 rms. TV TEL. 290–380 F ($55.10–$72.20) double. Breakfast 38 F ($7.20) extra. AE, DC, MC, V. Parking 50 F ($9.50).

This is actually a much better hotel than its boxlike exterior suggests. The four-story building has landscaped grounds and is near the busy road running in front of the church. You register in a lobby that has a raised hearth. Each room contains well-crafted reproductions of antique furniture. Traffic noise could be a problem here.

WHERE TO DINE

Auberge Bressane
166 bd. de Brou. ☎ **74-22-22-68.** Reservations recommended. Main courses 90–190 F ($17.10–$36.10); fixed-price menus 98 F ($18.60), 160 F ($30.40), 180 F ($34.20), 220 F ($41.80), and 290 F ($55.10). AE, DC, MC, V. Daily noon–1:30pm and 7:15–9:45pm. FRENCH.

Bresse poultry is the best in France, and chef Jean-Pierre Vullin specializes in succulent volaille de Bresse, served five ways. Of course the chef knows how to prepare other courses equally well. You may enjoy a gâteau of chicken liver, crayfish gratin, or sea bass with fresh basil. You can accompany these with such regional wines as Seyssel and Montagnieu. This venerated restaurant has recently been getting bad press because of the "chilly staff." On our latest visit, however, when we arrived with a party of friends from Lyon the *patronne* was a paragon of graciousness.

Ⓢ Au Chalet de Brou
168 bd. de Brou. ☎ **74-22-26-28.** Reservations recommended. Main courses 75–130 F ($14.25–$24.70); fixed-price menus 78 F ($14.80), 98 F ($18.60), 125 F ($23.75), 160 F

($30.40), and 220 F ($41.80). MC, V. Sat–Wed noon–2pm and 7–9:30am. Closed June 1–15 and Dec 23–Jan 23. FRENCH.

You'll find good food in this restaurant across from the church. The chef emphasizes regional products and fresh ingredients. Choices include poulet de Bresse with morels and chardonnay-cream sauce, terrine of artichoke hearts, and crêpes with mussels. One critic called the food "standard," but when you're in a gastronomic enclave, *standard* takes on a different meaning.

2 The Beaujolais Country

The vineyards of beaujolais start about 25 miles north of Lyon. This wine-producing region is small—only 40 miles long and less than 10 miles wide—yet it's one of the most famous areas in the nation and has become increasingly known throughout the world because of the "beaujolais craze" that began in Paris some 30 years ago. The United States is now one of the three big world markets for beaujolais. In an average year this region produces some 30 million gallons of wine, more than 190 million bottles.

Most people don't come to the beaujolais country to visit specific sites but rather to drink the wine. There are some 180 châteaux scattered throughout this part of France, and at many of these a wine devotee can stop and sample and/or buy bottles of the beaujolais.

VILLEFRANCHE—CAPITAL OF BEAUJOLAIS

Unlike Alsace with its wine road, the beaujolais country doesn't have a clearly defined route. Motorists branch off in many directions, stopping at whatever point or wine cellar intrigues them. However, in Villefranche we advise you to go to the **Office du Tourisme,** 290 rue de Thizy, 69400 Villefranche-sur-Saône (☎ 74-68-05-18), not far from the marketplace. There you can pick up a booklet on the beaujolais country containing a regional map and giving many itineraries; it also lists some 30 villages and the wine-tasting cellars open to the public.

In Le Beaujolais—the countryside, not the wine—you'll find a fascinatingly colorful part of France: not only vineyards on sunlit hillsides but also pleasant golden cottages where the vine growers live, as well as historic houses and castles. It has been called the Land of the Golden Stones.

ST-JULIEN-SOUS-MONTMELAS

This charming village is 6¹/₂ miles northwest of Villefranche. It was the home of Claude Bernard, father of physiology, who was born here in 1813. The small stone house in which he lived—now the **Musée Claude-Bernard** (☎ 74-67-51-44)—contains mementos of the great scholar, like instruments and books that belonged to him. The museum is open Tuesday to Sunday from 9am to noon and 2 to 6pm. Admission is 12 F ($2.30) for adults and 10 F ($1.90) for children.

SALLES

If you want specific sites to visit in the area, we suggest the monastery, **Le Prieuré,** at Salles (☎ 74-67-57-39), the church and the romanesque cloister built in the 11th and 12th centuries out of mellow golden stones, plus **Le Chapitre des Chanoinesses,** the chapter house of the canonesses, erected in the 18th century. The tour through the complex takes about 1¹/₂ hours; call ahead to request a guide. Admission is free. Salles lies northwest of Villefranche.

JULIENAS

This village produces a full-bodied robust wine. People here go to the **Cellier dans l'Ancien Eglise,** the old church cellar, to sip the wine. A statue of Bacchus with some scantily clad and tipsy girlfriends looks on from what used to be the altar. It's open daily from 9:45am to noon and 2:30pm to 6:30pm (closed Tuesday from October 1 to June 1).

CHENAS

At Chenas, 3 miles south of Juliénas, you might want to schedule a lunch stop at one the best dining rooms in beaujolais country.

WHERE TO DINE

⊗ Robin

Aux Deschamps, Chénas. ☎ **85-36-72-67.** Reservations required Sun. Main courses 100–150 F ($19–$28.50); fixed-price menus 120 F ($22.80), 150 F ($28.50), 180 F ($34.20), 220 F ($41.80), 240 F ($45.60), and 340 F ($64.60). AE, DC, MC, V. Sun–Tues and Thurs noon-2pm, Fri–Sat noon-2pm and 7–9:30pm. Closed Feb. FRENCH.

In a stone-sided farmhouse, this restaurant is surrounded by the the region's famous vineyards and is the domain of Daniel Robin, who trained with the great Alain Chapel. He prepares superb regional dishes, like Bresse chicken cooked in beaujolais and the finest andouillette (chitterling sausage) we've ever sampled. His gratin of crayfish and Charolais bourguignon have been praised by connoisseurs. Your only problem may be overcrowding on a summer weekend, when seemingly half of Paris shows up.

BAGNOLS

To reach Bagnols from Lyon, head north for 15 miles (about a half-hour drive): Take A6 to the Limonest exit, then follow the signs for Limonest/Le Bourg and turn left at the crossroads marked VILLEFRANCHE N6. Turn left once more onto D485 toward Lozanne/Le Bois d'Oingt. Go for 9 miles and take a right onto D38 heading for Bagnols.

WHERE TO STAY & DINE

✪ Château de Bagnols

69620 Bagnols. ☎ **74-71-40-00.** Fax 74-71-40-49. 12 rms, 8 suites. TV TEL. 2,000 F ($380.22) 2,500 (475.25) double; from 2,900 F ($551.30) suite. Breakfast 100 F ($19) extra. AE, DC, V. Closed Nov–Apr 24.

France's premier château/hotel, this was a Renaissance ruin that's been restored by 400 artisans and craftspeople for Helen Hamlyn and her husband, publisher/philanthropist Paul Hamlyn, who spent between $6 and $12 million on the project. You can wander around the mansion, filled with antiques, wall paintings, and art, much from the 17th century. Later you can retreat to one of the sumptuous rooms or suites; one suite is named for Mme de Sévigné, who spent a restless night there in 1673. This place is not for the young and restless—there are no gym and no tennis courts, for example. Elegant continental fare is served in the Guards Room, the main dining hall. This is lordly living on a grand and expensive scale.

VILLIE-MORGON

Heading south, you reach this village, which produces one of the greatest beaujolais wines. In the basement of the Hôtel de Ville, the **Caveau de Morgon** (☎ 74-04-20-99) is open daily from 9am to noon and 2 to 7pm; closed in January. Admission is free.

BELLEVILLE-SUR-SAONE

If you'd like another dining choice in the beaujolais country, we suggest driving south from Villié-Morgon to the junction with D37. Then head due east to Belleville-sur-Saône.

WHERE TO DINE

Le Rhône au Rhin

10 av. du Port. ☎ **74-66-16-23.** Reservations required. Main courses 80–130 F ($15.20–$24.70); fixed-price menus 125 F ($23.75), 155 F ($29.45), 195 F ($37.05), and 260 F ($49.40). AE, V. Tues–Sat noon–2pm and 7–9:30pm, Sun noon–2pm. FRENCH.

Chef Michel Debize operates this restaurant where the service and food are most impressive. A special feature is the wide selection of fixed-price menus, beginning inexpensively and climbing the scale for those who want to dine more elaborately. Appetizer specialties include raw salmon terrine and assiette of "fruits of the sea." Favored main courses include ris de veau (sweetbreads) au St-Véran. This restaurant doesn't seem to attract the press and guidebook acclaim it once did, but its cuisine remains as fine as ever.

3 Lyon

268 miles SE of Paris, 193 miles N of Marseille

At the junction of the turbulent Rhône and the tranquil Saône, a crossroads of Western Europe, Lyon is the third-largest city in France. It's a leader in book publishing and banking and is the world's silk capital. And it's also the gastronomic capital of France. Some of the most highly rated restaurants in the country, including Paul Bocuse, are found in and around Lyon. Such dishes as Lyon sausage, quenelles (fish balls), and tripe lyonnais are world famous. The region's succulent Bresse poultry is the best in France.

ESSENTIALS

GETTING THERE   There are three train stations in Lyon. If you're arriving from the north, don't get off at the first station, Gare La Part-Dieu; continue on to Gare de Perrache, where you can begin sightseeing. The high-speed TGV (*train à grande vitesse*) takes only two hours from Paris. Lyon makes a good stopover en route to the Alps or the Riviera.

Going by plane takes 45 minutes from Paris. Arrivals are at Aéroport Lyon-Satolas (☎ 72-22-72-21), 15¹/₂ miles east of the city. Buses run into the center of Lyon every 20 minutes during the day, taking 45 minutes and costing 50 F ($9.50) one way.

ORIENTATION   Lyon was founded on the long, narrow strip of land between the Rhône and Saône Rivers. Today, the city sprawls over many square miles, divided, like Paris, into arrondissements. The historic heart lies on both banks of the Saône, around the east bank's place Bellecour and the west bank's Primatiale St-Jean. The most central of Lyon's three railway stations is the Gare de Perrache, which deposits passengers at the frenetically busy **place Carnot,** three-quarters of a mile south of place Bellecour. The other railway stations (Gare des Brotteaux and the Gare La Part-Dieu) are in Lyon's commercial/industrial east end.

VISITOR INFORMATION   The Office de Tourisme is on place Bellecour (☎ 78-42-25-75).

TOURING THE TOWN

Begin your tour of Lyon at **place Bellecour,** one of the largest and most charming squares in France. A handsome equestrian statue of Louis XIV looks out on the encircling 18th-century buildings. Going down rue Victor-Hugo, south of the square, you reach the **Basilique Romane de St-Martin-d'Ainay,** rue Bourgelat (☎ 78-37-48-97), the oldest church in Lyon, dating from 1107. Admission is free and it's open Sunday to Friday from 8:30 to 11:30am and 3 to 6pm; closed in August. Back at the square, head north along rue de l'Hôtel-de-Ville, which leads to **place des Terreaux.** The Hôtel de Ville, one of the most beautiful in Europe, dominates the square. It dates from 1746—the outside is dark and rather severe, but the inside is brilliant.

SEEING THE TOP ATTRACTIONS

In the 1739 Lacroix-Laval mansion built by Soufflot (architect of the Panthéon in Paris), the **Musée des Arts-Décoratifs,** 30 rue de la Charité (☎ 78-37-15-05), contains furniture and objets d'art, mostly from the 17th and 18th centuries. The medieval and Renaissance periods also are represented. The collection includes a little bit of everything—from ivory-decorated rifles to four-posters draped in red velvet. One room, hung with Aubusson tapestries, displays Louis XIV furnishings. Look for a rare five-octave clavecin by Donzelague, the great 18th-century creator of musical instruments. The museum is open Tuesday to Sunday from 10am to noon and 2 to 5:30pm. Admission is 25 F ($4.75) for adults and 10 F ($1.90) for children; also good for the Musée Historique des Tissus (below).

Your ticket to the Musée des Arts-Décoratifs admits you to this even more interesting museum next door: the **Musée Historique ds Tissus,** 34 rue de la Charité (☎ 78-37-15-05), in the 1730 Palais de Villeroy. On view is a priceless collection of fabrics from all over the world, spanning 2,000 years. Some of the finest fabric made in Lyon from the 17th century to the present is displayed. The textiles embroidered with religious motifs in the 15th and 16th centuries are noteworthy, as are the 17th-century Persian carpets. Seek out the partridge-motif brocade by Philippe de la Salle for Marie Antoinette's bedchamber, as well as a brocaded satin woven for Queen Victoria of 150 colors with birds of paradise and orchids. The museum is open Tuesday to Sunday from 10:30am to 5:30pm. Admission is 25 F ($4.75) for adults and 12 F ($2.30) for children; also good for the Musée des Arts-Décoratifs (above).

On the south side of the square stands the Palais des Arts (also called the Palais de St-Pierre). This former Benedictine abbey was built between 1659 and 1685 in the Italian baroque style. Today it contains the **Musée des Beaux-Arts,** 20 place des Terreaux (☎ 78-28-07-66), with its outstanding collection of paintings and sculpture. You enter through a charming courtyard, graced with statuary and shade trees. On the ground floor is a display of Quattrocento paintings. The collection

Lyon

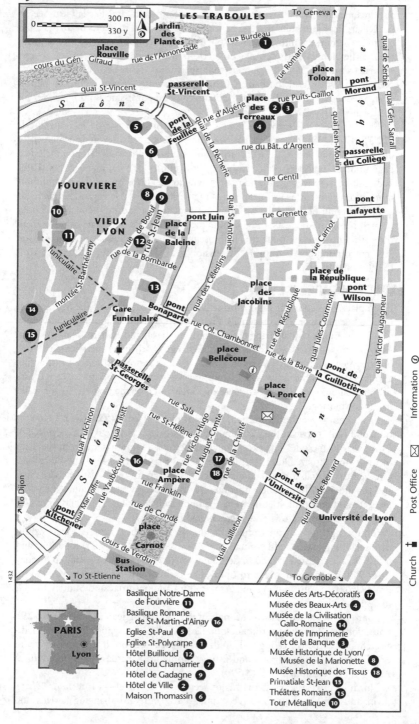

Basilique Notre-Dame de Fourvière **11**
Basilique Romane de St-Martin-d'Ainay **16**
Eglise St-Paul **5**
Eglise St-Polycarpe **1**
Hôtel Bullioud **12**
Hôtel du Chamarrier **7**
Hôtel de Gadagne **9**
Hôtel de Ville **2**
Maison Thomassin **6**

Musée des Arts-Décoratifs **17**
Musée des Beaux-Arts **4**
Musée de la Civilisation Gallo-Romaine **14**
Musée de l'Imprimerie et de la Banque **3**
Musée Historique de Lyon/ Musée de la Marionette **8**
Musée Historique des Tissus **18**
Primatiale St-Jean **13**
Théâtres Romains **15**
Tour Métallique **10**

Information ⓘ   Post Office ✉   Church ✝

PARIS — Lyon

1432

also includes Etruscan, Egyptian, Phoenician, Sumerian, and Persian art. See, in particular, Perugino's altarpiece. The top floor is devoted to works by artists ranging from Veronese, Tintoretto, and Rubens to Braque, Bonnard, and Picasso, with one of the richest 19th-century collections in France. Be sure to see Joseph Chinard's bust of Mme Récamier, the captivating Lyon beauty who charmed Napoleonic Paris, and the Fantin-Latour masterpiece *Reading*. The museum is open Wednesday to Sunday from 10:30am to 6pm; admission is 20 F ($3.80) for adults and 15 F ($2.85) for children.

The **Musée de l'Imprimerie et de la Banque,** 13 rue de la Poulaillerie (☎ 78-37-65-98), occupies a 15th-century mansion. It's devoted to mementos of Lyon's role in the world of printing and banking. Printing exhibits include a page from a Gutenberg Bible, 17th- to 20th-century presses, manuscripts, 16th- and 18th-century woodcuts, and many engravings. This is one of the most important printing museums in Europe, ranking with those at Mainz and Antwerp. It has a collection of books dating from "all epochs," including incunabula, books printed before Easter 1500. The banking section depicts Lyonnais banking from the 16th century to the present. The museum is open Wednesday to Sunday from 9:30am to noon and 2 to 6pm. Admission is 20 F ($3.80) for adults and 10 F ($1.90) for children.

EXPLORING VIEUX LYON

From place Bellecour, cross pont Bonaparte to the right bank of the Saône River or take bus no. 1 or 31 to reach ✪ **Vieux Lyon.** Covering about a square mile, Old Lyon contains an amazing collection of medieval and Renaissance buildings. Many of these houses were built five stories high by thriving merchants to show off their new wealth. After years as a slum, the area is now fashionable, attracting antiques dealers, artisans, weavers, sculptors, and painters, who never seem to tire of scenes along the characteristic **rue du Boeuf,** one of the best streets for walking and exploring.

First, stop to see the **Primatiale St-Jean,** place St-Jean (☎ 78-42-11-04), a cathedral built between the 12th and 15th centuries. Its apse is a masterpiece of Lyonnais romanesque. The exceptional stained-glass windows are from the 12th to the 15th century. Don't miss the flamboyant gothic chapel of the Bourbons. On the front portals are medallions depicting the signs of the zodiac, the Creation, and the life of St. John. The cathedral's 16th-century Swiss astronomical clock is intricate and beautiful; it announces the hour daily at noon, 2pm, and 3pm—in grand style a rooster crows and angels herald the event.

On the right side of the cathedral is the treasury, where rare pieces are exhibited, including jewels and Lyonnais silk. Admission is 16 F ($3.05) for adults and 5 F (95¢) for children 17 and under. The treasury is open Wednesday to Sunday from 9:30am to noon and 2 to 6pm. The cathedral itself is open Monday to Friday from 7:30am to noon and 2 to 7:30pm and Saturday and Sunday from 2 to 5pm; admission is free.

South of the cathedral is the **Manécenterie,** 70 rue St-Jean (☎ 78-92-82-29), noted for its 12th-century romanesque facade. The boys who sang in the medieval choir lived here, making it the oldest residence in Lyon. It's open Monday to Friday from 7:30am to noon and 2 to 7:30pm and Saturday and Sunday from 2 to 5pm. Admission is 10 F ($1.90).

North of the cathedral is the major sector of Old Lyon—a true *musée vivant* (living museum), with narrow streets, spiral stairs, courtyards, hanging gardens, and soaring towers. The most outstanding of the courtyards is the overhanging gallery of the **Hôtel Buillioud,** built in 1536 by Philibert Delorme.

At 14 rue de Gadagne stands the Hôtel de Gadagne, an early 16th-century residence housing the **Musée Historique de Lyon (☎ 78-42-03-61**), with interesting romanesque sculptures on the ground floor. Other exhibits include 18th-century Lyon furniture and pottery, Nevers ceramics, a pewter collection, and numerous paintings and engravings of Lyon vistas. Admission is free. It's open Wednesday to Monday from 10:45 to 6pm. In the same building is the **Musée de la Marionette** (same phone), which has three puppets by Laurent Mourguet, creator of Guignol, best known of all French marionette characters. The museum also has marionettes from other regions of France (including Amiens, Lille, and Aix-en-Provence) and important collections from around the world. It's open the same hours as the history museum.

While still in Vieux Lyon, make an attempt to see the exceptional gothic arcades of the 16th-century **Maison Thomassin,** place du Change; also the 16th-century **Hôtel du Chamarier,** 37 rue St-Jean, where the marquise de Sévigné lived; and, finally, the **Eglise St-Paul,** with its octagonal lantern tower from the 12th century.

CLIMBING FOURVIERE HILL

Rising to the west of Vieux Lyon on the west bank of the Saône is Fourvière Hill. This richly wooded hill—on which numerous convents, colleges, hospitals, two Roman theaters, and a superb Gallo-Roman museum have been established—affords a panoramic vista of Lyon, with its many bridges across two rivers, the rooftops of the medieval town, and (in clear weather) a view of the countryside extending to the snow-capped Alps.

Enthroned on its summit is the gaudy 19th-century **Basilique Notre-Dame de Fourvière,** 8 place de Fourvière (**☎ 78-25-51-82**), rising fortresslike with four octagonal towers and crenellated walls. Its interior is covered with richly colored mosaics. Adjoining is an ancient chapel. The belfry is surmounted by a gilded statue of the Virgin. Admission is free. It's open daily from 8am to noon and 2 to 6pm.

The **Gardens of the Rosary** extend on the hillside between the basilica and the 13th-century **Cathédrale St-Jean.** They're open daily between 8am and 6pm and provide a pleasant walk. A vast shelter for up to 200 pilgrims is found here. An elevator takes visitors to the top of the towers, and two funiculars service the hill.

In a park south of the basilica are the excavated **Théâtres Romains,** Montée de Fourvière, a Roman theater/odeum at 6 rue de l'Antiquaille. The theater is the most ancient in France, built by order of Augustus Caesar in 15 B.C. and greatly expanded during the reign of Hadrian. The odeum, reserved for musical performances, apparently was once sumptuously decorated. Its orchestra floor, for example, contains mosaics of such materials as brightly colored marble and porphyry. The third building in the sanctuary was dedicated in A.D. 160 to the goddess Cybele, or Sibella, whose cult originated in Asia Minor. All that remains are the foundations, though they seem to dominate the theater (175 feet by 284 feet). An altar dedicated to a bull cult and a monumental marble statue of the goddess are shown in the **Musée de la Civilisation Gallo-Romaine,** 17 rue Cléberg (**☎ 78-25-94-68**), a few steps from the archeological site. Admission is free; the site is open March to October only, Monday to Saturday from 9:30am to noon and 2 to 6pm and Sunday from 2 to 6pm. Guides are available on Sunday and holidays from 3 to 6pm. Performances are given at both theaters in summer.

NEARBY ATTRACTIONS

The **Amphithéâtre des Trois-Gauls** is built on the slope of Croix-Rousse, near Condate, a Gallic village where the Rhône and Saône rivers meet. This partly excavated amphitheater is known to have existed several centuries before the Romans arrived. Delegates from 60 tribes from all over Gaul met here in the earliest known example of a French parliamentary system. For this reason the 2,000th anniversary of France, its bimillennium, was celebrated in Lyon in 1989.

Across the Rhône, the 290-acre **Parc de la Tête** is the setting for a *son-et-lumière* program from June to October. The tourist office (see "Essentials," above) will supply details. Surrounded by a wealthy residential quarter, the park has a lake, illuminated fountains, a little zoo, a botanical garden with greenhouses, and a rose garden with some 100,000 plants.

In the tiny village of **Hauteville** near Lyon stands one of the strangest pieces of architecture in the world, representing the lifelong avocation of French postman Ferdinand Cheval: It's a palace of fantasy placed in a high-walled garden. During his lifetime M. Cheval was ridiculed by his neighbors as a crackpot, but his palace has been declared a national monument. The work was finished in 1912, when Cheval was 76; he died in 1925. The north end of the facade is in massive rococo style. The turreted tower is 35 feet tall, and the entire building is 85 feet long. The elaborate sculptural decorations include animals, such as leopards, and artifacts, such as Roman vases.

At Rochetaillée-sur-Saône, 7 miles north of Lyon on N433, the **Musée Français de l'Automobile "Henri Malartre"** is housed in the Château de Rochetaillée, 645 chemin du Musée (☎ 78-22-18-80). The collection includes an 1898 Peugeot, an 1908 Berliet, a 1900 Renault, and a 1938 Lancia-Astura. The château is surrounded by a large park. Admission to the museum and château is 25 F ($4.75) for adults; 17 and under free. Both are open daily from 9am to 5pm.

WHERE TO STAY
EXPENSIVE

✪ Cour des Loges

2468 rue du Boeuf, 69005 Vieux-Lyon. ☎ **78-42-75-75.** Fax 72-40-93-61. 53 rms, 10 suites. A/C MINIBAR TV TEL. 1,000–1,700 F ($190.10–$323.20) double; 2,000–3,000 F ($380.20–$570.30) suite. AE, DC, MC, V. Breakfast 105 F ($19.95) extra. Parking 120 F ($22.80). Bus 1 or 31.

This four-star luxury hotel in Old Lyon occupies several houses. It offers beautifully furnished rooms and suites—each equipped with a color TV with foreign channels, radio, and VCR. Because the streets are narrow, some of the rooms are a bit dark. The restaurant serves excellent food in an elegant setting. The hotel also offers a tapas bar, lounges, an indoor pool, a Jacuzzi, a dry sauna, terraced gardens, a wine cellar, and a private garage. Services include valet and 24-hour room service. The staff is courteous, highly efficient, and the most savvy in Lyon.

Pullman Perrache

12 cours de Verdun, 69002 Lyon. ☎ **72-77-15-00.** Fax 78-37-06-56. 127 rms. A/C MINIBAR TV TEL. 430–840 F ($81.70–$159.70) double. Breakfast 66 F ($12.55) extra. AE, DC, MC, V. Métro: Perrache.

This hotel near the Perrache train station offers some of Lyon's best rooms, with plush fabrics and inviting colors. The hotel is a monument to art nouveau and even has a winter garden. The hotel restaurant, Les Belles Saisons, does more than just cater to the tired business traveler who doesn't want to leave the premises at night. Its finely honed cuisine is often innovative and features continental and regional courses with flair.

MODERATE

⑤ Globe et Cécil

21 rue Gasparin, 69002 Lyon. ☎ **78-42-58-95**. Fax 72-41-99-06. 65 rms. TV TEL. 510 F ($96.90) double. Breakfast 48 F ($9.10) extra. AE, DC, V. Métro: Bellecour.

Near place Bellecour, this hotel is good value for Lyon, not only because of its location but also because of its attentive staff. The rooms are attractively furnished and comfortable. Owner Nicole Renart insisted that the rooms be individually decorated. Breakfast is the only meal served.

Grand Hôtel des Beaux-Arts

75 rue Président-Edouard-Herriot, 69002 Lyon. ☎ **78-38-09-50**. Fax 78-42-19-19. 79 rms. A/C TV TEL. 600 F ($114.05) double. Breakfast 55 F ($10.45) extra. AE, DC, V. Métro: Cordelier.

This has long been one of the leading moderately priced choices. The lobby evokes the 1930s, but not the rooms upstairs, done in no-nonsense modern style. Since this is a noisy part of the city, double glazing on the windows helps shut out traffic sounds; the quieter rooms are in the rear. A large breakfast is the only meal served here, though visitors often prefer having croissants and café au lait at one of the cafés along place Bellecour.

INEXPENSIVE

⑤ Bayard

23 place Bellecour, 69002 Lyon. ☎ **78-37-39-64**. Fax 72-40-95-51. 15 rms. TV TEL. 287–357 F ($54.55–$67.85) double. Breakfast 33 F ($6.25) extra. AE, V. Métro: Bellecour.

This town house is on the landmark place Bellecour. Don't be put off by the entrance, down a narrow hallway on the second floor. Inside you'll find special accommodations, each with a different name, price, and decor. This place is a discovery that should be better known, considering its rates.

⑤ Bellecordière

18 rue Bellecordière, 69002 Lyon. ☎ **78-42-27-78**. Fax 72-40-92-27. 45 rms. TV TEL. 320 F ($60.80) double. Breakfast 34 F ($6.45) extra. AE, V. Métro: Bellecour.

A savvy gourmet traveler we know always stays here, preferring to spend her money on Lyon's restaurants, not its hotel rooms. The accommodations here, often small, are of the no-frills variety, though each is reasonably comfortable. The helpful service and the politeness of the staff more than compensate. Breakfast is the only meal served, but many great restaurants are nearby.

WHERE TO DINE

The food in Lyon is among the finest in the world—and can be *very* expensive. However, we've found that a person of moderate means can often afford the most reasonable fixed-price menu at one of the following "expensive" restaurants.

EXPENSIVE

✪ Alain Chapel

N83 Mionnay, 01390 St-André-de-Corcy. ☎ **78-91-82-02**. Fax 78-91-82-37. Reservations required. Main courses 205–340 F ($38.95–$64.60); fixed-price menus 570 F ($108.35), 690 F ($131.15), and 790 F ($150.20); business menu (Wed–Fri) 310 F ($58.90). AE, DC,

MC, V. Tues 7:30–10:30pm, Wed–Sun 12:30–2pm and 7:30–10:30pm. Closed Jan. Take N83 12¹/₂ miles north of Lyon. FRENCH.

This three-star Relais Gourmand is a stylish place with a flower-garden setting. Alain Chapel was one of the world's premier chefs, and after he died many people claimed that the stellar reputation of his restaurant would tarnish, but under Philippe Jousse (who trained under Chapel) that hasn't been the case. Jousse not only learned the master's recipes and techniques but has actually improved on some. As an appetizer, we recommend the gâteau de foie blond, a hot mousse of chicken livers and marrow, pale gold, covered with a pink Nantua sauce. Or try the velvety eel pâté in puff pastry with two butter sauces. Delectable main courses include pan-fried skillet of fresh mushrooms and poulette de Bresse en vessie—truffled chicken poached and sewn into a pig's bladder (to retain its juices), baked, and served with a cream sauce with a bit of foie gras. Fresh vegetables such as turnips, parsnips, and carrots cooked al dente accompany many of the main courses.

The establishment also offers 14 beautiful rooms, with a double costing 750 to 800 F ($142.55 to $152.10), plus 87 F ($16.55) for breakfast. Parking is free.

✪ Léon de Lyon

1 rue Pleney. ☎ 78-28-11-33. Reservations required. Main courses 180–250 F ($34.20–$47.50); fixed-price meals 490–620 F ($93.10–$117.85). AE, MC, V. Mon–Sat noon–2pm and 7:30–10pm. Closed Aug 13–21. Métro: Hôtel-de-Ville. FRENCH.

Upstairs in this once private home, tables are placed in a series of small rooms decorated with culinary artifacts. The atmosphere may be traditional and typical, but the food isn't. Owner Jean-Paul Lacombe has been called a daring challenger to the top chefs of Lyon, serving both regional and modern cuisine with innovative flair. His brilliant use of Lyonnais offal might scare off the timid but will please the dedicated gastronome. Offerings might include oysters with Pouilly-Fuissé (dry white burgundy), pike quenelles, or lobster with asparagus. Seasonal offerings include snails bubbling in butter. More challenging fare includes terrine of sweetbreads with spinach and even quenelle of hare with turnip purée. His sorbets made with fresh fruits are a perfect ending.

✪ Paul Bocuse

Pont de Collonges, Collonges-au-Mont-d'Or. ☎ 72-42-90-90. Reservations required as far in advance as possible. Main courses 160–360 F ($30.40–$68.40); fixed-price menus 460 F ($87.45), 550 F ($104.55), 610 F ($115.95), 710 F ($134.95), and 740 F ($140.65). AE, DC, MC, V. Daily noon–2pm and 7–10pm. Take N433 5¹/₂ miles north of Lyon.

Paul Bocuse is the most famous contemporary chef in the world, and his restaurant is on the banks of the Saône at Collonges-au-Mont-d'Or. He specializes in regional cuisine, though long ago he was the leading exponent of *nouvelle cuisine* (which he later called "a joke"). Since Bocuse is gone so much of the time, the chefs he leaves behind must carry on preparing dishes the master created. It's as if Bocuse told them, "Don't cook anything that would destroy my legend!" Begin with the legendary black truffle soup, then perhaps try the perfumey Bresse chicken cooked in a pig's bladder.

✪ Nandron

26 quai Jean-Moulin. ☎ 78-42-10-26. Reservations recommended. Main courses 150–210 F ($28.50–$39.90); fixed-price menus 250 F ($47.50), 350 F ($66.50), and 450 F ($85.55). AE, DC, MC, V. Sun–Fri noon–2pm and 7:30–10pm. Closed Aug. Métro: Cordelier. FRENCH.

Bravo Bocuse

A resurgence in interest in chef Paul Bocuse swept across Lyon in 1994 when he bought Le Nord, a turn-of-the-century brasserie the master had worked in as a teenager. Menu prices here—about 180 F ($34.20) per person for a meal with wine and coffee—signaled that the last of the truly great chefs had finally succumbed to the appeal of the mass market. No one is complaining: The venue is the most popular in town for *les gens de bien*, particularly the bankers and merchants who seem to pack the place at lunch.

At least some of its success is derived from his name, for Bocuse is the most visible and enduring grand chef in France. His almost mythical restaurant in Lyon's suburb of Collanges-au-Mont-d'Or has earned a trio of Michelin stars (the top rating) every year since 1965. Less secure chefs might tremble at the thought of the public scrutiny this involves, fearing that the laurels thrown to him by culinary critics will be ripped away later. But Bocuse and his irrepressible ego seems to thrill year after year to the notion that he's without parallel.

Where, pray, might the master be at the time of your arrival in his *sanctum sanctorum?* Not necessarily at Collanges-au-Mont-d'Or or even in Lyon. Since creating some of the most awarded dishes in Europe (soupe de truffes, filet de loup en croûte, and chicken cooked in a pig's bladder), Bocuse has launched his own line of vacuum-packed foods, endorsed a string of bakeries in Japan, purchased a beaujolais vineyard, become interested in the French Pavilion at Disney World's Epcot Center in Florida, and helped develop a collection of compact discs (*Matins et Câlins*) designed to soothe the grumpy aftereffects of too much wine and foie gras. He's in demand everywhere from Chicago to Tokyo, and virtually every agent in Hollywood salivates at the thought of getting him to endorse anything and everything—from T-shirts to slotted spoons.

His team, however, quickly assures press and diners alike that though "temporarily absent," M. Bocuse is present "in spirit." And in this case, the spirit, as priests have affirmed for many years, is invariably stronger than the flesh.

In a stone-fronted house on the Rhône, this restaurant offers views of the river and pont Lafayette. There's a charming salon on the street level, but most people head upstairs for the large air-conditioned dining room. Gérard Nandron knows how to prepare both simple and complex dishes to perfection. The classic courses that made M. and Mme Nandron famous include pike quenelles with a tomato-cream sauce and casserole of calf's kidney and thyme. The excellent regional specialties include Bresse chicken cooked in tarragon vinegar and blanquette de volaille de Bresse. Some of the more challenging fare is *postnouvelle*: vegetable pâté with tomato mousse, sole or turbot simmered in court bouillon with herbs, and raw salmon with citron. Finding something reasonably priced on the wine list requires a bit of savvy. The waiters are helpful, and English is spoken here.

MODERATE

Bistrot de Lyon

64 rue Mercière. ☎ **78-37-00-62.** Reservations not required. Main courses 70–165 F ($13.30–$31.35); fixed-price lunch 130–150 F ($24.70–$28.50). AE, MC, V. Daily noon–2:30pm and 7pm–1:30am. Bus: 13 or 28. FRENCH.

This rendezvous for *le tout Lyon* is lively until early in the morning. It stands on a street of bistros, with several wine bars mixed in. The setting is elegant and traditional; the tables are marble-topped. Many dishes are offered, but you might stick to classic Lyonnaise fare, like poached eggs in red-wine sauce and pot-au-feu with fresh vegetables. Another classic is chicken with heaps of fresh pasta. This is a great place to people-watch.

Chez Gervais

42 rue Pierre-Corneille. ☎ **78-52-19-13.** Reservations recommdended. Main courses 80–130 F ($15.20–$24.70); fixed-price menus 150–185 F ($28.50–$35.15) (lunch only) and 185 F ($35.15). AE, MC, V. Mon–Sat 12:15–1:30pm and 8–9:30pm. Closed July. Métro: Avenue-Foche. FRENCH.

The classic cuisine of this restaurant is served in a fancifully green-lacquered decor; there are more tables on the second floor. After a friendly welcome, you choose among a selection of well-prepared specialties, such as warm asparagus in three sauces, stuffed turbot in champagne sauce, gratin of crayfish tails, and veal kidneys with white-port sauce. This is a place for the food-loving Lyonnais and makes no pretense at competing with the grand tables of the city.

INEXPENSIVE

⑤ Café des Fédérations

8 rue Major-Martin. ☎ **78-28-26-00.** Reservations recommended. Fixed-price menu 140 F ($26.60). AE, DC, V (accepted at dinner). Mon–Fri noon–2:30pm and 7–9:45pm. Closed Aug. Métro: Hôtel-de-Ville. FRENCH.

This is the city's best bistro, operated with panache by Raymond Fulchiron. A sawdust-covered tile floor and long sausages hanging from the ceiling set the tone, and the traditional food completes the picture. The host will help you choose from dishes like sliced pork sausages with boiled potatoes and watercress; tripe such as andouillettes, or tripe marinated, breaded, and grilled; and blood sausage with sautéed apples. You can end with some of the excellent cheeses or a fruit tart.

⑤ La Tassée

20 rue de la Charité. ☎ **78-37-02-35.** Reservations not required. Main courses 80–140 F ($15.20–$26.60); fixed-price menus 120 F ($22.80), 160 F ($30.40), 190 F ($36.10), and 280 F ($53.20). AE, DC, MC, V. Mon–Sat noon–2pm and 7–10:30pm. Closed Sat July–Aug. Métro: Bellecour. FRENCH.

The chef here isn't interested in fancy frills but believes in serving good food at prices most people can afford. Huge portions are dished out, and you might be offered anything from strips of tripe with onions to game or sole. The owners are Roger and Jean-Paul Borgeot. On our most recent visit we arrived here when the beaujolais nouveau had come in. It's a thin, sharp wine, bearing little resemblance to the real beaujolais. The dining room boasts noteworthy 19th-century frescoes.

4 Pérouges

288 miles SE of Paris, 22 miles NE of Lyon

The Middle Ages live on. Saved from demolition by a courageous mayor in 1909 and preserved by the government, this village of craftspeople often attracts movie crews; *The Three Musketeers* starring Michael York and *Monsieur Vincent* (1948) were filmed here. The town sits on what has been called an "isolated throne," atop a hill northeast of Lyon.

Follow rue du Prince, once the main business street, to **place du Tilleul,** at the center of which is a **Tree of Liberty** planted in 1792 to honor the Revolution. Nearby is the **Musée de Vieux-Pérouges,** place de la Halle (☎ 74-61-00-88), displaying such artifacts as hand-looms. It's open daily from 10am to noon and 2 to 6pm; closed Wednesday and Thursday morning from October to April. Admission is 15 F ($2.85). In the 13th century, weaving was the principal industry here and linen merchants sold their wares in the gothic gallery.

The whole village is a living museum, so wander at leisure. The finest house is on rue du Prince—the **Maison des Princes de Savoie**—and you can visit its watchtower; also ask to be shown the garden planted with "flowers of love." In the eastern sector of **rue des Rondes** are many stone houses of former hand-weavers. The stone hooks on the facades were for newly woven pieces of linen.

ESSENTIALS

GETTING THERE   It's easiest to drive to Pérouges, though the signs for the town, especially at night, are confusing. Remember as you drive that it lies northeast of Lyon, off Route 84, near Meximieux.

VISITOR INFORMATION   The Syndicat d'Initiative (tourist office) is at the Maison des Princes, rue du Prince (☎ 74-61-00-88).

WHERE TO STAY & DINE

✪ Hostellerie du Vieux-Pérouges

Place du Tilleul, 01800 Pérouges. ☎ **74-61-00-88.** Fax 74-34-77-90. 28 rms. TEL. 700–980 F ($133.05–$186.31) double. Breakfast 60 F ($11.40) extra. MC, V. Parking 40 F ($7.60). Hotel and restaurant both closed Thurs at lunch and on Wed Nov-Mar.

This is a treasure in a lavishly restored group of 13th-century timbered buildings. Georges Thibaut runs a museum-caliber inn furnished with polished antiques, cupboards with pewter plates, iron lanterns hanging from medieval beams, glistening refectory dining tables, and stone fireplaces. The restaurant is run in association with Le Manoir, where guests are accommodated. The food is exceptional, especially when it's served with the local wine, Montagnieu, a sparkling drink that's been compared to Asti-Spumante. Specialties include terrine truffée Brillat-Savarin, écrevisses (crayfish) pérougiennes, and galette pérougienne à la crème (a dessert crêpe). After dinner, ask for a unique liqueur made from a recipe from the Middle Ages: Ypocras. Meals cost 180 to 390 F ($34.20 to $74.10).

5 Roanne

242 miles SE of Paris, 54 miles NW of Lyon

On the left bank of the Loire, this is an industrial town often visited from Lyon or Vichy because it contains one of France's greatest three-star restaurants, the Hôtel des Frères-Troisgros (below).

In a beautiful neoclassic mansion built at the end of the 18th century, the **Musée Joseph-Déchelette,** 22 rue Anatole-France (☎ 77-71-47-41), offers an exceptional display of Italian and French earthenware from the 16th, 17th, and 18th centuries, as well as earthenware produced in Roanne from the 16th to the 19th century. This is the most important privately endowed museum in this part of France. Admission is 12 F ($2.30). The museum is open Wednesday to Monday from 10am to noon and 2 to 6pm.

The major church, **St-Etienne,** off place de Verdun, dates from the 13th and 14th centuries, with overhauls from the 19th century.

ESSENTIALS

GETTING THERE   There are train and bus connections to nearby cities, notably Lyon.

VISITOR INFORMATION   The Office de Tourisme is at cours de la République (☎ 77-71-51-77).

WHERE TO STAY & DINE

✪ Hôtel des Frères-Troisgros

Place de la Gare, 42300 Roanne. ☎ **77-71-66-97.** Fax 77-70-39-77. Reservations required. Main courses 190–260 F ($36.10–$49.40); fixed-price menus 520–660 F ($98.85–$125.45). AE, DC, MC, V. Wed 7:30–9:30pm, Thurs–Mon noon–1:30pm and 7:30–9:30pm. Closed Feb and Aug 1–15. FRENCH.

The restaurant in this railway-station hotel is one of the best in France. The dining room has been modernized and is decorated with contemporary art, and brothers Pierre and Michel Troisgros are the chefs. Their menu is a virtual celebration of the bounty of the countryside, and their appetizers include warm oysters in butter "in the style of Julia" and thin escalopes of salmon in a sorrel sauce. For a main course, we recommend duck legs served au vinaigre, thyme-scented ewe chops, Charolais beef with marrow in red-wine sauce, or superb squab. For dessert, try an assortment of cheese or a praline soufflé. The petits-fours with candied citrus peel may make you linger. The prices are high, but you're paying for acclaimed cuisine, beautiful service, and quality ingredients.

The hotel offers 19 well-furnished air-conditioned rooms, plus three suites. They cost 1,000 to 1,200 F ($190.10 to $228.10) for a double or 1,400 to 1,850 F ($266.15 to $351.70) for a suite, plus 100 F ($19) for breakfast.

NEARBY DINING & ACCOMMODATIONS

✪ Auberge Costelloise

2 av. de la Libération, Le Coteau. ☎ **77-68-12-71.** Reservations required. Main courses 90–155 F ($17.10–$29.45); fixed-price menus 115 F ($21.85), 185 F ($35.15), 250 F ($47.50), and 350 F ($66.50). AE, MC, V. Tues–Sat 12:15–2pm and 7:45–9pm. Closed Aug 1–21 and Dec 25–Jan 3. Bus 4. FRENCH.

Chef Daniel Alex and his wife, Solange, provide what this region needs: an attractive restaurant with fine cuisine and reasonable prices. Diners choose from one of the fixed-price à la carte menus, which change weekly; the cheapest one isn't available on Friday and Saturday nights. Popular dishes are gâteau of chicken livers with essence of shrimp, sole filet with confit of leeks, and pavé of Charolais bordelaise. You can order fine vintages of Burgundian wines by the pitcher. This is the place to head when you can't afford the dazzling but expensive food at Troisgros.

Hôtel Restaurant Artaud

133 av. de la Libération, 42120 Roanne, Le Coteau. ☎ **77-68-46-44.** Fax 77-72-23-50. Reservations recommended. Main courses 75–120 F ($14.25–$22.80); fixed-price menus 95 F ($18.05), 158 F ($30), 195 F ($37.05), and 350 F ($66.50). MC, V. Mon–Sat noon–2pm and 7:30–9pm. Closed July 25–Aug 15. Take N7 2 miles from the center of Roanne. Bus 4. FRENCH.

This is one of several restaurants in the satellite village of Le Coteau. In an elegant dining room, Nicole and Alain Artaud offer traditional French cuisine. Choices include monkfish salad with saffron, sautéed foie gras salad with strips of smoked duckling breast, beef from local farms, and a variety of desserts. There's also a good selection of French wines.

The hotel offers 25 well-appointed rooms; a double runs 180 to 400 F ($34.20 to $76), plus 30 F ($5.70) for breakfast.

6 Vienne

304 miles SE of Paris, 19 miles S of Lyon

Serious gastronomes know Vienne because it boasts one of France's leading restaurants, La Pyramide (below). But even if you can't afford to partake of the haute cuisine at that citadel, you may want to visit Vienne for its sights. On the left bank of the Rhône, it's a wine center, the southernmost Burgundian town.

Vienne contains many embellishments from its past, making it a *ville romaine et médiévale.* Near the center of town on place du Palais is the **Temple d'Auguste et de Livie,** inviting comparisons with the Maison Carrée at Nîmes. It was ordered built by Claudius and turned into a temple of reason during the Revolution. Another outstanding monument is the small **Pyramide du Cirque,** part of the Roman circus. Rising 52 feet, it rests on a portico with four arches and is sometimes known as the tomb of Pilate.

Take rue Clémentine to the **Cathédrale St-Maurice,** place St-Maurice, dating from the 12th century even though it wasn't completed until the 15th. It has three aisles but no transepts. Its west front is built in the flamboyant gothic style, and inside are many fine romanesque sculptures.

In the southern part of town near the river stands the **Eglise St-Pierre,** at place St-Pierre, a landmark that traces its origins to the 5th century, making it one of the oldest medieval churches in France. It contains a **Musée Lapidaire** (☎ 74-85-20-35) displaying architectural fragments and sculptures found in local excavations. The museum is open April to mid-October, Wednesday to Monday from 9am to 1pm and 2 to 6:30pm; mid-October to March, Wednesday to Saturday from 10am to noon and 2 to 5pm and Sunday from 2 to 5pm. Admission is 10 F ($1.90).

A large **Théâtre Romain,** 7 rue du Cirque (☎ 74-85-39-23), has been excavated east of town at the foot of Mont Pipet. Once theatrical spectacles were staged here for an audience of thousands. From April to October 15, you can visit Wednesday to Monday from 9:30am to 1pm and 2 to 6pm; October 16 to March, Wednesday to Saturday from 10am to noon and 2 to 5pm and Sunday from 1:30 to 5:30pm. Admission is 8 F ($1.50).

ESSENTIALS

GETTING THERE   Rail lines connect Vienne with the rest of France. Some trips require a transfer in nearby Lyon. After leaving Lyon, motorists take either N7 (more direct) or A7, an expressway meandering along the banks of the Rhône River.

VISITOR INFORMATION   The Office de Tourisme is at 3 cours Brillier (☎ 74-85-12-62).

WHERE TO STAY & DINE

⑤ Le Bec Fin

7 place St-Maurice. ☎ 74-85-76-72. Reservations required. Main courses 60–140 F ($11.40–$26.60); fixed-price menus 120 F ($22.80), 180 F ($34.20), 240 F ($45.60), and 320 F ($60.80). MC, V. Tues–Sat noon–2pm and 7–9pm, Sun noon–2pm. FRENCH.

The best-prepared and most generously served fixed-price meals in town are available in this rustic setting near the cathedral. A la carte specialties are somewhat more sophisticated, including salads laced with all the region's delicacies (foie gras, smoked duckling, and the like), breast of duckling with a truffled sauce, filet of turbot, and monkfish with saffron.

✪ La Pyramide Fernand-Point

14 bd. Fernand-Point, 38200 Vienne. ☎ 74-53-01-96. Fax 74-85-69-73. Reservations required. Main courses 185–360 F ($35.15–$68.40); fixed-price menus 270 F ($51.30), 420 F ($79.80), 520 F ($98.85), and 620 F ($117.85). AE, DC, MC, V. Thurs 7–9:30pm, Fri–Tues 12:30–2:30pm and 7–9:30pm. Closed Feb. FRENCH.

This is the premier place to stay and/or eat in the area, and for many it's their preferred stopover between Paris and the Riveria. The restaurant perpetuates the memory of a superb chef, Fernand Point; many of his secrets have been preserved, especially his sauces, touted as the best in the country. Specialties include turbot cooked in champagne, delectable sole with morels, and pike quenelles, that classic dish of Lyon. The chef can appeal to the tastes of both traditionalists and adventurers.

The hotel offers 21 air-conditioned rooms and four suites, all modern and decorated with oak. Doubles cost 880 F ($167.30) and suites are 1,300 F ($247.10), plus 80 to 100 F ($15.20 to $19) for breakfast.

NEARBY ACCOMMODATIONS & DINING

✪ Hostellerie Beau-Rivage

2 rue de Beau-Rivage, 69420 Condrieu. ☎ 74-59-52-24. Fax 74-59-59-36. 20 rms. MINIBAR TV TEL. 550–820 F ($104.55–$155.90) double. Breakfast 60 F ($11.40) extra. AE, DC, MC, V. Parking free. From Vienna, cross the Rhône on N86, then head south 7¹/₂ miles; pass through Condrieu and, on the southern outskirts, look for signs on the left.

A Relais & Châteaux, the inn offers well-furnished large rooms decorated with an old-fashioned touch. One of the accommodations is a former apartment, with lots of space and Renaissance decor. Virginia creeper covers the building's exterior, and the fast-flowing Rhône passes by the dining terrace. The cuisine here is exceptional and traditional—however, the prices are a bit hard to swallow. Try tarragon chicken cooked in a pig's bladder (to seal its juices), terrine of young rabbit, smoked salmon blinis, lobster bisque, or mousseline of lobster with chervil. The Côtes du Rhône wines complement the food well. Meals cost 275 to 400 F ($52.25 to $76). A *menu dégustation* goes for 600 F ($114.05).

7 Valence

417 miles SE of Paris, 62 miles S of Lyon

Valence stands on the left bank of the Rhône between Lyon and Avignon. A former Roman colony, it later became the capital of the Duchy of Valentinois, set up by Louis XII in 1493 for Cesare Borgia. The most interesting sight here is the

Cathédrale St-Apollinaire, consecrated by Urban II in 1095, though it's been much restored since. Built in the Auvergnat-romanesque style, the cathedral is on place des Clercs in the center of town. The choir contains the tomb of Pope Pius VI, who died here a prisoner at the end of the 18th century. It's open daily from 8am to 7pm.

Adjoining the cathedral is the **Musée Municipal,** 4 place des Ormeaux (☎ 75-79-20-80), noted for its nearly 100 red-chalk drawings by Hubert Robert done in the 18th century. It also has a number of Greco-Roman artifacts. It's open Monday, Tuesday, Thursday, and Friday from 2 to 6pm; Wednesday, Saturday, and Sunday from 9am to noon and 2 to 6pm. Admission is 12 F ($2.30) for adults; 15 and under free.

On the north side of the square, on Grand-Rue, you'll pass the **Maison des Têtes,** built in 1532 with sculpted heads of Homer, Hippocrates, Aristotle, and other Greeks.

ESSENTIALS

GETTING THERE There are fast and easy rail and highway connections to Lyon, Grenoble, and Marseille.

VISITOR INFORMATION The Office de Tourisme is on place du Général-Leclerc (☎ 75-43-04-88).

WHERE TO STAY & DINE

✪ Restaurant Pic

285 av. Victor-Hugo, 26000 Valence. ☎ **75-44-15-32.** Fax 75-40-96-03. Reservations required. Main courses 200–320 F ($38–$60.80); fixed-price menus 280 F ($53.20), 550 F ($104.55), 650 F ($123.55). AE, DC, MC, V. Mon–Tues and Thurs–Sat noon–2:30pm and 8–9:30pm, Sun noon–2:30pm. Closed Aug. FRENCH.

This is the least known of France's great three-star restaurants. Both the cooking and the wine list are exceptional, the latter featuring regional selections like Hermitage, St-Péray, and Côtes du Rhône. Alain Pic took over as chef when his renowned father, Jacques, died in 1992, and he performs admirably. This charming villa has a flower-garden courtyard and a dining room with big tables and ample chairs. Appetizers include ballotine of squab, pâté de foie gras en croûte, truffle-flecked émincé of duck, and breast of small game bird. For a main course we recommend the sea bass filet in velvety velouté, crowned by caviar; chicken cooked in a pig's bladder; sole filet in champagne; or lamb stew with basil, sweetbreads, and kidneys. In season, one of the chef's masterpieces is tender noisettes of venison served in a wine-dark sauce light as chiffon. The desserts are a rapturous experience, from the grapefruit sorbet to the cold orange soufflé.

Pic also rents three well-furnished doubles, costing 700 to 850 F ($133.05 to $161.60). Two suites, suitable for two, cost 1,000 F ($190.10). Reserve as far in advance as possible. Breakfast is 100 F ($19) extra.

8 The Ardèche

The Ardèche region became fashionable with foreign visitors only about a decade ago. Until then, it was almost unknown beyond the French borders, bypassed in favor of regions with more and better monuments and museums. Its wines are not the finest in France and its cuisine is the kind of fortifying country fare that nourishes the body but doesn't win awards. Though many districts of France contain buildings that have inspired architects around the world, the Ardèche is limited to stone-sided buildings of rustic but not grandiloquent charm. But as urbanites and visitors began seeking the pleasures of escapes to the wilderness or adventures like kayaking down sublimely beautiful cliff-edged canyons, the Ardèche finally came of age.

The Ardèche occupies the eastern flank of the Massif Central (see Chapter 19), a landscape of jagged, much-eroded granite and limestone highlands that ramble down to the western bank of the Rhône. It isn't the highest or most dramatic region—that honor goes to the Alps, whose peaks rise as much as three times higher. Although it defines itself as *Le Midi* (its southern border lies less than 25 and 31 miles from Avignon and Nîmes, respectively), its culture and landscape are more firmly rooted in the rugged uplands of France's central highlands.

Through its territory flow the streams and rivers that drain the snow and rain of the Massif Central. They include rivers with names like the Ligne, the Fontolière, the Lignon, the Tanargue, and, most important, the Ardèche. They flow beside, around, and through rocky ravines, ancient lava flows, feudal ruins, and stone-sided villages perched in high-altitude sites originally chosen for their medieval ease of defense.

The most famous and oft-visited section of the Ardèche is its southern extremity, with granite-sided ravines 1,000 feet deep, gouged by millions of springtime floodings of the Ardèche River—no wonder it's called the Grand Canyon of France. This area is the goal of thousands of motorists who, often with their children, take tours along the highways flanking the ravines.

We believe you should stop here to admire the gorges only briefly, on your way to somewhere else. An overnight in the less touristed northern reaches of the Ardèche is more rewarding than a view of the honky-tonk commercialism that sometimes pervades the southern reaches. In the northern Ardèche, in the 28 miles of hills and valleys separating the hamlets of Vals-les-Bains and Lamastre, is a soft and civilized wilderness, with landscapes that have been devoted to grape growing, sheepherding, and (more recently) hill trekking.

TOURING THE ARDECHE

The best way to appreciate the charms of the Ardèche is to take a morning's drive through the gorges of the southeastern edges and reserve your overnight stays and hill climbing for the less touristed northern edges. **Vallon-Pont-d'Arc,** the gateway to the gorges, was defined by one writer as a Gallic version "of honky-tonk Gatlinburg, Tennessee." Reserve your overnights for the two following towns. If you want to go kayaking in the gorges (early April to late November, when the waters are green and sluggish, safer than during the floods of winter and spring), you'll find at least three dozen rental agencies for everything from plastic kayaks to horses in Vallon-Pont-d'Arc.

One of the best-recommended outfits is **Adventure Canoë,** place du Marché (B.P. 27), 07150 Vallon-Pont-d'Arc (☎ **75-37-18-14**), which arranges rentals of canoes and kayaks for rides through the gorges. A three-hour *mini-descente* costs 195 F ($37.05) for two participants riding a 4-mile route from Vallon-Pont-d'Arc to the downstream hamlet of Chames. A full-day *grande descente* for two riding a l9-mile downstream route from Vallon-Pont-d'Arc to St-Martin d'Ardèche costs 320 F ($60.80). Prices include transport by minivan back to Vallon-Pont-d'Arc at the end of the ride. Lunch is not included, and participants must buy and

The Grand Canyon of France

Measuring no more than 119 miles in length, the Ardèche isn't the longest, mightiest, or most influential river in France, but it probably flows faster, with more geological aftereffects, than any of its more portentous rivals. Originating on the eastern edge of the Massif Central at about 5,000 feet above sea level, the Ardèche descends faster, over a shorter distance, than any of its mightier competitors. (In some sections it falls as much as 1 meter for every kilometer of its length, which by the standards of such relatively placid rivers as the Seine and the Loire is positively vertiginous.) These changes in altitude, combined with cycles of heavy rainfall and drought, result in what's probably the most temperamental and changeable waterway in France.

The resulting ebbs and flows have created what some visitors refer to as the Grand Canyon of France. Littered with alluvial deposits, strewn in ravines whose depth sometimes exceeds 950 feet, the river's lower extremity (its final 36 miles, before the waters dump into the Rhône) is one of the country's most unusual geological areas. A panoramic road (D290) runs along a rim of these canyons, providing views over an arid landscape of grasses, toughened trees, drought-resistant shrubs, and some of the most distinctively eroded deposits of granite, limestone, and basalt in Europe.

If you opt to drive along this route, expect some touristy silliness similar to the cheap motels, family-fun emporiums, and fast-food joints you'd expect near Yellowstone Park in the United States. There's no denying, however, the basic beauty of the site, which you can admire from a series of belvederes scattered along the highway. The highway runs in a meandering line that's approximately parallel to the bluffs and corniches of the river's northwestern edge. Many of the belvederes have brown-and-white signs that encourage motorists to stop and walk for a few minutes along some of the well-marked footpaths.

The route, which you can traverse in a few hours even if you stop frequently for sightseeing, stretches southeast to northwest between the towns of Vallon-Pont-d'Arc and Pont St-Esprit. Since the meandering corniche roads are a challenge to drive, be extra-careful. Particularly, beware of other vehicles, which may weave frighteningly out of their lanes as the drivers and passengers crane their necks to admire the beauty and snap photos furiously.

transport their own picnics, though the makings for this are available at dozens of bakeries and delicatessens near each point of origin.

Despite the appeal of kayaking, most travelers limit their exploration of the gorges to touring by car along their upper summits.

VALS-LES-BAINS
27 miles W of Montélimar, 86 miles SW of Lyon

In a depression of the valley of the Volane River, Vals-les-Bains is surrounded by about 150 freshwater springs whose existence was discovered relatively late—around 1600. Scientists have never really understood why each spring contains a different percentage of minerals: Most contain bicarbonate of soda, others are almost tasteless, and one—La Source Dominique—has such a high percentage of iron and arsenic it's considered poisonous. Waters from Dominique are piped away from the town center; others are funneled into a Station Thérmale adjacent to the town's casino.

From a position in the park outside the Station Thérmale, a *source intermittante* erupts, Old Faithful–style, to a height of around 25 feet at intervals of about six hours. Small crowds gather for eruptions at 5:30am, 11:30am, 5:30pm, and 11:30pm. A few steps away, the belle époque **casino,** Parc Thermale (☎ 75-37-49-21), is open daily from noon to 3am; entrance is free. The only casino between Lyon and Aigues-Mortes, it's mobbed weekends by local farmers and their families playing the slot machines. There's no restaurant on the premises, but there's a 600-seat theater for local acting companies, two movie theaters, and a disco (Le Must). Le Must opens at 10pm every night in summer and on Friday and Saturday from October to May. Women enter free, but men pay 50 F ($9.50), which includes the first drink.

Other than the surrounding scenery, the town's most unusual site is about 14 miles south, beside the highway to Privas. Here once stood a **ruined feudal château** that was richly embellished and enlarged in the 1700s, the home of the comtes du Valentinois. Ironically, it escaped the ravages of the Revolution only to fall into ruin in 1820, when its bankrupt owners sold its accessories and architectural ornaments to pay their debts. Today only the 16th-century entrance gate remains relatively unharmed. The views over the confluence of two ravines and the valley below is worth the detour.

Where to Stay

Grand Hôtel des Bains

3 Montée de l'Hôtel-des-Bains, 07600 Vals-les-Bains. ☎ **75-94-65-55.** Fax 75-37-67-02. 57 rms, 6 junior suites. TV TEL. 300–470 F ($57–$89.35) double; 600 F ($114.05) suite. AE, DC, MC, V.

This is the largest and best hotel in town, with a central wing built in 1860 in anticipation of a visit from Empress Eugénie. (Alas, Eugénie, finding she was comfortable in the nearby resort of Vichy, canceled her visit.) Despite the snub, the hotel added two additional wings in 1870 and has survived ever since, partly because of a cordial staff and well-maintained, conservatively furnished rooms. The restaurant charges 130 to 330 F ($24.70 to $62.70) for set menus, served daily at lunch and dinner.

Hôtel de l'Europe

86 rue Jean-Jaurès, 07600 Vals-les-Bains. ☎ **75-37-43-94.** Fax 75-94-66-62. 32 rms. TV TEL. 240–280 F ($45.60–$53.20) double. AE, DC, MC, V.

Built to house well-heeled patrons of the adjacent spa in 1805, this hotel retains memories of yesteryear's grandeur, despite an ongoing series of modernizations. There's no restaurant, but the rooms are large, high-ceilinged, and just dowdy enough to remind you of *la Belle France* of another era. The staff is as courtly and well mannered as the old-fashioned setting requires.

Where to Dine

Restaurant Mireille

3 rue Jean-Jaurès. ☎ **75-37-49-06.** Reservations recommended. Main courses 80–100 F ($15.20–$19); fixed price menus 70–160 F ($13.30–$30.40). MC, V. Thurs–Tues noon–2pm and 7:30–9pm. Closed two weeks in Apr and two weeks in Sept. FRENCH.

Containing only 26 seats, this restaurant occupies the space below vaulted stone ceilings that for centuries sheltered a herd of goats. Known for its earthy sense of warmth, the restaurant serves a carefully calibrated cuisine with an ambitious menu. It includes local pigeon roasted in honey sauce, mousse of flap mushrooms with scallops, and filet of turbot with beurre blanc.

LAMASTRE

26 miles N of Vals-les-Bains, 18 miles W of Valence

Near the Ardèche's northern frontier, the charming hamlet of Lamastre is known for its light industry (shoes, camping gear, furniture, and light machine tools). Many connoisseurs of Ardèche architecture view it as the most unaltered and evocative village in the district. Its most important site is its village church, in Macheville, in the hamlet's upper altitudes. Built of pink-toned stone in romanesque style, it boasts portions dating from the 12th century and is the frequent site of weddings, one of which you might get to view.

Don't expect lots of nightlife or razzle-dazzle here. The entertainment you provide is likely to be your own, though most visitors use the town as the daily debut of hill treks over the surrounding hills and valleys. A network of brown-and-white signs clearly marks each trail's direction and duration.

Where to Stay & Dine

Le Château d'Urbilhac

Rte. de Vernoux, 07270 Lamastre. ☎ 75-06-42-11. Fax 45-06-52-75. 12 rms. TEL. 1,100–1,150 F ($209.10–$218.60) double. Rates include half board. AE, DC, V. Closed Oct–Apr.

About a mile south of Lamastre's center, this is the only château (and only château-hotel) in the Ardèche. Built in the 1500s, it was renovated in the 19th century and is sheathed in a covering of pink-toned stucco. Rated three stars by the French government, it boasts a large outdoor pool and a tennis court, plus many of the slightly faded trappings of yesteryear. Its owner is Mme Marcelle Xampero, who prepares evening meals and maintains the 115 acres around the building. The restaurant is open only to hotel guests.

L'Hôtel du Midi

Place Seignobos, 07170 Lamastre. ☎ 75-06-41-50. Fax 75-06-49-75. 12 rms. TV TEL. 365–450 F ($69.35–$85.55) double. AE, DC, MC, V.

Built in 1925, with slightly faded rooms that retain a vague art deco allure, this place has been used as an overnight stop for both Charles de Gaulle and Elizabeth Bowes-Lyon, the Queen Mother of England. Maintained by members of the Perrier family, it's well known for its restaurant, which serves set menus priced at 165 to 395 F ($31.35 to $75.05). These are offered daily except Sunday night and all day Monday, from noon to 2pm and 7:30 to 9pm. The food is among the best in the region, much of it based on improvements of traditional regional specialties.

19 The Massif Central

In your race south to Biarritz or through the Rhône Valley to the Riviera, you'll penetrate the Massif Central, France's rugged agricultural heartland. Here you'll find ancient cities, lovely valleys, and a wonderful provincial cuisine. With its rolling farmland, isolated countryside, and châteaux and manor houses (in many of which you can stay and dine), this is one of the most unspoiled parts of France—your chance to see and be part of a life all too rapidly fading.

From the spa at Vichy to the volcanic *puys* of Auvergne, there's much of interest here and much to learn about the art of good living. We'll begin in the George Sand country in the old province of Berry, then proceed to the Auvergne and motor west to Limousin.

REGIONAL CUISINE Fans of this region's cuisine often praise it for its uncomplicated honesty and adherence to tradition; its critics claim it lacks finesse and creativity. Everyone, however, agrees that this is a rural, family-inspired tradition, based on generous quantities of fresh ingredients and few pretensions.

Characteristic dishes include soup (*un potée*) made with cabbage and about a dozen other ingredients (usually including both fresh and salted pork) and stuffed sheep's foot cooked inside a sheep's stomach. The region's cheeses include enormous wheels known as Cantal, bleu d'Auvergne, St-Nectair, and a goat's-milk cheese called *le cabecou*, which appears on cheese trays in grand restaurants throughout France. The Massif Central is famous for its desserts, including cherry tarts (sometimes with the cherry pits still in place) and many exceptional pastries.

The climate and soil are not conducive to grape growing, so most regional wines just pass for solid and uncomplicated table wine. The best local spirits are several types of distilled alcohol traditionally served after a meal. These are usually distilled from the fermented essence of flowers and herbs that include strawberries, raspberries, blossoms from the linden tree, myrtle, and a mountain flower called *gentiane*.

EXPLORING THE REGION BY CAR

Here's how to link together the best of the region if you rent a car.

Day 1 Begin in the ancient city of Bourges. Visit its cathedral and Palais Jacques-Coeur before driving southwest or southeast for an overnight stay at Nohant/La Châtre or Vichy. If you decide to spend

The Massif Central

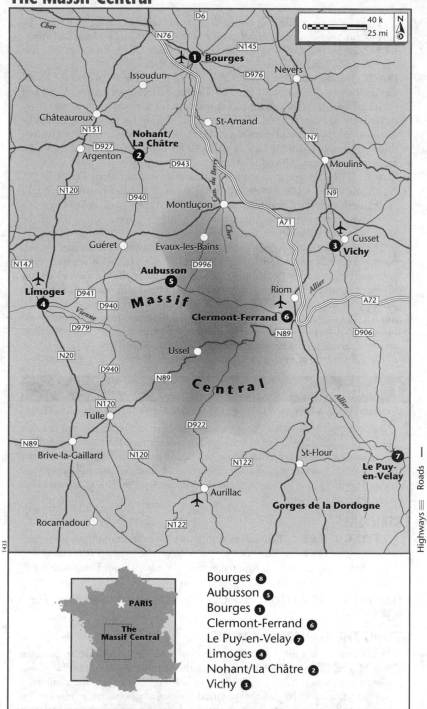

Bourges 8
Aubusson 5
Bourges 1
Clermont-Ferrand 6
Le Puy-en-Velay 7
Limoges 4
Nohant/La Châtre 2
Vichy 3

Highways ═ Roads ─

the night in Vichy, consider an hour's stopover in Nohant/La Châtre en route. Be alert to this town's name, as many maps refer to it for brevity's sake as La Châtre. From Bourges, Nohant/La Châtre lies 44 miles along D940; Vichy lies 90 miles away along N76 and N7.

Day 2   The following day, drive southwest from Vichy for 31 miles to the Massif Central's largest city: Clermont-Ferrand. The most direct route between Vichy and Clermont is D1093, though some motorists opt for a bypass south along D906, then a westward jog for a few miles along E70. Most of Clermont's sights can be seen in a densely scheduled morning, and because of this, we usually prefer to continue on to more charming Le Puy-en-Velay for the night. To do this, drive 65 miles southeast along N9 and N102.

Day 3   With Limoges as your final destination, head east along D590, D990, N122, and N120, a leisurely day's drive of about 175 miles. The road will take you through rock-filled pine forests and jagged landscapes, past some of France's least-developed countryside. About halfway along the route, stop at one of the Massif Central's most historic towns, Aurillac.

The town contains a rugged-looking castle, the Château de St-Etienne, which broods about half a mile north (☎ 71-48-49-09). It boasts a 13th-century dungeon and a dusty but oddly charming geological museum, the Musée des Volcans, in one of its wings. You can fortify yourself with a meal in Aurillac at Les Quatre Saisons, 10 rue Champeil (☎ 71-64-85-38). Meals are served at lunch and dinner, daily except Sunday night and all day Monday, from a centuries-old building. Set menus range from 75 to 200 F ($14.25 to $38). After Aurillac, continue driving northwest along N12 for 2 miles, when you'll reach Limoges, site of the manufacture of France's most famous porcelain. Spend the night here.

1 Bourges

148 miles S of Paris, 43 miles NW of Nevers, 95 miles NW of Vichy, 175 miles NW of Lyon

Once the capital of Aquitaine, Bourges lies in the heart of France, and you can visit here from Orléans at the end of your eastern trek through the Loire Valley. The commercial/industrial center of Berry, this regional capital is still off the beaten path for much tourism, even though it boasts a rich medieval past still in evidence today. Its history goes back far beyond the Middle Ages: In 52 B.C. Caesar called it the finest city in Gaul.

ESSENTIALS

GETTING THERE   There are good road and rail connections from Tours and other regional cities. For example, 13 trains arrive daily from Paris, taking $2^1/2$ hours. Sometimes a transfer is required at nearby Vierzon. From Tours, four trains a day arrive, taking 90 minutes.

VISITOR INFORMATION   The Office de Tourisme is at 21 rue Victor-Hugo (☎ 48-24-75-33).

SEEING THE TOP ATTRACTIONS

On the summit of a hill dominating the town, the ✪ **Cathédrale St-Etienne,** 9 rue Molière (☎ 48-65-49-44), is one of the largest and most beautiful gothic cathedrals in France. It was begun at the end of the 12th century and completed a century and a half later. Subsequent additions have been made. Flanked by asymmetrical towers, it has five magnificent doorways, including one depicting

What's Special About the Massif Central

Great Towns
- Bourges, the old capital of Aquitaine and geographical heart of France.
- Clermont-Ferrand, the ancient capital of the Auvergne, a double city on the Tiretaine River.
- Aubusson, *ville de la tapisserie*, celebrated for its carpets and tapestries.
- Limoges, the historical center of Limousin, known for its porcelain and enamel works.

Ancient Monuments
- Cathédrale St-Etienne, one of the most beautiful gothic cathedrals of France, at Bourges.
- Montferrand at Clermont-Ferrand, northeast of the city, a district of gothic and Renaissance buildings.

Literary Pilgrimages
- Château de Nohant, where novelist George Sand wrote and entertained the literati.

Special-Interest Museums
- Musée de Ranquet, at Clermont-Ferrand, with its exceptional collection of Gallo-Roman artifacts.
- Musée Départmental de la Tapisserie, at Aubusson, exploring five centuries of Aubusson carpetweaving.
- Musée National Adrien-Dubouche, at Limoges, the second great porcelain museum of France.

Festivals
- Foire des Vins (wine fair), the last weekend in August, at St-Pourçain-sur-Sioule.

Architectural Highlights
- Parc des Sources, a promenade walk at Vichy, the most fashionable promenade in the region.
- Cathédrale Notre-Dame, at Clermont-Ferrand, one of the great gothic churches of central France, from the 13th century.

episodes in the life of St. Stephen. With a high vaulted roof, the cathedral has five aisles and is remarkably long—407 feet deep. The cathedral is distinguished for its stained-glass windows, best viewed with binoculars. In rich blues and deep ruby reds, many of these windows were made between 1215 and 1225. One scene, *A Meal in the House of Simon*, is vividly colored, showing Jesus lecturing before Simon on the forgiveness of sins as Mary Magdalene repents at his feet.

To climb the north tower for a view of the cathedral and Bourges, you must obtain a ticket from the custodian, costing 20 F ($3.80) for adults and 13 F ($2.45) for children. The same ticket allows you to explore the 12th-century crypt, the largest in France. In the crypt rests the tomb (built between 1422 and 1438) of Jean de Berry, who ruled this duchy in the 14th century. Fanatically dedicated to art, he directed a "small army" of artisans, painters, and sculptors. The recumbent figure is the only part of the original tomb that has survived. The cathedral is open daily from 8am to 6:30pm, but the crypt cannot be visited on Sunday. Afterward, you may want to wander through the **Jardins de l'Archevêché,** the archbishop's gardens, credited to Le Nôtre. In these gardens you'll have a good view of the eastern side of the cathedral.

The **Palais Jacques-Coeur,** rue Jacques-Coeur (☎ 48-24-06-87), is one of the greatest secular gothic buildings in France. Take a guided tour through the four buildings around a central court, built about 1450 by finance minister/banker Jacques Coeur, who had amassed a fortune. Monsieur Coeur never got to enjoy the palace, however. After a trial by a jury of his creditors, he was tossed into prison by Charles VII and died there in 1456. His original furnishings no longer remain, but the decoration and wealth of detail inside the palace form a remarkable view of how opulent life could be in the 15th century. In the dining hall is a monumental chimneypiece, and in the great hall are sculptures from the 15th and 16th centuries. The palace is open daily: in July and August from 9am to 7pm; April to June, September, and October from 9am to noon and 2 to 6pm; and November to March from 9am to noon and 2 to 5pm. Admission is 26 F ($4.95) for adults and 17 F ($3.25) for ages 18 to 24 and over 60; 17 and under free.

The **Musée du Berry,** 4 rue des Arènes (☎ 48-57-81-15), is inside the elegant Hôtel Cujas, built about 1515. On display is a large collection of Celtic and Gallo-Roman artifacts. Especially impressive are the 280 funerary sculptures. Some rooms are devoted to finds from Egyptian archeological digs, along with medieval masterpieces of sculpture dating from around 1400. The museum is open Monday and Wednesday to Saturday 10am to noon and 2 to 6pm and Sunday from 2 to 6pm. Admission is 17 F ($3.25) for adults and 9 F ($1.70) for children.

The Renaissance **Hôtel Lallemant,** 6 rue Bourbonnoux (☎ 48-57-81-17), north of the cathedral, has been transformed into a museum of decorative art. The mansion was built for a textile merchant, and today its galleries display a colorful history of Bourges. Exhibits include china, objets d'art, ceramics, and a large display of antique furniture. The museum is open Tuesday to Saturday from 10am to noon and 2 to 6pm and Sunday from 2 to 6pm. Admission is 17 F ($3.25) for adults and 8.50 F ($1.60) for children.

WHERE TO STAY

✪ Bourbon et Restaurant St-Ambroix
Bd. de la République, 18000 Bourges. ☎ **48-70-70-00.** Fax 48-70-21-22. 59 rms. A/C TV TEL. 626 F ($118.95) double. AE, DC, V.

This has become *the* hotel for discriminating visitors to Bourges, and its cuisine is the finest in the entire area. A 16th-century abbey was converted into this first-class hotel with comfortable rooms that are well equipped but short on style. The refined cuisine of Christophe Langrée is the allure, even for locals. Under a vaulted ceiling of a former Renaissance chapel, you can select delectable main courses—perhaps baked saddle of lamb (pink and juicy) or escalope de foie gras de canard (duckling). The noix de ris de veau braisée (sweetbreads) is among the finest you're likely to sample anywhere. Meals range from 145 to 260 F ($27.55 to $49.40).

Le Christina
5 rue de la Halle, 18000 Bourges. ☎ **48-70-56-50.** Fax 48-70-58-13. 76 rms. TV TEL. 175–285 F ($33.25–$54.15) double; 275–315 F ($52.25–$59.85) triple. Breakfast 35 F ($6.65) extra. AE, MC, V. Parking 30 F ($5.70).

This is a simple inn, but the rooms at the Christina are comfortable and, in part, furnished with some stylish pieces. It's within an easy walk of the Palais Jacques-Coeur and the cathedral. Breakfast is the only meal served.

WHERE TO DINE

Jacques-Coeur

3 place Jacques-Coeur. ☎ **48-70-12-72.** Reservations required. Main courses 85–125 F ($16.15–$23.75); fixed-price menus 145 F ($27.55) and 180 F ($34.20). AE, DC, MC, V. Mon–Fri noon–2pm and 7:15–9:15pm, Sun noon–2pm. Closed July 21–Aug 21 and Dec 26–Jan 3. FRENCH.

François Bernard serves tasty traditional bourgeois cuisine amid a medieval decor. Specialties include veal kidneys berrichonne, fresh frogs' legs sautéed with herbs, scallops (available spring to October), and beef stew à la mode. The desserts are all homemade and tempting, and service is politely efficient. The featured wines from a balanced list are Quincy and Menetou-Salon. The competition for the dining franc in this town has heated up considerably in recent years, but this place continues rather smugly doing what it always did.

2 Nohant/La Châtre

180 miles S of Paris, 19 miles S of Châteauroux

George Sand was the pen name of Amandine Lucile Aurore Dupin, baronne Dudevant, the French novelist born in 1804. Her memory is forever connected to this little Berry hamlet near the Indre Valley.

In her early life she wrote bucolic tales of peasants but also penned romantic novels in which she maintained that women were entitled to as much freedom as men. Among 80 novels, some of her best known were *François le champi* and *La Mare au diable*. She was also known for her love affairs, her two most notorious being with poet Alfred de Musset, who journeyed with her to Venice, and composer Frédéric Chopin, who went with her to Majorca. By the time of her death in Nohant in 1876, George Sand had become a legend.

It was at the **Château de Nohant** (☎ **54-31-06-04**) that George Sand learned the ways and thoughts of the peasants. And in time she invited here some of the intellectual and artistic elite of Europe—Flaubert, Balzac, Delacroix, Liszt, and Gautier. The château dates from the late 1600s and was purchased in 1793 by the family of George Sand. Today it houses the mementos of Sand and her admirers and friends. You can see the boudoir where she wrote *Indiana*, the novel published when she was 28. You can also visit her private bedchamber/study. At Nohant, George Sand staged theatricals for her guests, dramatizing several of her novels—not very successfully, according to reports. Sometimes today *fêtes romantiques de Nohant* are staged, with an impressive list of musical performers.

The mansion tour takes about half an hour, and it's open April 1 to October 14, daily from 9:30 to 11:15am and 2:30 to 5:30pm; the rest of the year, daily from 10am to noon and 2 to 4pm. Admission is 27 F ($5.15) for adults and 13 F ($2.45) for children.

ESSENTIALS

GETTING THERE   The nearest train station is in Châteauroux; most visitors drive instead of relying on public transportation.

VISITOR INFORMATION   The nearest Office de Tourisme is on square George-Sand (☎ 54-48-22-64) in La Châtre, open daily year round.

WHERE TO STAY & DINE

Auberge de la Petite Fadette
Nohant-Vic, 35400 La Châtre. ☎ **54-31-01-48.** Fax 54-31-10-19. 11 rms. TV TEL. 290–350 F ($55.10–$66.50) double. MC, V.

This compound of 19th-century ivy-covered buildings abuts the château and is the focal point for one of the smallest villages in the region. Since 1890 the compound has been owned by four generations of the Chapleau family, and in 1995 it was renovated. A scattering of antiques decorates the interior, and the dining room serves set menus throughout the year to enthusiasts who come to worship at the shrine of Ms. Sand. Set menus cost 80 to 190 F ($15.20 to $36.10).

Château de la Vallée Bleue
Route de Verneuil, St-Chartier, 36400 La Châtre. ☎ **54-31-01-91.** Fax 54-31-04-48. 13 rms. MINIBAR TV TEL. 310–550 F ($58.90–$104.55) double. Breakfast 50 F ($9.50) extra. MC, V.

This château was built by Dr. Pestel so he could be close to his patient, George Sand. The doctor's home is now a hotel/restaurant owned by Gérard Gasquet. The rooms have been named after the doctor's former guests, including Musset, Delacroix, Flaubert, Chopin, and Liszt. There's also a 10-acre wooded park and a pool. The excellent regional specialties are characterized as *cuisine actuelle*, with an accent on presentation; they include goat cheese and carp with lentils and chicken à la George Sand (with a crayfish sauce). For dessert, try a delectable pear baked in pastry. Fixed-price menus cost 130 F ($24.70), 195 F ($37.05), and 250 F ($47.50), and nonguests can visit for meals (but should call for a reservation). The restaurant is open daily in summer but closed on Sunday evening and Monday from October to mid-April; it's closed completely in February.

3 Vichy

216 miles S of Paris, 33 miles NE of Clermont-Ferrand, 108 miles NW of Lyon

This world-renowned spa on the northern edge of the Auvergne, in the heart of Bourbon country, noted for its sparkling waters (said to alleviate liver and stomach ailments), looks in part as it did a century ago when princes and industrial barons filled its rococo casino. From 1861 Napoléon III was a frequent visitor, doing much to add to the spa's fame. However, by the 1980s the clients and their tastes had changed, but Vichy has begun a major step in sprucing up its hotels and modernizing its baths.

The city's current reputation for health and relaxation has been aided greatly by the Perrier craze that has swept throughout most of the world. The Perrier Company has a contract to bottle Vichy water for sale elsewhere and also runs the city's major attractions. Vichy is a sports-and-recreation center, boasting a casino, theaters, regattas, horse racing, and golf.

A promenade with covered walks, the **Parc des Sources** is the center of Vichy's fashionable life (May to the end of September). At night the spa's chief attraction is the brilliantly lit **Grand Casino,** 5 rue du Casino (☎ 70-97-93-37). Under high ceilings and immense chandeliers, gamblers come here from around the world to play blackjack and roulette. In the casino theater, Diaghilev produced his last ballet and Strauss directed *Salomé*. The Hall des Sources, the Galerie Napoléon, and the **Grand Etablissement Thermal** (the largest treatment center of its kind in Europe) are found here. The baths can be visited June to August, Wednesday, Thursday, and Saturday from 3 to 4:30pm.

ESSENTIALS

GETTING THERE   Vichy lies on the much-used Paris/Clermont-Ferrand rail line. Twenty trains per day arrive from Clermont-Ferrand (trip time: 30 min.), costing 46 F ($8.75) one way. From Paris eight trains per day arrive (trip time: 3½ hr.), costing 201 F ($38.20) one way.

VISITOR INFORMATION   The Office de Tourisme is at 19 rue du Parc (☎ 70-98-71-94).

WHERE TO STAY

Aletti Palace Hôtel

3 place Joseph-Aletti, 03200 Vichy. ☎ **70-31-78-77.** Fax 70-98-13-82. 54 rms, 14 suites. TV TEL. 650–760 F ($123.55–$144.45) double; 950–1,100 F ($180.55–$209.10) suite. Breakfast 70 F ($13.30) extra. AE, DC, MC, V.

This turn-of-the-century hotel contains all the grand vistas and elegant accessories you'd expect. The rooms are well furnished, many with balconies overlooking the wooded park and the casino; the baths are especially elegant. The hotel has a good restaurant and offers a bar and a terrace with a view of Vichy. Fixed-price meals cost 120 F ($22.80), 190 F ($36.10), and 250 F ($47.50).

Hôtel Chambord

84 rue de Paris, 03200 Vichy. ☎ **70-31-22-88.** Fax 70-31-54-92. 32 rms, 17 with bath (tub or shower). TV TEL. 180–260 F ($34.20–$49.40) double. Breakfast 30 F ($5.70) extra. AE, DC, MC, V.

This pleasant hotel is near the train station, and its rooms are comfortable though not stylish. The Escargot qui Tête restaurant offers good meals for reasonable prices, with fixed-price menus starting at 80 F ($15.20); it's open Tuesday to Sunday (closed Sunday night). In July and August, however, it's open daily. Many visitors find the restaurant more intriguing than the hotel.

✪ Pavillon Sévigné

50–52 bd. J.-F.-Kennedy/place Sévigné, 03200 Vichy. ☎ **70-32-16-22.** Fax 70-59-97-37. 43 rms, 4 suites. MINIBAR TV TEL. 680–1,300 F ($129.25–$247.10) double; 960–1,390 F ($182.50–$264.25) suite. Breakfast 75 F ($14.25) extra. AE, DC, MC, V. Parking 60 F ($11.40).

Renowned letter writer Mme de Sévigné stayed here when she was in Vichy for "the cure." This *grand Petit* offers gracious living near the thermal spa. The Pavillon has an ivory-colored brick exterior and ceramic parquet floors. The Empire-style rooms are individually decorated in pastel hues. The salon in which Mme de Sévigné stayed still evokes the 1600s, overlooking a courtyard. The restaurant is one of the finest in Vichy, decorated in the style of Napoléon III. Meals begin at 160 F ($30.40).

WHERE TO DINE

L'Alambic

8 rue Nicholas-Larbaud. ☎ **70-59-12-71.** Reservations required. Main courses 95–180 F ($18.05–$34.20); fixed-price menus 160–280 F ($30.40–$53.20). MC, V. Tues 7:30–10pm, Wed–Sun noon–2pm and 7:30–10pm. Closed Feb 4–27 and Aug 21–Sept 8. FRENCH.

There are only 20 places at this small restaurant, but they fill up quickly because the cuisine is the best in Vichy. Since 1989 Jean-Jacques Barbot has run a busy place, appealing to what one food critic called "the jaded palates of Vichy." In a pristinely elegant setting, you can enjoy ravioli stuffed with frogs' legs and herbs, ragoût of crayfish with wild mushrooms, roast pigeon, lobster bourguignon with baby vegetables, or beef filet grilled with marrow. The desserts are spectacular, including a gratin of pears grilled with almonds. The 280-F ($53.20) fixed-price menu is exceptional.

ⓢ Brasserie du Casino

4 rue du Casino. ☎ **70-98-23-06.** Reservations recommended at lunch. Main courses 65–110 F ($12.35–$20.90); fixed-price menus 98–145 F ($18.60–$27.55). AE, MC, V. Thurs–Mon noon–1:30pm and 7–10pm, Tues noon–1:30pm. Closed Nov. FRENCH.

This has been a thriving brasserie since the 1920s, and it's a preferred stopover for actors and musicians visiting from Paris to perform at the casino. The de Chassat family is charming and especially solicitous to foreigners dining at their restaurant, known for its sheathing of copper and art deco mahogany. At lunch it's busy, but the real charm comes out at night, when a pianist entertains. Specialties are sweetbreads with hazelnuts, paupiette of rabbit with shallots, and veal liver with fondue of onions.

4 Clermont-Ferrand

248 miles S of Paris, 110 miles W of Lyon

The ancient capital of the Auvergne, this old double city in south-central France has looked down on a long parade of history. On the small Tiretaine River, it was created in 1731 by a merger of two towns, Clermont and Montferrand. It's surrounded by hills, and in the distance is one of the great attractions of Auvergne, Puy-de-Dôme, a volcanic mountain.

ESSENTIALS

GETTING THERE   The Clermont-Aulnat airport is 4 miles east of town. Rail lines converge on Clermont-Ferrand from all parts of France, including Paris's Gare de Lyon, Marseille, and Toulouse. Trains from small towns in the Auvergne usually require a connection.

VISITOR INFORMATION   The Office de Tourisme is at 69 bd. Gergovia (☎ **73-93-30-20**).

EXPLORING THE TOWN

To begin your tour, head for the center of Clermont, the bustling **place de Jaude,** where you can sample a glass of regional wine at a café under the shade of a catalpa tree. When you're ready, take rue du 11-Novembre, which branches off from the main plaza. This street leads to **rue des Gras,** the most interesting artery of Clermont.

Most of the interesting old buildings are in Vieux-Clermont, whose focal point is place de la Victoire, site of the black-lava **Cathédrale Notre-Dame,** rue de la Cathédrale (☎ **73-92-46-61**), one of the great gothic churches of central France, dating primarily from the 13th and 14th centuries; it was added to in the 19th century. Its most outstanding feature is the series of stained-glass windows from the 13th and 14th centuries. Admission is free; it's open Monday to Saturday from 9:30am to noon and 2 to 5pm.

After leaving the cathedral, explore the buildings in this historic neighborhood. In particular, look for the **Maison de Savaron,** at 3 rue des Chaussetiers, constructed in 1513. It has a beautiful courtyard and a staircase tower.

Several blocks northest of the cathedral is the finest example of Auvergnat romanesque architecture, made of lava from volcanic deposits in the region: the **Eglise Notre-Dame-du-Port,** rue du Port (☎ 73-91-32-94). Dating from the 11th and 12th centuries, the church has four radiating chapels, and its transept is surmounted by an octagonal tower. The crypt holds a 17th-century "black Madonna." Admission is free; it's open daily from 8:30am to 6:30pm.

Between the two churches stands the Renaissance **Fontaine d'Amboise,** on place de la Poterne, its pyramid supporting a statue of Hercules. Nearby is **square Pascal,** commemorating the fact that Blaise Pascal was born here in 1623 in a house on rue des Gras. Regrettably, the house was demolished in 1958, but a statue honors the native son.

The wide range of exhibits at the **Musée Bargoin,** 45 rue de Ballainvilliers (☎ 73-91-37-31), includes some prehistoric objects, as well as wooden carvings and bronzes from the Gallo-Roman era. The museum also has interesting stained-glass windows, plus a wide range of paintings. The Flemish, French, and Italian masters range from the 17th to the 19th century, and there are contemporary artists as well. The museum is open May to September, Tuesday to Saturday from 10am to noon and 2 to 6pm and Sunday from 2 to 6pm; October to April, Tuesday to Saturday from 10am to noon and 2 to 5pm and Sunday from 2 to 6pm. Admission is 21 F ($4) for adults and 11 F ($2.10) for children.

Containing Gallo-Roman artifacts and local memorabilia, the **Musée de Ranquet,** 34 rue des Gras (☎ 73-37-38-63), is in the Maison des Architects, a Renaissance landmark. The collection includes regional furniture and workaday objects, like regional pottery from the 18th century. The museum owns two "arithmetical machines" that belonged to Pascal, the only two of their kind said to exist outside of private collections in France. There's also a room devoted to France's hero of the Battle of Marengo, Général Desaix. The museum is open May to September, Tuesday to Saturday from 10am to noon and 2 to 6pm and Sunday from 2 to 6pm; October to April, Tuesday to Saturday from 10am to noon and 2 to 5pm and Sunday from 2 to 6pm. Admission is 12 F ($2.30).

WHERE TO STAY

✪ Gallieni

51 rue Bonnabaud, 63000 Clermont-Ferrand. ☎ 73-93-59-69. Fax 73-34-89-29. 80 rms. MINIBAR TV TEL. 250–300 F ($47.50–$57) double. Breakfast 35 F ($6.65) extra. AE, DC, MC, V. Parking 20 F ($3.80). Bus 1, 2, 4, or 9.

This is not the best hotel in town, but many locals cite it as a good value. The rooms have recently been renovated, for the most part, and are comfortably furnished but somewhat uninspired. All are well maintained and clean, however. La Charade restaurant serves some of the most reasonably priced fare in town, with a fixed-price menu beginning at 90 F ($17.10).

Mercure Gergovie

82 bd. Gergovia, 63000 Clermont-Ferrand. ☎ 73-34-46-46. Fax 73-34-46-36. 124 rms. MINIBAR TV TEL. 445–485 F ($84.55–$92.15) double. Breakfast 52 F ($9.90) extra. AE, DC, MC, V. Parking 35 F ($6.65). Bus 1, 2, 4, or 9.

This modern hotel is near the lovely Jardin Lecoq. The rooms are well furnished and immaculate; most of them are rather spacious. Everything about the hotel is functional, not exciting, and many business travelers often stop off here if they're in town to do business with the Michelin company. La Retirade restaurant is a good choice, with meals starting at 115 F ($21.85).

WHERE TO DINE

Le Clavé

10–12 rue St-Adjutor. ☎ **73-36-46-30.** Reservations required. Main courses 110–160 F ($20.90–$30.40); fixed-price menus 100–380 F ($19–$72.20). MC, V. Mon–Fri noon–2pm and 8–10:30pm, Sat 8–10:30pm. Bus 1, 2, 4, or 9. FRENCH.

This well-known restaurant brings a big-city aesthetic to the heart of Clermont-Ferrand; the owner trained at Maxim's in Paris. Inside a 19th-century stone house, it contains two monochromatic dining rooms. Menu items are both classic and contemporary. Your meal may include foie gras en terrine or warm chiffonnade of crustaceans. If you like fish, try an old Mediterranean favorite, rascasse bonne femme or grilled filet of Atlantic perch, served with fennel and beurre blanc. If you prefer beef, try a pavé of beef with foie-gras sauce. Desserts, wheeled to your table on a trolley, vary with the chef's inspiration.

✪ Jean-Yves Bath

Place du Marché-St-Pierre. ☎ **73-31-23-23.** Reservations required. Restaurant, main courses 100–130 F ($19–$24.70); fixed-price menus 260–350 F ($49.40–$66.50). Brasserie, platters 45–55 F ($8.55–$10.45). AE, MC, V. Restaurant, Tues–Fri noon–2pm and 7:30–9:15pm, Sat 7:30–9:15pm. Brasserie, Tues–Sat noon–1am. Closed Feb and Nov. Bus 1, 2, 4, or 9. FRENCH.

Few pretensions and lots of wonderful flavors go into the locally inspired cuisine at Jean-Yves Bath's charming restaurant. The dining room looks as if it belongs on a yacht, thanks to liberal amounts of brass and mahogany. It's the perfect setting for a fish salad covered with truffles and vinaigrette. Other dishes include salad of rabbit with orange zest, fresh thyme, and tomato essence, as well as sweetbreads in puff pastry. Dessert might be strawberry ravioli. Cost-conscious meals are served throughout the day in the street-level brasserie, where the menu features heaping platters of bistro-style food (steaks, fish, and local sausages). The ground floor also contains a wine bar, where unusual local vintages are sold by the glass.

5 Le Puy-en-Velay

325 miles S of Paris, 80 miles SE of Clermont-Ferrand

The site of Le Puy-en-Veley (usually shortened to Le Puy) has been called one of the most extraordinary sights of France. The steep volcanic spires left from geological activities that ended millennia ago were capped with romanesque churches, a cathedral, and a collection of medieval houses that rise sinuously from the plain below. The history of Le Puy is centered around the cult of the Virgin Mary, which prompted the construction of many of the city's churches.

ESSENTIALS

GETTING THERE   St-Georges-d'Aurac is the nearest railway station, with connections from Nîmes and Clermont-Ferrand. From St-Georges-d'Aurac, a local train makes a slow and infrequent run into Le Puy. Trains from Lyon or St-Etienne are more direct.

VISITOR INFORMATION   The Office de Tourisme is on place du Breuil (☎ **71-09-38-41**).

SEEING THE TOP ATTRACTIONS

The romanesque **Cathédrale Notre-Dame,** place du For (☎ **73-62-11-45**), used to house many of the pilgrims heading to Santiago de Compostela in Spain. Marked by a vivid Oriental and Byzantine influence, it's worth a visit. You can also visit the adjoining cloisters; some of the carved capitals date from the Carolingian era. Your ticket to the cloisters also admits you to the Chapelle des Reliques et Trésor d'Art Religieux, which contains fabrics and gold and silver objects from the church treasury, as well as an unusual enameled chalice from the 12th century. The

---

Serving Up Volcanic Cones in the Auvergne

The region surrounding Clermont-Ferrand is one of France's most geologically distinctive. In 1977 the government designated 946,000 acres of its undulating, dark-stoned terrain as the Parc Naturel Régional des Volcans d'Auvergne. The park contains at least 150 villages as well as farms, with herds of cows and goats that produce the Auvergne's cheeses and *charcuteries.* However, scattered among them are are at least 90 extinct volcanic cones (*puys*), which rise dramatically and eerily above the pine forests.

The highest and oldest of these is **Puy-de-Dôme** (4,800 feet above sea level), a site used for worship since prehistoric times by the Gauls and the Romans. In 1648 Pascal used the mountaintop for experiments that proved Torricelli's hypothesis about how altitudes affect atmospheric pressure. And in 1911 one of the most dramatic events in French aviation occurred at Puy-de-Dôme when Eugène Renaux, with a passenger, flew nonstop from Paris in just over five hours, to land precariously on its summit and collect a 100,000-franc prize. From the summit, you'll have a panoramic view—on a clear day you can see all the way to Mont Blanc in the east. Shuttle buses run from the base to the summit, costing 18 F ($3.40) round-trip.

Areas of the park contain radically different features. **Les Puys** (also known as Monts Dômes) are a minichain of 112 extinct volcanoes (some capped with craters, some capped with rounded peaks) packed densely into an area 3 miles wide by 19 miles long. Each dome is unique: Some were built up by slow extrusions of upthrust rock; some were the source of vast lava flows. Those with craters at their summits were probably the site of violent explosions whose power stands in direct contrast to the region's peace and quiet today. The geological fury that created these hills ended between 5,000 and 6,000 years ago, but the rectangle of extinct volcanoes is aligned along what geologists define as one of the most potentially unstable fault lines in France, the San Andreas fault of the French mainland.

Because this region is relatively underpopulated, you might not be aware of the park's boundaries during your explorations, though details about trekking and camping are available from the **Parc Naturel Régional des Volcans d'Auvergne**, Montlosier, 63970 Aydat (☎ **73-65-67-19**), 12¹/₂ miles southwest of Clermont-Ferrand. A branch office is at 10 rue du Président-Delzons, 15000 Aurillac (☎ **71-48-68-68**). At least half a dozen guidebooks, publicizing individual treks through the park of between two and six hours' duration, are for sale at either branch—priced at 35 to 95 F ($6.65 to $18.05) each.

cathedral is open daily from 7am to 7pm. The cloisters and Chapel of Relics are open daily: July to September from 9:30am to 7pm, October to March from 9:30am to noon and 2 to 4:30pm, and April to June from 9:30am to noon and 2 to 6:30pm. Admission to the cathedral is free; to enter the cloisters and Chapel of Relics costs 20 F ($3.80) for adults and 13 F ($2.45) for children.

It's a very long climb up rocky stairs to reach the **Chapelle St-Michel-d'Aiguilhe,** atop the Rocher St-Michel, but when you get here you'll be struck by the Oriental influences in the floor plan, the arabesques, and the mosaics crafted from black stone. On view are some 12th-century murals and an 11th-century wooden depiction of Christ. It's open daily: mid-June to mid-September from 9am to 7pm, and mid-September to mid-June from 10am to noon and 2 to 5pm; closed mornings from December to February. Admission is 10 F ($1.90).

If you appreciate handcrafts, you'll enjoy the displays of lace, some from the 16th century, at the **Musée Crozatier,** in the Jardin Henri-Vinay (☎ **71-09-38-90**). Also here is a collection of carved architectural embellishments from the romanesque era and paintings from the 14th through the 20th century. It's open May to September, Wednesday to Monday from 10am to noon and 2 to 6pm; October to April, Monday and Wednesday to Saturday from 10am to noon and 2 to 4pm, Sunday from 2 to 4pm. Admission is 12 F ($2.30) for adults and 6 F ($1.15) for children.

WHERE TO STAY

Hôtel Chris'tel

15 bd. Alexandre-Clair, 43003 Le Puy CEDEX. ☎ **71-02-24-44.** Fax 71-02-52-68. 30 rms. TV TEL. 250–360 F ($47.50–$68.40) double. Breakfast 45 F ($8.55) extra. AE, DC, MC, V. Parking free.

This contemporary hotel in a good location offers comfortable rooms, each with a writing desk, an easy chair, and full-length windows that open onto a balcony. The hotel has a pleasant staff and an inviting dining room, serving only breakfast. It's 12 minutes from the town center.

WHERE TO DINE

Le Bateau Ivre

5 rue Portail-d'Avignon. ☎ **71-09-67-20.** Reservations recommended. Main courses 90–120 F ($17.10–$22.80); fixed-price menus 100 F ($19) (Tues–Thurs only), 145 F ($27.55), and 180 F ($34.20); *menu dégustation* 280 F ($53.20). V. Tues–Sat noon–2:30pm and 7:30–10pm. Closed June 11–21 and Nov 1–15. FRENCH.

This intimate dining room is in a pretty 19th-century house with lots of rustic detail. M. Datessen cooks and supervises the dining room. Specialties include salmon, snails, lamb cooked in wine, and a full array of other well-prepared French dishes. Dedicated pilgrims to Le Puy always seem to have this restaurant marked as the "serious" dining choice.

6 Aubusson

236 miles S of Paris, 55 miles E of Limoges, 59 miles NW of Clermont-Ferrand

In the Creuse Valley, the little market town of Aubusson enjoys world renown for its carpets and tapestries—in fact, it's called the *ville de la tapisserie.* Aubusson is characterized by clock towers, bridges, peaked roofs, and turrets—all of which inspired painter Gromaire's widely reproduced cartoon *View of Aubusson.* Against the gray granite, rainbow-hued skeins of wool hang from windows. The workshops of the craftspeople are spread throughout the town, and many are open to the public (inquire at the door).

The origin of the industry is unknown. Some credit the Arabs who settled here in 732. Others think that the craft came from Flanders in the Middle Ages. For years the favorite subject was *The Lady and the Unicorn*, the original of which was discovered in the nearby Château de Boussac. Many tapestry reproductions of the works of such 18th-century painters as Boucher and Watteau have also been made. Since World War II, designs by painters like Picasso, Matisse, and Braque have been stressed.

The **Musée Départemental de la Tapisserie,** Centre Culturel Jean-Lurçat, avenue des Lissiers (☎ **55-66-33-06**), has exhibits related to the six-century-long tradition of the Aubusson carpet-weaving industry. The displays also highlight the 20th-century rebirth of the Aubusson carpet and the art of tapestry weaving. It's open Friday to Wednesday from 9:30am to 12:30pm and 2 to 6pm; in summer, also on Thursday from 2 to 6pm. Admission is 18 F ($3.40) for adults and 12 F ($2.30) for children 11 to 16; 10 and under free.

La Maison du Vieux Tapissier, rue Vieille (☎ **55-66-32-12**), exhibits old carpets and displays a reconstruction of an old carpet-weaving studio.

ESSENTIALS

GETTING THERE   Aubusson has bus and rail service, much of it indirect, from Clermont-Ferrand and Paris, among other cities.

VISITOR INFORMATION   The Office de Tourisme is on rue Vieille (☎ 55-66-32-12).

WHERE TO STAY & DINE

Le Lion d'Or

Place du Général-Espagne, 23200 Aubusson. ☎ **55-66-13-88.** Fax 55-66-84-73. 11 rms. TV TEL. 250–300 F ($47.50–$57) double. AE, MC, V.

On the main square, this is a late 19th-century building whose modernization does not merge as authentically into the historic core as one would have wished. However, it's still the town's best hotel, with a polite but no-nonsense management by the Chaussoy family. The rooms are uncomplicated but comfortable; the street level contains a restaurant where set menus cost 85 to 240 F ($16.15 to $45.60). Between October 15 and April 15, no meals are served on Friday night and Saturday at lunch. In summer, meals are offered at lunch and dinner daily.

7 Limoges

246 miles S of Paris, 193 miles N of Toulouse

The ancient capital of Limousin, Limoges, in west-central France, is world-famous for its exquisite porcelain and enamel works, the latter a medieval industry revived in the 19th century. On the Vienne's right bank, the town historically has had two parts: the Cité, its narrow streets and old *maisons* on the lower slope, and the town proper at the summit.

ESSENTIALS

GETTING THERE   Limoges has bus and train service from all other regional cities, with direct trains from Toulouse, Poitiers, and Paris.

VISITOR INFORMATION   The Office de Tourisme is on boulevard de Fleurus (☎ 55-34-46-87).

SEEING THE TOWN

If you'd like to see an enameler or porcelain factory, ask at the tourist office for list of workshops (see "Essentials," above). Or go directly to the famous **Le Pavillon de la Porcelaine,** avenue John-Kennedy (☎ 55-30-21-86). Since 1842 Haviland has been exporting its porcelain to the United States and elsewhere. Over the years it has used the designs of artists like Gauguin and Dalí. You can see the masterpieces produced since 1842 in a museum. Later, visit an air-conditioned room where you can follow the manufacturing process with the help of a video on a giant screen. A large shop also sells the porcelain at factory prices. Admission is free. Le Pavillon is open daily: April to October from 8:30am to 7:30pm, and November to March from 8:30am to 7pm.

The **Musée National Adrien-Dubouché,** 8 bis place Winston-Churchill (☎ 55-77-45-58), displays a beautiful collection of Limoges china. In its porcelain collection the museum is second in France, bowing only to Sèvres. Its galleries trace the entire history of chinaware in the world. Whole dinner sets of noted figures are here. The main gallery also contains contemporary Limoges ware. Admission is 17 F ($3.25) for adults and 11 F ($2.10) for ages 18 to 25; 17 and under free. It's open in July and August, Wednesday to Monday from 10am to 5:15pm; September to June, Wednesday to Monday 10am to noon and 1:30 to 5:15pm.

The **Cathédrale St-Etienne,** place de la Cathédrale (☎ 55-34-17-38), was begun in 1273 but took many years to complete. The choir, for example, was finished in 1327, but work was going on in the nave until almost 1890. The cathedral is the only one in the old province of Limousin to be built entirely in gothic style. The main entrance is through Porte St-Jean, which has some beautiful carved wooden doors from the 16th century. The portal was constructed at the peak of the flamboyant gothic style. Inside, the nave appears so harmonious it's hard to imagine that its construction took six centuries. The rood screen is of interest, built in 1533 in the ornate style of the Italian Renaissance. The cathedral also contains some admirable bishops' tombs from the 14th to the 16th century. It's open daily from 9:30am to 6pm.

Adjoining the cathedral in the Jardins de l'Evêché—which offer a view of the Vienne and the Bridge of St. Stephen from the 13th century—the old archbishops' palace has been turned into the **Musée Municipal,** place de la Cathédrale (☎ 55-45-61-75). The 18th-century building, elegant in line, has an outstanding collection of Limoges enamels from the 12th century, as well as some enamel paintings by Leonard Limousin, who was born in 1505 in Limoges and went on to win world acclaim and the favor of four monarchs. Limoges was also the birthplace of Renoir, and the museum displays several works by this world-class artist. From June to September, the museum is open daily (except holidays) from 10am to noon and 2 to 6pm; October to May, Wednesday to Monday until 5pm. Admission is free.

Another church of interest is the **Eglise St-Michel-des-Lions,** at 11 rue Petitniauds-Beaupeyrat (☎ 55-34-18-13). Construction was launched in the 14th century and work continued into the 15th and 16th centuries. The church boasts late gothic stained glass, plus relics of St. Martial, including his head. It's open daily from 8am to 7pm.

If you're in the mood to stock up on local products, try these two **Prestige de Limoges** shops owned by the same company: At 2–13 bd. Louis-Blanc (☎ 55-34-44-15) you'll find Limoges's own "unblemished crystal," as well as crystal from Lalique, St. Louis, and Baccarat and silverware from Christofle and Puiforcat. At 27 bd. Louis-Blanc (☎ 55-34-58-61) you can buy porcelain from Haviland, Bernardaud, Raynaud, and Lafarge. There's also a collection of slightly damaged, imperfect seconds. Both shops are open Monday to Saturday from 9:15am to noon and 2 to 7pm.

WHERE TO STAY

La Caravelle

21 rue Armand-Barbès, 87000 Limoges. ☎ **55-77-75-29.** Fax 55-79-27-60. 37 rms. TV TEL. 370 F ($70.30) double. Breakfast 35 F ($6.65) extra. AE, DC, MC, V. Parking free.

Just north of the city center, this highly recommendable modern hotel is designed to stay young for years to come. It possesses a tranquil atmosphere, and guests receive a warm welcome. The rooms are simply furnished. Breakfast is the only meal served.

Royal Limousin

Place de la République, 87000 Limoges. ☎ **55-34-65-30.** Fax 55-34-55-21. 70 rms. MINIBAR TV TEL. 480–580 F ($91.20–$110.25) double. Breakfast 50 F ($9.50) extra. AE, DC, MC, V.

This modern oasis in a place of antiquity is near a municipal parking lot in the center of Limoges. The rooms are modish in chain-hotel style but generally large and sun-filled. The only drawback is that the hotel is often booked by summer group tours.

WHERE TO DINE

Philippe Redon

3 rue Aguesseau. ☎ **55-34-66-22.** Reservations recommended. Fixed-price menus 90 F ($17.10), 170 F ($32.30), 230 F ($43.70), and 290 F ($55.10). AE, DC, MC, V. Tues–Sat noon–2:30pm and 7–10pm. Closed Aug 1–15. FRENCH.

In a 19th-century house a few steps from the produce market, this restaurant is maintained by a youthful team of waiters headed by owner/chef Philippe Redon. It contains a 1930s art deco–style interior accented with exposed stone and flowers. Menu items are the personal statement of the chef and vary with the availability of local ingredients. Examples are crayfish with spices, turbot with girolle mushrooms, filet of monkfish marinated in Szechuan pepper, and codfish with truffles in puff pastry.

NEARBY ACCOMMODATIONS & DINING
IN ST-MARTIN-DU-FAULT

✪ La Chapelle St-Martin

87510 Nieul. ☎ **55-75-80-17.** Fax 55-75-89-50. 10 rms, 3 suites. A/C TEL. 580–950 F ($110.20–$180.60) double; 1,500 F ($285.15) suite. Half board 750–850 F ($142.50–$161.50) per person. AE, V. Closed: Hotel, Jan–Feb 15; restaurant, Mon year round. Parking free. Take N147 and D35 7 miles northeast from Limoges.

This is the best place to stay in the environs if you enjoy turn-of-the-century–style living and superb food in the tradition of the Relais & Châteaux group. The hotel is graciously situated in a private park with two ponds. Your host,

M. Dudognon, requests that you write or call well in advance. The rooms are individually decorated and tasteful, and some are suitable for the disabled. The food is excellent, the ingredients selected with care.

IN NIEUIL

To get to Nieuil, from Angoulême, take N141 in the direction of Limoges, making a left-hand turn at Suaux, heading toward Nieuil. Follow the signs for about a mile east of the village toward Fontafie. *Note:* Don't confuse Nieuil with La Chapelle St-Martin at Nieul (with a slightly different spelling).

✪ Château de Nieuil

16270 Nieuil. ☎ **45-71-36-38.** Fax 45-71-46-45. 11 rms, 3 suites. TEL. 820–1,250 F ($155.80–$237.60) double; 1,350–1,950 F ($256.65–$370.70) suite. Breakfast 70 F ($13.30) extra. AE, DC, MC, V. Parking free. Closed mid-Nov to late Apr.

This château, built in the 15th century as a hunting lodge for François I, was transformed in 1937 into the first château-hotel in France. Restored by the comte de Dampierre early in the 1800s after its destruction in the Revolution, it has remained in the antique-collecting family of Jean-Michel Bodinaud for the past three generations. Today, 400 acres of park and forest lead up to a series of beautifully maintained gardens, the pride of the owners. On the premises are tennis courts, a pool, and even an art and antiques gallery. The cuisine, supervised by Mme Luce Bodinaud, is superb, focusing on classic traditions and regional recipes. Typical dishes are stuffed cabbage, escalope of foie gras caramelized in port wine, filet of beef with mignonnette of pepper, and salmon cooked in court bouillon with sage. Fixed-price menus cost 230 to 300 F ($43.70 to $57). Nonguests can dine here if they call ahead.

The Dordogne & Périgord

Lovers of foie gras and truffles as well as lovers of nature have always sought out France's Dordogne and Périgord region. In this chapter we'll look at some capitals of provinces that long ago were subdivided into départements of France: Our first stop, Périgueux, was the capital of the old province of Périgord. After following the trail of the Cro-Magnon people, we'll visit Cahors, the ancient capital of Quercy, then Montauban, where the great painter Ingres was born.

However, in this region the towns themselves are not the stars—it's the unspoiled fertile countryside, of much hidden charm and antique character, that holds the fascination. In some villages the Middle Ages seem to live on. It's said there are no discoveries to be made in France, but you can defy the experts and make many discoveries if you give yourself adequate time to visit a region too often neglected by North Americans.

REGIONAL CUISINE   Ask gastronomes about the cuisine of the Dordogne and Périgord and the first thing to come to mind will be truffles, one of the most sought-after vegetables in France. The region produces more than 30 types, growing underground, without a root or stem, at the base of one type of oak tree in light soil of a certain degree of acidity. It gives off a distinctive odor, said by one 19th-century gastronome "to epitomize the perfumed soul of the Périgord." Because truffles grow underground (they're technically classified a "subterranean fungus"), truffle hunters have traditionally used carefully trained dogs to smell their location. Trained pigs have also been used to find them, but they tend to eat the truffle before it can be retrieved by the hunter.

Equally famous are the region's pâtés, which, when studded with "black diamonds" (truffles), have conquered many a resistant appetite. These are made from the enlarged livers of geese that have been force-fed a diet of rich corn. Some pâtés are still made of unadulterated goose liver, but the more frequently seen version is a ballotine of foie gras. This will usually have been prepared in a factory, where the goose liver is mixed with white turkey meat and then covered with meat gelatin.

One characteristic of the region's cuisine is the stuffing of many roasts and joints. The stuffing usually includes breadcrumbs, truffles, and segments of goose liver. The most famous sauce here is a sauce Périgueux, made from sweet madeira wine and truffles. Anything prepared *à la périgourdine* probably includes a garnish of truffles to which foie gras has been added. Another staple of the cuisine are *cèpes* (flap mushrooms). Other regional specialties are *bréjaude* (a cabbage/bacon soup served with rye bread) and *lièvre en chabessal* (freshly killed rabbit stuffed with highly seasoned pork, ham, and veal).

Rich in nutrients, the soil produces huge quantities of walnuts, vegetables, and fruits, plus some of the most succulent beef and veal from the limousin breed. This breed has been exported to Australia and South America, where it has thrived.

The most famous wines here are the red and white Bergerac, the red Pécharmant, and the deep-red Cahors. Cahors is best aged for a dozen years (some of them in an oaken cask) before reaching a suitable sophistication. The Montbazillac is a sweet, tawny dessert wine whose grapes have been deliberately permeated with a whitish-green mold known as noble rot (*pourriture noble*). When it's fermented, this improves the flavor of the wine, partly by reducing its acidity and partly because of a mystery that only Dionysus could fully understand.

EXPLORING THE REGION BY CAR

Here's how to link together the best of the region if you rent a car.

Day 1   Begin in the truffle capital of Europe, Périgueux, and spend the night there after a tour of the local sights.

Day 2   Drive 28 miles east on E70, detouring south at D704 for a visit to the prehistoric caves of Lascaux, near the village of Montignac. Unless you have an overwhelming interest in prehistory, continue 12¹/₂ miles southeast, following the course of the Vézère River. Stop for the night at Les Eyzies-de-Tayac.

Day 3   Rise early for a day of village-hopping from Les Eyzies to towns like Beynac-et-Cazenac (9 miles southeast of Les Eyzies) and Sarlat-la-Canéda (4¹/₂ miles northeast of Beynac). Both routes follow country roads marked only with signs leading to the above-mentioned destinations. Make a special effort to leave time for relaxing in the shadow of the Château de Beynac, where the aristocracy of Périgord used to gather. The castle is a 13th-century curiosity, but it's the view over the valley that makes a break here especially worthwhile. There's a worthy restaurant nearby, on the ground floor of a converted forge/blacksmith's shop transformed into the Hôtel Bonnet (☎ **53-29-50-01**); set menus range from 95 to 280 F ($18.05 to $53.20)

Unless you have time to linger, however, we recommend that you continue to Sarlat-la-Canéda, 6 miles northeast. There you'll find the unusual Cathédrale St-Sacerdos, and the Maison de la Boétie, place André Malraux, belonging to one of France's most famous Renaissance writers, Etienne de la Boétie. You might be tempted to enjoy a meal at one of the town's most endearing restaurants, the Hostellerie Marcel, 8 av. de Selves (☎ **53-29-21-98**). Meals are served at lunch and dinner daily, except Monday, and cost 90 to 200 F ($17.10 to $38).

Then embark on the day's final jaunt, a 25-mile excursion northeast along D704 and then along various well-signposted country roads to your night's stay at Colette's family homestead, the Château de Castel-Novel, in the town of Brive-La-Gaillard. (The town is also sometimes referred to as Varetz.) Retire early to rest up for a fully scheduled day tomorrow.

The Dordogne & Périgord

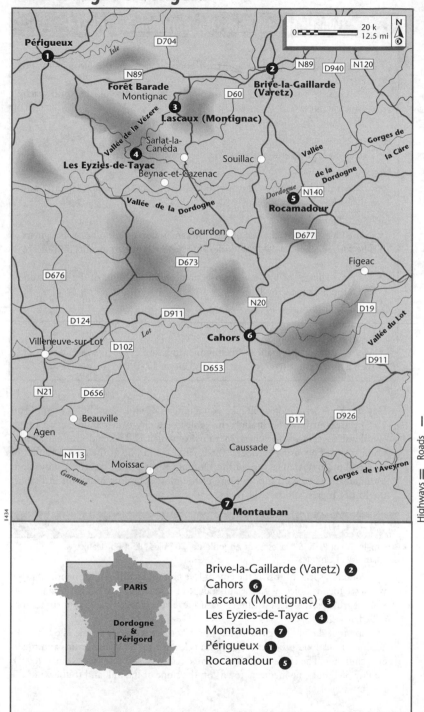

Highways = Roads —

Brive-la-Gaillarde (Varetz) ❷
Cahors ❻
Lascaux (Montignac) ❸
Les Eyzies-de-Tayac ❹
Montauban ❼
Périgueux ❶
Rocamadour ❺

What's Special About the Dordogne & Périgord

Great Towns
- Périgueux, city of foie gras and truffles and capital of the old province of Périgord.
- Les Eyzies-de-Tayac, called an archeologist's dream, one of the world's richest ancient sites.
- Rocamadour, another medieval town that defies gravity.

Ancient Monuments
- Grotte du Pech-Merle, a prehistoric cave near Cabrerets.

Literary Pilgrimages
- Château de Castel-Novel, former residence of French novelist Colette, now a Relais & Châteaux hotel.

Architectural Highlights
- Cathédrale St-Front, the last of the Aquitanian domed churches at Périgueux.
- The fortress castle at Les Eyzies-de-Tayac, now home to a collection of prehistoric relics.
- The "red village" of Collonges, with small mansions built of dark-red stone and a romanesque church.

Outstanding Museums
- Lascaux II, at Lascaux, displaying reproductions of the Sistine Chapel of prehistoric art.
- Musée Ingres, at Montauban, the premier museum of the province, with more than a dozen paintings by Ingres, born here in 1780.

Day 4 Your drive today will take you along an 80-mile southbound ramble on N20, with your final destination the pink-toned city of Montauban. En route, you'll visit several historic cities, foremost of which is Rocamadour, followed by Cahors, site of a worthy cathedral (St-Etienne), and one of the best examples of medieval military architecture in the Dordogne, the pont Valentré. Continue to Montauban, where you can visit one of the most appealing museums in France, the Musée Ingres, and stay the night.

1 Périgueux

301 miles SW of Paris, 53 miles SE of Angoulême, 70 miles NE of Bordeaux, 63 miles SW of Limoges

Gastronomes speak of this as the city of foie gras and truffles. Throughout France you'll see menu choices with the appendage of *à la périgourdine.* That means a garnish of truffles, the tastiest fungus nature ever provided. Foie gras is sometimes added as well.

Capital of the old province of Périgord, Périgueux stands on the Isle River. In addition to its food products, the region is known for its Roman ruins and medieval churches. The city's divided into three sections: the Cité (old Roman town), Le Puy St-Front (the medieval town) on the slope of the hill, and to the west, the modern town.

ESSENTIALS

GETTING THERE   Trains run frequently from Paris, Lyon, and Toulouse, plus many regional towns and villages. Six trains per day arrive from Paris (trip time: 6 to 7 hr.), four trains pull in from Lyon (trip time: 7 hr.), 10 trains per day from Bordeaux (trip time: 2¹/₂ hr.), and seven trains arrive from Toulouse (trip time: 4 hr.).

TOURING BY BIKE   One of the best ways to explore the surrounding district is by bike with a map obtained from the tourist office. Rentals are possible from **Au Tour de France,** 96 av. du Maréchal-Juin (☎ **53-53-41-91**), which charges 55 F ($10.45) for the first day, 40 F ($7.60) for each day following. Mountain bikes can be rented for 80 F ($15.20) for the first day, 60 F ($11.40) for each day thereafter. It's open Monday to Saturday from 9am to noon and 2 to 7pm.

VISITOR INFORMATION   The Office du Tourisme is at 26 place Francheville (☎ **53-53-10-63**).

SEEING THE TOP ATTRACTIONS

In Le Puy St-Front (the medieval quarter) rises the **Cathédrale St-Front,** at place de la Clautre (☎ **53-53-23-62**). It was built from 1125 to 1150, the last of the Aquitanian domed churches. Dedicated to St. Fronto, a local bishop, it's one of the largest churches in southwestern France. The cathedral's four-story bell tower rises nearly 200 feet, overlooking the marketplace; it's surmounted by a cone-shaped spire. With its five white domes and colonnaded turrets, St-Front evokes memories of Constantinople. The interior, somewhat bare, is built on the plan of a Greek cross, unusual for a French cathedral. Hearty visitors can apply to the sacristan (tip expected) for a tour of the roof. On this tour, you can walk between the domes and turrets, looking out over Vieux Périgueux with its old houses running down to the Isle.

The cathedral is open daily from 8am to noon and 2:30 to 7:30pm (closes at dusk in winter). You're admitted to the crypt and cloisters, dating from the 9th century, for 10 F ($1.90).

The other remarkable church—this one in the Cité area on rue de la Cité—is the **Eglise St-Etienne-de-la-Cité** (☎ **53-53-21-35**). This church was a cathedral until 1669, when it lost its position to St-Front. The church was built in the 12th century but has been much mutilated since. It contains a 12th-century bishop's tomb and a carved 17th-century wooden reredos depicting the Assumption of the Madonna. It's open daily from 8am to 5pm.

Built on the site of an Augustinian monastery, the **Musée de Périgord,** 22 cours Tourny (☎ **53-53-16-42**), has an exceptional collection of prehistoric relics as well as sculptures and Gallo-Roman mosaics. Many of the artifacts were recovered from digs in the Périgord region, which is rich in prehistoric remains. The museum is open Wednesday to Monday from 10am to noon and 2 to 6pm (to 5pm October to March). Admission is 10 F ($1.90) for adults and 6 F ($1.15) for children.

The **Tour de Vésone** stands 85 feet tall beyond the railway station, half a mile southwest of town. The *cella* of a Roman temple dedicated to the goddess Vesuna, it's all that remains to conjure up images of ancient rites.

The **Jardin des Arènes,** a vast eliptical amphitheater that once held as many as 22,000 spectators, is another reminder of Roman days. Now in ruins, the amphitheater, with a diameter of 1,312 feet, dates from the 2nd or 3rd century. The

No Stomach for Foie Gras

The taste of French gourmets for foie gras has inspired the vast numbers of dishes running the gamut from *traditionnelle* to *nouvelle*. Most of the delicacy is sold around Christmastime, when demand for the engorged livers of ducks or geese skyrockets.

Its preparation is distinctively French, with roots going back to the Middle Ages: First take an unsuspecting duck or goose. Then insert a coil down its throat and (in a process known as *gavage*) pour large amounts of corn directly into the bird's stomach two or three times a day. After about three weeks, the animal's liver expands to between 5 and 10 times normal size. The bird must then be slaughtered (and its liver preserved and prepared) just before it would otherwise die. The processed *foie gras* ("fat liver," because of the horrendous percentage of fat contained between the liver cells) sells for top-notch prices at supermarkets and gourmet outlets. Even in unpretentious shops the cost begins at around $20 for a mere 11 ounces.

Animal-rights activists consider the process an abomination, but their outcries tend to be ignored in a nation that looks upon the foodstuff with something like religious devotion. Despite opposition, France's National Society for the Defense of Animals buys frequent ads in national newspapers imploring boycotts of the product, calling it a "shameful and superfluous dish."

Foremost among the protesters is Brigitte Bardot, the 60-something veteran of films that helped create the stereotype of French women as sex kittens. Today, a tough-talking, no-nonsense Bardot has won world admiration as an international protector of kittens (and almost every creature, too) in her role as empress of animal rights. In a 1995 interview she cited her proudest achievement as the 1986 establishment of her foundation for the protection of animals; her most marked characteristic as courage; and the group of people she most despises as hunters. In the process, Bardot has endeared herself to new generations of fans and ensured a role for herself in the roster of world-class animal-rights activists.

Though Switzerland banned the production of foie gras in 1993 and despite of Bardot's formidable protest, production of the delicacy is rampant. As one social commentator noted, "What's the use of protesting? Denouncing foie gras in France is kind of like trying to ban beer in Germany or football in America."

admission-free site is open daily: May to August from 7:30am to 9pm, and September to April from 8am to 6pm. Near the arena are the remains of the **Château Barrière,** rue Turenne, built in the 11th or 12th century on Roman foundations.

WHERE TO STAY

Hôtel Bristol

39 rue Antoine-Gadaud, 24000 Périgueux. ☎ **53-08-75-90.** Fax 53-07-00-49. 29 rms. A/C MINIBAR TV TEL. 300–360 F ($57–$68.40) double. Breakfast 35 F ($6.65) extra. AE, MC, V. Parking free.

This modern three-star hotel is centrally located behind a small parking lot and offers comfortable, serviceable rooms, often with sleek styling. Breakfast is the only meal served, but it's only a five-minute walk to the town's best restaurants and major points of interest. The owners have spent much of their lives in North America and offer both a French and an English welcome to all international travelers.

WHERE TO DINE

La Flambée

2 rue Montaigne. ☎ **53-53-23-06.** Reservations recommended. Main courses 80–180 F ($15.20–$34.20); fixed-price menu 120 F ($22.80). AE, DC, MC, V. Mon–Sat noon–2pm and 6–10pm. FRENCH.

This restaurant is housed in a 250-year-old building with a high beamed ceiling and a staff that's been around for about 20 years. You'll be greeted cordially by the Thévenet family and treated to a rich cuisine using fresh local ingredients. They specialize in several foie gras dishes, but other popular choices are magrêt of duck, a variety of succulent grilled fish, tournedos Rossini, and lobster. The cookery is solid and reliable, though not the equal of L'Oison (below).

✪ L'Oison

In the Château des Reynats, at Chancelade, 24650 Périgueux. ☎ **53-03-53-59.** Fax 53-03-44-84. Reservations recommended. Main courses 130–180 F ($24.70–$34.20). AE, DC, MC, V. Tues–Sat noon–2pm and 8–10pm, Sun noon–2pm. FRENCH.

In 1995, the most acclaimed restaurant in Périgueux moved to the finest hotel, the 19th-century Château des Reynats, encircled by a manicured park. This slate-roofed manor offers an Empire dining room in which you can enjoy the *cuisine du marché* of talented chef Régis Chiorozas, who can do more with fresh ingredients than anyone else in the area. In landlocked Périgueux he concentrates on seafood—and does it taste fresh! But his menu also includes the traditional regional dishes, even a salad of fresh truffles that's among the most delectable we've ever sampled. In season, young partridge, roebuck, and hare are available. The desserts are sublime.

The château also rents 32 beautiful rooms, costing 590 F ($112.10) for a double.

2 Lascaux (Montignac)

308 miles SW of Paris, 29 miles SE of Périgueux

The Caves at Lascaux, near the Vézère River town of Montignac in the Dordogne region, contain the most beautiful and most famous cave paintings in the world. If you weren't among the fortunate thousands who got to view the actual paintings before 1963, you may be permanently out of luck. The drawings have been closed to the general public to prevent deterioration, but a replica gives you a clear picture of the remarkable works.

They were discovered in 1940 by four boys looking for a dog and were opened to the public in 1948, quickly becoming one of France's major attractions, drawing 125,000 visitors annually. However, it became evident that the hordes of tourists had caused atmospheric changes in the caves, endangering the paintings. Scientists went to work to halt the deterioration, known as "the green sickness."

ESSENTIALS

GETTING THERE   Train connections to Montignac are infrequent and inconvenient (there's only one train daily, from Brive). There are bus connections from Sarlat.

The easiest way to reach Montignac is driving northeast from Eyzies on N704 for 12 miles—from Eyzies, there are lots of signs to Brive.

VISITOR INFORMATION   The Syndicat d'Initiative (tourist office) is on place Léo-Magne (☎ 53-51-82-60), in Montignac.

EXPLORING THE CAVES

Visits to **Lascaux I** are by invitation only, and people in certain professions, such as those who work for museums or in science and journalism, are qualified to visit, if they obtain permission months in advance. If you think you might qualify, you can write to: Direction des Antiquités Préhistoriques d'Aquitaine, 6 bis cours de Gourgue, 33074 Bordeaux CEDEX (☎ 56-51-39-06).

A short walk downhill from the real caves leads to **Lascaux II** (☎ 53-51-45-03), an impressive reproduction in concrete, molded above ground. The 131-foot-long reproduction displays some 200 paintings so that visitors will at least have some idea of what the "Sistine Chapel of prehistory" looked like. Here you can see majestic bulls, wild boars, stags, "Chinese horses," and lifelike deer, the originals of which were painted by Stone Age hunters 15,000 to 20,000 years ago.

Lascaux II is open in July and August, daily from 9:30am to 7pm; off-season, Tuesday to Sunday from 10am to noon and 2 to 5:30pm. It's closed from the first week of January until February 3. Admission is 48 F ($9.10) for adults and 15 F ($2.85) for children 11 and under. Try to show up as close to opening time as possible—the number of visitors per day is limited to 2,000 and tickets are usually sold out within 2 hours of opening. During most of the year you can buy tickets directly at Lascaux II, but during July and August tickets are sold only from a kiosk at the Syndicat d'Initiative, place Léo-Magne, in Montignac. For information, call the number above.

With the same ticket you can visit a museum devoted to cave art: **Le Thot** (☎ 53-50-70-44), 4¹/₂ miles southwest of Montignac along D706 (follow the signs pointing to the hamlet of Les Eyzies). On the premises are a zoo with live animals, two projection rooms showing short films on the discovery of cave art at Lascaux, and exhibitions relating to prehistoric communities in the Dordogne. It's open during July and August from 9:30am to 7:30pm; the rest of the year, Tuesday to Sunday from 10am to noon and 2 to 5:30pm. After your visit, walk out on the terrace for a view of the Vézère Valley, the Lascaux hills, and an animal park.

About 500 yards uphill from the barricaded grotto of Lascaux, a narrow road branches off through a forest until it reaches **Site Préhistorique de Regourdou** (☎ 53-51-81-23). This site, discovered in 1954, produced a humanoid jawbone and other artifacts. Seasonal openings and hours are the same as those for Lascaux II. Admission costs 20 F ($3.80) for adults and 10 F ($1.90) for children 7 to 10; 6 and under free.

WHERE TO STAY & DINE

✪ Château de Puy Robert

Route 65, 24290 Montignac Lascaux. ☎ **53-51-92-13.** Fax 53-51-80-11. 33 rms, 5 suites. MINIBAR TV TEL. 610–1,180 F ($115.95–$223.20) double; 1,580 F ($300.35) suite. Breakfast 75 F ($14.25) extra. AE, DC, MC, V. Parking free. Closed Oct 15–May 5.

Set on 16 acres about a 10-minute walk from the grottoes, this was built in 1860 as a country home. The handsomely furnished and comfortable guest rooms offer views of the Vézère Valley, and on the premises is an outdoor pool; mountain bikes are available. Traditionalists prefer rooms in the château, though more modern rooms are found in the annex. The restaurant serves imaginative meals. Though chef Olivier Pons is relatively new, he's been good enough to retain the château's one Michelin star and delicately treads the border between regional/traditional and postnouvelle. Fixed-price menus range from 190 to 390 F ($36.10 to $74.10).

Soleil d'Or

16 rue du 4-Septembre, 24290 Montignac Lascaux. ☎ **53-51-80-22.** Fax 53-50-27-54. 28 rms, 4 suites. MINIBAR TV TEL. 295–405 F ($56.05–$76.95) double; 600 F ($114) suite. Breakfast 50–55 F ($9.50–$10.45) extra. AE, MC, V. Parking free.

In the heart of Montignac, this place functioned during the 1800s as a postal relay station, offering food and lodging to travelers and horses. Today, much improved, it offers traditionally furnished rooms. Facilities include an outdoor pool, a landscaped garden, a pub, and two restaurants. The less formal of these, Le Bistrot, offers salads, snacks, and simple platters priced at around 50 F ($9.50). The Restaurant serves traditional Dordogne fare like blanquettes of veal and daubes of beef as part of fixed-price meals costing 95 to 250 F ($18.05 to $47.50).

3 Les Eyzies-de-Tayac

331 miles SW of Paris, 28 miles SE of Périgueux

When prehistoric skeletons were unearthed in 1868, the market town of Les Eyzies was launched as an archeologist's dream. This area in the Dordogne Valley was found to be one of the richest in the world in ancient sites and deposits. Little by little, more and more caves were discovered in the region. In some of these caves our early ancestors had made primitive drawings going back some 30,000 years, the most beautiful and most famous, of course, at Lascaux. Many caves around Les Eyzies are open to the public.

ESSENTIALS

GETTING THERE   Local trains run from nearby Le Buisson, which has connections from larger cities like Bordeaux. The several daily trains from Périgueux are more direct.

TOURING BY BIKE   Bicycles are available for rent at the tourist office (below), costing from 30 F ($5.70) per half day or 40 F ($7.60) per full day. A 100-F ($19) deposit is required.

VISITOR INFORMATION   The Office de Tourisme, place de la Mairie (☎ 53-06-97-05), is open from March 15 to October only.

TOURING THE TOP ATTRACTIONS

Prehistoric artifacts from local excavations are on display in the **Musée National de Prehistoire** (☎ 53-06-97-03), occupying a late 16th-century fortress-castle on a cliff overlooking Les Eyzies. On the terrace is a statue of Neanderthal man created by Darde in 1930. One building displays a reconstructed Magdalenian tomb containing a woman's skeleton. The museum is open Wednesday to Monday from 9:30am to noon and 2 to 6pm (to 5pm December to March). Admission is 20 F ($3.80) for adults and 12 F ($2.30) for ages 18 to 25; 17 and under free.

THE CAVES

The **Grotte de Font-de-Gaume** (☎ 53-06-90-80) allows only a small group of visitors (perhaps 12) daily. Unfortunately, some of the markings you see were not from the Magdalenian ages, but from British students on a holiday back in the 18th century. Here bison, reindeer, and horses, along with other animals, reveal the skill of the prehistoric artists. Note that unless you show up very early or in off-season, it may be impossible to get a ticket to look at these remarkable drawings. In season, demand far exceeds the supply of tickets. The caves are open April to September, Wednesday to Monday from 9am to noon and 2 to 6pm; October to March, Wednesday to Monday 9:30am to noon and 2 to 5:30pm. Admission is 31 F ($5.90) for adults, 20 F ($3.80) for ages 18 to 25 and over 60, 7 F ($1.35) for children 7 to 17; 6 and under free.

Discovered at the turn of the century, the **Grotte des Combarelles** (☎ 53-06-97-72) has many drawings of animals, including musk oxen, horses, bison, and aurochs. Think of it as a gallery of Magdalenian art. To get here, take D47. Guided tours are available. It's open April to September, Thursday to Tuesday from 9am to noon and 2 to 6pm; October to March, Thursday to Tuesday from 10am to noon and 2 to 4pm. Admission is 31 F ($5.90) for adults, 20 F ($3.80) for ages 18 to 25 and over 60, 7 F ($1.35) for children 7 to 17; 6 and under free.

The most interesting cave is the **Grotte du Grand-Roc (Cave of the Big Rock)** (☎ 53-06-92-70). Upon entering you'll come on a tunnel of stalagmites and stalactites. The cave is northwest of the market town on the left bank of the Vézère (signs point the way on D47). It's open daily: June to September from 9am to 7pm, and off-season from 9:30am to 6pm. It's closed November 11 to March 30. Admission is 30 F ($5.70) for adults and 15 F ($2.85) for children.

WHERE TO STAY & DINE

✪ Le Centenaire

Rocher de la Penne, 24620 Les Eyzies-Tayac-Sireuil. ☎ **53-06-97-18.** Fax 53-06-92-41. 22 rms, 5 suites. MINIBAR TV TEL. 450–900 F ($85.55–$171.10) double; 1,200–1,500 F ($228.10–$285.10) suite. Breakfast 75 F ($14.25) extra. DC, MC, V. Parking free. Closed Nov–Apr 1.

Extensive renovation and smart decorating have made this a charming hotel with handsome but uninspired rooms. It offers a heated pool, health club, and shopping gallery. Talented chef Roland Mazère creates a light, modern French cuisine. His menu might include terrine of fresh foie gras, brochette of salmon (May to September only), noisettes d'agneau (lamb), young hare with onion purée, and lobster with truffles. The restaurant is closed Tuesday at lunch. Fixed-price menus cost 275 F ($52.25), 400 F ($76), and 500 F ($95.05).

⑤ Les Glycines

Route de Périgueux (D47), 24620 Les Eyzies-Tayac-Sireuil. ☎ **53-06-97-07.** Fax 53-06-92-19. 25 rms. TEL. 355–409 F ($67.45–$77.70) double. Half board 392–440 F ($74.50–$83.60) per person. AE, MC, V. Parking free. Closed late Oct to Apr 20.

Since 1862 this establishment has presented substantial regional cuisine, comfortable accommodations, and dozens of charming touches. Drinks are served on a veranda with a grape arbor. Henri and Christiane Mercat are the hard-working owners of this four-acre garden inn. In the restaurant, specialties include émincé of goose en confit. Fixed-price menus go for 135 F ($25.65), 180 F ($34.20), and 270 F ($51.30).

Pedal-Pushing Through the Dordogne

The Dordogne's rivers meander through countryside that's among the most verdant and historic in France. This area is relatively underpopulated but richer in monuments, feudal châteaux, 12th-century villages, and charming churches than other districts nearby.

Touring by bike will allow you to synchronize your travels and insights with the Dordogne's essentially rural character. Unlike in more pretentious regions of France, no château-hotel or inn will treat you disdainfully if your mode of arrival is on two rather than four wheels. (*Au contraire*, the staff will probably offer advice on suitable bike routes for your departure.) If you're ever in doubt about where your handlebars should lead you, know that you'll rarely go wrong if your route parallels the meandering riverbanks of the Lot, the Vézère, the Dordogne, or any of their ancient tributaries. Architects and builders since the 11th century have appreciated their charm and added greatly to the visual allure of their watersides.

The SNCF makes the transport of bicycles on the nation's railways almost as easy as transporting a suitcase. Barring the transport of your own wheels on the train from somewhere else, there's a wide assortment (everyone from Frère Jacques to his brothers) who can rent you a bicycle. For information on this, refer to the recommendations under "Essentials" in this chapter's sections on Périgueux, Les Eyzies-de-Tayac, and Montauban.

Alternatively, consider joining a group of cyclists whose activities are coordinated by the largest and most comprehensive organizer of sports/outdoor holidays: **Backroads,** 1516 5th St., Berkeley, CA 94710-1740 (☎ **800/462-2848**), offers an eight-day inn or camping trip through the Dordogne. Participants congregate in Bordeaux, then take a train to the hamlet of Tremolat, where they begin a 10-mile bike pedal, all before the end of the first day. Each day thereafter offers the option for itineraries of between 15 and 60 miles, depending on the endurance level of the participants. Accommodations include elegant châteaux-hotels, folkloric inns, and (for those willing to forgo a conventional bed), a network of campgrounds, each at a site of historic or cultural interest. Prices, depending on the degree of luxury, range from $1,090 to $2,700 per person, double occupancy, and don't include the $150 fee charged for the rental of a bicycle.

✪ Hôtel du Centre

Place de la Mairie, 24620 Les Eyzies-Tayac-Sireuil. ☎ **53-06-97-13.** Fax 53-06-91-63. 20 rms. TEL. 270–300 F ($51.30–$57) double. Breakfast 37 F ($7.05) extra. MC, V. Parking free. Closed mid-Nov to Mar.

Enjoy the rustic setting and riverside garden at this hotel, where Gérard Brun offers comfortable, provincial rooms. The cooking is unusually good, and M. Brun probably serves the best fixed-price menus in town, for 98 to 340 F ($18.60 to $64.60). His specialties include aiguillettes of duck with flap mushrooms, assiette périgourdine, ragoût of seafood, and soufflé aux noix. In season, enjoy your meal on a shaded terrace.

4 Brive-la-Gaillarde (Varetz)

302 miles SW of Paris, 56 miles S of Limoges

Three of the old provinces of France—Limousin, Quercy, and Périgord—met near here. At the crossroads, Brive "the bold" is an inviting town, with memories of the renowned French novelist Colette, who lived nearby when she was married to Henri de Jouvenel (see the Château de Castel-Novel under "Where to Stay," below). An important gastronomic center, Brive is a land of fine fruits, truffles, vegetables, and liqueurs, and in some of its shops you can buy a uniquely flavored local mustard.

In the town center is the **Musée de Brive,** in the Hôtel de Labenche, 26 bis bd. Jules-Ferry (☎ **55-24-19-05**). The 16th-century residence that houses the museum is one of Brive's most beautiful monuments. The art collections inside include objects from the prehistoric and Gallo-Roman periods, paintings, folk art, natural-history exhibits, and mementos of Brive's celebrated native daughters and sons. The museum is open April to October, Wednesday to Monday from 10am to 6:30pm; to 6pm off-season. Admission is 26 F ($4.95) for adults and 15 F ($2.85) for children.

Nearby is the **Eglise St-Martin,** place Charles-de-Gaulle (☎ **55-24-10-82**), a hodgepodge of architectural styles, with a romanesque transept and 14th-century aisles. It's open daily from 9am to 5pm.

ESSENTIALS

GETTING THERE   Brive has rail, bus, and highway connections from all other parts of France as it lies at the intersection of the Paris–Spain and Bordeaux–Lyon rail lines. The local airport, Laroche, is 3 miles west of the town center.

VISITOR INFORMATION   The Office de Tourisme is on place du 14-Juillet (☎ **55-24-08-80**).

WHERE TO STAY

✪ Château de Castel-Novel
19240 Varetz. ☎ **55-85-00-01**. 31 rms, 5 suites. TV TEL. 580–1,370 F ($110.25–$260.45) double; 1,550 F ($294.50) suite. Breakfast 75 F ($14.25) extra. AE, DC, MC, V. Parking free. Closed mid-Oct to Apr. Take D901 6¹/₂ miles northwest of Brive to a location half a mile outside Varetz.

The spirit of Colette lives on at this isolated old château on 25 acres. The French novelist often lived here when she was married to Henri de Jouvenel and drew many of the political and literary luminaries of her day to Varetz. This Relais & Châteaux is now run by Albert R. Parveaux. Ten new rooms are in the less luxurious annex, La Borderie, each with minibar and air conditioning. But literary fans prefer the main building. Colette's library has been turned into a charming salon, and the old stables are now a banqueting hall. Facilities include a pool and tennis courts.

In summer, lunch is prepared on a grill near the pool. In the restaurant, the cuisine includes temptations like three fish in roquefort-cream sauce, duckling stuffed with sorrel, ragoût of foie gras and truffles, and salad of flap mushrooms and gizzards. Fixed-price menus go for 260 F ($49.40), 310 F ($58.90), and 385 F ($73.15). Reservations are required.

Hôtel Ibis
32 rue Marcellin-Roche, 19100 Brive-la-Gaillarde. ☎ **55-17-62-62.** Fax 55-23-54-41. 48 rms.
TV TEL. 275 F ($52.25) double. Breakfast 35 F ($6.65) extra. AE, MC, V. Parking free.

A five-minute walk from the town center, this hotel was renovated in 1995. Since then, after several management changes, it has had three different names. The rooms are chain-hotel standardized, neutrally decorated, and comfortable but with few frills. The hotel has a bar but no restaurant; however, the independently run Bistro Cardinal occupies premises in the same building.

WHERE TO DINE

La Crémalllère
53 av. de Paris, 19100 Brive. ☎ **55-74-32-47.** Fax 55-17-91-83. Reservations required. Main courses 60–160 F ($11.40–$30.40); fixed-price menus 100–230 F ($19–$43.70). MC, V. Tues–Sat 12:30–1:30pm and 7:30–9:30pm, Sun 12:30–1:30pm. FRENCH.

Charlou Reynal is winning increasing acclaim as an inventive chef, and he's the darling of a thriving local art colony, who treat this place as their hangout. He knows how to take local produce and transform it into award-winning dishes. Specialties are egg in a coddler with purée of truffles and morels, flan of flap mushrooms with morels sauce, sliced filet of duck with cassisberry sauce, and puff pastry with marinated prunes and plum liqueur. The blood sausage with chestnuts might be too robust for most tastes.

Eight well-furnished rooms are available, costing 280 to 320 F ($53.20 to $60.80) double. Breakfast is 30 F ($5.70) extra. The hotel is closed Sunday night and Monday.

NEARBY ATTRACTIONS

If you have a car, we suggest you head south of Brive on D38 for the "red village" of **Collonges.** This hamlet contains petite mansions built of dark-red stone, including one corbelled house from the 16th century dedicated to the Siren. The church nearby is romanesque, built in the 11th and 12th centuries.

After leaving Collonges, you can continue south, passing the Puy Rouge, until you reach **Meyssac,** also built of red sandstone, known as "Collonges clay." The people here make a pottery out of this clay. The village is charming, with wooden buildings, some with porch roofs and antique towers.

From Meyssac, you can take D14, which becomes D96, until you reach the intersection with D20. Take D20, which becomes D8, leading north to Brive again. On the way back, you might like to stop at the tiny village of **Turenne,** its old houses evoking long-ago provincial France.

From there, continue along D8, passing through Nazareth, until you connect with D158 leading to **Noailles.** On a hillside, the Noailles church with its Limousin-style bell tower dominates the rolling green countryside. From Noailles, it's just a short drive back into Brive.

5 Rocamadour

336 miles SW of Paris, 41 miles SE of Sarlat-la-Canéda, 34 miles S of Brive, 39 miles NE of Cahors

The Middle Ages seem to live on here as they do in Sarlat. After all, Rocamadour reached the zenith of its fame and prosperity in the 13th century. Make an effort to see it even if it's out of your way. The setting is striking, one of the most unusual in Europe: Towers, old buildings, and oratories rise in stages up the side of a cliff on the right slope of the usually dry gorge of Alzou.

ESSENTIALS

GETTING THERE   Rocamadour and neighboring Padirac share a train station that isn't really convenient to either town—it's 3 miles east of Rocamadour on N140, serviced by infrequent trains from Brive in the north and Capdenac in the south. Most visitors avoid the inconvenience and drive. Call 65-33-63-05 for train schedules.

VISITOR INFORMATION   The Office de Tourisme, à la Mairie (☎ **65-33-62-59**), is open from March to November only.

SEEING THE TOWN

This gravity-defying village, with its single street (lined with souvenir shops), is boldly constructed. It's seen at its best when approached from the road coming in from the tiny village of L'Hospitalet. Once in Rocamadour, you can take a flight of steps from the lower town to the churches halfway up the cliff. The less agile would be advised to take the elevator instead, at a cost of 25 F ($4.75) for a round-trip ticket.

The entrance to the village is through the **Porte de Figuier (Fig Tree Gate),** through which many of the most illustrious Europeans of the 13th century passed. One of the oldest places of pilgrimage in France, Rocamadour became famous as a cult center of the black Madonna. It was supposedly founded by Zacchaeus, who entertained Christ at Jericho. He's claimed to have come here with a black wooden statue of the Virgin, though some authorities have suggested that this statue was carved in the 9th century.

At place de la Carreta is the entrance to the **Grand Escalier** (stairway) leading to the ecclesiastical center at the top, a climb of 216 steps. Even today, pilgrims make this difficult journey on their knees in penance. If you make it, you'll arrive at the **Parvis des Eglises,** place St-Amadour, with seven chapels. Guided tours of the chapels are conducted June 1 to September 15 only, Monday to Saturday from 9am to 6pm.

The **Musée-Tresor,** Parvis du Sanctuaire (☎ **65-33-63-29**), contains a gold chalice presented by Pope Pius II, among other treasures. The museum is open daily: in July and August from 9am to 6:30pm, and April to June and in September and October from 9am to noon and 2 to 6pm; closed December to March. Admission is 12 F ($2.30) for adults and 6 F ($1.15) for children.

Against the cliff, the **Basilique St-Sauveur,** place St-Amadour (☎ **65-33-62-61**), was built in the romanesque-gothic style from the 11th to the 13th centuries. It's decorated with paintings and inscriptions, recalling visits of celebrated persons, including Philippe the Handsome. In the Chapelle Miraculeuse, the "holy of holies," the mysterious St. Amadour (believed to be the publican Zacchaeus) is said to have carved out an oratory in the rock. Hanging from the roof of this chapel is one of the oldest clocks known, from the 4th century. Above the altar is the venerated statue of the Madonna. The romanesque Chapelle of St-Michel is sheltered by an overhanging rock; inside are two frescoes rich in coloring, dating (perhaps) from the 12th century. Above the door leading to the Chapelle Notre-Dame (☎ **65-33-63-29**) is a large iron sword that, according to legend, belonged to Roland. The basilica is open daily from 9am to 5pm.

Built on a cliff spur (reached by the curvy chemin de Croix Blanche) and now inhabited by chaplains, the **château** was medieval before its restoration. It's only of minor interest, but the view from its ramparts is panoramic. It's open daily: in July and August from 9am to 7pm; the rest of the year from 9am to noon and 1:30 to 6pm. Admission is 10 F ($1.90) for adults and 6 F ($1.15) for children 17 and under.

WHERE TO STAY & DINE

Beau-Site et Notre-Dame

Cité Médiévale, 46500 Rocamadour. ☎ **65-33 63-08.** Fax 65-33-65-23. 42 rms, 2 suites. TV TEL. 460 F ($87.45) double; 650 F ($123.55) suite. Breakfast 49 F ($9.30) extra. AE, DC, MC, V. Parking free. Closed Nov 12–Feb 12.

The stone walls here were built in the 15th century by an Order of Malta commander. Today the rear terrace provides visitors with a sweeping view of the Val d'Alzou. The reception area has heavy beams and a cavernous fireplace big enough to roast an ox. The guest rooms (in the main building and a less desirable annex) are comfortable; four are air-conditioned. The restaurant serves flavorful regional cuisine prepared by the Menot family, who have owned the place for many generations. Specialties include sautéed lamb with mustard flowers served with eggplant flan, duckmeat salad, raw marinated salmon with green peppercorns, and a dessert soufflé of caramelized walnuts. Fixed-price menus run 95 to 250 F ($18.05 to $47.50).

NEARBY ACCOMMODATIONS & DINING

Château de Roumégouse

N140, Rignac, 46500 Gramat. ☎ **65-33-63-81.** Fax 65-33-71-18. 14 rms, 2 suites. MINIBAR TV TEL. 600–980 F ($114.05–$186.30) double; 1,200 F ($228.10) suite. Breakfast 65 F ($12.35) extra. AE, DC, MC, V. Parking free. Closed Nov–Apr 1. Take N140 to Roumégouse, 2$^1/_2$ miles southeast of Rocamadour.

If you prefer to be away from the tourist bustle, try this Relais & Châteaux in Roumégouse. The 15th-century château overlooking the Causse is surrounded by 12 acres of parkland. Each room is unique, in both architecture and decor, and one has a private garden. In the lovely dining room fixed-price menus cost 170 to 320 F ($32.30 to $60.80); it's closed Monday at lunch and from December to the end of March. Even the scrambled eggs come with truffles.

6 Cahors

336 miles SW of Paris, 135 miles SE of Bordeaux, 55 miles N of Toulouse

The ancient capital of Quercy, Cahors was a thriving university city in the Middle Ages, and many antiquities from its illustrious past life remain. However, Cahors is known today mainly for the almost-legendary red wine that's made principally from the Malbec grapes grown in vineyards around this old city in central France. Firm but not harsh, Cahors is one of the most deeply colored of fine French wines.

The town is on a rocky peninsula almost entirely surrounded by a loop of the Lot River. It grew up near a sacred spring that, incidentally, still supplies the city with water. At the source of the spring, the **Fontaine des Chartreux** stands by the side of the **pont Valentré** (also called pont du Diable), a bridge with a trio of towers, a magnificent example of medieval defensive design erected between 1308 and

1380, then restored in the 19th century. The pont, the first medieval fortified bridge in France, is the most colorful site in Cahors, with crenellated parapets, battlements, and seven pointed arches.

Dominating the old town, the **Cathédrale St-Etienne,** 30 rue de la Chanterie (☎ **65-35-27-80**), was built in 1119 but reconstructed between 1285 and 1500. It was the first cathedral in the country to have cupolas, giving it a romanesque-Byzantine look. One remarkable feature is its finely sculptured romanesque north portal, carved about 1135 in the Languedoc style. Adjoining the cathedral are the remains of a gothic cloister from the late 15th century.

Cahors is a starting point for an excursion to the Célé and Lot valleys, a long journey that many French are fond of taking in summer, a round-trip of about 125 miles, lasting two days if you have plenty of time for sightseeing. The Office de Tourisme (see "Essentials," below) provides maps giving itineraries.

ESSENTIALS

GETTING THERE Cahors is serviced by train from Toulouse, Brive, and Montauban. You may have to transfer in neighboring towns. There is infrequent bus service from some of the outlying villages, several of which are of historic interest, but it's vastly easier to drive.

VISITOR INFORMATION The Office de Tourisme is on place Aristide-Briand (☎ **65-35-09-56**).

WHERE TO STAY

France

252 av. Jean-Jaurès, 46000 Cahors. ☎ **65-35-16-76.** Fax 65-22-01-08. 79 rms. MINIBAR TEL. 360 F ($68.40) double. Breakfast 40 F ($7.60) extra. AE, DC, MC, V. Parking 40 F ($7.60). Closed Dec 22–Jan 8.

This hotel, between pont Valentré and the train station, provides the best rooms in the town center. They're well furnished and well equipped, 38 with air conditioning. The room service is efficient. Breakfast is the only meal served.

Hôtel Terminus

5 av. Charles-de-Freycinet, 46000 Cahors. ☎ **65-35-24-50.** Fax **65-22-06-40.** 29 rms. TV TEL. 480–800 F ($91.25–$152.10) double. Breakfast 35 F ($6.65) extra. AE, MC, V. Parking free in an open courtyard, 45 F ($8.55) in a covered garage.

On the avenue leading from the railway station into the heart of town, this hotel still oozes the turn-of-the-century character of its original stone construction. The rooms are conservative and comfortable and were last renovated in 1994. On the premises is a well-recommended restaurant, Le Balandre. Even if you don't opt for one of a meal in its art deco dining room or on its outdoor terrace, you might want to step into its 1920s-style bar for a drink. Fixed-price meals cost 150 to 300 F ($28.50 to $57).

WHERE TO DINE

La Taverne

Place Escorbiac. ☎ **65-35-28-66.** Reservations recommended. Main courses 65–95 F ($12.35–$18.05); fixed-price menus 85 F ($16.15), 125 F ($23.75), and 185 F ($35.15). MC, V. Thurs–Tues noon–2pm and 7–9:30pm. Closed Feb and Sat–Sun nights in winter. FRENCH.

This restaurant serves outstanding local cuisine in a rustic atmosphere. The finely crafted cuisine of Quercy is featured here, along with other regional specialties.

Typical dishes are truffles in puff pastry, tournedos with foie gras and truffles, duck filet, breast of chicken with morels, and fresh fish.

AN EXCURSION TO GROTTE DU PECH-MERLE

The **Grotte du Pech-Merle** (☎ 65-31-27-05), a prehistoric cave near Cabrerets, 21 miles east of Cahors, was once used for ancient religious rites. The wall paintings, footprints, and carvings were discovered in 1922 and are approximately 20,000 years old. The cave may be explored only from Easter to the end of October, daily from 9:30am 6:30pm. Admission is 42 F ($8) for adults and 18 F ($3.40) for children. There are 2 miles of chambers and galleries open to the public. Aurignacian age art includes drawings of mammoths and bison. One cave is called the picture gallery, as it's decorated with the outlines of two horses.

7 Montauban

404 miles SW of Paris, 45 miles NW of Albi, 31 miles N of Toulouse

This pink-brick capital of the Tarn-et-Garonne is the city of the painter Ingres and the sculptor Bourdelle. Montauban, on the right bank of the Tarn, is one of the most ancient of southwest France's fortified towns. It's still dominated by the fortified **Eglise St-Jacques.** The most scenic view of Montauban is at the 14th-century brick bridge, **pont Vieux,** which connects the town to its satellite of Villebourbon. The bridge is divided by seven arches.

An admirer of Raphael and a student of David, Jean-Auguste-Dominique Ingres was born in 1780 in Montauban, the son of an ornamental sculptor/painter. The father recognized his son's artistic abilities early and encouraged him. Ingres lived for a time in Italy, seeking inspiration in classical motifs. He was noted for his nudes and historical paintings, which are now considered fine examples of neoclassicism. One of his first exhibitions of portraits in 1806 met with ridicule, but later generations have been more appreciative.

Though the Louvre in Paris owns many Ingres masterpieces, upon his 1867 death the artist bequeathed to Montauban more than two dozen paintings and some 4,000 drawings. These are displayed at the **Musée Ingres,** 19 rue de l'Hôtel-de-Ville (☎ 63-20-11-52), in a 17th-century bishops' palace. One painting in the collection is *Christ and the Doctors*, a work Ingres completed at 82. *The Dream of Ossian* was intended for Napoléon's bedroom in Rome. On the ground floor are works by Antoine Bourdelle, who was heavily influenced by Rodin. Two busts Bourdelle did, of Ingres and of Rodin, are particularly outstanding. The museum is open Tuesday to Sunday from 10am to noon and 2 to 6pm (in July and August, daily from 9:30am to noon and 1:30 to 6pm). Admission is 15 F ($2.85) for adults; children free.

For a final look at a masterpiece by Ingres, head for the **Cathédrale Notre-Dame,** place Roosevelt, a classical building framed by two square towers. In the north transept is the painting the church commissioned, *Vow of Louis XIII.* It's open daily from 8am to 7pm.

ESSENTIALS

GETTING THERE Seven to nine trains per day arrive from Paris (trip time: 5¹/₂ hr.), costing 313 F ($59.45) one way. Trains arrive every hour from Toulouse (trip time: 25 min.), costing 45 F ($8.55) one way.

If you're driving, RN20 (Paris–Toulouse–Andorra, Spain), RN113 (Bordeaux–Marseille), and the A61 motorway run through the Tarn-et-Garonne.

TOURING BY BIKE   Bicycles can be rented at **Gury,** 26 av. Gambetta (☎ 63-63-19-10), open Tuesday to Saturday from 8am to noon and 2 to 7pm. A deposit of 800 F ($152) is required.

VISITOR INFORMATION   The Office de Tourisme is on rue du Collège (☎ 63-63-60-60).

WHERE TO STAY

Hostellerie les Coulandriéres

Route de Castelsarrasin, 82290 Montauban. ☎ **63-67-47-47.** Fax 63-67-46-45. 22 rms. MINIBAR TV TEL. 290–380 F ($55.10–$72.20) double. Half board 400 F ($76) per person. AE, DC, MC, V. Parking free.

This inn 2 miles west of Montauban's center is most inviting. The lounges and dining room are traditionally furnished and the rooms are pleasant and comfortable. Facilities include a pool, bowling alley, volleyball court, and miniature-golf course. The inn also makes an excellent dining choice, as first-class ingredients are deftly handled by the chefs. In summer grills are a specialty.

Hôtel Ingres

10 av. Mayenne, 82000 Montauban. ☎ **63-63-36-01.** Fax 63-66-02-90. 31 rms. A/C MINIBAR TV TEL. 450 F ($85.55) double. Breakfast 60 F ($11.40) extra. AE, DC, MC, V. Parking free.

Many people rate the Ingres the town's finest place to stay. This contemporary hotel near the rail station has comfortable rooms, some overlooking a rear garden. Breakfast is the only meal served. This choice is more solid and reliable than exciting.

WHERE TO DINE

Hôtel Orsay et Restaurant la Cuisine d'Alain

Face Gare (across from the train station), 82000 Montauban. ☎ **63-66-06-66.** Fax 63-66-19-39. Reservations recommended. Main courses 100–130 F ($19–$24.70); fixed-price menus 120 F ($22.80), 180 F ($34.20), and 280 F ($53.20). AE, DC, MC, V. Mon 7:30–9:30pm, Tues–Sat 12:30–2pm and 7:30–9:30pm. Closed Dec 23–Jan 6 and the second and third weeks in Aug. FRENCH.

Restaurant la Cuisine d'Alain is the best restaurant in town, for chef Alain Blanc is talented and inventive. Try his terrine of lentils flavored with the neck of a fattened goose en confit, filet of beef with liver and apple flan, or escalope of grilled salmon in its own skin. The amazing dessert trolley offers plenty of choices.

Reasonably priced rooms also are available in the Hôtel Orsay. Doubles rent for 250 to 280 F ($47.50 to $53.20), plus 32 F ($6.10) for breakfast.

Bordeaux & the Atlantic Coast **21**

From historic La Rochelle to the bordeaux wine district, France's southwest is often glimpsed only briefly by those driving from Paris to Spain. However, this area is slowly gaining fame for its Atlantic beaches, medieval and Renaissance ruins, romanesque and gothic churches, vineyards, and charming old inns that serve up a splendid regional cuisine.

In our journey through this intriguing region, we won't stay entirely on the coastline but will also dip inland for a snifter of cognac in Cognac and trips to nearby art cities like Poitiers and Angoulême. Allow at least a week for this tour—just enough time to sample the wine, savor the cuisine's specialties, and see at least some of the major sights.

REGIONAL CUISINE Major specialties from this region are the *huîtres* (oysters) from Arcachon or Marennes, *jambon* (ham) from Poitou, *esturgeon* (sturgeon) or *saumon* (salmon) from the Gironde, *canard* (duck) from Challans, *chapon* (capon) or *poularde* (chicken) from Barbezieux, and *agneau* (lamb) from Pauillac.

Other specialties include *mouclade*, a mussel stew prepared with cream or white wine and shallots; *lamproie* or *l'anguille à la bordelaise* (lamprey eels from local rivers, served with a blood-enriched red-wine sauce); *entrecôte à la bordelaise* (steak in a wine-laced brown sauce with shallots, tarragon, and bone marrow)*; cèpes à la bordelaise* (flap mushrooms sautéed in oil and seasoned with chopped shallots and garlic); *escargots à la vigneronne* (snails simmered in a sauce of wine, garlic, and onions); and *chaudrée* (a local fish soup). The region's most famous cheese is chabichou, a variety of goat cheese, from Poitou; and its best chocolate is les duchesses d'Angoulême.

Bordeaux wines include everything from the finest French vintages to very ordinary table wines, which you'll find beneath plastic caps on supermarket shelves. Among the best are the incomparable wines from the Médoc and Graves. Other reds include St-Emilion and Pomerol.

EXPLORING THE REGION BY CAR

Here's how to link together the best of the region if you rent a car.

Day 1 Begin in Poitiers, home of the most famous woman of the Middle Ages, Eleanor of Aquitaine. After touring the old town, drive

What's Special About Bordeaux & the Atlantic Coast

Beaches
- Ile de Ré, an Atlantic island off the coast of La Rochelle, 19 miles long and surrounded by sandy beaches.

Great Towns
- Bordeaux, capital of old Aquitaine and center of the most important wine-producing area in the world.
- St-Emilion, an architectural gem of the Middle Ages and center of a famous wine district.
- La Rochelle, the French Geneva, a historic port and ancient city of sailors, with $3^1/2$ miles of fortifications.

Architectural Highlights
- Eglise St-Eutrope, at Saintes, built in the 1400s by Louis XI and one of the most important monuments in southwestern France.
- Esplanade des Quinconces, at Bordeaux, dating from 1818, a 30-acre square, the largest of its kind in Europe.
- Eglise Monolithe, at St-Emilion, the most important underground church in France.
- The Arena, at Saintes, from the 1st century, one of the oldest Roman amphitheaters in the world.

Wine Routes
- A tour of the Bordeaux vineyards, including Médoc, one of the most visited regions in southwestern France (tour highlight: the Château Mouton-Rothschild).

Events
- Bordeaux, a series of music weeks in May, the leading cultural event of the region.
- La Rochelle, sailing week in May, drawing boat devotees from around the world.

west 90 miles on A10 and E601 and spend the night in La Rochelle. While here, reflect on the fate of the Protestants who were starved into submission here in 1628 and of the fortified seaport's role in supplying French colonists in the nascent colony of Canada.

Day 2   Today you'll drive along the banks of the Charente River, with Angoulême, 80 miles southeast along N137 and N141, as your goal. En route, stop in Saintes, where monuments from nearly every civilization that ever thrived on French soil remain intact in the town center. (If you have enough time, consider adding a day to your itinerary and staying overnight in Saintes.) If you're pressed for time, continue southeast for a tour of the distillery town of Cognac. Here you can dine at the Hostellerie les Pigeons Blancs, 110 rue Jules-Brisson (☎ 45-82-16-36). Established in the 17th century as a coaching inn, it continues to offer well-prepared food and a worthy selection of the cognac distilleries. Continue on until you reach one of this region's most ancient towns, Angoulême, where you'll spend the night.

Bordeaux & the Atlantic Coast

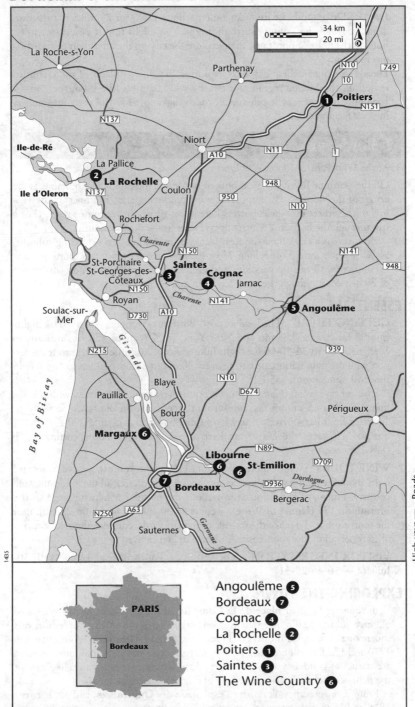

0 — 34 km
20 mi

N

La Roche-s-Yon
Parthenay
N10
749
Poitiers ❶
10
N151
N137
Niort
Ile-de-Ré
A10
N11
1
La Pallice
La Rochelle ❷
Coulon
948
Ile d'Oleron
N137
950
N10
Rochefort
Charente
N150
N141
948
St-Porchaire
St-Georges-des-Côteaux
Saintes ❸
Cognac ❹
Jarnac
Angoulême ❺
N150
Charente
N141
Royan
A10
Soulac-sur-Mer
D730
939
N215
Gironde
N10
D674
Blaye
Pauillac
Périgueux
Bay of Biscay
Bourg
Margaux ❻
N89
Libourne ❻
St-Emilion ❻
D709
Dordogne
Bordeaux ❼
D936
Bergerac
N250
A63
Garonne
Sauternes

Highways ══ Roads —

PARIS
Bordeaux

Angoulême ❺
Bordeaux ❼
Cognac ❹
La Rochelle ❷
Poitiers ❶
Saintes ❸
The Wine Country ❻

Day 3   Drive southeast from Angoulême along E606 for 75 miles toward Bordeaux and the wine country surrounding it. You might find it easiest to select a hotel in the heart of Bordeaux, then explore the city on the afternoon of your first day in town.

Days 4–5   Spend these two days exploring the alluvial plains of the Garonne, including the Médoc region and nearby wine hamlets like Libourne and St-Emilion. Spend the night either in Bordeaux again or at any of the wine-country inns we recommend.

1 Bordeaux

359 miles SW of Paris, 341 miles W of Lyon

On the Garonne River, the great port of Bordeaux, the capital of Aquitaine, is the center of the world's most important wine-producing area. It attracts many visitors to the offices of wine exporters here, most of whom welcome guests. (For a trip through the bordeaux wine country, refer to the next section.)

Bordeaux is a city of warehouses, factories, mansions, and exploding suburbs, as well as wide quays 5 miles long. Now the fifth-largest French city, Bordeaux was for 300 years a British possession, and even today it's called the most un-French of French cities, though the same has been said of Strasbourg.

ESSENTIALS

GETTING THERE   The local airport, Bordeaux-Mérignac, is served by flights from as far away as London and New York. It's 6³/₄ miles west of Bordeaux in Mérignac (☎ **56-34-50-00** for flight information). A shuttle bus connects the airport with the train station, departing every 30 minutes from 5:30am to 10pm (trip time: 40 min.), costing 35 F ($6.65) one way.

The railway station (Gare St-Jean) is on the west bank of the river, within a 30-minute walk (or 5-minute taxi ride) from the center of the old town. Some 10 to 14 trains from Paris arrive per day (trip time: 5 to 8 hr.), costing 290 F ($55.10) one way. However, the TGV from Paris arrives in just 3¹/₄ hours, costing 375 F ($71.25) one way.

WINE TOURS   Wine exporters welcome guests who come to sample wines and learn about the industry. In the next section, we'll take a tour of the bordeaux wine country. For maps and information about the popular wine routes, go to the **Maison du Vin (House of Wine),** 1 cours du 30-Juillet (☎ **56-00-22-66**), near the tourist office. To make the rounds of the vineyards, consider alternative forms of transportation: bus, houseboat, or horse-drawn caravan.

VISITOR INFORMATION   The Office de Tourisme is at 12 cours du 30-Juillet (☎ **56-44-28-41**).

EXPLORING THE TOWN

Your tour can begin at **place de la Comédie,** at the very heart of this venerated old city, a busy traffic hub that was once the site of a Roman temple. On this square one of the great theaters of France, the **Grand Théâtre,** was built between 1773 and 1780. A colonnade of 12 columns graces its facade. Surmounted on these are statues of goddesses and the Muses. Apply to the porter if you'd like to visit the richly decorated interior, a setting of elegance and refinement.

From here you can walk north to **esplanade des Quinconces,** laid out between 1818 and 1828, the largest square of its kind in Europe, covering nearly 30 acres.

Bordeaux

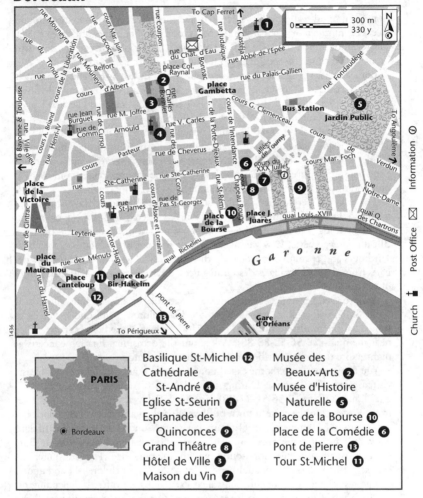

A smaller but lovelier square is **place de la Bourse,** bounded by quays opening onto the Garonne. It was laid out between 1728 and 1755, with a fountain of the Three Graces at its center. Flanking the square are the Custom House and the Stock Exchange.

The finest church in Bordeaux is the **Cathédrale St-André,** place Pey-Berland (☎ **56-52-68-10**), standing in the south of the old town. At the 13th-century Porte Royale (Royal Door), the sculptures are admirable; see also the 14th-century sculptures on the North Door. Separate from the rest of the church is the Tour Pey-Berland, a belfry begun in the 15th century and rising 155 feet. The church is open daily from 8 to 11am and 2 to 6pm.

Bordeaux has a second church with a separate belfry: the **Basilique St-Michel** with its Tour St-Michel. The belfry here is the tallest tower in the south of France. Rising 374 feet, it was erected in 1472. Once it was possible to climb the 228 steps for a panoramic view of the port, but you'll have to settle for a view of the tower from the ground, as the problems of safety and insurance have proven insurmountable. For information about any of the other four major churches of Bordeaux, you can telephone the Presbytère (☎ **56-94-30-50**), but only if you speak a little French. The church is open daily from 8am to noon and 2:30 to 5:30pm.

Bordeaux has yet another interesting church, the **Eglise St-Seurin,** whose most ancient sections, like its crypt, date from the 5th century. See the porch, left over from an earlier church; it has some capitals from the romanesque era. It's open daily from 8am to noon and 2:30pm to 5:30pm.

The **Musée des Beaux-Arts,** 20 cours d'Albret (Jardin du Palais-Rohan) (☎ **56-10-16-93**), has an outstanding collection ranging from the 15th to the 20th century. Works by Perugina, Titian, Rubens, Veronese, Delacroix, Gros, Redon, Marquet, and Lhote are displayed. The museum is open Wednesday to Monday from 10am to 6pm. Admission is 18 F ($3.40) for adults and 9 F ($1.70) for children.

The **pont de Pierre,** with 17 arches, stretches 1,594 feet across the Garonne and is one of the most beautiful bridges in France. Ordered built by Napoléon I in 1813, the bridge can be crossed on foot for a fine view of the quays and the port. But for an even better view we suggest a **tour of the port,** which lasts for about 1¹/₂ hours and encompasses a float up the river and all around the harbor. It departs from the Embarcadères des Quinconces, on quai Louis-XVIII in the center of town.

April to October, tours begin Monday to Saturday at 2:30 or 3pm. The cost is 55 F ($10.45) for adults and 45 F ($8.55) for children 9 and under. For exact times, call the tourism office (see "Essentials," above) or the boat captains' office near the quai (☎ **56-52-88-88**). Ask about the occasional floating concerts at night. Note that tours may be canceled without warning.

You may enjoy a waterborne expedition on one of France's mightiest (and least-visited) rivers, the Garonne. During July and August, **Alienor Loisirs,** Hangar 7, quai Louis-XVIII (☎ **56-51-27-90**), offers a Sunday-afternoon ride downriver from Bordeaux to the château town of Blaye. Boarding at the company's dock begins at around 11am before an 11:30am departure. Lunch is served on board, and between 2 and 4pm visitors enjoy a shore excursion in Blaye. The return to Bordeaux is usually scheduled for around 6:30pm the same day. The cost, lunch included, is 225 F ($42.75) for adults and 125 F ($23.75) for children 11 and under.

The rest of the year, roughly equivalent excursions are offered, depending on the number of prepaid advance reservations. For more information, call the Bordeaux tourist office or Alienor Loisirs.

WHERE TO STAY
VERY EXPENSIVE

Mercure Château Chartrons
81 cours St-Louis, 33300 Bordeaux. ☎ **56-43-15-00.** Fax 56-69-15-21. 138 rms, 6 suites. A/C MINIBAR TV TEL. 655–690 F ($124.50–$131.17) double; 850 F ($161.60) suite. Breakfast 55 F ($10.45) extra. AE, DC, MC, V. Parking free. Bus 7 or 8.

Operated by a prestigious wine exporter, La Maison Ginneste, this is probably Bordeaux's most talked-about hotel. Near the landmark place Tourny, it opened in 1991 behind the gracefully restored facade of an 18th-century mansion. The rooms are comfortable, outfitted with memorabilia of the wine trade. On the premises are a bar, with an impressive array of local vintages sold by the glass, and a restaurant, Le Cabernet, where well-prepared meals begin at 65 to 95 F ($12.35

to $18.05). A health club a few doors away (under separate management) opens its facilities to guests here.

Pullman Mériadeck

5 rue Robert-Lateulade, 33000 Bordeaux. ☎ **56-56-43-43.** Fax 56-96-50-59. 192 rms. A/C MINIBAR TV TEL. 450–800 F ($85.50–$152) double. Breakfast 55 F ($10.45) extra. AE, DC, MC, V. Bus 7 or 8.

The city's leading hotel, the Pullman offers modern comforts in a setting of antiquity facing a shopping mall. The well-furnished rooms attract vine growers and wine merchants from abroad; the best rooms are on the sixth floor (some are showing signs of wear and tear). Le Mériadeck, the main restaurant, is one of the finest hotel grills.

EXPENSIVE

Novotel Bordeaux Centre

45 cours du Maréchal-Juin, 33000 Bordeaux. ☎ **56-51-46-46.** Fax 56-98-25-56. 138 rms, 2 suites. A/C MINIBAR TV TEL. 490 F ($93.10) double; from 800 F ($152) suite. Children 15 and under stay free in parents' room. Breakfast 50 F ($9.50) extra. AE, DC, MC, V. Parking free. Bus 9.

This first-class hotel is a short walk from the thoroughfare of Sainte Catherine, quai des Chartrons, and the cathedral, in the heart of the city near the railway station. The rooms are well decorated and comfortably furnished, and some are suitable for the disabled. The hotel also offers laundry and room service.

MODERATE

Ⓢ Hôtel le Bayonne

15 cours de l'Intendance, 33000 Bordeaux. ☎ **56-48-00-88.** Fax 56-52-03-79. 36 rms. A/C MINIBAR TV TEL. 480 F ($91.20) double. Breakfast 55 F ($10.45) extra. AE, DC, MC, V. Parking 55 F ($10.45). Bus 7 or 8.

This restored 18th-century building has been turned into one of the most up-to-date three-star hotels in Bordeaux. The aura of the 1930s has been retained, and many comforts have been added. The soundproof rooms are furnished with color-coordinated fabrics and comfortable pieces. Many attractions, including several good restaurants and the Grand Théâtre, are nearby.

INEXPENSIVE

Etche-Ona

11 rue Mautrec, 33000 Bordeaux. ☎ **56-44-36-49.** Fax 56-44-59-58. 33 rms. TV TEL. 250–335 F ($47.50–$63.65) double. Breakfast 35 F ($6.65) extra. MC, V. Parking 52 F ($9.90). Bus 7, 8, or 26.

Small but tranquil and central, this hotel is one of the best bargains we've found in Bordeaux. It's within walking distance of many of the major attractions, including the Grand Théâtre, the cathedral, place de la Bourse, and the quays. The rooms are nicely but simply furnished. Breakfast is the only meal served.

Ⓢ Hôtel de Sèze

23 allées de Tourny, 33000 Bordeaux. ☎ **56-52-65-54.** Fax 56-44-31-83. 24 rms. MINIBAR TV TEL. 300–420 F ($57–$79.80) double. Breakfast 35 F ($6.65) extra. AE, DC, MC, V. Parking 40 F ($7.60). Bus 7 or 8.

This three-star hostelry occupies a building classified a historic monument. This reasonably priced hotel is such a well-known value that you should make reservations as early as possible. The rooms are well furnished: the cheapest with only a bed and bath (with shower), the most expensive with twin beds and bath (with a tub).

WHERE TO DINE
VERY EXPENSIVE

✪ La Chamade
20 rue des Piliers-de-Tutelle. ☎ **56-48-13-74.** Reservations required. Main courses 100–160 F ($19–$30.40); fixed-price menus 100 F ($19), 185 F ($35.15), 280 F ($53.20), and 320 F ($60.80). AE, MC, V. Mon–Sat 12:30–2pm and 7:30–10pm, Sun 7:30–10pm. Closed Sat–Sun July–Aug. Bus 7 or 8. FRENCH.

You'll have a delightful experience at La Chamade, in a vaulted 18th-century cellar of honey-colored stone. We highly recommend the monkfish salad, marinated and grilled and served with leeks and Greek-style artichokes. Other specialties include roasted foie gras with confit of leeks and poached duck thighs with baby vegetables. The fish are steamed to perfection and served simply, often with warm vinaigrette of tomatoes and basil. Owner Michel Carrère has an impressive collection of bordeaux.

✪ Le Chapon-Fin
5 rue Montesquieu. ☎ **56-79-10-10.** Reservations required. Main courses 160–240 F ($30.40–$45.60); fixed-price meals 220–400 F ($41.80–$76) at lunch, 250–400 F ($47.50–$76) at dinner. AE, DC, MC, V. Tues–Sat noon–2pm and 7:30–10pm. Bus 7 or 8. FRENCH.

Under the guidance of Francis Garcia from Barcelona, this is the leading restaurant in Bordeaux. His wife, Geraldine, helps manage the dining room, which boasts elaborate latticework and several banquettes in artificial stone grottoes. A pivoting skylight lets in summer breezes. The wines are usually selected from the most respected and expensive French vintages, and menu specialties are the best of the southwest. A meal might include truffle flan with essence of morels, gratin of oysters with foie gras, salmon steak grilled in its skin with pepper-flavored sabayon, and lobster gazpacho—followed by superb cheeses and desserts.

EXPENSIVE

✪ Le Vieux Bordeaux
27 rue Buhan. ☎ **56-52-94-36.** Reservations recommended. Main courses 100–180 F ($19–$34.20); fixed-price menus 150 F ($28.50), 200 F ($38), and 250 F ($47.50). AE, V. Mon–Fri noon–2pm and 8–10:15pm, Sat 8–10:15pm. Closed Aug 1–21. Bus 7 or 8. FRENCH.

One of the best-established restaurants in town, Le Vieux Bordeaux is nearly a neighborhood institution; the decor is an almost-incongruous mix of exposed wood and modern accents. Specialties include pavé of fresh salmon with warm oysters, roasted sweetbreads, turbot with buttered truffle sauce, and gratin of lobster with fresh noodles. The cookery seems to show more finesse as the years pass, except for some recent desserts.

MODERATE

La Tupina
6 rue de la Porte de la Monnaie. ☎ **56-91-56-37.** Reservations recommended. Main courses 75–120 F ($14.25–$22.80); fixed-price menu 220 F ($41.80). AE, DC, MC, V. Mon–Sat noon–2pm and 8–11pm. Bus 7 or 8. FRENCH.

One of Bordeaux's most talented chefs runs this cozy restaurant near the quai de la Monnaie. Jean-Pierre Xiradakis's specialty is duck, so your meal might begin with croûtons spread with duck rillettes, and his salads often use giblets, skin, and livers. The chef also prepares regional specialties, such as truffles and foie gras. A recently sampled potato salad contained slices of black truffles from Périgord. The foie gras often comes steamed en papillote. Sample one of the fine wines from the cellar.

INEXPENSIVE

✆ La Forge

8 rue du Chai-des-Farines. ☎ **56-81-40-96.** Reservations recommended. Main courses 50–90 F ($9.50–$17.10); fixed-price menus 75 F ($14.25), 100 F ($19), and 140 F ($26.60). AE, MC, V. Tues–Sat noon–1:30pm and 7:30–10:30pm. Closed mid-Aug to mid-Sept. Bus 7 or 8. FRENCH.

Jean-Michel Pouts, a former chef on the ocean liner *France*, owns this bistro. Well-prepared specialties include brochette of pork with gruyère, savory grilled meats, and an excellent cassoulet. The fixed-price menus are among the best in town for the price. The restaurant's devotion to a regional repertoire and attempts to keep prices down are most admirable. Everything is homemade.

NEARBY ACCOMMODATIONS & DINING

✪ Restaurant St-James/Hôtel Hautrive

3 place Camille-Hostein, 33270 Bouliac. ☎ **57-97-06-00.** Fax 56-20-92-58. Reservations required. Main courses 130–180 F ($24.70–$34.20); fixed-price menus 250–350 F ($47.50–$66.50). AE, DC, MC, V. Daily noon–2:30pm and 7–9:30pm. From Bordeaux, follow the signs to Toulouse/Bayonne, leading south, and when you reach the péripherique encircling Bordeaux, follow the signs to Paris; take Exit 23 and follow the signs to Bouliac. FRENCH.

This is the domain of Jean-Marie Amat, whose specialties are based on local seasonal ingredients. These may revolve around the abundances of cèpes (the district's meaty flap mushrooms), game (venison and pheasant), girolles (another kind of mushroom), and fruit. In an ultramodern dining room whose windows offer a view of some of the most famous vineyards in Europe, you can enjoy such dishes as civet of duck, oysters from Quiberon, tartare of salmon with olives, salad of marinated filets of quail, Pauillac lamb, and lamprey eels à la bordelaise.

Adjacent is the Hôtel Hautrive, whose 16 elegant rooms and two suites are scattered among four modern pavilions. Doubles go for 650 to 850 F ($123.50 to $161.50), and suites cost 1,150 to 1,350 F ($218.50 to $256.50), with breakfast 70 F ($13.30) extra.

2 The Wine Country

The major bordeaux wine districts are Graves, Médoc, Sauternes, Entre-deux-Mers, Libourne, Blaye, and Bourg. North of the city of Bordeaux, the Garonne River joins the Dordogne. This forms the Gironde, a broad estuary at the heart of the wine country. More than 100,000 vineyards produce some 70 million gallons of wine a year. And some of these are among the greatest red wines in the world. The white wines are lesser known, however.

WINE TOURS   Some of the famous vineyards are pleased to welcome visitors, providing they don't arrive at the busy harvest time. However, most vineyards are not likely to have a permanent staff to welcome you. Don't just show up—call first or check with local tourist offices about appropriate times to visit.

VISITOR INFORMATION   The best-respected source of information about the wines of Bordeaux (and French wines in general) is the **CIDD (Centre d'Information, de Documentation, & de Dégustation)**, 45 rue Liancourt, 75014 Paris (☎ 1/43-27-67-21; fax 1/43-20-84-00). Organized in 1982, this self-funded school presents about a dozen courses throughout the year addressing all aspects of wine tasting, wine producing, wine buying, and wine merchandizing. The organization offers a mine of information for anyone anticipating a tour of the vineyards and gives advice about vineyards that are particularly suited to tours.

MAP   Before heading out on this wine road, make sure you get a detailed map from the Bordeaux tourist office (above), since the "trail" is not well marked. Head toward Pauillac on D2, the wine road, called the *Route des Grands-Crus*.

MEDOC

The Médoc, an undulating plain covered with vineyards, is one of the most visited regions in southwestern France. Its borders are marked by Bordeaux and the Pointe de Grave. Throughout the region are many isolated châteaux producing grapes; only a handful of these, however, are worthy of your attention. The most visited château is that of Mouton-Rothschild, said to be an attraction in southwestern France second only to Lourdes, in spite of the red tape involved in visiting.

In Haut-Médoc, the soil is not especially fertile but absorbs much heat during the day. To benefit from this, the vines are clipped close to the ground. The French zealously regulate the cultivation of the vineyards and the making of the wine. Less than 10% of the wines from the region are called bordeaux. These are invariably red, including such famous labels as Châteaux Margaux, Château Latour, Châteaux Mouton, and Château Lafite. Most of these labels are from grapes grown some 3,000 feet from the Gironde River.

SEEING THE TOP ATTRACTIONS

Known as the Versailles of the Médoc, the Empire-style **Château Margaux,** 33460 Margaux (☎ **56-88-70-28**), on D2, was built in the 19th century near the village of Margaux. The estate covers more than 650 acres, of which some 187 produce Château Margaux and Pavillon Rouge du Château Margaux. Almost 30 acres are devoted to producing Pavillon Blanc du Château Margaux. The inhabitants of the château do not allow tours, but you may admire it from the outside. It's open Monday to Friday from 9am to 12:30pm and 2 to 5:30pm; closed August and during the harvest. To see the vat rooms and wine cellars, make an appointment by letter or phone.

The Grand Admiral of France, the duc d'Epernon, ordered the **Château de Beychevelle,** St-Julien, Beychevelle, 33250 Pauillac (☎ **56-59-23-00**), built in 1757 and commanded all ships to lower their sails as they passed by. (Beychevelle means "lowered sails.") The château, 10 miles beyond Margaux, is open Monday to Friday from 9:30am to noon and 2 to 6pm and Saturday from 9:30am to noon. Make an appointment through the Maison du Vin in Bordeaux (see "Bordeaux," above) or by calling direct.

Thousands of tourists visit the outstanding ✪ **Château Mouton-Rothschild,** Le Pouvalet, 33250 Pauillac (☎ **56-73-18-18**), one of the many homes of Baron Philippe de Rothschild and his American-born wife, Pauline. The baronne contributed greatly to the château's restoration. The welcoming room is beautifully furnished with part of the Rothschild collection of sculpture and paintings. A 16th-century tapestry depicts the harvesting of the grape. An adjoining museum, in former wine cellars (*chai*), has art from many eras—much of it related to the cultivation of the vineyards. Note the collection of modern art, including a statue by American sculptor Lippold. The wine produced in the surrounding vineyards was classified as *premier cru* in 1973. Before that it was labeled a "second growth." The château is open Monday to Thursday from 9:30 to 11:30am and 2 to 5pm and Friday from 9:30 to 11:30am and 2 to 4pm. Make an appointment by phone to see the cellars. It's closed in August and on holidays.

The **Château Lafite,** on D2 (☎ **56-59-01-74**), is second only to the nearby Château Mouton-Rothschild. Count on spending at least an hour here. The vinothèque contains many vintage bottles—several dating from 1797. The château was purchased in 1868 by the Rothschilds and is open Monday to Friday from 9 to 11am and 3 to 5pm. Make an appointment for a guided tour. It's closed on holidays and from mid-September to late November.

WHERE TO STAY & DINE

Auberge André

Le Grand Port, 33880 Cambes. ☎ **56-78-75-23.** Reservations recommended. Main courses 75–120 F ($14.25–$22.80); fixed-price menus 95–180 F ($18.05–$34.20). AE, DC, MC, V. Wed–Mon 12:30–3pm and 7:30–10pm. Closed Nov 1–15 and one week in Feb. FRENCH.

At the edge of Cambes, a village with no more than 100 residents, in a century-old farmhouse whose terrace offers a sweeping view of the Garonne, this is one of

---

Bordeaux's Red & White Gold

The lands bordering the Gironde flow with more than the alluvial runoffs from frequent rainfalls: Bordeaux and its region flow with wine from more than a quarter million acres of vineyards, affiliated with more than 3,000 châteaux.

The nuances of the product are more carefully documented than virtually any other foodstuff in France and are expedited to connoisseurs in about 150 countries around the globe. Foremost among the buyers is Belgium, followed by Germany. Tied for third place are the United Kingdom (where consumers have referred to red Bordeaux as "claret" since Elizabethan times) and the United States (where consumption has shifted away from hardcore spirits to a softcore allegiance to wine and beer).

Bordeaux whites are harmonious and stylish accompaniments for all kinds of food. Connoisseurs refer to them as "nervous" because of the way a tenuous variation in their bouquet can render them magnificent or ordinary. The most respected whites include sauternes, whose grapes grow in ancient vineyards and are left on the vine until the last possible moment. The "noble rot" (mold) permeating them enhances the fermentation process to standards that command premier prices virtually everywhere.

Despite the allure of Bordeaux whites, connoisseurs lust almost obsessively after the region's output of sophisticated reds. Rivaled only the earthy reds of Burgundy, these are claimed by enthusiasts to be better suited to aging than any other wine in the world. Whereas reds must never be drunk when young, whites should be drunk only when young.

the region's charming hideaways; it's owned by Patrick Dulou. Menu items might include filet of eel with parsley-butter sauce, lamprey bordelaise, confit de canard, filet of sea bass infused with essence of laurel, and salmon cooked with port.

The establishment also maintains four comfortable rooms upstairs, renting for 200 F ($38) double, with breakfast 25 F ($4.75) extra.

LIBOURNE

This is a sizable market town with a railway connection. At the junction of the Dordogne and Isle rivers, Libourne is roughly the center of the St-Emilion, Pomerol, and Fronsac wine districts. In the town, a large colonnaded square still contains some houses from the 16th century, including the Hôtel de Ville. In addition, you can explore the remains of 13th-century ramparts. In the town center is the **Office de Tourisme,** place Abel-Surchamp (☎ 57-51-15-04), where you can get information on visiting the Bordeaux vineyards.

WHERE TO STAY & DINE

Hôtel Loubat

32 rue Chanzy, 33500 Libourne. ☎ **57-51-17-58.** 25 rms. TV TEL. 250–270 F ($47.50–$51.30) double. Breakfast 30 F ($5.70) extra. AE, V.

This country inn, across from the railway station, is the town's leader, with reasonable rates and delicious meals. The rooms are French provincial and rather simple. The restaurant is open daily from noon to 2pm and 7 to 10pm; specialties are lamprey eels bordelaise, papillotte of salmon with crayfish, and sweetbreads with grapes and foie-gras sauce. Fixed-price menus run 85 to 200 F ($16.15 to $38), and there's also an à la carte menu.

NEARBY ACCOMMODATIONS & DINING

La Bonne Auberge

Rue du 8-Mai-1945 et av. John-Talbot, 33350 Castillon-la-Bataille. ☎ **57-40-11-56.** 10 rms. 250 F ($47.50) or 280 F ($53.20) double. Breakfast 25 F ($4.75) extra. AE, MC, V. Parking free. From Libourne, follow the signs pointing to Bergerac; take the highway for 18 miles to Castillon-la-Bataille, then continue to the far end of the village.

This family hotel is near an intersection of two busy highways. The rooms are simple but comfortable; the good food is plentiful. Serious diners go to the restaurant at the top of the exterior stairs; there's also a brasserie on the ground level. A fixed-price menu in the brasserie costs only 55 F ($10.45), and the fixed-price menu in the restaurant goes for 70 to 205 F ($13.30 to $38.95). Specialties are grilled salmon with shallot-flavored butter, omelets, lamb with parsley, sweetbreads with mushrooms, and entrecôte bordelaise. The restaurant is open daily from noon to 2pm and 7:30 to 9pm. The brasserie and restaurant are closed Saturday for lunch from November to March.

ST-EMILION

Surrounded by vineyards, St-Emilion is on a limestone plateau overlooking the Valley of the Dordogne; a maze of wine cellars has been dug out of the limestone underneath the town. The wine made in this world-famous district has been called "Wine of Honor," and British sovereigns nicknamed it "King of Wines." St-Emilion was named for an 8th-century Breton saint, a former baker who became a monk. The town, made mostly of golden stone and dating from the Middle Ages, is known for its macaroons.

St-Emilion maintains the ancient tradition of La Jurade. Members of this society wear silk hats and scarlet robes edged with ermine, and the Syndicat Viticole, which watches over the quality of wine, have all been around the world to promote the wines with this appellation. St-Emilion lies 22 miles northeast of Bordeaux between Libourne (5 miles away) and Castillon-la-Bataille (7 miles away). Its **Office de Tourisme** is on place des Créneaux (☎ 57-24-72-03).

Trains from Bordeaux make the 45-minute trip to St-Emilion twice per day.

SEEING THE TOP ATTRACTIONS

At the heart of St-Emilion is **place du Marché,** between two hills. An old acacia tree marks the center.

The **Eglise Monolithe** (☎ 57-24-72-03), the most important underground church in France, was carved out of limestone by the Benedictines during the 9th to 12th centuries. Its facade is marked by three 14th-century bay windows, and a sculpted portal from the same century depicts the Last Judgment and resurrection of the dead. The church is about 37 feet high, 67 feet wide, and 125 feet long. Tours leave from the tourist office every 45 minutes daily: April to October from 10am to 5:45pm; November to March from 10am to 5pm. Admission is 30 F ($5.70) for adults and 19 F ($3.60) for children. The church is closed December 24, 25, and 31, plus the first week of January.

Nearby is the grotto where it's believed that St. Emilion lived the quiet life of meditation and contemplation that led to his canonization. The grotto, said to contain the saint's bed, is below the **Chapelle de la Trinité,** from the 13th century—it's a rare structure in the southwest. Catacombs can be found nearby, and you can also view a spring of water surrounded by a 16th-century balustrade.

Finally, you may want to view the **Château du Roi,** founded by Henry III of the Plantagenet line in the 13th century. Until 1608 it was the town hall. From the top of the dungeon you can see St-Emilion, and, on a clear day, the Dordogne. You can wander about daily from 9am to 12:30pm and 2:30 to 6:30pm. Admission is 8 F ($1.50).

WHERE TO STAY

Hostellerie de Plaisance

Place du Clother, 33330 St-Emilion. ☎ **57-24-72-32.** Fax 57-74-41-11. 12 rms. A/C TEL. 790 F ($150.20) double. Breakfast 56 F ($10.65) extra. AE, DC, MC, V. Parking free. Closed Jan.

This is the best place to stay or dine in this medieval town. The well-styled rooms, some with views of stone monuments and towers, welcome the most sophisticated wine tasters and buyers; the best doubles have terraces where you can enjoy breakfast. Some rooms are quite small. The cuisine of Louis Quilain is the best known and most praised in the area. He's at his best when working with the region's bountiful seasonal ingredients.

WHERE TO DINE

⑤ Logis de la Cadene

Place Marché-au-Bois. ☎ **57-24-71-40.** Reservations not required. Main courses 60–90 F ($11.40–$17.10); fixed-price menus 90 F ($17.10), 120 F ($22.80), 150 F ($28.50), and 180 F ($34.20). AE, MC, V. Tues–Sat 12:30–2pm and 8–10pm, Sun 12:30–2pm. Closed Dec 24–Jan. FRENCH.

This 19th-century house has a pleasant vine-covered terrace, and the dining room has rustic decor. Specialties are often cooked on the grill over wood from local vineyards; many include flavorful local flap mushrooms (cèpes). The cuisine is based on market-fresh ingredients. "It's the cooking of the local people," said one habitué, "and we're proud of it."

3 Angoulême

275 miles SW of Paris, 72 miles NE of Bordeaux

Angoulême is on a hill between the Charente and Aguienne rivers, and you can easily visit it on the same day you visit Cognac. A "Balzac town," Angoulême first saw the novelist in 1831 when he came here and much admired his host's wife, Zulma Carraud.

The hub of the town is **place de l'Hôtel-de-Ville,** with its town hall erected from 1858 to 1866 on the site of the old palace of the ducs d'Angoulême, where Marguerite de Navarre, sister of François I, was born. All that remains of the ducal palace are the 15th-century Tour de Valois and the 13th-century Tour de Lusignan.

The **Cathédrale St-Pierre,** place St-Pierre (☎ 45-95-20-38), was begun in 1128 and was much restored in the 19th century. Flanked by towers, its facade boasts 75 statues—each in a separate niche—representing the Last Judgment. This is one of France's most startling examples of romanesque-Byzantine style. Some of its restoration was questionable, however. The architect, Abadie (designer of Sacré-Coeur in Paris), tore down the north tower, then rebuilt it with the original materials in the same style. In the interior you can wander under a four-domed ceiling.

Adjoining is the former Bishops' Palace, which has been turned into the **Musée Municipal,** 1 rue Friedland (☎ 45-95-07-69), with a collection of European paintings, mainly from the 17th to the 19th century. The most interesting exhibits are the African art and ethnological collections. It's open Wednesday to Monday from 10am to noon and 2 to 6pm. Admission is 15 F ($2.85) for adults; 17 and under free.

Finally, you can take the **promenade des Remparts,** boulevards laid down on the site of the town walls. Going along, you'll have a superb view of the valley almost 250 feet below.

ESSENTIALS

GETTING THERE Three regular trains per day arrive from Bordeaux (trip time: 1¹/₂ hr.), costing 100 F ($19) one way. However, 8 to 10 faster TGVs arrive from Bordeaux each day (trip time: 55 min.), costing 118 F ($22.40) one way, including the reservations fee.

VISITOR INFORMATION The Office de Tourisme is at 2 place St-Pierre (☎ 45-95-16-84).

WHERE TO STAY

Mercure Altea Hôtel de France

1 place des Halles, 16003 Angoulême CEDEX. ☎ **45-95-47-95.** Fax 45-92-02-70. 90 rms. TV TEL. 400–600 F ($76–$114.05) double. Breakfast 50 F ($9.50) extra. AE, DC, MC, V. Parking 40 F ($7.60).

This grand old hotel stands in the center of the old town on extensive grounds. The rooms are generally spacious, with high ceilings and French provincial furnishings. On the lobby level, a formal restaurant offers excellent food and polite service. Specialties include foie gras, sole meunière, and trout with almonds. Meals are served Monday to Friday from noon to 1:30pm and 7 to 9:15pm and Sunday from 7 to 9:15pm.

Novotel Angoulême Nord
Route de Poitiers, 16430 Champniers. ☎ **45-68-53-22.** Fax 45-68-33-83. 100 rms. A/C TV TEL. 350–390 F ($66.50–$74.10) double. Breakfast 50 F ($9.50) extra. AE, DC, MC, V. Parking free. Take N10 from Angoulême about 4 miles toward Poitiers.

This dependable hotel is the area's "family friendly" choice. The rooms are simple and chain uniform, each with a double bed and a single that transforms into a couch. The grounds are filled with evergreens and well-maintained lawns. The sunny modern restaurant serves a variety of local and international specialties, but the cuisine is not the reason to stay here.

WHERE TO DINE

La Ruelle
6 rue Trois-Notre-Dame. ☎ **45-92-94-64.** Reservations recommended. Main courses 70–180 F ($13.30–$34.20); fixed-price lunch 150 F ($28.50); fixed-price menus 140 F ($26.60), 160 F ($30.40), and 240 F ($45.60). V. Mon–Fri noon–2pm and 7:30–10pm, Sat 7:30–10pm. Closed Jan 1–7, Feb 19–25, Apr 8–14, and Aug 5–18. FRENCH.

This first-class restaurant, in the center of the oldest part of town, was once a pair of medieval houses separated by a narrow alley (a *ruelle*) that was covered over. Jean-François Dauphin is the proprietor and his wife, Véronique, the cook, and they're the only shining lights in Angoulême's dim culinary scene. The menus change with the chef's mood and the availability of ingredients, but you can count on classic French recipes given a modern twist. Specialties include sole with crayfish and cucumbers, gigot of lamb au Romarin, and filet of beef with pigs' feet in garlic-cream sauce. We especially recommend the fixed-price menus.

NEARBY ACCOMMODATIONS & DINING

✪ Le Moulin du Maine-Brun
RN141, Lieu-Dit la Vigerie, 16290 Asnières-sur-Nouère. ☎ **45-90-83-00.** Fax 45-96-91-14. 18 rms, 2 suites. MINIBAR TV TEL. 450–750 F ($85.50–$142.50) double; 1,000–1,300 F ($190.10–$247.10) suite. Breakfast 60 F ($11.40) extra. AE, DC, MC, V. Parking free. Drive 7 miles west of Angoulême (turn right at Vigerie); take RN141.

This Relais du Silence (part of a chain of hotels noted for their tranquillity) was originally a flour mill. In the early 1960s, Raymond and Irene Ménager acquired it and 80 acres of lowlands, about half of which are now devoted to the production of cognac. The maître d'hôtel's preferred brand is the one made in the hotel's distillery: Moulin du Domaine de Maine-Brun. These are the most luxurious accommodations in the area. The rooms are conservative and furnished with some antiques. The restaurant serves splendid fare; specialties usually include foie gras perfumed with house cognac. Fixed-price menus cost 180 F ($34.20), 280 F ($53.20), and 360 F ($68.40). The restaurant is open from 12:30 to 2pm and 7:30 to 9pm; it's closed November and December and Sunday night and Monday from January to April.

4 Cognac

297 miles SW of Paris, 23 miles NW of Angoulême, 70 miles SE of La Rochelle

The world enjoys 100 million bottles a year of the nectar known as cognac, which Victor Hugo called "the drink of the gods." Sir Winston Churchill required a bottle a day. It's worth a detour to visit one of the château warehouses of the great cognac bottlers. Martell, Hennessy, and Otard welcome visits from the public and will even give you a free drink at the end of the tour.

The best distillery tour is offered by ✪ **Hennessy,** 1 rue de la Richonne (☎ 45-35-72-68). It's open June 15 to September 15, Monday to Saturday from 9am to 5:30pm; and September 16 to June 14, Monday to Friday from 8:30 to 11am and 1:45 to 4:30pm.

At the **Musée de Cognac,** 48 bd. Denfert-Rochereau (☎ 45-36-53-77), you can see a collection including local artifacts, wine-industry exhibits, paintings, sculpture, furniture, and decorative art. Cognac is also the birthplace of the postcard, and the museum has some of the rarest and oldest examples. It's open Wednesday to Monday: June to September from 10am to noon and 2 to 6pm, and October to May from 2 to 5:30pm. Admission is 12 F ($2.30) for adults and 6 F ($1.15) for children.

Cognac has two beautiful parks: the **Parc François-Ier** and the **Parc de l'Hôtel-de-Ville.** The romanesque-gothic **Eglise St-Léger** is from the 12th century, and its bell tower is from the 15th century. François I was born in the now-dilapidated **château** in the town center; it dates from the 15th and 16th centuries and was a former residence of the House of Valois.

ESSENTIALS

GETTING THERE   Cognac's railway station is south of the town center. Five trains per day arrive from Angoulême (trip time: 1 hr.), costing 46 F ($8.75) one way, and six trains pull in from Saintes (trip time: 20 min.), costing 28 F ($5.30) one way. For rail schedules, call 45-82-03-29.

DISTILLERY TOURS   If you'd like to visit a distillery, go to its main office during regular business hours and request a tour. The staffs are generally receptive, and you'll see some brandies that have aged for as long as 50 or even 100 years. You can ask about guided tours at the tourist office.

VISITOR INFORMATION   The Office de Tourism is at 16 rue du 14-Juillet (☎ 45-82-10-71).

WHERE TO STAY

✪ Hostellerie les Pigeons Blancs

110 rue Jules-Brisson, 16100 Cognac. ☎ **45-82-16-36.** Fax 45-82-29-29. 7 rms. TV TEL. 280–450 F ($53.20–$85.55) double. Breakfast 42 F ($8) extra. AE, DC, MC, V. Parking free. Closed Jan.

This stylish hotel is named after the white pigeons that nest in the moss-covered stone walls. This angular farmhouse with sloping tile roofs was built in the 17th century as a coaching inn. For many years it was the home of the Tachets, until three of the siblings transformed it into a hotel/restaurant in 1973. It's a mile northwest of the center and has elegant guest rooms. (See "Where to Dine," below, for our restaurant recommendation.)

Ⓢ Hôtel Ibis/Hôtel Urbis

24 rue Elisée-Mousnier, 16100 Cognac. ☎ **45-82-19-53.** Fax 45-82-86-71. 39 rms, 1 suite. TV TEL. 295 F ($56.05) double; 400 F ($76) suite. Breakfast 35 F ($6.65) extra. AE, DC, MC, V. Parking 20 F ($3.80).

Clean, comfortable, and unpretentious, this hotel is identified by townspeople as either the Ibis or the Urbis, though management suggests the name Ibis will stick. There's a relaxed ambience in the public rooms, and the pleasant guest rooms are outfitted in a monochromatic standardized modern style; some overlook a garden. Breakfast is the only meal served, yet in certain circumstances simple platters can be prepared for guests who prefer to dine in.

WHERE TO DINE

Hostellerie les Pigeons Blancs

110 rue Jules-Brisson. ☎ **45-82-16-36.** Reservations recommended. Main courses 75–140 F ($14.25–$26.60); fixed-price menus 135 F ($25.65), 155 F ($29.45), and 200 F ($38). AE, DC, MC, V. Mon–Sat noon–2pm and 7–10pm, Sun noon–2pm. FRENCH.

This restaurant run by the Tachet family has two elegant dining rooms with ceiling beams and limestone fireplaces. Jacques is the chef, Jean-Michel the maître d', and Catherine the hostess. Menu listings depend on the availability of ingredients but might be warm oysters with Vouvray-flavored sabayon, rack of suckling pig with local wine, and sole filet steamed in cognac. The flavor combinations always seem successful here. (See "Where to Stay," above, for our hotel recommendation.)

La Marmite

14 rue St-Jean-du-Perot. ☎ **46-41-17-03.** Reservations required in summer. Main courses 98–290 F ($18.60–$55.10); fixed-price menus 180 F ($34.20), 295 F ($56.05), and 370 F ($70.30). AE, DC, MC, V. Thurs–Tues noon–2:30pm and 7–9:15pm. FRENCH.

Chef Louis Marzin is becoming better known all the time, though he's yet to be discovered by Michelin inspectors. His specialties are based on recipes he learned in his apprenticeships throughout the country; they include a plate of "fruits of the sea," grilled lobster, and monkfish with wild mushrooms. To these courses, he adds his special touches. The decor is a cross between a tavern and a café. In one corner is a small salon where you can order an apéritif.

NEARBY ACCOMMODATIONS & DINING

Moulin de Cierzac

Route de Barbezieux, Saint-Fort-sur-le-Né, 16130 St-Gonzac by Cognac. ☎ **45-83-01-32.** Fax 45-83-03-59. 10 rms. TV TEL. 280–520 F ($53.20–$98.80) double. Breakfast 60 F ($11.40) extra. AE, MC, V. Closed Jan 15–Feb 12. Parking free.

This former mill house, at the southern edge of the village beside a stream, has white shutters and lots of character. The guest rooms are comfortable, bright and functional. In the rustic dining room overlooking the park, specialties are steamed lobster in orange butter and filet of lamb in garlic-cream sauce. Local gastronomes flock to the place, noted for its accomplished classic cuisine.

5 Saintes

291 miles SW of Paris, 72 miles N of Bordeaux

The much-battered monuments of this town on the banks of the Charente River represent just about every civilization since the Romans, who made it the capital of southwestern France. Today, on the tree-lined streets bordered with shops, you're likely to enjoy an unusual stopover.

The ancient Roman city, called Mediolanum Santonus, was the place to which the Latin poet Ausone came to die at about the same time that St. Eutrope began to Christianize the town. This latter action led to repeated attacks by barbarians. During the Middle Ages the Plantagenets covered the city with religious monuments, many of which were visited by the pilgrims wending their way down to Santiago de Compostela in Spain.

During the 18th century and continuing into the 19th, the city witnessed the construction of many of its neoclassical buildings, such as the national theater and mansions erected by nobles as well as brigands. Saintes also was the birthplace of the 16th-century inventor of enameling, Bernard Palissy.

ESSENTIALS

GETTING THERE   Saintes is a railway junction for the surrounding region, and thanks to the nearby autoroutes, driving is easy. Seven or eight trains per day arrive from Bordeaux (trip time: 1¹/₄ hr.), and six trains per day pull in from Cognac (trip time: 20 min.).

VISITOR INFORMATION   The Office de Tourisme is in the Villa Musso, 62 cours National (☎ 46-74-23-82).

SEEING THE TOP ATTRACTIONS

Major attractions include the **Abbaye aux Dames,** 7 place de l'Abbaye (☎ 46-97-48-48), founded in 1047 by Geoffroi Martel, comte d'Anjou. It became a convent, attracting women from the finest families in France; daughters of the nobility, among whom was the future marquise de Montespan, were educated here. After the Revolution, so great was the hatred of the local people that the church was transformed into a dress shop. In 1942, after 20 years of restoration, the church was reconsecrated. The style is romanesque, though sections date from the 18th century. Every summer a festival of ancient music takes place here. The abbey's open daily from 9am to 5pm.

The **Arc de Germanicus,** on esplanade André-Malraux near the tourist office, was built in A.D. 19 of local limestone. In 1842 it was moved from a position near the end of a Roman bridge the authorities were demolishing to its present location on the right bank of the Charente. It's dedicated to Germanicus and Tiberius.

The **Cathédrale St-Pierre,** rue St-Pierre (☎ 49-41-23-76), was built on Roman foundations in the 12th century and greatly expanded in a flamboyant gothic style in the 15th century. Parts were destroyed by the Calvinists in 1568, but then rebuilt. The enormous organs date from the 16th and 17th centuries. It's open daily from 9am to 5pm. The Old City, an area of winding streets with a distinctly medieval flavor, surrounds the cathedral.

The **Eglise St-Eutrope,** rue St-Eutrope (☎ 46-93-71-12), is one of the most important monuments in southwestern France, in spite of the alterations to the nave that a misdirected series of architects performed in 1803. It was built in the 1400s by Louis XI, who revered St. Eutrope, believing the saint had cured him of a disease. The vast crypt is only half buried underground because of the slope of the land, and it's more a subterranean church than a crypt. The sarcophagus, said to contain the remains of St. Eutrope, is from the 4th century. In the crypt is a well nearly 150 feet deep, plus several Roman-era baptismal fonts. Admission is free, but it costs 2 F (40¢) to have the crypt illuminated. The church is open daily from 9am to 5pm.

The **Arènes Gallo-Romaines** is accessible from rues St-Eutrope and Lacurie. To visit it, ring the bell for the custodian. Built in the early 1st century, it's one of the oldest remaining Roman amphitheaters, though it's medium-size in comparison to others. Many of the seats are covered with wild shrubs and greenery, but in its heyday it could hold 20,000 spectators. A fountain has been built halfway up the slope of one of the sides, marking the spot where a disciple of St. Eutrope was beheaded. It's open June to September, daily from 9am to 8pm; October to May, daily from 9am to 6pm. Admission is free.

The town's homage to the acquisitive mania of one of its leading citizens can be admired in the **Musée Dupuy-Mestreau,** 4 rue Monconseil, adjacent to central place Blair (☎ **46-93-36-71**). The collection was once the property of M. Abel Mestreau and was later taken over by his grandson, Charles Dupuy, and then by the town of Saintes. Today it's the region's most eccentrically charming collection, a celebration of local folklore, history, and customs. You'll find 3,000 objects that include 19th-century dresses and lace headdresses, folkloric costumes, furniture, jewelry, and a poignant collection of early 20th-century objects carved from coconuts by prisoners incarcerated in the nearby prison at Rochefort.

From June 1 to September 1, a 90-minute tour, usually in rapid-fire French, is offered Wednesday to Monday at 11am and from 2 to 5pm. The rest of the year, when the building grows cold because of its lack of central heating, tours are conducted only Wednesday to Monday from 2 to 5pm. If a tour is in progress at the time of your arrival, a sign will instruct you to wait, usually for no more than 40 minutes, for the next tour. The cost is 10 F ($1.90) for adults; students and children 17 and under free.

WHERE TO STAY

Hôtel de l'Avenue

114 av. Gambetta, 17100 Saintes. ☎ **46-74-05-91.** Fax 46-74-32-16. 15 rms, 13 with bath (tub or shower). TV TEL. 168 F ($31.90) double without bath, 254–265 F ($48.25–$50.35) double with bath. Breakfast 32 F ($6.10) extra. MC, V. Parking free. Closed Dec 26–Jan 9 and Sun Oct–Apr 1.

This hotel was richly and comfortably renovated in 1991. Today the rooms are decorated with unusual lithographs and tasteful accessories and overlook a flowering courtyard or the garden in back. The Crozas family are the owners—they don't maintain a restaurant but will direct you to the adjacent Brasserie Louis (see "Where to Dine," below).

Relais du Bois St-George

Rue de Royan, 17100 Saintes. ☎ **46-93-50-99.** Fax 46-93-34-93. 21 rms, 10 suites. TV TEL. 600–750 F ($114.05–$142.55) double; from 1,100 F ($209.10) suite. Breakfast 70 F ($13.30) extra. MC, V. Parking free.

Off the Paris–Bordeaux motorway and only two minutes from the town center, this hotel is in the heart of a vast park with gardens and a small lake with ducks and swans. It's owned/managed by Jérôme Emery, who created it from the remains of an 11th-century farmhouse. The rooms are a well-balanced combination of modern comfort and antique furnishings, some with terraces overlooking the lake and garden. The restaurant is in a renovated farmhouse, with a view of the park and lake. The chef prepares savory specialties like suprême of turbot in langoustine sauce, filet of limousin beef with shallots, and a dessert trolley of home-made delicacies. Fixed-price menus are offered at 190 F ($36.10), 230 F ($43.70), and 480 F ($91.20).

WHERE TO DINE

Ⓢ Brasserie Louis

116 av. Gambetta. ☎ **46-74-16-85.** Reservations recommended. Main courses 55–130 F ($10.45–$24.70); fixed-price menus 68 F ($12.90) (Tues–Fri only) and 88–130 F ($16.70–$24.70). MC, V. Tues–Sun noon–2pm and 7–10pm. FRENCH.

This bustling brasserie is in a modern building whose interior is lined with mul-ticolored brick. About 100 places are available for those who look for honest, simple preparations of traditional recipes. There's also a terrace overlooking a gar-den, where some of the noise from the street is obscured. Menu items include plat-ters of shellfish, mussels prepared with white-wine or curry sauce, rack of lamb with herbs, and entrecôte of beef with french fries. It may not be the most inventive of cookery but it's soul-satisfying. If business merits it (it usually does), the place is open every day in July and August.

NEARBY DINING

Ⓢ La Vieille Forge

Route 137, vers La Rochelle. ☎ **46-92-98-30.** Reservations not required. Main courses 60–75 F ($11.40–$14.25); fixed-price menus 65 F ($12.35), 100 F ($19), and 130 F ($24.70). AE, DC, MC, V. Mon–Sat noon–1:45pm and 7–9:30pm. Take Route 137 to St-Georges-des-Coteaux, 3³/₄ miles northwest of Saintes. FRENCH.

Despite its relative isolation midway between the villages of St-Porchaire and Saintes, this is one of the busiest restaurants in the region. The dining room in the renovated building has a high-peaked roof and is decorated with bellows and iron tools used by 19th-century blacksmiths. Typical menu items include cèpes (flap mushrooms) bordelaise, brochette of magrêt of duckling with three kinds of pep-per, woodcocks with grapes, and house-style filet of sole. The restaurant's cook-ery is definitely grandmother style, but, in a bow to modern tastes, a grill and a pizzeria have been opened in another room.

6 La Rochelle

290 miles SW of Paris, 90 miles SE of Nantes, 100 miles S of Bordeaux, 88 miles NW of Angoulême

Once known as the French Geneva, La Rochelle is a historic Atlantic port and ancient sailors' city, formerly the stronghold of the Huguenots. It was founded as a fishing village in the 10th century on a rocky platform in the center of a huge marshland. Eleanor of Aquitaine gave La Rochelle a charter in 1199, freeing it from feudal dues. Becoming an independent city-state, the port capitalized on the wars between France and England. From the port sailed the founders of Montréal and others who helped colonize Canada. From the 14th to the 16th century La Ro-chelle enjoyed its heyday as one of France's great maritime cities.

As a hotbed of Protestant factions, it armed privateers to prey on Catholic ves-sels but was eventually besieged by Catholic troops. Two strong men led the fight—Cardinal Richelieu (with, of course, his Musketeers) and Jean Guiton, for-merly an admiral and then mayor of the city. Richelieu proceeded to blockade the port. Though La Rochelle bravely resisted, on October 30, 1628, Richelieu entered the city. From the almost 30,000 citizens of the proud city, he found only 5,000 survivors.

La Rochelle became the principal port between France and the colony of Canada, but France's loss of Canada ruined its Atlantic trade.

ESSENTIALS

GETTING THERE   La Rochelle–Laleu airport is on the coast, north of the city. Rail connections from Bordeaux and Nantes are frequent. Six to eight trains from Bordeaux arrive daily (trip time: 2 hr.), and four or five trains arrive from Nantes (trip time: 2 hr.). The TGV fast trains from Paris arrive seven to nine times per day (trip time: 3 hr.).

VISITOR INFORMATION   The Office de Tourisme is on place de la Petite Sirène (☎ 46-41-14-68).

SEEING THE TOP ATTRACTIONS

There are two aspects to La Rochelle: the old and unspoiled town inside the Vauban defenses and the tacky modern and industrial suburbs. Its **fortifications** have a circuit of $3^{1}/_{2}$ miles with a total of seven gates.

The town with its arch-covered streets will please the walker. The **port** is still a bustling fishing harbor and one of the major sailing centers in western Europe. Try to schedule a visit in time to attend a fish auction at the harbor. The **best streets for strolling** are rue du Palais, rue Chaudrier, and rue des Merciers with its ancient wooden houses. On the last, seek out the houses at nos. 17, 8, 5, and 3.

The **Hôtel de Ville,** place de la Mairie (☎ 46-41-90-44), in the city center, is constructed in a flamboyant 14th-century gothic style, with battlements. Inside you can admire the Henry II staircase with canopies and the marble desk of the heroic Jean Guiton. It's open Easter to late September, Monday to Friday from 9:30 to 11am and 2:30 to 5:30pm and Saturday from 2:30 to 5pm; late September to Easter, Sunday to Friday from 2:30 to 4:30pm. Admission is 15 F ($2.85) for adults and 8 F ($1.50) for children 4 to 12; 3 and under free.

Opposite the Tour de St-Nicolas (below), the **Tour de la Chaîne,** quai du Gabut (☎ 46-50-52-36), is named for the large chain that was fastened to it and pulled across the harbor to close it at night. The tower dates from the 14th century and is open May to September, daily from 9:30am to noon and 2 to 6:30pm; October to April, Saturday and Sunday from 10am to noon and 2 to 6:30pm. Admission is 20 F ($3.80) for adults and 10 F ($1.90) for children 15 and under.

The oldest tower in La Rochelle is the **Tour de St-Nicolas,** quai du Gabut (☎ 46-41-74-13), dating from 1371 or 1382. From its second floor you can enjoy a view of the town and harbor; however, from the top you can see only the old town and Ile d'Oléron. Opposite it, the **Tour de la Lanterne,** built between 1445 and 1476, was once a lighthouse but was used mainly as a jail —La Rochelle sergeants were imprisoned here in 1822. The towers are open June to August, daily from 9:30am to 7pm; in April, May, and September, Wednesday to Monday from 9:30am to 12:30pm and 2 to 6:30pm; October to March, Wednesday to Monday from 9:30am to 12:30pm and 2 to 5pm. Admission to both the Tour de St-Nicolas and the Tour de la Lanterne is 20 F ($3.80) for adults and 13 F ($2.45) for children.

French paintings are displayed in the **Musée des Beaux-Arts,** 28 rue Gargolleau (☎ 46-41-64-65), an episcopal palace built in the mid-18th century. The art spans the 17th to the 19th century, with works by Eustache Le Sueur, Brossard de Beaulieu, Corot, and Fromentin. Some 20th-century art is by Maillol and Lagar. It's open Wednesday to Monday from 2 to 5pm and charges 17 F ($3.25).

The most important artifacts pertaining to the history of La Rochelle and of ceramics are in the **Musée d'Obigny-Bernon,** 2 rue St-Côme (☎ 46-41-18-83). Included are painted porcelain from La Rochelle and other places throughout France. Established in 1917, the museum also houses a superb collection of Far Eastern art, compiled from the collections of several wealthy individuals who made donations. It's open Wednesday to Monday from 10am to noon and 2 to 6pm and charges 17 F ($3.25).

The **Musée du Nouveau-Monde,** in the Hôtel Fleuriau, 10 rue Fleuriau (☎ 46-41-46-50), traces the port's 300-year history with the New World. Exhibits start with the discovery of the Mississippi Delta in 1682 by LaSalle and end with the settling of the Louisiana territory. Other exhibits depict French settlements in the French West Indies, including Guadeloupe and Martinique. The museum is open Wednesday to Monday from 10:30am to 12:30pm and 1:30 to 6pm; it's closed Sunday morning. Admission is 16 F ($3.05) for adults; 17 and under free.

The **Musée Lafaille,** 28 rue Albert-Ier (☎ 46-41-18-25), is an ethnography/ zoology museum in a handsome 18th-century building surrounded by a garden; the original paneling has been preserved. Clement de Lafaille, a former comptroller of war, assembled much of the collection, which has been enlarged since he donated it to the city. Displays include rare shellfish, an idol from Easter Island, an embalmed giraffe given to Charles X (the first such specimen to be seen in France), and a parade boat encrusted with gems that was presented to Napoléon III by the king of Siam. It's open mid-June to mid-September, Tuesday to Saturday from 10am to noon and 2 to 6pm and Sunday from 2 to 6pm; off-season, Tuesday to Saturday from 10am to noon and 2 to 5pm and Sunday from 2 to 5pm; closed holidays. Admission is 14 F ($2.65) for adults; children free.

WHERE TO STAY

Hôtel François-I
13 rue Bazoges, 17000 La Rochelle. ☎ **46-41-28-46.** Fax 46-41-35-01. 38 rms. TV TEL. 215– 475 F ($40.85–$90.25) double. Breakfast 38 F ($7.20) extra. MC, V. Parking 38 F ($7.20).

This hotel seems to turn the clock back two centuries, but the plumbing is up-to-date. The service is efficient and kind, and the rooms are pleasantly furnished. Breakfast is the only meal served.

Hôtel les Brises
Chemin de la Digne-Richelieu, 17000 La Rochelle. ☎ **46-43-89-37.** Fax 46-43-27-97. 48 rms. TV TEL. 350–630 F ($66.50–$119.75) double. Breakfast 48 F ($9.10) extra. MC, V. Parking free.

Facing the sea, this hotel is most tranquil, opposite the new Port des Minimes and offering a view of the soaring 19th-century column dedicated to the Virgin. You can enjoy the view from the front balconies as well as the parasol-shaded patio. The immaculate rooms have cherrywood furniture. Breakfast is the only meal served.

Novotel La Rochelle Centre
1 av. de la Porte-Neuve, 17000 La Rochelle. ☎ **46-34-24-24.** Fax. 46-34-58-32. 94 rms. MINIBAR TV TEL. 650 F ($123.55) double. Breakfast 55 F ($10.45) extra. AE, DC, MC, V.

This hotel occupies a desirable verdant location in the Parc Charruyer, a greenbelt about a five-minute walk from La Rochelle. The rooms are monochromatic, standardized, and well maintained, with generous writing desks and big windows overlooking the park. There's also an outdoor pool. A charmless in-house restaurant serves drinks and platters throughout the day, with both regional and continental dishes.

WHERE TO DINE

⑤ Le Claridge

1 rue Admyrault. ☎ **46-50-04-19.** Reservations required. Main courses 80–130 F ($15.20–$24.70); fixed-price menus 98–165 F ($18.60–$31.35). AE, DC, MC, V. Mon–Fri 12:30–2pm and 8–10pm, Sat 8–10pm. FRENCH.

The cheaper fixed-price meal here is very popular. The restaurant is one floor above street level in a 17th-century building in the center of the old town. The dining room has a grand fireplace, heavy ceiling beams, and attractively decorated tables with lots of space. The cuisine is traditional—a typical meal often includes half a dozen oysters, confit of duckling house style, cheese, and dessert. The chef is particularly proud of his foie gras of duckling, smoked salmon of the house, feuilletté of scallops, and an assortment of fresh fish in a sauce consisting of a coulis of crayfish tails.

⑤ Les Quatre Sergents

49 rue-St-Jean-du-Pérot. ☎ **46-41-35-80.** Reservations required. Main courses 68–140 F ($12.90–$26.60); fixed-price menus 78 F ($14.80), 108 F ($20.50), 118 F ($22.40) and 168 F ($31.90). AE, DC, MC, V. Tues–Sat noon–2pm and 7:30–10pm, Sun noon–2pm. FRENCH.

This restaurant is housed in a fanciful art nouveau greenhouse that some visitors compare to the framework of the Eiffel Tower. Specialties include seafood ragoût, duxelles of turbot, mussels in curry sauce, and several regional recipes whose makeup hasn't changed much in about 100 years.

✪ Richard Coutanceau

Plage de la Concurrence. ☎ **46-41-48-19.** Reservations required. Main courses 125–195 F ($23.75–$37.05); fixed-price menus 200–400 F ($38–$76). AE, DC, MC, V. Mon noon–2pm, Tues–Sat noon–2pm and 7:30–9:30pm. FRENCH.

Delectable cuisine is served in this circular concrete pavilion in a pine-filled park. Half is devoted to a tea room, the rest to an elegant and informal dining room. Richard Coutanceau is both owner and chef; his "modernized" cuisine often includes fresh shellfish plucked from nearby waters, lobster-filled ravioli with zucchini flowers, roast bass, and Brittany lobster. Coutanceau is clearly an artist, and his cuisine is far superior to everything else in town.

NEARBY ATTRACTIONS

Clustered just to the north of the mouth of the Gironde lie at least five sandy islands, the biggest of which are Ile d'Oléron and Ile de Ré. Favored by French families who flock to their beaches, the islands are filled with pines, stone buildings, seasonal restaurants serving fresh local oysters, limestone outcroppings, and the ruins of very old windmills.

ILE D'OLERON   A bridge between the mainland and Ile d'Oléron makes access to the second-largest French offshore island (Corsica is bigger) relatively easy. The bridge is at Marennes, some 35 miles south from La Rochelle.

The Romans called Oléron Ularius, and for centuries it occupied a strategic position at the head of the Gironde estuary, between two of the major trading ports, La Rochelle and Bordeaux. Eleanor of Aquitaine lived in the island's château in 1199, just five years before she died. Notwithstanding her banishment, she imposed legal restraints on the island and helped create a maritime code that was used centuries later as the basis for France's law of the sea. For more insights into her life, you can visit the **Musée de l'Ile d'Oléron Aliénor-d'Aquitaine,** 37 rue Pierre-Loti, at St-Pierre-d'Oléron. It's open mid-June to mid-September only, daily from 10am to noon and 2:30 to 6:30pm. Admission is 20 F ($3.80).

Many visitors, however, prefer simply to drive around the island's perimeter, gazing at sparkling water, miles of oyster-laden salt flats, and old churches. For more information about Ile d'Oléron, contact the **Office de Tourisme,** place Gambetta, St-Pierre-d'Oléron (☎ 46-47-11-39); it's closed in October and every afternoon in winter.

ILE DE RE The more densely populated Ile de Ré endured the attempts for many centuries of England's imperialist yearnings, often submitting to attacks by Redcoats. In 1625 more than 2,000 English soldiers were slaughtered when the armies of Louis XIII attacked them simultaneously from two sides. One of the main products of the island today is wine, which French connoisseurs claim bears a subtle taste of algae.

In 1988 a bridge nearly 2 miles long was built to connect the Ile de Ré with the mainland. Ré has several information offices, the most convenient of which is the **Office de Tourisme,** place de la République, Rivedoux-Plage (☎ 46-09-80-62).

7 Poitiers

207 miles SW of Paris, 110 miles SE of Nantes

This city, the ancient capital of Poitou, the northern part of Aquitaine, is filled with history and memories. Everybody has passed through here—from England's Black Prince to Joan of Arc to Richard the Lion-Hearted.

Poitiers stands on a hill overlooking the Clain and Boivre rivers. It was this very strategic location that tempted so many conquerors. Charles Martel proved the savior of Christendom by chasing out the Muslims in 732 and perhaps altering the course of European civilization. Poitiers was the chief city of Eleanor of Aquitaine, who had her marriage to pious Louis VII annulled so she could wed England's Henry II.

For those interested in antiquity, this is one of the most fascinating towns in France. That battle we learned about in history books was fought on September 19, 1356, between the armies of Edward the Black Prince and those of King John of France. It was one of the three great English victories of the Hundred Years' War, distinguished by the use of the longbow in the skilled hands of English archers.

ESSENTIALS

GETTING THERE Rail service is available from Paris, Bordeaux, and La Rochelle. Some 14 of the fast TGV trains arrive from Paris daily (trip time: 1 1/2 hr.). Eight trains arrive daily from Bordeaux (trip time: 1 3/4 hr.), and seven pull in daily from La Rochelle (trip time: 2 hr.).

VISITOR INFORMATION The Office de Tourisme is at 8 rue des Grandes-Ecoles (☎ 49-41-21-24).

EXPLORING THE TOWN

In the eastern sector of Poitiers is the twin-towered **Cathédrale St-Pierre,** place de la Cathédrale (☎ 49-41-23-76), begun in 1162 by Henry II of England and

Eleanor of Aquitaine on the ruins of a Roman basilica. The cathedral was completed much later, but it has always been undistinguished architecturally. However, the interior, 295 feet long, contains some admirable stained glass from the early 13th century. It's open daily from 8am to 7pm.

From the cathedral you can walk to the **Baptistère St-Jean,** rue Jean-Jaurès, the most ancient Christian monument in France. It was built as a baptistery in the early 4th century on Roman foundations, then extended in the 7th century. It contains frescoes from the 11th to the 14th century and a collection of funerary sculpture. It's open in July and August, daily from 10:30am to 12:30pm and 3 to 6pm; April to June and September to October, Wednesday to Monday from 10:30am to 12:30pm and 3 to 6pm; November to March, Wednesday to Monday from 2:30 to 4:30pm. Admission is 8 F ($1.50).

A favorite place of pilgrimage in times gone by, the 11th-century **Eglise Ste-Radegonde,** in the eastern section of Poitiers, commemorates the patroness of Poitiers. In its crypt is her black marble sarcophagus. Radegonde, who died in 587, was the consort of Clotaire, king of the Franks.

Notre-Dame-la-Grande, place de Gaulle (☎ 49-41-22-56), is from the late 11th century, built in the romanesque-Byzantine style and richly decorated. See especially its west front, dating from the mid-12th century. Surrounded by an open-air market, the facade, carved like an ivory casket, is characterized by pinecone-shaped towers. Carvings on the doorway represent biblical scenes. It's open daily from 8am to 7pm.

From place du Maréchal-Leclerc, in the center of town, you can take rue Carnot to the romanesque **Eglise St-Hilaire-le-Grand,** rue St-Hilaire (☎ 49-41-21-57). The church dates from the 11th and 12th centuries; after much destruction, it was restored in the 19th century. It's open daily from 9am to 5pm.

The **Palais de Justice,** place Lepetit (☎ 49-52-24-63), incorporates the 14th-century keep and some other parts of a ducal palace. It was here that Joan of Arc was questioned by the doctors of the university who composed the French Court of Parliament, and also here that Richard the Lion-Hearted was proclaimed comte de Poitou and duc d'Anjou in 1170. It's open Monday to Friday from 9am to noon and 2 to 6pm.

The **Musée St-Croix,** accessible from 61 rue St-Simplicien (☎ 49-41-07-53), was built on the site of the old abbey of St-Croix, from which it takes its name. The museum has a fine-arts section devoted mainly to painting—especially Flemish art from the 16th and 17th centuries and Dutch paintings from the 16th to the 18th century. Several works by Bonnard, Sisley, and Oudot are displayed, along with a bronze, *The Three Graces,* by Maillol. A separate archeological section documents the history of Poitou, from prehistoric times to the Gallo-Roman era, the Renaissance, and up to the end of the 19th century. The museum is open Monday and Wednesday to Friday from 10am to noon and 1 to 6pm, and Saturday and Sunday from 10am to noon and 2 to 6pm. Admission is 15 F ($2.85).

In the environs, drawing some one million visitors annually, is **Futuroscope** (☎ 49-49-30-80), a science amusement park; it's 5¹/₂ miles north of Poitiers in Jaunay-Clan (take N10). This wonderland of technology offers you a chance to experience new sounds, images, and sensations. It has the world's most advanced film-projection techniques and largest screens. Exhibitions include "Kinemax" (a rock crystal covered with mirrors with a 400-seat cinema); "Omnimax" (films projected onto a gigantic dome via a special fish-eye lens, putting you into the heart of the action); *Le Tapis Magique* (a cinema that lets you fly above a continent with a monarch butterfly to guide you), and a 3-D cinema that puts you close to the lions on a safari. One park is devoted to children. From Poitiers, bus no. 16 runs to the park. The park is open in July and August, daily from 9am to 7pm; April to June and in September, daily from 9:30am to 6:30pm; and in October and November, daily from 9am to 6pm. Admission is 135 F ($25.65) for adults and 100 F ($19) for children.

WHERE TO STAY

Grand Hôtel de l'Europe

39 rue Carnot, 86000 Poitiers. ☎ **49-88-12-00.** Fax 49-88-97-30. 88 rms. TV TEL. 380–520 F ($72.20–$98.80) double. Breakfast 40 F ($7.60) extra. DC, MC, V. Parking 25 F ($4.75). Bus 1, 2, or 9.

Two hundred years ago this was a coaching inn; later the stables were transformed into additional rooms, 55 of which contain minibars. The field where the horses were watered is now a quiet courtyard with trees and shrubbery. The isolation of this place enhances its sense of 1930s civility. Breakfast is served in an old-fashioned dining room, with tall windows and an elaborate fireplace. Many of the rooms received major renovations in 1991 and are much more modern than the gracefully antique public rooms suggest.

⑤ Hôtel du Plat d'Etain

7 rue du Plat-d'Etain, 86000 Poitiers. ☎ **49-41-04-80.** Fax 49-52-25-84. 24 rms, 21 with bath (tub or shower). MINIBAR TV TEL. 225 F ($42.75) double without bath, 290 F ($55.10) double with bath. Breakfast 40 F ($7.60) extra. AE, MC, V. Parking 15 F ($2.85). Bus 2A.

One of the best bargains in Poitiers, this renovated hotel is on a narrow alley, a few steps from place du Maréchal-Leclerc. Many restaurants and sights are nearby. Several readers have commented on the warmth of the staff. Each functional, no-frills room has one or two double beds. There's a guarded parking area.

WHERE TO DINE

Aux Armes d'Obernai

19 rue Arthur-Ranc. ☎ **49-41-16-33.** Reservations required. Main courses 75–128 F ($14.25–$24.30); fixed-price menus 100 F ($19), 140 F ($26.60), and 210 F ($39.90). AE, DC, MC, V. Tues–Sat noon–1:45pm and 7:30–9:30pm, Sun noon–1:45pm. Closed 15 days in Feb, one week in March, and two weeks in Sept. FRENCH/POITEVIN.

This small restaurant is in the town center. Denise Husser, one of the region's outstanding chefs, is assisted by her husband, Louis. Specialties include lamb with thyme leaves, mignon of veal with honey and lemon, and sole with crayfish and fondue of leeks. Much of the cooking is in the traditional Poitevin style. The food is very good but not extraordinary, the cooking finely crafted. A few Alsatian dishes are also on the menu.

Maxime

4 rue St-Nicolas. ☎ **49-41-09-55.** Reservations recommended. Main courses 99–125 F ($18.80–$23.75); fixed-price menus 99 F ($18.80), 159 F ($30.20), 189 F ($35.90), and 245 F ($46.55). AE, V. Mon–Fri noon–2pm and 7:30–10pm. Closed Jan 5–15, July 10–20, and Aug 10–20. FRENCH.

Maxime is the most sophisticated restaurant in town and for some reason is completely ignored by the weekend crowds descending to visit Futuroscope. Perhaps begin with a before-dinner drink in the salon. The upstairs dining room has bourgeois warmth and a huge reproduction of a medieval battle scene from the tapestry of Bayeux. Christian Rougier is the charming and hardworking chef. The menu varies with the seasons but always includes ravioli with hot oysters and sometimes features râble of rabbit with forcemeat and chardonnay sauce, hot goat cheese in puff pastry, gigot of monkfish studded with garlic cloves, and succulent desserts. The chef's regional produce is first rate, and he lovingly fashions it into new and tempting dishes.

NEARBY ACCOMMODATIONS & DINING

⑤ Le Chalet de Venise

6 rue de Square (B.P. 4), 86280 St-Benoît. ☎ **49-88-45-07.** Fax 49-52-95-44. 10 rms. TEL. 380 F ($72.20) double. Breakfast 40 F ($7.60) extra. AE, DC, MC, V. Parking free. Closed Sept 4–10 and part of Feb. Take D88 south 2¹/₂ miles from Poitiers to St-Benoît or A10 to Exit 20, "Poitiers Sud."

Those who don't want to stay in the center of town will enjoy this reasonably priced inn surrounded by trees and shrubbery; its chalet opens onto the water. The rooms are simply furnished, clean, and comfortable, each with a distinct personality. The hotel and restaurant are warmly furnished and decorated with autumn colors. Drinks are served on a flagstone terrace, and the restaurant has a fireplace. The food is among the best in the Poitiers area, but dieters may find the portions large. Fixed-price menus are offered at 120 F ($22.80), 159 F ($30.20), 199 F ($37.80), and 280 F ($53.20)—but for many of the specialties of Poitou you'll have to order à la carte. The restaurant is open Tuesday to Sunday from noon to 2pm and 7:30 to 9pm; closed February.

22 The Basque Country & the Pyrénées

The chief interest in the Basque country, a land rich in folklore and old customs, is confined to a small corner of southwestern France, near the Spanish frontier. There you can visit the Basque capital, Bayonne, and explore the coastal resorts, chic Biarritz and St-Jean-de-Luz. In Bayonne's Roman arena in July and August you can see a real Spanish bullfight. The typical costume of the Basque—beret and cummerbund—isn't as evident as it once was, but you can still spot it here and there.

The vast Pyrenean region is a land of glaciers, summits, thermal baths, subterranean grottoes and caverns, winter sports centers, and trout-filled mountain streams. Pau is a good base for excursions in the western Pyrénées; and Lourdes is the major religious pilgrimage center in France.

REGIONAL CUISINE Several distinct culinary traditions have flourished in and around the Pyrénées: those of the Basque, the Béarn, the Catalàn, and the Landes region.

The food here is simple, hearty, and fresh, traditionally served on a table draped with the roughly woven, brightly striped cloths that have always been associated with the region. **Basque cuisine** transforms ordinary ingredients into aromatically tantalizing concoctions, usually with the liberal addition of pepper.

One savory delicacy is tuna grilled with local herbs over a wood fire and served with chopped garlic, parsley, vinaigrette sauce, and freshly pounded pepper. Other regional specialties include *bigorneaux* (periwinkles), which diners skewer from their shells with toothpicks; cèpes, meaty flap mushrooms braised with garlic andsprinkled with parsley; and lamb chops, pork chops, and Basque *bourrides* (fish stews), all with dollops of garlic. Basque bouillabaisse is called *ttoro*, and *chipirones* are cuttlefish, which the Basques stuff or stew after beating the flesh to break apart its toughness.

Basque country also produces *pipérade Basque*, scrambled eggs with tomatoes, onions, green peppers, and black pepper. Sausages popular here include *tripoxa*, made from calves' blood and hot peppers; *tripotcha*, from tripe of baby veal; and *loukinkas*, small garlic-laden sausages. A local sour cider is *pittara*, and the region's best wine is Irouléguy. Bayonne's chocolate is famous throughout France.

What's Special About the Basque Country & the Pyrénées

Beaches
- Grand Plage and Plage de la Côte des Basques, at Biarritz, among the most fashionable in the world.
- St-Jean-de-Luz, the second major French Basque resort, with a long curving beach of beautiful fine sand.

Great Towns
- Bayonne, the leading port and yacht basin on the Côte Basque.
- Biarritz, the premier Basque sea resort, the stamping ground of royalty.
- Lourdes, the major pilgrimage center for Catholics worldwide.

Architectural Highlights
- Cathédrale Ste-Marie, at Bayonne, a landmark gothic cathedral from the early 13th century.
- Château de Pau, at Pau, the Renaissance center of Marguerite de Navarre, known for her bawdy writings.
- Hôtel du Palais, at Biarritz, built by Napoléon III for Empress Eugénie and now a deluxe hotel.
- Boulevard des Pyrénées, at Pau, an esplanade built by Napoléon I and offering a famous panoramic view.

Gastronomic Pilgrimages
- Les Prés d'Eugénie, at Eugénie-les-Bains near Pau, center of the famous chef Michel Guérard, who gave us revolutionary *cuisine minceur*.

Festivals
- Summer Festival and regatta, in Biarritz, in July and August.

In **the Béarn,** centered around Pau, the wines are excellent and liberally consumed with the contents of the family *toupi* (soup pot). Many kinds of onion, beet, sorrel, chicory, bacon/cabbage, or garlic/tomato soup are prepared in this pot. Thick and aromatic stews are called *garbure,* and they're not considered suitable unless the ladle can stand upright in the pot. With bread and wine, the garbure is a full meal. The wines of the Béarn are better than those of the Basque county and include its most famous vintage, Jurançon. Sadly for its regional pride, though, sauce béarnaise was not created here—it was invented by a Basque chef in Paris.

The Pyrénées are also inhabited by the Catalans, who do much of their cooking in olive oil with generous amounts of garlic. The **Catalàn** national dish is *ouillade,* a constantly replenished pair of stewpots that are never emptied, washed, or cleaned. Catalan bouillabaisse is called *bouillinade* and is prepared with crayfish (among other fish) boiled in dry Banyuls wine.

Finally, in the northwestern Pyrénées, the traditional cooking medium is goose fat, which occasionally flavors the aromatic and delicious cassoulet. A cassoulet must always be cooked in a cassoule (earthenware pot), simmered in an oven for hours, and contain white beans and either goose meat, pork, lamb, partridge, or a combination of any of the above.

EXPLORING THE REGION BY CAR

Here's how to link together the best of the region if you rent a car.

Day 1   Begin in the district's eastern outpost, the pilgrimage site of Lourdes, to witness the debris of long-ago pilgrimages lining the town's churches and chapels. Then continue northwest for 18 miles along frequently signposted country roads to Pau, a forbidding fortress whose occupants altered the course of French history more than once. Spend the night here, or if you want to indulge yourself at one of the region's most elegant hotels, continue for another 25 miles north along N134 to Eugénie-les-Bains. Most of the allure of this town derives from chef Michel Guérard, so unless you plan to dine (or stay the night) at Les Prés d'Eugénie you might as well remain in Pau.

Day 2   From Pau, drive west along A64 for 56 miles to the medieval town of Bayonne. Wander through the town's medieval core, visiting the cathedral and the Musée Bonnat. Stop for an elegant evening meal at Cheval Blanc, 68 rue Bourgneuf (☎ **59-59-01-33**), in a 19th-century half-timbered stone house. Stay overnight here.

Day 3   Drive 6 miles southwest along N10 to one of the Basque country's two largest coastal resorts, Biarritz. This is a town where beachfront amusements, along with bars, cafés, and shops, hold more allure than historic sights, so for the moment abandon your cultural quests and have a good time. Stay out late and opt, the following day, to lie on the beach if that's your thing.

Day 4   Now drive southwest along the coastal road for about 9 miles, to a point just before the border of Spain. Check into any hotel in St-Jean-de-Luz, brush up on the Basque culture and its resistance movement, buy a beret, and ramble around the dozens of cafés and bars clogging the edges of the historic port.

1 Bayonne

478 miles SW of Paris, 114 miles SW of Bordeaux

The leading port/pleasure-yacht basin of the Côte Basque, divided by the Nive and Adour rivers, Bayonne is a cathedral city and capital of the Pays Basque. It's characterized by narrow streets, quays, and ramparts. Enlivening the scene are bullfights, *pelota* games (jai alai), and street dancing at annual fiestas. While here you may want to buy some of Bayonne's chocolate at one of the arcaded shops along rue du Port-Neuf, later enjoying a coffee at one of the cafés along place de la Liberté, the hub of town.

The old town, **Grand Bayonne**, is inside the ramparts of Vauban's fortifications, on the left bank of the Nive. This part of town is dominated by the early 13th-century ✪ **Cathédrale Ste-Marie**, rue d'Espagne (☎ **59-59-17-82**). This outstanding gothic building is distinguished by its nave's stained-glass windows, and many niches contain elaborate sarcophagi. From the 13th-century cloister you have a view of the cathedral's remarkable architecture. It's open Monday to Saturday from 7am to 12:30pm and 2:30 to 7:30pm and Sunday from 8am to 12:30pm and 3:30 to 7:30pm.

You might also like to visit the **Musée Bonnat**, 5 rue Jacques-Lafitte (☎ **59-59-08-52**), containing a collection of artwork painter Léon Bonnat donated to the city, including his own. Bonnat was especially fond of portraits, often of ladies in elegant 1890s dresses. In his own *Jacob Wrestling with the*

The Basque Country & the Pyrénées

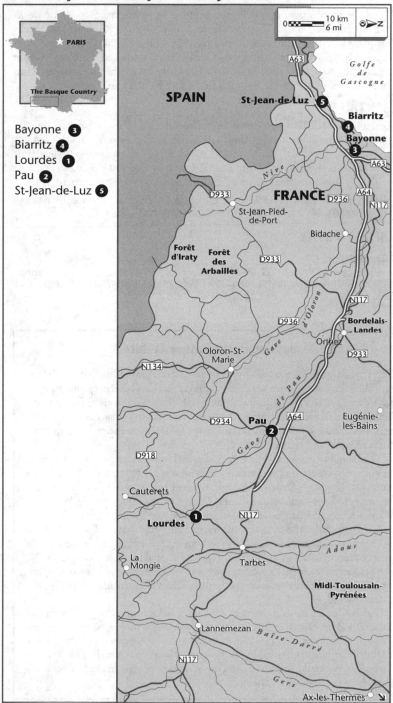

Angel, the angel is amazingly delicate and effete. Far greater painters whose works are represented include Degas, David, Goya, Ingres, Rubens, van Dyck, Rembrandt, Tiepolo, El Greco, even Leonardo. The museum is open June 15 to September 10, Wednesday to Monday from 10am to noon and 3 to 7pm (to 9pm Friday); the rest of the year, Saturday and Sunday from 10am to noon and 3 to 7pm. Admission is 15 F ($2.85) for adults and 5 F ($.95) for children.

ESSENTIALS

GETTING THERE   Bayonne is linked to Paris by 10 trains per day. Regular trains take nine hours, though the TGV arrives in five. Fares are 390 F ($74.10) one way, plus 36 to 90 F ($6.85 to $17.10) for a TGV reservation fee. Nine trains per day arrive from Bordeaux (trip time: $2^{1}/_{2}$ hr.), costing 130 F ($24.70) one way.

There's bus service from Biarritz and many outlying towns not serviced by train.

VISITOR INFORMATION   The Office de Tourisme is on place des Basques (☎ 59-46-01-46).

WHERE TO STAY

Le Grand Hôtel

21 rue Thiers, 64100 Bayonne. ☎ **59-59-14-61**, or 800/528-1234 in the U.S. and Canada. Fax 59-25-61-70. 56 rms. TV TEL. 480–630 F ($91.20–$119.70) double. Breakfast 45 F ($8.55) extra. AE, DC, MC, V. Parking 50 F ($9.50). Bus 7.

Basking in the Basque Culture

The Pays Basque (Basque country) is home to a unique culture rich in folklore, charm, and a sense of national destiny. Enterprising and seafaring, the Basques trace their roots to a pre–Indo-European people whose origins aren't fully known. The Basques resisted the incursions of both the ancient Romans and the Moors and later became known throughout Europe for their commercial zeal, capacity for hard work, and culinary skill.

The Basque language is a linguistic riddle that has puzzled ethnologists for years; its grammar, syntax, and vocabulary are in no way related to those of any other European language. Depending on the dialect being spoken, the language is known as Uskara, Euskara, or Eskuara. Though on the wane since the beginning of this century, the Basque language is now enjoying a modest renaissance.

Geographically, the Basque country straddles the western foothills of the Pyrénées, and the Basque people live in both France and Spain, in the latter in greater numbers than in the former. During the Spanish Civil War (1936–39) the Basques were on the Republican side and were defeated by Franco. Oppression during the Franco years has led to deep-seated resentment against the policies of Madrid.

The Basque separatist movement Euskadi ta Azkatasuna (Basque Nation and Liberty) and the French organization Enbata (Ocean Wind) engaged (unsuccessfully) in guerrilla activity in 1968 to secure a united Basque state. Despite the relative calm of recent years, many Basque nationalists fervently wish that the Basque people could be united into one autonomous state instead of being divided between France and Spain.

This hotel was built on the ruins of a medieval Carmelite convent around 1835. In 1991, after a total renovation, it attained four-star status as one of the town's best hotels. Its comfortably conservative rooms usually contain minibars as well as plushly upholstered furnishings. In the hotel's restaurant, Les Carmes, fixed-price meals cost 120 to 200 F ($22.80 to $38).

Mercure Agora

Av. Jean-Rostand, 64100 Bayonne. ☎ **59-63-30-90.** Fax 59-42-06-64. 109 rms. A/C TV TEL. 450 F ($85.50) double. Breakfast 55 F ($10.45) extra. AE, DC, MC, V. Parking free. Bus 7.

This modern chain hotel provides well-furnished rooms with river views. Drinks are served on the terrace, by the river near the wooded towpath. The restaurant's fixed-price menus begin as low as 90 F ($17.10), but the cuisine is not the reason to stay here.

WHERE TO DINE

✪ Cheval Blanc

68 rue Bourgneuf. ☎ **59-59-01-33.** Reservations recommended. Main courses 80–120 F ($15.20–$22.80); fixed-price menus 98 F ($18.60), 162 F ($30.80), and 232 F ($44.10). AE, DC, MC, V. July–Sept, daily noon–2:15pm and 7–9:30pm; Oct–June, Tues–Sat noon–2:15pm and 7–9:30pm, Sun noon–2:15pm. BASQUE.

The finest restaurant is in a 19th-century half-timbered stone house in the heart of the historic center. In a rustic/elegant dining room you can enjoy the cuisine of Jean-Claude Tellechea, which will be served by one of the most skilled maîtres d'hôtel in the Basque country, Robert Hualte. Menu items vary with the season but might include gazpacho of broad beans and baby peas, veal kidneys enhanced with veal drippings, and a supremely delicious dorado simmered in garlic and served with crépinette de marmitako (diced tuna with red and green peppers, bound by the lining of a pig's stomach). Dessert might be a pot of bittersweet chocolate with crème fraîche.

⑤ Euzkalduna

61 rue Pannecau. ☎ **59-59-28-02.** Reservations not required. Main courses 40–50 F ($7.60–$9.50). No credit cards. Mon–Sat noon–2:30pm. Bus 7. BASQUE.

This is the place to go for authentic Basque cuisine, but at lunch only. The chef doesn't offer a lot of seafood, though you can still order calamari. He prefers typically Basque dishes like pipérade, stuffed pimentos, and certain veal dishes. The cookery makes no pretense at refinement—it's the same hearty fare locals have been eating for decades.

2 Biarritz

484 miles SW of Paris, 120 miles SW of Bordeaux

One of the most famous seaside resorts in the world, Biarritz, in southwestern France, was once a simple fishing village near the Spanish border. Favored by Empress Eugénie, the Atlantic village soon attracted her husband, Napoléon III, who truly launched it. Later Queen Victoria showed up often, and her son, Edward VII, visited more than once.

In the 1930s the Prince of Wales (soon to be Edward VIII) and the woman he loved, Wallis Simpson, did much to make Biarritz even more fashionable, as they headed south with these instructions: "Chill the champagne, pack the pearls, and tune up the Bugatti." Biarritz became the pre–jet set's favorite sun spot, though those legends are long gone and aren't coming back. The resort is still fashionable, but the unthinkable has happened: It now offers surfing shops, tacky snack bars, and even some reasonably priced hotels. What would Mrs. Simpson say about that?

Today it's busy from July to September, quietly settling down for the rest of the year. We prefer Biarritz in June, when the prices are lower, the flowers are in bloom (especially the spectacular hydrangeas), and you can find space on the beach. Surf-boarding is most popular here, drawing many Stateside youths.

The original fishing village contains the oldest buildings, as well as the Casino Bellevue and the Hôtel du Palais (former villa of Empress Eugénie). The old town juts out between the **Grande Plage** and the **Plage de la Côte des Basques.** On the fringe of the Basque country, Biarritz has good wide sandy bathing beaches (the surf can be dangerous at times on the Grand Plage). Cliff walks, forming a grand promenade planted with tamarisks, are one of the most enduring attractions here. The most dramatic point is **Rocher de la Vièrge (Rock of the Virgin),** connected to the shore by a footbridge. Enclosed by jetties, **Port des Pêcheurs (Port of the Fishermen)** is yet another scenic spot.

ESSENTIALS

GETTING THERE   Ten trains arrive daily from Bayonne (trip time: 10 min.), which has rail links with Paris and other major cities in the south of France. The nearest rail station is 2 miles from the town center, in La Négresse. Buses carry passengers from the station to the center of Biarritz.

VISITOR INFORMATION   The Office de Tourisme is on Square d'Ixelles (☎ 59-24-20-24).

WHERE TO STAY
EXPENSIVE

✪ Château de Brindos
Lac de Brindos, 64600 Anglet. ☎ **59-23-17-68.** Fax 59-23-48-47. 12 rms, 2 suites. TV TEL. 1,000–1,500 F ($190.10–$285.15) double; 1,950 F ($370.70) suite. Breakfast 80 F ($15.20) extra. AE, DC, MC, V. Parking free.

With its own park and lake, this château, near the airport about 1 1/2 miles from Biarritz, is the most romantic stopover on the Côte Basque. The guest rooms and public rooms are beautiful. The pool is heated, private fishing can be arranged, six golf courses are close at hand, and tennis courts are on the premises. In a restaurant cantilevered over the lake, the Franco-Basque cuisine is superb, including foie gras soup, turbot mousseline in caviar sauce, duckling with small vegetables, and sea bass grilled with fennel. The finest regional foodstuff goes into the meals, which are both classic and innovative. The service is flawless yet not intimidating. Meals cost 250 F ($47.50) and up on the à la carte menu; call for a reservation.

✪ Hôtel du Palais
Av. de l'Impératrice, 64200 Biarritz. ☎ **59-41-64-00,** or 800/223-6800 in the U.S. and Canada. Fax 59-41-67-99. 90 rms, 30 suites. MINIBAR TV TEL. 1,450–2,750 F ($275.65–$522.80) double; 2,000–6,250 F ($380.20–$1,188.20) suite. Breakfast 110 F ($20.90) extra. AE, DC, MC, V. Parking free. Closed Feb. Bus 9.

This has been the grand playground for the international elite for the past century, built in 1854 by Napoléon III for Eugénie so that she wouldn't get homesick for Spain. He picked the most ideal beachfront, in view of the rocks and rugged shore-line. Of course, there are elaborately furnished suites here, but even the average rooms have period furniture, silk draperies, marquetry, and bronze hardware; 90 are air-conditioned. Try to get a room facing west to enjoy the sunsets. Le Grand Siècle, a gourmet restaurant with classic columns and chandeliers, serves excellent meals. Guests also dine at La Rotonde, enjoying typical Basque as well as international cuisine, and at lunch-only L'Hippocampe, a buffet restaurant around the heated seawater pool.

MODERATE

Hôtel Carlina

Bd. Prince-de-Galles, 64200 Biarritz. ☎ **59-24-42-14.** Fax 59-24-95-32. 31 rms, 2 suites. MINIBAR TV TEL. 350–450 F ($66.55–$85.55) double; 800–1,200 F ($152.10–$228.10) suite. Breakfast 20–70 F ($3.80–$13.30) extra. AE, DC, MC, V. Parking 30 F ($5.70). Bus 9.

This year-round hotel has an exceptional view of the Pyrénées and the Atlantic. The rooms are comfortable and well maintained if functional and uninspired, but price is the reason most guests are attracted to the place. Popular water sports are offered, including windsurfing. On the premises is a terrace bar and a solarium. A lackluster restaurant in the building is operated independently.

Hôtel Plaza

Av. Edouard-VII, 64200 Biarritz. ☎ **59-24-74-00.** Fax **59-22-22-01.** 60 rms. MINIBAR TV TEL. 595–820 F ($113.10–$155.90) double. Breakfast 58 F ($11) extra. AE, DC, MC, V. Parking free.

Near the casino and beach, this hotel offers pleasant amenities amid an art deco decor from 1928. Many of the large rooms have private terraces. Meals are served in a formal dining hall in summer and in a less formal pub the rest of the year. The Plaza is safe, reliable, but unexciting.

INEXPENSIVE

Hôtel du Fronton

35 av. du Maréchal-Joffre, 64000 Biarritz. ☎ **59-23-09-36.** Fax 59-23-22-07. 42 rms. TV TEL. 330 F ($62.70) double. Breakfast 33 F ($6.25) extra. MC, V. Parking free. Closed Mar 19–Apr 2 and Oct 22–Nov 26. Bus 9.

On a corner in the town center, this half-timbered hotel contains a bar and restaurant on its ground floor. The rooms, housed in a modern white-sided annex, have tall sliding windows and built-in wood-grained furniture. The restaurant, however, provides an old French provincial ambience, with large limestone hearths and beamed ceilings.

Hôtel du Port-Vieux

43 rue Mazagran, 64200 Biarritz. ☎ **59-24-02-84.** 18 rms, 14 with bath. TEL. 232–263 F ($44.10–$49.95) double without bath, 253–279 F ($48.05–$53) double with bath. Rates include continental breakfast. No credit cards. Closed end of Sept to Easter.

Finding a bargain in high-priced Biarritz takes some doing, but this serviceable in-season-only place is clean, comfortable, and well managed. Breakfast is the only meal served, but many cafés and restaurants are nearby. The staff remembers "a long time ago" when Michelin used to recommend them.

WHERE TO DINE

⑤ L'Auberge de la Negresse

10 bd. de l'Aérodrome. ☎ **59-23-15-83.** Reservations required. Main courses 40–60 F ($7.60–$11.40); fixed-price menus 57 F ($10.85), 81 F ($15.40), 132 F ($25.10), and

162 F ($30.80). MC, V. Tues–Sun noon–2:30pm and 7:15–10:15pm. Closed Oct. Bus 2. BASQUE.

Just 1¹⁄₂ miles south of Biarritz, this restaurant was named for a 19th-century slave who escaped from an American plantation by hiding in the bottom of a French ship. The inn she established on this site was used by Napoléon's army on its passage to Spain and eventually a railway station (Gare de la Négresse) was named in her honor. The inn doubles as a delicatessen, but the two dining rooms also serve flavorful meals. Typical dishes include salmon en papillotte, an array of homemade terrines, and fish. The food is simple and traditional.

✪ Café de Paris

5 place Bellevue, 64200 Biarritz. ☎ **59-24-19-53.** Fax 59-24-18-20. Reservations required. Restaurant, main courses 140–220 F ($26.60–$41.80); fixed-price menus 185–380 F ($35.15–$72.20). Bistro, main courses 75–115 F ($14.25–$21.85); fixed-price menu 145 F ($27.55). AE, DC, MC, V. Daily noon–2:30pm and 7–10pm. Closed Tues and Wed lunch in winter. Bus 2. BASQUE.

The supercharged chef here, Didier Oudill, is the hottest in town and has rescued the Café de Paris after its long decline. Oudill was the protégé of Michel Guérard and not only learned all that fabled chef had to teach but also has come up with many original creations. He's not afraid to use Bayonne ham, Spanish merluza (hake), or even earthy fava beans. The setting is naturally elegant, from the mirrors for looking at how glamorous you are to the inevitable palm trees. If you'd like to spend less, you can go to the bistro, where the menu changes often, though fish is always a feature.

In 1992, the establishment added 19 comfortable rooms, each with a sea view. Decorated in a conservatively traditional style, they cost 650 to 950 F ($123.50 to $180.50) for a double, with breakfast 85 F ($16.15) extra. Half board in the restaurant is available for an additional 300 F ($57) per person.

Les Flots Bleus

41 perspective des Côtes Basques. ☎ **59-24-10-03.** Reservations recommended. Main courses 50–82 F ($9.50–$15.60); fixed-price menus 80–164 F ($15.20–$31.15). AE, DC, MC, V. Daily noon–2pm and 7:30–9:30pm. BASQUE.

On the rocky coast a 10-minute walk from the town center, this restaurant has been the domain of Venice-born Arlette Casagrande and her congenial colleague, Mami, for nearly 30 years. The food is served in generous portions that brim with the full flavor of the Basque country. Choices include duck pâté, salade basquaise, roquefort salad, marinated mussels, richly aromatic fish soup, and dorado with garlic. This is a family-friendly place.

3 St-Jean-de-Luz

491 miles SW of Paris, 9 miles S of Biarritz

This Basque country tuna-fishing port/beach resort is the goal of many a person's dream of a beach vacation. St-Jean-de-Luz lies at the mouth of the Nivelle opening onto the Bay of Biscay, with the Pyrénées in the background.

In its principal church, the 13th-century **Eglise St-Jean-Baptiste,** at the corner of rue Gambetta and rue Garat (☎ 59-26-08-81), Louis XIV and the Spanish *infanta*, Marie-Thérèse, were married in 1660. The interior is among

Shopping Basque

Here are some shopping suggestions so you can bring some of your Basque experience home with you.

In St-Jean-de-Luz, ramble around the port, sip pastis in a harborfront café, and debate the virtues of the beret. Then scout out **Maison Adam,** which has sold almond-based confections since 1660 from a boutique at 6 place Louis-XIV (☎ **59-26-03-54**). Specialties include sugared macaroons, tournons (an almond-paste confection flavored with everything from chocolate to confit of berries), and canougat (soft caramels).

If you suddenly yearn for tea amid a landscape otherwise filled with cafés and bars, head for one of the region's oldest confiseries, tearooms, and pastry shops, **Dodin,** 7 rue Gambetta, in Biarritz (☎ **59-24-16-37**). You can carry your pastries away for consumption on the beach, but we prefer a cup of tea, priced at 20 F ($3.80), served in a street-level salon with a sea view.

To decorate your dinner parties back home, check out the napery at **Jean-Vier,** Ferme Berraine, Rte. Nationale 10, St-Jean-de-Luz (☎ **59-51-06-06**). Their bath, bedroom, and table linens are woven on the premises on old-fashioned looms, following traditional Basque patterns, and are among the most stylish and durable in the region.

If a bottle of souvenir spirits appeals to you, join the stream of artists, actors, and gourmands who value **Arosteguy,** 5 av. Victor-Hugo, in Biarritz (☎ **59-24-00-52**), as the most sophisticated purveyor of wine and eaux-de-vie in the region. Some of the vintages (the 1929 Haut-Brion burgundy, for example, or the 1890 Armagnac from Laberd'Olives) sell for as much as 6,000 F ($1,140.65). You can easily procure a more affordable wine or bottle of deceptively potent spirits distilled from pears, plums, or raspberries. Five generations of the same family have kept its inventory up to world-class standards since the place was founded in 1875.

And if Basque cuisine so envelops you in its charms, what should you use to serve your own pipérade Basque once you return home? Head for a 150-year-old shop in the shadow of Bayonne's cathedral, **La Maison Tajan,** 62–64 rue d'Espagne (☎ **59-59-00-39**), where you'll find the region's widest selection of glazed terra-cotta platters and pots, each oven- and microwave-proof and table-ready. Imported from nearby Spain and decorated only with a translucent earth-toned glaze, they're among the best accessories for the slow-cooking processes pivotal to Basque cuisine.

Incidentally, while you cook Basque at home you might as well wear appropriate footwear. Espadrilles, the canvas-topped, rope-bottomed slippers worn so fetchingly by local fisherfolk, are sold at virtually every souvenir shop and department store in the region. Upscale versions, however, are made to order at **Maison Garcia,** pont de Baskutenea, in Bidart, a hamlet midway between Biarritz and St-Jean-de-Luz (☎ **59-26-51-27**). A simple off-the-shelf model begins at a mere 47 F ($8.95), though espadrilles made to order (special sizes, special colors) rarely rise above 500 F ($95.05) per pair.

the most handsome of all Basque churches. Surmounting the altar is a statue-studded gilded retable. At the harbor, the brick-and-stone **Maison de l'Infante,** in the Louis XIII style, sheltered the Spanish princess.

The Sun King, meanwhile, dreamed of another woman at **La Maison de Louis XIV** (also known as the **Château Lohobiague**), on place Louis-XIV, the center of the old port (☎ 59-26-01-56). The noble facade is distinguished by small towers built into each corner. The interior is in old Basque style, with beams and iron nails still visible. The second-floor stairwell leads to the apartments where the widow of the original builder received Louis XIV on his marriage journey. Don't miss the large kitchen with its large fireplace. It's open June to September only, Monday to Saturday from 10:30am to noon and 2:30 to 5:30pm and Sunday from 2:30 to 5:30pm (until 6pm in July and August). Admission is 15 F ($2.85) for adults and 12 F ($2.30) for children.

This port's many narrow streets flanked by old houses are great for strolling. If possible try to attend a fish auction. Livening up the resort are pelota, fandangos, and a celebration beginning on June 24 called **Toro del Fuego.** Highlight of the festivities is when a snorting papier-mâché bull is carried through town. The towns-people literally dance in the streets.

ESSENTIALS

GETTING THERE   Some 10 trains per day arrive from Biarritz (trip time: 15 min.), a one-way ticket costing 14 F ($2.65). There are also 10 trains per day from Paris, a regular train taking 10 hours and the TGV arriving in only 5. One-way tickets from Paris cost 360 F ($68.40), plus 30 to 90 F ($5.70 to $17.10) for TGV reservations.

VISITOR INFORMATION   The Office de Tourisme is on place du Maréchal Foch (☎ 59-26-03-16).

WHERE TO STAY
EXPENSIVE

✪ Grand Hôtel
43 bd. Thiers, 64500 St-Jean-de-Luz. ☎ **59-26-35-36.** Fax 59-51-19-91. 43 rms. A/C TV TEL. 1,400 F ($266.15) double. Breakfast 100 F ($19) extra. AE, MC, V.

After a massive renovation, this small luxury hotel is now the finest in the town center, though it's even better known for its restaurant, the only place at the resort ranking a Michelin star. Perhaps as a sign of changing times, its former night-club has been turned into a fitness center. Air conditioning has been installed and the pool heated. The rooms to go for are those opening onto panoramic views of the Bay of Biscay or the beach. Many patrons, however, visit only for La Coupole restaurant, with panoramic bay views. The cuisine often includes innovative dishes inspired by the bounty of the region. Pyrénées lamb, for example, is casserole roasted and so tender the meat falls from the bone. Red mullet filets are stuffed with squid, and prawns are roasted with sesame seeds. A supreme strawberry soufflé is served from June to the end of September.

✪ Hôtel de Chantaco
Golf de Chantaco, 64500 St-Jean-de-Luz. ☎ **59-26-14-76.** Fax 59-26-35-97. 20 rms, 4 suites. TV TEL. 1,000–1,500 F ($190.10–$285.15) double; 1,100–1,600 F ($209.10–$304.15) suite. Breakfast 80 F ($15.20) extra. AE, DC, MC, V. Parking free. Closed Nov–Mar. Take D918 a mile from the town center.

Surrounded by an 18-hole golf course and gardens, this hotel a mile from the ocean resembles a country château, with Moorish arches, a side patio garden, and a refined decor. The rooms are luxurious and well equipped, and most have been modernized. Breakfast is served on a patio with wisteria-covered arches and a fountain. The hotel's restaurant, El Patio, serves excellent regional and international cuisine. The welcome is as gracious as the cuisine, and garden dining is possible in fair weather.

MODERATE

La Devinière
5 rue Loguin, 64500 St-Jean-de-Luz. ☎ **59-26-05-51.** 8 rms. TEL. 550–650 F ($104.55–$123.55) double. Breakfast 50 F ($9.50) extra. MC, V.

Originally a private town house, La Devinière is an antiques-filled modernized hotel with well-maintained rooms. Breakfast is the only meal served, but the staff will direct you to nearby restaurants for other meals. There's also a tranquil garden.

INEXPENSIVE

La Fayette
18–20 rue de la République, 64500 St-Jean-de-Luz. ☎ **59-26-17-74.** Fax 59-51-11-78. 18 rms. TV TEL. 350 F ($66.50) double. Breakfast 35 F ($6.65) extra. AE, DC, MC, V.

This hotel/restaurant occupies a central position near place Louis-XIV. Its rooms evoke a dignified (and slightly battered) earlier age, but the restaurant is one of the most reliable in town. The regional specialties and classic French dishes include seafood casseroles, grilled duck, sea bass with thyme and lemon-butter sauce, and roast rack of lamb.

ⓢ Villa Bel-Air
Promenade Jacques-Thibaud, 64500 St-Jean-de-Luz. ☎ **59-26-04-86.** Fax 59-26-62-34. 19 rms. TV TEL. 395–470 F ($75.05–$89.35) double. Breakfast 39 F ($7.40) extra. Half board 416–436 F ($79.05–$82.85) per person. MC, V. Parking free. Closed mid-Nov to mid-Apr.

This hotel offers clean and comfortable accommodations with a sea view and a restaurant serving lunch and dinner from June to October. In good weather, enjoy a meal on the terrace. Most guests stay on the half-board plan. The place won't thrill you but is one of the most reliable choices, offering good value.

WHERE TO DINE

The only really grand cuisine in town is served at the Hôtel Grand (above).

Auberge Kaïku
17 rue de la République. ☎ **59-26-13-20.** Reservations recommended. Main courses 65–140 F ($12.35–$26.60); fixed-price menus 135 F ($25.65), 180 F ($34.20), and 240 F ($45.60). AE, MC, V. Daily noon–2pm and 7–11pm. Closed Nov 12–Dec 22, Mon lunch June 15–Sept 15, and Wed Sept 16–June 14. BASQUE.

On a narrow street off place Louis-XIV, the Auberge Kaïku is the best restaurant in town outside the hotels. The structure, with hand-hewn beams and chiseled masonry, dates from 1540 and is said to be the oldest in town. The auberge is run by Emile and Jeanne Ourdanabia, who serve a lightened regional cuisine. You might enjoy John Dory with fresh mint, grilled shrimp, filet of beef with essence of truffles, and duckling in honey.

⑤ Chez Maya (Petit Grill Basque)

4 rue St-Jacques. ☎ **59-26-80-76.** Reservations recommended. Main courses 46–86 F ($8.75–$16.35); fixed-price menu 92 F ($17.50). MC, V. Thurs–Tues noon–2pm and 7–10pm. Closed Dec 20–Jan 20. BASQUE.

This small auberge is highly acclaimed for quality and value. Specialties include a delectable fish soup and paella. Its fixed-price menu is the best value at the resort. Chefs cook as their grandparents did, including all those old favorites (squid cooked in its own ink), and no one here seem to know that various food revolutions have come and gone.

La Vieille Auberge

22 rue Tourasse. ☎ **59-26-19-61.** Reservations required. Main courses 75–100 F ($14.25–$19); fixed-price menus 69 F ($13.10), 99 F ($18.80), 112 F ($21.30), and 122 F ($23.20). AE, MC, V. Tues noon–2pm, Thurs–Mon noon–2pm and 7–10pm. Closed Nov 12–Apr 1. BASQUE.

This Basque tavern specializes in seafood, and the owners claim the fish soup is second to none. Monsieur and Madame Daniel Grand offer good-value fixed-price menus, the most expensive of which is enormous. Generally the recipes are part Basque/part Landaise, and each dish goes well with the vin du pays, especially mussels à la crème.

4   Pau

477 miles SW of Paris, 122 miles SW of Toulouse

High above the banks of the Gave de Pau River, this year-round resort is a good halting point in your trek through the Pyrénées. The British discovered Pau in the early 19th century, launching such innovative practices here as fox hunting, a custom that's lingered. Even if you're just passing through, go along **boulevard des Pyrénées,** an esplanade erected on Napoléon's orders, for the most famous panoramic view in the Pyrénées.

ESSENTIALS

GETTING THERE   Pau-Uzein airport is 7¹/₂ miles north of town. Call 59-33-21-29 for flight information. There are good train connections from Biarritz (six per day taking two hours); a one-way ticket costs 85 F ($16.15).

VISITOR INFORMATION   The Office de Tourisme is on place Royale (☎ 59-27-27-08).

SEEING THE TOP ATTRACTIONS

The heart of the commercial district is busy **place Clemenceau,** out of which radiate at least five boulevards. At the western end of town stands the **Château de Pau,** 2 rue du Château (☎ 59-82-38-00), dating from the 12th century and still steeped in the Renaissance spirit of the bold Marguerite de Navarre, who wrote the bawdy *Heptaméron* at 60. The castle has seen many builders and tenants. Louis XV ordered the bridge that connects the castle to the town, while the great staircase hall inside was commissioned by Marguerite herself. Louis-Philippe had all the apartments redecorated around 1840. Inside are many souvenirs, including a crib made of a single tortoise shell for Henri de Navarre, who was born here. There's also a splendid array of Flemish and Gobelins tapestries. The great rectangular tower, Tour de Gaston Phoebus, is from the 14th century.

On the château's third floor is a **Musée Regional** containing ethnographical collections of the Béarn, the old name of the country of which Pau was the capital. Finally, you may want to walk through the beautiful **Parc National,** the gardens (or what's left of them) that surrounded the château in the 16th century.

The château and museum are open daily from 9:30 to 11:45am and 2 to 5:15pm. Admission is 27 F ($5.15) for adults and 18 F ($3.40) for children 17 and under.

The **Musée des Beaux-Arts,** rue Mathieu-Lalanne (☎ **59-27-33-02**), displays a collection of European paintings, including Spanish, Flemish, Dutch, English, and French masters, such as El Greco, Zurbarán, Degas, and Boudin. It's open Wednesday to Monday from 9am to noon and 2 to 6pm. Admission is 12 F ($2.30) for adults and 6 F ($1.15) for children.

WHERE TO STAY
MODERATE
Hôtel Continental

2 rue du Maréchal-Foch, 64000 Pau. ☎ **59-27-69-31.** Fax 59-27-99-84. 80 rms. MINIBAR TV TEL. 450 F ($85.55) double. Continental breakfast 40 F ($7.60) extra; buffet breakfast 60 F ($11.40) extra. AE, DC, MC, V. Parking free. Bus 1.

The centrally located Continental is the main hotel in the town center and is regarded as the best of a lackluster lot. The rooms are stylishly decorated, modernized, and soundproof; some are suitable for the disabled. There's a garage on the premises.

Hôtel de Gramont

3 place Gramont, 64000 Pau. ☎ **59-27-84-04.** Fax 59-27-62-23. 36 rms, 2 suites. TV TEL. 280–495 F ($53.20–$94.05) double; 495 F ($94.05) suite. Breakfast 35 F ($6.65) extra. AE, DC, MC, V. Parking free. Bus 1.

Within walking distance of the château and the railroad station, this hotel is one of the most impressive buildings in town. The four-story châteaulike structure has street-level arcades and high-ceilinged soundproof rooms, 10 of which are air-conditioned and some of which are suitable for the disabled.

INEXPENSIVE
Hôtel-Restaurant Corona

71 av. du Général-Leclerc, 64000 Pau. ☎ **59-30-64-77.** Fax 59-02-62-64. 20 rms. TV TEL. 200–260 F ($38–$49.40) double. Breakfast 28 F ($5.30) extra. AE, MC, V. Bus 1.

The French architect who designed this hotel had completed many commissions in Montréal. In honor of them, he added what were considered at the time many Canada-inspired touches, like the ample use of exposed pinewood. About a mile east of the center of Pau, it offers comfortable accommodations and ample portions of food in its two dining rooms. The more formal of the two is the restaurant, where fixed-price meals cost 140 to 180 F ($26.60 to $34.20). A less expensive meal is offered in the evening, but not at lunch, for 80 F ($15.20). There's also a brasserie, where *plats du jour* begin at around 41 F ($7.80). Both restaurants (but not the hotel) are closed Friday night, all day Saturday, and from December 20 to January 10.

⑤ Le Postillon

Place de Verdun, 10 cours Camou, 64000 Pau. ☎ **59-72-83-00.** Fax 59-72-83-13. 28 rms. TV TEL. 265 F ($50.35) double. Breakfast 32 F ($6.10) extra. MC, V. Bus 1.

This is a cozy hotel, with French provincial decor and a flower-filled courtyard. The rooms are comfortably furnished, but no one thinks about style here. It's the reasonable price that keeps the place full. Breakfast is the only meal served, but there's a choice of restaurants nearby.

WHERE TO DINE

⑤ Au Fin Gourmet

24 av. Gaston-Lacoste. ☎ 59-27-47-71. Reservations recommended. Main courses 70–120 F ($13.30–$22.80) ; fixed-price menus 85–160 F ($16.15–$30.40). AE, DC, MC, V. Tues–Sun noon–2:15pm and 7–10pm. Bus 1. BASQUE.

This restaurant is maintained by Christian, Laurent, and Patrick, sons of the since-retired founder, Clément Ithuriague. It offers an outdoor terrace for warm-weather dining and a cuisine based almost exclusively on regional ingredients. Menu items include marinated codfish with herbs "from the kitchen garden" and bouillon-flavored potatoes, rack of lamb flavored with herbs from the Pyrénées in a parsley-enriched crust, sliced and sautéed foie gras, and braised stuffed trout. This restaurant's 85-F ($16.15) fixed-price menu is a crowd-pleaser and one of Pau's best dining values.

✪ Chez Pierre

16 rue Louis-Barthour. ☎ 59-27-76-86. Reservations required. Main courses 80–150 F ($15.20–$28.50). AE, DC, MC, V. Mon–Fri noon–2:30pm and 7–10pm, Sat 7–10pm. Bus 1. BEARNAISE.

Chez Pierre turns regional products into extraordinary creative dishes. In air-conditioned comfort, you can sit downstairs at one of the eight tables or upstairs in one of three tiny salons. Chef Raymond Casau is among the finest around, and his specialties are sole with white mushrooms and small new cucumbers, fresh salmon braised with Jurançon (a rather sweet golden Pyrenean wine), and cassoulet with white beans. Year after year, we're always served our finest meal in Pau at this establishment.

La Gousse d'Ail

12 rue du Hédas. ☎ 59-27-31-55. Reservations not required. Main courses 80–102 F ($15.20–$19.40); fixed price menus 98 F ($18.60), 125 F ($23.75), and 185 F ($35.15). MC, V. Mon–Fri noon–1:30pm and 7–10:30pm, Sat 7–10:30pm. Bus 1. BASQUE.

A few blocks from the château, this restaurant has a stone, brick, and stucco interior with ceiling beams and a fireplace. Meals might include a gâteau of shell-fish with essence of crab; a tart of puff pastry with gruyère, tomato, and basil; a mixture of monkfish with salmon and wild mushrooms; cream of mussel soup; and an onglet of beef with mustard grains and a marmalade of shallots. The specialties of the southwest are deftly handled.

NEARBY ACCOMMODATIONS & DINING

A century ago Empress Eugénie came to Eugénie-les-Bains to "take the cure." Now some of the world's most discerning people follow in her footsteps, though for a different attraction. About 33 miles north of Pau is the marvelous domain of Michel Guérard. The town has has no rail station, so most people drive from Pau.

✪ Les Prés d'Eugénie (Michel Guérard)

Eugénie-les-Bains, 40320 Beaune. ☎ 58-05-06-07. Fax 58-51-13-59. Reservations required. Main courses 195–360 F ($37.05–$68.40); fixed-price menus 390 F ($74.10), 490 F ($93.15), and 650 F ($123.55). AE, MC, V. Fri 12:30–2pm, Thurs–Tues 12:30–2pm and 7:30–10pm. BASQUE.

This Relais & Châteaux is the creation of Michel Guérard, the master chef whose *cuisine minceur* started a culinary revolution in the early 1970s. Built during the 19th century as a spa where Empress Eugénie could take a rest cure, it attracts a stream of clients who appreciate the calm, the much-publicized cooking, and the endless business expansions of its owner. Offered here are both *cuisine minceur*, so calorie counters can still enjoy well-seasoned flavors and fresh ingredients, and the heartier *cuisine gourmand*, whose traditions are influenced by Basque and classic French recipes. Specialties are cream of crayfish soup, whiting in white-wine sauce, mullet steamed with seaweed and oysters, lamb steamed with fennel, and a wide variety of simply steamed fish with fresh vegetables.

Besides the 28 rooms and 7 suites in the main building, 8 accommodations are in an outlying annex, La Couvent des Herbes. These rent for 800 to 1,650 F ($152 to $313.50) for a double and 1,000 to 2,000 F ($190 to $380) for a suite. Breakfast costs 90 F ($17.10) extra. Less expensive are the 27 rooms and 5 apartments in La Maison Rose, where the half board—700 to 800 F ($133 to $152) per person—focuses on *cuisine minceur*.

Those unwilling to pay the stratospheric prices in the main restaurant sometimes select a table in a satellite restaurant operated by M. Guérard, **La Ferme aux Grives.** The cuisine here focuses on specialties of the region as part of a fixed-price menu costing 180 F ($34.20). Comfortable and rustically elegant, La Ferme aux Grives is open for lunch and dinner daily except Tuesday at lunch and all day Monday.

5 Lourdes

497 miles SW of Paris, 25 miles SE of Pau

Muslims turn to Mecca, Hindus to the Ganges, but for Catholics Lourdes is the world's most beloved shrine. Nestled in a valley in the southwestern part of the Hautes-Pyrénées, it's the scene of pilgrims gathering from all over the world. Be sure to nail down your hotel reservation in overcrowded August.

On February 11, 1858, the Virgin is believed by the Roman Catholic world to have revealed herself to a poor shepherd girl, Bernadette Soubirous. Eighteen such apparitions were reported. Bernadette, subject of the film *Song of Bernadette,* died in a convent in 1879. She was beatified in 1925, then canonized in 1933.

Her apparitions literally put Lourdes on the map. The town has subsequently attracted millions of visitors, the illustrious and the poverty-stricken. The truly devout are often disheartened at the tawdry commercialism of Lourdes today. And some holiday-seekers are acutely disturbed by the human desperation of victims of various afflictions spending their hard-earned savings seeking a "miracle," then having to return home without a cure. However, the church has recognized many "cures" that took place after patients bathed in the springs, labeling them "true miracles."

ESSENTIALS

GETTING THERE   Train passengers headed for Lourdes from Bayonne or Biarritz must transfer in Pau. Trip time to Pau is 30 minutes. A one-way ticket costs 36 F ($6.85). There are also connections from Toulouse and Paris.

VISITOR INFORMATION   The Office de Tourisme is at place du Champs-Commun (☎ 62-94-15-64).

EXPLORING THE TOWN

From July 1 to September 20, tourists and pilgrims can join the ✪ **Day Pilgrims,** a pilgrimage (in English) that gathers at 9am at the statue of the Crowned Virgin for a prayer meeting in the meadow facing the Grotto. The services include a 9:30am Stations of the Cross and an 11am mass. In the afternoon, assembling at the same spot at 2:30pm, pilgrims are taken on a guided visit to the Sanctuaries, or places associated with Bernadette. At 4:30pm there's a Procession of the Blessed Eucharist, starting from the Grotto. The 8:45pm Marian cele-bration, rosary, and torchlight procession all start from the Grotto as well. In the Sanctuaries you'll be told the story of Lourdes and of Bernadette, complete with a free slide show (in English) that runs about 15 minutes.

At the **Grotto of Massabielle** the Virgin is said to have appeared 18 times to Bernadette between February 11 and July 16, 1858. This venerated site is acces-sible to pilgrims both day and night, and a Holy Mass is celebrated there every day. The Statue of Our Lady depicts the Virgin in the posture she is said to have taken in the place she reputedly appeared, saying to Bernadette in Pyrenean dialect, "I am the Immaculate Conception."

At the back of the Grotto, on the left of the altar, is the **Miraculous Spring** that reportedly welled up on February 25, 1858, during the ninth apparition, when Bernadette scraped the earth as instructed. The Virgin is said to have commanded her, "Go and drink at the spring and wash there." The water from this spring is collected in several reservoirs, from which you can drink.

Other sanctuaries associated with St. Bernadette include the crypt, the first chapel built on top of the Grotto, the Basilica of the Immaculate Conception, the Rosary Basilica, and the underground Basilica of St. Pius X. In town, there are the house where Bernadette lived, the Cachot, the baptismal font in the parish church, and the hospital chapel where she made her first communion.

The **Upper Basilica,** at place du Rosaire, was built in the 13th-century ogival style but wasn't consecrated until 1876. It contains one nave split into five equal bays. Lining its interior are votive tablets. On the west side of the square is the **Rosary Basilica,** with two small towers. It was built in 1889 in the Roman-Byzantine style and holds up to 4,000. Inside, 15 chapels are dedicated to the "mysteries of the rosary."

The oval **Basilica of Pius X** was consecrated in 1958. An enormous under-ground chamber covered by a concrete roof, it's 660 feet long and 270 feet wide, holding as many as 20,000. After St. Peter's in Rome, it is the world's largest church.

Nearby, the **Musée Bernadette** (☎ 62-94-13-15) contains scenes represent-ing the life of the saint; it's open daily from 9am to noon and 2 to 6pm. True Bernadette devotees will also seek out the **Moulin de Boly,** rue Bernadette-Soubirous (☎ 62-94-23-53), where the saint was born on January 7, 1844, the daughter of a miller. Her former home is open Easter to October only, daily from 8am to 7:30pm. This was actually her mother's house. Bernadette's father, François Soubirous, had his family home in another mill, **Moulin Lacadé,** at 2 rue Bernadette-Soubirous (☎ 62-96-22-51). You can visit daily from 9am to 12:15pm and 2:15 to 7pm. None of these attractions charges admission.

You can visit the privately owned wax museum, **Musée Grévin,** 87 rue de la Grotte (☎ 62-94-33-74), where displays retrace not only Bernadette's life but also the life of Christ, with a reproduction of Leonardo da Vinci's *Last Supper.* This museum in the center of Lourdes is open daily from 9 to 11:30am and 1:30 to 6pm (in July and August, also from 8:30 to 10pm). Adults pay 32 F ($6.10) and children 6 to 12 are charged 16 F ($3.05); 5 and under free.

If you want a panoramic view, take an elevator up to the terrace of the **Château-Fort de Lourdes,** an excellent example of medieval military architecture. The castle contains the **Musée Pyrénéen,** 25 rue du Fort (☎ **62-94-02-04**), with a collection of regional handcrafts and costumes, including a collection of dolls in nuns' habits. In the courtyard are scale models of different styles of regional architecture. Both the château and the museum may be visited April to mid-October, daily from 9 to 11am and from 2 to 6pm; off-season, it closes at 5pm and is also closed Tuesday. Admission is 25 F ($4.75) for adults and 12 F ($2.30) for children 6 to 12; 5 and under free.

EXPLORING THE PYRENEES

Lourdes is a great base for exploring the Pyrénées. You can take tours into the snowcapped mountains across the border to Spain or go horseback riding near Lac de Lourdes, 2 miles northwest of town. Outstanding sites include Bagnères-de-Bigorre, a renowned thermal spa; Pic du Jer, for a panoramic vista; Béout, for a view and an underground cave where prehistoric implements have been found (reached by funicular); Pibeste, for another sweeping view; the Caves of Medous, an underground river with stalactites; and for a full-day tour, the Heights of Gavarnie, at 4,500 feet, one of France's great natural wonders.

WHERE TO STAY
EXPENSIVE

Gallia et Londres
26 av. Bernadette-Soubirous, 65100 Lourdes. ☎ **62-94-35-44.** Fax 62-94-53-66. 90 rms. A/C TV TEL. 800 F ($152.10) double. Rates include breakfast. AE, V. Parking 50 F ($9.50). Closed Oct 20–Mar 28. Bus 2.

This old-fashioned four-star hotel is among the most patronized in Lourdes, retaining its provincial flavor for many religious groups that seem to check in en masse. The rooms are decorated in a period style and often have balconies; some are suitable for the disabled. Its restaurant is solidly reliable throughout the year, serving fixed-price menus. The hotel has a garden, plus a bar and a pub.

MODERATE

Galilée et Windsor
10 av. Peyramale, 65100 Lourdes. ☎ **62-94-21-55.** 168 rms. A/C. 400–450 F ($76–$85.55) double. Rates include breakfast. AE, DC, MC, V. Closed from the end of Oct to Mar. Parking free. Bus 2.

This hotel is traditional with a modernized interior. The rooms are pleasant, though they often contain plastic furnishings. The restaurant frequently serves regional and continental meals to religious groups and offers nothing to challenge the tastebuds.

Grand Hôtel de la Grotte
66–68 rue de la Grotte, 65000 Lourdes. ☎ **62-94-58-87.** Fax 62-94-20-50. 80 rms, 3 suites. A/C MINIBAR TEL. 425–480 F ($80.75–$91.25) double; 1,200 F ($228.10) suite. Half board 345–420 F ($65.55–$79.80) per person. AE, DC, MC, V. Parking free. Closed Oct 22–Good Fri. Bus 2.

The Grand Hôtel de la Grotte is an old favorite, well furnished with a typical upper-bourgeois French decor that's being slowly updated. Its restaurant, open to the public, offers regional meals. If you can get a room on an upper floor, you'll have one of the most panoramic views in town, of not only the sanctuaries and the river but also the mountains. Rooms on the basilica side seem to be noisy. The hotel has a garden by the Adour.

INEXPENSIVE

Hôtel Adriatic

4 rue Baron-Duprat, 65100 Lourdes. ☎ **62-94-31-34.** Fax 62-42-14-70. 85 rms. TEL. 340–420 F ($64.60–$79.80) double. Breakfast 35 F ($6.65) extra. MC, V. Parking free. Bus 2.

With a bright English-speaking staff, this hotel offers clean and traditional rooms; about 25 also offer TVs and minibars. The in-house restaurant serves fine regional cuisine. The hotel is close to the shrines, the home of St. Bernadette, the parish church, and the town's fortified castle.

Notre-Dame de France

8 av. Peyramale, 65100 Lourdes. ☎ **62-94-91-45.** Fax 62-94-57-21. 76 rms. A/C TEL. 350 F ($66.50) double. Breakfast 30 F ($5.70) extra. Half board 280 F ($53.20) per person. AE, MC, V. Closed Oct 15–Mar 15. Bus 2.

Next to the Galilée et Windsor (above), the Notre-Dame de France is another good budget choice, with clean rooms and simple furnishings. Meals are a good buy, with regional cuisine offered.

WHERE TO DINE

Relais de Saux

Route de Tarbes (N21), 65100 Lourdes. ☎ **62-94-29-61.** Fax 62-42-12-64. Reservations recommended. Fixed-price menus 140 F ($26.60) (lunch only), and 180 F ($34.20), 230 F ($43.70), and 310 F ($58.90). AE, DC, MC, V. Daily noon–1:45pm and 7:15–9:30pm. Take D914 1¹/₂ miles northeast of Lourdes to the village of Saux. BASQUE.

This is the best restaurant in the area. However, unless you're staying at the hotel you can visit only for lunch—dinner is reserved for guests. It's housed in an ivy-covered manor. Inside, the collection of carved-wood fireplaces complements the beamed ceilings, silk-upholstered walls, and rustic artifacts. Meals are supervised by innkeeper Madeleine Heres and her husband, Bernard. Specialties include a warm seafood salad with marjoram, escalope of duck liver with caramelized pears, filet of beef with flap mushrooms, and roast lobster with butter mousse.

Upstairs are seven guest rooms, some with large windows overlooking the garden. Doubles cost 500 F ($95.05). Half-board terms are 850 F ($161.60) for two.

ⓢ Taverne de Bigorre et Hôtel d'Albret

21 place du Champs-Commun, 65100 Lourdes. ☎ **62-94-75-00.** Fax 62-94-78-45. Reservations recommended. Fixed-price menus 62 F ($11.80), 85 F ($16.15), 130 F ($24.70), and 170 F ($32.30). AE, MC, V. Daily noon–1:30pm and 7–9pm. Closed Jan 6–Feb 9 and Nov 20–Dec 23. Bus 2. BASQUE.

This restaurant has some of the best food in town, with tournedos with flap mushrooms a specialty. You can also order such country dishes as the chef's salad with smoked magrêt, escalope of warm duck foie gras with apples, and sautéed tornedos in cream sauce. Mountain trout is especially good here.

The Hôtel d'Albret is one of the best budget hotels in Lourdes, with 27 comfortabe rooms. Half-board rates are 193 to 242 F ($36.65 to $46) per person.

Languedoc, Roussillon & the Camargue

Languedoc, one of southern France's great old provinces, is a loosely defined area encompassing such cities as Nîmes, Toulouse, and Carcassonne. It's one of the leading wine-producing areas and is fabled for its art treasures.

The coast of Languedoc—from Montpellier to the Spanish frontier—might be called France's "second Mediterranean," first place naturally going to the Riviera. A land of ancient cities and a generous sea, it's less spoiled than the Côte d'Azur, with an almost-continuous strip of sand stretching west from the Rhône and curving snakelike toward the Pyrénées. Back in the days of de Gaulle, the government began an ambitious project to develop the Roussillon-Languedoc coastline, and it's been a booming success, as the miles of sun-baking bodies in July and August testify.

Ancient Roussillon is a small region of greater Languedoc, forming the Pyrénées Orientales département. This is the French Catalonia, inspired more by Barcelona in neighboring Spain than by remote Paris. Over its long and colorful history it has known many rulers. Legally part of the French kingdom until 1258, it was surrendered to James I of Aragón. Until 1344 it was part of the ephemeral kingdom of Majorca, with Perpignan as the capital. By 1463 Roussillon was annexed to France again. Then Ferdinand of Aragón won it back, but by 1659 France had it again. In spite of local sentiment for reunion with the Catalans of Spain, France still firmly controls the land.

The Camargue is a marshy delta between two arms of the Rhône. South of Arles is cattle country. Strong wild black bulls are bred here for the arenas of Arles and Nîmes. The small white horses, amazingly graceful, were said to have been brought here by the Saracens. They're ridden by *gardiens*, French cowboys, who can usually be seen in wide-brimmed black hats. The whitewashed houses, plaited-straw roofs, pink flamingos who inhabit the muddy marshes, vast plains, endless stretches of sandbars—all this qualifies as Exotic France.

REGIONAL CUISINE The cuisine of Languedoc/Roussillon is heavily influenced by garlic, olive oil, and strong flavors. The region has plentiful game, trout, succulent lamb, and seafood, usually prepared with local herbs, wine, and garlic.

One of the region's legendary dishes is usually prepared on a brazier in a boat on the open sea: the tripe (intestines) of tuna mixed with white wine and herbs, accompanied by a glass of seawater, whose salt alleviates some of the unpleasantness. A vastly more palatable dish is *pouillade*, which requires the simultaneous preparation of two pots of soup (one made with cabbage, the other with white beans). Just before serving, the contents are mixed together in a serving bowl.

Other regional specialties include excellent fish stews, foie gras, truffles, escargots, exotic mushrooms from the north-central areas, pâté of thrush from Rodez, cherries from Lodève, *aigo bouillido* (a soup made with garlic, eggs, aromatic herbs, and croûtons), *aligot* (a cheese dish made with garlic-laced cream, butter, potatoes, and cheese), and cassoulet of white beans and various meats. The region's most famous cheese is *pélardon*, made from goat's milk. The most famous pastry is the *Alleluia*.

As for wine, Hérault, Aude, and Garde rank first, second, and third in total wine production in France. Most of this is ordinary table wine. A few, however, have been granted an *Appellation d'Origine Controlée*. Some of the best are Fitou, produced in the Hautes-Corbières district near Narbonne, and Minervois, from west and northwest of Narbonne.

EXPLORING THE REGION BY CAR

Here's how to link together the best of the region if you rent a car.

Days 1–2   Begin in Toulouse, ancient capital of Languedoc and France's fourth-largest city. On the second day here, consider a detour to Auch, 43 miles west along N124, for a meal at the Hôtel de France. If the idea of spending time in a major urban center like Toulouse doesn't appeal to you, consider spending only one night, skipping Auch, and proceeding with the rest of this tour.

Day 3   From Toulouse, drive northeast on N88 and D922 for 43 miles to Cordes, a medieval village perched on a rocky hilltop. After your visit, drive southeast on D600 to Albi, site of the fortified Eglise Ste-Cecilia and one of the bloodiest religious massacres in French history. Spend the night here.

Day 4   Drive south for 25 miles on N112 for a visit to the brooding medieval city of Castres. Then continue 40 miles south on D112 and D118 for a tour of one of the most spectacular fortified sites in Europe, Carcassonne, where you'll stay the night.

Day 5   The day's final destination is Perpignan, but rather than reaching it via high-speed superhighways, we prefer to drive south and then west along D118 and D117. Spend the afternoon exploring Perpignan but retire early with the expectation of some complicated driving (and serious sunbathing) tomorrow.

Day 6   Your day's final destination is Collioure, but en route we recommend a mountain detour to the hamlet of Céret. (Reach Céret from Perpignan by driving south—toward Spain—along A9, then exiting after about 12 miles and driving west for 4 miles along D115.) Céret is well suited to a quiet hour or two in the sun, and you may decide to dine at La Terrasse au Soleil, route de Fontfrède, whose restaurant is a cost-conscious hideaway once favored by Salvador Dalí.

After your meal, drive east along D618 for 20 miles to the seaside hamlet of Collioure. Shaped like a half moon and flanked by a fortified château, it resembles St-Tropez before that town's tourist invasion. It was favored by artists during the Fauve period of early modern art. Spend the night here near what's the most charming village on the Côte Vermeille.

Languedoc, Roussillon & the Camargue

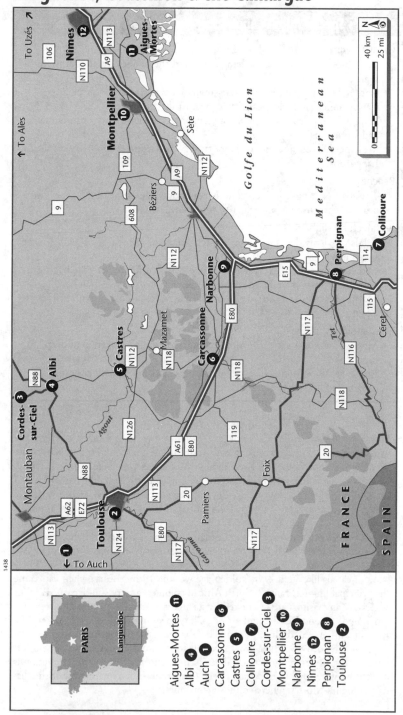

To Uzès

Nîmes **12**

106

N113

Aigues-Mortes

N110

A9

11 Aigues-Mortes

↑ To Alès

Montpellier **10**

109

Sète

A9

N112

Golfe du Lion

9

Béziers

608

N112

Mediterranean Sea

Perpignan

114

7 Collioure

9

Narbonne **9**

E15

8 Perpignan

E80

115

Céret

9

Mazamet

N117

Tet

Castres **5**

N112

N118

Carcassonne **6**

N118

N116

4 Albi

N88

3 Cordes-sur-Ciel

119

N118

Montauban

N88

Agout

N126

A61

E80

20

Foix

N113

20

Pamiers

2 Toulouse

A62

E72

N124

E80

N117

Garonne

N117

FRANCE

SPAIN

1 ↓ To Auch

N113

N

40 km

25 mi

0

PARIS

Languedoc

Aigues-Mortes **11**
Albi **4**
Auch **1**
Carcassonne **6**
Castres **5**
Collioure **7**
Cordes-sur-Ciel **3**
Montpellier **10**
Narbonne **9**
Nîmes **12**
Perpignan **8**
Toulouse **2**

1438

What's Special About Languedoc, Roussillon & the Camargue

Great Towns
- Toulouse, ancient capital of Languedoc and the major city of southwestern France.
- Cordes, built like an eagle's nest, a town of arts and crafts.
- Carcassonne, a great fortress city set against the Pyrénées.
- Perpignan, the "second capital" of Catalonia, an ancient city of monuments and attractions.
- Montpellier, an ancient university city and capital of Mediterranean Languedoc.

Beaches
- The coast of Languedoc, a second Mediterranean and one of the great European beaches, from Montpellier to the Spanish frontier.

Architectural Highlights
- Palais des Rois de Majorque, former palace of the kings of Majorca, at Perpignan.
- Cathédrale Ste-Marie, at Auch, from the 15th century, one of the handsomest gothic churches in the south of France.
- Maison Carrée, at Nîmes, one of the best-preserved Roman temples in Europe.

Outstanding Museums
- Musée Toulouse-Lautrec, at Albi, the most important collection of his paintings.
- Musée Fabre, at Montpellier, one of the most acclaimed provincial art galleries of France, filled with masterpieces.

Day 7 This is your day to beach-hop. Stop for a swim or a snack wherever the view inspires you but keep moving with your final destination in mind: Narbonne, 50 miles north of Collioure. Even though A9 can get you there most efficiently, we suggest that you at least begin the day by driving north along the narrow coastal road, admiring the string of fast-developing beach resorts. If traffic is dense, you can detour inland 7 miles, then continue along A9. Spend the night in Narbonne.

Day 8 Now you can explore the Camargue, a grass-covered wetland. Your first destination is canal-sided Sète, 50 miles northeast of Narbonne. Drive along A9, then detour through Agde along N112. Follow N112 east to Sète, built on a network of canals like Venice. Its golden age was the 19th century, when it became the principal link to France's North African colonies; a ferry still departs daily for Algeria. Many visitors are fascinated by its architecture, a somewhat bizarre combination of Second Empire and art deco. Try to stop for a meal at Restaurant La Rotonde, in Le Grand Hôtel, 17 quai de Tassigny (☎ 67-46-12-20).

From Sète, drive on the coastal road off to the northeast. Your route will follow a string of interconnected barrier islands and lead you through wetlands favored by waterfowl to the heart of the Camargue. The crown jewel of the district is Aigues-Mortes, where you'll stay overnight.

Day 9   Backtrack westward 20 miles on D62 for a view of the ancient Roman town of Montpellier. Know in advance that despite the town's *charme méridionale*, traffic is going to be dense. Tour the town, then drive 31 miles northeast along A9 to visit Nîmes, where you'll spend the night.

1 Auch

451 miles SW of Paris, 126 miles SE of Bordeaux

On the west bank of the Gers, in the heart of the ancient duchy of Gascony, of which it was the capital, the town of Auch is divided into an upper and a lower quarter, connected by several flights of steps. In the old part of town the narrow streets are called *pousterles*. These streets center on **place Salinis,** from which there's a good view of the Pyrénées. Branching off from here, the **Escalier Monumental** leads down to the river, a descent of 232 steps.

On the north of the square is the **Cathédrale Ste-Marie,** at place de la Cathédrale (☎ **62-05-22-89**). Built from the 15th to the 17th century, this is one of the handsomest gothic churches in the south of France. It has 113 Renaissance choir stalls made of carved oak, and a custodian will let you in for 5 F (95¢). The stained-glass windows, also from the Renaissance, are impressive. Its 17th-century organ was one of the finest in the world at the time of Louis XIV. The cathedral is open daily from 7:30am to noon and 2 to 7pm (closes at 5:30pm in winter).

Next to the cathedral stands an 18th-century archbishop's palace with a 14th-century bell tower, the **Tour d'Armagnac,** which was once a prison.

ESSENTIALS

GETTING THERE   Seven trains per day run between Toulouse and Auch (trip time: 1¹/₂ hr.). A one-way ticket costs 70 F ($13.30).

Six to eight SNCF buses arrive in Auch daily from Agen. The trip takes 1¹/₂ hours and costs 55 F ($10.45) one way.

VISITOR INFORMATION   The Office de Tourisme is at 1 rue Dessoles (☎ **62-05-22-89**).

WHERE TO STAY & DINE

✪ Hôtel de France (Restaurant André-Daguin)
Place de la Libération, 32003 Auch CEDEX. ☎ **62-61-71-84.** Fax 62-61-71-81. 27 rms, 2 suites. MINIBAR TV TEL. 600–970 F ($114–$184.30) double; 1,500–2,500 F ($285–$475) suite. Breakfast 80 F ($15.20) extra. AE, DC, MC, V. Parking free.

Built around the much-modernized 16th-century core of an old inn, this hotel in the center of town offers comfortable, conservative rooms (14 air-conditioned) and one of the most famous restaurants in France. The cuisine is called "innovative within traditional boundaries." Menu choices include an assortment of preparations of foie gras from Gascony, brochette of oysters with foie gras, a duo of magrêts de canard cooked in a rock-salt shell and served with papillotte of vegetables, and stuffed pigeon roasted with spiced honey. The desserts include a platter of four chocolate dishes and café au café, a presentation of mousses and pastries unified by their coffee content. Over the years we've had some of our most memorable meals in France here, yet there have also been disappointments. The restaurant is open for lunch Tuesday to Sunday and dinner Tuesday to Saturday; it's closed in January.

⑤ Le Relais de Gascogne

5 av. de la Marne, 32000 Auch. ☎ **62-05-26-81**. Fax **62-63-30-22**. 38 rms. A/C TV TEL. 335 F ($63.65) double. Breakfast 31 F ($5.90) extra. MC, V. Parking 30 F ($5.70). Closed Dec 22–Jan 12.

This hotel offers economical accommodations and meals. The rooms have been modernized and are comfortably furnished. The food is often quite good, especially the salad of duck breast, foie gras of duck, and hearty cassoulet. This place, though small, remains a stronghold of Gascon gastronomy.

2 Toulouse

438 miles SW of Paris, 152 miles SE of Bordeaux, 60 miles W of Carcassonne

The old capital of Languedoc and France's fourth-largest city, Toulouse (known as La Ville Rose) is cosmopolitan in flavor. The major city of the southwest, filled with gardens and squares, it's the gateway to the Pyrénées. Toulouse is also an artistic and cultural center. It's had a stormy history, playing many roles—once it was the capital of the Visigoths and later the center of the comtes de Toulouse.

GETTING THERE   The Toulouse-Blagnac airport lies in the city's northwestern suburbs, 7 miles from the center. Call 61-42-44-00 for flight information.

Nine trains per day arrive from Paris (trip time: 7 hr.), 8 from Bordeaux (trip time: 2¹/₄ hr.), and 11 from Marseille (trip time: 4¹/₂ hr.).

The Canal du Midi links many of the region's cities with Toulouse by waterway.

VISITOR INFORMATION   The Office de Tourisme is in the Donjon du Capitole, rue Lafayette (☎ **61-11-02-22**).

SEEING THE TOP ATTRACTIONS

The city's major monument is the ✪ **Basilique St-Sernin,** 13 place St-Sernin (☎ **61-21-80-45**). Consecrated in 1096, this is the largest and finest romanesque church extant. One of its most outstanding features is the Porte Miègeville, opening onto the south aisle and decorated with 12th-century sculptures. The door opening into the south transept is the Porte des Comtes, its capitals depicting the story of Lazarus. Nearby are the tombs of the comtes de Toulouse. Entering by the main west door, you can see the double side aisles that give the church five naves, an unusual feature in romanesque architecture. An upper cloister forms a passageway around the interior. Look for the romanesque capitals surmounting the columns.

In the axis of the basilica, 11th-century bas-reliefs depict *Christ in His Majesty.* The ambulatory leads to the crypt (ask the custodian for permission to enter), containing the relics of 128 saints, plus a thorn said to be from the Crown of Thorns. In the ambulatory, the old baroque retables and shrine have been reset; the relics here are those of the Apostles and the first bishops of Toulouse. The ambulatory and crypt may be visited July to September only, Monday to Saturday from 10am to 5:30pm and Sunday from noon to 5:30pm. The basilica can't be visited during services. Admission is 10 F ($1.90).

Opposite St-Sernin is the **Musée St-Raymond,** place St-Sernin (☎ **61-22-21-85**), housed in a college reconstructed in 1523. It contains one of the finest collections of Imperial busts outside Rome and is open Monday and Wednesday to Saturday from 10am to noon and 2 to 6pm and Sunday from 10am to noon. Admission is 10 F ($1.90) for adults and 5 F (95¢) for children.

Toulouse

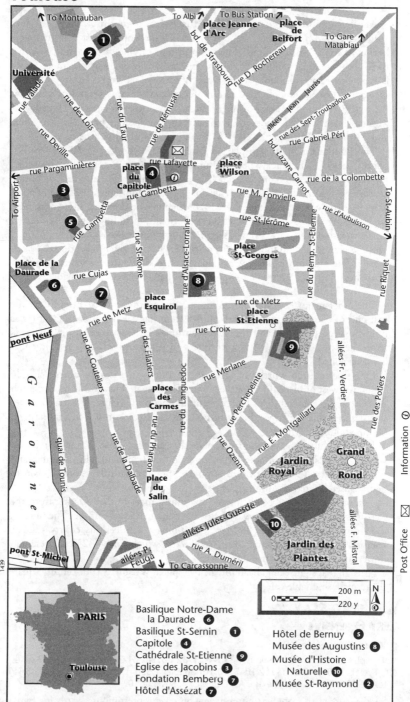

↖ To Montauban · To Albi ↗ · To Bus Station ↗

place Jeanne-d'Arc

place de Belfort

To Gare Matabiau ↑

Université

bd. de Strasbourg · rue D. Rochereau · allées Jean Jaurès · rue des Sept-Troubadours

rue Valade · rue des Lois · rue du Taur · rue de Remusat

rue Deville · rue Gabriel Péri

rue Pargaminières

← To Airport

rue Lafayette

place du Capitole ④ ⓘ · **place Wilson** · rue de la Colombette

rue Gambetta · bd. Lazare Carnot · To St-Aubin ↗

③

rue M. Fonvielle

⑤ · rue St-Jérôme · rue d'Aubuisson

rue Gambetta · rue St-Rome · rue d'Alsace-Lorraine · **place St-Georges** · rue du Remp. St-Etienne · rue Riquet

place de la Daurade

⑥ · rue Cujas · ⑦ · ⑧

place Esquirol

rue de Metz · **place St-Etienne**

pont Neuf

rue de Metz · rue Croix · ⑨ · allées Fr. Verdier

Garonne

rue des Couteliers · rue des Filatiers · rue du Languedoc · rue Merlane · rue Perchepeinte · rue des Potiers

quai de Tounis

place des Carmes

rue du Pharaon · rue Ozenne · rue E. Montgaillard

rue de la Dalbade

Jardin Royal · **Grand Rond** · allées F. Mistral

place du Salin

allées Jules-Guesde

⑩

pont St-Michel

allées P. Feuga · rue A. Duméril

↓ To Carcassonne

Jardin des Plantes

1459

Post Office ⊠   Information ⓘ

★ PARIS

● Toulouse

Basilique Notre-Dame la Daurade ⑥
Basilique St-Sernin ①
Capitole ④
Cathédrale St-Etienne ⑨
Eglise des Jacobins ③
Fondation Bemberg ⑦
Hôtel d'Assézat ⑦

Hôtel de Bernuy ⑤
Musée des Augustins ⑧
Musée d'Histoire Naturelle ⑩
Musée St-Raymond ②

0 ▭▬▭▬ 200 m / 220 y   N

Another important museum is the **Musée des Augustins,** 21 rue de Metz (☎ 61-22-21-82). In its 14th-century cloisters is the world's most important collection of romanesque capitals. The sculptures or carvings are magnificent, and there are some fine examples of early Christian sarcophagi. On the upper floors is a large painting collection, with works by Murillo, Toulouse-Lautrec, Gérard, Delacroix, Rubens, and Ingres. The museum also contains several portraits by Antoine Rivalz, a local artist of major talent. The museum is open Thursday to Monday from 10am to noon and 2 to 6pm and Wednesday from 10am to noon and 2 to 10pm. Admission is 10 F ($1.90) for adults; children free.

The **Fondation Bemberg,** place d'Assézat, rue de Metz (☎ 61-12-06-89), opened in 1995 and quickly became one of the city's most important museums. Housed in the Assézat mansion from 1555, the museum offers an overview of five centuries of European art. The nucleus of the collection represented the lifelong work of George Bemberg, collector extraordinaire, who donated 331 works. The largest bequest was 28 paintings by Pierre Bonnard, including his *Moulin Rouge.* Bemberg also donated works by Pissarro, Matisse (his *Vue d'Antibes*) and Monet, plus the Fauves. The foundation also owns Canaletto's much-reproduced *Vue de Mestre.* The museum is open Wednesday to Monday: June to September from 10am to 6pm, and October to May from 10am to 5pm. Admission is 25 F ($4.75).

The other major ecclesiastical building is the **Cathédrale St-Etienne,** at the east end of rue de Metz (☎ 61-52-03-82). It has a bastardized look (it was built between the 11th and the 17th century). The rectangular bell tower is from the 16th century. It has a unique ogival nave to which a gothic choir has been added.

One final church worthy of attention is the **Eglise des Jacobins,** in Old Toulouse, west of place du Capitole along rue Lakanal. This gothic brick church dates from the 13th century. The convent, daring in its architecture, has been restored and forms the largest block of buildings in France in use as a monastery. Visiting hours are erratic.

In civic architecture, the **Capitole,** place du Capitole (☎ 49-52-24-63), is outstanding. Built in 1753, it houses the Hôtel de Ville (city hall), plus a theater, and is open Monday to Friday from 8:30pm to 5pm and Saturday from 8:30am to noon; closed holidays. Admission is free.

Toulouse has a number of fine old mansions, most of them dating from the Renaissance, when Toulouse was one of the richest cities of Europe. The finest is the **Hôtel d'Assézat,** on rue de Metz, containing a 16th-century courtyard. The mansion houses the Académie des Jeux-Floraux, which since 1323 has presented flowers made of wrought metal to poets.

After all that sightseeing, head for the oval **place Wilson,** a 19th-century square sheltering fashionable cafés.

WHERE TO STAY
VERY EXPENSIVE

✪ Grand Hôtel de l'Opéra

1 place du Capitole, 31000 Toulouse. ☎ **61-21-82-66.** Fax 61-23-41-04. 40 rms, 9 suites. A/C TV TEL. 800–1,000 F ($152.10–$190.10) double; 1,350–1,500 F ($256.65–$285.15) suite. Breakfast 82 F ($15.60) extra. AE, DC, MC, V. Bus 5 or 10.

The owners of this opulent hotel have won several prestigious awards for transforming a 17th-century building (once a convent) into a sophisticated new ensemble. The public rooms contain early 19th-century antiques and Napoleonic-inspired tenting over the bars. Some guest rooms have urn-shaped balustrades overlooking formal squares, and all have high ceilings and modern amenities. The hotel runs the town's most prestigious restaurant (see "Where to Dine," below), plus a brasserie and an indoor restaurant. Facilities include an indoor pool, a Jacuzzi, and a health club.

MODERATE

Hôtel des Beaux-Arts

1 place du Pont-Neuf, 31000 Toulouse. ☎ **61-23-40-50.** Fax 61-22-02-27. 20 rms. A/C TV TFl 450–900 F ($85.55–$171.10) double. Breakfast 65–75 F ($12.35–$14.25) extra. AE, DC, MC, V. Parking 70 F ($13.30).

Occupying a richly dignified pink-brick villa built 250 years ago on the banks of the Garonne, this is a charming hotel in the heart of town. Despite the historic facade, the well-equipped and soundproof rooms are somberly modern and comfortable. Breakfast is the only meal served; diners often head for the Brasserie des Beaux-Arts (see "Where to Dine," below), in the same building, with an entrance around the corner.

Sofitel Toulouse Centre

84 allée Jean-Jaurès, 31000 Toulouse. ☎ **61-10-23-10.** Fax 61-10-23-20. 105 rms, 14 suites. A/C MINIBAR TV TEL. 850 F ($161.60) double; 1,550 F ($294.65) suite. Breakfast 80 F ($15.20) extra. AE, DC, MC, V. Parking 80 F ($15.20). Bus 148.

This soaring 18-story hotel is probably the best in Toulouse. Set adjacent to place Wilson, the hotel employs a charming bilingual staff and offers rooms for handicapped travelers and suites that are outfitted for use either as mini-offices or as lodgings for families. The hotel has 24-hour room service, an in-house parking garage (much needed in this congested neighborhood), a bar, and a bustling brasserie.

INEXPENSIVE

⑤ Hôtel Raymond-IV

16 rue Raymond-IV, 31000 Toulouse. ☎ **61-62-89-41.** Fax 61-61-38-01. 38 rms. MINIBAR TV TEL. 330–380 F ($62.70–$72.20) double. Breakfast 40 F ($7.60) extra. AE, DC, MC, V. Parking 25 F ($4.75); free weekends. Bus 5, 10, 14, or 16.

On a quiet street close to the town center and the rail station, this antique building contains pleasantly decorated rooms, which are sometimes discounted on weekends. The location means you're within walking distance of the historic quarter, with its theaters, shops, and nightclubs. Though breakfast is the only meal served, the English-speaking staff will direct you to nearby restaurants.

WHERE TO DINE
VERY EXPENSIVE

✪ Vanel

22 rue Maurice-Fontvieille. ☎ **61-21-51-82.** Reservations required. Main courses 130–320 F ($24.70–$60.80); fixed-price menus 200 F ($38) (lunch, with wine and coffee), 250 F ($47.50), and 500 F ($95.05) (with champagne). AE, MC, V. Mon–Sat 12:15–1:30pm and 7:30–10pm. Closed Aug 1–15. Bus 5, 10, 14, or 16. BASQUE.

The chef here creates scrumptious meals, giving new meaning to regional courses and often discovering new taste sensations. The choices include stuffed pigeon or pigeon roasted with spices and honey, pigs' feet stuffed with sweetbreads and foie gras, and sea bass with baby vegetables. The wine list is well balanced, with many interesting selections, including Cahors and Côtes de Duras. The service is impeccable. Also on the premises is the Bistrot Vanel, with fixed-price menus for 98 ($18.60) and 120 F ($22.80).

EXPENSIVE

✪ Les Jardins de l'Opéra

In the Grand Hôtel de l'Opéra, 1 place du Capitole. ☎ **61-23-07-76.** Reservations required. Main courses 150–260 F ($28.50–$49.40); fixed-price menus 290 F ($55.10) and 480 F ($91.20). AE, DC, MC, V. Mon–Sat noon–2pm and 8–10pm. Closed Jan 2–7 and Aug 6–29. Bus 5, 10, 14, or 16. FRENCH.

Toulouse-Lautrec: A Giant of a Talent

Though painter Henri de Toulouse-Lautrec spent his most creative years in Paris, his name still evokes the pink-walled city of southwestern France that clings tenaciously to his legacy. Never growing taller than 5 feet, he was famous for his unfettered portraits of prostitutes and cabaret entertainers and for his brilliantly vicious caricatures of belle époque pretensions.

Despite his physical shortcomings, no one can debate the titanic dimensions of Toulouse-Lautrec's art. In a span of less than 20 years he executed 737 canvases, 275 watercolors, 363 prints and posters, more than 5,000 drawings, some ceramics and stained-glass windows, and more than 300 artworks classified as "pornography."

Born into a much-intermarried family of aristocrats whose ancestors could be traced back to Charlemagne, he was the only surviving child of his parents' union and the cousin of several children with epilepsy, dwarfism, neurological disorders, and alarming skeletal malformations. Toulouse-Lautrec grew into a short but relatively normal-looking young man, but his later years were marred by changes in his appearance that included violent toothaches, repeated fractures in the bones of his legs, and eventually a growth in the side of his nose and lips that led to frequent drooling.

Geneticists blame some of his problems on his genetic makeup and its propensity for pycnodysostosis (*pick*-no-did-os-*to*-sis), a sometimes painful form of dwarfism attended by such complications as underdeveloped facial bones, incomplete closure of the "soft spots" between the plates of the skull, short fingers and toes, and easily decayed teeth. But despite the cogency of scientific reasoning, no one will ever know for sure why Toulouse-Lautrec suffered as he did: His descendents have repeatedly refused their permission to either be genetically tested for the disorder or to have the artist's corpse exhumed.

The family's **Château du Bosc** (also known as the Fortresse Berenger-Bosc, owned during his life by the artist's grandmother) (☎ **65-69-20-83** or 65-72-26-16) is 29 miles from Toulouse, reached from Albi by N88. Built in 1180 and renovated in the 1400s, the château is midway between Albi and Rodez (also spelled Rodes) and is open to visitors daily from 9am to 7pm. Admission is 25 F ($4.75). The present owner, Mlle de Céleran, is most gracious to those interested in Toulouse-Lautrec's life. It's polite to precede a visit here with a phone call, but it's not required.

Ironically, Toulouse-Lautrec's 1901 death at age 36 had little to do with his dwarfism: The cause was acute alcoholism.

The entrance to the city's best restaurant is in the 18th-century Florentine courtyard of the Grand Hôtel. The dining area is a series of intimate salons, several of which face a winter garden and a reflecting pool. You'll be greeted by the gracious Maryse Toulousy, whose husband, Dominique, prepares what critics have called the perfect combination of modern and old-fashioned French cuisine. The outstanding menu listings are likely to include rack of lamb with garlic croquettes and a "cake" of eggplant and anchovies, shellfish salad with artichoke hearts, blond chicken livers with caramelized port-wine sauce, and ravioli stuffed with foie gras and a distillation of truffles.

MODERATE

⊛ Brasserie des Beaux-Arts

1 quai de la Daurade. ☎ **61-21-12-12.** Reservations recommended. Main courses 70–110 F ($13.30–$20.90); fixed-price menus 99–141 F ($18.80–$26.80). AE, DC, MC, V. Daily noon–3:30pm and 7pm–1am. Bus 5, 10, 14, or 16. FRENCH.

This turn-of-the-century brasserie was designed by entrepreneur Jean-Paul Bucher, who has made a career of restoring art nouveau brasseries. The decor includes walnut paneling and many mirrors, and the cuisine emphasizes well-prepared fresh fish and seafood, along with a scattering of regional courses. Try the foie gras or country-inspired sauerkraut, accompanied by the house riesling, served in a pitcher. During warm weather, eat on the terrace. A menu for 95 F ($18.05) is served from 10pm on.

Chez Emile

13 place St-Georges. ☎ **61-21-05-56.** Reservations recommended. Main courses 98–130 F ($18.60–$24.70); fixed-price menus 115–150 F ($21.85–$28.50) at lunch, 210–230 F ($39.90–$43.70) at dinner. AE, DC, MC, V. Tues–Sat noon–2:30pm and 7–9:30pm. TOULOUSIEN.

In an old-fashioned house on one of the most beautiful squares of Toulouse, this restaurant offers the specialties of chef François Ferrier. In winter, meals are served one floor above street level in a cozy enclave overlooking the square; in summer, the venue moves to the street-level dining room because of its access to a flower-filled terrace. Menu choices include cassoulet toulousain, magrêt de canard traditional style, and parillade of grilled fish with a pungently aromatic cold sauce of sweet peppers and olive oil. The wine carte is filled with intriguing surprises.

NEARBY ACCOMMODATIONS & DINING

Hôtel de Diane

3 route de St-Simon, or 296 chemin de Tucaut, 31100 Le Mirail. ☎ **61-07-59-52.** Fax 61-68-38-94. 35 rms. MINIBAR TV TEL. 460–520 F ($87.40–$98.80) double. Breakfast 45 F ($8.55) extra. AE, DC, MC, V. Parking free. Take D23 for 5 miles from Toulouse to Exit 27.

This hotel/restaurant surrounded by a 5-acre park is the most tranquil retreat near Toulouse. The turn-of-the-century villa offers well-decorated rooms, 13 of which are air-conditioned; some rooms are in annexes. The restaurant, Saint-Simon, offers a choice of meals in the garden or the Louis XV–style dining room. The fixed-price menus, at 105 to 180 F ($19.95 to $34.20), offer the best value. The restaurant serves lunch Monday to Friday and dinner Monday to Saturday until 9:30pm. In spite of the impeccable service and gracious welcome, our recent meal was flawed—one dish would arrive perfect but the next would be underseasoned or soggy. The bordeaux, however, was wonderful.

3 Albi

433 miles SW of Paris, 47 miles NE of Toulouse

The "red city" (for the color of the building stone) of Albi straddles both banks of the Tarn River and is dominated by its brooding 1282 **Cathédrale Ste-Cécile** (☎ 63-54-15-11), near place du Vigan, the medieval center of town. Fortified with ramparts and parapets and containing transepts and aisles, it was built by local bishops during a power struggle with the comtes de Toulouse. Try not to miss the exceptional 16th-century rood screen. The cathedral is open daily: June to August from 8:30am to 7pm, and September to May from 9 to 11:30am and 2 to 5:30pm. Admission is 2 F (40¢).

Opposite the north side of the cathedral is the Palais de la Berbie (Archbishop's Palace), another fortified structure dating from the late 13th century. Inside, the **Musée Toulouse-Lautrec** (☎ 63-54-14-09) contains the world's most important collection of that artist's paintings, more than 600 specimens. His family bequeathed the works remaining in his studio. Toulouse-Lautrec was born at Albi on November 24, 1864. Crippled in childhood, his legs permanently deformed, he lived in Paris most of his life and produced posters and sketches of characters in music halls and circuses. His satiric portraits of the turn-of-the-century demimonde were both amusing and affectionate. The museum also owns paintings by Degas, Bonnard, Matisse, Utrillo, and Rouault. It's open April to September, daily from 9am to noon and 2 to 6pm; October to March, Wednesday to Monday from 10am to noon and 2 to 5pm. Admission is 20 F ($3.80) for adults and 10 F ($1.90) for children.

Toulouse-Lautrec was born in the **Hôtel Bosc** in Albi; it's still a private home and cannot be toured, but there's a plaque on the wall of the building, on rue Toulouse-Lautrec (no number) in the historic town core.

ESSENTIALS

GETTING THERE   Fifteen trains per day link Toulouse with Albi (trip time: 1 hr.); the one-way fare is 60 F ($11.40). There's also a direct Paris–Albi night train.

Motorists from Paris can take RN20 via Cahors and Caussade; from Bordeaux, take the Autoroute des Deux Mers, exiting at Montauban.

VISITOR INFORMATION   The Office de Tourisme is in the Palais de la Berbie, place Ste-Cécile (☎ 63-54-22-30).

WHERE TO STAY

Hostellerie St-Antoine
17 rue St-Antoine, 81000 Albi. ☎ **63-54-04-04.** Fax 63-47-10-47. 47 rms. A/C TV TEL. 950 F ($180.50) double. Breakfast 60 F ($11.40) extra. AE, DC, MC, V. Parking free.

This 250-year-old hotel has been owned by the same family for five generations; today it's managed by Jacques and Jean-François Rieux. Their mother focused on Toulouse-Lautrec when designing the hotel, since her grandfather was a friend of the painter and was given a few of his paintings, sketches, and prints. Several are in the lounge, which opens onto a rear garden. The rooms have been delightfully decorated, with a sophisticated use of color, good reproductions, and occasional antiques. Even if you're not spending the night, consider dining here: The Rieux culinary tradition is revealed in their traditional yet creative cuisine, and everything tastes better washed down with Gaillac wines.

Mercure Altéa
41 rue Porta, 81000 Albi. ☎ **63-47-66-66.** Fax 63-46-18-40. 56 rms. MINIBAR TV TEL. 440–510 F ($83.60–$96.90) double. Breakfast 55 F ($10.45) extra. AE, DC, MC, V. Parking free.

The modern Altéa is one of the best places to stay in Albi. It was built in an 18th-century mill on the edge of the Tarn, and the facade and huge entryway were preserved. The rooms are well equipped, 28 with air conditioning. A little rejuvenation is needed in the baths, though. The first-class restaurant serves superb meals—both regional and continental. Tables are set on the terrace in summer.

✪ La Réserve
Route de Cordes à Fonvialane, 81000 Albi. ☎ **63-60-80-80.** Fax 63-47-63-60. 24 rms, 4 junior suites. MINIBAR TV TEL. 850 F ($161.50) double; from 1,000 F ($190) suite. Breakfast 70 F ($13.30) extra. AE, DC, MC, V. Parking free. Closed Nov–Apr.

This country-club villa on the outskirts of Albi, a mile west of the center, is managed by the Rieux family, who also run the Hostellerie St-Antoine (above). It was built in the Mediterranean style, with a pool and a fine garden in which you can dine. The rooms, well furnished and color coordinated, contain imaginative decorations (but avoid those over the kitchen); the upper-story rooms have sun terraces and French doors. In the restaurant, specialties include pâté de grives (thrush), carré d'agneau aux cèpes (lamb with flap mushrooms), and tournedos Périgueux. Even if you're not a guest, consider a visit. The wine carte is rich in bordeaux, and the prices per bottle are reasonable.

WHERE TO DINE

Jardin des Quatre Saisons
19 bd. de Strasbourg. ☎ **63-60-77-76.** Reservations recommended. Fixed-price menus 120 F ($22.80) and 150 F ($28.50). AE, MC, V. Tues–Sun 12:30–2pm and 7:30–10pm. FRENCH.

The best food in town is served by Georges Bermond, who believes that menus, like life, should change with the seasons—and that's how the restaurant got its name. The service is always competent and polite in a winter-garden setting much appreciated by locals who dine here on special occasions. Visitors are always welcome. You might enjoy gratinée of mussels in a compote of fish, anchovy ravioli with essence of anise-scented tomatoes, or pot-au-feu of the sea. The chef gives finesse and harmony to his cuisine. His wine carte is the finest in Albi.

4 Cordes-sur-Ciel

421 miles SW of Paris, 15¹/₂ miles NW of Albi

This site is remarkable, like an eagle's nest on a hilltop, opening onto the Cérou valley. The name Cordes is derived from the textile and leather industries that thrived here during the 13th and 14th centuries. It became a fortified Protestant refuge during the wars of religion.

In the 14th century when the town's troubles eased, artisans working with linen and leather prospered. It also became known throughout France for its brilliantly colored silks. In the 15th century, however, plagues and religious massacres reduced the city to a minor role. A brief renaissance occurred in the 19th century, when automatic weaving machines were introduced.

Today Cordes is an arts-and-crafts city, and many of the ancient houses on the narrow streets contain artisans plying their skills—blacksmiths, enamelers, graphic artists, weavers, engravers, sculptors, and painters. You park outside, then go under an arch leading to the old town.

ESSENTIALS

GETTING THERE   If coming by train, you'll have to get off in nearby Vindrac and either rent a bicycle or take a taxi the remaining 2 miles to Cordes.

VISITOR INFORMATION   The Syndicat d'Initiative (tourist office) is in the Maison du Grand-Fauconnier (☎ **63-56-00-52**).

SEEING THE TOP ATTRACTIONS

Often called "the city of a hundred gothic arches," Cordes contains numerous **old houses** built of pink sandstone. Many of the doors and windows are fashioned of pointed (broken) arches that still retain their 13th- and 14th-century grace. Some of the best-preserved ones line the Grande-Rue, also called rue Droite.

The **Musée Charles-Portal,** le Portail-Peint (☎ **63-56-00-40**), is named after the archivist of the Tarn region who was also an avid historian of Cordes. It contains everyday artifacts of the textile industry of long ago, old farming measures, samples of local embroidery, a reconstructed peasant home interior, and other medieval memorabilia. It's open in July and August, daily from 2 to 6pm; in May, June, September, and October, Sunday only from 2 to 5pm. Admission is 10 F ($1.90) for adults and 5 F (95¢) for children.

The Maison du Grand-Fauconnier (House of the Falcon Master) is named for the falcons carved into the stonework of the wall. A grandly proportioned staircase in the building leads to the **Musée Yves-Brayer,** Grande-Rue (☎ **63-56-00-40**). Yves Brayer came to Cordes in 1940 and became well known. After watching Cordes fall gradually into decay, he renewed interest in its restoration. The museum is open in July and August, daily from 10am to noon and 2 to 6pm; April to June and September to November, Monday to Friday from 8:30am to noon and 1:30 to 6pm and Sunday and holidays from 2 to 6pm; December to March, daily from 8:30am to noon and 1:30 to 6pm. Admission is 5 F (95¢).

The **Eglise St-Michel,** Grande-Rue, dates from the 13th century, though many alterations have been made since. The view from the top of the tower encompasses much of the surrounding area. Much of the lateral design of the side chapels probably comes from the cathedral at Albi. Before being shipped here, the organ (dating from 1830) was in Notre-Dame de Paris. Visiting hours are erratic. If the church is closed, ask at the *tabac* (tobacco shop) across from the front entrance.

WHERE TO STAY & DINE

Hostellerie du Parc

Les Cabannes, 81170 Cordes. ☎ **63-56-02-59.** Fax 63-56-18-03. Reservations recommended. Main courses 70–120 F ($13.30–$22.80); fixed-price menus 130 F ($24.70), 160 F ($30.40), 195 F ($37.05), and 280 F ($53.20). AE, DC, V. Mon-Sat noon–2pm and 7–10pm, Sun noon–2pm. Closed Mon Nov–Mar. FRENCH.

About a mile west of the town center, on route de St-Antonin (D600), this century-old stone house offers generous meals in a wooded garden or paneled dining room. The specialties include homemade foie gras, duckling, poularde occitaine, rabbit with cabbage leaves, and calf's sweetbreads with morels. Claude Izard is the amiable owner/director.

The hotel offers 14 simply furnished rooms, a double costing 260 to 290 F ($49.40 to $55.10), plus 33 F ($6.25) for breakfast.

✪ Maison du Grand Ecuyer

Rue Voltaire, 81170 Cordes. ☎ **63-56-01-03.** Fax 63-56-16-99. Reservations required. Main courses 120–200 F ($22.80–$38); fixed-price menus 170 F ($32.30), 290 F ($55.10), and 360 F ($68.40). AE, DC, MC, V. Tues 7–9:30pm, Wed–Sun noon–2pm and 7–9:30pm. Closed Oct 15–Easter. FRENCH.

The restaurant of this ancient hotel is a national historic monument. Chef Yves Thuriès prepares platters that have made his restaurant an almost mandatory stop during a visit to Cordes. Specialties include three confits of lobster, salad of red mullet with fondue of vegetables, and noisette of lamb in orange sauce. The dessert selection is about the grandest and most overwhelming in this part of France. As a novelty, the 290-F ($55.10) menu reproduces the meal served to Mitterrand during his visit, the 320-F ($60.80) duplicates the food offered Elizabeth II, and the grandest of all, the 360-F ($68.40) menu presents what was dished up for the emperor of Japan.

The hotel is in the 15th-century hunting lodge of Raymond VII, comte de Toulouse. There are 11 rooms, all with antiques. Doubles cost 450 to 850 F ($85.50 to $161.50), plus 70 F ($13.30) for a superb breakfast. The most-desired room, honoring former guest Albert Camus, has a four-poster bed and a fireplace.

5 Castres

Built on the bank of the Agout River, Castres is the point of origin of trips to the Sidobre, the mountains of Lacaune, and the Black Mountains. Today the wool industry, whose origins go back to the 14th century, has made Castres one of France's two most important wool-producing areas. The town was formerly a Roman military installation. A Benedictine monastery was founded here in the 9th century, and the town fell under the comtes d'Albi in the 10th century. During the wars of religion, it was Protestant.

ESSENTIALS

GETTING THERE   From Toulouse, there are eight trains per day (trip time: 1 hr.), costing 70 F ($13.30) one way. From Albi (above), there are seven trains via St-Sulpice (trip time: 20 min.), costing 70 F ($13.30) one way.

VISITOR INFORMATION   The Syndicat d'Initiative (tourist office) is in the Théâtre Municipal, place de la République (☎ **63-71-56-58**).

TOURING THE TOP ATTRACTIONS

The ✪ **Musée Goya**, in the Jardin de l'Evêché (☎ **63-71-59-27**), is in the town hall, an archbishop's palace designed by Mansart in 1669. Some of the spacious public rooms have ceilings supported by a frieze of the archbishop's coats-of-arms. The collection includes 16th-century tapestries and the works of Spanish painters from the 15th to the 20th century. Most notable, of course, are the paintings of Francisco de Goya y Lucientes, all donated to the town in 1894 by Pierre Briguiboul, son of Castres-born artist Marcel Briguiboul. *Les Caprices* is a study of figures created in 1799, after the illness that left Goya deaf. Filling much of an entire room, the work is composed of symbolic images of demons and monsters, a satire of Spanish society.

The museum is open June to August, Monday to Saturday from 9am to noon and 2 to 6pm and Sunday from 10am to noon and 2 to 6pm; it's closed Monday in April, May, and September, and from October to March it closes at 5pm. Admission is 20 F ($3.80) for adults and 10 F ($1.90) for children.

A few rooms of the former archbishop's palace are reserved for the **Musée Jean-Jaurès,** 2 place Pélisson (☎ **63-72-01-01**). This museum is dedicated to the workers' movements of the late 19th and early 20th centuries. It gathers printed material issued by various Socialist factions in France during this era. See, in particular, an issue of *L'Aurore* containing Zola's famous "J'accuse" article from the Dreyfus case. Paintings, sculptures, films, and slides round out the collection. The museum is open in July and August, daily from 9am to noon and 2 to 6pm; April to September 21, Tuesday to Sunday from 9am to noon and 2 to 6pm; September 22 to March, Tuesday to Sunday from 9am to noon and 2 to 5pm. Admission is 10 F ($1.90) for adults; children free.

Architect Caillau began construction of the **Eglise St-Benoêt,** place du 8-Mai-1945 (☎ **63-59-05-19**), in 1677, on the site of a 9th-century Benedictine abbey. The baroque structure was never completed according to its original plans, however. The painting at the far end above the altar was executed by Gabriel Briard in the 18th century. It's open daily from 9am to 5pm.

WHERE TO STAY

Le Grand Hôtel
11 rue de la Libération, 81103 Castres CEDEX. ☎ **63-59-00-30.** Fax 63-59-03-50. 40 rms. MINIBAR TV TEL. 210–280 F ($39.90–$53.20) double. Breakfast 35 F ($6.65) extra. AE, DC, MC, V. Parking 30 F ($5.70). Closed Dec 22–Jan 10. Bus 10.

This traditional hotel, owned by three generations of the same family since it was built in 1860, is one of the best of the moderately priced establishments in town. Half its comfortably furnished rooms open onto the river. In spite of its name, the Grand is no longer the hotel of choice for Castres, a position it has lost to the Renaissance (below).

Hôtel Renaissance
17 rue Victor-Hugo, 81100 Castres. ☎ **63-59-30-42.** Fax 63-72-11-57. 10 rms, 4 suites. TV TEL. 265–315 F ($50.35–$59.85) double; 470–570 F ($89.35–$108.35) suite. Breakfast 35 F ($6.65) extra. AE, MC, V.

The Renaissance is the best hotel in Castres. It was built in the 17th century as the courthouse, then functioned as a colorful but rundown hotel throughout most of the 20th century—until 1993, when it was discreetly restored. Today you'll see a severely dignified building composed, depending on which part you look at, of *colombages*-style half-timbering, with a mixture of chiseled stone blocks and bricks. Some rooms have exposed timbers; all are clean and comfortable, evoking the crafts of yesteryear. Simple platters can be prepared for guests wishing to eat in their rooms, though plans for a restaurant are in effect.

WHERE TO DINE

La Mandragore
1 rue Malpas. ☎ **63-59-51-27.** Reservations recommended. Main courses 85–120 F ($16.15–$22.80); fixed-price menus 70 F ($13.30) (with wine, served at lunch only), 85 F ($16.15), 130 F ($24.70), 155 F ($29.45), and 240 F ($45.60). AE, DC, MC, V. Mon 7–10pm, Tues–Sat noon–2pm and 7–10pm. LANGUEDOCIEN.

On an easily overlooked narrow street, this restaurant occupies a small section of one of the many wings of the medieval château-fort of Castres. The decor is consciously simple, perhaps as an appropriate foil for the stone walls and overhead beams. Sophie (in the dining room) and Jean-Claude (in the kitchens) Belaut prepare a regional cuisine that's among the best in town. Served with charm and tact, it might include lasagne of foie gras, roast pigeon stuffed with foie gras and served with gâteau of potatoes and flap mushrooms, petits encornets (local squid) stuffed with tomatoes and saffron, and grilled fresh fish.

6 Carcassonne

495 miles SW of Paris, 57 miles SE of Toulouse

Evoking bold knights, fair damsels, and troubadours, the greatest fortress city of Europe rises against a background of the snow-capped Pyrénées. Floodlit at night, it captures fairy-tale magic, but back in its heyday in the Middle Ages all wasn't so romantic. Shattering the peace and quiet were battering rams, grapnels, a mobile tower (inspired by the Trojan horse), catapults, flaming arrows, and the mangonel.

Carcassonne consists of two towns: the **Ville Basse** (Lower City) and the medieval **Cité.** The former has little interest, but the latter is among the major attractions in France, the goal of many a pilgrim. The fortifications consist of the inner and outer walls, a double line of **ramparts.** The inner rampart was built by the Visigoths in the 5th century. Clovis, king of the Franks, attacked in 506 but failed. The Saracens overcame the city in 728, until Pepin the Short (father of Charlemagne) drove them out in 752. During a long siege by Charlemagne, the populace of the walled city was starving and near surrender until Dame Carcas came up with an idea. According to legend, she gathered up the last remaining bit of grain, fed it to a sow, then tossed the pig over the ramparts. It's said to have burst, scattering the grain. The Franks concluded that Carcassonne must have unlimited food supplies and ended their siege.

Carcassone's walls were further fortified by the vicomtes de Trencavel in the 12th century and Louis IX and Philip the Bold in the following century. However, by the mid-17th century its position as a strategic frontier fort was over and the ramparts were left to decay. In the 19th century the builders of the Lower Town began to remove the stone for use in new construction. But interest in the Middle Ages revived, and the government ordered Viollet-le-Duc (who restored Notre-Dame in Paris) to repair and where necessary rebuild the walls. Reconstruction continued until very recently.

Enclosed in the walls is a small populace. The **Cathédrale St-Nazaire,** La Cité (☎ 68-25-27-65), dates from the 11th and 12th centuries, containing some beautiful stained-glass windows and a pair of rose medallions. The nave is in the romanesque style, but the choir and transept are gothic. The organ, one of the oldest in southwestern France, is from the 16th century. The tomb of Bishop Radulph is well preserved, dating from 1266. The cathedral is open daily from 9am to noon and 2 to 6pm. Admission is free.

ESSENTIALS

GETTING THERE   Carcassonne is a major stop for trains between Toulouse and destinations south and east. Two dozen trains from Toulouse pass through daily (trip time: 50 min.), costing 72 F ($13.70) one way. There are 14 trains per day from Montpellier (trip time: 2 hr.), costing 110 F ($20.90) one way, and 12 trains per day from Nîmes (trip time: 2¹/₂ hr.), costing 135 F ($25.65) one way.

VISITOR INFORMATION The Office de Tourisme is at 15 bd. Camille-Pelletan (☎ 68-25-07-04).

WHERE TO STAY
IN THE CITE

Cité
Place de l'Eglise, 11000 Carcassonne. ☎ **68-25-03-34.** Fax 68-71-50-15. 23 rms, 3 suites. A/C TV TEL. 1,020–1,250 F ($193.90–$237.60) double; from 1,600 F ($304.15) suite. Breakfast 90 F ($17.10) extra. AE, DC, MC, V. Parking 40 F ($7.60). Bus 4.

This former pope's palace has long been the most desirable place to stay in the old city. Massively renovated, it's now luxurious, built within the actual walls, adjoining the cathedral. You enter into a long gothic corridor/gallery leading to the lounge. Many rooms open onto the ramparts and a garden and feature antiques or reproductions. Modern equipment has been discreetly installed, and there's also a heated pool. The hotel is renowned for its restaurant, La Barbacane, with its mock gothic windows and golden fleurs-de-lis shield and lion motifs. Chef Michel del Burgo trained under two of France's greatest, Alain Ducasse and Michel Guérard, and his imaginative cuisine incorporates the region's flavors. He's known for "celebration courses" of the southwest, like sautéed foie gras with liquid polenta that contains a thigh confit and duck hearts, a dish better tasted than described.

Ⓢ Hôtel des Remparts
3–5 place du Grand-Puits, 11000 Carcassonne. ☎ **68-71-27-72.** 18 rms. TEL. 280–330 F ($53.20–$62.70) double. Breakfast 35 F ($6.65) extra. MC, V. Parking 20 F ($3.80). Bus 4.

An abbey in the 12th century, this building was converted into a charming hotel in 1983 after major repairs to the masonry and roof. it's located at the edge of a stone square in the town center. The rooms contain no-frills furniture. The owners are most proud of the massive stone staircase that twists around itself. Make reservations at least two months ahead if you plan to stay here during summer.

AT THE ENTRANCE TO THE CITE

Ⓢ Hôtel du Donjon
2 rue du Comte-Roger, 11000 Carcassonne. ☎ **68-71-08-80,** or 800/528-1234 in the U.S. and Canada. Fax 68-25-06-60. 36 rms, 2 suites. MINIBAR TV TEL. 505 F ($96) double; 850 F ($161.60) suite. Continental breakfast 52 F ($9.90) extra. AE, DC, MC, V. Parking 40 F ($7.60). Bus 4.

This little hotel is big on charm, the best value in the moderate range. Built in the style of the old Cité, it has a honey-colored stone exterior with iron bars on the windows. The interior is a jewel, reflecting the sophistication of owner Christine Pujol. Elaborate Louis XIV–style furniture graces the reception lounges. A newer wing contains additional rooms in a medieval architectural style, and the older rooms have been renewed; 22 are air-conditioned. Their furnishings are in a severe style. The hotel also runs a restaurant nearby, the Brasserie le Donjon.

IN VILLE-BASSE

Hôtel Terminus
2 av. du Maréchal-Joffre, 11001 Carcassonne. ☎ **68-25-25-00.** Fax 68-72-53-09. 110 rms. TEL. 250–400 F ($47.50–$76) double. Breakfast 30 F ($5.70) extra. AE, DC, MC, V. Parking 30 F ($5.70). Bus 4.

This old-style hotel has many antique furnishings. Most rooms are spacious, with views of the mountains, the old city, or the river. The restaurant, Relais de l'Ecluse, offers very good meals in a grand setting, with fixed-price menus at 95 F ($18.05), 145 F ($27.55), and 200 F ($38). An air-conditioned minibus shuttle takes guests to the Cité twice a day.

WHERE TO DINE

Auberge du Pont-Levis

La Cité. ☎ 68-25-55-23. Reservations recommended. Main courses 70–150 F ($13.30–$28.50); fixed-price menus 130 F ($24.70), 195 F ($37.05), and 250 F ($47.50). AE, DC, MC, V. Tues–Sat noon–1:30pm and 8–9:30pm, Sun noon–1:30pm. Bus 4. FRENCH.

This auberge is at the entrance to the medieval city near Porte Narbonnaise. Its foundations are almost as old as the city. Dine either in a room one floor above street level or on a terrace ringed with flowers. Owner/chef Henri Pautard is aided by his wife, Andrée. They serve generous portions of roast pigeon in garlic purée, filet of sole with velouté of lobster, filet of sea bass with cabbage and smoked salmon, and hearty cassoulet. Much of the food shows a respect for tradition, and all the regional courses made with duck appear throughout the year, including the classic breast of duck with foie gras. But some courses are more imaginative, like leek-and-artichoke terrine.

Au Jardin de la Tour

11 rue Porte-d'Aude, Cité de Carcassonne. ☎ 68-25-71-24. Reservations recommended in summer. Main courses 70–140 F ($13.30–$26.60); fixed-price menus 140–220 F ($26.60–$41.80). AE, DC, MC, V. Daily noon–2pm and 8–10pm. Closed Wed Nov Easter. Bus 4. FRENCH.

A culinary team labors to create an authentic Languedoc cuisine. This restaurant is in the oldest part of the Cité, at the end of a long corridor. Menu choices include a large selection of salads, stuffed chicken, onglet of beef with shallots, confit of duckling, and the inevitable cassoulet, everybody's favorite.

❾ Le Languedoc

32 allée d'Iéna. ☎ 68-25-22-17. Reservations recommended. Main courses 90–140 F ($17.10–$26.60); fixed-price menus 130 F ($24.70), 175 F ($33.25), 220 F ($41.80), and 260 F ($49.40). AE, DC, MC, V. Tues–Sat noon–2:30pm and 7:30–9:30pm, Sun noon–2:30pm. Closed Dec 20–Jan 20. Bus 4. FRENCH.

Lucien Faugeras and his son, Didier, are both excellent chefs (they also own the Hôtel Montségur). The dining room has a warm Languedoc atmosphere, the proper setting for their culinary repertoire, achieved by rough plaster walls, ceiling beams, an open brick fireplace, and provincial cloths over peasant tables. The specialty is cassoulet au confit de canard (the famous stew made with duck cooked in its own fat). The pièce de résistance is tournedos Rossini, with foie gras truffé and madeira sauce. A smooth dessert is crêpes flambées Languedoc. In summer, dine on a pleasant patio or in the air-conditioned restaurant.

NEARBY ACCOMMODATIONS & DINING

✪ Domaine d'Auriac

Route St-Hilaire, 11000 Carcassonne. ☎ 68-25-72-22. Fax 68-47-35-54. 23 rms. MINIBAR TV TEL. 630–1,430 F ($119.75–$271.85) double. Breakfast 80 F ($15.20) extra. AE, DC, MC, V. Parking free. Closed Jan 8–Feb 2. Take D104 about 2 miles from Carcassonne.

The premier place for food and lodging is this moss-covered 19th-century manor house, boasting gardens with reflecting pools and flowered terraces. The uniquely decorated rooms in this Relais & Châteaux have a certain photo magazine glamour; some are in an older building with high ceilings, and others have a more modern decor. Renovations are ongoing. Bernard Rigaudis sets a grand table in his lovely dining room. In summer, meals are served beside the swimming pool on the terraces. The menu changes about five or six times yearly but might include truffles and purple artichokes with essences of pears and olives. Meals cost 190 to 390 F ($36.10 to $74.10). The restaurant is open daily from 12:30 to 2pm and 7:30 to 9:15pm. Reservations are required.

7 Collioure

577 miles SW of Paris, 17 miles SE of Perpignan

You may recognize this port and its sailboats from the Fauve paintings of Lhote and Derain. It's said to resemble St-Tropez before it was spoiled, attracting, in days of yore, Matisse, Picasso, and Dalí. Collioure is the most authentically alluring port of Roussillon, a gem with a vivid Spanish and Catalàn image and flavor. Some visitors believe it's the most charming village on the Côte Vermeille.

The two curving ports are separated from each other by the heavy masonry of the 13th-century **Château Royale,** place du 8-Mai-1945 (☎ **68-82-06-43**). The château, now a museum of modern painting and sculpture, is open June 20 to September, Wednesday to Monday from 10:30am to 6:30pm; March to June 19 and in October and November, Wednesday to Monday from 2 to 6pm (closed the rest of the year). Admission is 20 F ($3.80) for adults and 14 F ($2.65) for children. Also try to visit the **Musée Jean-Peské,** route de Port-Vendres (☎ **68-52-05-66**), with its collection of works by artists who migrated here to paint. It's open June to September, daily from 3 to 8pm; October to May, Wednesday to Monday from 2 to 7pm. Admission is 15 F ($2.85).

The town's sloping narrow streets, charming semifortified church, antique lighthouse, and eerily introverted culture make it worth an afternoon stopover.

ESSENTIALS

GETTING THERE   Collioure is serviced by frequent train and bus connections, especially from Perpignan. Many visitors drive along the coastal road (N14) leading to the Spanish border.

VISITOR INFORMATION   The Office de Tourisme is on place du 18-Juin (☎ **68-82-15-47**); closed in January.

WHERE TO STAY

☉ Les Caranques
Route de Port-Vendres, 66190 Collioure. ☎ **68-82-06-68.** Fax 68-82-00-92. 16 rms, 14 with bath. TEL. 530 F ($100.75) double without bath, 650 F ($123.55) double with bath. Rates include half board. AE, MC, V. Parking free. Closed Oct 10–Mar.

This hotel is well-scrubbed, comfortably furnished, personalized, and one of the best bargains in town. The terrace opens onto a view of the old port. The restaurant is for guests only, almost all of whom elect to stay on the half-board plan.

✪ Relais des Trois Mas et Restaurant la Balette
Route Port-Vendres. 66190 Collioure. ☎ **68-82-05-07.** Fax 68-82-38-08. 19 rms, 4 suites. A/C TV TEL. 850 F ($161.60) double; 995–1,680 F ($189.15–$319.40) suite. Breakfast 68 F ($12.90) extra. Closed Nov 13–Dec 15.

This premier hotel in town is also the restaurant of choice. The hotel honors the famous artists who've lived at Collioure in the decoration of its beautiful rooms, which lead to spacious baths. The rooms open onto views of the water. Even if you aren't a guest, you may want to take a meal in the dining room, with its views of the harbor. Christian Peyre is unchallenged as the lead chef of town. His cooking is inventive, often simple and refined.

WHERE TO DINE

Ⓢ La Pérouse

6 rue de la République. ☎ 68-82-05-60. Reservations recommended. Main courses 110–140 F ($20.90–$26.60); fixed-price menus 98 F ($18.60), 135 F ($25.65), and 198 F ($37.60). AE, MC, V. July–Sept, daily noon–2pm and 7–9:30pm. Closed Nov 26–Dec 26 and Tues in winter. FRENCH.

This restaurant occupies the whitewashed cellar of a building in the heart of town. Small windows illuminate the enormous antique barrels and the bullfighting accessories in back, though some visitors prefer a seat on the glassed-in veranda instead. The kitchens make few concessions to modern cuisine; instead, food is prepared with solid authenticity, following regional traditions. Menu items might include salade catalán, panaché of anchovies, spicy preparations of scallops, and bouillabaisse. Dessert might be a simple but satisfying crème caramel.

8 Perpignan

562 miles SW of Paris, 229 miles NW of Marseille

At Perpignan you may think you've crossed the border into Spain, for it was once Catalonia's second city, after Barcelona. Even earlier it was the capital of the kingdom of Majorca. But when the Roussillon—the French part of Catalonia—was finally partitioned off, Perpignan became French forever, authenticated by the Treaty of the Pyrénées in 1659. However, Catalàn is still spoken here, especially among the country people.

Perpignan derives its name from the legend of Père Pinya, a plowman said to have followed the Têt River down the mountain to the site of the town today, where he started cultivating the fertile soil, with the river carrying out its promise to water the fields.

ESSENTIALS

GETTING THERE   Six trains per day arrive from Paris (trip time: 10 hr.) and 12 trains from Marseille (trip time: 4 hr.). There are also five trains per day from Nice (trip time: 7 hr.).

If they're already on the French Riviera, motorists can continue west along A9 to Perpignan.

VISITOR INFORMATION   The Office Municipal du Tourisme is at the Palais des Congrès, place Armand-Lanoux (☎ 68-66-30-30).

SEEING THE TOP ATTRACTIONS

Among the chief sights, the **Castillet** (castle) is a machicolated and crenellated redbrick building that's a combination gateway and fortress from the 14th century. If you ask the keeper, you can climb the tower for a good view of the town. The Castillet houses **La Casa Païral**, place de Verdun (☎ 68-35-42-05), which has exhibitions of Catalàn regional artifacts and folkloric items, including typical dress. Admission is free, and it's open Wednesday to Monday: June to mid-September from 9:30 to 11:30am and 2:30 to 6:30pm, and mid-September to May from 9am to noon and 2 to 6pm.

The **Cathédrale St-Jean,** rue de l'Horloge (☎ 68-51-33-72), dates from the 14th and 15th centuries and has an admirable nave and interesting 17th-century retables. Leaving via the south door, you'll find on the left a chapel with the *Devout Christ,* a magnificent wood carving depicting Jesus contorted with pain and suffering—his head, crowned with thorns, drooping on his chest. The cathedral is open daily from 8am to noon and 2 to 7pm.

At the top of the town, the Spanish citadel encloses the **Palais des Rois de Majorque** (Palace of the Kings of Majorca), rue des Archers (☎ 68-34-48-29). This structure from the 13th and 14th centuries, built around a court encircled by arcades, has been restored by the government. You can see the old throne room with its large fireplaces and a square tower with a double gallery; from the tower there's a fine view of the Pyrénées. A guided tour—in French only—is mandatory and departs every 30 minutes, costing 20 F ($3.80) for adults and 10 F ($1.90) for students; children 7 and under free. It's open daily: June to September from 10am to 6pm, and October to May from 9am to 5pm.

WHERE TO STAY

Hôtel de la Loge

1 rue des Fabriques Nabot, 66000 Perpignan. ☎ **68-34-41-02.** Fax 68-34-25-13. 22 rms. MINIBAR TV TEL. 350 F ($66.50) double. Breakfast 35 F ($6.65) extra. AE, DC, MC, V.

This beguiling little place dates from the 16th century but has been renovated to become a modern three-star hotel. It's located right in the heart of town, near not only the Loge de Mer, from which it takes its name, but also the Castillet. It's also near a canal outlet of the Têt. The cozy rooms are attractively furnished.

Park Hotel

18 bd. Jean-Bourrat, 66000 Perpignan. ☎ **68-35-14-14.** Fax 68-35-48-18. 67 rms. A/C MINIBAR TV TEL. 260–500 F ($49.40–$95.05) double. Breakfast 40 F ($7.60) extra. AE, DC, MC, V. Parking 30 F ($5.70).

This hotel faces the Jardins de la Ville, and its rooms are well furnished and soundproof. A first-class cuisine is served in the restaurant, Le Chapon Fin, which offers both à la carte choices and fixed-price menus. Chef Eric Lecerf is the finest in the area, and he uses prime regional produce to turn out postnouvelle choices like roast sea scallops flavored with succulent sea urchin velouté, various lobster dishes, and penne with truffles. As an accompaniment, try a Collioure or Côtes du Roussillon. The restaurant is open for lunch Monday to Saturday and dinner Monday to Friday. The hotel also houses Le Bistrot du Park, specializing in seafood.

WHERE TO DINE

⑤ L'Apero

40 rue de la Fusterie. ☎ **68-51-21-14.** Reservations required. Main courses 60–90 F ($11.40–$17.10); fixed-price menus 69 F ($13.10) (lunch Mon–Fri only), 110 F ($20.90), and 160 F ($30.40). AE, DC, MC, V. Mon–Wed noon–2pm, Thurs–Sun noon–2pm and 7–11pm. FRENCH.

We've always found that this informal bistro serves the best-value menus in town. Most diners visit for lunch and its bargain menu of 69 F ($13.10) is only available then. This is "a nice little place," known for traditional cooking and a convivial atmosphere. Chef/owner Jean-Pierre Mariné offers such dishs as basil-stuffed salmon, filet of trout with sorrel, lamb cutlets in garlic-cream sauce, and tournedos in roquefort sauce.

Festin de Pierre

7 rue du Théâtre. ☎ **68-51-28-74.** Reservations required. Main courses 105–110 F ($19.95–$20.90); fixed-price menu 150 F ($28.50). AE, DC, MC, V. Thurs–Mon noon–2pm and 7–9:30pm, Tues noon–2pm. Closed Feb 8–28 and June 15–30. FRENCH.

This restaurant attracts a conservative and socially prestigious clientele who dine under a Renaissance-era ceiling. The excellent cuisine is traditional—no frivolity. In a clublike atmosphere, patrons enjoy offerings like red mullet cutlets with watercress salad, filet of turbot in champagne sauce, and veal kidneys in an aged sweet-wine sauce.

9 Narbonne

525 miles SW of Paris, 38 miles E of Carcassonne

Medieval Narbonne was a port to rival Marseille in Roman times, its "galleys laden with riches." It was the first town outside Italy to be colonized by the Romans, but the Mediterranean, now 5 miles away, left it high and dry. For that reason it's an intriguing place, steeped with antiquity.

ESSENTIALS

GETTING THERE Narbonne has rail, bus, and highway connections with other cities on the Mediterranean coast and with Toulouse. Rail travel is the most popular means of transport, with 14 trains per day arriving from Perpignan (trip time: 45 min.), 13 per day from Toulouse (trip time: 1½ hr.), and 12 per day from Montpellier (trip time: 55 min.).

VISITOR INFORMATION The Office de Tourisme is on place Roger-Salengro (☎ **68-65-15-60**).

TOURING THE TOP ATTRACTIONS

All the museums below sell a **global ticket** costing 10 F ($1.90) and entitling visitors to enter them over a period of 48 hours.

Construction of the **Basilique St-Just,** place de l'Hôtel-de-Ville (☎ **68-32-09-52**), began in 1272 but was never finished. Only the transept and a choir were completed; the choir is 130 feet high, built in the bold gothic style of northern France. At each end of the transept are 194-foot towers from 1480. There's an impressive collection of Flemish tapestries. The cloisters are from the 14th and 15th centuries and connect the cathedral with the Archbishops' Palace. It's open Tuesday to Sunday: March to October from 9:30am to 12:30pm and 3 to 7pm, and November to February from 10am to noon and 2 to 5pm. The **Palais des Archevêques (Archbishops' Palace)** (☎ **68-90-30-30**) is fortified, with three towers from the 13th and 14th centuries. The Old Palace on the right is from the 12th century and the so-called New Palace on the left is from the 14th. The neo-gothic **Hôtel de Ville** (town hall), part of the complex, was constructed by Viollet-le-Duc from 1845 to 1850.

The archbishops of Narbonne lived elegantly in the **Palais Neuf (New Palace).** The archbishops' rooms are reached by climbing 88 steps up the monumental Louis XIII staircase. It's said that the old archbishops were hauled up the stairs on mules. Today these apartments have been converted into museums.

The **Musée Archéologique** (☎ 68-90-30-30) has prehistoric artifacts, Bronze Age tools, 14th-century frescoes, and Greco-Roman amphorae. Several of the sarcophagi date from the 3rd century, and some of the mosaics are of pagan origin. It's open Tuesday to Sunday: May to October from 9:30am to 12:30pm and 3 to 7pm, and November to April from 10am to noon and 2 to 5pm. The **Musée d'Art et d'Histoire** (☎ 68-90-30-30) is three floors above street level in the former private apartments, the rooms in which Louis XII stayed during his siege of Perpignan. Their coffered ceilings are enhanced with panels depicting the nine Muses. A Roman mosaic floor and 17th-century portraits are on display. There's also a collection of antique porcelain, enamels, and a portrait bust of Louis XIV. This museum has the same hours as the Musée Archéologique. The **Donjon Gilles-Aycelin,** from the late 13th century, has a lofty observation platform with a view of the cathedral, the surrounding plain, and the Pyrénées.

You can see Roman artifacts at the **Musée Lapidaire,** place Lamourguier (☎ 68-65-53-58), in the 13th-century Eglise de Lamourguier. The broken sculptures, Roman inscriptions, and relics of medieval buildings make up one of the largest such exhibits in France and one of the most important. It's open Monday to Saturday from 10 to 11:50am and 2 to 6pm.

The early gothic **Basilique St-Paul-Serge,** rue de l'Hôtel-Dieu (☎ 68-41-09-82), was built on the site of a 4th-century necropolis. It has an elegant choir with fine Renaissance wood carving and some ancient Christian sarcophagi. The chancel from 1229 is admirable. The north door leads to the Paleo-Christian Cemetery, part of an early Christian burial ground. It's open daily from 9am to 5pm.

WHERE TO STAY

Languedoc
22 bd. Gambetta, 11100 Narbonne. ☎ **68-65-14-74.** Fax 68-65-81-48. 42 rms, 4 suites. TEL. 290–380 F ($55.10–$72.20) double; 480 F ($91.20) suite. Breakfast 38 F ($7.20) extra. AE, DC, MC, V. Parking 30 F ($5.70).

This modernized hotel is near the canal de la Rhône. Owned by the Lion family, it offers well-equipped rooms and a restaurant serving regional specialties. Typical Languedoc dishes include grilled salmon with anchovy butter, tender lamb cooked with beans, veal liver provençal, and sautéed chicken chasseur. The hotel's English Pub is open daily from 6pm to 2am.

⑤ La Résidence
6 rue du 1er-Mai, 11100 Narbonne. ☎ **68-32-19-41.** Fax 68-65-51-82. 26 rms. A/C TV TEL. 450–490 F ($85.55–$93.15) double. MC, V. Parking 50 F ($9.50).

Our favorite hotel in Narbonne is near the Cathédrale St-Just. The 19th-century La Résidence is comfortable and decorated with antiques. It doesn't have a restaurant but offers breakfast. The welcome is gracious.

WHERE TO DINE

L'Alsace
2 av. Pierre-Sémard. ☎ **68-65-10-24.** Reservations recommended. Main courses 120–160 F ($22.80–$30.40); fixed-price menus 98 F ($18.60), 120 F ($22.80), and 150 F ($28.50). AE, DC, MC, V. Mon 12:30–2pm, Wed–Sun 12:30–2pm and 7:30–9:30pm. FRENCH.

Across from the railroad station, this restaurant is one of the best in Narbonne. The comfortable dining room is done in an English style, with a long menu. In spite of the name of the restaurant, the cuisine is not of Alsace-Lorraine in eastern France, but more typical of the food of western France. The Sinfreus, the owners, offer a fry of red mullet, a savory kettle of bourride, and magrêt of duck with flap mushrooms. One specialty is assiette des pêcheurs, containing grilled portions of many kinds of fish, plus a lobster salad.

Aux 3 Caves

4 rue Benjamin. ☎ **68-65-28-60.** Reservations required. Main courses 82–110 F ($15.60–$20.90); fixed-price menus 98 F ($18.60), 160 F ($30.40), and 215 F ($40.85). AL, DC, V. Wed 7–9:30pm, Thurs–Mon noon–2pm and 7–9:30pm. FRENCH.

This excellent restaurant is in restored romanesque cellars. The owners offer an elegant decor and present a classic menu, their repertoire focusing on popular platters from the region. They're known for their traditional cassoulet but also prepare confit of duckling with garlic, platters of fresh sardines cooked in white wine, grilled turbot, and gratin of snails.

10 Montpellier

471 miles SW of Paris, 100 miles NW of Marseille, 31 miles SW of Nîmes

The capital of Mediterranean (or Lower) Languedoc, this ancient university city is still renowned for its medical school, founded in the 13th century. Nostradamus qualified as a doctor here, and even Rabelais studied at the school. Petrarch came to Montpellier in 1317, staying for seven years.

ESSENTIALS

GETTING THERE   Twenty trains per day arrive from Avignon (trip time: 1 hr.), 8 from Marseille (trip time: $1^3/4$ hr.), 1 per hour from Toulouse (trip time: 2 hr.), and 10 per day from Perpignan (trip time: $1^1/2$ hr.). Nine trains per day arrive from Paris, calling for a change in Lyon (trip time: 5 hr.). Two buses a day arrive from Nîmes (trip time: $1^3/4$ hr.). For motorists, Montpellier lies off A9 heading west.

VISITOR INFORMATION   The Office de Tourisme is at 78 av. du Pirée (☎ 67-22-06-16).

EXPLORING THE TOWN

Paul Valéry met André Gide in the **Jardin des Plantes** (☎ 67-63-43-22), and you might begin there, as it's the oldest such garden in France, from the 15th century. Reached from boulevard Henri-IV, this botanical garden, filled with exotic plants, was opened in 1593. Admission is free, and it's open daily from 9am to noon and 2 to 5pm. Nearby is the **Cathédrale St-Pierre,** on place St-Pierre (☎ 67-66-04-12), founded in 1364. Once the church of a Benedictine monastery, the cathedral suffered badly in religious wars. (After 1795 the monastery was occupied by the medical school.) Today it has a somewhat-bleak west front with two towers and a canopied porch.

Called the Oxford of France, Montpellier is a city of young people, as you'll notice if you sit at a café opening onto the heartbeat **place de la Comédie,** admiring the Théâtre, the 18th-century Fountain of the Three Graces, or whatever else amuses you. It's the living room of Montpellier, the meeting place of students from all over the world who study here.

The ✪ **Musée Fabre,** 39 bd. Bonne-Nouvelle (☎ 67-66-06-34), is one of France's great provincial art galleries, occupying the former Hôtel de Massilian, where Molière once played for a season. The origins of the collection were an exhibition of the Royal Academy that was sent to Montpellier by Napoléon in 1803. The most important works of the collection, however, were given by François Fabre, a Montpellier painter, in 1825. After Fabre's death, many other paintings from his collection were donated to the gallery. Several of these he painted himself, but the more important works were ones he had acquired—including Poussin's *Venus and Adonis* and Italian paintings like *The Mystical Marriage of Saint Catherine.* This generosity was followed by donations from other parties, notably Valedau, who in 1836 left his collection of Rubens, Gérard Dou, and Téniers. The museum is open Tuesday to Friday from 9am to 5:30pm and Saturday and Sunday from 9:30am to 5pm. Admission is 16 F ($3.05).

Before leaving town, take a stroll along the 17th-century **promenade du Peyrou,** a terraced park with views of the Cévennes and the Mediterranean. This is a broad esplanade constructed at the loftiest point of Montpellier. Opposite the entrance is an Arc de Triomphe, erected in 1691 to celebrate the victories of Louis XIV. In the center of the promenade is an equestrian statue of Louis XIV, and at the end, the **Château d'Eau,** a monument to 18th-century classicism, a pavilion with Corinthian columns. Water is brought here by a conduit, nearly 9 miles long, and an aqueduct.

WHERE TO STAY
EXPENSIVE

Alliance-Métropole
3 rue Clos-René, 34000 Montpellier. ☎ **67-58-11-22.** Fax 67-92-13-02. 81 rms, 4 suites. A/C MINIBAR TV TEL. 580 F ($110.25) double; 680–880 F ($129.25–$167.30) suite. Breakfast 70 F ($13.30) extra. AE, DC, MC, V. Parking 40 F ($7.60). Bus 7 or 9.

Superior rooms in the heart of Montpellier can be found at the Métropole, which has been completely brought up-to-date while retaining a certain nostalgia. The agreeably decorated rooms are well equipped and have marble baths. Ask for one of the rooms overlooking the unusual interior garden, as these have a pleasant view and are quieter.

Sofitel Antigone
1 rue Pertuisanes, 34000 Montpellier. ☎ **67-65-62-63.** Fax 67-65-17-50. 90 rms, 1 suite. A/C TV TEL. 715 F ($135.90) double; 1,400 F ($266.15) suite. Breakfast 80 F ($15.20) extra. AE, DC, V.

In the heart of Montpellier, this hotel is the obvious favorite of the traveling businessperson. However, in summer it does quite a business with the tourists. It's particularly distinguished for its hotel pool, of which there aren't many. The rooms are chain format but first class. The best accommodations are on a floor known as Privilège, and here you get such extras as an all-marble bath. Some rooms are suitable for the disabled. It's a winning choice, with the most efficient staff in the city.

MODERATE

Hôtel George-V
42 av. St-Lazare, 34000 Montpellier. ☎ **67-72-35-91.** Fax 67-72-53-33. 39 rms. TV TEL. 360 F ($68.40) double. Breakfast 45 F ($8.55) extra. AE, DC, MC, V. Parking free. Bus 7 or 9.

Located near a park on the northern edge of the city, this well-managed hotel offers traditionally furnished rooms. Some wear and tear shows, but it's a good value nevertheless. The bar is for guests only.

INEXPENSIVE

⑤ Les Arceaux

33–35 bd. des Arceaux, 34000 Montpellier. ☎ **67-92-03-03.** Fax 67-92-05-09. 18 rms. TV TEL. 275–315 F ($52.25–$59.85) double. Breakfast 33 F ($6.25) extra. MC, V. Parking free. Bus 9.

A hotel has been here since the turn of the century. Its location is excellent, right off the renowned promenade du Peyrou. The rooms are pleasantly but simply furnished, and a shady terrace adjoins the hotel. Breakfast is the only meal served.

WHERE TO DINE

Le Chandelier

Immeuble La Coupole Antigone. ☎ **67-92-61-62.** Reservations required. Main courses 120–200 F ($22.80–$38); fixed-price menus 150 F ($28.50) (lunch only), 250 F ($47.50), 300 F ($57), and 360 F ($68.40). AE, DC, MC, V. Mon 7:30–9:30pm, Tues–Sat noon–1:30pm and 7:30–9:30pm. Bus 7 or 9. FRENCH.

This is a modern showcase for the cuisine of Gilbert Furland, a panoramic restaurant with large windows and even private parking. He searches for "temptations of the palate," which means you'll find some unusual flavor combinations. The ragoût of lobster is perhaps his most delightful dish. His menu changes frequently but may include smoked eel mousse with mint-flavored mussels, lamb sweetbreads with crayfish in vinaigrette sauce, veal kidneys in basil, and a mosaic of hare with foie gras.

✪ Jardin des Sens

11 av. St-Lazare. ☎ **67-79-63-38.** Reservations required. Main courses 120–225 F ($22.80–$42.75); fixed-price weekday lunch 165 F ($31.35); fixed-price menus 270–430 F ($51.30–$81.70). AE, V. Mon–Sat noon–2:30pm and 7–10pm. Closed Jan 2–15 and July 25–Aug 15. FRENCH.

If we could award more than one star, we'd grant two to this citadel of fine cuisine. Twin chefs Laurent and Jacques Pourcel have taken Montpellier by storm. Michelin has awarded them two stars, thus bestowing its divine blessing. Postnouvelle reigns here. The rich bounty of the Languedoc is served, but only after going through a process designed to enhance its natural flavor. The meals at times seem flawless, and no wonder restaurateurs of Montpellier are wishing these twins had settled in some other city. The cuisine could be almost anything, depending on where the twins' imaginations roam. A mackerel tart we sampled one late autumn day was truly memorable. So was a bacon-flavored fricassée of langoustines and lamb sweetbreads.

✪ L'Olivier

12 rue Aristide-Olivier. ☎ **67-92-86-28.** Reservations not required. Main courses 98–145 F ($18.60–$27.55); fixed-price menus 145–187 F ($27.55–$35.55). AE, DC, MC, V. Tues–Sat noon–1:30pm and 7:30–9:30pm. Closed Aug 6–Sept 3. Bus 7 or 9. FRENCH.

Perhaps no restaurant, with the exception of Jardin des Sens, has improved more than this. Chef Michel Breton is making his name known in the restaurant guides to the south of France. The decor is something out of a 1950s boudoir, but they don't come here for background—they want to try Breton's "creative statements."

Some courses that might appear regularly are salmon with oysters, fricassée of lamb with thyme, warm monkfish terrine, and salad of lamb sweetbreads with extract of truffles. The welcome is warm-hearted and sincere.

11 Aigues-Mortes

466 miles SW of Paris, 39 miles NE of Sète

South of Nîmes you can explore a lot of the Camargue by car. The most rewarding target is Aigues-Mortes, the city of the "dead waters." In the middle of dismal swamps and melancholy lagoons, Aigues-Mortes is France's most perfectly preserved walled town. Four miles from the sea, it stands on four navigable canals. Once Louis IX and his crusaders set forth from Aigues-Mortes, then a thriving port, the first in France on the Mediterranean. The walls, which still enclose the town, were constructed between 1272 and 1300. The **Tour de Constance** (☎ **66-53-61-55**) is a model castle of the Middle Ages, its stones looking out on the marshes. At the top, which you can reach by elevator, a panoramic view unfolds. Admission is 26 F ($4.95) for those 25 or older, 17 F ($3.25) for those 18 to 24, and 7 F ($1.35) for children 17 and under. The monument is open daily: June to September from 9am to 7pm, and October to March from 9:30am to noon and 2 to 4:30pm.

ESSENTIALS

GETTING THERE   Five trains per day connect Aigues-Mortes and Nîmes (trip time: 40 min.), and four buses per day arrive from Nîmes (trip time: 55 min.).

VISITOR INFORMATION   There's an Office de Tourisme at porte de la Gardette (☎ **66-53-73-00**).

WHERE TO STAY

Hostellerie des Remparts

6 place d'Armes, 30220 Aigues-Mortes. ☎ **66-53-82-77.** 19 rms. TEL. 280–380 F ($53.20–$72.20) double. Breakfast 37 F ($7.05) extra. AE, DC, V. Parking free.

Established about 300 years ago, this weather-worn inn is at the foot of the Tour de Constance, adjacent to the fortifications. Popular and often fully booked (especially in summer), it has a narrow stone staircase and rooms with simple furniture; 10 contain TVs. Breakfast is the only meal served.

St-Louis

10 rue de l'Admiral-Courbet, 30220 Aigues-Mortes. ☎ **66-53-72-68.** Fax 66-53-75-92. 22 rms. MINIBAR TV TEL. 490 F ($93.15) double. Breakfast 45 F ($8.55) extra. AE, DC, MC, V. Parking 45 F ($8.55). Closed Jan–Mar 14.

This small inn near place St-Louis offers attractively furnished but somewhat basic rooms—nevertheless it's one of the most desirable addresses in town. The restaurant serves good regional food, with meals costing 100 to 180 F ($19 to $34.20).

WHERE TO DINE

Restaurant les Arcades

23 bd. Gambetta, 30220 Aigues-Mortes. ☎ **66-53-81-13.** Fax 66-53-75-46. Reservations recommended. Main courses 75–165 F ($14.25–$31.35). AE, DC, MC, V. Tues 7:30–9:30pm, Wed–Sun noon–2pm and 7:30–9:30pm. Closed Feb 15–Mar 15 and two weeks in Nov. FRENCH.

This restaurant has several formal sections with ancient beamed ceilings or intricately fitted stone vaults. Almost as old as the nearby fortifications, the place is especially charming on sultry days, when the thickness of the masonry keeps the interior cool. Good food is served at reasonable prices and is likely to include lobster fricassée, bouillabaisse, and grilled duckling.

The owner also rents six large comfortable rooms upstairs, with doubles costing 450 F ($85.50); three guests in the same room cost 500 F ($95.05). Breakfast is 60 F ($11.40) extra.

12 Nîmes

440 miles S of Paris, 27 miles W of Avignon

Nîmes, the ancient Nemausus, is one of the finest places in the world for wandering among Roman relics. A busy industrial city today, it's the gateway to the Rhône Valley and Provence.

ESSENTIALS

GETTING THERE Nîmes has bus and train service from the rest of France and is near several autoroutes. It lies on the main rail line between Marseille and Bordeaux. Six trains a day arrive from Paris, taking $4^1/_2$ hours.

VISITOR INFORMATION The Office de Tourisme is at 6 rue Auguste (☎ 66-67-29-11).

EXPLORING THE TOWN

The pride of Nîmes is the **Maison Carrée,** place de la Comédie (☎ 66-36-26-76), built during the reign of Augustus. On a raised platform with tall Corinthian columns, it's one of the most beautiful and certainly one of the best-preserved Roman temples of Europe. It inspired the builders of the Madeleine in Paris as well as Thomas Jefferson. Contemporary art exhibits are staged here. It's open daily: June to September from 9am to 7pm, and October to May from 9am to 5:30pm. Admission is free. Across the square stands its twin, the **Carreé d'Art,** an architectural study in glass and aluminum, from 1985. It houses a library and the **Musée d'Art Contemporain** (☎ 66-76-35-70), with seasonal exhibits of contemporary art. It's open Tuesday to Sunday from 11am to 7pm, charging 20 F ($3.80) for adults and 15 F ($2.85) for children.

The elliptically shaped **Amphithéâtre Romain,** place des Arènes (☎ 66-76-72-77), a twin to the one at Arles, is far more complete than the Colosseum of Rome. It's two stories high, each story with 60 arches, and was built of huge stones fitted together without mortar. One of the best preserved of the arenas from ancient times, it held more than 20,000 spectators who came to see gladiatorial combats and wolf or boar hunts. Today it's used for everything from ballet recitals to bullfights and is open daily: June to September from 9am to 7pm, and October to May from 9am to noon and 2 to 5:30pm. Admission is 20 F ($3.80) for adults and 15 F ($2.85) for children.

The **Jardin de la Fontaine,** at the end of quai de la Fontaine, was laid out in the 18th century, using the ruins of a Roman shrine. It was planted with rows of chestnuts and elms, adorned with statuary and urns, and intersected by grottos and canals—making it one of the most beautiful gardens in France. Adjoining it is the ruined Temple of Diana and the remains of some Roman baths. Over the park towers **Mont Cavalier,** surmounted by the Tour Magne, the city's oldest Roman monument, which you can climb for a panoramic view.

Nîmes has a number of museums. Our favorite is the **Musée des Beaux-Arts,** rue Cité-Foulc (☎ 66-67-38-21), containing French paintings and sculptures from the 17th to the 20th century as well as Flemish, Dutch, and Italian works from the 15th to the 18th century. Seek out in particular one of G. B. Moroni's masterpieces, *La Calomnie d'Apelle*, and a well-preserved Gallo-Roman mosaic. The museum is open Tuesday to Sunday from 11am to 6pm. Admission is 20 F ($3.80) for adults and 15 F ($2.85) for children. If time allows, visit the **Musée du Vieux-Nîmes,** place de la Cathédrale (☎ 66-36-00-64), housed in an episcopal palace from the 1600s. It's rich in antiques, including pieces from the 17th century. The museum is open Tuesday to Sunday from 11am to 6pm, charging 20 F ($3.80) for adults and 15 F ($2.85) for children.

One of the city's busiest thoroughfares, boulevard de l'Amiral-Courbet, leads to the **Porte d'Arles**—the remains of a monumental gate built by the Romans during the reign of Augustus. Farther along are the **Musée de Préhistoire et d'Histoire Naturelle,** the **Musée Archéologique,** and the **Musée Taurin,** devoted to bullfighting and its memorabilia. All three are housed in the former Collège des Jésuites, whose church was once one of the region's Catholic strongholds.

Outside the city, the Roman **Pont du Gard** spans the Gard River and was built without mortar; its huge stones have stood the test of time. Consisting of three tiers of arches, it dates from about 19 B.C. Frédéric Mistral recorded a legend claiming that the devil constructed the bridge providing he could claim the soul of the first person to go across. To visit it, take N86.

WHERE TO STAY
EXPENSIVE
Imperator Concorde
Quai de la Fontaine, 30900 Nîmes. ☎ **66-21-90-30.** Fax 66-67-70-25. 65 rms, 3 suites. A/C MINIBAR TV TEL. 530–1,000 F ($100.70–$190) double; 1,800 F ($342) suite. Breakfast 65 F ($12.35) extra. AE, DC, MC, V. Parking 70 F ($13.30). Bus 3 or 5.

This leading hotel is near the Roman monuments, opposite the Jardin de la Fontaine. With a recent major renovation, it has been much improved. You can order lunch in the hotel's enticing rear gardens. The best rooms have Provençal pieces; others have been renewed in a traditional way to preserve their character.

Mercure Nîmes-Ouest
Parc Hôtellier Ville Active, 30900 Nîmes. ☎ **66-84-14-55.** Fax **66-38-01-44.** 98 rms. A/C MINIBAR TV TEL. 460 F ($87.40) double. Breakfast 50 F ($9.50) extra. AE, DC, MC, V. Parking free. Bus 4.

This hotel is outside the city but only a five-minute drive from the arena and Maison Carrée. The design is contemporary, and the furnishings are attractive. There are also an adjoining pool area, a sun terrace, and a tennis court. The hotel restaurant, Le Mazet, serves grilled meats and regional dishes. Though motorists find it convenient, don't come here seeking old-world charm.

MODERATE
Le Louvre
2 square de la Couronne, 30000 Nîmes. ☎ **66-67-22-75.** Fax 66-36-07-27. 31 rms, 2 suites. TV TEL. 380 F ($72.20) double; 450 F ($85.50) suite. Breakfast 35 F ($6.65) extra. AE, DC, MC, V. Parking 75 F ($14.25). Bus 3 or 5.

Nîmes

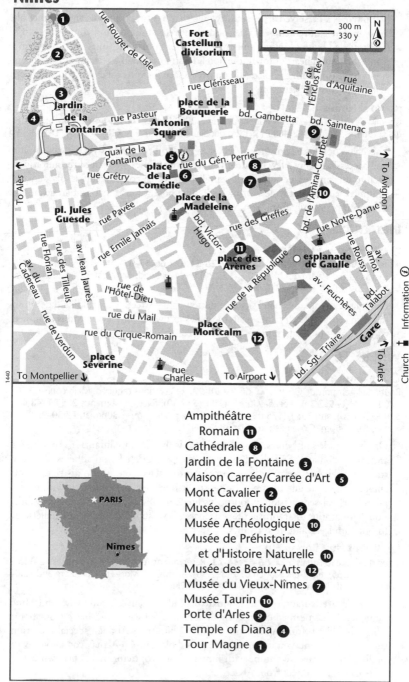

Ampithéâtre Romain ⑪
Cathédrale ⑧
Jardin de la Fontaine ③
Maison Carrée/Carrée d'Art ⑤
Mont Cavalier ②
Musée des Antiques ⑥
Musée Archéologique ⑩
Musée de Préhistoire et d'Histoire Naturelle ⑩
Musée des Beaux-Arts ⑫
Musée du Vieux-Nîmes ⑦
Musée Taurin ⑩
Porte d'Arles ⑨
Temple of Diana ④
Tour Magne ①

Le Louvre is a preserved 17th-century villa that has functioned as an inn since almost anyone can remember. The rooms are well equipped and comfortable, if a bit tarnished, some looking out over an inner courtyard lined with flowering plants. Set in the heart of town, the hotel doesn't maintain a restaurant but directs guests to nearby dining choices. If you need space for your car, reserve it when you make your room reservation.

Novotel Nîmes

Chemin de l'Hostellerie, bd. Périphérique Sud, 30000 Nîmes. ☎ **66-84-60-20.** Fax 66-38-02-31. 96 rms. A/C TV TEL. 480 F ($91.25) double. Breakfast 48 F ($9.10) extra. AE, DC, MC, V.

This chain hotel is one of the city's best, if you don't demand style and charm. It's easily accessible, only a few hundred feet from the Nîmes Sud exit of the autoroute. Each room contains a double bed, a single bed (which converts into a sofa), a well-equipped bath, and a wide writing desk. The hotel offers a bar and an attractive restaurant open daily from 6am to midnight.

INEXPENSIVE

⑤ Hôtel l'Amphithéâtre

4 rue des Arènes, 30000 Nîmes. ☎ **66-67-28-51.** Fax **66-67-07-79.** 18 rms. TV TEL. 220–260 F ($41.80–$49.40) double; 280 F ($53.20) triple or quad. Breakfast 33 F ($6.25) extra. MC, V. Closed Dec 22–Jan 28. Bus 3 or 5.

Behind the Arènes, this hotel sits on a narrow, quiet street. The building dates from the 18th century. Each rather plain room has its own color scheme and is furnished with antiques or modern pieces.

WHERE TO DINE

✪ Alexandre

Route de l'Aéroport de Garons. ☎ **66-70-08-99.** Reservations required. Main courses 130–170 F ($24.70–$32.30); weekday lunch 170 F ($32.30); fixed-price menus 255 F ($48.45), 320 F ($60.80), and 395 F ($75.05). AE, MC, V. Tues–Sat noon–1:30pm and 7:30–9:30pm, Sun noon–1:30pm. Closed Feb 26–Mar 13. FRENCH.

On the outskirts of Nîmes, near the airport, is this fine restaurant. It's the elegant and rustic domain of Michel Kayser, an exceptional chef who adheres to classic tradition. The dessert tray is one of the most delectable in the district. Menu choices might include rillette of home-smoked eel or flan of foie gras with truffle juice. Chef Kayser's version of tournedos Frédéric-Mistral has won culinary awards. Equally tempting is ambrosia of gamecock with Chinese cabbage and gallette of turbot with leeks and fresh truffles.

Le Bistrot du Chapon Fin

3 rue du Château-Fadaise. ☎ **66-67-34-73.** Reservations required. Main courses 72–115 F ($13.70–$21.85); fixed-price lunch 68 F ($12.90). AE, MC, V. Mon–Fri noon–2pm and 7:30–10pm, Sat 7:30–10pm. Closed Aug. Bus 3 or 5. FRENCH.

This tavern/restaurant, on a little square behind St. Paul's, is run by M. and Mme Grangier. It has beamed ceilings, small lamps, and a white-and-black stone floor. Mme Grangier is from Alsace, and the menu has many Alsatian specialties. From the à la carte menu you can order foie gras d'oie-truffé d'Alsace, coq au vin with riesling, and entrecôte flambé with morels. The proprietor makes his own confit d'oie from geese direct from Alsace.

San Francisco Wine Bar

11 place de la Couronne. ☎ 66-76-19-59. Reservations not required. Main courses 50–120 F ($9.50–$22.80); fixed-price lunch 77 F ($14.65). AE, DC, MC, V. Tues–Sat noon–2pm and 7pm–midnight, Sun noon–2pm. Bus 3 or 5. FRENCH.

This is the most famous and creative American eatery in the south of France. The place is paneled with mahogany and has leather banquettes you might've found in a turn-of-the-century California saloon. An array of salads and platters are served, and at lunch you can order a quick menu, including an appetizer, a garnished main course, and two glasses of wine. Typical dishes are magrêt of duckling and contrefilet of steak with roquefort sauce. There are more than 300 varieties of wine, by the glass or pitcher.

24 Provence

Provence has been called a bridge between the past and present, where yesterday blends with today in a quiet, often melancholy way. Peter Mayle's best-selling *A Year in Provence* (as well as the TV movie based on the book) has played no small part in the burgeoning popularity this sunny corner of southern France has enjoyed during recent years.

The Greeks and Romans first filled the landscape with cities boasting Hellenic theaters, Roman baths, amphitheaters, and triumphal arches. These were followed in medieval times by romanesque fortresses and gothic cathedrals. In the 19th century Provence's light and landscapes attracted illustrious painters like Cézanne and van Gogh. Despite the changes over the years, the howling mistral will forever be heard through the broad-leaved plane trees.

Provence has its own language and its own customs. The region is bounded on the north by the Dauphine, the west by the Rhône, the east by the Alps, and the south by the Mediterranean. We'll focus in the next chapter on the part of Provence known as the glittering Côte d'Azur.

REGIONAL CUISINE   Part of Provence's charm lies in its distinctive cuisine, which successfully marries the traditions of mountains and seaside. The earliest contributors to this were probably the ancient Italians, for strong comparisons can be made between the Provençal and the Italian emphasis on fresh fish and vegetables, olive oil, and garlic.

The best of Provençal produce includes melons from Cavaillon and elongated tube-shaped onions known as *éschalotes-bananes*. The most famous vegetable dish is *ratatouille*, a stew of tomatoes, garlic, eggplant, zucchini, onions, and peppers, liberally sprinkled with olive oil and black pepper. A slightly different version is *soupe au pistou*, with the addition of basil, pounded garlic, vermicelli, strong beans, and grilled tomatoes.

Each town along the Provence coast seems to have a fish-stew specialty: In Nice stockfish is used in *stocaficada*. *Bourride* is made with whitefish, garlic, onions, tomatoes, herbs, egg yolks, saffron, and grated orange rind. Toulon has its *esquinado*, with saltwater crabs, vinegar, water, and pulverized mussels. And the best and most authentic *bouillabaisse* is from Marseille.

Provence

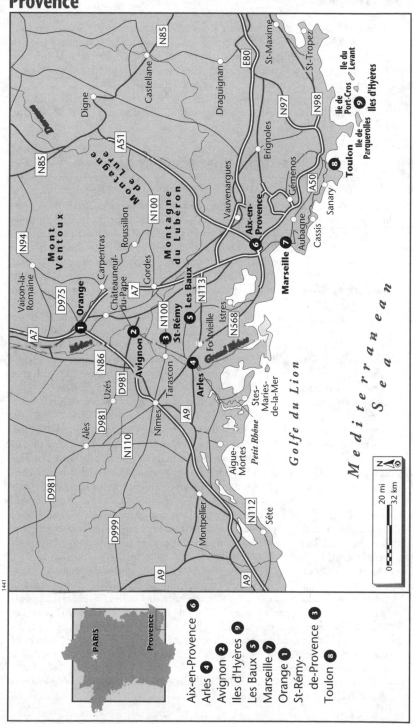

Aix-en-Provence ⑥
Arles ④
Avignon ②
Iles d'Hyères ⑨
Les Baux ⑤
Marseille ⑦
Orange ①
St-Rémy-
de-Provence ③
Toulon ⑧

PARIS

Provence

N85
N85
N94
A51
Montagne de Lure
Digne
Castellane
E80
St-Maxime
St-Tropez
Ile du Levant
Draguignan
N97
N98
Ile de Port-Cros
⑨ Iles d'Hyères
Mont Ventoux
Vaison-la-Romaine
D975
Orange
Carpentras
Châteauneuf-du-Pape
Roussillon
N100
Gordes
Montagne du Lubéron
Vauvenargues
Brignoles
⑧ Toulon
Ile de Parquerolles
A7
N86
A7
③ N100
St-Rémy
⑤ Les Baux
N113
Istres
N568
Aix-en-Provence ⑥
⑦ Marseille
Gémenos
A50
Aubagne
Cassis
Sanary
Uzés
D981
D981
Avignon
② Tarascon
① Durance
④ Arles
Fontvieille
Grand Rhône
Alès
N110
Nîmes
A9
Stes-Maries-de-la-Mer
Petit Rhône
Golfe du Lion
Mediterranean Sea
D981
Aigue-Mortes
D999
Montpellier
N112
Sète
A9
A9

N
20 mi
32 km
0

Several Provençal meat dishes are welcome substitutes for the ubiquitous fish: *daube de boeuf* (beef stew); *fricassée de pintade* (guinea fowl), perhaps served with a mild purée of sweet garlic; and a fricassée or *ragoût de cabri* (goat). Provence boasts scores of savory cheeses, among them Picadon, Pélardon, and St-Félicien; dozens of pastries and breads; and many scented honeys.

The regional wines are almost as diverse as the cuisine. They include the vast family of the Côtes-du-Rhône, the Gigondas, the Châteauneuf-du-Pape, and the Château de Fonsalette.

EXPLORING THE REGION BY CAR

Here's how to link together the best of the region if you rent a car.

Day 1   Begin in Orange, with Roman ruins and *charme méridionale*. After touring the monumental zone, continue south for 8 miles along A9 to Châteauneuf-du-Pape, where you can dine at the Hostellerie du Château des Fines-Roches, route d'Avignon (☎ 90-83-70-23). Though it was built in the 19th century, it looks feudal, thanks to its many medieval features. The hostelry offers overnight accommodation, but we suggest you stop only for lunch. Then continue on to Avignon, 8 miles south along any of at least three highways (each marked "Avignon"), and spend the night there.

Day 2   From Avignon, drive 13 miles south to St-Rémy de Provence. Leave Avignon along N570, then detour east along country roads signposted for the destination. When you get there, it might be time for lunch at the Bar/Hôtel/Restaurant des Arts, 32 bd. Victor-Hugo (☎ 90-02-08-50). It's not the most elegant dining spot in town, but it wonderfully evokes the "bohemian" spirit that drew many painters to St-Rémy. Now continue southwest for another 15 miles along roads signposted to "Arles." Look for a view of one of the town's romanesque highlights—the Eglise St-Trophime. Spend the night in Arles.

Day 3   From Arles, drive northeast for 6 miles along country roads to Fontveille, where the collection at the Musée Alphonse-Daudet will appeal to aficionados of French literature. From here, drive northeast 9 miles to Les Baux de Provence. This town makes a fine overnight stop, but after you've toured its feudal ramparts, consider extending your day by continuing for an overnight trip (or making a round-trip twilight excursion) to Gordes, about 27 miles northeast; your excursion will give you a glimpse of Provençal countryside you might not otherwise have seen. (There are about five ways to reach Gordes from Les Baux: A suitably scenic route takes you back to St-Rémy, east along D99, then over country roads whose signs point toward Coustellet and Gordes.)

Day 4   Today's final destination is Aix-en-Provence, one of the region's centerpieces of art, commerce, and culture. If you spent the night in Les Baux and didn't make it to Gordes, make it a point today to visit Gordes, its château, and its Vasarely museum as part of an early-morning excursion. To reach Aix from Les Baux de Provence, head east along D5, E80, and then A8 for 40 miles. To reach Aix from Gordes, head southwest from Gordes for 11 miles to the hamlet of Cavaillon (the name of the town is signposted from Gordes), then drive southwest along A8 for 32 miles to Aix.

Once you've toured Aix, consider an excursion to the Château de Vauvenarges, site of Pablo Picasso's last home. Reach it from Aix by traveling 10 miles east on

What's Special About Provence

Beaches
- Ile de Porquerolles, off the coast, whose northern shore is made up of herb-bordered beaches.

Architectural Highlights
- Cours Mirabeau, the main street of Aix-en-Provence, one of the most beautiful in Europe.
- Pont St-Bénézet, at Avignon, the famous bridge of the ditty "Sur le Pont d'Avignon."

Great Towns
- Marseille, capital of Provence, the largest French seaport and the second-largest city of France.
- Avignon, "city of the popes," surrounded by nearly intact ramparts.
- Aix-en-Provence, a historic city of monuments, museums, and memories of famous painters.
- Arles, the former capital and a typical Roman city of Provence.
- Les Baux, the most spectacular village of Provence, "a nesting place for eagles."

Ancient Monuments
- Château d'If, off the coast of Marseille, an ancient fortress used as the setting for *The Count of Monte Cristo.*
- Roman Theater and Amphitheater, at Arles, two great classical monuments.
- Le Palais des Papes, at Avignon, the ancient seat of the popes during the "Babylonian captivity."
- Le Théâtre Antique, at Orange, an 8,000-seat theater from the days of Hadrian.

Festivals
- Festival of Avignon, held from early June to early August, a month of great theater and cultural performances.
- International Music Festival, in Aix-en-Provence, in July and August, one of the best on the Continent.

D10. The château's interior cannot be visited, but Picasso's body, along with that of one of his wives, Jacqueline Roche, is buried nearby. If you opt for a day trip from Aix, you might appreciate a meal at Au Moulin de Provence, rue des Maquisards (☎ 42-66-02-22).

Day 5   Your itinerary today depends on your preferences and on how much you're trying to escape urban congestion. If you're not bothered by potential traffic jams and crowds, opt for a night in Marseille, as the port there offers lots of raffish local color and a history going back to the days of the Phoenicians. If the congestion of Marseille doesn't appeal to you, consider a night in Toulon, a port evoking some aspects of Marseille but on a smaller, more manageable scale. (Regardless of where you stay, we suggest that you order bouillabaisse for supper.)

Day 6   This day is devoted to whatever offbeat adventure you like. Consider a boat ride to the Iles d'Hyères (boats depart several times a day from Toulon) or a leisurely drive east to St-Tropez (for more information, see Chapter 25).

1 Iles d'Hyères

24 miles ESE of Toulon, 74 miles SW of Cannes

Off the Riviera in the Mediterranean is a little group of islands enclosing the southern boundary of the Hyères anchorage. During the Renaissance they were called the Iles d'Or from a golden glow sometimes given off by the rocks in the sunlight. The tranquil islands today give no reflection of the periods of attacks by pirates and Turkish galleys, British fleet activity, and landing of Allied troops during World War II.

ESSENTIALS

GETTING THERE There's ferry service to the Ile de Porquerolles from one of four ports along the Côte d'Azur. It's a 15-minute ride from the harbor of La Tour Fondue, on the peninsula of Gien, 20 miles east of Toulon, with 5 to 20 daily departures. For information, call the Transports Maritimes et Terrestres du Littoral Varois, in La Tour Fondue (☎ 94-58-21-81). Other, less frequent midsummer routes include a 50-minute boat ride from Le Lavandou, a 90-minute ride from Cavalaire, and a 50-minute ride from Toulon. For information on crossings from Toulon, call the Trans-Med 2000, quai Stalingrad, Toulon (☎ 94-92-96-82).

The most popular maritime route to the Ile de Port-Cros is the 30-minute crossing from Le Lavandou, departing three to nine times daily. For information, call the Compagnie Maritime des Vedettes "Iles d'Or" et Le Corsaire, in Le Lavandou (☎ 94-71-01-02). There's also a one-hour crossing from Cavalaire and a 75-minute crossing from Hyères-Plage.

VISITOR INFORMATION There are no tourist bureaus on the islands, but the tourist offices in Toulon and Hyères try to fill in the gaps. Contact the Office de Tourisme, Rotonde J-Salusse, avenue de Belgique, Hyères (☎ 94-65-18-55), or the Office de Tourisme, 8 av. Colbert, Toulon (☎ 94-22-08-22).

ILE DE PORQUEROLLES

This is the largest and westernmost of the Iles d'Hyères, with a rugged south coast, the north strand being made up of sandy beaches bordered by heather, scented myrtles, and pine trees. The island is about 5 miles long and 1¼ miles wide and is 3 miles from the mainland. You can get here by ferryboat from many of the seaports along the Côte d'Azur. For example, between mid-June and October 1, two or three daily one-hour trips are made from Toulon. The round-trip fare is 80 F ($15.20). Information is available from **Trans-Med 2000,** quai Stalingrad, in Toulon (☎ 94-92-96-82).

WHERE TO STAY & DINE

✪ Mas du Langoustier
83400 Porquerolles. ☎ **94-58-30-09.** Fax 94-58-36-02. 60 rms. TV TEL. 1,735 F ($329.65) double. Rates include half board. AE, DC, MC, V. Closed Oct 18–Apr.

In a large park on the island's western tip, this is a tranquil resort hotel with tennis courts and a view of a lovely bay ringed with pines. Employees greet guests in a covered wagon by the jetty. Should you visit only for a meal, prices begin at 300 F ($57). Try the loup (sea bass) with Noilly Prat in puff pastry or tender kid with dried tomatoes roasted in casserole. Chef Joël Guillet is a rising star here. The house wine is an agreeable rosé. You can drink and dine on the terraces.

Le Relais de la Poste

Place des Armes, 83540 Porquerolles. ☎ **94-58-30-26.** Fax 94-58-33-57. 30 rms. TEL. 496-716 F ($94.25-$136.05) double. Rates include continental breakfast. No credit cards. Closed late Sept to Apr 1.

On a small square, this pleasant little hotel offers Provençal-style rooms, with loggias. It's a rather simple place and full of people who don't have the funds—or the desire—to sample the food and lodgings at the rather grand Mas du Langoustier (above). The hotel has a crêperie and mountain bicycle rentals.

ILE DE PORT-CROS

Lush subtropical vegetation reminiscent of a Caribbean island's makes this a green paradise, 3 miles long and 1¼ miles wide. No cars are allowed on the island. Take a ferry from one of three ports: From Le Lavandou, between Easter and October 20, there are 2 to 12 daily 50-minute crossings; from October 21 to Easter, there are only 3 trips per week. For information, contact **Cie Maritime des Vedettes "Iles d'Or"** in Le Lavandou (☎ **94-71-01-02**). Between June 10 and September 15, there's one crossing per day from Cavalaire, taking just over an hour; contact Cie Maritime des Vedettes "Iles d'Or" in Cavalaire (☎ **94-64-08-04**). From Port de la Plage d'Hyères, up to four crossings per day are made, in 1¼ hours. For information in Port d'Hyères, contact **Transports Maritimes et Terrestres du Littoral Varois** (☎ **94-57-44-07**).

WHERE TO STAY & DINE

Le Manoir

83400 Ile de Port-Cros. ☎ **94-05-90-52.** Fax 94-05-90-89. 23 rms. TEL. 1,360–1,900 F ($258.40–$361) double. Rates include half board. DC, MC, V. Closed Oct–May 1.

This 18th-century colonial-style mansion set in a park is the best place to stay on the island. The terrace overlooks the bay of Port-Cros, shaded by bamboo, eucalyptus, and oleander. Chef Gérard Ré serves lobster-and-fish terrine, several seasoned meats, and fresh local fish with baby vegetables, as well as regional goat cheese and velvety mousses. The Buffets charge 250 F ($47.50) for a fixed-price menu. Dinner is served daily from 8 to 9:30pm.

2 Toulon

519 miles S of Paris, 79 miles SW of Cannes, 42 miles E of Marseille

This fortress and modern town is the principal naval base of France—the headquarters of the Mediterranean fleet, some of whom can be seen wandering the streets. A beautiful harbor, it's surrounded by hills and crowned by forts. The place is protected on the east by a large breakwater and on the west by the great peninsula of Cap Sicié. Separated by the breakwater, the outer roads are known as the Grande Rade and the inner roads the Petite Rade. On the outskirts is a winter resort colony. Though not as dangerous or as intriguing as Marseille, Toulon also has a large Arab population from North Africa. Note that there's racial tension here, worsened by the closing of the shipbuilding yards.

ESSENTIALS

GETTING THERE   From Marseille (below), trains arrive about every 30 minutes in Toulon (trip time: 1 hr.). If you're on the Riviera, frequent trains arrive from Nice (trip time: 2 hr.) and from Cannes (trip time: 80 min.). Three buses per day arrive from Aix-en-Provence (trip time: 75 min.).

VISITOR INFORMATION   The Office de Tourisme is at 8 av. Colbert (☎ 94-22-08-22).

EXPLORING THE TOWN

In **Vieux Toulon**, between the harbor and boulevard de Strasbourg (the main axis of town), are many remains of the port's former days. Visit the **Poissonerie,** the typical covered market, bustling in the morning with fishmongers and buyers. Another colorful market, the **Marché,** spills over onto the narrow streets around cours Lafayette. Also in old Toulon is the **Cathédrale Ste-Marie-Majeure** (St. Mary Major), built in the romanesque style in the 11th and 12th centuries, then much expanded in the 17th. Its badly lit nave is gothic, and the belfry and facade are from the 18th century. It's open daily from 9am to 5pm.

In contrast to the cathedral, tall modern buildings line quai Stalingrad, opening onto **Vieille d'Arse.** On place Puget, look for the *atlantes* (caryatids), figures of men used as columns. These interesting figures support a balcony at the Hôtel de Ville and are also included in the facade of the naval museum.

The **Musée de la Marine,** place du Ingénieur-Général-Monsenergue (☎ 94-02-02-01), contains many figureheads and ship models and is open daily from 10am to noon and 2:30 to 7pm. Admission is 24 F ($4.55) for adults and 12 F ($2.30) for children. The **Musée de Toulon,** 113 bd. du Général-Maréchal-Leclerc (☎ 94-93-15-54), contains both old and contemporary works, ranging from the 16th century to the present. There's a particularly good collection of Provençal and Italian paintings, as well as religious works. The latest acquisitions include New Realism pieces and minimalist art. It's open daily from 1 to 7pm; admission is free.

Once you've covered the top attractions, we suggest taking a drive, an hour or two before sunset, along the **corniche du Mont-Faron.** It's a scenic boulevard along the lower slopes of Mont Faron, providing views of the busy port, the town, the cliffs, and, in the distance, the Mediterranean.

Earlier in the day, consider boarding a funicular near the Altéa La Tour Blanche Hôtel. This *téléphérique* (cable car) operates daily from 9 to 11:45am and 2:15 to 6:30pm, costing 40 F ($7.60) for adults and 25 F ($4.75) for children round-trip. Once you get to the top, enjoy the view and then visit the **Memorial National du Débarquement,** Mont Faron (☎ 94-88-08-09), which documents, among other exhibits, the Allied landings in Provence in 1944. It's open Tuesday to Sunday from 9 to 11:45am and 2 to 6:45pm in summer, from 9 to 11:30am and 2 to 5:45pm in winter. Admission is 24 F ($4.55) for adults and 10 F ($1.90) for children 5 to 12; 4 and under free.

WHERE TO STAY

La Corniche

1 littoral Frédéric-Mistral at Le Mourillon, 83000 Toulon. ☎ **94-41-35-12.** Fax 94-41-24-58. 22 rms, 4 suites. A/C MINIBAR TV TEL. 450–510 F ($85.55–$96.95) double; from 610 F ($115.95) suite. Breakfast 50 F ($9.50) extra. AE, DC, MC, V. Parking 40 F ($7.60). Bus 3.

An attractive hotel with an interior garden, a café, and a restaurant, La Corniche offers some accommodations with sea views and loggias, and room decoration is in the Provençal style. The dining room, which has ivy extending through the ceiling, offers a sea view. A trio of pine trees grow right through the restaurant. A fairly good but limited wine list complements the food, which is perfectly adequate but not something to savor.

New Hôtel Tour Blanche
Bd. de l'Amiral-Vence, 83299 Toulon. ☎ **94-24-41-57.** Fax 94-22-42-25. 92 rms. A/C MINIBAR TV TEL. 395 F ($75.05) double. Breakfast 50 F ($9.50) extra. AE, DC, MC, V. Parking free. Bus 3.

With excellent modernized accommodations, attractive gardens with terraces, and a pool, this is the best hotel at the naval port. Some rooms have balconies opening onto the water. The restaurant with a panoramic view serves a fixed-price menu at 90 F ($17.10). The food is inspired by Provence and the Midi, and there's a good selection of wines from Provence. The hotel is about 1 1/2 miles north of the center of Toulon, at the foot of the cable car.

WHERE TO DINE

Le Dauphin
21 bis rue Jean-Jaurès. ☎ **94-93-12-07.** Reservations required. Main courses 125–160 F ($23.75–$30.40); fixed-price menu 120 F ($22.80). AE, MC, V. Mon–Fri noon–1:45pm and 7:30–9:30pm, Sat 7:30–9:30pm. Closed Aug 1–15. Bus 3. PROVENÇAL.

Le Dauphin serves some of the best food in Toulon, though it's in a seedy part of the city. Chef Alain Biles has worked at the most prestigious restaurants in Paris, and his *cuisine moderne* is rich and varied. Consider one of his *suggestions du jour* as well as one of the wines from the well-stocked cellar. He always has a selection of fish, such as scallops, filets of red mullet (often flavored with thyme, basil, and fondue of tomatoes), salmon, and poissons du jour. His meat selections range from duck breast to pigeon to filet of beef, often served with foie gras.

3 Marseille

479 miles S of Paris, 116 miles SW of Nice

Bustling Marseille is the third-largest city in France but the premier port. A crossroads of world traffic—Dumas called it "the meeting place of the entire world"—the city is ancient, founded by Greeks from the city of Phocaea, near present-day Izmir, Turkey, in the 6th century B.C. The city is a place of unique sounds, smells, and sights. It has seen wars and much destruction, but trade has always been its raison d'être.

Perhaps its most common association is with the national anthem of France, "La Marseillaise." During the Revolution, 500 volunteers marched to Paris, singing this rousing song along the way. The rest is history.

ESSENTIALS

GETTING THERE   The Marseille airport (☎ **42-89-09-74**) accepts international flights from all over Europe and several weekly flights from New York.

Marseille has rail connections from hundreds of European cities, with especially good connections to and from Italy. Marseille is also the terminus for the TGV bullet train, which departs daily from Paris's Gare de Lyon (trip time: 4 3/4 hr.). Local trains leave Paris almost every hour, making a number of stops before reaching Marseille.

Warning: Throughout the world, Marseille has a seamy reputation. It's considered dangerous, the center of a rich crime empire, a seat of drug smuggling and prostitution. So exercise caution.

VISITOR INFORMATION The Office de Tourisme is at 4 La Canebière (☎ 91-54-91-11).

EXPLORING THE CITY

Many visitors never bother to visit the museums, preferring to absorb the unique spirit of the city as reflected on its busy streets and at its sidewalk cafés, particularly those along the main street, **Canebière.** Known as "can of beer" to World War II GIs, it is the spine and soul of Marseille, but the seediest main street in France. Lined with hotels, shops, and restaurants, the street is filled with sailors of every nation and a wide range of foreigners, especially Algerians. In fact, some 100,000 North Africans live in the city and its tenement suburbs, often in souklike conditions. The Canebière winds down to the **Vieux-Port,** dominated by the massive neoclassic forts of St-Jean and St-Nicholas. The port is filled with fishing craft and yachts and ringed with seafood restaurants.

Motorists can continue along to the **corniche Président-J-F-Kennedy,** a promenade running for about 3 miles along the sea. You pass villas and gardens along the way and have a good view of the Mediterranean. To the north, the **Port Moderne,** the "gateway to the East," is man-made. Its construction began in 1844, and a century later the Germans destroyed it. Motorboat trips are conducted along the docks.

A BOAT RIDE TO CHÂTEAU D'IF From quai des Belges at Vieux-Port you can take one of the motorboats on a 20-minute ride to Château d'If (☎ 91-59-02-30), for 40 F ($7.60) round-trip. Boats leave about every 15 minutes. Contact **GACM** (☎ 91-55-50-09), whose office on quai des Belges is open daily from 7am to 7pm.

On the sparsely vegetated island of **Château d'If,** François I built a fortress to defend Marseille, the place later housing a state prison; carvings by Huguenot prisoners can still be seen inside some of the cells. Alexandre Dumas used the château as a setting for *The Count of Monte Cristo*, though the adventure never took place. Its most famous association—with the legendary *Man in the Iron Mask*—is also apocryphal. The château is open daily: April to September from 9am to 7pm, and October to March from 9am to 1pm and 2 to 5:30pm. Admission is 26 F ($4.95) for adults and 17 F ($3.25) for children.

SEEING THE TOP ATTRACTIONS

One of the most scenic oases here is the **Palais Longchamp,** place Bernex, with its spectacular fountain and colonnade, built during the Second Empire. Housed in a northern wing of the palace is the **Musée des Beaux-Arts** (☎ 91-62-21-17), displaying a vast array of paintings, both foreign and domestic, from the 16th to the 19th century. They include works by Corot, Millet, Ingres, David, and Rubens. Some 80 sculptures and objets d'art were bequeathed to the museum as well, and particularly interesting is a gallery of Pierre Puget sculpture. One salon is devoted to Honoré Daumier, born in Marseille in 1808. The museum is open daily from 10am to 5pm. Admission is 12 F ($2.30) for adults and 6 F ($1.15) for children; ages 65 and older free.

Nearby is the **Musée Grobet-Labadié,** 140 bd. Longchamp (☎ 91-62-21-82), containing a private collection that was bequeathed to the city in 1923. It possesses exquisite Louis XV and Louis XVI furniture, as well as an outstanding collection of medieval Burgundian and Provençal sculpture. Other exhibits include 17th-century Gobelins tapestries, 15th-century German and Flemish paintings, and

17th-century faïence. It's open Wednesday from 2 to 6:30pm and Thursday to Monday from 10am to noon and 2 to 6pm. Admission is 12 F ($2.30); children free.

At the **Musée Cantini,** 19 rue Grignan (☎ 91-54-77-75), the temporary exhibitions of contemporary art are often better than the permanent collection. This museum is devoted to modern art, with masterpieces by Derain, Marquet, Ernst, Masson, Balthus, and others. It also owns a selection of important young international artists. The museum is open Wednesday to Monday from 11am to 6pm. Admission is 17 F ($3.25) for adults and 10 F ($1.90) for students; ages 65 and over and 10 and under free.

The **Musée du Vieux-Marseille,** in the Maison Diamantée, 2 rue de la Prison (☎ 91-55-10-19), near the city hall, is a history and folklore museum known for its *santons*—little statuettes made of colored clay representing characters of the Nativity. Santons are traditionally made by a few families on the town outskirts, the models and molds passed down from generation to generation. They appear at a traditional fair in December in Marseille. Other exhibits include furniture, pottery, old maps, engravings, and 19th-century paintings by Provençal artists. It's open Tuesday to Sunday from 10am to 5pm. Admission is 12 F ($2.30) for adults and 6 F ($1.15) for children.

The **Musée d'Histoire de Marseille,** Centre Bourse, square Belsunce (☎ 91-90-42-22), is unusual. You're allowed to wander through an archeological garden where excavations are still going on, as scholars attempt to learn more about the ancient town of Massalia, founded by Greek sailors. Of course, many of the exhibits, such as old coins and fragments of pottery, only suggest their former glory. To help you more fully realize the era, you're aided by audiovisual exhibits, and the museum has a free exhibition room. You can also see what's left of a boat that was dug up on the site. The museum is open Tuesday to Saturday from 10am to 4:45pm. Admission is 12 F ($2.30) for adults and 6 F ($1.15) for children.

For a city as ancient as Marseille, antique ecclesiastical monuments are few. However, the seemingly fortified **Basilique St-Victor,** quai de Rive-Neuve (☎ 91-33-25-86), has a crypt from the 5th century, when the church and abbey were founded by St. Cassianus. The crypt, which also reflects work done in the 10th and 11th centuries, may be visited Monday to Saturday from 10 to 11am and 3 to 6pm and Sunday from 3 to 6pm. Admission to the crypt is 10 F ($1.90). You reach it by going out quai de Rive-Neuve (near the Gare du Vieux-Port).

Two cathedrals are on place de la Major, near Old Marseille, with domes and cupolas that may remind you of Istanbul. (For information on both, call 94-92-28-91.) The **Ancienne Cathédrale de la Major** dates chiefly from the 12th century, having been built on the ruins of a Temple of Diana. In its left aisle is the Chapelle St-Lazare, in the early Renaissance style. Nearby is a Lucca della Robbia bas-relief. The cathedral is open Wednesday to Monday from 9am to noon and 2 to 6:30pm; admission is free. The newer **Cathédrale de la Major** was one of the largest built in Europe in the 19th century, some 450 feet long. Its interior is adorned with mosaic floors and red-and-white marble banners, and the exterior is in a bastardized romanesque-Byzantine style. This cathedral is open Wednesday to Monday from 9am to noon and 2 to 6:30pm; admission is free.

The landmark **Basilique Notre-Dame de la Garde,** place du Colonel-Edon (☎ 91-37-42-82), crowns a limestone rock overlooking the southern side of Vieux-Port. It was built in the romanesque-Byzantine style popular in the 19th century and was topped by a 30-foot gilded statue of the Virgin. Visitors come here not so much for the church as for the view—best seen at sunset—from its terrace. Spread out before you are the city, the islands, and the sea.

Another vantage point for those seeking a panoramic view is **Parc du Pharo,** a promontory facing the entrance to Vieux-Port. You stand on a terrace overlooking the Château du Pharo, built by Napoléon III for his empress Eugénie. Fort St-Jean and the old and new cathedrals can be seen clearly.

WHERE TO STAY
VERY EXPENSIVE

✪ Résidence le Petit Nice

Corniche Président-J-F-Kennedy/Anse-de-Maldormé, 13007 Marseille. ☎ **91-59-25-92.** Fax 91-59-28-08. 17 rms, 2 suites. A/C MINIBAR TV TEL. 1,900 F ($361.20) double; from 3,900 F ($741.40) suite. Breakfast 110 F ($20.90) extra. AE, DC, MC, V. Parking 100 F ($19). Bus 83.

The best in Marseille, the Résidence opened in 1917, when the Passédat family joined two suburban villas. The narrow approach to the establishment will take you past what looks like a row of private villas, in a secluded area below the street paralleling the beach. The rooms are in the main building or an annex. The restaurant is beautiful, with a view of the Marseille shore and the rocky islands off its coast. It's run by Jean-Paul Passédat and Gerald, his son, whose imaginative culinary successes include royal daurade with confit of eggplant, vinaigrette of rascasse (hogfish), and sea devil with saffron and garlic. They run the finest restaurant in Marseille, a city where dinner often means a bowl of fish soup or a plate of couscous. The restaurant is open Tuesday to Sunday; from early October to the end of March, it's closed Sunday and on Monday at lunch.

EXPENSIVE

Sofitel Marseille Vieux-Port

36 bd. Charles-Livon, 13007 Marseille. ☎ **91-52-90-19.** Fax 91-31-46-52. 127 rms, 3 suites. A/C MINIBAR TV TEL. 630–930 F ($119.75–$176.80) double; from 1,750 F ($332.70) suite. Breakfast 70 F ($13.30) extra. AE, DC, MC, V. Parking 35 F ($6.65). Bus 83.

This seven-story, chain hotel, with its many windows, looms above the massive embankments. Depending on the exposure, the rooms may look out on the boulevard traffic or on one of the best panoramic views of the port of Old Marseille. They're fairly generous in size, up-to-date, and comfortable, but unimaginative in decor. In 1987 its owner, the Accor hotel giant, turned over 93 rooms to a new 3-star Novotel (below). Today two entrances, staffs, and dining/drinking facilities exist in the same building. There are also a pool, an elegant bar, and Les Trois Forts, a restaurant with views of the harbor and its defenses. Meals are served daily from noon to 2pm and 7 to 9:30pm.

MODERATE

⑤ Novotel Marseille Centre

36 bd. Charles-Livon, 13007 Marseille. ☎ **91-59-22-22.** Fax 91-31-15-48. 90 rms. A/C TV TEL. 490–580 F ($93.15–$110.25) double. Breakfast 50 F ($9.50) extra. AE, DC, MC, V. Parking 35 F ($6.65).

As mentioned for the Sofitel above, this Novotel was created in 1987. In typical Novotel format, you don't receive the services offered at the Sofitel, but if that doesn't bother you this is one of the best and most reasonably priced hotels in town. Each room contains a double and a single bed (which serves, thanks to bolster cushions, as a couch) and a desk; some, however, look a little tired. Those with views of the Old Port tend to fill up first. The lattice-decorated restaurant serves good basic meals, beginning at 115 F ($21.85), daily from 6am to midnight.

INEXPENSIVE

✪ Grand Hôtel Genève-Vieux-Port

3 bis rue Reine-Elisabeth, 13001 Marseille. ☎ **91-90-51-42.** Fax 91-90-76-24. 493 rms. A/C MINIBAR TV TEL. 370 F ($70.30) double. Breakfast 45 F ($8.55) extra. AE, DC, MC, V. Parking 60 F ($11.40) nearby. Bus 83.

Near the port, this stylish hotel is a good value, especially since it was massively renovated in 1995. The most expensive rooms have views of the port. Breakfast is the only meal served as there's no restaurant on the premises.

⑤ La Residence du Vieux-Port

18 quai du Port, 13001 Marseille. ☎ **91-91-91-22.** Fax 91-56-60-88. 52 rms. A/C TV TEL. 350–500 F ($66.50–$95) double. Breakfast 30 F ($5.70) extra. AE, DC, MC, V. Parking 50 F ($9.50). Bus 83.

This is highly recommended for those who want to be in the center of Marseille's waterfront life. A café and a breakfast room are on the second floor, while a bar is behind the lobby. The rooms have loggia-style terraces opening onto the port—many show their age but are still serviceable.

WHERE TO DINE
EXPENSIVE

✪ Au Pescadou

19 place Castellane. ☎ **91-78-36-01.** Reservations recommended. Main courses 98–210 F ($18.60–$39.90); fixed-price menus 160–200 F ($30.40–$38). AE, MC, V. Mon–Sat noon–2pm and 7–11pm, Sun noon–2pm. Closed July 21–Aug. Bus 83. SEAFOOD.

Maintained by three multilingual sons of Barthélémy Mennella, the original owner, this is one of the finest seafood restaurants in Marseille. Beside a busy traffic circle downtown, it overlooks a fountain, an obelisk, and its sidewalk display of fresh oysters. For an appetizer, try almond-stuffed mussels or "hors d'oeuvres of the fisherman." Main-dish specialties are bouillabaisse de Marseille, gigot de lotte (monkfish stewed slowly in cream sauce with fresh vegetables), and scallops cooked with morel.

Next to the main restaurant and under the same management are two informal newcomers, with rapid service and low prices. In **Le Coin Bistrot,** simple platters are served to a mostly youthful clientele at around 65 F ($12.35) each. In **La Brasserie,** platters of nonfish dishes are the norm, with menu items like blanquettes of veal, steak à la pizzaiola, and pastas, costing around 100 F ($19) per meal. Note that only the formal Au Pescadou receives the Frommer star.

✪ Le Jambon de Parme

67 rue de La-Palud. ☎ **91-54-37-98.** Reservations not required. Main courses 100–150 F ($19–$28.50); fixed-price menu 180 F ($34.20). AE, DC, MC, V. Tues–Sat noon–2pm and 8–10:15pm, Sun noon–2pm. Closed July 15–Aug 29. Bus 83. ITALIAN.

Le Jambon de Parme is not only the best Italian restaurant in Marseille but also the best restaurant outside the hotels. The cuisine of Lucien Giravalli is both classic and original, and the wine list is extensive. The atmosphere is exquisite, with a Louis XVI decor complemented by framed engravings of Italian towns. The fried scampi and homemade ravioli are as good as any you'll find in Italy. You might try the tortellini in smooth cream sauce or filets of capon cooked with champagne. And the veal kidneys in marsala sauce and the soup with truffles are exceptional.

MODERATE

Brasserie Vieux-Port New-York

33 quai des Belges. ☎ **91-33-91-79.** Reservations recommended at lunch. Main courses 85–150 F ($16.15–$28.50); fixed-price menu 145 F ($27.55). AE, DC, MC, V. Brasserie, daily noon–2:30pm and 7:30–11:30pm. Bar and café, daily 6:30am–3:30am. FRENCH/PROVENÇAL.

This time-honored brasserie sits on one of the quays overlooking the city's ancient harbor. Many locals consider it their favorite café, taking advantage of its dawn-to-dusk hours for a glass of midmorning wine, afternoon coffee, or whatever. Amid a battered art deco interior, you can enjoy farci du jour (stuffed vegetable of the day, tomatoes, peppers, or onions, usually served as part of a main course), grilled fish, côte du boeuf with marrow sauce, bouillabaisse, and a wide array of grilled meats. Wines focus on the vintages of Provence.

INEXPENSIVE

⊛ Chez Angèle

50 rue Caisserie. ☎ **91-90-63-35.** Reservations recommended. Main courses 45–100 F ($8.55–$19); fixed-price menu 90 F ($17.10). V. Tues–Sun noon–2:30pm and 7–11pm. Closed Sun July–Aug. Bus 83. PROVENÇAL/ITALIAN.

A local friend guided us here, and though most of Marseille's cheap eating places are not recommendable, this one is worthwhile if you're watching your francs. It's small, with a typical bistro ambience, and is usually filled with locals. You can come here for pizza or well-prepared ravioli, tagliatelle, osso buco, escargots Provençal, and Marseille-style tripe.

NEARBY ACCOMMODATIONS & DINING

Relais de la Magdeleine

13420 Gemenos. ☎ **42-32-20-16.** Fax 42-32-02-26. 24 rms, 1 suite. TV TEL. 530–800 F ($100.70–$152) double; 990–1,200 F ($188.10–$228) suite. Breakfast 68 F ($12.90) extra. MC, V. Parking free. Closed Dec–Mar 15. Head east of Marseille for 14 miles along A50.

In a country mansion at the foot of the Ste-Baume mountain range, the Relais de la Magdeleine is surrounded by parks and woodlands, near the venerated spot where Mary Magdalene is believed to have died. The inn has pleasant architectural details, with a carving of the Virgin and Child above the fireplace. The guest rooms are pleasant and personal. The relais also serves good meals, with lunches beginning at 160 F ($30.40) and dinner beginning at 250 F ($47.50). Specialties include lamb cooked with Provençal herbs and filet of sole Beau Manoir. There's a good-size pool, tennis courts are 10 minutes away, a golf course is 20 minutes away, and the beach is 15 minutes away.

4 Aix-en-Provence

469 miles S of Paris, 50 miles SE of Avignon, 20 miles N of Marseille

Founded in 122 B.C. by a Roman general, Caius Sextius Calvinus, who named it Aquae Sextiae after himself, Aix was first a Roman military outpost and then a civilian colony, the administrative capital of a province of the later Roman Empire, the seat of an archbishop, and the official residence of the medieval comtes de Provence. After the union of Provence with France, Aix remained until the Revolution a judicial and administrative headquarters.

The celebrated son of this old capital city of Provence, Paul Cézanne, immortalized the countryside nearby. Just as he saw it, Montagne Ste-Victoire looms over the town, though a string of high-rises has now cropped up on the landscape. The most charming center in all Provence, this faded university town was once a seat of aristocracy, its streets walked by counts and kings.

ESSENTIALS

GETTING THERE   At a rail and highway junction, the city is easily accessible, with trains arriving hourly from Marseille, taking 40 minutes. Independent bus companies service Aix-en-Provence. SATAP (☎ **42-26-17-43**) operates four buses a day to and from Avignon, taking 1½ hours.

VISITOR INFORMATION   The Office de Tourisme is at 2 place du Général-de-Gaulle (☎ **42-16-11-61**).

SPECIAL EVENTS   The highlight of the season is the annual music festival, one of the best on the Continent.

EXPLORING THE CITY

Cours Mirabeau, the main street, is one of the most beautiful in Europe. Plane trees stretch their branches across the top to shade it from the hot Provençal sun like an umbrella, filtering the light into shadows that play on the rococo fountains below. On one side are shops and sidewalk cafés, on the other richly embellished sandstone *hôtels particuliers* (mansions) from the 17th and 18th centuries. Honoring Mirabeau, the revolutionary and statesman, the street begins at the 1860 landmark fountain on place de la Libération.

The **Cathédrale St-Sauveur,** place des Martyrs de la Résistance (☎ **42-23-45-65**), is dedicated to Christ under the title St-Sauveur (Holy Savior or Redeemer). Its Baptistery dates from the 4th and 5th centuries, but the architectural complex as a whole has seen many additions. It contains a brilliant Nicolas Froment triptych, *The Burning Bush*, from the 15th century. One side depicts the Virgin and Child, the other Good King René and his second wife, Jeanne de Laval. It's open Wednesday to Monday from 8am to noon and 2 to 6pm.

You might also visit the **Chapelle Penitents-Bleus,** 2 bis rue du Bon-Pasteur, a 16th-century chapel built to honor St. Joseph on the ancient Roman Aurelian road linking Rome and Spain. The chapel was restored by Herbert Maza, founder and former president of the Institute for American Universities. It's open Monday to Friday from 9am to noon and 2 to 6pm.

Nearby in a former archbishop's palace is the **Musée des Tapisseries,** 28 place des Martyrs de la Résistance (☎ **42-23-09-91**). Lining its gilded walls are three series of tapestries from the 17th and 18th centuries collected by the archbishops to decorate the palace: *The History of Don Quixote* by Notoire, *The Russian Games* by Leprince, and *The Grotesques* by Monnoyer. In addition, the museum exhibits rare furnishings from the 17th and 18th centuries. Charging 13 F ($2.45) for admission, it's open daily from 10am to noon and 2 to 5:45pm.

Up rue Cardinale is the **Musée Granet,** place St-Jean-de-Malte (☎ **42-38-14-70**), which owns several Cézannes but not a very typical collection of the great artist's work. Matisse donated a nude in 1941. Housed in the former center of the Knights of Malta, the fine-arts gallery contains work by van Dyck, van Loo, and Rigaud; portraits by Pierre and François Puget; and (the most interesting) a *Jupiter and Thetis* by Ingres. Ingres also did an 1807 portrait of the museum's namesake, François Marius Granet. Granet's own works abound. The museum is open Wednesday to Monday from 10am to noon and 2:30 to 6pm; closed January. Admission is 25 F ($4.75) for adults and 15 F ($2.85) for children.

Outside town, at 9 av. Paul-Cézanne, is the **Atelier de Cézanne** (☎ 42-21-06-53), the studio of the painter considered to be the major forerunner of cubism. Surrounded by a wall, the house was restored by American admirers. Repaired again in 1970, it remains much as Cézanne left it in 1906, "his coat hanging on the wall, his easel with an unfinished picture waiting for a touch of the master's brush," as Thomas R. Parker wrote. It may be visited Wednesday to Monday from 10am to noon and 2 to 5pm (to 6:30pm June to September). Admission is 14 F ($2.65) for adults and 8 F ($1.50) for children.

Perhaps the best thing to do in Aix is to walk along the ✪ **route de Cézanne** (D17), which winds eastward through the Provençal countryside toward the Ste-Victoire. From the east end of cours Mirabeau, take rue du Maréchal-Joffre across boulevard Carnot to boulevard des Poilus, which becomes avenue des Ecoles-Militaires and finally D17. The stretch between Aix and the hamlet of Le Tholonet is full of twists and turns where Cézanne often set up his easel to paint. It may be a longish hike (3¹/₂ miles), but it's possible to do it leisurely by starting early in the morning. Le Tholonet has a café or two where you can refresh yourself while waiting for one of the frequent buses back to Aix.

WHERE TO STAY
EXPENSIVE

✪ Mercure Paul-Cézanne
40 av. Victor-Hugo, 13100 Aix-en-Provence. ☎ **42-26-34-73.** Fax 42-27-20-95. 55 rms, 1 suite. A/C MINIBAR TV TEL. 380–490 F ($72.20–$93.15) double; 750 F ($142.55) suite. Breakfast 50 F ($9.50) extra. AE, DC, MC, V. Bus 27, 42, or 51.

On a street of sycamores, the Mercure has a refined interior. The lounge seems more like a private sitting room than the lobby of a hotel. The rooms may have mahogany Victorian furniture, Louis XVI chairs, marble-top chests, gilt mirrors, and oil paintings. All baths have hand-painted tiles. The small breakfast room opens onto a rear courtyard.

✪ Villa Gallici
Av. de la Violette (impasse des Grands Pins), 13100 Aix-en-Provence. ☎ **42-23-29-23.** Fax 42-96-30-45. 15 rms, 2 suites. A/C MINIBAR TV TEL. 850–1,750 F ($161.60–$332.70) double; 1,750–2,350 F ($332.70–$446.75) suite. Breakfast 95 F ($18.05) extra. AE, DC, MC, V. Parking free.

This elegant inn is the most stylishly decorated hotel in Aix, created by a trio of architects and interior designers (Mssrs Dez, Montemarco, and Jouve). Each room contains a private safe and an individualized decor of subtlety and charm, richly infused with the decorative traditions of Aix. The villa sits in a large enclosed garden in the heart of town, close to one of the best restaurants, Le Clos de la Violette (see "Where to Dine," below). Simple meals can be ordered from this restaurant and served at lunchtime beside the Villa's pool. On the premises are a limited array of spa facilities as well.

MODERATE

Novotel Aix-en-Provence Sud

Périphérique Sud, arc de Méyran, 13100 Aix-en-Provence. ☎ **42-16-09-09.** Fax 42-26-00-09. 80 rms. A/C MINIBAR TV TEL. 440 F ($83.60) double. Breakfast 48 F ($9.10) extra. AE, DC, MC, V. Parking free. Take the ring road 2 miles south of the town center (exit at Aix-Est 3 Sautets).

At the end of a labyrinthine but well-marked route, this clean chain hotel offers some of the largest accommodations in town. The rooms have been designed for European business travelers or the traveling family in summer, each with one single and one double bed and a fully accessorized bath. The hotel offers one of the most pleasant dining rooms in the suburbs, with big windows overlooking Rivière arc de Méyran and an ivy-covered forest.

If this hotel is full, rooms are usually available at the slightly newer **Novotel Aix-Beaumanoir,** périphérique Sud, 13100 Aix-en-Provence (☎ **42-27-47-50;** fax 42-38-46-41), where the rooms are similar and the rates are the same.

INEXPENSIVE

Hôtel de France

63 rue Espariat, 13100 Aix-en-Provence. ☎ **42-27-90-15.** Fax 42-26-11-47. 27 rms. MINIBAR TV TEL. 276–376 F ($52.45–$71.45) double. Breakfast 35 F ($6.65) extra. AE, DC. Bus 27, 42, or 51.

At place des Augustins, around the corner from cours Mirabeau, this two-star 19th-century building has a glass-and-wrought-iron canopy and modernized rooms. Those with streetside exposure tend to be noisy.

Hôtel la Caravelle

29 bd. du Roi-René, 13100 Aix-en-Provence. ☎ **42-21-53-05.** Fax 42-96-55-46. 32 rms. TV TEL. 270–395 F ($51.30–$75.05) double. Breakfast 34 F ($6.45) extra. AE, DC, MC, V. Bus 27, 42, or 51.

A three-minute walk from the center at cours Mirabeau is this conservatively furnished three-star hotel with a bas-relief of a three-masted caravelle on the beige stucco facade. The hotel is run by M. and Mme Henri Denis, who offer breakfast in the stone-floored lobby. The majority of the rooms were restored in 1995; they have double-glazed windows to help muffle the noise.

WHERE TO DINE

EXPENSIVE

✪ Le Clos de la Violette

10 av. de la Violette. ☎ **42-23-30-71.** Reservations required. Main courses 160–190 F ($30.40–$36.10); fixed-price lunch 200 F ($38); fixed-price menus 320–450 F ($60.80–$85.55). AE, V. Mon noon–1:30pm, Tues–Sat noon–1:30pm and 7:30–9:30pm. Closed Oct 22–Nov 6. Bus 27, 42, or 51. FRENCH.

In an elegant residential neighborhood, which most visitors reach by taxi, Le Clos de la Violette is the most innovative restaurant in town. This imposing Provençal villa has an octagonal reception area and several modern dining rooms. The food produced by Jean-Marc and Brigitte Banzo has been called a "song of Provence." Typical dishes include an upside-down tart of snails with parsley juice, fricassée of sole with lobster, filet of pigeon with foie gras, and a sumptuous array of desserts. The service is extremely professional and even gracious.

MODERATE

⊕ Brasserie Royale

17 cours Mirabeau. ☎ **42-26-01-63.** Reservations required. Main courses 50–95 F ($9.50–$18.05); fixed-price meals 75 F ($14.25), 90 F ($17.10), and 100 F ($19). MC, V. Daily noon–2pm and 7pm–1am. Bus 27, 42, or 51. FRENCH.

This informal brasserie offers excellent, unpretentious regional cooking at moderate prices. It's an animated crowded restaurant with an interior dining room and a glass-enclosed section on the sidewalk. You're served hearty fare like tripe Provençal, daube Provençal, and bourride Provençale. The chef is known for his *plats du jour*, which on our last visit included lapin (rabbit) chasseur, paella, osso buco, and couscous. If you're dining light, you might enjoy one of four kinds of omelets. Wines of Provence come by the half or full bottle. The brasserie is a glacier during the afternoon, serving several ice-cream specialties and milkshakes and Irish coffee.

Note that one small section of the brasserie is identified as a "restaurant," where prices are a bit higher but the quality and ambience are not significantly different.

Chez Maxime

12 place Ramus. ☎ **42-26-28-51.** Reservations recommended. Main courses 90–120 F ($17.10–$22.80); fixed-price menus 120–160 F ($22.80–$30.40). MC, V. Mon 8–11pm, Tues–Sat noon–2pm and 8–11pm. Closed Jan 15–31. FRENCH.

In the pedestrian zone, this restaurant specializes in regional dishes. There's an terrace on the sidewalk in front, plus a wood-trimmed stone interior where the most important element is the cuisine. Specialties are cassolette of mussels; côte de boeuf with truffle juice or bone marrow; salmon, sole, or filet of rascasse with pistou; and several preparations of lamb cooked over an oakwood fire. (If you request it, a resident butcher will dress the lamb's carcass adjacent to your table, an experience some locals consider entertaining.)

INEXPENSIVE

⊕ Le Bistro Latin

18 rue de la Couronne. ☎ **42-38-22-88.** Reservations recommended. Main courses 75–112 F ($14.25–$21.30); fixed-price menus 125 F ($23.75), 185 F ($35.15), and 260 F ($49.40). AE, DC, MC, V. Tues–Sat noon–2pm and 7–10:30pm. Bus 27, 42, or 51. FRENCH.

The best little bistro in Aix-en-Provence—for the price, that is—is run by Bruno Ungaro, who prides himself on his fixed-price menus. He offers two intimate dining rooms, decorated with antiques. The staff is young and enthusiastic, and Provençal music plays in the background. Try the chartreuse of mussels, one of the meat dishes with spinach-and-saffron cream sauce, or crêpe of hare with basil sauce. We've enjoyed the classic cuisine on all our visits, particularly the scampi risotto.

5 Arles

450 miles S of Paris, 22 miles SW of Avignon, 55 miles NW of Marseille

Arles has been called "the soul of Provence," and art lovers, archeologists, and historians are attracted to this town on the Rhône. Many of its scenes, painted so luminously by van Gogh in his declining years, remain to delight. The great Dutch painter left Paris for Arles in 1888, the same year he cut off part of his left ear. But he was to paint some of his most celebrated works in this Provençal town, including *Starry Night, The Bridge at Arles, Sunflowers,* and *L'Arlésienne.*

The Greeks are said to have founded Arles in the 6th century B.C. Julius Caesar established a Roman colony here in 46 B.C. Under Roman rule Arles prospered. Constantine the Great named it the second capital in his empire in 306, when it was known as "the little Rome of the Gauls." It wasn't until 1481 that Arles was incorporated into France.

ESSENTIALS

GETTING THERE   Arles lies on the Paris–Marseille and the Bordeaux–St-Raphaël rail lines, so has frequent connections from most cities of France. Ten trains arrive daily from Avignon (trip time: 20 min.) and 10 per day from Marseille (trip time: 1 hr.). From Aix-en-Provence, 10 trains arrive per day (trip time: $1^3/4$ hr.).

There are about five buses per day from Aix-en-Provence (trip time: $1^3/4$ hr.).

VISITOR INFORMATION   The Office de Tourisme, where you can buy a *Billet Globale,* is on the esplanade des Lices (☎ 90-18-41-20).

SEEING THE TOP ATTRACTIONS

First go to the tourist office (above), where you can purchase one of three *Billets Globales* (passes), depending on your time and interests: *Forfait 1* admits you to the town's museums and costs 25 F ($4.75) for adults and 19 F ($3.60) for children; *Forfait 2* provides access to the Roman monuments only, costing 30 F ($5.70) for adults and 20 F ($3.80) for children; and *Forfait 3* admits you to all the major attractions, at a cost of 44 F ($8.35) for adults and 31 F ($5.90) for children.

The town is full of monuments from Roman times. The general vicinity of the old Roman forum is occupied by **place du Forum,** shaded by plane trees. Once the Café de Nuit, immortalized by van Gogh, stood on this square. Two columns in the Corinthian style and pediment fragments from a temple can be viewed at the corner of the Hôtel Nord-Pinus. South of here is **place de la République,** the principal plaza, dominated by a 50-foot-tall blue porphyry obelisk. On the north is the impressive Hôtel de Ville (town hall) from 1673, built to Mansart's plans and surmounted by a Renaissance belfry.

On the east side of the square is the **Eglise St-Trophime** (☎ 90-49-36-36), noted for its 12th-century portal, one of the finest achievements of southern romanesque style. In the pediment Christ is surrounded by the symbols of the Evangelists. Frederick Barbarossa was crowned king of Arles on this site in 1178. The cloister, in both the gothic and romanesque styles, is noted for its medieval carvings. The church is open daily from 8am to 7pm and admission is free. The cloister's hours are 9 to 11:30am and 2 to 4:30pm daily, with an admission of 15 F ($2.85) for adults and 10 F ($1.90) for students.

The **Museon Arlaten** (☎ 90-96-08-23) is entered at 29 rue de la République—its name is written in old Provençal style. It was founded by Frédéric Mistral, the Provençal poet and leader of a movement to establish Modern Provençal as a literary language, using the money from his Nobel Prize for literature in 1904. This is really a folklore museum, with regional costumes, portraits, furniture, dolls, a music salon, and one room devoted to mementos of Mistral. Among its curiosities is a letter (in French) from President Theodore Roosevelt to

In Search of van Gogh's "Different Light"

Before the impressionists found refuge in Provence, the district had already attracted many artists. During the pope's residency at Avignon, a flood of Italian artists frescoed the papal palace in a style worthy of St. Peter's, and even after their departure, Provençal monarchs like King René imported painters from Flanders and Burgundy to adorn his public buildings. This continued to the 18th and 19th centuries, as painters drew inspiration from the dazzling light of Provence, but it wasn't until the age of the impressionists that the role of Provence as an artistic catalyst became fully recognized.

Dutch-born Vincent van Gogh (1853–90) moved to Arles in 1888 and spent two years migrating through the historic towns of Les Baux, St-Rémy, and Stes-Maries, recording through the filter of his neuroses dozens of impressionistic scenes now prized by museums everywhere. His search, he said, was for "a different light," which led to the generation of masterpieces like *Starry Night*, *Cypresses*, *Olive Trees*, and *Boats Along the Beach*.

Van Gogh wasn't alone in his pursuit of Provençal light: Gaugin joined him eight months after his arrival, and soon thereafter engaged him in a violent quarrel, which reduced the Dutchman into a morbid depression that required his hospitalization in a local sanitarium. Within two years van Gogh returned to Paris, where he committed suicide in July 1890.

Things went somewhat better for Cézanne, who was familiar with the beauties of Provence thanks to his childhood in Aix-en-Provence. He infuriated his father, a prominent Provençal banker, by abandoning his studies to pursue painting. Later, his theories about line and color were publicized around the world. Though he migrated to Paris, he rarely set foot outside Provence from 1890 until his 1904 death. Some critics have asserted that Cézanne's later years were devoted to one obsession: recording the line, color, and texture of Montagne-St-Victoire, a rocky knoll a few hours' horse ride east of Aix. He painted it more than 60 times without ever grasping its essence the way he'd hoped. The bulk of the Provençal mountain, however, as well as the way shadows moved across its rocky planes, were decisive in affecting the cubists, whose work Cézanne directly influenced.

Mistral, bearing the letterhead of the Maison Blanche in Washington, D.C. Admission is 15 F ($2.85) for adults and 10 F ($1.90) for children. The museum is open April to October, daily from 9am to noon and 2 to 7pm; November to March, Tuesday to Sunday from 9am to noon and 2 to 5pm.

The two great classical monuments are the **Théâtre Antique,** rue du Cloître (☎ 90-96-93-30), and the Amphitheater. The Roman theater, begun by Augustus in the 1st century, was mostly destroyed and only two Corinthian columns remain. Now rebuilt, the theater is the setting for an annual drama festival in July. The theater was where the *Venus of Arles* was discovered in 1651. Take rue de la Calade from the town hall. The theater is open daily: June to September from 8:30am to 7pm, in March and October from 9am to 12:30pm and 2 to 6pm. in April from 9am to 12:30pm and 2 to 6:30pm, in May from 9am to 12:30pm and 2 to 7pm, and November to February from 9am to noon and 2 to 4:30pm. Admission is 15 F ($2.85) for adults and 9 F ($1.70) for children.

Nearby, the **Amphitheater,** Rond-Pont des Arènes (☎ **90-96-03-70**), also built in the 1st century, seats almost 25,000 and still hosts bullfights in summer. The government warns you to visit the old monument at your own risk. For a good view, you can climb the three towers that remain from medieval times, when the amphitheater was turned into a fortress. It keeps the same hours as the Roman theater (above). Admission is 15 F ($2.85) for adults and 9 F ($1.70) for children.

Perhaps the most memorable sight in Arles is **Les Alyscamps,** rue Pierre-Renaudel, once a necropolis established by the Romans, converted into a Christian burial ground in the 4th century. As the latter, it became a setting for legends in epic medieval poetry. Today it's lined with poplars as well as any remaining sarcophagi. Arlesiens escape here to enjoy a respite from the heat. Another ancient monument is the **Thermes de Constantín,** rue Dominique-Maisto, near the banks of the Rhône. Today only the baths (*thermae*) remain of a once-grand imperial palace. Visiting hours are the same as at the Amphitheater, and admission is 15 F ($2.85) for adults and 9 F ($1.70) for children.

Nearby, with an entrance at 10 rue du Grand-Prieuré, is the Musée Réattu (☎ **90-96-37-68**), with the collection of local painter Jacques Réattu. The museum has been updated with more recent works, including etchings and drawings by Picasso, some depicting bullfights. Other works are by Gauguin, Dufy, Utrillo, and Léger. Note the Arras tapestries from the 16th century. It's open daily: June to September from 9am to 12:30pm and 2 to 7pm, October to January from 10am to 12:30pm and 2 to 5pm, and February to May from 10am to 12:30pm and 2 to 7pm. Admission is 15 F ($2.85) for adults and 9 F ($1.70) for children.

WHERE TO STAY

Calendal
22 place Pomme, 13200 Arles. ☎ **90-96-11-89.** 27 rms. TEL. 320–350 F ($60.80–$66.50) double. Breakfast 32 F ($6.10) extra. AE, DC, MC, V. Closed late Jan to Feb 15. Bus 4.

On a quiet square not far from the arena, the Calendal offers rooms that have Provençal decor and some antiques, most with views of the shaded garden. A buffet breakfast is the only meal served. The Calendal has long been the bargain hunter's favorite in Arles, and the rooms have recently been redecorated.

Hôtel d'Arlatan
26 rue du Sauvage, 13631 Arles. ☎ **90-93-56-66.** Fax 90-49-68-45. 33 rms, 7 suites. MINIBAR TV TEL. 450–695 F ($85.55–$132.10) double; 795–1,350 F ($151.10–$256.65) suite. Breakfast 58 F ($11) extra. AE, DC, MC, V. Parking 55 F ($10.45). Bus 4.

In the former residence of the comtes d'Arlatan de Beaumont, near place du Forum, this hotel has been managed by the same family since 1920. It was built in the 15th century on the ruins of an old palace ordered by Constantine—in fact, there's still a wall from the 4th century. The rooms are furnished with authentic Provençal antiques, the walls covered with tapestries in the Louis XV and Louis XVI styles. Try to get a room overlooking the garden; 25 rooms are air-conditioned.

⑤ Hôtel le Cloître
16 rue du Cloître, 13200 Arles. ☎ **90-96-29-50.** Fax 90-96-02-88. 33 rms. TEL. 210–310 F ($39.90–$58.90) double; 400 F ($76) triple. Breakfast 33 F ($6.25) extra. AE, MC, V. Parking 30 F ($5.70). Bus 4.

Between the ancient theater and the cloister, this hotel is one of the best-value stops in Arles. The restored old house has a Provençal atmosphere, pleasant rooms, and a TV lounge, though 17 rooms have their own TVs. Parking is available nearby.

WHERE TO DINE

⑤ La Côte d'Adam (Adam's Rib)

12 rue de la Liberté. ☎ **90-49-62-29.** Reservations required in summer. Main courses 50–67 F ($9.50–$12.75); fixed-price menus 69 F ($13.10), 84 F ($15.95), and 99 F ($18.80). AE, MC, V. Tues–Sun noon–2pm and 7:15–9:30pm. Closed Nov 15–30. Bus 4. PROVENÇAL.

In the historic center of town, this restaurant has a rustic interior with a beamed ceiling and a high carved-stone fireplace. It holds 40 and serves such dishes as fish filets with shellfish and duckling ragoût in white wine. Many of them are imbued with fragrant olive oil. In summer it's likely to be open daily.

⑤ Hostellerie des Arènes

62 rue du Refuge. ☎ **90-96-13-05.** Reservations required. Main courses 40–75 F ($7.60–$14.25); fixed-price menus 80 F ($15.20) and 99 F ($18.80). MC, V. Wed–Mon noon–2pm and 7–9pm. Closed Jan 10–Feb 20. Bus 4. PROVENÇAL.

Close to the arena, the hostellerie offers Provençal meals whose well-prepared specialties include seafood in puff pastry, braised duckling laced with green peppercorns, brochette of mussels with tartar sauce, and veal marengo. In warm weather, meals are served on the terrace. Owner/chef Maurice Naval offers inexpensive wines by the carafe or the bottle.

Le Vaccarès

Place du Forum, 9 rue Favorin. ☎ **90-96-06-17.** Reservations required. Main courses 65–155 F ($12.35–$29.45); fixed-price menus 135 F ($25.65), 175 F ($33.25), and 235 F ($44.65). MC, V. Tues–Sat noon–2pm and 7:30–9:30pm. Closed Jan 15–Feb 15. Bus 4. PROVENÇAL.

Le Vaccarès offers southern French elegance and the finest food in town, in a setting opening onto the market of Arles. Bernard Dumas uses unusual ingredients to create innovative Provençal dishes. Specialties include sauté of lamb with pistou, sucarello of mussels with herbs, sea-devil soup, steamed sea bass, and émincé of beef with Châteauneuf. Its selection of wines is impressive (especially the Rhône Valley and Var).

6 Les Baux

444 miles S of Paris, 12 miles NE of Arles, 50 miles N of Marseille and the Mediterranean

Cardinal Richelieu called Les Baux a nesting place for eagles. In its lonely position high on a windswept plateau overlooking the southern Alpilles, Les Baux is a mere ghost of its former self. Once it was the citadel of the powerful seigneurs of Les Baux, who ruled with an iron fist and sent their conquering armies as far as Albania. The town is just 50 miles north of Marseille and the Mediterranean, nestled in a valley surrounded by mysterious, shadowy rock formations. In medieval times troubadours from all over Europe came to this "court of love," where they recited Western Europe's earliest-known vernacular poetry. Eventually, the notorious "Scourge of Provence" ruled Les Baux, sending his men throughout the land to kidnap people. If no one would pay ransom for one of his victims, the poor wretch was forced to walk a gangplank over the cliff's edge.

Fed up with the rebellions against Louis XIII in 1632, Richelieu commanded his armies to destroy Les Baux. Today the castle and ramparts are a mere shell, though you can see remains of great Renaissance mansions.

ESSENTIALS

GETTING THERE   From Arles you can take one of four daily buses (trip time: 30 min.), costing 25 F ($4.75) one way, or from Avignon three per day (June to August), taking 35 minutes and costing 38 F ($7.20) one way.

VISITOR INFORMATION   The Office de Tourisme is on impasse du Château (☎ 90-54-34-39), open Easter to October.

WHERE TO STAY
VERY EXPENSIVE

✪ L'Oustaù de Beaumanière

Les Baux, 13520 Maussane-les-Alpilles. ☎ **90-54-33-07.** Fax 90-54-40-46. 12 rms, 8 suites. A/C MINIBAR TV TEL. 1,150 F ($218.50) double; 1,400–2,100 F ($266–$399) suite. Breakfast 100 F ($19) extra. Half board 2,700–3,300 F ($513–$627) double. AE, DC, MC, V. Parking free. Closed Jan 10–Mar 3 and Nov 15–Dec 7 in winter, (restaurant closed all Wed and Thurs lunch).

This Relais & Châteaux is in the valley at the foot of Les Baux de Provence. Opened by the late Raymond Thuilier after the war, it quickly developed a loyal following and continues under Jean-André Charial, Thulier's grandson. This place consists of four separate houses, with guest rooms dating from the 16th and 17th centuries. In the stone-vaulted dining room, the chef serves specialties like lobster soufflé, mullet cooked in red wine and served on a bed of leeks, and gigot d'agneau (lamb) en croûte, followed by a soufflé of red fruits. Fixed-price menus cost 460 F ($87.40) and 720 F ($136.80). Service is daily from noon to 3pm and 7:30pm to midnight. Reservations are essential.

MODERATE

Auberge de la Bevengudo

Vallon de l'Arcoule, route d'Arles, 13520 Les Baux. ☎ **90-54-32-54.** Fax 90-54-42-58. 17 rms, 3 suites. A/C TV TEL. 520–670 F ($98.80–$127.30) double; 800–930 F ($152–$176.70) suite. Breakfast 58 F ($11) extra. AE, MC, V. Parking free outside, 50 F ($9.50) inside. Closed Nov–Feb 1.

This auberge is a tastefully converted 19th-century farmhouse surrounded by sculptured shrubbery, towering trees, and parasol pines, a mile from the village. Extras include a pool, a tennis court, and an expansive terrace. An annex contains attractive modern rooms, some with antique four-poster beds, each with a terrace. The inn serves a delectable cuisine, with menu items including pigeon roasted with black mushrooms, grilled lamb chops with ratatouille, Mediterranean sole filet fried with rosemary, and magrêt of duckling with pink peppercorns. The fixed price menus change daily and cost around 230 F ($43.70).

INEXPENSIVE

⑤ Hostellerie de la Reine-Jeanne

Grand-Rue, 13520 Les Baux. ☎ **90-54-32-06.** Fax 90-54-32-33. 11 rms. TEL. 260–330 F ($49.40–$62.70) double. Breakfast 35 F ($6.65) extra. MC, V. Closed late Nov to Feb 1 (restaurant closed Tues mid-Oct to late Nov and Feb 2 to mid-Mar).

This warm immaculate inn is the best bargain in Les Baux. Guests enter through a typical provincial French bistro where they're welcomed by Alain Guilbard. All the rooms are very comfortable, and three have their own terraces. Fixed-price menus cost 105 F ($19.95) and 150 F ($28.50).

WHERE TO DINE

✪ La Riboto de Taven

Le Val d'Enfer, 13520 Les Baux. ☎ **90-54-34-23.** Fax 90-54-38-88. Reservations required. Main courses 140–180 F ($26.60–$34.20); fixed-price menus 198 F ($37.60) (lunch only) and 280–420 F ($53.20–$79.80). AE, DC, MC, V. Tues noon–2pm, Thurs–Mon noon–2pm and 7:30–10pm. Closed Jan 5–Mar 15. FRENCH.

This 1835 farmhouse outside the medieval section of town has been owned by two generations of the Novi family, of which Christine and Philippe Theme are the English-speaking daughter and son-in-law. In summer, you can sit outdoors at the beautifully laid tables, one of which is a millstone. Menu items may include sea bass in olive oil, fricassée of mussels flavored with basil, and lamb en croûte with olives—plus homemade desserts. The cuisine is a personal statement of Jean-Pierre Novi, whose cookery is filled with brawny flavors and the heady perfumes of Provençal herbs.

It's also possible to rent two rooms so large they're like suites, each at 900 F ($171.10), plus 80 F ($15.20) for breakfast.

7 St-Rémy-de-Provence

438 miles S of Paris, 16 miles NE of Arles, 8 miles N of Les Baux

Nostradamus, the French physician/astrologer whose reputation is enjoying great vogue today, was born here in 1503. Nostradamus also has his detractors, like those who denounce the astrologer and his more than 600 obscure verses as "psychotic." In 1922 Gertrude Stein and Alice B. Toklas found St-Rémy after "wandering around everywhere a bit," Ms. Stein wrote to Cocteau. But mainly St-Rémy is associated with van Gogh. He committed himself to an asylum here in 1889 after cutting off his left ear. Between moods of despair, he painted such works as *Olive Trees* and *Cypresses.*

GETTING THERE   There are local buses from Avignon, taking 45 minutes and costing 26 F ($4.95) one way.

VISITOR INFORMATION   The Office de Tourisme is at place Jean-Jaurès (☎ **90-92-05-22**).

SEEING THE TOP ATTRACTIONS

The cloisters of the asylum van Gogh made famous in his paintings can be visited at the 12th-century **Monastère de St-Paul-de-Mausolée** (☎ **90-92-02-31**). Now a psychiatric hospital, the former monastery is east of D5, a short drive north of Glanum (see "Nearby Attractions," below). The cell in which this genius was confined from 1889 to 1890 cannot be visited, but it's still worth coming here to explore the romanesque chapel and cloisters with their circular arches and columns, which have beautifully carved capitals. The cloisters are open daily from 9am to noon and 2 to 6pm. On your way to the church you'll see a bust of van Gogh. Admission is 12 F ($2.30).

In the center of St-Rémy, the **Musée Archéologique**, in the Hôtel de Sade, rue du Parage (☎ **90-92-13-07**), displays both sculptures and bronzes excavated at Glanum. It's open June to October, daily from 9am to noon and 2 to 6pm; and in April and May, Monday to Friday from 3 to 6pm and Saturday and Sunday from 10am to noon. Admission is 12 F ($2.30) for adults and 6 F ($1.15) for children.

WHERE TO STAY

Les Antiques

15 av. Pasteur, 13210 St-Rémy-de-Provence. ☎ **90-92-03-02.** Fax 90-92-50-40. 27 rms.
MINIBAR TEL. 370–600 F ($70.30–$114.05) double. Breakfast 62 F ($11.80) extra. AE, DC,
MC, V. Parking free. Closed Oct 21–Apr 8.

This moderately priced stylish 19th-century villa is in a seven-acre park with a pool.
It contains an elegant reception lounge, which opens onto several salons. All furnishings are Napoléon III. Some of the accommodations are in a private modern
pavilion, with direct access to the garden. The rooms are handsomely furnished,
usually in pastels or rose. In summer, guests have breakfast (the only meal served)
in what used to be the Orangerie.

⊛ Château de Roussan

Route de Tarascon, 13210 St-Rémy-de-Provence. ☎ **90-92-11-63.** Fax 90-92-50-59. 21 rms,
18 with bath (tub or shower). TEL. 360–380 F ($68.40–$72.20) double without bath, 440–
750 F ($83.60–$142.55) double with bath. Breakfast 60 F ($11.40) extra. AE, MC, V. Park-
ing free.

This château's most famous resident, Renaissance psychic Nostradamus, lived in
a rustic outbuilding a few steps from the front door. Today guests pass beneath
an archway of 300-year-old trees leading to the neoclassical facade, which was constructed of softly colored local stone in 1701. As you wander around the grounds
you'll be absorbed in the history, especially when you come on the baroque sculptures lining the basin, fed by a stream. The restaurant is open for dinner, plus Sunday lunch; it's closed on Wednesday. Fixed-price menus begin at 120 F ($22.80).

✪ Vallon de Calrugues

Chemin Canto-Cigalo, 13210 St-Rémy-de-Provence. ☎ **90-92-04-40.** Fax 90-92-44-01.
41 rms, 12 suites. MINIBAR TV TEL. 980 F ($186.30) double; from 1,480 F ($281.35) suite.
Breakfast 105 F ($19.95) extra. AE, DC, MC, V. Parking free.

Surrounded by a park, this stylish Mediterranean hotel has the best accommodations and restaurant in town. Owners Françoise and Jean-Michel Gallon offer
beautifully furnished rooms and suites, all with built-in safes. The rooms have been
recently enlarged and renovated, with marble baths added. The dining terrace alone
may compete with the cuisine, which under young Gilles Blandin is winning early
praise for his innovative, light dishes. Facilities include a pool, tennis courts, a
sauna and gym, and horseback riding (for which you pay extra).

WHERE TO DINE

⊛ Bar/Hôtel/Restaurant des Arts

32 bd. Victor-Hugo, 13210 St-Rémy-de-Provence. ☎ **90-92-08-50.** Reservations recommended. Main courses 70–140 F ($13.30–$26.60). AE, DC, MC, V. Wed–Mon noon–2pm
and 7:30–9:30pm. Closed Feb and Nov 1–12. FRENCH.

This old-style café/restaurant and hotel is on the east side. The wait for dinner can
be as long as 45 minutes, so you may want to spend some time in the bar, with
its wooden tables and slightly faded decor. The restaurant is time-tested, with pine
paneling, copper pots, and original paintings. The menu lists specialties like rabbit terrine, steak au poivre with champagne, tournedos with madeira and mushrooms, duckling in orange sauce, and trout served three ways. By special order the
chef will serve crayfish, lobster, and game dishes.

If you want to spend the night, the 17 rooms upstairs are basic, some in
Provençal style, with rustic ceiling beams and exposed timbers; 8 have baths. A

room without bath costs 185 F ($35.15), rising to 328 F ($62.30) with bath, plus 40 F ($7.60) for breakfast.

Le Jardin de Frédéric

8 bd. Gambetta. ☎ **90-92-27-76.** Reservations required. Main courses 90–110 F ($17.10–$20.90); fixed-price menu 165 F ($31.35). AE, DC, MC, V. Thurs–Tues noon–2pm and 7:30–9:30pm. Closed Feb. FRENCH.

Housed in a small villa close to the town center, this popular bistro is the best restaurant around. The family-run restaurant offers rabbit with plums, terrine de canard, onion tart, gigot with roquefort, and poached turbot with sorrel. It's almost the type of food you'd be served in a local Provençal home. In summer guests can dine at tables in front of the house.

NEARBY ATTRACTIONS

A mile south of St-Rémy on D5 is **Ruines de Glanum,** avenue Vincent-van-Gogh (☎ **90-92-23-79**), a Gallo-Roman city (follow the signs to "Les Antiques"). Its historical monuments include an Arc Municipal, a triumphal arch dating from the time of Julius Caesar, and a cenotaph called the Mausolée des Jules. Garlanded with sculptured fruits and flowers, the arch dates from 20 B.C. and is the oldest in Provence. The mausoleum was raised to honor the grandsons of Augustus and is the only extant monument of its type. In the area are entire streets and foundations of private residences from the 1st-century town. Some remains are from an even earlier Gallo-Greek town dating from the 2nd century B.C. Admission is 28 F ($5.30) for adults and 16 F ($3.05) for ages 18 to 24 and over 60; 17 and under free. The excavations are open daily: April to September from 9am to 7pm, and October to March from 9am to noon and 2 to 5pm.

8 Avignon

425 miles S of Paris, 50 miles NW of Aix-en-Provence, 66 miles NW of Marseille

In the 14th century, Avignon was the capital of Christendom; the popes lived here during what the Romans called the Babylonian Captivity. The legacy left by that "court of splendor and magnificence" makes Avignon one of the most interesting and beautiful of Europe's cities of the Middle Ages.

ESSENTIALS

GETTING THERE   Avignon is a junction for bus routes throughout the region and train service from other towns is frequent. The TGV trains from Paris arrive 13 times per day (trip time: 4 hr.), and 17 trains per day arrive from Marseille (trip time: $1^1/_2$ hr.).

VISITOR INFORMATION   The Office de Tourisme is at 41 cours Jean-Jaurès (☎ 90-82-65-11).

EXPLORING THE TOWN

Even more famous than the papal residency is the ditty "Sur le pont d'Avignon, l'on y danse, l'on y danse," echoing through every French nursery and around the world. Ironically, **pont St-Bénézet** was far too narrow for the danse of the rhyme. Spanning the Rhône and connecting Avignon with Villeneuve-lèz-Avignon, the bridge is now only a fragmented ruin. According to legend, it was inspired by a vision a shepherd named Bénézet had while tending his flock. Actually, the bridge

A Tale of Two Papal Cities

In 1309 a sick man named Pope Clement V, nearing the end of his life, arrived in Avignon. Lodged as a guest of the Dominicans, he died in the spring of 1314 and was succeeded by John XXII. The new pope, unlike the previous Roman popes, lived modestly in the Episcopal Palace. When Benedict XII took over, he enlarged and rebuilt the palace. Clement VI, who followed, built an even more elaborate extension called the New Palace. After Innocent VI and Urban V, Pope Gregory XI did no building. Inspired by Catherine of Siena, he wanted to return the papacy to Rome and succeeded. In all, seven popes reigned at Avignon. Under them, art and culture flourished, as did vice. Prostitutes blatantly went about peddling their wares in front of cardinals, rich merchants were robbed, and innocent pilgrims from the hinterlands were brutally tricked and swindled.

From 1378, during what's known as the Great Schism, one pope ruled in Avignon, another in Rome. The reign of the pope and the "antipope" continued, one following the other, until both rulers were dismissed by the 1417 election of Martin V. Rome continued to rule Avignon until it was joined to France at the time of the Revolution. The ramparts (still standing) around Avignon were built in the 14th century and are characterized by their machicolated battlements, turrets, and old gates.

was built between 1117 and 1185 and suffered various disasters from then on. In 1669 half the bridge toppled into the river. On one of the piers is the two-story Chapelle St-Nicolas—one story in romanesque style, the other in gothic. The bridge is open daily: April to September from 9am to 6:30pm, and October to March from 9am to 5pm. Admission is 10 F ($1.90).

Dominating Avignon from a hill is the **Palais des Papes,** place du Palais-des-Papes (☎ **90-27-50-71**). You're shown through on a guided tour, usually lasting 50 minutes. The tour is somewhat monotonous, as most of the rooms have been stripped of their finery. The exception is the Chapelle St-Jean, known for its beautiful frescoes attributed to the school of Matteo Giovanetti and painted between 1345 and 1348. These frescoes present scenes from the life of John the Baptist and John the Evangelist. More Giovanetti frescoes can be found above St. John's Chapel in the Chapelle St-Martial. The frescoes depict the miracles of St. Martial, the patron saint of Limousin.

The Grand Tinel (banquet hall) is about 135 feet long and 30 feet wide, and the pope's table stood on the southern side. The pope's bedroom is on the first floor of the Tour des Anges. Its walls are entirely decorated in tempera with foliage on which birds and squirrels perch. Birdcages are painted in the recesses of the windows. In a secular vein, the Stag Room—the study of Clement VI—was frescoed in 1343 with hunting scenes. Added under the same Clement, who had a taste for grandeur, the Great Audience Hall contains frescoes of the prophets, also attributed to Giovanetti and painted in 1352.

The palace is open daily: July to September from 9am to 7pm, April to June and in October from 9am to 12:15pm and 2 to 6pm, and November to March from 9am to noon and 2 to 5pm. Admission is 38 F ($7.20) for adults and 29 F

($5.50) for children and those over 65. Guided tours in English depart daily at 10am and 3pm, costing 46 F ($8.75) for adults and 37 F ($7.05) for children.

Near the palace is the 12th-century **Cathédrale Notre-Dame,** place du Palais-des-Papes, containing the flamboyant gothic tomb of John XXII, who died at age 90. Benedict XII is also buried here. Crowning the top is a gilded statue of the Virgin from the 19th century. The cathedral is open daily from 11am to 6pm and admission is free. From the cathedral, enter the promenade du Rocher-des-Doms to stroll through its garden and enjoy the view across the Rhône to Villeneuve-lèz-Avignon.

The **Musée du Petit-Palais,** place du Palais-des-Papes (☎ **90-86-44-58**), contains an important collection of paintings from the Italian schools from the 13th to the 16th century, including works from Florence, Venice, Siena, and Lombardy. In addition, salons display 15th-century paintings done in Avignon and several galleries are devoted to Roman and gothic sculptures. It's open Wednesday to Monday from 9:30 to 11:50am and 2 to 6pm. Admission is 18 F ($3.40) for adults and 9 F ($1.70) for children.

The **Musée Calvet,** 67 rue Joseph-Vernet (☎ **90-86-33-84**), is housed in an 18th-century mansion displaying prehistoric stoneware, Greek marbles, Egyptian monuments, and many paintings. Our favorite oil is by Brueghel (the younger), *Le Cortège Nuptial* (The Bridal Procession). Look for a copy of Bosch's *Adoration of the Magi* as well. Other works are by David, Manet, Delacroix, Daumier, and Renoir. It's open daily from 10am to noon and 2 to 6pm. Admission is 20 F ($3.80) for adults and 10 F ($1.90) for children.

The **Musée Lapidaire,** entered at 18 rue de la République (☎ **90-85-75-38**), is in a 17th-century Jesuit church displaying an important collection of Gallo-Roman sculptures. It's open Wednesday to Monday from 10am to noon and 2 to 6pm. Admission is 15 F ($2.85) for adults; children free.

SEEING VILLENEUVE-LEZ-AVIGNON

A 45-F ($8.55) ticket—available at the sights below—gains you admission to all the town's attractions. The modern world is impinging on Avignon, but across the Rhône at Villeneuve-lèz-Avignon the Middle Ages slumber on. When the popes lived in exile at Avignon, wealthy cardinals built palaces (*livrées*) across the river. Many visitors prefer to stay or dine there rather than in Avignon (see our recommendations, below).

However, even if you're staying at Avignon or just passing through, you'll want to visit Villeneuve, especially to see its Carthusian monastery, **Chartreuse du Val-de-Bénédiction,** 60 rue de la République (☎ **90-25-05-46**). France's largest charterhouse, it's now a cultural center, where artistic events are organized throughout the year.

Pope Innocent VI (whose tomb can be viewed) founded this charterhouse, which became the most powerful in the country. Inside, a remarkable *Coronation of the Virgin* by Enguerrand Charonton is enshrined; painted in 1453, the masterpiece contains a fringed bottom that's Bosch-like in its horror, representing the denizens of hell. The 12th-century graveyard cloister is lined with cells where the former fathers prayed and meditated. The charterhouse is open daily: April to September from 9am to 6:30pm, and October to June from 9:30am to 5:30pm.

Crowning the town is **Fort St-André** (☎ **90-25-45-35**), founded in 1360 by Jean-le-Bon to serve as a symbol of might to the pontifical powers across the river.

The Abbaye St-André, now owned privately, was installed in the 18th century. You can visit the formal garden encircling the mansion. The mood here is tranquil, with a rose-trellis colonnade, fountains, and flowers.

The grounds are open daily: April to September from 9am to noon and 2 to 6:30pm, and October to March from 10am to noon and 2 to 5pm. Admission costs 8 F ($1.50). You can also visit the twin towers, with their impressive rooms and terraces with panoramic views. The towers are open daily: April to September from 9:30am to 12:30pm and 2 to 6:30pm, and October to March from 10am to noon and 2 to 5pm.

Last, visit the **Eglise Notre-Dame,** place Meissonier, founded in 1333 by Cardinal Arnaud de Via. Its proudest possession is a 14th-century Virgin of Ivory, one of the great French treasures. It's open Wednesday to Monday: April to September from 10am to noon and 3 to 7:30pm, and October to March from 10am to noon and 2 to 5pm. Admission is free.

WHERE TO STAY
VERY EXPENSIVE

✪ La Mirande
4 place Amirande, 84000 Avignon. ☎ **90-85-93-93.** Fax 90-86-26-85. 20 rms, 1 suite. A/C MINIBAR TV TEL. 2,100 F ($399.20) double; 2,600 F ($494.30) suite. Breakfast 95 F ($18.05) extra. AE, DC, V.

In the heart of Avignon, this restored 700-year-old town house is one of the grand little luxuries of France. Behind the Palais des Papes, the hotel treats you to two centuries of decorative art in France—from the 1700s Salon Chinois to the Salon Rouge, its striped walls in Rothschild red. In 1987 the house was acquired by Achim and Hannelore Stein who, with their son and daughter and a Paris decorator, transformed it into a citadel of luxury. The most sought-out room is no. 20, opening onto the garden. But all the rooms are stunning, with huge tubs. The restaurant earns its one star in Michelin and is among the finest in Avignon. Chef Eric Coisel has a light, sophisticated touch. But since our last meal there had two outstanding dishes and one far off target, we prefer to give the Frommer star to the hotel, not the restaurant.

EXPENSIVE

Hôtel d'Europe
12 place Grillon, 84000 Avignon. ☎ **90-82-66-92.** Fax 90-85-43-66. 44 rms, 3 suites. A/C TV TEL. 780–1,600 F ($148.25–$304.15) double; 2,300 F ($437.25) suite. Breakfast 90 F ($17.10) extra. AE, DC, MC, V. Parking 50 F ($9.50).

The vine-covered Hôtel d'Europe has been in operation since 1799. You enter through a courtyard, where tables are set in the warmer months. The grand hall and salons boast tastefully arranged antiques and decorative elements, such as Aubusson tapestries. The good-size guest rooms have handsome decorations, period furnishings, and tile or marble baths. Three suites are perched on the roof with views of the Palais des Papes. In some twin-bedded rooms the beds are a bit narrow. Its restaurant, La Vielle Fontaine, is the most distinguished in Avignon, but not the best. Meals are served in elegant dining rooms or in a charming inner courtyard. The wine list is impressive but celestial in price, and the cookery ranges from sublime to off-the-mark.

MODERATE

Mercure Palais-des-Papes

Quartier de la Balance, rue Ferruce, 84000 Avignon. ☎ **90-85-91-23.** Fax 90-85-32-40. 86 rms. A/C TV TEL. 460–560 F ($87.45–$106.45) double. Breakfast 50 F ($9.50) extra. AE, DC, MC, V. Parking 50 F ($9.50). Bus 11.

This chain hotel is one of the best in Avignon. It lies within the city walls, at the foot of the Palace of the Popes. The rooms are well furnished, though functional and without any particular style. There's a small bar but no restaurant, as breakfast is the only meal served. Avoid the skimpy room service tray and head for the buffet breakfast.

INEXPENSIVE

Hôtel d'Angleterre

29 bd. Raspail, 84000 Avignon. ☎ **90-86-34-31.** Fax **90-86-86-74.** 40 rms, 35 with bath (tub or shower). TEL. 250–360 F ($47.50–$68.40) double with bath. Breakfast 35 F ($6.65) extra. MC, V. Parking free. Closed Dec 22–Jan 15. Bus 11.

Near the heart of Avignon, this classical structure is the best budget hotel. The rooms are comfortably but basically furnished, 35 with TVs. Breakfast is the only meal served.

Hôtel Danieli

17 rue de la République, 84000 Avignon. ☎ **90-86-46-82.** Fax 90-27-09-24. 29 rms. TV TEL. 390–470 F ($74.10–$89.35) double. Breakfast 35 F ($6.65) extra. AE, DC, MC, V. Bus 11.

This hotel's Italian influence is clear in its arches, chiseled stone, tile floors, and baronial staircases. It's small and informal. The rooms combine modern furnishings with touches of art deco, yet are not particularly special, though they're well-maintained. Breakfast is the only meal served.

WHERE TO DINE

✪ Christian Etienne

10 rue Mons. ☎ **90-86-16-50.** Reservations recommended. Main courses 120–290 F ($22.80–$55.10); fixed-price lunch (Mon–Fri) 160 F ($30.40); fixed-price menus 280 F ($53.20), 290 F ($55.10), 400 F ($76), and 480 F ($91.25). AE, MC, V. July, daily noon–2:30pm and 8–10:30pm; the rest of the year, Mon–Sat noon–2:30pm and 8–10:30pm. FRENCH.

The stone house containing this restaurant was built just before the Palais des Papes (next door) and was used as the office of the building supervisor. The dining room contains very old ceiling and wall frescoes honoring the marriage of Anne de Bretagne to the French king in 1491. Several of the fixed-price menus present specific themes: For example, the one at 290 F ($55.10) features only vegetables, the one at 400 F ($76) offers preparations of lobster, and the one at 480 F ($91.25) relies on the discretion of the chef (*un menu "confiance"*). A la carte specialties include fennel soup with sea barnacles, terrine of foie gras cooked with sauterne, roast pigeon with escalope of foie gras, and filet of sole cooked with dill and stuffed with compôte of eggplant. Christian Etienne is enjoying his reign as the star chef of Avignon. Throughout the year, based on what's available, he shows the full range and depth of his culinary repertoire and is always adding to it.

ⓢ La Fourchette II

7 rue Racine. ☎ **90-85-20-93.** Reservations not required. Main courses 70–100 F ($13.30–$19); fixed-price lunch 100 F ($19); fixed-price menus 110–145 F ($20.90–$27.55). MC, V. Mon–Fri noon–2pm and 7:30–9:30pm. Closed Aug 12–27. Bus 11. FRENCH.

This bistro offers creative cooking at a moderate price. There are two dining rooms, one like a summerhouse with walls of glass, the other more like a tavern with oak beams. You might begin with parfait of chicken liver with spinach flan or mousseline of fish in saffron sauce. Fresh sardines marinated with citrus also are served. Two specialties are daube of beef avignonnaise style with macaroni and the grilled lambs' liver with raisins.

✪ Hiély-Lucullus

5 rue de la République. ☎ **90-86-17-07.** Reservations required. Fixed-price menus 140 F ($26.60), 210 F ($39.90), and 310 F ($58.90). AE, MC, V. Mon 7:30–9:30pm, Wed–Sun noon–2pm and 7:30–9:30pm. Closed Jan 10–24 and June 19–July 4. Bus 11. FRENCH.

This Relais Gourmand is wonderful. The town's most fabled chef, Pierre Hiély, has retired, though he drops in occasionally to check up on how his former sous-chef, André Chaussy, is doing. He's doing just fine and is still offering those reasonably priced fixed-price menus (no à la carte). The same cuisine is offered, with occasional creative touches added. Try one of his special appetizers, such as petite marmite du pêcheur, a savory fish soup ringed with black mussels. A main-dish specialty is pintadeau (young guinea hen) with peaches. The pièce de résistance is agneau des Alpilles grillé (alpine lamb) sur feu de bois. Carafe wines include Tavel Rosé and Châteauneuf-du-Pape.

WHERE TO STAY & DINE IN VILLENEUVE-LEZ-AVIGNON

ⓢ Hôtel de l'Atelier

5 rue de la Foire, 30400 Villeneuve-lèz-Avignon. ☎ **90-25-01-84.** Fax 90-25-80-06. 19 rms. TV TEL. 220–420 F ($41.80–$79.80) double. Breakfast 38 F ($7.20) extra. AE, DC, MC, V. Parking free on street, 45 F ($8.55) in nearby garage.

Villeneuve's budget offering is this 16th-century village house that has preserved much of its original style. Inside is a tiny duplex lounge with a large stone fireplace. Outside, a sun-filled rear garden, with potted orange and fig trees, provides fruit for the breakfast. The immaculate accommodations are comfortable and informal, though a bit dowdy. In the old bourgeois dining room, a continental breakfast is the only meal served.

✪ La Magnaneraie Hostellerie

37 rue Camp-Bataille, 30400 Villeneuve-lèz-Avignon. ☎ **90-25-11-11.** Fax 90-25-46-37. 25 rms, 2 suites. A/C MINIBAR TV TEL. 600–1,100 F ($114.05–$209.10) double; 1,500 F ($285.15) suite. Breakfast 75 F ($14.25) extra. AE, DC, MC, V. Parking free.

One of the most charming accommodations in the region is on 2 acres of gardens under the direction of Gérard and Eliane Prayal. Tastefully renovated and enlarged with a new wing in the 1980s, the place is furnished with antiques and good reproductions. Many guests here arrive for only one night but remain for many days, to enjoy the good food, atmosphere, garden, tennis court, and landscaped pool. In 1993, the government rating of this inn was increased to four stars, mostly because of M. Prayal's excellent cuisine. His fixed-price menus range from 170 F ($32.30) for a celebration of traditional Provençal recipes to 330 F ($62.70) for a *menu dégustation*. Menu items might include zucchini flowers stuffed with mushroom-and-cream purée, petit feuilleté of foie gras and truffles, croustillant of red snapper with basil and olive oil, and rack of lamb with thyme. Dessert might be gratin of seasonal fruits with sabayon of lavender-flavored honey.

9 Orange

409 miles S of Paris, 34 miles NE of Nêmes, 75 miles NW of Marseille, 16 miles S of Avignon

Orange gets its name from the days when it was a dependency of the Dutch House of Orange-Nassau. Overlooking the Valley of the Rhône, the city tempts visitors with the third-largest triumphal arch extant in Europe and the best-preserved Roman theater in Europe. Louis XIV, who toyed with the idea of moving the theater to Versailles, said: "It is the finest wall in my kingdom."

In the southern part of town, the ✪ **Théâtre Antique,** place des Frères-Mounet (☎ 90-51-80-06), dates from the days of Augustus. Built into the side of a hill, it once held 8,000 spectators in tiered seats divided into three sections based on class. Carefully restored, the nearly 350-foot-long and 125-foot-high theater is noted for its fine acoustics and is used today for outdoor entertainment. It's open daily: April to September from 9am to 6:30pm, and October to March from 9am to noon and 1:30 to 5pm. Admission is 25 F ($4.75) for adults and 20 F ($3.80) for children.

To the west of the theater once stood one of the biggest temples in Gaul, which, with a gymnasium and the theater, formed one of the greatest buildings in the empire. Across the street at place des Frères-Mounet, the **Musée Municipal d'Orange,** place du Théâtre-Antique (☎ 90-51-80-06), displays fragments excavated in the arena. Your ticket to the ancient theater will also admit you to this museum, which is open Monday to Saturday: April to September from 9am to 6:30pm, and October to March from 9am to noon and 1:30 to 5:30pm.

Even older than the theater is the **Triumphal Arch** on avenue de l'Arc-de-Triomphe. It has decayed, but its sculptural decorations and other elements are still fairly well preserved. Built to honor the conquering legions of Caesar, it rises 72 feet and is nearly 70 feet wide. Composed of a trio of arches held up by Corinthian columns, it was used as a dungeon for prisoners in the Middle Ages.

Before leaving Orange, head for the hilltop park, **Colline St-Eutrope,** for a view of the surrounding valley with its mulberry plantations.

ESSENTIALS

GETTING THERE   Orange sits on some of the major French north-south rail and highway arteries, making arrivals by train, bus, or car convenient. Twenty trains per day arrive from Avignon (trip time: 17 min.), costing 27 F ($5.15) one way. From Marseille there are 14 trains per day (trip time: 1¹/₂ hr.), costing 100 F ($19) one way. From Paris there are 14 trains per day (trip time: 4¹/₂ hr.), costing 335 F ($63.65) one way.

VISITOR INFORMATION   The Office de Tourisme is on cours Aristide-Briand (☎ 90-34-70-88).

SPECIAL EVENTS   At the end of July, a drama, dance, and music festival called **Les Chorégies d'Orange** takes place at the Théâtre Antique. For information or tickets, call 90-34-15-52.

WHERE TO STAY

ⓢ Hôtel Louvre et Terminus
89 av. Frédéric-Mistral, 84100 Orange. ☎ **90-34-10-08.** Fax 90-34-68-71. 32 rms, 2 suites.
TEL. 320 F ($60.80) double; 390 F ($74.10) suite. Breakfast 38 F ($7.20) extra. AE, MC, V.
Parking 38 F ($7.20). Closed Dec 20–Jan 5.

Surrounded by a garden terrace, this conservatively decorated hotel, a Logis de
France, offers good value. Here, 12 rooms have minibars, 34 contain TVs, and 16
are air-conditioned. The hotel also has a good restaurant, serving meals daily beginning at 90 F ($17.10). It also has a pool.

Mercure Altea Orange
80 route de Caderousse, 84100 Orange. ☎ **90-34-24-10.** Fax 90-34-85-48. 99 rms.
MINIBAR TV TEL. 440 F ($83.60) double. Breakfast 52 F ($9.90) extra. AE, DC, MC, V. Parking free.

This is a comfortable modern hotel outside the edge of the city. Its well-furnished
rooms are arranged around a series of gardens, the largest of which contains a pool.
Fixed-price menus in the poolside restaurant go from 70 to 160 F ($13.30 to
$30.40).

WHERE TO DINE

Le Parvis
3 cours Pourtoules. ☎ **90-34-82-00.** Reservations required. Main courses 60–110 F ($11.40–
$20.90); fixed-price menus 98 F ($18.60), 128 F ($24.30), 152 F ($28.90), and 205 F
($38.95). AE, DC, MC, V. Tues–Sat noon–2:30pm and 7–9:30pm, Sun noon–2:30pm. Closed
Nov 17–Dec 3. FRENCH.

Jean-Michel Berengier sets the best table in Orange, though the dining room is
rather austere. He bases his cuisine on not only well-selected vegetables but also
the best ingredients from "mountain or sea." Try his escalope of braised sea bass
with fennel or feuilleté of asparagus. Lamb is a specialty, but the way it's cooked
depends on the season. Service is efficient and polite. A special children's menu
is offered for 60 F ($11.40).

NEARBY ACCOMMODATIONS

Château de Rochegude
26790 Rochegude. ☎ **75-04-81-88.** Fax 75-04-89-87. 25 rms, 4 suites. A/C MINIBAR
TV TEL. 650–1,500 F ($123.55–$285.15) double; 1,800–2,500 F ($342.20–$475.25) suite.
Breakfast 80 F ($15.20) extra. AE, DC, MC, V. Parking free. Closed Jan–Feb. Take D976
toward Gap for 9 miles.

This Relais & Châteaux stands on 20 acres of parkland. The stone castle is at the
edge of a hill, surrounded by Rhône vineyards. Throughout its history this 11th-
century turreted residence has been renovated by a series of distinguished owners,
ranging from the pope to the dauphin. The current owners have made many 20th-
century additions, but ancient touches still survive. Each room is done in a period
style, such as Napoléon III or Louis XVI. The food and service are exceptional.
You can enjoy meals surrounded by flowering plants in the stately dining room.
There are also a barbecue by the pool and sunny terraces where refreshments are
served. In the restaurant, fixed-price menus cost 200 F ($38) at weekday lunches;
other menus (available at both lunch and dinner) cost 280 to 480 F ($53.20 to
$91.25).

25 The French Riviera

It's been called the world's most exciting stretch of beach and "a sunny place for shady people." Every habitué has a favorite oasis here and will try to convince you of its merits: Some say "Nice is passé." Others maintain that "Cannes is queen." Others shun both in favor of Juan-les-Pins, and still others would winter only at St-Jean-Cap-Ferrat. If you have a large bankroll you may prefer Cap d'Antibes, but if money is short you can try the old port of Villefranche.

Each resort on the Riviera, known as the Côte d'Azur (Azure Coast)—be it Beaulieu by the sea or eagle's-nest Eze—offers its unique flavor and special merits. Glitterati and eccentrics have always been attracted to this narrow strip of fabled real estate, less than 125 miles long, between the Mediterranean and a trio of mountain ranges. Perhaps the Russians were the most eccentric, fleeing winter's fury for clear skies, blue waters, and orange groves.

A trail of modern artists attracted to the brilliant light and setting of the Côte d'Azur have left a rich heritage: Matisse in his chapel at Vence, Cocteau at Menton and Villefranche, Picasso at Antibes and seemingly everywhere else, Léger at Biot, Renoir at Cagnes, and Bonnard at Le Cannet. The best collection of all is at the Maeght Foundation in St-Paul-de-Vence.

The Riviera's high season used to be winter and spring only. However, with changing tastes, July and August have long been the most crowded months, and reservations are imperative. The average summer temperature is 75°F; the average winter temperature, 49°F.

The Corniches of the Riviera, depicted in countless films, stretch from Nice to Menton. The Alps here drop into the Mediterranean, and roads were carved along the way. The lower road, about 20 miles long, is the **Corniche Inférieure.** Along this road are the port of Villefranche, Cap-Ferrat, Beaulieu, and Cap-Martin. Built between World War I and the beginning of World War II, the **Moyenne Corniche** (Middle Road), 19 miles long, also runs from Nice to Menton, winding spectacularly in and out of tunnels and through mountains. The highlight is at mountaintop Eze. The **Grande Corniche**—the most panoramic—was ordered built by Napoléon in 1806. La Turbie and Le Vistaero are the principal towns along the 20-mile stretch, which reaches more than 1,600 feet high at Col d'Eze.

The French Riviera

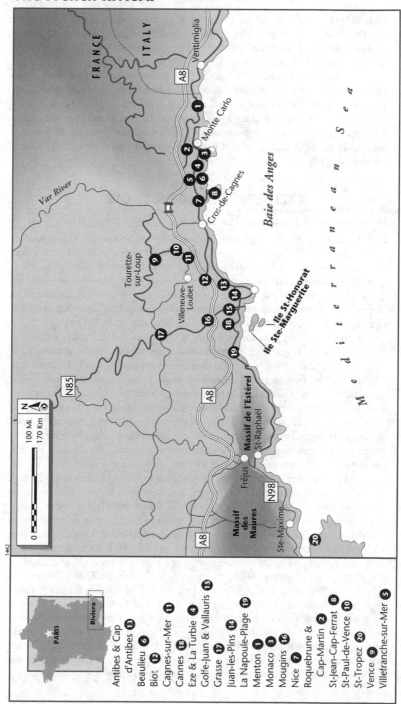

Antibes & Cap
d'Antibes ⓭

Beaulieu ⓺

Biot ⓬

Cagnes-sur-Mer ⓫

Cannes ⓲

Eze & La Turbie ⓸

Golf-Juan & Vallauris ⓯

Grasse ⓱

Juan-les-Pins ⓮

La Napoule-Plage ⓳

Menton ❶

Monaco ❸

Mougins ⓰

Nice ❼

Roquebrune &
Cap-Martin ❷

St-Jean-Cap-Ferrat ❽

St-Paul-de-Vence ⓾

St-Tropez ⓴

Vence ❾

Villefranche-sur-Mer ❺

REGIONAL CUISINE In the 19th century an undeveloped coastal strip of eastern Provence was deemed "the Riviera." Technically, the Riviera is part of Provence, and all the culinary traditions of that region (see Chapter 24) apply to it, albeit in slightly diluted forms.

The Riviera houses some of the bastions of French cuisine alongside budget eateries catering to culinary fads, juxtaposed in sometimes-uncomfortable proximity. Outside Paris, the Riviera probably has more types of restaurants and greater numbers of "theme restaurants" than anywhere else in France. In other words, expect a generalized context of Provençal cuisine, with generous doses of the kinds of international sophistication you'd expect to find in Paris, New York, Rome, London, or Tokyo.

EXPLORING THE REGION BY CAR

Here's how to link together the best of the Riviera if you rent a car.

Day 1 Begin at the Riviera's westernmost outpost, St-Tropez, where you can explore the sensual charms of a town whose world publicity began long before Brigitte Bardot made it cinematically famous. Stay the night here.

Days 2–4 Drive southeast along the coastal road (N98) for 47 miles, with the intention of settling in for the night at either Cannes or its satellite resort of La Napoule. Test your luck in any of the resort's casinos and explore what many Parisians consider the most culturally absorbing large city of the Riviera.

Use your hotel as a base for exploring at least four of the attractions nearby: Mougins (a stone town, 5 miles north of Cannes, famous for the restaurants of Roger Vergé); Grasse (whose perfume distilleries were praised by the French kings, 11 miles north); Biot (site of the Léger museum, 9 miles northeast), and Golfe-Juan and Vallauris (a hamlet made famous for its pottery by Picasso, 4 miles east).

Day 5 Now head farther east. Make an early-morning start so you can visit Cap d'Antibes (a *très* chic resort with some of the most expensive hotels in Europe), Antibes (site of the Picasso museum, a once-sleepy fishing village with reasonably priced hotels), and Juan-les-Pins (a middlebrow resort that attracts lots of families but can still be lots of fun). Since all three are less than 4 miles from one another, select a hotel in one or another, but make it a point to at least drive through the other two. At some point we suggest you stop for a meal at Restaurant de Bacon, boulevard de-Bacon, Cap d'Antibes (☎ **93-61-50-02**). It's one of the few places in France where bouillabaisse is a legend unto itself (almost everyone orders it). Skip the gussied-up versions made with lobster and order *bouillabaisse nature*, which despite its apparent simplicity will set you back 450 F ($85.50) per person.

Day 6 Today you can explore three towns within 5 miles of one another: Cagnes-sur-Mer (site of a hilltop fortress where Simone de Beauvoir wrote *Les Mandarins*), St-Paul-de-Vence (a "perched village" fortified during the early Middle Ages to protect its residents from Saracen raids), and Vence (legendary site of a buried treasure that's never been found). From Antibes, drive 7 miles northeast to reach Cagnes-sur-Mer, where your exploration begins. Regardless of the town you select, remember that in St-Paul-de-Vence is the Fondation Maeght and in Vence is the Matisse museum. You'll have a busy day just making it to the top sights, and if you want to luxuriate in the region, you might devote two days to its charms.

What's Special About the French Riviera

Outstanding Museums
- Musée Ile-de-France, at St-Jean, with the collection of the baronne de Rothschild.
- The Maeght Foundation, at St-Paul-de-Vence, a distinguished modern-art collection.
- Matisse Chapel, not a museum but the artist's final masterpiece, at age 77.

Great Towns
- Roquebrune, a restored medieval hill village.
- St-Paul-de-Vence, a fortified hill village favored by artists.
- Eze, on a rocky outcrop above the sea.
- St-Jean-Cap-Ferrat, a peninsula for the glitterati.

Great Resorts
- Monte Carlo/Monaco, the Côte d'Azur at its most glamorous and expensive—with casino action.
- Nice, still the reigning resort, but now a little tarnished.
- Cannes, for the trappings of ultra-sophistication.
- St-Tropez, the *only* place to be if you look like Bardot did when she filmed *Et Dieu créa la femme* (*And God Created Woman*) here.

Events & Festivals
- Monte Carlo Motor Rally, in mid- to late January, one of the world's most famous races.
- Carnival of Nice, mid- to late February, France's major carnival.
- Cannes Film Festival, mid- to late May, a parade of flesh, genius, and dashed hopes.

Beaches
- Cannes, with a bikini-clogged sandy beach, at La Croisette; the Hôtel Carlton has the most fashionable strip.
- St-Tropez, with sandy beaches running for 4 miles—all topless and some bottomless, where exotic hedonism reigns.

Days 7–8 Your drive on Day 7 marks your transition from the western to the eastern Riviera, a mountainous region greatly influenced by neighboring Italy. The best resorts are confusingly scattered in a random pattern around Nice, so we propose that you drive southeast to Nice. (Regardless of which town you choose for your overnight on Day 6, your early-morning drive won't involve a distance of more than 14 miles.) Use Nice as a base for exploring St-Jean-Cap-Ferrat (6 miles east), Villefranche-sur-Mer (4 miles east), Beaulieu (6 miles east), and Eze and La Turbie (7 miles northeast). By the time you reach Roquebrune, signs pointing to nearby Monaco will become increasingly visible, but since Monaco deserves a full day, return to Nice for the night and delay your immersion into the glitter (and urban congestion) of Monaco for the following day.

Day 9 Drive 11 miles east of Nice for a full day in Monaco. Check into a hotel as early as the staff will allow, then plan on visits to the Grimaldi family palace (open only from June to September) and its museum (open all year), the oceanographic museum, and the casinos.

Day 10   Leave Monaco, heading 3 miles northeast for Roquebrune, with its château and satellite resort of Cap-Martin, then head east for 5 miles to Menton, a sleepy border town whose sun-flooded allure is more Italianate than French. Spend the night here or, for an added adventure (if your passport and the rental contract for your car allow you to do so), continue driving into Italy, where the hotels, restaurants, and *dolce vita* of the Italian Riviera beckon. For details on coverage beyond the French-Italian border, refer to *Frommer's Italy '96*.

1 Menton

596 miles S of Paris, 39 miles NE of Cannes, 5 miles E of Monaco

Menton is more Italianate than French. Right at the border of Italy, Menton marks the eastern frontier of the Côte d'Azur. Its climate, incidentally, is the warmest on the Mediterranean coast, a reputation that attracts a large, rather elderly British colony throughout the winter. Menton experiences a foggy day every 10 years—or so they say.

According to a local legend, Eve was the first to experience Menton's glorious climate. Expelled from the Garden of Eden along with Adam, she tucked a lemon in her bosom, planting it at Menton because it reminded her of her former stamping ground. The lemons still grow in profusion here, and the fruit of that tree is given a position of honor at the **Lemon Festival** in February. Actually, the oldest Menton visitor may have arrived 30,000 years ago. He's still around—or at least his skull is—in the Municipal Museum (below).

Don't be misled by all those "palace-hotels" studding the hills. No longer open to the public, they've been divided and sold as private apartments. Many of these turn-of-the-century structures were erected to accommodate elderly Europeans, mainly English and German, who arrived carrying a book written by one Dr. Bennett in which he extolled the joys of living at Menton.

ESSENTIALS

GETTING THERE   There are good bus and rail connections that make stops at each resort along the Mediterranean coast, including Menton. Many visitors arrive by car along one of the corniche roads. Two trains per hour arrive from Nice (trip time: 35 min.), and two trains per hour from Monte Carlo (trip time: 10 min.). A local company, Autocars Broch, also runs buses between Nice and Menton, one almost every hour. The same frequent bus service is offered between Monte Carlo and Menton.

VISITOR INFORMATION   The Office de Tourisme is in the Palais de l'Europe, 8 av. Boyer (☎ **93-57-57-00**).

SEEING THE TOP ATTRACTIONS

On the Golfe de la Paix (Gulf of Peace), Menton, which used to belong to Monaco, is on a rocky promontory, dividing the bay in two. The fishing town, the older part with narrow streets, is in the east; the tourist zone and residential belt is in the west.

Writer/artist/filmmaker Jean Cocteau liked this resort, and the **Musée Jean-Cocteau,** Bastion du Port, quai Napoléon-III (☎ **93-57-72-30**), in a 17th-century fort, contains the death portrait of Cocteau sketched by MacAvoy, as well as MacAvoy's portrait of Cocteau. Some of the artist's memorabilia is here—stunning charcoals and watercolors, ceramics, signed letters, and 21 brightly colored pastels. The museum is open Wednesday to Sunday: June 15 to September 15 from 10am to noon and 3 to 6pm, and September 16 to June 14 from 10am to noon and 2 to 6pm. Admission is free.

At **La Salle des Mariages,** in the Hôtel de Ville, rue de la République (☎ 93-57-87-87), Cocteau painted frescoes depicting the legend of Orpheus and Eurydice, among other things. A tape in English helps explain them. The room contains red-leather seats and leopard-skin rugs and is used for civil marriage ceremonies. It's open Monday to Friday from 8:30am to 12:30pm and 1:30 to 5pm. Admission ia 5 F (95¢).

The **Musée de Préhistoire Régionale,** rue Lorédan-Larchey (☎ 93-35-84-64), presents human evolution on the Côte d'Azur for the past million years. It emphasizes the prehistoric era, including the head of Grimaldi Man, found in 1884 in the Baousse-Rousse caves. Audiovisual aids, dioramas, and videocassettes enhance the exhibition. It's open Wednesday to Monday: June 15 to September 15 from 10am to noon and 3 to 7pm, and September 16 to June 14 from 10am to noon and 2 to 6pm. Admission is free.

The **Musée des Beaux-Arts,** Palais Carnoles, 3 av. de la Madone (☎ 93-35-49-71), contains 14th-, 16th-, and 17th-century paintings from Italy, Flanders, Holland, and the French schools, as well as modern paintings, including works by Dufy, Valadon, Derain, and Leprin—all acquired by a British subject, Wakefield Mori. The museum is open Wednesday to Monday: June 15 to September 15 from 10am to noon and 3 to 7pm, and September 16 to June 14 from 10am to noon and 2 to 6pm. Admission is free.

WHERE TO STAY

⑤ Le Dauphin

28 av. du Général-de-Gaulle, 06500 Menton. ☎ **93-35-76-37.** Fax 93-35-31-74. 30 rms. TV TEL. 350–500 F ($66.50–$95.00) double; 600 F ($114) triple. Rates include continental breakfast. AE, MC, V. Parking free (only small cars). Closed Oct 20–Dec 20. Bus 3.

This affable hotel lies just off the beach. The double-insulated rooms are bright and uncluttered, each with a balcony opening onto the mountain range or the sea. Multilingual owner/director Jacques Ridès is a classical-music buff who has created a unique hotel feature: two acoustically inviting practice studios—the Apollo, with a baby grand piano, and the Dionysos, for round-the-clock rental. The attentive staff is wonderfully welcoming. Three meals per day are served, a prix fixe costing only 80 F ($15.20). In the afternoon the restaurant is transformed into a tea salon.

Hôtel Princess et Richmond

617 promenade du Soleil, 06500 Menton. ☎ **93-35-80-20.** Fax 93-57-40-20. 45 rms. A/C MINIBAR TV TEL. 375–505 F ($71.25–$95.95) double. Rates include continental breakfast. AE, DC, MC, V. Parking 35 F ($6.65). Closed Nov 5–Dec 19. Bus 3.

At the edge of the sea near the commercial district, this hotel boasts a facade of warm Mediterranean colors, with a sunny garden terrace. The owner rents comfortable soundproof rooms with modern and French traditional furnishings and balconies. Drinks are served on the roof terrace, where you can enjoy a view of the curving shoreline. In the evening a small snack can be served in your room. There's also an open-air Jacuzzi, plus a small fitness room in the solarium. The staff organizes sightseeing excursions.

WHERE TO DINE

⑤ La Calanque

13 square Victoria. ☎ **93-35-83-15.** Reservations not required. Main courses 65–150 F ($12.35–$28.50); fixed-price menus 90 F ($17.10), 120 F ($22.80), and 135 F ($25.65). AE, DC, MC, V. Tues–Sun noon–2pm and 7:15–9:30pm. Bus 4. FRENCH/ITALIAN.

Of the restaurants along the port, La Calanque is the best for the budget. In fair weather, tables are set under shade trees in full view of the harbor. We recommend the spaghetti napolitaine, tripe niçoise, soupe de poissons, and fresh sardines (grilled over charcoal and very savory), with the focus on locally harvested seafood. Two specialties are bouillabaisse and barba giuan, small biscuits cooked in olive oil after having been stuffed with a variety of local greens.

Petit Port

1 place Fontana. ☎ **93-35-82-62.** Reservations recommended. Main courses 100–110 F ($19–$20.90); fixed-price menus 100–130 F ($19–$24.70). AE, MC, V. Thurs–Tues noon–3pm and 7pm–midnight. FRENCH.

Small and charming, employing many members of an extended family, this restaurant serves well-prepared portions of fresh fish in a century-old house near the medieval port. Everything is homemade, even the bread. Specialties include grilled sardines (succulent and increasingly difficult to find), fish soup, several kinds of grilled meats, and (in honor of the northern France origins of its owner) tripe in the style of Caen. The place prides itself on its location—less than a mile from the Italian border.

2 Roquebrune & Cap-Martin

Roquebrune: 592 miles S of Paris, 3 miles W of Menton
Cap-Martin: 3 miles W of Menton, 1¹/₂ miles W of Roquebrune

Roquebrune, along the Grande Corniche, is a charming mountain village with vaulted streets. The only one of its kind, the **Château de Roquebrune** (☎ 93-35-07-22) was originally a 10th-century Carolingian castle; the present structure dates in part from the 13th century. Dominated by two square towers, it houses a historical museum. From the towers, there's a panoramic view along the coast to Monaco. The castle gates are open daily from 10am to noon and 2 to 6pm; admission is 10 F ($1.90) for adults and 6 F ($1.15) for children.

Three miles west of Menton, **Cap-Martin** is a satellite of the larger resort that's been associated with the rich and famous since Empress Eugénie wintered here in the 19th century. In time, the resort was honored by the presence of Sir Winston Churchill. Don't think you'll find a wide sandy beach—you'll encounter plenty of rocks, against a backdrop of pine and olive trees.

ESSENTIALS

GETTING THERE   Cap-Martin has train and bus connections from the other cities of the Mediterranean coast, including Nice and Menton. To reach Roquebrune, you'll have to take a taxi or bus from the station at Cap-Martin or Menton.

VISITOR INFORMATION   The Office de Tourisme is at 20 av. Paul-Doumer in Roquebrune (☎ 93-35-62-87).

WHERE TO STAY

Hôtel Victoria
7 promenade du Cap, 06190 Roquebrune/Cap-Martin. ☎ **93-35-65-90.** Fax 93-28-27-02.
32 rms. A/C MINIBAR TV TEL. 348–518 F ($66.10–$98.45) double. Breakfast 35 F ($6.65)
extra. AE, DC, MC, V. Parking 30 F ($5.70). Closed Jan 5–Feb 5.

This rectangular building is set behind a garden in front of the beach. The rooms
are well furnished. You can have a drink at the bar decorated with a sweeping
mural of the Alps. Breakfast is the only meal served. This long-enduring favorite
is considered the second-best hotel in town, though not in the same league as the
Vista Palace (below).

Hôtel Vista Palace
Grande Corniche, 06190 Roquebrune/Cap-Martin. ☎ **92-10-40-00,** or 800/223-6800 in the
U.S. Fax 93-35-18-94. 42 rms, 26 suites. A/C MINIBAR TV TEL. 1,200–2,400 F ($228.10–
$456.25) double; 1,200–5,000 F ($228.10–$950.55) suite. Breakfast 100 F ($19) extra.
AE, DC, MC, V. Parking 100 F ($19).

This extraordinary hotel/restaurant stands on the outer ridge of the mountains
running parallel to the coast, giving an "airplane view" of Monaco that's spectacular. And the design of the Vista Palace is just as fantastic: Three levels are cantilevered out into space so that every room seems to float. Nearly all the rooms have
balconies facing the Mediterranean. If you don't want to stay here, at least consider stopping by for a meal—it's expensive but worth it. Le Vistaero is open daily
from 12:15 to 2:15pm and 8 to 10pm; three fixed-price menus are available, at
200 F ($38), 300 F ($57), and 560 F ($106.45). The Mediterranean cuisine is
envied by the region's restaurateurs. Facilities here include a pool, a sauna, massage, an indoor squash court, and a fitness center.

WHERE TO DINE

Au Grand Inquisiteur
8 rue du Château. ☎ **93-35-05-37.** Reservations required. Main courses 77–140 F ($14.65–
$26.60); fixed-price menus 145 F ($27.55) and 215 F ($40.85). MC, V. Tues 7:30–10pm,
Wed–Sun noon–1:30pm and 7:30–10pm. Closed Mar 21–31 and Nov 2–Dec 25. FRENCH.

This culinary find is a miniature restaurant in a two-room cellar near the top of
the medieval mountaintop village of Roquebrune. On the steep, winding road to
the château, this building is made of rough-cut stone, with large oak beams. The
cuisine, though not the area's most distinguished, is quite good, like the chef's duck
special or salad made with sweetbreads. Most diners, however, wisely opt for one
of the fresh seafood choices. The wine list is exceptional—some 150 selections,
most at reasonable prices.

3 Monaco

593 miles S of Paris, 11 miles E of Nice

The outspoken Katharine Hepburn once called Monaco "a pimple on the chin of
the south of France." She wasn't referring to the principality's lack of beauty but
rather to the preposterous idea of having a little country, a feudal anomaly, taking up some of the choicest coastline along the Riviera. Hemmed in by France on
three sides and facing the Mediterranean, tiny Monaco staunchly maintains its

independence. Even Charles de Gaulle couldn't force Prince Rainier to do away with his tax-free policy. As almost everybody in an overburdened world knows by now, the Monégasques do not pay taxes. Part of their country's revenue comes from tourism and gambling.

Monaco—or rather its capital of Monte Carlo—has for a century been a symbol of glamour. Its legend was further enhanced by the 1956 marriage of the man who was at that time the world's most eligible bachelor, Prince Rainier III, to American actress Grace Kelly. She had met the prince when she was in Cannes for the film festival to promote the Hitchcock movie she made with Cary Grant, *To Catch a Thief*; a journalist friend had arranged a photo shoot with the prince— and the rest is history. A daughter, Caroline, was born to the royal couple in 1957; a son, Albert, in 1958; and finally a second daughter, Stephanie, in 1965. The Monégasques welcomed the birth of Caroline, but went wild at the birth of Albert, a male heir. According to a 1918 treaty, Monaco would become an autonomous state under French protection should the ruling dynasty become extinct. However, the fact that Albert is still a bachelor has the entire principality concerned.

Though not always happy in her role, Princesse Grace soon won the respect and adoration of her people. In 1982, a sports car she was driving, with daughter Stephanie as a passenger, plunged over a cliff, killing Grace instantly. The Monégasques still mourn her death.

Monaco became a property of the Grimaldi clan, a Genoese family, as early as 1297. With shifting loyalties, it has maintained something resembling independence ever since. In a fit of impatience, the French annexed it in 1793, but the ruling family recovered it in 1814, though the prince at the time couldn't bear to tear himself away from the pleasures of Paris for "dreary old Monaco."

ESSENTIALS

GETTING THERE   Monaco has rail, bus, and highway connections from other coastal cities, especially Nice. Trains arrive every 30 minutes from Cannes, Nice, Menton, and Antibes. There are no border formalities for anyone entering Monaco from mainland France.

SPECIAL EVENTS   For car-racing fans, there's the **Rallye and Grand Prix** in May.

VISITOR INFORMATION   The Direction du Tourisme is at 2A bd. des Moulins (☎ **92-16-61-16**).

EXPLORING THE PRINCIPALITY

The second-smallest state in Europe (Vatican City is the tiniest), Monaco consists of four parts: The old town, **Monaco-Ville,** on a promontory, the Rock, 200 feet high, is the seat of the royal palace and the government building, as well as the Oceanographic Museum. To the west of the bay, **La Condamine,** the home of the Monégasques, is at the foot of the old town, forming its harbor and port sector. Up from the port (walking is steep in Monaco) is **Monte Carlo,** once the playground of European royalty and still the center for wintering wealthy, the setting for the casino and its gardens and the deluxe hotels. The fourth part, **Fontvieille,** is a surprisingly neat industrial suburb.

Ironically, **Monte-Carlo Beach,** at the far frontier, is on French soil. It attracts a chic crowd, including movie stars in the skantiest bikinis and thongs. The resort has a freshwater pool, an artificial beach, and a sea-bathing establishment.

Monaco

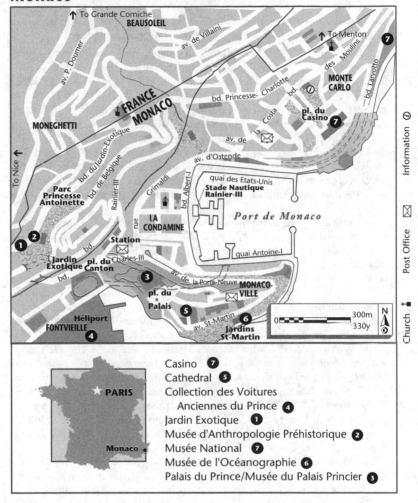

No one used to go to Monaco in summer, but now that has totally changed—in fact, July and August tend to be so crowded it's hard to get a room. Further, with the decline of royalty and multimillionaires, Monaco is developing a broader base of tourism (you can stay there moderately—but it's misleading to suggest that you can stay there cheaply). The Monégasques very frankly court the affluent visitor. And at the casinos here you can also lose your shirt. "Suicide Terrace" at the casino, though not used as frequently as in the old days, is still a real temptation to many who have foolishly gambled away family fortunes.

Life still focuses around the **casino,** which has been the subject of countless legends and the setting for many films. High drama is played to the fullest here. Depending on the era, you might've seen Mata Hari shooting a tsarist colonel with a jewel-encrusted revolver when he tried to slip his hand inside her bra to discover her secrets—military, not mammary. The late King Farouk, known as "The Swine," used to devour as many as eight roast guinea hens and 50 oysters before losing thousands at the table. *Chacun à son goût.* Richard Burton presented Elizabeth Taylor with the obscenely huge Koh-i-noor diamond here.

SEEING THE TOP ATTRACTIONS   During summer, most visitors—many over from Nice for the day—want to see the Italianate home of Monaco's royal family, the **Palais du Prince,** dominating the principality from "The Rock." When touring Les Grands Appartements du Palais, place du Palais (☎ 93-25-18-31), you're shown the Throne Room and allowed to see some of the art collection, including works by Brueghel and Holbein, as well as Princesse Grace's stunning state portrait. The palace was built in the 13th century, and part of it dates from the Renaissance. You're also shown the chamber where England's George III died. The ideal time to arrive is 11:55am to watch the 10-minute changing of the guard. The palace is open June to September, daily from 9:30am to 6:30pm; in October, daily from 10am to 5pm. Admission is 30 F ($5.70) for adults and 15 F ($2.85) for children.

In a wing of the palace, the **Musée du Palais Princier** (Souvenirs Napoléoniens et Collection d'Archives), place du Palais (☎ 93-25-18-31), contains a collection of mementos of Napoléon and Monaco itself. When the royal residence is closed, this museum is the only part of the palace that the public can visit. It's open December to May, Tuesday to Sunday from 10:30am to 12:30pm and 2 to 5pm; June to September, daily from 9:30am to 6:30pm; in October, daily from 10am to 5pm. Admission is 20 F ($3.80) for adults and 10 F ($1.90) for children.

The **Jardin Exotique,** boulevard du Jardin-Exotique (☎ 93-30-33-65), was built on the side of a rock and is known for its cactus collection. The gardens were begun by Prince Albert I, who was both a naturalist and a scientist. He spotted some succulents growing in the palace gardens, and knowing that these plants were normally found only in Central America or Africa, he created the garden from them. You can also explore the grottoes here, as well as a **Musée d'Anthropologie Préhistorique** (☎ 93-15-80-06). The view of the principality is splendid. The museum is open daily: June to September from 9am to 7pm, and October to May from 9am to 6pm. Admission is 35 F ($6.65) for adults and 17 F ($3.25) for children 6 to 18; 5 and under free.

The **Musée de l'Océanographie,** avenue St-Martin (☎ 93-15-36-00), was founded by Albert I, great-grandfather of the present prince. In the main rotunda is a statue of Albert in his favorite costume—that of a sea captain. Displayed are specimens he collected during 30 years of expeditions aboard his oceanographic boats. The aquarium—one of the finest in Europe—contains more than 90 tanks.

Prince Albert's collection is exhibited in the zoology room. Some of the exotic creatures here were unknown before he captured them. You'll see models of the oceanographic ships, aboard which he directed his scientific cruises from 1885 to 1914. Albert's last cruises were on board the *Hirondelle II.* The most important part of its laboratory has been preserved and reconstituted as closely as possible. The cupboards contain all the equipment and documentation necessary for a scientific expedition. Skeletons of specimens are on the main floor, including a giant whale that drifted ashore at Pietra Ligure in 1896—it's believed to be the same one the prince harpooned earlier that year. The skeleton is remarkable for its healed fractures sustained when a vessel struck the animal as it was drifting asleep on the surface. An exhibition devoted to the Discovery of the Ocean is in the physical-oceanography room on the first floor. In addition, underwater movies are shown continuously in the lecture room.

The Oceanography Museum is open daily: in July and August from 9am to 8pm; in April, May, and September from 9am to 7pm; in March and October from 9:30am to 7pm; and November to February from 10am to 6pm. Admission is 60 F ($11.40) for adults and 30 F ($5.70) for children 6 to 18; 5 and under free.

In the **Collection des Voitures Anciennes du Prince,** Les Terraces de Fontvieille (☎ **92-05-28-56**), Prince Rainier has opened a showcase of his private collection of 85 exquisitely restored vintage autos, including the 1956 Rolls-Royce Silver Cloud that carried the prince and his princess on their wedding day. It was given to the royal couple by Monaco shopkeepers as a wedding present. A 1952 Austin Taxi on display was once used as the royal "family car." Other exhibits are a Woodie, a 1937 Ford station wagon once used by Prince Louis II when on hunting trips, and a 1925 Bugatti 35B, winner of the Monaco Grand Prix in 1929. The museum is open daily: April to October from 10am to 7pm, and November to March from 10am to 6pm. Admission is 30 F ($5.70) for adults and 15 F ($2.85) for students.

The **Musée National,** 17 av. Princesse-Grace (☎ **93-30-91-26**), features "automatons and dolls of yesterday," along with sculptures in the rose garden. In a villa designed by Charles Garnier (architect of the Opéra Garnier in Paris), this museum houses one of the world's greatest collections of mechanical toys and dolls. See especially the 18th-century Neapolitan crib, which contains some 200 figures. This collection, assembled by Mme de Galea, was presented to the principality in 1972; it stemmed from the 18th- and 19th-century trend of displaying new fashions on doll models. The museum is open daily: Easter to September from 10am to 6:30pm, and October to Easter from 10am to 12:15pm and 2:30 to 6:30pm. Admission is 26 F ($4.95) for adults and 16 F ($3.05) for children 6 to 16; 5 and under free.

DAYTIME SWIMMING   On French soil, **Monte-Carlo Beach** adjoins the Monte-Carlo Beach Hôtel, avenue Princesse-Grace (☎ **93-78-21-40**). The beach club becomes an integral part of the social life of Monaco (especially for the international set). In addition to the artificial beach, there are two pools, one for children.

Built to overlook the yacht-clogged harbor, the stupendous **Stade Nautique Rainier-III,** quai Albert-Ier, at La Condamine (☎ **93-15-28-75**), a pool frequented by Monégasques, was a gift from the prince to his loyal subjects. It's open daily: in July and August from 9am to midnight, and March to June and September to November from 9am to 6pm. Admission is 22 F ($4.20).

WHERE TO STAY
VERY EXPENSIVE

✪ Hôtel de Paris
Place du Casino, 98000 Monaco. ☎ **92-16-30-00.** Fax 93-16-38-49. 206 rms, 41 suites. A/C MINIBAR TV TEL. 2,200–2,700 F ($418.25–$513.30) double; from 5,700 F ($1,083.65) suite. Breakfast 140 F ($26.80) extra. AE, DC, MC, V. Parking 120 F ($22.80). Bus 1 or 2.

On the main plaza, opposite the casino, this is one of the most famous hotels in the world. At least two dozen movie companies have used its lobby as a background. The ornate facade has marble pillars, and the impressive lounge has an art nouveau rose window at the peak of the dome. The hotel is furnished with a dazzling decor of marble pillars, statues, crystal chandeliers, sumptuous carpets, Louis XVI chairs, and a wall-size fin-de-siècle mural. The guest rooms are fashionable and, in many cases, sumptuous. Unlike most hotels, rooms opening onto the sea aren't as spacious as those in the rear.

Dining/Entertainment: The evening usually begins in the bar. On top of the Hôtel de Paris, the Louis XIV royal galley–style Le Grill has an impressive sliding roof. While dining you can watch the arrival and departure of the world's greatest yachts. In addition to the distinguished cuisine, the hotel has a collection of rare fine wines kept in a dungeon chiseled out of the rocks. In Le Grill, a complete meal begins at 400 F ($76). The elegant Le Louis XV is recommended under "Where to Dine," below. The Côte Jardin offers a daily lunch buffet of Mediterranean specialties, with a terrace opening onto a view of the sea.

Facilities: Thermes Marins spa, between the Hôtel de Paris and the Hôtel Hermitage, with complete cures of thalassotherapy under medieval supervision, including "antismoking," "anti-heavy legs," and "postnatal" cures; large indoor pool; two saunas; fitness center; beauty center.

✪ Hôtel Hermitage

Square Beaumarchais, 98005 Monaco CEDEX. ☎ **92-16-40-00.** Fax 93-50-82-06. 240 rms, 25 suites. A/C MINIBAR TV TEL. 1,450–2,800 F ($275.50.65–$532.20) double; from 4,200 F ($798.45) suite. Breakfast 140 F ($26.60) extra. AE, DC, MC, V. Parking 120 F ($22.80). Bus 1 or 2.

Picture yourself sitting in a wicker armchair, being served drinks under an ornate stained-glass dome with an encircling wrought-iron balcony. You can do this at the clifftop Hermitage, with its "wedding cake" facade. The "palace" was the creation of Jean Marquet (who created marquetry). Large brass beds are in the rooms, where decoratively framed doors open onto balconies. You have a choice of rooms in the Prince wing, where accommodations are more traditionally old-fashioned, or in the more modern Costa or Excelsior wing, with a choice of either contemporary or period furnishings. The most expensive rooms open onto the water. High-season rates are charged during Christmas, New Year's, Easter, July, and August. The stylish dining room has Corinthian columns and chandeliers, serving a refined contemporary cuisine. Fixed-price menus begin at 310 F ($58.90). The Bar Scorpion is a chic rendezvous that at night is a piano bar.

EXPENSIVE

Hôtel Mirabeau

1 av. Princesse-Grace, 98000 Monaco. ☎ **92-16-65-65.** Fax 93-50-84-85. 93 rms, 10 suites. A/C MINIBAR TV TEL. 1,000–2,000 F ($190.10–$380.20) double; from 3,000 F ($570.30) suite. Breakfast 140 F ($26.60) extra. AE, DC, MC, V. Parking 115 F ($21.85). Bus 1 or 2.

This attractive hotel is next to the Monte Carlo Casino and also opens onto a noisy street. Two elevators descend to ground level at the sea. Its well-decorated rooms received a rejuvenation in 1993; many have balconies with views of the sea or garden. La Coupole, one of the best restaurants on the Côte d'Azur, is capped with a glass canopy and has a fashionable bar. In summer, guests linger over breakfast or a buffet lunch (May to September) in the Café Mirabeau.

MODERATE

Hôtel Alexandra

33 bd. Princesse-Charlotte, 98000 Monaco. ☎ **93-50-63-13.** Fax 92-16-06-48. 56 rms. A/C TV TEL. 780 F ($148.25) double. Breakfast 56 F ($10.65) extra. AE, DC, MC, V. Bus 1 or 2.

This hotel is in the center of the business district, on a busy and often-noisy street corner. Its comfortably furnished guest rooms don't generate much excitement, but they're reliable and respectable. The Alexandra knows it can't compete with the giants of Monaco and doesn't even try. But it attracts those who'd like to visit the principality without spending a fortune.

INEXPENSIVE

Ⓢ Hôtel Cosmopolite
4 rue de la Turbie, 98000 Monaco. ☎ **93-30-16-95.** 24 rms, none with bath. 200 F ($38) double. Breakfast 32 F ($6.10) extra. No credit cards. Parking free on street. Bus 1, 2, or 4.

This century-old hotel is down a set of steps from the train station. Madame Gay Angèle, the English-speaking owner, is proud of her "Old Monaco" establishment. Her more expensive rooms have showers, but the cheapest way to stay here is to request a room without shower—there are adequate facilities in the hallway.

Ⓢ Hôtel de France
6 rue de la Turbie, 98000 Monaco. ☎ **93-30-24-64.** 26 rms. TEL. 350 F ($66.50) double; 390 F ($74.10) triple. Breakfast 35 F ($6.65) extra. V. Parking 40 F ($7.60). Bus 1 or 2.

Not all Monégasques are rich, as a stroll along this street will convince you. Here you'll find some of the cheapest living and eating establishments in the high-priced principality. This 19th-century hotel, three minutes from the rail station, has modest furnishings but is clean and comfortable.

WHERE TO DINE
VERY EXPENSIVE

Le Grill de l'Hôtel de Paris
Place du Casino. ☎ **92-16-30-00.** Reservations required. Main courses 190–620 F ($36.10–$117.80). AE, DC, MC, V. Daily noon–2:30pm and 7:30–10pm. Closed Jan 8–31. FRENCH.

There's no swankier place here than the rooftop of the Hôtel de Paris. The view alone is worth the expense, with the turrets of the fabled casino on one side and the yacht-clogged harbor of Old Monaco on the other. In fair weather and in summer, the ceiling opens to reveal the starry sky. The fine cuisine is backed up by one of the Riviera's finest wine lists, with some 20,000 bottles; the wine cellar is carved out of the rock below. In a soft, elegant atmosphere, an array of temptations is presented. Les poissons de la Méditerranée feature the inevitable loup (sea bass), which can be grilled for one or two diners, as can the daurade. Lamb from the Alps is featured in a number of ways and various beef dishes, like côte de boeuf du Charolais, also tempt diners.

✪ Le Louis XV
In the Hôtel de Paris, place du Casino. ☎ **92-16-30-01.** Reservations recommended. Jacket and tie required at dinner. Main courses 330–360 F ($62.70–$68.40); fixed-price menus 760–850 F ($144.50–$161.60). AE, DC, MC, V. July–Aug, Wed 8–10pm, Thurs–Mon noon–2pm and 8–10pm; Sept–June, Thurs–Mon noon–2pm and 8–10pm. Bus 1 or 2. FRENCH/ITALIAN.

The arrival of culinary star Alain Ducasse in this restaurant's kitchen was greeted with ethusiasm, especially by Prince Rainier, who'd invited him here. On the lobby level of the five-star Hôtel de Paris, Le Louis XV offers what one critic called "down-home Riviera cooking within a Fabergé egg." Despite the place's regal trappings (or as a reaction against them?), Ducasse creates a simple cuisine. Everything is light, attuned to the seasons, with an intelligent and modern interpretation of both Provençal and northern Italian courses. The service is superb.

EXPENSIVE

L'Argentin

In the Loews Monte-Carlo, 12 av. des Spélugues. ☎ **93-50-65-00.** Reservations recommended. Main courses 150–270 F ($28.50–$51.30); fixed-price menu 295 F ($56.05). AE, DC, MC, V. Daily 7:30pm–4:30am. Bus 1 or 2. ARGENTINIAN.

Conceived with panache by the developers of one of the brassiest hotels on the Riviera, L'Argentin is unique. One of the largest restaurants in town, it's banked with windows facing the sea and has the most impressive grills anywhere. Uniformed chefs tend three blazing fires, from which diners are protected by a thick sheet of glass. The decor was inspired by the Argentinian pampas and has gaucho accessories, such as cowskin-draped banquettes. Gamblers appreciate the late-night suppers (after 1am, with a limited menu). Much of the beef is imported from America; menu choices include Texas pork ribs, a mixed grill called parillada Argentine, sizzling contrefilet or filet steaks, and a Spanish-inspired seafood zarzuela.

Le Café de Paris

Place du Casino. ☎ **92-16-20-20.** Reservations not required. Main courses 70–180 F ($13.30–$34.20). AE, DC, MC, V. Daily 8am–4am. Bus 1 or 2. INTERNATIONAL.

This is the Monte Carlo counterpart of Paris's Café de la Paix, and everyone seems to drop in at least once a day. Opposite the casino and the Hôtel de Paris, the café provides a front-row seat for the never-ending spectacle of Monte Carlo. It's owned by the Société des Bains de Mer and was completely rebuilt in the late 1980s, when a belle époque–style brasserie was created. The Grand Café with its terrace and adjacent bar are still there, as are several boutiques and a Parisian-style "drugstore." One room is devoted to "one-armed bandits." Around six *plats du jour* are offered, and the cuisine is international with a varied menu. You get top quality at reasonable prices. The chefs are best with their fresh seafood. A limited supper menu is offered after 2am.

INEXPENSIVE

Pizzeria Monégasque

4 rue Terrazzani. ☎ **93-30-16-38.** Reservations not required. Pizzas 45–60 F ($8.55–$11.40); main courses 55–120 F ($10.45–$22.80); fixed-price lunch 70–90 F ($13.30–$17.10); fixed-price menu 130 F ($24.70). AE, MC, V. Mon–Fri noon–2:30pm and 7:30pm–12:30am, Sat 7:30pm–12:30am. Closed Dec 25–Jan 1. Bus 1 or 2. FRENCH/ITALIAN.

This luxurious pizzeria is the melting pot of Monte Carlo. Almost anyone might arrive—in a limousine or on a bicycle—even members of the royal family. The owner has grown accustomed to seeing all the follies and vanities of this town pass through his door; he serves pizzas, fish, and grilled meats to whomever shows up. Specialties include magrêt du canard (duckling), grilled scampi, carpaccio, and beef tartare.

Stars 'n Bars

6 quai Antoine-Ier. ☎ **93-50-95-95.** Reservations not required. Dinner salads, burgers, and platters 65–128 F ($12.35–$24.30). MC, V. Tues–Sun noon–5pm and 7pm–midnight. AMERICAN.

This place deliberately revels in the cross-cultural differences that have contributed so much to Monaco's recent history. Modeled on the kind of sports bars growing popular in large U.S. cities, it features two distinct dining and drinking areas; a blues bar with live music performed most evenings from 9:45pm to around 2am; and a sports bar with memorabilia donated by every athlete of note. No one will mind if you drop in to either place just for a drink, but if you're hungry, menu items read like an homage to the macho-American experience. Try an Indy 500 or a Triathlon salad, a Wimbledon or a Slam Dunk sandwich, or a breakfast of champions (eggs and bacon and all the fixings) priced at 65 F ($12.35); and if your children happen to be in tow and are feeling nostalgic for the ballpark back home, order a little leaguer's platter, designed for those under 12.

AFTER DARK

The **Loews Casino,** 12 av. des Spélugues (☎ 93-50-65-00), is a huge room filled with the one-armed bandits, adjoining the lobby in the Loews Monte-Carlo. It also features blackjack, craps, and American roulette. Additional slot machines are available on the roof starting at 11am—for those who want to gamble with a wider view of the sea. It's open daily from 4pm to 4am (to 5am for slot machines). Admission is free.

A speculator, François Blanc, made the ✪ **Monte Carlo Casino,** place du Casino (☎ 92-16-21-21), the most famous in the world, attracting Sarah Bernhardt, Mata Hari, King Farouk, and Aly Khan (Onassis used to own a part-interest). The architect of Paris's Opéra Garnier, Charles Garnier, built the oldest part of the casino, and it remains an extravagant example of period architecture. The new grand dukes are fast-moving international businessmen on short-term vacations. Baccarat, roulette, and chemin-de-fer are the most popular games, though you can play "le craps" and blackjack as well.

Different parts of this famous building open at different times. The Salle Américaine, containing only Las Vegas–style slot machines, opens at noon, as do doors for roulette and trente-quarente. A section for roulette and chemin-de-fer opens at 3pm. The hottest action begins at 4pm when the full casino swings into action, with more roulette, craps, and blackjack. The gambling continues until very late/early, the closing depending on the crowd. The casino classifies its "private rooms" as those areas not reserved for slot machines. To enter the casino, you must carry a passport, be at least 21, and pay an admission of 50 to 100 F ($9.50 to $19) if you want to enter the private rooms. In lieu of a passport, an identity card or driver's license will suffice.

The foremost winter establishment, under the same ownership, is the **Cabaret** in the Casino Gardens, where you can dance to the music of a smooth orchestra. A good cabaret is featured, often with ballet numbers. It's open from mid-September until the end of June, but closed Tuesday. From 9pm you can enjoy dinner at a cost of 400 F ($76). Drinks ordered separately begin at 140 F ($26.60). For reservations, call 92-16-36-36.

In the **Salle Garnier** of the casino, concerts are held periodically; for information, contact the tourist office (see "Essentials," above). The music is usually classical, featuring the Orchestre Philharmonique de Monte Carlo.

The casino also contains the **Opéra de Monte-Carlo,** whose patron is Prince Rainier. This world-famous house, opened in 1879 by Sarah Bernhardt, presents a winter and spring repertoire that traditionally includes Puccini, Mozart, and Verdi. The famed Ballets Russes de Monte-Carlo, starring Nijinsky and Karsavina, was created in 1918 by Sergei Diaghilev. The national orchestra and ballet company of Monaco appear here. Tickets may be hard to come by; your best bet is to ask your hotel concierge. You can make inquiries about tickets on your own at the

Atrium du Casino (☎ 92-16-22-99), open Tuesday to Sunday from 10am to 12:30pm and 2 to 5pm. Standard tickets generally cost 100 to 500 F ($19 to $95).

4 Eze & La Turbie

585 miles S of Paris, 7 miles NE of Nice

The hamlets of Eze and La Turbie, though 4 miles apart, have so many similarities that most of France's tourist officials speak of them as if they're one. Both boast fortified feudal cores high in the hills overlooking the Provençal coast, and both were built during the early Middle Ages to stave off raids from corsairs who wanted to capture harem slaves and laborers. Clinging to the rocky hillsides around these hamlets are upscale villas, many of which were built by retirees from colder climes since the 1950s. Closely linked, culturally and fiscally, to nearby Monaco, Eze and La Turbie have full-time populations of fewer than 3,000, and the medieval cores of both contain art galleries, boutiques, and artisans' shops that have been restored.

Eze is accessible via the Moyenne (Middle) Corniche, La Turbie via the Grande (Upper) Corniche. Signs are positioned along the coastal road indicating the direction motorists should take to reach either of the hamlets.

The leading attraction in Eze is the **Jardin Exotique,** boulevard du Jardin Exotique (☎ 93-41-10-30), a lushly landscaped showcase of exotic plants. Entrance is 12 F ($2.30). It can be visited daily: March to October from 9am to 8pm, and November to February from 9am to noon and 2 to 8pm.

La Turbie boasts a ruined monument erected by ancient Roman emperor Augustus in 6 B.C., the **Trophy of the Alps.** (Many locals call it La Trophée d'Auguste.) It rises near a rock formation known as La Tête de Chien, at the highest point along the Grand Corniche, 1,500 feet above sea level. The monument, restored with funds donated by Edward Tuck, was erected by the Roman Senate to celebrate the subjugation of the people of the French Alps by the Roman armies. A short distance from the monument is the **Musée du Trophée des Alps** (☎ 93-41-10-11), a minimuseum containing finds from archeological digs nearby and information about the monument's restoration. It's open daily: April to September from 9am to 7pm, and October to March from 9:30am to 5pm. Entrance costs 21 F ($4) for adults and 15 F ($2.85) for children.

ESSENTIALS

GETTING THERE Eze (also known as Eze-Village) is most easily reached by car via the Moyenne (Middle) Corniche road.

VISITOR INFORMATION The Office de Tourisme is on place du Général-de-Gaulle, Eze-Village (☎ 93-41-26-00), open March to October.

WHERE TO STAY & DINE

Auberge le Soleil

44 av. de la Liberté, 06360 Eze-Bord-de-Mer. ☎ **93-01-51-46.** Fax 93-01-58-40. 10 rms. MINIBAR TEL. 280 F ($53.20) double. Rates include half board. AE, DC, MC, V. Parking free. Closed mid-Nov to Dec 1.

This pink stucco villa is a few steps from the Basse Corniche. It has a quiet rear terrace, and the interior is filled with rattan chairs, exposed brick, and lots of brass. The simply furnished doubles draw mainly a summer crowd, though the inn is open most of the year. Half board is a good deal here—the meals are satisfying.

✪ Hostellerie du Château de la Chévre d'Or

Rue du Barri, 06360 Eze-Village. ☎ **93-41-12-12.** Fax 93-41-06-72. 30 rms, 8 suites. A/C TV TEL. 1,800–2,600 F ($342.20–$494.25) double; 3,300 F ($627.35) suite. Breakfast 100 F ($19) extra. AE, MC, DC, V. Parking free. Closed late Nov to Mar 1.

This is a miniature village retreat built in the 1920s in neo-gothic style, but without a beach. On the side of a stone village off the Moyenne Corniche, this Relais & Châteaux is a complex of village houses, all with views of the coastline. The owner has had the interior of the "Golden Goat" flawlessly decorated to maintain its old character while adding modern comfort. Even if you don't stop in for a meal or a room, try to visit for a drink in the lounge, which has a panoramic view.

Fresh salads and original fruit cocktails are served in the Café du Jardin, which overlooks the Mediterranean. Le Grill du Château is a more traditional restaurant where you can enjoy grilled fish and meat. Other choices are Chez Justin, for informal meals, and La Chèvre d'Or, known for its *menu gastronomique* at 560 F ($106.50).

5 Beaulieu

583 miles S of Paris, 6 miles E of Nice, 7 miles W of Monte Carlo

Protected from the cold north winds that blow down from the Alps, Beaulieu-sur-Mer is often referred to as "La Petite Afrique" (Little Africa). Like Menton, it has the mildest climate along the Côte d'Azur and is especially popular with wintering wealthy. Originally, English visitors staked it out, after an English industrialist founded a hotel here between the rock-studded slopes and the sea. Beaulieu is graced with lush vegetation, including oranges, lemons, and bananas, as well as palms.

The **Beaulieu Casino** fronts La Baie des Fourmis, the beautiful gardens that attract the evening promenade crowd.

The **Villa Kérylos,** rue Gustave-Eiffel (☎ 93-01-01-44), is a replica of an ancient Greek residence, painstakingly designed and built by archeologist Theodore Reinach. Inside, the cabinets are filled with a collection of Greek figurines and ceramics. But most interesting is the reconstructed Greek furniture, much of which would be fashionable today. One curious mosaic depicts the slaying of the minotaur and provides its own labyrinth (if you try to trace the path, expect to stay for weeks). It's open daily: in July and August from 10am to 5pm, in September and October from 10am to noon and 2 to 5:30pm, and December to June from 10:30am to 12:30pm and 2 to 6pm. Admission is 35 F ($6.65) for adults and 15 F ($2.85) for children and seniors over 65.

The **golf course** of Mont Agel is 10 minutes from the resort.

ESSENTIALS

GETTING THERE   Rail service connects Beaulieu with Nice, Monaco, and the rest of the Côte d'Azur. Most visitors drive from Nice via the Moyenne Corniche or the coastal highway.

VISITOR INFORMATION   The Office de Tourisme is on place Georges-Clemenceau (☎ 93-01-02-21).

WHERE TO STAY
VERY EXPENSIVE

✪ Le Métropole
15 bd. du Général-Leclerc, 06310 Beaulieu-sur-Mer. ☎ **93-01-00-08.** Fax 93-01-18-51. 50 rms, 3 suites. A/C TV TEL. 1,465–1,975 F ($278.50–$375.45) per person. Rates include half board. AE, MC, V. Parking free. Closed Oct 20–Dec 20.

This fin-de-siècle Italianate villa offers the most luxurious accommodations along the Côte d'Azur. It's classified as a Relais & Châteaux and set on 2 acres of grounds. Here you'll enter a world of polished French elegance, with lots of balconies opening onto sea views. The use of marble and Oriental carpets sets the class note, and the lounge fronts the sea. The guest rooms are furnished in tasteful fabrics and flowery wallpapers. The baths are elegantly spacious, most often tiled, and have double sinks.

Dining/Entertainment: The food is the best in the area, winning one star from Michelin. The restaurant has a seaside terrace/bar, which elegantly retreats inside when the weather turns chilly. Chef Gilbert Roubat's cuisine is classic, and only the finest—also the most expensive—ingredients are used.

Services: 24-hour room service.

Facilities: Concrete jetty for sunning, heated pool; tennis and golf nearby.

✪ La Réserve
5 bd. du Général-Leclerc, 06310 Beaulieu-sur-Mer. ☎ **93-01-00-01.** Fax 93-01-28-99. 40 rms, 3 suites. A/C MINIBAR TV TEL. 2,000–4,000 F ($380.20–$760.45) double; 4,200–5,400 F ($798.45–$1,026.60) suite. Breakfast 120 F ($22.80) extra. AE, DC, MC, V. Parking free. Closed Nov–Mar.

One of the Riviera's most famous hotels, this pink-and-white fin-de-siècle palace is on the Mediterranean. Here you can sit having an apéritif watching the sun set over the Riviera while a pianist treats you to Mozart. A number of the public lounges open onto a courtyard with bamboo chairs, grass borders, and urns of flowers. The social life centers around the main drawing room, much like the grand living room of a country estate. The hotel has been rebuilt in stages, so the rooms range widely in size and design; however, all are deluxe and individually decorated and each has a beautiful view of either the mountains or the sea.

Dining/Entertainment: The dining room has a coved frescoed ceiling, parquet floors, crystal chandeliers, and picture windows facing the Mediterranean. Specialties include sea bass with thin slices of potatoes in savory tomato sauce, sea bream stuffed with local vegetables, and roast rack of lamb.

Facilities: Private harbor for yachts, submarine fishing gear, sauna, thalassotherapy, seawater pool (heated Oct–May).

EXPENSIVE

Hôtel Frisia
Bd. Eugène-Gauthier, 06310 Beaulieu-sur-Mer. ☎ **93-01-01-04.** Fax 93-01-31-92. 32 rms. MINIBAR TV TEL. 420–680 F ($79.80–$129.25) double. Breakfast 45 F ($8.55) extra. AE, V.

This small hotel has been owned by the same family since 1907. In 1994 the rooms were renovated and a bath installed in each. In 1996 plans call for all the rooms to be air-conditioned as well. Its well-furnished rooms, decorated in a modern style, most often open onto views of the harbor, with sea-view rooms the most expensive. English is spoken, and foreign guests are made especially welcome. The hotel has a sunny garden and comfortable, inviting lounges.

Breakfast is the only meal served, but many reasonably priced dining places are within walking distance.

⊛ Hôtel Marcellin

18 av. Albert-ler, 06310 Beaulieu-sur-Mer. ☎ **93-01-01-69.** Fax 93-01-37-43. 21 rms, 15 with bath; 1 suite. TEL. 260 F ($49.40) double without bath, 300 F ($57) double with bath; from 500 F ($95.05) suite. Breakfast 32 F ($6.10) extra. MC. Parking free.

A good budget selection in an otherwise high-priced resort, the Marcellin rents restored rooms with homelike amenities, each with a southern exposure. It's been run by the same family since 1938. The hotel is welcoming and has a little outside terrace. The government has given the Marcellin two stars.

WHERE TO DINE

La Pignatelle

10 rue de Quincenet. ☎ **93-01-03-37.** Reservations recommended. Main courses 55–130 F ($10.45–$24.70); fixed-price menus 80 F ($15.20), 130 F ($24.70), 160 F ($30.40), and 200 F ($38). MC, V. Thurs–Tues 12:15–1:30pm and 7:15–9:30pm. Closed mid-Oct to mid-Nov. FRENCH.

Even in this superexpensive resort, you can find an excellent and affordable Niçois bistro—La Pignatelle. After all, the locals have to eat somewhere and not all visitors can afford the higher-priced places. This family-run restaurant is the most popular dining room in town, and it's usually crowded. Specialties include the inevitable salade niçoise, soupe de poissons (fish), cassolette of mussels, fresh lobster, daurade, three kinds of sole, scampi provençal, and tripe niçoise. It's very basic and robust food, and that's why it's so popular with locals.

6 St-Jean-Cap-Ferrat

583 miles S of Paris, 6 miles E of Nice

This has been called Paradise Found. Of all the oases along the Côte d'Azur, no place has the snob appeal of Cap-Ferrat. It's a 9-mile promontory sprinkled with luxurious villas, outlined by sheltered bays, beaches, and coves. The vegetation is lush. In the port of St-Jean, the harbor accommodates yachts and fishing boats.

The Italianate **Musée Ile-de-France,** avenue Denis-Séméria (☎ 93-01-33-09), affords you a chance to visit one of the most legendary villas along the Côte d'Azur, built by the Baronne Ephrussi, a Rothschild. She died in 1934, leaving the building and its magnificent gardens to the Institut de France on behalf of the Académie des Beaux-Arts. The wealth of her collection is preserved: 18th-century furniture; Tiepolo ceilings; Savonnerie carpets; screens and panels from the Far East; tapestries from Gobelins, Aubusson, and Beauvais; original drawings by Fragonard; canvases by Renoir, Sisley, and Boucher; rare Sèvres porcelain; and more. Covering 12 acres, the gardens contain fragments of statuary from churches, monasteries, and torn-down palaces. One entire section is planted with cacti.

The museum and its gardens are open daily: in July and August from 10am to 7pm, and September to June from 10am to 6pm. Admission to the museum and gardens is 38 F ($7.20) for adults and 25 F ($4.75) for children. To visit just the gardens is 12 F ($2.30).

ESSENTIALS

GETTING THERE Most visitors drive or take a taxi from the rail station at nearby Beaulieu. There's also bus service from Nice.

VISITOR INFORMATION The Office de Tourisme is on avenue Denis-Séméria (☎ 93-76-08-90).

WHERE TO STAY
VERY EXPENSIVE

○ Grand Hôtel du Cap-Ferrat
Bd. du Général-de-Gaulle, 06290 St-Jean-Cap-Ferrat. ☎ **93-76-50-50.** Fax 93-76-04-52. 59 rms, 11 suites. A/C MINIBAR TV TEL. 950 F ($180.60) double; from 2,700 F ($513.30) suite. Rates include continental breakfast. AE, DC, MC, V. Parking free.

One of the best features of this turn-of-the-century palace is its location—at the tip of the peninsula in the midst of a 14-acre garden of semitropical trees and manicured lawns. It has been the retreat of the international elite since 1908. Parts of the exterior have open loggias and big arched windows, and guests enjoy the views from the elaborately flowering terrace over the sea. The guest rooms are conservatively modern with dressing rooms, and rates include admission to the pool, Club Dauphin. The beach is accessible via funicular from the main building. The hotel is open year round.

Dining/Entertainment: The hotel's indoor/outdoor restaurant serves *cuisine du marché*, which might include salad of warm foie gras and chanterelles, nage of crayfish and lobster, or breast of duckling with honey and cider vinegar. The dining room is one of the last of the great belle époque palaces on the Côte d'Azur. The meals and service are flawless but come at a very high price. A la carte meals cost 390 to 500 F ($74.10 to $95.05). The American-style bar opens onto the garden.

Services: 24-hour room service, same-day laundry.

Facilities: Olympic-size heated pool, tennis courts, hotel bicycles.

○ La Voile d'Or
31 av. Jean-Mermoz, St-Jean-Cap-Ferrat, 06230 Villefranche-sur-Mer. ☎ **93-01-13-13.** Fax 93-76-11-17. 50 rms, 5 suites. A/C MINIBAR TV TEL. 1,400–3,400 F ($266.15–$646.35) for two. Rates include half board. No credit cards. Parking free. Closed Nov–Mar 12.

The Golden Sail is a brilliant tour de force and offers intimate luxury in a villa converted into a hotel. Antique collector turned hôtelier Jean R. Lorenzi owns this hotel at the edge of the little fishing port and yacht harbor, with a panoramic view of the coast. The guest rooms, the lounges, and the restaurant open onto terraces. The rooms are individually decorated with hand-painted reproductions of antiques, carved gilt headboards, baroque paneled doors, parquet floors, antique clocks, and paintings.

Dining/Entertainment: Guests gather on the canopied outer terrace for lunch, and in the evening they dine in a stately room with Spanish armchairs and white wrought-iron chandeliers. The sophisticated menu offers regional specialties and a few international dishes, as well as the classic French cuisine. The drawing room is richly decorated. Most intimate is a little bar, with Wedgwood-blue paneling and antique mirroring.

Facilities: Two pools.

MODERATE

○ Brise Marine
Av. Jean-Mermoz, St-Jean-Cap-Ferrat, 06230 Villefranche-sur-Mer. ☎ **93-76-04-36.** Fax 93-76-11-49. 16 rms. TV TEL. 695 F ($132.10) double. Breakfast 55 F ($10.45) extra. MC, V. Closed Nov–Jan.

A bargain paradise, this villa with a front and rear terrace is on a hillside. A long rose arbor, beds of subtropical flowers, palms, and pines provide an attractive setting. The atmosphere is casual and informal, and the rooms are comfortably but simply furnished. Guests have breakfast either in the beamed lounge or under the rose trellis. The little corner bar is for afternoon drinks.

§ Hôtel Clair Logis

12 av. Centrale, 06230 St-Jean-Cap-Ferrat. ☎ **93-76-04-57.** Fax 93-76-11-85. 18 rms. TEL. 390–640 F ($74.10–$121.60) double. Breakfast 45 F ($8.55) extra. AE, DC, MC, V. Parking free. Closed Jan–Feb 15 and Nov–Dec 15.

A rare find here, this hotel occupies what was a 19th century villa surrounded by 2 acres of semitropical gardens. The pleasant rooms are scattered over three buildings within the confines of the garden. The hotel's most famous guest was General de Gaulle, who lived in a room called "Strelitzias" (Bird of Paradise) during many of his retreats from Paris. Each room is named after a flower. The most romantic and most spacious accommodations are in the main building; the rooms in the annex are the most modern but have the least character.

WHERE TO DINE

✪ Le Provençal

2 av. Denis-Séméria. ☎ **93-76-03-97.** Reservations required. Fixed-price menus 250 F ($47.50), 350 F ($66.50), and 550 F ($104.55). MC, V. Apr–Sept, Tues–Wed 7:30–9:30pm; Thurs–Mon noon–2:30pm and 7:30–9:30pm; Oct, Tues–Sat noon–2:30pm and 7:30–9:30pm, Sun noon–2:30pm. Closed Nov–Mar. FRENCH.

In this Provence-inspired dining room high above the village, with a sweeping panorama, you can enjoy marinated artichoke hearts with half a lobster, John Dory roasted in fig leaves and served with fresh figs, roast pigeon with cinnamon, a classic bourride Provençal, and a choice of five "petits desserts" that might be macaroons with chocolate or crème brûlée. The cooking seems more inspired than ever, though French gastronomic books often omit mention of it (Michelin, however, awards it a star). The food is solemnly served, as if part of a grand ritual.

Le Sloop

Au Nouveau Port. ☎ **93-01-48-83.** Reservations recommended. Main courses 110–125 F ($20.90–$23.75); fixed-price menu 155 F ($29.45). AE, DC, MC, V. June–Sept, Wed 7–9:30pm, Thurs–Tues noon–2:30pm and 7–9:30pm; Oct–Nov 15 and Dec 15–May, Thurs–Tues noon–2:30pm and 7–9:30pm. Closed Nov 15–Dec 15. FRENCH.

This is the most popular, and most reasonably priced, bistro in this very expensive area. Outfitted in blue and white, it sits directly at the edge of the port, overlooking the yachts in the harbor. The best of regional produce is handled deftly by the chefs, who present dishes like salmon tartare with baby onions; warm salad of red mullet; salad composed of fresh mozzarella, avocados, and lobster; John Dory with fresh pasta and basil; turbot with lobster sauce and calamari; and filet of veal with basil sauce. The regional wines are reasonably priced.

7 Villefranche-sur-Mer

581 miles S of Paris, 4 miles E of Nice

According to legend, Hercules opened his arms and Villefranche was born. It sits on a big blue bay that looks like a gigantic bowl, large enough to attract U.S. Sixth Fleet cruisers and destroyers. Quietly slumbering otherwise, Villefranche takes on the appearance of an exciting Mediterranean port when the fleet's in. Four miles from Nice, it's the first town you reach along the Lower Corniche.

Once popular with such writers as Katherine Mansfield and Aldous Huxley, it's still a haven for artists, many of whom take over the little houses—reached by narrow alleyways—that climb the hillside. **Rue Obscure** is vaulted, one of the strangest streets in France (to get to it, take rue de l'Eglise). In spirit it belongs more to a North African casbah. People live in tiny houses on this street, protected from the elements. Occasionally, however, there's an open space, allowing for a tiny courtyard.

One artist who came to Villefranche left a memorial: Jean Cocteau decorated the 14th-century romanesque **Chapelle St-Pierre,** quai de la Douane (☎ 93-01-73-92), presenting it to "the fishermen of Villefranche in homage to the Prince of Apostles, the patron of fishermen." One panel pays homage to the gypsies of the Stes-Maries-de-la-Mer. In the apse is a depiction of the miracle of St. Peter walking on the water, not knowing that he's supported by an angel. On the left side of the narthex Cocteau honored Villefranche's young women in their regional costumes. The chapel, which charges a 14-F ($2.65) admission, is open Tuesday to Sunday: July to September from 9:30am to noon and 3 to 7pm, October to March from 9:30am to noon and 2 to 5pm, and April to June from 9:30am to noon and 2 to 6pm; closed mid-November to mid-December.

ESSENTIALS

GETTING THERE   Trains arrive from most towns on the Côte d'Azur, especially Nice (every 30 min.), but most visitors drive via the Corniche Inférieure (Lower Corniche).

VISITOR INFORMATION   The Office de Tourisme is on Jardin François-Binon (☎ 93-01-73-68).

WHERE TO STAY

Versailles

Av. Princesse-Grace-de-Monaco, 06230 Villefranche-sur-Mer. ☎ **93-01-89-56.** Fax 93-01-97-48. 46 rms, 3 suites. A/C MINIBAR TV TEL. 860 F ($163.50) double. AE, DC, MC, V. Breakfast 50 F ($9.50) extra. AE, DC, MC, V. Parking 50 F ($9.50). Closed Nov–Dec.

Several blocks from the harbor and outside the main part of town, this location gives you a perspective of the entire coastal area. The hotel offers comfortably furnished rooms with big windows for a good view. Guests congregate on the roof terrace, where they can order breakfast or lunch under an umbrella. In the dining room, meals begin at 170 F ($32.30). The pool has a terrace and is surrounded by palms and bright flowers.

Welcome

1 quai Courbet, 06230 Villefranche-sur-Mer. ☎ **93-76-76-93.** Fax 93-01-88-81. 32 rms. A/C MINIBAR TV TEL. 660–890 F ($125.45–$169.20) double. Breakfast 50 F ($9.50) extra. AE, DC, MC, V. Closed Nov 15–Dec 20.

Involving you instantly in Mediterranean port life, the Welcome was a favorite of Jean Cocteau. It's a six-floor villa hotel with shutters and balconies where everything has recently been modernized. Try for a fifth-floor room overlooking the water. Once Pope Paul III embarked from this site with Charles V, but nowadays the departures are more casual—usually for fishing expeditions. The sidewalk café is the focal point of town life. The lounge and the restaurant, St-Pierre, have open fireplaces and fruitwood furniture; meals begin at 170 F ($32.30).

WHERE TO DINE

La Mère Germaine

Quai Courbet. ☎ **93-01-71-39**. Reservations recommended. Main courses 68–135 F ($12.90–$25.65); fixed price menu 195 F ($37.05). AE, MC, V. May–Oct, daily noon–2pm and 7–10pm; Nov 1–14 and Dec 16–Mar, Thurs–Tues noon–2pm and 7–10pm. Closed Nov 15–Dec 15. FRENCH/SEAFOOD.

Plan to relax here over lunch while watching fishers repair their nets. One of the best of a string of restaurants on the port, this place is popular with U.S. Navy officers, who've discovered the bouillabaisse made with tasty morsels of freshly caught fish and mixed in a caldron with savory spices. We also recommend the grilled loup (bass) with fennel, salade niçoise, sole Tante Marie (stuffed with mushroom purée), and beef filet with three peppers. The wonderful carré d'agneau (lamb) is for two.

La Trinquette

Port de la Darse. ☎ **93-01-71-41**. Reservations recommended. Main courses 75–160 F ($14.25–$30.40); fixed-price meals 100 F ($19), 150 F ($28.50), and 200 F ($38); bouillabaisse 280 F ($53.20). No credit cards. Thurs–Tues noon–2:15pm and 7:30–10pm. Closed Dec–Jan. PROVENÇAL/SEAFOOD.

Charming and traditional, a few steps from the harborfront, this restaurant prides itself on its fish. You can choose from among about 15 to 20 kinds, all fresh, prepared any way you specify, with a wide variety of well-flavored sauces. One of these might be aïoli, the region's garlic-enriched mayonnaise.

8 Nice

577 miles S of Paris, 20 miles NE of Cannes

The Victorian upper class and tsarist aristocrats loved Nice in the 19th century, but it's solidly middle class today. In fact, of all the major resorts of France, from Deauville to Biarritz to Cannes, Nice is the least expensive. It's also the best excursion center on the Riviera, especially if you're dependent on public transportation. For example, you can go to San Remo, the queen of the Italian Riviera, returning to Nice by nightfall. From the Nice airport, the second largest in France, you can travel by bus along the entire coast to resorts like Juan-les-Pins and Cannes.

Nice is the capital of the Riviera, the largest city between Genoa and Marseille (also one of the most ancient, having been founded by the Greeks, who called it "Nike," or Victory). Because of its brilliant sunshine and relaxed living, artists and writers have been attracted to Nice for years. Among them were Matisse, Dumas, Nietzsche, Apollinaire, Flaubert, Hugo, Sand, Stendhal, Chateaubriand, and Mistral.

ESSENTIALS

GETTING THERE Visitors who arrive at **Aéroport Nice–Côte d'Azur** (☎ **93-21-30-30**) can take an airport bus departing every 20 minutes to the Station Centrale in the city center. Buses run from 6am to 10:30pm and cost 8 F ($1.50). For 25 F ($4.75) you can take a *navette* (airport shuttle) that goes several times a day from the train station or the airport. A taxi ride into the city center will cost at least 180 F ($34.20).

Trains arrive at **Gare Nice-Ville,** avenue Thiers (☎ **93-87-50-50**). From here you can take frequent trains to Cannes, Monaco, and Antibes, among other destinations. An information office at the station is open Monday to Saturday from 8am to 7pm and Sunday from 8am to noon and 2 to 7pm. If you face a delay, you can take showers at the station and eat at the cafeteria. The *navette* travels several times a day from the train station to the city center for 25 F ($4.75).

VISITOR INFORMATION   The Office de Tourisme is on avenue Thiers, at the Station Centrale (☎ 93-87-07-07), near place Masséna; it's open Monday to Saturday from 8:45am to 12:30pm and 2 to 6pm. This office will make you a hotel reservation; the fee depends on the classification of the hotel.

GETTING AROUND   Most buses in Nice leave from the **Station Centrale,** 10 av. Félix-Fauré (☎ 93-80-08-70), in the vicinity of place Masséna. Take bus no. 12 to the beach. To save money, purchase a *carnet* of five tickets for 31 F ($5.90), available at the tourist offices (see "Visitor Information," above).

You can rent bicycles and mopeds at **Nicea Rent,** 9 av. Thiers (☎ 93-82-42-71), near the Station Centrale. March to October, it's open daily; November to April, Monday to Saturday from 9am to noon and 2 to 6pm. The cost begins at 120 F ($22.80) per day, plus a 2,000-F ($380) deposit. Credit and charge cards are accepted.

SPECIAL EVENTS   At certain times of year, Nice is caught up in frenzied carnival activities. The **Nice Carnival** draws visitors from all over Europe and North America to this ancient spectacle. The Mardi Gras of the Riviera begins 12 days before Shrove Tuesday, celebrating the return of spring with parades, floats (*corsi*), masked balls (*veglioni*), confetti, and battles in which young women toss flowers—and only the most wicked throw rotten eggs instead of carnations. Climaxing the event is a fireworks display on Shrove Tuesday, lighting up the Bay of Angels. King Carnival goes up in flames on his pyre but rises from the ashes the following spring.

EXPLORING THE CITY

In 1822 the orange crop at Nice was bad and the workers faced a lean time. So the English residents put them to work building **boulevard des Anglais,** which remains a wide boulevard fronting the bay and, split by "islands" of palms and flowers, stretches for about 4 miles. Fronting the beach are rows of grand cafés, the Musée Masséna, villas, and hotels—some good, others decaying.

Crossing this boulevard in the briefest of bikinis or thongs are some of the most attractive people in the world. They're heading for the beach—"on the rocks," as it's called here. Tough on tender feet, the beach is shingled, one of the least attractive (and least publicized) aspects of the cosmopolitan resort city. Many bathhouses provide mattresses for a charge.

In the east, the promenade becomes **quai des Etats-Unis,** the original boulevard, lined with some of the best restaurants in Nice, each specializing in bouillabaisse. Rising sharply on a rock is the **château,** the spot where the ducs de Savoie built their castle, which was torn down in 1706. The steep hill has been turned into a garden of pines and exotic flowers. To reach the château, you can take an elevator; actually, many prefer to take the elevator up, then walk down. The park is open May to August, daily from 10am to 7:30pm (off-season, to 4:30pm).

At the north end of Castle Hill is the famous old **graveyard** of Nice, visited primarily for its lavishly sculpted monuments that form their own enduring art statement. It's the largest one in France and the fourth largest in Europe. To reach it, you can take a small canopied "toy train," which will take you to the Bar du Donjon where you can enjoy a drink or a meal.

Nice

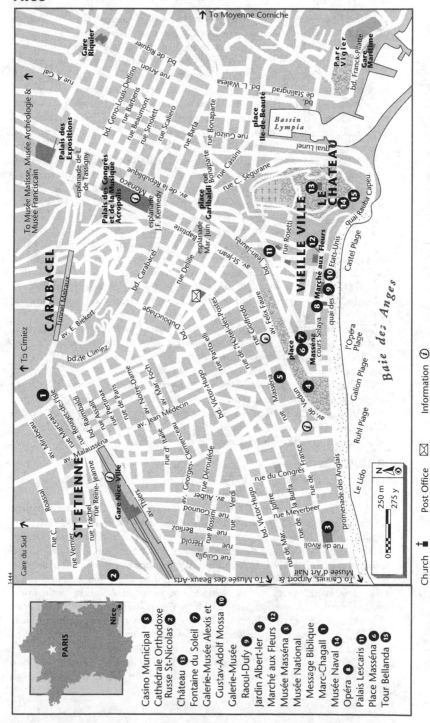

To Moyenne Corniche

To Cimiez

To Musée Matisse, Musée Archéologie & Musée Franciscain

CARABACEL

ST-ETIENNE

VIEILLE VILLE

LE CHÂTEAU

Bassin Lympia

Baie des Anges

Parc Vigier

Gare Riquier

Gare Maritime

Gare du Sud

Gare Nice-Ville

Palais des Expositions

Palais des Congrès et de la Musique Acropolis

place Garibaldi

place Masséna

place Ile-de-Beauté

Marché aux Fleurs

To Cannes, Airport & To Musée des Beaux-Arts

Musée d'Art Naïf

Le Lido

Ruhl Plage

Galion Plage

l'Opéra Plage

Castel Plage

0 | 250 m
0 | 275 y

N

Church

Post Office ☒

Information ℹ

Casino Municipal ⑤
Cathédrale Orthodoxe Russe St-Nicolas ②
Château ⑬
Fontaine du Soleil ⑦
Galerie-Musée Alexis et Gustav-Adolf Mossa ⑩
Galerie-Musée Raoul-Dufy ⑨
Jardin Albert-Ier ④
Marché aux Fleurs ⑫
Musée Masséna ③
Musée National Message Biblique Marc-Chagall ①
Musée Naval ⑭
Opéra ⑪
Palais Lescaris ⑥
Place Masséna ⑥
Tour Bellanda ⑮

PARIS

Nice

In the Tour Bellanda is the **Musée Naval (Naval Museum),** Parc du Château (☎ **93-80-47-61**), sitting on "The Rock." The tower stands on a precariously perched belvedere overlooking the beach, the bay, the old town, and even the terraces of some of the nearby villas. Of the museum's old battle prints, one depicts the exploits of Caterina Segurana, the Joan of Arc of the Niçois. During the 1543 siege by Barbarossa, she ran along the ramparts, raising her skirts to show her shapely bottom to the Turks as a sign of contempt, though the soldiers were reported to have been more excited than insulted. The museum is open May to September, Wednesday to Monday from 10am to noon and 2 to 7pm (off-season, to 5pm); it's closed from November 15 to December 15.

Continuing east from The Rock you reach **the harbor,** where the restaurants are even cheaper and the bouillabaisse just as good. While sitting here lingering over an apéritif at a sidewalk café, you can watch the boats depart for Corsica (perhaps take one yourself). The port was excavated between 1750 and 1830. Since then an outer harbor—protected by two jetties—has also been created.

The "authentic" Niçois live in **Vieille Ville,** the old town, beginning at the foot of The Rock. Under sienna-tiled roofs, many of the Italianate facades suggest 17th-century Genoese palaces. The old town is a maze of narrow streets, teeming with local life and studded with the least expensive restaurants in Nice. Buy an onion pizza (*la pissaladière*) from one of the local vendors. Many of the old buildings are painted a faded Roman gold, and their banners are multicolored laundry flapping in the sea breezes.

While there, try to visit the **Marché aux Fleurs,** the flower market at cours Saleya. The vendors start setting up their stalls at noon and the market opens from 2 to 4pm. A flamboyant array of carnations, violets, jonquils, roses, and birds of paradise is wheeled in on carts.

The center of Nice is **place Masséna,** with pink buildings in the 17th-century Genoese style and the Fontaine du Soleil (Fountain of the Sun) by Janoit, dating from 1956. Stretching from the main square to the promenade is the **Jardin Albert-Ier,** with an open-air terrace and a Triton Fountain. With palms and exotic flowers, it's the most relaxing oasis at the resort.

TOP MUSEUMS

If the pebbles of the beach are too sharp for your tender toes, you can escape into some of the finest museums along the Riviera.

The partner of the Galerie-Musée Raoul Dufy (below), the **Galerie-Musée Alexis et Gustav-Adolf Mossa,** 59 quai des Etats-Unis (☎ **93-62-37-11**), was inaugurated in 1990. Here, admire the dynamic lines of a veritable family dynasty of Nice-born artists. Among them is Alexis Mossa, famous for local landscapes and scenes of the Nice carnival. He's considered one of the early symbolist painters, a representative of a movement that brought a definitive end to the romantic movement of the late 19th century and a harbinger of surrealism. Also here are the works of Alexis's son, Gustav-Adolf Mossa, who continued his father's work. One series of works executed between 1903 and 1919, gracefully serves as a precursor to surrealism. The museum is open Tuesday to Saturday from 10am to noon and 2 to 6pm and Sunday from 2 to 6pm. Admission is free. Take bus no. 8.

La Galerie des Ponchettes, inaugurated in 1950 by Matisse, became, in 1990, the **Galerie-Musée Raoul-Dufy,** 77 quai des Etats-Unis (☎ **93-62-31-24**), in an annex of the Musée des Beaux-Arts (below). It presents one of the most beautiful collections by the "Havrais" artist (that means he comes from Le Havre) who lived from 1877 to 1953. Most of the collection was bequeathed to the museum by his widow. The extremely diversified works include 28 oils, 15 watercolors, 88 drawings, 3 ceramics, a tapestry, and 15 proposals for fabric designs commissioned by legendary couturier Paul Poiret. In its new setting, Dufy is immortalized, facing the waters of the Baie des Anges, which his works helped immortalize. The museum is open Tuesday to Saturday from 10am to noon and 2 to 6pm. and Sunday from 3 to 6pm. Admission is free. Take bus no. 8.

The ✪ **Musée des Beaux-Arts,** 33 av. des Baumettes (☎ **93-44-50 72**), is housed in the former residence of Ukrainian Princess Kotchubey. Its construction began in 1878 and was completed by a later owner, American James Thompson. It has an important gallery devoted to the masters of the Second Empire and Belle Epoque, with an extensive collection of the 19th-century French experts. The gallery of sculptures includes works by J. B. Carpeaux, Rude, and Rodin. Note the important collection by a dynasty of painters, the Dutch Vanloo family. One of its best-known members, Carle Vanloo, born in Nice in 1705, was Louis XV's "Premier Peintre." A fine collection of 19th- and 20th-century art is displayed, including works by Ziem, Raffaelli, Boudin, Renoir, Monet, Guillaumin, and Sisley. The museum is open Tuesday to Sunday: May to September from 10am to noon and 3 to 6pm, and October to April from 10am to noon and 2 to 5pm; closed three weeks in November. Take bus no. 3, 7, 12, 18, or 38.

The **Musée International d'Art Naïf Anatole-Jakovsky (Museum of Naïve Art),** av. Val-Marie (☎ **93-71-78-33**), is housed in the beautifully restored Château Ste-Hélène, on avenue Val-Marie in the Fabron district. The collection was once owned by the namesake of the museum, for years one of the world's leading art critics. His 600 drawings and canvases was turned over to the institution and made accessible to the public. Artists from more than two dozen countries are represented here—from primitive painting to contemporary 20th-century works. The museum is open Wednesday to Monday: May to September from 10am to noon and 2 to 6pm, and October to April from 10am to noon and 2 to 5pm. Admission is free. Take bus no. 9, 10, or 12.

The fabulous villa housing the **Musée Masséna,** 65 rue de France (☎ **93-88-11-34**), was built in 1900 in the style of the First Empire as a residence for Victor Masséna, the prince of Essling and grandson of Napoléon's marshal. The city of Nice has converted the villa, next door to the Hôtel Negresco, into a museum of local history and regional art. A remarkable First Empire drawing room furnished in the opulent taste of that era, with mahogany-veneer pieces and ormolu mounts, is on the ground floor. Of course there's the representation of Napoléon as a Roman Caesar and a bust by Canova of Marshal Masséna. The large first-floor gallery exhibits a collection of Niçois primitives and also has a display of 14th- and 15th-century painters, as well as a collection of 13th-century masterpieces of plates and jewelry decorated with enamel (Limoges). There are art galleries devoted to the history of Nice and the memories of Masséna and Garibaldi. Yet another gallery is reserved for a display of views of Nice during the 19th century. The museum is open Tuesday to Sunday: May to September from 10am to noon and 3 to 6pm, and October to April from 10am to noon and 2 to 5pm; closed holidays. Admission is free. Take bus no. 3, 7, 8, 9, 10, 12, 14, or 22.

MORE ATTRACTIONS

Ordered built by none other than Tsar Nicholas II, the **Cathédrale Orthodoxe Russe St-Nicolas à Nice,** av. Nicolas-II (off boulevard du Tzaréwitch) (☎ **93-96-88-02**), is the most beautiful religious edifice of the Orthodoxy outside Russia and is the most perfect expression of Russian religious art abroad. It dates from the Belle Epoque, when some of the Romanovs and their entourage turned the Riviera into a stamping ground. Everyone from grand dukes to ballerinas walked the promenade. The cathedral is richly ornamented and decorated with lots of icons. You'll easily spot the building from afar because of its collection of ornate onion domes. Church services are held on Sunday morning. The cathedral is open daily: June to September from 9am to noon and 2:30 to 6pm, and October to May from 9:30am to noon and 2:30 to 5pm. Admission is 12 F ($2.30). From the central rail station along avenue Thiers, head west to boulevard Gambetta; then go north to avenue Nicolas-II.

The baroque **Palais Lascaris,** 15 rue Droite (☎ **93-62-05-54**), is intimately linked to the Lascaris-Vintimille family, whose recorded history predates the year 1261. Built in the 17th century, it contains elaborately detailed ornaments. An intensive restoration undertaken by the city of Nice in 1946 brought back its original beauty, and the palace is now classified a historic monument. The most elaborate floor is the *étage noble*, retaining many of its 18th-century panels and plaster embellishments. A circa-1738 pharmacy, complete with many of the original Delftware accessories, is on the premises. The palace is open Tuesday to Sunday from 9:30am to noon and 2:30 to 6pm; closed in November. Take bus no. 1, 2, 3, 5, 6, 14, 16, or 17.

The **Parc des Miniatures,** avenue de l'Impératrice-Eugénie (☎ **92-44-67-74**), is one of France's oddest theme museums, a world where everything has been reduced to a size suited to an eagle's-eye view from above. It celebrates Nice's history and culture, from prehistoric times to the present, and contains hundreds of well-crafted monuments and buildings. Each is filled with and/or surrounded by miniature people and set in a 6-acre park dotted with flower beds, lakes, and fountains, 3 miles west of Nice's center. Allow between 60 and 90 minutes for a visit. It's open March to October, daily from 9:30am to 6:30pm; the rest of the year, hours are Saturday and Sunday from 9:30am to 6:30pm and Wednesday from 2 to 6:30pm.

In the parc's administration building is an independent museum founded/maintained by a retired airline pilot and Vietnam veteran, Eric Huitric. The **Musée des Trains Miniatures** (☎ **93-97-41-40**) has one of the world's most comprehensive collections of miniature trains plus an impressive number of accessories made in France, Germany, Denmark, and the United States between 1910 and the present. Its eight complete track layouts represent all the major railway guages of Europe and North America. In 1994 the museum attracted more than 30,000 visitors, making it the 23rd most frequently visited museum along the Côte d'Azur. It's open daily from 9:30am to 6:30pm.

Admission to the Parc des Miniatures costs 47 F ($8.95) for adults and 30 F ($5.70) for children 4 to 12. Admission to the Musée des Trains Miniatures costs 30 F ($5.70) for adults and 20 F ($3.80) for children 4 to 12. A combined ticket costs 60 F ($11.40) for adults and 445 F ($84.55) for children 4 to 12. Children 3 and under enter free.

NEARBY ATTRACTIONS IN CIMIEZ

In the once-aristocratic hilltop quarter of Cimiez, Queen Victoria wintered at the Hôtel Excelsior and brought half the English court with her. Founded by the Romans, who called it Cemenelum, Cimiez was the capital of the Maritime Alps province. To reach this suburb, take bus no. 15 or 17 from place Masséna. Recent excavations have uncovered the ruins of a Roman town, and you can wander among the diggings. The arena was big enough to hold at least 5,000 spectators, who watched contests between gladiators and wild beasts shipped in from Africa.

The **Monastère de Cimiez** (Cimiez Convent), place du Monastère (☎ **93-81-55-41**), embraces a church that owns three of the most important works from the primitive painting school of Nice by the Brea brothers. See the carved and gilded wooden main altarpiece. In the sacristy, frescoes are of a peculiar style, with symbolic and esoteric pictures. Most of these works are in the sacristy, and many other works can be seen only on guided tours. In a restored part of the convent, the **Musée Franciscain** is decorated with 17th-century frescoes. Some 350 documents and works of art from the 15th to the 18th century are displayed, and a monk's cell has been re-created. See also the 17th-century chapel. In the gardens you can get a panoramic view of Nice and the Bay of Angels. Matisse and Dufy are buried in the cemetery. The monastery and museum are open Monday to Saturday from 10am to noon and 3 to 6pm. Tours are given Monday to Friday at 10 and 11am and 3, 4, and 5pm. Admission is free.

The **Musée Matisse,** in the Villa des Arènes-de-Cimiez, 164 av. des Arènes-de-Cimiez (☎ **93-81-08-08**), honors the great artist who spent the last years of his life in Nice; he died here in 1954. Seeing his nude sketches today, you'll wonder how early critics could've denounced them as "the female animal in all her shame and horror." The museum has several permanent collections, most painted in Nice and many donated by Matisse and his heirs. These include *Nude in an Armchair with a Green Plant* (1937), *Nymph in the Forest* (1935/1942), and a chronologically arranged series of paintings from 1890 to 1919. The most famous of these is *Portrait of Madame Matisse* (1905), usually displayed near another portrait of the artist's wife, by Marquet, painted in 1900. There's also an ensemble of drawings and designs (*Flowers and Fruits*) he prepared as practice sketches for the Matisse Chapel at Vence. Probably the most famous are *The Créole Dancer* (1951), *Blue Nude IV* (1952), and around 50 dance-related sketches he did between 1930 and 1931. The museum is open Wednesday to Monday: April to September from 11am to 7pm, and October to March from 10am to 5pm. Admission is 25 F ($4.75) for adults and 10 F ($1.90) for children.

In the hills of Cimiez above Nice, the **Musée National Message Biblique Marc-Chagall** (Chagall Museum), av. du Docteur-Ménard (☎ **93-81-75-75**), is devoted to Marc Chagall's treatment of biblical themes. The handsome museum is surrounded by shallow pools and a garden planted with thyme, lavender, and olive trees. Born in Russia in 1887, Chagall became a French citizen in 1937. The artist and his wife donated the works—the most important collection of Chagall ever assembled—to the French state in 1966 and 1972. Displayed are 450 of his oils, gouaches, drawings, pastels, lithographs, sculptures, and ceramics; a mosaic; three stained-glass windows; and a tapestry. A splendid concert room was especially decorated by Chagall with outstanding stained-glass windows. Temporary exhibitions are organized each summer about great periods and artists of all times.

Special lectures in the rooms are available in both French and English (call for an appointment). The museum is open Wednesday to Monday: July to September from 10am to 7pm, and October to June from 10am to noon and 2 to 5:30pm. Admission is 17 F ($3.25) for adults and 8 F ($1.50) for ages 18 to 24 and over 60; 17 and under free. Fees may be higher for special exhibitions.

WHERE TO STAY
VERY EXPENSIVE

✪ Hôtel Négresco

37 promenade des Anglais, 06007 Nice CEDEX. ☎ **93-88-39-51.** Fax 93-88-35-68. 132 rms, 18 suites. A/C MINIBAR TV TEL. 1,300–2,350 F ($247–$446.50) double; from 3,750 F ($712.50) suite. Breakfast 120 F ($22.80) extra. AE, DC, MC, V. Parking free. Bus 8.

The Négresco is one of the many super-glamorous hotels along the French Riviera. Jeanne Augier has taken over the place and has triumphed. This Victorian wedding-cake hotel is named after founder Henry Negresco, a Romanian, who died franc-less in Paris in 1920. It was built on the seafront, in the "French château" style, with a mansard roof and domed tower, and its interior design was inspired by the country's châteaux and museums. The decorators of the guest rooms scoured Europe to gather antiques, tapestries, paintings, and art. Some rooms have personality themes, like the Louis XIV chamber, which has a green-velvet bed under a brocaded rose canopy. The Chambre Impér-atrice Joséphine 1810 regally re-creates an Empire bedroom, with a huge rosewood "swan bed" set in a fleur-de-lis–draped recess. The Napoléon III room has swagged walls and a half-crowned canopy in pink, with a leopard-skin carpet. The most expensive rooms with balconies face the Mediterranean. The staff wears 18th-century costumes. Less expensive meals are served in La Rotonde, though the featured restaurant—one of the greatest on the Riviera—is Chantecler (see "Where to Dine," below).

✪ Palais Maeterlinck

Basse Corniche, 06300 Nice. ☎ **90-00-72-00.** Fax 92-06-18-10. 22 rms, 6 suites. A/C MINIBAR TV TEL. 1,650–2,900 F ($313.50–$551) double; from 2,700 F ($513) suite. Breakfast 110 F ($20.90) extra. AE, DC, MC, V. Parking free. Closed Nov–Mar 1. Drive 4 miles east of Nice along the Basse Corniche.

On 9 landscaped acres east of Nice, this deluxe hotel—"the jewel of the Côte d'Azur"—is a sumptuous palace. It was built as a villa for Maurice Maeterlinck, the Belgian writer and winner of the Nobel Prize for literature. In a garden setting, filled with banana trees, olive trees, and cypresses, the writer lived between the two world wars. From the lofty grounds, guests can take a funicular down to the rock-strewn beach, complete with a marina. The elegant rooms, one with mirrored walls, have terraces opening onto views of such chic enclaves as Cap d'Antibes and Cap-Ferrat. The hotel's two restaurants offer excellent French and international cuisine, with Provençal specialties. Meals go for 160 to 240 F ($30.40 to $45.60), but there's no service on Sunday night or Monday. A buffet lunch is served on the terrace.

EXPENSIVE

Hôtel Abela

223 promenade des Anglais, 06200 Nice. ☎ **93-37-17-17.** Fax 93-71-21-71. 321 rms, 12 suites. A/C MINIBAR TV TEL. 920–1,120 F ($174.80–$212.80) double; from 2,550 F ($484.50) suite. Breakfast 90 F ($17.10) extra. AE, DC, MC, V. Parking 100 F ($19). Bus 8.

Alongside the major beachside thoroughfare, this streamlined contemporary hotel is one of the most alluring palaces in town. In 1992 it was acquired by a consortium of Lebanese and French investors who maintain high standards. A discreet portico leads into the sun-flooded lobby. Most of the attractive guest rooms open onto the promenade des Anglais, with balconies fronting the sea; they're filled with amenities. Visitors enjoy soft piano music in the sophisticated piano bar in the lobby. Les Mosaïques offers a gastronomic French cuisine and Lebanese specialties, with full meals at 25 to 175 F ($23.75 to $33.25) per person, without wine. Between June and September, one of the most sumptuous lunch buffets in Nice is served beside the pool.

Westminster Concorde

27 promenade des Anglais, 06000 Nice. ☎ **93-88-29-44.** Fax 93-82-45-35. 105 rms, 8 suites. A/C MINIBAR TV TEL. 500–1,000 F ($95.05–$190.10) single or double; from 1,300 F ($247.10) suite. Breakfast 70 F ($13.30) extra. AE, DC, MC, V. Parking 65 F ($12.35). Bus 8.

This 1880 hotel stands prominently along the famous promenade. Its elaborate facade was restored in 1986 to its former grandeur, and many renovations were made, including the installation of air conditioning. The contemporary rooms are comfortable and have soundproof windows; a few open onto balconies. The dining and drinking facilities include plant-ringed terraces with a view of the water and Le Farniente restaurant, where a fixed-price lunch or dinner begins at 160 F ($30.40).

MODERATE

Busby

36–38 rue du Maréchal-Joffre, 06000 Nice. ☎ **93-88-19-41.** Fax 93-87-73-53. 80 rms. A/C TV TEL. 550–650 F ($104.55–$123.55) double. Breakfast 35 F ($6.65) extra. AE, DC, MC, V. Closed Nov 15–Dec 20. Bus 9, 10, 12, or 22.

This place should please you if you want an elegant central hotel that has all the modern amenities. Totally renovated, the hotel has kept its old Niçois facade, with balconies and shutters at the tall windows. The guest rooms are dignified yet colorful, and some contain pairs of mahogany twin beds and two white-and-gold wardrobes. The bar is cozy, and the long dining room has marble columns, mirrors, and ladderback chairs. The restaurant is open from December 15 to May.

Grand Hôtel Aston

12, av. Félix-Fauré, 06000 Nice. ☎ **93-80-62-52.** Fax 93-80-40-02. 156 rms. 650–1,100 F ($123.55–$209.10) double. Breakfast 80 F ($15.20) extra. AE, DC, MC, V. Parking 90 F ($17.10).

One of the most alluring in its price bracket, this elegantly detailed 19th-century hotel has been radically renovated. Most rooms overlook the splashing fountains of the city's showcase, the Espace Masséna, a few blocks from the water. The rooftop garden offers dance music and a bar on summer evenings and has a panoramic coastline view.

INEXPENSIVE

⊛ Hôtel Alize

65 rue Buffa, 06000 Nice. ☎ **93-88-99-46.** 11 rms. A/C TEL. 240–280 F ($45.60–$53.20) double; 320–350 F ($60.80–$66.50) triple. Breakfast 25 F ($4.75) extra. V. Bus 8.

Right off the promenade des Anglais and boulevard Gambetta, this is a modest hotel that's completely well maintained. The rooms are comfortably furnished,

often in bright colors. Near the chic Négresco, this hotel is a bargain. Breakfast is
the only meal served, but the rooms are air-conditioned.

⑤ Hôtel Canada

8 rue Halévy, 06000 Nice. ☎ **93-87-98-94.** Fax 93-87-17-12. 18 rms. TV TEL. 210–330 F
($39.90–$62.70) double, 270–360 F ($51.30–$68.40) double with kitchenette. Breakfast
30 F ($5.70) extra. AE, DC, MC, V. Bus 12 from the train station to Grimaldi.

Nearby are some expensive neighbors, but the Canada is a bargain, popular with
families who like to reserve one of the rooms with kitchenettes. Near the sea, the
hotel is in a pedestrian zone. Many Canadians are attracted to it because of its
name, though it's French run. Each room is comfortably furnished. Decorative
touches abound, including an occasional brass headboard on a bed. The most expensive rooms, with the kitchenettes, are also air-conditioned. Reservations are
needed in summer—as far in advance as possible.

⑤ Villa Eden

99 bis, promenade des Anglais, 06000 Nice. ☎ **93-86-53-70.** Fax 93-87-17-12. 15 rms,
6 with shower only. TEL. 170 F ($32.30) double without shower, 360 F ($68.40) double with
shower. Breakfast 30 F ($5.70) extra. AE, MC, V. Parking free. Bus 8.

In 1925, an exiled Russian countess built this art deco villa on the seafront, surrounded it with a wall, and planted a tiny garden. The villa still remains, despite
the construction of much-taller modern buildings on both sides. You can enjoy the
ivy and roses in the garden and stay in old-fashioned partly modernized rooms
whose sizes vary greatly. The owner maintains a wry sense of humor and greets
guests at breakfast, the only meal served.

WHERE TO DINE
VERY EXPENSIVE

✪ Chantecler

In the Hôtel Négresco, 37 promenade des Anglais. ☎ **93-88-39-51.** Reservations required.
Main courses 180–250 F ($34.20–$47.50); fixed-price menus 390 F ($74.10), 430 F ($81.70),
490 F ($93.10), and 550 F ($104.50). AE, DC, MC, V. Daily 12:30–2:30pm and 7:30–
10:30pm. Closed mid-Nov to mid-Dec. Bus 8. FRENCH.

Of all France's great palace hotels, none has a chef to equal Dominique Le Stanc—
for this culinary genius merits high praise. Beautifully restored and redecorated,
this restaurant is a delight. You know you're in for a treat when the waiter comes
around with a dozen homemade breads for your selection. Monsieur Le Stanc's
cuisine is excellent and attractively presented. To begin, try one of his specialties:
ravioli stuffed with a small lobster, asparagus, and artichokes. He also does a "symphony" of truffles, scallops, potatos, and leeks in a feathery-thin "potato hamburger," as one food critic called it. You might also want to try his fricassée of
sweetbreads with morels. This is one of the few restaurants on the Riviera where
every dish is likely to be great, especially the desserts.

✪ Le Florian

22 rue Alphonse-Karr. ☎ **93-88-86-60.** Reservations recommended. Main courses 100–
240 F ($19–$45.60); fixed-price menus 189 F ($35.90), 250 F ($47.50), and 350 F ($66.50).
MC, V. Mon–Fri noon–2pm and 7:30–10pm, Sat 7:30–10pm. Closed July–Aug. Bus 9, 10,
or 12. FRENCH.

This art deco restaurant occupies half the ground floor of a turn-of-the-century
apartment building. Amid mahogany paneling and a vivid sense of the 1930s, chef
Claude Gillon prepares such dishes as shellfish-stuffed ravioli served with lobster
bouillon and cream sauce, oxtail with foie-gras sauce, stuffed pigs' feet, suckling

lamb with lima beans, and Challons duckling with red-wine sauce. The food is professionally prepared, and each item we've sampled has been profoundly flavorful. Restrained and dignified, the restaurant is sometimes confused with its less formal partner, Le Bistrot du Florian, next door.

MODERATE

Chez Michel (Le Grand Pavois)

11 rue Meyerbeer. ☎ **93-88-77-42.** Reservations required. Main courses 120–190 F ($22.80–$36.10); bouillabaisse 300–450 F ($57–$85.50); fixed-price menus 195–250 F ($37.05–$47.50). AE, DC, MC, V. Daily noon–2:30pm and 7–11pm. Bus 8. SEAFOOD.

Chez Michel is nestled under an art deco apartment building near the water. The brass-trimmed ship's steering wheel adds to the nautical decor—as you'd expect, this is a seafood restaurant. One of the partners, Jacques Marquise, is from Golfe-Juan, where for 25 years he managed the famous fish restaurant Chez Tétou. It was known for its bouillabaisse, which M. Marquise now prepares at Chez Michel. Other delectable specialties are baked sea bass in white wine, herbs, and lemon sauce and grilled flambé lobster. The wine list has a number of reasonably priced bottles.

⑤ La Toque Blanche

40 rue de la Buffa. ☎ **93-88-38-18.** Reservations not required. Main courses 120–200 F ($22.80–$38); fixed-price menus 140 F ($26.60), 160 F ($30.40), and 290 F ($55.10). AE, MC, V. Tues–Sat 12:30–2pm and 7:30–9:30pm, Sun 12:30–2pm. Bus 8. FRENCH.

La Toque Blanche has only about a dozen tables amid its winter-garden decor. Owners Denise and Alain Sandelion pay particular attention to their shopping and buy only very fresh ingredients. The cuisine is skillfully prepared—try their sea bass roasted with citrus juice, sautéed sweetbreads with crayfish, or salmon prepared with fresh shrimp. The set menus are a particularly good value.

INEXPENSIVE

Flo

2–4 rue Sacha-Guitry. ☎ **93-13-38-38.** Reservations recommended. Main courses 54–116 F ($10.25–$22.05); fixed-price menus 99 F ($18.80) and 141 F ($26.80). AE, DC, MC, V. Daily noon–3pm and 7pm–12:30am. Bus 1, 2, or 5. FRENCH.

In 1991 one of the most successful chains of historic brasseries bought the premises of a once-stylish restaurant and transformed it into this brasserie, modeled after its Paris namesake (the Brasserie Flo). The high ceilings are covered with their original frescoes, but the venue is brisk, stylish, and fun. Menu items include an array of grilled fish, choucroute (sauerkraut) in the Alsatian style, and steaks with brandied pepper sauce.

⑤ La Nissarda

17 rue Gubernatis. ☎ **93-85-26-29.** Reservations recommended. Main courses 45–78 F ($8.55–$14.80); fixed-price menus 78–138 F ($14.80–$26.20). AE, DC, MC, V. Mon–Sat noon–2pm and 7–10pm. Closed Aug. NIÇOISE/NORMAN.

About a 10-minute walk from place Masséna, this restaurant is maintained by a Normandy-born family (the Pruniers) who work hard to maintain the aura and some of the culinary traditions of Nice. In an intimate setting lined with old engravings and photographs of the city, the place serves local versions of ravioli, lasagne, spaghetti carbonara, and grilled salmon with herbs. A handful of Norman-based specialties also manage to creep into the menu, like escalopes of veal with cream sauce and apples.

⑤ Restaurant l'Estocaficada

2 rue de l100 Hôtel-de-Ville. ☎ **93-80-21-64.** Reservations recommended. Main courses 50–95 F ($9.50–$18.05); fixed-price menus 58–78 F ($11–$14.80); pizzas 30–45 F ($5.70–$8.55). AE, MC, V. Mon–Fri noon–2pm and 7–10pm, Sun 7–10pm. Bus 1, 2, or 5. NIÇOIS.

Estocaficada is the Provençal word for stockfish, the ugliest fish in Europe. You can see one for yourself—there might be a dried-out, balloon-shaped version on display in the cozy dining room. Brigitte Autier is the owner/chef, whose busy kitchens are visible from virtually everywhere in the dining room. Descended from a matriarchal line (since 1958) of mother-daughter teams who have managed this place, she's devoted to the preservation of recipes prepared by her Niçois grandmother. Examples include gnocchis, beignets, several types of farcies (tomatoes, peppers, or onions stuffed with herbed fillings), grilled sardines, bouillabaisse served as a main course or in a mini-version, and faux-filets with black pepper or Calvados. As a concession to popular demand, the place also serves pizzas and pastas.

AFTER DARK

Nice has some of the most active nightlife along the Riviera, with evenings usually beginning at a café. A quarterly booklet, *L'Infor,* available free at the tourist office, lists the city's cultural attractions. You can also pick up a copy of *La Semaine des Spectacles,* outlining the week's nighttime diversions.

The major cultural center along the Riviera is the **Opéra de Nice,** 4 rue St-François-de-Paule (☎ **93-85-67-31**), with a busy season in winter. A full repertoire is presented, including both operas and the popular French Opéra Comique. In one season you might see *La Bohème, Tristan und Isolde,* and *Carmen,* as well as a *saison symphonique,* dominated by the Orchestre Philharmonique de Nice. The opera hall is also the major venue for concerts and recitals. The box office is open Tuesday to Saturday from 11am to 7pm. Tickets range from 50 to 240 F ($9.50 to $45.60).

9 St-Paul-de-Vence

575 miles S of Paris, 14 miles E of Grasse, 17 miles E of Cannes, 19 miles N of Nice

Of all the perched villages of the Riviera, St-Paul-de-Vence is the best known. It was popularized in the 1920s when many noted artists lived there, occupying the 16th-century houses flanking the narrow cobblestone streets. The feudal hamlet grew up on a bastion of rock, almost blending into it. Its ramparts (allow about 30 minutes to encircle them) overlook a peaceful setting of flowers and olive and orange trees. As you make your way through the warren of streets you'll pass endless souvenir shops, a charming old fountain carved in the form of an urn, and a gothic church from the 13th century.

ESSENTIALS

GETTING THERE   Some 20 buses per day leave from Nice's *gare routière,* taking 55 minutes and costing 28 F ($5.30) one way.

VISITOR INFORMATION   The Office de Tourisme is at Maison Tour, rue Grande (☎ **93-32-86-95**).

SEEING THE TOP ATTRACTION

The most important attraction of St-Paul-de-Vence lies outside the walls at **Fondation Maeght** (☎ **93-32-81-63**), one of the most modern art museums in

Europe. On a hill in pine-studded woods, the Maeght Foundation is like a Shangri-la. Not only is the architecture avant-garde, but also the building houses one of the finest collections of contemporary art on the Riviera. Nature and the creations of men and women blend harmoniously in this unique achievement of architect José Luís Sert. Its white concrete arcs give the impression of a giant pagoda.

A stark Calder rises like some futuristic monster on the grassy lawns. In a courtyard, the elongated bronze works of Giacometti form a surrealistic garden, creating a hallucinatory mood. Sculpture is also displayed inside, but it's at its best in a natural setting of surrounding terraces and gardens. The museum is built on several levels, its many glass walls providing an indoor-outdoor vista. The foundation, a gift "to the people" from Aimé and Marguerite Maeght, also provides a showcase for new talent. Exhibitions are always changing. Everywhere you look, you see 20th-century art: mosaics by Chagall and Braque, Miró ceramics in the "labyrinth," and Ubac and Braque stained glass in the chapel. Bonnard, Kandinsky, Léger, Matisse, Barbara Hepworth, and many other artists are well represented.

There are a library, a cinema, and a cafeteria here. In one showroom you can buy original lithographs by artists like Chagall and Giacometti and limited-edition prints. Admission is 45 F ($8.55) for adults and 35 F ($6.65) for children. It's open daily: July to September from 10am to 7pm, and October to June from 10am to 12:30pm and 2:30 to 6pm.

WHERE TO STAY
VERY EXPENSIVE

✪ Le Mas d'Artigny
Route de la Colle et des Hauts de St-Paul, 06570 St-Paul-de-Vence. ☎ **93-32-84-54.** Fax 93-32-95-36. 53 rms, 29 suites. A/C MINIBAR TV TEL. 885–1,830 F ($168.25–$347.90) double; from 2,680 F ($509.50) suite. Breakfast 115 F ($21.85) extra; half board 400 F ($76) per person extra. MC, V. Parking 75 F ($14.25).

This hotel might remind you of a sprawling Provençal homestead set in an acre of pine forests. It's about 2 miles from St-Paul, at the end of a winding road. Semitropical plants surround the outside. In the lobby is a constantly changing exhibition of art. Each of the comfortably large rooms has its own terrace or balcony. Private suites (with a private pool) are on a slope below the blue-tile pool of the hotel, with hedges for privacy. For such an elegant Relais & Châteaux, the restaurant is a bit lackluster in decoration, but a compensating factor is its views of the garden. Chef Arthur Dorschner regales guests with his flavors of Provence, everything tasting as if it's ripened in the sun. Only quality ingredients are used to shape this harmonious and rarely complicated cuisine. The wine cellar deserves a star for its vintage collection, but watch those prices!

EXPENSIVE

✪ Hôtel le St-Paul
86 rue Grande, 06570 St-Paul-de-Vence. ☎ **93-32-65-25.** Fax 93-32-52-94. 15 rms, 3 suites. A/C MINIBAR TV TEL. 600–1,900 F ($114.05–$361.20) double; 1,200–1,700 F ($228.10–$323.20) suite. Breakfast 90 F ($17.10) extra; half board 390 F ($74.10) per person extra. AE, DC, MC, V.

Converted from a 16th-century Renaissance residence and retaining many original features, this four-star Relais & Châteaux is in the heart of the medieval village. The guest rooms, decorated in a sophisticated yet Provençal style, have safe-deposit boxes, satellite TV, and many extras. One woman wrote us that sitting on the balcony of Room 30 she understood why Renoir, Léger, Matisse, and even Picasso were inspired by Provence. Many rooms enjoy a view of the valley with the Mediterranean in the distance. The restaurant has a flower-bedecked terrace sheltered by the 16th-century ramparts as well as a superb dining room with vaulted ceilings. Menus might include locally inspired dishes like cream of salt cod with a thin slice of grilled pancetta, risotto of crayfish and broadbeans, roast veal chop with morels and barley, and a delightful crème brûlée with a hint of rosemary.

MODERATE

Les Orangers

Chemin des Fumerates, route de la Colle (D107), 06570 St-Paul-de-Vence. ☎ **93-32-80-95.** Fax 93-32-00-32. 7 rms, 2 suites. TEL. 490–580 F ($93.15–$110.25) double; 690 F ($131.15) suite. Breakfast 40 F ($7.60) extra. MC, V. Parking free.

Monsieur Franklin has created a beautiful "living oasis" in his villa less than half a mile from the village. The scents of roses, oranges, and lemons waft through the air. The main lounge is impeccably decorated with original oils and furnished in a provincial style. Expect to be treated like a guest in a private home here. The rooms, with antiques and Oriental carpets, have panoramic views. On the sun terrace are banana trees, flower beds, and climbing geraniums.

INEXPENSIVE

⑤ Les Bastides St-Paul

880 route des Blaquières (route de Vence), 06570 St-Paul-de-Vence. ☎ **92-02-08-07.** Fax 93-20-50-41. 17 rms. MINIBAR TEL. 450–550 F ($85.55–$104.55) double; 650 F ($123.55) triple. Breakfast 45 F ($8.55) extra. AE, DC, MC, V. Parking free.

This hotel is in the hills outside town, a mile south of St-Paul and 2¹/₂ miles south of Vence. Divided into three buildings, it offers clean and comfortably carpeted rooms, each accented with regional artifacts. On the premises is a pool shaped like a cloverleaf, a cozy breakfast area, and a sensitive management staff headed by long-time hoteliers Marie José and Maurice Giraudet. Breakfast is served anytime a client wants it.

WHERE TO DINE

La Colombe d'Or

1 place du Général-de-Gaulle. ☎ **96-32-80-02.** Reservations required. Main courses 100–250 F ($19–$47.50). AE, DC, MC, V. Daily noon–2:30pm and 7–10:30pm. Closed Nov 5–Dec 19. FRENCH.

The Golden Dove, for decades the most celebrated restaurant in St-Paul, always seems to appear as a setting for every film ever shot on the Riviera. Famous for its remarkable art collection, it offers dining to guests who can also enjoy Miró, Picasso, Klee, Dufy, Utrillo, and Calder. In fair weather, everyone tries for a seat on the terrace—to soak up the view. You might begin with smoked salmon or a plate of foie gras from Landes if you've recently won at the casino. Otherwise, you can generally count on a soup made with the fresh vegetables of the season. One of the best fish dishes is poached sea bass with mousseline sauce. You can also order daurade grilled to your specifications. Tender beef comes with gratin dauphinois (potatoes), or you may prefer lamb from Sisteron. A classic finish to any meal is a soufflé flambé au Grand-Marnier.

10 Vence

575 miles S of Paris, 19 miles N of Cannes, 15 miles NW of Nice

Travel up into the hills northwest of Nice—across country studded with cypresses, olive trees, and pines, where bright flowers, especially carnations, roses, and oleanders, grow in profusion—and Vence comes into view. Outside the town, along boulevard Paul-André, two olive presses carry on with their age-old duties. But the charm lies in the **Vieille Ville (Old Town).** Visitors invariably have themselves photographed on place du Peyra in front of the urn-shaped Vieille Fontaine (Old Fountain), a background shot in several motion pictures. The 15th-century square tower is also a curiosity.

If you're wearing the right kind of shoes, the narrow, steep streets of the old town are worth exploring. Dating from the 10th century, the cathedral on place Godeau is unremarkable except for some 15th-century gothic choir stalls. But if it's the right day of the week, most visitors quickly pass through the narrow gates of this once-fortified walled town to where the sun shines more brightly:

It was a beautiful golden autumn along the Côte d'Azur. The great Henri Matisse was 77, and after a turbulent introspective time he set out to create his masterpiece—"the culmination of a whole life dedicated to the search for truth," as he said. Just outside Vence, Matisse created the ✪ **Chapelle du Rosaire,** avenue Henri-Matisse (☎ 93-58-03-25), for the Dominican nuns of Monteils. From the front you might find it unremarkable and pass it by—until you spot a 40-foot crescent-adorned cross rising from a blue-tile roof.

Matisse wrote: "What I have done in the chapel is to create a religious space ... in an enclosed area of very reduced proportions and to give it, solely by the play of colors and lines, the dimensions of infinity." The light picks up the subtle coloring in the simply rendered leaf forms and abstract patterns: sapphire blue, aquamarine, and lemon yellow. In black-and-white ceramics, St. Dominic is depicted in only a few lines. The most remarkable design is in the black-and-white tile Stations of the Cross, with Matisse's self-styled "tormented and passionate" figures. The bishop of Nice came to bless the chapel in the late spring of 1951 when the artist's work was completed. Matisse died three years later.

The chapel is open December 13 to October, Tuesday and Thursday from 10 to 11:30am and 2:30 to 5:30pm. Admission is free; donations are welcomed.

ESSENTIALS

GETTING THERE   Frequent buses from Nice take one hour and cost 20 F ($3.80) one way.

VISITOR INFORMATION   The Office de Tourisme is on place Grand-Jardin (☎ 93-58-06-38).

WHERE TO STAY
VERY EXPENSIVE

✪ Le Château du Domaine St-Martin

Route de Coursegoules, 06140 Vence. ☎ 93-58-02-02. Fax 93-24-08-91. 14 rms, 10 suites. A/C MINIBAR TV TEL. 1,370–2,300 F ($260.30–$437) double; 2,700–3,200 F ($513–$608) suite. Breakfast 105 F ($19.95) extra. AE, DC, MC, V. Parking free. Closed Nov 15–Mar 15.

This château, a complex of Mediterranean-style buildings in a 35-acre park 2 miles outside Vence, was built in 1936 on the grounds where the "Golden Goat treasury" was reputedly buried. When the Genève family purchased the estate, they had to sign a bill of sale agreeing to share the treasure, if found, with the previous owners. A complex of tile-roofed villas with suites was built in the terraced gardens. You can walk through the gardens on winding paths lined with tall cypresses, past the ruined chapel and olive trees. The guest rooms are finely furnished. The glass-enclosed restaurant has a view of the coast and a superb French cuisine. In summer many guests prefer the grill at poolside. Nonguests who make reservations are welcome. Fixed-price menus range from 300 F ($57) at lunch to 420 to 480 F ($79.80 to $91.25) at dinner.

MODERATE

Le Floréal
Av. Rhin-et-Danube, 06140 Vence. ☎ **93-58-64-40.** Fax 93-58-79-69. 43 rms, 2 suites. A/C MINIBAR TV TEL. 450 F ($85.55) double; from 650 F ($123.55) suite. Breakfast 50 F ($9.50) extra. MC, V. Parking free.

On the road to Grasse is this pleasant, comfortable hotel with a view of the mountains. Many of the well-furnished rooms look out on the large pool in the well-kept garden, where orange trees and mimosa add fragrance to the breezes. The hotel has parking, air-conditioned lounges, and a bar.

INEXPENSIVE

Ⓢ Auberge des Seigneurs (Inn of the Noblemen)
Place du Friene, 06140 Vence. ☎ **93-58-04-24.** Fax 93-24-08-01. 8 rms. TEL. 300–350 F ($57–$66.50) double. Breakfast 50 F ($9.50) extra. AE, DC, MC, V. Parking free. Closed July 1–10 and Nov 15–Dec 15.

This 400-year-old stone hostelry lets you experience Old Provence. Inside is a long wooden dining table, in view of an open fireplace with a row of hanging copper pots and pans. The cuisine of François I is served in an antique atmosphere with wooden casks of flowers and an open spit for roasting and grilling. Fascinating decorative objects and antiques are everywhere. The food is superb, with fixed-price menus costing 200 to 230 F ($38 to $43.70).

WHERE TO DINE

Ⓢ La Farigoule
15 rue Henri-Isnard. ☎ **93-58-01-27.** Reservations recommended. Fixed-price menus 115–140 F ($21.85–$26.60). AE, MC, V. Sat 7–10pm, Sun–Thurs 12:30–2pm and 7–10pm. Closed Nov 10–Dec 15. FRENCH.

During summer you can enjoy regional cuisine in the garden under a rose arbor. Chef Georgette Gastaud grills much of the food on an open fire. A long line forms on Sunday afternoon. The least expensive fixed-price menu may include fish soup, trout meunière, a vegetable, and cheese or dessert—service and drinks extra. The most expensive fixed-price menu is far more enticing and might include asparagus vinaigrette, mussels marinara, a tender rabbit with seasonal vegetables, cheese and dessert—drinks and service extra. There is no à la carte.

11 Cagnes-sur-Mer

570 miles S of Paris; 13 miles NE of Cannes

Cagnes-sur-Mer, like the Roman god Janus, has two faces. Perched on a hill in the "hinterlands" of Nice, **Le Haut-de-Cagnes** is one of the most charming spots on the Riviera. Naomi Barry wrote that it "crowns the top of a blue-cypressed hill like a village in an Italian Renaissance painting." At the foot of the hill is an old fishing port and rapidly developing beach resort called **Cros-de-Cagnes,** between Nice and Antibes.

For years Le Haut-de-Cagnes attracted the French literati, including Simone de Beauvoir, who wrote *Les Mandarins* here. A colony of painters also settled here; Renoir said the village was "the place where I want to paint until the last day of my life." Today the racecourse is one of the finest in France.

ESSENTIALS

GETTING THERE Buses from Nice and Cannes stop at Cagnes-Ville and at Béal/Les Collettes, within walking distance of Cros-de-Cagne. The climb from Cagnes-Ville to Le-Haut-de-Cagnes is very strenuous, so there's a minibus running about every 45 minutes from place du Général-de-Gaulle, in the center of Cagnes-Ville to Le-Haut-de-Cagnes.

VISITOR INFORMATION The Office de Tourisme is at 6 bd. Maréchal-Juin, Cagnes-Ville (☎ **93-20-61-64**).

SPECIAL EVENTS The **International Festival of Painting** is presented by the Musée d'Art Moderne Méditerranéen from July to September; 40 nations participate. For information, call 93-20-85-57.

SEEING THE TOP ATTRACTIONS

The orange groves and fields of carnations of the upper village provide a beautiful setting for the narrow cobblestone streets and 17th- and 18th-century homes. Drive your car to the top, where you can enjoy the view from **place du Château** and have lunch or a drink at a sidewalk café.

While in Le Haut-de-Cagnes, visit the **fortress** on place Grimaldi. It was built in 1301 by Rainier Grimaldi I, a lord of Monaco and a French admiral (see the portrait inside). Charts reveal how the defenses were organized. In the early 17th century the dank castle was converted into a more gracious Louis XIII château.

The château contains the **Musée de l'Olivier (Museum of the Olive Tree)** and a **Musée d'Art Moderne Méditerranéen (Museum of Modern Mediterranean Art)**, 7 place Grimaldi (☎ **93-20-85-57**). The ethnographical museum shows the steps in the cultivating and processing of the olive. The modern-art gallery displays work by Kisling, Carzou, Dufy, Cocteau, and Seyssaud, among others, with temporary exhibitions. In one salon is an interesting trompe-l'oeil fresco, *La Chute de Phaeton,* by Carlone, an Italian. From the tower you get a panoramic view of the Côte d'Azur. The museum is are open Wednesday to Monday: June 15 to September from 10am to noon and 2 to 6pm, and October 1–14 and November 16 to June 14 from 10am to noon and 2 to 5pm; closed October 15 to November 15. Admission is 6 F ($1.15) for adults and 3 F (55¢) for children. The International Festival of Painting takes place here (see "Essentials," above).

WHERE TO STAY
IN LE HAUT-DE-CAGNES

✪ Le Cagnard

Rue du Pontis-Long, Le Haut-de-Cagnes, 06800 Cagnes-sur-Mer. ☎ **93-20-73-21.** Fax 93-22-06-39. 18 rms, 10 suites. MINIBAR TV TEL. 380–900 F ($72.20–$171.10) double; 1,100–1,500 F ($209.10–$285.15) suite. Breakfast 70 F ($13.30) extra. AE, DC, MC, V. Parking free. Closed Nov–Dec 18.

Several village houses have been joined to form this handsome hostelry owned by Felix Barel. The dining room is covered with frescoes, and there's also a vine-draped terrace. The rooms and salons are furnished with family antiques, such as provincial chests, armoires, Louis XV chairs, and copper lavabos. Each room has its own style—some are duplexes; others have terraces and views of the country-side. The cuisine of chef Jean-Yves Johany is reason enough to make the trip here. Fresh ingredients are used in delectable dishes placed on one of the finest tables set in Provence. This talented chef features Sisteron lamb (carré d'agneau) spit-roasted with Provençal herbs for two, as well as wonderfully tender côte de boeuf. The pièce de résistance dessert is the extravagantly prepared mousseline de glace aux charmeuses de bois. Fixed-price menus begin at 320 to 380 F ($60.80 to $72.20); à la carte meals average 530 F ($100.75).

IN CROS-DE-CAGNES

⑤ Hôtel le Minaret

Av. Serre, 06800 Cros-de-Cagnes. ☎ **93-20-16-52.** 20 rms. TV TEL. 300 F ($57) double. Breakfast 25 F ($4.75) extra. MC, V.

This two-star hotel has a courtyard with tables in the front and a hard-working staff. It once sported a decorative minaret in the North African style. Though it was removed in a restoration, the name has remained. Fifty yards from the beach, Le Minaret also has a shaded garden filled with mimosa, orange trees, and palms. Some rooms have terraces or balconies; all have kit-chenettes. There's a bar on the premises, but no restaurant, though several are within walking distance.

WHERE TO DINE
IN LE HAUT-DE-CAGNES

Josy-Jo

8 place du Planastel. ☎ **93-20-68-76.** Reservations required. Main courses 130–160 F ($24.70–$30.40). AE, MC, V. Mon–Fri noon–2pm and 7:30–10pm, Sat 7:30–10pm. Closed Aug 1–15. FRENCH.

Sheltered behind masses of vines and flowers, this restaurant on the main road to the château used to be the home and studio of Modigliani and Soutine during their hungriest years. Today it belongs to the charming and cheerful Bandecchi family, who have lined the dining room with art. Their cuisine is simple, fresh, and excellent. You can enjoy brochette of gigot of lamb with kidneys, four succulent varieties of steak, calves' liver, a homemade terrine of foie gras of duckling, an array of salads, and Irish coffee. Meats are roasted over an open grill flaming with Portuguese charcoal.

Restaurant des Peintres

71 montée de la Bourgade. ☎ **93-20-83-08.** Reservations required. Main courses 150–210 F ($28.50–$39.90); fixed-price menus 200–300 F ($38–$57). AE, DC, V. July 14–Aug, Mon and Wed 7–10pm, Tues and Thurs–Sun noon–2:30pm and 7–10pm; Sept–July 13, Thurs–Tues noon–2:30pm and 7–10pm. FRENCH.

Alain Llorca is a young chef who ranks among our top discoveries along the Côte d'Azur. He received his training under such famous chefs as Le Stanc, the finest chef on the Riviera today, working out of the Négresco in Nice. Though Llorca learned many of Le Stanc's "secrets," he has also forged ahead with his own tal-ent and inventiveness. His cuisine is enough to dazzle: It's light, filled with flavor, and endlessly satisfying. Spit-roasted lamb is roasted with aromatic fennel and local artichokes. Be prepared to be seduced by this fine and original cookery—perhaps by the chestnut cream with poached truffles. In spring he does amazing things with asparagus and makes a carpaccio of tuna. The wine list is reasonable in price, and proprietors Jacques and Claudie extend a warm welcome.

IN CROS-DE-CAGNES

✪ Loulou (La Réserve)

91 bd. de la Plage. ☎ **93-31-00-17.** Reservations recommended. Main courses 135–195 F ($25.65–$37.05). AE, MC, V. Mon–Fri noon–2:30pm and 7–9:45pm, Sat 7–9:45pm. Closed July 15–Aug 3 and for lunch Aug 3–31. FRENCH.

Named for a famous long-departed chef, this restaurant is across from the sea. In front is a glassed-in veranda perfect for people-watching. Chef Eric Campo is noted for his fresh fish, as well as for rockfish soup (in season), aiguillettes of duckling with herbs, and a selection of grilled meats. We were slow to catch on to just how talented Campo is in the kitchen, and in this edition we award a long-overdue Frommer star. Though many of the French gastronomic guides continue to ignore this talented chef, Michelin has bestowed a star, of which Campo is rightly proud. Everything is solid and reliable, yet he also knows how to be inventive in bringing out the inherent flavor in every dish.

A NEARBY ATTRACTION

Les Collettes, 19 chemin des Collettes (☎ **93-20-61-07**), has been restored to what it looked like when Renoir lived here from 1908 until his death in 1919. He continued to sculpt here, even though he was crippled by arthritis and had to be helped in and out of a wheelchair. He also continued to paint, with a brush tied to his hand and with the help of assistants. One of his last paintings, *Rest After Bathing,* can be seen in the Louvre.

The house was built in 1907 in an olive and orange grove. There's a bust of Mme Renoir in the entrance room. You can explore the drawing room and dining room on your own before going up to the artist's bedroom. In his atelier are his wheelchair, easel, and brushes. From the terrace of Mme Renoir's bedroom is a stunning view of Cap d'Antibes and Le Haut-de-Cagnes. Although Renoir is best remembered for his paintings, it was in Cagnes he began experimenting with sculpture. The museum has 20 portrait busts and portrait medallions, most of which depict his wife and children. The curators say they represent the largest collection of Renoir sculpture in the world. On a wall hangs a photograph of one of Renoir's sons, Pierre, as he appeared in the 1932 film *Madame Bovary.* The house is open May to October 14, daily from 10am to noon and 2 to 5pm; October 15–29 and December to April, Wednesday to Monday from 10am to noon and 2 to 5pm; closed October 30 to November 30. Admission is 20 F ($3.80) for adults and 10 F ($1.90) for children.

12 Biot

570 miles S of Paris; 6 miles E of Cagnes-sur-Mer; 4 miles NW of Antibes

Biot has been famous for its pottery ever since merchants began to ship earthenware jars to Phoenicia and destinations throughout the Mediterranean. Biot was originally settled by Gallo-Romans and has had a long war-torn history. Somehow the potters still manage to work at their ancient craft. Biot is also the place Fernand

Léger chose to paint until the day he died. The greatest collection of his work is on display at a museum here.

In the late 1940s glassmakers created a bubble-flecked glass known as *verre rustique*. It comes in brilliant colors like cobalt and emerald and is displayed in many store windows on the main shopping street. The town also is known for its carnations and roses, sold on the arcaded square. Flowers also are flown to the capitals of northern Europe.

ESSENTIALS

GETTING THERE   The train station is 2 miles from the town center. There's frequent service from Nice and Antibes. The bus from Antibes is even more convenient than the train.

VISITOR INFORMATION   The Office de Tourisme is on place de la Chapelle (☎ 93-65-05-85).

SEEING THE TOP ATTRACTION

The most popular attraction in town is the **Musée National Fernand-Léger,** chemin du Val-de-Pome (☎ **93-65-63-61**), opened in 1960. The collection was assembled by his widow, Nadia Léger. The stone-and-marble facade is enhanced by Léger's mosaic-and-ceramic mural. On the grounds is a polychrome ceramic sculpture, *Le Jardin d'Enfant.* Inside are two floors of geometrical forms in pure flat colors. The collection includes gouaches, paintings, ceramics, tapestries, and sculptures—showing the development of the artist from 1905 until his death. His paintings abound with cranes, acrobats, scaffolding, railroad signals, buxom nudes, casings, and crankshafts. From his first cubist paintings, Léger was dubbed a "Tubist." Perhaps the most unusual work depicts a Léger *Mona Lisa* contemplating a set of keys, a wide-mouthed fish dangling at an angle over her head.

The museum is open Wednesday to Monday from 10am to noon and 2 to 6pm (to 5pm in winter). Admission is 30 F ($5.70) for adults and 20 F ($3.80) for ages 18 to 24 and over 60; 17 and under free.

WHERE TO DINE

✪ Les Terraillers

11 route du Chemin-Neuf. ☎ **93-65-01-59.** Reservations required, as far in advance as possible. Main courses 150–190 F ($28.50–$36.10); fixed-price menus 170 F ($32.30), 260 F ($49.40), 300 F ($57), and 350 F ($66.50). AE, V. Thurs–Tues noon–2pm and 7–10pm. Closed Nov. MEDITERRANEAN.

This 16th-century studio that produced clay pots and ceramics has been transformed into a premier restaurant. The menu may include terrine of foie gras with Armagnac, lobster-stuffed ravioli, and rabbit with wild mushrooms. Chef Claude Jacques displays amazing culinary skill, delighting all with his Provençal/Mediterranean cuisine. There are those who say his cookery could use a bit of simplication, but that didn't prevent Michelin from awarding him a star.

13 Antibes & Cap d'Antibes

567 miles S of Paris, 13 miles SW of Nice

On the other side of the Bay of Angels, across from Nice, is the port of Antibes. This old Mediterranean town has a quiet charm, unique on the Côte d'Azur. Its little harbor is filled with fishing boats and pleasure yachts. The marketplaces are full of flowers, mostly roses and carnations. If you're in Antibes in the evening, you can watch fishermen playing the popular Riviera game of *boule.*

Spiritually, Antibes is totally divorced from Cap d'Antibes, a peninsula studded with the villas and pools of the haut monde. In *Tender Is the Night* F. Scott Fitzgerald described it as a place where "old villas rotted like water lilies among the massed pines." Photos of film stars lounging at the Eden Roc have appeared in countless Sunday supplements.

ESSENTIALS

GETTING THERE   Trains from Cannes arrive every 30 minutes (trip time: 16 min.), costing 16 F ($3.05) one way, and trains from Nice arrive every 30 minutes (trip time: 18 min.), costing 19 F ($3.60) one way.

VISITOR INFORMATION   The Office de Tourisme is on place du Général-de-Gaulle (☎ 92-90-53-00).

TOURING THE TOP ATTRACTIONS

On the ramparts above the port is the Château Grimaldi, place du Château, which contains the ✪ **Musée Picasso** (☎ 92-90-54-20). Once the home of the princes of Antibes of the Grimaldi family, who ruled the city from 1385 to 1608, today it houses one of the greatest Picasso collections in the world. Picasso came to the small town after his bitter war years in Paris and stayed in a small hotel at Golfe-Juan until the museum director at Antibes invited him to work and live at the museum. Picasso then spent 1946 painting at the museum. When he departed he gave the museum all the work he'd done that year—two dozen paintings, nearly 80 pieces of ceramics, 44 drawings, 32 lithographs, 11 oils on paper, 2 sculptures, and 5 tapestries. In addition, a gallery of contemporary art exhibits Léger, Miró, Ernst, and Calder, among others. For contrast there's an exhibit of Ligurian, Greek, and Roman artifacts. The museum is open Tuesday to Sunday: July to September from 10am to 7pm, and October to June from 10am to noon and 2 to 6pm. Admission is 22 F ($4.20) for adults and 12 F ($2.30) for ages 18 to 24 and over 60; 17 and under free.

Cap d'Antibes has the **Musée Naval et Napoléonien,** Batterie du Grillon, boulevard J-F-Kennedy (☎ 93-61-45-32). This ancient military tower has an interesting collection of Napoléonic memorabilia, naval models, paintings, and mementos. A toy-soldier collection depicts various uniforms, including one used by Napoléon in the Marengo campaign. A wall painting on wood shows Napoléon's entrance into Grenoble; another tableau shows him disembarking at Golfe-Juan on March 1, 1815. In contrast to Canova's Greek-god image of Napoléon, a miniature pendant by Barrault reveals the Corsican general as he really looked, with pudgy cheeks and a receding hair-line. In the rear rotunda is one of the many hats worn by the emperor. You can climb to the top of the tower for a view of the coast that's worth the price of admission. The museum is open Monday to Saturday: April to October from 10am to noon and 3 to 7pm, and December to March from 9:30am to noon and 2:15 to 4pm. Admission is 15 F ($2.85) for adults and 7 F ($1.35) for children 9 and under.

WHERE TO STAY
VERY EXPENSIVE

✪ Hôtel du Cap–Eden Roc

Bd. J-F-Kennedy, 06601 Cap d'Antibes. ☎ **93-61-39-01.** Fax 93-67-76-04. 130 rms, 10 suites. A/C TEL. 2,300–3,000 F ($437.25–$570.35) double; from 4,000 F ($760.45) suite. Breakfast 120 F ($22.80) extra. No credit cards. Parking free. Closed mid-Oct to mid-Apr. Bus A2.

This Second Empire hotel, opened in 1870, is surrounded by 22 splendid acres of gardens. It's like a great country estate, with spacious public rooms, marble fireplaces, scenic paneling, chandeliers, and clusters of richly upholstered armchairs. Some rooms and suites have regal period furnishings. The staff is famed for its snobbery. But regardless of who you are, they can always claim they've dealt with bigger and more famous names. The world-famous Pavillon Eden Roc, near a rock garden apart from the hotel, has a panoramic Mediterranean view. Venetian chandeliers, Louis XV chairs, and elegant draperies add to the drama. Lunch is served on an outer terrace, under umbrellas and an arbor. Dinner specialties include bouillabaisse, lobster Thermidor, and sea bass with fennel.

MODERATE

⑤ Auberge de la Gardiole

Chemin de la Garoupe, 06600 Cap d'Antibes. ☎ **93-61-35-03.** Fax 93-67-61-87. 21 rms. MINIBAR TV TEL. 440–480 F ($83.60–$91.25) per person. Rates include half board. AE, DC, MC, V. Closed Nov 4–Dec 10. Bus A2.

M. and Mme Courtot run this country inn with a delightful personal touch. The large villa, surrounded by gardens and pergola, is in an area of private estates. The charming rooms, on the upper floors of the inn and in the little buildings in the garden, contain personal safes; 15 are air-conditioned. The owners buy the food and supervise its preparation; the cuisine is French/Provençal. The cheerful dining room has a fireplace and hanging pots and pans, and in good weather you can dine under a wisteria-covered trellis. Fixed-price menus cost 120 to 170 F ($22.80 to $32.30) for nonguests.

⑤ Manoir Castel Garoupe Axa

959 bd. de la Garoupe, 06600 Antibes. ☎ **93-61-36-51.** Fax 93-67-74-88. 27 apts. MINIBAR TV TEL. 640–930 F ($121.65–$176.80) apt for two. Rates include continental breakfast. MC, V. Parking free. Closed Nov 15–Mar 15. Bus A2.

We highly recommend this Mediterranean villa, on a private lane in the center of the cape, because it offers apartments for the price of hotel rooms elsewhere. It has a tile roof, private balconies, arches, shuttered windows, and a tranquil garden. Facilities include a freshwater pool and a tennis court. The rooms are nicely appointed.

INEXPENSIVE

⑤ Le Cameo

Place Nationale, 06600 Antibes. ☎ **93-34-24-17.** 8 rms, 3 with shower only, 5 with bath. TEL. 220 F ($41.80) double with shower only, 280 F ($53.20) single or double with bath. Rates include breakfast. DC, MC, V. Closed Jan–Feb. Bus A2.

On a historic square, this 19th-century Provençal villa is the best-known inn in the center of town. The rooms are old-fashioned and admittedly not for everyone, perhaps typical of the place where Picasso might've stayed when he first hit town. Local residents gather every afternoon and evening in the bar, often taking a meal in the adjacent home-style dining room. Amid bouquets of flowers and crowded tables, you'll enjoy local fish, stuffed mussels, bouillabaisse, and fried scampi. Fixed-price menus are offered for 85 F ($16.15), 120 F ($22.80), and 165 F ($31.35). The restaurant is open Saturday to Thursday from noon to 2pm and 7 to 10:30pm.

WHERE TO DINE

La Bonne Auberge
Quartier de Brague, route N7. ☎ **93-33-36-65.** Reservations required. Fixed-price menu 185 F ($35.15). MC, V. May–Sept, daily noon–2pm and 7–10:30pm; Oct–Nov 14 and Dec 16–Apr, Tues–Sun noon–2pm and 7–10:30pm. Closed Nov 15–Dec 15. Take the coastal highway (N7) 2¹/₂ miles from Antibes. FRENCH.

For many years following its 1975 opening, this was one of the most famous restaurants on the French Riviera. In 1992, following the death of its famous founder, Jo Rostang, his culinary heir, Philippe Rostang, wisely limited its scope and transformed it into a worthwhile but less ambitious restaurant. The menu offers a wide selection of dishes at a fixed price of 185 F ($35.15) per person, plus wine. Choices vary but may include a Basque-inspired pipérade with poached eggs, savory swordfish tart, chicken with vinegar and garlic, and quenelles de brochet Jo Rostang. Dessert might be an enchanting peach soufflé.

✪ Restaurant de Bacon
Bd. de Bacon. ☎ **93-61-50-02.** Reservations required. Fixed-price menus 250–400 F ($47.50–$76). AE, DC, MC, V. Tues–Sun 12:30–2pm and 8–10pm. Closed Nov–Feb 1. SEAFOOD.

Among some of the most expensive residences in the world, this restaurant on a rocky peninsula has a panoramic view of the coast. Bouillabaisse aficionados claim that Bacon's offers the best version in France. This fish stew, conceived centuries ago as a simple fisher's supper, is now one of the world's great dishes. In its deluxe version, saltwater crayfish float atop the savory brew; we prefer the simple version—a waiter adds the finishing touches at your table. If bouillabaisse is not to your liking, try a fish soup with the traditional garlic-laden rouille sauce, fish terrine, sea bass, John Dory, or something from an exotic collection of fish unknown in North America. These include sar, pageot, and denti, prepared in several ways. Many visitors are confused by the way fish dishes are priced by the gram. A guideline to remember is that light lunches here cost around 350 to 450 F ($66.50 to $85.55); substantial dinners go for 450 to 880 F ($85.55 to $167.30).

Les Vieux Murs
Promenade de l'avenue de l'Amiral-de-Grasse. ☎ **93-34-06-73.** Reservations recommended. Main courses 130–220 F ($24.70–$41.80); fixed-price menu 200 F ($38). AE, MC, V. Daily noon–2pm and 7:30–10pm. FRENCH/SEAFOOD.

This charming Provençal tavern occupies a room inside the 17th-century ramparts that used to fortify the old seaport. The space contains soaring stone vaults and a simple decor painted for the most part in white. There's also a glassed-in front terrace that offers a pleasant view of the water. Menu specialties include a warm salad of mullet, oysters baked in champagne sauce, and very fresh filets of such fish as daurade, rascasse, sole, salmon, and rougeot, prepared dozens of ways. Suzanne and Georges Romano often have more hungry diners than tables, so try to book early.

Their 200-F ($38) fixed-price menu is one of the best values on the coast. Their culinary creations may not leave you speechless, but they'll undoubtedly impress with their distinctive flavors and aromatic spices.

14 Juan-les-Pins

567 miles S of Paris, 6 miles S of Cannes

This suburb of Antibes is a resort that was developed in the 1920s by Frank Jay Gould. At that time, people flocked to "John of the Pines" to escape the "crassness" of nearby Cannes. In the 1930s Juan-les-Pins drew a chic crowd during the winter. Today it attracts young Europeans from many economic backgrounds.

Juan-les-Pins is often called a honky-tonk town or the "Coney Island of the Riviera," but anyone who calls it that hasn't seen Coney Island in a long time. One newspaper writer called it "a pop-art Monte Carlo, with burlesque shows and nude beaches"—a description much too enticing for such a middle-class resort.

The town offers some of the best **nightlife** on the Riviera, and the action reaches its frenzied height during the July jazz festival. Many revelers stay up all night in the smoky jazz joints, then sleep the next day on the beach. The **casino,** in the town center, offers cabaret entertainment, often until daybreak. During the day, skin-diving and waterskiing predominate. The pines sweep down to a good beach, crowded with summer sunbathers, most often in skimpy beachwear.

ESSENTIALS

GETTING THERE Juan-les-Pins is connected by rail and bus to most other Mediterranean coastal resorts, especially Nice, from which frequent trains arrive throughout the day (trip time: 30 min.).

VISITOR INFORMATION The Office de Tourisme is at 51 bd. Charles-Guillaumont (☎ **92-90-53-05**).

SPECIAL EVENTS The **jazz festival** is in July. The tourist office (above) will supply the details, which change from year to year.

WHERE TO STAY
EXPENSIVE

Belles-Rives

Bd. Baudoin, 06160 Juan-les-Pins. ☎ **93-61-02-79.** Fax 93-67-43-51. 41 rms, 4 suites. A/C MINIBAR TV TEL. 1,500–2,680 F ($285.15–$509.50) double; 4,100–4,880 F ($779.25–$927.75) suite. Half board 410 F ($77.90) per person extra. AE, MC, V. Closed Oct 8–Mar.

This is one of the fabled addresses on the Riviera. Once it was a holiday villa occupied by Zelda and F. Scott Fitzgerald, and the scene of many a drunken brawl. In the following years it hosted the illustrious, like the duke and duchess of Windsor, Josephine Baker, and even Edith Piaf. A certain 1930s aura still lingers in the decor. The views of the sea that those celebrities enjoyed is still there to enchant. A major restoration began in 1988 but has slowed because of the economic downturn. The best accommodations are half a dozen sea-view rooms sparked up in 1990; some, however, remain a tad behind the times. Double-glazing and a new air-conditioning system help a lot. The lower terraces are devoted to garden dining rooms and a waterside aquatic club with a snack bar/lounge and a jetty extending into the water. Dinners are served in a romantic setting on the terrace with a panoramic view of the bay. Meals begin at 230 F ($43.70). Also on premises are a private beach and a landing dock.

Hôtel Juana

La Pinède, av. Gallice, 06160 Juan-les-Pins. ☎ **93-61-08-70.** Fax 93-61-76-70. 45 rms, 5 suites. A/C TV TEL. 850–1,950 F ($161.60–$370.70) double; 1,800–3,500 F ($342.20–$665.40) suite. Breakfast 95 F ($18.05) extra; half board 390 F ($74.10) per person extra. MC, V. Closed Nov–Mar.

This balconied art deco building, owned by the Barache family since 1931, is separated from the sea by the park of pines that gave Juan-les-Pins its name. The hotel has a private swimming club where guests can rent a "parasol and pad" on the sandy beach at reduced rates. Nearby is a park with umbrella tables and shady palms. It's constantly being refurbished, as reflected by the rooms, which are very attractive, with mahogany pieces, well-chosen fabrics, tasteful carpets, and large baths in marble or tile imported from Italy. The rooms also have such extras as safes and (in some) balconies. We discuss La Terrasse restaurant under "Where to Dine," below. There's a bar in the poolhouse. Also on premises are a private beach and a heated outdoor pool.

MODERATE

Hôtel des Mimosas

Rue Pauline, 06160 Juan-les-Pins. ☎ **93-61-04-16.** Fax 92-93-06-46. 36 rms. MINIBAR TEL. 470–650 F ($89.35–$123.55) double. Breakfast 50 F ($9.50) extra. AE, MC, V. Parking free. Closed Sept 30–Apr 15.

Five minutes from the town center, this elegant 1870s-style villa sprawls in a tropical garden on a hilltop. Michel and Raymonde Sauret redesigned the interior with the help of an architect who trained in the United States. The decor is a mix of high-tech and Italian-style comfort, with antique and modern furniture. There's a bar, but no restaurant. The rooms have balconies. A pool is set, California style, amid huge palm trees. The hotel is fully booked in summer, so reserve far in advance.

Hôtel le Pré Catelan

22 av. des Palmiers, 06160 Juan-les-Pins. ☎ **93-61-05-11.** Fax 93-67-83-11. 18 rms TEL. 350–450 F ($66.50–$85.55) double. Breakfast 35 F ($6.65) extra. AE, MC, V. Parking free.

In a residential area near the town park, this Provençal villa has a garden with rock terraces, towering palms, lemon and orange trees, large pots of pink geraniums, trimmed hedges, and outdoor furniture. The atmosphere is casual. The more expensive rooms have terraces, and the furnishings are rather basic. The hotel and restaurant are open all year.

INEXPENSIVE

⑤ Hôtel Cecil

Rue Jonnard, 06160 Juan-les-Pins. ☎ **93-61-05-12.** Fax 93-67-09-14. 21 rms. TV TEL. 280–380 F ($53.20–$72.20) double. Breakfast 30 F ($5.70) extra. MC, V. Parking 50 F ($9.50). Closed Oct 15–Jan 15.

Located 50 yards from the beach, this well-kept hotel is one of the best bargains in Juan-les-Pins. Owner/chef Michel Courtois provides a courteous welcome and good meals. The rooms are well worn yet clean. In summer, guests may dine on a patio.

WHERE TO DINE

⑤ Auberge de l'Esterel

21 rue des Iles, 06160 Juan-les-Pins. ☎ **93-61-86-55**. Fax 93-61-08-67. Reservations recommended. Fixed-price menus 120–160 F ($22.80–$30.40). AE, MC, DC, V. July–Aug, daily 12:30–2pm and 7:30–9:30pm; Sept–Oct and Dec–June, Tues–Sat 12:30–2pm and 7:30–9:30pm, Sun 12:30–2pm. Closed Nov 11-Dec 11. FRENCH.

The dining room of this hotel combines charm with simplicity and good food, plus a beautiful garden set up with tables for outdoor dining during clement weather. The prices, given the neighborhood and the demand, are reasonable. Everything is ordered as part of fixed-price meals. Specific courses might include brouillade of eggs with truffles and foie gras, varied hors d'oeuvres that reflect the culinary breadth of the chefs, osso buco of lotte with fresh spaghetti, and rack of lamb with Provençal herbs.

The inn rents 14 comfortably furnished rooms, costing 260 to 380 F ($494 to $72.20) for a double, plus 30 F ($5.70) for breakfast. The inn was completely renovated in 1995.

✪ La Terrasse

In the Hôtel Juana, La Pinède, av. Gallice. ☎ **93-61-20-37**. Reservations required. Main courses 240–350 F ($45.60–$66.50); fixed-price menus 250 F ($47.50), 390 F ($74.10), 430 F ($81.70), 480 F ($91.25), and 590 F ($112.15). MC, V. July–Aug, daily 12:30–2pm and 7:30–10:30pm; Apr–June and Sept–Oct, Thurs–Tues 12:30–2pm and 7:30–10:30pm. Closed Nov–Mar. FRENCH.

Bill Cosby loves this gourmet restaurant so much that he's been known to fly chef Christian Morisset and his Dalí mustache to New York to prepare dinner for him. Morisset, who trained with Vergé and Lenôtre, cooks with a light, precise, and creative hand. His cuisine is the best in Juan-les-Pins. The ideal place to dine in summer is the terrace, among a lively, sophisticated crowd. The chef interprets traditional dishes and creates his own. Milk-fed veal, John Dory, and scampi-stuffed ravioli—all we've sampled has been delectable. We have to mention the "baby vegetables" served here, for eating baby vegetables is what distinguishes the rich from the rest of us, according to the late Truman Capote.

15   Golfe-Juan & Vallauris

Golfe-Juan: 567 miles S of Paris, 4 miles E of Cannes
Vallauris: 565 miles S of Paris, 4 miles E of Cannes

Napoléon and 800 men landed at Golfe-Juan in 1815 to begin his Hundred Days. Protected by hills, Golfe-Juan was also the favored port for the American navy, though it's primarily a family resort known for its beaches. It contains one notable restaurant: Chez Tétou (below). A short road leads from Golfe-Juan to Vallauris. Once merely a stopover along the Riviera, Vallauris (noted for its pottery) owes its reputation to Picasso, who "discovered" it. The master came to Vallauris after World War II and occupied a villa known as "The Woman from Wales."

ESSENTIALS

GETTING THERE   Buses travel to both Vallauris and Golfe-Juan from Cannes, and other buses connect the two towns.

VISITOR INFORMATION   There's an Office de Tourisme at 84 av. de la Liberté in Golfe-Juan (☎ **93-63-73-12**) and another on square 8-Mai in Vallauris (☎ **93-63-82-58**).

SEEING THE TOP ATTRACTIONS

Ceramics and souvenirs—many the color of rich burgundy—line the street. Frankly, most of the ware displayed in shops is in poor taste. One notable exception is at **Galerie Madoura** (☎ 93-64-66-39), the only shop licensed to sell Picasso reproductions. The master knew and admired the work of the Ramie family, who founded Madoura, open Monday to Friday from 9:30 am to 12:30pm and 2:30 to 7pm. Some of the reproductions are limited to 25 to 500 copies.

Picasso's *Homme et Mouton* (*Man and Sheep*) is the outdoor statue where Aly Kahn and Rita Hayworth were married. The council of Vallauris had intended to ensconce this statue in a museum, but Picasso insisted it remain on the square "where the children could climb over it and the dogs water it unhindered."

At place de la Libération stands a chapel of rough stone shaped like a Quonset hut. It houses the **Musée National de Picasso,** place de la Libération (☎ 93-64-18-05). Picasso decorated the chapel with two paintings: *La Paix* (*Peace*) and *La Guerre* (*War*). The paintings offer contrasting images of love and peace on the one hand and violence and conflict on the other. In 1970 a house painter gained illegal entrance to the museum one night and substituted one of his own designs, after whitewashing a portion of the original. When the aging master inspected the damage, he said, "Not bad at all." The museum is open Wednesday to Monday from 10am to noon and 2 to 6pm. Admission is 8 F ($1.50) for adults and 4 F (75¢) for children.

WHERE TO DINE

✪ Chez Tétou

Av. des Frères-Roustand, sur la Plage, Golfe-Juan. ☎ 93-63-71-16. Reservations required. Main courses 320–470 F ($60.80–$89.35); bouillabaisse 395–470 F ($75.05–$89.35). No credit cards. Thurs–Tues noon–2:30pm and 8–10pm. Closed Nov. SEAFOOD.

In its own amusing way, this might be one of the most famous restaurants along the Côte d'Azur, capitalizing richly on the glittering *beau monde* who frequented it during the 1950s and 1960s. Retaining its Provençal earthiness despite its high prices, it has thrived in a white-sided beach cottage for more than 65 years. It still serves a bouillabaisse often remembered years later by non-French visitors who consider it superb. Other items on the deliberately limited menu include grilled sea bass with tomatoes Provençal, sole meunière, and several preparations of lobster. The list of appetizers is extremely limited (platters of charcuterie or several almost-perfect slices of fresh melon), because most diners head for the house specialty, bouillabaisse. Your dessert might be a special powdered croissant with grandmother's jams (winter) or homemade raspberry and strawberry tarts (summer).

16 Mougins

561 miles S of Paris, 7 miles S of Grasse, 5 miles N of Cannes

This once-fortified town on the crest of a hill provides an alternative for those who want to be near the excitement of Cannes but not in the midst of it. Picasso and other artists appreciated the rugged, sun-drenched hills covered with gnarled olive trees. Gentle streams flow in the little valleys. Mougins is the perfect haven for those who feel the Riviera is overrun, spoiled, and overbuilt. It preserves the quiet life very close to the international resort. The wealthy come from Cannes to golf here.

ESSENTIALS

GETTING THERE There's limited daily bus service from Cannes. The bus from Cannes to Grasse stops a mile from Mougins.

VISITOR INFORMATION The Syndicat d'Initiative (tourist office) is at 15 av. Jean-Charles-Mallet (☎ 93-75-87-67).

WHERE TO STAY

Manoir de l'Etang

Aux Bois de Font-Merle, allée du Manoir, 06250 Mougins. ☎ 93-90-01-07. Fax 92-92-20-70. 14 rms. TV TEL. 600–950 F ($114.05–$180.60) double. Breakfast 55 F ($10.45) extra. AE, V. Parking free. Closed Feb and Nov.

In the midst of olive trees and cypresses, this is one of the choice places to stay on the Riviera, housed in a 19th-century Provençal building. It has all the romantic extras associated with some Riviera properties, including "love goddess" statuary in the garden and candlelit dinners around a pool, but it charges reasonable rates for these pleasures. The rooms are bright and modern—you'll feel almost as if you're staying in a private home, which this place virtually is. Some rooms are extremely spacious. In winter, meals are served around a wood-burning fireplace. The chef bases his menu on the freshest ingredients available in any season.

WHERE TO DINE

L'Amandier de Mougins Café-Restaurant

Place du Commandant-Lamy. ☎ 93-90-00-91. Reservations recommended. Main courses 75–95 F ($14.25–$18.05). AE, DC, MC, V. Daily noon–2:15pm and 8–10pm. NIÇOISE/ PROVENÇAL.

The illustrious founder of this relatively inexpensive bistro is the world-famous Roger Vergé, whose much more expensive Moulin de Mougins is described below. Conceived as a mass-market satellite to its exclusive neighbor, this restaurant serves relatively simple platters in an airy stone house in the village center. Specialties are usually based on traditional recipes and might include salmon carpaccio; tagliatelli with olives; michette of tomatoes, zucchini, and mozzarella; grilled skewers of chicken with local herbs; and John Dory with lime sauce.

Moulin de Mougins

Notre-Dame de Vie, 06250 Mougins. ☎ 93-75-78-24. Fax 93-90-18-55. Reservations required. Main courses 180–230 F ($34.20–$43.70); fixed-price menus 585–700 F ($111.20–$133.05). AE, DC, MC, V. Tues–Wed and Fri–Sun noon–2:15pm and 8–10pm, Thurs 8–10pm. Closed Feb 4–Mar 7. FRENCH.

This is among France's top 20 restaurants or an overpublicized citadel that's in serious decline, depending on which critic you read. Michelin still awards it two stars, however. A 10-foot-wide stone oil vat, complete with a wooden turnscrew and a grinding wheel, is near the entrance. This culinary kingdom belongs to Roger Vergé, the *maître cuisinier de France*. His specialties include filets de rougets (red mullet) de roche en barigoule d'artichaut as well as noisettes d'agneau (lamb) de Sisteron with eggplant cake in thyme-flavored sauce. His forte is fish from the Mediterranean, bought each morning fresh. Monsieur Vergé offers a lot of fantastic, even historic wines, but he also has a good selection of local vintages. The meal was uneven during our last visit, though one dish, prepared just for that day, was sublime. The problem may be that Vergé's celebrity causes him to be away for a great part of the time. We know him to be one of France's grandest chefs, once viewed as today's Escoffier. And he still is—when he's there.

The old mill offers five beautiful air-conditioned suites, honeymoon lairs with provincial beds, Louis XVI chairs and chests, bay windows, and matching flowered toile coverings for furniture and beds. A double costs 800 to 1,300 F ($152.10 to $247.10), plus 75 F ($14.25) for breakfast.

17 Grasse

563 miles S of Paris, 11 miles N of Cannes

Grasse is the most fragrant town on the Riviera. Surrounded by jasmine and roses, it has been the capital of the perfume industry since the 19th century. It was once a famous resort, attracting such royalty as Queen Victoria and Princess Pauline Borghese, Napoléon's lascivious sister.

ESSENTIALS

GETTING THERE Some 21 buses per day pull in from Cannes (trip time: 45 min.), costing 20 F ($3.80) one way, and 15 per day from Nice (trip time: 1¹/₂ hr.), costing 30 F ($5.70) one way.

VISITOR INFORMATION The Office de Tourisme is on place de la Foux (☎ 93-36-03-56).

SEEING THE TOP ATTRACTIONS

One of the best-known perfume factories is the **Parfumerie Fragonard,** 20 bd. Fragonard (☎ 93-36-44-65), named after the 18th-century French painter. An English-speaking guide will show you how "the soul of the flower" is extracted. After the tour, you can explore the museum of perfumery, which displays bottles and vases that trace the industry back to ancient times. It's open daily, including holidays, from 9am to 6pm.

The **Musée d'Art et d'Histoire de Provence,** 8 place du Sours (☎ 93-36-01-61), is in the Hôtel de Clapiers-Cabris, built in 1771 by Louise de Mirabeau, the marquise de Cabris and sister of Mirabeau. The collection includes paintings, four-poster beds, marquetry, ceramics, brasses, kitchenware, pottery, urns, even archeological finds. It's open June to September, daily from 10am to noon and 2 to 7pm; October and December to June, Wednesday to Sunday from 10am to noon and 2 to 5pm. Admission is 12.60 F ($2.40) for adults and 6.30 F ($1.20) for children.

Nearby is the **Villa Fragonard,** 23 bd. Fragonard (☎ 93-36-01-61), whose collection includes the paintings of Jean-Honoré Fragonard; his sister-in-law, Marguerite Gérard; his son, Alexandre; and his grandson, Théophile. Fragonard was born in Grasse in 1732. The grand staircase was decorated by Alexandre. It's open Wednesday to Sunday: June to September from 10am to noon and 2 to 6pm, and October and December to June from 10am to noon and 2 to 5pm. Admission is 10 F ($1.90) for adults and 5 F (95¢) for children.

Another popular place to visit is the **Parfumerie Molinard,** 60 bd. Victor-Hugo (☎ 93-36-01-62). The firm is well known in the United States and its products are sold at Saks, Neiman Marcus, and Bloomingdale's. In the factory, you can witness the extraction of the essence of the flowers, and the process of converting flowers into essential oils is explained in detail. You'll discover why turning flowers into perfume has been called a "work of art" and can admire a collection of antique perfume-bottle labels as well as see a rare collection of Baccarat and Lalique. It's open Monday to Saturday from 9am to 6:30pm and Sunday from 9am to noon and 2 to 6pm.

WHERE TO STAY

⑤ Les Arômes
Route de Cannes, 06130 Grasse. ☎ **93-70-42-01.** 7 rms. TV TEL. 300 F ($57) double. Breakfast 25 F ($4.75) extra. AE, MC, V. Parking free.

Although Les Arômes is near a noisy highway between Grasse and Cannes, privacy and calm are guaranteed by the surrounding wall and gravel courtyard. Half a mile south of the center of Grasse, this modern building was designed in a Provençal style, with beige stone, pink stucco, and terra-cotta tiles. The dining room, with three large arched windows overlooking the courtyard, is open daily except Saturday lunch from noon to 2pm and 7:30 to 9:30pm. It's also open to nonguests, who pay 90 F ($17.10), 130 F ($24.70), and 180 F ($34.20) for a fixed-price menu.

Hôtel Panormama
2 place du Cours, 06130 Grasse. ☎ **93-36-80-80.** Fax 93-36-92-04. 36 rms. MINIBAR TV TEL. 305–480 F ($57.95–$91.25) double. Breakfast 40 F ($7.60) extra. AE, DC, MC, V. Parking free at night.

This centrally located hotel has a facade in a sienna hue that its owners call "Garibaldi red." The more expensive rooms have balconies, southern exposure, and views of the sea; 20 have air conditioning. The furnishings are basic and simple. There's no bar or restaurant, but food is brought to your room on request.

WHERE TO DINE

Restaurant Amphitryon
16 bd. Victor-Hugo. ☎ **93-36-58-73.** Reservations recommended. Main courses 88–165 F ($16.70–$31.35); fixed-price menus 118 F ($22.40), 154 F ($29.25), and 268 F ($50.90). AE, DC, MC, V. Mon–Sat noon–1:30pm and 7:30–9pm. Closed Aug 15–Sept 15. FRENCH.

The buildings that line this street, including this restaurant, were stables in the 19th century. Today, in a modern ambience of fabric-covered walls, you can enjoy the cuisine of Michel André, who serves the best food in Grasse. The fixed-price menus are a bargain. The cuisine is inspired by southwestern France, with plenty of foie gras and duckling, as well as lamb roasted with thyme. Also recommendable is the Mediterranean fish soup with Provençal rouille.

18　Cannes

562 miles S of Paris, 101 miles E of Marseille, 16 miles SW of Nice

When Coco Chanel went here and got a suntan, returning to Paris bronzed, she startled ladies of society. Nonetheless they quickly began copying her, abandoning their heretofore fashionable peach complexions. Today the bronzed bodies—in nearly nonexistent swimsuits—that line the sandy beaches of this chic resort continue the late fashion designer's example.

Popular with celebrities, Cannes is at its most frenzied during the **International Film Festival** at the Palais des Festivals on promenade de la Croisette. Held in either April or May, it attracts not only film stars but those with similar aspirations. On the seafront boulevards flashbulbs pop as the starlets emerge—usually wearing what women will be wearing in 1999 (did you see buxom Pamela Anderson prancing around in black leather as the paparrazzi flashed and beckoned?). International regattas, galas, *concours d'élégance,* even a Mimosa Festival in February—something is always happening at Cannes, except in November, traditionally a dead month.

Sixteen miles southwest of Nice, Cannes is sheltered by hills. For many it consists of only one street, **promenade de la Croisette,** curving along the coast and split by islands of palms and flowers. It's said that the prince of Wales (before he became Edward VII) contributed to its original cost. But he was a Johnny-come-lately to Cannes. Setting out for Nice in 1834, Lord Brougham, a lord chancellor of England, was turned away because of an outbreak of cholera. He landed at Cannes and liked it so much he decided to build a villa there. Returning every winter until his death in 1868, he proselytized it in London, drawing a long line of British visitors. In the 1890s Cannes became popular with Russian grand dukes (it's said that more caviar was consumed here than in all of Moscow). One French writer claimed that when the Russians returned as refugees in the 1920s, they were given the garbage-collection franchise.

A port of call for cruise liners, the seafront of Cannes is lined with hotels, apartment houses, and chic boutiques. Many of the bigger hotels, some dating from the 19th century, claim part of the beaches for the private use of their guests. But there are also public areas.

ESSENTIALS

GETTING THERE   Cannes is connected to each of the Mediterranean resorts, Paris, and the rest of France by rail and bus lines. Cannes lies on the major coastal rail line along the Riviera, with trains arriving frequently throughout the day. From Antibes to Cannes by rail takes only 15 minutes, or 35 minutes from Nice. The TGV from Paris going via Marseille also services Cannes. Buses pick up passengers at the Nice airport every 40 minutes during the day, delivering them to Cannes, and service is also available from Antibes at one bus every half an hour. The international airport at Nice is only 20 minutes northeast.

VISITOR INFORMATION   The Office de Tourisme is on esplanade du Président-Georges-Pompidou (☎ **93-39-24-53**).

SPECIAL EVENTS   The world-famous International Film Festival is held in April or May.

TOURING THE TOP ATTRACTIONS

Above the harbor, the old town of Cannes sits on Suquet Hill, where you'll see a 14th-century tower, which the English dubbed the **Lord's Tower.**

Nearby is the **Musée de la Castre,** in the Château de la Castre, Le Suquet (☎ **93-38-55-26**), containing fine arts, with a section on ethnography. The latter includes relics and objects from everywhere from the Pacific islands to Southeast Asia, including both Peruvian and Mayan pottery. There's also a gallery devoted to relics of ancient Mediterranean civilizations, from the Greeks to the Romans, from the Cypriots to the Egyptians. Five rooms are devoted to 19th-century paintings. The museum is open Wednesday to Monday: April to June from 10am to noon and 2 to 6pm, July to September from 10am to noon and 3 to 7pm, and October to March from 10am to noon and 2 to 5pm. Admission is 10 F ($1.90).

Another museum of note, the **Musée de la Mer,** Fort Royal (☎ 93-38-55-26), displays artifacts from Ligurian, Roman, and Arab civilizations, including paintings, mosaics, and ceramics. You can also see the jail where the Man in the Iron Mask was incarcerated. Temporary exhibitions of photography are also shown here. Open June to September only, the museum can be visited daily from 10am to noon and 2 to 6pm. Admission is 10 F ($1.90).

WHERE TO STAY
VERY EXPENSIVE

✪ Hôtel Carlton Intercontinental
58 bd. de la Croisette, 06400 Cannes. ☎ **93-06-40-06,** or 800/327-0200 in the U.S. Fax 93-06-40-25. 326 rms, 28 suites. A/C MINIBAR TV TEL. 1,360–3,690 F ($258.55–$701.50) double; from 4,830 F ($918.20) suite. Breakfast 145 F ($27.55) extra. AE, DC, MC, V. Parking 150 F ($28.50). Bus 11.

Cynics say that one of the most amusing sights in Cannes is the view from under the vaguely art deco and very grand gate of the ornate Carlton. There you'll see vehicles of every description pulling up to drop off huge amounts of baggage and vast numbers of fashionable guests who've made this one of the most colorful hotels in Cannes. It's the epitome of belle époque luxury and has become such a part of the heartbeat of the city that to ignore it would be to miss the spirit of the resort. The twin gray domes at either end of the facade are often the first things recognized by the various starlets planning their grand entrances, grand exits, and grand scenes in the hotel's public and private rooms.

Shortly after it was built in 1912, the Carlton attracted the most prominent members of the *haut monde* of Europe, including members of royal families. They were followed decades later by the most important screen personalities. Today you'll find both industrial conventions and tour groups—nonetheless, in summer (especially during the film festival) the public rooms still are filled with all the voyeuristic and exhibitionistic fervor that seems so much a part of the Riviera. The guest rooms here were renovated in 1990. Double-glazing, big combination baths with hairdryers, and luxurious appointments are part of the features. The most spacious rooms are generally in the west wing, and many of the upper-floor rooms open onto balconies fronting the sea. You never know who your next-door neighbor will be.

Dining/Entertainment: The Carlton Casino Club is a casino that opened in 1989. La Côte restaurant is one of the most distinguished along the Riviera. Though the restaurant had fallen into decline, chef Sylvain Duparc has awakened sleepy tastebuds again with his profound affinity for the flavors of Provence. He's been called "a culinary troubador." The seventh floor has been reconstructed and now shelters another stunning restaurant, La Belle Otéro, which Michelin rewards with two stars, giving only one to La Côte. In our opinion, the awards should be reversed.

Facilities: Private beach, health club with spa facilities, glass-roofed indoor pool.

✪ Hôtel Martinez
73 bd. de la Croisette, 06400 Cannes. ☎ **92-98-73-00.** Fax 93-39-67-82. 418 rms, 12 suites. A/C MINIBAR TV TEL. 960–3,300 F ($182.50–$627.35) double; from 5,500 F ($1,045.60) suite. Breakfast 110 F ($20.90) extra. AE, DC, MC, V. Parking 100 F ($19). Bus 1.

When this landmark art deco hotel was built in the 1930s, it rivaled any other hotel along the coast in sheer size alone. Over the years, however, it has fallen into disrepair and closed and reopened several times. But in 1982 the Concorde chain returned the hotel and its restaurants to their former luster, and today it competes with the Carlton and Majestic. Despite its grandeur, the hotel is a little too convention-oriented for our tastes, but the rooms remain in good shape. The aim of the decor was a Roaring 20s style, and all units are well appointed with private safes, marble baths, wood furnishings, tasteful carpets, and pastel fabrics.

Dining/Entertainment: La Palme d'Or, among the finest restaurants in Cannes, is recommended under "Where to Dine," below. The poolside restaurant, L'Orangerie, serves light, low-calorie meals in a decor of azure and white lattices.

Services: 24-hour room service, same-day laundry/valet.

Facilities: Private beach, waterskiing school, cabañas, octagonal pool, seven tennis courts.

EXPENSIVE

Hôtel Gray-d'Albion
38 rue des Serbes, 06400 Cannes. ☎ **92-99-79-79.** Fax 93-99-26-10. 172 rms, 14 suites. A/C MINIBAR TV TEL. 700–1,600 F ($133.05–$304.15) double; 2,400–6,000 F ($456.25–$1,140.65) suite. Breakfast 95 F ($18.05) extra. AE, DC, MC, V. Bus 1.

The smallest of the major hotels here is not on the Croisette, but this building contains pastel-colored rooms, each outfitted with all the luxury a modern hotel can offer—some critics consider the Gray-d'Albion among the most luxurious hotels in France. Groups form a large part of its clientele, but it also caters to the individual guest. Rooms on the 8th and 9th floors have views of the Mediterranean. Dining selections include Le Royal Gray, one of the best in Cannes (see "Where to Dine"), a beach-club restaurant, and a brasserie that features special courses from Lebanon.

MODERATE

Hôtel le Fouquet's
2 rond-point Duboys-d'Angers, 06400 Cannes. ☎ **93-38-75-81.** Fax 92-98-03-39. 10 rms. A/C MINIBAR TV TEL. 480–980 F ($91.25–$186.30) double. Breakfast 50 F ($9.50) extra. AE, DC, MC, V. Parking 50 F ($9.50). Closed Nov–Dec 8. Bus 1.

This is an intimate, select hotel drawing a discreet clientele, often from Paris, who'd never think of patronizing the grand palace hotels, even if they could afford them. Very "Riviera French" in design and decor, it's several blocks from the beach. Each of the attractive, airy rooms is decorated in bold colors, containing a loggia, a dressing room, and a hairdryer. Most rooms are spacious. There's no restaurant.

Hôtel Splendid
Allée de la Liberté (4 et 6 rue Félix-Fauré), 06400 Cannes. ☎ **93-99-53-11.** Fax 93-99-55-02. 64 rms, 2 suites. A/C TV TEL. 690–970 F ($131.15–$184.40) double; from 1,300 F ($247.10) suite. Rates include continental breakfast. AE, DC, MC, V.

This is a good, conservative hotel—a favorite of academicians, politicians, actors, and musicians. Opened in 1871, it's one of the oldest hotels at the resort. An ornate white building with sinuous wrought-iron accents, the Splendid looks out onto the sea, the old port, and a park. The rooms boast antique furniture, paintings, and videos; 40 of them have kitchenettes. The more expensive rooms have sea views.

INEXPENSIVE

Hôtel de Provence

9 rue Molière, 06400 Cannes. ☎ **93-38-44-35.** Fax 93-39-63-14. 30 rms. A/C MINIBAR TV TEL. 380–490 F ($72.20–$93.15) double. Breakfast 38 F ($7.20) extra. AE, MC, V. Parking 30 F ($5.70). Bus 1.

In 1992 the rooms at this family-owned hotel were renovated into a comfortably uncluttered format of well-scrubbed convenience. Most have private balconies, and many overlook the garden. The hotel stands in its own walled garden of palms and flowering shrubs on a quiet inner street. In warm weather, breakfast is served out under the vines and flowers of an arbor, and *plats du jour* are usually available at dinner for 55 to 60 F ($10.45 to $11.40). Nonguests can eat here at dinner only.

⑤ Le St-Yves

49 bd. d'Alsace, 06400 Cannes. ☎ **93-38-65-29.** Fax 93-68-50-67. 10 rms, 2 suites. TV TEL. 350–450 F ($66.50–$85.55) double; from 650 F ($123.55) suite. Breakfast 35 F ($6.65) extra. DC. Parking free. Bus 1.

Set back from the busy coastal boulevard by a garden and a grove of palm trees, this villa is a historical monument. English-speaking Marylene Camplo owns the villa, part of which she has converted into private apartments that can be rented by the week or the month. However, she has kept some rooms to rent for short periods. The rooms differ in size and are pleasantly furnished, mainly with odds and ends accumulated over the years. Breakfast includes fresh croissants, country butter, and rich jam.

WHERE TO DINE
EXPENSIVE

✪ La Palme d'Or

In the Hôtel Martinez, 73 bd. de la Croisette. ☎ **92-98-74-14.** Reservations required. Main courses 180–350 F ($34.20–$66.50); fixed-price menus 295 F ($56.05), 330 F ($62.70), and 550 F ($104.55). AE, DC, MC, V. Tues 7:30–10:30pm, Wed–Sun 12:30–2pm and 7:30–10:30pm. Closed Nov 18–Dec 15. Bus 1. FRENCH.

When this hotel was renovated by the Taittinger family (of champagne fame), one of their primary concerns was to establish a restaurant that could rival the tough competition in Cannes. And they've succeeded. The result was a light-wood–paneled, art deco marvel overlooking the pool and La Croisette. The room is hung with pictures of Hollywood stars. Alsatian-born chef Christian Willer has worked at some of the greatest restaurants in France. Here his sublime specialties include warm foie gras with fondue of rhubarb, nage of sole with Bellet wine, slightly warm salad of monkfish with a hint of pepper, and salmon with caviar-cream sauce. Many find it hard to pass up the bouillon of lobster with basil and fresh vegetables or the palate-cleansing sorbet flavored with white cheese. Service is excellent without being stiff.

Le Royal Gray

In the Hôtel Gray-d'Albion, 38 rue des Serbes. ☎ **93-68-54-54.** Reservations required. Main courses 120–165 F ($22.80–$31.35); fixed-price menus 148 F ($28.10) and 260 F ($49.40). AE, DC, MC, V. June–Sept, Mon 8-10:30pm, Tues–Sat noon–2pm and 8-10:30pm; Oct–May, Tues–Sat noon–2pm and 8-10:30pm. Bus 1. FRENCH.

Hailed until quite recently as the most distinguished restaurant in Cannes, Le Royal Gray is now in a period of transition and the word won't be in on it for many months yet. Chef Jacques Chibois brought the restaurant its initial fame, but he's now moved on to open his own place; however, he remains as a consultant to the new chef, Michel Bigot. Michelin not only removed its two stars, but has removed its recommendation altogether. Bigot ("with a name like that, you've got to be good") has not yet recaptured Chibois's glory, but he's making a valiant attempt by offering an innovative interpretation of French classic fare.

While seated on the restaurant's fabled terrace, you can peruse the menu listing such delectables as salad of endives, sautéed turnips with goose filets, and nuts or the quail salad. The gratinated oysters with champagne and truffles is among the more enticing appetizers. Main courses might include everything from leg of lamb filet with lentils and curry to calf's liver with grilled potatoes. The menu is often surprisingly simple. Service is first class.

MODERATE

Gaston-Gastounette

7 quai St-Pierre. ☎ 93-39-49-44. Reservations required. Main courses 150–200 F ($28.50–$38); fixed-price meals 120–165 F ($22.80–$31.35) at lunch, 195 F ($37.05) at dinner. AE, DC, MC, V. Daily noon–2pm and 7–11pm. Closed Dec 1–18 and Jan. Bus 1. FRENCH.

This is the best restaurant to offer views of the marina. Located in the old port, it has a stucco exterior with oak moldings and big windows and a sidewalk terrace surrounded by flowers. Inside you'll be served bouillabaisse, breast of duckling in garlic-cream sauce, grilled sea bass with herbs, stuffed mussels, pot-au-feu de la mer, and such fish platters as turbot and sole. Sorbet, after all that savory Mediterranean food, is appropriate for dessert.

La Mère Besson

13 rue des Frères-Pradignac. ☎ 93-39-59-24. Reservations required. Main courses 95–140 F ($18.05–$26.60); fixed-price menus 90 F ($17.10) at lunch, 140–170 F ($26.60–$32.30) at dinner. AE, DC, MC, V. Mon–Fri 12:15–2pm and 7:30–10:30pm, Sat 7:30–10:30pm. Bus 1. FRENCH.

The culinary traditions of Mère Besson are carried on in one of Cannes's favorite restaurants. All the specialties are prepared with consummate skill, especially the Provençal dishes featured daily. Most delectable is estouffade Provençal—beef braised with red wine and rich stock flavored with garlic, onions, herbs, and mushrooms. Specialties include soupe au pistou and soupe de poissons. Every Wednesday you can order lou piech, a Niçoise name for veal brisket stuffed with white-stemmed vegetables, peas, ham, eggs, rice, grated cheese, and herbs. The meat is cooked in salted water with vinegar, carrots, and onions, like a stockpot, then served with thick tomato coulis.

INEXPENSIVE

ⓢ Au Mal Assis

15 quai St-Pierre. ☎ 93-39-13-38. Reservations required. Main courses 75–190 F ($14.25–$36.10); fixed-price menu 150 F ($28.50). AE, MC, V. Daily 8am–11pm. Closed Nov. Bus 1. FRENCH.

For unpretentious and appealingly earthy Provençal charm, this is our choice. Relatively moderate in its pricing, especially when compared to many of the resort's more expensive choices, it was established in 1949 and has done a thriving business since. You can order moules (mussels) Provençal, sole meunière, bourride, a wide array of fresh fish, several versions of lobster, and a succulent version of bouillabaisse for two. Its deliberately ambiguous name is a source of endless local humor, because it translates either as "at the place where guests are badly seated" or "at the place where men but not women are seated." The fixed-price menu is especially good, considering what it contains.

⑤ Le Monaco

15 rue du 24-Août. ☎ **93-38-37-76.** Reservations required. Main courses 50–90 F ($9.50–$17.10); fixed-price menus 85–110 F ($16.15–$20.90). MC, V. Mon–Sat noon–2pm and 7–10pm. Closed Nov 10–Dec 15. Bus 1. FRENCH/ITALIAN.

This workingperson's favorite eatery, crowded but always cheap, is conveniently near the train station. The likeable ambience features closely placed tables, clean napery, and a staff dressed in bistro-inspired uniforms. Menu choices include generous portions of osso buco with sauerkraut, spaghetti bolognese, trout with almonds, and minestrone with basil. Paella and couscous are very popular. Another specialty is grilled sardines, which many restaurants won't serve anymore, considering them too messy and old-fashioned.

AFTER DARK

On the eighth floor (seventh, in France) of the Carlton International, 50 bd. de la Croisette, **Le Casino du Carlton** (☎ 93-68-00-33) was established in 1988. Considerably smaller than its major competitor (the Casino Croisette, below), its modern decor nonetheless draws its share of devotees. Jackets are required for men, and a passport or government-issued identity card is required for admission. It's open daily from 4pm to 4am. Admission is 65 F ($12.35).

The largest and most legendary casino in Cannes, the **Casino Croisette,** in the Palais des Festivals, 1 jetée Albert-Edouard (near promenade de la Croisette) (☎ 93-68-00-07), moved into a new building set on piers over the old port in 1983. Within its glittering confines you'll find all the gaming tables you'd expect—open daily from 5pm to 4 or 5am—and one of the best nightclubs in town, **Jimmy's de Régine,** completely outfitted in shades of red. Jimmy's is open Wednesday to Sunday from 11pm until dawn; drinks begin at 70 F ($13.30). You must present your passport to enter the gambling room.

A glamorous restaurant, Le Restaurant des Jeux, occupies one semicircular end of the gaming floor, a format that successfully combines classic French cuisine with casino-watching. Dinner begins at around 350 F ($66.50), and jackets for men are requested. The restaurant is open daily from 8pm to 3am.

Admission to the gambling areas is 70 F ($13.30); admission to Jimmy's is 130 F ($24.70), including one drink.

AN EASY EXCURSION TO THE ILES DE LERINS

Across the bay from Cannes, the Lérins Islands are the most interesting excursion from the port. A boat leaves frequently from the harbor, taking 15 minutes to reach Ile Ste-Marguerite and 30 minutes to Ile St-Honorat. For information, call 93-39-11-82. The round-trip fare to Ile Ste-Marguerite is 40 F ($7.60); to St-Honorat, 45 F ($8.55); or 60 F ($11.40) round-trip to both.

ILE STE-MARGUERITE   The first island is named after St. Honorat's sister, Ste. Marguerite, who lived here with a group of nuns in the 5th century. Today this is a youth center whose members (when they aren't sailing and diving) are dedicated to the restoration of the fort. From the dock where the boat lands, you can stroll along the island (signs point the way) to the **Fort de l'Ile,** built by Spanish troops from 1635 to 1637. Below is the 1st-century B.C. Roman town where the unlucky man immortalized in *The Man in the Iron Mask* was imprisoned.

One of French history's most perplexing mysteries is the identity of the man who wore the *masque du fer,* a prisoner of Louis XIV who arrived at Ste-Marguerite in 1698. Dumas fanned the legend that he was a brother of Louis XIV, and it has even been suggested that the prisoner and a mysterious woman had a son who went to Corsica and "founded" the Bonaparte family. However, the most common theory is that the prisoner was a servant of the superintendent, Fouquet, named Eustache Dauger. At any rate, he died in the Bastille in Paris in 1703.

You can visit his cell at Ste-Marguerite, in which every visitor seemingly has written his or her name. As you stand listening to the sound of the sea, you realize what a forlorn outpost this was.

The **Musée de la Mer,** Fort Royal (☎ **93-43-18-17**), traces the history of the island, displaying artifacts of Ligurian, Roman, and Arab civilizations, plus the remains discovered by excavations. These include paintings, mosaics, and ceramics. It's open June to September, daily from 10am to noon and 2 to 6pm (to 5pm off-season); closed in January. Hours vary, depending on the arrival of the boats. Admission is 10 F ($1.90).

ILE ST-HONORAT   Only a mile long, Ile St-Honorat is even lonelier. St. Honorat founded a monastery here in the 5th century. Since the 1860s the Cistercians have owned the ecclesiastical complex, consisting of both an old fortified monastery and a contemporary one. You can spend the day wandering through the pine forests on the west side of the island, the other part being reserved for silent prayer.

19   La Napoule-Plage

560 miles S of Paris, 5 miles W of Cannes

This secluded resort is on the sandy beaches of the Golfe de la Napoule. In 1919 the once-obscure fishing village was a paradise for eccentric sculptor Henry Clews and his wife, an architect. Fleeing America's "charlatans," whom he believed had profited from World War I, the New York banker's son emphasized the fairy-tale qualities of his new home. His house is now the **Musée Henry-Clews**—an inscription over the entrance reads "Once upon a time."

The **Château de la Napoule,** boulevard Henry-Clews (☎ **93-49-95-05**), was rebuilt from the ruins of a medieval château. Clews covered the capitals and lintels with his own grotesque menagerie—scorpions, pelicans, gnomes, monkeys, lizards—the revelations of a tortured mind. Women, feminism, and old age are recurring themes in the sculptor's work, as exemplified by the distorted suffragette depicted in his *Cat Woman.* The artist was preoccupied with old age in both men and women and admired chivalry and dignity in man as represented by Don Quixote—whom he likened to himself. Clews died in Switzerland in 1937 and his body was returned to La Napoule for burial. Mrs. Clews later opened the château to the public. Guided visits are possible Wednesday to Monday: March to November at 3pm, 4pm, and 5pm, and December to February at 3pm and 4pm. Admission is 28 F ($5.30) for adults and 20 F ($3.80) for children.

ESSENTIALS

GETTING THERE   La Napoule-Plage lies on the bus and train routes between Cannes and St-Raphael.

VISITOR INFORMATION   The Office de Tourisme is at 274 bd. Henry-Clews (☎ **93-49-95-31**).

WHERE TO STAY

⑤ La Calanque

Bd. Henry-Clews, 06210 La Napoule. ☎ **93-49-95-11.** 17 rms, 11 with bath (tub or shower). TEL. 570 F ($108.35) double without bath, 580–620 F ($110.25–$117.85) double with bath. Rates include half board. MC, V. Parking free. Closed Nov–Mar.

The foundations of this charming hotel date from the Roman Empire, when an aristocrat built a villa here. The present hotel looks like a hacienda, with pink stucco walls and shutters. Register in the bar in the rear (through the dining room). The restaurant is garden style, with an outdoor terrace, and offers the cheapest fixed-price meal in La Napoule. Nonguests are welcome.

Le Royal Hôtel & Casino

605 av. du Général-de-Gaulle, 06212 Mandelieu La Napoule. ☎ **92-97-70-00.** Fax 93-49-51-50. 185 rms, 25 suites. A/C MINIBAR TV TEL. From 640 F ($121.65) double; from 2,500 F ($475.25) suite. Breakfast 95 F ($18.05) extra. AE, DC, MC, V. Parking 60 F ($11.40).

This Las Vegas–style hotel is on the beach near an artificial harbor, about 5 miles from Cannes. It was the first French hotel to include a casino and the last establishment (just before the building codes changed) to be allowed to have a casino directly on the beach. The hotel has one of the most contemporary designs on the Côte d'Azur. The interior is dramatically contemporary, filled with plush touches, warm shades, and lots of marble. Most of the attractive modern rooms are angled toward a view of the sea. Those facing the street are likely to be noisy in spite of soundproofing. Le Féréol is recommended under "Where to Dine," below. An informal café serves both Tex-Mex and specialties of Provence, and a nightclub on the premises offers live music. The casino offers blackjack, craps, and roulette. It's open daily from 8pm to 4am. Facilties here include a pool, tennis courts, a sauna, a private beach, and a 27-hole golf course.

WHERE TO DINE

Le Féréol

In Le Royal Hôtel & Casino, bd. Henry-Clews. ☎ **92-97-70-00.** Reservations recommended. Main courses 90–140 F ($17.10–$26.60); buffet lunch 190 F ($36.10); fixed-price dinners 205–250 F ($38.95–$47.50). AE, DC, MC, V. Daily noon–3:30pm and 7:30pm–1am. FRENCH.

This well-designed restaurant services all the culinary needs of the largest hotel (and the only casino) in town. Expanded in 1991 with the addition of a large outdoor terrace, it offers one of the most impressive lunch buffets in the neighborhood, with an usually large selection of hors d'oeuvres. At night the place becomes candlelit and more elegant. Menu items include filet of beef gourmandine, served with a filling of duck liver and fricassée of flap mushrooms; a traditional version of bourride Provençal; noisettes of lamb with an olive sauce; and a wide array of grilled meats and fish.

✪ L'Oasis

Rue Honoré-Carle. ☎ **93-49-95-52.** Reservations required. Main courses 200–260 F ($38–$49.40); fixed-price menus 350 F ($66.50), 450 F ($85.55), and 550 F ($104.55). AE, DC, MC, V. Apr–July 14 and Sept–Oct, daily noon–1:30pm and 8–10pm; July 15–Aug, daily 8–10pm; Nov–Mar, Mon 8–10pm, Tues–Sat noon–1:30pm and 8–10pm, Sun noon–1:30pm. FRENCH.

At the entrance to the harbor of La Napoule, in a 40-year-old house with a lovely garden and an unusual re-creation of a mock-medieval cloister, this restaurant became world-famous under the tutelage of the now retired Louis Outhier. Today chef Stephane Raimbault prepares the most sophisticated cuisine in La Napoule. Presumably, Raimbault has learned everything Outhier had to teach him and today charts his own culinary course. Because Raimbault cooked in Japan for nine years, many of his dishes are of the "East Meets West" variety. In summer, meals are served beneath the shade of the plane trees in the garden. Menu specialties may include taboulette of crayfish with tamarind juice, warm foie gras of duckling with verdure de blettes (a Provençal vegetable similar to spinach), turbot en meunière with beets and capers, filet of pork with sage oil, and John Dory roasted with herbs in the traditional style. The wine cellar houses one of the finest collections of Provençal wines anywhere.

20 St-Tropez

543 miles S of Paris, 47 miles SW of Cannes

Sun-kissed lasciviousness is rampant in this carnival town, but the true Tropezian resents the fact that the port has such a bad reputation. "We can be classy too," insisted one native. Creative people in the lively arts along with ordinary folk create a volatile mixture. One observer said that St-Tropez "has replaced Naples for those who accept the principle of dying after seeing it. It is a unique fate for a place to have made its reputation on the certainty of happiness."

St-Tropez was greatly popularized by Bardot in *And God Created Woman*, but it's been known for a long time. Colette lived here for many years. Even the late diarist Anaïs Nin, confidante of Henry Miller, posed for a little cheesecake on the beach here in 1939 in a Dorothy Lamour bathing suit. Earlier, St-Tropez was known to Guy de Maupassant, Signac, Matisse, and Bonnard.

Artists, composers, novelists, and the film colony are attracted to St-Tropez in summer. Trailing them is a line of humanity unmatched anywhere else on the Riviera for sheer flamboyance. Some of the most fashionable yachts bringing the chicest people anchor here in summer, disappearing long before the dreaded mistral of winter.

ESSENTIALS

GETTING THERE   The nearest railway station is in St-Raphaël, a neighboring resort; at the *vieux port*, four or five boats per day leave the Gare Maritime de St-Raphaël, rue Pierre Auble (☎ 94-95-20-00), for St-Tropez (trip time: 50 min.), costing 100 F ($19) round-trip. Some 15 Sodetrav buses per day, leaving from the *gare routière* in St-Raphaël (☎ 94-95-24-822), go to St-Tropez, taking 1¹/₂ to 2¹/₄ hours, depending on the bus. A one-way ticket costs 45 F ($8.55). Buses run directly to St-Tropez from Toulon and Hyères.

If you drive, you'll have to squeeze your car into impossibly small parking spaces wherever you can find them. One large parking lot lies just south of place des Lices/place du XVe Corps, several blocks inland from the port.

VISITOR INFORMATION   The Office de Tourisme is on quai Jean-Jaurès (☎ 94-97-45-21).

VISITING THE TOP ATTRACTIONS

Near the harbor is the **Musée de l'Annonciade,** at place Georges-Grammont (☎ 94-97-04-01), installed in the former chapel of the Annonciade. As a legacy

from the artists who loved St-Tropez, the museum shelters one of the finest modern-art collections on the Riviera. Many of the artists, including Paul Signac, depicted the port of St-Tropez. Opened in 1955, the collection includes such works
as Van Dongen's yellow-faced *Women of the Balustrade* and paintings and sculpture by Bonnard, Matisse, Braque, Dufy, Utrillo, Seurat, Derain, and Maillol. The
museum is open Wednesday to Monday: June to September from 10am to noon

The Chic & the Restless

It was named after an obscure saint, a 1st-century Christian soldier martyred by
Nero, whose headless body, set adrift at sea, landed on the rocky shore of what is
now known as St-Tropez. (According to legend, the cock and the dog that accompanied the corpse refused to devour it, proving to the fisherfolk who discovered the boat's strange cargo that God had indeed favored the earthly remains of
his martyr.)

During the 19th century geography kept the town in relative obscurity, even
when such resorts as Nice were booming. Isolated at the tip of a rocky peninsula,
inconveniently far from sandy beaches and a railway station, it's the only north-
facing town on the Côte d'Azur, unpleasantly exposed to winter storms and—at
least to the Victorians—too earthy, too fishy, and too cold for a proper midwinter haven. Those drawbacks were considered virtues by artistic iconoclasts like
Paul Signac, who began wintering here in 1892. Matisse, Dongen, Seurat, and
Bonnard soon gravitated here, and by the 1920s Colette could be spotted here
in shorts! After his abdication and their marriage, the duke of Windsor and his
American duchess, the "wicked" Wallis Warfield Simpson, dallied around the
port as well, much to the delight and occasional shock of stargazers.

During World War II, the American army used St-Tropez as an embarkation
point, and later Françoise Sagan and the chauvinistic musical diva of the existentialists, Juliette Greco, announced their approval of the place. The resort's fame
was sealed in 1956 with Roger Vadim's *And God Created Woman*, starring sex
goddess Brigitte Bardot, which elevated St-Tropez into a playground for French-
speaking versions of James Dean. Perhaps Bardot's most memorable moment
here was when she publicly removed her brassiere in a café on an otherwise un-
eventful morning and announced it was time to wake up sleepy old St-Tropez.

She certainly succeeded, as evidenced by a higher percentage of expensive yachts
in the harbor than of fishing craft. Since the town has no railway station (the
SNCF arrives at neighboring St-Raphaël), unless you can arrive by parachute,
midsummer traffic jams make glamorous arrivals and departures impossible.

What seems to be the most fashionable thing to do in St-Tropez? You must
declare loudly to all who'll listen that this is the absolute last year you'll be spending
your holiday here. And who are the newest celebrities to lend their *cachet* to the
place? They include Giorgio Armani, Princess Caroline of Monaco (with her
chauffeur/lover), decorator to the stars Jacques Grange, and novelist/actor
(author of *The Hairdresser of St-Tropez*) Rupert Everett.

And where should an aspiring nudist go to make a splash in a town jaded by
the sight of too much flesh? Try virtually any beach outside town, most notably
Pampelonne (3 miles southwest) or Tahiti Beach, a concession-loaded strip of
golden sand that's long been favored by exhibitionists wearing next to nothing.

and 4 to 8pm, and in October and December to May from 10am to noon and 2 to 6pm. Admission is 22 F ($4.20) for adults and 11 F ($2.10) for children.

Two miles from St-Tropez, **Port Grimaud** makes an interesting outing. If you approach the village at dusk, when it's softly bathed in Riviera pastels, it'll look like some old hamlet, perhaps from the 16th century. But this is a mirage. Port Grimaud is the dream-fulfillment of its promoter, François Spoerry, who carved it out of marshland and dug canals. Flanking these canals, fingers of land extend from the main square to the sea. The homes are Provençal style, many with Italianate window arches. Boat owners can anchor right at their doorsteps. One newspaper called the port "the most magnificent fake since Disneyland."

WHERE TO STAY
VERY EXPENSIVE

✪ Byblos
Av. Paul-Signac, 83990 St-Tropez. ☎ **94-56-68-00.** Fax 94-56-68-01. 47 rms, 55 suites. A/C MINIBAR TV TEL. 1,080–2,380 F ($205.30–$452.45) double; from 2,450 F ($465.75) suite. Breakfast 120 F ($22.80) extra. AE, DC, MC, V. Parking free. Closed Nov–Mar.

The builder said he created "an anti-hotel, a place like home." That's true if your home resembles a palace in Beirut with salons decorated with Phoenician gold statues from 3000 B.C. On a hill above the harbor, this deluxe complex has intimate patios and courtyards. There are seductive retreats filled with antiques and rare decorative objects, many brought from Lebanon, including polychrome carved woodwork on the walls, marquetry floors, and a Persian-rug ceiling. Every room is unique. In one, for example, there's a fireplace on a raised hearth, paneled blue-and-gold doors, and a bed recessed on a dais. Le Hameau contains 10 duplex apartments built around a small courtyard with an outdoor spa. Some rooms have balconies overlooking an inner courtyard; others open onto a terrace of flowers.

Dining/Entertainment: You can dine by the pool at Les Arcades, enjoying Provençal food, or try an Italian restaurant offering an antipasta buffet, many pasta courses, and other typical fare from France's neighbor. Later in the evening you can dance on a circular floor surrounded by bas-relief columns in the hotel's nightclub, Caves du Roy. There are also two bars.

Services: 24-hour room service, same-day laundry/valet, beauty salon.

Facilities: "High-fashion" pool, sauna.

✪ Résidence de la Pinède
Plage de la Bouillabaisse, 83990 St-Tropez. ☎ **94-97-04-21.** Fax 94-97-73-64. 36 rms, 6 suites. A/C MINIBAR TV TEL. 800–2,915 F ($152–$553.85) double; 2,050–7,150 F ($389.70–$1,359.30) suite. Breakfast 115 F ($21.85) extra. AE, DC, MC, V. Parking free. Closed Oct 16–Mar.

This four-star luxury hotel was constructed around an existing tower once used to store olives. Jean-Claude and Nicole Delion own this seaside Relais & Châteaux. The airy, spacious rooms are decorated in pastels; they open onto balconies or terraces with a view over the bay of St-Tropez. All were recently redecorated. The hotel is the finest in St-Tropez after the Byblos (above).

Dining/Entertainment: Excellent food, especially seafood, is served in the dining room or on the terrace under the pine trees. In the past, mainly residents of the hotel dined here. However, the cuisine of Hervé Quesnel, who worked at the deluxe Hôtel Crillon in Paris, has drawn Tropéziens anxious to sample his refined cooking with a Provençal flavor.

Services: 24-hour room service, same-day laundry/valet.
Facilities: Kidney-shaped pool, beach.

EXPENSIVE

✪ La Bastide de St-Tropez

Route des Carles, 83990 St-Tropez. ☎ **94-97-58-16.** Fax 94-97-21-71. 20 rms, 6 suites. A/C MINIBAR TV TEL. 950–1,900 F ($180.60–$361.15) double; 2,100–3,400 F ($399.20–$646.35) suite. Breakfast 60–100 F ($11.40–$19) extra. AE, DC, MC, V. Parking free. Closed Jan.

Near the landmark place des Lices, this tile-roofed manor looks deliberately severe, but the interior is far more opulent. A grand staircase leads from a sun-filled living room to the upper floors. The rooms are named according to their unique decor, including "rose of Bengal" and "tangerine dawn." Each has a terrace or private garden, and some have Jacuzzis. Several, however, are quite small. The hotel is noted for its restaurant, l'Olivier.

Hôtel Résidence des Lices

135 av. Augustin-Grangeon, 83900 St-Tropez. ☎ **94-97-28-28.** 41 rms. A/C TV TEL. 590–1,150 F ($112.15–$218.60) double. Breakfast 55 F ($10.45) extra. AE, MC, V. Parking free. Closed Jan 4–Easter and Oct 31–Dec 26.

One consistently reliable bet for lodgings in St-Tropez is this modern hotel in its own small garden close to place des Lices. The nicely furnished rooms are tranquil, overlooking either the pool or garden; their rates vary widely according to their view and size. Breakfast is the only meal served, though afternoon snacks are provided beside the pool.

MODERATE

Hôtel Ermitage

Av. Paul-Signac, 83990 St-Tropez. ☎ **94-97-52-33.** Fax **94-97-10-43.** 26 rms. TEL. 590–790 F ($112.15–$150.20) double. Breakfast 55 F ($10.45) extra. AE, DC, MC, V. Parking free.

Attractively isolated amid the rocky heights of St-Tropez, this hotel was built in the 19th century as a private villa. Today its red-tile roof and green shutters shelter a plush hideaway. A walled garden is illuminated at night, and a cozy corner bar near a wood-burning fireplace takes the chill off blustery evenings. The rooms are pleasantly but simply furnished, and the staff can be charming. Breakfast is the only meal served.

Hôtel la Tartane

Route des Salins, 83990 St-Tropez. ☎ **94-97-21-23.** Fax 94-97-09-16. 14 rms. A/C TV TEL. 750–900 F ($142.55–$171.10) double. Breakfast 70 F ($13.30) extra. AE, V. Parking free. Closed Oct 15–Mar 15.

This hotel is midway between the center of St-Tropez and the Plage des Salins, about a three-minute drive from each. There's a stone-rimmed pool set into the garden and attractively furnished public rooms with terra-cotta floors. The guest rooms are well-furnished bungalows centered around the pool. Breakfasts are elaborate and attractive, and lunch is offered between 1 and 3pm; dinner is served between 7:30 and 9:30pm nightly. Bouillabaisse and fresh fish from the Mediterranean are the specialties.

La Ponche

3 rue des Remparts, 83990 St-Tropez. ☎ **94-97-02-53.** Fax 94-97-78-61. 18 rms. A/C TV TEL. 800–2,200 F ($152.10–$418.25) double. Breakfast 60 F ($11.40) extra. AE, MC, V. Closed Nov–Mar 15.

Overlooking the old fishing port, this has long been a cherished address, run by the same family for more than half a century. The hotel is filled with the original, airy paintings of Jacques Cordier, which adds to the elegant atmosphere. Each room has been newly redecorated and is well equipped, opening onto views of the sea. The hotel restaurant is big on Provençal charm and cuisine and a sophisticated crowd can be found on its terrace almost any night in fair weather.

WHERE TO DINE

EXPENSIVE

✪ Le Bistrot des Lices

3 place des Lices. ☎ **94-97-29-00.** Reservations required in summer. Main courses 190-210 F ($36.10–$39.90); fixed-price menus 175 F ($33.25) at lunch, 260–380 F ($49.40–$72.20) at dinner. AE, MC, V. Daily noon–2pm and 7:30pm–midnight. Closed Thurs in winter and Jan–Feb. FRENCH.

Don't let the "bistrot" in the name fool you. This is a first-class restaurant, with the most celebrated cuisine in St-Tropez and a glamorous clientele. There's a glass-enclosed outdoor café, and a piano bar/café in the outer room. In summer tables are placed in the rear garden. Chef Laurent Tarridec features a menu filled with Provençal flavor. He's known for his creative use of local produce in its prime. Aïoli, the garlicky mayonnaise sauce of Provence, is delectable with certain fresh fish courses, like John Dory. The classic vegetable medley, ratatouille, appears with oven-roasted turbot. Even young rabbit is sometimes offered with fresh herbs. Pig's foot in a casserole doesn't sound too enticing but is absolutely delectable. Some of the finest wines of Provence, many of them reasonably priced, appear on the menu.

Les Mouscardins

16 rue Portalet. ☎ **94-97-01-53.** Reservations required. Main courses 125–235 F ($23.75–$44.65); fixed-price menu 170 F ($32.30). AE, MC, V. Daily noon–2:30 and 7:30–11:30pm. Closed Nov–Mar 15. FRENCH.

At the end of the harbor, this restaurant has won awards for culinary perfection. The dining room is in formal Provençal style with an adjoining sun room under a canopy. The menu includes classic Mediterranean dishes, and as an appetizer we recommend moules (mussels) marinières. The two celebrated fish stews of the Côte d'Azur are offered: bourride Provençal and bouillabaisse. The fish dishes are excellent, particularly the loup (sea bass). The chef prepares two dessert specialties—soufflés made with Grand Marnier or Cointreau.

MODERATE

L'Echalotte

35 rue Allard. ☎ **94-54-83-26.** Reservations recommended in summer. Main courses 80–130 F ($15.20–$24.70); fixed-price menu 150 F ($28.50). AE, MC, V. Fri–Wed 12:30–2pm and 8–11:30pm. Closed Nov 15–Dec 15. FRENCH.

This charming restaurant, with a tiny garden and clean dining room, serves consistently good food for moderate prices. You can enjoy lunch on the veranda or dinner indoors. The tables may be difficult to get, especially in peak summer weeks. The cuisine is solidly bourgeois, including grilled veal kidneys, crayfish with drawn-butter sauce, and filet of turbot with truffles. The major specialty is several kinds of fish, like sea bass and daurade royale cooked in a salt crust.

INEXPENSIVE

Boeuf sur la Place

3 place des Lices. ☎ **94-97-60-50.** Reservations not required. Main courses 80–138 F ($15.20–$26.20); fixed-price lunch 85 F ($16.15). MC, V. Daily noon–2:30pm and 7–10:30pm. Closed Wed in winter. STEAKS.

A newcomer to the historic place des Lices lies adjacent to the Bistro des Lices (above) and is owned by the same management. Specializing only in flavorful cuts of meat, it offers well-prepared steaks and chops best consumed with a bottle of hearty red wine. Menu choices include carpaccio (thinly sliced raw marinated beef laden with garlic and herbs), "brochettes of the butcher," filets and faux-filets in several styles, and a wide array of desserts. This restaurant remains open throughout the year.

AFTER DARK

Located below the Hôtel Sube, the **Café de Paris,** sur le Port (☎ **94-97-00-56**), is one of the most consistently popular hangouts in town. An attempt has been made to glorify a fairly utilitarian room with turn-of-the-century globe lights, an occasional 19th-century bronze, masses of artificial flowers, and a long zinc bar. The crowd is irreverent and animated. It's busy even in winter, after the yachting crowd departs. It's open daily: June to September from 8am to 3am, and October to May from 8am to 7pm.

Reporter Leslie Maitland once described the kind of clientele attracted to the **Café Sénéquier,** sur le Port (☎ **94-97-00-90**), at cocktail hour: "What else can one do but gawk at a tall, well-dressed young woman who appears *comme il faut* at Sénéquier's with a large white rat perched upon her shoulder, with which she occasionally exchanges little kisses, while casually chatting with her friends?" This is one of many oddities at this anything-goes café. All the tables, chairs, and stools are red. There's a panoramic view of the port from under the canopy. During the summer, yacht-watching is a favorite pastime here. It's open June to September, daily from 8am to 1am; off-season, daily from 8am to 7pm; closed November 11 to December 20.

Appendix: Menu Savvy

à la "in the manner of" or "accompanied by"

alsacien or **à l'alsacienne** in the style of Alsace (usually with sauerkraut, foie gras, or sausage)

à l'ancienne old-fashioned, "in the style of grandmother"

à point medium rare

aiguillettes long thin slivers, usually of duck

aïoli garlic-laced mayonnaise

amuse-gueule or **amuse-bouche** a preappetizer

andouillette chitterling or tripe sausage

apéritif before-dinner libation said to "awaken" the appetite

assiette du pêcheur mixed seafood plate

baguette the famous long loaf of crusty French bread

ballottine deboned, stuffed, and rolled poultry

basquais or **à la basquaise** Basque-style (usually with tomatoes, red peppers, and ham)

béarnaise sauce made with egg yolks, shallots, white wine, vinegar, butter, and tarragon

béchamel buttery white-flour sauce flavored with onion and herbs

beurre blanc "white butter" sauce with white wine, butter, and shallots

bigarade bitter-orange sauce, often served with duck

blanc de volaille breast of hen

blanquette stewed meat with white sauce, enriched with cream and eggs

boeuf à la mode marinated beef braised with red wine and served with vegetables

boeuf en daube beef stew with red wine

bordelais or **à la bordelaise** in the style of Bordeaux (usually accompanied with a wine-laced brown sauce flavored with shallots, tarragon, and bone marrow)

boudin noir blood sausage

bouillabaisse Mediterranean fish soup made with tomatoes, garlic, saffron, and olive oil

bourguignon or **à la bourguignonne**   in the style of Burgundy (usually with red wine, mushrooms, bacon, and onions)

bourride   Mediterranean fish soup with aïoli, served over slices of bread

breton or **à la bretonne**   in the style of Brittany, often with white beans

brunoise   tiny cut-up vegetables

canard à la presse   duck killed by suffocation, then pressed to extract the blood and juices, which are simmered with cognac and red wine

canard sauvage   wild duck

carbonnade   beef stew, originally from Flanders, often cooked with beer

carré d'agneau   crown roast or loin of lamb

cassolette   dish served in a small casserole

cassoulet   Toulousien specialty of white beans cooked with preserved goose or duck, pig's trotters, sausages, carrots, and onions

céleri rémoulade   shredded celery root with tangy mayonnaise

cèpes à la bordelaise   large, meaty wild boletus mushrooms cooked with oil, shallots, and herbs

choucroute garni   Alsatian sauerkraut garnished with pork products and boiled potatoes

cochon de lait   roast suckling pig

confit   meat (usually duck or goose) cooked and preserved in its own fat

coq au vin   chicken stewed with mushrooms and red wine

côte d'agneau   lamb chop

côte de boeuf   rib steak

court bouillon   a broth with white wine, herbs, carrots, and soup greens in which poultry, fish, or meat is cooked

crème brûlée   thick custard dessert with a caramelized topping

crème chantilly   sugared whipped cream

crème fraîche   sour heavy cream

crème pâtissière   custard filling for cakes

croque monsieur   toasted sandwich containing cheese and ham; if prepared with a fried egg on top, it's a *croque madame*

darne   a slice of fish steak, usually salmon

daurade   prized sea bream (similar to porgy)

demoiselles de Cherbourg   small Norman lobsters in court bouillon

diable   deviled and peppery

digestif   any after-dinner liqueur (like Armagnac) that's presumed to aid the digestive processes

dijonnais or **à la dijonnaise**   denotes the presence in a dish of mustard, usually Dijon

duxelles   chopped shallots and mushrooms sautéed and mixed with rich cream

eau-de-vie   "water of life"— brandy distilled from fruit or herbs; usually has a very high alcohol percentage and is consumed at the end of a meal

écrevisse   freshwater crayfish

escabèche   Provençal dish of small fish (often sardines) browned in olive oil, marinated, and served cold

escargots de Bourgogne   land snails prepared with garlic, parsley, and butter

estoficado purée of dried codfish, tomatoes, olive oil, onions, and herbs; a specialty of Nice

faisan pheasant

farci stuffed

feu de bois, au cooked over a wood fire

fraises des bois wild strawberries

française, à la garnish of peas with lettuce, pearl onions, and herbs

fricassée braised meat or poultry stew; any medley of meat, even fish, that's stewed or sautéed

friture fried food

fromage blanc white cheese (like cottage cheese)

fumet fish-based stock

galantine classic dish of cooked meat or fowl, served cold in jelly aspic

galette flat round cake or pastry; in Brittany, a crêpe of buckwheat flour

garni garnished

gâteau cake

gelée jelly or aspic

gibelotte rabbit fricassée in wine sauce

gigot haunch (or leg) of an animal, almost always that of lamb or mutton

glaces ice in general; ice cream in particular

glaçons ice cubes

gratin brown crust that forms on top of a dish when it's oven-browned; a dish that's covered with breadcrumbs and melted cheese

grenouilles frogs' legs

grillé grilled

herbes de Provence a medley of rosemary, summer savory, bay leaf, and thyme

hollandaise yellow sauce of egg yolk, butter, and lemon juice whipped smooth

homard à l'armoricaine lobster browned and simmered with shallots, cognac, white wine, and onions

hors d'oeuvres appetizers

huile d'olive olive oil

île flottante "Floating Island," a rich dessert of a kirsch-soaked biscuit dressed with maraschino cherries and whipped cream

jambon de Bayonne salt-cured ham from the Basque region

jardinière garnish of freshly cooked vegetables

julienne cut into thin strips

jus juice; *"au jus"* means with natural, unthickened gravy

landais or **à la landaise** in the style of Landes—a garnish of goose fat, pine nuts, and garlic

langouste clawless spiny lobster or rock lobster

langoustine clawed crustacean (in Britain, a prawn)

lardons cubes of bacon, often served with soups and salads

léger or **légère** light in texture, flavor, and calories

légume vegetable

limande lemon sole

lotte monkfish or angler fish

lou magrêt breast of fattened duck

loup de mer wolf-fish, a Mediterranean sea bass

lyonnais or **à la lyonnaise** white-wine sauce with shredded and sautéed onions

macédoine medley of diced vegetables or fruits

marchand de vins wine merchant; also implies a rich sauce made from shallots and red wine

marmite thick soup made from beef and vegetables, simmered for hours on a low fire; the pot in which the soup is cooked. A *marmite des pêcheurs* refers to a fish soup, or stew, prepared in a marmite.

ménagère, à la "housewife style"—accompanied with potatoes, onions, and carrots

meunière, à la "In the style of the miller's wife"—rolled in flour and sautéed in butter

meurette a red-wine sauce, often served with poached eggs and freshwater fish; any wine sauce

mignonette a substance (usually beef) cut into small cubes

millefeuille a napoleon

mirepoix minced onions, ham, and carrots sautéed in butter and flavored with herbs

mornay béchamel sauce flavored with cheese

moules à la marinière mussels in herb-flavored white wine with shallots

nage, à la an aromatic court bouillon used for poaching

Nantua pink sauce made of white wine, crayfish, and tomatoes

navarin mutton prepared with potatoes and turnips

normande sauce of eggs, cream, and mushrooms, in the style of Normandy; meat or fish flavored with Calvados

oeufs à la neige "eggs in snow"—beaten egg whites poached in milk and served with vanilla-flavored custard

omelette norvegienne Baked Alaska *à la française*

pain bread

palourde clamlike mollusk, most often stuffed

pamplemousse grapefruit

panaché any mixture

papillote, en cooked in parchment paper

parfait layered ice-cream dessert

parisienne, à la with leeks and potatoes

Parmentier a dish with potatoes

pâté minced meat that's spiced and baked in a mold and served either hot or cold; sometimes made from fish or vegetables

pâté feuilletée puff pastry

paysanne chicken or meat braised and garnished with vegetables

périgourdine, à la sauce usually made with foie gras and truffles

pipérade classic Basque dish of scrambled eggs with onions, tomatoes, peppers, and ham

piquante tangy sauce made with shallots, vinegar, herbs, small pickles, and white wine

pistou sauce of garlic, fresh basil, and olive oil, from Provence

plat du jour the daily special

poêlé pan-fried

poisson fish—*de mer* is from the ocean; *de lac* from the lake; *de rivière* from the river

poivrade peppery brown sauce made with wine and vinegar

pomme apple

pomme de terre Potato—*pommes de terre* is frequently shortened to *pommes*, as in *pommes frites* (french fries)

porc pork; *porc salé* is salt pork

pot-au-feu "pot on the fire"—meat stew cooked in an earthenware pot

poulet, poularde chicken—*poulet fermier* is free-range; *poussin* is a chick

pré salé seaside meadow whose grasses are said to be especially beneficial for the pasturing of lambs or sheep; flesh from lambs raised in these meadows is especially succulent

pressé pressed or squeezed, as in fresh orange juice

prix fixe   a set meal with a fixed price

profiteroles   small cream puffs of chou pastry with a filling of whipped cream or custard

provençal or **à la provençale**   in the style of Provence, most often with garlic, tomatoes, and onion

purée   mashed or forced through a sieve

quenelles   rolls of pounded and baked fish, often pike, usually served warm; can also be made from chicken or veal

ragoût   stew, usually made from beef

rascasse   a scorpion fish in Mediterranean bouillabaisse

ratatouille   a Mediterranean medley of peppers, tomato, eggplant, garlic, and onions

ravigote   sauce made with vinegar, lemon sauce, white wine, shallot butter, and herbs

rémoulade   cold mayonnaise flavored with mustard

rillettes   minced pork spread popular in Tours

rognons   kidneys, usually veal

ris de veau   veal sweetbreads

rosé   meat or poultry cooked rare

rôti   roasted

rouennaise (canard à la . . .)   duck stuffed with its liver in a blood-thickened sauce

rouille   olive oil–based mayonnaise, with peppers, garlic, and fish broth, served with bouillabaisse in Provence

roulade   meat or fish roll, most often stuffed

sabayon   egg custard flavored with marsala wine

saignant or **saignante**   "bleeding"—referring to anything cooked rare, especially roast beef

salade lyonnaise   green salad flavored with cubed bacon and soft-boiled eggs

salade niçoise   salad made with tomatoes, green beans, tuna, black olives, potatoes, artichokes, and capers

salade verte   green salad

sandre   pickerel; a perchlike river fish

saucisse   French pork sausage

sole cardinal   poached filet of sole with crayfish-flavored cream sauce

sommelier   wine steward

sorbet   sherbet, usually flavored with fresh fruit

soubise   béchamel sauce with onion

soufflé   "blown up" fluffy baked egg dish flavored with almost anything, from cheese to Grand Marnier

steak au poivre   pepper steak, covered with fresh peppercorns, with cognac flambé

suprême   white sauce made with heavy cream

table d'hôte   fixed-price preselected meal, usually offering a limited (if any) choice of dishes

tartare   any preparation of cold chopped raw meat flavored with piquant sauces and spices (including capers and onions)

tartare (sauce)   cold mayonnaise spiced with herbs, vinegar, and mustard

tarte tatin   caramelized upside-down apple pie

tartine   open-face sandwich, or bread slathered with jam and butter

terrine   potted meat in a crock

timbale   fish or meat dishes cooked in a casserole

tournedos Rossini   beef filet sautéed in butter with pan juices, served with foie-gras garnish

tripes à la môde de Caen   beef tripe cooked in Calvados with carrots, leeks, onions, herbs, and spices

truite au bleu   fish that's gutted moments before being plunged into boiling vinegar and water, which turns the flesh blue

vacherin   ice cream in a meringue shell; a rich cheese from eastern France

velouté   classic velvety sauce, thickened with a roux of flour and butter

Véronique, à la   garnished with peeled white grapes; usually applies to filet of sole

Vichy   with glazed carrots

vichyssoise   creamy potato-and-leek soup, served cold

vinaigrette   oil-and-vinegar dressing flavored with herbs and perhaps a hint of mustard

vol-au-vent   puff-pastry shell

Xérès, vinaigre de   sherry-flavored vinegar

zeste   citrus peel without its white pith, twisted and used to flavor drinks, such as vermouth

Index

NOTES

NOTES

NOTES

NOTES

NOTES

The following Frommer's guides are available from your favorite bookstore, or you can use the order form on the preceding page to request them as part of your membership in Frommer's Travel Book Club.

FROMMER'S COMPLETE TRAVEL GUIDES

(Comprehensive guides to sightseeing, dining and accommodations, with selections in all price ranges—from deluxe to budget)

Acapulco/Ixtapa/Taxco, 2nd Ed.	C157	Jamaica/Barbados, 2nd Ed.	C149
Alaska '94-'95	C131	Japan '94-'95	C144
Arizona '95	C166	Maui, 1st Ed.	C153
Australia '94-'95	C147	Nepal, 3rd Ed. (avail. 11/95)	C184
Austria, 6th Ed.	C162	New England '95	C165
Bahamas '96 (avail. 8/95)	C172	New Mexico, 3rd Ed.	C167
Belgium/Holland/Luxembourg,		New York State, 4th Ed.	C133
4th Ed.	C170	Northwest, 5th Ed.	C140
Bermuda '96 (avail. 8/95)	C174	Portugal '94-'95	C141
California '95	C164	Puerto Rico '95-'96	C151
Canada '94-'95	C145	Puerto Vallarta/Manzanillo/	
Caribbean '96 (avail. 9/95)	C173	Guadalajara, 2nd Ed.	C135
Carolinas/Georgia, 2nd Ed.	C128	Scandinavia, 16th Ed.	C169
Colorado '96 (avail. 11/95)	C179	Scotland '94-'95	C146
Costa Rica, 1st Ed.	C161	South Pacific '94-'95	C138
Cruises '95-'96	C150	Spain, 16th Ed.	C163
Delaware/Maryland '94-'95	C136	Switzerland, 7th Ed.	
England '96 (avail. 10/95)	C180	(avail. 9/95)	C177
Florida '96 (avail. 9/95)	C181	Thailand, 2nd Ed.	C154
France '96 (avail. 11/95)	C182	U.S.A., 4th Ed.	C156
Germany '96 (avail. 9/95)	C176	Virgin Islands, 3rd Ed.	
Honolulu/Waikiki/Oahu, 4th Ed.		(avail. 8/95)	C175
(avail. 10/95)	C178	Virginia '94-'95	C142
Ireland, 1st Ed.	C168	Yucatán '95-'96	C155
Italy '96 (avail. 11/95)	C183		

FROMMER'S $-A-DAY GUIDES

(Dream Vacations at Down-to-Earth Prices)

Australia on $45 '95-'96	D122	Ireland on $45 '94-'95	D118
Berlin from $50, 3rd Ed.		Israel on $45, 15th Ed.	D130
(avail. 10/95)	D137	London from $55 '96	
Caribbean from $60, 1st Ed.		(avail. 11/95)	D136
(avail. 9/95)	D133	Madrid on $50 '94-'95	D119
Costa Rica/Guatemala/Belize		Mexico from $35 '96	
on $35, 3rd Ed.	D126	(avail. 10/95)	D135
Eastern Europe on $30, 5th Ed.	D129	New York on $70 '94-'95	D121
England from $50 '96		New Zealand from $45, 6th Ed.	D132
(avail. 11/95)	D138	Paris on $45 '94-'95	D117
Europe from $50 '96		South America on $40, 16th Ed.	D123
(avail. 10/95)	D139	Washington, D.C. on $50	
Greece from $45, 6th Ed.	D131	'94-'95	D120
Hawaii from $60 '96 (avail. 9/95)	D134		

FROMMER'S COMPLETE CITY GUIDES

(Comprehensive guides to sightseeing, dining, and accommodations in all price ranges)

Amsterdam, 8th Ed.	S176	Minneapolis/St. Paul, 4th Ed.	S159
Athens, 10th Ed.	S174	Montréal/Québec City '95	S166
Atlanta & the Summer Olympic		Nashville/Memphis, 1st Ed.	S141
Games '96 (avail. 11/95)	S181	New Orleans '96 (avail. 10/95)	S182
Atlantic City/Cape May, 5th Ed.	S130	New York City '96 (avail. 11/95)	S183
Bangkok, 2nd Ed.	S147	Paris '96 (avail. 9/95)	S180
Barcelona '93–'94	S115	Philadelphia, 8th Ed.	S167
Berlin, 3rd Ed.	S162	Prague, 1st Ed.	S143
Boston '95	S160	Rome, 10th Ed.	S168
Budapest, 1st Ed.	S139	St. Louis/Kansas City, 2nd Ed.	S127
Chicago '95	S169	San Antonio/Austin, 1st Ed.	S177
Denver/Boulder/Colorado Springs,		San Diego '95	S158
3rd Ed.	S154	San Francisco '96 (avail. 10/95)	S184
Disney World/Orlando '96 (avail. 9/95)	S178	Santa Fe/Taos/Albuquerque '95	S172
Dublin, 2nd Ed.	S157	Seattle/Portland '94–'95	S137
Hong Kong '94–'95	S140	Sydney, 4th Ed.	S171
Las Vegas '95	S163	Tampa/St. Petersburg, 3rd Ed.	S146
London '96 (avail. 9/95)	S179	Tokyo '94–'95	S144
Los Angeles '95	S164	Toronto, 3rd Ed.	S173
Madrid/Costa del Sol, 2nd Ed.	S165	Vancouver/Victoria '94–'95	S142
Mexico City, 1st Ed.	S175	Washington, D.C. '95	S153
Miami '95–'96	S149		

FROMMER'S FAMILY GUIDES

(Guides to family-friendly hotels, restaurants, activities, and attractions)

California with Kids	F105	San Francisco with Kids	F104
Los Angeles with Kids	F103	Washington, D.C. with Kids	F102
New York City with Kids	F101		

FROMMER'S WALKING TOURS

(Memorable strolls through colorful and historic neighborhoods, accompanied by detailed directions and maps)

Berlin	W100	Paris, 2nd Ed.	W112
Chicago	W107	San Francisco, 2nd Ed.	W115
England's Favorite Cities	W108	Spain's Favorite Cities (avail. 9/95)	W116
London, 2nd Ed.	W111	Tokyo	W109
Montréal/Québec City	W106	Venice	W110
New York, 2nd Ed.	W113	Washington, D.C., 2nd Ed.	W114

FROMMER'S AMERICA ON WHEELS

(Guides for travelers who are exploring the U.S.A. by car, featuring a brand-new rating system for accommodations and full-color road maps)

Arizona/New Mexico	A100	Florida	A102
California/Nevada	A101	Mid-Atlantic	A103

FROMMER'S SPECIAL-INTEREST TITLES

Arthur Frommer's Branson!	P107	Frommer's Where to Stay U.S.A.,	
Arthur Frommer's New World		11th Ed.	P102
of Travel (avail. 11/95)	P112	National Park Guide, 29th Ed.	P106
Frommer's Caribbean Hideaways		USA Today Golf Tournament Guide	P113
(avail. 9/95)	P110	USA Today Minor League	
Frommer's America's 100 Best-Loved		Baseball Book	P111
State Parks	P109		

FROMMER'S BEST BEACH VACATIONS

(The top places to sun, stroll, shop, stay, play, party, and swim—with each beach rated for beauty, swimming, sand, and amenities)

California (avail. 10/95)	G100	Hawaii (avail. 10/95)	G102
Florida (avail. 10/95)	G101		

FROMMER'S BED & BREAKFAST GUIDES

(Selective guides with four-color photos and full descriptions of the best inns in each region)

California	B100	Hawaii	B105
Caribbean	B101	Pacific Northwest	B106
East Coast	B102	Rockies	B107
Eastern United States	B103	Southwest	B108
Great American Cities	B104		

FROMMER'S IRREVERENT GUIDES

(Wickedly honest guides for sophisticated travelers and those who want to be)

Chicago (avail. 11/95)	I100	New Orleans (avail. 11/95)	I103
London (avail. 11/95)	I101	San Francisco (avail. 11/95)	I104
Manhattan (avail. 11/95)	I102	Virgin Islands (avail. 11/95)	I105

FROMMER'S DRIVING TOURS

(Four-color photos and detailed maps outlining spectacular scenic driving routes)

Australia	Y100	Italy	Y108
Austria	Y101	Mexico	Y109
Britain	Y102	Scandinavia	Y110
Canada	Y103	Scotland	Y111
Florida	Y104	Spain	Y112
France	Y105	Switzerland	Y113
Germany	Y106	U.S.A.	Y114
Ireland	Y107		

FROMMER'S BORN TO SHOP

(The ultimate travel guides for discriminating shoppers—from cut-rate to couture)

Hong Kong (avail. 11/95)	Z100	London (avail. 11/95)	Z101